The SCRIBNER ENCYCLOPEDIA *of*

AMERICAN LIVES

The SCRIBNER ENCYCLOPEDIA *of*

AMERICAN LIVES

THE 1960s

VOLUME ONE

A–L

WILLIAM L. O'NEILL
VOLUME EDITOR

KENNETH T. JACKSON
SERIES EDITOR IN CHIEF

CHARLES SCRIBNER'S SONS®

THOMSON
™
GALE

New York • Detroit • San Diego • San Francisco • Cleveland • New Haven, Conn. • Waterville, Maine • London • Munich

Charles Scribner's Sons
An imprint of The Gale Group
300 Park Avenue South, 9th floor
New York, NY 10010

Library of Congress Cataloging-in-Publication Data

The Scribner encyclopedia of American lives. The 1960s / edited by
William L. O'Neill.
     p.   cm.
    Includes bibliographical references and index.
    ISBN 0-684-80666-5 (set : alk paper)
    ISBN 0-684-31221-2 (v. 1)   ISBN 0-684-31222-0 (v. 2)
    1. United States—Biography—Dictionaries. 2. Biography—20th century.
  I. O'Neill, William L.
CT213.S374   2003
920.073'09'046—dc21   2002012581
                                         CIP

1 3 5 7 9 11 13 15 17 19 20 18 16 14 12 10 8 6 4 2
PRINTED IN THE UNITED STATES OF AMERICA

EDITORIAL *and* PRODUCTION STAFF

Project Editor
NEIL SCHLAGER

Editorial Assistants
KELLY BAISELEY BETH RICHARDSON VANESSA TORRADO-CAPUTO

Copy Editors, Researchers
JANET BALE MARY GILLASPY JUDSON KNIGHT
MARCIA MERRYMAN MEANS MADELINE PERRI SUSAN SCHARPF
TERESA BARENSFELD JAMES DeWAYNE CRAWFORD LINDA FORTIN
CYNTHIA GIUDICI HARRABETH HAIDUSEK MARGERY HEFFRON
ANNE LESSER TARA MANTEL CHRIS ROUTLEDGE LISA WOLFF

Proofreaders
DENISE EVANS CAROL HOLMES WILLIAM JENSEN KYUNG LIM KALASKY

Picture Researchers
KATHLEEN DROSTE

Designer
BRADY McNAMARA

Compositor
IMPRESSIONS BOOK AND JOURNAL SERVICES, INC.

Project Manager
SARAH FEEHAN

Senior Editor
JOHN FITZPATRICK

Publisher
FRANK MENCHACA

PREFACE

The Scribner Encyclopedia of American Lives: The 1960s is published in two alphabetically arranged volumes containing the biographies of 647 notable figures who were active in the 1960s. After *SEAL: Sports Figures,* it is the second in a series of *SEAL* thematic volumes dedicated to a specific topic in United States history.

We have followed the successful format of previous volumes in the *SEAL* series. Entries begin with an opening paragraph that highlights some of the subject's most important achievements and are accompanied in most instances by a photograph of the subject. Articles are signed by their authors, and the back matter in Volume 2 identifies authors by institutional or occupational affiliation in addition to listing all entries by field or occupation.

Many of the 201 contributors to these two volumes have previously written for *SEAL* and, before that, for the *Dictionary of American Biography,* also published by Scribners. Contributors include authors who have written full length biographies of their subjects, journalists, historians, scholars in other fields, and professional writers. We are gratified that authors who have worked with us in the past have chosen to stay on board for this project; this Scribner endeavor, however, is an entirely new venture with all entries written specifically for the *SEAL 1960s* volumes. In addition to thorough reviews of secondary source material, authors have often interviewed family members, journalists, other authorities, and in some cases the subjects themselves. Both the *Dictionary of American Biography* and previous *SEAL* volumes limited entries to Americans who were deceased. *SEAL 1960s,* which continues to include subjects in business, government, the arts, and every other important area in American life, includes both the living and the dead.

The process of selecting the 647 subjects that appear in *SEAL 1960s* was a difficult one, and we are aware that informed readers might have made different choices. Weighing the relative merits of figures from different fields is exponentially more problematic than comparing figures in the same field, and that of course is itself often a cause of controversy, as evidenced by the annual debates about awards given by the Pulitzer Prize committee, the Academy of Motion Picture Arts and Sciences, and the numerous other bodies that recognize eminence in our designated categories. The biographical concentration of *SEAL 1960s* is on Americans, but we have included persons of other nationalities, exemplified by the poet W. H. Auden and the film director Alfred Hitchcock, who had long periods of residence in the United States and significantly influenced American art and culture.

Many subjects are *of* the 1960s in that they helped define it or in some other way are connected to it in the public's mind. Two of the four presidents included, John F. Kennedy and Lyndon B. Johnson, fall into this category. President Dwight D. Eisenhower has no entry because he spent only one year of office in the 1960s and was clearly *of* the 1940s and 1950s. President Richard M. Nixon does warrant a long entry because the events we associate with the 1960s extended into the 1970s—the war in Vietnam, the antiwar and student movements, and, certainly, Watergate. The Reverend Martin Luther King, Jr., Malcolm X, and other figures of the civil rights movement are self-evidently of the 1960s. So also are leaders of the various youth movements, such as Tom Hayden and Abbie Hoffman. Many entertainers will be forever associated with period despite having long post-1960s careers. Bob Dylan, Brian Wilson and the Beach Boys, and Jerry Garcia and the Grateful Dead belong to this category.

The 1960s was the most turbulent period in the second half of the twentieth century and indelibly marked the decades that came after it. Even today the United States owes many of its characteristics, good and bad, to changes that began in this decade. Yet, unlike during World War II, occurrences associated with the 1960s— war, civil unrest, reform and revolutionary movements—did not overwhelm the nation. Such commonplace activities as making and selling goods, producing art and music, doing research, and playing and viewing sports were often little affected by even the most sensational events. Because we wanted to provide a cross section of American life, many entries are thus on subjects who were not *of* the period in the sense of helping to shape it. Including such figures as businessman J. Paul Getty, actor Rock Hudson, and the Reverend Norman Vincent Peale, prophet of positive thinking, reminds us that a strange feature of the age had to do with the often sharp divisions between epochal events and daily life. Other entries feature subjects who did not do their most significant work during the decade. This is the case with many Nobel Prize–winning scientists, for example, who usually received their awards for research conducted earlier. Omitting such figures would have denied readers information on the greatest scientists of the period. Ultimately, although we conferred with numerous experts, the final responsibility for selection rests entirely with the editors.

Most entries date the 1960s loosely. Few subjects fit neatly within the precise dates of 1960 and 1969. For Nixon, as an example, the "1960s" ended with his resignation in 1974. Similarly, most of the athletes in *SEAL 1960s* had careers that overlapped with the 1950s or the 1970s, and sometimes both. For the artist Louise Nevelson, the relevant era began in 1958 when she exhibited her painted black wood environment, *Moon Garden + One*. Consequently, the scope of each entry varies, in some cases limited to only a few years, in others spanning several decades.

Unlike the standard *SEAL* volumes, which evenly cover in detail the subject's entire life, *SEAL 1960s* focuses specifically on the subject's activities during the decade of the 1960s. Many subjects, from the entertainer Frank Sinatra to the author Saul Bellow to the actor-turned-politician Ronald Reagan, had long careers before or after the 1960s, and in many cases both. In such instances, however, contributors have devoted more than half of the text to the subjects' activities during the 1960s, providing only the key points of their lives before or after the decade. While *SEAL 1960s* may not be the source for a comprehensive profile on the subject, we believe these articles are uniquely valuable in offering a sharply focused view of the figures who defined the decade, or who were influential at the time.

There are many to acknowledge in an undertaking of this dimension. At the heart of these volumes are dedicated photo and copy editors and hundreds of talented writers. Sarah Feehan, Associate Editor at Scribners, provided the strongest possible support, guidance, and encouragement. Words cannot express our gratitude to Neil Schlager of the Schlager Group, who oversaw the production of this immense and complex enterprise with speed, efficiency, and good humor. Tracy Eddy contributed valuable research assistance, and we thank Richard H. Gentile for continuing to lend insight and historical expertise as he has done since *SEAL* first began.

William L. O'Neill, Volume Editor
Kenneth T. Jackson, Series Editor in Chief

CONTENTS

VOLUME 1

VOLUME 2

The SCRIBNER ENCYCLOPEDIA *of*

AMERICAN LIVES

A

AARON, Henry Louis ("Hank") (*b.* 5 February 1934 in Mobile, Alabama), baseball legend, executive, and career home-run record holder, who rose to sports celebrity status during the height of the civil rights movement in the Jim Crow South.

Aaron, the third of eight children born to Herbert Aaron, a boilermaker's assistant, and Estella Aaron, a homemaker, began his baseball career playing fast-pitch softball because his schools did not have organized baseball teams. Aaron attended Central High School in Mobile, but transferred during his junior year to the Josephine Allen Institute, which had a baseball program. Baseball became the center of young Aaron's life, and his education decidedly took a backseat to the game, much to his mother's dismay. In 1951 Aaron played shortstop for the semiprofessional Mobile Black Bears. Then in 1952 the Indianapolis Clowns, a professional Negro League team, offered Aaron a contract for $200 a month. Aaron made a deal with his mother to finish school in the off-season, and she agreed to allow him to turn professional.

Major League Baseball (MLB) was actively recruiting African-American players in the early 1950s, and it quickly noticed Aaron. He signed with the Boston Braves on 14 June 1952 and was sent to their minor league team in Eau Claire, Wisconsin, where he won Rookie of the Year. Despite the MLB effort to integrate the sport, the South remained strongly segregationist and firmly entrenched

by Jim Crow legislation. In 1953 the Braves sent Horace Garner, Felix Mantilla, and Aaron to its South Atlantic (Sally) League Class A farm club in Florida, the Jacksonville Suns, making them reluctant pioneers to integrated baseball in the South. Only nineteen years old, Aaron entered one of the two remaining all-white baseball circuits.

Although Aaron led the Sally League with a .362 batting average and 125 runs batted in (RBI), he also endured racism and discrimination exceeding anything he had experienced in Mobile. Spectators yelled obscenities, sent hate mail, and even threatened violence. Aaron, Garner, and Mantilla often stayed with an African-American family when they traveled and ate on the bus because of "white only" restaurant restrictions. Even when the team won, segregation kept them from attending victory parties. Aaron responded with a quiet stoicism. His 1954 rookie season as a right fielder with the Milwaukee Braves was a success. In 1957 Aaron batted .322 with forty-four home runs, was voted the Major League Most Valuable Player (MVP), and led the Braves to their only World Series title—a seven-game victory over the New York Yankees.

As the 1960s approached, and the civil rights movement gained momentum, Aaron's success and confidence grew, and his patience with racism and discrimination lessened. Although playing baseball kept African-American players from being active participants in the civil rights movement, Aaron, along with fellow player Bill Bruton, supported sympathetic politicians. They even campaigned for John F.

Hank Aaron. ARCHIVE PHOTOS, INC.

Kennedy in 1960. Aaron participated in civil rights causes throughout Atlanta and often involved teammates, but he did so without fanfare. Aaron and Bruton also sought to change things within their own sphere of influence. In 1961 Aaron, along with two teammates, pressured the Braves general manager, John McHale, to have all race signs removed in Brandenton Park, the training camp facility for the Braves near Sarasota, Florida. *Jet* magazine reported that the Milwaukee Braves were the first to "hit the Jim Crow ball head-on." The next issue Aaron addressed was hotel segregation. The problem was not with the Braves but with the Brandenton hotels. When Aaron pressed the issue, the Braves found a hotel just outside Brandenton that accepted the whole team. Aaron also started reading the works of James Baldwin and Martin Luther King, Jr.

In 1966 the Braves franchise moved to Atlanta. Although Atlanta was a "New South" city with a moderate mayor, Ivan Allen, who supported civil rights, Aaron was apprehensive about moving back to the South. Once again he started receiving hate mail, some of which threatened his family, and was subjected to abusive name-calling. Aaron's stoicism, however, was beginning to erode and he spoke out more often. He began to publicly support and stress in interviews the importance of having African-American managers in the Major Leagues. Then, in 1966 at Wrigley Field, a reporter for *Jet* caught Aaron at just the right mo-

ment. In the resulting article, "Hank Aaron Blasts Racism in Baseball," Aaron gave the writer a litany of ways in which baseball discriminated against African-American players. The Braves also put Aaron in the spotlight. During a 1966 baseball promotion Aaron traveled on a seventeen-day trip to Vietnam that ended with a meeting with President Lyndon B. Johnson at the White House.

Along with professional concerns over the relocation to Atlanta, Aaron also had intense personal concerns about moving his family back to the South. Aaron had married Barbara Lucas on 3 October 1953, and they had five children. He now had a family of his own, as well as taking in his brothers and sisters. Aaron bought a house on two acres of land in a segregated neighborhood. Aaron was also concerned for his family's safety at ballgames. Often they endured verbal abuse from fans calling Aaron derogatory names.

Aaron was under constant pressure in Atlanta. He knew the team was playing not only to win ball games, but also to win over the South. Despite the pressures of Atlanta, segregation, and racism, Aaron continued to excel as a ballplayer. He was the first player ever to have his own night in Atlanta-Fulton County stadium after his 500th home run, and he received admiration and accolades from mayor Ivan Allen for his role in helping to end segregation in the South. In 1969 he was still hitting .300 even though he was approaching the traditional retirement age and suffering from back problems. Aaron was also getting closer and closer to Babe Ruth's career record of 714 home runs.

In the early 1970s people began to speculate that Aaron had the potential to beat Ruth's record. Despite the stress of his divorce from Barbara Lucas in 1971, and receiving an estimated 3,000 letters per day, including hate mail, Aaron's performance on the field was solid. The hate mail was so cruel that the Braves hired personal security for Aaron. The Federal Bureau of Investigation (FBI) became involved to screen his mail and to trace threatening telephone calls. An FBI investigation also uncovered a plot to kidnap Aaron's daughter, who was then a student at Fisk University. In November 1973 Aaron married Billye Suber; they had one child. On opening day in 1974 Aaron finally hit his 714th home run, and on 8 April 1974 in Atlanta, Aaron became the home-run king, earning the nickname, "Hammerin' Hank." Then at the end of the 1974 season, at the age of forty, Aaron was traded to the Milwaukee Brewers, to the city where his professional career started. He played two more years, mostly as a designated hitter, before retiring in 1976.

Aaron returned to Atlanta as vice president and director of player development under the Braves new owner Ted Turner, making him one of the first African-American executives in Major League Baseball. Aaron was inducted into the National Baseball Hall of Fame in 1982 during his first year of eligibility. He was selected for a record twenty-four All-Star teams and won three Gold Gloves awards. He was the first player in baseball history to amass 500 home runs and 3,000 hits in a career. As well as his home-run total of 755, he also holds records for career RBI with 2,297; total bases with 6,856; and games played with 3,298. Aaron is active in charity work with organizations such as Big Brothers/Big Sisters of America, the Boy Scouts of America, the American Cancer Society, the National Easter Seal Society, and the Leukemia Society of America. Amazingly, despite being baseball's home-run king and a goodwill ambassador for the sport, Aaron still receives some hate mail.

★

Aaron has written several biographies, including *Aaron, r.f.* (1968), with Furman Bisher, later revised as *Aaron* (1974); *I Had a Hammer: The Hank Aaron Story* (1991), with Lonnie Wheeler; and *Home Run: My Life in Pictures* (1999), with Dick Schaap. Biographies include Al Hirshberg, *Henry Aaron: Quiet Superstar* (1969); Stan Baldwin and Jerry Jenkins, *Bad Henry: In Collaboration with Hank Aaron* (1974); Dan Schlossberg, *Hammerin' Hank! The Henry Aaron Story* (1974); George Plimpton, *One for the Record: The Inside Story of Hank Aaron's Chase for the Home-Run Record* (1974); and Don Money and Herb Anastor, *The Man Who Made Milwaukee Famous: A Salute to Henry Aaron* (1976). Two articles of note are "Henry Aaron's Golden Autumn," *Time* (24 Sept. 1973), and "End of the Glorious Ordeal," *Sports Illustrated* (15 Apr. 1974).

LISA A. ENNIS

ABRAMS, Creighton William, Jr. (*b.* 15 September 1914 in Springfield, Massachusetts; *d.* 4 September 1974 in Washington, D.C.), army officer who commanded U.S. forces in Vietnam from 1968 to 1972.

Abrams was the oldest of three children born to Creighton William Abrams, a railroad repairman, and Nellie Randall, a homemaker. Abrams graduated as valedictorian and senior class president of Agawam High School in Agawam, Massachusetts, a community just south of Springfield, in 1932. Abrams then graduated from the U.S. Military Academy and was commissioned a second lieutenant in the cavalry in 1936. On 30 August that same year, Abrams married Julia Harvey; they had six children. Following service with the 1st Cavalry Division, he was assigned to the 1st Armored Division in 1940, before being transferred to the 4th Armored Division in April 1941. After briefly serving as commander of a battalion in the 37th Armored Regiment and then as executive officer of the regiment, he was named commander of the 37th Tank Battalion with the rank of lieutenant colonel in September 1943.

Abrams was a demanding leader who emphasized hard

Creighton Abrams. THE LIBRARY OF CONGRESS

training and strict discipline. Stocky, plainspoken, gruff, and noted for his short fuse, he ran his battalion in a businesslike fashion, although he always evidenced a heartfelt concern for the well-being of his men. After three years of training in the United States and England, Abrams and the 4th Armored Division landed in Normandy in July 1944. During the next ten months, as commander of the 37th Tank Battalion and for a time Combat Command A and Combat Command B, he was often in the division's vanguard as it drove across France and Germany as part of the Third Army, commanded by General George Patton, Jr. Displaying tactical acumen and usually leading from his own tank, dubbed "Thunderbolt," Abrams earned a reputation as one of the U.S. Army's outstanding tank commanders. The high point in his World War II service came during the Battle of the Bulge in December 1944, when he led the task force that broke through the German lines to relieve U.S. units bottled up in Bastogne, Belgium.

After the war Abrams held a variety of staff and troop assignments in which he enhanced his reputation as an expert on armored warfare. He also graduated from the Command and General Staff College in 1949 and the Army War College in 1953. During the final stage of the Korean War he served successively as chief of staff of I Corps, IX Corps, and X Corps, helping plan defenses against the last major Communist attacks. Abrams was promoted to brigadier general in 1956 and to major general in 1960. While attached to the office of the army chief of staff he commanded the troops deployed to the University of Mississippi in 1962 to quell the riots that broke out after the admission of an African-American student. A year later he commanded the troops alerted for possible intervention in Tuscaloosa and Birmingham, Alabama, at a time of tense racial unrest. Impressed by Abrams's sensitive handling of these controversial affairs and the high regard other generals had for him, Secretary of Defense Robert McNamara in 1964 appointed Abrams vice chief of staff of the army; he also was promoted to full general. As vice chief of staff, Abrams worked with Chief of Staff General Harold K. Johnson to direct the army's buildup for the Vietnam War, a task complicated by President Lyndon B. Johnson's refusal to mobilize the reserves and the National Guard. This experience convinced Abrams that, in the future, reserve components must be integrated into the army structure in a way that ensured their availability in a conflict.

In April 1967 Abrams was appointed deputy commander of U.S. Military Assistance Command, Vietnam (MACV), with the expectation he would eventually succeed General William C. Westmoreland as MACV commander. Abrams's primary responsibility was to improve the military effectiveness of the Army of the Republic of Vietnam (ARVN). To this point ARVN, plagued by weak leadership, inadequate training, a high desertion rate, shortages of military equipment, corruption, and excessive involvement in politics, had generally performed poorly in battles with Viet Cong (VC) and North Vietnamese main-force units and in the pacification campaign that was designed to eliminate VC insurgents from the countryside and provide protection for the rural population. Optimistic about the fighting ability of the South Vietnamese soldier and able to work with Vietnamese authorities, Abrams tried to make up for ARVN's ills, focusing primarily on its leadership and logistical shortcomings. When ARVN performed much better than anticipated during the Communist Tet offensive in early 1968, Abrams received much of the credit.

During the Tet offensive, Westmoreland, lacking confidence in the local field commanders, made Abrams temporary commander of the I Corps area in northern South Vietnam. The heaviest fighting centered on the city of Hue, and by insisting that his mixed force of U.S. and ARVN troops had plentiful firepower and logistical support, Abrams was able to clear the city of North Vietnamese and VC forces.

Following Westmoreland's departure to become the army's chief of staff, Abrams became commander of MACV on 3 July 1968, a job he had unofficially been performing since the Tet offensive. He quickly made major changes in the conduct of the war. Westmoreland had emphasized a two-war strategy: U.S. forces engaged in large-scale search-and-destroy missions to destroy main-force enemy units,

while the South Vietnamese focused on local security. Implementing many of the recommendations of "A Program for Pacification and Long-Term Development of South Vietnam," a study prepared in the army chief of staff's office in 1965–1966 that argued that control of the population was the key to victory, Abrams initiated a one-war operational strategy. He ended Westmoreland's division of missions between U.S. and South Vietnamese combat forces and instructed all units to concentrate on providing protection for South Vietnam's villages.

Massive sweep operations were downgraded, and primacy was given to small-unit patrols and ambushes to cut off the Communists' access to the population, interdict their movement, and locate and destroy their supply caches. These tactics were complemented by incursions into Cambodia in 1970 and Laos in 1971 to push the Communists away from the borders of South Vietnam and to destroy supplies, and by pacification programs meant to eliminate the Communist infrastructure in South Vietnam's villages and hamlets. Nation-building programs were instituted to improve South Vietnam's educational, medical, transportation, and agricultural systems. Before long, statistical indicators showing reduced VC activity among the population seemed to indicate that pacification was succeeding, although the heavy losses suffered by VC forces during the Tet offensive might have been as important as Abrams's efforts.

In the spring of 1969 Abrams was charged with carrying out President Richard M. Nixon's policy of Vietnamization, which prescribed the unilateral withdrawal of U.S. troops from South Vietnam and assigned South Vietnamese forces greater responsibility for the conduct of the war. Abrams doubted that the South Vietnamese could deal with North Vietnamese forces by themselves in the foreseeable future and believed they would need residual U.S. combat and material support for years. Nevertheless he was loyal to his superiors in Washington. While cautioning Nixon not to move too quickly in deescalating U.S. involvement, he vigorously followed through with Vietnamization, virtually ending major U.S. field operations by the fall of 1969. Abrams directed the withdrawal of U.S. forces, which decreased from approximately 550,000 troops in early 1969 to 24,000 at the end of 1972, and oversaw a vast increase in the size of South Vietnamese forces and programs to improve their leadership, training, and arms.

Abrams's efforts to prepare the South Vietnamese to fight alone had their deficiencies. He did not insist that they free up more of their regular forces from static security missions so they could be organized into a mobile strategic reserve; he was slow to make plans for more heavy equipment for ARVN; and he failed to take a hard-nosed stand on the need for South Vietnam to improve its high-level military leadership. Yet to many, Abrams's efforts seemed reasonably successful when the South Vietnamese, with the crucial assistance of U.S. airpower and advisors, repelled a major North Vietnamese offensive in the spring of 1972.

In June 1972 Abrams left Vietnam and returned to the United States to become army chief of staff in October of that year. During the next two years he devoted himself to rebuilding an army that was demoralized by its Vietnam ordeal and, when Nixon ended conscription, converting it into an all-volunteer force. Stressing combat readiness, the integration of reserve forces into the active force structure, greater attention to the welfare of soldiers and their families, the need for the most modern weapons, and new doctrines of air-land warfare, he helped lay the foundation for the professional army that performed superbly in the Gulf War in 1991. The M1 battle tank, the backbone of the modern U.S. Army armored division, is named after Abrams. Abrams died of complications from surgery for lung cancer and was buried with full military honors in Arlington National Cemetery in Washington, D.C.

Abrams was one of the outstanding soldiers of his era. An aggressive and inspiring leader who epitomized professionalism and integrity, he had the difficult tasks of orchestrating the withdrawal of the United States from an unpopular war and giving the South Vietnamese at least a chance for survival once U.S. military participation had ended. Although South Vietnam collapsed in 1975, Abrams fulfilled his rearguard mission as skillfully as could be expected, given his diminishing resources and South Vietnam's fundamental political and military flaws. An admiring diplomat perhaps best summarized Abrams's role in Vietnam when he remarked that Abrams, a fighting soldier and a master of offensive warfare, "deserved a better war."

★

Abrams's papers are at the U.S. Army Military History Institute, Carlisle Barracks, Pennsylvania. Lewis Sorley provides an admiring view of Abrams in *Thunderbolt: General Creighton Abrams and the Army of His Times* (1992), and *A Better War: The Unexamined Victories and Final Tragedy of America's Last Years in Vietnam* (1999). See also Bruce Palmer, Jr., *The 25-Year War: America's Role in Vietnam* (1984), and Jeffrey J. Clarke, *The United States Army in Vietnam: Advice and Support: The Final Years, 1965–1973* (1988). An obituary is in the *New York Times* (4 Sept. 1974).

JOHN KENNEDY OHL

ABZUG, Bella (*b.* 24 July 1920 in New York City; *d.* 31 March 1998 in New York City), politician, activist, and lawyer who became a leading figure in the feminist and antiwar movements.

Abzug was born the second daughter of Emmanuel Savitsky, a butcher who emigrated from Russia in 1905 after the outbreak of the Russo-Japanese War, and Esther Tank-

Bella Abzug. THE LIBRARY OF CONGRESS

lefsky. Her father, who died when she was thirteen, was a pacifist, and his ideas had a strong impact on Abzug.

After receiving a B.A. at Hunter College of the City University of New York in 1942, Abzug earned a scholarship to attend the Columbia University School of Law, where she was one of only six women. She received her LL.B. in 1947. During her early days as a female lawyer, she began wearing her trademark wide-brimmed hats. She once recalled, "When I was a young lawyer, I would go to people's offices and they would always say, 'Sit here. We'll wait for the lawyer.' Working women wore hats. It was the only way they would take you seriously." She continued to wear a hat throughout her career, and was particularly happy to do so after her election to Congress, since "they didn't want me to wear it." Some of her hats have been donated to the Smithsonian Institution.

While attending Columbia, she met Martin Abzug, an aspiring novelist and businessman, and they married on 4 June 1944. Though they had two daughters, it was agreed early in their relationship that she would pursue her legal career even after they had children.

Abzug first came to national attention in 1951 when she traveled to Mississippi to defend Willie McGee, a black man accused of raping a white woman with whom he had consensual sex. She succeeded in obtaining two stays of execution, but he was eventually executed. Abzug was pregnant at the time, and according to her daughter, Liz, she miscarried late in that pregnancy because of the efforts she exerted during the trial.

During the McCarthy hearings of the 1950s, Abzug defended the civil rights of several individuals indicted for leftist activities. At the same time she counseled tenants and minorities, and her work had considerable influence upon the Civil Rights Act of 1964 and the Voting Rights Act of 1965. Her social activism in the fifties spilled over into antiwar activism in the sixties. Abzug wrote in her book *Gender Gap,* "As an instinctive feminist all my life, I came to political feminism by way of activities in the women's peace movement and involvement in Democratic Party reform politics."

Abzug's true political involvement began in the 1960s, when the Soviet Union and the United States resumed nuclear testing. With former Hunter College colleagues Mim Kelber, Amy Swerdlow, and Judy Lemer, she cofounded Women Strike for Peace (WSP) in 1961. WSP, which actively demanded a comprehensive nuclear test ban, was the first national group to draw massive attention to the danger of radioactive material in milk. Abzug later remarked, "We held one demonstration after another at the United Nations and at the White House, and we lobbied in Congress. I served as both political action director and legislative director." In 1963 the limited nuclear test ban treaty was signed, and WSP later expanded its mission. It began protesting the war in Vietnam, and Abzug soon became a prominent speaker against the poverty, racism, and violence that, as Swerdlow wrote, "mocked the promise of democracy in America."

In New York City, Abzug organized groups to work for the election of peace candidates; most prominent was Paul O'Dwyer, who was defeated in his run for the Senate in 1968. Abzug was appalled that President Lyndon B. Johnson, who was elected in 1964 on a pledge of "no wider war," escalated the war in Southeast Asia, and she took center-stage among New York Democrats in the "Dump Johnson" movement of 1967 and 1968. She mobilized peace forces to campaign for the evacuation of troops from Vietnam.

Subsequent to Johnson's fall from power, Abzug founded the Coalition for a Democratic Alternative, which supported the antiwar presidential candidacies of senators Robert Kennedy and Eugene McCarthy. In the summer of 1968 she helped form the Coalition for an Open Convention. After the Democratic defeat in 1968, she founded the New Democratic Coalition. In 1969, when the Republican Party denied renomination to the liberal New York mayor John Lindsay, Abzug organized a coalition to help him gain the right to run on an independent ballot line on which antiwar, pro–civil rights Democrats could vote for him. Regarding her participation in the peace movement, the columnist Jimmy Breslin remarked, "Some came early, others came late. Bella has been there forever."

In 1970 Abzug ran for Congress after experiencing her own personal "click," her feminist epiphany. She observed, "I had been working hard all those years to elect men who weren't any more qualified or able than I, and in some cases they were less so." When she ran for Congress, there were only nine women among the 435 members of the House, and Abzug's rallying cry was, "This woman belongs in the House—The House of Representatives." After an energetic campaign, Abzug defeated Barry Farber, the popular host of a local radio show in New York City. In Congress, Abzug immediately began her campaign to get the troops out of Vietnam. During six years in Washington, she helped found the National Women's Political Caucus, authored such landmark legislation as the Freedom of Information Act and the first gay rights bill, cosponsored the Equal Rights Amendment, and was the first to call for President Richard M. Nixon's resignation.

The media never tired of Abzug and her plain-talking, good-natured style. Calling her "Battling Bella," "Mother Courage," and "Hurricane Bella," they enjoyed inventing new epithets to describe her bellicose personality. In 1976 she gave up her safe congressional seat to run for the Senate and lost by only one percentage point to Daniel Patrick Moynihan. Abzug never again held political office, but she continued to practice law and work for women's groups. She started a lobbying group called Women U.S.A. and founded the Women's Environment and Development Organization (WEDO).

Abzug died at the age of seventy-seven from complications following heart surgery. She was eulogized for three hours and five minutes at Riverside Memorial Chapel in New York City by many of her compatriots from the 1960s, including Jane Fonda, Betty Friedan, and Gloria Steinem. Joseph Bologna, the actor, lovingly predicted that Ms. Abzug's first action would be "to immediately begin petitioning God for better conditions—for the people in hell." Abzug is buried in Old Mount Carmel Cemetery in Glendale, New York.

★

Some material derived from an interview with Liz Abzug, younger daughter of Bella S. Abzug. Autobiographies include *Bella! Ms. Abzug Goes to Washington* (1972), and (with Mim Keller) *Gender Gap* (1984). Interesting biographical articles include Esther Stineman, *American Women in Politics: Contemporary and Historical Profiles* (1980), and Gloria Steinem, "Bella Abzug," *Ms* (Jan. 1996). Tributes at the time of her death include Adam Nagourney, "Recalling Bella Abzug's Politics and Passion," *New York Times* (3 Apr. 1998), and Gloria Steinem, "Born to Be a World Leader," *Ms.* (July.–Aug. 1998). Obituaries are in the *New York Times* (1 Apr. 1998) and the *Nation* (20 Apr. 1998).

MARGARET GARRY BURKE

AGNEW, Spiro Theodore (*b.* 9 November 1918 in Baltimore, Maryland; *d.* 17 September 1996 in Berlin, Maryland), governor of Maryland and vice president of the United States who became known for his bombastic and divisive speeches attacking the media and liberal protesters.

The son of homemaker Margaret Akers Pollard and her second husband, Greek immigrant and restaurateur Theodore Spiro Agnew (formerly Anagnostopoulous), Agnew grew up with his older half brother W. Roy Pollard in Baltimore. After graduating from Forest Park High School in 1937, he began chemistry studies at Johns Hopkins University. In 1940, having lost interest in chemistry, Agnew left the university without a degree and enrolled in night classes at the University of Baltimore Law School. During the day he worked as a legal aide, an assistant personnel manager, and an insurance investigator. Agnew married Elinor Isabel ("Judy") Judefind on 27 May 1942; they had four children.

In September 1941 Agnew was drafted into the U.S. Army and served as a second lieutenant with the 10th Armored Division in France and Germany. He received the Bronze Star, and upon his discharge as captain in 1945, he completed his LL.B. in 1947 at Baltimore and then earned an LL.D. in 1949 from the University of Maryland. Admitted to the bar in 1949, Agnew practiced briefly with a Baltimore law firm before striking out on his own. His fledgling law office quickly failed, and Agnew joined Lumbermen's Mutual Insurance Company.

Agnew had registered his political party affiliation as a Democrat, following in the footsteps of his ward leader father, but the opportunities for Democrats in Maryland were few. Switching to the Republican Party, he joined the Baltimore County zoning appeals board in 1957 and became chairman one year later. After Agnew mounted a failed campaign for a judgeship in 1960, the Democrats decided to remove him from the Democrat-dominated zoning board in 1961. The publicity generated by this crude ejection cast Agnew as an honest man wronged by machine politics and helped propel him into the post of Baltimore County executive. Sworn in on 1 December 1962, Agnew had campaigned as a civil libertarian who opposed discrimination for moral, not political, reasons.

Notoriously thin-skinned and insensitive to the inflammatory impact of his words, Agnew soon made enemies. In the spring and summer of 1963, civil rights activists demonstrated to persuade a Baltimore-area amusement park to desegregate. Agnew created a civil rights commission to settle racial disputes, but worried the activists would undermine his efforts to reach a settlement with the park. Seemingly oblivious to the patience long exhibited by African Americans in the face of discrimination, Agnew publicly stated, "It is my earnest hope that there will be no outbursts of dem-

Spiro T. Agnew. THE LIBRARY OF CONGRESS

onstrations, no intemperate haste . . . no rash actions to jeopardize the advances possible if we exercise statesmanship and strength." The civil rights activists continued marching.

Running for governor of Maryland in 1966, Agnew had the immense good luck to have a rabid segregationist as an opponent. "This state must not be controlled by a devil that sits holding a two-pronged pitchfork of bigotry and hatred," Agnew declared before coasting to an easy victory. Once in office he initiated tax reform, increased aid to antipoverty programs, established the strictest state law against water pollution in the country, repealed the state law against racial intermarriage, supported open housing, and pushed for the liberalization of abortion laws.

An ardent proponent of legal proceduralism, Agnew took a strong stand for law and order, categorizing peaceful demonstrations as "militant pushing." In 1968 he ordered the arrest of 227 trespassing Bowie State University students who were holding a sit-in to protest the dilapidated buildings at the predominantly African-American campus. "I refuse to knuckle under to the demands of students no matter how justified they are," Agnew explained. When Baltimore erupted in flames after the 1968 assassination of Dr. Martin Luther King, Jr., Agnew arranged a meeting with 100 moderate black leaders who had tried to restore calm by walking the streets during the rioting. Agnew opened the meeting by insulting the leaders: "I did not request your presence to bid for peace with the public dollar." Demanding that African Americans repudiate radicals like Stokely Carmichael, Agnew then gave a speech described as "punitive" and "condescending" by one angry attendee, who walked out along with seventy others.

A centrist who did not have enough star power to outshine Richard M. Nixon, Agnew became the Republican choice for vice president in 1968 and was sworn into office on 20 January 1969. Assigned to the National Security Council and chairing the National Aeronautics and Space Council among his many duties, Agnew quickly developed a reputation for candor and inflammatory statements. He often said what Nixon felt but could not publicly express. Agnew attacked student protesters as "spoiled brats who never have had a good spanking" and "who take their tactics from Gandhi and their money from Daddy." He informed the poor and young, "We will listen to your complaints. You may give us your symptoms [but] we will make the diagnosis and . . . will implement the cure." Blaming the conduct of anti-Vietnam protesters on an "overly permissive society," Agnew added, "I wanted to do a lot of silly things when I was that age too, but my parents wouldn't let me." On 13 November 1969 the vice president vehemently denounced television newscasters as a hostile "unelected elite" who subjected Nixon's speeches to instant analysis. He raised the possibility of greater government regulation of this "virtual monopoly," a suggestion that many in television took as a threat to freedom of speech.

One of the most popular Republicans in the nation, Agnew's comments struck a chord with many Americans. Returned to office with Nixon in 1972, he learned soon after that he was the target of a grand jury investigation for accepting bribes from construction firms seeking state contracts and for taking kickbacks after he had become vice president. Agnew pleaded no contest to tax evasion, receiving probation and a fine. He resigned from office on 10 October 1973, was disbarred in Maryland in 1974, and spent his remaining years firmly out of the public eye. Undiagnosed acute leukemia claimed his life at a Berlin, Maryland, hospital. He is buried in Dulaney Valley Memorial Gardens in Timonium, Maryland, north of Baltimore.

Agnew's legacy is not a positive one. By fostering divisiveness, he contributed to the disillusionment with the political process that marked the end of the 1960s. His betrayal of the public through bribe taking, after he had loudly proclaimed the values of law and order, added mightily to the cynicism with which Americans have subsequently viewed politicians.

★

Agnew's papers are at the University of Maryland Archives and Manuscripts Department in College Park. In *Go Quietly . . . Or Else* (1980), he wrote of his days as vice president and the scandal that brought him down. Joseph Albright paints a highly critical portrait of the vice president in *What Makes Spiro Run* (1972). More balanced examinations of Agnew can be found in Theo Lippman, *Spiro Agnew's America*, and Jules Witcover, *White Knight: The Rise of Spiro Agnew* (both 1972). Agnew's controversial relationship with the press is addressed in John R. Coyne, Jr., *The Impudent Snobs: Agnew vs. the Intellectual Establishment* (1972), and the best account of Agnew's fall from grace is in Richard M. Cohen and Jules Witcover, *A Heartbeat Away: The Investigation and Resignation of Vice President Spiro T. Agnew* (1974). Obituaries are in the *New York Times* and *Washington Post* (both 19 Sept. 1996).

CARYN E. NEUMANN

AIKEN, George David (*b.* 20 August 1892 in Dummerston, Vermont; *d.* 19 November 1984 in Montpelier, Vermont), U.S. senator from Vermont from 1941 to 1975 who was one of the leading opponents of U.S. intervention in Southeast Asia.

Aiken was the son of Edward Webster Aiken, a farmer, and Myra Cook. Shortly after his birth, the family moved to Putney, Vermont, where Aiken attended school. There he graduated from Brattleboro High School in 1909, ending his formal education. In 1912, at the age of twenty, Aiken and a friend borrowed $100 to purchase land for planting raspberries. A few years later, he increased the parcel to 500 acres that included a nursery. Aiken's interest in cultivation remained throughout his life, and was reflected in his sponsorship and support for legislation regarding farms and agriculture.

Before entering politics, Aiken served for seventeen years as the school director for the town of Putney. His first attempt at election to Vermont's house of representatives in 1922 failed, but he ran again for the same position and was elected in 1930. Three years later, he became speaker of the state house of representatives. Elected lieutenant governor of Vermont in 1935, Aiken later won election as the state's governor, a position he held from 1937 to 1941.

Aiken was elected U.S. Senator from Vermont in 1941, and remained in the Senate until his retirement in 1975. Throughout his time in the Senate, Aiken was a member of the Agriculture and Forestry Committee, and in 1954, he gave up thirteen years of seniority on the Labor and Public Welfare Committee in order to fill a vacancy on the Foreign Relations Committee. Had he not done so, the seat would have gone to Senator Joseph McCarthy of Wisconsin, for whom Aiken did not attempt to hide his distaste. By the 1960s, Aiken had become a most vocal and respected member of this committee. In 1958 Aiken became chair of the Subcommittee on Canada, a position he held until his

Senator George Aiken, conducting a speech in which he insited that U.S. involvement in Vietnam was undermining credibility abroad, 1968. © BETTMANN/CORBIS

retirement, and in 1959, he was appointed to the Joint Committee on Atomic Energy.

Although he represented a small rural state, Aiken was an internationalist who supported the notion of the United Nations (UN) as a peacekeeping organization. In 1960, President Dwight D. Eisenhower appointed him delegate to the fifteenth session of the UN General Assembly. Ten years later, President Richard M. Nixon appointed Aiken to the President's Commission for the Observance of the Twenty-fifth Anniversary of the United Nations.

Aiken believed that U.S. foreign policy should be formulated in conjunction with Congress and the executive branch. In 1968 he voted for Senator J. William Fulbright's resolution that required the president to seek consent from Congress before making "national commitments" to other nations. Aiken also believed that foreign policy issues should be approached in a spirit of bipartisanship.

Consistent with this principle, Aiken supported President Lyndon B. Johnson, a Democrat, when he sent 20,000 troops to stabilize the government of the Dominican Republic in 1965. He believed that this action prevented bloodshed, protected U.S. investments, and stopped the spread of similar rebellions to other Caribbean and Latin American countries.

Likewise in the early 1960s Aiken supported Johnson's policy on the Vietnam War. In 1964 he voted for the Gulf of Tonkin resolution, which gave the president more power to increase U.S. troops in Vietnam. As the war escalated, however, Aiken became an opponent of Johnson on the issue of Southeast Asia. He later voted for the Cooper-Church Amendment, which called for a gradual withdrawal of U.S. troops from Vietnam.

In 1966 Aiken made his famous proclamation, "if a face-saving device was needed to pull out of the fighting, President Johnson should simply declare the United States the winner and begin de-escalation." Senate majority leader Mike Mansfield called Aiken the "wise old owl" as opposed to the "hawks who wanted victory in Vietnam and the doves who wanted to pull out of the region." Aiken supported President Richard M. Nixon's Vietnam policy of bombing Hanoi, which he hoped would quickly put an end to the war. When Nixon in 1973 negotiated a withdrawal from Vietnam, which eventually led to a Communist takeover of the country, Aiken noted: "What we got was essentially what I recommended six years ago—we said we had won, and we got out."

As the ranking Republican on the Agriculture and Forestry Committee, Aiken in 1965 introduced the Aiken Rural Water and Sewer Act, which provided federal assistance for rural water and sewage systems. Among his other agriculture legislation was the Talmadge-Aiken Act, adopted in 1962, which coordinated federal and state laws dealing with the flow of farm products to consumers. This law was expanded in 1967 to include meat products. Aiken also continually promoted rural electrification in Vermont. He was a great supporter of the Vermont Electric Co-op, and helped place the Vermont Yankee Nuclear Power Plant in Vernon in 1972.

Aiken admired President Johnson's social programs and his fight against poverty. In 1964, he helped sponsor the Food Stamp Act, a program he had hoped to make permanent three decades earlier when it was first introduced by the administration of President Franklin D. Roosevelt during the period from 1939 to 1943. Johnson also turned to Aiken in the writing of a compromise to the 1964 Civil Rights Bill, when the longest filibuster in Senate history threatened to prevent the enaction of the most far-reaching civil rights legislation passed since the Reconstruction. Aiken's contribution to the public accommodation section, which was known as the "Mrs. Murphy's Boarding House," because Aiken insisted that small businesses (like "Mrs. Murphy's boarding house") remain exempt from federal regulation, helped in the passage of this bill.

Aiken ran for his last term as senator in 1968, and during that final stint on Capitol Hill, he supported Nixon throughout the Watergate scandal. His last term was noted for his environmentalist legislation, including sponsorship of the Eastern Wilderness Areas Act in 1974.

From 1914 until her death in 1966, Aiken was married to Beatrice Howard, with whom he had four children, including a son who was killed in a 1959 plane crash. He married Lola Pierotti, his longtime administrative assistant, in 1967. Books by Aiken include *Pioneering with Fruits and Berries* (1936), *Speaking from Vermont* (1938), *Pioneering with Wildflowers* (1968), and *Aiken: Senate Diary, January 1972–January 1975* (1976).

★

A collection of Aiken's papers is at the Bailey/Howe Library at the University of Vermont at Burlington, Vermont. An informative source on Aiken's last term in the Senate is his own *Aiken: Senate Diary, January 1972–January 1975* (1976). Twenty-four interviews with Aiken recorded from 1975 to 1980 are part of an oral history collection at the Bailey/Howe Library at the University of Vermont. An obituary is in the *New York Times* (20 Nov. 1984).

MARGALIT SUSSER

Alvin Ailey. THE LIBRARY OF CONGRESS

AILEY, Alvin (*b.* 5 January 1931 in Rogers, Texas; *d.* 1 December 1989 in New York City), African-American choreographer, modern dance innovator, and founder of the Alvin Ailey American Dance Theater.

Ailey was born to Alvin Ailey and Lula Elizabeth Cliff Cooper, and grew up picking cotton in rural southern Texas. His father left when Ailey was six months old. Ailey later considered the poverty and racism of 1930s Texas "an enormous stain" on his life. The rousing spirituals he heard in the region's Baptist churches, and the blues he listened to in its nightclubs, influenced Ailey in a more positive way. Ailey was twelve when he and his mother moved to Los Angeles, where he saw performances by Billie Holiday, Duke Ellington, the Ballet Russe de Monte Carlo, and dancer Katherine Dunham's revues *Tropics* and *Le Jazz Hot.* Years later, he met and collaborated with Ellington on *My People* and *The River,* and dedicated the dance *Pas de Duke* to him. He also restaged one of Dunham's revues with his own company. His mother married in 1945 and Ailey's stepbrother, Calvin, was born in 1953.

Ailey began studying modern dance at age eighteen with modern dance pioneer Lester Horton, whose integrated dance troupe was a rarity in its day. From Horton, Ailey learned a wide range of dance forms, including Japanese theater and Native American dances. When Horton died in 1953, Ailey took over the company, but his nontraditional education influenced him to develop his own dance style. Ailey's first choreographed pieces were *Afternoon Blues* in 1953, *According to St. Francis* (a tribute to Horton), *La Creation du Monde* (Creation of the World), and *Mourning Morning,* all in 1954.

Ailey danced in local nightclubs as part of the duo "Al and Rita" with fellow dance student Marguerite Angelos, who later achieved fame as the poet Maya Angelou. He became fascinated with the entire theatrical presentation of the dance—the music, costumes, lights, and themes. He studied languages in college at the University of California at Los Angeles (1949 to 1950), Los Angeles City College (1950 to 1951), and San Francisco State College (1952 to 1953), but dropped out to pursue dance in New York City. There, Ailey studied dance with modern dance legend

Martha Graham, as well as Hanya Holm and Karel Shook. He appeared with Dorothy Dandridge in the film *Carmen Jones* (1954). He also performed with Harry Belafonte in *Sing, Man, Sing* (1956), and with Lena Horne in *Jamaica* (1957), and acted in plays, including *Carefree Tree* (1955), and the short-lived Broadway production *Tiger, Tiger, Burning Bright* (1962).

Ailey struggled to put together his own troupe, Alvin Ailey American Dance Theater (AAADT), which rehearsed wherever it could. His inaugural concert, featuring all Ailey originals, took place on 30 March 1958, and his *Ode and Homage, Redonda,* and *Blues Suite* won enthusiastic approval from the audience. Ailey danced his own *Ariette Oubliee* to Debussy music in a second concert that year. In his third concert, he unveiled *Revelations,* which remained a cornerstone dance for his troupe more than forty years later. The Ailey company of the 1950s and 1960s included many of Horton's former students. Ailey also choreographed pieces for other companies: *Feast of Ashes* for the Joffrey Ballet, three pieces for the Harkness ballet, and *Anthony and Cleopatra* for the Metropolitan Opera at Lincoln Center in New York City.

Revelations debuted in 1960 and was the product of endless research, countless hours of listening to music, and extensive soul-searching for Ailey. He recalled sleepy Sundays in church with his mother. The dance is built around spirituals sung by a live choir, including "I Been 'Buked, I Been Scorned," and follows a chronological flow of sorts. It is simple, direct, and powerful. The opening segment features the dancers dressed in simple, earth-tone costumes, signifying sorrow and a sense of rootedness in the soil. The opening stance, with a group of dancers close together, arms stretched to the sky, is among the most memorable in modern dance. It exemplifies the plainness and simplicity that gave Ailey's work an air of truth. The second section represents baptism, and dancers in pure white and blue tones. Ailey re-created onstage his own baptism, which had taken place in a snake-infested pond behind a church in his hometown. The final scene echoes the energy of a gospel church, with bright yellows and browns, the women carrying small fans. It has been said that more people have seen *Revelations* than any other ballet created in the twentieth century.

After two years of "station wagon tours," as Ailey called them, AAADT made a home for itself in a New York City YWCA in 1960. The troupe and its supporters converted the space into a 450-seat theater, rehearsal space, and costume house. It was called Clark Center for Performing Arts after the family that had donated funds to the renovation. At the Clark Center, Ailey found complete acceptance for what he was—an African American, a homosexual, and an incredibly talented and inspired artist. The place became a friendly hangout for African-American theater performers, dancers, and musicians. Six dancers filled the small stage

for the first performance in November 1960, which included Lester Horton's *Beloved* and *Revelations.* Ailey was known for producing works by little-known choreographers, many of whom were competitive with him. He believed strongly that the work of choreographers who lacked their own companies would likely be lost without an effort to preserve those pieces, and that modern dance needed a living repository of both its classic and lesser-known dances.

Ailey's vision of what dance should be—"a popular form, wrenched from the hands of the elite"—appealed to increasingly larger audiences, although he always felt he had to make an extra effort to attract African Americans to the theater. He once estimated that only 20 percent of his audiences were black. He made a "social and political statement" with his primarily black dance troupe, as African Americans were not accepted in most other classical or concert dance companies. In the more militant 1960s, however, he was criticized for allowing whites and Asians to dance with his company.

The troupe found a more receptive audience in Europe, where it was met with hour-long standing ovations. Fueled in part by the universal popularity of the music in *Revelations,* the U.S. State Department invited the Ailey company to perform on an extensive and highly acclaimed 1962 tour of Southeast Asia, Ailey's first trip abroad. AAADT's international destinations also included Brazil and Africa, and, in 1970, Ailey's became the first American troupe to tour the Soviet Union.

Ailey managed the troupe's cash-strapped operations while dancing and choreographing, often disbanding the company when finances ran out, only to regroup. He lost dancers after every show because, he said, even faithful performers need to eat. Ailey constantly had to worry about money, and this, he felt, limited him artistically. He wanted the best in designers, music, and rehearsal spaces, and wanted to keep his dancers happy. It confounded him that the bulk of contributions went to classical ballet troupes.

In 1965 Ailey left the dancing to his dancers and the running of the business to a team of devoted supporters while he narrowed his focus to concentrate solely on choreography. By this time, the Ailey family included the dance theater, its training company, the Alvin Ailey Repertory Ensemble, and the Alvin Ailey American Dance Center. Dancer Judith Jamison joined the troupe in 1965, danced for fifteen years, then took over as artistic director.

Given to fits of temper and passionate outbursts, Ailey was notoriously difficult to work with. "I sacrifice everything to stay in dance," he wrote in his autobiography, and he expected those around him to do the same. He hired dancers who were temperamental, too, because he preferred their instincts and expressiveness. He chose round, full women along with the typical long, lean dancers, but detested the blank faces and cookie-cutter bodies that were the preference and trademark of the legendary ballet choreographer George Balanchine. "Come dancers," he would say as his dancers gathered around him the first day of a rehearsal for a new piece, to hear his ideas. His rehearsals were as much about acting as dancing, a method which took some getting used to.

Revelations launched a decade that was filled with a whirlwind of events and achievements for Ailey. He performed lead roles off and on Broadway, appeared with his company at the two most prestigious American dance festivals, and toured the world. He choreographed sixteen dances in the 1960s, including *Quintet* and the raw *Masekela Langage,* the latter about South African trumpet player Hugh Masekela, who was exiled for criticizing apartheid. The troupe performed at the White House for President Lyndon B. Johnson in 1968. Ailey choreographed *The River* for the American Ballet Theatre in 1970. His famous *Cry,* which was a birthday present to his mother and a tribute to all black women, debuted in 1971, and became an instant classic. He watched his company grow in size and prestige, even as it often mirrored the complexities of race issues in the United States.

The late 1970s saw the deaths of many of Ailey's close friends, including Duke Ellington and former Horton dancer Joyce Trisler. Ailey turned to drugs and was hospitalized for depression. He cleaned up his life, continued to choreograph, and kept the company together. By 1984, when Ailey and the troupe celebrated their twenty-fifth anniversary at the New York City Center, the Alvin Ailey Dance Theater had performed before some 15 million people in 44 countries on 6 continents. Ailey died of complications from AIDS, and is buried at Rose Hills Memorial Park in Whittier, California.

★

Writings on Ailey include his own *Revelations: The Autobiography of Alvin Ailey* (1995), as well as Jack Mitchell, *Alvin Ailey American Dance Theater* (1993), and Jennifer Dunning, *Alvin Ailey: A Life in Dance* (1996).

BRENNA SANCHEZ

AL-MIN, Jamil Abdullah. *See* Brown, Hubert Gerold.

ALBEE, Edward Franklin, III (*b.* 12 March 1928 in Virginia), Pulitzer Prize–winning playwright whose controversial work during the 1960s was both celebrated for its intensity and originality and reviled for its honest, graphic nature.

Albee, born somewhere in Virginia, was adopted by Reed Albee, the owner of the Keith-Albee chain of vaudeville theaters, and Frances Cotter. He grew up in Westchester County, New York, a pampered only child whose every wish was indulged. There was little communication with

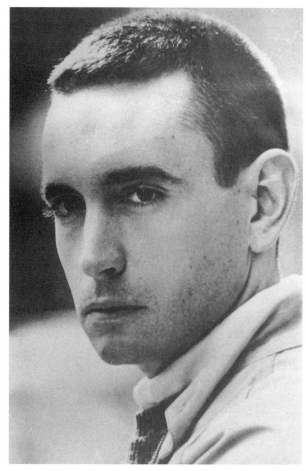

Edward Albee. THE LIBRARY OF CONGRESS

his parents; his domineering mother, when angry, reminded him he was adopted. A loner, Albee grew up with a beloved governess and other parental surrogates, including his maternal grandmother.

Albee's first theatrical experiments were with a young playmate who tied him up with imaginary ropes during one of their improvisations; his terrified screams brought both children's nannies running. Albee and his nanny were often driven by the family chauffeur into New York City to catch Broadway matinees. Albee wrote his first play, a three-act sex farce called *Aliqueen,* at age twelve. His parents' winter trips to the South interrupted Albee's primary schooling, and he became a troublesome student who was expelled from two private boarding schools before graduating in 1948 from the Choate School in Wallingford, Connecticut.

Choate was Albee's first intellectual home, and he became a prolific poet there. At age seventeen he wrote his first novel, *The Flesh of Unbelievers,* and his first professional publication, a poem, appeared in the Texas monthly *Kaleidograph.* After three halfhearted semesters at Trinity College in Hartford, Connecticut, Albee ended his formal education, becoming one of many contemporary playwrights who lacked a college education but were known for their brilliant dialogue.

Albee's paternal grandmother left him a small trust fund when she died in 1949, and Albee used this money to leave his parents' home and move to New York City's Greenwich Village. He then traveled to Italy, where he wrote a novel. He met the poet W. H. Auden in New York and the novelist and playwright Thornton Wilder, who encouraged him to write plays, in New Hampshire. Albee started furiously writing plays, many of which were never published or produced. His personal history figured strongly in most of the story lines. Albee, an admitted homosexual from the age of thirteen, was once engaged, but never married or had children. He lived with the composer William Flanagan from 1952 to 1959, and Jonathan Thomas, a Canadian sculptor, from 1971. He also had significant relationships with the playwright Terrence McNally and the decorator William Pennington.

As Albee's thirtieth birthday approached, he felt intensely dissatisfied. In February 1958 he quit his messenger job with Western Union—taking plenty of paper and a typewriter with him—and wrote *The Zoo Story* in just three weeks. *The Zoo Story* is a searingly confessional and darkly humorous exchange between a disturbed outcast and a conventional, middle-class family man. With this work, Albee transcended the artificiality that marked his previous plays and achieved a new level of intense realism. Unable to find a U.S. producer for *The Zoo Story*, Albee premiered the work in Berlin in 1959. It debuted off Broadway in New York City in 1960, when theater in the United States was beginning to examine a seamier and more graphic slice of American culture and values. Albee's *The Sandbox, The Death of Bessie Smith, Fam and Yam,* and *The American Dream* were all produced in 1960 and 1961. Some critics identified Albee with the "theater of the absurd" (avant-garde theater made up of pointless scenes meant to express isolation and frustration), although he considered the characterization absurd.

Albee's first full-length play, *Who's Afraid of Virginia Woolf?* (1962), is about two couples—one older and mutually abusive, one younger—who come together in a harrowing, drunken, late-night journey into truth and illusion. It debuted on Broadway and earned the Tony Award and the New York Drama Critics Circle Prize as best play of the year. Audiences both laughed and gasped at the play's passion and maliciousness. In one of many controversies surrounding *Who's Afraid of Virginia Woolf?,* which some considered a "filthy" play, Albee was denied a Pulitzer Prize for drama by a censorious Pulitzer board. The film version of *Who's Afraid of Virginia Woolf?* (1966) was as groundbreaking as the stage play and won several Academy Awards. It proved to be a cornerstone in the careers of the first-time director Mike Nichols and the actors Richard Burton, Elizabeth Taylor, George Segal, and Sandy Dennis. Although Albee was not involved with the production, he was relieved to find that the screenplay was true to his play.

By 1963 Albee was the most acclaimed young playwright in the United States. He was featured on the cover of *Newsweek* as the "Odd Man In." By the mid-1960s he was second only to William Shakespeare on the list of the most frequently performed playwrights in college theaters. Albee continued to experiment. His adaptation for Broadway of Carson McCullers's *The Ballad of the Sad Cafe* (1963) was his first such effort and received only lukewarm reviews. *Tiny Alice* (1964), Albee's highly anticipated second full-length, original play, was produced on Broadway and became his problem play. It was questioned endlessly, and even Albee could not satisfactorily explain the play's meaning and intention.

Malcolm, another adaptation, and *A Delicate Balance* were both on Broadway in 1966. *Malcolm* was a disaster, but *A Delicate Balance* was one of Albee's best plays and earned him his first Pulitzer Prize. He reworked Giles Cooper's *Everything in the Garden* (1967) into a suburban tale of a woman who is offered a job as a prostitute when she and her husband are down on their luck. Next in line were two interrelated plays, *Box* and *Quotations from Chairman Mao Tse-Tung* (1968), which were his most abstract works.

Albee's influence on American theater during the 1960s resulted in a shift from the gay and optimistic productions of the 1950s. He was a pioneer of a new and sometimes disturbing vérité that took hold of American playwrights of the era, and remains evident in contemporary theater. Although he never repeated the success of *Who's Afraid of Virginia Woolf?,* Albee never stopped writing plays as he pleased and endured critical buffeting. He won two more Pulitzer Prizes, for *Seascape* (1975), and *Three Tall Women* (1994). Of all of his autobiographical story lines, none was as personal as *Three Tall Women,* written after his mother's death in 1989 about their troubled relationship. Albee lectured, taught playwriting, and served as the head of the U.S. chapter of the International Theater Institute. In 1993 a good number of his plays, including several premieres, were staged in New York City, including a year-long festival of his work. Forty years after his first great success, Albee was once again the toast of Broadway, as his *The Goat, or Who Is Sylvia?* won the Tony Award for best play of 2002.

★

Biographies of Albee include Ruby Cohn, *Edward Albee* (1969), and Mel Gussow, *Edward Albee: A Singular Journey* (1999). Reviews include Brooks Atkinson, "Theatre: A Double Bill Off Broadway," *New York Times* (15 Jan. 1960); Thomas Lask, "Dramatist in a Troubled World," *New York Times* (22 Jan. 1961); Howard Taubman, "Theatre: Intense Hour," *New York*

Times (2 Mar. 1961); "The Theater: Albee's 'Who's Afraid,'" *New York Times* (15 Oct. 1962); Peter Kihss, "Albee Wins Pulitzer Prize; Malamud Novel Is Chosen," *New York Times* (2 May 1967); Mel Gussgow, "Edward Albee, Elder Statesman, Is in a State of Professional Reprise," *New York Times* (1 Dec. 1993); and Steven Drukman, "Edward Albee: Who's Afraid of Controversy? Not This Playwright," *Interview* (Mar. 2002).

BRENNA SANCHEZ

ALI, Muhammad (Cassius Clay)   (*b.* 17 January 1942 in Louisville, Kentucky), three-time heavyweight champion boxer, Olympic gold medalist, and outspoken champion of African-American rights who risked jail for his antiwar beliefs and brought the political controversies of the 1960s into the sporting arena.

Born Cassius Marcellus Clay, Jr., one of two sons of Cassius Clay, a sign painter, and Odessa Grady, a household domestic worker, Ali grew up amid the racial discrimination then ubiquitous in the southern United States. Ali graduated from DuValle Junior High School and Central High School in Louisville. A poor student, he began boxing as a teenager and found in the sport an outlet for his physical energy as well as an arena for his extrovert personality. Ali won 100 bouts as an amateur, two National Golden Gloves championships, and two American Athletic Union championships. At the 1960 Olympic Games in Rome, he won

Muhammad Ali. CORBIS CORPORATION (BELLEVUE)

the gold medal in the Light Heavyweight Division and turned professional soon thereafter.

Between 1960 and 1964, under the training of Angelo Dundee, Ali barnstormed the United States, winning a reputation as an agile, if unorthodox, fighter and a boastful big-mouth who ballyhooed his matches with predictions and rhymes. Inspired by the professional wrestler Gorgeous George, he dubbed himself "The Greatest." Ali's verbal wit, vibrant personality, and clean-cut good looks made him ideal television material, and at this stage he was welcomed by members of the boxing establishment concerned with the sport's sleazy, old-fashioned image.

Unbeknownst to them, this promising heavyweight contender was growing more impatient with American racism. As Ali later explained, "I won a gold medal representing the United States at the Olympic Games, and when I came home to Louisville, I still got treated like a nigger."

In 1961 or 1962, Ali came into contact with the Nation of Islam, popularly known as the "Black Muslims," the longest-established and most well-known Black Nationalist organization in the United States. As a separatist group that rejected white society, the Nation of Islam was reviled by whites and many African Americans, including the leadership of the civil rights movement. The young boxer kept his links to the organization secret for more than two years. During this period he formed a friendship with Malcolm X, who was among the first to grasp that Ali was more than a clown, that he represented a new type of African-American sports star with a new relationship to his people.

Ali's antics helped win him a shot at the World Heavyweight Championship, then held by the fearsome Sonny Liston. In the run-up to the fight, the underdog Ali spent time in private with Malcolm X, then under suspension by Elijah Muhammad, the Nation's Supreme Minister, for his caustic remarks on the Kennedy assassination. Rumors of Ali's association with Malcolm X and the Nation nearly led to the cancellation of the fight, which was held in Miami on 25 February 1964. In the end, Ali shocked the pundits by dominating Liston from the outset, dancing and jabbing his way to the title at the age of twenty-two. That night he spent a quiet evening with a select group of friends—including Malcolm X, the singer Sam Cooke, and the football player Jim Brown—and the following day informed the press that he was a member of the Nation of Islam. Citing the violence unleashed against African-American civil rights protesters in the South, Ali announced: "I'm not a Christian anymore. I know where I'm going and I know the truth, and I don't have to be what you want me to be. I'm free to be what I want." This announcement was a ground-breaking declaration of independence, personal and political, by a young African-American sports star, and it was greeted with nearly universal hostility by the mainstream media and the political and boxing establishments, a hostility that was to endure throughout the decade.

In the week following his victory over Liston, Ali and Malcolm X toured Harlem and visited the United Nations, where they made plans for a visit to Africa. On 6 March 1964 Elijah Muhammad awarded the new champion an "original name"—a great honor in the Nation of Islam—announcing that from now on he would be known as Muhammad Ali. Two days later, when Malcolm X made his public break with the Nation of Islam, the new heavyweight champion chose to remain with Elijah Muhammad, and denounced his former mentor and friend.

In 1964 it was considered provocative and eccentric for African Americans to adopt Islamic or African names, and Ali had to battle for many years to force the media to accept it. His commitment to the name and the identity it represented was deepened by his first trip to Africa in May and June 1964. Ali met Kwame Nkrumah, the anticolonialist revolutionary and president of Ghana, and Egyptian president Gamal Abdul Nasser, both stalwarts of the Non-Aligned Movement, and thus deeply suspect in the eyes of the U.S. State Department. For the first time, Ali heard his new name chanted by large crowds of poor people.

Back home, however, Ali was still regarded as a bad example to his people and his generation, and was regularly upbraided for his religious and political views. His second fight with Sonny Liston, held in Lewiston, Maine, on 25 May 1965, did little to improve his image. There was much controversy over the "phantom punch" that put Liston out in the first round. Ali's next fight, against former world champion Floyd Patterson, took on a highly politicized coloring after Patterson declared that he wanted to beat Ali in order to "take the title back for America." When the two met in the ring on 22 November 1965, a supremely confident Ali toyed with and taunted Patterson, shouting at him, "Come on, white America!" Sportswriters decried Ali's performance as mean-spirited.

These criticisms were merely a prelude to the avalanche of condemnation that was to break over Ali's head in 1966. Early that year, the Pentagon had expanded the draft, and as a result Ali was reclassified from "1-Y" to "1-A," thus becoming eligible for military service. Pressed by reporters for his response to the news, Ali declared on 17 February 1966: "I ain't got no quarrel with them Vietcong." Later that day, he explained his feelings to Robert Lipsyte of the *New York Times*: "I'm no longer a Cassius Clay, a Negro from Kentucky. I belong to the world, the black world. I'll always have a home in Pakistan, in Algeria, in Ethiopia. This is more than money."

Ali was denounced as a traitor and a coward, and under pressure from politicians and newspapers, promoters in state after state refused to stage his fights. He was forced to travel abroad—fighting in London (twice), Toronto,

and Frankfurt over the next few months—and in the process expanding his fan base outside the U.S. borders. Indeed, for most of his career, and certainly throughout the second half of the 1960s, Ali was far more popular abroad than at home.

In the seven title bouts he fought between February 1966 and his banishment from the ring in March 1967, Ali was at the peak of his form, combining speed, strength, power, and tactical guile. In this period he reached his height as a stylist in the ring, although his most dramatic and heroic fights were to come years later.

In late March 1967 Ali returned to Louisville to support a campaign for housing desegregation led by Dr. Martin Luther King, Jr., who had backed Ali's stand on the draft and cited him as a model for American youth. On 29 March 1967 Ali explained to reporters why he would not serve in the armed forces: "Why should they ask me to put on a uniform and go ten thousand miles from home and drop bombs and bullets on brown people in Vietnam while so-called Negro people in Louisville are treated like dogs and denied simple human rights? . . . [T]he real enemy of my people is right here."

On 28 April 1967, in Houston, Ali refused induction into the U.S. armed forces and was charged with violation of the Federal Selective Service Act. Boxing authorities immediately stripped Ali of his title and his license to fight. On 25 June he was tried, convicted, and sentenced to the maximum of five years imprisonment and a $10,000 fine. Ali was released on bail pending appeal and never served his jail sentence, but his passport was confiscated. Unable to travel abroad, unable to fight at home, Ali began a three-and-a-half-year exile from the ring, while his lawyers mounted a prolonged legal appeal.

During this period Ali supported his family by undertaking speaking engagements at colleges across the country. Bemused by his conservative homilies on sex and drugs, young people responded enthusiastically to his jokes and his denunciations of white racism and the war. Through the years of official opprobrium, Ali had been acquiring a huge army of grassroots supporters, both black and white. His symbolic centrality in the black insurgency of the era was illustrated in the 1968 Olympics in Mexico City, where African-American sprinters greeted the U.S. national anthem with Black Power salutes. Foremost among their demands—even before a boycott of apartheid South Africa—was the restoration of Ali's heavyweight title.

The rising tide of antiwar protest made it more difficult to jail Ali, who had become an icon of both the black and youth revolts. On 28 September 1970 a New York State court ordered the State Athletic Commission to restore Ali's boxing license. His conviction was finally quashed by the U.S. Supreme Court on 28 June 1971.

In Atlanta, on 26 October 1970, in his first comeback

fight, Ali defeated Jerry Quarry in front of a glittering audience of African-American celebrities. But on 8 March 1971 Ali suffered his first-ever professional defeat at the hands of the reigning heavyweight champion Joe Frazier. He then set about an arduous climb back to the top. Over the next three years he fought thirteen times (losing once, to Ken Norton), before his rematch with Frazier on 28 January 1974. This time Ali emerged the victor, setting up the classic confrontation with the new heavyweight champion George Foreman.

Known as the "Rumble in the Jungle," the fight was staged in Kinshasa, then Zaire (now once again the Democratic Republic of the Congo), under the aegis of the dictator Mobutu Sese Seko and the promoter Don King. Ali's return to Africa after his years of persecution and exile was emotionally charged, both for the fighter and his global legion of fans. Few gave the now thirty-two-year-old Ali any chance against the young power-puncher Foreman. But on 30 October 1974, in one of the greatest upsets in the history of modern sport, Ali knocked out Foreman in the eighth round to reclaim the heavyweight title of the world, seven and a half years after it had been taken away from him because of his political and religious beliefs.

Vindicated in the ring, Ali basked in a new popularity and respectability. With the end of the Vietnam War, and the retreat of African-American political activism, he seemed a less threatening figure. In 1975, in what was widely reported as a gesture of political, racial, and generational reconciliation, a laying to rest of the ghosts of the 1960s, Ali was finally invited to the White House by President Gerald R. Ford. Also that year, Ali was selected as the 1974 *Sports Illustrated* Sportsman of the Year.

Ali triumphed again in his third and final bout with Frazier, a punishing encounter on 30 September 1975 dubbed the "Thrilla' in Manila," but after that his powers declined. Ali lost the heavyweight title to Leon Spinks on 15 February 1978 and then regained the title for the third time in a rematch with Spinks in 1979. His attempted comebacks in 1980 and 1981 were disastrous, and took a heavy toll on his physique. Ali retired with a 56-5 record; his final bout was a loss to Trevor Berbick in 1981.

In the 1980s, Ali became ill with Parkinson's disease, which some speculate was induced by head trauma in the ring. He broke his remaining links with the family of Elijah Muhammad and converted to orthodox Sunni Islam. He reemerged as a public figure in the 1990s, disabled but still active in a variety of humanitarian causes. Ali is a United Nations Messenger of Peace and a spokesperson for the National Parkinson's Foundation, and has also worked for the Sisters of the Poor, UNICEF, and the campaign to cancel Third World debt. He lit the torch at the 1996 Atlanta Olympic Games, where he was presented with a replacement of his 1960 gold medal. *When We Were Kings:*

The True Story of the "Rumble in the Jungle," a documentary film of the Kinshasa fight, won an Academy Award for best feature documentary in 1997. In 2001 Ali's career was the subject of a big-budget Hollywood feature, *Ali,* starring Will Smith. Ali was inducted into the U.S. Olympic Hall of Fame in 1983, the Boxing Hall of Fame in 1987, and the International Boxing Hall of Fame in 1990. He remains one of the world's most widely known and well-liked celebrities.

Ali has been married four times: first to Sonji Roi (1964 to 1965), then to Belinda Boyd (1967 to 1976), Veronica Porche (1977 to 1986), and Yolanda "Lonnie" Williams (19 November 1986 to the present). Ali and Williams live at Ali Farm in Berrien Springs, Michigan. He has six children by his four marriages, as well as two other children whom he recognizes as his own.

In fusing the personal with the political, surreal humor with moral earnestness, popular culture with social criticism, Ali proved an archetypal 1960s figure. Adept at exploiting the electronic media, he projected to a mass audience radical ideas about African-American identity, about war and the role of the United States abroad, that only a few years before had been considered the preserve of an extremist minority.

★

Ali's official autobiography, *The Greatest: My Own Story* (1975), by Ali and Richard Durham, has inaccuracies, gaps, and some inventions; Ali's actual involvement in it was minimal. Biographies include Robert Lipsyte, *Free to be Muhammad Ali* (1978); David Remnick, *King of the World: Muhammad Ali and the Rise of an American Hero* (1998); and Thomas Hauser, *Muhammad Ali: His Life and Times* (1991), which remains the most comprehensive and reliable biography. Gerald Early, ed., *The Muhammad Ali Reader* (1998), collects articles by prominent writers from the early 1960s to the mid-1990s. Mike Marqusee, *Redemption Song: Muhammad Ali and the Spirit of the Sixties* (1999), analyzes Ali's political context and global impact.

MIKE MARQUSEE

ALLEN, Stephen Valentine Patrick William ("Steve") (*b.* 26 December 1921 in New York City; *d.* 30 October 2000 in Encino, California), comedian, writer, composer, lyricist, actor, concert artist, and lecturer who composed over 7,900 songs and was the author of fifty-four published books.

Allen was the son of Carroll Allen, who performed vaudeville under the stage name Billy Allen, and comedienne Isabelle Donohue, whose stage name was Belle Montrose Allen. Allen's father died before he was two, and Allen spent much of his childhood traveling with his mother from city to city. He attended seventeen different schools, ending up at Union High School in Phoenix, where his mother had taken him for the sake of his health. He was, he said later, "a pampered, sickly beanpole, too weak for athletics and too asthmatic for the army," but he loved writing, learned to play the piano by ear, and began to develop his remarkable talent for comedic ad-libbing.

In 1941 Allen enrolled at Drake University in Des Moines, Iowa, but as his asthma became worse he returned to Phoenix. After a brief spell at the State Teachers College of Arizona in Tempe, in 1942, he was offered an opportunity to work in the radio business. Allen worked at KOY radio in Phoenix as announcer, writer, pianist, and producer. He was drafted into the U.S. Army in 1943, but asthma continued to plague him, so he was discharged after only five months and returned to KOY. Here his ad-libbing skills became evident.

On 23 August 1943 Allen married Dorothy Goodman, whom he had met while attending the State Teachers College of Arizona. They had three children and divorced in 1952. That same year, Allen found himself at a dinner party seated next to actress Jayne Meadows, who, appalled by his gaping at her, said, "Mr. Allen, you're either the rudest man I ever met or the shyest." They married on 31 July 1954, and had one son.

In 1944 Allen moved to Los Angeles and continued his radio career. He joined the Hollywood station KNX in 1948 as a disc jockey with a midnight time slot, but his chat between records soon proved to be a bigger draw than the music. Allen expanded his comedic audience and transferred his ad-lib abilities to television. By 1954 he was working at the National Broadcasting Company (NBC), where he created and hosted the *Tonight Show*, which became the standard for late-night television comedy programs. He left the *Tonight Show* in 1956 in order to concentrate on the *Steve Allen Show* (which aired on NBC from 1956 to 1960), introducing talented new entertainers to prime-time television viewers.

By 1960 Allen had established himself as one of the top television and radio personalities in the United States. Although primarily known for his comedy, Allen introduced and helped make popular many of the famous comedians and entertainers of the 1960s: singers such as Andy Williams, Steve Lawrence, and Eydie Gorme, and comedians such as Louis Nye, Don Knotts, Tom Poston, Tim Conway, Steve Martin, and Jackie Mason. Allen was "hip" long before most Americans knew what the word meant.

After leaving the *Tonight Show,* Allen moved to the American Broadcasting Company (ABC) to do a syndicated show (the *Steve Allen Show*) from 1961 until 1964. He hosted *I've Got a Secret* for CBS from 1964 to 1967. From 1968 to 1972, with his wife Jayne Meadows, he did a syndicated version of the *Steve Allen Show* (CBS). He continued to campaign against coarse language on televi-

Steve Allen. ASSOCIATED PRESS AP

sion, blowing a whistle to drown out any mild epithet uttered on his shows, which at that time were primarily broadcast live.

Throughout his life Allen pursued his interest in writing, developing new concepts and ideas, and writing books that required the reader to think. His works include a novel, *Not All of Your Laughter, Not All of Your Tears* (1962), the nonfiction book *Letter to a Conservative* (1965), and the poetry collection *Flash of Swallows* (1969).

After the 1960s Allen continued his television career. Half talk show, half historical review, the Emmy-winning *Meeting of Minds* ran on the Public Broadcasting System (PBS) from 1977 to 1981. The show featured actors playing historical figures such as the Chinese revolutionary leader Sun Yat-sen, the political philosopher Machiavelli, and the poet Elizabeth Barrett Browning from their differing perspectives. They debated history and society, with Allen as moderator. Allen's later career also included several motion pictures, including *The Benny Goodman Story* (1955) and *The Sunshine Boys* (1975), in which he played a cameo role as himself.

In 1986 Allen was inducted into the Television Hall of Fame. In later years Allen backed the Parents Television Council, a watchdog group, by sponsoring advertisements urging broadcasters and parents to exercise responsibility.

He commented, "It saddens me that television, which was once wholesome, instructive and entertaining, has now become so vulgar and violent." Allen died of an apparent heart attack after carving pumpkins with his grandchildren, and is buried at Forest Lawn Hollywood Hills, in Los Angeles.

Known variously as "Mr. Midnight," television's "Renaissance Man," and "the thinking man's comic," Allen parlayed five decades in show business into a string of successes in almost every entertainment medium. His droll sense of humor, talent for improvisation, knack for patter, and style as an interviewer inspired the successful formula for numerous television talk shows. "He was an icon, an original," said comedian Milton Berle. Johnny Carson added, "He was a most creative innovator and brilliant entertainer."

★

Allen's autobiographies include *Mark It and Strike It* (1960) and *Hi-Ho Steverino!: My Adventures in the Wonderful Wacky World of TV* (1992). Articles about Allen are in *Time* (23 Nov. 1953), *America* (14 Nov. 1964), *Psychology Today* (Aug. 1982), and the *Los Angeles Times* (15 Apr. 1982 and 6 Oct. 1985). Obituaries are in the *New York Times, Washington Post, Chicago Tribune,* and *Los Angeles Times* (all 1 Nov. 2000), and the (London) *Times* (2 Nov. 2000). An oral history interview by Ronald Davis, "Reminiscences of Steve Allen," done on 18 November 1975 for the *New York Times* Oral History Program and Southern Methodist University Oral History Project on the Performing Arts, no. 96, is a good source for information about Allen's life in the entertainment business up to 1975.

JOAN GOODBODY

ALLEN, Woody (*b.* 1 December 1935 in Brooklyn, New York), prominent filmmaker who evolved during the 1960s from a stand-up comic and writer of humorous sketches to an actor, director, and writer of an ongoing body of film reflecting his unique vision of modern life in general and New York City in particular.

Allen was born Allen Stewart Konigsberg, the only child of Martin Konigsberg, a waiter and jewelry engraver, and Nettie Cherry, a housewife. His early passions included magic and card tricks, the clarinet (which he continues to play), movies, and sports. While a student at Brooklyn's Midwood High School (1949–1953), Allen sent jokes to columnists such as Earl Wilson and Walter Winchell, who paid him per joke and then attributed them to public personalities. This was also the period in which he dropped his birth name for "Woody Allen," a nickname given to him because he always brought the stick to neighborhood stickball games.

Allen was a notably poor student, both in high school

Woody Allen, 1967. THE KOBAL COLLECTION

and later during brief stints in 1953 at New York University and at City College (now the City University of New York). His early writing was deemed "dirty" by his high school teachers, and his mother was often called to the principal's office because of her son's truancy, bad marks, and habit of causing disturbances. New York University expelled him for poor marks, and he dropped out of City College.

In 1952, while still in high school, Allen had joined the National Broadcasting Company (NBC) as a staff writer. Two years later he married his childhood sweetheart, Harlene Rosen (they divorced in 1960), and left home to make a living from peddling one-liners and writing for a variety of television shows, including Sid Caesar's *Your Show of Shows* (1950–1954) on NBC, where Allen competed for attention with the likes of Mel Brooks and Neil Simon. The freewheeling atmosphere was not congenial to the characteristically shy Allen. He was in much more control working as a comedian in Greenwich Village nightclubs, where he began performing in 1960 and developed his comic persona as a bumbling, anxiety-ridden loser. Allen's bespectacled, sad countenance was a perfect match for his neurotic observations about life. His early models were Mort Sahl, a satiric commentator on the political scene, and Bob Hope, a joke teller with impeccable timing.

Allen peppered his stand-up routines with observations about how guilt-ridden he was. He would describe, for example, stealing second base in a ball game and then, overwhelmed by remorse, returning to first. Rather than working as a "stand-up" comic, Allen usually performed—like

Sahl—by sitting on a high stool and moving nervously from one bit of autobiographical confession to another. Many wrongly confused this persona, the "mask," with Allen himself. He was meticulous about his material, just as he was later meticulous about his films. Above all else, Allen the artist was in control, even if his character often seemed on the edge of a nervous breakdown.

Allen's comedy struck a chord that was just right for the early 1960s: hip, irreverent, and packing just enough psychic truth to make it interesting. If the tall tales of nineteenth-century American humor featured characters who were long on boast and brag, Allen's persona turned those exaggerated claims on their head. Instead of evoking a swaggering frontiersman who could outrun, outride, outshoot, and beat up any man in the house, Allen boasted that he was the weakest, most sensitive person on the planet. In addition, he was often characterized as a man who was the architect of his own misfortune in the mold of the classical schlemiel.

During the mid-1960s Allen began writing humorous sketches for *The New Yorker,* and a collection of those pieces appeared as *Getting Even* in 1971. Comic revenge was crisply parceled out to those who had bedeviled his childhood and early adolescence. A wide range of authority figures, from parents and teachers to the culture in general, was lambasted. Parody was one of Allen's favorite techniques because it allowed him to play against a recognizable target. In the lexicon of prizefighters, he was a counterpuncher—someone who waited for his opponent's punch and then nailed him with an unexpected right cross.

In 1964 Allen was discovered by the producer Charles Feldman and given a chance to write the screenplay for the film *What's New, Pussycat?* (1965). It is the story of a man who cannot stay faithful to the woman he loves and seems, in retrospect, the perfect fit for Allen's temperament and talent. The film marked Allen's acting debut, as a psychiatric patient, and further enhanced his growing reputation as an overly sensitive, screwed-up plant.

What's New, Pussycat? was a financial success, but Allen was not pleased with the finished project. The problem, largely the same one that had plagued his days as a staff writer for television shows, was control. In 1964 he acquired the rights to a dreadful Japanese spy film (*Dagi no Kagi*), reedited it, and dubbed in a sound track written and performed by himself, Louise Lasser (whom he married on 2 February 1966 and divorced in 1969), Frank Buxton, and Len Maxwell. The result may technically have been a collaborative effort, but its signature thumbprint was all Allen. In *What's Up, Tiger Lily?* (1966), written and performed by Mickey Rose, the quest is for *the* perfect egg-salad recipe. Over the ensuing years, the film became a cult classic and remains a lively, very funny example of Allen's early years as a filmmaker.

Much the same can be said of *Take the Money and Run* (1969), a mock documentary about Virgil Starkwell (played by Allen), a flop as a criminal. In one scene, Virgil hands a bank teller a note demanding money that ends with, "I have a gun." Unfortunately Virgil, ever the schlemiel, has such poor penmanship that the teller thinks he has written, "I have a gu*b*." In another scene, he fashions a gun from a bar of soap (shades of the legendary bank robber Willie Sutton) and is almost free, when a sudden downpour turns his fake gun into soapsuds. During the 1960s, Allen also wrote for the Broadway stage, with *Don't Drink the Water*, opening in 1966, and *Play It Again, Sam*, opening in 1969.

Allen's career as one of America's most impressive auteur filmmakers continued from the 1970s into the early 2000s, with a new film nearly every year. In terms of box office success, most were on the modest side—with the notable exception of *Annie Hall* (1977), which won an Academy Award for best picture. In the 1990s Allen's cinematic efforts were often overshadowed by drama in his personal life. His long-term relationship with the actress Mia Farrow, which produced a son in 1987, ended bitterly in 1992. He married Soon-Yi Previn, one of Farrow's adopted daughters, in 1997. In the new century, Allen continued to follow his own creative instincts and to exercise unparalleled control over his many artistic projects.

★

Useful books about Allen's life and career include: Bill Adler and Jeff Feinman, *Woody Allen: Clown Prince of American Humor* (1975); Eric Lax, *On Being Funny: Woody Allen and Comedy* (1975); Lee Guthrie, *Woody Allen: A Biography* (1978); and Foster Hirsch, *Love, Sex, Death, and the Meaning of Life: Woody Allen's Comedy* (1981).

SANFORD PINSKER

ALSOP, Joseph Wright, V (*b.* 10 October 1910 in Avon, Connecticut; *d.* 28 August 1989 in Washington, D.C.), journalist, author, and syndicated columnist whose conservative, anti-Communist writings during the Vietnam War cemented his reputation as an erudite political reporter.

Alsop was one of two sons of Joseph Wright Alsop, IV, an insurance executive, "gentlemen farmer," and member of the Connecticut General Assembly, and Corinne Douglas (Robinson) Alsop, who also served in the Connecticut General Assembly. He graduated from the Groton School in 1928 and from Harvard University with a B.A. in English literature in 1932. That same year Alsop obtained a job with the *New York Herald Tribune*. Three years later his coverage of the murder trial of the alleged kidnapper and killer of the infant son of the famous aviator Charles Lindbergh earned him a promotion to Washington, D.C., to cover national news stories.

Joseph Alsop. © BETTMANN/CORBIS

In Washington, Alsop was assigned to Capitol Hill, where he reported on the 1935 Nye Committee hearings, in which the committee investigated charges that the United States had been drawn into World War I by international arms merchants who stood to gain from increased weapons sales. He also covered the Franklin D. Roosevelt administration's 1937 "court-packing scheme" and wrote a book about the crisis, *The 168 Days* (1938), with Turner Catledge. Alsop left the *Tribune* in 1937 and, with Robert Kintner as his collaborator, wrote a syndicated column called "Capital Parade" for the North American Newspaper Alliance until 1940. In 1941 Alsop suspended his column to join the U.S. Navy as a lieutenant junior grade. He became an intelligence officer and was sent to Bombay, India, as a naval observer. Disappointed by what promised to be an unexciting and war-length tour of duty, Alsop arranged a transfer to China, where he joined the Flying Tigers, a volunteer air force led by Colonel (later General) Claire L. Chennault, as a "lend-lease administrator." Alsop served as a captain in the Fourteenth Air Force in China under Chennault from 1943 to 1945.

Alsop left China in August 1945; returned to the United States; and teamed up with his brother, Stewart, to revive his column for the *New York Herald Tribune* from 1946 to 1958. The title of the column, "Matter of Fact," was not chosen idly but rather reflected Alsop's belief, recounted in

his autobiography *I've Seen the Best of It*, that he was a "reporter first and foremost" and was therefore determined "never to write about overseas problems" unless he had "at least gone overseas myself for long enough to smell the weather in the streets." Consistent with this conviction, Alsop journeyed abroad regularly until he retired in 1974. From 1958 to 1974 Alsop worked for the *Los Angeles Times* syndicate. In 1950, for instance, he spent four months from July to October in Korea traveling with combat units. At various times over the next decade he reported from England, Taiwan, Thailand, Burma, Singapore, and the Soviet Union. He also went to Vietnam in 1953 and 1954, when the Viet Minh, a politico-military organization of nationalists and Communists aimed at liberating Vietnam, challenged French control. These two trips were his introduction to the Vietnam crisis that was to consume him for the next two decades.

Although he was a New Deal Democrat domestically, Alsop took an increasingly more conservative, anti-Communist stance abroad. He was an early advocate of using American troops to prevent a French defeat in Vietnam. After the French withdrawal from Vietnam in 1954, Alsop supported the employment of American forces to resist a Communist takeover in Southeast Asia. By the time President John F. Kennedy came into office in January 1961, the threat from the Vietcong, the Communist guerrilla forces of North Vietnam, was such that in Alsop's calculations, the prospect of America's "fighting a full scale" war in Vietnam "was by no means unthinkable."

Alsop's view of what was at stake in Southeast Asia was rooted in both ideology and geopolitics. In ideological terms, he envisioned the conflict in the region as one between totalitarian Communism and the democratic system of the West. From a geopolitical perspective, he favored a heightened U.S. presence in Vietnam to preserve America's place as a Pacific power. Alsop predicted that the Pacific was "due to become another great world lake on a par with the Atlantic." Given such deeply held assumptions, Alsop never wavered in his near-obsession that not only must America resist surrender in Vietnam, but it also must provide its fighting forces with the adequate military and popular support to assure at least a stalemate. In arguing thus, Alsop, like other pundits, underestimated the resilience and perseverance of the North Vietnamese in their pursuit of national unity.

Throughout the presidencies of Lyndon B. Johnson and Richard M. Nixon, Alsop used his column to prod the chief executives to greater effort in Vietnam. In June 1964, for example, Walter Lippmann, a respected and widely read columnist, urged Johnson to withdraw from Vietnam and the entire Asian mainland as "part of some much larger and more elaborate diplomatic proposal and action." Alsop saw the situation very differently. The president, he argued, "had the means to avert defeat" but seemed unable to muster the necessary resolve. In Alsop's estimation, however, Johnson "had no way out any longer, except to try to deal with the war crisis first," leaving other matters for later consideration. He urged Johnson, who was enraged by Alsop's hard-line hectoring, to recognize that "all that the American interest demands—and demands imperatively—is avoidance of defeat in the war, and this simply means prevention of a Communist takeover." He then warned Johnson in a 23 December 1964 *Herald* article that "if strong measures are not taken . . . the U.S. is almost certainly doomed to suffer the greatest defeat in American history." He went on to say, "Pearl Harbor, after all, was a mere episode, whose ultimate sequel was victory around the world, but defeat here will be both shattering and final," and "its character and its consequences will make it a bitter new experience for the United States." He concluded, with gloomy censoriousness, "It will be his [Johnson's] defeat."

Nixon was also the recipient of Alsop's unsolicited advice. In an article entitled "The Viet Cong Is Losing Its Grip," in the December 1968 issue of *Reader's Digest,* Alsop, after a month-long survey of conditions throughout South Vietnam, informed the newly elected president that the Tet offensive had been "a disaster for Hanoi" and the "real turning point" of the war. (The Tet offensive was a massive assault undertaken in 1968 by the North Vietnamese against cities in the South. It proved to be a military triumph for the North.) The Vietcong's "days are numbered," Alsop concluded, "unless President Nixon is finally driven to throw in the sponge." Three years later, with criticism of the war mounting, Alsop's position stiffened. He wrote, bitterly, in the *Washington Post* (29 Aug. 1971) that critics of the war were "downright eager to be proved right by an American defeat." Alsop, however, was backing a losing cause. The last of America's troops exited Vietnam in March 1973, and by early 1975 Hanoi had extended its control over all of South Vietnam.

Ground down by the "tragic" defeat in Vietnam and depressed by his separation from Susan Mary Jay Patten, whom he had married on 16 February 1961, Alsop decided to close down his column in December 1974. Alsop was a homosexual, and his marriage was a platonic social partnership. Alsop and Patten, who had no children, separated in 1973 and divorced in 1978. In retirement he remained active, publishing *The Rare Art Tradition* (1982) and *FDR—1882–1945: A Centenary Remembrance* (1982). An erudite and companionable host, he also continued to entertain friends, as he had for years, in his Washington, D.C., home. He died at home of complications from lung cancer, anemia, and emphysema.

Alsop's journalistic standing was compromised seriously by his intractable position on Vietnam—"the hinge," as David Marsh observed, "on which Alsop's reputation

swung." Still, over the course of his full career, Alsop's accomplishments were impressive. In particular, as is pointed out in his *Los Angeles Times* obituary, "he helped to invent the political column in its modern form." He did so by conscientious "foot-leather" journalism; skillful writing; and, as another reminiscence observes, "standards of independence and courage that set him apart" from his peers (*New Republic*). One suspects, then, with the perspective purchased by time, that Alsop will find his place among the leading journalists of the twentieth century.

★

Alsop's papers are in the Library of Congress, and the Special Collections Library at Boston University holds the papers of his brother, Stewart Alsop. Joseph Alsop and Adam Platt, *I've Seen the Best of It: Memoirs* (1992), presents Alsop's account of his life and career. Revealingly, the book closes with the assassination of President Kennedy. Joseph and Stewart Alsop, *The Reporter's Trade* (1958), is a collection of Alsop's views on journalism and reprints of his articles from the previous twelve years. Biographical information is in Leann Grabavoy Almquist, *Joseph Alsop and American Foreign Policy: Journalist as Advocate* (1993), and Edwin Yoder, *Joe Alsop's Cold War: A Study of Journalistic Influence and Intrigue* (1995). Robert W. Merry, *Taking on the World: Joseph and Stewart Alsop—Guardians of the Twentieth Century* (1996), is a dual biography of the brothers. Obituaries are in the *Washington Post, New York Times, Chicago Tribune,* and *Los Angeles Times* (all 29 Aug. 1989); the *Boston Globe* and *Daily Telegraph* (London) (both 30 Aug. 1989); and the *New Republic* (18 Sept. 1989).

RICHARD P. HARMOND

ALVAREZ, Luis Walter (*b.* 13 June 1911 in San Francisco, California; *d.* 1 September 1988 in Berkeley, California), experimental physicist who won the 1968 Nobel Prize for developing the liquid hydrogen bubble chamber and detecting new resonant states (short-lived subatomic particles occurring only in high-energy nuclear collisions) in particle physics.

Alvarez was one of four children born to Walter Clement Alvarez, a physician, and Harriet Skidmore (Smythe) Alvarez. He attended grammar school and the Polytechnic High School in San Francisco before his father accepted a position at the Mayo Clinic in Rochester, Minnesota. Alvarez graduated from Rochester High School in 1928. He initially attended the University of Chicago to study chemistry, but changed his major to physics, earning a B.S. in 1932, an M.S. in 1934, and a Ph.D. in 1936, all in physics. Alvarez married Geraldine Smithwick in 1937; they had two children and later divorced. On 28 December 1958 Alvarez married Janet L. Landis, with whom he had two children.

In 1936 Alvarez worked at the Ernest O. Lawrence Radiation Laboratory at the University of California, Berkeley,

Luis W. Alvarez. THE LIBRARY OF CONGRESS

and except for occasional and temporary stints at other laboratories, he spent the rest of his career there. He became a professor of physics in 1945, and served in that position until 1978, when he became a professor emeritus.

In 1937 Alvarez discovered that the capture of electrons by the nucleus (K-electron capture) is a beta-decay process and, with Robert Cornog, proved that the helium 3 isotope is stable, but the hydrogen 3 isotope is radioactive. Alvarez also made important contributions to the study of the spin dependence of nuclear forces, and he helped to produce the first mercury 198 lamp, a device developed by the Bureau of Standards into its present form as the universal standard of length for that particular wavelength of light. In 1939 he and Felix Bloch made the first measurement of the magnetic moment of the neutron, a characteristic of the strength and direction of the particle's magnetic field.

From 1940 to 1943 Alvarez worked at the Massachusetts Institute of Technology in Cambridge, Massachusetts, where he developed radar systems. His team created the VIXEN radar system for the airborne detection of submarines, a phased-array radar, the ground-controlled-approach (GCA) radar that allowed aircraft to land in poor visibility, as well as microwave beacons and linear antenna arrays. Alvarez received the 1946 Collier Trophy, the U.S. government's most prestigious aviation award, for these achievements.

Alvarez also worked on the atomic bomb project with Enrico Fermi at the metallurgical laboratory at the University of Chicago from 1943 to 1944, and in the explosives division at Los Alamos, New Mexico, from 1944 to 1945 on the Hiroshima project. He developed the detonators for the plutonium bomb, and flew as a scientific observer at both the Alamogordo and Hiroshima explosions.

After the end of World War II, Alvarez returned to Berkeley and designed the Berkeley forty-foot proton linear accelerator, completing it in 1947. He also invented the tandem electrostatic accelerator and devised the microtron for accelerating electrons. In 1951 Alvarez published the first suggestion for charge exchange acceleration that led to the development of the Tandem Van de Graaff accelerator.

In 1953 Alvarez met Donald Glaser, the inventor of the bubble chamber detector for particle physics, who in 1960 would win the Nobel Prize for physics. Alvarez built a massive (72 in [183 cm]) bubble chamber, eight times the size of the Berkeley chamber, containing liquid hydrogen harnessed to a proton synchrotron that generated particles. When the particles passed through the chamber they left a trail of ions, which triggered vaporization. The vapor trails (trails of bubbles) were recorded on cameras and analyzed using automatic scanning and measuring equipment developed by Alvarez. The data from these tests were stored on punch cards and submitted for computer analysis. The study of the trails as they curved under the effect of magnetic fields provided crucial information about the nature of the particles. Alvarez received the 1968 Nobel Prize in physics for this particle research.

The bubble chamber was used to discover a large number of new, short-lived particles, including the K (the first meson resonance) and the omega meson, discoveries that were crucial in the development of the eightfold way model of elementary particles, and subsequently the theory of quarks. The number of known elementary particles rose from about 30 to more than 100 during the 1960s, and Alvarez and his team are credited with discovering about half of the new ones.

Later in his life Alvarez devoted his time to a wide array of intellectual endeavors, including the study of cosmic rays using high-altitude balloons and superconductive magnets. He used cosmic rays to assist in the search for hidden chambers in the pyramids in Egypt, and he utilized shock wave technology to reexamine the evidence from the assassination of President John F. Kennedy in 1963. These episodes are described in his autobiography, *Alvarez: Adventures of a Physicist* (1987).

Alvarez held patents for more than thirty inventions, mainly in electronics and optics. Among his many awards were the Medal for Merit (1947), California Scientist of the Year for his work on high-energy physics (1960), Einstein Medal for his contribution to physical sciences (1961), Pioneer Award of the AIEEE (1963), National Medal of Science for contributions to high-energy physics (1964), and Michelson Award (1965). Alvarez's valuable contributions in fundamental physics, accelerator development, and radar technology are recognized in several branches of science.

Alvarez retired in 1978, but continued to lead an active life, regularly working in the laboratory. In 1980 he proposed, with his son Walter Alvarez, that unusually high levels of iridium at the boundary between Cretaceous and Tertiary rocks indicated a major meteor impact with Earth about 65 million years ago, and suggested that this might explain the mass extinction of the dinosaurs—a plausible but debated theory. Alvarez died at the age of seventy-seven at his home in Berkeley of complications from esophageal cancer.

★

Alvarez's autobiography is *Alvarez: Adventures of a Physicist* (1987). Biographical information is also in Peter W. Trower, ed., *Discovering Alvarez: Selected Works of Luis W. Alvarez, with Commentary by His Students and Colleagues* (1987), and Corinn Codye, *Luis W. Alvarez* (1989). See also Matt S. Meier, Conchita Franco Serri, and Richard A. Garcia, eds., *Notable Latino Americans: A Biographical Dictionary* (1997), and Kay Porter and Marilyn Ogilvie, eds., *The Biographical Dictionary of Scientists,* 3rd ed., vol. 1 (2000). Obituaries are in the *New York Times* (2 Sept. 1988) and the *Washington Post* (3 Sept. 1988).

MARIA PACHECO

ANDEL, Jay Van. *See* DeVos, Richard Marvin, and Jay Van Andel.

ANDREWS, Julie (*b.* 1 October 1935 in Walton-on-Thames, Surrey, England), singer and actress who, during the 1960s, became one of the biggest Broadway and Hollywood stars of all time but then suffered from upheavals in the film industry and changing public tastes.

Andrews was born Julia Elizabeth Wells, the elder of two children of Edward Wells, a teacher, and Barbara Morris Wells, a pianist. She was called "Julie" from birth and acquired the last name "Andrews" after her mother divorced her father to marry a vaudeville singer named Ted Andrews, and the girl joined her mother and stepfather's act. Gifted from an early age with a striking soprano voice, Andrews attended a professional children's school, then took voice lessons and studied with a governess until she was fifteen.

As a teenager Andrews's talent eclipsed her mother and stepfather's. She made her solo debut in 1947 in London and toured in vaudeville and pantomime. At almost nineteen, she was chosen as the lead for the New York production of *The Boy Friend* (1954), a musical that originated in London. After a year in that role, she was selected to play Eliza Doolittle in *My Fair Lady,* Alan Jay Lerner and Frederick Loewe's musical adaptation of George Bernard Shaw's *Pygmalion* (1916). During her two years in this musical (1956–1958), Andrews proved herself as an actress, moving with seeming ease from a cockney flower girl to a grand lady.

After marrying her childhood sweetheart, the theatrical designer Tony Walton, on 10 May 1959, Andrews starred as Guinevere in Lerner and Loewe's next production, *Cam-*

Julie Andrews *(right)* with Richard Burton in a 1967 performance of *Camelot.* CORBIS CORPORATION (BELLEVUE)

elot (1960–1962). Although this reworking of the Arthurian legend received slightly less glowing reviews than *My Fair Lady,* it brought success to its creators and stars, and Andrews was the darling of Broadway.

While appearing in stage productions, Andrews had ventured into television. She costarred with Bing Crosby in the television musical "High Tor" (1956), and she was picked by Richard Rodgers and Oscar Hammerstein II to star in their television version of "Cinderella" (1957). In 1962 Andrews teamed with her friend Carol Burnett for "Julie and Carol at Carnegie Hall," an hour of comedy and music that highlighted the contrast between the informal American comedienne and her "refined" English chum. Despite these successes and her theatrical fame, Andrews was not thought of as a natural for motion pictures, and all three of her Broadway roles went to other actresses when the plays were adapted for the large screen. The animation kingpin Walt Disney was not concerned with using established film stars, however, and after seeing *Camelot* he asked Andrews to take the title role in his live action/ animation amalgam *Mary Poppins* (1964). As an incentive, he asked Walton to serve as the film's production designer. The pair, who had just had a daughter in 1962, journeyed to California for the film, in which Andrews portrayed a stern yet fanciful English nanny who won the hearts of her charges (and the viewing public).

The role gained Andrews an Academy Award for best actress (rumored to have been accorded her partly in sympathy for the loss of the *My Fair Lady* movie lead to nonsinger Audrey Hepburn) and the leads in two other films. In *The Americanization of Emily* (1964), she had her first nonsinging role as a young Englishwoman in World War II who dates a coward in order to avoid heartbreak. The film's antiwar message delighted some viewers and confused others.

Andrews's talent was more prominently displayed in a film that echoed *Mary Poppins* in its wholesomeness and musicality, but became even more popular. For *The Sound of Music* (1965), director Robert Wise reworked Rodgers and Hammerstein's romantic musical play about nuns and Nazis in the Austrian Alps with scenic locations and added Andrews's forceful presence. The film made Andrews an eternal star—and typecast her as an optimistic virgin. *The Sound of Music* was the largest grossing film of all time for ten years, and proved one of Hollywood's most enduring musicals. It also proved one of the last.

Andrews's next films, although successful, were less well made and less popular. *Torn Curtain* and *Hawaii* (both 1966), drew on her dramatic abilities, but neither gave her a showy role. *Thoroughly Modern Millie* (1967), directed by George Roy Hill, returned Andrews to her musical-comedy roots as a Midwestern lass turned flapper in the 1920s; it also gave her a chance to perform with theatrical legends Beatrice Lillie and Carol Channing. Nevertheless, it revealed fissures in the film community. According to Andrews's biographer Robert Windeler, Hill wanted to make the film short and light, but was induced by his studio to inflate it into a "prestige" road show production.

Andrews's next two films also followed the prestige route—straight into bankruptcy. In the 1960s major studios began to embrace the blockbuster mentality, hoping to recuperate losses with big films that would, like *The Sound of Music,* make enough money to save whole corporations. To do the executives justice, it is hard to see how anyone could have predicted that public taste would turn away from big-budget musicals—and from Andrews. Nevertheless, the costly *Star!* (1968), in which Andrews played the writer Gertrude Lawrence, and *Darling Lili* (1970), in which she portrayed a fictitious singing spy in World War I, lost money.

Biographers are torn in accounting for this change in the public's affections. Some accounts suggest that viewers did not want to see the "pure" star of *The Sound of Music* play a real woman with feet of clay or a spy. Others argue that as moviegoers became more cynical, they turned against the wholesomeness Andrews and musicals seemed to represent. In any case, her association with the decade's most popular film harmed her future acting prospects, and Andrews retired temporarily from moviemaking.

She returned to film from time to time—mainly with the writer-director of *Darling Lili,* Blake Edwards, whom she had married on 12 November 1969, after divorcing Walton in 1968. The couple adopted two children, and Andrews became a stepmother to Edwards's two children from a previous marriage. Edwards tried to expand Andrews's persona by making films in which she appeared sexy and even bawdy. The most successful of these, *Victor/ Victoria* (1982), was transformed into a stage play, and Andrews found herself back on Broadway in 1995. Despite the loss of much of her singing voice after a throat operation in 1997, she continued to perform in occasional nonsinging roles in film and television.

Andrews never quite managed to move beyond her image of the 1960s, however. For good or ill, she would always be associated in the public mind with *Mary Poppins*'s "Spoonful of Sugar" and *The Sound of Music*'s "Favorite Things," with a perky sweetness that peaked and then quickly entered the realm of nostalgia during that decade of change.

★

Andrews has received surprisingly little serious coverage from biographers. Robert Windeler, *Julie Andrews: A Life on Stage and Screen* (1997), is the most comprehensive work, followed by Les Spindle, *Julie Andrews: A Bio-Bibliography* (1989). James Arntz and Thomas S. Wilson, *Julie Andrews* (1995), is mainly a picture book with extended captions. An example of the adoring press coverage of Andrews during her heyday in the 1960s is "The Now and Future Queen," *Time* (23 Dec. 1966). Also helpful is the Public Broadcasting Service *Great Performances* presentation "Julie Andrews: Back on Broadway" (1995).

TINKY "DAKOTA" WEISBLAT

ARBUS, Diane (*b.* 14 March 1923 in New York City; *d.* 26 July 1971 in New York City), photographer known for her spare and often startling portraiture who came into her own as an artist during the 1960s.

Born Diane Nemerov, Arbus was the daughter of David Irwin Nemerov and Gertrude "Buddy" Russek. She was raised in privilege in New York City, where her family owned and operated a well-known furrier and department-store chain. Her siblings included an older brother, Howard, who became a lauded poet, and a younger sister, Reneé, who become a noted sculptor.

Both parents were distant to their children, and a nanny tended both Arbus and her siblings during their childhood. Arbus was shy, and closest to her brother. She was educated at the Ethical Culture and Fieldston schools, where she developed an interest in art, first sketching, then studying oil painting and collage. She was also a voracious reader, as she would be her entire life. Her favorite books included *Alice in Wonderland,* gothic novels such as *Jane Eyre* and *Wuthering Heights,* as well as mythological tales.

She met Allan Franklin Arbus while they both worked at her family's store, and they reportedly instantly fell in love. Despite her parents' interventions and objections, they married on 10 April 1941, shortly after Arbus reached her eighteenth birthday. They eventually had two daughters, Doon and Amy. With the advent of World War II, Allan Arbus enlisted in the Signal Corps and was assigned to photography school. He shared what he was learning with his wife, before being shipped to Burma in 1944.

After Allan returned to the United States in the late 1940s, the couple decided to start a fashion photography studio. Although they shared duties, Diane was stylist for the sessions. The studio eventually expanded into advertising photography, with clients such as Maxwell House Coffee and General Electric.

Although successful, Arbus wished to further explore photography as art. She was given her independence to pursue art photography in about 1957, since Allan wanted to study acting. The Arbus's studio continued operations, and they agreed to remain partners. Her most influential teacher was Lisette Model, a photographer who challenged and encouraged her to explore so-called "freaks" as subjects for her portraits. Among her other mentors were Marvin Israel, Richard Avedon, and Walker Evans.

During the 1960s, the world of art experienced a movement away from fixed tradition. Certainly none of Arbus's

Diane Arbus. MR. STEPHEN FRANK

subject matter could be considered conventional. She plunged headlong into exploring the seamy side of life, and acknowledged her direct photographs of street people, dwarves, and transvestites as trophies or documents of her adventures. Arbus is often quoted as having said, "A photograph is a secret about a secret. The more it tells you, the less you know." From 1962 through 1967, she photographed nudes at naturist camps throughout New Jersey and Pennsylvania in hopes of publishing a book, but it was never released. Late in her career, she photographed residents in a home for the developmentally disabled. This book was released after her death.

The years between 1962 and 1964 are acknowledged to have been Arbus's most productive. She was awarded Guggenheim fellowships in 1963 and 1966 and continued to receive assignments from magazines such as *Esquire, New York, Nova,* and the *Sunday Times* (London) *Magazine.* It was on these assignments that Arbus photographed leaders of the decade, including F. Lee Bailey, Coretta Scott King, and Abbie Hoffman. With these more conventional subjects, she was said to have behaved "like the first paparazzi." The writer Norman Mailer once said "giving a camera to Diane Arbus is like putting a live grenade in the hands of a child." Throughout her adult life, Arbus had problems with depression. This was exacerbated by ongoing problems with hepatitis, which began in 1966. Also during this period Arbus was asked to participate in the Museum of Modern Art "New Documents" show, for which three of her photos were selected in 1965. Concerned about the photographs initially selected, she balked at inclusion in the exhibit. Ultimately the museum agreed to display more recent work with which she was satisfied. The 1967 exhibit included thirty pieces, and was recognized as the high point in her career.

In 1969 the Diane and Allan Arbus Studios closed, and the couple, although separated for years, formally divorced. Allan remarried and moved to California, where he continued to pursue an acting career. (His most popular role was that of Dr. Sidney Freedman in the television program *M*A*S*H*.)

Arbus taught and lectured at schools throughout the 1960s, including Cooper Union and Rhode Island School of Design. Her final residence was an artists' community known as Westbeth, where she had moved in January 1970. She committed suicide in her own apartment.

Arbus's photographs never failed to get a reaction. One reviewer likened the conflicting sensations to those experienced when passing an accident: the curious person is both compelled to look and revulsed at the same time. Her subject matter was often viewed as perverse because the subjects in her most confrontational photographs were people on society's fringes, but Arbus seemed to relish confrontation with anything approaching conformity or societal normalcy. Because she sought to capture people at their most intimate or revealing moments, Arbus was alternately praised for investing her subjects with dignity, and reviled for exploiting them. In retrospect, she has been hailed for her ability to capture psychologically telling images.

Arbus was productive in her short career. Much of her work was not shown or released until after her death, perhaps in large part because she rarely seemed sufficiently satisfied with her work, but also because her contribution to modern photography was not sufficiently appreciated until then. Her work was shown posthumously at various museums throughout the world. One of the first such retrospectives was mounted by the Museum of Modern Art in New York, and the exhibit eventually toured throughout the United States. Arbus was also the first American photographer to be selected for the Venice Biennale exhibit. Works by Arbus are in the permanent collections of the Museum of Modern Art, New York City, and the George Eastman House, Rochester, New York.

★

Biographical sources on Arbus include Patricia Bosworth, *Diane Arbus: A Biography* (1984). For autobiographical material see Diane Arbus, *Diane Arbus* (1972); and Diane Arbus, *Magazine Work*, Doon Arbus and Marvin Israel, eds. (1984); and Diane Arbus, *Untitled*, edited and designed by Doon Arbus and Yolanda Cuomo (1995). An article on Arbus is Hal Hinson, "Arbus in Wonderland," *The Atlantic Monthly* 254 (Nov. 1984): 129–130.

LINDA DAILEY PAULSON

ARENDT, Hannah (*b.* 14 October 1906 in Hannover, Germany; *d.* 4 December 1975 in New York City), political philosopher, professor, and author of *Eichmann in Jerusalem* (1963), an account and assessment of the trial of the Nazi leader.

Arendt was the only child of secular Jewish parents, Paul Arendt, an engineer, and Martha (Cohn) Arendt, a homemaker. At age fifteen Arendt entered the University of Berlin, studying classics and Christian theology. After two years she transferred to Marburg University, where she studied philosophy with the eminent philosopher Martin Heidegger. Two years later she moved to Heidelberg to study with Karl Jaspers, the existentialist philosopher. While studying with Jaspers she wrote her doctoral dissertation on the concept of love in St. Augustine's thought. She received her doctorate in 1928 at age twenty-two.

In 1930 she married Günther Stern, a Jewish philosopher, with whom she fled to Paris in 1933 when the German dictator Adolf Hitler came to power. In 1936 Arendt met Heinrich Blücher, a German political refugee. She and Stern were divorced in 1939, and she married Blücher in 1940. After the outbreak of war they were interned in a detention camp for enemy aliens. They escaped and fled to the United States in 1941.

Arendt became a U.S. citizen in 1951, the same year that saw the publication of *The Origins of Totalitarianism*, her first major political work. Widely praised, the book firmly established her reputation as a writer and scholar. The book

Hannah Arendt. AP/WIDE WORLD PHOTOS

analyzed the two major forms of twentieth-century totalitarianism, Nazism and Communism, and sought to establish their genesis in the anti-Semitism and imperialism of the nineteenth century.

Arendt had not previously succeeded in finding teaching positions at American universities, but the stature she achieved through her book's critical acclaim changed that. Over the next two decades she taught at the University of California, Berkeley, the University of Chicago, Brooklyn College, and Columbia, Northwestern, and Cornell Universities. In 1959 she became the first woman to attain a full professorship at Princeton University. In 1967 Arendt was named university professor of political philosophy at the New School for Social Research in New York City, a position she held until her death.

On Revolution, published in 1963, was a rethinking of the causes and results of modern revolutions, notably those in the United States and France. Generally well received, this book was eclipsed, however, by the publication of Arendt's most influential work, *Eichmann in Jerusalem: A Report on the Banality of Evil* (1963). In 1961 Arendt had accepted an assignment from the *New Yorker* to cover the trial in Jerusalem of Adolph Eichmann, accused of implementing the Nazi genocide of the Jews of Europe. Her coverage of the trial was serialized in the magazine and later expanded and published in book form.

Eichmann in Jerusalem was widely read and highly controversial. Many readers misinterpreted her thesis, thinking that by describing Eichmann as banal, Arendt meant he was normal, thus exonerating him. However, Arendt saw Eichmann as an illustration of the problem of a human being within a modern totalitarian system. Bruno Bettelheim, in the *New Republic*, pointed out that "because of her concentration on the injustice bred by totalitarianism, Arendt at times creates an ambiguity in the evaluation of guilt."

Jewish readers were particularly outraged by her criticism of the state of Israel, the Israeli prime minister David Ben-Gurion, and the Israeli attorney general Gideon Hausner, as well as her assessment that the Jews of Europe were complicit in their own slaughter during the Third Reich by passively marching to their deaths.

The Eichmann trial was widely perceived as a model of fairness and justice. Arendt took issue with that perception, delving into the nature of the judicial process and comparing the need for justice with the need for punishment.

Arendt herself asserted she was trying to calmly analyze the situation, to get beyond the emotions, even the hysteria, the trial evoked. She found that, far from being a monster of evil, Eichmann was simply a glorified clerk who was too morally stunted to perceive the impact of his actions. Those who wanted to focus on Eichmann as the principal creator of the Holocaust were disappointed in Arendt's assessment. But she held her ground, commenting, "If you kill a mon-

ster you can go to bed and sleep, for there aren't many of them. But if Eichmann was normality, then this is a far more dangerous situation."

The phrase that made her name something of a household word was "the banality of evil," which Arendt used to distinguish Eichmann's actions from a malevolent delight in murder. Rather, she believed, Eichmann arrived at his willing involvement in the Nazis' so-called final solution through a failure or absence of sound thinking and judgment.

During the last decade of her life, Arendt became increasingly concerned with thinking and judgment as political faculties, themes that had interested her throughout her career. Her projected trilogy, *The Life of the Mind*, was incomplete at the time of her death. The first two volumes, *Thinking* and *Willing*, were published posthumously in 1978. She had just begun work on the third volume, *Judging*, when she died. In 1982 her *Lectures on Kant's Political Philosophy* were published, delineating her reflections on political judgment.

Arendt was widely recognized for her achievements. She was awarded honorary degrees from Princeton, Dartmouth, Smith, Notre Dame, Yale, and the New School. In 1975 she became the first woman and the first U.S. citizen to be awarded Denmark's Sonning Prize for contributions to European civilization.

Arendt died in 1975 of a heart attack in her New York City apartment. Her ashes are buried at Bard College, New York City. A longtime friend said of her after her death, "There was a supreme relevance in what she had to say. Whether you thought her right or wrong, what she had to say was invariably important."

★

See Bhikhu Parkh, *Hannah Arendt and the Search for a New Political Philosophy* (1981), and Dana Villa, ed., *The Cambridge Companion to Hannah Arendt* (2000), for a deeper understanding of Arendt's political philosophy. Reviews of *Eichmann in Jerusalem* are in the *New York Times* (19 May 1963), the *Christian Science Monitor* (23 May 1963), the *New Republic* (15 June 1963), and *Commentary* (Sept. 1963). An obituary is in the *New York Times* (6 Dec. 1975).

NATALIE B. JALENAK

ARMSTRONG, Neil Alden (*b.* 5 August 1930 in Wapakoneta, Ohio), astronaut and commander of *Apollo 11* who became the first man to walk on the Moon on 20 July 1969.

Armstrong was the eldest of three sons born to Stephen Armstrong and Viola Engel. The family traveled extensively because Stephen Armstrong was an auditor of county records in Ohio, but settled in Wapakoneta when Armstrong was

Neil Armstrong.

the first to lock onto a craft in space, but a jet thruster malfunctioned after they had collared onto the rocket, and the two vehicles spun out of control for thirty minutes. "With extraordinary piloting skill," a NASA press release later maintained, Armstrong was able to detach *Gemini* from the rocket and regain pilot control. He and Scott were forced to abort the three-day mission little more than ten hours after liftoff, but they landed safely in the Pacific Ocean.

Most Americans were not privy to the extremely dangerous tasks the astronauts faced as they tried to secure U.S. superiority in space, but the stark reality hit home on 7 January 1967, when Virgil Grissom, Edward White, and Roger Chaffee died in a launch pad fire. In May 1968 Armstrong was test-piloting a jet-propelled moon-landing vehicle when he ejected only 200 feet from the ground, parachuting to safety as the vehicle crashed. On 11 and 12 October 1968, the U.S. program rebounded from these disasters and near-disasters with the successful launch of *Apollo 7,* followed by *Apollo 8, Apollo 9,* and *Apollo 10,* each of which accomplished ever more complex tasks, from sophisticated docking procedures to lunar orbits, in an effort to land a man on the Moon.

On 16 July 1969 a Saturn 5 rocket blasted off for a sixty-hour journey to the Moon. Aboard were Armstrong, the commander, lunar module pilot Edwin Aldrin, Jr., and command module pilot Michael Collins. After they were pulled into lunar orbit on 19 July, Armstrong and Aldrin entered their lunar module *Eagle* while Collins piloted the command module *Columbia.* On 20 July Armstrong and Aldrin unlocked the *Eagle* and descended toward the lunar surface. The original landing site was littered with enormous boulders, so Armstrong switched to the semimanual guide system and steered the module to a safer site in the Sea of Tranquility. He had twenty seconds worth of fuel left before an automatic abort would have eliminated the possibility of a landing.

Armstrong was dressed in a space suit that, with its electricity, water, oxygen, and two-way radios, weighed 350 pounds on Earth, but which was less than sixty pounds on the Moon. In this cumbersome suit, Armstrong emerged from the *Eagle,* slowly descended the ladder, and at 10:56 P.M., stepped onto the Moon's surface. With 600 million people watching and listening, he stated, "That's one small step for [a] man, one giant leap for mankind." Within the half-hour, Aldrin joined him for a moonwalk that lasted twenty-one hours and thirty-seven minutes. They set up television cameras and planted the U.S. flag on the Moon's surface, signifying to the world that Armstrong's one "small" step put the United States ahead of the Soviet Union in the race for superiority in space. The astronauts took photographs, collected soil and rock samples, and set up a solar wind collector, a seismic instrument, and a laser reflector. With each step, the astronauts seemed to bounce

thirteen. By the age of fourteen, Armstrong was flying from the Wapakoneta Airport (later renamed for him), and by sixteen he had earned his pilot's license. Armstrong graduated from Blume High School in Wapakoneta in 1947, and attended Purdue University in Indiana, where he studied aeronautical engineering. He left college to serve in the Korean War, during which he flew seventy-eight missions and was shot down twice, receiving the Air Medal and two Gold Stars. He completed his B.A. degree in aerospace engineering at Purdue in 1955, and in January 1956 married Janet Shearon, with whom he had two sons.

Also in 1956, Armstrong joined the National Advisory Committee for Aeronautics (NACA). In this capacity, he served as test pilot for supersonic F-100A, F-100C, F-101, F-104A, X-1B, X-5, F-105, 106, B-47, KC-135, and Paresev jets, and flew X-15s up to 4,000 miles per hour, forty miles high. He was also a pilot for the experimental Dynasoar, a craft designed to orbit Earth and reenter the atmosphere, landing like a plane.

In September 1962 Armstrong was accepted into the second team in the nation's new space program, the National Aeronautics and Space Administration (NASA), and became backup command pilot for the *Gemini V* mission. On 16 March 1966, Armstrong was the command pilot for the *Gemini VIII–Titan* mission. With copilot Major David R. Scott, he orbited Earth three times and captured a prearranged target, the Agena rocket. Armstrong and Scott were across the Moon's tan and gray, dusty surface, scarred and pitted with craters and boulders. They left a plaque that reads, "Here men from the plant Earth first set foot on the Moon—July 1969 A.D.—We came in peace for all mankind." As Armstrong implied with his first memorable words on the Moon, space exploration is not just the privilege or right of any one nation, but offers an extended sense of meaning for human beings, who living on a small planet, now have the possibility of forming extraterrestrial colonies. On 21 July Armstrong and Alden lifted off the Moon's surface to rendezvous with Collins, and on 22 July the *Columbia* blasted out of lunar orbit and headed for Earth. It splashed down in the Pacific Ocean on 24 July at 12:50 P.M., and the *Apollo 11* crew were picked up by the USS *Hornet*. President Richard M. Nixon greeted them, and as the 1960s came to a close, Armstrong and his crew were honored with parades and ceremonies around the United States and the world.

Armstrong went back to school to earn his M.A. degree in aerospace engineering at the University of Southern California in 1970. He worked for NASA until 1971 as deputy associate administrator for aeronautics. He then taught aeronautical engineering at the University of Cincinnati until 1979, and went on to serve as the chairman of the Presidential Advisory Committee for the Peace Corps (1971–1973) and chairman of computing technologies for Aviation, Inc. (1982–1992). He was a member of the National Commission on Space (1985 to 1986), vice-chairman of the Presidential Commission on the Space Shuttle *Challenger* Accident (1986), and chairman of AIL Technologies, Inc. (2000). In addition to the Presidential Medal of Freedom and the Congressional Space Medal of Honor, Armstrong received numerous honorary degrees and other awards in the United States, as well as seventeen awards from foreign countries. When he landed the *Eagle* and took those first brave steps on the Moon, not only did Armstrong capture the very best of the spirit of the 1960s, but he widened horizons for all mankind.

★

Neil Armstrong, Michael Collins, and Edwin E. Aldrin, Jr., *First on the Moon,* with Gene Farmer and Dora Jane Hambin (1970), gives an excellent firsthand account of *Apollo 11.* Armstrong's introduction to Alan Shepard and Deke Slayton, *Moon Shot: The Inside Story of American's Race to the Moon* (1994), offers his insights into the race to the Moon. Andrew Chaikin, *A Man on the Moon: The Voyages of the Apollo Astronauts* (1994), gives a good account of the *Apollo* missions.

JANE FRANCES AMLER

ASH, Mary Kay (*b.* 12 May 1918 in Hot Wells, Texas; *d.* 22 November 2001 in Dallas, Texas), founder and flamboyant business leader of Mary Kay Cosmetics, a company she built

up from a Dallas storefront in 1963 with nine saleswomen "beauty consultants," to a direct-marketing Fortune 500 company with over 800,000 independent beauty consultants in thirty-seven countries.

Born Mary Kathlyn Wagner, Ash was the youngest of four children of Edward Alexander Wagner and Lula Vember Hastings, who operated a hotel in Hot Wells, a spa town twenty-five miles northwest of Houston. Two years after she was born, her father developed tuberculosis, and the family moved to Houston's disadvantaged Sixth Ward. Her mother had to support the family while Ash took care of her father, an experience she later credited with giving her self-assurance. Her mother kept encouraging her, saying, "You can do it!" Ash continued this theme in the famous motivational seminars she eventually held each year for her "troops," beginning with the first anniversary of the founding of Ash Cosmetics in 1963.

Although Ash had been an outstanding student, who in 1935 had graduated at the head of her class at Reagan High School in Houston and aspired to become a doctor, lack of family funds made college impossible. She married Ben Rogers, an aspiring musician and gas station attendant, right out of school in 1935. In 1936 at age seventeen, Ash gave birth to a daughter, and later had two sons.

Ash, who excelled at extemporaneous speaking in school, joined Stanley Home Products in direct sales in 1938 to earn enough money to move her family out of her mother's house. She tried college briefly in the early 1940s, but she soon recognized that medicine was not her calling. Ash's talents were in selling. When her husband came home in 1945 after serving three years in the U.S. Army during World War II, he asked for a divorce. Ash was left with three children to support, and she began working full-time for Stanley Home Products in direct sales.

Always very competitive, Ash won the title of Miss Dallas during her second year with the company. Her success at Stanley was renowned, but she left in 1953 when a man she had trained was promoted to a management position over her. Ash immediately joined World Gift Company, another direct-sales company. Again her enthusiasm and talent brought success. One year she was responsible for a 53 percent increase in sales at the company. Ash was made the national training director for World Gift Company in 1959, but she quit in 1963 when she found out the men she was training were earning twice her salary. Of her decision to quit, she said, "I couldn't believe God meant a woman's brain to bring fifty cents on the dollar."

After twenty-five years in direct sales, Ash briefly retired in 1963. Planning to write a book, she began compiling lists of what worked and what did not work in her experiences in direct sales. Soon she realized what she was actually doing was outlining a "dream company," one that would give women an "open-end opportunity." The 1960s may have been a period of social revolution in many senses, but real business opportunities were not generally available to women, especially to married women. Ash decided she would open a company based on "the golden rule and a philosophy of God first, family second, career third."

Ash now had a plan for a company; all she needed was a line of products to sell. She remembered a beauty cream she had received from a Texas hide tanner's daughter when hosting a sales party for Stanley Home Products. The cream was very good, but it had an unpleasant odor. In 1963 Ash bought the formula and had it reformulated to have a nice smell. She had it packaged in pink and gold, so the product would look attractive displayed in the all-white bathrooms so popular in 1963.

In July 1963 Ash married George Hallenbeck, who also had experience in direct sales, and he became her partner in planning the new company. Together they invested their entire assets of $5,000 and decided to open "Beauty by Mary Kay" in a storefront in Dallas, where Hallenbeck would handle the business end, and she would focus on products and sales.

On 13 August 1963, Hallenbeck died of a heart attack at the breakfast table while going over the final balance sheet for the opening of the new company. With everything she had invested in the plans, Ash opened her business on 13 September 1963 with the help of her youngest son, twenty-year-old Richard Rogers. They started with one shelf of pink-packaged cosmetics and a dynamic plan. Ash built her business from nothing to sales of $34,000 within months of opening the store.

Ash built her empire on her remarkable people skills and woman's intuition. She recruited women to join a sales force as independent consultants—not employees—who were trained by the company in dynamic sales techniques. She believed other women would be as motivated as she was when her mother told her, "You can do it!" She also believed in what she called "Cinderella gifts," rewards to recognize sales achievements. She held the first motivational convention on 13 September 1964, one year after starting the business.

In 1968 Ash ordered a pink Cadillac as her personal business car. It made such a sensation that she decided the use of a pink Cadillac should be the ultimate reward for her top beauty consultants. The first pink Cadillac was awarded in 1969. At the time of Ash's death there were about 1,600 pink Cadillacs on the road.

On 6 January 1966 Ash married Mel Ash. She established a charitable foundation that provides funding for cancer research, particularly breast cancer, and for the prevention of violence against women. Ash received many awards in recognition of her achievements and contributions, including one for "most outstanding woman in busi-

ness in the twentieth century" from Lifetime Television in 1999. Ash died of natural causes.

★

Autobiographies of Ash include *Mary Kay* (1981) and *Mary Kay You Can Have It All* (1995). Additional information on Ash can be found in her file at the Barker Texas History Center, University of Texas at Austin (2001). Obituaries are in the *New York Times* and *Dallas Morning News* (both 23 Nov. 2001).

M. C. NAGEL

ASH, Roy Lawrence (*b.* 20 October 1918 in Los Angeles, California), corporate manager, financier, and government official, who built Litton Industries into a modern conglomerate enterprise; directed the Office of Management and Budget for two presidents; helped introduce modern accounting methods to government work; and advised President Richard M. Nixon to create the Environmental Protection Agency.

Ash was born the son of Charles K. Ash, a grain and hay broker, and Fay E. (Dickinson) Ash. Ash attended public schools in Los Angeles, including George Washington High School and Manual Arts High School, graduating in 1935. He then landed a job with the Bank of America Trust and Savings Association in Los Angeles, where he worked for the cash collection department, eventually moving to administrative positions.

In 1942 Ash joined the U.S. Army and attended its officer's candidate school. There he was selected to join the U.S. Army Air Corps' statistical control division, which was headed by Charles B. Thornton. Ash's genius for managing a diverse inventory was important to modernizing the management techniques of the air corps. On 13 November 1943 Ash married Lila Marie Hornbek, with whom he had five children. When he was discharged from the army in 1945, he held the rank of captain.

Thornton and many who had served under him joined the Ford Motor Company after the war, becoming known as the "whiz kids," but Ash chose to go to school instead. He had been based at Harvard University, and he was admitted to Harvard's Graduate School of Business Administration on the strength of his work in the army, even though he did not have a bachelor's degree. He received his M.B.A. in 1947.

Ash then went to San Francisco to work at Bank of America's headquarters as its chief of statistical control. Meanwhile, Thornton had taken a job with Hughes Aircraft Company, and he persuaded Ash to join him in 1949. In 1953 they pooled their resources and founded their own company, Electro-Dynamics Corporation. Ash used his little corporation as a base for soliciting investors, each of whom purchased $29,200 in stock. He used the investors' money to leverage bank loans, and in 1953, he and Thornton purchased Litton Industries, an electronics company that was doing about three million dollars per year in sales.

This was the beginning of what business historians consider the modern age of conglomerates and mergers. Throughout the 1950s Litton Industries, under the guidance of Thornton and Ash, purchased technology companies that were often bigger than Litton Industries. For instance, in 1958, they bought a controlling interest in Monroe Calculating Machines Company, which then had annual sales of $45 million per year, compared to Litton Industries' receipts of only $30 million per year.

Litton Industries entered the 1960s with annual sales of $245 million and forty-eight factories in nine nations. By then, the original fifty investors from 1953 had made more than $4 million each on their investments. In 1960 Ash was named president of Litton Systems, Inc., the subsidiary that focused on military contracts. In 1961 Thornton stepped down from the presidency of Litton Industries, while retaining his position as the corporation's chief executive officer (CEO), and Ash received formal recognition of his contribution to the company's success by becoming its president.

Litton Industries thrived in the 1960s by making each of its many divisions—fifty by 1966—an independent enterprise. The leaders of each division were entrepreneurs who made their own decisions about what to manufacture and how to sell it without having to consult with Thornton or Ash. The idea was to let every manager spread his entrepreneurial wings and thrive; but this experience and training resulted in many other corporations hiring away Litton Industries' managers, creating corporate executives known as "Lidos," for "Litton Industries Dropouts."

By the end of 1966 Litton Industries had annual sales in excess of $1 billion, with net earnings of $55 million. It made over six thousand products in factories around the world. The expertise of Litton Industries' leaders was in demand for virtually every kind of large enterprise. The United States government hired the corporation to train candidates for the Job Corps, and it was even hired by the government of Greece to manage the industrial and economic development of the island of Crete. Yet in the last quarter of 1967 and the first quarter of 1968, Litton Industries' earnings dropped, and its stock prices soon dropped as well. The problem was partly the drain of good management talent, the "Lidos," which hurt the growth of some of the corporation's subsidiaries, and partly a result of the general economic malaise engendered by the inflationary factors of high domestic spending programs and the expense of the Vietnam War. However, Ash was able to reenergize the Royal typewriter division, in particular, and by 1969, Litton Industries had resumed growing.

In 1968 Richard M. Nixon was elected president of the United States, and he appointed Ash as the Director of the Office of Management and Budget (OMB). The OMB kept track of government spending, detecting waste by auditing various parts of the government, and Ash proved brilliant at this. He remained as director during both the Nixon and Ford administrations. He had direct access to the president and was called upon to advise him on how to solve problems in administering government programs. Nixon had extensive ambitions for solving America's domestic problems. His political instincts forced him to lend an ear to those who had concerns about issues like affirmative action and the environment, even though these were areas of less interest to him than foreign affairs. Ash recommended that a special agency devoted to preserving the health of the American environment be created. This was the beginning of what the Nixon administration named the Environmental Protection Agency.

Ash made the biggest public gaffe of his career when in 1972 he told a journalist that he believed that in twenty years the world's economy would be controlled by one central authority. For the rest of his life, he regretted this remark, which seemed to imply that the United States and other nations would lose their economic independence.

Ash continued his involvement in public service by helping to organize the Los Angeles Summer Olympics of 1984. From 1977 to 1980 he was an adviser to the Republican National Committee. As well as serving as a board member for several charities and colleges, he worked as an adviser for several corporations. During the 1980s, when Bank of America was in serious fiscal difficulty because of bad loans and loan defaults, he helped put the bank back in financial order and served as a public spokesperson who reassured investors that the bank would survive.

★

There are no autobiographies or biographies of Ash. Works examining Litton Industries and industrial conglomerates include Beirne Lay, Jr., *Someone Has to Make It Happen: The Inside Story of Tex Thornton—The Man Who Built Litton Industries* (1969); Robert Sobel, *The Rise and Fall of the Conglomerate* (1984); and Jeffrey L. Rodengen and Melody Maysonet, *The Legend of Litton Industries* (2000), focus more on Thornton than on Ash.

KIRK H. BEETZ

ASHBERY, John Lawrence (*b.* 28 July 1927 in Rochester, New York), prolific poet who led the avant-garde New York school of poets during the 1960s and whose work is known for being somewhat abstract, even "difficult"; he is regarded as a leader in American letters.

Ashbery was one of two children of Chet Ashbery, a farmer, and Helen Lawrence, a biology teacher, and grew up on a fruit farm near Lake Ontario, where he worked in the or-

John Ashbery. AP/WIDE WORLD PHOTOS

chards during the summers. In his teens Ashbery read such poets as W. H. Auden, Dylan Thomas, and Wallace Stevens, but his first ambition was not to write, but to paint. Nevertheless, he won spelling bees and went on a national radio show as a "quiz kid." He wrote poems good enough to be published in *Poetry* while in prep school, but they were stolen and published under a pseudonym by a former roommate. He graduated from Harvard University in 1949 and moved to New York City, where he worked in publishing from 1951 to 1955. Ashbery received a master's degree from Columbia University in New York in 1951. Ashbery's first volume, *Turandot and Other Poems,* appeared in 1953.

W. H. Auden had enormous importance for Ashbery, who wrote an undergraduate honors thesis on the elder poet, and Ashbery's second collection of poems, *Some Trees* (1956), was chosen by Auden for inclusion in a Yale University young poets' series. Ashbery left that summer to spend a year in France on a Fulbright scholarship. He remained in Paris for the next ten years, except for the 1957

to 1958 school year, when he returned to New York City as a graduate student of French literature at New York University. He published *The Poems* in 1960.

The New York school of poets was an intensely creative and prolific band of friends and artistic collaborators during the 1960s, and was considered "the last authentic avant-garde movement that we have had in American poetry." The four core members were Ashbery, Kenneth Koch, Frank O'Hara, and James Schuyler. According to his peers, Ashbery came closest to approaching the ideal: "John's the poet," O'Hara once declared. With their start in the early 1950s, during the Korean War and the era of McCarthyism, these poets bucked the literary establishment. They fought the anxieties of the age by fully investing their energies in their work. They also were aligned with the second generation of the New York school painters, which included the abstract expressionists of New York's Tibor de Nagy Gallery: Fairfield Porter, Jane Freilicher, Nell Blaine, and Larry Rivers. John Bernard Myers, the gallery's director, named the New York school of poets in 1961, teamed them with the artists of his gallery, and promoted and published them.

In 1960, while still in Paris, Ashbery accepted a friend's offer to replace her as the weekly art critic for the Paris *Herald Tribune.* At the time, he saw the job as little more than a paycheck in a city where finding work was difficult for Americans. The job developed into a career, and Ashbery worked as an art critic for the next twenty-five years for publications such as *ArtNews, Newsweek,* and *New York.* The editorial freedom Ashbery enjoyed at the *Herald Tribune* allowed him to determine his own subject matter, style, and approach. In his first year alone he wrote about Brazilian painting, Bulgarian art, Italian sculpture, Japanese photography, American abstractions, Flemish primitives, Barbizon landscapes, and the Gustave Moreau Museum. He wrote not as an expert, but as an informed observer who was interested in what was worth seeing, ignoring issues of theory, practice, or methodology.

Ashbery may have fallen into his career as a critic, but it was nonetheless significant in his development as a poet. The regular deadlines associated with journalism, the obligation to "grind out several pages" and "produce an article . . . rain or shine, exhibition or no exhibition" built his discipline as a poet. It showed him that he could "sit down the same way with a poem." It is interesting, too, that the painters Ashbery has been most interested in, including Giorgio De Chirico, Fairfield Porter, and R. B. Kitaj, are either particularly literary artists, or have written extensively about themselves. Ashbery borrowed freely from the traditions of the French surrealist movement. His writings on art attempted to encourage cross-pollination between art and poetry.

Visual art was a profound influence on the New York

school of poets, which was named so in 1961. But it can be said that it began in 1948, when Ashbery, just through his junior year at Harvard, wrote "The Painter" and mailed it to his friend, Harvard graduate and fellow poet Kenneth Koch, then living in New York. "The Painter," a sestina, was the first of many poems in which these poets aligned themselves with modern painters in their personal and artistic crises and conflicts, and their sense of artistic and romantic possibility. The group gelled in 1951. During his Paris years, Ashbery often regretted being so far away from the thriving New York art scene, but he was proud that he stayed away. He saw Paris as a "neutral climate" that allowed him to work as he chose.

Ashbery's poetry and "experiments with language" during this era were less influenced by his studies in French literature than they were by the work of Gertrude Stein, the avant-garde American writer whose Paris home was a salon for leading artists and writers of the period between the two World Wars. In a 1957 review of Stein's *Stanzas in Meditation,* Ashbery virtually described the poetry he later came to write, though he was describing Stein's work. He said Stein's poetry was "comforting or annoying or brilliant or tedious. Like people, [her poems] sometimes make no sense and sometimes make perfect sense. . . ." Stein could not have described his own work more precisely. His work was rarely autobiographical; rather, his poems fit anyone's biography. Some analysts see this as Ashbery's escape from the details of his own daily and professional lives. His early published poems took the form, cadence, and look of traditional poems, but did not serve their stated subjects. "The Portrait of Little J.A. in a Prospect of Flowers" would seem, by its title, to be autobiographical, but Ashbery reveals nothing about himself in the work.

At the time, Ashbery described the poems in his 1962 collection *The Tennis Court Oath* as having parallels with abstract expressionism, a statement that came to haunt him. He later became known for his evasiveness; he was convinced that he was bound to be misinterpreted, and resisted being labeled in any way. The poems in *The Tennis Court Oath* were syntactically, grammatically, and metaphorically disjointed. Ashbery put these poems together like a collage painter might; stray bits from newspapers, broken phrases from children's books, lines from bad poetry, and loose phrases floating in his own mind went into the poems of *The Tennis Court Oath.* About the poem "Europe," Ashbery once commented, "I didn't know what I wanted to do, but I did know what I didn't want to do." The book found favor with young, experimental poets, while establishment critics preferred his later work. For poets coming of age in the 1960s, the Ashbery of *The Tennis Court Oath* and *Rivers and Mountains* (1966) was the initiating experience, while the critical reaction to Ashbery during these years was al-

most reflexively hostile. His subsequent works of the era include *Selected Poems* (1967), *Three Madrigals* (1968), *Sunrise in Suburbia* (1968), and *Fragment* (1969).

Ashbery is a dense and intricate poet. His metaphors can be elusive, even frustrating. For Ashbery, poems are made not of ideas, but of words and names. He often found titles and phrases for his work in snippets of overheard conversations. Ashbery's work has been compared to abstract painting—fractured and indistinct. He contorts syntax, changes tense or person, uses endless parenthetical remarks and ellipses; his style has been likened to a roller coaster of associative thoughts. Ashbery's admirers admit they can find him undecipherable when they are tired or impatient, but that when "the frequencies meet . . . it is a form of trance." He is comfortable using the everyday language of the street, of advertising, of nursery rhymes. Ashbery's language is more familiar to most readers than that of the typical poet, though he never ventures into the realm of conversation; the reader never forgets he is reading poetry. Ashbery once claimed that he rarely rewrites; he believed that the meaning of his poems is automatically "there" when the words are put to paper. He often begins writing with a title. Ashbery is open about his homosexuality, although some critics claim he has evaded his gay identity in his work.

The 1975 publication of Ashbery's *Self Portrait in a Convex Mirror* established him as the preeminent poet of the United States. It won the "triple crown" of American poetry prizes: the Pulitzer Prize, the National Book Award, and the National Book Critics Circle Award. Among countless other grants and fellowships, Ashbery earned the MacArthur Foundation "genius grant" in 1985. In 1995, Ashbery received the Poetry Society of America's Robert Frost Medal, and in 1997, he received the American Academy of Arts and Letters' Gold Medal for poetry. He has written over twenty books of poetry and teaches at Bard College.

★

Further readings on Ashbery include the collection of art criticism by John Ashbery, *Reported Sightings: Art Chronicles, 1957–1987* (1989), and David Lehman, *The Last Avant-Garde: The Making of the New York School of Poets* (1998). Criticism of his work includes Robert Richman, "Our Most Important Living Poet," *Commentary* (July 1982), and Steven Meyer, "Ashbery: Poet for All Seasons," *Raritan* (fall 1995).

BRENNA SANCHEZ

ASHE, Arthur Robert, Jr. (*b.* 10 July 1943 in Richmond, Virginia; *d.* 6 February 1993 in New York City), first African-American male professional tennis player to win a Grand Slam tournament.

Ashe was the son of Arthur Robert Ashe, Sr., and Mattie Cordell Cunningham. His father was a parks superintendent and his mother was a homemaker. He had a younger brother, Jimmy. His mother died in 1950 at the tragically young age of twenty-seven. In 1955 his father married Lorraine Kimbrough. Ashe's father in 1947 was assigned to a security role with the Richmond park district with supervisory responsibilities at the eighteen-acre Brookfield Playground. Young Ashe was fascinated watching the tennis exploits of Ron Charity, a successful African-American athlete who became Ashe's first instructor. Later, Ashe was mentored by Dr. R. W. Johnson. At the age of twelve Ashe was excluded from taking part in a Richmond tennis tournament because of the park's "whites only" policy, an experience that is said to have had a great impact on him.

Slim and slight of physique, Ashe took to tennis. He won age-group American Tennis Association (ATA) national championships in 1955, 1958, 1959, and 1960. From 1960 to 1963 he was the ATA men's singles champion. Ashe, however, only entered his first nonsegregated tournament as a sixteen-year-old in 1959.

Ashe eventually completed his high school education in St. Louis, Missouri. As a result of his stellar tennis apprenticeship and excellent school performance, he received a 1961 scholarship to the University of California, Los Angeles (UCLA), the first ever granted to an African-

American tennis player. The significance of this happening at the beginning of the decade is colossal: while athletes of color were being recruited in significant numbers for college sports such as football, basketball, and track and field, tennis, with its history of "whiteness" and association with the upper classes—very similar to golf—stood as a symbol of racial division and social exclusion.

David K. Wright's biography comments on aspects of Ashe's college experience. "California had a more tolerant view of race," Wright observed, "yet barriers remained. Ashe was not allowed to play at an exclusive club. Interracial dating was accepted by students, but not by everyone else. One young woman's mother did not learn that Ashe was African American until she saw him on television. The daughter had not mentioned the color of her boyfriend's skin in telling her mother about him."

At UCLA, Ashe pursued three professional avenues: tennis, business administration, and U.S. Army Reserve Officers Training Corps (ROTC). In 1963 Ashe's U.S. amateur ranking was six, but two years later, he was in second place. He was only twenty-one when he won the U.S. intercollegiate singles championship. He graduated from UCLA in 1966, and a year later was commissioned as a second lieutenant in the U.S. Army. In 1968 he won both the U.S. Amateur championship and the U.S. Open at Forest Hills, New York. The year's high point, however, was when he led the United States team to triumph with the Davis Cup.

Thoughtful, insightful, and a resolute critic of racism, Ashe believed in dialogue, communication, and reasoned discourse. Ashe's way was not that of John Carlos and Tommie Smith, who electrified a world audience at the 1968 Olympic Games in Mexico City by throwing clenched fists skywards to indicate their contempt for the status quo. Nor was Ashe a trailblazer in the same way that Jackie Robinson was in baseball, a sport that experienced an influx of black athletes in the 1960s. According to Ashe biographer Marvin Martin, "Nothing similar happened with Ashe in tennis. Whereas Robinson soon had lots of company, Ashe remained the lone black male playing at the top level of tennis. And little changed in that regard in the decades that followed."

In 1966 *Current Biography* profiled Ashe, and the composite picture that emerged is an intriguing one. It reveals that the six-foot, one-inch, 150-pound tennis player had a repertoire of sixteen different backhands and survived through, but was not insensitive to, the ironies and dissonance of his role as a black celebrity in a white sports subculture. He was referred to in one *Sports Illustrated* interview as experiencing genuine angst while playing in a Long Island tennis tournament where he did not see one other African American except for the waiters and locker-room attendants. On the other hand, Ashe was cognizant of the many opportunities presented to him because of his extraordinary

Arthur Ashe holds his Wimbledon trophy, 1975. CORBIS CORPORATION (BELLEVUE)

tennis skills. He had a retainer to promote Coca-Cola and endorsed Clark Gum and American Safety Razors for Philip Morris. Ashe also felt moved to comment on situations that reflected well on race relations within the United States. In a *New York Times* piece, Ashe is quoted about his 1966 Davis Cup sleeping arrangements "when they [the rest of the world] see two guys from the South like Cliff Richey and me, one white and one colored, both sharing a room and being close friends, it must do a little good."

Ashe left the military in 1969 and enjoyed a top-five world tennis ranking until 1975. In 1970 a visit to South Africa brought him face to face with the ugliness of apartheid, and for the rest of his life he was a stern critic of the system. In 1973 he was the first athlete of color to play in a major South African tennis tournament.

In 1975 Ashe defeated fellow American Jimmy Connors in four sets to win the Wimbledon singles championships, and in 1977 he won the Australian Open. Ashe married New York photographer Jeanne-Marie Moutoussamy on 20 February 1977; the couple had one child.

In 1979 Ashe experienced a series of heart attacks, and these resulted in his tennis retirement in 1980. These health concerns did not stop him from captaining the U.S. Davis Cup team to two championships in 1980 and 1985. He then went to work as a commentator for Home Box Office (HBO) and the American Broadcasting Company (ABC).

In 1988 Ashe published *A Hard Road to Glory*, a pioneering three-volume series of black sports history. Sadly, brain surgery in 1988 revealed that Ashe had contracted AIDS as a result of a tainted blood transfusion in 1983.

Ashe died of AIDS-related pneumonia at the age of forty-nine. He was inducted into the International Tennis Hall of Fame in 1985. The central stadium at the National Tennis Center in Flushing Meadow, New York, the site of the U.S. Open, was renamed the Arthur Ashe Stadium. He is buried at Woodland Cemetery in Richmond.

In 1992 *Sports Illustrated* made Ashe the Sportsman of the Year, and although his thirty-three tennis championships are noteworthy, Ashe is best remembered for his courage, character, and quiet resolve. Eleven thousand people attended his funeral in Richmond and his memorial service in New York City. Andrew Young, former U.S. delegate to the United Nations, said of him, "He took the burden of race and wore it as a cloak of dignity." Ashe himself, assessing his own career with regard to that of a leading statesman of the twentieth century, said, "Compared to [Nelson] Mandela's sacrifice my own life . . . has been one of almost self-indulgence. When I think of him, my own political efforts seem puny."

★

Ashe biographies include David K. Wright, *Arthur Ashe: Breaking the Color Barrier in Tennis* (1996), and Marvin Martin, *Of Tennis and the Human Spirit* (1999). A profile of Ashe by Miriam F. Shelden is in David L. Porter, ed., *African-American Sports Greats* (1995). Brad Herzog's essay on Ashe in *The Sports 100* (1995) is a glorious evocation of a political athlete who made protests persuasive rather than polemical protestations. Obituaries are in the *Washington Post* and *New York Times* (both 7 Feb. 1993) and the London *Times* (8 Feb. 1993).

SCOTT A. G. M. CRAWFORD

ASHMORE, Harry Scott (*b.* 28 July 1916 in Greenville, South Carolina; *d.* 20 January 1998 in Santa Barbara, California), and **William Calhoun ("Bill") BAGGS** (*b.* 22 September 1922 in Atlanta, Georgia; *d.* 7 January 1969 in Miami, Florida), editors of metropolitan newspapers whose views contrasted sharply with those held by many of their fellow southerners. During two missions to North Vietnam in the late 1960s, they spoke with that country's leader, Ho Chi Minh, in an attempt to end America's conflict with his regime.

Ashmore, the younger son of William Green Ashmore and Elizabeth (Scott) Ashmore, worked his way through Clemson College in South Carolina after his father's shoe store failed in the Great Depression. After earning his B.A. degree from Clemson in 1937, he reported for several hometown newspapers. In the course of his work he observed signs of discontent among African Americans in the region. On 2 June 1940 he married Barbara Edith Laier, a Boston native teaching at Furman University in Greenville; they had one child, a daughter. In 1941 he was named a Nieman Fellow at Harvard University in Cambridge, Massachusetts, but the U.S. entry into World War II interrupted his fellowship. Ashmore was commissioned as a reserve officer at Clemson and served as a staff officer in the European theater.

After being discharged as a lieutenant colonel in 1945, he worked as an associate editor of the *Charlotte News* in North Carolina. Ashmore's advocacy of civil rights for African Americans caused *Time* magazine to call him "one of the South's most realistic and readable editorial writers." In 1947 he moved to Little Rock, Arkansas, where he soon became the editor of the *Arkansas Gazette*. There he continued to criticize racial discrimination, became nationally active in the Democratic Party, and challenged the governor's attempt to block integration of Little Rock's Central High School in 1957. The Pulitzer Prize committee awarded the *Arkansas Gazette* the prestigious public service award for 1958, and Ashmore won the 1958 prize for editorial writing. Opposition to the paper's position and to him personally persuaded Ashmore to leave the *Gazette* in 1959 and accept a post as a senior fellow at the Center for the Study of Democratic Institutions (CSDI) in Santa Barbara, California.

In 1959 the CSDI was contracted to revise the structure of the *Encyclopaedia Britannica,* and Ashmore worked as the project's editor until 1963. At that point he began to devote his full attention to the center's efforts to ease world tension by bringing people together to discuss issues central to world harmony. Under the auspices of the CSDI, 2,000 delegates from twenty nations met in New York City in February 1965. Neither they nor those who attended a second meeting two years later accomplished much; however, the effort put into organizing these conferences prompted Ashmore and his friend Bill Baggs, a center director, to travel to Hanoi, where they spoke with Ho Chi Minh in January 1967. They believed the North Vietnamese leader sought negotiations to end the war and were convinced their attempt to facilitate his overture was sabotaged by the administration of President Lyndon B. Johnson, which bitterly opposed their intervention. Ashmore and Baggs publicly criticized their government and published an account of U.S. "double-dealing" in *Mission to Hanoi: A Chronicle of Double Dealing in High Places* (1968). Despite the Johnson administration's angry reaction, the U.S. State Department authorized a second trip in March 1968; by this time Johnson was eager to negotiate with North Vietnamese leaders. Both men believed their second visit "opened the way to the Paris peace talks."

As public attention shifted away from civil rights and the Vietnam War, Ashmore became less personally involved nationally, although he remained active in the affairs of the CSDI. At age eighty-one, on 9 January 1998, he suffered a stroke from which he never regained consciousness. His body was cremated, and his ashes were scattered in the Pacific Ocean near Santa Barbara.

Baggs was the son of Crawford C. Baggs, a Ford car dealer, and Kate May (Bush) Baggs. The youngest of four children, he moved to Colquitt, Georgia, to live with his mother's family after the death of both parents. There he completed high school and turned down an appointment to the U.S. Naval Academy. Confined to bed for a year by illness, Baggs read extensively; after recovering and feeling that he had learned more while ill than in school, he decided not to attend college. Instead, he went to Panama in 1941 and worked for the *Panama Star and Herald.* When the United States entered World War II, Baggs joined the Army Air Corps and flew B-24s from North Africa and Italy.

Baggs was discharged in 1945 and married Joan Orr of Athens, Georgia, on 7 July 1945. In 1946 he became a reporter for the *Miami News,* the Cox Newspaper Group's lackluster evening paper. Baggs polished his craft in Miami, where his skill and personality earned him promotion to a political columnist by 1949. Early in his journalistic career, Baggs met the U.S. financier and presidential adviser Bernard Baruch. The elder statesman opened doors that proved invaluable to the young newsman. During the administrations of John F. Kennedy and Lyndon B. Johnson, Baggs had widespread contacts in the United States and abroad.

In 1957 Cox Newspapers appointed Baggs as the editor of the *Miami News,* passing over journalists with more experience. By releasing underperforming staff and promoting the talented, the new editor revived the paper. Although he could not overcome the dominance of the *Miami Herald,* he made the *News* more vibrant and provocative. *Time* magazine observed, "By almost any measure, Baggs's *Miami News* is the best second-best newspaper in the U.S." As the editor, Baggs used humor to challenge racial discrimination, promote civic improvement, and question the nation's foreign policy. Conservative southerners found his outlook repellant and barraged him with critical, and occasionally threatening, letters. He replied with gentle humor even when someone fired a bullet into his office wall. His White House connections enabled the *News* to scoop the competition during the Cuban Missile Crisis in 1962, when the United States and the Soviet Union nearly went to war because of the Soviets' installation of nuclear missiles in Cuba. Baggs's access to Washington insiders also smoothed the way for the *News* reporter Hal Hendrix, who in 1963 won the Pulitzer Prize for international reporting. Baggs's successful campaign to preserve southern Key Biscayne as a public park prompted the governor of Florida to name the site Bill Baggs Cape Florida State Park.

Baggs's final foray into public service teamed him with his longtime friend Ashmore; they were determined to help find a way out of America's involvement in the Vietnam War. Baggs felt that Johnson's escalation of the war had brought the nation no closer to victory, created growing discord at home, and drained resources that could have been better used for peaceful purposes. In January 1967 Baggs and Ashmore embarked on the first of two trips to Hanoi. Overworked by the demanding schedule imposed by his job, Baggs contracted influenza and died at age forty-six. His body was cremated, and his ashes were scattered in the Atlantic Ocean off Key Biscayne.

Unlike their colleagues in broadcast journalism, Baggs and Ashmore worked in relative obscurity. Neither is the subject of a full biography or is even mentioned in surveys of the 1960s, but both left their mark on the era. Their campaign on behalf of civil rights for all Americans strengthened the assault on discrimination in the South. If they did not eliminate prejudice, their public opposition helped to make it unfashionable, even in the heart of Dixie. Their questioning of U.S. involvement in Southeast Asia did not end the conflict, but both believed it played a significant role in launching the talks that eventually extricated the United States from the long, bloody Vietnam War.

★

Material relating to Ashmore's association with the Center for the Study of Democratic Institutions is held by the library at the University of California, Santa Barbara. Two books written by

Ashmore, *Hearts and Minds: The Anatomy of Racism from Roosevelt to Reagan* (1982) and *Civil Rights and Wrongs: A Memoir of Racism and Politics, 1944–1996* (1997), contain autobiographical material. Obituaries are in the *New York Times* and *Arkansas Times Gazette* (both 22 Jan. 1998). The William C. Baggs Papers, a collection of correspondence, photographs, and writings from the 1940s through 1969, are held by the Otto G. Richter Library, University of Miami. Biographical sketches of Baggs were published in *Newsweek* (12 Aug. 1957) and *Time* (16 Nov. 1962). The *New York Times, Miami News,* and other newspapers covered the Baggs-Ashmore trips to Hanoi. The *Saturday Evening Post* (16 Dec. 1967) featured Baggs's account of his talk with Ho Chi Minh, and *Time* (29 Sept. 1967) and *Newsweek* (2 Oct. 1967) ran articles on the mission. Obituaries are in the *Miami News* and *New York Times* (both 8 Jan. 1969).

BRAD AGNEW

AUBREY, James Thomas, Jr. (*b.* 14 December 1918 in La Salle, Illinois; *d.* 3 September 1994 in New York City), media executive and producer credited with improving the financial fortune of the Columbia Broadcasting System (CBS) television network in the early 1960s.

Aubrey, the oldest of four sons of advertising executive James T. Aubrey and homemaker Mildred Stever, spent his childhood in the Chicago area and New York City. A privileged child, the tall, athletic Aubrey was educated at Phillips Exeter Academy in New Hampshire (1934–1938) and graduated cum laude from Princeton in 1941 with a B.A. in English. During World War II he served as a test pilot with the U.S. Air Force, achieving the rank of major. In 1944 Aubrey married actress Phyllis Thaxter. They had two children, Susan Schuyler Aubrey, who as Skye Aubrey enjoyed a brief performing career, and a son. Aubrey and Thaxter divorced in 1963.

In 1946 Aubrey settled in Los Angeles, where he sold advertising for Condé Nast publications before joining the local CBS radio and television affiliates in 1948 as an account executive. Thus began his association with the company where he would see his biggest successes and his most prominent failure.

In the mid-1950s, Aubrey was hired as a programmer for CBS television, where he helped develop the popular western series *Have Gun, Will Travel* (1957–1963). CBS executives were slow to appreciate the programmer's gifts, however, and in 1956 Aubrey accepted a position as vice president in charge of programs and talent at the American Broadcasting Company (ABC). In two short years he was able to turn the fledgling network into a worthy rival of CBS and the National Broadcasting Company (NBC), in part by introducing such successful series as *The Real Mc-Coys,* which aired on ABC from 1957 to 1962, and on CBS from 1962 to 1963.

Having demonstrated a flair for programming, Aubrey returned to CBS in April 1958 and within a year succeeded Louis Cowan as network president. A tireless executive who by the 1959–1960 season toiled twelve hours a day, six days a week, Aubrey had a clear set of standards for all CBS programs. The shows had to feature a big-name star, they needed to have a workable format, and creative control had to be ceded to CBS. Additionally, and most important for the financial health of CBS, Aubrey presold all half-hour programs to no more than two advertising sponsors with contracts that ran for fifty-two weeks at full price. By contrast, other networks were selling one-minute spots on their shows in thirteen-week increments.

Aubrey came to be noted for his infallible instinct for popular television shows. Although some within the company questioned the lowbrow nature of some of the programs, fearing they might tarnish CBS's reputation as the "Tiffany" network, the public embraced such oddball offerings as a program about a talking horse (*Mr. Ed,* 1961–1965), and another about a family of backwoods millionaires (*The Beverly Hillbillies,* 1962–1971). Much of this success was credited to Aubrey's willingness to embrace the burgeoning audience of young families. He was also said to be a master of audience flow, programming new or struggling series in time slots after hit series to create new hits. A prime example of this was *The Dick Van Dyke Show* (1961–1966), which struggled until Aubrey aired it after *The Beverly Hillbillies.*

Not all the programs Aubrey championed were ratings bonanzas. Tiffany Network shows such as *The Defenders* (1961–1965) and *East Side/West Side* (1963 to 1964) garnered critical acclaim and even Emmy Awards but struggled in the ratings. Still, their presence demonstrated Aubrey's principle of balance in programming. The press liked to tout CBS as "the comedy network," but Aubrey could point to the one-hour dramas as examples of the network's commitment to diversity.

As network president from 1959 to 1965, Aubrey also concentrated on CBS's daytime lineup, a mix of soap operas and audience participation shows that earned strong ratings and large profits. During Aubrey's presidency, the combined revenue for CBS nearly doubled, rising from $25 million to $49.6 million. CBS also dominated the Nielsen ratings, placing six shows in the top ten from 1960 to 1964. And during the 1963–1964 season, the network enjoyed the then unprecedented feat of airing fourteen of the fifteen highest-rated shows on television.

From the start of his presidency at CBS, Aubrey came under criticism for his somewhat abrasive managerial style. He was noted for his brusque demeanor that often bruised the egos of the top talent. Aubrey clashed openly with Jack

Benny, whose ratings were slipping, over the decision to move the comedian's show from Sunday nights to Tuesdays. Benny eventually took the series to rival NBC when his contract was up in 1964, but Aubrey's instincts proved sound when the show's ratings rose during the 1962–1963 season.

Although there was some carping in the media over the quality of CBS programs and there were disgruntled producers and performers (the film producer and character actor John Houseman reputedly dubbed Aubrey "the Smiling Cobra"), Aubrey remained in favor with CBS chairman William S. Paley as long as the revenues grew. But just months after Aubrey graced the cover of *Business Week,* his career began a downward trajectory. For nearly four years Aubrey had creative control, which included the network's investments in the shows it produced with an eye to reaping money from syndication, but during the 1964–1965 season Aubrey agreed to air three new series produced by former actor Keefe Brasselle without even viewing a pilot episode. Each series failed, and, coupled with a slippage in network income and his growing negative reputation (his critics in the media variously described him as "imperious," "arrogant," "ruthless" and "a monster," and his personal life provided endless fodder for the gossip columns), Paley had no choice but to replace Aubrey. His contract at CBS was terminated in February 1965.

After a protracted dispute over his stock options, Aubrey walked away with a settlement in excess of $1 million. Investing wisely, Aubrey spent from February to October 1965 traveling, dabbling in the operations of an import-export firm, and heading Aubrey Productions, which reportedly had deals with several studios for film and television projects, although nothing was ever produced.

In a move that surprised some in the entertainment industry, billionaire Kirk Kerkorian appointed Aubrey president of Metro-Goldwyn-Mayer (MGM) in October 1969. Kerkorian had purchased the studio primarily for its name recognition and planned to build a hotel in Las Vegas. When Aubrey assumed control of MGM, it had not had a hit film since 1965 and it was deeply in debt. Employing his "ruthless" business style, Aubrey took a bottom-line approach, instituting a complete restructuring of the studio and its divisions, laying off almost half of its staff and selling off many of the studio's assets, including property in Southern California and England. In an even more controversial move, Aubrey sold over forty-five years' worth of costumes and props. MGM had an operating loss of $8 million in 1970, but the sale of $9.8 million in assets put it back in the black for the first time in four years. And after the costly failure in 1970 of *Ryan's Daughter,* Aubrey instituted a budgetary cap of $2 million per picture.

However, while MGM was now fiscally sound, the artistic reputation of the once great studio was in decline.

Many filmmakers complained of Aubrey's interference in production and of his propensity to edit out any controversial material that might lead to a "restricted" rating. MGM continued to post an operating profit, but that was mainly due to the annual sale of assets (overseas theater chains, music companies, and so on) and not because of hit movies. By the time Aubrey departed in 1973, the MGM Grand was set to open in Las Vegas and MGM had ceased to be a major distributor of motion pictures. Aubrey returned to independent producing, with only a handful of projects, such as the 1976 feature *Futureworld* and the 1979 ABC television movie *The Dallas Cowboys Cheerleaders,* making any impact. Aubrey died of a heart attack and was buried in Westwood Memorial Park, in Los Angeles.

★

There is no official biography of Aubrey, although he is a key character in Merle Miller's memoir, with Evan Rhodes, *Only You, Dick Darling!: Or How to Write One Television Script and Make $50,000,000* (1964), and reportedly served as the fictional inspiration for the main characters in Keefe Brasselle, *The Cannibals: A Novel About Television's Savage Chieftains* (1968), and Jacqueline Susann, *The Love Machine* (1969). Aubrey features prominently in William S. Paley, *As It Happened: A Memoir* (1979), Lewis J. Paper, *Empire: William S. Paley and the Making of CBS* (1987), and Sally Bedell Smith, *In All His Glory: The Life of William S. Paley, the Legendary Tycoon and His Brilliant Circle* (1990). Articles about Aubrey's career include "Number 1 Supplier of TV News," *Business Week* (25 Apr. 1964); Max Lerner, "The Aubrey Story," *New York Post* (5 Mar. 1965); Robert Windeler, "Motion Pictures: Analysis: Aubrey's Appointment at MGM—Why?" *Entertainment World* (31 Oct. 1969); and Jodi Lawrence, "Jungle Jim and the MGM Acid Test: An Exclusive Interview with Jim Aubrey," *Today's Film Maker* (Feb. 1972). Obituaries are in the *New York Times* and *Variety* (both 12 Sep. 1994).

TED MURPHY

AUDEN, W(ystan) H(ugh)   (*b.* 21 February 1907 in York, England; *d.* 29 September 1973 in Vienna, Austria), poet, playwright, librettist, critic, translator, editor, lecturer, and teacher.

The youngest of three sons of George Augustus Auden and Constance Rosalie Bicknell, Auden was brought up in Birmingham, England, where his father was a school medical officer and later a professor of public health and where his mother was a college-educated nurse who raised the family in the Anglican tradition. As a boy attending schools in Surrey and Norfolk, Auden was fascinated by machines, medicine, and geology. At Christ Church, Oxford University, he studied science but then switched to English, graduating in 1928. At Oxford, he became known as one of the best poets of a generation that included the top left-wing writers of the 1920s.

Rebelling against his traditional background, Auden explored the ideas of Marx and Freud and, with his father's help, spent the year after college in Germany, where the writer Christopher Isherwood, a former schoolmate, visited him. In Berlin, Auden felt freer to apply his radicalism, developing a homosexual lifestyle that expressed his identity. In 1935, aware of the growing menace of Nazism, he married the writer Erika Mann (daughter of the author Thomas Mann), but the union was only a formal arrangement. The British passport Mann acquired upon her marriage enabled her to leave Germany for England. From 1930 to 1935 Auden worked as a schoolmaster in England, where he cofounded the Group Theatre in 1932 and worked with the General Post Office film unit in 1935.

Auden's early writings and plays, some of which were collaborations with Isherwood, established him as a skilled writer. In 1936 and 1937 Auden traveled to Iceland and then drove an ambulance in Spain during that country's civil war. He and Isherwood visited China in 1938 to report on the war there. In 1939 the two went to the United States, where Auden met a bright young student from Brooklyn College named Chester Kallman. "Mr. Right," as Auden called Kallman, became his life companion. In 1946 Auden became a naturalized U.S. citizen, settling in New York City with Kallman.

Auden found success on both the academic scene and in publishing. Among his teaching assignments were stints at the New School for Social Research (1940–1941 and 1946–1947), the University of Michigan in Ann Arbor (1941–1942), Swarthmore College (1942–1945), Bennington College (1946), Barnard College (1947), Smith College (1953), and finally, back in England, at Oxford University (1956–1961). Auden's main interest was writing, however, and his most notable publications are *The Collected Poetry of W. H. Auden* (1945), the Pulitzer Prize–winning *Age of Anxiety* (1947), *The Enchafed Flood* (1950), and *The Shield of Achilles* (1955). During the 1960s Auden published prolifically, including *Homage to Clio* (1960); *A Book of Aphorisms* (1960, with Louis Kronenberger); *The Dyer's Hand* (1962), a collection of essays and lectures; *About the House* (1965); *Collected Shorter Poems, 1927–1957* (1966); *Collected Longer Poems* (1968); *Secondary Worlds* (1968), his T. S. Eliot Memorial Lectures from the University of Kent; *City Without Walls and Many Other Poems* (1969); and *A Certain World: A Commonplace Book* (1970).

By 1960 Auden's writing already had brought him an ample harvest of awards, including the King's Gold Medal for poetry (1937), Guggenheim Fellowships (1942 and 1945), the Award of Merit Medal from the American Academy of Arts and Letters (1945), the Pulitzer Prize in poetry (1948), the Bollingen Prize in poetry (1954), the National Book Award (1956), the Feltrinelli Prize (1957), and the Guinness Poetry Award (1959, shared with Robert Lowell

W. H. Auden. CORBIS CORPORATION (BELLEVUE)

and Edith Sitwell). With money from the Feltrinelli Prize, Auden bought a farmhouse outside Vienna and spent most of his summers there from 1957 on, wintering in New York City at 77 Saint Mark's Place, between First and Second Avenues, where he remained until 1972.

Auden also made significant contributions as a translator. With the Scandinavian scholar Leif Sjöberg, he produced *Markings,* the journal of UN Secretary General Dag Hammarskjöld (translated from the Swedish and published in 1964), and translations of other Swedish poets, including Pär Lagerkvist and Gunnar Ekelöf. He cotranslated works by the writer Johann Wolfgang von Goethe and the playwright Bertolt Brecht from German, the philosopher Søren Kierkegaard from Danish, and other works from French and Old Norse.

Auden's relationship with Kallman was not as successful as his career, and by 1941 it became clear that the men were neither sexually compatible nor monogamous. By 1963 Kallman, who was disappointed with his own career as a poet, no longer wanted to spend winters in New York City with Auden, preferring to live with lovers in Athens. In despair, in September 1964 Auden went to Berlin to live for half a year, but the city had changed, and his spirits were not lifted. Despite their unhappiness, Auden and

Kallman's relationship lasted thirty-four years. Auden had enhanced his love of music through Kallman, and some of their most positive moments had been spent collaborating on opera libretti, including one for *The Rake's Progress,* by Igor Stravinsky (premiered in Venice in 1951), and another for *The Bassarids,* by Hans Werner Henze (premiered at the Salzburg Festival in 1966).

Auden became deeply disillusioned with politics, not least during the U.S. presidential campaigns of 1964, when his poem "September 1, 1939" was misquoted and used out of context in a television advertisement by Lyndon B. Johnson, accusing his opponent of supporting the Vietnam War. In 1968 Auden claimed that if he were forced to choose between voting for Johnson and for Richard Nixon, he could vote for neither. Nevertheless, he never gave up on politics and wrote frequently about the perversion of language by politicians. Although he was surrounded in the 1960s by hippies in his neighborhood on Saint Mark's Place, he said that he admired their spirit but feared that they had not read any of his poems (except perhaps "The Platonic Blow," published without permission in the magazine *Fuck You*).

Oddly enough, although Auden had felt obliged through most of his adult years to express his homosexual desires only through his poetry, the 1967 passage of social reforms in Britain decriminalizing homosexuality impressed him little: most gays had managed all right, he thought, without such a law. Earlier, when the English paperback edition of the British writer D. H. Lawrence's erotic novel *Lady Chatterley's Lover* was prosecuted for obscenity in 1960, he had wanted to testify that the novel was pornographic.

Auden had been seriously addicted to cigarettes, alcohol, and amphetamines for years, and these substances began to take their toll. Friends noticed that in his later years Auden's appearance changed dramatically, another result of a health problem he had endured since early adulthood. Touraine-Solente-Gole syndrome had a thickening and wrinkling effect on the skin of his forehead, face, scalp, hands, and feet. It did not threaten his mental faculties, but there was no treatment. Auden's friend, the influential thinker Hannah Arendt, was concerned about him. She had just been widowed when, in November 1970, he asked her to marry him. (Erika Mann had died in 1969.) It saddened Arendt to decline, but she knew that it was not a feasible suggestion, as did a male acquaintance in New York whom Auden asked to move in with him. Auden soon found himself living alone, which did not appeal to him, and he accepted the position that Oxford University offered him in 1972, to move back as an honorary fellow of Christ Church. But the university life there no longer suited him, and the academic community found his unconventional ways unacceptable.

In the summer of 1973 Auden returned to his house in Kirchstetten, Austria, where he had summered since 1948, and on 28 September gave a successful poetry reading in Vienna for the Austrian Society for Literature. Sometime that night, in his hotel room, Auden died in his sleep from heart failure. He was discovered in his hotel room by Chester Kallman. The older poet, who was scheduled to return to Oxford that day, had never failed to love or support his life partner and did so also in his will. Kallman, who was in poor health, died fifteen months later, at age fifty-four. Auden was buried in Austria.

★

Auden's papers are housed at the Berg Collection of the New York Public Library. Various manuscripts are also housed in collections at Swarthmore College in Swarthmore, Pennsylvania; the Bodleian Library of Oxford University; the British Museum; the Lockwood Memorial Library in Buffalo, New York; and the Humanities Research Center at the University of Texas. Biographies include Humphrey Carpenter, *W. H. Auden: A Biography* (1981). Full-length books about Auden include Richard Davenport-Hines, *Auden* (1996); Stan Smith, *W. H. Auden* (1997); John Fuller, *W. H. Auden: A Commentary* (1998); and Edward Mendelson, *Early Auden* (2000) and *Later Auden* (2000). For information about specific time periods or events in Auden's life, see Dorothy J. Farnan, *Auden in Love: The Intimate Story of a Lifelong Love Affair* (1984); Katharine Bucknell and Nicholas Jenkins, eds., *The Map of All My Youth: Early Works, Friends and Influences* (1990); and Norman Page, *Auden and Isherwood: The Berlin Years* (2000). Articles of particular interest include Richard R. Bozorth, "Auden's Games of Knowledge," *Between Men—Between Women: Lesbian and Gay Studies* (2001). Web sites include the Auden Society at http://www.audensociety.org. Obituaries are in the *New York Times* (30 Sept., 4 Oct., and 5 Oct. 1973), the *Detroit Free Press* (30 Sept. 1973), and *Time* (8 Oct. 1973).

VERNE MOBERG

AVALON, Frankie (*b.* 18 September 1940 in Philadelphia, Pennsylvania), and **Annette Joanne FUNICELLO** (*b.* 22 October 1942 in Utica, New York), singers and actors who came to prominence as teen idols in the 1950s, then costarred in the successful *Beach Party* series of teen films in the 1960s.

Avalon was born Francis Thomas Avalone. He began his show business career as a child trumpet player, appearing on *The Jackie Gleason Show* and other programs and recording two instrumental records, "Trumpet Sorrento" and "Trumpet Tarantella," for X-Vik Records, an RCA subsidiary; both records were released in 1954. Avalon then joined the band *Rocco and the Saints*, whose lineup included the drummer Robert Ridarelli (later a teen idol himself, as Bobby Rydell). In 1957, while still in high school in Philadelphia, Avalon signed with Peter De Angelis and Robert Marcucci, songwriters who also managed Chancellor Records. At the end of the year Avalon released "DeDe Dinah," which became his first Top Ten hit.

Avalon's success coincided with the rise of the "teen idols," a crop of pleasant, nonthreatening male singers such as Bobby Rydell, Bobby Vinton, and Fabian, who represented a safe alternative to the wildness of the original rock-and-roll stars such as Elvis Presley. From 1958 to 1959 Avalon had Top Ten hits with the songs "Venus," which was his biggest hit, selling more than one million copies in less than one week; "Why," which topped the charts; "Ginger Bread"; "Bobby Sox to Stockings"; and "Just Ask Your Heart." After 1960 his records charted increasingly lower, but by then he had moved into films. He made his screen debut performing the song "Teacher's Pet" in *Jamboree* (1957), and later appeared in *The Alamo* (1960), *Voyage to the Bottom of the Sea* (1961), *Panic in the Year Zero* (1962), *Sail a Crooked Ship* (1962), *Drums of Africa* (1963), and *Operation Bikini* (1963).

Funicello was the only girl of three children born to Joe Funicello, a mechanic, and Virginia Albano, a homemaker. When Funicello was four years old the family moved from New York across the country to the San Fernando Valley outside Los Angeles. She began taking music and dancing lessons, and in 1955 she was discovered by Walt Disney, who saw her performing the lead role in *Swan Lake* in an amateur dance revue at the Starlight Bowl in Burbank, California. That same year he cast her in his new television program, the *Mickey Mouse Club,* where she quickly became the most popular "Mouseketeer" and even had her own line of licensed merchandise. Funicello subsequently appeared in the Disney television serials *Adventures of Spin and Marty* (1955) and *Zorro* (1957), as well as the Disney films *The Shaggy Dog* (1959) and *Babes in Toyland* (1961). She launched her singing career on the Disneyland and Buena Vista labels, having Top Twenty hits with "Tall Paul" (1959) and "O Dio Mio" and "Pineapple Princess" (both 1960). Her albums *Annette Sings Anka* and *Hawaiiannette* (both 1960) and *Annette's Beach Party* (1963) all charted in the Top Forty. She received a high school diploma in 1960.

In 1963 Avalon and Funicello were cast as the stars of the American International Pictures (AIP) film *Beach Party.* Seeking to capitalize on the success of the teen comedies *Where the Girls Are* and *Gidget, Beach Party* stuck to a basic formula: the on-again/off-again relationship of "Frankie" (Avalon) and "Dolores" or "Dee Dee" (Funicello), set against a backdrop of teen exploits including surfing or drag racing. There were guest spots from adult actors such as Don Rickles and Buddy Hackett, and plenty of dancing, to the music of *Dick Dale and the Del Tones* and "Little" Stevie Wonder. Although promoted with titillating advertisements

Frankie Avalon and Annette Funicello. AP/WIDE WORLD PHOTOS

("When 10,000 biceps go around 5,000 bikinis . . . you KNOW what's gonna happen!"), the proceedings were invariably wholesome; even the obligatory biker gang proved to be ludicrously inept. The initial film was highly successful, and a series of sequels was produced.

Muscle Beach Party, Bikini Beach (both 1964), and *Beach Blanket Bingo* and *How to Stuff a Wild Bikini* (both 1965) adhered to the basic scenario of *Beach Party.* Occasionally the storyline did move off the beach, as in *Pajama Party* (1964) and *Ski Party* and *Dr. Goldfoot and the Bikini Machine* (both 1965). *Fireball 500* (1966), set in the world of drag racing, was the last AIP feature in which Avalon and Funicello costarred; the film also starred Fabian.

Funicello's other films in the 1960s include the Disney films *The Misadventures of Merlin Jones* (1964); *The Monkey's Uncle* (1965); another drag racing film, *Thunder Alley* (1967); and the off-beat feature *Head* (1968), starring the musical group the Monkees. She then largely curtailed her career to raise a family. Funicello married her manager, Jack Gilardi, on 9 January 1965; they had three children.

Funicello continued to do television work and became a spokesperson for the Skippy brand of peanut butter, among other endorsements.

Avalon appeared in light comedies and teen exploitation films during the 1960s, including *I'll Take Sweden* and *Sergeant Deadhead* (both 1965), *The Million Eyes of Sumuru* (1967), *Skidoo* (1968), which was Groucho Marx's last film, and the thriller *Horror House* (1969). In 1976 he released a disco version of "Venus," which peaked at number forty-six on the pop chart. In 1978, in a gentle parody of his teen-idol persona, he appeared in the successful musical *Grease,* and in 1985 he toured with Rydell and Fabian in a show billed as the "Golden Boys of *Bandstand.*"

Following the tour he reunited with Funicello, and they were coexecutive producers of the 1987 film *Back to the Beach,* which spoofed their beach-party films and poked fun at Funicello's Skippy peanut butter endorsements. The two made further appearances parodying their wholesome personas in the television show *Pee-Wee Herman's Christmas Special* (1988) and the feature film *Troop Beverly Hills* (1989).

Funicello divorced Gilardi in 1981 and married Glen Holt, a horse trainer and breeder, on 5 March 1986. She was diagnosed with multiple sclerosis in 1987, though she did not announce the condition publicly until 1992. She told her story in her 1994 book *A Dream Is a Wish Your Heart Makes* and later appeared in the television film based on the book. As she fought the disease, Funicello launched two new ventures, the Teddy Bear Company and a perfume, "Cello, by Annette." Funicello also set up the Annette Funicello Research Fund for Neurological Diseases, which receives a portion of the profits of her businesses. Avalon married Kay Diebel in 1962; they have eight children. He continues to make public appearances, and his company, Frankie Avalon Products, sells a variety of health supplements.

★

There are no biographies of Avalon. Funicello's autobiography, written with Patricia Romanowski, is *A Dream Is a Wish Your Heart Makes: The Annette Funicello Story* (1994). An interview with Funicello is "Mighty Mouse," *Los Angeles Magazine* (1 Apr. 1994). She also wrote the foreword to Lorraine Santoli, *The Official Mickey Mouse Club Book* (1995). The late 1950s to early 1960s rock period is detailed in Ed Ward, Geoffrey Stokes, and Ken Tucker, eds., *Rock of Ages: The Rolling Stone History of Rock and Roll* (1986). Detailed information on the *Beach Party* films is in David Ehrenstein and Bill Reed, *Rock on Film* (1982), and Marshall Crenshaw, *Hollywood Rock: A Guide to Rock 'n Roll in the Movies* (1994).

GILLIAN G. GAAR

B

BAEZ, Joan Chandos (*b*. 9 January 1941 in New York City), folksinger, songwriter, and antiwar and human rights activist who began her career in the tumultuous 1960s. Her clear, soaring soprano voice was the clarion call for thousands of disaffected American youth during that decade.

Baez was the middle of three daughters born to Albert Baez, a Mexican-born physicist, and Joan Bridge, a homemaker of Scottish-English ancestry. Both parents came from a strong religious background; their fathers were both ministers. The Baez family converted to the Quaker faith, and their daughters were raised in a strong moral climate. This pacifistic faith was the foundation for the family's activism. The father's work as a researcher, teacher, and consultant took the family to Baghdad, Paris, and many cities in the United States.

Baez was an indifferent student who suffered bouts of anxiety that often kept her at home or in the nurse's office. Her Mexican heritage had given her a dark skin color, which made her feel self-conscious and unattractive. In 1954, when Baez was thirteen, her aunt took her and her younger sister, Mimi, to a concert by the legendary folk singer Pete Seeger in the Palo Alto High School gym. It was reportedly a revelation for Baez, the moment when she realized she could be a professional singer. The Baez girls were all musical, but Joan's musical talent became an opportunity for her to shine, to become the center of attention, and to be well liked. Both Joan and Mimi progressed from

ukulele to guitar. Baez graduated from Palo Alto High School as a talented artist who attracted increasing attention for her natural guitar ability and her beautiful soprano voice.

The family returned to the East Coast after Baez's graduation, settling in Belmont, Massachusetts. In the fall of 1958 she enrolled at Boston University. At freshman orientation Baez met some students playing the guitar and found friends who could teach her new songs and guitar techniques. She was soon skipping most of her classes and hanging out with students who were part of the growing coffeehouse scene in Cambridge, Massachusetts. She dropped out of Boston University before the end of her second semester.

Committed to a career as a folksinger, Baez appeared regularly at Club 47, drawing increasingly larger crowds of collegians. She received good reviews in the *Harvard Crimson* and recorded on the local Cambridge label, Veritas. She also attracted the attention of Albert Grossman, a Chicago club owner and personal manager who later signed Bob Dylan and Janis Joplin. Grossman booked Baez for a two-week engagement in June 1959 at his Chicago club, Gate of Horn. Grossman sensed that Baez had star quality and was eager to sign her. However, Baez preferred working with Manny Greenhill.

At the Gate of Horn, Baez met the folk singers Bob Gibson and Odetta, and Gibson invited Baez to share his stage time at the Newport (Rhode Island) Folk Festival in July

Joan Baez. THE LIBRARY OF CONGRESS

1959. The festival, in its fifth year, drew an audience of 13,000 college-age fans. Such folk festivals were an outgrowth of jazz festivals that had originated in the early 1950s.

It rained the first day of the concert, and Baez spent the day backstage to see and meet the performers. Her clothes were soaked, her hair stringy, and her bare feet were covered with mud from her walk over to the tent when Gibson invited her onstage to sing a duet. Then he turned a microphone over to her for a solo. Standing still, with her arms at her side, Baez electrified the crowd of thousands with the power and intensity of her voice, and they erupted in applause. She was the hit of the festival. She signed a recording contract with Vanguard, a small, low-key folk artist label, which had also signed Odetta. Her first album, *Joan Baez* (1960), became a huge success without promotion or a supporting tour.

Baez met Bob Dylan in April 1961 at the Folk City coffeehouse in Greenwich Village, New York City, and they soon became romantically involved. Baez's 1968 album, *Any Day Now*, is a collection of Dylan's songs. Dylan had been scuffling around the coffeehouses, singing without much success, and wanted to meet Baez, who already had a successful debut album and was performing to sold-out concerts around the country. In the early 1960s thousands of young people across the country were mobilizing,

editorializing, participating in Freedom Marches, and assisting in voter registration in the South. Folk songs like those of Baez were their anthems.

At the Monterey Folk Festival (like Newport, a spin-off from a jazz festival) Baez and Dylan performed together in May 1963. Initially, Dylan was poorly received; his voice was harsh and his guitar-playing discordant. However, Baez joined him to sing and urged the crowd to listen because his songs spoke to all people who wanted a better world. The press anointed them the reigning Queen and Prince of Folk Music. The previous November, Baez had been the cover subject of a *Time* magazine issue. Baez toured with Dylan in 1965. She was nominated for a Grammy in the best folk recording category and gave her first major concert in Europe at London's Royal Albert Hall.

President John F. Kennedy was tentative about civil rights legislation. On 28 August 1963, following his somewhat belated package of antidiscrimination legislation (subsequently signed by President Lyndon B. Johnson), the Freedom March in Washington drew 250,000 protesters. Baez and Dylan sang "We Shall Overcome" at the foot of the Lincoln Statue, but they soon took different paths. Dylan had little interest in social issues, and Baez became even more involved in them. In 1964, as a protest against U.S. involvement in the Vietnam War, she withheld the part of her income taxes she believed were designated for military spending—ultimately a symbolic gesture, as the Internal Revenue Service simply placed a lien on her assets. Baez was invited to sing at a salute to President Johnson on 26 May 1964 at the National Guard Armory in Washington. She took the opportunity to urge Johnson to withdraw troops from Vietnam; at the same time, she bolstered his support for civil rights. Her own efforts in support of civil rights included participating in the August 1963 march from Selma to Montgomery, Alabama. Baez often marched with her arms linked with those of Dr. Martin Luther King, Jr.

While attending Quaker meetings when the Baez daughters were teenagers, the Baez family had become friends with Ira Sandperl, a West Coast pacifist. Baez felt her sense of philosophy was naive and unfocused, which made her feel inadequate. She asked Sandperl to tutor her in pacifist social and political philosophy. In the summer of 1963 the two founded the Institute for the Study of Nonviolence at Baez's home in Carmel Valley, California. Sandperl ran the Institute (now known as the Resource Center for Nonviolence) for over ten years.

In October 1967 Baez and her mother were arrested in Oakland, California, for blocking the entrance to the Armed Forces Induction Center, and each served two sentences in Santa Rita Rehabilitation Center. During the October sit-in Baez met David Harris, a former Stanford University student body president and now a draft resistance organizer. Baez and Harris married on 26 March 1968 while touring together in support of resistance to the draft. Harris was later sentenced to three years in prison for refusing induction into the armed forces. After the birth of their son in December 1969, Baez resumed touring and made talk show appearances with a renewed and articulate confidence while Harris served twenty months in prison. In 1971 the two wrote *Coming Out*, a book of photographs taken on draft resistance tours after Harris was released. The couple separated soon afterward and divorced in January 1974.

Baez's music and albums initially comprised traditional folk songs, but by her fourth album (1962) she was using some of Dylan's material. However, throughout the decades she has sung a variety of material, acquiring a musical balance, but she has rejected rock and roll.

From Birmingham to Bosnia to Berkeley, Baez has used her voice to draw people into the protest movements or humanitarian causes. Czech president Václav Havel credited her with influencing his country's Velvet Revolution. She traveled to Vietnam in December 1972 to deliver mail and presents to U.S. prisoners during the bombing of Hanoi. During concerts in South America she received death threats and required police surveillance.

Baez has continued to sing and speak out, raising money for humanitarian causes and singing in fund-raisers such as Live Aid and on tours around the world. The "barefoot madonna" endures as a celebrated and significant activist of our time.

★

Baez has written two autobiographies, *Daybreak* (1968) and *And a Voice to Sing With: A Memoir* (1987). Additional information on Baez can be found in David Hajdu, *Positively 4th Street: The Lives and Times of Joan Baez, Bob Dylan, Mimi Baez Fariña, and Richard Fariña* (2001); and Ray B. Browne, Marshall Fishwick, and Michael T. Marsden, eds., *Heroes of Popular Culture* (1972).

ROSEMARIE S. CARDOSO

BAGGS, William Calhoun. *See* Ashmore, Harry Scott, and William Calhoun ("Bill") Baggs.

BAILYN, Bernard (*b.* 10 September 1922 in Hartford, Connecticut), historian of early U.S. history, Harvard professor of history, two-time winner of the Pulitzer Prize in history, winner of the Bancroft Prize, and former president of the American Historical Association.

Bailyn was born to Charles Manuel Bailyn and Esther Schloss, and was raised in Hartford. In the fall of 1940, Bailyn entered Williams College, where he studied history, literature, and philosophy. During his junior year Bailyn joined the U.S. Army, serving in the Signal Corps and the Army Security Agency during World War II. In 1945, while still in the army, Bailyn completed the requirements for a B.A. degree in English literature from Williams College. After leaving the army the following year, Bailyn began graduate studies in history at Harvard University. Reflecting on his decision to enter graduate school, Bailyn remembered that he was interested in studying three facets of history: the relationship between Europe and the United States, the evolution of the world from a premodern to modern society, and the interplay between social and intellectual history. Bailyn's early queries into history served as the foundation for his entire academic career.

Specializing in the early social and economic history of the United States, as well as the history of Rome and medieval Europe, Bailyn earned his M.A. in 1947, and his Ph.D. in 1953. On 18 June 1952 he married Lotte Lazarsfeld; they have two sons. Proving his merits as a student, Bailyn became an instructor at Harvard in 1949, an associate professor with tenure in 1958, and a full professor in 1961. In 1966 he was named the Winthrop Professor of History and in 1981 became the Adams University Professor. Between 1962 and 1970, he served as editor-in-chief of the John Harvard Library, a series of modern editions of classic works by American authors. Between 1967 and 1977 (and again from 1984 to 1986), Bailyn worked as the co-editor of *Perspectives in American History,* a collection of essays published by the Charles Warren Center. As well as carrying out his professional duties at Harvard, Bailyn has been an active member of the American Historical Association, serving as president in 1981.

In the early 1960s, Bailyn established himself as a pre-eminent social and intellectual historian in the field of U.S. colonial history, with the publication of two significant works: *Education in the Forming of American Society: Needs and Opportunities for Study* (1960), and "Political Experience and Enlightenment Ideas in Eighteenth-Century America," an article in the *American Historical Review* (1962). In the former, Bailyn revealed that education is more than simply a formal institution of learning; it is a process in which culture transmits itself from one generation to the next. Bailyn noted that in early colonial education, the family unit was responsible for educating the children, aided by the apprentice system, the church, and the local community. However, Bailyn discovered that education in British North America slowly began to take on a distinctive American character as colonial society matured. As labor shortages, the abundance of land, and religious pluralism became commonplace in the British colonies, the number of schools rapidly increased. As a result, colonial society, as well as colonial education, became more American than European. *Education in the Forming of American Society* solidified Bailyn's place as a prominent social historian of early U.S. history.

Bailyn furthered his reputation as a social historian with

the article "Political Experience," which portrayed the American colonial experience as being distinctively different from its European counterpart. This brief article suggested that the American Revolution was not the result of social upheaval as many progressive historians had defined it, but it was instead a contest of ideas. Unlike many scholars writing about the Revolutionary period, Bailyn did not see Enlightenment political philosophies, England's common-law tradition, or the appeal of antiquity as the driving force behind the activities of the revolutionaries; rather, he characterized the Americans as being loyal to the republican experiments of the seventeenth century and suspicious of the rise of ministerial power and influence in the eighteenth century.

In the early 1960s Bailyn would further refine his interpretations of the American Revolution by editing a large collection of Revolutionary pamphlets for the John Harvard Library. As he culled through over 400 pamphlets dating from 1750 to 1776, Bailyn came to a greater understanding of the Revolutionary period. In 1965 Bailyn explained his findings in a lengthy introduction ("The Transforming Radicalism of the American Revolution") to the first published volume of pamphlets, *Pamphlets of the American Revolution, 1750–1776*, for which he won the Harvard Faculty Prize. Bailyn introduced the idea that the American Revolution is best understood as a constitutional dispute between the British colonies and the British government. Bailyn believed that the colonial arguments presented in the edited pamphlets were not merely rhetorical rationalizations used by radical colonial leaders to overshadow their material interests, but expressed the convictions and principles that lay at the heart of the Revolutionary movement.

Bailyn's introduction was separately published in 1967 as *The Ideological Origins of the American Revolution*. This was undoubtedly the most important work Bailyn published in the 1960s, and its arguments greatly affected American and British scholars who studied the causes of the American Revolution. Bailyn asserted that American leaders during the late colonial period were committed to the ideals of the radical Whig Party, an association politically opposed to the absolute authority of the British crown in seventeenth-century England. According to Bailyn, strict adherence to the Whig philosophy caused Americans to see British rule in the colonies from 1763 to 1776 as sinister and maligned. In fact, Bailyn claimed that the colonials were so dedicated to the idea of protecting civil and political rights from governmental tyranny that they became firmly convinced that the British government was engaged in a corrupt plan designed to rob them of their most basic rights as Englishmen.

Although Bailyn's findings concerning the conservative characteristics of the colonists were important in understanding the causes of the American Revolution, he placed an equal if not greater emphasis on understanding the consequences of the Revolutionary movement, which proved to be more radical in nature. Bailyn suggested that American society in the years following 1765 was completing a period of transformation that had been slowly taking place since the British first colonized North America. American political leaders became increasingly willing to adopt more radical positions pertaining to issues such as representation in government, natural rights of citizens, constitutional construction, and political sovereignty. Additionally, Bailyn argued that Revolutionary ideology served as a challenge to many social institutions in the colonies, especially the legitimacy of slavery, the right of states to establish and maintain an official religion, and the need to adhere to the policy of deference to social superiors. Counter to traditional interpretations of the Revolution, Bailyn argued that the radicalism of the Revolutionary period was not the result of economic distress or social upheaval, but was caused by a new radical ideology that was opposed to all practices that restricted human liberties. The fact that *The Ideological Origins of the American Revolution* won both the Pulitzer Prize and the Bancroft Prize in 1968 suggests how important Bailyn's contribution was to the historical community. Bailyn continued to examine the influence of radical Whig thought in the colonies in *The Origins of American Politics* (1968), which was the Harvard professor's last major publication in the 1960s.

As a whole, Bailyn's publications in the 1960s significantly contributed to the development of a new body of historical literature that focused on the idea of republicanism and pushed scholars to consider how ideology influences society. Bailyn continued to make valuable contributions to the study of early U.S. history in the decades following the 1960s. His work on the Royalist governor of Massachusetts, *The Ordeal of Thomas Hutchinson* (1974), won the 1975 National Book Award in history. Proof of his enormous influence on the historical community was evident when he won his second Pulitzer Prize for *Voyagers to the West: A Passage in the Peopling of British North America on the Eve of the Revolution* (1986), a study that examines the dramatic upsurge in emigration from Britain to the North American colonies prior to the Revolution. Although Bailyn has enjoyed a long and influential career, his most valuable and enduring insights into early U.S. history came in the 1960s.

★

Biographical information on Bailyn is in James A. Henretta, Michael G. Kammen, and Stanley N. Katz, eds., *The Transformation of Early American History: Society, Authority, and Ideology* (1991); and Robert Allen Rutland, ed., *Clio's Favorites: Leading Historians of the United States, 1945–2000* (2000). Analyses of Bailyn's views are in John A. Garraty, *Interpreting American History:*

Conversations with Historians, Part I (1970); Karen J. Winkler, "Wanted: A History that Pulls Things Together—An Interview with Bernard Bailyn," *Chronicles of Higher Education* 20 (July 1980): 3; A. Roger Ekirch, "Sometimes an Art, Never a Science, Always a Craft: A Conversation with Bernard Bailyn," *William and Mary Quarterly* (Oct. 1994): 625–658; and Edward Connery Lathem, *Bernard Bailyn: On the Teaching and Writing of History: Responses to a Series of Questions* (1994). Examinations of Bailyn's influence on intellectual historiography are in Robert Shalhope, "Toward a Republican Synthesis: The Emergence of an Understanding of Republicanism in American Historiography," *William and Mary Quarterly* 29 (Jan. 1972): 49–80; and Shalhope, "Republicanism and Early American Historiography," *William and Mary Quarterly* 39 (Apr. 1982): 334–356.

KENNETH WAYNE HOWELL

BAKER, Carroll (*b.* 28 May 1931 in Johnstown, Pennsylvania), actress whose promising film career in the 1960s was derailed when she was unable to shake her sex goddess image.

Baker, one of two daughters of William W. Baker and Virginia Duffy, attended Greensburg High School in Pennsylvania, graduating in 1949, and Saint Petersburg Junior College in Florida. After settling in New York City, she married furrier Louis Ritter in 1952 and divorced him the same year. In 1953 she began attending Lee Strasberg's Actors Studio. She appeared in two stage productions in New York, making her Broadway debut in 1954 in the hit show *All Summer Long*. In 1955 she married Jack Garfein; they had two children.

Established as a credible young actress, Baker began to receive major offers from Hollywood. Finally she accepted the role of Luz Benedict, the daughter of Elizabeth Taylor's and Rock Hudson's characters in George Stevens's *Giant* (1956). Only three weeks after completing *Giant,* she started shooting Elia Kazan's controversial *Baby Doll* (1956). Kazan cast Baker in the leading role, which was created by the playwright Tennessee Williams. Starring as a young Mississippi wife in a film written by one of the most important playwrights of the period was intended to give Baker success; however, it marked her as just another sexy blonde for the rest of her career.

Tellingly, despite Baker's largely unsuccessful attempts to play down the sexual frankness of her screen image in the next few films she made, the name "Baby Doll" remained with her. Even her 1983 autobiography is titled *Baby Doll*. In her autobiography, Baker complains that the attention she received from the public and the press because of the film, and the controversy it caused with the Catholic Legion of Decency, was "a confusing, disillusioning, distasteful, and even abhorrent experience." Yet the title of the book points to her willingness, almost three decades after

Carroll Baker, 1962. THE KOBAL COLLECTION

the film, to build her success on the very image that the film and the press created. The cover photos on the paperback edition of the book also indicate this continuity between Baker and her famous screen role. One portrays Baker at the time the book was written, while the other depicts her in the famous Baby Doll posture of sucking her thumb in a crib.

During the late 1950s and the early 1960s, Baker tried to find roles that would be a complete departure from her role in *Baby Doll*. She joined the all-star cast of William Wyler's *The Big Country* (1958), accepting the role of a wealthy ranch owner's daughter who is in love with Gregory Peck. This ambitious Western epic, however, failed to revive Baker's star image. As the film ran over schedule and over budget, Baker was released when her contract expired; her character quickly dropped out of sight in the movie without much explanation.

Baker next pursued her detachment from the Baby Doll image with Irving Rapper's *The Miracle* (1959), which was based on a Spanish legend about a nun who runs away from the convent after asking the Virgin Mary to step in for her. Baker admitted that the film was not her cup of tea; after seeing a sneak preview in New York City, she "got into a huff" and asked her agents to buy back her contract from Warner Brothers. This was the first of several wrong choices that eventually led Baker away from Hollywood. That same year she starred in Paramount's *But Not for Me,* an undistinguished comedy that did little to create a new screen image for her. She commented, "I'd taken a gigantic step backwards, committed a type of professional suicide, and suddenly I was stricken by the horror of what it means to be no longer in demand. No offers came my way: three months, four months, six months."

When offers did start to come again, they were for films that all seemed promising to Baker, who was facing severe depression and financial problems, but they failed to be particularly exciting or rewarding. Her next four films included the unsuccessful Method experiment *Something Wild* (1961), in which Baker played a rape victim; *Bridge to the Sun* (1961); *How the West Was Won* (1962); and *Station Six-Sahara* (1963). Henry Hathaway and John Ford's *How the West Was Won* was the sole success, but because it had such a large cast, it did little to rekindle Baker's fame.

Baker's career had taken a downward turn and become artistically unremarkable. Only eight years after her overnight stardom with Baby Doll, Baker was seeking a "comeback" vehicle and accepted a role in *The Carpetbaggers* (1964). Although the film briefly restored Baker's star status, it did not help her escape from her sex symbol image. The success of *The Carpetbaggers* limited Baker once and for all to the stereotype of the blonde goddess and did nothing to alter either the critics' or the public's perception of her.

After starring in Ford's *Cheyenne Autumn* (1964), and Stevens's *The Greatest Story Ever Told* (1965), Baker stopped trying to change her screen image, but her choices had ruinous effects on her career. She agreed to be photographed for *Playboy* magazine and then played the title roles in *Sylvia* (1965) and *Harlow* (1965), films that banked on her sexual appeal. Ironically, when Baker finally accepted roles modeled on the part that had made her famous, she was unable to turn them into box-office hits. In particular, the highly publicized *Harlow* failed badly with audiences and critics alike. The financial losses were so catastrophic that the Paramount producer Joseph E. Levine canceled Baker's seven-year contract. Suddenly, she again found herself unemployed. To avoid another nervous breakdown, she joined the comedian Bob Hope in 1966 for a tour to entertain U.S. soldiers in Vietnam.

In 1969 Baker divorced Garfein and moved to Italy. She remained there throughout the 1970s, starring in several B movies, mainly erotic thrillers and melodramas. In 1982 she married the actor and art director Donald Burton. Although Baker did not appear again in leading roles, from the late 1970s to the early 2000s she acted in supporting roles in U.S. productions on stage, in film, and on television. Her screen image finally became diversified, albeit at the price of reduced visibility. Baker appeared in art-house releases such as Andy Warhol's *Bad* (1977) and Bob Fosse's *Star 80* (1983), in social problem films such as *Native Son* (1986) and Hector Babenco's *Ironweed* (1987), and in blockbusters such as *Kindergarten Cop* (1990) and *The Game* (1997).

Baker's career and star image embodied the difficulty experienced by many actresses in the 1960s in finding a way of sustaining their initial success in Hollywood. Film historians are still debating the extent to which this difficulty was due to the changing modes of production in the movie industry, the shifting taste of audiences, or the development of countercultural values among certain social strata in the final years of the era. Baker's screen personae from *Baby Doll* to *Harlow*, and the exploitation films she made in Italy through the late 1960s and the 1970s, also appear in constant negotiation with the related stereotypes of the "Hollywood Lolita" and the blonde sex goddess. Baker was initially able to exploit the "nymphet syndrome" in the movies, and the title role in *Baby Doll* launched her as a major star. Yet, in the end, such stereotypes proved limiting for Baker, and movies such as *Sylvia* and *Harlow*, in which she completely surrendered to the role of the sex object, were disastrously received by critics and audiences alike.

★

Baker published her autobiography *Baby Doll* (1983), the sentimental memoir *To Africa with Love* (1985), and the novel *A Roman Tale* (1986). Some parts of the study by Marianne Sinclair, *Hollywood Lolitas: The Nymphet Syndrome in the Movies* (1988), are devoted to an analysis of Baker's screen personae.

LUCA PRONO

BALANCHINE, George (*b.* 22 January 1904 in Saint Petersburg, Russia; *d.* 30 April 1983 in New York City), ballet dancer, instructor, and choreographer who by the 1960s was generally acknowledged as the world's greatest living choreographer and whose ballets and teaching style have affected generations of students and professionals ever since.

Born Georgi Melitonovitch Balanchivadze, Balanchine was one of three children born to Meliton Balanchivadze and Maria Nikolayevna Vassilyeva. His father, a Georgian, was a composer and failed businessman; his Russian mother, a bank employee. When Balanchine was still small, the family moved to Lounatiokki, now in Finland, and there he began piano lessons. Although his parents had planned a military career for him, he was accepted into the Maryinsky Theatre (Imperial Ballet) School in Saint Petersburg at the age of nine, where he received a free education as well as classical ballet instruction. He graduated in 1921 and was

George Balanchine *(center)*. ARCHIVE PHOTOS, INC.

admitted to the resident company the Soviet State Ballet, at the same time enrolling in the Petrograd Conservatory of Music to study piano and composition.

When Balanchine was sixteen he created his first choreography, and during the 1920s he prepared a series of programs to showcase his own ballets. He was joined by Tamara Gevergeva (later "Geva"), his first wife, whom he married in 1922, and Alexandra Danilova, with whom he later lived after Geva had left him. By 1923 the group had so outraged the ballet establishment that it eagerly accepted an opportunity to tour Germany for the summer of 1924. That fall, Serge Diaghilev saw the troupe perform, and in December hired it to dance with his Ballets Russes.

As soon as the troupe joined the Ballets Russes, Diaghilev (who renamed Balanchivadze "Balanchine") asked Balanchine if he could create ballets for the opera "very fast." Balanchine complied, and soon became the company ballet master and chief choreographer. In 1925 he created dances for twelve operas and choreographed his first ballet, *Le Chant du Rossignol*, to music by Igor Stravinsky. In 1928 he created *Apollon Musagète* (later, *Apollo*), and in 1929, the year Diaghilev died, *Prodigal Son*. Both ballets are still considered masterpieces.

Years after, reflecting on the profoundest influences on his artistic life, Balanchine named two. The first was his training at the Maryinsky, where he was taught its "strict discipline . . . its classicism, the basis of all ballet [and] its . . . tradition." The second was Diaghilev, from whom "I learned to recognize what was great and valid in art . . . and to be . . . an artist."

In 1933 Balanchine formed his own, short-lived troupe, Les Ballets 1933, and that same year he met Lincoln Kirstein, the wealthy son of a Boston family. Kirstein had dreamed of establishing an "American" ballet company and had already seen several of Balanchine's choreographies. Balanchine was interested in working with Kirstein, but insisted "first, a school," to which Kirstein agreed. Balanchine came to New York City on 18 October 1933; the School of American Ballet opened on New Year's Day 1934. Their American Ballet company began in March 1935, but folded in 1938.

During the following decade, Balanchine created dances for musical comedies and Hollywood films and worked in Europe. He married Vera Zorina (born Brigitta Hartwig) on 24 December 1938 and became a U.S. citizen in 1939. He later divorced Zorina and married Maria Tallchief in 1946, the year that he and Kirstein formed the Ballet Society. In 1948 Morton Baum of New York's City Center saw the company, and asked Kirstein: "How would you like the idea of having the Ballet Society become the New York City Ballet?" Thus in 1948 the group was officially renamed and accorded the status of a public institution.

The New York City Ballet (NYCB), at City Center, thrived under Balanchine's artistic direction during the 1950s. He created at least thirty-seven new dances during the decade, including *La Valse* (1951), *The Nutcracker* (1954), *Western Symphony* (1954), *Allegro Brillant* (1956), *Agon* (1957), and *Stars and Stripes* (1958). The school, generally intended to provide a source of new dancers for the company, also flourished, becoming, as *Time* magazine noted in 1954, "the best and busiest in the U.S."

By the 1960s the reputations of the company, school, and Balanchine personally were firmly established. In a biography of Balanchine, Bernard Taper said that the company was giving an average of 150 performances a year, up from twenty-four during its first year at City Center. In 1964 music critics Rosalyn Krokover and Harold Schonberg wrote that the NYCB now "dominates the scene to the exclusion of any other group." Another critic added in 1966 that the school was "harder to get into than Radcliffe."

The introduction to a 1961 *Horizon* interview with Balanchine stated that he was already a "choreographer without peer," and in 1964 British dance critic Clive Barnes said that he was "very possibly the most remarkable creative force ballet has ever known." In 1960 Balanchine choreographed *Monumentum pro Gesualdo,* called in a 1972 *Saturday Review* article a "major" work that extended "the range, the scope and the style of formal expressive movement." It was compared to *Agon,* one of his so-called "plotless" ballets, for which he had been frequently criticized over the years. These two works, along with the now famous *Apollo,* were all set to music by Stravinsky.

Balanchine's choreography was always cradled in the classic ballet style he was taught at the Maryinsky, and the choreographers who most influenced him—Marius Petipa and Kasyan Goleizovsky—came from this tradition, the latter advocating the art of pure dance and exulting in the potential of the human body. Balanchine expanded this concept. "To him the classical technique was not a constriction but a liberation," wrote Taper, and quoted Balanchine as saying: "I would like to show that these bodies of ours . . . can be beautiful." Unlike his contemporaries Martha Graham and Anthony Tudor, Balanchine did not feel that emotion or story line was the impetus of dance. He made dance itself the center of his ballets, often eschewing even costume and decor to focus more fully on the dancing.

Music, however, was essential, and Balanchine, a fine musician himself, would choreograph a ballet directly on the dancers only after listening to the music and examining its score. Although he loved Mozart, Balanchine favored modern composers, especially Stravinsky, with whom he often worked. He said about Stravinsky, "(M)usic is time. . . . I couldn't make a ballet without music [because] I am not a creator of time myself. . . . Stravinsky is."

In 1963 Balanchine made his first ballet *Movements for*

Piano and Orchestra (again Stravinsky) for Suzanne Farrell, with whom he was obsessed. Although he did not believe in the "star" system of ballet (Tallchief, whose marriage to Balanchine was annulled in 1952, would leave in 1965 over this issue), he did choreograph pieces for his current favorites. He wrote *Don Quixote,* in which he danced the title role opening night, for Farrell in 1965. In 1969 Balanchine divorced his fourth wife, Tanaquil LeClercq, whom he had married on 31 December 1952, in the hope Farrell would marry him. She did not and soon left the company.

On 16 December 1963 the Ford Foundation gave $7,756,750 to support American ballet, and the bulk, to be distributed over about ten years, went to the NYCB, the School of American Ballet, and other companies and schools with Balanchine connections. Not surprisingly, there was an outcry from other choreographers and companies—most notably, the American Ballet Theatre and Agnes de Mille, Martha Graham, and Ted Shawn—who claimed that "true American dance" was being "crucified." In actual fact, this grant focused attention on the financial needs of American dance in general, and several donors soon stepped in to help those not given Ford money.

The Ford Foundation grant also permitted a number of small, regional, Balanchine-related companies to develop into prestigious organizations such as the Boston and Pennsylvania Ballets, to which Balanchine donated some of his masterpieces, including his first American ballet *Serenade* (1935), for their own repertories. It also allowed the New York school to continue to offer scholarships—a practice begun in 1941 that helped the dancers Tanaquil LeClercq, Jacques d'Amboise, and Edward Villella to attend in the 1940s. Farrell came to the school on a scholarship, and then joined the company in the early 1960s, dancing with d'Amboise, Villella, Tallchief, Erik Bruhn, Melissa Hayden, Allegra Kent, Patricia McBride, Arthur Mitchell, and Violette Verdy.

"It's all yours, George. Take it from here," said Philip Johnson, architect for Lincoln Center's New York State Theater. The laconic reply: "Just what I always wanted." This exchange marked the opening night of the $19.3 million theater, considered by many to be the first expressly designed for a choreographer, on 23 April 1964. The theater did indeed contain elements dear to Balanchine's heart—a vast stage with excellent footing, large practice rooms, and good acoustics. Lincoln Center itself grew out of a desire by the Metropolitan Opera and the Philharmonic Society for new buildings, and Kirstein wrote that if "the Met by itself could have built a new home . . . there would have been no great need . . . for Lincoln Center." As it turned out, Kirstein and Balanchine were able to nominate their own architect, for whom they were his "single client," even though the theater was to be shared with the New York City Opera. The three principles agreed "to the smallest detail" on their architectural tastes, and Balanchine was an active participant in much of the design, including the floors of the practice studios, which were woven in a system he developed. Since, as Kirstein added, New York at that time had no appropriate space for welcoming heads of state, the promenade and theater interior were designed with great elegance for just such purposes.

Opening night was celebrated with a full-length *Midsummer Night's Dream,* which Balanchine had first presented in 1962. Balanchine had always imagined a company like the Maryinsky that could present large, elaborate ballets—a vivid contrast to his many spare, uncostumed choreographies—and he later created such dances as *Harliquinade* (1965), *Don Quixote* (1965), and *Jewels* (1967) for the new theater.

In 1969 Jerome Robbins, whom Balanchine had made associate artistic director in 1949, returned to the company as ballet master, having spent over a decade working mostly in musical comedy. More than thirty years before, Balanchine had choreographed *Slaughter on Tenth Avenue* (1936) for Richard Rodgers's *On Your Toes,* which had integrated classical ballet into musical comedy for the first time, and he produced a new version of *Slaughter* for the State Theater. It premiered on 2 May 1968, the same day as his *Requiem Canticles,* created in memory of Dr. Martin Luther King, Jr.

The 1970s brought a mix of acclaim and criticism to both company and choreographer. On one hand, some thought his new ballets inferior and the dancing sloppy. On the other, he staged a week of dances, most of them new, for a 1972 Stravinsky Festival, and his company continued to boast many of the finest dancers in the country, now including Gelsey Kirkland, Mikhail Baryshnikov, and Peter Martins. By 1979, 400 students were enrolled in the school, where Balanchine himself continued to teach.

A dark, wiry, always dapper man of immense energy, Balanchine suffered his first heart attack in 1978. By 1982 his health was failing quickly, and he entered Roosevelt Hospital in November. He died there of pneumonia brought on by Creutzfelt-Jakob Disease, a rare, fatal brain disorder that is one of the human variants of the so-called "mad cow" disease. Balanchine was devoutly religious, and his huge funeral was held at the Russian Orthodox Cathedral of Our Lady of the Sign in New York City. He is buried in Sag Harbor, Long Island.

Balanchine's City and Lincoln Center years represented the apogee of ballet in the United States. He raised choreography to an independent art form, and devotees flocked to see his choreography as much as his troupe's extraordinary dancing. In 1973 Deborah Jowitt hailed Balanchine as a "living national treasure." Six years later Walter Terry observed that "after creating more than 100 ballets for the NYCB and its companies . . . [Balanchine] would now

appear to be an American choreographer." Edwin Denby agreed that he was "more than anyone else, the real founder of the American classic style. . . . He changed the way we look at dance. Very few people in the history of any art have that kind of impact."

★

The best full-length biography is Bernard Taper, *George Balanchine: A Biography* (1984). Don McDonagh, *George Balanchine* (1983), focuses more on his choreographies than his life. There are essays by Lincoln Kirstein in *Portrait of Mr. B.: Photographs of George Balanchine* (1984), and interviews edited by Francis Mason in *I Remember Balanchine: Recollections of the Ballet Master by Those Who Knew Him* (1991). Other books of note are Lincoln Kirstein, *The New York City Ballet* (1973), and Jennifer Dunning, *"But First a School": The First Fifty Years of the School of American Ballet* (1985). A plethora of journal and newspaper articles have been written about Balanchine. The best of those dealing most specifically about him in the 1960s and after are Ivan Nabokov and Elizabeth Carmichael's interview in *Horizon* (Jan. 1961): 44–56; Rosalyn Krokover and Harold C. Schonberg, "Ballet in America: One-Man Show?," *Harper's Magazine* (Sept. 1964): 92–96; Hubert Saal, "Caution: Choreographer at Work," *New York Times Magazine* (11 Sept. 1966); Lincoln Kirstein, "Balanchine and Stravinsky: The Glorious Undertaking," *Dance Magazine* (June 1972); Dale Harris, "Balanchine: The End of a Reign?," *Saturday Review* (15 July 1972); Deborah Jowitt, "Balanchine & Co. at 40, 20 and 10," *The New York Times Magazine* (11 Nov. 1973); Walter Terry, "Formidable Balanchine: The Long Reign of America's Ballet Master," *Saturday Review* (29 Sept. 1979); and "Encounters with Balanchine," *Dance Magazine* (July 1983). Obituaries are in the *New York Times, Chicago Tribune,* and *Los Angeles Times* (all 1 May 1983), and in *Newsweek* and *Time* (both 9 May 1983).

SANDRA SHAFFER VANDOREN

BALDWIN, James Arthur (*b.* 2 August 1924 in New York City; *d.* 1 December 1987 in Saint-Paul de Vence, France), essayist, social critic, playwright, novelist, and activist who shaped public debate on justice and American democracy in the 1960s. His polemical writings on racial discrimination, gay consciousness, personal alienation, and black liberation fused art and activism, anticipated the social challenges the United States would come to face, and raised the bar on the nation's call to conscience.

Raised by his mother, Emma Berdis Jones, a domestic worker, and his stepfather, David Baldwin, Sr., a clergyman and factory worker, Baldwin was the oldest of nine children and the only one born out of wedlock. His mother was single at the time of his birth and married his stepfather in 1927, when Baldwin was three years old. He never knew

James Baldwin, 1964. Hulton-Deutsch Collection/Corbis

his biological father. His illegitimacy was the first in a long line of obstacles that Baldwin would endure in his life. He survived the unforgiving conditions of his childhood (the Great Depression, malnutrition, an overbearing and mentally deteriorating stepfather, and the oppression of African Americans) by finding validation outside his home, first through education and then in the black church, which he viewed as a separate experience from white Christianity.

Baldwin's voracious appetite for books and penchant for ideas distinguished him academically at an early age. He attended Public School 24 and then Frederick Douglass Middle School. Dewitt Clinton High School in the Bronx, one of the city's elite institutions, eventually selected him to attend, and Baldwin graduated in 1942. His teachers were a unique gathering of New York's most progressive literary, educational, and activist minds. Countee Cullen, who produced one of the great poems of the Harlem Renaissance period, "Yet, Do I Marvel," served as instructor and mentor for the young Baldwin during his years at Douglass Middle School. Cullen encouraged Baldwin's writing as a way for him to organize the world and discover himself. Outside approval greatly mattered to the gangly youngster, who was becoming increasingly uncertain about his sexuality as he matured.

Baldwin grew up in Harlem during the waning years of its literary Renaissance. Premised upon the philosopher Alain Locke's contention that the twentieth century witnessed a new and gifted generation of African Americans (termed the New Negro), the Harlem Renaissance produced intellectuals who considered literature and the arts as the vehicle for social change. Although Baldwin had marginal ties to the literati of the Renaissance, he may have

been their most penetrating and uncompromising heir.

Even in the years of this literary flowering, Harlem's prospects were narrow for Baldwin. Moreover, he was growing increasingly estranged from his stepfather. During the 1930s, David Baldwin fell deeply into paranoia and depression, which strained all aspects of their relationship Small differences of opinion degenerated into prodigious battles of will. The stress compelled Baldwin to become a boy preacher in the Pentecostal Mount Calvary Church at the age of fourteen. His escape to religion foreshadowed future defections when Baldwin could not manage the crises in his life. Avoidance was both a defense mechanism and a vital step on his path to becoming a writer. In 1943 the urge forced him out of his home, away from the church, and into a brief stint as a bohemian in Greenwich Village. Baldwin left the United States altogether for Paris, France, in 1948.

The search to discover himself, beyond his domineering stepfather, outside his race, and without the questions of his sexuality led Baldwin to become an expatriate. In Paris, Baldwin launched his publishing career in earnest, producing a polemical essay, "Everybody's Protest Novel" (1949), and then a series of pathbreaking novels, *Go Tell It on the Mountain* (1953), *Notes of a Native Son* (1955), and the monumental *Giovanni's Room* (1956). By 1960 many recognized Baldwin as the premier black writer of his time. His writings anticipated the tone, content, and emotion of the civil rights movement in the United States. Race conflict pervaded his writings in the 1950s, a consequence of his own identity crises and his journalistic assignments in the American South. Recording the lives of southerners brought Baldwin in contact with the spiritual figurehead of the civil rights movement, the Reverend Martin Luther King, Jr. It also introduced him to the Student Nonviolent Coordinating Committee (SNCC) and the Congress of Racial Equality (CORE).

Writing about race relations presented Baldwin with a distinct philosophic dilemma. He had proclaimed in "Everybody's Protest Novel" that writers should not subscribe to ideology, nor should they write for propaganda, a stance that separated him in many ways from most African-American writers since the Harlem Renaissance. Nevertheless, Baldwin felt compelled to defend his expatriate status against charges that he had abandoned America to live a raceless existence in Europe. Although they were never resolved, these concerns made the 1960s the most productive and publicly visible period of his life. Moreover, the decade catapulted Baldwin into the role he himself disparaged, that of an antagonist for race consciousness and equal rights in America.

Baldwin's first writing of the 1960s was a collection of essays, *Nobody Knows My Name: More Notes of a Native Son* (1961). The essays were his most conscious meditations on the question of race to that date, written with a touch of irony reminiscent of the writer Ralph Ellison (in his *Invisible Man*), which attributed black invisibility to white intransigence. In 1962 Baldwin published the novel *Another Country*, a self-reflective exploration of racism and homosexuality. To Baldwin, *Another Country* was an existential parable on racial reconciliation, driven by the sacrifice of its central character, Rufus. The book received mixed reviews, but Baldwin was working toward his monumental social commentary, *The Fire Next Time* (1963).

By this time Baldwin was deeply involved in the civil rights movement and was frustrated by government inaction. *The Fire Next Time* pressed for more urgency and warned Americans that humanistic love was the only option available outside a racial apocalypse. *Blues for Mr. Charlie*, a 1964 play, reiterated Baldwin's prophecy concerning the potential for violence should mainstream Americans ignore the righteous indignation of oppressed African Americans. Brutal acts of hatred, such as the murder of the civil rights leader Medgar Evers in June 1963 in Mississippi and the deaths of four black girls, bombed in a Birmingham church on September 15 the same year, provided the tragic inspiration for the play.

Blues for Mr. Charlie used the black theater to confront the demons plaguing race politics and the civil rights movement. The play announced the Janus-faced logic of black militancy that blamed white false consciousness and vacillation for the inability to overcome injustice. With searing clarity, Baldwin prophesied the radicalization of the civil rights movement and the possibility that white liberals would abandon the cause. Left in the wake, he warned, would be the original intent of the civil rights movement and passive resistance, the notion that the human capacity for love is a greater force than the propensity to hate. *Blues for Mr. Charlie* was even more of a tinderbox than *The Fire Next Time,* because it left the moral questions dangling with no solution.

Four years later Baldwin again tried his hand at drama with *The Amen Corner*. Although Baldwin published *The Amen Corner* in 1968, it had been playing at theaters throughout the nation since the late 1950s. The play examined the inner conflict between love and isolation, the chaos of unimpeded personal choice, and the dull consistency of safety. Baldwin's final major literary work of the 1960s was *Tell Me How Long the Train's Been Gone* (1968), which critics in the United States derided as fixed in the politics of the civil rights movement and devoid of artistic interpretation. Some readers (mostly Europeans), however, viewed the book in biographical terms. These critics believed the protagonist Leo Proudhammer's journey from a social philosophy of Christian love to militant nationalism to be similar to Baldwin's own metamorphosis during the decade.

By 1968 writers and critics became increasingly concerned that Baldwin had transgressed the unspoken line between life and art. Quite simply, they thought that he spent too much of his time proselytizing for civil rights. Baldwin, however, saw no distinction between life and art. His development as an artist came from the civil rights movement and unresolved identity issues from his childhood. He simply could not escape his duty to defend black liberation in the United States. Additionally, Baldwin knew that his work was useful. His writing about the pervasive nature of white supremacy in the United States and the dissonance it created across racial lines gave the civil rights movement intellectual balance and validity. It was the appropriate complement to Dr. King's social philosophy.

In the 1960s Baldwin became involved in quite a few campaigns for civil and human rights that spanned the decade and took many forms. The Federal Bureau of Investigation monitored him for his support of the Fair Play for Cuba Committee, a leftist association that advocated for Communist Cuba. When the University of Mississippi denied James Meredith, a black Mississippian, admission in 1962, Baldwin gave a series of protest lectures throughout the South for CORE that exposed him to the horror of the Jim Crow South. It also introduced him to Evers.

By then famous for *The Fire Next Time,* Baldwin preached a gospel of liberation to his audience that called for whites to relinquish their myths about the past and African Americans. Doing this, he argued, was their surest way to free themselves from the legacy of white supremacy. In support of King's campaign in Birmingham, Baldwin drafted a letter to U.S. Attorney General Robert Kennedy, chastising the administration for not taking up the civil rights movement's moral challenge to the nation. Baldwin's efforts culminated in the famous meeting on civil rights between the Kennedy administration and artists and a few activists, which took place on 24 May 1963, a few months before the March on Washington.

Despite his conspicuous political acts and the national consensus that he was the most absorbing speaker on the question of race, African-American leaders gave Baldwin no significant part in the 28 August 1963 March on Washington, a rally where more than 200,000 people gathered in support of equal rights for all. The decision of the march leaders foreshadowed Baldwin's estrangement from the civil rights community. One can assume that there were reservations among the planners about having a gay man take such a visible role in the event, but the fact that Baldwin's rhetoric was becoming more radical also may have influenced the decision. Baldwin admired Dr. King and was a staunch advocate of integration, but he increasingly began to see that moral persuasion alone would not balance the social scale. His time as an expatriate had sensitized him to the idea that African Americans existed as a colony of the Western world. White supremacy, Baldwin found, had created structures and rituals akin to the empires of Europe. As such, it required an anticolonial response. Similarly, he agreed with the urgency and uncompromising posture of the activist Malcolm X but disagreed with Malcolm X's commitment to separation from whites.

After race riots in Watts, Los Angeles, in 1964, the civil rights movement split between passive resisters and Black Power advocates. The division put Baldwin in the unusual position of being sympathetic to both sides. Baldwin was a significant force in the development of Black Power's rhetoric and ideas, but he distrusted the agenda of its leadership. Nevertheless, like King and Malcolm X, Baldwin developed a relationship with the members of CORE, the Black Panther Party, and SNCC. To some degree, his alliance with the radicals appeared natural, because both doubted the commitment of white liberals, on whom the civil rights community depended to promote change.

Throughout the late 1960s Baldwin showed his support by speaking and writing on behalf of the militants, even though there was a faction among them that questioned his place in black liberation, owing to his commitment to integration and his homosexuality. Baldwin's harshest critic among the radicals was Eldridge Cleaver, a former inmate who had become a writer and minister of information for the Black Panthers, who equated Baldwin's homosexuality with race hatred and suicide. Nevertheless, Baldwin forged an uneasy bond with the Black Power activists, because they represented to him an answer to the inherent weakness of King's political philosophy.

By the end of the 1960s, the alliance between Baldwin and the black militants became more strained as the militants increasingly used Baldwin's celebrity to promote their own brand of revolution. *The Fire Next Time* and subsequent writings had argued that while blacks could not trust a white Christian God to deliver the United States from its nightmare of oppression, neither could they rely upon a black God. This stance alienated Baldwin from Elijah Muhammad and the Nation of Islam (a radical religious movement, also known as the Black Muslims, that espoused racial separation) in the early 1960s. To Baldwin, a black cult built upon a fictional past and myths about the present was just as toxic as western lies. Baldwin's final separation from the civil rights movement came with the assassination of Dr. Martin Luther King, Jr., on 4 April 1968.

Baldwin did not drift into obscurity in the 1970s; he continued to have a very productive writing career until his death from stomach cancer at the age of sixty-three. He is buried in Ferncliff Cemetery in Hartsdale, New York. The 1960s undoubtedly stand as Baldwin's golden moment, a time when he helped set the national agenda and defined the structure of the discussion that formed the civil rights revolution.

★

Some of Baldwin's papers and letters are at the Schomburg Center for Research in Black Culture in New York City. Biographies include Louis Hill Pratt, *James Baldwin* (1978); Lisa Rosset, *James Baldwin* (1989); Quincy Troupe, ed., *James Baldwin: The Legacy* (1989); James Campbell, *Talking at the Gate: A Life of James Baldwin* (1991); David A. Leeming, *James Baldwin: A Biography* (1994); and Randall Kenan, *James Baldwin* (1994). Other helpful insights are in Fern Marja Eckman, *The Furious Passage of James Baldwin* (1966); Stanley Macebuh, *James Baldwin: A Critical Study* (1973); Ernest A. Champion, *Mr. Baldwin, I Presume: James Baldwin–Chinua Achebe, A Meeting of the Minds* (1995); Rosa Bobia, *The Critical Reception of James Baldwin in France* (1997); Ross Posnock, *Color and Culture: Black Writers and the Making of the Modern Intellectual* (1998); Dwight McBride, ed., *James Baldwin Now* (1999); Katherine L. Balfour, *The Evidence of Things Not Said* (2001); and Keith Clark, *Black Manhood in James Baldwin, Ernest J. Gaines, and August Wilson* (2002). Obituaries are in the *Times* (London), *New York Times, Detroit Free Press, Chicago Tribune, Philadelphia Inquirer,* and *USA Today* (all 2 Dec.1987).

CHRISTOPHER T. FISHER

BALL, George Wildman (*b.* 21 December 1909 in Des Moines, Iowa; *d.* 26 May 1994 in New York City), undersecretary of state for economic affairs, January–November 1961; undersecretary of state, 1961–1966; and the most prominent and consistent advocate of U.S. nonintervention in Vietnam during the Kennedy and Johnson administrations.

Ball was the third and youngest son of Amos Ball, Jr., a Standard Oil of Indiana vice president, and Edna Wildman, a teacher. Educated at public schools in Evanston, Illinois, Ball obtained bachelor's and law degrees from Northwestern University in 1930 and 1933 and, after a spell in the U.S. Treasury Department, practiced law in Chicago until the early 1940s. In 1932 Ball married Ruth Sneathen Murdoch, a social worker from Pittsburgh; the couple adopted two sons, Douglas Bleakly and John Colin.

During World War II Ball held government positions with the Office of Lend-Lease Administration and the Foreign Economic Administration. Arthur Schlesinger, Jr., who met Ball in 1943, found him "a delight . . . a wonderfully spirited, resourceful, joyous, imperturbable, elegant man." After the war Ball moved to Washington, where he helped found the international law firm Cleary, Gottlieb, Steen, and Ball. The firm represented the French government and the European Coal and Steel Community—later the European Economic Community (EEC)—and Ball became a dedicated, lifelong supporter of freer international trade, which he believed was an engine of economic growth and political progress. In the 1950s he also helped establish the Bilderberg Group, which organized annual meetings of prominent Western political and business leaders. Four mentors greatly influenced Ball: his Chicago law partner, the liberal Democrat Adlai Stevenson, who became governor of Illinois; Jean Monnet, the French architect of postwar European unity and Ball's greatest role model, whom he met during World War II; Dean Acheson, Harry Truman's assertive and Atlanticist secretary of state from 1949 to 1953; and the preeminent Washington journalist, Walter Lippmann.

Ball worked for Stevenson in both his unsuccessful 1952 and 1956 presidential campaigns and initially supported his 1960 bid for the Democratic nomination. When John F. Kennedy became the nominee, Ball made speeches and wrote articles on his behalf and prepared foreign policy position papers. Kennedy was sufficiently impressed to invite Ball to become undersecretary of state for economic affairs, the third-ranking post in the Department of State. Ball quickly assembled a well-qualified staff, some experienced departmental officers, others talented outsiders, who greatly enhanced his own bureaucratic effectiveness. So did the close relationship he developed with the reserved Secretary of State, Dean Rusk. The two men often shared an evening scotch or bourbon and, despite their major policy differences over Vietnam, Ball paid warm tribute to Rusk in his memoirs. Rusk never developed similar rapport with his own deputy, Chester Bowles, an idealistic and somewhat ineffective liberal who concentrated on American relations with Asia, Africa, and Latin America, whereas throughout his career Ball believed that his country's primary international interests lay in its relationship with Europe. After ten months Ball replaced Bowles, becoming undersecretary for political affairs in the November 1961 "Thanksgiving Day massacre" reorganization of top State Department personnel. From then on Ball's responsibilities were far more extensive, and in Rusk's absence he often served as acting secretary. Immensely energetic and hardworking, Ball also became an administration troubleshooter, making numerous trips to such problem areas as Pakistan, Congo, the Dominican Republic, Korea, Cyprus, and Greece. He generally sought peaceful resolution of conflicts and disliked American endorsement of regimes not firmly based on popular political participation.

Before his promotion, Ball focused primarily on his economic responsibilities, and he did not attend top-level meetings on political and military strategy. Ball argued forcefully that a major downward revision of American tariff rates and greater presidential flexibility on economic issues were needed to resolve the persistent balance-of-payments deficit and other trade difficulties he anticipated would occur after Britain's expected entry into the European Common Market. He was heavily involved in drafting the 1962 Trade Expansion Act, which slashed tariffs on many foreign goods and gave the president great discretionary authority to take retaliatory measures against foreign protectionism. Ball also successfully supported the use of United Nations and United States forces to prevent the Belgian-backed secession of the copper-rich Katanga province from the newly independent Congo.

Ball accorded high priority to furthering European economic integration through Britain's membership in the EEC. He believed that a strong and economically interdependent and prosperous Europe was crucial to U.S. alliance policies. Like Acheson, he trenchantly argued that since World War II, too often with American backing, Britain had myopically tried to maintain the illusion that it was still an independent great power rather than moving to become the leader of Europe. Ball also thought greater British influence in Europe was desirable to offset that of West Germany. In 1965 Ball termed French president Charles de Gaulle "a self-centered nationalist" for vetoing Britain's application to join the Common Market, and briefly contemplated a contingency plan for a limited confederation of the English-speaking peoples in the United States, Britain, Canada, Australia, and New Zealand. The plan included amalgamating those areas of the world whose

George Ball. ARCHIVE PHOTOS, INC.

currencies were linked to either the dollar or the pound sterling, a scheme he soon abandoned as impracticable.

During the Cuban Missile Crisis, Kennedy included Ball in the Executive Committee (ExCom) of senior officials who met regularly to discuss the U.S. response. Ball advised following the less drastic course of a naval blockade or quarantine rather than launching surprise air strikes. After the crisis Ball wrote a legal justification for the U.S. decision and made arrangements to inform American allies of it. After Kennedy's death Ball worked on White House transition arrangements for the Lyndon B. Johnson administration.

Despite his multifarious responsibilities, Ball was best known for his consistent opposition to U.S. intervention in Vietnam. Tall, burly, forceful, and well read, Ball could be a formidable opponent, but on Vietnam he failed to convince his fellow officials. In November 1961 Ball dissented when General Maxwell D. Taylor and the economist Walt W. Rostow returned from Vietnam recommending an increased commitment of U.S. aid, advisers, and, if possible, troops. Over two years the Kennedy administration gradually increased the number of American advisers in Vietnam from a few hundred to 16,000, with Ball always on the losing side. Ball was greatly influenced by his memories of France's failure to sustain a quasicolonial Vietnamese government during the 1950s but also believed that Vietnam, and indeed all of Asia, was an area of peripheral importance to the United States. In addition, Ball considered President Ngo Dinh Diem's government in South Vietnam both corrupt and incompetent, incapable of winning the war. On 24 August 1963 Ball, together with State Department officials Michael V. Forrestal and Roger Hilsman, drafted a cable instructing Henry Cabot Lodge, the American ambassador to South Vietnam, to respond favorably to enquiries by Vietnamese generals whether the United States would welcome a coup against Diem and recognize the resulting government. In November 1963 Diem was overthrown and assassinated, an event Ball always maintained made no difference to the eventual outcome of the war in Vietnam.

Ball found Johnson personally more congenial than Kennedy and later suggested that, whereas Johnson tolerated his repeated private questioning of administration policies on Vietnam, Kennedy would probably have been far less patient and would have eventually demanded his resignation. Some, however, felt that Ball was the "house dove" or "devil's advocate," his dissent acceptable because his presence in discussions on Vietnam proved that all options had been thoroughly considered. As American involvement in Vietnam escalated, with large-scale bombing raids on North Vietnam launched after the August 1964 Tonkin Gulf incident and the commitment of American ground forces in May 1965, Ball repeatedly submitted lengthy memoranda questioning almost every prevailing

assumption on the conflict. He argued from European experience that the domino theory (which suggested that a single communist Asian country would "infect" its neighbors) was unfounded and contended that, rather than considering U.S. involvement in Vietnam proof of American anticommunist resolve, the West European allies would regard it as a major error that would call into question American officials' prudence and judgment. Ball also warned that war in Vietnam might easily dilute support for Johnson's Great Society domestic reform programs. Drawing on his World War II service with the U.S. Strategic Bombing Survey and on his report that concluded that heavy bombing of German cities had failed to destroy popular morale and the will to fight, Ball contended that American bombing of North Vietnam would be no more effective in persuading Hanoi to cease its campaign against the South. He maintained these positions even when Johnson forced him to admit that American withdrawal would probably lead to the collapse of South Vietnam and to a communist takeover. Ball also recommended increased U.S. trade with and recognition of mainland China as well as its admission to the United Nations. Between October 1964 and July 1965 Ball submitted eight lengthy memoranda urging American withdrawal from Vietnam, all of which the president ignored.

Although Ball based his opposition on pragmatic considerations, on moral grounds the death and suffering caused by the war distressed him deeply. In September 1966 Ball, weary of publicly defending policies he privately deplored, and under financial pressure, resigned to become a senior partner in Lehman Brothers, a top New York investment bank. He never questioned fellow officials' good faith on Vietnam, merely their judgment, and, following the gentleman's code, he remained silent on Vietnam, later stating, "I could not share the confidence of my colleagues for a sustained period, then go out and denounce them." Only with the 1971 publication of the Pentagon Papers did his dissent become common knowledge.

Ball became one of the senior advisers, or "wise men," whom Johnson occasionally consulted on major foreign policy issues and in January 1968 chaired a committee to investigate the *Pueblo* Incident, when North Korea seized an American intelligence-gathering vessel. As before, he advocated that the United States cut its losses and leave Vietnam; at a November "wise men" meeting Ball bitterly assailed his colleagues for their indifference to rising American casualty figures. After the disastrous Tet offensive early in 1968, Ball's fellow advisers finally swung around to his perspective, and Johnson publicly announced that he would open negotiations and would not seek reelection. In the following months, however, Ball felt Johnson's peace policies were far too half-hearted. In spring 1968 Johnson prevailed upon a reluctant Ball to become U.S. ambassador to the United Nations, an assignment that bored him and one he left after three months to campaign aggressively for Hubert Humphrey, the Democratic presidential nominee, who might well have named him secretary of state. Ball had ably positioned himself for this office by publishing *The Discipline of Power* (1968), which forcefully assailed the growing isolationist trend in the United States. The victory of Republican Richard Nixon, whom Ball despised for his use of McCarthyite smear tactics in the 1950s, effectively relegated him to private life.

Ball remained with Lehman until he retired in 1982, cultivating international business contacts in Europe and the Middle East. In 1978 President Jimmy Carter asked Ball to report on the growing troubles in Iran, and he presciently but unavailingly recommended that only democratic reforms would prevent the ouster of Shah Mohammed Reza Pahlavi. From the early 1970s Ball criticized Israel's post-1967 annexation of Palestinian territory and called for reduced American support of Israel, a controversial stance that made him politically unacceptable to many Democrats. Until his death in 1994 of abdominal cancer, he spoke and wrote extensively on foreign affairs.

Elitist, ambitious, and Eurocentric, Ball nonetheless demonstrated not merely bureaucratic effectiveness but a reflective streak that distinguished him from most of his contemporaries. When convinced of a position's validity, he argued for it with stubborn conviction and tenacity regardless of its unpopularity. Unlike most of his peers, he preferred long-term analyses to short-term, ad hoc crisis management. It may be no exaggeration to term him the greatest secretary of state the United States never had.

★

Ball's personal papers were deposited in the Seeley G. Mudd Memorial Library of Princeton University. He donated relatively small collections of his official papers to the National Archives II, College Park, Maryland; the John F. Kennedy Presidential Library, Boston, Massachusetts; and the Lyndon B. Johnson Presidential Library, Austin, Texas. Many of his papers were published in the appropriate volumes of the series *Foreign Relations of the United States*. Ball wrote his own memoirs, *The Past Has Another Pattern* (1982), and reflected on some of the lessons of office in *The Discipline of Power* (1968). The fullest biography is James A. Bill, *George Ball: Behind the Scenes in U.S. Foreign Policy* (1997). Ball's position on Vietnam is fully covered in David L. DiLeo, *George Ball, Vietnam, and the Rethinking of Containment* (1991). Arthur Schlesinger, Jr., wrote a revealing memorial of Ball for the *Century Association Yearbook* (1995). Obituaries are in the *New York Times* (28 May 1994); the *Washington Post* (29 May 1994); the *Times* (London) (30 May 1994); and the *Daily Telegraph* (31 May 1994). Ball recorded oral histories for the Kennedy and Johnson presidential libraries.

PRISCILLA ROBERTS

BANCROFT, Anne (*b.* 17 September 1931 in New York City), award-winning stage, film, and television actress who first came to national prominence during the 1960s with her portrayal of Annie Sullivan in *The Miracle Worker* (1962), and for her unforgettable performance as Mrs. Robinson in *The Graduate* (1967).

Born Anna Maria Louisa Italiano, daughter of Michael Italiano and Mildred di Napoli, Bancroft grew up in the Bronx, and began taking acting and dancing lessons when she was only four years old. She attended P.S. 12 and Christopher Columbus High School in the Bronx. After graduating from high school, Bancroft enrolled at the American Academy of Dramatic Arts (AADA) in Manhattan, where she studied acting from 1948 until 1950. Upon leaving AADA in 1950, she found work in television dramas, appearing under the name Anne Marno.

In 1952 Bancroft made her way to Hollywood. She signed a contract with Twentieth Century–Fox and began a largely unremarkable career in second-rate films, mostly westerns and crime dramas. The first of her films for Fox during this period was *Don't Bother to Knock* (1952), which costarred Marilyn Monroe and Richard Widmark and was a notable exception to the mostly undistinguished fare that

Anne Bancroft in a scene from *The Graduate*, 1967. THE KOBAL COLLECTION/EMBASSY PICTURES

followed. Bancroft married Martin A. May, a building contractor, on 1 July 1953, but they divorced four years later on 13 February 1957. Dissatisfied with the direction her career was taking in Hollywood, Bancroft headed back east in 1957, determined to make a name for herself on the stage. That same year, she studied with famed acting coach Herbert Berghof in New York. The following year, she landed a starring role in *Two for the Seesaw* on Broadway, a performance that won for her the Antoinette Perry (Tony) Award as Best Actress. In 1960 Bancroft enjoyed another major Broadway triumph, winning a New York Drama Critics Award and her second Tony for her role as Sullivan, private tutor to a young Helen Keller in William Gibson's stage production of *The Miracle Worker.*

On the strength of her Broadway triumphs, Bancroft returned to Hollywood in the early 1960s to reprise her portrayal of Sullivan in director Arthur Penn's film adaptation of *The Miracle Worker* (1962). She starred opposite Patty Duke as the young Helen Keller, a role that Duke had played in the Broadway production of Gibson's play. Although the film was not a financial success, it scored big with the critics, almost all of whom lavished praise on Bancroft's performance. Looking back on her first major film success on the fortieth anniversary of its release, Bancroft fondly remembered the help she had received from the film's director. "Arthur Penn taught me everything," she told Richard Ridge of *Broadway Beat.* "He really was . . . more help to me in my acting than any other person alive or dead. He's just an extraordinary teacher, and I was a good student just like Annie and Helen. That was Arthur and me. Everything he taught me I learned."

Not all of Bancroft's memories about the filming of *The Miracle Worker* were fond ones. In a May 2000 interview with the *Calgary Sun,* she recalled some of the contrasts between toiling on an independent production and acting in a major studio's film. "It was the first movie I did that wasn't a big studio film, and it was the first time I saw the future of showbiz and what would happen with these independent movies. You got so spoiled by the big studios. Now you have a trailer instead of having your own dressing room on the lot. And being a princess at heart, it was very difficult for me."

Despite her newfound success in motion pictures, Bancroft was hardly ready to turn her back on Broadway, which had done so much to resuscitate her career. After she completed work on *The Miracle Worker,* she returned to the New York stage to appear in a revival of Bertolt Brecht's *Mother Courage and Her Children* (1963). Her appearance on Broadway, however, prevented Bancroft from attending the Academy Awards presentation when she was up for Best Actress for her performance in *The Miracle Worker.* Asked to select someone to receive the Oscar for her should she win, Bancroft told Van Wyk, "I said I'd like

one of the greats like Joan Crawford or Bette Davis, somebody like that. But I didn't know that Bette Davis and Joan Crawford were having a feud. Obviously lots of people did, but I didn't. So the fact that Bette Davis was also nominated meant she couldn't pick up my Oscar, so they got Joan Crawford to pick it up. And I won and Joan Crawford walked out on stage and picked up the Oscar, and there was Bette Davis so angry at Joan Crawford and me!"

Bancroft's work in *The Miracle Worker* was the first of several motion picture successes for the actress during the 1960s. In 1964, fewer than two years after the release of *The Miracle Worker,* she received her second Academy Award nomination as Best Actress for her role in *The Pumpkin Eater* (1964), a British film with a screenplay by Harold Pinter. Bancroft portrayed the mother of several young children who leaves her second husband to marry a promising scriptwriter, played by Peter Finch. Over time she begins to disintegrate mentally as she gradually becomes aware of her husband's infidelities. *Variety's* reviewer wrote: "The role may sound conventional enough, but not as played by Bancroft; she adds a depth and understanding which puts it on a higher plane." Although Bancroft lost her Oscar bid to Julie Andrews, she did win the British Academy Award as Best Actress for her performance in film.

In 1964, Bancroft married comedy writer/director Mel Brooks. The couple first met when they both appeared as guests on a television talk show in the early 1960s. Brooks paid a staffer on the show to tell him which restaurant Bancroft was planning to eat in after the show so that he could "accidentally" bump into her and strike up a conversation. After a brief courtship, they married in New York's City Hall with a passerby serving as their witness.

Bancroft portrayed an American mission doctor in *Seven Women* (1966), the final film from director John Ford. The story line chronicles the indignities suffered by the female members of an American mission team in northern China after they are taken captive by bandits. Bancroft's character, smoldering with worldly cynicism, clashes with the rigidly moralistic head of the mission, played by Margaret Leighton. According to the review in *Variety,* "Bancroft endows her character with some authority." Bancroft also starred as Inga Dyson in *The Slender Thread* (1965), which costarred Sidney Poitier and marked the directorial debut of Sidney Pollack.

Perhaps Bancroft's greatest cinematic triumph of the 1960s came with her role as the unforgettable, "man-eating" Mrs. Robinson in 1967's *The Graduate,* directed by Mike Nichols. In a reappraisal of the film some thirty years after its release, *Chicago Sun-Times* reviewer Roger Ebert wrote that, although the film seemed decidedly dated three decades later, Bancroft's Mrs. Robinson survives as its "most sympathetic and intelligent character." In Ebert's view, "Mrs. Robinson is the only person in the movie who is not playing old tapes. She is bored by a drone of a husband, she drinks too much, she seduces Benjamin [played by Dustin Hoffman in his screen debut] not out of lust but out of kindness or desperation. . . . She is also sardonic, satirical and articulate—the only person in the movie you would want to have a conversation with." Certainly there is no other role in her career with which Bancroft is more closely identified than Mrs. Robinson, a figure who has become something of an icon for the 1960s. Bancroft was nominated for the Best Actress Oscar for her role in *The Graduate* but lost to Katharine Hepburn.

Since the 1960s, Bancroft has continued to work steadily in film and television, appearing in such films as *The Turning Point* (1977), for which she received an Academy Award nomination; *Agnes of God* (1985), which earned her another nomination from the Academy; as well as *84 Charing Cross Road* (1986), *Honeymoon in Vegas* (1992), and *Heartbreakers* (2001). An actress of uncommon talent, Bancroft has entertained audiences for more than half a century, and is still going strong. Although her very earliest films were not particularly memorable, no one was more keenly aware of this than the actress herself. In the years since *The Miracle Worker,* Bancroft has created a long string of memorable characters. One of the greatest actresses working today, Bancroft continues to impress audiences with the breadth of her acting ability. Although probably best known for her work in film, she has made a significant contribution to the Broadway stage and television drama as well.

★

An excellent overview of the lives and careers of Bancroft and her husband, Mel Brooks, can be found in Will Holtzman, *Seesaw: A Dual Biography of Anne Bancroft and Mel Brooks* (1979). Also helpful are Karen Arthur, "Anne Bancroft: She Paid Her Dues," in *Close-Up: The Movie Star Book* (1978), Danny Perry, ed.; J. R. Haspiel, "Anne Bancroft: The Odyssey of Ruby Pepper," *Films in Review* (Jan. 1980); and Anika Van Wyk, "Bancroft's Royal Role," *Calgary Sun* (2 May 2000).

DON AMERMAN

BANKS, Dennis J. (*b.* 12 April 1937 on the Leech Lake Indian Reservation, Minnesota), charismatic social activist who cofounded and helped to lead the American Indian Movement, which was established in 1968 to raise awareness concerning the struggles and issues of Native Americans.

Banks, whose Native American name is Nowacumig, is a member of the Chippewa or Ojibwa people (sometimes called the Anishinabi or Original Woodland people). At age five, Banks was sent to the Pipestem Indian School, more than 400 miles from his home. Students attending the school, which was run by the Bureau of Indian Affairs (BIA), were forced to speak English and punished when

Dennis Banks. AP/WIDE WORLD PHOTOS

they spoke in their native language. He attended Pipestem for nine years, then went on to two more schools. In 1953 Banks joined the U.S. Air Force and served in Japan and Korea. Five years later he was discharged and returned to Minnesota.

Banks was unable to find steady work. He became involved with alcohol and petty crime and was jailed for burglary in 1964. His white accomplice received probation, but Banks spent almost three years in prison. Once he was paroled, he became involved in the community and helped to set up Little League baseball teams with George Mitchell, a future cofounder of the American Indian Movement (AIM). He returned to crime, however, and was convicted of forgery, for which he served a six-month sentence. While on probation, Banks violated his parole and was sent to Minnesota's Stillwater State Prison in 1967. At Stillwater he gained a reputation as an uncooperative inmate, spent time in solitary confinement, and read voraciously about the civil rights movement, the antiwar movement, the Black Panthers, Students for a Democratic Society, and Indian treaties.

Banks left prison with a new focus and a determination to improve the life of Native Americans. In 1968 he landed a job with the Honeywell Corporation and recruited other Native American employees for the company. Honeywell provided financial support for Banks's community projects and even granted him leave to form an Indian political movement. However, when Banks publicly criticized Honeywell's involvement in a number of defense contracts for manufacturing antipersonnel weapons and refused to recruit for the company, his employment ended.

In July 1968 Banks, Eddie Benton Banai, George Mitchell, Clyde Bellecourt, and 200 other Native Americans met in Minnesota and established AIM. Modeled on the Black Panther movement, AIM was born from rage fueled by federal government programs that required Indians to leave their ancestral lands and move into urban areas. The group chose an international symbol of distress for their official emblem: the upside-down U.S. flag. AIM's main goals were to increase employment opportunities, improve housing, and provide culturally appropriate primary and secondary education for Native Americans. AIM also sought to address the problem of police harassment of Indians. The group videotaped arrests and educated Indians about basic legal rights and procedures. The beatings and harassment that had been common declined; moreover, Indians began suing police for verbal abuse.

AIM made national headlines when a group of 200 Indians, with Banks as their spokesman, "reclaimed" Alcatraz Island in San Francisco Bay as Indian Territory; the occupation lasted from November 1969 to June 1971. Other AIM protests included a day of mourning on the *Mayflower* replica at Plymouth, Massachusetts, on Thanksgiving Day in 1970. When authorities failed to charge two white brothers who had beaten and murdered Raymond Yellow Thunder, Banks and two other men led a caravan in protest. As a result, the brothers became the first white men sentenced to prison for the murder of an Indian. Before the 1972 presidential election, Banks led another, larger AIM caravan—the Trail of Broken Treaties—which traveled to Washington, D.C. When officials refused to meet with the group, the caravan participants took over the BIA office for six days and renamed it the Native American Embassy.

Banks was a primary leader of AIM's most famous protest, the standoff at Wounded Knee, South Dakota, on 28 February 1973. With the help of Vietnam veterans, the group captured and fortified the town, the location of the infamous 1890 massacre of Native Americans by U.S. forces. Federal marshals and Federal Bureau of Investigation (FBI) agents immediately surrounded the protestors, creating a blockade. When the standoff ended on 9 May 1973, two Indians were dead, and several protestors and a marshal were wounded. Banks and another AIM leader, Russell Means, were arrested and prosecuted for their roles in the takeover. After a sensational, eight-month-long trial, the charges were dismissed on the grounds of prosecutorial misconduct. As a result of the stand at Wounded Knee,

Banks became the most popular spokesman for Native Americans in the country.

Banks faced prosecution again for his participation in a courthouse riot in Custer, South Dakota, during the trial of a white man accused of murdering an Indian. This time Banks fled from his scheduled 1975 sentencing hearing. He surfaced in California, where he received amnesty from Governor Jerry Brown. Banks received an associate of arts degree from the University of California, Davis, and served as the chancellor of Deganawidah-Quetzecoatl (D-Q) University, a small, two-year college in Yolo County dedicated to the education of Native Americans. He also lectured locally and organized a spiritual run from Davis to Los Angeles. When Brown left office in 1983, Banks fled again, this time to the Onondaga Reservation in New York, where he remained for more than a year and organized the Great Jim Thorpe Longest Run from New York City to Los Angeles. Weary of isolation from his family and his people, Banks surrendered to the South Dakota authorities and served eighteen months of a three-year sentence.

Since his release in 1985, Banks has worked as a drug and alcohol counselor, persuaded Honeywell to build a computer factory in Oglala, South Dakota, headed the effort to free Leonard Peltier (who was convicted of the 1975 murder of two FBI agents at Pine Ridge, near where the Wounded Knee incident took place in 1973), and helped to protect Indian burial grounds. Since 1978 Banks has served as the director and coach of the Sacred Run, an international organization dedicated to the sacredness of all living things. He has also had minor roles in three films: *War Party* (1989), *Thunderheart* (1992), and *The Last of the Mohicans* (1992). Inspired by the revolutionary movements of the 1960s, Banks emerged from BIA schools and prison to become an influential and charismatic leader of the most significant Native American Movement in history.

★

Banks's autobiography is *Sacred Soul* (1988). Biographical information on Banks is included in Peter Matthiessen, *In the Spirit of Crazy Horse* (1992), and Paul Chaat Smith and Robert Allen Warrior, *Like a Hurricane* (1996). See also *Current Biography Yearbook*, vol. 53 (1992).

LISA A. ENNIS

BARNETT, Ross Robert (*b.* 22 January 1898 in Standing Pine, Mississippi; *d.* 6 November 1987 in Jackson, Mississippi), governor of Mississippi from 1960 to 1964 and a staunch segregationist who defied the federal government in September 1962 when he blocked the admission of James Meredith to the University of Mississippi.

Barnett was born in rural Leake County, Mississippi, the tenth child in a family he described as "poor, poor." His father, John William Barnett, was a veteran of the Confederate Army, a cotton farmer, and a sawmill operator. His mother, Virginia Ann Chadwick, was a schoolteacher. He earned a B.A. from Mississippi College in 1922 and an LL.D. from the University of Mississippi School of Law in 1926. He supported himself in school as a janitor, barber, and traveling salesman of aluminum cookware, then established a successful legal practice in Jackson specializing in damage suits. In 1926 he married Mary Pearl Crawford. They had three children: Ross, Jr., Virginia, and Ouida. He was president of the Mississippi State Bar Association in 1943 and 1944.

In 1951 Barnett entered Mississippi's Democratic gubernatorial primary, finishing fourth. He ran again in 1955 with the same result. In the 1959 primary, however, he was the largest vote-getter in a four-man field. Barnett's success was largely due to support from the Citizens' Council, an organization dedicated to the preservation of white supremacy. Barnett made no bones about his views. "God was the original segregationist," he declared. "He made the white man white and the black man black, and he did not intend for them to mix." During the run-off election he attacked his opponent, Lieutenant Governor Carroll Gartin, for his "moderation" on racial issues. He defeated Gartin by 37,000 votes.

Much of Barnett's term as governor was devoted to defending segregation. Each legislative session passed bills intended to frustrate federal desegregation moves and thwart the nascent civil rights movement. Most infamous was Senate Bill 1923, passed in 1960, permitting districts to close public schools if they were ordered to integrate. Unhappy with the Democratic Party's civil rights plank, Barnett organized an unpledged slate that won Mississippi's eight electoral votes in the 1960 presidential election.

During the Barnett administration, the Citizen's Council enjoyed unprecedented access to state government. Council president Bill Simmons became an adviser to the governor on race relations. Barnett authorized direct payments of $5,000 per month to support the council's programs and increased appropriations for the council-dominated Mississippi State Sovereignty Commission.

Barnett won a victory of sorts when the Freedom Riders arrived in Jackson on 24 May 1961 to test compliance with the 1960 *Boynton* v. *Virginia* ruling prohibiting segregated transportation facilities. The protestors were promptly arrested, convicted, and sent to prison. By avoiding bloodshed, Barnett avoided a direct confrontation with federal authorities and negative publicity for his state.

Barnett's most notable clash with the federal government occurred in September 1962, when James Meredith

Governor Ross Barnett testifying before the Sate Commerce Committee, 1963. ASSOCIATED PRESS AP

attempted to matriculate at the University of Mississippi (Ole Miss). On 13 September Barnett urged Mississippians to resist the federal government: "I now call on every public official and every private citizen of our great state to join with me in refusing . . . to submit to illegal usurpation of power by the Kennedy administration." While Barnett was denouncing the government, he was engaged in secret negotiations with the White House, attempting to arrange a face-saving compromise.

On 20 September Barnett personally refused to enroll Meredith. Five days later, using the discredited legal doctrine of interposition, he blocked the door when Meredith arrived at the university trustees' office in Jackson. The next day Lieutenant Governor Paul Johnson again rebuffed Meredith. The United States Court of Appeals for the Fifth Circuit then cited Barnett and Johnson for contempt of court.

On Saturday, 29 September, the Ole Miss football team faced the University of Kentucky at Memorial Stadium in Jackson. A capacity crowd of 41,000 Confederate flag-waving fans cheered wildly as Barnett strode to a microphone installed at midfield and delivered an emotional address: "I love Mississippi. I love her people—her customs. I love and respect her heritage." With his arm extended and his fist clenched above his head, he was a picture of defiance.

The following day Meredith arrived on the Ole Miss campus. While President John F. Kennedy pleaded with Mississippians to refrain from violence, several thousand angry people massed in front of the Lyceum Building. The mob tossed rocks and bottles at federal marshals, who responded with tear gas. In the ensuing riot two bystanders were killed and 375 persons were injured. Kennedy dispatched army troops and federalized Mississippi National Guardsmen to restore order. On 1 October Meredith was enrolled, becoming the university's first known African-American student.

Barnett left the governor's mansion and returned to the practice of law in 1964. When asked to list his accomplishments, he proudly pointed to the 440 industries that located in Mississippi during his term. Barnett expressed few regrets: "Generally speaking, I'd do the same things again." Barnett sought the Democratic gubernatorial nomination again in 1967 but finished fourth in the primary. He remained a popular figure in Mississippi, making speeches across the state and each August entertaining visitors at the Neshoba County Fair. He died of heart failure in 1987 and was buried in the family plot in Leake County.

Along with Orville Faubus of Arkansas and Alabama's George Wallace, Barnett tried to turn back the tide of racial integration and preserve "the southern way of life." Ironically, Barnett's actions helped advance the cause he so fiercely opposed. By forcing a reluctant Kennedy to take decisive action, Barnett focused national attention on the Magnolia State and helped set in motion a chain of events that resulted in greatly expanded civil rights for African Americans.

★

Barnett's gubernatorial papers are held by the Mississippi State Department of Archives and History. James Silver, *Mississippi: The Closed Society* (1966), contains a critical account of the Ole Miss crisis by a former history professor at the university. Chapter 4 of *Kennedy Justice* (1971) by Victor Navasky includes transcripts of Barnett's phone conversations with Attorney General Robert Kennedy. A sympathetic account of Barnett's political career is found in Erle Johnston, *I Rolled with Ross: A Political Biography* (1980). William Doyle, *An American Insurrection: The Battle of Oxford, Mississippi, 1962* (2001), presents a detailed account of the integration of the University of Mississippi. Episode Two of the PBS video series *Eyes on the Prize: America's Civil Rights Years, 1954–1965* (1987) includes footage of Barnett's efforts to prevent Meredith's admission. Obituaries are in the *Clarion-Ledger* and *Jackson Daily News* (both 7 Nov. 1987) and the *New York Times* (8 Nov. 1987).

PAUL T. MURRAY

BARTH, John Simmons (*b.* 27 May 1930 in Cambridge, Maryland), fiction writer whose novels are both complex human tales and investigations into the nature of fiction.

The son of John Jacob Barth and Georgia Simmons, Barth was born in the Maryland Tidelands area that has been the scene of most of his fiction. He had an older brother and a twin sister, and indeed, twins became a theme in his writing.

After graduating from high school, Barth went to study music at Julliard High School in New York City, where he soon realized that he did not have the ability to become a professional musician. He returned to Maryland and attended Johns Hopkins University in Baltimore, attaining an A.B. in 1951 and an M.A. in 1952. On 11 January 1950 he married Anne Strickland, with whom he had two sons and a daughter. He remained at Johns Hopkins as a junior instructor until 1953, then moved to Pennsylvania State University, where he moved up the academic ladder to the rank of associate professor. In 1965 he went to the State University of New York at Buffalo as a full professor.

His first two novels, both brief, amusing, nihilistic tales, were published in the1950s: *The Floating Opera* in 1956 and

John Barth. ALEX GOTFRYD/CORBIS

End of the Road in 1958. (A revised edition of the latter, published in 1967, was called *The End of the Road.*) These did not prepare the reader for his next work, in 1960.

The Sot-Weed Factor (its title is an archaic term for a tobacco merchant) is an 800-page mock epic, mostly set in late-seventeenth-century Maryland. Its protagonist, Ebenezer Cooke (based on a historical figure of that name), is described throughout as "poet and virgin." In the former role, Cooke sets out to write an epic *Marylandiad,* about the newly discovered land; in the latter, he sets out as an innocent, like Voltaire's Candide, and encounters even more sex, violence, and disillusionment than his predecessor. Cooke is guided by the utterly corrupt Henry Burlingame, a trickster who impersonates many other people during the book, and thus sets a theme of the untrustworthiness of all information, from texts to the evidence of the senses. *The Sot-Weed Factor* has stories within stories, including the epic Cooke is writing and the remarkably obscene alleged diary of Captain John Smith. The doubt cast upon all these sources leaves the reader with little or no certainty about anything that has happened.

Barth's next novel, *Giles Goat-Boy; Or, the Revised New Syllabus* (1966), managed to be even stranger than its predecessor. With some simplification, it may be described as an allegorical gospel about a half-man half-goat who discovers his humanity and becomes a savior in a university that represents the universe. Barth, who denied that the book was his own work, presented it as a computer tape given to him, but the book includes an (alleged) note from the publisher to the effect that Barth really did write it. In the course of his quest, Giles must fulfill all of the traditional hero roles. (In fact, Barth has admitted that he referred to Joseph Campbell's *The Hero with a Thousand Faces* to ensure that he included all the stages.) Eventually, Giles has to find three separate answers to the central riddle of life. The book also includes parodic references to the Bible (both testaments) and many ancient myths, as well as a full-length play, *Taliped Decanus,* which is *Oedipus Rex* translated to the university setting. At the end, the reader is left even more uncertain than in *The Sot-Weed Factor* as to what is true in the context of the book.

Having seemingly exhausted the possibilities of the long novel, Barth turned to short stories, publishing the collection *Lost in the Funhouse* in 1968. These stories likewise turned away from traditional narrative. The book largely focuses on Ambrose, a writer, beginning with "Night-Sea Journey," the saga of the sperm that will unite with an egg to become him. In the title story Ambrose finds the experience of being in the funhouse so daunting that he decides to become an artist, one who creates funhouses for others, and the author demonstrates his ability to create such complex wonders. One tour de force, "Menelaid," includes seven levels of quotation (quotes within quotes), yet remains clear.

Another important Barth work of the 1960s was an essay, "The Literature of Exhaustion" (first printed in the *Atlantic,* 1967). The essay was widely considered to be a statement of "the death of the novel": the belief that it no longer was possible to write meaningful novels. Barth has insisted that he was merely making clear that a particular stage in history was passing, and pointing to possible directions from there. He later wrote a follow-up essay, "The Literature of Replenishment" (1979), to clarify the point.

At the end of the decade Barth went through personal changes. He and his wife divorced in 1969, and the following year, on 27 December 1970, he married Shelly Rosenberg. In 1973 he returned to Johns Hopkins as a professor. He has written eight more books of fiction, including the remarkable *Letters* (1979), in which he brings back the central characters from his six previous books.

Barth is often considered one of the patron saints of postmodernism because of the way his fiction calls its own existence into question, leaving the work not a self-contained whole with its own internally consistent truth, but an entity in multiple dialog with the author, the reader, and the rest of literature—perhaps the rest of the universe. The multiple frauds and impostures in *The Sot-Weed Factor* and the complex apparatus surrounding the central tale in *Giles Goat-Boy* admirably serve this purpose. Barth should not, however, be seen as merely the constructor of funhouses, complex but ultimately lifeless. He is a writer of wit and grace, and his self-referential structures are inhabited by living beings.

★

Barth's manuscripts are kept in the Library of Congress and the libraries of Pennsylvania State and Johns Hopkins Universities. He discusses his life in *The Friday Book* (1984), particularly in the essay "Some Reasons Why I Tell the Stories I Tell the Way I Tell Them Rather than Some Other Stories Some Other Way." There is no full biography of Barth. Important studies of his life and writing include David Morrell, *John Barth: An Introduction* (1976); Max F. Schulz, *The Muses of John Barth: Tradition and Metafiction from Lost in the Funhouse to The Tidewater Tales* (1990); and Alan Lindsay, *Death in the Funhouse: John Barth and Poststructural Aesthetics* (1995).

ARTHUR D. HLAVATY

BARZUN, Jacques Martin (*b.* 30 November 1907 in Créteil, France), cultural historian, educator, and college administrator best known for his wide-ranging scholarship and his consistent defense of the liberal arts and the humanist tradition.

The son of Henri Martin Barzun and Anna-Rose Barzun, Barzun was initiated into the life of the mind at a very early age. His father, a noted literary scholar, was a member of the Abbaye group, which included such renowned French men of letters as Jules Romains and Georges Duhamel. In the years before World War I, Barzun attended the Lycée Janson de Sailly in Paris. The shortage of teachers caused by the war compelled administrators to adopt the Lancaster system, in which the older students instructed the younger. Barzun thus received his first experience as a teacher at the age of nine.

Barzun's father came to the United States on a diplomatic mission in 1917, and Barzun followed two years later. In 1923, when he had not yet passed his sixteenth birthday, Barzun enrolled in Columbia University. Initially preparing for a career in law and the foreign service, Barzun eventually became captivated by the study of history, earning a B.A. in 1927, an M.A. in 1928, and a Ph.D. in 1932. He joined the faculty at Columbia in 1929, before completing his degree, and served as an instructor in history until 1937. Promoted to assistant professor in 1938, Barzun became an associate professor in 1942 and a full professor in 1945. In 1960 he was appointed Seth Low Professor of History, a chair he occupied until 1967, when he became University Professor of History, a position he held until his retirement in 1975. Between 1955 and 1958 Barzun was dean of graduate faculties at Columbia, and was subsequently dean of faculties and provost until 1967, then professor emeritus

Jacques Barzun. CORBIS CORPORATION (BELLEVUE)

until 1975. Barzun became a naturalized U.S. citizen in 1933, and married Marianna Lowell in August 1936; they had three children. Barzun's first wife died in 1979, and in June 1980 Barzun married Marguerite Davenport.

Although Barzun's rate of publication during the 1960s did not match his output during the 1940s and 1950s, he nonetheless produced several important and controversial books. In 1961 he reissued *Classic, Romantic, and Modern,* which had originally appeared in 1943 under the title *Romanticism and the Modern Ego.* A defense of the romantic sensibility, *Classic, Romantic, and Modern* also exemplifies Barzun's attempt to recover the ideas he still considered of value to contemporary society. The romantics, Barzun argued, were neither sentimental nor insipid. Rather, in answer to the numbing rationalism and scientism of the Enlightenment and the unsettled aftermath of the Napoleonic Wars, they sought to fashion a new world through the robust application of intellect and imagination to a host of social, political, intellectual, and aesthetic problems. This thesis paralleled Barzun's conclusion in *Science: The Glorious Entertainment* (1964) that not all aspects of human experience could be illuminated by the scientific method.

According to Barzun, romanticism "expresses and exalts [man's] energetic, creative, expansive tendencies by recognizing that, although he is but a feeble creature lost in the universe, he has unpredictable powers that develop under stress of desire and risk." The destruction of romanticism in the twentieth century, as Barzun lamented in the epilogue to the revised edition of *Classic, Romantic, and Modern,* ensured "the elimination not alone of romanticist art and its sequels, but of all high art of the last five centuries." Anti-intellectual, sensational, and technical, modern art, Barzun contended, embraced an aesthetic of annihilation.

The publication of *The American University: How It Runs, Where It Is Going* (1968) earned Barzun both devoted partisans and embittered antagonists. Reiterating a defense of the liberal arts tradition that he had first articulated in *The Teacher in America* (1945), Barzun reaffirmed that the purpose of the university is to sustain "the unity of knowledge, the desire and power to teach, and the authority and skill to pass judgment on what claims to be knowledge. . . ." The operation of the university, however, is not, and can not be, democratic. Occupying different stations, teachers and students are not equals and it is dishonest and dangerous to pretend that they are. "Only rarely," Barzun wrote, does a teacher learn from a student, "a fact he does not know or a thought that is original and true. . . . [T]o make believe that their knowledge and his are equal is an abdication and a lie."

Barzun reserved special ire for radical students who sought the drama of "revolutionary experience" by replacing the true university with a "stimulation palace." Displaying an "indifference to clothes and cleanliness, a distrust and neglect of reasoning, [and] a freedom in sexuality," young militants demanded immediate "relevance" in their education or else pursued a "new religion" designed to resolve all "the perplexities of life." Some went further, envisioning the university as an experimental utopian society organized explicitly to advance black power, free love, or popular revolution. None of these objectives, Barzun attested, is compatible with the real aims of a university.

Most undergraduates, Barzun suggested, want not freedom but order in their lives. To enable them to escape "fever and frenzy," the university has to become a place of "respite and meditation." Radical critics such as Martin Duberman assailed Barzun's image of the university as well as his apparent disdain for students. Duberman and others insisted that Barzun focused so exclusively on grooming, hygiene, and manners that he had lost sight of the merits that the younger generation possessed: their sense of justice, their determination that the United States live up to its finest ideals, and their quest for meaning. To many who were part of the academic leftist movement of the 1960s, Barzun's criticisms of student attitudes and conduct seemed so inconsequential and idiosyncratic that they hardly merited a response. Yet, Duberman wrote, "Mandarins like Barzun . . . are so certain of the rightness of their own patterns of thought and action and so eager to denounce all deviations by the young from those patterns that they blind themselves (and others) to the serious questions this new generation has raised. . . ."

In addition to the titles previously mentioned, Barzun's essential works are *Race: A Study in Modern Superstition* (1937); *Darwin, Marx, Wagner: Critique of a Heritage* (1941); *Berlioz and the Romantic Century* (1950); *God's Country and Mine: A Declaration of Love Spiced with a Few Harsh Words* (1954); *The House of Intellect* (1959); *The Use and Abuse of Art* (1974); *Clio and the Doctors: Psycho-History, Quanto-History, and History* (1974); *A Stroll with William James* (1983); *A Word or Two Before You Go. . . .* (1986).

Since the 1960s, Barzun has continued his extraordinary career, translating, editing, or writing more than twenty books. The most recent, *From Dawn to Decadence: 500 Years of Western Cultural Life, 1500 to the Present,* was published in 2000 when Barzun was ninety-three years old. It became a surprise best-seller, thereby confirming his reputation as one of the most eminent men of letters in the modern world.

★

There is no biography of Barzun. Critical assessments of Barzun's scholarship during the 1960s include Victor Lange, "Romanticism and the Modern Ego," *New Republic* (18 Dec. 1961); Frank Kermode, "Europe by Candlelight," *New Statesman* (31 Aug. 1962); Martin Duberman, "On Misunderstanding Student Rebels," *The Uncompleted Past* (1969); Paul Wilkinson, "Redefinition and Defence: Jacques Barzun on the American University," *Contemporary Review* (Jan. 1970).

MARK G. MALVASI

BATE, Walter Jackson (*b.* 23 May 1918 in Mankato, Minnesota; *d.* 26 July 1999 in Boston, Massachusetts), professor, Pulitzer Prize–winning biographer, and humanist.

Bate was one of two children of William G. Bate, a school superintendent, and Isabel Melick. His father encouraged him to read a prepared list of biographies by paying him ten cents for every book, and Bate spent his profits at motion picture matinees. He attended public schools in Richmond, Indiana.

At age five, Bate was injured in a hit-and-run accident that permanently damaged his sympathetic nervous system. He later underwent a new surgical procedure that severed parts of that system called a "sympathectomy," which was conducted in the amphitheater of Massachusetts General Hospital and observed by doctors and residents. The operation disqualified him for military service and he suffered the aftereffects throughout his life. His participation in the procedure placed his religious views in direct opposition to those of his mother, a Christian Scientist who refused treatment for diabetes. Bate blamed his mother's dogmatic faith for the deaths of both his parents during his early twenties. He ultimately believed in the transcendent power of love, and inclination of the universe toward a higher order, with the cooperation of sentient individuals exercising their free will.

Bate worked his way through Harvard University by washing dishes and working in Widener Library. Author Roger Rosenblatt described him as representing "all the greatness and the lunacy of the English department as it once had been . . . he became one of an entirely new breed of English professors—those who worked for pay." Bate received his B.A. summa cum laude in 1939, his M.A. in 1940, and his Ph.D. in 1942. His senior honors essay about the poet John Keats's phrase "negative capability" was published in book form, establishing Bate's work in the field of romantic studies. Bate taught history and literature at Harvard between 1946 and 1986 and chaired the Harvard English department from 1955 to 1962. He was Abbot Lawrence Lowell Professor of the Humanities from 1962 to 1979 and Kingsley Porter University Professor of the Humanities from 1980 to 1986.

Bate criticized the Harvard English department's graduate training that focused primarily on philology and details of ancient and obscure "other recondite tongues." Recalling a comment made by former Harvard English professor

William Allan Neilson that it only took the Egyptians five weeks to make a mummy, but the Harvard English department required five years, Bate appreciated language studies that employed imagination and subjectivity. He feared imitation of scientific applications would fragment, trivialize, and sterilize the humanities. He taught the humanities as broadly conceived, including philosophy, linguistics, religion, history, music, and art.

In his biographical research, Bate reflected on personal existence, which resulted in his unique ability to tease out universal threads of humanness, as well as to bridge the gap between academic and popular authorship. Howard Moss of the *New York Times* later wrote that Bate had a remarkable understanding of Keats's development as a man, thinker, poet, and technician. "He has the uncommon ability to hold these four difficult facets—each requiring the specialized knowledge of the psychologist, the philosopher, the critic and the prosodist." Embracing the ordinary in search of the seeds of greatness, Bate said, "If there can be a facing up to the essentials of common experience, the humanities can shake themselves into sanity," and "[Samuel Johnson] was always turning a thing upside down and shaking the nonsense out of it."

Having begun his studies of Keats and Johnson early in his graduate career, Bate continued them throughout his academic life, producing a number of award-winning publications. Bate's *John Keats* (1963), garnered numerous awards, including the 1964 Pulitzer Prize for biography and the Christian Gauss Award of Phi Beta Kappa. Bate's *Samuel Johnson* (1977), a reworking of his earlier *The Achievement of Samuel Johnson* (1955), won the 1978 Pulitzer Prize for biography, the National Book Award, and the National Book Critics Circle Award.

Bate hearkened to Keats's "immortal freemasonry" of great expressive spirits who could serve as guides, as sources of hope, to individuals faced with challenges and adversity. Themes that permeated his scholarship included the psychology of achievement, the intimidating pressures of past achievements, the relation of literature to personal experience, and the paradoxical relationship between the ordinary and fallible qualities in individual lives and their subsequent rise to greatness. Quoting Johnson, Bate said, "The first step in greatness is to be honest." Looking to universal truths led to fulfilling one's own nature and becoming human. Bate's *Coleridge* (1968), was not a full-scale biography, but experts hailed it as the best introduction to Coleridge's varied achievements and difficulties.

Bate's most popular Harvard enterprise was a course about Johnson that he taught for thirty years; it seemed to nourish a student generation that was groping for meaning and challenging every available convention. Students remembered Bate as the best teacher they knew, recalling his unassuming, yet stimulating teaching style. They described him as friendly, mischievous and decent, engaging and emotional, but not histrionic. At Harvard, Bate lived in undergraduate dormitories and conversed daily with the students. In the late 1960s the Harvard student "Confidential Guide" referred to him as "the great Bate."

In keeping with the political tone of the period, Bate disliked the smugness of Harvard's Cambridge circles, yet he admired Robert Kennedy. He hated the lies of the administration of President Richard M. Nixon, and he worried about the widening global economic disparities.

Bate died of heart failure at Beth Israel Deaconess Medical Center in Boston six days after surgery for esophageal cancer. His body was cremated without funeral services, and his ashes were scattered on his New Hampshire farm in Amherst by his surviving sister and his eleven nieces and nephews. An avid conservationist, Bate bequeathed his farm to the Amherst Conservation Commission.

Bate's closest colleagues said, "He gave his students . . . the gift of hope: that human nature can overcome its frailties and follies and . . . carve out something lasting and worthwhile, even something astonishing." Bate was a model mentor for children of the 1960s. He rebelled against conventions, did not serve in the military, came from the working class, and was perceived to be a little crazy. It would seem that Bate furnished what the youth of the 1960s craved: real answers to life's questions, hypocrisy stripped bare, and genuine love and concern for his fellow human beings.

★

The prefaces to Bate's *John Keats* (1963) and *The Achievement of Samuel Johnson* (1955) furnish Bate's own insights to his craft. Biographical information is in Roger Rosenblatt, *Coming Apart: A Memoir of the Harvard Wars of 1969* (1997), and "Faculty of Arts and Sciences—Memorial Minute—W. Jackson Bate," *Harvard University Gazette* (1 June 2000). Obituaries are in the (London) *Independent* (31 July 1999); the *New York Times*, *Washington Post*, *Los Angeles Times*, and *North American Society for the Study of Romanticism* (all 28 July 1999); and the (London) *Times* (30 July 1999).

LERI M. THOMAS

BEATTY, (Henry) Warren (*b.* 30 March 1937 in Richmond, Virginia), motion-picture actor, director, producer, and screenwriter who, as a megastar of the 1960s, was notorious for his arrogance and innumerable love affairs, but who matured later in his career to become a respected member of Hollywood's artistic community.

Beaty, who later added a *t* to his last name, and his older sister, Shirley MacLaine, were born into a solid, middle-class family with some show business experience. Their father, Ira O. Beaty, was a public school administrator who had been a violinist and a drummer in his own band, and their mother, Kathlyn MacLean Beaty, was a former actress and drama coach.

As a child "Little Henry" loved reading and playing the piano. A loner, he spent hours pantomiming celebrities such as Milton Berle and Al Jolson. Beatty attended Washington and Lee High School in Arlington, Virginia, where his father was the principal. He was the star of the football team and president of the senior class. After graduating in 1955 and turning down many offers of football scholarships, Beatty chose to attend Northwestern University in Evanston, Illinois, enrolling in the School of Speech and Drama in 1955.

Disappointed with the curriculum, Beatty left college after his freshman year and moved to New York City to study with acting teacher Stella Adler. Subsisting on peanut butter sandwiches in a cheap apartment on Manhattan's West Side, he paid for his acting lessons with odd jobs, such as dishwasher, sandhog, and piano player at a local bar.

In February 1957 Beatty landed his first job on a television show, which was followed by acting jobs on soap operas, supplemented by stage appearances in summer stock. In one of these performances he was spotted by director Joshua Logan and invited to take a screen test. Metro-Goldwyn-Mayer (MGM) executives were impressed with the handsome young actor and offered him a contract. In 1959 he moved to Hollywood, where he dated the actress Joan Collins and accepted the role of handsome, arrogant Milton Armitage on the Colombia Broadcasting System (CBS) sitcom *The Many Loves of Dobie Gillis.*

In September 1959 Beatty was offered a lead role on Broadway in William Inge's *A Loss of Roses.* During rehearsals he exhibited the bad-boy behavior that became his trademark in the 1960s. He habitually arrived late without an excuse, argued constantly with the director, Daniel Manne, and often with Inge himself over changes in the script, and disrupted rehearsals by inviting his girlfriend, Collins, to attend. The play closed on 19 December 1959 after only twenty-five performances. Beatty was the only cast member whose reviews were excellent.

In 1960 Beatty was in the headlines and gossip columns even before he made his first film. He and Collins were an item, fighting for space in the gossip columns with Elizabeth Taylor and her new husband, Eddie Fisher.

Even though he knew from firsthand experience how difficult Beatty could be, William Inge was impressed by Beatty's ability and recommended him for the lead male role, opposite Natalie Wood, in the film *Splendor in the Grass,* for which he wrote the screenplay. At the time Wood and her husband, Robert Wagner, were considered the perfect Hollywood couple. The passionate love scenes in the

Warren Beatty. ARCHIVE PHOTOS, INC.

film seemed a little too well rehearsed to Wagner, and he and Wood separated. Beatty immediately moved in with the beautiful actress. Released in October 1961, *Splendor in the Grass* was enormously popular, especially among teenagers. It was the film that made Beatty a star.

Beatty's career soared with the release of three important films over twelve months. As well as the success of *Splendor in the Grass,* Beatty received good reviews for another Inge film, *All Fall Down* (1962), and for his portrayal of an Italian gigolo in *The Roman Spring of Mrs. Stone* (1961). At the same time that Wood was nominated for an Oscar for *Splendor,* she received critical praise for her work in *West Side Story*, and she was preparing for the lead role in *Gypsy.* The media frenzy over the two attractive stars was exceeded only by that over Elizabeth Taylor and Richard Burton. Beatty, an unknown, had become famous. His fame increased when Woody Allen took Beatty's real-life opening line with girls, "What's new, pussycat?" as the title for his 1965 movie, which in turn provided a hit for Tom Jones. Carly Simon, a 1970s companion, wrote the hit song "You're So Vain" about Beatty.

After the release of *All Fall Down,* Beatty stopped working. He turned down over seventy scripts and lost millions of dollars of potential salary, along with the leading roles in successful films such as *Barefoot in the Park, The Leopard,*

Act One, and *PT109.* He and Wood were too busy traveling and having fun.

By 1963 Beatty found himself in serious debt. He returned to work and made *Lilith* (1964), the filming of which was disturbed by frequent clashes between the egocentric star and director Robert Rossen. The movie received poor reviews, as did Beatty's next effort, *Mickey One* (1965). By this time Beatty and Wood were fighting constantly. In 1964 the couple broke up, and Beatty flew into the arms of the beautiful French actress Leslie Caron, whose husband named Beatty as corespondent in his divorce case. Caron had little notion at the time that she was just one in a long list of beautiful women with whom Beatty formed romantic liaisons, including Diane Ladd, Jane Fonda, Vivian Leigh, Judy Carne, Julie Christie, Britt Ekland, Madonna, and Diane Keaton. Worried about his career after these box office flops, Beatty took matters into his own hands and decided to produce his next film himself. At lunch one day with Caron and Francois Truffaut, the French director told him about a new script that related the story of Depression-era gangsters Bonnie Parker and Clyde Barrow in a violent but sympathetic way. Choosing an unknown fashion model–turned-actress, Faye Dunaway, for his costar, Beatty produced and starred in *Bonnie and Clyde.* Released in 1967, the film received bad reviews, but audiences loved it, particularly the slow-motion splatter of blood and bullets in the final scene. Beatty's portrayal of the antiheroic, sociopathic Barrow endeared the film to youthful, rebellious, antiauthoritarian audiences of the late 1960s.

Beatty promoted the film almost completely by himself. By Academy Award time, *Bonnie and Clyde* had earned ten Oscar nominations, including best actor for Beatty and best actress for Dunaway. Beatty collected over $6 million and, having proved that he was a superior actor/producer/businessman, became the toast of the town. Soon he began a four-year liaison with actress Julie Christie, whom he had met in London in 1966.

Because he was so wrapped up with Christie and with working only on his own terms, Beatty turned down offers most other stars would have grabbed. He passed on *Butch Cassidy and the Sundance Kid*; he turned down an opportunity to produce *The Godfather* and to star in the part eventually given to Al Pacino. After making a poorly received film, *The Only Game in Town* (1969), Beatty traveled the world with Christie for two years. Both stars refused interviews during this period.

In 1975 Beatty hoped to repeat his *Bonnie and Clyde* success. He produced *Shampoo,* which he coauthored. The film won several awards, including an Oscar for best supporting actress, and it became Columbia Pictures' top-grossing film of the year. He followed this success with another, producing and cowriting *Heaven Can Wait* (1978), which earned nine Oscar nominations and grossed over $120 million.

Beatty then began to produce and direct his masterpiece, *Reds* (1981), the story of journalist John Reed and the radical movement in the United States. On the set Beatty was a taskmaster, insisting on retakes of almost every scene. The film earned twelve Academy Award nominations and earned Beatty an Oscar for best director. The playboy had finally been vindicated. Six years later, however, he produced and starred in one of the biggest flops in Hollywood history, *Ishtar* (1987).

In 1990 Beatty produced, directed, and played the title role in *Dick Tracy.* The following year, while coproducing and starring in *Bugsy,* the story of notorious gangster Bugsy Siegel, he fell in love with his costar, Annette Bening, whom he married in 1992. The couple starred together again in the romance *Love Affair* (1994). A long-time political activist, Beatty played an apolitically correct senator in *Bulworth* (1998), a film he wrote, directed, and produced.

In 2001 Beatty rekindled memories of Ishtar as he starred in another phenomenal bust, *Town and Country.* Budgeted at $90 million and earning a miserable $6.7 million during its brief theatrical run, *Town and Country* was released three years after completion and pulled from theaters after a mere four weeks, moving critics to rank it among the biggest flops in movie history.

Beatty, who is called by his nickname, Pro, lives with Bening and their four children in Beverly Hills, California. The actor still disdains the press, articulating his distaste for giving personal interviews by saying, "In a way, I'd rather ride down the street on a camel than give what is sometimes called an in-depth interview. I'd rather ride down the street on a camel nude. In a snowstorm. Backwards."

Beatty has been nominated for an Academy Award fourteen times, but only four of those nominations have been for best actor. He is the only person in cinema history to get Academy nods as producer, director, writer, and actor in the same film. Beatty has achieved this level of excellence twice, first with *Heaven Can Wait* in 1978, and then with *Reds* in 1981. In 2000 the Motion Picture Academy of Arts and Sciences honored Beatty with the Irving G. Thalberg Award, a prize given to directors and producers to recognize a lifetime body of work. Beatty was honored for the range and scope of his cinema projects and his dedication to approaching the business of movies with intelligence and integrity.

★

James Spada, *Shirley and Warren* (1985), explores the relationship between Beatty and his sister and spends considerable time describing the actor's childhood. John Parker, *Warren Beatty: The Last Great Lover of Hollywood* (1993), concentrates on Beatty's life and career in the 1960s and describes the actor's contributions to the film industry. Ellis Amburn, *The Sexiest Man Alive: A Biography of Warren Beatty* (2002), goes into great detail about the actor's amorous activities. Stephanie Zacharek's lengthy article, "Warren Beatty," Salon.com (20 Mar. 2000), forsakes exploring Beatty's personal life and concentrates instead on examining his creative abilities.

JOHN J. BYRNE

BECK, Julian (*b*. 31 May 1925 in New York City; *d*. 14 September 1985 in New York City), founder of the avant-garde The Living Theatre in 1947 with wife Judith Malina.

Born in Manhattan's Washington Heights district, Beck was the younger of two boys born to Irving Beck, a motorcycle parts business owner and salesman, and Mabel Lucille Blum, a teacher. From an early age, he showed an interest in the theater and enjoyed being taken to plays, concerts, and operas by his parents. Beck attended the privileged Horace Mann School, where his classmates included William F. Buckley, Jr., and Jack Kerouac. At Horace Mann, Beck acted in numerous theatrical productions and began writings plays, stories, and poems. In 1942, he was admitted to Yale University, but dropped out in his first year. He later attended City College of New York from 1946 to 1949.

In 1943, at the age of eighteen, Beck met Judith Malina through a mutual acquaintance. The two became partners in both life and work. They married on 30 October 1948, and later had two children. Beck and Malina's dream was to start an experimental repertory company in which they could direct and act. In 1947 they legally incorporated The Living Theatre, which they launched using an inheritance of $6,000. They staged several productions by experimentalist writers such as Paul Goodman, Gertrude Stein, Luigi Pirandello, and others. The Living Theatre stages included the home of the Becks on West End Avenue, the Cherry Lane Theatre, a loft on 100th Street, and a building at 14th Street and Sixth Avenue in New York City.

In 1957 Beck and Malina spent thirty days in jail for refusing to participate in an air-raid defense drill, the first of twelve incidents in which they were arrested for various acts of civil disobedience. In 1961 Malina conceived the idea of a General Strike for Peace, which took place on 29 January 1962. The strike lasted a few days, as participants marched to the New York Office of the Atomic Energy Commission and to the United Nations, where the strikers spoke to U.S. and Soviet officials. Other Strike for Peace rallies occurred in the next few years, and Beck and Malina would be arrested at several of these demonstrations.

In the 1960s Beck and Malina formulated the mission of their theater. Their presentations would be imaginative, the casts would improvise, and the themes would reflect Beck and Malina's view of anarchy and pacifism. The *Village Voice*, which in 1959 awarded them the Lola D'Annunzio Award for their decade-long contribution to the off-Broadway movement, was a staunch supporter, and gave Living Theatre productions numerous positive reviews.

In 1961 The Living Theatre was asked to participate in the Theatre des Nations festival in Paris, where they staged their play *Connection*, in which a young actor by the name of Martin Sheen performed. The company won the Grand Prix of the Theatre des Nations, and the cast won a medal from the Paris Theatre Critics Circle for best acting. A year later, Beck and Malina's company went to the Theatre des Nations again. The French loved The Living Theatre productions, especially those in which the actors mingled with the audience before and during the performance. The mingling between cast and audience was to become a trademark of The Living Theatre, which in 1962 toured other European cities and established a European base.

In 1963 Malina directed *The Brig*, which dealt with the harsh life of a military prison. The play reinforced Beck's belief in the French visionary Antonin Artaud's idea of "the theatre of cruelty" ("a theatre in which the actors are like victims burning at the stake, signaling through the flames"), and confirmed The Living Theatre as a repertory company with a social and political agenda.

Beck and Malina had a strong following for their pro-

Julian Beck *(right)*, with Judith Malina in his arms. CORBIS CORPORATION (BELLEVUE)

ductions by the 1960s, but their theater was constantly in debt, and their actors were underpaid. Although Beck was able to obtain a nonprofit status on donations for The Living Theatre, he still needed to pay tax on ticket admissions, and ended up owing federal, state, and city taxes. By 1963, The Living Theatre was in financial trouble, owing monies to the landlord, the local power company, and the Internal Revenue Service (IRS). Beck and Malina protested the federal government's seizure of theater properties for back payment of taxes, and their acts of civil disobedience again landed them in jail. In 1964 Beck and Malina were given an eleven-count felony indictment for preventing IRS agents from performing their duties.

Beck and Malina left the United States in 1964 to stage their production of *The Brig* in several European cities. Other productions performed by Beck and Malina's company in Europe were *Mysteries and Smaller Pieces, The Maids, Frankenstein,* and *Antigone.* While in Europe, Beck appeared as an actor in such films as *Living and Glorious* (1965), *Amore, Amore* (1966), *Agonia* (1967), *Oedipus Rex* (1967), *Le Compromis* (1968), *Etre Libre* (1968), and *Paradise Now* (1969).

Paradise Now was conceived in 1968 and was to be a whole new experience for The Living Theatre. Before it was filmed, it was performed on stage. It dealt with such topics as loss of Eden and the "resurrection of Native Americans," and included audience participation. In 1968 Beck and Malina, with their repertory company, returned to the United States for a two-week engagement at Yale. *Paradise Now* involved nudity both from the actors and audience, and after a performance, Beck, other actors, and some audience members were arrested for indecent exposure.

During the 1960s, Beck published the poetry collections *Songs of the Revolution: One to Thirty-five* (1963) and *Twenty-one Songs of the Revolution* (1969). Other writings included *Revolution and Counterrevolution* (1968), and *Conversations with Julian Beck and Judith Malina* (1969), edited by Jean-Jacques Lebel.

The Living Theatre company returned to Europe in 1969, and in the 1970s performed in Morocco, Brazil, and Mexico, where they were either received openly and praised for their productions or found themselves in trouble with the authorities. They continued to have money problems, and were bailed out by various supporters. They also remained politically active and returned to the United States in 1971 to perform in various cities. After more than seven years in Europe, from 1975 to 1983, The Living Theatre returned to New York. Beck had been diagnosed with cancer, but was well enough to film *The Cotton Club,* a Francis Ford Coppola film. Despite his illness, Beck appeared in a 1984 episode of the television show *Miami Vice,* and in the film *Poltergeist II: The Other Side* (1986). Beck died of abdominal/colon cancer. Malina remarried in 1988 to Hanon Reznikov, and continued to run The Living Theatre in the early twenty-first century.

★

Writings on Beck and his career include John Tytell, *The Living Theatre: Art, Exile, and Outrage* (1995). Also useful is Jean-Jacques Lebel, ed., *Conversations with Julian Beck and Judith Malina* (1969). An obituary is in the *New York Times* (17 Sept. 1985).

MARGALIT SUSSER

BÉKÉSY, Georg von (György) (*b.* 3 June 1899 in Budapest, Hungary; *d.* 13 April 1972 in Honolulu, Hawaii), physiologist and physicist who won the Nobel Prize in physiology or medicine in 1961 for his pioneering work on the human auditory system.

Békésy was the son of Alexander, a diplomat, and Paula Mazaly von Békésy. The diplomatic life meant living in many countries, and Békésy's early education took place in Munich, Germany; Constantinople, Turkey; Budapest, Hungary; and Zurich, Switzerland. He studied chemistry at the University of Berne and graduated with a baccalau-

Georg von Békésy. THE LIBRARY OF CONGRESS

reate degree in 1920. In 1926 he earned a Ph.D. from the University of Budapest for the development of a fast method for determining molecular weight. Békésy worked at the Hungarian Telephone and Post Office Laboratory from 1928 to 1945 as a communications engineer and taught experimental physics at Pázmány Péter University in Budapest from 1939 to 1945.

His research at the Hungarian laboratory, originally intended to improve telephone communications, resulted in Békésy's discovery of the physical mechanism of stimulation within the cochlea. By developing anatomical dissection techniques using the low-powered microscope and inventing a special grinding mechanism, which operated in a water bath, he determined the mechanical characteristics of neural transduction in the inner ear. This technique allowed rapid, nondestructive dissection of the cochlea, so sound waves could be observed in the basilar membrane. Silver particles were sprinkled on the nearly transparent basilar membrane and examined stroboscopically. This was the foundation of the traveling-wave theory: sound impulses produce a wave sweeping along the basilar membrane. As the wave travels through the membrane, the amplitude increases until it reaches a maximum and then falls off sharply until the wave dies out. That point at which the wave reaches its greatest amplitude is where the frequency of the sound is detected. As Hermann von Helmholtz had postulated, Békésy found that the high-frequency tones are perceived near the base of the cochlea and the lower frequencies toward the apex.

In 1946 Békésy emigrated to Sweden to work at the Karolinska Institute. There he developed the Békésy audiometer. In 1947, invited by S. S. Stevens, Békésy came to the United States to run the Psycho-Acoustic Laboratory at Harvard University. While at Harvard he became a naturalized citizen. He continued his work on the perception of the senses, culminating in the publication of *Experiments in Hearing* (1960). Békésy won the Nobel Prize in physiology or medicine in 1961 for this landmark research and the complete publication of his research works and publications in one volume. By developing the model of the inner ear and devising methods to research how the neural system works in hearing, Békésy laid the foundation for subsequent work on sound and hearing in the 1960s. He also developed new techniques that led to a clearer understanding of hearing problems in humans and devised instruments that enabled researchers to do more precise work.

After receiving the Nobel Prize, he became concerned with the biophysics of sense organs and with perception and worked in this area for the rest of the 1960s. His scientific objective was to understand all of the common biological processes of perception. In the academic year 1965–1966, Békésy became professor of sensory sciences at the University of Hawaii in Honolulu, after mandatory retirement from Harvard and the loss by fire of the Psycho-Acoustic Laboratory. His research at the university, from 1966 until his death in 1972, involved the creation of many microscopic devices to aid in precision work. Hawaiian Telephone sponsored some of his research.

In addition to the Nobel Prize, Békésy received several scientific distinctions and honorary doctorates from seven universities, including the University of Medical Sciences in Budapest. Several laboratories in the world are named for him in recognition of his pioneering work. He never married or had children. Békésy is also well known for his collection of art, which he left to the Nobel Foundation after his death, and his love of music and antiques. His passion for research was a driving force throughout his life.

★

The Library of Congress has Békésy's collections of manuscripts, movies, and photographs. In addition to E. G. Weaver, trans., *Experiments in Hearing* (1960), he published *Sensory Inhibition* (1967). A brief autobiographical sketch appears in "Some Biophysical Experiments from Fifty Years Ago," *Annual Review of Physiology* (1974), and S. S. Stevens, Fred Warshofsky, and others, *Sound and Hearing* (1970). His obituary is in the *New York Times* and the *Washington Post* (both 16 June 1972).

KIM LAIRD

BELL, Daniel (*b.* 10 May 1919 in New York City), sociologist, author, educator, and cofounder, with Irving Kristol, of the magazine *The Public Interest* in 1965.

Bell was the second son born to Benjamin Bell and Anna Kaplan, both of whom were garment workers. His father died in the influenza epidemic of 1920. Until the age of six, Bell spoke only Yiddish, but by the time he was thirteen he had mastered English and was reading the works of Karl Marx, John Stuart Mill, and other political theorists. He graduated from high school at age sixteen and entered City College of New York.

There he participated in the "alcove," a gathering of left-wing intellectuals that included Bell's Trotskyite classmates Irving Howe, Nathan Glazer, Seymour M. Lipset, and Irving Kristol. The group argued politics and together formulated their opposition to Stalinism. Although Bell was wary of ideological dogma, he joined the Young People's Socialist League, or "Yipsels," a group concerned with programs for social reform. Reflecting on his college years, Bell would later note that he was a socialist with a small *S*.

Bell graduated from City College in 1939 with a B.S. in sociology, and then enrolled in graduate courses in sociology at Columbia University, where he would eventually earn his Ph.D. in 1960.

Married three times, Bell wed his first wife, Nora

Daniel Bell. THE LIBRARY OF CONGRESS

Potashnick, on 20 September 1943. The couple had one daughter and later divorced. His second marriage, to Elaine Graham on 13 April 1949, also ended in divorce. Finally, in November 1960 Bell married Pearl Kazin, with whom he had a son.

A prolific essayist, Bell was a staff writer for *The New Leader* from 1939 to 1941 and its managing editor from 1941 to 1944. In 1945 he became editor of *Common Sense,* and he taught at the University of Chicago from 1945 to 1948. *Fortune* magazine employed him as its labor editor from 1948 to 1958, during which time he also served as a part-time lecturer in sociology at Columbia University. Also during the 1950s, Bell edited *The New American Right* (1955), a collection of essays by historians and sociologists on the rise of the conservative political movement following World War II. In 1963 he would expand and update the book under the title *The Radical Right.*

Following his resignation from *Fortune,* Bell returned to Columbia in 1959 as an associate professor of sociology. After completing his doctorate, he was promoted to the rank of full professor. He also served as chairman of Columbia's sociology department. During the student uprisings at Columbia in 1968, Bell played an important role as a negotiator between students and the administration and was instrumental in providing guidelines for restructuring educational policy at the university.

In 1960 Bell published *The End of Ideology: On the Exhaustion of Political Ideas in the Fifties,* which became one of the most important books of the decade and solidly established his reputation as one of the country's leading intellectuals. *The End of Ideology* consists of sixteen essays that Bell had published earlier in various journals over a ten-year period. The book subsequently became the source of a decade-long debate. Defining ideology as "the conversion of ideas into social levers," Bell welcomed the apparent drift away from "extreme" political ideologies that had characterized Western intellectuals in the 1940s and 1950s, but he also decried the loss of vitality in American political thought. He argued that the catastrophes associated with the Moscow show-trials, the Nazi-Soviet pact, the concentration camps, and the suppression of the Hungarian worker's revolt, had dealt a lethal blow to intellectuals' faith in the old ideologies. Traditional systems of thought, he asserted, had been "exhausted" and had lost their "power to persuade."

During the 1960s Bell's arguments divided intellectuals as they questioned whether there had been an "end of ideology," and if so, whether this was a sign of progress or decline. Bell, in turn, looked forward to a future when intellectuals would approach political life with a modesty shorn of grand hopes for change, committed to carefully measuring the consequences of their political activity. He argued that intellectuals had betrayed their responsibilities in earlier decades by surrendering critical thinking to the appeal of mass movements and dogmatic ideologies. Although Bell celebrated the end of ideologies, he also decried the trend toward bureaucratic rationality, as well as communal decay that made it difficult to define the "public interest." Bell rejected the belief that the alleged objectivity of the social sciences could replace conflict in the making of policy. Rather, he insisted that social problems were profoundly moral in character, and the reduction of the social sciences to a value-free method was part of the problem with modern bureaucratic society—not part of the solution to that problem.

To advance the ideas in *The End of Ideology,* Bell, along with Irving Kristol, founded *The Public Interest* in 1965, with the aim to "transcend ideology through reasoned public debate and disinterested inquiry into public policy," and to promote rational choice in social planning. The magazine encouraged nonideological analysis and sought to influence policy makers, not politicians. During the course of the next eight years, its circulation rose from 5,000 to 11,000 by 1973. Although Bell was not a political activist, he insisted on his identity as a liberal, and as his disagreements with the conservative-minded Kristol increased, he eventually resigned as coeditor of the quarterly in 1973. He withdrew from its publications committee in 1982.

During the same year that Bell cofounded *The Public Interest,* he published the results of a yearlong study of undergraduate education on college campuses. Entitled *The Reforming of General Education* (1965), the report argued for the traditional values of the liberal arts and eschewed the trend to shorten undergraduate programs. The college experience, argued Bell, "should be four years of unforced maturation." He advanced support for a liberal arts curriculum that would inform the student's understanding of history and Western civilization before the concentration on a specific discipline began. Bell was concerned that education was becoming so functional that it was in danger of producing highly trained but intellectually impoverished specialists. He also contended that campus unrest constituted a rebellion by students against the "organizational harness" that had been forced on them at an early age.

In addition to his concern about the future of higher education, Bell was also interested in the use of sociology for social prediction. Appointed chairman of the American Academy of Arts and Sciences Commission on the Year 2000, he convened its first meeting in October 1965, and its subsequent deliberations became the basis for his book *Toward the Year 2000* (1968), in which Bell noted that "The function of prediction is not, as is often stated, to aid social control, but to widen the spheres of moral choice." Because of the opportunity for collaborating with other scholars on problems of social prediction, Bell moved in 1969 from Columbia to Harvard University, where he collaborated with academic futurists on studies for the commission. His book *The Coming of Post-Industrial Society* (1973) was the result of his venture in social forecasting.

In 1976 Bell published *The Cultural Contradictions of Capitalism,* which, along with *The End of Ideology,* appeared on the *Times Literary Supplement* list of the 100 most important books of the second half of the twentieth century. At the beginning of the twenty-first century, Bell was the Henry Ford II Professor Emeritus of the Social Sciences at Harvard, as well as scholar in residence of the American Academy of Arts and Sciences. Summing up his career, Bell described himself as a liberal in politics, a socialist in economics, and a conservative in culture.

★

There is no biography of Bell. The best sources can be found in magazine articles and fragments in books that deal with the 1960s, including William H. Honan, "They Live in the Year 2000," *New York Times Magazine* (9 Apr. 1967); Jay Nuechterlein, "The Good Liberal," *National Review* 42, no. 9 (14 May 1990): 42–45; Howard Brick, *The Age of Contradiction: American Thought and Culture in the 1960s* (1998); and Joseph Dorman, *Arguing the World* (2002).

JACK FISCHEL

BELLOW, Saul (*b.* 10 June 1915 in Lachine, Quebec, Canada), Nobel Prize–winning novelist, several of whose novels— *The Adventures of Augie March, Seize the Day, Henderson the Rain King, Herzog,* and *Mr. Sammler's Planet*—have secured for him a place in the American literary canon.

Bellow was the youngest of four children born to Abraham Bellow and Liza Gordon, Russian Jewish immigrants who arrived in Canada two years before his birth. The father was a businessman, often unsuccessful, whose lines of trade were many, not all of them legal. He moved the family to Chicago when Bellow was nine, and by the time Bellow graduated from Tuley High School and entered the University of Chicago in 1933, the father was the owner of the Carroll Coal Company. A suit against the temporarily uninsured company, following the death of one of its workers, saddled the family with long-term debt, and forced Bellow to withdraw from the university. He picked up his studies first at the University of Wisconsin and then at Northwestern University, from which he graduated with a degree in anthropology in 1937.

Between Bellow's taking of his degree and the period of his greatest success, the 1960s, he worked at making himself a writer. In 1941 *Partisan Review* published his first story, "Two Morning Monologues," and in 1943 it published an excerpt from Bellow's novel in progress, *Dangling Man,* itself published in 1944. In its opening pages, the book famously put the Hemingway cult of reserve and silence to

Saul Bellow. THE LIBRARY OF CONGRESS

rest: "If you have difficulties, grapple with them silently, goes one of their commandments. To hell with that! I intend to talk about mine, and if I had as many mouths as Siva has arms and kept them all going at the same time, I still could not do myself justice." It was Bellow's first public act of braying, something that he turned into an art form in succeeding novels such as *The Victim* (1947), *The Adventures of Augie March* (1953), *Seize the Day* (1956), and *Henderson the Rain King* (1959).

Bellow's contribution to our understanding of the 1960s is chiefly connected with the publication of two novels, *Herzog* (1964) and *Mr. Sammler's Planet* (1970). About the former, it has been said that "the prose is charged, rich, full of the specifics and precisely defined impressions that create the feel of the mid-1960s American life." Of the latter, a critic has written, "Bellow captures better than anyone the feel of American society in the late 1960s, with its blend of social rebellion, sexuality, racial unrest, and personal aggrandizement."

The 1960s also saw Bellow try his hand at drama, with the Broadway production of *The Last Analysis* in 1964 and the Spoleto, London, and New York productions of *Under the Weather* (1966), a group of three short plays (*A Wen, Orange Soufflé, Out from Under*). *The Last Analysis* is the story of a formerly successful comedian, Bummidge, who attempts to resuscitate not so much his career as his life by engaging "on an expedition to recover the forgotten truth," and in the process sets out to hold up a mirror to society's unspoken desperation and angst: "*Only* a comic," Bummidge muses. "Bummidge—he doesn't know Greek or calculus. But he knows what he knows. Have you ever watched audiences laughing? You should see how monstrous it looks; you should listen from my side of the footlights. Oh, the despair, my son! The stale hearts! The snarling and gasping!" The play failed to find an audience, closing after twenty-eight performances. Its failure with both audiences and critics led Bellow to rewrite and publish it in book form, and to try to defend it. "*The Last Analysis,*" he wrote, "is not simply a spoof of Freudian psychology, though certain analysts have touchily interpreted it as such. Its real subject is the mind's comical struggle for survival in an environment of Ideas—its fascination with metaphors, and the peculiarly literal and solemn manner in which Americans dedicate themselves to programs, fancies, or brainstorms."

As for *Under the Weather,* the most notable of its three one-act plays, *A Wen,* concerns a Nobel Prize–winning physicist, Solomon Ithimar, whose obsessive recall of a high-school sweetheart's birthmark upon her thigh compels him to seek her out. Middle-aged, heavy-set, and married to a chiropodist, she clearly is no longer the woman of his fantasies, but she is part of his past and the play is as much about the longing for this, his past, as it is for the birthmark

itself. The critics, however, thought no better of *Under the Weather* than they did of *The Last Analysis.* Edith Oliver, writing in the *New Yorker,* tartly remarked: "Apparently, Mr. Bellow believes that it is a good idea to earn while you learn, and although his first full-length exercise, 'The Last Analysis,' was a full-blown disaster when exhibited on Broadway in 1964, he has gamely come on once again to show us how he is progressing in his studies." Thus, playwriting proved for Bellow what it had also proved for Henry James, who also famously suffered a serious defeat when he took it up in mid-career.

Bellow's dramatic successes during this period were not recorded in the theater but in fiction, especially with the phenomenally successful *Herzog,* which his biographer James Atlas refers to as the author's "passport to great fame and wealth." For good reason: the novel was on the bestseller list for forty-two weeks, selling 142,000 copies in hardcover. It also earned the author his second National Book Award. Part *roman à clef,* part cultural critique, the novel struck a nerve in the American psyche, anticipating, as the critic Keith Opdahl writes, "the mood of the coming decade." What it especially anticipated was the faltering collapse of marriage as the centerpiece of American social existence—as well as the centrality that divorce itself would assume in the American realistic novel of the last third of the twentieth century. The eminent critic Tony Tanner has said of the eighteenth- and nineteenth-century realistic novel that in it one finds testimony to the fact that "For bourgeois society marriage is the all-subsuming, all-organizing, all-containing contract. It is the structure that maintains the Structure." By contrast, its late-twentieth-century counterpart offers itself as testimony to a contrary truth: the fissiparous nature of contemporary life. "Things fall apart," wrote Bellow, echoing the poet W. B. Yeats's "Second Coming," in *Mr. Sammler's Planet*; and the thing most noticeably falling apart, in both the contemporary world and novel, is marriage. It comes as no surprise, then, to hear that upon the publication of *Herzog,* Bellow "received two or three thousand letters from people pouring out their souls to me, saying, 'This is my life, this is what it's been like for me.' "

It was also like that for Bellow himself, now in his second marriage, for the impulse for the novel sprang from Bellow's rage at being cuckolded by a man, Jack Ludwig, whom he had thought of as his best friend. Not without cause, then, does the novel begin, "If I am out of my mind, it's all right with me, thought Moses Herzog." Alternating between third person and first person, the novel ostensibly takes place in Herzog's head, as he recalls the events surrounding his own cuckolding by Valentine Gersbach and sends off letters to friends and foes, famous and not, living and dead, to anyone who might help him achieve escape and relief from the state of being "incoherent with anger." In time, Herzog does come down from the heights of his rage, and the novel ends with him deciding to write no more letters, a sign of his sanity reasserting itself: "Perhaps, he'd stop writing letters. Yes, that was what was coming, in fact. The knowledge that he was done with these letters. Whatever had come over him during these last months, the spell, really seemed to be passing, really going." But before the novel concludes, Bellow, in the voice of Herzog, offers up a picture of contemporary American reality that is inimically opposed to the integrity of the individual soul, to its cries for meaning.

Mr. Sammler's Planet picks up this theme, viewing a late 1960s urban culture—that of New York City—through the eyes of an aging Holocaust survivor, the eponymous Mr. Arthur Sammler. The culture itself is found enmeshed in a Bataille-like notion of the real, wherein sex and violence are understood as authenticity's fundamental factors. Mr. Sammler has experienced evil firsthand, not only by being forced to dig his own grave, but also by being shot by the German guards and then, after his miraculous escape from amidst the freshly buried corpses (including that of his wife), by being hounded in the forests by Polish resistance fighters. And having experienced evil as such, he thinks it neither "banal"—the term applied to it by the American philosopher Hannah Arendt—nor emancipatory, in the spirit of the French intellectual Georges Bataille. (Both thinkers are mentioned, and dismissed, in the novel.) In fact, "like many people who had seen the world collapse once, Mr. Sammler entertained the possibility that it might collapse twice."

And late 1960s New York provides its full share of evidence to influence apocalyptic thoughts: "New York makes one think about the collapse of civilization, about Sodom and Gomorrah, the end of the world. The end of the world wouldn't come as a surprise here. Many people already bank on it." Mr. Sammler doesn't bank upon it; his spiritual longing for completion won't permit such an acquiescence to despair. But he is frightfully taken aback by a culture that does not acknowledge that one can become the prisoner of one's vaunted freedoms, of one's appetites and lusts. Released from feelings of puritanical guilt, cosmopolitan culture offers up manifest examples of why it might benefit from reinstating guilt to its proper place in defining human nature: "The labors of Puritanism now was ending. The dark satanic mills changing into light satanic mills. The reprobates converted into children of joy, the sexual ways of the seraglio and of the Congo bush adopted by the emancipated masses," ending in a scenario of "libidinous privileges, the right to be uninhibited, spontaneous, urinating, defecating, belching, coupling in all positions, tripling, quadrupling, polymorphous, noble in being natural, primitive, combining the leisure and luxurious inventiveness of Versailles with the hibiscus-covered erotic ease of Samoa."

Mr. Sammler speaks in the thinly veiled voice of Bellow himself, and the novel has often been singled out as offering a too reactionary view of 1960s culture. Yet when read many decades later, the novel, so independently conceived, seems remarkably acute in its social critique, more penetrating than many a novel whose author simply purveyed the decade's shibboleths. It is for his independent spirit that Bellow is valued, the spirit that writes out of the conviction "that the truth is not loved because it is improving or progressive. We hunger and thirst for it—for its own sake." It is the conviction that Mr. Sammler, praying over the corpse of his dead nephew, memorably voices at novel's end: "He was aware that he must meet, and he did meet—through all the confusion and degraded clowning of this life through which we are speeding—he did meet the terms of his contract. The terms which, in his inmost heart, each man knows. As I know mine. As all know. For that is the truth of it—that we all know, God, that we know, that we know, we know, we know."

By the time of *Mr. Sammler's Planet*'s publication, and certainly by 1975, with the publication of *Humboldt's Gift,* Bellow's reputation had solidified. He was among the pantheon of great American novelists, as well as a leading figure in the subset of American Jewish novelists, whose notables included Bernard Malamud, Philip Roth, and Norman Mailer. He was awarded the Nobel Prize in 1976. Other books would follow, including *The Dean's December* (1982), *Him with His Foot in His Mouth, and Other Stories* (1984), *More Die of Heartbreak* (1987), and *Ravelstein* (2000). They have been fine additions to a magnificent oeuvre.

★

Biographies of Bellow include Ruth Miller, *Saul Bellow: A Biography of the Imagination* (1991), and James Atlas, *Bellow* (2000). Studies of Bellow's work include Tony Tanner, *Saul Bellow* (1965); Keith Opdahl, *The Novels of Saul Bellow: An Introduction* (1967); Irving Malin, *Saul Bellow's Fiction* (1969); Sarah Blacher Cohen, *Saul Bellow's Enigmatic Laughter* (1974); G. I. Porter, *Whence the Power?* (1974); John Jacob Clayton, *Saul Bellow: In Defense of Man* (1979); Daniel Fuchs, *Saul Bellow: Vision and Revision* (1984); Jeanne Brahm, *A Sort of Columbus: The American Voyages of Saul Bellow's Fiction* (1984); Ellen Pifer, *Saul Bellow: Against the Grain* (1990); and Peter Hyland, *Saul Bellow* (1992).

CHRISTOPHER J. KNIGHT

BENNETT, Tony (*b.* 3 August 1926 in Long Island City, New York), singer who, after an earlier career as a successful pop singles artist in the 1950s, reestablished himself in the 1960s as a masterful balladeer and concert performer, producing a series of highly regarded and commercially successful albums that flew in the face of the dominant rock music of the era.

Tony Bennett, 1965. HUTTON-DEUTSCH/CORBIS

Bennett was born Anthony Dominick Benedetto, the second son and third child of John Benedetto, a grocer, and Anna Suraci, a homemaker who later became a seamstress. He began singing in amateur contests as a teenager, worked as a singing waiter, and began to get jobs in local clubs. Bennett attended but did not graduate from the High School of Industrial Arts in New York City.

Turning eighteen during World War II, Bennett joined the U.S. Army and spent two years in the infantry, seeing combat in Europe. After returning to the United States he studied at the American Theatre Wing and came in second to Rosemary Clooney on Arthur Godfrey's talent show. In 1949, while appearing with the singer Pearl Bailey in Greenwich Village, he was spotted by the entertainer Bob Hope, who put him into his show and suggested the stage name of Tony Bennett.

In 1950 Bennett signed a contract with Columbia Records. The following year he scored his first hit when "Because of You" reached number one on the pop charts in September. It was succeeded at the top of the charts by his next single, a cover of Hank Williams's "Cold, Cold Heart." More hits followed before Bennett returned to number one in November 1953 with "Rags to Riches," followed by "Stranger in Paradise" in early 1954. With the rise of rock 'n' roll at mid-decade, musical tastes changed,

and there was less of a market for the kind of big-voiced pop tenor represented by Bennett and others. He responded by moving more toward jazz and standards and began performing in nightclubs, where he was accompanied by the pianist Ralph Sharon. As he made the transition, his record sales fell, but he eventually found a whole new audience.

Bennett married Patricia Beech, with whom he had two children, on 12 February 1952. They divorced in 1971, and he married Sandra Grant on 29 December of that year. That marriage, which also produced two children, likewise ended in divorce, in 1984.

In the late 1950s and early 1960s Bennett released several impressive albums, including *In Person!*, recorded with Count Basie and His Orchestra, in 1959, and *Tony Bennett Sings a String of Harold Arlen* in 1960, neither of which reached the charts. It was at this point that Sharon showed him "I Left My Heart in San Francisco," a song written in 1954 by Douglass Cross and George Cory. Bennett recorded it in January 1962, and Columbia released it as a single. Coming from an artist whose career on the charts had seemed to be over, it took a long time to catch on, and even then succeeded across the country on a regional basis, achieving only a top twenty ranking, even though it remained on the charts for almost nine months. Meanwhile, the *I Left My Heart in San Francisco* LP became a gold-selling top five hit, and *Tony Bennett at Carnegie Hall*, a live double album also containing the song, reached the top forty. Bennett won Grammy Awards for record of the year and best solo vocal performance for the single.

Coming more than a decade after Bennett's initial success, "I Left My Heart in San Francisco" not only gave his career a second wind but also pushed it to a higher level. He was restored to commercial success on records, quickly scoring two more top-forty singles, "I Wanna Be Around" and "The Good Life," as well as the top-five LP *I Wanna Be Around,* and he was achieving this success with high-quality material. The arrival of the Beatles in February 1964 signaled another change in the direction of popular music, but Bennett at first continued to score with top-forty singles such as "Who Can I Turn To (When Nobody Needs Me)," from the musical *The Roar of the Greasepaint, The Smell of the Crowd;* and "If I Ruled the World," from the musical *Pickwick,* and such top-twenty LPs as *The Many Moods of Tony* and *The Movie Song Album.*

In 1965 Bennett temporarily split with Sharon and attempted to launch a movie career. But *The Oscar,* a universally panned flop released in 1966, turned out to be his only job as an actor. By 1967 the major record labels, recognizing the increased popularity of rock music, began to neglect classic pop artists such as Bennett. At Columbia Records company president Clive Davis encouraged the label's roster of pop singers to record contemporary material written by younger musicians. By 1969 Bennett was recording albums such as *I've Gotta Be Me* and *Tony Sings the Great Hits of Today,* which featured songs by Burt Bacharach and Hal David, Jimmy Webb, and John Lennon and Paul McCartney. They did not restore his commercial fortunes, however, and in the early 1970s he parted ways with Columbia. At first he signed to MGM Records, then founded his own label, Improv. When it foundered, he stopped recording, although he continued to tour successfully during the rest of the 1970s and into the 1980s.

In 1986, managed by his son Danny Bennett, Bennett re-signed to Columbia and issued his first album in nine years, *The Art of Excellence.* By now his cheery demeanor, classy appearance, and continuing affection for pop standards were able to attract a whole new audience and launch a third stage of his lengthy career. *Perfectly Frank,* a tribute album to Frank Sinatra released in 1992, went gold, as did the following year's *Steppin' Out,* a tribute to Fred Astaire. In 1994 Bennett appeared on MTV's *Unplugged* series with Elvis Costello and k. d. lang, and the resulting platinum recording won the Grammy for album of the year. In 2001 Bennett toured the country with lang and celebrated his seventy-fifth birthday by releasing a duets album, *Playin' with My Friends: Bennett Sings the Blues.*

In a sense, Bennett in the 1960s can be thought of as a throwback to an earlier time, given that the main trend in popular music was toward rock, with which he had no affinity. In fact, however, he achieved even greater renown during the decade than he had in the 1950s; he continued to find contemporary songs that benefited from his musical approach; and his commitment to quality allowed him to maintain his audience and, eventually, attract a new one not yet born or in its infancy in the 1960s.

★

Bennett told his own story in *The Good Life* (1998), written with Will Friedwald. Tony Jasper, *Tony Bennett* (1984), is a reasonable account of his life, although it misses his late renaissance. Whitney Baillett's excellent profile of Bennett, first published in *The New Yorker,* is reprinted in his book *American Singers* (1988). The author's own biographical article, "Tony Bennett: Forty Years of 'Pure American Music,'" appeared in *Goldmine* (10 Jan. 1992).

WILLIAM RUHLMANN

BERRIGAN, Daniel Joseph (*b.* 9 May 1921 in Virginia, Minnesota), and **Philip Francis BERRIGAN** (*b.* 5 October 1923 in Two Harbors, Minnesota), first Roman Catholic priests to receive federal prison sentences for antiwar activities during the Vietnam conflict. Daniel was ordained as a Jesuit and became a poet, educator, and peace activist; his brother, a former Josephite, became an author and nonviolent resister.

Daniel and Philip Berrigan are the youngest of six sons born to Thomas W. Berrigan, a second-generation Irish American, and Frieda (Fromhart) Berrigan, whose family emigrated from Germany to the Midwest in the 1890s. Their father worked as a railroad engineer until he was fired because of his Socialist Party affiliation. In the early years of the Great Depression the family moved back to Thomas's hometown of Syracuse, New York, where he found work at the Niagara-Mohawk electrical plant. A devout Catholic, Thomas was active in local church council initiatives and in union politics.

The Berrigans lived on a ten-acre farm near Onondaga Lake. After graduating from high school in 1939, Daniel entered Saint Andrew-on-Hudson Seminary near Poughkeepsie, New York. For the next thirteen years he studied for the priesthood; he also earned a B.A. degree from the seminary in 1946 and a M.A. degree from Woodstock College in 1952. His seminary training was marked by work at a local mental hospital, teaching French, English, and Latin at Saint Peter's Preparatory School in Jersey City, New Jersey, and three years of theological studies at West College in Massachusetts. On 19 June 1952 he was ordained as a Jesuit. His primary ambition was to work in civil rights causes.

Philip spent one semester at Saint Michael's College in Toronto before being drafted into the army in 1943. He was commissioned as a second lieutenant while serving in Europe during World War II. When the war ended, he enrolled in 1946 at the College of the Holy Cross in Worcester, Massachusetts, and received his B.A. in 1950. After graduation he surprised his family and friends by announcing his intention to enter the priesthood. The racial hatred he saw during basic training was the deciding factor. He entered the Society of Saint Joseph, a Catholic missionary order "devoted to the spiritual care of black Americans."

Daniel and Philip's commitment to serving the dispossessed intensified during the 1950s. In 1953–1954 Daniel spent a year studying in a small town near Lyons, France, where he met members of the worker-priest movement who had taken factory jobs. In the autumn of 1954 he returned to New York and taught French and theology at Brooklyn Preparatory School for the next three years, while also working with groups such as the Young Christian Workers and the Walter Ferrell Guild promoting social justice for the poor, especially African Americans and Puerto Ricans. Daniel also wrote poetry, and in 1957 won the Lamont Poetry Award for his first collection, *Time Without Number.* That same year he was appointed as a professor of New Testament studies at Le Moyne College in Syracuse, where he remained until 1963, when older faculty members complained of his "'unprofessional' relationship to students and his daring innovations in liturgy."

Philip, meanwhile, was ordained as a Josephite priest in 1955. He then spent a year at an African-American church in Washington, D.C., and five years teaching at an African-

Philip Berrigan *(far left)* and Daniel Berrigan *(far right)*, photographed in King of Prussia, Pennsylvania. AP/Wide World Photos

American high school in New Orleans. In the early 1960s Philip joined civil rights groups like the Urban League and the Congress of Racial Equality. His New Orleans Catholic Sodality chapter constantly called for racial integration and equality. Perhaps to a greater degree than Daniel, he fully immersed himself into the civil rights struggles of that era. During his time in New Orleans, Philip earned two degrees: a B.S. from Loyola University in 1960 and an M.A. from Xavier University in 1963.

By the early 1960s the brother priests "began to practice a unified spiritual and political activism during the civil rights struggles." At the same time, they expanded their concerns to address the rising danger of nuclear war. They were deeply influenced by the Trappist monk Thomas Merton's view that "the country was slipping into a moral decline as a result of its indifference toward domestic demands for justice and its preoccupation with confronting the Soviet Union." In 1964 the Berrigans joined with other activists to form the Catholic Peace Fellowship, which was affiliated with the well-known religious-pacifist organization the Fellowship of Reconciliation. The two brothers perceived "the budding American Catholic peace movement as a new force in the Church's effort at reintegrating prayer and social action into the mature Christian life."

The mid-1960s marked a turning point in their activism. Influenced by the civil disobedience practices employed by Martin Luther King, Jr., and Dorothy Day's Catholic Worker Movement, the Berrigans increasingly turned to active nonviolence in response to the escalation of U.S. military involvement in Vietnam. When Daniel returned to the United States in 1964 after a year's sabbatical in Europe, he commented, "We were spoiling for a fight; we were determined not to yield before a poor and despised people, whose 'underdeveloped, non-white status' made them 'prime expendable targets' . . . . I began . . . , as loudly as I could, to say 'no' to the war." He started participating in antiwar protests, as well as fasting, picketing, and engaging in sit-ins and teach-ins as part of his civil disobedience actions. In the summer of 1965, much to the chagrin of the hawkish Francis Cardinal Spellman, Daniel helped to found the interdenominational Clergy and Laity Concerned about Vietnam.

Philip, who was now working in an African-American parish in Baltimore, joined with local clerical and lay supporters in conducting a sit-in at Fort Myer, Virginia. He also began to turn toward a more dramatic form of protest: resistance. On 27 October 1967 he and three associates carried out a planned raid upon an inner-city draft board. The "Baltimore Four" entered the office and grabbed a number of records and poured containers of duck blood on Selective Service files.

Initially, Daniel had expressed serious reservations over the tactics of the Baltimore Four, although he had already been arrested and jailed during the October 1967 March on the Pentagon. But shortly after accompanying the historian and activist Howard Zinn to Hanoi, North Vietnam, to assist in obtaining the release of three U.S. pilots, Daniel joined his brother and seven other activists in destroying Selective Service files in Catonsville, Maryland. After alerting the media about their raid, on 17 May 1968 the "Catonsville Nine" entered the draft board and seized some 1-A files. They escaped to an adjacent parking lot, placed the documents in trash containers they had brought, and burned the files using homemade napalm while reciting the Lord's Prayer. The police rushed in to arrest them, and the raid gained national attention.

Daniel was now fully committed to a life of resistance, while on 7 April 1969 Philip secretly married one of the protestors, Elizabeth McAlister, a nun who taught art history at Marymount Manhattan College; the couple eventually had three children. The marriage was not formally announced until four years later, thus ending Philip's ministry as a Catholic priest. Scheduled to report to federal authorities on 9 April 1970 for their Catonsville activities, the brothers chose to go underground. Daniel had been sentenced to three years in jail; Philip was given three and one-half years, to run concurrently with the six years he had already begun serving for his first draft board incident. After only twelve days Philip, along with a companion from the Baltimore Four, was picked up by authorities. Daniel was later arrested on Block Island (off Rhode Island), having avoided capture for several months. The Berrigans were paroled in 1972.

Throughout the 1970s and the following decades, the Berrigans continued their antiwar resistance. Philip and Elizabeth joined other activists in establishing a resistance community, Jonah House, in Baltimore. Daniel and Philip were arrested numerous times for protest actions at weapons manufacturers and other sites and both were active in the antinuclear Plowshares movement. Along with living a life of nonviolent civil disobedience, the brothers have been prolific writers. Daniel has written more than fifty books and four films. Philip has authored six books and numerous articles. The Berrigan brothers began their adult lives devoted to God's calling in the ministry; by the 1960s they were transformed into nonviolent revolutionaries and remain so today.

★

A number of works written by the Berrigans offer insights into their words and deeds. Philip's *No More Strangers* (1965) discusses his shift from civil rights to antiwar activism. Daniel's *To Dwell in Peace: An Autobiography* (1987) represents an extension of his earlier *No Bars to Manhood* (1970). Philip's more recent autobiographical work is *Fighting the Lamb's War: Skirmishes with the American Empire* (1996). A compelling testimonial account of the actions of the Catonsville Nine is Daniel's *The Trial of the Catonsville Nine* (1970). A personal account of Philip Berrigan's and Elizabeth McAlister's antiwar activism is *The Time's Discipline: The Beatitudes and Nuclear Resistance* (1989). Francine du Plessix Gray, *Divine Disobedience: Profiles in Catholic Radicalism* (1970), represents a spirited account of their activism as does Patricia McNeal, *Harder than War: Catholic Peacemaking in Twentieth-Century America* (1992). A penetrating reflection on the dissident priests can be found in William Van Etten Casey and Philip No-

bile, eds., *The Berrigans* (1971). The rise and fall of the Berrigan-influenced Catholic resistance is examined in Charles A. Meconis, *With Clumsy Grace: The American Catholic Left, 1961–1975* (1979). Murray Polner and Jim O'Grady, *Disarmed and Dangerous: The Radical Lives and Times of Daniel and Philip Berrigan* (1997), provides provocative and telling insights. An important bibliographical reference work is Anne Klejment, *The Berrigans: Bibliography of Published Works by Daniel, Philip, and Elizabeth McAlister Berrigan* (1979). Klejment has also written a useful essay, "The Berrigans: Revolutionary Christian Nonviolence," in *Peace Heroes in Twentieth-Century America,* ed. Charles DeBenedetti (1986).

CHARLES F. HOWLETT

BERRYMAN, John Allyn (*b.* 25 October 1914 in McAlester, Oklahoma; *d.* 7 January 1972 in Minneapolis, Minnesota), Pulitzer Prize-winning poet and critic known for bringing American idioms to poetry, and for creating Henry, the despairing protagonist of *77 Dream Songs* (1964).

Berryman was the only child of John Allyn Smith, and Martha Little, and was first named John Allyn Smith, Jr. His father was a bank clerk in a series of small Oklahoma towns, and his mother a teacher, but in 1925 the family moved to Tampa, Florida, where they opened a restaurant.

John Berryman. MR. JERRY BAUER

Within a year the restaurant folded, and Berryman's parents separated. Deep in debt from failed land speculations, Berryman's father committed suicide on 26 June 1926, an event that would trouble the poet for the rest of his life. When his mother remarried in September the same year and moved to Manhattan, Berryman took the name of his stepfather, John Angus McAlpin Berryman, a New York bond broker. He adopted the name legally in 1936.

Perhaps as a consequence of his unsettled background, Berryman was an outsider at South Kent School in Connecticut, where he entered as a boarder in 1928. He excelled in class, coming first through four consecutive years, but was bullied because he was an inept sportsman. Entering Columbia College, New York, in 1932, Berryman began to show promise as a poet. Under the watchful eye of poet Mark van Doren, Berryman won college poetry prizes, was published in *The Nation* in 1935, and graduated Phi Beta Kappa with a B.A. in English. He subsequently spent two years as a Kellett Fellow graduate student at Clare College, Cambridge, in England. He married Eilleen Patricia Mulligan on 24 October 1942, the same year that his first individual collection of poems, *Poems,* appeared.

By the early 1950s Berryman was a popular visiting lecturer at universities around the United States, and was gaining stature as a poet. *Homage to Mistress Bradstreet,* which first appeared in *Partisan Review* in 1953, won the University of Chicago's prestigious Harriet Monroe Poetry Prize in 1957. Told in the voice of Anne Bradstreet, the seventeenth-century poet, *Homage* anticipates Berryman's use of borrowed identities in his masterpiece, *The Dream Songs* (1964).

Berryman began working on *The Dream Songs* in 1955 while living in Minneapolis, but the early parts of the sequence were first published in 1964 as *77 Dream Songs.* The final part of the sequence, *His Toy, His Dream, His Rest,* was published in 1968. In fact, *The Dream Songs* make most sense in terms of 1960s culture. Their protagonist, Henry, is a hero for the age. He is despairing, morally confused, and beyond salvation. Though chronologically part of a generation of poets who favored short, descriptive, fragmentary poems, Berryman's work in the 1960s is on a large scale. He is often labeled a "confessional" poet, along with Robert Lowell and Sylvia Plath. Confessional poetry tends to consist of personal recollections and expressions of feeling, features that allow it to meet the individualistic mood of the period. But unlike most other confessional poets, Berryman distances himself from the subject of the poetry by using narrative, and developing it in the voice of fictionalized characters. In the case of *The Dream Songs,* one of these alter egos is a white man made up as a black, who acts as an alter ego for Henry and his life of trivial excess. Through these other voices, and his challenging use of idiomatic American English, Berryman manages to ex-

press not only his own despair, but also the troubled spirit of the times.

With his large beard and thick glasses, Berryman was a well-known figure in literary circles in the 1960s. *77 Dream Songs* won the Pulitzer Prize for poetry in 1965, placing Berryman among the top rank of American poets. By 1969, when the entire series was published as *The Dream Songs,* the sequence ran to 385 songs, each composed in a three-stanza, eighteen-line rhyming format.

As he became more famous, Berryman's already shaky mental health grew increasingly unstable. He had divorced his first wife on 19 December 1956, and married twenty-four-year-old Elizabeth Ann Levine just a week later. They had one son, but Berryman's frequent infidelities, developing alcoholism, and repeated hospitalizations for nervous exhaustion brought the marriage to an end in 1959. Yet, as his health declined, Berryman's work seemed to improve. After his second divorce he taught at the University of California, Berkeley, and at Brown University, where he was considered a brilliant teacher, and continued to write scholarly articles and books. He married again on 1 September 1961, to twenty-two-year-old Kate Donahue; they had two daughters.

Although he had worked as an academic at the University of Minnesota since 1955, and would continue to do so until his death in 1972, after the success of *77 Dream Songs* in 1964, Berryman was free to travel and write. He completed the remaining 308 sections of *The Dream Songs* on a Guggenheim Fellowship, traveling to Ireland, and continuing to drink heavily even while undergoing treatment for alcoholism. By the mid-1960s, Berryman's hospital treatment for nervous exhaustion was an almost annual event, yet between 1967 and 1970 he won the Academy of American Poets Award (1967), the National Endowment for the Arts Award (1967), the National Book Award (1969), and shared the Bollingen Prize (1969) with Karl Shapiro. In what would turn out to be the last few years of his life, Berryman had become a major figure in American literature, and an important influence on American poetry. Berryman reached his academic peak when he was named Regents' Professor of Humanities at the University of Minnesota, Minneapolis, in 1969.

Yet, despite his success, and the relative stability of his home life, Berryman continued his alcoholic decline. By 1969 he was obsessed with his father's suicide to the point of breakdown. That year he began treatment for alcoholism on three separate occasions, and in 1970 experienced what he called a "religious conversion" to a form of Catholicism, his father's religion. Berryman completed two more volumes of poetry, *Love & Fame* (1970) and *Delusions, Etc.* (1972). Berryman was one of the most innovative and perceptive poets of the human condition after World War II. In particular *The Dream Songs,* with their multiple voices, dynamic linguistic styles, and wild stories, express the tension between freedom and terror that characterizes the postmodern culture of the 1960s. For Berryman himself such despair was much more than a literary argument. He killed himself by jumping from the Washington Avenue Bridge in Minneapolis. He is buried in Saint Paul, Minnesota.

★

Berryman's papers are at the University of Minnesota, Minneapolis. His essays and short stories are published in *The Freedom of the Poet* (1976), and his letters are published as *We Dream of Honor: John Berryman's Letters to His Mother* (1988). Berryman's autobiographical account of his rehabilitation is *Recovery: A Novel* (1973). Biographies include William J. Martz, *John Berryman* (1969); J. M. Linebarger, *John Berryman* (1974); John Haffenden, *The Life of John Berryman* (1982); and Paul L. Mariani, *Dream Song: The Life of John Berryman* (1990). Peter Stitt's interview with Berryman, "The Art of Poetry," in *Paris Review* 53 (winter 1972), has special impact because of its closeness to the date of the poet's suicide. An obituary is in the *New York Times* (8 Jan. 1972).

CHRIS ROUTLEDGE

BISHOP, Elizabeth (*b.* 8 February 1911 in Worcester, Massachusetts; *d.* 6 October 1979 in Cambridge, Massachusetts), prize-winning poet, translator, and fiction writer whose small body of verse during the 1960s perfected the intimate, observant voice of her earlier work and certified her place among the great American poets of the twentieth century.

Bishop was the only child of William Thomas Bishop and Gertrude May Bulmer. Though born in Massachusetts, she joined her maternal grandparents in Great Village, Nova Scotia, a few years after her father's unexpected death and her mother's precipitous mental decline. Bishop delighted in Nova Scotia's rural atmosphere, which provided a setting for several of her most famous poems, but her father's wealthy parents eventually removed their granddaughter to the more "proper" environs of Worcester. The resulting sense of loss and homelessness became a central theme in her writings and contributed to the depression, asthma, and alcoholism that troubled Bishop much of her life.

While a senior at Vassar College in 1934, Bishop befriended the poet Marianne Moore, who became a model for the young poet and encouraged her to pursue a life of writing. By nature shy and careful, Bishop showed similar qualities as a writer, revising drafts endlessly and never rushing to publish, though her work was soon appearing in *The New Yorker* and *The Partisan Review*. During the 1940s, she began summering in New York City and wintering in Key West, Florida, a pattern her first two books of poetry, *North & South* (which won the Houghton Mifflin Poetry Award for 1946), and *North & South—A Cold Spring*

(which won the Pulitzer Prize in 1955), reflected in the varied geographies and carefully detailed landscapes of those two parts of the United States.

In 1951, anxious to escape New York's competitive atmosphere and disappointed after a planned trip to Italy to visit friend and fellow poet Robert Lowell fell through, Bishop sailed for South America on a round-the-world cruise. In Pétropolis, Brazil, while visiting the aristocrat Lota de Macedo Soares, she suffered a violent allergic reaction to the local cashew fruit. Soares's care of Bishop during her protracted illness sparked a romantic relationship that would continue for fifteen years.

Life in Brazil proved an anodyne for the ever-wandering Bishop. By 1953, she had settled happily into Soares's rural estate, with its panoply of adoptive children and animals, and felt at ease with her lesbian identity as she never had in the United States. Although removed from the social changes taking place back home, she kept abreast of developments in poetry, but the trend toward free verse and confessionalism conflicted with her more classical sensibilities. Her experience of the Brazilian landscape and culture during the late 1950s and early 1960s helped Bishop compose the poems that would form her third book, *Questions of Travel* (1965). Dividing the book into two sections, "Brazil" and "Elsewhere," she seemed to suggest that her new home, so unlike her childhood Nova Scotia and New England, had provided the grounding Bishop needed to explore regions of memory that proximity had denied her.

Bishop's characteristic eye for detail and her preference for questions rather than answers in her poetry thrived on her experience of Brazil. In the poem "Questions of Travel," she asked of her lifelong wanderings, "What childishness is it that while there's a breath of life / in our bodies, we are determined to rush / to see the sun the other way around? / The tiniest green hummingbird in the world?" The second half of the volume explores autobiographical elements the poet's earlier work avoided. "Sestina" recalls a moment with Bishop's maternal grandmother that entwines domestic comfort and sadness, presumably at the absence of a daughter/mother). Characteristically linking the familiar and the strange to achieve emotional resonance, Bishop described her grandmother's teacup as "full of dark brown tears."

Although her emphasis on controlled syntax and tone made Bishop's poetry seem conservative in comparison to other poetry of the 1960s, the book *Questions of Travel* demonstrated a new richness of diction, an increasing wonder at encounters with the natural world, and a comfort with direct statement that would influence such varied poets as John Ashbery (an experimentalist), James Merrill (a formalist), and Adrienne Rich (a feminist poet).

In 1961 Bishop's stable life began unraveling after Soares accepted a government position in Rio de Janeiro,

Elizabeth Bishop. AP/Wide World Photos

overseeing the construction of Flamingo Park. At first, Bishop and Soares were excited by the prospect of relocating to the city. But Bishop's dealings with Time–Life Books, for whom she was writing a guide to Brazil (published in 1962), became an increasing source of frustration, and Rio's busy environs, as well as a military coup in 1964, contrasted harshly with their tranquil country life.

Bishop began to drink heavily, and though she tried writing poems and translations from the short stories of Clarice Lispector, which allegorize the experience of being a woman in a man's world, things soon fell apart. Returning to Brazil after a one-year teaching appointment at the University of Washington in 1966, where she had begun an affair with a younger woman named Suzanne Bowen, Bishop found Soares jealous and distraught. In spite of efforts at reconciliation, the two women grew further apart, and in 1967, after joining Bishop on a visit to New York City, Soares overdosed on sedatives and died a few days later.

Inconsolable, Bishop sought refuge in Bowen, who took her to San Francisco in 1968. There Bishop met such poets as Thom Gunn and Robert Duncan, and even interviewed the wife of Eldridge Cleaver, but she found the changed social mores troubling to her sense of decorum. Soon after,

the two women moved into an eighteenth-century country house in the Brazilian village of Ouro Prêto. However, Bishop would never regain the peace and ease she had enjoyed with Soares, and in 1970 she and Bowen separated. Their parting, however, freed Bishop to complete her first original poems in three years, including the famous "In the Waiting Room," a reflection on the poet's girlhood awakening to the fact of her own identity.

In 1970 Bishop's *Collected Poems* received a National Book Award, and Robert Lowell offered Bishop his teaching post at Harvard while he spent a year abroad. She accepted and later chose to remain in Boston. While there, she completed a small volume of poems that would become her most critically acclaimed book, *Geography III* (winner of the National Book Critics Circle Award in 1976), in which her characteristic gentle humor and clarity of vision were shown to have survived a lifetime of upheaval and loss. Bishop died of an embolism, and is buried in the Bishop family plot in Worcester, Massachusetts.

Though physically and politically removed from the United States for much of the 1960s, Bishop composed during this time a body of poetry that not only received the accolades of contemporaries, but greatly influenced American poetry for the remainder of the century. An easy blending of precise sensory detail, lively phrasing, and complex prosody resulted in poems that allowed Bishop to consider such personal issues as her own alcoholism, sense of homelessness, and lesbian identity, without succumbing to the confessionalism that dominated the 1960s. For a time the accolade "a poet's poet" distanced Bishop from other poets of the 1960s, but her poetry continues to demonstrate a capacity for both addressing and transcending the issues of its day.

★

Autobiographical works about Bishop include her own selected letters, *One Art* (1994). Biographical works include David Kalstone, *Becoming a Poet: Elizabeth Bishop with Marianne Moore and Robert Lowell* (1989); Brett C. Miller, *Elizabeth Bishop: Life and the Memory of It* (1993); and Gary Fountain, *Remembering Elizabeth Bishop: An Oral Biography* (1994).

Temple Cone

BLASS, William Ralph ("Bill") (*b.* 22 June 1922 in Fort Wayne, Indiana; *d.* 12 June 2002 in New Preston, Connecticut), fashion designer known for elegantly feminine dresses and dashing sporty clothes, as well as for establishing clean, modern, and impeccable style for women and men.

The only son of Ralph Blass, a hardware wholesaler, and Ethyl Keyser, a dressmaker, Blass longed to escape his small-town childhood. His father committed suicide when

Blass was only five. "My mother never discussed it," he told a reporter later, and neither did he. Growing up during the Great Depression, Blass frequented the local movie theater and was inspired by the glamour of such Hollywood stars as Marlene Dietrich and Greta Garbo. "Something about glamour interested me," he later commented. "All my schoolbooks had drawings of women on terraces with a cocktail and a cigarette." His favorite glamour queen was Carole Lombard, whose family home was just down the street from his. "She inspired me to get out of Indiana."

By his early teens, Blass was selling fashion sketches to New York City fashion designers. He graduated from Fort Wayne High School in 1939, moved to New York City, and studied for six months at Parsons School of Design. He then worked as a sketch artist in the sportswear firm of David Crystal.

With the outbreak of World War II, Blass enlisted in the U.S. Army and was assigned to a secret camouflage unit known as the "Shadow Army," which was made up of architects and artists, including the future abstractionist Ellsworth Kelly. The unit set up fake artillery installations with inflatable tanks and with recordings of marching soldiers. Later Blass was a combat engineer and saw action at the Battle of the Bulge.

In 1945 Blass returned to New York and worked briefly with future archrival Anne Klein, who soon fired him. Blass then designed for Anna Miller through the 1950s. In 1959 he joined the firm of Maurice Rentner and quickly became head designer. The label was popular with wealthy dowagers, but Blass's designs for younger women expanded the line and instantly increased sales. He simplified previous designs, eliminated clutter of line, and included bold color. His 1960 spring collection combined two brilliant colors such as a hot pink suit with a bright turquoise hat. Smock dresses were belted with bow-tied leather sashes. A pink linen jacket was worn over a navy blue woolen dress.

The 1961 collection continued bold color and fabric combinations, and added embellishments, most notably ruffles. The dress line broke with the severe look of the 1950s, and it created a softer appearance and mood. For the 1962 fall collection, Blass created a soft basic dress under a jacket or coat of tailored precision.

Blass's designs for spring 1963 became his breakthrough collection, and won him his second of eight Coty awards. With soft and bright fabric, both the neckline and dress hem were ruffled. The dress became the best seller in the firm's history, as well as a hit with fashion critics. Eugenia Sheppard noted how it made both a woman's face and feet appear more becoming. A variant of the design in 1965 included jeweled buttons.

Blass's classic ruffled and soft-fabric dress became his trademark look throughout the 1960s. It created an elegant and feminine appearance that was appropriate for society

Bill Blass *(right)*, shown with a model wearing clothes that he designed, October 1961. © BETTMANN/CORBIS

ladies, and stood in opposition to the 1963 "mod" miniskirt of Mary Quant. For his part, Blass considered the mod look a "frantic youth kick."

Blass's 1966 spring collection emphasized two extremes: brilliant prints and soft, slinky crepes on the one hand, and simple white with daisies on the other. The summer collection included short, revealing evening dresses with deep slits in long sheaths. The provocative bare shoulders and low necklines were a part of that year's trend, but Blass never raised the hemline more than a few inches above the knee. Also that year Blass created a one-of-a-kind beige chantilly lace dress for model Jean Shrimpton, who wore it in a Revlon cosmetics ad, eliciting so much demand that the firm put the design into high production. Thus couture became ready-to-wear.

Blass introduced his menswear line in 1967. Deliberately styled to break away from the traditional gray flannel suit, his first year's look featured light fabrics, boldly colored shirts, and plaids. He won a 1968 Coty Award for these clothes, which are now the standard in men's wear.

In 1970 Blass bought out Rentner's firm and renamed it Bill Blass Ltd. It was then rare for an American designer to own his own firm. His mix-and-match chic of ruffled dresses and boldly colored evening dresses became a part of a turning point in fashion history. In 1973 the French fashion industry staged at Versailles a Franco-American showcase at which, after a tired show of French couture, Blass and other American designers caused a sensation. Blass became internationally renowned, and began the highly successful and lucrative licensing of his name on dozens of products, from luggage to perfume.

By courting society women and catering to their sense of elegant taste, Blass made a career of designing completely feminine clothes. "Women will look to the designer who interprets clothes in the way they like," Blass once commented. "I love his clothes," former first lady Nancy Reagan said, "because they are comfortable, wearable and pretty." Blass retired in 1999. He died of cancer in 2002, and his body was cremated.

★

Blass's memoir is *Bare Blass* (2002). See also Bernadine Morris, "Fashion Is Back in Fashion," *New York Times* (8 Dec. 1976); Samantha Miller, "A Touch of Blass," *People Weekly* (6 Dec. 1999); and Eric Wilson, "Bill Bares All," *Womens Wear Daily* (2 Feb. 2002). Obituaries are in the *New York Times* and *Los Angeles Times* (both 13 June 2002).

PATRICK S. SMITH

BLOCH, Konrad Emil   (*b*. 21 January 1912 in Neisse, Germany [now Poland]; *d*. 15 October 2000 in Burlington, Massachusetts), Nobel Prize–winning scientist whose discovery of the basic steps in cholesterol synthesis would ultimately lead to a lowering of the death rate from coronary artery disease.

The son of Fritz Bloch and Hedwig Streimer, Bloch studied at the Technische Hochschule in Munich, Germany, where he was drawn to organic chemistry, especially the structure of natural products. Bloch, who was Jewish, left Munich in 1934, the year after Adolf Hitler became chancellor of Germany and the Nazi authorities told him that he must end his studies. With a degree in chemical engineering (1934), he moved to Davos, Switzerland, and worked in a tuberculosis sanitarium, where he investigated the phospholipids of tubercle bacilli.

After immigrating to the United States in 1936, Bloch joined the Department of Biochemistry at Columbia University and studied under Hans T. Clarke. He received his Ph.D. in 1938, joined Rudolf Schoenheimer's laboratory, and became interested in intermediary metabolism and problems of biosynthesis. The following year, Bloch and collaborator David Rittenberg initiated the work on the biological synthesis of cholesterol that was to occupy much of his subsequent career. Naturalized as a U.S. citizen in 1944, Bloch accepted an appointment at the University of Chicago in 1946. In 1954 he was appointed Higgins Professor of Bio-

Konrad E. Bloch. AP/WIDE WORLD PHOTOS

chemistry in the Department of Chemistry at Harvard University, and became chairman of the department in 1968.

Bloch and Feodor Lynen, who was on the faculty of the Max Planck Institute in Munich, received the Nobel Prize in medicine and physiology in 1964 for their work on cholesterol and fatty acid metabolism. Although cholesterol had been isolated nearly 200 years earlier from human gallstones and its chemical structure had been elucidated during the first two decades of the twentieth century, scientists knew little about how cholesterol is formed.

Bloch's research focused on the biosynthesis within the body that turned acetic acid into cholesterol. Using the radioisotope carbon-14, Bloch, in collaboration with David Rittenberg, confirmed that cholesterol was, in part, derived from the two-carbon acetate molecule. In experiments with rat livers, Bloch and colleagues identified the hydrocarbon squalene, which is produced in the liver, as an intermediate in cholesterol synthesis. A terpene (a hydrocarbon found in essential oils) with an open chain of thirty carbon atoms, squalene begins the folding necessary to produce the four rings of cholesterol. Bloch also discovered many of the other thirty-six overall steps needed to convert acetate (a salt or ester of acetic acid) into cholesterol. These steps are of vital importance, because malfunctions in the process of formation and metabolism of lipids are at the root of many cardiovascular diseases. At the time, death from cardiovascular disease was reaching what would turn out to be an all-time high. As a result, the Nobel Prize citation read, in part: "Circulatory diseases are the foremost cause of death in many parts of the world and the therapy against these diseases will in the future rest upon the firm foundation laid by professors Bloch and Lynen."

Bloch's research would be a vital factor in the 40 to 50 percent decrease in coronary heart disease that occurred in the United States after the late 1960s. For example, Bloch's discoveries concerning the steps that lead from the production of acetic acid to the production of cholesterol were of fundamental importance in the subsequent discovery of drugs called statins, which are used to treat high cholesterol by interfering with cholesterol synthesis. Bloch's research also showed that cholesterol is a vital component of all body cells and that it is a precursor of bile acids and one of the female sex hormones.

After winning the Nobel Prize, Bloch, an extremely modest man, refused to have his picture taken in front of a sign that read, "Hooray for Dr. Bloch!" Nevertheless, Bloch's extraordinary contribution to science and mankind was also recognized in 1964 with the Fritzsche Award from the American Chemical Society, as well as the Distinguished Service Award from the University of Chicago School of Medicine. In 1965, the University of Notre Dame honored him with the Centennial Science Award, and the Lombardy Academy of Sciences awarded him the Cardano Medal.

Despite his commitment to research, Bloch avoided the competition and animosity that often results from scientists "competing" to make new and important discoveries. His daily routine included visiting the laboratories of his co-workers to talk about their work and latest findings and to foster a spirit of cooperation. Bloch was also a dedicated teacher throughout the 1960s and beyond. Thousands of Harvard students took his basic biochemistry course, and many of them went on to become scientists and scholars.

Bloch continued to conduct research into the biosynthesis of cholesterol and other substances, including glutathione, a substance used in protein metabolism; the metabolism of olefinic fatty acids; and comparative and evolutionary biochemistry. A former associate editor of the *Journal of Biological Chemistry,* Bloch authored hundreds of scientific papers dealing with the metabolism of proteins and amino acids. He also wrote the popular 1997 book *Blondes in Venetian Paintings, the Nine-banded Armadillo, and Other Essays in Biochemistry,* in which he discussed various aspects of biochemistry and explained the chemical basis for numerous biological processes.

Bloch died at the age of eighty-eight in a Massachusetts hospital due to complications from congestive heart failure. He was survived by his wife of fifty-nine years, Lore, a Munich native to whom he was married on 15 February 1941. They had two children.

★

A source of information on the specifics of Bloch's cholesterol research is E. P. Kennedy and F. H. Westheimer, "Nobel Laureates: Bloch and Lynen Win Prize in Medicine and Physiology," *Science* (23 Oct. 1964): 504–506. A detailed description of the cholesterol research conducted by Bloch and colleagues can be found in Bloch's article "Summing Up," *Annual Reviews of Biochemistry* 56 (1987): 1–19. An obituary is in *Nature* 409 (Feb. 2001).

DAVID PETECHUK

BLOCK, Herbert Lawrence ("Herblock") (*b.* 13 October 1909 in Chicago, Illinois; *d.* 7 October 2001 in Washington, D.C.), one of the foremost American political cartoonists of the twentieth century; throughout the 1960s the widely syndicated cartoons of the four-time Pulitzer Prize winner documented a political scene that passed from the peace of the Eisenhower years through the turmoil of the Vietnam War, while never overlooking the many unfolding controversies within American society.

The youngest son of David Julian Block, a chemical engineer, and Theresa "Tessie" Lupe, a homemaker, Block

Herbert L. Block. THE LIBRARY OF CONGRESS

grew up on Chicago's far north side with his two brothers. Demonstrating artistic talent early, Block received a scholarship to the School of the Art Institute of Chicago at age twelve, and while attending Nicholas Senn High School he began contributing cartoons to suburban newspapers under the pen name of "Herblock," which he continued to use throughout his career. After graduating from Senn in 1927, he attended Lake Forest College for two years, where he studied English and political science before dropping out to become an editorial cartoonist for the *Chicago Daily News* newspaper in 1929. His first illustration, on forestry conservation, appeared in the *News* on 24 April 1929.

In 1933 Block became a syndicated editorial cartoonist for the Newspaper Enterprise Association (NEA) in Cleveland, where he remained for ten years. During that period he supported such domestic issues as the New Deal, antismoking, and government funding of the arts, while also maintaining an ongoing stream of cartoons that warned of the approaching dangers posed by the Soviet dictator Joseph Stalin, the German dictator Adolf Hitler, Japan, and Italy. After receiving his first Pulitzer Prize for editorial cartooning in 1942, Block entered the U.S. Army in 1943, where he rose to the rank of sergeant in the Information and Education Division.

Leaving military service at the end of 1945, Block joined the struggling *Washington Post* newspaper in January 1946 as an editorial cartoonist; his work at the *Post* would eventually be syndicated in more than 300 newspapers. Block worked for the *Post* for the next fifty-five years. During his first decade in Washington, Block continued to gain recognition as one of the foremost political cartoonists in the United States, winning a second Pulitzer Prize in 1954 for a drawing of Stalin, although his support of Adlai Stevenson's 1952 presidential bid brought him into serious conflict with the *Post*'s publisher. He was a firm opponent of Senator Joseph McCarthy's conduct while in quest of Communist conspirators, and Block is credited with coining the phrase "McCarthyism" in a cartoon that appeared on 29 March 1950.

After recovering from a heart attack in late 1959, Block returned to work in January 1960. He originally supported Hubert Humphrey for the 1960 Democratic presidential nomination but eventually came to respect John F. Kennedy, although he was never particularly friendly with Kennedy's brother Robert, who became attorney general. Richard M. Nixon's recognition of the cartoonist's influence was such that the Republican candidate believed that erasing, in the minds of voters, Block's artistic image of Nixon as an unshaven and suspicious-looking character was a key to the 1960 election. After Kennedy won the presidency, Block criticized him occasionally on some issues; one of his best-known cartoons appeared on 1 No-

vember 1962 and portrayed Kennedy and the Soviet leader Nikita Krushchev struggling to contain the "monster" of nuclear war.

Block displayed mixed attitudes toward President Lyndon B. Johnson, but his artwork definitely expressed support for Johnson's efforts in the 1960s on behalf of programs such as civil rights, the Great Society, and the War on Poverty. One of his most well-known pieces on civil rights, entitled "House Divided," appeared on 5 March 1968, and his ongoing editorial commentary in the 1960s included societal concerns such as gun control, aid to education, antismoking, and environmental protection. In recognition of Block's support on these many issues, he was commissioned by Postmaster General Lawrence O'Brien in 1966 to design the United States commemorative stamp in honor of the 175th anniversary of the Bill of Rights.

Block's commentary on gun control escalated in 1968, fueled in part by the assassinations of Dr. Martin Luther King, Jr., and Robert Kennedy. On 20 March 1968 he released his well-known cartoon entitled "Shooting Gallery," which pictured American citizens as the targets in the gallery. His most controversial cartoon was in 1968; entitled "The Vote to Kill," it listed the names of eighteen senators who had voted against a gun control bill. The cartoon drew protests from the U.S. Congress and the National Rifle Association.

Throughout the 1960s Block, initially a "hawk" on the Vietnam War, increasingly questioned President Johnson's conduct of the war and his growing hostility toward the press and other critics. A low point in their relationship came when Johnson was extremely angered by the cartoon "Happy Days on the Old Plantation" on 30 June 1965, in which Block contradicted the White House public-relations efforts to portray the president as a sensitive, cultivated, and warm-hearted man.

The political journalist Walter Lippmann's criticism of the war also came under attack from Johnson. In 1967 Block wrote an article for the *Post* in which he defended Lippmann; a cartoon showing an angered president hurling lightning bolts at the journalist accompanied the article. Block's questioning of the war was highlighted by cartoons that showed Johnson on an upward-bound Vietnam escalator (17 June 1965), Uncle Sam neck-deep in a forbidding swamp called Asia (28 January 1968), and a beleaguered general in Vietnam still pumping out favorable news dispatches from his destroyed headquarters (1 February 1968).

Despite his criticisms of Johnson, Block dreaded the ascendancy of Richard M. Nixon to the presidency in 1969. The cartoonist's distrust of Nixon dated back to the late 1940s, and one of Block's most famous works had appeared on 29 October 1954, depicting a suitcase-touting Nixon emerging from an open sewer. Block continued to criticize the war, including the apparent contradiction in Nixon's planning to win the war while also building an undisclosed peace plan, and these criticisms would eventually include the escalation of the bombing in Cambodia in 1971. He regularly attacked Nixon and Vice President Spiro Agnew for their attempts to censor the war news, and Agnew once denounced the cartoonist as a "master of sick invective." Block continued to produce editorial cartoons into the 1970s on the conduct of the war, and he was one of the most active commentators on the unfolding scandals of the Nixon administration, including Watergate.

Over the next three decades Block continued to cover the administrations of several more presidents, during which time he received numerous awards in recognition of his place among the U.S.'s most important and influential political commentators of the twentieth century. These honors included winning his third individual Pulitzer Prize for cartooning in 1979, after he had shared a Pulitzer Prize in 1973 as a member of the *Washington Post* team covering the Watergate scandal. Block also received a total of five honorary degrees as well as the Presidential Medal of Freedom from President William J. Clinton in 1994. A very private person with a gentle and unassuming personality, Block never married. His last cartoon appeared on 26 August 2001, and while on vacation he contracted pneumonia and passed away at Sibley Memorial Hospital in Washington, D.C., at the age of ninety-one.

★

Block's work is on permanent exhibit in the Rosenwald Collection of the National Gallery of Art in Washington, D.C. Some of his original drawings are gifted to the Library of Congress. Between 1952 and the end of his career Block wrote twelve books, liberally illustrated with political cartoons, including his autobiography, *Herblock: A Cartoonist's Life* (1993). Further autobiographical material can be found in an article by Block, "Five Decades of Herblock," in the *Washington Post* (31 Dec. 1995), in which he reviewed the political highlights of his career with the newspaper. David Von Drehl, "Humility Through a Well-Founded Confidence," *Washington Post* (8 Oct. 2001), reviews Block's career. Obituaries are in the *Washington Post* and *New York Times* (both 8 Oct. 2001); *The Economist* (13 Oct. 2001); and *U.S. News and World Report* (22 Oct. 2001).

RAYMOND SCHMIDT

BLOUGH, Roger Miles (*b.* 19 January 1904 in Riverside, Pennsylvania; *d.* 8 October 1985 in Hawley, Pennsylvania), in true Horatio Alger fashion rose from the humblest of beginnings to become a captain of industry—president and board chairman of U.S. Steel.

Blough was born in a community that is described as both a section of Johnstown (famous for the 1889 killer flood) and a small village outside the western Pennsylvania city.

His father, Christian Emanuel Blough, a truck farmer and greenhouse operator, and his mother, Viola Nancy (Hoffman) Blough, a nurse, were of modest means. Because of the family's finances, Blough, the fifth of seven children, planned to attend school no further than eighth grade, a fairly common practice at the time. His teachers, realizing his academic abilities, encouraged him to continue his education. He first worked his way through Susquehanna Academy (affiliated with Susquehanna University, located in Selinsgrove, Pennsylvania) and then the university itself. He enrolled in 1920, but dropped out for the 1923–1924 academic year to earn money to continue. He graduated with a B.A. in 1925. While at Susquehanna, the five-foot, eleven-inch, 175-pound Blough earned multiple letters in football, basketball, and tennis. A serious student, he was also active on campus and well liked. *The Lanthorn* (the Susquehanna yearbook) said of him, "Those of us who know Roger best have learned that behind that kind smile and laughing eyes there lies a character containing those elements of greatness before which the world will someday bow in awe."

Blough secured a teaching (mathematics and science) and coaching (basketball) position in Hawley in northeastern Pennsylvania. On 13 June 1928 he married a fellow teacher, Helen Martha Decker. They had twin daughters. His wife's father was Hawley's leading attorney. Influenced by his father-in-law, Blough enrolled at Yale Law School. His brilliant academic record continued—he was editor of the *Yale Law Journal*. In the depth of the Great Depression, Blough graduated in 1931. He applied at New York's leading Wall Street law firm, White and Case, and was offered a $200-a-month position. George Case noted on his application, "First class chap, clean, good-looking. I like him."

Heading a team of twenty lawyers in defending U.S. Steel on monopoly charges during a congressional hearing in 1939 and 1940, Blough impressed the steel giant's president, Benjamin F. Fairless. He was made U.S. Steel's general solicitor in 1942. He rose through the ranks and succeeded Fairless as president in 1955.

Blough presided over the smoothly run Big Steel firm, but in 1962 he locked horns with President John F. Kennedy over increases in steel prices. At the time U.S. Steel was by far the largest producer of steel in the United States. The company was, in fact, the nation's third-largest corporation, behind only General Motors and Standard Oil of New Jersey.

On 31 March 1962 an agreement was reached between the United Steelworkers of America (the union) and the steel industry. The union felt the agreement gave liberal concessions to Big Steel as far as wages were concerned. This was done, as the industry said, to keep the overall cost of steel production low and competitive with foreign markets. Kennedy and the government, in general, were pleased with the agreement and viewed it as an inflation-

Roger Blough presenting before a House-Senate joint economic committee, 1971. © BETTMANN/CORBIS

fighting measure. But just ten days later, on 10 April 1962, Blough flew to Washington, D.C., and personally handed Kennedy a press release stating that U.S. Steel had raised the price of its steel by $6 a ton. To make matters worse for the young president and his battle against inflationary trends, Bethlehem Steel, the nation's second-largest producer, immediately followed with a price increase of its own. Kennedy was incensed over the price increase.

Over the next three days, the government flexed its collective muscles. Four antitrust investigations into the steel industry and its business practices were instituted. Consideration was given to legislation that would roll back the price of steel to levels prior to the controversial increases. Price and wage controls were threatened and discussed. Even the FBI got into the act, questioning the news media on U.S. Steel's action in an attempt to determine possible collusion and price-fixing. Perhaps the most serious ramification was the government's decision to divert Department of Defense contracts away from Blough's firm. Kennedy stated that he felt the steel industry had "double-crossed" him and the increase was "unjustifiable and irresponsible," and added that the steel executives had "utter contempt for their fellow countrymen."

When Blough left the White House, the president was said to have remarked, "My father always told me they [big-business executives] were sons of bitches, but I never believed him—until now." Kennedy was not the only one to hold a news conference. On the fourth day of the crisis, 14 April 1962, Blough addressed the media, defending the price increase as "necessary to finance modernization of the industry to maintain competitiveness." One day before

Blough's news conference, three other large steel producers—Inland, Kaiser, and Armco—indicated they would not be joining U.S. Steel and Bethlehem in upping steel prices. First, Bethlehem reversed its action on the increase, and "by sunset," as *New York Times* obituary writer Daniel J. Cuff put it, "U.S. Steel caved in."

A few days later, on 18 April 1962, Blough placed a call to the White House in an attempt to mend fences. The conversation was described as being "useful and cordial." But not all hard feelings were erased. Businessmen from many industries in addition to steel were irate at what they considered the government's involvement with the private sector.

The 1960s were not entirely controversial for Blough. He served out the decade, somewhat out of the spotlight, retiring as CEO in 1969. He remained a U.S. Steel board member until 1976—while working once again for White and Case—and then retired fully to the hamlet of Hawley. In 1963 he was presented the National Football Foundation's highest award—the Gold Medal. It was an honor that had previously been given to Dwight D. Eisenhower, Herbert Hoover, Douglas MacArthur, and later, ironically, to John F. Kennedy. Blough was also honored as Industrialist of the Year in 1967.

Blough died of heart failure, was cremated, and is buried in Green Gate Cemetery in Hawley.

With one notable exception, the affable Blough led an industrial giant for several decades of prosperity with little fanfare. He once said, "I was pretty lucky. I can't remember any serious reverses." Intellect, hard work, and dedication also had something to do with his rise to prominence.

★

Blough's personal and corporate papers are housed in the Susquehanna University Library (Selinsgrove, Pennsylvania), which bears his name. Three books by Blough give insight into his thinking: *Free Man and the Corporation* (1959); *Government Wage-Price Guideposts in the American Economy* (1967), with George Meany and Neil H. Jacoby; and *The Washington Embrace of Business* (1975). An obituary is in the *New York Times* (10 Oct. 1985).

JIM CAMPBELL

BOHLEN, Charles Eustis ("Chip") (*b.* 30 August 1904 in Clayton, New York; *d.* 1 January 1974 in Washington, D.C.), professional diplomat and Soviet expert who served as ambassador to France (1962–1968) during the administrations of John F. Kennedy and Lyndon B. Johnson.

Bohlen was the second of three sons born to Charles Bohlen, a banker and prominent sportsman, and Celestine Eustis, a New Orleans socialite whose father served as American ambassador to France in the 1890s. He was educated at Saint Paul's School in Concord, New Hampshire, and Harvard University, from which he received a bachelor's degree in European history in 1927. Joining the Foreign Service in 1929, Bohlen was among the first small group of American diplomats, including his lifelong friend George F. Kennan, trained as Russian experts. In the 1930s, after the United States resumed diplomatic relations with the Soviet Union, Bohlen spent two tours of duty (1934–1935 and 1938–1940) in junior positions in the American embassy in Moscow. In 1935 he married Avis Thayer, the sister of a colleague; the couple had two daughters, Avis and Celestine, and a son, Charles. He attended the Moscow, Cairo, Teheran, and Yalta conferences, the last two as an adviser and translator for President Franklin D. Roosevelt. He impressed presidential aide Harry Hopkins, at whose insistence Bohlen also took on State Department liaison duties with the White House. He continued to serve in the Truman administration and was involved in drawing up the blueprints for both the Marshall Plan and the North Atlantic Treaty Organization. From 1953 to 1957 Bohlen was ambassador to the Soviet Union, until Secretary of State John Foster Dulles, often unsympathetic to his advice, relegated him to the Philippine embassy.

In 1959 Christian A. Herter, the new secretary of state, brought Bohlen back as his special assistant, a position he retained through the 1961 transition to the Kennedy administration. Throughout his career Bohlen consistently believed that the nature of the Soviet power structure and considerations of ideology and national interest often made the Soviet Union's dealings with Western powers difficult, but that, provided the United States took a firm line, negotiations and a degree of mutual understanding were feasible. Preparing for the May 1960 Soviet-American summit,

Charles E. Bohlen. ARCHIVE PHOTOS, INC.

he advised President Dwight D. Eisenhower to remain resolute over West Berlin, which the Soviet Union was threatening to take over. Bohlen accompanied Eisenhower to this meeting, which was cut short after Soviet forces shot down an American U-2 spy plane over Russian territory, an incident Bohlen suspected provided a welcome excuse for the domestically insecure Soviet general secretary, Nikita Khrushchev, to abort the summit.

Six feet tall, slim, handsome, and socially adept, in style Bohlen fit almost ideally into the incoming Kennedy administration. Offered a top European embassy by Secretary of State Dean Rusk, he chose to remain in the State Department in Washington as Rusk's assistant for over a year in order to familiarize himself with the new regime's outlook. From the beginning Kennedy consulted him on numerous issues. With W. Averell Harriman and Llewellyn Thompson, in February 1961 Bohlen spent two days briefing Kennedy on the Soviet Union. Bohlen felt that only at a summit meeting would Kennedy fully comprehend the nature of the Soviet leadership, so he endorsed plans for a meeting in Vienna in June 1961, to which he accompanied the president. Khrushchev's bellicose bluster on disarmament and Berlin left the inexperienced Kennedy somewhat shaken. When soon afterward Khrushchev ordered the construction of the Berlin Wall, Bohlen initially suggested a measured response rather than the full domestic mobilization and American troop deployments to Berlin urged by other senior advisers. Characteristically, Kennedy followed a middle position, drafting additional troops and requesting increased military appropriations. After a visit to Berlin in August 1961, Bohlen warned Kennedy that the United States must respond forcibly, swiftly, and decisively to any future Soviet attempt to intimidate American allies, particularly over Berlin. The uncompromising Soviet stance at the Geneva arms limitation talks Bohlen and Rusk attended in March 1962 further convinced him that Russia remained intransigent.

In his administration's first weeks, Kennedy consulted Bohlen on plans inherited from Eisenhower to mount an invasion of Cuba to overthrow Fidel Castro's anti-American and pro-communist government. To his subsequent regret, Bohlen did not express his misgivings about this venture. Instead, he merely stated that, given the island's strategic insignificance to the Soviet Union, Khrushchev was unlikely to intervene militarily, though the Russians might provide Castro with arms and supplies and would undoubtedly exploit any invasion for propaganda purposes. His failure to oppose the invasion plan forthrightly revealed the occasional limitations of Bohlen's belief that professional diplomats should function primarily as technical experts rather than policymakers.

In October 1962, when Soviet missiles were discovered in Cuba, Bohlen counseled Kennedy to combine firmness and restraint. He suggested that Kennedy first correspond sternly but privately with Khrushchev, advice the president ignored, and then declare a naval blockade of the island, the course ultimately chosen. Bohlen was about to leave for France, to which he had been appointed ambassador, so attended only the first two days of meetings of the executive committee of senior advisers who handled the crisis, for fear that postponing his departure would alert the Soviets to the missiles' discovery.

Bohlen considered French president Charles de Gaulle one of the twentieth century's few genuinely great men. However, as ambassador he struggled with the difficulties caused by de Gaulle's determination to enhance France's international stature, first by excluding the British from the European Economic Community and then by removing France from the North Atlantic Treaty Organization (NATO) in 1966 and demanding the withdrawal of all American forces and the closure of NATO bases on French soil by April 1967. Bohlen convinced the Johnson administration to accede to these demands, as any other course would be counterproductive. He also, unsuccessfully, advised the administration that its strategy of bombing North Vietnam to force Hanoi's leadership to negotiate a settle-

ment to the war was likely to prove ineffective, particularly given the lack of public support.

In 1967 Bohlen declined to return to Moscow as ambassador, whereupon Rusk appointed him deputy undersecretary of state for political affairs. He concentrated on Soviet and East European affairs, calling for the expansion of American trade with the Soviet bloc, as this was likely to weaken Soviet control over Eastern Europe. Watching the developing Czechoslovak crisis of 1967–1968, Bohlen failed to anticipate the Soviet military intervention of August 1968 but advised that the United States restrict its response to diplomatic protests. Bohlen retired from the State Department in 1969 as its highest-ranking career officer. He became president of the investment company Italamerica, wrote his memoirs, and lectured extensively on U.S. foreign policy. In 1974 Bohlen died of cancer in Washington, D.C., and was buried in Laurel Hill Cemetery in Philadelphia, Pennsylvania.

Bohlen's attitude toward the Soviet Union consistently mingled suspicion with the belief that the United States must be firm in defending its interests. In a 1969 survey professional State Department personnel picked Bohlen as their model of an ideal and effective diplomat, one who observed the conventions but whose abilities and readiness to innovate transcended the limitations career foreign service personnel often face.

★

Bohlen's personal papers are in the Manuscripts Division of the Library of Congress. Many of his official papers are included in the records of the Department of the State in the National Archives II, College Park, Maryland; the holdings of the John F. Kennedy Presidential Library, Boston, Massachusetts; and the Lyndon B. Johnson Presidential Library, Austin, Texas. Many documents from his official career are also included in the series *Foreign Relations of the United States*. Bohlen wrote *The Transformation of American Foreign Policy* (1969) and his memoirs, *Witness to History, 1929–69* (1973). T. Michael Ruddy wrote the biography *The Cautious Diplomat: Charles E. Bohlen and the Soviet Union, 1929–1969* (1986). Bohlen is one of the protagonists of Walter Isaacson and Evan Thomas, *The Wise Men: Six Friends and the World They Made: Acheson, Bohlen, Harriman, Kennan, Lovett, McCloy* (1986). His career during the Eisenhower, Kennedy, and Johnson administrations is covered in articles in Eleanora W. Schoenebaum, ed., *Political Profiles: The Eisenhower Years* (1980), and Nelson Lichtenstein, ed., *Political Profiles: The Kennedy Years* (1976), and *Political Profiles: The Johnson Years* (1976). Obituaries are in the *New York Times* and *Washington Post* (both 2 Jan. 1974) and the London *Times* (3 Jan. 1974). Bohlen recorded oral history interviews for Columbia University, the John F. Kennedy Presidential Library, and the Lyndon B. Johnson Presidential Library.

PRISCILLA ROBERTS

BOND, (Horace) Julian (*b.* 14 January 1940 in Nashville, Tennessee), leader of Atlanta sit-ins and a founder of the Student Nonviolent Coordinating Committee (SNCC) who served as SNCC's communications director until his election to the Georgia state legislature.

Bond was the middle of three children born to a distinguished family of African-American educators. His father, Horace Mann Bond, was a college dean and president. His mother, Julia Washington Bond, was a librarian. He grew up in Pennsylvania on the campus of Lincoln University. At age twelve he was enrolled in the George School, where he was one of two African-American students. "I never really lived the life of a southern Negro kid," he observed.

In 1957 the family moved to Atlanta, where Bond attended Morehouse College. In February 1960 Bond helped organize students for lunch-counter sit-ins along the lines of those occurring in Greensboro, North Carolina. Students from Atlanta's black colleges formed the Committee on Appeal for Human Rights. On 15 March 1960 Bond led demonstrators at the City Hall cafeteria. They were arrested and held in jail for ten hours, Bond's only arrest during the 1960s. Rich's department store soon became the students' principal target. Demonstrations continued for nearly eighteen months until Rich's capitulated.

Bond was among 120 protest leaders who gathered at Shaw University in Raleigh, North Carolina, on Easter weekend in 1960. They formed an independent organization to coordinate their movement, the Student Nonviolent Coordinating Committee (SNCC). For the first issue of SNCC's newsletter Bond contributed a poem and an article on the Atlanta sit-ins. He also worked as a reporter for the *Atlanta Inquirer.*

On 28 July 1961 Bond married Spelman College student Alice Clopton. The next year she delivered their first child. With all his outside interests, Bond's grades suffered. He reflected, "You'd try for a long time to balance school work and this kind of work [protest]. It was something I couldn't balance." In the spring of 1962 he dropped out of college.

James Forman, SNCC's executive secretary, hired Bond as the organization's director of communications. Bond's coworker, Mary King, profiled the young activist in her autobiography, *Freedom Song:* "Slender, debonair, and six feet one and a half inches tall, Julian had a polish that belied his youth. . . . Imperturbable and urbane, he had a wry sense of humor."

Bond seldom was found on the front lines at protests. He worked behind the scenes, managing communications with roving organizers and sending stories to contacts in the national press. In his history of SNCC, *In Struggle,* Clayborne Carson described Bond as "an atypical SNCC worker. . . . His position in the Atlanta headquarters, cou-

Julian Bond. THE LIBRARY OF CONGRESS

pled with the responsibility of providing for a wife and children, had isolated him from SNCC's field operations. Nonetheless, he was greatly respected within the organization for his dedication and intelligence."

As the pace of movement activity quickened, the scope of Bond's public relations work increased. His job involved "feeding those tapes to radio stations, handouts to reporters, tearing around the South," he recalled, on fast-moving expeditions to local outposts. "SNCC had twenty projects in Mississippi and I'd hit them all in the course of a week and then go into Arkansas, Louisiana, Tennessee, and Georgia." As a result of these travels Bond was well known within SNCC. When internal ideological conflicts became intense, he remained on good terms with everyone. Mary King recalled, "he almost never took a hard stance or positioned himself on one side or another of any raging SNCC issue; if pushed to speak on a policy issue, he would most likely respond with an observation."

In 1965, with a third child on the way (he and Alice would eventually have five), Bond began looking for a better-paying job. The Georgia legislature had redistricted, and he became a candidate from the 136th legislative district, which represented Atlanta. Utilizing the organizing skills of SNCC volunteers, Bond ran a grassroots campaign emphasizing economic issues. He won the primary and handily defeated his Republican opponent with 82 percent of the vote.

When it came time to take his seat, however, Bond encountered stiffer opposition. Days before the swearing-in ceremony, SNCC issued a statement condemning the Vietnam War and encouraging black men to resist the draft. When asked if he supported the statement, Bond replied, "I concur fully. I would not burn my own draft card, but I admire the courage of those who do." His remarks touched off a firestorm of criticism. The Georgia House voted 184 to 12 to expel him. Bond won in two subsequent special elections. Meanwhile, his lawyers challenged the legislature's action. On 5 December 1966 Supreme Court Chief Justice Earl Warren ordered that Bond be seated.

In August 1968 Bond arrived at the Democratic Convention to challenge the seating of Georgia's mostly white "regular" delegation. The convention voted to give half of the state's seats to Bond's "insurgents." This victory elevated his standing among liberal delegates. He gave a seconding speech for Senator Eugene McCarthy, and his name was placed in nomination for vice president. He received 48.5 votes before withdrawing, noting that he was seven years shy of the constitutionally mandated minimum age of thirty-five.

In 1975 Bond was elected to the Georgia state senate, where he would remain until 1987. In 1986 he ran for the U.S. House of Representatives against his former SNCC colleague, John Lewis, to whom he lost in a bitter run-off election marked by allegations that Bond had used cocaine. Alice, who divorced Bond in 1989, told police that her husband was a cocaine addict but later retracted her statement.

Bond remained active in media projects, including narrating the Public Broadcasting System (PBS) history of the civil rights movement, *Eyes on the Prize*. He also wrote a syndicated newspaper column and hosted a television program, *America's Black Forum*. Bond has held academic appointments at Harvard University, American University, and the University of Virginia, among others. In 1998 he was elected chairman of the board of the National Association for the Advancement of Colored People (NAACP).

A leader of the sit-in movement who played an important role in SNCC, Bond was at the center of the 1960s freedom struggle. He was also the first of his generation to make the successful transition from protest to electoral politics. As one of the most prominent African-American politicians of the decade, he became a national spokesman for young people disenchanted with the established order.

★

Three books published in 1971 focus on Bond's early career: George R. Metcalf, *Up from Within: Today's New Black Leaders;* John Neary, *Julian Bond: Black Rebel;* and Roger M. Williams, *The Bonds: An American Family.* Clayborne Carson, *In Struggle: SNCC and the Black Awakening of the 1960s* (1981), places Bond's

work within the larger perspective of SNCC and the civil rights movement. Mary King, *Freedom Song: A Personal Story of the 1960s Civil Rights Movement* (1984), also focuses on SNCC.

PAUL T. MURRAY

BONO, Sonny. *See* Sonny and Cher.

BOULDING, Kenneth Ewart (*b.* 18 January 1910 in Liverpool, England; *d.* 18 March 1993 in Boulder, Colorado), internationally known economist, philosopher, social science theorist, author, peace activist, and witty poet.

Boulding was the only child of William Couchman Boulding, a plumber and Methodist lay preacher, and Elizabeth ("Bessie") Ann (Rowe) Boulding, a homemaker. When he was approximately nine years old, Boulding's parents took him out of his crowded Church of England school and entered him in a more desirable, originally Unitarian school, which prepared him for the examinations to gain a scholarship into the Liverpool Collegiate, a local day school from which Boulding graduated in 1928. He won a chemistry scholarship to New College, Oxford University, in 1928, but after a year he switched to the School of Politics, Philosophy, and Economics and graduated in 1931, earning a first-class degree in economics. He also earned an M.A. in 1939 from the same institution. In his biography he was quoted as saying, "At that time the great problems of the human race seemed to be economic." At the age of twenty-two, he published his first paper in *The Economic Journal*, edited by John Maynard Keynes. Fellowships at Harvard University and the University of Chicago followed.

Boulding taught for three years, from 1934 to 1937, at the University of Edinburgh in Scotland, and then he moved to the United States. He taught at Colgate University in New York from 1937 to 1941 and became a naturalized U.S. citizen in 1948. The bulk of his teaching career was spent at two institutions: the University of Michigan in Ann Arbor from 1949 to 1968, and the University of Colorado from 1968 to 1980. (In the latter year he was named professor emeritus.)

An active Methodist in his youth, Boulding wanted to model his life on the teachings of Christ. He stated that he "was flooded by a strong feeling that if I was going to love Jesus, I could neither kill anybody nor participate in war." He became interested in the Quaker religion and eventually joined the Society of Friends (Quakers), which became a major part of his life. Boulding met his wife, Elise Bjorn-Hansen, a sociologist and peace activist, in 1941 at a Quaker meeting in Syracuse, New York, and they were married within three months on 31 August 1941. They had five children.

Being a scholar and a Quaker, Boulding was committed

Kenneth Boulding. Mr. Kenneth Abbott

to the doctrine of peace and worked for it throughout his life. From the last half of 1941 through the first of half of 1942, Boulding was an economist with the Economic and Financial Section of the League of Nations at Princeton, New Jersey. After being warned that he would be fired if he and his wife sent out a planned statement on disarmament, he resigned his wartime post and then distributed the letter. He also planned to go to jail or be deported rather than serve in World War II. After interviews with psychiatrists, he was classified 4-F, or unfit for service.

Another facet of his personality was the need for order. His biographer quotes him as saying, "I have a secret and insidious passion for generality and for system." By 1949 he was working ardently on integrating the social sciences, theorizing that all the social sciences were studying the same thing. He had come to believe in a harmonious world order using this transdisciplinary approach. With the tumultuous social change of the 1960s, his views became more popular, and he increased his efforts to effect social change. He was an early nonviolent protestor.

In 1955 Boulding helped create the *Journal of Conflict Resolution,* and in 1959, the Center for Research on Conflict Resolution, which lasted for twelve years until 1971. In 1958 he began a vigil at the University of Michigan's flagpole, a campus focal point, in response to nuclear testing. In 1960 he stood at the Pentagon, protesting military aggression along with other Quakers. In 1961 he rejected an attractive visiting university position in Hawaii because it required a strict loyalty oath, and Quakers do not swear oaths.

In 1962 two books of his, *Social Justice* and *Conflict and Defense: A General Theory*, were published. The second of these explored the way that economics influences the fields of peace and conflict studies. That year, he and his wife helped start the International Peace Research Association, and in 1963, Boulding edited the book *Disarmament and the Economy.* In March of 1965 Boulding helped organize the early "teach-ins" at the University of Michigan to oppose the Vietnam War, a form of protest that spread to other campuses.

In the early days of the Students for a Democratic Society, Boulding gave them inspiration and encouragement. In 1965 Boulding published an article, "Reflection on Peace: Protesting Love Without Knowledge," in which he rejected "love acting without knowledge." In 1967 he wrote a memo on proposing to refuse paying taxes in protest against the Vietnam War. In 1971 he admonished a meeting of peace-research organizations, declaring that "there was too much creativity and not enough discipline."

Boulding once said, "They thought I was a dangerous radical. Actually, I am a dangerous conservative." Truthfully, Boulding had respect and faith for all humanity, and he believed that if individuals espoused his transdisciplinary philosophy, they could understand how to help all human beings live together peacefully in the future. When others turned to violence to make their point, Boulding turned to knowledge and activism. In the mid-1960s he successfully delved into grants investigation and helped found the Association for the Study of the Grants Economy. He stated that this interest arose from his ideas of conflict management and "why some conflicts were fruitful and others were not."

Boulding won the John Bates Clark Medal in 1949 and was President of the American Association of Economics, the American Association for the Advancement of Science, the Society for General Systems Research, and the Peace Research Society International. He also was awarded numerous honorary doctorates. Boulding also wrote many books, including *The Economics of Peace* (1945); *Disarmament and the Economy* (1963); *The Meaning of the Twentieth Century: The Great Transition* (1964); *Environmental Quality in a Growing Economy* (1968); *Beyond Economics: Essays on Society, Religion, and Ethics* (1970); *Economics as a Science* (1970); *Economics of Pollution* (1971); *The Economy of Love and Fear* (1972); and *Peace and War Industry* (1972). He published more than one thousand articles, books, book reviews, monographs, and pamphlets in thirty-one, self-defined categories. The topics about which he wrote most often were the economics of peace and war; peace and conflict; and knowledge, information and education. During the 1960s he added "dynamics/development/future." Boulding contributed his valuable insights to fields such as economics, ecology, human behavior, and general system theory, and he inspired his colleagues to question their own belief systems. He once stated, "If my life philosophy can be summed up in a sentence, it is that I believe that there is such a thing as human betterment." Boulding died peacefully after a long bout with cancer at the age of eighty-three in Boulder, Colorado, where he was known as the "Boulding of Boulder."

★

Six volumes of Boulding's writings are in Fred R. Glahe and Larry D. Singell, *Collected Papers of Kenneth E. Boulding* (1971–1986). Boulding's biography is Cynthia Earl Kerman, *Creative Tension: The Life and Thought of Kenneth Boulding* (1974). Kerman wrote a chapter in the 1973 book *Peace Movements in America* on Boulding's achievements. Boulding wrote "A Bibliographical Autobiography" for his 1992 book, *Towards a New Economics*, and an autobiographical chapter, "From Chemistry to Economics and Beyond," for the book *Exemplary Economists* (2000), edited by Roger Backhouse and Roger Middleton. A bibliography of Boulding's writing is Vivian L. Wilson, *Bibliography of Published Works by Kenneth E. Boulding* (1985). Biographical information is also in Robert Wright, *Three Scientists and Their Gods: Looking for Meaning in an Age of Information* (1988). Articles about Boulding include Tracy Mott, "Kenneth Boulding, 1910–1993," *The Economic Journal* 110 (June 2000): F430–F444; and an entry written by Anatol Rapoport in *The New Palgrave: A Dictionary of Economics* (1987), edited by John Eatwell, Murray Milgate, and Peter

Newman. Obituaries are in the *New York Times* and *Washington Post* (both 20 Mar. 1993), the *Chicago Tribune* (21 Mar. 1993), and the *American Economist* (22 Sept. 1993).

GWYNETH H. CROWLEY

BOWLES, Chester Bliss ("Chet") (*b.* 5 April 1901 in Springfield, Massachusetts; *d.* 25 May 1986 in Essex, Connecticut), liberal Democratic politician who served as undersecretary of state, Kennedy's special representative and adviser for Asian, African, and Latin-American affairs, and U.S. ambassador to India during the 1960s.

Bowles was born into a prominent New England family in Springfield, Massachusetts, the third child and second son of Charles Allen Bowles, a paper manufacturer, and Nellie Harris Bowles, a homemaker. He was educated at two Connecticut private schools, Choate and Roxbury, and graduated from Yale University's Sheffield Scientific School with a B.S. in 1924. In 1925 he married a Springfield debutante, Julia Fisk, with whom he had two children, Chester, Jr., and Barbara. From 1925 Bowles worked in New York City in advertising, and in 1929 with William Benton he established the agency of Benton and Bowles, serving as its chief executive from 1936 to 1941. Bowles's first marriage ended in 1932, and in 1934 he remarried, to Dorothy ("Steb") Stebbins, a Smith College graduate in social work who was often credited with awakening his social conscience, and with whom he had three children, Cynthia, Sally, and Sam. During World War II Bowles joined the government, heading the federal Office of Price Administration (1943–1946); he later became a Democratic governor of Connecticut (1949–1951), ambassador to India and Nepal (1951–1953), and a congressional representative (1959–1961).

In 1960 Bowles supported John F. Kennedy's presidential campaign, hoping in return to become secretary of state. Kennedy shared Bowles's interest in gaining third world loyalties but not his New Dealer's preference for economic aid over military coercion, nor the low priority Bowles accorded relations with the Soviet Union and Europe and his lack of interest in nuclear policy. Six feet four, lanky in youth, hulking in middle age, Bowles lacked the sense of humor and social sophistication needed to survive in the highly polished, intellectually rarefied, and sometimes cruelly competitive Kennedy administration circles—the milieu Jacqueline Kennedy, the president's widow, subsequently termed "Camelot." He accepted the lesser position of undersecretary of state but lacked rapport with Secretary Dean Rusk and swiftly became known as a poor administrator—in one colleague's words, "a pleasant idealistic fellow, naive and wordy." Bowles's opposition to the bungled March 1961 Bay of Pigs invasion of Cuba and, worse still, widely circulated press reports of his dissent soon alienated the influential attorney general, the president's brother Robert.

A staunchly anticolonial Wilsonian, Bowles urged American support for emerging nations in Africa, even when such states adopted cold war nonalignment. In 1961 he deplored European backing for the secessionist regime of Moise Tshombe in the Katanga province in the former Belgian Congo, and he welcomed its collapse when assailed by United Nations forces. From the early 1950s Bowles urged that the United States move toward improving relations with China, with the ultimate objective of recognizing both China and Taiwan. As undersecretary he unsuccessfully suggested the relaxation of trade and travel controls against China and the extension of food aid, ideas Kennedy and Rusk quickly squelched. Bowles opposed the growing U.S. troop commitment to Laos and Vietnam, arguing that this might provoke Chinese intervention—almost certainly exaggerating, as he had since the 1950s, the potential Chinese military threat. He recommended instead that all Indochina be neutralized under international guarantees, a suggestion probably unworkable given North Vietnamese determination to destabilize the South.

Fired in November 1961, Bowles took the vague, essentially honorific post of special presidential representative to Latin America, Africa, and Asia. He continued to advocate a "Peace Charter for Southeast Asia," effectively his earlier neutralization scheme, and massive economic aid for that region. He resigned in January 1963, but later that year Kennedy, recognizing Bowles's genuine talent for handling third world countries, appointed him ambassador to India, a post he held until 1969.

Bowles hoped to repeat the triumphs of his first ambassadorial assignment, when his efforts eventually facilitated substantial long-run increases in American economic aid to India, but found his second mission more difficult. Prime Minister Jawaharlal Nehru, with whom his relationship had been close, was ill when Bowles arrived, and he died in 1964. Nehru's successor, Lal Bahadur Shastri, served less than two years, a period dominated by the 1965 Indo-Pakistan War, before dying in office. Nehru's daughter and Shastri's successor, Indira Gandhi, was cool toward Bowles, greatly resenting his unsolicited avuncular advice. Bowles strongly admired President Lyndon Johnson's domestic civil rights stance and War on Poverty programs, but unlike Kennedy, who appreciated Bowles's empathy with developing countries, Johnson and many of his officials found his identification with India irritating and often ignored him. Even so, Bowles's rejection of the ambassadorial mansion in favor of a modest bungalow, his obvious distaste for diplomatic socializing, and the warm respect he and his wife, who frequently wore saris, showed ordinary Indians were long remembered in his host country.

Bowles always deplored the 1954 U.S. military alliance

Chester Bowles, June 1963. © BETTMANN/CORBIS

with India's neighbor Pakistan, and before Kennedy's assassination in November 1963 submitted to him a scheme whereby the United States would give both nations limited military assistance, provided they observed ceilings on defense spending and sought no additional weaponry from other countries. When India and Pakistan went to war in 1965, both employing American weapons, the United States initially halted all further military aid to both nations and later drastically cut all military programs. More fruitfully, Bowles backed major agricultural reforms that brought about the "Green Revolution," which ultimately made India self-sufficient in food grains. Johnson's policy of deliberately doling out food aid in small installments, which appalled Bowles, may well have been one incentive impelling India to implement such measures.

Bowles had only limited success in winning Indian support for American policies in Vietnam, one major reason for Johnson's disenchantment with Indira Gandhi. Privately Bowles continued to advocate a major economic aid program for Southeast Asia and to support a halt to bombing and the opening of peace negotiations; publicly he remained silent as the Johnson administration ignored his dissenting advice. In January 1968 Bowles represented the United States in talks with Prince Norodom Sihanouk of Cambodia, his objectives being to reach an understanding with Cambodia over American pursuit of Viet Cong forces, limit U.S. military incursions into Cambodia, and so preserve the country's neutrality and integrity. Though initially successful, these talks failed to prevent a subsequent full-scale American invasion of Cambodia. Bowles also helped orchestrate the 1967 defection from India to the United States of Svetlana Alliluyeva, daughter of the Russian dictator Josef Stalin.

Retiring in 1969, Bowles published somewhat anodyne memoirs. In 1971, the year they were published, he welcomed the separation of Bangladesh from Pakistan. In 1986 Bowles died of Parkinson's disease, which had been diagnosed in 1965, and was buried in Essex, Connecticut. His considerable abilities notwithstanding, Bowles's liberal, noninterventionist, and non-Europeanist outlook, decidedly at odds with the prevailing post-1945 foreign policy consensus, and his fondness for lofty, idealistic, and rhetorical generalities precluded his wielding greater influence within the administrations he served.

★

Bowles left his personal papers to Yale University Library. Many of his official papers are among the records of the Department of State in the National Archives II, College Park, Maryland; the John F. Kennedy Presidential Library, Boston, Massachusetts; and the Lyndon B. Johnson Library, Boston, Massachusetts. Some documents from his official career have been published in the series *Foreign Relations of the United States.* In retirement Bowles published his rather unrevealing memoirs, *Promises to Keep: My Years in Public Life 1941–1969* (1971). Although written by a diplomatic protégé and associate, his only biography, Howard B. Schaffer's *Chester Bowles: New Dealer in the Cold War* (1993), is a balanced and fair assessment of his public career. Brief accounts of Bowles's service under Kennedy and Johnson are given in Nelson Lichtenstein, ed., *Political Profiles: The Kennedy Years* (1976), and *Political Profiles: The Johnson Years* (1976). Obituaries are in the *New York Times* and *Washington Post* (both 26 May 1986). Bowles recorded oral histories for Columbia University, the Kennedy Presidential Library, the Johnson Presidential Library, and the Jawaharlal Nehru Memorial Library, New Delhi, India.

PRISCILLA ROBERTS

BRADBURY, Ray (*b.* 22 August 1920 in Waukegan, Illinois), prolific author noted for his fantastic fiction, often set in science-fictional settings. His best-known works are *The Martian Chronicles* (1950), *Dandelion Wine* (1953), and *Fahrenheit 451* (1957).

Ray Bradbury was the third son of Leonard Spaulding and Esther Moberg. His older brother had a twin who died before Bradbury was born, and Bradbury's younger sister Elizabeth died when Bradbury was seven. Bradbury, who even as a child was noted for his highly impressionable and vivid imagination, grew up in the small town of Waukegan,

Illinois, a peaceful place that later appeared in his stories as "Green Town, Illinois." His Aunt Neva, who gave him books of fairy tales and took him to see the films *The Hunchback of Notre Dame* and *The Wizard of Oz,* did much to encourage his imaginative life. Bradbury's teenage years were marked by the Great Depression, which drove his father west in search of work. The family lived in Arizona from 1926 to 1927, and from 1932 to 1933; in 1934, they moved to Los Angeles, where Bradbury has lived ever since. Bradbury graduated from Los Angeles High School, and after graduating, lived with his family and found work delivering newspapers.

Bradbury began publishing stories in amateur science-fiction magazines in the mid-1930s, and in 1941, with the encouragement of the well-known science-fiction writers Leigh Brackett and Robert Heinlein, he sold three stories of the fifty-two he had written that year. With this success, he decided to become a writer, and quit his job as a newspaper salesperson to begin a prolific career.

On 27 September 1947 Bradbury married Marguerite Susan McClure, with whom he had four daughters between 1949 and 1958. Bradbury, who was the only science-fiction writer of the time to be published in higher-paying, mainstream periodicals, supported his family through selling his stories; in 1944 he made $800 from the sale of forty stories.

During the late 1950s Bradbury published some of his best-known works: *The Martian Chronicles* (1950), *The Illustrated Man* (1951), *Fahrenheit 451* (1953), and *Dandelion Wine* (1957), as well as several story collections. Bradbury's introduction to the literary mainstream came in 1950, when writer Christopher Isherwood "discovered" *The Martian Chronicles,* a lyrical account of human exploration on Mars, and wrote a highly favorable review of it in *Tomorrow* magazine. Isherwood, like many other mainstream readers, had assumed that all science fiction was bad by definition, and was delighted to discover that this book was marked by a vivid and original style, as well as sensitivity and imagination. "His is a very great and unusual talent," Isherwood wrote of Bradbury.

Bradbury also worked on films, writing the treatment that later became the script for the first 3-D science-fiction film, *It Came from Outer Space* (1953). Also in 1953, John Huston hired him to write the script for the film *Moby Dick,* released in 1956.

Although *Fahrenheit 451* appeared in 1953, it presaged many issues of the 1960s. In the book, set in an undetermined future era, fireman Guy Montag and his colleagues no longer put out fires, but start them for the purpose of burning books. The book examines issues of free speech, the proper authority of the government, and individualism versus conformity. Although Bradbury told Everett T. Moore in the *ALA Bulletin* that the novel was inspired by

Ray Bradbury. THE LIBRARY OF CONGRESS

the repressive events of the McCarthy era, its themes were still relevant in the 1960s, when social forces, including the antiwar movement, the civil rights movement, and the hippie subculture, emphasized personal freedom, social justice, and antiauthoritarianism. Montag, in fact, goes through clear phases of rebellion and consciousness-raising. He begins as a loyal and unquestioning fireman following orders. Gradually, he begins to examine his actions and wonder why the system is so repressive. Over time, he realizes that as a book burner, he is destroying the shared heritage and consciousness of his community. He calls in sick to work, an act of passive resistance similar to those used by 1960s social demonstrators, who favored peaceful refusal to cooperate over violent rebellion. As the book progresses, Montag moves more and more to the fringe of his society, living among other outcasts and misfits.

As Wayne L. Johnson noted in *Ray Bradbury,* some of the characters and events in the novel "might have been drawn from the turbulent political events of the sixties," including the portrayal of Montag's wife, who spends all her time doing drugs and watching television; Clarisse, a young woman who prefigures the "flower children" of the 1960s; and an old woman, who resists the firemen by pouring kerosene not only over her books, but also over her body before lighting a match, just as Buddhist monks did in the 1960s to protest the Vietnam War.

In 1962 Bradbury published *Something Wicked This Way Comes,* a novel that in setting and theme is similar to his earlier *Dandelion Wine.* Set in idyllic Green Town, Illinois, a fictionalized version of Bradbury's hometown, the novel explores life-changing events in the lives of two friends, Jim Nightshade and William Halloway, when "Cooper and Dark's Pandemonium Shadow Show," a mysterious carnival, comes to town. Emphasizing themes of coming-of-age, as well as good versus evil, the novel contrasts the wholesome nature of the town with the evil brought by the supernatural carnival people, who feed on fear and spiritual pain.

Bradbury has also written screenplays, plays, and poetry, as well as a book on creative writing. A prolific writer, he writes every day. He has received the World Fantasy Award for Lifetime Achievement (1977), the Grand Master Nebula Award from the Science Fiction and Fantasy Writers of America (1988), the Horror Writers' Association Bram Stoker Award and lifetime achievement award (1989). Bradbury received an Emmy award for his teleplay *The Halloween Tree,* and was nominated for an Academy Award for his animated film *Icarus Montgolfier Wright* (1961). His influence on other writers was honored in a collection, *The Bradbury Chronicles: Stories in Honor of Ray Bradbury* (1991). Perhaps the greatest tribute Bradbury received came in 1971, when the *Apollo 15* crew named a lunar crater Dandelion Crater in honor of Bradbury's *Dandelion Wine.*

Bradbury, who claimed to recall everything that had happened to him since the moment of his birth, as well as every book he ever read and every movie he had ever seen, drew on his memories of small-town Midwestern childhood, as well as images in popular movies and books of his youth, to create his own fiction. Although his books are often categorized as science fiction, critics continue to argue to what genre his work belongs; he has been highly honored by mainstream literary critics, and at the same time, often disowned by the science-fiction community. In *Dream Makers,* Bradbury told Charles Platt that the rift between him and other science-fiction writers occurred because "I left the family, you see. And that's a danger . . . to [science-fiction writers]. Because they haven't got out of the house."

David Mogen observed in *Ray Bradbury* that throughout Bradbury's career, many critics within science fiction have commented that his "values and philosophy are fundamentally opposed to the ethos of true 'science fiction'," a reference to his apparent distrust of machinery, his lack of detailed scientific knowledge, and his emphasis on a nostalgic past rather than the future.

In *The Universe Makers,* Donald A. Wollheim examined Bradbury's work and noted that he was not a science fiction writer, because "His stories are stories of people—real and honest and true in their understanding of human nature—but for his purposes the trappings of science fiction are sufficient—mere stage settings." Unlike the stories of other science fiction writers, Bradbury's works do not have an underpinning of solid science or a logical extrapolation. For example, as Wollheim noted, "His Mars bears no relation to the astronomical planet," but is largely derived from the imagined Mars of 1930s pulp novels and horror movies. However, Wollheim wrote, Bradbury is "a mainstream fantasist of great brilliance."

★

David Mogen, *Ray Bradbury* (1986), provides details on Bradbury's life and work, and Robin Anne Reid, *Ray Bradbury: A Critical Companion* (2000), examines each of his works and provides varying critical interpretations. Donald A. Wollheim, *The Universe Makers* (1971), includes a profile of Bradbury, and Charles Platt, *The Dream Makers* (1980), features an interview. *Fahrenheit 451* is discussed in Wayne L. Johnson, *Ray Bradbury* (1980), as well as in Everett T. Moore, "A Rationale for Bookburners: A Further Word from Ray Bradbury," *ALA Bulletin* 55, no. 5 (May 1961): 403–404.

KELLY WINTERS

BRADLEY, William Warren ("Bill") (*b.* 28 July 1943 in Crystal City, Missouri), professional basketball player and Hall of Famer who was also a Rhodes scholar and U.S. senator.

Bradley was the only child of Warren, a banker, and Susan (Crowe) Bradley, a junior high school teacher, and he grew up in both Crystal City, a small town on the banks of the Mississippi about thirty-five miles south of St. Louis, and West Palm Beach, Florida, where the family had a second home. He was an outstanding student as well as one of the top high school basketball players in the country at Crystal City High School, where he scored over 3,000 points between 1957 and 1961. Bradley led his team to the Final Four of the Missouri state tournament three times and was voted All-State twice as well as *Parade* Magazine All-America twice. Initially he signed a letter of intent to attend Duke University, but he changed his plans and enrolled at Princeton University in the fall of 1961. Bradley had been to Europe and visited Oxford University, which had made a great impression upon him. He set his sights on a Rhodes scholarship and felt that his chances for obtaining one were much greater by attending Princeton.

Bradley began his varsity career the next year, as freshmen were ineligible for varsity play at that time. In his sophomore year he led the Tigers to the Ivy League title, averaging 27.3 points per game and just over 12 rebounds per game. Bradley, a versatile six-foot, five-inch player, was

Bill Bradley in 1970, the first year he led the Knicks to the NBA championship. ASSOCIATED PRESS AP

a great shooter, good ball handler, and deft passer who saw the floor well and involved all of his teammates in the game. He was voted All-Ivy in 1963 as well as the next two years. The Tigers made the NCAA tournament by defeating Yale in a playoff after the two teams tied for the title with 11–3 records (only league champions were eligible to play in the tournament then), but they lost in the first round to Saint Joseph's (Pennsylvania), 82–81. The next year, the Tigers were 12–2 in the league and again won the league title. They won their first-round game against VMI but lost to Connecticut, 52–50, before defeating Villanova in the Eastern Consolation round. (These rounds have been eliminated since the NCAA expanded its field to sixty-five teams from what was originally eight in 1939. There were a number of expansions of the field with sixty-four teams being invited starting in 1985 and sixty-five starting in 2000). Bradley was a First Team All-America player and won a slot on the U.S. Olympic team, of which he was subsequently named captain. Behind Bradley the squad continued its dominance in Olympic basketball, going undefeated and capturing the gold medal in Tokyo in 1964.

Bradley and the 1964–1965 Princeton team had a storybook season. The team went 13–1 to again win the Ivy League title, then defeated Penn State, North Carolina State, and Providence to advance to the Final Four. Their opponent was Michigan. Earlier in the season at the Holiday Festival Tournament in New York, Princeton had led Michigan and its star, Cazzie Russell, 75–63, when Bradley fouled out after scoring 41 points. The Tigers lost 80–78. In the NCAA tournament, Michigan won by a greater margin, 93–76. At that time a third-place game was played, and Princeton met Wichita State. In that contest Bradley set an NCAA tournament record with 58 points, breaking the record of Oscar Robertson, as the Tigers won, 118–82. Bradley was named Most Valuable Player of the NCAA tournament and, later that year, became the first basketball player ever to win the Sullivan Award as the top amateur athlete in the United States. In three college seasons, Bradley scored 2,503 points, an average of 30.2 points per game. He was again a First Team All-America in 1965 as well as Associated Press, United Press International, and United States Basketball Writers Association Player of the Year. Bradley graduated from Princeton with a B.A. in history in 1965.

Drafted by the New York Knickerbockers, Bradley instead chose to defer a professional basketball career and accept a Rhodes scholarship to Oxford, from which he eventually earned an M.A. degree (cum laude) in English in 1967. During his first year at Oxford, Bradley also played for the Olympia Simmenthal team in Turin, Italy, on weekends. In his second year Bradley played little basketball but reported to the Knicks in midseason in 1967–1968 after completing his degree at Oxford and nearly six months of active duty in the Air Force Reserve from July to December of 1967. He completed his service in 1973 with the rank of first lieutenant.

Upon joining the Knicks during the 1967–1968 season, Bradley played in forty-five games, averaging 8 points, 3 assists, and just over 2 rebounds a game. The statistics were not exactly auspicious, but Bradley had been away from the game nearly a full year, and the team finished the season at 43–39, their first winning record since 1959. The next season Bradley became a starter, with his old college rival, Cazzie Russell, coming off the bench. The Knicks went 54–28 and upset the Baltimore Bullets in the first round of the playoffs before losing to the Boston Celtics and Bill Russell, the eventual champions. Bradley averaged 12.4 points, just over 4 rebounds, and just under 4 assists per game. In the playoffs he improved to 16 points and 7 rebounds per game. Bill Russell retired the next season, 1969–1970, and the young Knicks became the best team in the NBA, with a 60–22 record. They defeated Baltimore and Milwaukee, the latter led by Lew Alcindor (later Kareem Abdul-Jabbar), to win the Eastern Division series, then edged the Los Angeles Lakers four games to three to bring New York its first NBA championship. Every starter on the team averaged at least 14 points per game. Bradley had 14.5 and was second on the team with 4 assists per game. The Knicks won the Eastern Division title again in 1970–1971 but lost in the second round of the playoffs to the Baltimore Bullets. In 1971–1972 they went to the NBA finals but lost to the Lakers before winning the NBA title once more in 1972–1973. During those three seasons, Bradley averaged 12.4, 15.1, and 16.1 points per game.

On 14 January 1974 Bradley married Ernestine Schlant, a college professor; they have one daughter. Bradley retired after the 1977 season with 9,217 points, an average of 12.4 per game. In 1978 he ran successfully for the United States Senate as a Democrat from New Jersey and was reelected in 1984 and 1990 before announcing his retirement from the Senate in 1995. In 2000 he mounted a bid for the Democratic presidential nomination but lost to Al Gore. In 1983 he was enshrined in the Naismith Memorial Basketball Hall of Fame.

★

Bradley's career with the Knicks is best captured in his book *Life on the Run* (1976). His autobiography, *Time Present, Time Past: A Memoir* (1996), focuses more on his senatorial rather than his basketball career. John McPhee, *A Sense of Where You Are* (1965), follows Bradley while at Princeton. Both the 18 Jan. 1965 and the 20 Mar. 1965 issues of *Sports Illustrated* have stories on Bradley and his Princeton team.

MURRY R. NELSON

BRENNAN, William Joseph, Jr. (*b.* 25 April 1906 in New-ark, New Jersey; *d.* 24 July 1997 in Arlington, Virginia), justice of the U.S. Supreme Court whose liberalism, keen intellect, and leadership were responsible for more than 1,300 written opinions, many of them key majority opinions concerning individual rights.

Brennan was the first of eight children—four boys and four girls—of William J. Brennan, Sr., an Irish immigrant who became a labor leader and city representative, and Agnes McDermott, also an Irish immigrant. He grew up in the Vailsburg section of Newark, attending Barringer High School, from which he graduated in 1924. Brennan then attended the Wharton School of the University of Pennsylvania in Philadelphia, graduating in 1928 with a B.S. in economics. On 5 May 1928 Brennan married Marjorie Leonard; they had three children. Brennan earned an L.L.B. at Harvard Law School, where his teachers included Felix Frankfurter, with whom he would later sit on the U.S. Supreme Court. After graduating in 1931 Brennan returned to Newark. When World War II broke out several years later he joined the U.S. Army as legal counsel for the

William J. Brennan, Jr. SUPREME COURT OF THE UNITED STATES

Ordnance Department and achieved the rank of full colonel. He also attracted the attention of Arthur T. Vanderbilt, the chief justice of New Jersey, who, after World War II, was responsible for Brennan being named as an associate in his court.

Vanderbilt was rumored to be in position for a seat on the U.S. Supreme Court when he asked Brennan to substitute for him at a conference on law reform, at which some of President Dwight D. Eisenhower's top justice officials were present. Brennan so impressed U.S. Attorney General Herbert Brownell that when Eisenhower decided he wanted a Roman Catholic on the Court, Brownell recommended Brennan.

Brennan was nominated as a recess appointment in 1956 and later was confirmed by the Senate. Brennan at once connected with the Eisenhower-appointed chief justice, Earl Warren. Brennan's first significant opinion was delivered in *Roth* v. *United States* (1957), which established the community standards doctrine—specifically, that to be pornographic "the dominant theme of the material as a whole" must appeal "to the prurient interest" as judged by "contemporary community standards"—that continues to govern obscenity charges in the twenty-first century.

Brennan delivered his most significant opinion in 1962 when he spoke for the Court in *Baker* v. *Carr*, which addressed legislative apportionment schemes whereby state monies are distributed; in this case, rural populations were weighted more heavily than urban ones and consequently received a higher per capita proportion of state funds. Previously the court had refused to enter what Frankfurter had termed the "political thicket" of the apportionment of state or federal legislative districts. But in *Baker*, Brennan brushed aside this objection and ruled that the Fourteenth Amendment forbade legislative districts that were not of essentially equal population, or (as Justice Douglas later framed it) "one person who has one vote" for elected officials. The decision at once nullified schemes that gave rural areas with tiny populations one member in the lower branch of the state house while vastly larger cities got only one or two representatives. Eventually the Court expanded its ruling to include districts of members of the federal House of Representatives and both chambers of state bodies.

The Warren court also instituted sweeping reforms in the procedures used in bringing criminal cases to court and reforms in admitting evidence. Brennan voted for most of these reforms, which included the now-famous Miranda warnings and the changes in search and seizure rules that police chiefs complained would hamstring their investigations. In May 1965 Billy Joe Wade had been placed without benefit of counsel in a suspect lineup for a robbery committed in September 1964. He filed suit. Chief Justice Warren was wary of requiring a lawyer for a lineup proceeding, as delay could weaken the memory of an identifying witness, but in *United States* v. *Wade* (1967), Brennan overcame Warren's objection and authored the Court's majority opinion, which ruled in favor of requiring the assistance of counsel in criminal matters at every "critical stage" of a prosecution, not only at the trial.

In the 1960s federal courts had elaborate barriers to hearing complaints about civil rights violations. Cases had to be "ripe" for review (meaning no outstanding issues could be involved except those requiring immediate resolution by the U.S. Supreme Court) and, despite the ancient use of habeas corpus attacks after an initial appeal on criminal convictions, were limited. (Habeas corpus is the doctrine, dating from the Middle Ages, that a prisoner can immediately question the legality of his detention without waiting for the usual criminal processes.) In *Fay* v. *Noia* (1963) and *Dombrowski* v. *Pfister* (1965), Brennan attacked procedural barriers preventing the hearing of federal civil rights claims. In 1968 Brennan ruled that the Bill of Rights required that the confession of a criminal codefendant must be subject to cross-examination in order to be admissible against the primary defendant.

In 1967 Brennan's political reform views took another turn. *New York Times* v. *Sullivan* was a libel case involving a Montgomery, Alabama, town commissioner accused of using tear gas at an Alabama college. Normally the courts would uphold a libel suit only if negligent falsehood and subsequent injury were involved. But in *Sullivan*, Brennan held that in the case of a "public figure" the courts would require that a plaintiff show that a defendant possessed a reckless disregard for the truth, a decision that made it harder for political leaders and other notables to threaten members of the press by pursuing them with a libel suit. Brennan eventually opened the entire range of Bill of Rights civil liberties to those seeking redress from both state and federal governments. In 1972 Brennan joined the majority in *Roe* v. *Wade*, which held that a woman was constitutionally entitled to an abortion during the first trimester of pregnancy.

As the years went on, Brennan found himself swimming against the tide in the Court. The ailing Warren was replaced by Warren Burger, and in the 1980s Ronald Reagan appointed justices who were opposed to much of the Warren court's thinking, particularly with respect to the federal government's exercise of judicial power.

Brennan became senior associate justice in 1975, and as such he could name the writer for court opinions when the chief justice disagreed with him—a power Burger reportedly tried to undermine. On 1 December 1982 Brennan's wife died; the following March he married his secretary, Mary Fowler. Brennan spent much of his energy during his last years on the bench in an effort to permanently abolish the death penalty, which had been suspended with his support in 1972.

Brennan retired in 1990, and President George H. W. Bush appointed David Souter in his place. The next appointee to the Court after Souter was Ruth Bader Ginsburg, who had once taught law a few yards from where Brennan was born.

Brennan died in a nursing home in Arlington, Virginia, of complications from a fractured hip. He is buried in Arlington National Cemetery.

★

Brennan's personal papers are at the Library of Congress. Studies of his life and theoretical thinking are numerous. Kim Isaac Eisler, *A Justice for All* (1991), is an adoring tribute that argues that Brennan was the technician behind many of the landmark decisions of the Warren court. See also E. Joshua Rosenkranz and Bernard Schwartz, *Reason and Passion: Justice Brennan's Enduring Influence* (1997). Studies of Brennan's opinions as a separate body of jurisprudence include David E. Marion, *The Jurisprudence of William J. Brennan, Jr.: The Law and Politics of "Libertarian Dignity"* (1967). Official memorials to Brennan are in 158 *New Jersey Reports* (1999) and 115B *Supreme Court Reports* (2000). An obituary is in the *New York Times* (25 July 1997).

JOHN DAVID HEALY

BREWSTER, Kingman, Jr. (*b.* 17 June 1919 in Longmeadow, Massachusetts; *d.* 8 November 1988 in Oxford, England), president of Yale University noted for his somewhat liberal views and for expanding the faculty and instituting policy changes that increased opportunities for women.

The third child, and second to survive to adulthood, of Kingman Brewster, a lawyer, and Florence Foster Besse, Brewster was raised just outside Boston. When he was six years old, his parents divorced, and Brewster and his older sister Mary went to live with their mother and new stepfather Edward Ballantine, a professor of music at Harvard University.

Brewster was educated at The Belmont Hill School from 1930 to 1936, where he served on the debate team and worked on the school newspaper. In his junior year, he received tutoring so that he could spend what would have been his senior year traveling Europe with his mother, stepfather, and sister. After that year abroad, Brewster enrolled at Yale College, from which he graduated in 1941. He then worked as a special assistant coordinator for economics in the U.S. Office of Inter-American Affairs before joining the U.S. Navy as an aviator on antisubmarine patrol in the north and south Atlantic. Discharged with the rank of lieutenant in 1945, Brewster enrolled at Harvard Law School, where he served as treasurer and note editor of the *Harvard Law Review* before earning his law degree in 1948. For one

Kingman Brewster, Jr. THE LIBRARY OF CONGRESS

year, he worked in Paris as an assistant to Harvard professor Milton Katz, a special representative of the U.S. Marshall Plan. Upon his return to the United States, Brewster taught briefly at the Massachusetts Institute of Technology before joining the faculty at Harvard Law School in 1950. He spent a decade there teaching law, achieving the rank of full professor in 1953.

As the 1960s dawned, Brewster resigned from Harvard and was appointed provost-designate of his undergraduate alma mater. By fall 1961 he had succeeded Norman S. Buck as provost and had joined the faculty at the Yale Law School. As provost, Brewster undertook a somewhat controversial set of policies designed to increase the size and improve the caliber of the Yale teaching staff. Brewster's tripartite program included appointing newly hired faculty jointly to the undergraduate college and graduate school; establishing a university-wide faculty committee to evaluate and rule on tenure, thereby creating overall standards; and reconfiguring the budget to allow for increases in faculty salaries.

Following the death of Yale president A. Whitney Griswold in spring 1963, Brewster was named president effective that October, and was formally inaugurated on 11 April 1964. The first lawyer to serve as Yale president, Brewster

was also the first man without a Ph.D. since 1900 to be appointed to that position. Over the summer of 1963, he established a three-person commission to investigate complaints of racial discrimination in university employment. Hand in hand with his expansion of the university's faculty, Brewster instituted new undergraduate-admission policies meant to attract the best students from around the world regardless of wealth and status, rather than merely selecting from the families of alumni. In keeping with this policy of opening up the school to the best minds, Brewster began to lay the groundwork for perhaps his most controversial decision—allowing the admission of women to Yale. Negotiations began with Vassar College to become the sister institution along the lines of the model of Harvard and Radcliffe, but the Vassar administration eventually balked at the idea of relocating to New Haven, Connecticut. Nevertheless, Brewster pushed for the admission of women, and in the fall of 1969 some 500 female students were accepted.

Several other program areas were formed, expanded, or rejuvenated under the Brewster presidency. In 1965 the Yale School of Medicine became affiliated with the Grace–New Haven Medical Community Hospital, resulting in a world-class institution for medical instruction, research, and practice. The following year, the Yale School of Drama benefited from the appointment of Robert Brustein as its dean, as well as the establishment of the Afro-American studies and computer science departments. Both an undergraduate college seminar program and a five-year bachelor of arts degree program (which included a junior year abroad) were initiated, and there was an overhaul of the grading system and the credit requirements for graduation.

Despite his self-description as a supporter of moderate Republican political philosophy, Brewster openly spoke out in opposition to U.S. involvement in Vietnam and the inequities in the military draft. His liberal stance kept the Yale community relatively unscathed during the turbulent 1960s and the rise of the antiwar movement. The few student demonstrations that did take place were generally dealt with in an orderly and swift manner.

Although Brewster continued to champion innovations into the 1970s, the more conservative members of the alumni began to reduce their financial support, to the extent that, by 1976, the university began to face a deficit. Brewster decided to step down as president almost simultaneously with his appointment by President Jimmy Carter to serve as U.S. ambassador to Great Britain, a post he held from 1977 until 1981. He then joined the law firm of Winthrop, Stimson, Putnam, and Roberts, and in 1984 became resident partner of its London office. In 1986 Brewster accepted a five-year term as master of University College, Oxford, where he served until his death of a heart attack. He is buried at Grove Street Cemetery in New Haven.

Brewster married Mary Louise Phillips, with whom he would have five children, on 30 November 1942. He authored several articles and books, most notably *Antitrust and American Banking Abroad* (1958).

Brewster was one of the most influential and progressive academics of the 1960s. His administration at Yale had the primary objective of improving the university's academic standards even though it required a substantial overhaul of the existing policies, as well as an expansion of programs, schools and departments. Although some of the more conservative alumni were vocal in their opposition to Brewster, citing his liberal policies and the resulting budget deficits, he was admired by faculty, staff, and students, and his innovations paved the way for Yale to reemerge as an influential and important academic institution.

★

The Kingman Brewster, Jr., Collection is housed at the Manuscripts and Archives at the Sterling Memorial Library, Yale University. A profile of Brewster is John Bainbridge, "Our Far-Flung Correspondents: Excellency," *New Yorker* (12 Dec. 1977). An obituary is in the *New York Times* (9 Nov. 1988).

TED MURPHY

BRINKLEY, David. *See* Huntley, Chester Robert ("Chet"), and David McClure Brinkley.

BROOKE, Edward William, III (*b.* 26 October 1919 in Washington, D.C.), lawyer and liberal Republican politician who made history in 1966 when he became the first African American elected to the U.S. Senate by popular vote.

Brooke is the youngest of three children and the only son of Edward William Brooke, Jr., an attorney with the Veterans Administration, and Helen Seldon, a homemaker. Raised in a middle-class household in the self-contained African-American community of segregated Washington, D.C., he grew up relatively unscarred by white prejudice. Handsome, personable, and athletic, Brooke was a popular figure at Dunbar High School, the most prestigious black high school in the country, and at all-black Howard University, from which he graduated in 1936. As a premed student at Howard, he grew bored with his course of study, and he had abandoned the idea of becoming a surgeon by the time he received his B.S. degree in 1941.

Shortly after the United States entered World War II, Brooke was inducted into the U.S. Army and commissioned a second lieutenant in the all-black 366th Combat Infantry Regiment. Sent to northern Italy in 1944, he attained the rank of captain, participated in an attack on a heavily fortified artillery battery and was awarded the Bronze Star. Having learned to speak Italian, Brooke also served as liaison officer to local partisans fighting behind

Edward Brooke. ASSOCIATED PRESS AP

enemy lines in the Po Valley. At the war's end, he met Remigia Ferrari-Scacco, the daughter of a Genoese businessman, whom he married on 7 June 1947. They had two daughters.

Brooke developed a serious interest in law when he was assigned to defend soldiers from his regiment at courts-martial proceedings. In 1946, following his discharge, he enrolled at Boston University Law School. Functioning in a predominantly white world for the first time, Brooke became editor of the law review. He earned his LL.B. degree in 1948, and his LL.M. a year later. After passing the bar examination in 1948, Brooke opened a one-man practice in Roxbury, a racially mixed Boston neighborhood. In 1950 his friends convinced him to run for state representative. He "cross-filed" (a practice no longer allowed) as a candidate in both the Republican and Democratic party primaries, and won the Republican nomination, but lost the general election even though he captured more votes in his district than any earlier African-American candidate. After another setback as a Republican legislative candidate in 1952, Brooke did not seek public office for eight years.

As part of an effort by party leaders to bring more diversity to the Massachusetts Republican ticket in 1960, Brooke was nominated for secretary of state. Although he was defeated, his energetic campaign garnered over one million votes, an impressive total for a candidate running statewide for the first time, and in a state that was 98 percent white. In 1961 Republican governor John A. Volpe appointed Brooke chairman of the Boston Finance Commission, a body charged with investigating city finances and administration. At a time when government scandals dominated the headlines in Massachusetts, Brooke held highly publicized hearings, exposed malfeasance in a number of city departments, and established a reputation as a fighter of corruption.

In 1962 Brooke challenged and upset Elliot L. Richardson, a pillar of the Boston Brahmin establishment, in a tight, often bitter race for the Republican nomination for state attorney general. He then won election over Democrat Francis E. Kelly by nearly 260,000 votes out of 2.1 million cast. The only victorious member of his ticket, Brooke became the first African American elected to a major state-wide office in the United States.

As attorney general, Brooke gained greater stature as a crusader against public corruption. Over the next four years, he became a familiar visage on television, announcing developments in his large-scale investigation of crime in state government and proposing remedies for corruption-tainted agencies. Before he left office, Brooke had secured more than one hundred indictments against eighty individuals and corporations. He had also obtained major convictions against loan company executives and state regulators for a bribery scheme to raise interest rates, and against a judge and two others for larceny of public funds from the Boston Common underground garage project.

On the national stage, Brooke joined fellow moderate Republicans in a last-ditch attempt to prevent the nomination of Senator Barry Goldwater of Arizona, a hard-line conservative who had voted against the recently passed Civil Rights Act, as the party's candidate for president in 1964. After the effort fizzled at the Republican National Convention, Brooke withheld his support from the national ticket, a position that—along with his record in office—gained him strong approval from the Bay State electorate. He won reelection by a margin of over 797,000 votes, while Goldwater lost Massachusetts to President Lyndon B. Johnson by more than 1.2 million votes.

As his party's best vote-getter and a figure of growing national repute, Brooke was the logical choice of Republicans to replace the incumbent U.S. Senator Leverett Saltonstall when he announced he would not seek a fifth term in 1966. The overwhelming favorite from the outset, Brooke ran a nearly flawless campaign. Addressing the racial tensions of the 1960s in a characteristically moderate tone, he denounced the confrontational tactics of both the Black Power advocate Stokely Carmichael and the white segregationist Lester Maddox. On the thorny issue of U.S. involvement in Vietnam, Brooke adopted a mildly dovish position, favoring a negotiated settlement of the war. His defeat of Democratic former governor Endicott Peabody by

over 438,000 votes made him the first African-American U.S. senator since Reconstruction.

Brooke—whose 1966 book *The Challenge of Change: Crisis in Our Two-Party System* called upon Republican leaders to embrace large-scale government programs for rehabilitation of the poor, education, and urban renewal—fit comfortably into his party's liberal wing in the Senate. He took a particular interest in foreign affairs and housing issues. On the former, he promoted increased aid to underdeveloped countries, and on the latter, he sponsored a 1969 amendment that limited to 25 percent the amount of income public housing tenants had to pay for rent. Although he also cosponsored an open housing amendment (with Democrat Walter Mondale of Minnesota) that became the basis for the landmark Fair Housing Act of 1968, Brooke was never considered a leading civil rights figure in Congress.

In 1968 Brooke supported the bid of New York Governor Nelson A. Rockefeller for the Republican presidential nomination, but, in contrast to 1964, he endorsed and campaigned with the party's eventual nominee, Richard M. Nixon. Nonetheless, Brook did become disenchanted with what he regarded as the divisive "law and order" rhetoric of Nixon and running mate Spiro T. Agnew. Following Nixon's election, Brooke was offered the ambassadorship to the United Nations and other posts, but preferred the independence of the Senate. He exhibited that independence in 1969 by strongly opposing Nixon's Safeguard antiballistic missile (ABM) system and his nomination of southern conservative Clement Haynsworth to the Supreme Court.

Brooke was easily reelected in 1972 (while Nixon lost Massachusetts, the only state he did not win in that year's presidential election), but his political career ended in defeat in 1978, following revelations that he misrepresented his finances in a deposition during divorce proceedings. Brooke and his first wife divorced that year, and in 1979 he married Anne Fleming, with whom he had a son.

Brooke saw himself as a politician who happened to be black, rather than as a black politician, and generally eschewed the role of civil rights leader. In the 1960s, he was most important as a symbol, and indeed an embodiment, of the ability of talented middle-class African Americans to gain mainstream acceptance.

★

Brooke's papers are deposited in the Manuscript Division of the Library of Congress in Washington, D.C. A memoir, *Edward W. Brooke: A Senator's Life in Black and White,* is forthcoming. Early biographical efforts are John Henry Cutler, *Ed Brooke: Biography of a Senator* (1972), and Elinor C. Hartshorn, "The Quiet Campaigner: Edward W. Brooke in Massachusetts" (Ph.D. diss., University of Massachusetts, 1973). Bryant Rollins, "Life Story of

Ed Brooke," a sixteen-part series in the *Boston Globe* (27 June–12 July 1965), discusses Brooke's early years. Short accounts of his life and career are in Stephen Hess and David S. Broder, *The Republican Establishment: The Present and Future of the G.O.P.* (1967); Alec Barbrook, *God Save the Commonwealth: An Electoral History of Massachusetts* (1973); Nelson Lichtenstein, ed., *Political Profiles: The Johnson Years* (1976); and Eleanora Schoenebaum, ed., *Political Profiles: The Nixon-Ford Years* (1979). Important articles include Edward R. F. Sheehan, "Brooke of Massachusetts: A Negro Governor on Beacon Hill?," *Harper's Magazine* (June 1964); John F. Becker and Eugene E. Heaton, Jr., "The Election of Senator Edward W. Brooke," *Public Opinion Quarterly* 31 (fall 1967); Judson L. Jeffries, "U.S. Senator Edward W. Brooke and Governor L. Douglas Wilder Tell Political Scientists How Blacks Can Win High-Profile Statewide Office," *PS: Political Science and Politics* 32 (Sept. 1999); and Sally Jacobs, "The Unfinished Chapter," *Boston Globe Magazine* (5 Mar. 2000).

RICHARD H. GENTILE

BROOKS, Gwendolyn Elizabeth (*b.* 7 June 1917 in Topeka, Kansas; *d.* 3 December 2000 in Chicago, Illinois), poet, writer, and the first African American to win the Pulitzer Prize (1950), who in the 1960s committed herself to the theme of black pride.

Daughter of David Anderson Brooks and Keziah Corinne Wims, Brooks grew up in Chicago. Her mother was a former schoolteacher, her father a mechanic and insurance broker and the son of a runaway slave. When Brooks was thirteen, her poem "Eventide" was published in *American Childhood.* After attending two high schools, she graduated in 1934 from a third, integrated Englewood High, and went on to Woodrow Wilson Junior College, from which she graduated in 1936. By then she was a regular contributor to a weekly column in the Chicago *Defender,* an African-American newspaper. Brooks did publicity for the National Association for the Advancement of Colored People (NAACP) Youth Council and worked as a typist and for a spiritualist at the Mecca, an apartment complex and the site of one of her major poems.

On 1 September 1939 Brooks married Henry Blakely II, a writer and insurance adjustor. The couple, who had two children, separated in 1969 but reunited in 1974.

As a young wife and mother, Brooks took a poetry course at Chicago's South Side Community Arts Center. In 1943 she won the Midwestern Writers' Poetry Award and in 1945 published *A Street in Bronzeville,* whose title referred to Chicago's south side ghetto. Brooks's second poetry collection, *Annie Allen,* won the Eunice Tietjens Prize from *Poetry* Magazine (1949) and the 1950 Pulitzer Prize, making her the first African-American writer to be so honored. *Maud Martha,* her only novel, appeared in 1953.

Gwendolyn Brooks. AP/WIDE WORLD PHOTOS

Poems in *The Bean Eaters* (1960) range from the eponymous one about a couple subsisting on beans to "We Real Cool," about younger pool-hall habitués, and from "The Lovers of the Poor," about the white Ladies Betterment League, to "The Last Quatrain of the Ballad of Emmett Till," about a murdered black man. Writing realistic and unsentimental poetry about poor African Americans, Brooks was veering from domestic concerns to political issues.

However, "the real turning point" in Brooks's radicalization came in 1967 with her participation in the Second Black Writers' Conference at Fisk University in Nashville, Tennessee. In the presence of such spirited young black students and writers as LeRoi Jones (later Amiri Baraka), Brooks was awakened to a new consciousness of black selfhood, womanhood, and the arts. Thereafter she changed her hairstyle, loosened her writing, and employed less elevated language in her work. She later wrote in *Primer for Blacks,* "Blackness / is a title, / is a preoccupation / is a commitment Blacks / are to comprehend," and in *A Capsule Course in Black Writing,* she expressed her allegiance to "the new black ideal of black identity and solidarity."

In the Mecca (1968) is dedicated "to the memory of Langston Hughes, and to James Baldwin, LeRoi Jones, and Mike Alexandroff, educators extraordinaire." First conceived as a novel, these 807 lines of free verse with shifting narrators follow Mrs. Sallie Smith, mother of nine, as she searches for her missing daughter, Pepita, through the Mecca, a vast architectural showpiece turned slum (1891–

1952) filled with myriad personalities. The section "After Mecca" includes poems on the assassinated civil rights leaders Medgar Evers and Malcolm X. Except for the compilation *The World of Gwendolyn Brooks,* this was Brooks's last book published by Harper and Row (her publisher since 1945), as she switched her allegiance to small black publishing houses, an adherence to principle that cost her financial gain and reviews. For example, *Riot,* Brooks's reaction to the disturbances following the assassination of the Reverend Martin Luther King, Jr., was published by Broadside Press in 1969.

In poetry that celebrated both Chicago's Wall of Respect (for the Artists Workshop of the Organization of Black American Culture) and a Picasso statue in the city's Daley Plaza, Brooks promoted black pride rather than white hatred. She protested injustice by refocusing her writing, increasing her community participation, supporting the Black Arts movement, and encouraging young black artists. She became involved with the Blackstone Rangers, teaching poetry to this Chicago gang and editing their anthology *Jump Bad*. Named Poet Laureate of Illinois (1969) after the death of Carl Sandburg, she used that office to promote poetry, establishing the Annual Poet Laureate Award, a monetary reward for elementary and high school students. She also designated "Significant Illinois Poets"; conducted poetry workshops; visited prisons, drug centers, and hospitals; created mentoring programs; and attended poetry "slams" (readings). Previously afraid of flying, Brooks traveled to East Africa in 1971 to rediscover her black heritage.

Brooks read her poetry at the Library of Congress (1962) and taught at various institutions, including Columbia College in Chicago; the University of Chicago Leadership Program; the University of Wisconsin–Madison, where she served as Rennebohm Professor of English; and City College of New York, where she served as distinguished professor of the arts. After a mild heart attack in 1971, she gave up most teaching.

In addition to receiving honorary degrees from dozens of American universities, Brooks's many honors included two Guggenheim Fellowships (1946, 1947). She was the first African-American woman appointed to the American Academy of Arts and Letters (1976) and became National Endowment for the Humanities Jefferson Lecturer for Distinguished Intellectual Achievement in the Humanities (1994). "Eighty Gifts," a public reading in Chicago, celebrated her eightieth birthday. Brooks died of cancer in her home. Following a funeral service on 10 December 2000 at Rockefeller Memorial Chapel of the University of Chicago, Brooks was interred at Lincoln Cemetery.

While writing poetry about the lives of poor blacks in Chicago, Brooks addressed the universal themes of life and death. The first African American to win the Pulitzer Prize, this author of more than twenty books committed herself in the 1960s to being a model for black identity and solidarity. Poet, humanist, and honored American, a shy girl who transformed herself into a literate voice for poetry and African Americans, Brooks became "poet laureate of the black spirit" in America's post–Harlem Renaissance and civil rights eras.

★

Brooks's papers are collected at Bancroft Library, University of California, Berkeley. Her *Report from Part One* (1972) includes childhood reminiscences, interviews, photos, and poetry explication, while *Report from Part Two* (1996) continues her memoir. George E. Kent, *A Life of Gwendolyn Brooks* (1989), is a biography (up to 1978) based on personal association, interviews, records, and analysis of Brooks's poetry. D. H. Melhem, *Gwendolyn Brooks: Poetry and the Heroic Voice* (1987), is a discussion of her life built around her major works. The eighteen essays in Maria K. Mootry and Gary Smith, eds., *A Life Distilled: Gwendolyn Brooks, Her Poetry and Fiction* (1987), assess her work. An obituary is in the *New York Times* (3 Dec. 2000).

RACHEL SHOR

BROWN, Claude (*b.* 23 February 1937 in New York City; *d.* 2 February 2002 in New York City), author of *Manchild in the Promised Land* (1965) and lecturer, freelance journalist, and social critic writing for *Esquire, Life, The New York Times Magazine,* and *The Saturday Evening Post.*

Like many African Americans before and after them, in 1935 Henry Lee, a railroad worker, and Ossie (Brock) Brown, a domestic worker, migrated to New York City from the rural South in the hopes of finding a "promised land" where they and their four children would prosper. Trading South Carolina and their families for a tenement at 146th Street and Eighth Avenue in Harlem, the Browns worked in menial positions. Brown, the third child, was born in a community characterized by extreme poverty, crime, violence, and drugs.

Early on, the young Brown's playground was the street; he reported being an accomplished petty thief by the age of six, and he was eager to start school so his older friends could teach him to play hooky. By 1945 he had joined a gang, and by February 1946 he had been expelled from four schools. A year with his grandparents in South Carolina did nothing to curb his wildness, and in February 1948 he was sentenced to two years in the Wiltwyck School for emotionally troubled boys in Ulster County, New York. There he met Wiltwyck's cofounder, Eleanor Roosevelt, whom he thought a "crazy-acting old lady," though he later dedicated his book to her. Importantly, he also formed a lasting relationship with the school's director and psychologist, Dr. Ernest Papanek, which later proved seminal in the course of his life. When Brown was released in August

1950, his primary goal was to try the drug everyone was talking about: heroin. A violent physical reaction spared him the addiction that cost so many of his friends their lives in what he called a "plague" attacking Harlem and its residents. His luck did not prevent him from getting shot in the abdomen during an attempted burglary, and he soon was serving time at the Warwick School for Boys in Orange County, New York. He was released briefly, then reincarcerated until July 1953.

Brown's release from Warwick did not mark the end of his criminal activity, but it did mark the beginning of his transformation from petty thief and dealer to educated writer. Exposed while in detention to history, art, and music, in 1954 Brown began attending night school at Washington Irving High School, enrolling in academic courses that he had been steered away from previously. After his younger brother's incarceration, Brown enrolled in courses at Howard University in Washington, D.C., in 1959. During his first year at Howard, Papanek requested that Brown write an article on Harlem for *Dissent*, an established quarterly political magazine. An editor at Macmillan read the piece and offered Brown a $2,000 advance on a book about his youth. It took two years—during which time Brown studied writing under the writer and scholar Toni Morrison and others—but in 1963 he finally delivered a 1,500-page manuscript, only to have it shelved for a year until a new editor uncovered it. Published as *Manchild in the Promised Land* in 1965, the book was an instant success. It is the second best-selling book that Macmillan has ever published, after *Gone with the Wind*.

Brown's childhood and teenage years provided the basis of his autobiographical novel, which has proved an American classic. Over four million copies have been sold, even though at the time of its publication it generated a variety of extreme reactions. The novel introduced most white readers to the intimate reality of the life of impoverished urban African Americans for the first time with compassion and insight. Many African Americans wrote Brown to thank him "for writing our story," and he did it often in the language of the streets. This language resulted in censorship and even the firing of teachers who insisted on introducing the book to their students, though some academics were entranced by the linguistic flow and rhythm of the contemporary urban black vernacular. In *Manchild in the Promised Land*, Brown paints a portrait of a child confronted with tremendous obstacles. His father, frustrated by circumstances, is violent and abusive, while his mother is exhausted by work and the difficulties of raising children in a hostile environment.

Lauded for its realistic portrait of Harlem life, Brown's novel is, in part, so compelling because of the detailed descriptions and compassion with which he treats many of his subjects. Pimps, prostitutes, junkies, and thieves are not

Claude Brown testifying before the U.S. Senate, August 1966. © BETT-MANN/CORBIS

defined by what they do but by who they are, who their families are, and how they treat people. As Brown asserts, "you can't stop loving a woman because she's a whore." Nor is the book a portrait only of those engaged in illegal activity: Brown also documents the rituals and beliefs of families transplanted from the South, the storefront religion in which many sought solace, the attractiveness of Coptic and Muslim faiths to urban African Americans, the jazz scene of late 1950s New York, and the struggle to survive debilitating poverty by whatever means necessary. His curiosity about the differences between people and their experiences allows him to learn a great deal, which he then shares with his reader. And while he expresses anger at the wrongs done to people, black and white, never once does Brown apologize for the criminal antics that seem inevitable given the story he tells of his upbringing. This matter-of-fact approach, combined with the urban black vernacular, has the potential to undermine the exceptionality of his experiences for the reader unfamiliar with his world; indeed, this seems exactly what Brown intended—to downplay the potential for sensationalism in exchange for the possibility of understanding. The result, for Brown's 1960s reader, was a portrait of an urban black man and his world in stark contrast to the image of the culturally bereft Bigger Thomas of Richard Wright's popular *Native Son* (1940). This black man did not struggle toward thought, as many whites still held; indeed, he was already there. Remarked Brown in

1965, "I'm trying to show more than anything else the humanity of the Negro . . . Somebody has to stop problemizing and start humanizing the Negro."

For many liberal 1960s readers, Brown's perspective and insights were earth-shattering in representing urban African Americans. Brown was invited to testify as an expert witness before congressional inquiries, lecture to national organizations, and write for a number of popular presses.

Brown graduated from Howard with a B.A. degree in liberal arts the same year *Manchild* was published, and studied law first at Stanford University, then at Rutgers University. But he gave up legal studies when he discovered that he could earn more as a lecturer, leaving him time to pursue his writing and ongoing activism for the reform of the juvenile justice system. On 9 September 1961 Brown married Helen Jones Brown; they had one child and later divorced. In 1976 Brown published *Children of Ham*, which detailed the lives of young African Americans in New York who successfully kick heroin. In 2000 a Los Angeles–based theater company that works with youth dramatized *Manchild* for a contemporary audience, many of whom would have read the book as a mandatory text in high school or college. Two years later Brown died of a lung condition, leaving unfinished his manuscript on the crack epidemic that further devastated Harlem in the 1980s. Brown left behind his companion, Laura Higgins, with whom he had one child.

★

Claude Brown, "The Language of Soul," in *Mother Wit from the Laughing Barrel: Readings in the Interpretation of Afro-American Folklore* (1973), edited by Alan Dundes, provides insights on black language and usage. Joseph Keller, "Black Writing and the White Critic," *Negro American Literature Forum* 3, no. 4 (winter 1969): 103–110, surveys 1960s perspectives on black authors, including Brown. Obituaries are in the *New York Times* (6 Feb. 2002), *Detroit News* (7 Feb. 2002), *Time* (18 Feb. 2002), and *Jet* (25 Feb. 2002).

JENNIFER HARRIS

BROWN, Helen Gurley (*b.* 18 February 1922 in Green Forest, Arkansas), influential writer and magazine editor whose work in the 1960s celebrated the pleasures of being a single woman.

Brown was born to Arkansas schoolteachers Ira M. Gurley and Cleo Sisco. Her father, who had also served as a state legislator, died when she was ten years old. After her sister developed polio, her family's modest lifestyle became even more spartan. Brown attended Texas State College for Women but opted to move to Los Angeles in 1941 to start a secretarial career. She graduated from Woodbury Business College in 1942 and also took writing courses through

Helen Gurley Brown, January 1965. © BETTMANN/CORBIS

the University of California, Los Angeles, extension school. She worked as a secretary and advertising copywriter until 1962.

Brown describes having transformed herself into a confident, financially secure, and independent woman during this period. "I once had the world's worst case of acne. . . . I grew up in a small town. I didn't go to college. My family was, and is, desperately poor, and I have always helped support them." She married the motion picture executive David Brown on 25 September 1959. They had no children.

With her husband's encouragement, she wrote *Sex and the Single Girl* (1962). Based on her own experiences, the book celebrates the single lifestyle and provides honest advice on everything from sex to entertaining. It became an instant best-seller. Brown's aim was to remove the stigma placed on the single life and give women a guide for staying single "in superlative style." At the time, women were expected to desire marriage and children rather than the single life, and to be single in one's thirties was viewed as a particularly awful predicament.

Although happily married when she wrote her book, Brown touted her thirty-seven years of being single as qualifying her as an expert. She tackled topics from fashion and lifestyle to domestic life and career in 267 pages.

The book was considered sensational at the time. Its

candor, particularly regarding sex, generated condemnation. Who would have considered advocating relationships between married men and single women—even tips on spotting homosexual men—as appropriate? Although the 1960s were noted as a period when sexual freedoms were explored and celebrated, frank discussions of sexuality—especially women's sexuality—were still taboo early in the era. It was a popularly held belief that "nice girls" remained virgins until their wedding night. Brown knew better. The book filled a void in providing information to young women, causing *Sex and the Single Girl* to remain on best-seller lists into 1963. With the success of the book, Brown started writing a syndicated newspaper column, "Woman Alone."

Letters poured in from readers of *Sex and the Single Girl*. The Browns discussed how out of touch most contemporary women's magazines seemed and began concocting plans to start their own publication, devoted in great part to answering some of the questions readers continued to ask. Brown's publisher put her in contact with executives at the Hearst Corporation. The company, although unwilling to finance a new publication, decided to hire Brown. In 1965 she was named editor-in-chief of *Cosmopolitan*.

The magazine, originally founded in 1886 as a general interest publication, was one of the oldest magazines in the United States. In 1964 its sales were off by 20 percent, and Brown was brought in to revamp the magazine. During the process she invented the image of the ideal contemporary woman, the "*Cosmo* girl." Each magazine cover featured one of these *Cosmo* girls—beautiful, provocatively clad women oozing confidence and sexuality.

Much like her book, Brown focused the editorial content of *Cosmopolitan* on advice for single women. Brown envisioned her prototypical reader as a youthful career woman, interested in topics from fashion to—of course—sex. Each issue included information about how to have a successful career as well as how to attract and keep a man. This feminine approach to feminism stood in stark contrast to those advocating radical political change for women in the late 1960s and 1970s. The magazine's circulation began steadily improving.

Feminist activists opposed Brown and differed with her opinions, arguing vehemently that she was setting the women's movement back by failing to be more overtly feminist in the magazine's content. They went so far as to organize a sit-in in 1970 at the *Cosmopolitan* offices.

Brown says feminists objected to the magazine because "they feel that *Cosmo* panders to men, that we try to make life comfortable for men, and you can't do that and be a feminist. I say you absolutely can." Rather than vilifying men, Brown espoused the beliefs that feminists could like men and that being a sex object was fine. "If you're not a sex object, you're in trouble. You want to be known for your brain, but to have somebody want you sexually is the best thing there is. You can still look pretty and smell pretty and achieve."

Brown also endured criticism from other quarters, especially from parents and others concerned about the morality of messages the magazine was sending young women. She said the assumption has been made "that *Cosmo* and I are leading their daughters astray. We aren't. . . . We say do your own work, . . . use your talent, live up to your potential."

In reflection Brown considers her tenure at *Cosmopolitan* her greatest professional success. "The next biggest success is my first book, *Sex and the Single Girl*, from which *Cosmo* stemmed. There wouldn't be any new *Cosmo* if it hadn't been for that book." Brown supervised her final issue of *Cosmopolitan* in February 1997.

★

Autobiographical information about Brown can be found in *Sex and the Single Girl* (1962). See also "Bad Girl Helen Gurley Brown, the Original Cosmo Girl, Defies Every Label You Want to Pin on Her," *Psychology Today*, 27, no. 2 (Mar.–Apr. 1994): 22–26.

LINDA DAILEY PAULSON

BROWN, Hubert Gerold ("H. Rap") (*b.* 4 October 1943 in Baton Rouge, Louisiana), political activist and head of the Nonviolent Action Group (NAG), who in 1967 was elected chairman of the Student Nonviolent Coordinating Committee (SNCC), but became increasingly militant and was listed on the Federal Bureau of Investigation's Ten Most Wanted Fugitives list in 1970.

Brown was the youngest of three children of Eddie C. Brown and Thelma Warren. His father was on active duty in the U.S. military during World War II when Brown was born, and later went to work for Esso Standard Oil Company as a laborer. Brown acquired the nickname "Rap" as a youngster. He became politically involved as a high school student in 1960, when he led his class in a protest march to the campus of Howard University in Washington, D.C., an effort for which the entire high school class received a two-day suspension.

Brown enrolled at Southern University in Baton Rouge at age fifteen and came to odds with school administrators very quickly. During this time he gained notoriety as a civil rights organizer and later as a black militant, going by the name of H. Rap Brown. In 1962 he spent the summer in Washington, D.C., with a group of students who formed the core of the SNCC, among them Stokely Carmichael. During the summer of 1963 Brown spent a week in Cam-

H. Rap Brown, August 1967. ASSOCIATED PRESS AP

bridge, Maryland, where the Cambridge Revolt, a civil rights movement led by Gloria Richardson, was under way.

In 1964, when the SNCC initiated the Mississippi Summer Project, a voter-registration drive, Brown spent approximately four weeks in Holmes County. He attended the Democratic National Convention in Atlantic City later that summer in a show of support for the Mississippi Freedom Democratic Party (MFDP), which was based on a platform that challenged the Democratic party of Mississippi for failing to represent the state's African-American population. Brown was outraged when the Democrats refused to seat MFDP delegates at the convention. In the fall of 1964 he abandoned college and returned to Washington, D.C., to work at the Department of Agriculture.

With the civil rights movement spreading throughout the United States, Brown spent a great deal of time shuttling back and forth from Washington to SNCC national headquarters in Atlanta. He was elected in 1965 to serve as chairman of NAG, an organization closely affiliated with Howard University, and in that capacity headed delegations to see U.S. Attorney General Nicholas Katzenbach and President Lyndon B. Johnson. These meetings raised ire on both sides of the table and led columnist Drew Pearson to note Brown's "ill abuse" toward Johnson.

Brown worked with the United Planning Organization in Washington in 1964, and was later reassigned to work with a police–community relations program, where he proved particularly charismatic in improving dialogue between the two sides. Nevertheless, Brown believed that only so-called Uncle Tomism could motivate African Americans to serve in law enforcement. Annoyed by social programs that appeared to patronize minority interests, he withdrew from involvement with all such programs by the end of 1965. Highly antagonistic toward the white race, members of which he habitually called "honky," Brown made generous use of crude and obscene rhetoric in stating his case, and grew increasingly militant, threatening to "Burn America down." By 1968, he had attained the status of justice minister in the militant Black Panther Party.

Brown was arrested on a concealed weapons charge in 1966, in what was the first in an ongoing series of skirmishes with law-enforcement officers. He secured his own release and moved to Greene County, Alabama, to oversee the Greene County Project, a voter registration drive. In May 1967 he was elected chairman of SNCC, and at the end of July he revisited Cambridge, Maryland, where he spoke at an event orchestrated by Gloria Richardson. After his speech, for which he was accused of inciting a riot, FBI agents apprehended Brown at the airport in Washington, as he attempted to depart for New York City. Brown was then held in jail in Alexandria and subsequently charged with inciting a riot in Cambridge. During that incarceration he wrote the first of his "Letters from Jail." Among the thoughts expressed in these writings, Brown wrote, "I consider myself neither morally nor legally bound to obey laws which were made by a group of white 'lawmakers' who did not let my people be represented in making those laws."

Brown was released, but was arrested again for carrying a rifle en route to Baton Rouge from New York City. In February 1968 in New Orleans he began a hunger strike from his prison cell and penned a second "Letter from Jail" on 21 February, stating: "No slave should die a natural death. There is a point where caution ends and cowardice begins." A third letter, dated 2 March 1968, follows the same tone as the two prior letters and closes with "Yours in Revolution, H. Rap Brown." Brown spent a total of forty-three days in jail in New Orleans, and fasted the entire time. Eventually his bond was reduced from $100,000 to $30,000, but only to facilitate his extradition to Virginia, where he was held in an underground cell with daylight visible only from an overhead grate. This incident, in the wake of the assassination of Dr. Martin Luther King, Jr., served to indicate the extent to which state and federal governments feared a possible uprising among the African-American population.

Brown was convicted of armed robbery in 1973 and paroled in 1976. While in prison in the early 1970s, Brown embraced the religion of Islam, changing his name to Jamil Abdullah Al-Amin. Considerably subdued and reinvented as a Muslim cleric, he moved to Atlanta upon his release. There he operated the Community Store until he was arrested in April of 2000 and charged with murdering a police officer. Brown was convicted of the crime in 2002.

Brown married Lynne Doswell, a schoolteacher, on 3 May 1968. The marriage ended, and he took a second wife, Karima, with whom he fathered two children.

★

Brown's autobiography, *Die, Nigger, Die* (1969), was republished in 2002, with an updated foreword by Ekwueme Michael Thelwell. In 1993 Brown wrote a book of Islamic philosophy, *Revolution by the Book: The Rap Is Live.* See also Jack E. White, "Dividing Line: Rap Brown's Deadly Return: A Legendary Black Militant Is Accused of Murder," *Time* (3 Apr. 2000), and "H. Rap Brown Arrested, Charged With Killing Sheriff's Deputy in Atlanta," *Jet* (10 Apr. 2000).

GLORIA COOKSEY

BROWN, James Joe, Jr. (*b.* 3 May 1933 in Augusta, Georgia), highly influential singer and pioneer first of rhythm and blues and later of funk, known variously as the "Hardest-Working Man in Show Business," "Soul Brother Number 1," and the "Godfather of Soul."

Son of Joe Gardner Brown, a turpentine worker, and Susie Behlings, Brown was born in poverty. His parents split when he was four years old, and he lived for many years with his father in turpentine shacks. He learned to play the harmonica at age five. In Augusta, Brown danced for nickels for servicemen from nearby Fort Gordon and learned the blues from the veteran composer and singer Tampa Red. He also learned shouting technique at Pentecostal churches. Despite positive influences, Brown took up petty theft and was arrested and sentenced to eight to sixteen years in jail. He became so adept at singing and dancing in prison that he was nicknamed Music Box. Released on parole at nineteen, he joined a gospel group headed by Bobby Byrd. He married Velma Warren on 19 June 1953.

Despite his religious affiliation, Brown was drawn to secular music. He studied the styles of popular black artists, especially Hank Ballard and the Midnighters. Brown formed a band called the Flames and recorded "Please, Please, Please," with King Records in 1956. The raw emotion and shouting style of the song made it a million-seller. Brown and the Flames began a virtually constant tour, doing as many as 350 one-night stands a year. Eventually this schedule, along with the overwhelming flow of his shows, which invariably ended with him covered with a cape after

James Brown perfoming at the March Against Fear rally at Tugaloo University, 1966. FLIP SCHULKE/CORBIS

an exhausting, sweaty rendition of hits, won him the sobriquet "Hardest-Working Man in Show Business." Brown allegedly lost seven pounds during each performance.

As the 1960s opened Brown had a strong collection of hits and a well-honed band, now known as the Famous Flames. He lobbied the King Records management to record him live at the legendary Apollo Theater in New York, and when they declined, he paid for the recording himself. The resulting 1963 album, *Live at the Apollo,* became a classic of live performance; it brought him to the attention of the white audience and still sells well. To advance his career Brown moved to New York City, signed a contract with Smash Records, and released another classic, "Out of Sight," in the summer of 1964.

As Brown contended in his autobiography, *James Brown: The Godfather of Soul,* he and his band now established "all kinds of rhythms at once," making for spellbinding dance music. A reconstituted James Brown Revue became a tightly knit ensemble anchored by a powerful horn section headed by Fred Wesley and the incomparable

Maceo Parker. As "Out of Sight" roared up the charts, young whites created a crossover market for Brown. His song lyrics entered popular slang, and his music was inescapable. Although contract disputes with King temporarily hampered his recording career, Brown made numerous television appearances. He appeared in the TAMI International Show, taped in Santa Monica in November 1964 and released a few months later. Though the lineup featured Chuck Berry, the Supremes, the Rolling Stones, Smokey Robinson and the Miracles, Lesley Gore, and Marvin Gaye, Brown dominated the show.

Now commanding 10 percent royalties and enjoying ever-greater artistic freedom, Brown released a series of archetypal songs including "Papa's Got a Brand New Bag" (July 1965), "I Got You (I Feel Good)" (November 1965), "Prisoner of Love" (March 1966), "It's a Man's Man's Man's World" (March 1966), and "Don't Be a Drop Out" (October 1966). He toured England and the United States incessantly and released more live albums.

Brown had a polyvalent political appeal. Black militants endorsed him because of his strong, masculine roots music. They were less enthusiastic about his association with mainstream leaders and even taunted him as an Uncle Tom. Brown went to Vietnam to entertain U.S. troops, and upon his return responded with another paradigmatic song, "(Say It Loud) I'm Black and I'm Proud" (August 1968).

National political figures sought Brown's endorsement. He was invited to the White House in 1968 and, when summoned to Vice President Hubert Humphrey's table, he declined, but suggested they meet halfway across the room, an offer Humphrey accepted. Brown later endorsed Humphrey's presidential bid. Also in 1968, when Dr. Martin Luther King, Jr., was assassinated, Boston authorities pleaded with Brown to go forward with a planned performance as a means of helping keep the streets quiet. Brown put on the show before a capacity crowd, and his presence that night helped make Boston one of the few major American cities that did not erupt with rioting and looting following the assassination. The tape of this extraordinary show, in which Brown expressed his grief for the slain leader, became an underground classic. Brown angered many militants and others by performing at Richard Nixon's inaugural in January 1969; refusing to be pigeonholed, he later endorsed Nixon in the latter's successful 1972 presidential reelection bid.

Now known as the "Godfather of Soul" and "Soul Brother Number One," Brown began extending the length of his songs, creating dance classics with powerful rhythmic grooves, a style known as *funk*, which he virtually invented. Released on King and on Polydor Records, examples include "Give It Up or Turn It a Loose" (January 1969), "(Get Up, I Feel Like Being a) Sex Machine" (July 1970), and "Super Bad" (October 1970). Brown accumulated ninety-four Top 100 *Billboard* singles and recorded over 800

different songs on his many albums, all done in the midst of a grueling touring schedule. Brown's touring band became a research university for young black musicians, the most prominent being William "Bootsy" Collins. Parker and Wesley later propelled the music of Prince in the 1980s before starting solo careers of their own.

Brown's first marriage ended in divorce in 1968, and later that year Brown married a second wife, Deirdre. That marriage also ended in divorce, and in September 1984 Brown married Adrienne Lois Rodriguez, a hairstylist and makeup artist. In addition to a deceased son from his first marriage, Brown has six children.

Brown continued to make influential dance tracks throughout the 1970s and was able to survive the disco revolution by his contributions to movie soundtracks, most notably "Living in America" from *Rocky IV* (1985). As rap and hip-hop began to dominate black music in the 1980s, Brown joined hip-hop pioneer Afrika Bambaataa for a duet in 1983. He was inducted into the Rock and Roll Hall of Fame in 1986. Increasingly Brown was drawn into drugs and by 1990 returned to prison for several years after an arrest for possession of PCP ("angel dust"). Nevertheless, his music continues to appeal across the generations and is still a staple of radio selections.

★

Biographical information about Brown is in his autobiography, *James Brown: The Godfather of Soul* (1990). A biographical profile of Brown is in *St. James Encyclopedia of Popular Culture* (2000). For additional information, see Philip Gourevitch, "Mr. Brown: On the Road with His Bad Self," *New Yorker* (29 July 2002).

GRAHAM RUSSELL HODGES

BROWN, James Nathaniel ("Jim") (*b.* 17 February 1936 in Saint Simons Island, Georgia), superbly talented pro football star who dominated his sport as few, if any, have, while speaking out and acting on behalf of America's black minority.

Brown grew up in relative isolation on Saint Simons Island, just off Brunswick, Georgia. Early on, he was essentially raised by his great-grandmother. His father, Swinton Brown, a small-time boxer and laborer, deserted the family soon after Brown's birth. His mother, Theresa Brown, left Brown in his great-grandmother's care and went north to work as a domestic in Manhasset, New York. She sent for Brown when he was seven years old. The transition from rural southern poverty to northern suburban affluence was startling. (The Browns themselves were not affluent, but they lived with the well-to-do family for whom Brown's mother worked.) Brown quickly became involved in athletics and excelled at every sport he tried. While completing his tenure at Manhasset High School, from which he graduated in 1953, Brown received nearly fifty football

Jim Brown. ASSOCIATED PRESS AP

scholarship offers from various big-time schools, but a local lawyer, Ken Molloy, wanted Brown to attend his alma mater, Syracuse University. Syracuse was less than enthusiastic about Brown, and he matriculated there in 1953 only after Molloy and Manhasset businessmen, along with friends and neighbors, paid Brown's tuition—something that would be a violation of NCAA rules today but was legal then.

Brown, because he was the only African American and non-scholarship athlete, was virtually ignored by his freshman team coaches. However, his athletic ability was simply too spectacular to overlook. By his sophomore season, he saw considerable playing time. He blossomed as a junior and senior, earning unanimous All-America halfback honors in 1956, his final season; in an eight-game schedule (Syracuse won seven), Brown gained 986 yards. His 6.2 yards-per-carry average was the nation's best. But football was not Brown's only sport. His size (six feet, two inches tall and 218 pounds—he later added ten pounds as a pro) and speed made him what some of the sport's most astute observers call "the greatest lacrosse player ever." He also was stellar in baseball, basketball, and track and field. It has been said that had he trained for it, he could have become the world's heavyweight boxing champion.

When Brown graduated from Syracuse with a B.A. in physical education in 1957, he led the degree recipients in the graduation parade dressed in his Army ROTC uniform. A bona-fide All-America in college, Brown reached superstardom as a professional. During and after his pro football career, he was generally conceded to be the best-ever player—regardless of position.

The Cleveland Browns of the National Football League (NFL) took Brown as their first-round draft choice for the 1957 season. He was an immediate sensation, leading the league in rushing (942 yards) and touchdowns (19). Brown was so fast and powerful, defensive back Don Burroughs once remarked, "Every time I tackle him it feels like there's a dice game going on in my mouth." For the remainder of his brilliant nine-year career, Brown led the league *and* rushed for 1,000 or more yards all but once. In 1958 he set an NFL record by gaining 1,527 yards—eclipsing Steve Van Buren's old mark by 381 yards. That same year, he again led the NFL in rushing and touchdowns—14. In 1959 Brown was again a 1,000-yard rusher (1,329 and 14 touchdowns). By 1960, after leading the league in rushing yards and touchdowns in each of his first three seasons, Brown was acknowledged as the NFL's brightest star. In 1960 and 1961 he produced two more 1,000-yard seasons—1,257 and 1,408 respectively. He missed the 1,000-yard milestone, a benchmark for all great runners, in 1962—but just barely, with 996 yards. It later came out that Brown played all season with an injured wrist that prevented him from using his lethal stiff-arm to ward off would-be tacklers. It was the only season in which he did not lead the NFL in rushing.

As a team the Browns were winning games but not championships. Critics felt that Paul Brown, the team's founding coach, had lost his magic touch. His tactics and rigid rules, which had won so many championships in the 1950s, were no longer working. The game, they said, had passed him by. In 1962 a new owner, Art Modell, took over the team. Perhaps to ingratiate himself with the players, Modell listened to their complaints about the coach. During a Cleveland newspaper strike in 1962–1963—his critics say the timing was chosen to avoid adverse publicity—Modell fired the legendary Paul Brown. Jim Brown, who was said to favor a more wide-open offense (Paul Brown called every play), was accused by some of orchestrating the future Pro Football Hall of Fame coach's ouster. The star runner denied influencing Modell's decision both at the time and later.

Under new coach Blanton Collier, Brown and the Browns responded in 1963. Given the ball on pitch-outs, tosses, and power sweeps—outside running plays designed to take advantage of his sprinter's speed—the healthy halfback responded by gaining over a mile and setting an NFL rushing record: 1,863 yards at a 6.4-yard average. The team finished in second place. In 1964 the whole package came together. The Browns won the NFL championship in convincing style, 27–0, over the Baltimore (now Indianapolis) Colts. Brown's league-leading rushing total was 1,446 yards. He led Cleveland to the championship game the next season, too, but Vince Lombardi's Green Bay Packers defeated them, 23–12.

Two off-field activities took much of Brown's time in the 1960s—films and minority business concerns. In 1964 Brown had a role in the feature film *Rio Concho*. He was filming *The Dirty Dozen* in England in the summer of 1966 when filming delays prevented him from reporting to the Browns' training camp. At the top of his game, Brown simply walked away from football. Unlike the many stars who linger a year or two too long, Brown undoubtedly could have played outstanding football for several more years. He said at the time, "I had played all the football I wanted to and was ready to move on." Brown made over twenty-five feature films, including *100 Rifles* and *Ice Station Zebra*, as well as blaxploitation films.

Having worked in public relations for Pepsi-Cola during his playing days, Brown founded the Black Economic Union (BEU) in 1966 in an effort to foster black-owned enterprise. Four hundred companies got their start with help from the BEU.

Brown's outspokenness earned him a reputation as a militant and probably cost him endorsement dollars as

companies chose not to be associated with him. He explained his attitude this way: "It's a matter of choosing between total manhood and freedom and your economic welfare and prosperity. I have made the choice."

In June 1958 Brown and Sue Jones were married. The couple had three children and divorced in 1972. After retiring from the NFL, Brown was involved in several assault incidents, usually involving women. One such incident involved his second wife, Monique Gunthrop, whom he married in June 1999. Rather than accept a sentence that included forty hours of community service picking up trash, Brown went to jail for six months in 2002. He argued, perhaps legitimately, that his longtime work with Amer-I-Can, an organization that deals with at-risk youth and "gangbangers," far exceeded forty hours.

Though Brown has been outspoken, complex, and controversial, his athletic brilliance remains unchallenged—he still holds a half-dozen NFL records. Brown is a member of the college football, pro football, and lacrosse halls of fame—the only athlete to be inducted into all three institutions.

★

The most insightful of Brown's several autobiographies is *Out of Bounds* (1989), written with Steve Delshon; another, written with Myron Cope, is *Off My Chest* (1964). A different perspective is offered in James Toback, *Jim: The Author's Self-Centered Memoir on the Great Jim Brown* (1971). Larry Klein, *Jim Brown: The Running Back* (1965), and Stan Isaacs, *Jim Brown: The Golden Year of 1964* (1970), provide further information.

JIM CAMPBELL

BROWNE, Malcolm Wilde (*b.* 17 April 1931 in New York City), Pulitzer Prize–winning journalist who made his mark in the 1960s by covering South America and Southeast Asia, specifically Vietnam.

Browne is the son of Douglas Granzow Browne, an architect, and Dorothy Rutledge Wilde, a Quaker pacifist, and grew up in Greenwich Village in New York City. Browne attended Swarthmore College from 1948 to 1950 and New York University from 1950 to 1951. He was a laboratory chemist for five years before stumbling into journalism when, as an enlisted GI in postwar Korea, he walked into an army press-relations office that sought someone who could write and type. From 1956 to 1958 he worked in Korea as a U.S. Army correspondent for the *Pacific Stars and Stripes*. Disliking the olive drab uniform he had to wear, Browne bought all the red socks on sale at the 8th Army post exchange in Korea. He has worn red socks ever since.

After completing his enlistment in Korea, Browne returned to New York, where he became the editor of the

Middletown Daily Record (1958–1960). He then became an Associated Press (AP) reporter, first in Baltimore and then as Vietnam correspondent from 1961 to 1965. He continued to report on Vietnam from 1965 to 1966 for the American Broadcasting Company (ABC), and then as a freelance writer from 1966 to 1968. Browne was one of the first reporters in the early 1960s, along with David Halberstam of the *New York Times* and Neil Sheehan and Peter Arnett of United Press International (UPI), to question U.S. involvement in Vietnam under the administration of President John F. Kennedy. Browne was one of the first American journalists to settle in Saigon when U.S. involvement in Vietnam was at an "advisory" level. And as AP bureau chief, Browne saw firsthand the corrupt South Vietnamese government, which consisted of President Ngo Dinh Diem, his brother, and his brother's wife Madame Nhu, who was known as the "Dragon Lady."

In 1961 while at Bien Hoa, the headquarters of the South Vietnamese Air Force, Browne reported that U.S. Air Force pilots were serving in other than an advisory capacity. He photographed U.S. pilots being used for combat duty, an activity the Kennedy administration denied was taking place. In his memoir *Muddy Boots and Red Socks: A Reporter's Life* (1993), Browne recounts glancing "into the cockpits of some taxiing T-28 two-seat fighter planes—and [seeing] Caucasians behind the controls. Here, then, was visual proof. They were actively fighting, not just advising." However, Browne was unable to photograph this particular incident, as U.S. and South Vietnamese soldiers had confiscated his camera.

Two years later Browne photographed the suicide by burning of a Buddhist monk in protest of the corrupt government of South Vietnam. This photo won Browne the World Press Photo Contest in 1963, and China used the photo as propaganda against U.S. involvement in the region. The publicity surrounding the photo was also a factor in ending the Kennedy administration's support of Diem's government.

In 1964 Browne's dispatches from Vietnam won a Pulitzer Prize for international reporting. His stories on Vietnam were hidden in old newspapers and smuggled out by travelers who were leaving the region. Much of Browne's reporting on Vietnam can be found in *Reporting Vietnam: American Journalism, 1959–1969* (part one, 1998).

During the final years of the 1960s, Browne reported for the *New York Times* from Buenos Aires, Argentina; his reports covered topics such as the newly elected Marxist government of Chile. Other stories included those on Ernesto "Che" Guevara and Fidel Castro of Cuba, and South American guerrilla groups. Browne also wrote about Latin America being a haven to war criminals from World War II, and included reports on the government-sanctioned attacks on Argentina's Jewish communities. Browne's stint

Malcolm Browne, May 1964. ASSOCIATED PRESS AP

in South America was the longest assignment of his reporting career.

Browne's ease with languages, including French, German, Spanish, Russian, Japanese, and Vietnamese, helped in his reporting of foreign affairs. He won many awards in the 1960s for his news coverage of Southeast Asia and Latin America. As well as the Pulitzer Prize and World Press Photo Award, in 1964 he won the Overseas Press Club Award, the Sigma Delta Chi Award, and the Associated Press Managing Editors Award. In 1966 he received the Edward R. Murrow Memorial Fellowship from the Council on Foreign Relations.

In the first half of the 1970s Browne covered other hot spots for the *New York Times*. He was correspondent for the Pakistan-Iran-Afghanistan region from 1971 to 1972, and correspondent for Indochina from 1972 to 1973. Then he became correspondent in Belgrade, Yugoslavia. He returned to Saigon in 1975 as bureau chief for the *Times*. Browne was one of the last American journalists to leave Saigon as it fell to North Vietnam, and reported on Saigon's frantic last days as South Vietnamese were trying to evacuate the city.

Browne returned to the United States in 1977 and became a science correspondent for the *Times*. In 1981 he left the paper to work as senior editor for *Discover Magazine,* before returning to the *Times* in 1985 as a science writer until his retirement in 2000. He had one last stint as foreign correspondent when he covered the Persian Gulf War in 1991 for the *New York Times.* From 1995 to 1996 Browne served as McGraw Professor of Writing at Princeton University, in New Jersey.

Browne married his third wife, Huynh thi Le Lieu, on 18 July 1966. He has two children, one each from his previous two marriages. In addition to his autobiography, Browne published *The New Face of War* in 1965. His work on Vietnam can be found in *Reporting Vietnam: American Journalism 1969–1975* (part two, 1998).

★

Browne's autobiography is *Muddy Boots and Red Socks: A Reporter's Life* (1993). Articles about Browne and his career include Scott Sherman, "David Halberstam, Malcolm Browne: Seeing the War," *Columbia Journalism Review* 40, no. 4 (Nov./Dec. 2001): 56.

MARGALIT SUSSER

BRUBECK, David Warren ("Dave") (*b.* 6 December 1920 in Concord, California), pianist and composer who helped popularize "cool" jazz among white audiences in the 1950s and 1960s.

Brubeck was the youngest of three sons born to Howard "Pete" Brubeck, a cattle wrangler and championship roper, and Elizabeth Ivey, a pianist and piano teacher. Brubeck played the piano from the age of four. By the time he was twelve, the family moved from the San Francisco suburb of Concord to a remote ranch managed by his father outside Ione, California.

Brubeck majored in veterinary medicine his first year at College of the Pacific in Stockton, California, but soon switched to music. He practiced, and experimented with, the time signatures of swing music on an old upright piano in a basement flat he and his buddies called the "Bomb Shelter." Brubeck met Iola Marie Whitlock, a drama major, and on 21 September 1942—several weeks after Brubeck graduated and enlisted in the army—he and Iola married. The couple eventually had six children.

For two years in the army, Brubeck served band duty at Riverside's Camp Haan. In 1944 he formed the Wolf Pack, an integrated army band, while serving in the Third Army under General George Patton in Germany. After his discharge in 1946 he studied counterpoint and polytonality under Darius Milhaud at Mills College in Oakland, California.

Several years of struggle followed, until 1949, when San Francisco disc jockey Jimmy Lyons began broadcasting recordings by Brubeck's group, then called the Dave Brubeck Trio. Also in 1949, fans polled in *Down Beat* and *Metronome* voted the Dave Brubeck Trio the best new instru-

Dave Brubeck. AP/WIDE WORLD PHOTOS

mental group of the year. After adding alto saxophonist Paul Desmond to the mix, the new Dave Brubeck Quartet's first album on Columbia, *Jazz Goes to College,* became one of the ten top-selling albums of 1954, and later that year Brubeck appeared on the cover of *Time* magazine.

The U.S. State Department sent the quartet to eighteen countries in Europe and the Middle East in 1958, a tour that gave Brubeck the idea of recording an album with unusual time signatures. Over the strong objections of Columbia's marketing department, *Time Out,* featuring Brubeck's "Blue Rondo a La Turk" in 9/8 time and Desmond's "Take Five" in 5/4 tempo, was produced in 1959. It would go on to sell one million copies.

At the start of the 1960s Brubeck was America's biggest-selling jazz musician. He persuaded Columbia Records president Goddard Lieberson to release a single of "Take Five" and "Blue Rondo" for radio and jukebox play. Conscious of how easily a listener might lose his way in a quintuple meter, Brubeck played a constant vamp figure, improvising accompaniment throughout "Take Five." Desmond then tamed the 5/4 time signature with a sweet sound listeners likened to the taste of a dry martini. Critics maintained that jazz could not be performed with such esoteric meters, but fans disagreed, pushing the single in 1961 to the top of the charts and making it the first jazz single to become a gold record.

"Creating a hit with 'Take Five,'" Brubeck admitted, "was the furthest thing from any of our minds. It was never supposed to be a hit. It was supposed to be a Joe Morello . . . drum solo, but the catchy melody and the insistent rhythm, I guess, is what got them." The 1960s seemed ready for innovation in jazz, he thought, and for a relaxation of previous distinctions between purely popular music and jazz improvisation. "In other countries folk music was not limited to 4/4," he said, "and I sensed that was now true in America too."

The Dave Brubeck Quartet remained the most popular jazz group of the sixties, topping the *Down Beat* readers' polls in 1962, 1963, 1964, and 1965, as well as *Billboard*'s disc jockey poll in 1962 and its reader's polls in 1965 and 1966. Throughout the period the quartet continued recording, and played up to 250 shows a year. Brubeck communicated with college-age audiences, the jazz historian Stanley Crouch suggested, "because of his individual, improvisational style. When you hear him playing the piano, you know that's Dave Brubeck." Ted Gioia, an authority on West Coast jazz, maintained that 1960s youth culture was ready to embrace a style they saw as "quintessentially American, upbeat, all-embracing and forward-looking."

The quartet's enthusiastically received concert at Carnegie Hall in February 1963 demonstrated the fact that people of all ages were turning on to Brubeck's music. *Jazz Impressions of New York* (1964) sold well and widely and was followed by the quartet's appearance in the Lincoln Center's "Great Performers" series of April 1966. In December 1967, after an exultant European tour, the Dave Brubeck Quartet was officially disbanded because its leader had wearied of the grueling schedule and wanted to spend more time with Iola and their six children. The pause also gave him time to explore his spiritual sensitivities. *The Light in the Wilderness* was a sixty-three-minute oratorio, based on the teachings and temptations of Christ, for which Iola provided the libretto. In March 1969 the Cincinnati Symphony premiered the piece, which the Columbia Broadcasting System (CBS) television network broadcast on Easter morning.

The Gates of Justice, a jazz cantata that musically linked the Old Testament with the speeches of Martin Luther King, Jr., also debuted in 1969. A *Fugal Fanfare,* commissioned by the Cincinnati Symphony on its seventy-fifth anniversary, was first performed 27 January 1970. Brubeck dedicated *Truth Is Fallen,* scored for orchestra, chorus, and rock band, to the students killed at Kent State and Jackson State universities in 1970. In the 1970s and 1980s Brubeck was back on the road, performing and recording his classical and jazz pieces with a new group. Four of his children often joined the tour: Darius on electronic keyboard, Chris on electric bass and trombone, Danny on drums, and Matthew on cello.

Brubeck produced more than 500 jazz and classical pieces, entertained seven U.S. presidents, and played for Pope John Paul II. Brubeck's status as a national treasure was confirmed in 1994 when he was awarded the National Medal of Arts. By then he had helped build a worldwide following for jazz. Brubeck found his sixty-year climb to the jazz heights an exercise in surprising self-discovery. "In jazz you perform as you compose," he told an interviewer; this made the music "a place to go beyond myself." In moments of inspiration, "I'm the happiest guy in the world," he said, because "when it's all working there's nothing better in this world."

★

Many of Brubeck's manuscripts and photographs, along with his correspondence, both business and personal, are held in the Dave Brubeck Institute for Jazz Studies at the University of the Pacific, Stockton, California. A biography is Fred M. Hall, *It's About Time: The Dave Brubeck Story* (1996), which includes a discography through the summer of 1997. Brubeck's contribution to easing cold war tensions is analyzed in Ilse Storb and Klaus-Gotthard Fischer, *Dave Brubeck: Improvisations and Compositions, The Idea of Cultural Exchange* (1994). Brubeck discusses his life and art with Leonard Lyons in *The Great Pianists: Speaking of Their Lives and Music* (1983), and with Hedrick Smith in *Rediscovering Dave Brubeck,* produced by South Carolina Educational Television in 2001 and aired on the Public Broadcasting System.

BRUCE J. EVENSEN

BRUCE, David Kirkpatrick Este (*b.* 12 February 1898 in Baltimore, Maryland; *d.* 5 December 1977 in Washington, D.C.), prominent United States diplomat who served from 1961 to 1969 as ambassador to Great Britain and headed the U.S. delegation to the Paris peace talks on Vietnam from 1970 to 1971.

Bruce was the fourth and youngest son of William Cabell Bruce, a Virginia plantation owner and lawyer, and Louise Este Fisher, daughter of a socially prominent Baltimore lawyer. He was educated at the private Gilman Country School in Baltimore before pursuing undergraduate studies at Princeton University from 1915 to 1917. From 1917 to 1919 he served in the American Expeditionary Force, the army the United States raised to participate in the European conflict after entering World War I, an experience that precipitated his enduring fascination with Europe. After returning from the war, at parental insistence he studied law at the University of Virginia (1919–1920) and the University of Maryland (1920–1921), passing the Maryland bar examination in November 1921. Tall, handsome, and cultivated, in 1926 Bruce married wealthy heiress Ailsa Mellon, whom he divorced in 1945 to marry Evangeline

David Bruce, March 1961. © BETTMANN/CORBIS

Bell. He had one daughter, Audrey, with his first wife, and three children, Alexandra (Sasha), David Surtees, and Nicholas Cabell, with his second.

In 1939 the outbreak of war in Europe launched Bruce on a career of public service that, with occasional short breaks, continued until two years before his death. He was elected to the Virginia House of Delegates in 1939, where he served until 1942. As head of the Economic Cooperation Administration in Paris (1948–1949) and U.S. ambassador to France (1949–1952), he was heavily involved in Europe's postwar reconstruction, subsequently serving as undersecretary of state (1952–1953), U.S. representative to the nascent European Coal and Steel Community (1953–1954), and U.S. ambassador to West Germany (1957–1959).

The fervently pro-Allied Bruce had spent the 1940 blitz in London heading the American Red Cross War Mission, and his dispatches home helped to develop American support for Britain. In 1941 he had begun a four-year spell directing the London mission of the Office of Strategic Services, where he worked closely with the British Special Operations Executive and also met his half-British second wife. Bruce's wartime experiences, during which he gathered a vast array of influential British friends, led many Britons to consider him an "honorary Englishman." Bruce, a lifelong Democrat whose father served a term as senator for Maryland, had hoped that his party's victory in 1960 would bring his appointment as secretary of state. Instead, in 1961 President John F. Kennedy offered him the London

embassy, where Bruce remained until 1969, that post's longest-serving incumbent.

The Bruces quickly became fixtures on the London social scene, entertaining the British royal family and the political and cultural elite, together with such distinguished visitors as first lady Jacqueline Kennedy and her sister, Lee Radziwill, with Evangeline's legendary elegance and stylish aplomb. Privy to many details of the 1963 Profumo affair, when Britain's secretary of state for war, John Profumo, resigned over his relationship with a call girl, Bruce attracted FBI criticism for failing to give the Kennedy administration sufficient warning of the developing scandal, whose ramifications some suspected might involve the American president. In 1963 Bruce found particularly depressing the untimely deaths of two men he greatly admired, President Kennedy, who was assassinated, and Philip Graham, the publisher of the *Washington Post*, who committed suicide. Personal tragedy struck closer to home in 1967, when Audrey Currier, his elder daughter, and her husband died in a Caribbean airplane crash.

Both Kennedy and his successor, Lyndon B. Johnson, respected and valued Bruce's literate, acutely analytical dispatches as ambassador. Although somewhat closer to Britain's Conservative Party politicians, Bruce was on sufficiently good terms with their socialist counterparts to negotiate a smooth transition without difficulty when the Labour Party took power in 1964. Bruce had to alleviate the tensions generated by Kennedy's sudden cancellation in December 1962 of the Skybolt missile program, which British leaders had anticipated using to deploy their own nuclear warheads, and to mediate the often strained relationship between Johnson and Labour's Harold Wilson, Britain's prime minister from 1964 to 1970.

When necessary, Bruce had the confidence to act independently. Disturbed by British street protests against the American decision to blockade Cuba during the October 1962 missile crisis, without obtaining State Department authorization Bruce released to the British press intelligence photographs of Soviet missile installations on Cuba. More sympathetic to British imperialism than many Americans, Bruce warned that Britain should not be pressured to decolonize her remaining empire too quickly, and regretted Wilson's 1968 decision to withdraw British military forces east of Suez, which he considered strategically detrimental to the United States as well as Britain.

Despite his Anglophile outlook, Bruce feared that British leaders failed to realize their country was living well beyond its means and frequently predicted economic collapse. His gloomy dispatches on Britain's economic problems became notorious within the U.S. State Department. Much influenced by his lengthy friendship with Jean Monnet, the "father of the Common Market," Bruce was a committed advocate of postwar European integration. He therefore welcomed Britain's 1961 decision to apply for membership in the European Economic Community, which he hoped might ultimately also promote closer links between the United States and Europe, and deplored French president Charles de Gaulle's veto of the British request.

Dealings between Wilson and Johnson became particularly acerbic over growing American involvement in Vietnam, an issue that became increasingly prominent in Anglo-American relations. Dubious as to the wisdom of American backing of Vietnam, Laos, and Cambodia, initially Bruce nonetheless felt that his country should keep its pledged faith to these states. He privately questioned the accuracy of reports of the August 1964 Tonkin Gulf Incident, but in public he loyally supported and defended his country's position. Massive popular protests against the Vietnam War, particularly the violent demonstrations in which both the London embassy and his Georgetown home became targets, and such Vietnam-related episodes as the defacement of the British memorial to Kennedy at Runnymede repelled a man who valued decorum and restraint. Bruce's growing private fears that American victory was unattainable and concern over the war's damaging domestic and international impact on the United States led him to favor a negotiated settlement. As ambassador Bruce supported and sought to facilitate various proposals intended to accomplish this. The most prominent among them was a peace effort devised in 1967 by Wilson in collaboration with the visiting Soviet premier, Aleksei Kosygin, but aborted in part by Johnson's intransigent refusal to extend a bombing pause then in effect. Predictably, Bruce welcomed Johnson's March 1968 decision to seek peace and American withdrawal.

After leaving the embassy, the Bruces broke with diplomatic convention by leasing a stylish London flat, from which Evangeline Bruce conducted a well-publicized feud with Lee Annenberg, her successor as ambassador's wife in the American embassy. From 1970 to 1971 Bruce headed the American delegation at the largely nonsubstantive Paris peace talks on Vietnam, until ill health and frustration brought about his resignation. Bruce's penultimate assignment was as first chief of the United States Liaison Office to the People's Republic of China (1973–1974), a largely symbolic position in which his seniority, ability, and charm facilitated a crucial stage in the reopening of Sino-American relations. He retired after one last stint as United States ambassador to NATO (1974–1976). In 1977 Bruce died of heart failure in Washington, D.C., and was buried at Oak Hill Cemetery in Maryland. Early in 1978 the British held an official memorial service in Westminster Abbey for him, the first American since Kennedy so honored.

Elegant, cultivated, witty, discreet, and able, a consummate insider blessed with immense stamina, Bruce embodied both the virtues and limitations of the U.S. diplomatic establishment that dominated the making of his country's mid-twentieth-century foreign policy. His years in London coincided with the Vietnam-generated loss of confidence in that elite's foreign policy tradition and to a broader loss of civility and restraint he found deplorable.

★

Bruce's personal papers are held by the Virginia Historical Society, Richmond, Virginia. The originals of his diaries, together with numerous official cables and other correspondence, are in National Archives II, College Park, Maryland; many of his official communications are also published in the series *Foreign Relations of the United States*. Archival materials on his years in London are in the British Foreign Office Files on the United States in the Public Records Office, Kew, United Kingdom. The only full biography is Nelson D. Lankford, *The Last American Aristocrat: The Biography of Ambassador David K. E. Bruce* (1996). Philip M. Kaiser, *Journeying Far and Wide: A Political and Diplomatic Memoir* (1992), portrays Bruce as ambassador in London. Bruce's assignments London and at the Paris peace negotiations are covered in the articles on him in Nelson Lichtenstein, ed., *Political Profiles: The Kennedy Years* (1976), and *Political Profiles: The Johnson Years* (1976); and Eleanora Schoenebaum, ed., *Political Profiles: The Nixon/Ford Years* (1979). A tribute to Bruce is in the *Century Association Yearbook 1978*. Obituaries are in the *New York Times* and *Washington Post* (both 6 Dec. 1977). Bruce recorded oral history interviews for the John F. Kennedy Presidential Library, Boston, Massachusetts, and the Lyndon B. Johnson Presidential Library, Austin, Texas.

PRISCILLA ROBERTS

BRUCE, Lenny (*b.* 13 October 1925 in Mineola, New York; *d.* 3 August 1966 in Los Angeles, California), innovative comedian who served as catalyst for an emerging counterculture by challenging obscenity laws and probing cultural pieties. He paved the way for a new kind of comedy.

Possessed by a fierce sense of moral outrage, Bruce, born Leonard Alfred Schneider, developed an arsenal of caustic social commentary. He was the only child of an odd couple. His mother, Sadie Kitchenburg, later Sally Marr, preferred show business to child nurture, while his father, Myron "Mickie" Schneider, a podiatrist, provided the principal parenting. Only five when his parents parted, Bruce led a nomadic life. The only Jew in his class in Bellmore, Long Island, a predominantly German community, he dropped out of high school. Bereft of moorings, Bruce went to sea, joining the navy in 1942 and securing a discharge four years later by feigning homosexuality.

Upon liberation, between stints at sea working as a deckhand, Bruce did odd jobs and briefly studied acting at the Geller Dramatic Workshop in Los Angeles. Starting as a comic in Brooklyn, New York, he introduced strip acts and impersonated movie stars. Winning a contest on Arthur

Lenny Bruce. AP/WIDE WORLD PHOTOS

Godfrey's *Talent Scouts* program, a radio-television simulcast, in 1949, he launched his career as a wandering Jewish comic. On the road he met a twice-divorced, once-arrested, bisexual stripper, Honey Harlowe (born Harriet Lloyd), and they married on 15 June 1951. They had one child and divorced in 1957; Bruce never remarried. As Pygmalion to her Galatea, Bruce failed to transform Harlowe into a successful *chanteuse*. After a near fatal car wreck, Bruce tried to raise money for a mythical charity (a leper colony in Africa) as a fake priest, Father Mathias. Exposed but not punished for this hustle, Bruce returned to the legitimate theater.

Success arrived in the late 1950s as the young comic, inspired by the improvisational style of Mort Sahl, abandoned schlock in favor of shock in his assault on the conventional pieties and hidden hypocrisies embedded in American culture. He gained many loyal fans at Enrico Banducci's San Francisco club, the Hungry I. As the 1960s dawned, Bruce earned more than $3,000 per week and sold 190,000 records. Drug addiction and his broken marriage, however, led to *tsores* (trouble).

Bruce oscillated between a wish for sainthood and an inescapable sense of his own corruption. He confessed, "I can't get worked up about politics. I grew up in New York and I was hip as a kid that I was corrupt and the mayor was corrupt. I have no illusions." In his quest for sainthood, Bruce essayed many roles—hipster, underground man, counterculture hero, hustler, junkie, gadfly, victim, litigant,

priest, Jew, comic—before he self-destructed on a toilet in his California dream house.

In his bits Bruce targeted the hustler in advertising, show business, and, most dangerously, organized religion. Invidiously, he contrasted the ubiquitous Christian God—represented on rocks, on bank buildings, in museums, on crucifixes, in movies, in musicals, in cars—with the little Jewish God confined to the *mezuzah* box in the doorways of Jewish homes. However, Bruce identified the following as fellow Jews: residents of big cities, Italians, African Americans, Dylan Thomas, Count Basie, Eugene O'Neill, mouths, bosoms, rye bread, macaroons, chocolate, and "tushy kissers." According to Bruce, in ancient Egypt, before Charlton Heston a.k.a. Moses liberated them, to avoid backbreaking, ball-busting pyramid construction, Jews gravitated to show business. He noted that although both rabbis and priests defecate, only one, in theory at least, copulates. In the Jewish tribe, he joked, there is no merit badge for abstinence; thus rabbis are notoriously big *shtuppers*. Animated by a penchant for deflating authority, Bruce identified with outcasts and losers. He belligerently used Yiddish phrases, hip argot, and obscene language to shock Americans into an awareness of their prejudices as evidenced in his hilarious over the top routine: "Just How Do You Relax Colored People at Parties?"

Beginning in 1958 Bruce imparted his comic bits on LP records. They won friends and influenced enemies. *Time* magazine appended the label "Sick Comic." Bruce inspired many comedians in the 1960s as he perfected a unique form of humor that shocked as it amused. Speaking for many peers, Redd Foxx said, "Lenny Bruce was the greatest human being I ever met. He was honest . . . He was crucified for telling the truth. He was a great influence on me." On sex and race and choosing a lifetime partner, the allegedly sick Bruce posed a sane alternative: Lena Horne over Kate Smith; Harry Belafonte over Charles Laughton. Such ruminations inspired later comics such as Richard Pryor, George Carlin, and Robert Klein and the writer Norman Lear.

Arguably, Bruce's greatest triumph arrived at Carnegie Hall on 2 May 1961. A full house roared with laughter, especially at his "Christ and Moses" bit. Later that year he was arrested for drug possession in Philadelphia. Whether over drugs or obscenity, confrontations with the law continued in San Francisco, Los Angeles, Chicago, London, and New York. Unable to control his demons, the self-destructive comic obsessively and compulsively turned to narcotics. Egged on by intellectuals and "America Firsters" (First Amendment advocates) to combat repression, Bruce proved unsuited for this heavy role. He grew flabby from too many candy bars, colas, and controlled substances. His mind drifted. Despite personal failure, however, Bruce left a salutary stir in his wake.

Prior to Bruce, American humor had defined limits: sexual innuendo, booze, and evacuation. In the 1960s Bruce went beyond the fringe to zero in on spiritual fakers. He coupled pacifism and pornography to turn on a generation of rebels. Ralph Gleason called him the leader of the first wave of America's social and cultural revolution, whose followers recognized that the ultimate obscenity is war, not love. Socratically, Bruce questioned the meaning of obscenity. Subversively, he explored the chasm between churches and Christianity, synagogues and Judaism, love and marriage, law and lawyers, fantasy and reality.

Busted many times for alleged obscenity, usually at the behest of clerics, Bruce, had he lived, might have enjoyed the last laugh as sex scandals came to plague certified celibates. Opposed to the religious bureaucracy (letter) but not its ideals (spirit), he challenged obsolete laws, libidinal repression, and what the sociologist C. Wright Mills aptly called "crackpot reality." Bruce died of an overdose of morphine. He is buried in Eden Memorial Park in San Fernando, California. An exorcist of society's demons, Bruce could not control his own. Death at age forty, the writer Dick Schaap observed, is the ultimate obscenity.

★

Among the various biographies, Albert Goldman, *Ladies and Gentlemen—Lenny Bruce!!* (1974), is the most comprehensive, if not always the most accurate. Goldman's analysis of Bruce, especially in his shorter articles, eclipses all other contributors: Frank Kofsky, *Lenny Bruce: The Comedian as Social Critic and Secular Moralist* (1974); Sanford Pinsker, "Lenny Bruce: Shpritzing the Goyim/Shocking the Jews," in Sarah Blacher Cohen, ed., *Jewish Wry: Essays on Jewish Humor* (1987); and Joseph Dorinson, "Lenny Bruce: A Jewish Humorist in Babylon," in *Jewish Currents* 35, no. 2 (Feb. 1981). Though Lenny Bruce, *How to Talk Dirty and Influence People: An Autobiography* (1966), is informative, the best primary source remains John Cohen, ed., *The Essential Lenny Bruce* (1967).

JOSEPH DORINSON

BUCKLEY, William F(rank), Jr. (*b.* 24 November 1925 in New York City), journalist and author whose writings in the 1950s and 1960s are credited with giving the American conservative movement its intellectual inspiration as well as helping political conservatives move into the mainstream of late-twentieth-century and early-twenty-first-century American politics.

Buckley was born into a wealthy family, the sixth of ten children of William Frank Buckley, Sr., a lawyer who had led an adventurous life building an oil empire in seven countries, especially Mexico, and New Orleans–born Aloise (Steiner) Buckley. Buckley's father was a tough man who was determined that his children not grow up spoiled and elitist. Buckley attended schools in France and England and graduated from Millbrook School in Millbrook, New York, in 1943. In 1944 he attended the University of Mexico for a semester and then joined the U.S. Army, serving in the infantry and leaving as a second lieutenant in 1946. He then entered Yale University. Buckley had been raised to be self-confident and to trust his own judgment, which created conflict. He discussed this in his first book, *God and Man at Yale: The Superstitions of Academic Freedom* (1951); he readily debated Marxists and atheists, proving to have a deadly wit and a devastating delivery while advocating his conservative Roman Catholic principles. In 1950 he graduated with a B.A. While he was an undergraduate, in 1947, he was appointed to teach beginning Spanish, and he remained in that post for a year after graduation.

God and Man at Yale elicited bitter, hateful reviews from left-wing writers. Meanwhile, Buckley joined the Central Intelligence Agency (CIA) and was assigned to Mexico; his supervisor was the novelist and eventual Watergate conspirator E. Howard Hunt. (During the 1972 presidential campaign burglars broke into the Watergate offices of the Democratic Party; their connections were traced back to the White House and the committee to reelect Richard Nixon.) In 1952 Buckley left the CIA to pursue journalism, joining the staff of the *American Mercury* only to leave it because of its anti-Semitic editorial stance. He was a supporter of Senator Joseph McCarthy's well-publicized, often cruel effort to reveal the Communist threat to America.

Buckley's declaration that he wanted to "revitalize the conservative position" in the United States seemed outrageous in 1955. With McCarthy's eventual disgrace, political conservatism seemed almost dead and was held in disrepute. But Buckley founded the *National Review* in 1955 with every intention of making his moralistic brand of conservatism a force in American politics; this was brash and suggested an overweening self-importance, but it also happened, and Buckley had much to do with how it happened.

The *National Review* featured essays, sometimes polemics, and straightforward journalism. By 1964, when the conservative senator Barry Goldwater was nominated for president, the magazine had a paid circulation of more than 125,000. (The number of subscribers drifted down to about 100,000 in 1980 but received a boost when President Ronald Reagan declared in 1983 that he read it and awaited each issue eagerly.) In 1960 Buckley helped found the Young Americans for Freedom; to the puzzlement of leftist writers, the organization attracted thousands of poor and lower-middle-class young people who found Buckley's moralistic view of politics appealing. The organization, which worked as a lobbying group and as support for conservative causes, had a membership near fifty-five thousand by 1969. In 1961

William F. Buckley, Jr. ARCHIVE PHOTOS, INC.

Buckley helped form the Conservative Party in New York, perhaps hoping to inspire a mass movement. Although Buckley lost his bid for mayor of New York in 1965 on the Conservative ticket, finishing third behind the Republican John Lindsay and the Democrat Abraham Beame with 13.4 percent of the vote, the Conservative Party did not prove irrelevant. Buckley's brother James was elected U.S. senator for New York as a Conservative Party candidate in 1970.

In 1962 Buckley began his newspaper column "On the Right," which was syndicated to more than three hundred newspapers in the 1980s. This column and Buckley's *National Review* helped give his conservatism legitimacy in the eyes of mainstream voters during the 1960s. Buckley's opposition to bigotry, especially anti-Semitism, and the *National Review*'s exposure of antidemocratic rightist movements encouraged people to see conservatism as rational and honest. When the *National Review* exposed the right-wing John Birch Society as anti–civil rights, the journal and its editor, Buckley, showed principle. Indeed, Buckley insisted all his career that conservatism means conserving civil rights—or, more plainly, protecting civil rights.

In 1966 Buckley began hosting a weekly interview show, *Firing Line*, on a local television station. The show's producer did a good job of finding such provocative guests as the atheist Madalyn Murray O'Hair, the Black Panther ac-

tivist Huey Newton, the boxer Muhammad Ali, the Russian writer Aleksandr Solzhenitsyn, and the British journalist Malcom Muggeridge. Buckley, already notorious but a vague figure for many people outside New York, became a superstar. His odd habit of leaning his head back to stare down his nose at his guests, his lapboard covered with papers, his slow speech, and his biting humor as well as his sudden smiles combined to make him endearing as a personality, whatever his views. *Firing Line* won an Emmy in 1969. In 1971 the Public Broadcasting Service picked up the show, giving it exposure on more than 170 television stations. It remained popular until Buckley retired from it in 1999.

In 1969 President Richard Nixon appointed Buckley one of five members of the Advisory Commission of the U.S. Information Agency. Buckley resigned from the position in 1972 to protest what he viewed as Nixon's betrayal of conservatism by instituting wage and price controls to combat inflation. Even so, he accepted an appointment to the American delegation to the United Nations for 1973; he made his presence known, denouncing the anti-Americanism of many delegates. His book *United Nations Journal: A Delegate's Odyssey* (1974) made plain his objections to what he observed, even while asserting that America's participation in the United Nations was worthwhile.

Buckley married Patricia Austin Taylor in 1950. They had one son. After the 1960s Buckley wrote a series of best-selling novels about the secret agent Blackford Oakes and devoted much of his time to writing nonfiction about sailing as well as social commentaries that emphasized a need for Americans and all people to lead moral lives. It was the explosion of activity in the 1960s that set most of the pattern for his later life and fixed in the minds of most observers an image of Buckley as honest, friendly, and brilliant, even among those who disagreed with his political views.

★

Buckley's nonfiction is rife with anecdotes about himself, but *Nearer, My God: An Autobiography of Faith* (1997) stands out because it gives a good explanation of the beliefs that form the foundation of his political and social views. Other significant autobiographical works include *The Unmaking of a Mayor* (1966), about running for mayor of New York, and *Overdrive: A Personal Documentary* (1983), about a day in his frenetic life; both offer insights into the gusto with which he lives. Charles Lam Markmann, *The Buckleys: A Family Examined* (1973), portrays the Buckleys as analogous to the Kennedys, with William F. Buckley the counterpart of John Fitzgerald Kennedy; the analogy does not hold up. He depicts Buckley as crude, vitriolic, and half-witted. John Judis, *William F. Buckley, Jr.: Patron Saint of the Conservatives* (1988), is the only full-length biography.

KIRK H. BEETZ

BUMBRY, Grace (*b.* 4 January 1937 in St. Louis, Missouri), operatic mezzo-soprano and dramatic soprano who was the first African-American artist to appear at the Wagner Festival in Bayreuth, Germany, debuting in 1961 as Venus in Richard Wagner's *Tannhäuser*.

The youngest of three children, Bumbry grew up with her brothers in a religious and musical family in St. Louis. Her father Benjamin was a freight handler for the Cotton Belt Route railroad, and her mother, Melzia Walker, was a schoolteacher from Mississippi. Encouraged by her Sumner High School voice teacher, Kenneth Billups, and her church choir director, Sarah Hopes, in 1954 Bumbry entered a teenage talent contest sponsored by local radio station KMOX and won first prize, including a scholarship to the St. Louis Institute of Music. At that time, however, the Institute did not admit African-American students, and Bumbry, with the agreement of her parents and teachers, rejected the offered compromise of segregated private lessons. Supportive KMOX executive Robert Hyland then arranged for Bumbry to appear on the nationally televised *Arthur Godfrey Talent Scouts* program, where in 1954, Bumbry sang "O don fatale" from Verdi's *Don Carlos*. She won first prize, and her performance brought her several scholarship offers.

Bumbry graduated from Sumner High School in Jan-

uary 1954. She studied briefly at Boston University that year, then transferred to Northwestern University in 1955. Also in 1955 she sang in master classes for the noted German soprano Lotte Lehmann, an opportunity that resulted in more than three years of intensive study at the Music Academy of the West in Santa Barbara, California, with Lehmann, who categorized Bumbry's voice as mezzo-soprano, and coach Armand Tokatyan, who classified it as dramatic soprano. Lehmann persuaded the young singer to focus her career away from the concert stage and toward opera. In 1957 Bumbry received a Marian Anderson Scholarship and the John Hay Whitney Award, and in 1958 she was joint semifinalist with Martina Arroyo in the Metropolitan Auditions of the Air. These awards enabled her to travel abroad to study French art song repertoire with Pierre Bernac, a French baritone and vocal coach known for his interpretation of French song. She graduated from the Music Academy of the West in 1959.

Bumbry inaugurated her professional career in Europe, believing that an African-American classical singer would improve her chance of career success overseas. She was one of several African-American singers of the 1960s who turned to Europe for opportunities unavailable in the United States. In June 1959 she gave her first concert abroad at London's Wigmore Hall, then traveled to Paris for several favorably reviewed concerts. In 1960 she made

Grace Bumbry. AP/WIDE WORLD PHOTOS

her international operatic debut as Amneris in *Aida* at the Paris Opera, where she received a standing ovation for her performance in the "Judgement Scene." She subsequently signed a multiyear contract with the Basel Opera House.

Bumbry's emerging reputation brought her to the attention of Wieland Wagner, grandson of Richard Wagner, who shocked traditionalists by auditioning and selecting her in the spring of 1961 to sing the role of Venus, conventionally a blonde and blue-eyed Nordic archetype, in *Tannhäuser* at the annual Wagner Festival in Bayreuth. The scandal caused by Wagner's decision to use an African-American singer in what was considered the shrine to the Aryan ideal was reflected in the international press. "Die schwarze Venus" (the Black Venus) became a cause célèbre, and Wagner declared in a newspaper interview, "I shall bring in black, yellow, and brown artists if I feel them appropriate. I require no ideal Nordic specimens. My grandfather wrote for vocal colours, not skin colours." With her radiantly self-assured premiere performance on 23 July 1961, costumed in gold lamé, Bumbry reached true international status. The performance garnered forty-two curtain calls during a thirty-minute ovation, with the loudest outbursts of applause reserved for Bumbry. The European press hailed her as "an authentic goddess with a radiant noble voice." The *New York Herald Tribune* stated, "The voice is ravishing . . . she is a dramatic soprano of the first quality."

In August 1961 the impresario Sol Hurok recruited Bumbry to his high-profile stable of performing artists, and she signed a five-year, $250,000 contract for recordings, television appearances, and opera and concert engagements. Hurok arranged to have Bumbry return to Washington, D.C., in February 1962, to sing at a formal state dinner at the White House as the guest of President and Mrs. John F. Kennedy. The audience at the performance included Vice President Lyndon B. Johnson, Speaker of the House John McCormack, and Chief Justice Earl Warren. At the conclusion of her performance, President Kennedy led Bumbry by the hand from the dais to a standing ovation.

That fall she toured Japan with the Paris Opera, singing the role of Carmen, and in November 1962 began a nine-week tour of the United States, which consisted of a concert debut at Carnegie Hall and twenty-five performances in twenty-one cities. Her performances brought rave reviews. The *New York Times* hailed her as "A superbly gifted artist . . . a gorgeous, clear, ringing voice . . . a regal bearing and a thoroughly winning stage presence."

In 1963 Bumbry debuted at Covent Garden as Princess Eboli in *Don Carlos,* and the Chicago Lyric Opera featured her in *Tannhäuser.* On 6 July 1963 she married the Polish-born tenor Erwin Andreas Jaeckel, whom she had met in Basel and who eventually became her manager. The couple had no children. Bumbry returned to the Basel Opera

House and acquired a villa in nearby Lugano. She also bought homes in New York and California, furs, and several cars, including a Jaguar and an orange Lamborghini for auto racing, her new hobby. In 1965 she debuted at the Metropolitan Opera as Princess Eboli in *Don Carlos,* and the press proclaimed her "an exciting, magnetic, dynamic singer." Bumbry subsequently chose to concentrate on the soprano repertoire; when she and her husband/manager disagreed on this decision, the marriage ended in divorce. In 1970 Bumbry debuted in a soprano role as Salomé in London's Covent Garden. The *Financial Times* reported, "Miss Bumbry has the compass and the power for the role. The ease and smoothness of her singing . . . were a constant pleasure." Contributing equally to her Covent Garden success was her "dance of the seven veils," choreographed with Arthur Mitchell of the Dance Theatre of Harlem.

Bumbry distinguished herself artistically from the earliest days of her career. Not only has she performed many of the great mezzo-soprano roles, but her forays into the soprano operatic repertoire have been applauded. She appeared or recorded with legendary conductors including Claudio Abbado, Leonard Bernstein, Karl Böhm, Christoph von Dohnanyi, Herbert von Karajan, James Levine, Seiji Ozawa, Giuseppe Patané, Wolfgang Sawallisch, and Georg Solti. Her extensive discography includes recordings of opera, lieder, and oratorio on the Phillips, EMI, Decca, RCA, and Sony labels. In the 1990s she founded the Black Musical Heritage Ensemble and was appointed a UNESCO Goodwill Ambassador. She makes her home in the United States and Switzerland.

★

Rosalyn M. Story, *And So I Sing: African-American Divas of Opera and Concert* (1990), and Helena Matheopoulos, *Diva: Great Sopranos and Mezzos Discuss Their Art* (1991), each include a chapter on Bumbry with information about her activities during the 1960s. *Blacks in Classical Music: A Bibliographical Guide to Composers, Performers, and Ensembles* (1988), compiled by John Gray; and *Black Music in America: A Bibliography* (1981), compiled by JoAnn Skrowronski, provide many citations for articles about Bumbry in journals and reference works.

CHRISTINE WONDOLOWSKI GERSTEIN

BUNDY, McGeorge (*b.* 30 March 1919 in Boston, Massachusetts; *d.* 16 September 1996 in Boston, Massachusetts), Harvard University academic who served as special assistant for national security affairs to presidents John F. Kennedy (1961–1963) and Lyndon B. Johnson (1963–1966), after which he headed the Ford Foundation until 1979.

One of five siblings, Bundy was the third and youngest son and third child of Harvey Hollister Bundy, a leading

Boston corporate lawyer, and Katharine ("Kay") Lowell Putnam, a homemaker and the daughter of one of Boston's most prominent families. He grew up in a family ethic of public service, intensified first by his father's and (later) his own conscious adherence to the tradition of assertive but principled U.S. internationalism that dated back to President Theodore Roosevelt, and was best represented in their lives by Henry L. Stimson (secretary of state under Herbert Hoover and secretary of war under both William Howard Taft and Franklin D. Roosevelt), under whom Bundy's father served in both the state and war departments. Bundy, who attended Dexter Lower School in Boston, Groton, an elite Massachusetts private school, and Yale University, his father's alma mater, invariably excelled academically, leaving Groton at age sixteen with perfect marks and graduating first in his Yale class in 1940 with a B.A. degree in mathematics. Elected to the Harvard Society of Fellows in 1941, after one year Bundy joined the U.S. Army, deciphering intelligence intercepts for Admiral Alan Kirk, the commander of U.S. naval forces in the Sicily and Normandy invasions of World War II. Bundy, who rose to the rank of captain and was discharged in 1945, assisted in the planning of the Sicily and Normandy invasions.

After the war, for two years Bundy helped the elderly Stimson research and write his memoirs, *On Active Service in Peace and War* (1948), which laid out for future generations that influential statesman's worldview. Soon after, Bundy edited a volume of the official speeches of Secretary of State Dean Acheson, his brother William's father-in-law. Although Bundy had only an undergraduate degree, he switched fields from mathematics in 1949 to teach government and international affairs at Harvard University. In 1950 Bundy married Mary Buckminster Lothrop, a fellow Bostonian, with whom he had four sons. In 1953 Harvard appointed Bundy, now age thirty-four, as Dean of Arts and Sciences. He remained in the position until 1961, attracting such nationally known scholars as sociologist David Riesman to Harvard. Bundy was known for his intellectual brilliance, energy, swift assimilation of information, and wit, though his critics subsequently suggested that in Bundy's roles as dean and public official these superficial qualities masked an absence of deeper reflection and a tendency to accept prevailing conventional cold war wisdom.

Though nominally a Republican, Bundy was close to center-left Harvard liberals such as the historian Arthur M. Schlesinger, Jr., and the economist John Kenneth Galbraith, and like them Bundy supported and advised John F. Kennedy, his local Democratic senator, in Kennedy's 1960 campaign. In 1961 Kennedy appointed Bundy to the White House as presidential assistant for national security affairs, where his ambition, intellectual brilliance, and empathy with the president allowed him to greatly overshadow the secretary of state, Dean Rusk. Bundy's critics argue that he

McGeorge Bundy. THE LIBRARY OF CONGRESS

lacked a firm moral compass and often accorded overly high priority to pragmatic considerations of political expediency, as when he supported increases in strategic nuclear missiles he knew were unnecessary and a civil defense program whose ineffectiveness he recognized. Bundy's acquiescence reflected the degree to which he thought it his function to be a competent manager rather than an innovative formulator of policy. As Kennedy's gatekeeper on foreign affairs, Bundy controlled the access of both information and individuals to the president, prepared the agenda for National Security Council meetings, and selected the personnel for the task forces Kennedy established to handle specific foreign policy problems. Both Bundy and Kennedy shared a lively appreciation of the central significance of U.S. power and the need to employ it in situations—Cuba, Berlin, and Vietnam, for example—where U.S. interests or prestige might be at stake. Bundy considered it his role to ensure that the president was briefed on both sides of any issue and to this end sometimes played devil's advocate. Even so, within a few weeks of taking office, he approved the disastrous March 1961 failed Bay of Pigs invasion, an attempt to overthrow the pro-Communist Cuban government of Fidel Castro that ended in fiasco and brought international humiliation to the United States.

Bundy was involved in every aspect of foreign policy formulation and implementation, including the Cuban Missile Crisis of October 1962, when the United States discovered that the Soviet Union had installed nuclear-armed missiles on Cuba and demanded their withdrawal. It fell to Bundy to inform Kennedy that American intelligence overflights had detected the presence of these weapons. Surprisingly indecisive, Bundy initially supported airstrikes to destroy the missiles, subsequently endorsed the naval quarantine option Kennedy eventually selected, yet then switched once more to airstrikes. When the Soviet leader Nikita Khrushchev sent two somewhat contradictory responses to the United States' ultimatum on Cuba, it was Bundy who suggested replying only to the first, less confrontational message. Reflecting later on this crisis, in his book *Danger and Survival: Choices About the Bomb in the First Fifty Years* (1988), Bundy suggested that Kennedy employed "a certain excess of rhetoric," when more moderate language would have been less alarming to Americans. It also seems that, to resolve the 1958–1963 crisis over Berlin, Bundy would have welcomed a U.S. agreement with the Soviet Union whereby both recognized the separate existence of West and East Germany and their post–World War II boundaries and the two Germanies signed a nonaggression pact, suggestions prefiguring détente and *Ostpolitik,* but Bundy accepted without demur Kennedy's decision that such moves were politically infeasible. Bundy and Kennedy both emphasized that the United States would react forcibly should the Soviet Union or East Germany try to annex West Berlin—it was Bundy who drafted Kennedy's 1961 speech proclaiming *Ich bin ein Berliner*—but acquiesced in the Soviet decision that year to staunch the hemorrhage of East German refugees to the West by erecting the Berlin Wall.

By far the most controversial aspect of Bundy's government service was his responsibility for the escalation of the U.S. involvement in Vietnam. Dissenters pilloried both Bundy and his brother William, assistant secretary of state for East Asia under President Lyndon B. Johnson, for their part in the growing U.S. entanglement. As early as 1961 Bundy suggested a limited deployment of U.S. combat troops to South Vietnam, though Kennedy sent further military advisers instead, and in the following two years Bundy endorsed various paramilitary operations. When army officers opposed to South Vietnamese president Ngo Dinh Diem planned a coup in autumn 1963, Bundy acquiesced and kept himself closely informed of their developing plans. After Kennedy's assassination in November 1963, Bundy continued to serve President Johnson. Convinced by early 1964 that South Vietnam's government was ineffective and corrupt and that victory in the war would demand major domestic political reforms within South

Vietnam, Bundy volunteered to go there himself as U.S. ambassador, an offer Johnson declined. Despite some personal misgivings over its likely success, Bundy acquiesced in Johnson's decision to react to the August 1964 Tonkin Gulf incident with a gradually escalating bombing campaign, accepting that the president best comprehended the political implications. In early 1965 Bundy visited Vietnam for the first time, a trip that coincided with Viet Cong attacks on U.S. Air Force personnel based at Pleiku. Bundy immediately demanded heavy U.S. retaliation through an escalated bombing campaign of "sustained reprisals" against North Vietnam. Despite some doubts about the efficacy of large troop deployments, in mid-1965 Bundy accepted Johnson's decision to commit U.S. ground forces. Bundy himself later suggested that, had Kennedy lived, he would have avoided full-scale American intervention, but that in mid-1965 political and psychological considerations made Johnson so determined to commit troops, he would have ignored whatever arguments his advisers made to the contrary. Critics, however, assailed Bundy's own contemporaneous failure to undertake any serious efforts to dissuade Johnson.

Personal incompatibility with Johnson led Bundy to leave his administration in January 1966 to head the Ford Foundation. He remained until 1979, moving that institution to support aggressive and often controversial policies on race relations, the environment, the creation of public television, and ethical investing. Yet Vietnam perennially dogged Bundy, effectively destroying his chances of becoming secretary of state or president of a major university. Following the gentleman's code in which he was reared, Bundy refused either to defend his record or to publicly criticize Johnson administration policies, and for the rest of his life rarely even discussed them. Until early 1968 he supported the war, albeit in March 1967 warning against any further escalation and in November 1967 advising Johnson to persevere but gradually to de-escalate the U.S. commitment while enhancing South Vietnamese self-reliance. After the massive early 1968 Tet Offensive, Bundy finally advocated a bombing halt. Shortly afterward, with most of the other "Wise Men" the administration consulted, Bundy told a shocked Johnson that victory was unattainable and recommended that the United States open peace negotiations with North Vietnam. While defending the war's conduct to date, in October Bundy publicly called for steady U.S. troop withdrawals until 100,000 were left in place, if necessary indefinitely, and a bombing halt. In 1971, moreover, Bundy testified before Congress in favor of limiting presidential power to fight wars without congressional consent, an indirect commentary on Johnson's behavior in 1965. For ten years, from 1979, he taught at New York University, writing on nuclear policy. In 1982, together with George

F. Kennan, Robert S. McNamara, and Gerard Smith, he called for no U.S. first-use of nuclear weapons. Bundy died suddenly of heart failure in Boston and was buried at Saint John's Church, Beverly Farms, Massachusetts.

Bundy embodied the strengths, virtues, limitations, and weaknesses of the U.S. foreign policy establishment, whose heir he considered himself, and the credibility of whose outlook the Vietnam War helped to destroy. Although preeminent among those whom journalist David Halberstam termed "the best and the brightest," despite his outstanding ability and intelligence Bundy was unwilling to question conventional wisdom beyond certain limits. His lengthy and distinguished subsequent career notwithstanding, his reputation never entirely recovered from the damage wreaked by his perceived responsibility for Vietnam, and until his death this record made him a controversial figure.

★

Collections of Bundy's papers are at the John Fitzgerald Kennedy Library in Boston and the Lyndon Baines Johnson Library at the University of Texas at Austin. Additional manuscript material on his time in government service is in records of the Department of State in the National Archives II, College Park, Maryland. The Ford Foundation Archives, New York City, contain his records as president of the foundation. The relevant volumes of the series *Foreign Relations of the United States* contain numerous materials produced by Bundy, and his evolving position during the Cuban Missile Crisis may be followed in Ernest R. May and Philip D. Zelikow, eds., *The Kennedy Tapes: Inside the White House During the Cuban Missile Crisis* (1997). Bundy reflects on various aspects of his government service in *Danger and Survival: Choices About the Bomb in the First Fifty Years* (1988), and also in David A. Welch and James G. Blight, eds., *On the Brink: Americans and Soviets Reexamine the Cuban Missile Crisis* (1989). The only biography is Kai Bird, *The Color of Truth: McGeorge Bundy and William Bundy: Brothers in Arms: A Biography* (1998). Shorter assessments include Joseph Kraft, *Profiles in Power: A Washington Insight* (1966); and Arthur M. Schlesinger, Jr., "A Man Called Mac," *George* (Dec. 1996). David Halberstam, *The Best and the Brightest* (1972), focuses heavily on Bundy's responsibility for Vietnam. Bundy features extensively in numerous other works on the Kennedy and Johnson administrations, including David M. Barrett, *Uncertain Warriors: Lyndon Johnson and His Vietnam Advisers* (1993); Lloyd C. Gardner, *Pay Any Price: Lyndon Johnson and the Wars for Vietnam* (1995); and Lawrence Freedman, *Kennedy's Wars: Berlin, Cuba, Laos, and Vietnam* (2000). Bundy's activities at the Ford Foundation may be followed in that institution's Annual Reports from 1966 through the 1970s; they are also discussed in Waldemar A. Nielsen, *The Golden Donors: A New Anatomy of the Great Foundations* (1985). Among tributes to Bundy are Peter Solbert in the *Century Association Yearbook* (1997): 272–275, and Francis M. Bator, "Glimpses of Mac,"

Groton School Quarterly (May 1997). Bundy recorded oral histories for the Kennedy and Johnson Libraries. Obituaries are in the *New York Times* and *Washington Post* (both 17 Sept. 1996), and the *Daily Telegraph* and the (London) *Times* (both 18 Sept. 1996).

PRISCILLA ROBERTS

BUNKER, Ellsworth (*b.* 11 May 1894 in Yonkers, New York; *d.* 27 September 1984 in Brattleboro, Vermont), powerful business executive and U.S. ambassador to several countries during the 1950s to 1970s, including to South Vietnam during the Vietnam War.

Bunker's father, George Raymond Bunker, was one of the founders of the National Sugar Refining Company, a massive, wealthy firm; his mother, Jean Polhemus Cobb, was a housewife. Bunker grew up at the family home in Yonkers, along with his younger brother and sister and an older half brother. He attended private schools, eventually graduating from the Mackenzie School in Dobbs Ferry, New York, in 1912. He then attended Yale College in New Haven, Connecticut, majoring in history and economics and graduating with a B.A. in 1916. At Yale he participated in the Reserve Officers Training Corps, although he never saw active duty.

Ellsworth Bunker, April 1965. © BETTMANN/CORBIS

After graduating from Yale, Bunker took a job with the National Sugar Refining Company unloading shipments at a dock. He slowly worked his way through the sugar business, taking assignments of ever-greater responsibility to gain firsthand knowledge of the many aspects of the business. He even learned Spanish and Portuguese because some of the company's most important suppliers were in Argentina and Brazil. Bunker's experience in South America, as well as his knowledge of Latin American languages, proved to be of great importance in his later diplomatic career. On 24 April 1920 he married Harriet Allen Butler; they had three children.

In the mid-1920s Bunker became the manager of Warner Sugar Refining Company, a subsidiary of National Sugar. He joined the National Sugar board of directors in 1927 and soon showed he had a sharp but flexible mind and excellent business instincts. He became secretary in 1931 and eventually became a company vice president and treasurer in 1934. During the 1940s Bunker's responsibilities widened as he took positions on the boards of directors of other sugar companies in Puerto Rico, Mexico, and Cuba. In 1940 he became the president of National Sugar, serving in that capacity until 1948, when he became the company's chief executive officer, serving in that capacity to 1951.

In the early 1950s the U.S. Secretary of State Dean Acheson advised President Harry Truman to appoint Bunker as the ambassador to Argentina. Acheson had met Bunker at Yale, and knew he had a knack for solving difficult problems and had dealt with many officials in Argentina—skills that were needed to untangle a web of distrust between the United States and Argentina's Perónist regime. After taking up the ambassadorship in 1951, Bunker mollified the government of Juan Domingo Perón and smoothed relations between the two countries.

In 1952 Bunker was sent as the U.S. ambassador to Italy, which was still suffering from the effects of World War II and years of fascist rule. The Italian government was unstable, and Bunker worked to help the country remain democratic. A lifelong member of the Democratic Party, he left his post in 1953 when Dwight Eisenhower became president and replaced Bunker with Clare Boothe Luce. Bunker was still on National Sugar's board of directors and served as the president of the American Red Cross from 1954 to 1956.

In 1956 Eisenhower asked Bunker to serve as a representative to the United Nations General Assembly; he liked Bunker's performance and appointed him to be U.S. ambassador to India and Nepal. Bunker served as ambassador to Nepal until 1959 and to India until the start of President John F. Kennedy's administration in 1961. Bunker was well liked in India, where his tact, gentle presentation of his views, and honesty were appreciated. After leaving India

he became a diplomatic troubleshooter for the United States. As such, in 1962 he mediated a dispute between the Netherlands and Indonesia over the Dutch dependency Irian Barat (also known as West Irian), preventing a war by arranging a United Nations–sponsored plebiscite in Irian Barat and persuading the Netherlands to surrender the dependency to Indonesia when the vote went against the Netherlands. For his efforts, Bunker was awarded the Presidential Medal of Freedom in 1963. In that year, Yemen was in the midst of a civil war, and the United Arab Republic's president Gamal Abdel Nasser had sent troops to fight for the communists, while Saudi Arabia's prime minister Prince Faisal had sent troops to support the royalists. Acting as a representative of Secretary of State Dean Rusk, Bunker persuaded Nasser and Faisal to withdraw their troops and call a truce. The agreement did not last long, collapsing only days after Bunker had finished his work. He was appointed as the U.S. representative to the Organization of American States (OAS) in January 1964, was elected to the chairmanship of the OAS in November 1964, and spent much of his time defusing potential wars.

Bunker's work was complicated by the U.S. invasion of the Dominican Republic, which President Lyndon B. Johnson had ordered in April 1965 to prevent a violent communist takeover of the country. Even though Johnson's actions angered some members of the OAS, Bunker managed to persuade the OAS nations to form a coalition that sent troops to the Dominican Republic to keep the peace and help conduct an unsullied election. In 1967 he was awarded his second Presidential Medal of Freedom for this work. Another of his tasks while serving in the OAS was to put a peaceful end to the rioting against Americans in Panama. Bunker successfully worked out an agreement acceptable to both sides, although he eventually returned to Panama in the 1970s to resolve disagreements over ownership of the Panama Canal.

In 1966 Bunker left his position on National Sugar's board of directors, probably because of the demands made on him as a troubleshooting negotiator for the United States. On 6 October 1966 President Johnson made Bunker an ambassador-at-large; on 25 April 1967 Bunker became U.S. ambassador to South Vietnam. Letters written by Bunker to Johnson, made public by the *New York Times,* reveal that Bunker told the president from the start of his service in Vietnam that the war was a quagmire. He considered the South Vietnamese government to be corrupt and knew that people in the countryside favored the Vietcong. Even so, he tried to find ways to secure the safety of the South Vietnamese people and to win their support against North Vietnam and the Vietcong.

By 1967 Bunker believed he was making headway. To reduce the corruption in the South Vietnamese government, he persuaded Premier Nguyen Cao Ky not to run for president in the 1967 elections and to accept the lesser post of vice president. Further, he persuaded Nguyen Van Thieu to run for the presidency. When Thieu won the election, disappointed rivals suggested his victory had been rigged by the United States, although many U.S. politicians believed the election was fraudulent. On 3 January 1967 Bunker married Carol Clendening Laise (his first wife had died in 1964); Laise was U.S. ambassador to Nepal and eventually became the general director of the U.S. Foreign Service.

Even though Bunker and Thieu worked closely together, Bunker was unable to persuade Thieu to join the peace talks that had started in November 1968 between the United States and North Vietnam. Eventually, in spite of Thieu's intransigence, the United States and North Vietnam reached an agreement to end aggression and make peace. It did not seem to matter to those involved that the North Vietnamese government had no intention of honoring the peace accords. Once the agreement was signed in January 1973, Bunker resigned as U.S. ambassador to South Vietnam on 30 March 1973, believing that his work was done.

In September 1973 President Richard Nixon reappointed Bunker as a U.S. ambassador-at-large. In that capacity, Bunker negotiated with Israel and its neighbors to try to prevent another war in the Middle East; he was not successful. Bunker also was asked to settle the dispute over the Panama Canal between the United States and the Panamanian dictator Omar Torrijos Herrera. To put the Panamanians at ease, he agreed to hold negotiations on Panamanian soil. For more than three years, Bunker and the Panamanian negotiators wrestled with the intricacies of the old 1903 Hay-Bunau-Varilla treaty that gave the United States total control over the Panama Canal forever.

The U.S. government was worried that, without its troops there to protect the canal, the strategically important shipping zone would be vulnerable to enemy attack. The Panamanians wanted more of the money the canal earned, using the argument of sovereignty over the canal to stir up nationalistic sentiment among the Panamanian population. Eventually, after years of persuasion by Bunker, the Panamanian government agreed to a U.S. military presence to help protect the canal and to a gradual turnover of canal operations to Panamanians by the beginning of 2000. The United States agreed to pay Panama more of the canal's income and to gradually relinquish control. The countries signed the agreement on 10 August 1977.

Bunker retired from the foreign service in 1978 and maintained residences in both Washington, D.C., and Putney, Vermont. He was the founding chairman of Georgetown University's Institute for the Study of Diplomacy. Bunker died at age ninety in Brattleboro Memorial Hospital of a viral infection and is buried in Dummerston, Vermont.

He left a legacy of great achievements and profound failures. In business, he was a tough negotiator, helping his company prosper, and he was a sensible, sharp advisor to other corporations. He was more famous for his efforts to negotiate agreements between nations that were potentially going to war against each other, and he gained his greatest notoriety from his term as the U.S. ambassador to South Vietnam in the late 1960s and early 1970s. Those who worked with Bunker noted that he was a hard but fair negotiator, who did not allow personality differences to distract him from the objectives of his negotiations. During his time in Vietnam, Bunker became known as "the Refrigerator" because of his imperturbable demeanor, even in crises.

★

"Bunker, Ellsworth" in *Current Biography Yearbook* (1978) offers a good overview of Bunker's work as an ambassador. *The Bunker Papers: Reports to the President from Vietnam, 1967–1973,* Douglas Pike, ed. (1990), reveals some of Bunker's influence on how the war in Vietnam was conducted, as well as his frankness in presenting his views to President Johnson. Obituaries are in the *New York Times* (28 Sept. 1984), and the *National Review* (2 Nov. 1984). The Lyndon Baines Johnson Library oral history collection in Austin, Texas, includes enlightening interviews with Bunker, which also are available on the library's website at <www.lbjlib.utexas.edu>.

KIRK H. BEETZ

BURGER, Warren Earl (*b.* 17 September 1907 in Saint Paul, Minnesota; *d.* 25 June 1995 in Washington, D.C.), judge on the U.S. Court of Appeals for the District of Columbia Circuit, then fifteenth chief justice of the United States, known during the 1960s for his conservative critique of changes in criminal law.

Burger was the fourth of seven children born to Charles Joseph Burger and Katharine Schnittger. Charles Burger owned a truck farm and worked as a railroad cargo inspector and traveling salesman. In 1925 Burger completed John A. Johnson High School in Saint Paul, but financial need prevented him from taking advantage of the partial scholarship he won to Princeton University. Instead, he worked as an insurance agent and took night classes at the University of Minnesota. In 1927, while continuing his job with the Mutual Life Insurance Company, he enrolled in the Saint Paul College of Law (now William Mitchell College of Law), from which he earned the LL.B. *magna cum laude* in 1931.

From 1931 to 1953 Burger practiced law in St Paul. He married Elvera Stromberg in 1933, a union that produced two children and lasted until Elvera's death sixty-one years later. Burger was an active Republican, most notably as a

Warren E. Burger. ARCHIVE PHOTOS, INC.

supporter of the progressive Harold Stassen. Burger was an advisor to Stassen during the latter's successful campaign for governor of Minnesota in 1938, and in both 1948 and 1952 Burger represented Stassen at the Republican National Convention. At the convention in 1952 Burger, on Stassen's behalf, turned the votes of Minnesota's delegation over to Dwight D. Eisenhower.

In 1953 Burger was appointed assistant attorney general in charge of the Claims Division (now the Civil Division), which brought the federal government's civil suits in federal court. Burger argued several cases before the Supreme Court, including *Peters* v. *Hobby* (1955), in which he defended a controversial decision of the government's Loyalty Review Board when the solicitor general refused to do so. In the same year President Eisenhower nominated Burger to the Court of Appeals for the District of Columbia (D.C.) Circuit, on which Burger took his seat in April 1956.

For the next thirteen years, until 1969, Burger was a judge on an appellate court that has often been considered the most important in the nation because it so often handles the significant federal issues originating in decisions by federal agencies. However, the D.C. Circuit also served as the appellate court for the District of Columbia itself, so the court saw many common civil and criminal cases ordinarily reviewed by state courts. Burger became known in the field

of general criminal law, especially because of his disagreements with liberal colleagues such as Judges David Bazelon and J. Skelly Wright.

For example, the traditional test for the insanity defense was, according to *M'Naghten's Case* (1843), whether the defendant, when he acted, knew the difference between right and wrong. In 1954, however, in *Durham* v. *United States*, the D.C. Circuit created a new test whereby the defendant could be excused if his action were the product of a mental disease or defect. No other court accepted this innovation, which made judgment turn on the credibility of expert psychiatric testimony rather than moral culpability. Burger became the court's leading critic of the *Durham* test, and in 1962 he wrote the opinion in *McDonald* v. *United States* that limited the scope of "mental disease or defect" by narrowing its definition. By 1972 the court had abandoned the *Durham* test altogether.

Burger dissented from the court's opinion in *Killough* v. *United States* (1962), which reversed a conviction for murder because the defendant had been held for thirty-six hours before arraignment, during which time the defendant had confessed. Burger believed the contemporary rule that criminal defendants be brought to court "without unnecessary delay," *Mallory* v. *United States* (1957), had to be balanced by society's interest in protecting itself from criminals, an interest that sometimes outweighed technical procedure. Burger later became a critic of the decision handed down by the Supreme Court in *Miranda* v. *Arizona* (1966), that suspects in police custody were not to be interrogated without first being apprised of their constitutional rights, including the privilege against self-incrimination.

By the late 1960s Burger was a prominent "law-and-order" judge. He gained national attention when excerpts of a speech he delivered to the Ripon Society in Wisconsin were published in *U.S. News and World Report* (August 1967, reprinted June 1969). In the speech, Burger compared the U.S. criminal justice system unfavorably with the system in Scandinavian countries. Crime, Burger argued, was exacerbated by the long delay between suspects' arrests and trials, by the length of the trials themselves, by the numerous appeals granted to convicted criminals, and by the inadequate effort to rehabilitate prisoners. The speech was later quoted by Republican presidential candidates, including Richard M. Nixon, who, soon after he took office, nominated Burger on 21 May 1969 to replace the retiring Chief Justice Earl Warren. Burger had judicial experience, a conservative view of criminal law, and a "strict constructionist" approach to the Constitution. After a swift confirmation, Burger took his seat on 23 June 1969.

Burger was expected to reverse the liberal tide of the Warren Court, which had played such an activist role in the field of civil rights. Yet, Burger joined the majority in a number of the Supreme Court's most activist decisions, including *Swann* v. *Charlotte-Mecklenburg Board of Education* (1971), which authorized busing in order to effect desegregation of schools, and *Roe* v. *Wade* (1973), which abrogated state laws on abortion. The most important of Burger's own opinions concerned the separation of powers in federal government, including *United States* v. *Nixon* (1974), which rejected President Nixon's claim to executive privilege and ordered him to comply with a subpoena issued during the investigation of the Watergate burglary. *I. N. S.* v. *Chadha* (1983) struck down Congress's use of the legislative veto. Burger, who was the longest-serving chief justice of the twentieth century, retired in 1986 to chair the Commission on the Bicentennial of the United States Constitution. He died of congestive heart failure, and is buried in Arlington National Cemetery in Arlington, Virginia.

During the 1960s Burger gained a reputation as a conservative appellate judge, one who was committed to an efficient criminal justice system that worked to the benefit of both society and convicted criminals. It was this reputation that brought Burger to the attention of President Nixon at the end of the decade and that secured his nomination to be chief justice.

★

Burger's professional and personal papers and memorabilia are housed in a special collection at the Earl Gregg Swem Library of the College of William and Mary, at Williamsburg, Virginia. Biographical material and information on Burger's most important decisions as chief justice can be found in *The Justices of the United States Supreme Court: Their Lives and Major Opinions* (1997), Leon Friedman and Fred L. Israel, eds. Tributes upon Burger's retirement from the Supreme Court appear in the *Harvard Law Review* 100, no. 8 (1987): 969–1001. Tributes *in memoriam* appear in the *William Mitchell Law Review* 22, no. 1 (1996): 1–65; and *Texas Law Review* 74, no. 2 (1995): 207–236. A respectful obituary is in *the Guardian* (27 June 1995).

ANDREW J. CARRIKER

BURNETT, Carol (*b.* 26 April 1933 in San Antonio, Texas), popular comic actress who set the standard for comedy-variety television shows with her long-running *Carol Burnett Show,* arguably the most successful show of its kind in television history.

Daughter of Joseph "Jody" Thomas Burnett, the manager of a movie theater, and Louise Creighton, a publicity writer for a Hollywood movie studio, Burnett was raised almost from birth by her maternal grandmother, Mabel Eudora White, whom she called "Nanny." Burnett's alcoholic parents left her in the care of Nanny and set off for Hollywood in search of fame and fortune, which proved elusive. Her parents split up while Burnett was still in elementary

Carol Burnett in character for the musical comedy *Once upon a Mattress,* 1960. © BETTMANN/CORBIS

school, and she and Nanny moved west to live with Burnett's mother in a cramped one-bedroom apartment. Louise Burnett gave birth to another daughter, Christine, a product of her relationship with a married man, when Burnett was eleven years old.

An inconsistent student at best, Burnett found solace in her Hollywood neighborhood's many movie theaters, where she saw all of the classic films of the day, and in occasional trips with Nanny to nearby Grauman's Chinese Theater for movie premieres. After finishing her studies at Le Conte Junior High School, Burnett entered Hollywood High School, from which she graduated in 1951. Interested in pursuing a career in journalism, she enrolled in the University of California at Los Angeles (UCLA) in 1953, but soon changed her major to theater arts. She met fellow student Don Saroyan, and in 1995 the two left school and traveled to New York City in search of a career in musical theater. Burnett and Saroyan married on 17 December 1955, a day that also marked her television debut, on a children's program known as the *Winchel–Mahoney Show.* Burnett next landed a major part on the ill-fated Buddy Hackett situation comedy called *Stanley,* which ran from September 1956 until March 1957. At about the same time, she began making occasional appearances on the Columbia Broadcasting System (CBS) *Garry Moore Show,* and in 1958 was signed as a regular. In April 1959 she opened in an off-Broadway production of *Once Upon a Mattress,* based on the *Princess and the Pea* fairy tale. The play proved so popular that it moved to Broadway before the end of the year.

Burnett made a huge impact on the national entertainment scene in the 1960s. Her appearances on the *Garry Moore Show* earned her an Emmy Award in 1962, and she grabbed another Emmy the following year for her television special with Julie Andrews, *Julie and Carol Live at Carnegie Hall.* Even as her career soared, Burnett's marriage to Saroyan was undergoing severe strains. The couple separated amicably in 1960 and divorced in 1962. Her popularity on the *Garry Moore Show* persuaded CBS executives to sign Burnett to a ten-year contract. In 1963 Burnett married Joe Hamilton, producer of the *Garry Moore Show.* That same year, Burnett appeared in her first motion picture, *Who's Been Sleeping in My Bed?* However, her special magic seemed not to work as well on the big screen as it did in the smaller, more intimate world of television.

Burnett's first star vehicle for CBS was a variety series entitled *The Entertainers* that debuted in 1964. She was, along with Bob Newhart and Caterina Valente, one of the show's three rotating hosts. Unfortunately, the show failed to catch on with television viewers, and was cancelled early in the following year. Burnett's contract with CBS called for her to do one special a year and make at least two guest appearances on other network shows. Although company executives encouraged her to take on another sitcom, Burnett adamantly resisted, reasoning, "They would probably name me Gertrude or Agnes, and that's all I'd be forever."

So popular were Burnett's occasional variety specials that CBS eventually began pushing her to host a regular weekly show in this genre. She learned some important lessons about what works and what does not in a 1967 special called *Carol + 2,* which paired her with guests Lucille Ball and Zero Mostel. Probably the least successful of Burnett's specials, the show featured skits that somehow never got off the ground, as well as generally unsatisfying performances from all involved. When she finally succumbed to the network's pressure and agreed to host the weekly *Carol Burnett Show,* Burnett insisted that the project be put in the hands of a brand-new production company. Joe Hamilton was signed as producer.

Burnett's weekly variety show debuted with a splash on 11 September 1967, with Jim Nabors, star of the popular sitcom *Gomer Pyle,* as guest star. The show was added to the already popular CBS Monday night lineup that included *Gunsmoke, The Lucy Show, The Andy Griffith Show,* and *Family Affair.* Burnett's initial show proved such a big hit with audiences that for most of its eleven-year run she insisted on Nabors as her guest star for the opening show of each subsequent season. Good-luck charm or not, Nabors

was probably less central to the show's success than the regular team of supporting players, which included Harvey Korman, Lyle Waggoner, and a young unknown named Vicki Lawrence. While still a senior in high school, Lawrence sent Burnett a local newspaper clipping that remarked on the teenager's uncanny resemblance to the actress. In an accompanying letter, Lawrence invited Burnett to come see her perform at the local fire company's "Miss Fireball Contest." Since Burnett was engaged in a search for an actress to play her younger sister on her variety show, she made plans to attend the event. Impressed with Lawrence's talent, Burnett signed her for the show, and Lawrence remained for the full eleven-year run.

As able as Burnett's team of supporting players was, in the final analysis, the show's success could be credited mostly to Burnett's uniquely intimate relationship with not only the studio audience, but with the nationwide television audience as well. A star of undeniable brilliance, she somehow managed to come across as "just plain folks" with audiences. Although Burnett prefers to be known as an actress who does comedy, she is also an undeniably brilliant comedienne. This became clear in her stand-up routines at the beginning of every show. Her acting skills were equally apparent in the zany collection of characters she created during the run of her show. The heart of the Burnett show was sketch comedy, peopled with unforgettable characters such as burned-out film actress Nora Desmond, hapless secretary Mrs. Wiggins, and the cleaning lady, perhaps the most poignant of all Burnett's characters. Burnett also showed a particular talent for spoofing movies. The show's send-up of *Gone with the Wind,* entitled "Went with the Wind," is as dead-on a parody as one is ever likely to see. Equally hilarious was the Burnett team's take on soap opera melodrama, which was dubbed "As the Stomach Turns."

Burnett's variety hour soon became the most popular show of its type in television history. Largely on the strength of its success, Burnett in 1968 won the Golden Globe Award as Best Female Television Star and in 1969 was named Harvard University's Hasty Pudding Woman of the Year. One of the most enduring of the Burnett show's creations was the dysfunctional Harper family, forever squabbling in the fictional blue-collar town of Raytown. This recurring sketch on the weekly variety show featured Burnett as woebegone Eunice, married to good-for-nothing Ed (Korman), and forever bedeviled by her mother Thelma, who was played masterfully by Lawrence. So successful was the Harper family saga that it lived beyond the run of the Burnett variety show as a thirty-minute weekly sitcom entitled *Mama's Family.* Burnett was no longer a regular cast member in the spin-off, but she returned occasionally as Eunice.

Despite pressure from CBS to go for another season,

Burnett wisely opted to take her wildly successful weekly variety show off the air in 1978 before it began to wear thin with its audience. Although the show remained popular, the departures of some original cast members had taken some of the magic out of the show's trademark comedy sketches. Yeoman efforts by Tim Conway and Dick Van Dyke helped to keep things working, but the show's finest hours had passed.

Burnett made several films during the 1970s, and in the 1980s even returned to the stage, appearing in a number of Stephen Sondheim musicals. Efforts to recapture the magic of her 1967–1978 variety show, however, proved elusive. In the summer of 1979 she returned to television with an American Broadcasting Company (ABC) series entitled *Carol Burnett and Company*, which featured Lawrence and Conway but failed to win favor with viewers. A somewhat more successful effort, *Carol and Company,* went on the air on the National Broadcasting Company (NBC) in March 1990. Though well received by critics, the NBC half-hour show never won much of an audience, and was cancelled in 1991. A CBS variety series bearing the same title as Burnett's successful 1967–1978 show lasted only seven weeks in late 1991. However, *Showstoppers,* a November 2001 reunion of the regulars from Burnett's long-running variety show, attracted nearly 30 million viewers—the best performance in that time period that CBS had seen in more than a decade.

When Burnett married Hamilton in 1963, she found herself playing mother to her husband's eight children from a previous marriage, and before long, she and Hamilton added three daughters to the family. The marriage became troubled during the mid-1970s, and the couple separated in 1982. They divorced in 1984, and Hamilton died in 1991. When her eldest daughter Carrie was only thirteen, she became heavily addicted to alcohol and drugs. Burnett battled for the next four years to release her daughter from the grip of addiction, a struggle that was ultimately successful. During the process mother and daughter became closer than ever. In November 2001, Burnett married forty-five-year-old Brian Miller, a music contractor for the Hollywood Bowl Orchestra. Tragedy struck only a couple of months later in late January 2002, when Carrie succumbed to lung and brain cancer. Before Carrie's death, mother and daughter collaborated on *Hollywood Arms,* a play scheduled to open on Broadway in the fall of 2002.

Burnett's contributions to television and sketch comedy are incalculable. Those of the television viewing public who were fortunate enough to see them will never forget the zany characters she created. And Burnett's work is far from finished. In the early years of the new millennium, she continued to delight audiences on stage, screen, and television. Whether for her awe-inspiring Tarzan yell or her poignant portrayal of the cleaning lady, Burnett has made

an indelible impression upon popular culture. Her long-running television variety show was the best of its kind, its clever comedy skits earning Burnett the title of "Queen of Comedy." Perhaps more notably, her unique rapport with the audience has made her one of the best-loved entertainers of our time.

★

Burnett's autobiography, *One More Time* (1986), provides valuable insight into the early life of the actress, covering her childhood and very early career through her debut on Broadway. Helpful biographies include George Carpozi, *The Carol Burnett Story* (1975); C. B. Church, *Carol Burnett: Star of Comedy* (1976); Caroline Latham, *Carol Burnett: Funny Is Beautiful* (1986); J. Randy Taraborrelli, *Laughing Till It Hurts: The Complete Life and Career of Carol Burnett* (1988); and James Howe, *Carol Burnett: The Sound of Laughter* (1988).

DON AMERMAN

BURNS, Arthur Frank (*b.* 27 April 1904 in Stanislau, Austria [now Ukraine]; *d.* 26 June 1987 in Baltimore, Maryland), economist, and chairman of the U.S. Federal Reserve Board, who held that the government should fight inflation and unemployment by cutting taxes while maintaining the value of the dollar.

Burns was born Arthur Frank Burnseig, the only child of Nathan Burnseig and Sarah Juran, immigrants from eastern Europe who lived in Bayonne, New Jersey. His father worked as a painting contractor. An outstanding student at high school, Burns received a scholarship to Columbia University; he worked his way through school in a series of jobs that included painter, sailor, waiter, postal clerk, and shoe salesman. At Columbia he earned his B.A. in 1921, his M.A. in 1925, and his Ph.D. in economics in 1934. Meanwhile, in 1927 he began teaching economics at Rutgers University, which he continued doing until 1944.

In 1930 Burns began two associations that would last him the remainder of his life. He married Helen Bernstein on 25 January; they had two sons. Also that year he became a research associate at the National Bureau of Economic Research (NBER). In 1944 he forged yet another lifelong association when he went to work at Columbia as a professor of economics. That position lasted until 1959, whereupon he became John Bates Clark Professor of Economics (1959 to 1969), and finally an emeritus professor (1969 to 1987).

At the NBER, Burns came under the influence of economist Wesley Clair Mitchell, noted for his studies of business cycles. Later, he and Mitchell coauthored *Measuring Business Cycles* (1946). Burns rejected the ideas of the prominent British economist John Maynard Keynes, whose policies of large-scale government spending programs and increased money supplies were then being implemented

Arthur F. Burns. ARCHIVE PHOTOS, INC.

through President Franklin D. Roosevelt's New Deal programs. By the time he replaced Mitchell as director of research at the NBER in 1945, Burns had concluded that governments should maintain high employment levels but should restrict inflation.

During the 1950s Burns had an opportunity to put his ideas to work as chairman of the Council of Economic Advisors under President Dwight D. Eisenhower from 1953 to 1956. He would not hold such a prominent position in the realm of national economic policy again until his appointment as economic counselor to Richard M. Nixon in 1969, but he did serve as a member of the President's Advisory Committee on Labor-Management Policy from 1961 to 1966 under John F. Kennedy and Lyndon B. Johnson.

Ironically, Burns, an economic conservative whose most significant work was performed under Republican presidents, was nominally a Democrat. Though he was the most conservative member of the committee, he found support from Kennedy, who in 1962 called for tax cuts as a means of stimulating the economy. Kennedy also sought to index wage increases to increases in labor productivity, a policy Burns himself later imitated as Federal Reserve ("Fed") chairman under Nixon. Additionally, Kennedy and Johnson,

with Burns's support, put together a tax-cut plan, which was passed by Congress in 1964.

Burns favored making annual tax cuts, but by the time of Nixon's election in 1968 the human and economic toll of the Vietnam War had brought about a change of priorities. No longer was there the need to stimulate a good economy; rather, it was now a matter of rescuing a flagging economy from further decline. Not only had the war cost the nation heavily in terms of lives lost, but it had proved an enormous financial drain, bringing about the largest budget deficit since the end of World War II. This had in turn spawned high inflation, which, combined with the general crisis of confidence taking hold of the United States in the wake of the war, led to an erosion of faith in the government's ability to jump-start the economy.

Already by 1965 a word describing the resulting economic conditions had entered the language: *stagflation.* Though Burns did not coin the term, which refers to a situation of continuing inflation, relatively high unemployment, and stagnant consumer demand and economic growth, he famously warned against it in a 1970 speech. A year earlier Nixon had appointed him counselor, a position with a rank equivalent to that of a cabinet secretary, and in that capacity he held wide responsibilities in domestic affairs. An even more significant appointment followed in 1970, when Nixon chose him to chair the Fed.

To combat stagflation, Burns recommended the federal government cut back on spending and the Fed work to slow the growth of the money supply. These measures, he believed, would put the brakes on inflation without causing a recession. Nixon accepted the ideas in broad terms and incorporated them into his New Economic Policy, introduced after a meeting at Camp David on 15 August 1971. However, where the value of the dollar was concerned, Nixon rejected the advice of Burns and others, who favored stabilization of the currency, and instead brought an end to fixed exchange rates. In so doing, the president was following the advice of Undersecretary of the Treasury Paul Volcker, who in turn had been influenced by University of Chicago economist Milton Friedman—one of Burns's own students from Rutgers.

As a result of the Volcker measures, the value of the dollar fell against that of the Japanese yen and the West German deutschmark. At the same time, Burns's Fed tightened the money supply, sending interest rates skyrocketing and helping bring about a recession even as inflation continued to climb. Stagflation thus became a full-scale reality in the aftermath of Nixon's 1972 reelection, which ultimately brought about an even more serious crisis in the form of the Watergate scandal.

Although Burns had a reputation as a conservative and a dubious attitude toward government intervention in the economy, in a number of particulars he actually supported an activist role for the federal government. This was evident during Nixon's truncated second term, when Burns seemed to reverse many of the policies he had maintained in the first term, especially expanding the money supply to boost the economy. Yet signs of this changing attitude were already apparent in 1970 and 1971.

After the economic collapse of the Penn Central Railroad in 1970, Burns announced that the Fed would provide funds necessary to prevent a panic. During this time Burns began to support wage and price guidelines, and he influenced Nixon's implementation of these measures in 1971. In this year he first expanded the supply of currency, reinforcing the economy and helping ensure Nixon's 1972 landslide victory against South Dakota Senator George McGovern.

Nixon resigned in 1974, but Burns remained as Fed chairman under the administration of Gerald R. Ford and continued the policies of government intervention introduced under the Nixon administration. After President Jimmy Carter declined to reappoint him, Burns resigned from the Fed on 31 January 1978. Eighteen months later, following the brief tenure of G. William Miller, Volcker took office as Fed chairman.

Meanwhile, Burns had become involved with the American Enterprise Institute, which would establish the Arthur F. Burns Memorial Lecture series after his death. In 1981 he was appointed ambassador to the Federal Republic of Germany by President Ronald Reagan. He resigned in 1985 at the conclusion of Reagan's first term and in April 1987 underwent triple bypass heart surgery at Johns Hopkins Hospital in Baltimore. Burns died of complications from this surgery; he was honored with a memorial service held by the American Enterprise Institute.

During his career Burns published a dozen books and pamphlets and contributed to other works. His most significant publication, inasmuch as it is an overview of his ideas during the most important phase of his career, is *Reflections of an Economic Policy Maker: Speeches and Congressional Statements, 1969–1978* (1978). Notable publications during the 1960s include *The Management of Prosperity* (1966) and *The Business Cycle in a Changing World* (1969).

German chancellor Helmut Schmidt, who became a close friend during Burns's tenure as ambassador, called him "the Pope of Economics." Certainly Burns looms as large in national history as any Fed chairman, but observers are far from unanimous in their assessments of his legacy. In the view of some, Burns helped maintain economic stability during troubled times. Supporters point to his calm in the face of the Penn Central crisis, which not only served to allay fears but also advanced his personal prestige and the power of his office.

Detractors maintain that by reversing the free-market policies of his early career, Burns made a bad situation worse. Economic historians across a broad political spectrum have judged Nixon's wage and price controls a failure, and because Burns was one of the leading architects of that policy, some of the blame falls to him. Critics and admirers alike, however, agree that Burns was a strong leader in the Fed. Whereas his predecessor, William McChesney Martin, had led by consensus, Burns proposed that the chairman vote first, rather than last, so as to establish confidence in his leadership. By so doing he helped establish the national prominence of the Fed, paving the way for strong leadership by Alan Greenspan at the end of the twentieth century.

★

Burns's papers from his years in public service and academe are found in two collections. The larger of the two, at the Gerald R. Ford Library in Ann Arbor, Michigan, contains materials from Burns's tenure on the Federal Reserve Board, as well as documents concerning both domestic and international economic affairs. The Dwight D. Eisenhower Library in Abilene, Kansas, contains many of Burns's unpublished works, including speeches and lectures, notes from trips, and drafts for the book *Measuring Business Cycles.* Wyatt C. Wells addresses a key phase of Burns's career in *Economist in an Uncertain World: Arthur F. Burns and the Federal Reserve, 1970–78* (1994). Analyses of his work and ideas appear in Edward S. Flash, Jr., *Economic Advice and Presidential Leadership* (1965); Herbert Stein, *The Fiscal Revolution in America* (1969); and William Breit and Roger Ransom, *The Academic Scribblers* (1971). William Safire, *Before the Fall: An Inside View of the Pre-Watergate White House* (1975), contains information on Burns's role in the Nixon administration. Richard D. Bartel conducted a lengthy interview with Burns, published as "An Economist's Perspective over Sixty Years," *Challenge* 27 (Jan.–Feb. 1985): 17–25. An obituary is in the *New York Times* (27 June 1987).

JUDSON KNIGHT

BURROUGHS, William S(eward) (*b.* 5 February 1914 in St. Louis, Missouri; *d.* 2 August 1997 in Lawrence, Kansas), Beat generation novelist who authored *Naked Lunch* (1959) and served as a counterculture icon for the hippie and punk-rock movements.

The second of two sons born to Mortimer Perry Burroughs, a businessman, and Laura Lee, a descendent of Confederate general Robert E. Lee, William was named after his paternal grandfather, the man who perfected the adding machine and set up the Burroughs Corporation. Raised in an affluent household, Burroughs attended private schools in St. Louis and Los Alamos, New Mexico, before entering Harvard University in 1932. After receiving his B.A. in English in 1936, Burroughs studied medicine briefly at the University of Vienna. There he met Ilse Klapper, a

William S. Burroughs. HULTON/ARCHIVE BY GETTY IMAGES

German-Jewish refugee, whom he married in 1937 in order to help her escape from Nazi Germany. Although Klapper immigrated to the United States, she and Burroughs never lived together as man and wife and divorced in 1946.

After his return to the United States, Burroughs took courses in psychology and anthropology at Harvard and Columbia. In the summer of 1942 he was drafted, but he was honorably discharged in September after the Army reviewed his psychiatric history because of his mother's influence. Back in New York City in 1944, he met Jack Kerouac and Allen Ginsberg. Together they launched the "Beat generation," the most significant literary movement in the second half of the twentieth century. With their rejection of middle-class America's 1950s conformist values and their stress on the importance of individual freedom and expanded consciousness, Ginsberg's "Howl" (1956), Kerouac's *On The Road* (1957), and Burroughs's *Naked Lunch* (1959), inspired a generation of 1960s rebels bent on political, social, and spiritual reform.

Like the 1960s, however, the Beat movement had its dark side. In August 1944 Burroughs and Kerouac were arrested as material witnesses in a murder case involving two friends, Lucien Carr and David Kammerer. Carr had fatally stabbed Kammerer, a homosexual stalker who had relentlessly pursued him. Around this time Burroughs became addicted to morphine.

Living at 119 West 115th Street in 1945, in a large apartment he shared with Kerouac and his new bride Edie

Parker, Burroughs met Parker's roommate Joan Vollmer Adams. Although Burroughs's orientation was homosexual, he and Joan entered into a common-law marriage and she bore him a son, William Burroughs, Jr., in 1947 (he died in 1981). Burroughs and Adams remained together, both heavily abusing drugs, until September 1951 in Mexico City. At a drinking party, Adams challenged Burroughs to shoot a glass off her head in imitation of the legendary William Tell, and he shot her dead.

After Adams's death, Burroughs explored South America in search of the hallucinogenic drug Yage, before settling in Tangier in 1954. For the next few years he struggled with his drug habit and the writing of *Naked Lunch*, which was published first by Olympia Press in Paris in 1959, and then by Grove Press in the United States in 1962. A savage attack on all forms of power and control, the widely reviewed book was both lavishly praised and roundly condemned. Poet Karl Shapiro declared it to be "one of the most important pieces of literature in our time," while novelist John Wain viewed it as "the merest trash. . . ." To Norman Mailer, Burroughs was "the only American novelist living today who may conceivably be possessed of genius," but to the state of Massachusetts he was a pornographer. The obscenity trial that followed the publication of the book made *Naked Lunch* a best-seller. The Massachusetts Supreme Court decision on 7 July 1966, clearing the novel of the obscenity charge, marked a watershed in the history of literary censorship in the United States.

During the early 1960s Burroughs lived mostly in Paris and London. Working with the artist Brion Gysin, he discovered a new method of composition he called the "cut-up." This involved cutting up his own texts as well as others and randomly pasting them together. The process yielded interesting, sometimes startling results. With the cut-up method, Burroughs believed he had found a way to bypass the ultimate source of control—language itself. He used the cut-up heavily in *The Soft Machine* (1961), *The Ticket That Exploded* (1962), and *Nova Express* (1964), a trilogy devoted to an alien Nova mob and their plan to conquer planet Earth. By the end of the decade the United States was to land a man on the Moon. Burroughs sought to create a new mythology commensurate with America's quest for a "New Frontier": "This is the space age," he proclaimed, "we are here to go. . . ."

In the late 1960s London was a mecca for experimental arts. Burroughs took a flat at 8 Duke Street and remained there for the next eight years. Through his friend Ian Sommerville, he met Paul McCartney, and in 1967 he appeared on the album cover of the Beatles' *Sgt. Pepper's Lonely Hearts Club Band*.

In August 1968 *Esquire* magazine asked Burroughs to cover the Democratic National Convention in Chicago, along with Terry Southern and Jean Genet. The delegates were meeting at the Conrad Hilton Hotel to choose between Hubert H. Humphrey and Eugene McCarthy, but the real drama took place in Chicago's streets, as 20,000 police and National Guard troops clashed with Yippie (Youth International Party) demonstrators, led by Jerry Rubin and Abbie Hoffman, who had come to protest the Vietnam War and celebrate a "festival of life." The confrontation turned into a nationally televised bloodbath. Burroughs joined his friend Allen Ginsberg in the front lines of the march from Lincoln Park, although he had little faith in either the Yippie's provocative theatrics or Ginsberg's "flower power" as effective agents of political change. Before returning to London, Burroughs saw Jack Kerouac one last time. The "king of the Beats" died on 21 October 1969.

Burroughs remained productive throughout the 1970s and 1980s. Following *The Wild Boys: A Book of the Dead* (1971), he began work on the Red Night trilogy, which included *Cities of the Red Night* (1981), *The Place of the Dead Roads* (1984), and *The Western Lands* (1987). He returned to New York City in 1973 and taught writing in the master of fine arts program at City College in fall 1974. From 1975 to 1981 Burroughs lived at "the Bunker" at 222 Bowery. His proximity to the music club CBGB's put him in close touch with the punk-rock scene. In 1981, at the urging of his secretary, James Grauerholz, Burroughs moved to Lawrence, Kansas, where he lived quietly until his death of heart failure. He is buried in Bellfontaine Cemetery in St. Louis.

Writing in the *New York Times Book Review*, critic Perry Meisel remarked, "By the time the counterculture of the 1960s succeeded the Beats, license had become law, and Mr. Burroughs had become a principal avatar of the liberationist esthetic he helped create." Burroughs's contempt for authority, combined with his surreal treatment of violence, homosexuality, and drug addiction, appealed to young people, particularly musicians. The bands Soft Machine, the Mugwumps, and Steely Dan all derived their names from his books. He collaborated with a host of rock stars including Laurie Anderson, Kurt Cobain, U2, and Tom Waits, and is credited with coining the term "heavy metal" to describe this subgenre of rock music. Burroughs's pervasive influence on popular culture, however, was not without its price. Ironically, his growing popularity, which led to television and film appearances, even a Nike commercial, helped turn a literary outlaw into a pop icon.

★

Manuscripts and papers relating to Burroughs are in the libraries of Ohio State University, Columbia University, and Arizona State University. Biographies include Ted Morgan, *Literary Outlaw: The Life and Times of William S. Burroughs* (1988), a detailed, well-researched work written with Burroughs's cooperation; and Barry Miles, *William Burroughs: El Hombre Invisible* (1993). Jennie Skerl, *William S. Burroughs* (1985), also contains biographical material. Published correspondence includes *The Yage Letters,* with Allen Ginsberg (1963); *Letters to Allen Ginsberg 1953–1957* (1982); and *The Letters of William S. Burroughs 1945–1959* (1993). *The Job* (1970, revised and enlarged edition 1974), interviews with Daniel Odier, is a good source on Burroughs's life and art through the 1960s. *Conversations with William S. Burroughs* (1999), and *Burroughs Live 1960–1999* (2001), contain the collected interviews from 1960 onward. The latter is more extensive and includes Conrad Knickerbocker, *Paris Review* (fall 1965) interview. Victor Bockris, *With William Burroughs: A Report From the Bunker* (1981), contains interviews and dinner conversations with literary and artistic friends including Allen Ginsberg, Andy Warhol, and Mick Jagger. *Last Words* (2000), is a journal recording Burroughs's final thoughts between 14 November 1996 and 29 July 1997. *Word Virus: The William S. Burroughs Reader* (1999), excerpts from a lifetime's work, includes valuable biographical introductions for each section by Burroughs's longtime companion and literary executor James Grauerholz, as well as an accompanying compact disc of Burroughs reading from his work. His unique voice, a cross between T. S. Eliot and W. C. Fields, is preserved on numerous other recordings, including *Call Me Burroughs* (1965), *Dead City Radio* (1990), and *Spare Ass Annie and Other Tales* (1993). Howard Brookner, *Burroughs: The Movie* (1983), is an informative and entertaining documentary film. Obituaries are in the *New York Times,* (London) *Guardian*, and *Washington Post* (all 4 Aug. 1997).

WILLIAM M. GARGAN

C

CAGE, John Milton, Jr. (*b.* 5 September 1912 in Los Angeles, California; *d.* 12 August 1992 in New York City), pioneer in experimental music and performance art, regarded as one of the most influential avant-garde composers of the 1960s.

Cage was the only child of John Milton Cage, an inventor, and Lucretia Harvey, a columnist for the *Los Angeles Times*. Cage graduated as the class valedictorian from Los Angeles High School in 1928 and entered Pomona College in Claremont, California, but left school for Europe in 1930. He returned to the United States in 1931 and studied composition with Richard Buhlig, Adolph Weiss, Henry Cowell, and Arnold Schoenberg. On 7 June 1935 Cage married Xenia Andreyevna Kashevaroff, one of the six daughters of an Alaskan Russian Orthodox priest. They divorced in 1945.

Cage discovered he had little interest in traditional composition but was fond of experimenting with new methods. His first major experiment was *Bacchanale* (1938) for what he called the "prepared piano"—a piano with objects such as paper and nails inserted between the strings to produce a percussive sound. In 1943 the League of Composers presented a concert featuring works by Cage and others at the Museum of Modern Art in New York. The concert was warmly received and established Cage's place as a leading avant-garde composer. In 1949 his most famous work for the prepared piano, *Sonatas and Interludes* (1946–1948), de-

buted and was well received. He was recognized by the National Academy of Arts and Letters "for having thus extended the boundaries of musical art." In the 1950s, influenced by the *I Ching* (the Chinese *Book of Changes*), Cage began to employ chance operations to eliminate the subjective elements from his compositions. He abandoned traditional music structure such as form and harmony and used pitches that were randomly selected. His *Imaginary Landscape No. 4* (1951) and *Music of Changes* (1951) illustrate his idea of indeterminacy and unpredictability. In August 1952 in Woodstock, New York, Cage's famous silent piece *4'33"* was premiered by David Tudor, who sat at the piano for exactly four minutes, thirty-three seconds without playing. Any sound, including noise from the audience, was considered part of the performance.

The 1960s marked an important stage in Cage's life. He had often dreamed of establishing a center for experimental music in a college or university or with corporate sponsorship. This became a reality in 1960 when he was appointed a fellow of the Center for Advanced Studies at Wesleyan University in Middletown, Connecticut. During his residency (1960–1961, 1970) he was able to concentrate on experimental music and summarize his philosophy. Commissioned by the Montreal Festivals Society in 1961, Cage created an orchestra piece, *Atlas Eclipticalis* (1961–1962), by consulting astronomical charts. When the piece was performed by Leonard Bernstein with the New York Philharmonic at Lincoln Center in February 1964, not only the

John Cage. CORBIS CORPORATION (BELLEVUE)

audience but also some of the performers disliked it. Some critics were not in favor of Cage's work. The composer Aaron Copland once questioned whether the random nature of Cage's music could "hold the continuing interest of the rational mind." The trend of the counterculture in the 1960s, however, brought an awareness and understanding of Cage's ideas of Eastern philosophy and aesthetics in his musical creation. Cage's six-week concert tour of Japan with Tudor in 1962 and a world tour with the Cunningham Dance Company in 1964 were more successful stories. He became president of the Cunningham Dance Foundation and director of the Foundation for Contemporary Performing Arts in 1965.

In 1962 Cage founded the New York Mycological Society with Lois Long, Esther Dam, Guy G. Nearing, and Ralph Ferrara. He had become interested in mushroom study back in the 1950s when he lived in Stony Brook, New York. He developed his expertise in mycology and even used his knowledge to win a grand prize in an Italian television game-show contest in 1958. Cage was also interested in language in the late 1960s, particularly letters, words, and syllables.

A distinguishing feature of Cage's compositions in the 1960s was his increasingly complex performances that resulted in musical events as opposed to traditional concerts. Such performances required a long time, usually months, to prepare the scores and performing materials. When Cage served as composer in residence at the University of Cincinnati, he produced *Musicircus* (1967), a mixed-media hap-pening involving dancers, mimes, singers, rock musicians, jazz performers, and pianists who performed simultaneously with films and slide shows. He was also appointed research professor and associate of the Center for Advanced Study at the University of Illinois (1967–1969) and artist in residence at the University of California at Davis (1969). His *HPSCHD* (pronounced "harpsichord," 1969, in collaboration with the University of Illinois composer Lejaren Hiller, Jr.) was an astonishing multimedia event combining performances of computer-modified works of Mozart, Beethoven, Chopin, Schoenberg, Hiller, and Cage by seven harpsichordists together with electronic tapes, amplifiers, speakers, films, slides, and colored lights. In *Cheap Imitation* (1969), his typical work prepared using the *I Ching*, Cage replaced the original pitches (based on *Socrate* by the French composer Erik Satie) with randomly selected notes.

The publication of Cage's writings accelerated in the 1960s. Wesleyan University Press published two important books, *Silence* (1961) and *A Year from Monday* (1967). The books contained two collections of Cage's essays, lectures, and personal memoirs that reflected his thoughts, ideas, aesthetics, and philosophy. "This is a book," wrote reviewer B. D. Henry, referring to *A Year from Monday*, "which should be read by everyone who wants to know what the arts of today are about." Cage's philosophy was well stated in *Silence*: "Our intention is to affirm this life, not to bring order out of chaos or to suggest improvements in creation, but simply to wake up to the very life we're living, which is so excellent once one gets one's mind and one's desires out of the way and lets it act of its own accord." Other notable books published in this decade included *Diary* (1967–1968); *Notations* (1969, with Alison Knowles), which included photographs of his collection of autographs from more than 300 composers; and *To Describe the Process of Composition Used in Not Wanting to Say Anything About Marcel* (1969). In recognition of his achievements, Cage was elected to the National Institute of Arts and Letters in 1968 and awarded the Thorne Music Grant in 1969.

In the 1970s and 1980s, some of Cage's compositions showed a tendency toward the traditional. His *Etudes Australes* (1974–1975) employed conventional instrumentation and notation, and *Thirteen Harmonies* (1984) even revealed a concern for harmony. In 1987 his opera, *Europera*, premiered in Frankfurt, Germany. Among numerous awards, Cage was elected to the American Academy of Arts and Sciences (1978), made Commandeur de l'Ordre des Arts et Lettres by the French Ministry of Culture (1982), appointed Charles Eliot Norton Professor of Poetry at Harvard University (1988–1989), inducted into the American Academy of Arts and Letters (1989), and awarded the Kyoto Prize (1989).

Six feet tall, with a craggy face, Cage was charming, witty, and friendly toward young musicians and critics. In his late years Cage was troubled by arthritis, but he acted with the grace of his youthful appearance. Before his eightieth birthday, the music world planned a series of celebrations, concerts, symposia, and exhibitions, but Cage died of a stroke at Saint Vincent's Hospital in New York City. His body was cremated and the ashes scattered at sea.

A leading avant-garde musical artist, Cage had an extraordinary influence on composers of his generation. His music and ideas were controversial but also opened a wide range of new artistic possibilities. His unconventional musical concepts and methods were widely used by other avant-garde composers such as Philip Glass and Steve Reich. Perhaps Cage's impact in the 1960s was best described in Peter Yates's review of *Imaginary Landscape No. 5* in 1963: "John Cage would appear to be the most influential living composer today—whatever opinion you or I may hold about his music."

★

Cage's "An Autobiographical Statement," delivered in Kyoto, Japan, in November 1989 when he received the Kyoto Prize, was published in the *Southwest Review* (winter 1991). Robert Dunn, *John Cage* (1962), is a bibliography of Cage's works along with a brief biography. Calvin Tomkins, *The Bride and the Bachelors: The Heretical Courtship in Modern Art* (1965), offers more detailed biographical information. Richard Kostelanetz, a renowned Cage expert, published numerous works on Cage, including *John Cage* (1970), a compilation of writings by and about Cage; *Writings About John Cage* (1993), a collection of essays by prominent au-

thors such as Henry Cowell, Virgil Thomson, and Peter Yates; and "The American Avant-Garde, Part II: John Cage," *Stereo Review* (May 1969). Other current readings include David Revill, *The Roaring Silence: John Cage, A Life* (1992), and Marjorie Perloff and Charles Junkerman, eds., *John Cage: Composed in America* (1994). Obituaries are in the *New York Times* (13 Aug. 1992) and *Billboard* (22 Aug. 1992).

DI SU

CALLEY, William Laws, Jr. (*b.* 8 June 1943 in Miami, Florida), second lieutenant in the U.S. Army and, after the longest court-martial in military history, the only U.S. soldier convicted of a crime in the My Lai massacre during the Vietnam War.

Calley was the second of four children of William Laws Calley, who sold heavy construction equipment until his business went bankrupt, and his wife. He grew up in a relatively prosperous middle-class home and was characterized as somewhat of a loner and as a below-average student. During his high school years he attended Florida Military and Georgia Military Academies before graduating from Miami Edison Senior High School in 1962. After high school he spent one year at Palm Beach Junior College. He flunked out in 1963 and worked at odd jobs, including dishwasher, railroad switchman, and insurance appraiser. In 1964, as railroad switchman, Calley was arrested for allowing a forty-seven-car freight train to block traffic for nearly thirty minutes during rush hour at several downtown intersections, but he was cleared of the charges. Calley tried to enlist in the U.S. Army in 1964 but was rejected because of hearing problems. He wandered around doing other odd jobs before finding his roots in 1966 as an enlisted man in the army. (During the conflict in Vietnam, the army decided to reclassify certain formerly ineligible potential recruits.) His mother died of cancer shortly after he went into the army.

Calley's military career began in July 1966 with basic training in Fort Bliss, Texas, after which he was transferred to Fort Lewis, Washington, where he trained as a clerk-typist. On 16 March 1967 he went to the Fort Benning School for Boys in Fort Benning, Georgia, to attend Officers Candidate School (OCS), where, according to Calley, he learned to kill. OCS was a struggle for Calley, but training was accelerated in the summer, when the battalion was to be deployed earlier than had been expected. After OCS, Calley joined Charlie Company, First Battalion, Twentieth Infantry, in Hawaii, under the command of Captain Ernest Medina. He was given charge of the rifle company's first platoon. On 1 December 1967 Calley, now a lieutenant in the Eleventh Infantry, landed in Vietnam and immediately began to conduct patrol missions in the hills of northern

William L. Calley, Jr., during the My Lai court-martial proceedings, 1971.
ASSOCIATED PRESS AP

South Vietnam. On 16 March 1968 Calley led a patrol into the village of My Lai in the Quang Ngai Province and participated in what became known as the largest massacre ever perpetrated by U.S. soldiers.

Knowing very little about combat, Calley, along with about eighty men of Company C, led search-and-destroy missions to force the Forty-eighth Vietcong to move. Calley's first platoon led the sweep into the hamlet of My Lai, an alleged Vietcong stronghold, and attacked the village shortly after sunrise. In the course of combat, villagers were gathered and taken to Calley for questioning before the alleged killings began on the early afternoon of 16 March 1968. Estimates of the number of people killed varied, but the final army estimate was 347. The five-foot, three-inch, twenty-four-year-old platoon leader, who wanted to make the military his career, stormed his way into international history by way of what came to be called My Lai Four (after the tiny hamlet where the massacre took place), an event that had an immeasurable impact on the 1960s, a decade labeled as the "decade of tumult and change."

The actions at My Lai received only a passing mention at the weekly Saigon military meeting in March 1968. In April the army looked into the rumors of civilian deaths in My Lai but found nothing to warrant disciplinary measures. Months after the My Lai massacre, the American public learned of what happened when the returning Vietnam veterans and news reporters began to piece together reports from Vietnamese refugees and U.S. soldiers who

had been eyewitnesses to or heard of the massacre. According to these reports, the U.S. troops in My Lai encountered little if any hostile fire, found virtually no enemy soldiers in the village, and suffered only one casualty.

Soon after the My Lai massacre, Captain Medina had promoted Calley to first lieutenant, and Calley stayed in Vietnam on search-and-destroy missions for another year. He requested and received a transfer out of Charlie Company to Company G of the Seventy-fifth Rangers. Soon, however, a series of letters by a former soldier to government officials forced the army to take action. Early in June 1969, a month before his tour ended, Calley was pulled out of Vietnam and sent to Fort Benning, Georgia, with special orders to report to Washington, D.C. Accordingly, his request for a third tour of Vietnam was turned down. On 19 June 1969 Calley was advised that he might be charged with murder for his actions at My Lai Four.

In September 1969, to Calley's surprise, he was formally charged with the murder of civilians. In November 1969 the story of the My Lai massacre was on the front pages of newspapers and magazines around the world. Calley's court-martial began in November 1970. As he testified, "I was ordered to . . . destroy the enemy. I did not sit down and think in terms of men, women, and children. They were all classified the same, . . . just enemy soldiers." On 29 March 1971 six army combat veterans found Calley guilty of the premeditated murder of at least twenty-two civilians and sentenced him to life imprisonment at hard labor. His sentence was later reduced to ten years, and in September 1974 a federal district court overturned the conviction. Released on parole in November and given a dishonorable discharge, Calley became a free man. He is the manager of a jewelry store in Columbus, Georgia.

Some say that what happened at My Lai was in part due to U.S. military policy. Moralists would claim Calley's actions were unconscionable. Still others would make the case that Calley was merely obeying orders—to destroy My Lai and everything in it. Although the My Lai massacre will remain in the historical records, the magnitude of its horror seems to have faded with the passing of the years.

★

Biographical information on Calley can be gleaned from various sources. John Sack, *Lieutenant Calley: His Own Story* (1971), gives Calley's thoughts on his life before My Lai through his trial for the massacre. Pertinent biographical information can be found in Richard Hammer, *The Court-Martial of Lt. Calley* (1971). Wayne Greenshaw, *The Making of a Hero: The Story of Lieutenant William L. Calley, Jr.* (1971), provides details on Calley's emergence as a hero and discusses the reasons why some people consider him one.

JOYCE K. THORNTON

CALVIN, Melvin (*b.* 8 April 1911 in Saint Paul, Minnesota; *d.* 8 January 1997 in Berkeley, California), biochemist who received the 1961 Nobel Prize for chemistry for his discovery of the chemical pathways of photosynthesis.

Calvin was the son of Elias Calvin, a factory worker originally from Lithuania, and Rose Irene (Hervitz) Calvin, a homemaker originally from what is now the nation of Georgia. Calvin attended public schools and graduated from Central High School in Detroit, Michigan, in 1927. He received his B.Sc. in chemistry in 1931 from the Michigan College of Mining and Technology (now the Michigan Technological University) in Houghton, Michigan, where he was the college's first chemistry major, and his Ph.D. in chemistry in 1935 from the University of Minnesota. His doctoral work was under the direction of George A. Glocker, and his dissertation examined the electron affinity of halogens—that is, the means by which elements in the halogen family (including chlorine and fluorine) exert the strong chemical bonding forces that they do. Calvin was awarded a Rockefeller Foundation fellowship, and from 1935 to 1937 worked with Michael Polanyi, a Hungarian-born physical chemist best known for his work on adsorption processes and his philosophy of science and society, at the University of Manchester, England. While studying in Manchester, Calvin developed an interest in coordination catalysis, especially metalloporphyrins (organic molecules producing chlorophyll and hemoglobin).

Calvin's academic career started in 1937 at the University of California, Berkeley, as an instructor, at the invitation of Gilbert N. Lewis. He was the first non-Berkeley graduate to be hired by the Department of Chemistry in more than twenty-five years and was one of the first chemists to join Ernest O. Lawrence's Radiation Laboratory. Calvin became assistant professor in 1941, associate professor in 1945, full professor in 1947, and university professor of chemistry in 1971. He developed an interest in the theoretical aspects of organic molecular structure and behavior. (The term *organic* in chemistry refers to the study of carbon-containing compounds.) His two main publications during his early years at Berkeley were *The Color of Organic Substances* (1939), with G. N. Lewis, and *The Theory of Organic Chemistry* (1941), with G. E. K. Branch.

His career was interrupted from 1941 to 1945 as he worked on government projects during World War II, including the National Defense Research Council and two years on the Manhattan Project. On 4 October 1942 Calvin married Marie Genevieve Jemtegaard; they had two daughters and one son.

Calvin's work in photosynthesis (the process by which green plants use solar energy to convert water and carbon dioxide into carbohydrates and oxygen) began in the mid-1940s. Calvin was awarded the 1961 Nobel Prize in chem-

Melvin Calvin. THE LIBRARY OF CONGRESS

istry for his explanation of the process of photosynthesis. He developed a system using carbon-14, utilizing the newly available radioisotopes from the Hanford and Oak Ridge National Laboratories, as a tracer in the green algae *Chlorella*. He and his team mapped the complete route that carbon travels through a plant during photosynthesis, starting from its absorption as atmospheric carbon dioxide to its conversion into carbohydrates and other compounds. His experiments consisted of arresting *Chlorella*'s growth at various stages and measuring the amount of radioactive material present, thus being able to identify most of the reactions involved in the intermediate steps of photosynthesis.

Calvin's work showed that sunlight acts on the chlorophyll in a plant to fuel the manufacture of organic compounds other than just carbon dioxide, as previously believed. It was already known that there were two interdependent processes in photosynthesis: the light reaction, in which a plant captures energy from sunlight, and the dark reaction, in which carbon dioxide and water combine to form carbohydrates such as sugar and starch. Calvin's work on photosynthesis concentrated on the light-independent reaction, previously referred to as the dark reaction. Calvin used paper chromatography (a method used to analyze complex mixtures by separating them into the chemicals from which they are made, with paper used as a stationary phase), to identify ten intermediate products generated by the photosynthetic process. This cycle of reactions is now referred to as the Calvin Cycle.

Calvin was director of the organic chemistry group in the Lawrence Radiation Laboratory from 1946, and he established the laboratory's Chemical Biodynamics Division, which he directed for twenty years.

A new, three-story building was opened on the Berkeley campus in 1963 to house his research group. The doughnut-shaped structure, designed by Calvin, had an open interior with radial lab benches, all intended to foster an atmosphere of cooperative teamwork. Upon Calvin's retirement, the unique, circular building was renamed the Melvin Calvin Laboratory.

Calvin received numerous awards and honorary degrees during his lifetime, including election to the National Academy of Sciences, the American Philosophical Society, the American Academy of Arts and Sciences, the Royal Society of London, the Royal Netherlands Academy of Sciences and Letters, and the German Academy of Scientists. Calvin wrote more than 500 papers and seven books, including *Chemical Evolution* (1969). Calvin received the Davy Medal from the Royal Society of London (1964), the Priestley Medal from the American Chemical Society (1978), the Gold Medal from the American Institute of Scientists (1979), and the National Medal of Science (1989).

From 1963 to 1966, during the administration of President Lyndon B. Johnson, Calvin was a member of the President's Science Advisory Committee, and in 1975, under President Gerald R. Ford, he served on the President's Advisory Group on Major Advances in Science and Technology. Calvin also advised the National Aeronautics and Space Administration (NASA) and the Department of Energy. Both NASA's moon missions and its search for extraterrestrial life were influenced by Calvin's input. His efforts included protecting the Moon against biological contamination from Earth during the Apollo landings; preventing cross-contamination between the Moon and Earth; searching for organic and biological compounds in lunar samples; and planning for the search for biological compounds on other planets.

In 1980, after stepping down from the directorship of the laboratory of chemical biodynamics, Calvin directed a small research group in the chemistry department until 1996, studying artificial photosynthesis and plant-produced fuel and chemical feedstock substitutes. He maintained a lifelong interest in adapting photosynthetic techniques for energy production.

After years of failing health, Calvin died at the age of eighty-five from a heart attack. On 25 January 1997 a memorial service was held for him at Hertz Hall at Berkeley. Calvin's alma mater, Michigan Technological University, established the Melvin Calvin Nobel Laureate Lecture in

1997. In 2002 Berkeley announced the creation of the Melvin Calvin Distinguished Professorship in the department of chemistry.

★

Biographical information about Calvin is in Eduard Farber, *Nobel Prize Winners in Chemistry, 1901–1961* (1963); David W. Swift, *SETI Pioneers: Scientists Talk About Their Search for Extraterrestrial Intelligence* (1990): 116–135; and David H. and Diane W. Husic, *Nobel Laureates in Chemistry, 1901–1992* (1993): 423–425. Obituaries are in the *New York Times* and the *San Francisco Chronicle* (both 10 Jan. 1997) and the *Los Angeles Times* (11 Jan. 1997).

MARIA PACHECO

CAMPBELL, Joseph John (*b.* 26 March 1904 in New York City; *d.* 30 October 1987 in Honolulu, Hawaii), mythologist, storyteller, and educator who applied the insights of depth psychology to comparative religion and popularized the approach in the 1960s.

Campbell was the oldest of three children born to Charles Campbell, a traveling salesman, and Josephine Lynch. As a boy he saw the totem poles at the Museum of Natural History and Buffalo Bill's Wild West Show at Madison Square Garden, and became intensely interested in Native American culture. Campbell was not merely curious about Native Americans; he identified with them. He liked to tell the story of a family walk on Riverside Drive during which a woman stopped and remarked, "What nice little boys!" He looked up at her seriously and said, "I have Indian blood in me." Not to be outdone, his brother added, "I have dog blood in me."

In 1921 Campbell enrolled at Dartmouth College, but a year later he transferred to Columbia University. At Columbia he studied literature, ran track, and played the saxophone in jazz bands. He earned his A.B. in 1925. In 1926 he wrote his master's thesis, *A Study of the Dolorous Stroke*, on Wasteland imagery in the Arthurian legends. (The Wasteland is a place or state of spiritual desolation.) Between 1927, when he earned his M.A. at Columbia, and 1929, he studied medieval French at the University of Paris and Sanskrit at the University of Munich. While in Europe he also encountered the ideas of the Austrian psychoanalyst Sigmund Freud and the Swiss psychiatrist Carl Jung, and the novels of James Joyce and Thomas Mann.

In 1929, frustrated by the narrowness of academic curricula, Campbell rented a cabin in Woodstock, New York, and continued reading on his own. In 1934 he took a job with the literature department at Sarah Lawrence College, a position he would hold for thirty-eight years. On 5 May 1938 he married Jean Erdman, a former student and a member of the Martha Graham Dance Company. They had no children.

During his first years at Sarah Lawrence, Campbell met the Indologist Heinrich Zimmer and, after Zimmer's death, edited his unpublished writings. In 1949 he finished his classic *The Hero with a Thousand Faces*. In this book Campbell drew on Jung's theory of archetypes, elementary figures of the human unconscious that guide behavior. He argued that all heroic tales have the same underlying structure and that they are not idle fantasies, but useful guides to life. In his words, "The latest incarnation of Oedipus, the continued romance of Beauty and the Beast, stand this afternoon on the corner of Forty-second Street and Fifth Avenue, waiting for the traffic light to change."

The 1960s were the hinge of Campbell's career. During that decade he completed *The Masks of God* (1959–1968), a four-volume compilation of his college lectures on religion. Although he made use of Jungian archetypes in this series, he also maintained that some mythological themes, such as the widespread story of the serpent and the maiden, were diffused from culture to culture. In the final volume, *Creative Mythology* (1968), Campbell argued that science and technology had made traditional religious systems obsolete and that modern people should construct new myths from their own experiences. Invoking the Arthurian legends, he offered his readers a choice between the Grail Quest—the life-affirming path to personal fulfillment—and dead parochial faiths leading into a spiritual Wasteland.

During the 1960s Campbell presented his ideas in a variety of forums. He lectured at the Cooper Union in New York City; at the Foreign Service Institute in Washington, D.C.; and at the Esalen Institute, a New Age growth center in Big Sur, California. Also, in 1960 he became a trustee of the Bollington Foundation, a Jungian society in Switzerland. Finally, in 1969 he published *The Flight of the Wild Gander,* a cross-cultural study of the origin and function of myth.

Despite his individualism, Campbell was very uneasy with the culture of the 1960s. Particularly misguided, in his opinion, were communism and experimental drug use. Behind the former's promise of material happiness, he saw a new, even more oppressive kind of orthodoxy. In the latter he detected an immature attempt to skip necessary steps on the way to wisdom. When a young woman told him that her generation was able to go from childhood straight to enlightenment, he replied, "But, my dear, then all you've missed is life."

Campbell was also troubled by personal issues during the 1960s. In 1964 he lost both his brother, who suffered from alcoholism, and his friend and editor Pascal Covici. Meanwhile, his wife traveled abroad to put on her play *The Coach with Six Insides*. Although this separation preserved a measure of romance in the marriage, it also made both

Joseph Campbell. © BETTMANN/CORBIS

Campbell and Jean lonely. To make matters worse, Campbell continued to face criticism of his work. A negative review of *Occidental Mythology* (1964), the third volume of *The Masks of God*, occasioned a particularly unpleasant episode. In an uncharacteristically bellicose series of letters, Campbell went on the offensive, impugning the reviewer's credentials and even his intelligence.

It is to Campbell's credit that he did not play the curmudgeon or force his political views on his students. Patiently, he endured a Vietcong flag and a portrait of the Chinese leader Mao Zedong in the room above his office. His entire life was a testimony to the importance of "following one's own bliss," a phrase associated with Campbell. Still, he always recognized the benefit of collective rituals. After President John F. Kennedy's assassination in 1963, he thought the United States needed "a compensatory rite to re-establish the sense of solidarity," and he was deeply moved by the president's funeral.

Campbell reached the height of his popularity in the 1970s and 1980s, in part because of the movie director George Lucas, who wanted his *Star Wars* saga to be a modern myth and used the blueprint in *The Hero with a Thousand Faces* to construct its plot. Also, Lucas's Skywalker Ranch in Nicasio, California, was the setting for some of Bill Moyers's interviews of Campbell in 1985. In 1987, the year Campbell died of cancer of the esophagus, these interviews aired on Public Television as *The Power of Myth*. They are available on audiocassette and videotape and in print. For many, they have served as an introduction to Campbell's ideas. Campbell is buried in Oahu Cemetery in Hawaii.

★

Campbell's papers are located at Pacifica Graduate Institute, Carpinteria, California. His authorized biography is Stephen and Robin Larsen, *Joseph Campbell: A Fire in the Mind* (1991). The best interview with Campbell is Bill Moyers, *The Power of Myth* (1988). A wealth of information may also be found in Phil Cousineau, *The Hero's Journey: Joseph Campbell on His Life and Work* (1990). Campbell's *Myths to Live By* (1972), a collection of his lectures from the Cooper Union, is an excellent introduction to his ideas.

STEVEN M. STANNISH

CAPOTE, Truman Garcia (*b.* 30 September 1924 in New Orleans, Louisiana; *d.* 25 August 1984 in Los Angeles, California), flamboyant novelist, journalist, playwright, screenwriter, and short-story writer, known for the precision of his prose and his ostentatious lifestyle, who is often credited with creating the genre of the nonfiction novel with the publication of *In Cold Blood* (1966).

Capote was born Truman Streckfus Persons, the son of Archulus "Arch" Persons and Lillie Mae Faulk (later Nina Capote). As a child, Capote saw little of his parents. His father was frequently off chasing get-rich-quick schemes that never panned out. His mother was often away pursuing her fervent desire for a grander life, leaving Capote in the care of relatives in Monroeville, Alabama, where he became childhood friends with (Nelle) Harper Lee, who would eventually write the highly acclaimed *To Kill a Mockingbird*. Lee was only the first of the famous people Capote would become acquainted with during the course of his life.

In 1931 Capote's mother moved to New York City to live with Joseph Garcia Capote, a successful businessman. She divorced Arch Persons, married Joe Capote, and discarded the name "Lillie Mae" for the more sophisticated "Nina." In 1932 Capote joined his mother and her new husband in New York. Joe Capote legally adopted Truman on 14 February 1935, and Truman Persons became Truman Capote.

Convinced at an early age that he wanted to be a writer, Capote was a disinterested student, and when the opportunity presented itself, he abandoned school for a position as a copyboy with *The New Yorker*. By the mid-1940s, he had begun to publish short stories in respected periodicals

Truman Capote. GETTY IMAGES

such as *Harper's Bazaar* and *Mademoiselle*. His work was well received, and in 1946 he won the O. Henry Memorial Award for "Miriam."

By the time Capote's first novel, *Other Voices, Other Rooms,* found print in 1948, literary circles in New York were already buzzing with rumors about his talent, and Capote, always the *homme d'esprit* (witty gentleman), had ingratiated himself into New York society's inner circle. Capote continued to publish fiction, essays, plays, and screenplays throughout the 1950s, but two events occurred in the 1960s that made that decade the pinnacle of his life and career.

The first was the result of a single-column story in the 16 November 1959 edition of the *New York Times* titled "Wealthy Farmer, 3 of Family Slain." The story about the murder of a farmer, his wife, and his two children in a small town in Holcomb, Kansas, took possession of Capote, and he was compelled to write about the incident. Originally planning to write a short piece for *The New Yorker,* Capote, accompanied by Harper Lee, traveled to the small town to interview people who had known the murdered family. After a rocky start, Capote managed to penetrate the small town culture of Holcomb, despite his boyish appearance, effeminate mannerisms, and high-pitched voice. When the two murderers were arrested in late 1959, Capote began adding their story to his work.

Obsessed with the story and aware of its potential to result in a literary masterpiece, Capote maintained an ongoing relationship with both killers until their executions in 1965. The resulting book, *In Cold Blood,* which was published in January 1966, was indeed hailed as a masterpiece and brought Capote both the critical and popular success he had imagined when he first began to write. It was Capote himself who coined the term "nonfiction novel" to describe what he considered a new literary form. Most literary scholars disagreed that it was a new genre, but that did not deter them from admitting the book's brilliance. Noel Coward called it a masterpiece, as did Conrad Knickerbocker in his review for the *New York Times Book Review.* Readers fought over copies. Irving "Swifty" Lazar smashed a glass over Otto Preminger's head at the 21 Club when the two fought after Lazar backed out of a promise to sell the film rights to Preminger for a Frank Sinatra vehicle. Capote's biographer Gerald Clarke put it succinctly when he wrote, "Nineteen sixty-six was . . . [Capote's] year."

The publication of *In Cold Blood* made Capote a household name—a widely recognized figure in American literature and culture, but the next monumental event in Capote's life during the 1960s doubled his fame and made him a legend. Partly as an offering to the hundreds of rich, famous, and influential people who had befriended him throughout his life, and partly to further his own more mature image, Capote planned and executed the single most important social event of the 1960s—the Black and White Ball in honor of *Washington Post* publisher Katherine Graham at the Plaza Hotel in New York City on 28 November 1966. Capote's planning was as meticulous as his writing. His exclusive guest list included some of the most influential people in the world: writers such as Norman Mailer, Edward Albee, Philip Roth, and Tennessee Williams; celebrities such as Tallulah Bankhead, Frank Sinatra and Mia Farrow, Lauren Bacall, Douglas Fairbanks, Jr., Andy Warhol, and Greta Garbo; a broad assortment of royalty; and a gathering of Vanderbilts, Rothschilds, and Rockefellers. The event drew so much attention that the *New York Times* printed the guest list on its front page.

For the remainder of the 1960s, Truman Capote was "omnipotent" (as *Women's Wear Daily* claimed). "His mere presence . . . virtually guaranteed the success of any event he attended," said Kay Meehan. A society reporter for the *New York Times* claimed that Capote's "name on an invitation . . . [was] as potent as a Rockefeller signature on a check."

Capote's fame turned to infamy in the 1970s. The main focus of his writing was *Answered Prayers,* a novel he had first imagined in 1958. Capote thought *Answered Prayers* would establish him as the American Proust, but despite the promise of the early chapters, *Answered Prayers,* a roman

à clef that exposed the secrets of his high society friends, became his undoing. When chapters of the work in progress were published in *Esquire* in the mid 1970s, they prompted outrage from Capote's influential friends. Capote was shunned in many social circles. Despondent over the loss of most of his longtime affiliations, Capote sank further into alcohol and drug abuse and became a caricature of his former self. He died of a "cardiac rhythm disorder" as a "result of drug overload" in 1984, without completing what promised to be his greatest work. He was cremated, and his ashes were scattered near his Long Island home.

★

Much relevant information about Capote's life in Brooklyn in the 1950s and 1960s can be gleaned from his own *A House on the Heights* (reprinted 2002). The most comprehensive biography of Capote is Gerald Clarke, *Capote* (1988). See also George Plimpton, *Truman Capote* (1997); Lawrence Grobel, *Conversations with Capote* (2000); and Marie Rudisill with James C. Simmons, *The Southern Haunting of Truman Capote* (2000).

KEVIN ALEXANDER BOON

CARMICHAEL, Stokely (Kwame Touré, Kwame Turé)

(*b.* 29 June 1941 in Port-of-Spain, Trinidad; *d.* 15 November 1998 in Conakry, Guinea), radical African-American civil rights leader, a fiery speaker who coined the widely used phrase "black power" and personified the face of black militancy in the 1960s.

Carmichael was the son of Adolphus Carmichael, a carpenter and cab driver, and Mabel Charles, a steamship stewardess. His parents emigrated from Trinidad to the United States when Carmichael was a toddler. Until he was ten or eleven Carmichael was raised by his grandmother; he then joined his parents in Harlem in 1952. The family soon moved to an all-white neighborhood in the Bronx, and he entered the elite Bronx High School of Science, a public school for gifted children.

While still in high school Carmichael heard about the sit-ins at segregated lunch counters in the South and became inspired to join the movement for racial equality. He rejected scholarships from several mostly white universities and enrolled instead at Howard University in Washington, D.C., in 1960. He joined the Congress of Racial Equality (CORE) Freedom Riders, a group of students of varying ethnicities who took dangerous bus trips that challenged the segregated transportation system in the South, and on these rides he was jailed several times.

In the spring of 1964 Carmichael graduated from Howard with a B.A. in philosophy and joined the Student Nonviolent Coordinating Committee (SNCC), which was organizing volunteers for "Freedom Summer," a massive voter registration campaign in the South. Tall, lanky, out-

Stokely Carmichael, June 1966. ASSOCIATED PRESS AP

spoken, and charismatic, Carmichael became a campaign leader. Colleague Mike Miller described him as "bold, audacious, fun-loving, with an infectious grin; his presence filled a room." Phil Hutchings, an organizer with SNCC, later wrote: "It was impossible not to like him even if you disagreed with him." Serving as SNCC field organizer in Lowndes County, Alabama, Carmichael helped swell black voter rolls from seventy to 2,600. When the Democratic and Republican parties failed to enthusiastically support the voter drive, Carmichael organized his own party, the Lowndes County Freedom Organization, which adopted a black panther as its symbol. Huey Newton and Bobby Seale would later adopt the symbol as the name for the Black Panther Party.

Radicalized by dozens of arrests, Carmichael, after repeatedly seeing peaceful protesters brutalized, became impatient with the tactics of the nonviolent civil rights movement leadership. Instead of mobilizing blacks to win concessions from the federal government, he sought to organize them to take political power into their own hands. In 1966 he succeeded John Lewis as chairman of SNCC and within a month broke completely with the mainstream civil rights movement. At a rally in Greenwood, Mississippi, on 16 June 1966, Carmichael shouted: "We've been saying 'Freedom' for six years. What we are going to start saying now is 'Black Power!'" The crowd of supporters chanted the phrase, and it caught on quickly, even though the Reverend Martin Luther King, Jr., criticized the phrase as an "unfortunate choice of words." It galvanized many young people but struck fear into the hearts of some whites supportive of more moderate aims and tactics.

Carmichael became the best-known and most visible ad-

vocate of militant tactics and goals. His "Black Power!" slogan turned into a crusade that demanded more than just civil rights and integration into the mainstream of American society—it demanded real political power for black Americans. A mesmerizing speaker, his goal was to use the white-owned media to reach black Americans and change their consciousness.

In 1967 Carmichael explained his views in the book *Black Power: The Politics of Liberation in America,* coauthored by the political scientist Charles Hamilton. Carmichael wrote that black power was "a call for black people to define their own goals, to lead their own organization." But in speeches that same year, Carmichael said black power meant "building a movement that will smash everything Western civilization has created." In a speech in Havana, Cuba, Carmichael spoke of "preparing groups of urban guerillas" for "a fight to the death" in the inner cities of the United States.

Carmichael's fierce rhetoric made many people uncomfortable. In 1967 SNCC severed ties with him, and Carmichael joined the Black Panther Party, becoming its honorary prime minister. In an interview with *Der Spiegel,* he identified bank robberies as one source of potential income for Panther activities. But his relationships with the Panthers soon soured. Even though the Panthers openly advocated armed resistance and militant action, they continued to seek support among whites. Carmichael denounced this practice and publicly resigned from the Panthers.

In April 1968 Carmichael married the South African singer Miriam Makeba and moved to Guinea, where he and Makeba lived in a seaside villa in Conakry, the capital. The deposed head of state of Ghana, Kwame Nkrumah, was his next-door neighbor. Carmichael soon began calling himself Kwame Ture, to honor Nkrumah and the Marxist leader of Guinea, Kwame Toure, who also befriended him. Carmichael later divorced Makeba and married a Guinean doctor named Marlyatou Barry; they also divorced. He had two sons.

By the end of the 1960s Carmichael became an emissary of the All African Peoples Revolutionary Party, lecturing worldwide. At speeches on American campuses and in cities, he called for black Americans to join him in a mass emigration to Africa to create a pan-African black socialist state, saying that such a step was the only means for achieving black power. But his crusade attracted few adherents in the United States or Africa, and Carmichael quickly became a fringe figure.

Carmichael lived the rest of his life in Guinea and was a staunch supporter of President Toure. He often dressed in fatigues and carried a pistol. In 1986 he was briefly jailed by a military government that took power after Toure's death. He remained staunch in his views to the end of his life, saying his fatal prostate cancer "was given to me by the forces of American imperialism and others who conspired with them." He died at age fifty-seven and was buried in Conakry.

More than any black leader, Carmichael was the personification of black militancy during the 1960s, even though his period of fame was relatively short. He never relinquished that militant stance. He also refused to see the 1960s as a closed chapter and a period of successful change. Until his death he continued to answer his phone with the phrase, "Ready for the revolution!" He wrote to Miller after a 1988 SNCC reunion that "Many you know have already accepted their laurels and do not even pretend to see the need for further reforms. For them the '60s put everything in place and they did it. Well, I still see Revolution and continue to work for it."

★

Before his death Carmichael was working on an autobiography, but it was never published. Short biographies include Jacqueline Johnson, *Stokely Carmichael: The Story of Black Power* (1990). Discussions of Carmichael's life and politics appear in *Social Policy* (winter 1998) and the *Economist* (21 Nov. 1998). An obituary is in *The New York Times* (16 Nov. 1988).

MICHAEL BETZOLD

CARPENTER, (Malcolm) Scott (*b.* 1 May 1925 in Boulder, Colorado), naval test pilot and electronics expert who was one of the first seven astronauts chosen for the U.S. space program and is best known for his harrowing 1962 flight in the Mercury program, in which he became the second American to orbit Earth.

Carpenter was the son of Marion Scott Carpenter, a chemist, and Florence Kelso (Noxon) Carpenter, a homemaker. His parents divorced when he was three years old; shortly afterward, his mother was hospitalized with tuberculosis, and his grandfather Victor Noxon took over his care. Carpenter remembers being a ne'er-do-well youth who goofed off in school and was a thief and a drifter.

Inspired by a motion picture, he decided to become a pilot. After graduating from high school in 1943, he entered the wartime naval flight training program at Colorado College in Colorado Springs. In 1944 he attended the preflight school at Saint Mary's College of California in Moraga; after six months he went for primary flight training in Ottumwa, Iowa. However, World War II ended before he could complete his training, and the navy discontinued the V-5 program in which Carpenter had enrolled.

By the mid-1940s Carpenter had a deep passion for flying. He began attending the University of Colorado at Boulder in 1945 and earned a B.S. in aeronautical engineering in 1949. During his college years, on 9 September 1948, Carpenter married Rene Louise Price; they eventually had four children and later divorced. In 1949 Carpenter was accepted by the navy and was sent to train in Pensacola, Florida, and then in Corpus Christi, Texas (November 1949 to April 1951). Later in 1951 he studied at the Fleet Airborne Electronics Training School in San Diego, California, and also trained on Whidbey Island, Washington.

As part of the Korean War effort, from 1951 to 1954

Scott Carpenter, 1962. ASSOCIATED PRESS AP

Carpenter served in Patrol Squadron Six on antisubmarine patrols and shipping surveillance. In 1954 he was accepted for training at the test pilot school in Patuxent River, Maryland, where he flew several different kinds of aircraft and continually honed his skills by taking additional courses in electronics and intelligence. In 1958 he was assigned to be the air intelligence officer on the aircraft carrier *Hornet*. He then received orders to report to Washington, D.C., for a secret assignment.

This assignment turned out to be testing to become one of America's first seven astronauts. After undergoing many unpleasant examinations, Carpenter was named on 9 April 1959 as one of the Mercury Seven. His special contributions to the astronaut program were in electronics and navigation. Carpenter's supervisors also were impressed by his intense focus on problems and tasks. Donald K. Slayton was scheduled to be America's fourth person in space, but he was grounded by heart disease, and Carpenter was named to replace him. Carpenter called his Mercury capsule *Aurora 7* because "aurora" means "dawn," and he saw his flight as part of a new dawn for the United States.

Carpenter was launched into space on 24 May 1962. Part of his mission was to duplicate John Glenn's earlier orbiting of Earth by orbiting three times. Another part was to discover how well an astronaut could accomplish tasks and research while weightless. Most of the experiments went well, but a large balloon failed to deploy fully. Carpenter was supposed to observe the multicolored balloon trailing behind his craft and to note which colors were easiest to see, to help determine the most visible colors for space docks; he saw enough to settle on orange.

Through a mistake, Carpenter expended too much fuel, perhaps leaving too little for slowing *Aurora 7* for reentry into Earth's atmosphere. When he retrofired to slow the craft, the attitude device malfunctioned, putting the nose too high. Then the retro-rockets failed to fire to begin the process of slowing down. After one second had passed, Carpenter pressed a button to manually fire the rockets; two seconds after that, they fired. Also, the balloon had failed to release from the capsule. Further, the capsule was see-sawing, and only by expending fuel could Carpenter partially stabilize *Aurora 7*. The parachutes for slowing the descent did not deploy properly, and Carpenter had to work intensely to get the main chute to deploy at all. Communications depended on line-of-sight transmission, and the craft went under the line of sight, so its weak transmissions could not be heard. For forty minutes, Carpenter was lost to the world. His craft hit the ocean so hard that it submerged completely, slowly rising back to the surface, with water leaking into it, and far off course. Rather than open the escape hatch and risk sinking the capsule, Carpenter crawled perilously out of an opening in the nose; he then

inflated a life raft, wrestled it upright in the water, turned on a homing beacon, and awaited rescue.

Carpenter's efforts and unflappability in the face of near death seemed heroic, but officials from the National Aeronautics and Space Administration (NASA) blamed him for the problems with the flight and told him he would never be allowed into space again. In 1963 Carpenter helped to design the lunar module part of the Apollo spacecraft and was the executive assistant to the director of the Manned Spaceflight Center in Houston, Texas.

Carpenter lost his flight status after suffering serious injuries in a motorcycle accident on 16 July 1964. The next summer, on leave from NASA, he became an aquanaut for the navy project SEALAB II, serving as the chief officer of the diving crew and spending thirty days submerged while carrying out experiments on the ocean floor near La Jolla, California. Carpenter earned the Distinguished Flying Cross and the navy's Legion of Merit for his work on SEALAB II. He then returned to NASA and was put in charge of providing underwater zero-gravity training for astronauts (for "neutral buoyancy"). On 10 August 1967 he left NASA and became the director of aquanaut operations for SEALAB III, conducting research that led to the development of new deep-sea diving and rescue techniques.

Carpenter retired from the navy on 1 July 1969, and from then into the early twenty-first century was working as an engineering consultant. In 1972 he married Maria Roach; they had two children. Carpenter and Roach divorced, and in 1988 he married Barbara Curtin. They had one child and later divorced. In the 1990s Carpenter published two novels, the *Steel Albatross* (1990) and *Deep Flight* (1994), both of which are technological thrillers that draw on his knowledge of deep-sea diving.

Carpenter remains a hero in the public imagination, not only for his 1962 spaceflight but for his public service in deep-sea research after his flying days were over. He helped to determine how much water an astronaut should drink and that it was safe to eat solid foods in space. Additionally, he helped to develop the lunar module that carried astronauts to the surface of the Moon, pioneered underwater rescue techniques that have saved many lives, and helped to open the deep ocean to exploration.

★

Current Biography Yearbook (1962) offers details about Carpenter's early life. Douglas B. Hawthorne, *Men and Women of Space* (1992) provides a brief account of Carpenter's accomplishments. Carpenter and his fellow astronauts wrote *We Seven, by the Astronauts Themselves* (1962). Carpenter wrote two other books in the 1960s about his experiences, *Exploring Space and Sea* (1967) and *Inner Space* (1969).

KIRK H. BEETZ

CARROLL, Diahann (*b.* 17 July 1935 in New York City), regarded as one of the United States' most talented singers and actresses, a pioneer for blacks in the entertainment business in 1960s, and the first African-American woman to have her own weekly television series.

Born Carol Diann Johnson, Carroll is the elder of two daughters of John Johnson, a subway conductor, and Mabel Faulk, a nurse. She was raised in Harlem and the Bronx in New York City. Carroll began singing at Harlem's Abyssinian Baptist Church at the age of six. While still attending the High School of Music and Art, she worked in nightclubs and auditioned as "Diahann Carroll" on the television show *Arthur Godfrey's Talent Scouts.* After finishing high school Carroll enrolled at New York University, majoring in psychology. In 1954 she won a singing contest on television and came to prominence in *Carmen Jones.* Carroll left New York University that same year to star in *House of Flowers,* for which she was nominated for a Tony Award. In September 1956 Carroll married the casting director of the *House of Flowers,* Monte Kay; they had one daughter. In 1959 she costarred in *Porgy and Bess* with the actor Sidney Poitier, with whom she fell in love and began an affair.

In the early 1960s Carroll continued to sing and play supporting roles in films. In 1961 she made two films, *Paris Blues* (with Poitier) and *Goodbye Again.* In the early 1960s she also became a regular guest on the *Tonight Show,* hosted by Jack Paar and airing on the National Broadcasting Company (NBC).

Having seen Carroll in *House of Flowers* and impressed by her talents, Richard Rodgers, one of the greatest writers in American musical theater, cast Carroll in the starring role of the Broadway musical *No Strings* in 1961. Carroll played Barbara Woodruff, a fashion model involved in an interracial romance. Her performance ran for more than a year, and she won (with another actress) the coveted Tony Award in 1962 for best female performance in a musical. Despite the disappointment of not being cast in the movie version of the play, Carroll was undaunted in her pursuit of success and turned her attention to film. In 1962 *No Strings* finished its New York run and began a nationwide tour, which Carroll joined.

Carroll left the cast of *No Strings* when she became engaged to Poitier, but they broke off the relationship several months later. In 1966, between her acting roles, Carroll resumed her nightclub singing. She played at the Persian Room at the Plaza Hotel in New York City twice a year and often performed in San Francisco, Washington, D.C., and Las Vegas. By the mid-1960s she was also a frequent guest on a number of television shows, including the *Danny Kaye Show,* the *Carol Burnett Show, Hollywood Palace,* and specials with Dean Martin and Frank Sinatra. She ap-

Diahann Carroll, 1968. © BETTMANN/CORBIS

peared in the movie drama *Hurry Sundown* with Jane Fonda in 1967 and the crime caper *The Split* in 1968.

Although Carroll had previously appeared on a number of shows, television was not a major aspect of her career. However, in 1968 she left for Beverly Hills to star in *Julia,* and in doing so became the first African American to star in a weekly television situation comedy. Carroll played Julia Baker, a middle-class Vietnam War widow raising her five-year-old son. The success of *Julia* was remarkable, and it helped change the image of black Americans on television, paving the way for such later hits as the *Cosby Show.* Carroll said in her autobiography: "It was such a wonderful feeling to know that I was accepted into millions of homes every Tuesday." Carroll received an Emmy nomination and won a Golden Globe for the best newcomer in television for her role in *Julia* in 1968.

There were, however, some unexpected problems. The popular show, produced by Hal Kanter, was an attempt to forward the cause of mutual understanding in the highly charged, racially tense atmosphere of the time. Ironically, the popularity of the show brought heightened exposure for Carroll and pressured her to respond to the racial tensions that had arisen in the wake of the assassination of the civil rights leader the Reverend Martin Luther King, Jr. Carroll was stung by criticism of the authenticity of Julia's single motherhood, her affluent lifestyle, and the lack of a strong male role model. In addition, the white press expected Carroll to act as a spokesperson for black America. The show was acknowledged by many as breakthrough and seen by others as a betrayal.

Although *Julia* was controversial, the media storm did not affect the ratings. The show was first aired in September 1968, and by October it had become the highest rated show on the air. The show gained considerable attention, but the change in Carroll's image from glamorous to maternal later diluted her nightclub image. After playing the role of a nurse on television, Carroll discovered that her nightclub career had withered, as fans replaced their old image of the glamorous singer with a new one. In an effort to regain an audience, Carroll began to make her shows more elaborate. In 1970, when the time came for Carroll to renew her contract, she requested to be released from *Julia*.

In 1972 Carroll returned to singing, and on 21 February 1973 she married her second husband, Freddie Glusman. She starred in the feature film *Claudine* (1974), for which she received an Oscar nomination. In 1976 she married Robert Deleon, who later died in a car crash. Carroll hosted her own show, starred in television movies such as *Roots, the Next Generations* (1979) and *I Know Why the Caged Bird Sings* (1979). She also starred in the stage version of *Agnes of God* (1982), published her autobiography (1986), and played the role of Dominique Deveraux in the popular television series *Dynasty* (1984–1987). In January 1987 she married the singer Vic Damone (they divorced in 1996), and in 1989 she appeared on the television series *A Different World* and *Dead of Night*. Carroll was diagnosed with breast cancer in 1994, but she overcame the disease with an aggressive treatment program. In 1996–1997 she appeared in Andrew Lloyd Webber's musical *Sunset Boulevard,* and in 1997 she launched her own clothing line.

Carroll has received numerous awards and honors. She was inducted into the Black Filmmaker's Hall of Fame in 1976 and was honored as the best actress at the National Association for the Advancement of Colored People's Eighth Annual Image Awards, also in 1976. She has been featured at the Lincoln Center for the Performing Arts and the Kennedy Center in Washington, D.C.

Carroll's life is a story of triumph and perseverance. She aspired beyond her childhood Harlem, but she found herself in an industry whose doors opened only slowly for African Americans. While building her career, Carroll confronted and fought racism and triumphed over considerable obstacles to become an accomplished artist.

★

A clipping file on Carroll is in the Billy Rose Theatre Collection, New York Public Library for the Performing Arts, New York City. Carroll's autobiography, *Diahann! An Autobiography* (1986), written with Ross Firestone, provides intimate details of her personal life and career. Donald Bogle, *Blacks in American Film and Television: An Encyclopedia* (1988), contains critical reviews of Carroll's major films plus a brief but informative biographical sketch. For more biographical information see "Diahann Carroll Talks about Her Life, Love, and Career in a Revealing Interview," *Jet* (23 Dec. 1985), and "Diahann Carroll and Vic Damone: New Marriage and New Career on Stage," *Jet* (26 Jan. 1987).

NJOKI-WA-KINYATTI

CARSON, John William ("Johnny") (*b.* 23 October 1925 in Corning, Iowa), comedian and host of *The Tonight Show Starring Johnny Carson* throughout most of the 1960s.

Carson was the second of three children born to Homer ("Kit") Carson, a power company manager, and Ruth Hook. Growing up in Iowa and Nebraska, his major interests were magic, ventriloquism, and radio comedy. He spent hours studying the comedy of Bob Hope, Fred Allen, and especially Jack Benny. He began performing his magic act publicly as "The Great Carsoni" as a teen and expanded his repertoire to include ventriloquism while in the U.S. Navy from 1943 to 1946, and at the University of Nebraska at Lincoln from 1946 to 1949.

After earning his B.A. in radio and speech, Carson took a job with WOW radio in Omaha, where by the end of 1949 he had his own program, *The Johnny Carson Show*. A predictor of things to come, the show was dominated by Carson's comedy routines and jokes, which illustrated the fact that his distinctive style of easy, accessible humor with just a pinch of the risqué was already developed. Carson married Joan ("Jody") Wolcott, with whom he would have three sons, in 1949. Soon he had his own TV show, *The Squirrel's Nest* (1949–1951), where he further honed the personality for which he would later become so famous on *The Tonight Show*.

During the 1950s Carson moved up through the television ranks with a series of shows. In 1951 he joined KNXT-TV in Los Angeles as an announcer, and by 1952 he had his own show, *Carson's Cellar*. In 1954 Carson began working on network television as the host of the short-lived prime-time game show, *Earn Your Vacation,* followed by *Carson's Coffee Break* and a stint writing for *The Red Skelton Show*. When Carson substituted for Skelton, he gained so much recognition that the Columbia Broadcasting System (CBS) introduced *The Johnny Carson Show* (1955), as a summer replacement. The show was not successful in prime time, however, and was cancelled the next year. Carson returned immediately to daytime television with a show of the same name, but in 1957 moved to New York

City and the American Broadcasting Company (ABC) for the game show *Who Do You Trust?*.

In 1958 Carson substituted for Jack Paar on *The Tonight Show*, a successful National Broadcasting Company (NBC) program that had been hosted by Steve Allen from 1954 to 1957, and by Paar since then. Paar, who continually pushed the boundaries of acceptability in late 1950s and early 1960s late-night television, departed in 1962. NBC invited Carson, who was still hosting *Who Do You Trust?*—also a highly successful show—to take his place. On 1 October 1962 Carson debuted as host of *The Tonight Show,* which aired from 11:15 P.M. to 1:00 A.M. He brought with him Ed McMahon, who had served much the same function on *Who Do You Trust?* as he would on the new show. Skitch Henderson returned to *The Tonight Show* to act as musical director, as he had when Steve Allen was host. (Carl "Doc" Severinsen replaced Henderson in 1967.)

Significant parts of Carson's act were clearly derivative. He had several of Jack Benny's mannerisms and facial expressions, and his Carnac the Magnificent was very much like Steve Allen's The Answer Man, while Aunt Blabby was a close cousin of Jonathan Winters's Maude Frickert. The Mighty Carson Art Players had their antecedents in Fred Allen's Mighty Allen Art Players. Nevertheless, Carson adapted these ideas in such a way as to make them distinctively his own. Like Paar, he began each show with a monologue, but not with the highly personal, often controversial tone Paar had used. Like Steve Allen, Carson had musical numbers, skits, and stunts, but these were performed by different guests every night and not, as on Allen's show, by a troupe of regular performers. Carson interviewed famous guests, but they were generally show business personalities plugging some book or new project; he was not running the intellectual salon Paar had been hosting.

Carson had a special predilection for eccentrics, the elderly, young children, and animals of all sorts, and he frequently featured them on the show. He was also known for remarks tinged with sexual innuendo, and for commenting on social and political issues of the day. But unlike Paar, Carson did not so much push the limits of current public tastes as he reflected changes to the limits of those tastes. In the 1960s and beyond, Carson turned *The Tonight Show* into a sort of "cultural cornerstone" and himself into a video-age Will Rogers.

In spite of his tremendous popularity, Carson did have several major conflicts with NBC during the 1960s. In 1964 NBC frequently interrupted *The Tonight Show* for news reports during the Republican and Democratic conventions, which led to a showdown between Carson and the news division of NBC. For better or worse, ratings prevailed over news, and Carson came out on top. By 1965 Carson was fed up with the fact that *The Tonight Show*

Johnny Carson. ARCHIVE PHOTOS, INC.

began at 11:15 P.M., and that many stations were not picking the show up until 11:30, thus cutting out Carson's entire monologue. He began a one-man strike and simply refused to show up until 11:30, thereby successfully pressuring NBC to change the starting time. When NBC showed reruns of *The Tonight Show* during a 1967 strike by Carson's union, the American Federation of Television and Radio Artists (AFTRA), this engendered such ill will that Carson remained on strike even after other AFTRA members went back to work. Carson returned only after contract renegotiations won him vastly greater control over the show, and over time, he became legendary for working fewer and fewer nights for more and more money.

In 1964 *The Tonight Show* began the practice of week-long special visits to Los Angeles, and in April 1972 it moved there permanently. Some of the most notable events on *The Tonight Show* took place during the 1960s, among them the 1965 tomahawk incident in which Ed Ames emasculated a plywood "sheriff" while demonstrating tomahawk throwing. The highest-rated *Tonight Show* ever took place in 1969, when the eccentric singer Tiny Tim married "Miss Vicki" Budinger on the show.

During Carson's tenure, *The Tonight Show* became a major showcase for musical acts and especially comedians. After *The Ed Sullivan Show* went off the air in 1974, a booking on Carson's became a symbol of success. Comedy greats such as Woody Allen, George Carlin, Richard Pryor, Redd Foxx, Bill Cosby, Don Rickles, and Joan Rivers came into national prominence based largely on their *Tonight Show* appearances.

Throughout the 1960s Carson was active beyond *The Tonight Show*. For example, when he played Las Vegas in 1963, he broke the opening night record at the Sahara Hotel's Congo Room set by Judy Garland. He performed at President Lyndon B. Johnson's inaugural gala in 1965, and published two books, *Happiness Is a Dry Martini* (1965) and *Misery Is a Blind Date* (1967). Carson made the cover of *Time* magazine on 19 May 1967, and in 1969 tried his hand at an unsuccessful prime-time variety special.

His greatest achievement, however, was *The Tonight Show*, which proved such a success that other networks jumped on the late-night bandwagon with their own shows. Les Crane (1964–1965), Joey Bishop (1967–1969), Dick Cavett (1969–1974), David Frost (1969–1972), and Merv Griffin (1969–1972) all went up against Carson, but none could dent his ratings.

During his time on *The Tonight Show,* Carson went through several changes in his personal life. He and Wolcott divorced in 1963. He married Joanne Copeland in 1963; they divorced in 1972. He and Joanna Holland married in 1972 and divorced in 1983. He married his fourth wife, Alexandra ("Alexis" or "Alex") Mass, in 1987. His second son Rick died in a traffic accident in 1991. Carson spoke of retiring several times, but was coaxed into continuing until May 1992, when he left after three decades as host.

In the 1960s Carson perfected the model for the late-night talk show, and the format he developed—the opening monologue, the live band, the studio audience, taped stunts and skits, novelty guests and animal acts, even the set with its couch and desk—would remain in place decades later. Carson's own monologue style was reflected in the stand-up performances of later comedians such as Dennis Miller and Bill Maher, and his topical and slightly off-color humor led the way to increased political and sexual content on television.

★

Biographies of Carson include Nora Ephron, *And Now Here's Johnny* (1968); Douglas Lorence, *Johnny Carson: A Biography* (1975); Paul Corkery, *Carson: The Unauthorized Biography* (1987); and Laurence Leamer, *King of the Night: The Life of Johnny Carson* (1989).

PATRICIA L. MARKLEY

CARSON, Rachel Louise (*b.* 27 May 1907 in Springdale, Pennsylvania; *d.* 14 April 1964 in Silver Spring, Maryland), scientist and writer whose book *Silent Spring* (1962) activated public concern over the use of pesticides and inspired a new environmental consciousness in the 1960s.

Carson was the youngest of three children born to Robert Carson and Maria McLean. Her father purchased their home, a farm, with plans to subdivide and sell, but made few sales over the years. Instead he worked as a traveling salesman, electrician, and a utility-company employee, among other jobs, and the family often struggled for enough money to survive. Her mother was a thirty-eight-year-old homemaker with two children already in school when Carson was born. McLean had a keen interest in nature and a love of reading that she shared with her youngest daughter. She and Carson were inseparable, spending endless hours wandering the outdoors. On one of these walks, Carson discovered a fossilized fish in the cliffs near her home, sparking a special interest in scientific discovery.

From her youngest years, Carson pursued writing. Her first story was published in the September 1918 issue of *St. Nicholas*, a popular children's literary magazine. A shy, slim, introverted girl, Carson was an excellent student and was accepted on partial scholarship to Pittsburgh's Pennsylvania College for Women (later Chatham College). Carson began college as an English major, but under the influence of Mary Scott Skinker, who taught her in a biology class and became her mentor and friend, she switched to science in her third year. After graduating on 10 June

Rachel Carson. AP/WIDE WORLD PHOTOS

1929 Carson left for a summer internship at the Marine Biology Laboratory in Woods Hole, Massachusetts. Enamored with the sea, she continued her studies at Woods Hole during the summers and completed her master's degree in zoology at Johns Hopkins University in Baltimore.

Throughout her life, Carson experienced demanding familial obligations. As a college student, she cared for nieces and nephews in her crowded family home during the summer. Family responsibilities prevented her from pursuing a doctorate, and as she began to make a living, she provided a home for her parents and at times her siblings and their offspring.

Carson taught zoology at the University of Maryland for a few years, before beginning a fifteen-year career as a scientist and editor for the U.S. government in 1936. She became the first female biologist ever hired by the U.S. Bureau of Fisheries. Her final government position was as editor-in-chief at the U.S. Fish and Wildlife Service.

While earning her living as a government employee, Carson began submitting nature articles for publication. In time, she completed two books about the sea: *Under the Sea-Wind* (1941) and *The Sea Around Us* (1952). Writings from her second book had been rejected by fifteen magazines, but once it was published, the work became hugely popular and stayed on the best-seller lists for eighty-six weeks. Not only did the book earn Carson national prominence as a naturalist and writer, it also allowed her to leave her job, devote all her time to writing, and buy a summer home in Maine. Carson, whose writing was praised for its clarity and elegance of style, completed her trilogy of sea books with *The Edge of the Sea* in 1955.

Carson tended to her sister, niece, and mother during their failing health and subsequent deaths, and adopted her grandnephew Roger when her niece died. Thus at age forty-eight, she became mother to a five-year-old boy. In 1957 local and state governments sprayed a combination of fuel oil and the insecticide DDT over portions of the northeastern United States. Carson had friends in Massachusetts and Long Island who witnessed the wildlife damage that resulted, and she was persuaded to write an article in protest. She had considered writing on the subject as early as 1945, even suggesting such an article to *Reader's Digest,* whose editors failed to show interest. But by 1958 Carson felt compelled to change directions in her writing, and to begin researching the effects of pesticides on wildlife as the subject of her next book. "The more I learned about the use of pesticides, the more appalled I became," she later said. "I realized that here was the material for a book. What I discovered was that everything which meant most to me as a naturalist was being threatened, and that nothing I could do would be more important."

In the 1950s and early 1960s, Americans generally embraced pesticides and chemicals as boons to human civilization, believing them responsible for increased agricultural production and for easing the nuisance and destruction from uncontrolled insects. And in light of the cold war and the rush to win the "space race" against the Soviets, technological advancements by the United States were seen as patriotic. For these reasons, the publication of Carson's *Silent Spring* in 1962 was highly controversial. Knowing criticism was inevitable, Carson was meticulous in her research, calling upon her extensive contacts in government, academia, and conservation groups for accurate data, and devoting a fifty-five-page appendix to her principal sources.

Portions of *Silent Spring* first appeared in the *New Yorker* in June 1962. Carson used the title to bring up images of a world absent of birds as a result of chemical poisoning. Even before the book was published, chemical companies threatened lawsuits and began attacking Carson rather than her facts. When the book was released on 27 September 1962, the National Agricultural Chemicals Association spent over $250,000 on a public-relations campaign to discredit Carson. They painted her as an alarmist and a hysterical female. A letter from former Secretary of Agriculture Ezra Taft Benson to President Dwight D. Eisenhower, in which he expressed the opinion that Carson might be a Communist, and questioned why "a spinster with no children" would be so concerned about genetics, was widely quoted.

But *Silent Spring* was a runaway best-seller, and sales were probably helped by the criticism it attracted. The book spoke of the connection between cancer and pesticides, raising issues of public health. President John F. Kennedy's interior secretary Stewart Udall took an early interest in the book, and used it to advocate pesticide regulation within the government. A shift in the public attitude toward the environment was meanwhile taking place. As Carson stated in a speech to the National Parks Association, the public no longer "assumed that someone was looking after things—that the spraying must be all right or it wouldn't be done."

Two days before Carson appeared on the Columbia Broadcasting System's *CBS Reports* in April 1963, three of the five largest commercial sponsors withdrew their advertising. Nevertheless, the network broadcast the show and Carson came across as dignified, calm, polite, and concerned, thus easily vindicating herself from personal attacks. On 15 May 1963 President Kennedy's Science Advisory Committee released the report "The Uses of Pesticides," which formalized support for Carson's findings. During her June 1963 testimony before the Senate Commerce Committee, chaired by Senator Abraham Ribicoff of Connecticut, Carson provided ideas for reform, and called for the formation of an independent board or commission within the executive branch of government.

Vice President Al Gore later credited Carson with inspiring the formation of the Environmental Protection Agency (EPA), as well as leading himself and millions of others to an environmental consciousness.

At the time of her death, only Carson's closest friends were aware of the tremendous pain and physical strain she had faced in her last few years. Carson had been battling cancer throughout the writing of *Silent Spring*. She never publicly suggested a link between her cancer and an agricultural-research facility near her home, but privately she suspected it. Carson died from a coronary heart attack. She had requested cremation, and that her ashes be scattered off the coast of Maine near her home, but against her wishes, her brother Robert held a large funeral for her at the National Cathedral in Washington, D.C. Later, her friends observed her original request.

Considered one of the most influential books of the twentieth century, *Silent Spring* had far-reaching effects. At a time when the American public began questioning the government's decision to fight the Vietnam War, they also began rethinking the human relationship to nature. Because of Carson, words such as "ecology" and "environment" entered the public vocabulary. No one could have predicted the impact that one woman, described by naturalist Louis Halle as "quiet, diffident, neat, proper and without affectation," could have on society. Carson herself did not live long enough to observe the impact of her book. After she completed writing *Silent Spring* she wrote in a letter: "I have felt bound by a solemn obligation to do what I could—if I didn't at least try I could never again be happy in nature. But now I can believe I have at least helped a little. It would be unrealistic to believe one book could bring a complete change."

★

Carson's personal papers are at Yale University in New Haven, Connecticut. Two significant biographies are Paul Brooks, *The House of Life: Rachel Carson at Work* (1972), and Linda Lear, *Rachel Carson: Witness for Nature* (1997). Martha Freeman, ed., *Always, Rachel* (1995), offers an intimate view of Carson through the letters she exchanged with her friend Dorothy Freeman. Peter Matthiessen wrote a good brief biography for *Time* magazine's "100 People of the Century" issue (29 Mar. 1999), and Stewart Udall, one of the first politicians to become interested in Carson's work, discussed her in "How the Wilderness Was Won," *American Heritage* (Feb.–Mar. 2000). The Web site http://www.rachelcarson.org is also a good source for information.

JANET INGRAM

CASH, John R. ("Johnny") (*b*. 26 February 1932 in Kingsland, Arkansas), country music legend, songwriter, and actor, known for hits like "Folsom Prison Blues" and "I Walk the Line."

Cash, the fourth of seven children born to sharecroppers Ray Cash and Carrie Rivers, grew up with cotton fields and Southern Baptists, music and religion. Cash was already singing and writing songs when he was twelve years old. Everyone in the Cash family sang, but, according to Johnny's mother, he had "the gift," and so she did laundry to earn money for his singing lessons.

In 1950 Cash joined the U.S. Air Force and was sent to radio operator school. Stationed in Landsberg, Germany, with the Security Service as a radio intercept operator, he demonstrated a special talent for Russian Morse Code. The air force promoted him to staff sergeant early in hopes of enticing him to reenlist, but the strategy did not work, and Cash was honorably discharged in 1954.

Once back in the United States, Cash married Vivian Liberto, with whom he had corresponded during his time in Germany. The couple moved to Memphis, Tennessee, and Cash took a job as a salesman. Miserable in that career, he continued to pursue music. In 1954 he took his first steps toward a music career when he traveled to Corinth, Mississippi, to see John Bell of WMCA radio. Even though Cash had no experience, Bell was polite and encouraged him to attend Keegan's School of Broadcasting in Memphis. Cash took Bell's advice and enrolled part time. At this same time, Cash's brother introduced him to two other aspiring musicians, Marshall Grant and Luther Perkins. Soon the trio was playing local events in North Memphis.

In 1955 the group took their music to Sam Phillips's Sun Records and eventually earned a contract. Cash's first two songs, "Hey Porter" and "Cry, Cry, Cry," were hits. In 1956 he finally achieved national recognition with "I Walk the Line" and began a string of television appearances.

In 1958 Cash signed with Columbia Records in order to record more gospel and moved his family to Ventura, California. He had taken his first "pep pill" in 1957 and had become addicted to amphetamines by 1960. The drugs Cash took were common prescription medicines, but he took so many it created a powerful psychological dependence. Cash believed the pills (usually diet pills) gave him the energy and confidence to be a better performer. As he took more pills, he found he needed barbiturates to come down from the effects of the amphetamines. His drug abuse worsened, and Cash became moody and unpredictable. Unable to sleep or eat, at six feet, one inch tall, Cash dropped to 155 pounds. Despite the drugs, Cash recorded seven albums in the 1960s, and his hit "Ring of Fire" (1963), went to number one on the pop and country and western charts. His musical success, however, was marked with profound personal difficulties.

Early in the 1960s he moved back to Nashville, leaving his wife and their four daughters in California. As Cash began to exhibit the symptoms of addiction, his friends began to try to help him. In particular, June Carter, a member

Johnny Cash in the recording studio. THE LIBRARY OF CONGRESS

of a popular music family that Cash often toured with, took a special interest in his health, often throwing his pills away. During the 1960s Cash wrecked every car he owned (and some he did not). In 1965 U.S. Customs officials saw him buy drugs from a heroin dealer just across the Mexican border and arrested him; he received a suspended sentence and a fine. A regular at the Grand Ole Opry, Cash was told not to come back after he threw the microphone down and broke stage lights one night in 1965. Later that same night, he wrecked the Cadillac he was driving, breaking his nose and jaw. The drugs also caused Cash to develop severe cases of laryngitis, and he began to cancel entire tours. In 1966 his wife filed for divorce.

Also in the 1960s, Cash was criticized for perceived controversy in his songs. Radio stations refused to play "The Ballad of Ira Hayes," about the Native-American Marine and hero who helped raise the U.S. flag over Iwo Jima during World War II. In 1964 Cash bought a full-page ad in *Billboard* chastising those disc jockeys. He also wrote songs about the civil rights movement, and in 1966 the Ku Klux Klan began publishing propaganda pieces about Cash and his wife. Despite threats of violence Cash sued the Klan for slander. Cash was also criticized for his explicit lyrics about drugs and violence. Cash's fans paid little attention to the Klan, however, and his career continued to flourish.

His style and lyrics were especially popular with convicts, who were his favorite audience. Sympathetic from his few run-ins with the law, Cash performed in prisons throughout his career. When a Georgia prison offered Cash $5,000 to come to sing, he said he would perform free if they would spend the $5,000 on the men.

In 1967 Cash was near death. June Carter and her parents Maybelle and E. J. moved in with him, and stayed through his withdrawal from drugs. The Carters feared for Cash's life and used a mixture of tough love and faith in God to get Johnny through his withdrawals. June threw out all his pills, and when he yelled at her she would calmly read his favorite Bible passages aloud. Once he was thinking clearly again, Cash realized how much the Carters, and June in particular, cared for him, and with their love and a strong faith Cash began to fight his addiction with a new determination. Cash's first performance after his recovery was for a high school fundraiser; it was a success. He continued to stay off drugs, and in 1968 he asked June to marry him during a London, Ontario, concert of 5,000 people. The couple married 1 March 1968 and added a son, John Carter Cash, to the family that included Cash's daughters Rosanne, Kathy, Cindy, and Tara, as well as June's two daughters Carlene and Rosey. Intensely religious, the family took a vacation to Israel and studied the Bible and Jewish history.

In 1968 Cash recorded the live album *At Folsom Prison*. Bob Dylan invited him to sing a duet and write liner notes for his album *Nashville Skyline,* and in June 1969 Dylan appeared in the first segment of the American Broadcasting Company (ABC) television show *The Johnny Cash Show,* which lasted for two years. Also in 1969, "A Boy Named Sue" went to number two and was named single of the year by the Country Music Association (CMA); his album *Johnny Cash at San Quentin* was number one for four weeks and was named album of the year by CMA; and Cash was named CMA's entertainer of the year. Cash's appeal had spread from country and folk music to rock and pop.

While touring military bases in Vietnam in 1969, Cash caught a fever and was prescribed the same pills he had been addicted to; he subsequently suffered a relapse of his addiction. Exceeding his dosage, drinking, and continuing work, Cash developed pneumonia, but June helped him get healthy again.

During the 1970s Cash's music career continued to flourish. He and June made a documentary, *Gospel Road,* in Israel (1971), and his hit songs included "A Thing Called Love" (1972) and "One Piece at a Time" (1976). Cash, Carl Perkins, and Jerry Lee Lewis recorded *The Survivors* in 1982, and, Cash, Kris Kristofferson, Waylon Jennings, and Willie Nelson recorded *Highwayman* in 1985, and *Highwayman 2* in 1990. He also starred in a number of westerns for television and movies.

Cash was inducted into the Rock and Roll Hall of Fame

in 1992, the first performer inducted into both the Rock and Roll Hall of Fame and Country Music Hall of Fame, and the only one until Elvis Presley was elected to the Country Music Hall of Fame in 1998. He has won eleven Grammys, including the 1999 Lifetime Achievement Award and the 2002 shared Grammy for best country album. Two of his Grammys came for writing liner notes, for his *At Folsom Prison* album and Bob Dylan's *Nashville Skyline*.

Cash had another, nearly deadly, case of pneumonia in 1998. In 2001, after a series of misdiagnoses (including Parkinson's disease and the similar Shy-Drager Syndrome) doctors said that Cash suffers from a nervous-system disorder known as autonomic neuropathy, a group of symptoms involving the central nervous system that leaves him extremely vulnerable to pneumonia.

★

Cash has written two autobiographies: *Man In Black* (1975) and *Cash: The Autobiography,* with Patrick Carr (1997). Biographies include Christopher Wren, *Winners Got Scars Too: The Life and Legend of Johnny Cash* (1971); Cindy Cash, *The Cash Family Scrapbook* (1997); and Frank Moriarty, *Johnny Cash* (1997).

LISA A. ENNIS

CASTANEDA, Carlos César Salvador Arana (*b.* 25 December 1925? in either Cajamarca, Peru, or São Paulo, Brazil; *d.* 27 April 1998 in Los Angeles, California), author of autobiographical anthropology, later considered metaphor, allegory, or literary hoax, who was called by *Time* magazine the "Godfather of the New Age."

Great uncertainty overshadows facts about the origins, identity, and exact name of Carlos Castaneda and the existence of his mentor, Don Juan Matus. Castaneda's U.S. immigration records cite his birthdate as 25 December 1925, in Cajamarca, Peru, but other sources say that he was born in São Paulo, Brazil, in either 1931 or 1935. Controversy also exists about whether Castaneda signed his will three days before his death and cremation. In one of the rare interviews he permitted, Castaneda told *Time* that to use statistics to authenticate biographical facts was similar to using science to substantiate sorcery. He never permitted anyone to make audiotapes or video recordings of him, and photographs always show his hands or hat in front of his face.

In 1955 Castaneda enrolled in Los Angeles Community College, taking courses in psychology and creative writing; he received an A.A. in psychology in 1959 and applied for U.S. citizenship that year. In 1960 he married Margaret Runyon. He enrolled at the University of California, Los Angeles (UCLA), and received a B.A. in anthropology in

1962 and then entered UCLA's graduate program. In the introduction to *The Teachings of Don Juan: A Yaqui Way of Knowledge* (1968), Castaneda said that he had met Don (a title of respect) Juan in 1960 in a bus station in Nogales, Arizona, while Castaneda was seeking information about peyote cactus. He visited Don Juan in Arizona and Mexico periodically from June 1961 to September 1965 and reorganized his notes and conversations into this first book.

The book has two sections: Castaneda's field notes on "the subjective version of what [he] perceived while undergoing the experience" of using peyote and a "structural analysis" of these data. The paperback edition of *Teachings of Don Juan* sold 300,000 copies. J. R. Moehringer wrote that this book struck "just the right note at the peak of the psychedelic 1960s." As a "strange alchemy of anthropology, allegory, parapsychology, ethnography, Buddhism and perhaps great fiction," it "made . . . Castaneda a cultural icon." Don Juan led his apprentice, Castaneda, into paranormal experiences through various hallucinogenic drugs—peyote, jimson weed, and psilocybin mushrooms. The widespread acceptance of this book coincided with the hallmarks of the 1960s: alienation and frustration; respect for eccentric, unusual persons, especially those with a non-white worldview; drug cults; definitions of differing realities in a backlash against science; and love of nature, especially the earth.

In the 1971 sequel, *A Separate Reality: Further Conversations with Don Juan*, Castaneda implied that the use of peripheral vision, the finding of a "seat of power," and the chewing or smoking of a mixture containing psilocybin mushrooms would show readers the path to knowledge. Castaneda stated that Don Juan "succeeded in pointing out to me that my view of the world cannot be final because it is only an interpretation." *Journey to Ixtlan: The Lessons of Don Juan* (1972), the third volume in the series, includes a variety of drugless techniques through which the apprentice can gain "new-age" consciousness. This third volume, with a brief introduction and new title, served as a doctoral thesis and completed the work for Castaneda's Ph.D. from UCLA in 1973. The fourth volume, *Tales of Power*, focuses more on Castaneda's dealings with the unknown than with lessons taught by Don Juan.

Many of the millions of readers of the four volumes believed them to be literally true. On 5 March 1973, *Time* noted that the strength of the books lay in the fact that Castaneda kept "voluminous and extraordinarily vivid notes" of his efforts at Socratic dialogue with Don Juan; the article questioned, however, whether the books could be considered scientific anthropology. William Kennedy wrote in the *New Republic*, "The whole work is . . . an elaborate and admirably detailed metaphor with the aim of guiding the reader out of the humdrum and into self-awareness." He went on to call Castaneda a "cult figure . . . especially with the young."

In subsequent years, however, readers and scholars began to doubt that Castaneda's experiences were real and, eventually, to question Don Juan's existence. The botanist Weston LaBarre stated that *Teachings of Don Juan* is "pseudo-profound, sophomoric, and deeply vulgar," further labeling it "frustratingly and tiresomely dull, posturing pseudoethnography and, intellectually, kitsch." Richard de Mille suggested that Castaneda used "the anthropology hoax" as a means of getting published, consistent with his lifelong pattern of playing tricks. De Mille documented contradictions in Castaneda's "field reports," noting their lack of convincing detail (for example, lack of Yaqui or other Indian names for plants), and he cited plagiarism of English-language sources for what were presented as Don Juan's words.

Although Castaneda, through Don Juan, described drug and nondrug paths to knowledge, the drug cults of the 1960s sometimes took these books as a measure of societal and even academic approval. The psychological and spiritual search for different realities, as in science fiction and comparative mythology, had great appeal to readers' imaginations. Above all, the ability of drugs to open the mind to increased perceptions was widely accepted at the time.

In 1993 Castaneda started the Tensegrity movement, a cult based on meditation and movement exercises, somewhat like kung fu. The corporation Cleargreen surrounded and cared for Castaneda in his final years, selling books and mementos and giving Tensegrity seminars at which Castaneda occasionally appeared. Castaneda died from complications of liver cancer in Westwood, a well-to-do suburb of Los Angeles, and was cremated within a few hours of death. His death was not reported for two months.

Was Castaneda's work science or fiction? In contrast to the Western tradition of rationalism and scientific method, the Don Juan books describe an alternate reality with its equally valid way of thinking and acting. As to the physical reality of Don Juan himself, we might equally ask whether Virgil really appeared in the flesh to guide Dante through the Inferno to Paradise. Sam Keen wrote in *Psychology Today* that the more important question is: "What does Don Juan tell us about ourselves, about the millions in this country and abroad, who have read his words?"

With eight million books sold in seventeen languages, Castaneda perpetually created "a separate reality" and perhaps could not draw clear lines between fact and fiction, metaphor and hallucinogenic experience. The eminent comparative mythologist Joseph Campbell was not attacked for his frequently repeated advice to "follow your bliss." Castaneda's definitions of reality and bliss, which were different from those of Western-trained intellectuals like Campbell, were eagerly read by young people in the 1960s

Carlos Castaneda. AP/WIDE WORLD PHOTOS

as another avenue to "truth." The "New Age" owes much to Castaneda's perceptions and the Cleargreen movement, with its crystals, chimes, and feathers. Jeremy Narby and Francis Huxley perhaps stated it most accurately: "Using literary devices, Castaneda played shaman-style tricks on his readers, astounding people by sleight-of-hand to free their minds from their preconceptions of reality."

★

Kenneth E. St. Andre's article on Castaneda in the *Scribner Encyclopedia of American Lives*, vol. 5, 1997–1999, gives acceptable data concerning Castaneda's birth, death, and other statistics; it also cites the best sources for Castaneda's evaluation. More recent studies include Weston LaBarre's botanical analysis in *The Peyote Cult* and "Stinging Criticism from the Author of 'The Peyote Cult'" (1972), in Daniel C. Noel, ed., *Seeing Castaneda: Reactions to the "Don Juan" Writings of Carlos Castaneda* (1976); and Jeremy Narby and Francis Huxley, eds., *Shamans Through Time: 500 Years on the Path to Knowledge* (2001). See also Ronald Sukenick, "Don Juan and the Sorcerer's Apprentice," *Time* (5 Mar. 1973); William Kennedy, "Fact or Fiction," *New Republic* (16 Nov. 1974): 28–30; Michael Mason, *New Statesman* (27 June 1975); J. R. Moehringer, "A Hushed Death for Mystic Author Carlos Castaneda," *Los Angeles Times* (19 June 1998); and Martin Goodman continues the discussion with *I Was Carlos Castaneda: The Afterlife*

Dialogues (2001). Obituaries are in the *New York Times* (19 and 20 June 1998).

DESSA CRAWFORD

CAVETT, Richard Alva ("Dick") (*b.* 19 November 1936 in Gibbon, Nebraska), comedian and writer who, beginning in the late 1960s, was a prominent talk show host known for his acerbic wit and droll manner and for his literate and provocative guests.

Cavett, the only child of Alva B. Cavett and Eva Richards, both schoolteachers, grew up in Gibbon and then in nearby Grand Island, Nebraska. His mother died when he was ten; later, his father remarried another schoolteacher and moved the family to Lincoln. As a child, Cavett wanted to be a comedian, and his childhood heroes included Stan Laurel, Groucho Marx, and Fred Allen. He also greatly appreciated the style and grace of Fred Astaire.

While attending Lincoln High School he excelled in gymnastics and acted, along with his classmate Sandy Dennis, in school plays as well as in local stock productions. Like his later rival, talk show host Johnny Carson, Cavett

Dick Cavett. THE KOBAL COLLECTION

performed magic shows interspersed with comic gags. If Carson could not perform in his hometown of Omaha, Cavett was booked as a replacement.

Cavett attended Yale University on a scholarship. At first majoring in English literature, he switched to drama his senior year, and frequented New Haven's Schubert Theatre, ingratiating himself with show business people, including Moss Hart and Basil Rathbone. On weekends he went to New York City, where he met and became friends with Fred Allen and Groucho Marx. After graduating from Yale in 1958 with a B.A. degree, Cavett did summer stock theater and then moved to New York. Because he could not support himself with occasional bit parts on television, he worked as a copyboy at *Time* magazine.

While working at *Time,* Cavett discovered that the talk show host Jack Paar spent his entire day worrying about his nightly opening monologue. Cavett wrote two pages of comic material. When he delivered it, he had the good fortune to bump into Paar himself, who used the material that night. Soon afterward Cavett was hired as a regular staff writer for Paar.

Back in 1954, Steve Allen had looked into a television camera and said, "First the good news . . . this show is going on forever." Allen, as the first host of a national night-owl talk show (1954–1957), was poking fun at a new format that has now become a fixture in broadcasting. Allen's successor at *The Tonight Show* was Paar, who abandoned Allen's sketch comedy and variety show format for the now standard opening of an urbane monologue followed by a sofa-and-desk routine in which a supporting sidekick and guests talked. Paar left the show in 1962, but Cavett remained on the staff, writing for interim hosts like Groucho Marx. He left to write briefly for Jerry Lewis, then returned to write for Johnny Carson, who became the longtime permanent host (1962–1992).

Encouraged by Woody Allen to move from writing comedy to performing, as he himself had done, Cavett left *The Tonight Show* in 1964 and started a stand-up comedy act. He appeared in coffeehouses and nightclubs, including the Bitter End, the hungry i, and the Blue Angel. He also appeared regularly on television panel shows like *What's My Line?,* and on radio. In 1967 Cavett and Yale classmate Tony Converse successfully packaged a talk show for the American Broadcasting Company (ABC) that placed Cavett in a morning slot ordinarily occupied by a soap opera.

For his first talk show, Cavett deliberately chose guests who ordinarily never chatted on television, such as the design engineer Buckminster Fuller. The actress Patricia Neal detailed her struggle learning to talk again after a stroke. "He has the virtue of being a good listener," noted critic Jack Gould, "before phrasing his next inquiry." Instead of watching a soap opera, viewers could enjoy the Beat poet Allen Ginsberg debating the philosopher Paul

Weiss or the liberal folk singer Joan Baez confronting the conservative hawk Louis Nizer about the Vietnam War. Cavett's show won an Emmy for outstanding daytime programming but was canceled due to low ratings.

In 1969 Carson's *Tonight Show* had two rivals. Many Columbia Broadcasting System (CBS) affiliates ran the syndicated talk show hosted by Merv Griffin, on which Cavett had made his television debut as a stand-up comedian in 1964. ABC's nighttime talk show slot was hosted by the Rat Pack comic Joey Bishop. Bishop's show had dreadfully low ratings. In fact, over forty affiliates dropped it and ran old movies instead. ABC management had been impressed by Cavett's low-key, conversational style and realized his alternative roster of guests was unsuitable for daytime fare. Cavett replaced Bishop, resulting in an immediate bounce in the network's ratings. In fact, the show's audience increased almost 50 percent in the top five markets.

The Dick Cavett Show continued its host's earlier approach of focusing beyond the usual starlets, comics, and singers who were the common fare of nightly chat. Critics again praised his lineup of showbiz luminaries (Laurence Olivier, Katharine Hepburn, and Noel Coward), authors (Norman Mailer and Joseph Heller), and other personalities (the psychologist B. F. Skinner, the *Playboy* publisher Hugh Hefner, and the conservative politician Barry Goldwater). A *New York Times* column by the critic Christopher Porterfield ran under the headline "O.K., You Folks Who Don't Watch TV, Cavett's Back."

Although columnists like Earl Wilson urged him to "dumb it up," Cavett remained dedicated to hosting literate and mesmerizing combinations (the actress Raquel Welch with the author Truman Capote) or a single guest for an entire show (the actor-director Orson Welles or the dancer Fred Astaire). ABC's new show was considered a class act, and Cavett's ratings were competitive with Carson and Griffin in urban markets. He won a second Emmy in 1972.

Cavett was willing to deal with controversial issues and became, on occasion, a target of political pressure. For instance, he was blamed for the Senate defeat of federal support of Boeing's supersonic transport because various guests had opposed it. Yet Cavett gave a Boeing spokesman more than equal time to defend the company. ABC blocked an appearance by the radical African American Angela Davis, and a show about censorship was itself censored.

Even though Cavett's show had a large and loyal audience, ABC cut it to two nights and then dropped it in 1974 because of less-than-satisfactory ratings. After that Cavett did occasional primetime interview specials, a Broadway play (*Otherwise Engaged*), and talk shows on public and cable outlets. He married actress Carrie Nye in 1964; they live in New York City and Montauk Point, Long Island.

Cavett's wry and sophisticated manner made for not just thinking-people's television but for a highly entertaining and overdue corrective to the usual fare of a talk show.

★

Cavett wrote two memoirs with Christopher Porterfield: *Cavett* (1974) and *Eye on Cavett* (1983). See also Jack Gould, "TV: Dick Cavett Offers Housewives Second Coffee," *New York Times* (5 Mar. 1968); Nora Ephron, "Dick Cavett Reads Books," *New York Times* (2 June 1968); and Christopher Porterfield, "O.K., You Folks Who Don't Watch TV, Cavett's Back," *New York Times* (28 Dec. 1969).

PATRICK S. SMITH

CERF, Bennett Albert (*b.* 25 May 1898 in New York City; *d.* 27 August 1971 in Mount Kisco, New York), publisher, writer, and television personality who played a major role in the publishing revolution of the 1960s that, over the remainder of the century, transformed a business of gentlemen into a mass marketing enterprise dominated by communications industry conglomerates.

Cerf was the only child of Gustave Cerf, a lithographer, and Frederika (Wise) Cerf. Growing up in Manhattan, he graduated from Columbia University (1919) with a B.A. degree and membership in Phi Beta Kappa; he then earned

Bennett Cerf, 1965. © BETTMANN/CORBIS

a B.Litt. from Columbia's School of Journalism in 1920. Five years later, in partnership with his close friend Donald Klopfer, he purchased the Modern Library—a line of 109 classic books—from the cash-strapped publishing house of Boni and Liveright for $250,000. Royalty-free and widely used in schools and colleges in the days before paperback books, Modern Library titles were hugely profitable. Within three years the partners earned back their purchase costs.

In 1927 Cerf and Klopfer decided to publish new books "at random" in addition to the Modern Library. Calling their firm Random House, they initially produced elegant (and expensive) limited editions of classics—an enterprise that failed with the Wall Street crash in 1929—but by the mid-1930s they were publishing thirty or so trade books a year by some of the century's leading writers. In 1933 Cerf successfully challenged a federal law banning the importation of James Joyce's *Ulysses*—in a landmark case based on the First Amendment—and established his reputation for defending liberal causes and encouraging literary freedom.

On the cusp of the 1960s Cerf was the proud and energetic president of a medium-size publishing house, best known for its well-edited books and two strong children's lines: Landmark Books (principally history) for teenagers, and Beginner Books (featuring Dr. Seuss), both of which had been developed by Cerf's second wife, Phyllis Fraser, whom he had married in September 1940 and with whom he had two sons. (Cerf was married briefly to the actress Sylvia Sydney in 1935.) In 1959 Random House went public, offering 30 percent of its stock to investors, with Cerf and Klopfer retaining equal shares of the remainder.

The sale of Random House shares on the New York Stock Exchange was part of the dramatic change that had come to publishing since World War II. Once a small-market world of gentlemen publishers, bookselling by 1960 was big business. Sales of individual titles reached into the millions in hardcover and paperback as books were sold in drugstores, airline terminals, and supermarkets as well as traditional bookshops. With fortunes to be made, publishing stocks were the darlings of Wall Street.

Cerf had anticipated much of this as early as 1944, when he had written Klopfer, then serving with the army in England, that the "future of the book business lies in . . . mass markets," and despite a wistful glance at the past that had given them "days of easy living," he and Klopfer successfully moved Random House through this maze of changes. By 1960 they had increased the number and diversity of titles on their annual list and updated the Modern Library (now numbering more than 450 titles), which they offered in paperback editions. They added new departments, notably a reference division that published *The Random House Dictionary of the English Language* in 1966 in a direct and successful challenge to Merriam-Webster.

What made this smooth (and lucrative) transition possible was the remarkable business friendship that Cerf and Klopfer sustained for forty-five years. They were, an editor wrote, "opposites in temperament and taste" who sat across from each other at matching desks, sharing the same room and the same secretary and drawing the same salary and benefits. At the outset in 1925 they agreed that the mercurial, dynamic Cerf would handle editorial and promotional matters and the soft-spoken, self-effacing Klopfer would manage production and sales, but in practice their roles were interchangeable. Between them they created what many editors believed was the best publishing climate in the country, as Cerf had a talent for selecting first-rate editors and giving them a free hand to operate.

In 1960 Cerf effected a merger with Alfred A. Knopf, whose imprint was arguably the most distinguished in America, with a strong history list and writers like Albert Camus and André Gide. In a kind of last hurrah for traditional publishing practices, the sale was initiated by the principals over lunch at the Stork Club and sealed by a handshake in Knopf's office. In 1961 Cerf acquired Pantheon (the publisher of Boris Pasternak and Mary Renault) and three smaller specialized houses. Five years later RCA purchased Random House for $40 million and a guarantee of editorial independence.

For Cerf the 1960s were a celebratory and, as it turned out, valedictory decade. He was easily the best-known publisher in America (perhaps, some said, the *only* publisher in America with instant recognition) because of his role as a principal performer, since 1951, on *What's My Line?*, a highly popular television game show. (The show ended in 1967.) He appeared regularly in advertising (donating the money to charity; what he wanted, he wrote, was his picture in print). His daily collection of jokes and puns was syndicated in more than 300 papers nationwide, and through the 1960s he continued to turn out a steady stream of best-selling joke books, riddles, and puns, which, by the time of his death in 1971, numbered more than twenty titles, with total sales in excess of five million copies. In the 1960s he edited three collections of contemporary plays (his "secret love," he told an interviewer).

Despite his reputation as a literary boulevardier—Cerf made no secret of his desire for celebrity status and his longing to be part of the glamorous world of Hollywood and Broadway—he took his publishing duties seriously, taking great pride in the quality of his books and the authors who had come to Random over the years: from Eugene O'Neill in the 1920s to William Faulkner in the 1950s to popular writers like James Michener and literary figures like William Styron in the 1960s. In interviews and his own writings, he celebrated both the joy he found in living and his contributions to publishing and, by extension, America's cultural life.

★

The Bennett Cerf/Random House papers are in the Rare Book and Manuscript Library at Butler Library, Columbia University, where the Oral History Research Office has several hours of taped interviews, portions of which were transcribed in *At Random: The Reminiscences of Bennett Cerf* (1977), edited by Phyllis Cerf and Albert Erskine. For the relationship between Cerf and Donald Klopfer, see *Dear Donald, Dear Bennett: The Wartime Correspondence of Bennett Cerf and Donald Klopfer* (2002), and Hiram Haydn, *Words and Faces* (1974). For a brief history of Random House, see John W. Tebbel, *A History of Book Publishing in the United States,* vol. 3 (1978) and vol. 4 (1981). An obituary is in the *New York Times* (29 Aug. 1971).

ALLAN L. DAMON

CHALL, Jeanne Sternlicht (*b.* 1 January 1921 in Shendishov, Poland; *d.* 27 November 1999 in Cambridge, Massachusetts), psychologist, leading expert in reading research and instruction for more than fifty years, and professor at the Harvard Graduate School of Education.

Chall was the youngest of five children of Hyman and Eva (Kreinik) Sternlicht. At the age of seven, Chall moved with her brother and three sisters to New York, where she met her father for the first time. (Chall's father had left Poland for New York in 1920.) The Yiddish-speaking Sternlicht children attended New York City public schools, learning English at a time when no bilingual programs existed. Chall was the first in her family to attend college. Gail Kearns, a former student and friend of Chall's, wrote, "Jeanne Chall could have been considered a 'poster child' for free higher education." She was able to study at City College of the City University of New York because it charged nothing for tuition; her older sister helped pay for her transportation. In 1941 Chall graduated from City College cum laude. She later earned an M.A. (1947) and a Ph.D. (1952) from Ohio State University. In 1946 she married Leo P. Chall; they had no children and divorced in 1964.

From 1943 to 1945 Chall worked in New York City at Teacher's College, Columbia University, as an assistant to Irving Lorge, an early pioneer in intelligence testing. Here Chall discovered her love for, and the importance of, comprehensive research. At Ohio State she first applied this love for research, developing, with Edgar Dale, the Dale-Chall readability formula. The formula quickly became (and still is) one of the most widely used guides for matching texts to readers. Between 1950 and 1965 Chall taught at City College, where she published her first book, *Readability: An Appraisal of Research and Application* (1958). During this period she also took visiting positions at the State Univer-

sity of New York at New Paltz (summers 1954, 1955, and 1956) and at Columbia University (summers 1958 and 1960; fall 1960; spring 1961). Chall first taught at Harvard University's Graduate School of Education in 1963 as a visiting associate professor. In 1965 she accepted Harvard's offer of a full professorship.

During the 1960s many educators were calling for a change in the ways in which children were taught to read. While some moved blindly ahead with the latest trends in education (including the dismissal of phonics, often in favor of the "look-see" method), Chall asked why such innovations were employed before research evidence supporting their effectiveness was developed. In *Learning to Read: The Great Debate* (1967), she argued that the teaching of phonics was necessary in reading instruction. In preparation for the book, Chall reviewed hundreds of research studies done between 1910 and 1965; she also visited classrooms and interviewed teachers and textbook publishers. Chall's book reminded readers that pedagogical innovation should be based on sound research, not on the latest fad.

Chall was prolific throughout her career. In addition to *Learning to Read,* in the 1960s she wrote more than twenty articles and, with Shirley C. Feldmann, a research report entitled "A Study in Depth of First Grade Reading: An Analysis of the Interactions of Proposed Methods, Teacher Implementation and Child Background" (1966) for the U.S. Office of Education. She was the consulting editor for *Folktales of Other Lands* (published in eight volumes between 1963 and 1964), and she was a developer of the *Roswell-Chall Auditory Blending Test* (1962). Altogether, Chall wrote, co-wrote, or edited more than twenty books; the total number of her articles, tests, research reports, and interviews exceeds two hundred.

In her research and writing Chall expressed a commitment to helping all people improve their reading skills. In "Attitudes of Children from a Deprived Environment Toward Achievement-Related Concepts," in the *Journal of Educational Research* (October 1965), Chall and her co-authors argued for the importance of improving the reading abilities of low-income minority children. She also demonstrated a concern for adult literacy, a concern whose beginnings might be traced to the part she played as a grade-school student in helping her mother learn English so that she could pass the citizenship exam. The extent of Chall's concern is expressed in such articles as "Estimating the Size of Vocabularies of Children and Adults: An Analysis of Methodological Issues" in the *Journal of Experimental Education* (winter 1963).

In 1966 Chall founded the Harvard Reading Lab (now named after her) and served as its director for more than twenty-five years. Her other professional commitments were extensive. She acted as secretary-treasurer (1963) and president (1965 to 1966) of the National Conference on

Research in English. From 1962 to 1965 she sat on the board of directors for the International Reading Association. Also in the 1960s Chall was asked to join a number of advisory committees, among them, the Steering Committee, Project Literacy, U.S. Office of Education (1964 to 1970); National Advisory Committee on Dyslexia and Related Reading Disorders, U.S. Department of Health, Education, and Welfare (1968 to 1970); Advisory Council for Title III, ESEA (Elementary and Secondary Education Act, enacted in 1965), Commonwealth of Massachusetts (1968 to 1972); and Advisory Board, Children's Television Workshop (1968 to 1999). In all she was affiliated with nine professional associations, eighteen advisory committees, and five editorial boards, including the board of the *Journal of Educational Psychology*.

Chall was the recipient of the most distinguished honors in the field of education. Her more than fifty years of professional work did not cease until her death at the age of seventy-eight from congestive heart failure. Less than two weeks earlier, with the help of Mary E. Curtis, Chall had finished *The Academic Achievement Challenge: What Really Works in the Classroom*. Returning to the question that sparked much of her research and writing—Why are so many educational innovations adopted before research supports their effectiveness?—Chall concluded that the traditional approach to teaching (as opposed to the student-led, hands-on approach) produces higher academic achievement, especially for low-income children. She spent much of her career making the connection between good research and good practice, citing that educational innovation should be based on solid research.

★

Information about Chall is in Gail Kearns, "Jeanne S. Chall: A Memorial Tribute" and "Practical Tools for Teachers: A Selected Reference List of Resources by Jeanne S. Chall," both in *Perspectives: Journal of the International Dyslexia Association* (2000); the Gale Group's *Contemporary Authors Online* (2000; <http://galenet.galegroup.com>); and William Dee Nichol's website about Jeanne Chall at <http://education.uncc.edu/wdnichol/Chall.html>.

CANDICE MANCINI-KNIGHT

CHAMBERLAIN, Wilton Norman ("Wilt") (*b.* 21 August 1936 in Philadelphia, Pennsylvania; *d.* 12 October 1999 in Los Angeles, California), legendary seven-foot, one-inch center whose on-court style influenced the evolution of basketball to a sport dominated by tall, powerful, but highly mobile players.

The eighth of eleven children born to William Chamberlain, a handyman and janitor, and Olivia, a domestic worker, Chamberlain was by far the tallest member of his

family. He was sufficiently outstanding in his basketball career at Overbrook High School in Philadelphia that Eddie Gottlieb, owner of the local Philadelphia Warriors, was able to acquire draft rights to Chamberlain after high school under a new rule, awarding "territorial rights" to local teams. After a three-year apprenticeship at the University of Kansas (1956–1958), where he endured racist taunts from fans and opposing players, and a year with the Harlem Globetrotters (1958–1959), Chamberlain was able to join the Warriors.

Armed with an annual salary estimated at around $65,000, Chamberlain was ready to establish himself as the best in the game, to win championships, and to make bushels of money. In fact, he continued touring with the Globetrotters during the summers until 1968. He succeeded in his personal and financial goals, but with the omnipotent Boston Celtics (led by center Bill Russell) in the way, championships eluded the Warriors, and Chamberlain had difficulty shaking a noxious "loser" label. That aspersion was not evident in his first season. After stunning the New York Knicks with 43 points in his first professional game on 24 October 1959, Chamberlain roared through the season. He was named rookie of the year and Most Valuable Player (MVP), after a year in which he broke league records for minutes played (3,388), scoring average (37.6 points per game), rebounding (26.9 rebounds per game), and five other categories. In a pattern repeated over the next five years, however, the Celtics ousted Philadelphia in the play-offs in six games. Russell had lower statistics than Chamberlain, but his team invariably won, as critics castigated Chamberlain's failure to produce a miracle. Chamberlain threatened to retire after this first year, but was enticed to return by a three-year $350,000 contract.

Chamberlain established himself as the dominant player in the game by his second season. On 24 November 1960 he grabbed an NBA record fifty-five rebounds in one game against Russell's Celtics, an achievement that has never been successfully challenged. However, Syracuse ousted Philadelphia in the first round of the play-offs.

Frank McGuire, Chamberlain's new coach for the 1961–1962 season, convinced him to score even more, arguing that the team won when the center scored fifty or more points per game. McGuire devised an offense that focused almost entirely on Chamberlain, who played an extraordinary season in which he scored an average of 50.4 points per game, played 79 complete games, and had 63 games in which he scored 40 points or more. He capped this incredible season with a 100-point outburst against the New York Knicks on 4 March 1962. Almost as amazingly, Chamberlain was not chosen as the first team all-star center or season MVP; both honors went to Russell. Philadelphia lost in the divisional play-offs to Boston in a controversial seventh game in Boston in which the official Mendy Rudolph was accused of throwing the game to the Celtics.

Wilt Chamberlain. CORBIS CORPORATION (NEW YORK)

After the season Gottlieb sold the team to San Francisco financiers, who moved the Warriors west. McGuire declined to go, and Chamberlain, induced by a contract at $100,000 a year, went only briefly.

Chamberlain piled up individual honors over the next two years, but there were no play-off successes. In January 1965 the San Francisco Warriors traded him to the Philadelphia 76ers. Again, Chamberlain was frustrated by the Celtics, whose John Havlicek won yet another championship for the team with a clutch steal as time ran out in the seventh game. Not until 1967 would Chamberlain's team end the Boston dynasty. After beating the Celtics in the divisional play-offs, Philadelphia finally won a championship—ironically, by conquering Chamberlain's former team, the San Francisco Warriors, in six games in 1967. Chamberlain, always defensive and aloof, was reluctant to enjoy the victory, although he later wistfully noted that he had finally made "it all the way."

His triumph was short-lived. In the next season, though he was named league MVP for the second year in a row (he won again the following year), the Celtics once more ousted Philadelphia in another memorable play-off. Over the summer of 1968 the Los Angeles Lakers acquired Chamberlain for three players plus cash. Lakers owner Jack Kent Cooke was determined to produce a winner in Los Angeles and paid Chamberlain $200,000 a season plus lucrative benefits. (Chamberlain is an unsung contributor to the rise in player salaries in this era.) Chamberlain liked Cooke and was willing to overlook cliques on the team, which was headed by the star forward Elgin Baylor. The Lakers steamrolled through the regular season, but the Celtics denied Chamberlain a second championship.

Among the most durable players in the league, Chamberlain tore a tendon inside his kneecap and missed most of the 1969–1970 season. He returned late in the season and led the Lakers into the play-offs, but the New York Knicks beat them in seven games for the championship. The next year Chamberlain became the first NBA player to accumulate 30,000 points for his career, a mark only surpassed much later by Kareem Abdul-Jabbar. More importantly, Chamberlain and the Lakers surpassed the Knicks in the championship finals.

Chamberlain played one more season with the Lakers, briefly retired, then emerged with the San Diego Clippers in the upstart American Basketball Association. Later, he sponsored a woman's volleyball team and lived in quiet luxury in Los Angeles. He never married. An extraordinary athlete, Chamberlain nearly boxed Muhammad Ali in an exhibition and was considered one of the strongest men in sports. Sensitive about the "loser" label, he was proud of his innumerable records and his wealth. Physically fit, his death from a heart attack in 1999 shocked and saddened the sports world.

★

Chamberlain wrote two autobiographical works: *Wilt: Just Like Any Other Seven-Foot Millionaire Who Lives Next Door* (1974) and *A View from Above* (1991). See also Bill Libby, *Goliath: The Wilt Chamberlain Story* (1977). An obituary is in the *New York Times* (13 Oct. 1999).

GRAHAM RUSSELL HODGES

CHAMPION, Gower (*b.* 22 June 1919 in Geneva, Illinois; *d.* 25 August 1980 in New York City), noted dancer, choreographer, and director of stage, screen, and television.

Born to John W. Champion, an advertising executive, and Beatrice Carlisle, a custom dressmaker, Champion was raised by his mother in Los Angeles after his parents divorced. He studied dance and, at the age of seventeen, quit Fairfax High School to spend the next six years, 1936 to 1942, touring fashionable cabarets with his dancing partner, Jeanne Tyler. Billing themselves as "Gower and Jeanne, America's Youngest Dancers," the pair eventually made their way to Hollywood, where they had cameo roles in the films *Streets of Paris* (1939), *The Lady Comes Across* (1942), and *Count Me In* (1942).

During World War II, Champion briefly left the stage to enlist in the U.S. Coast Guard. After the war he returned to film and in 1947 found a new dance partner in his childhood sweetheart, Marge Belcher, who became his wife on 5 October 1947; the couple had two children and divorced in 1973. The Champions' stylish and energetic performances were especially suited to the new medium of television, and they appeared on virtually every TV variety show of the 1950s. They also appeared in a number of big-screen movie musicals, including *Show Boat* (1951) and *Jupiter's Darling* (1955). By the late 1950s Champion made the decision to return to Broadway—where, almost a de-

Gower Champion, August 1967. ASSOCIATED PRESS AP

cade earlier, he had successfully choreographed and directed his first musical stage production.

At first glance Champion's choice for his return to Broadway appeared doubtful. The 1960 production of *Bye, Bye Birdie* was a first-time effort not only for its producer but for its lyricist, composer, and many cast members as well. But under Champion's sure-handed direction, the production maintained an energy that was punctuated by stirring and stunning choreography. One opening-night critic found the play "the funniest, most captivating and most expert musical comedy one could hope to see in several seasons of showgoing." Others agreed; Champion was awarded two Tonys, one for direction, the other for choreography, for *Bye, Bye Birdie*.

From this point on Champion was known not only for his superb direction of farce but also his ability to entertain audiences. His productions had more in common with the Hollywood musicals of the 1940s and 1950s, in that they were often comedic, light in tone, and colorful in presentation. Like Jerome Robbins, also active in the theater at this time, Champion looked for so-called triple-threat performers—those who could sing, act, and dance—rather than those whose talents were limited to the chorus line. Also like Robbins, Champion relentlessly worked to design sets that provided a seamless flow from scene to scene, as in films.

Throughout the 1960s Champion produced hit after hit. His successes rank among the greatest musicals of the American theater, including *Carnival!* (1961), *Hello, Dolly!* (1964), for which Champion won two more Tony Awards, and *I Do! I Do!* (1966). He did some of his most notable work in collaboration with the producer David Merrick, with whom he had a fruitful if stormy relationship for nearly two decades.

With *Carnival!*, Champion tried a different approach in his direction. His decision to make the audience participants in the show allowed them to experience much of the same enchantment the main character, Lili, has for the traveling carnival troupe. The technique also succeeded in creating an intimate rapport with the cast and audience. Champion heightened the intimacy by doing away with the curtain and the opening overture and by having some of the actors make their entrances and exits via the theater aisles. Both critics and audiences responded enthusiastically to Champion's innovations; *Carnival!* was one of the season's biggest hits.

Hello, Dolly! was another rousing success for Champion, who took what many thought was an uninspired and disjointed story and turned it into one of Broadway's most memorable productions of the decade. Carol Channing's starring performance and the show's score were so memorable that Champion's direction and wildly exciting choreography were often overlooked by critics. But with *I Do!*

I Do!, Champion once more directly enjoyed the critics' toasts to his fast-paced direction and choreography.

In 1966 Champion took on the production of *The Happy Time*, which had enjoyed a run on Broadway in 1950. To make the production more current and more of a concept musical, Champion employed a triple-tiered revolving stage. The stage allowed the actors to move seamlessly from one scene to the next without breaking the play's continuity or flow. These smooth onstage transitions gave the effect of watching a series of "photographs" as the storyline progressed. Champion also took advantage of the sophisticated film effects used in IMAX productions. While a bold move on Champion's part, the technology dwarfed the performers and contributed to the play's failure. When *The Happy Time* opened in 1968, critics praised Champion's direction but found the play sentimental and old-fashioned. Champion nevertheless won a Tony for the play's choreography. The following year he experienced yet another disappointment with the doomed production of *A Flea in Her Ear.* By the end of the decade it was clear Champion was out of step with the times; he had become a handsome anachronism.

Unfortunately, the successes Champion enjoyed on the Broadway musical stage never translated in his attempts to direct drama or films, which were often critical and commercial failures. The irony is that many of his stage productions of the 1960s relied on cinematic techniques such as the close-up, flashback, and cross-fade. Champion's directorial work was a great influence on the imminent technological revolution of the Broadway stage in the coming decades; as one artistic director noted, "He modernized the old Broadway style."

In 1980, after an absence of nearly five years from the director's chair, Champion agreed to choreograph and direct a theatrical adaptation of the 1933 movie musical *42nd Street.* Even though he was not Merrick's first choice as the director, Champion proved to be the right choice in directing the old-fashioned musical. However, he was suffering from a rare blood disorder and was supposed to cut back on his activities. As the task of directing rehearsals took its toll, Champion was no longer able to conceal his illness. Instead, he pushed Merrick to hasten production of *42nd Street.*

On 25 August 1980, only hours before the play opened, Champion died. The ordinarily reclusive Merrick came on stage after the numerous curtain calls to make the announcement. Champion's death only heightened the play's own tale of show business, adversity, and the old adage "The show must go on." Although he was never considered a choreographic or directorial innovator after the fashion of Robbins or Bob Fosse, Champion left his own imprint. His productions were elegant and sophisticated yet unpretentious. While his plays tended to avoid social commentary or taboo subjects, they did help to break new ground in their use of technology and staging and set a new direction in American theater.

★

There is no biography of Champion, but see William Goldman, *The Season* (1969); David Payne-Carter, "Gower Champion and the American Musical Theater" (Ph.D. diss., New York University, 1989); and Robert Emmet Long, *Broadway, the Golden Years: Jerome Robbins and the Great Choreographer-Directors 1940 to the Present* (2001). See also Jess Gregg, "Scenes from a Memoir," *Dance Magazine* 73, no. 9 (Sept. 1999). An obituary is in the *New York Times* (27 Aug. 1980).

MEG GREENE

CHANEY, James Earl (*b.* 30 May 1943 in Meridian, Mississippi; *d.* 21 June 1964 in Neshoba County, Mississippi), **Andrew GOODMAN** (*b.* 23 November 1943 in New York City; *d.* 21 June 1964 in Neshoba County, Mississippi), and **Michael Henry SCHWERNER** (*b.* 6 November 1939 in New York City; *d.* 21 June 1964 in Neshoba County, Mississippi), civil rights workers whose abduction and murder by Ku Klux Klan members during the first days of Mississippi's Freedom Summer project drew national attention to the violence directed against the civil rights movement in the Deep South.

Chaney was the second of five children born to Ben Chaney, an itinerant plasterer, and Fannie Lee Roberth Chaney, a domestic worker. After being expelled from high school he worked for his father before joining the Congress of Racial Equality (CORE) in the winter of 1964 as an unpaid staff member.

Goodman was the middle son of Robert, a contractor, and Carolyn Goodman. He attended the Walden School, a progressive private school in Manhattan with a mostly Jewish student body. There he became involved in liberal political causes. At the time he joined the Mississippi Freedom Summer project, Goodman had completed his junior year at Queens College, where he was an anthropology major.

Schwerner was the second son of Nathan, a partner in a wig manufacturing company, and Anne Schwerner, a high school biology teacher. He attended Cornell University, graduating with a degree in rural sociology in 1961. He enrolled in Columbia University's School of Social Work but dropped out in June 1962 to take a job as a settlement house worker. The same month he married Rita Levant. In 1963 the couple became active in protests against racial discrimination, and that fall they applied to CORE to go south to work in the freedom movement. On 16 January 1964 they arrived in Mississippi—the first full-time white civil rights workers in the state—and were sent to Meridian, where they operated a community center. Cha-

Michael Schwerner *(left)*, James Chaney *(center)*, and Andrew Goodman *(right)*. © Bettmann/Corbis

ney assisted Schwerner in Meridian, frequently driving Schwerner over the back country roads he knew well. Despite his Ivy League background, Schwerner developed an easy rapport with the black youths who flocked to the center. His visibility made him a prime target for the Ku Klux Klan, whose members tagged him with the code name "Goatee."

In June 1964 Schwerner and Chaney traveled to Oxford, Ohio, where recruits for the Mississippi Freedom Summer were being trained. The project involved sending nearly a thousand volunteer civil rights workers, most of them white college students, into Mississippi to increase voter registration, develop political organization, and conduct "Freedom Schools," which were designed to teach basic academic skills to African-American children in order to supplement their woefully inadequate public school curriculum. On 20 June 1964 Schwerner and Chaney returned to Mississippi with Goodman, who had been assigned to Meridian. The next day they drove to the Longdale community in Neshoba County to investigate the burning of Mount Zion Methodist Church. The church had been offered as a site for a Freedom School, and this made it a target for Klan reprisal. After leaving Longdale they were arrested for speeding by Deputy Sheriff Cecil Price and taken to the county jail in Philadelphia, Mississippi. The three men were released from jail at 10:30 P.M. after paying a $20 fine. Ten miles outside of town, Price again stopped their blue station wagon and turned them over to a gang of Klansmen. The young men were murdered by the side of the road; their car was burned and their bodies buried.

When Goodman, Chaney, and Schwerner failed to return to Meridian, CORE staffers notified the Federal Bureau of Investigation (FBI) and state police. The disappearance became national news the following day. Civil rights forces were convinced they had been killed, but local authorities claimed the trio had staged their own kidnapping to garner publicity. President Lyndon Johnson ordered a massive manhunt to locate the men. A force of FBI agents descended on the state to investigate. On 4 August 1964 the badly decomposed bodies were discovered beneath fifteen feet of earth in a farm pond dam. Autopsies revealed all three had been shot at close range and Chaney had been brutally beaten. The parents tried to hold an integrated funeral for their martyred sons but learned that Mississippi law did not permit it.

Chaney is buried in Okatibee Cemetery, Lauderdale County, Mississippi; Goodman is buried in Mount Judah Cemetery, Queens, New York; and Schwerner was cremated in New York City.

On 4 December 1964 nineteen men, including Price and Sheriff Lawrence Rainey, were arrested on federal charges of violating the victims' civil rights. After nearly three years of legal maneuvering, thirteen men were tried, and on 20 October 1967 seven were convicted and sentenced to prison terms ranging from three to ten years. It was the first time Mississippi white men were found guilty of lynching. On 19 March 1970, after exhausting their appeals, the seven convicted men entered federal custody. No prosecution on state charges of murder was ever initiated.

Goodman, Chaney, and Schwerner symbolize the idealistic youths who challenged the entrenched power of white supremacy in the Deep South. If their killing was intended to intimidate movement forces, it had the opposite effect. Activists "invaded" the state that summer, and Mississippi was permanently changed. In his history of the Mississippi civil rights movement, John Dittmer describes the visibility the murders brought to the Klan's activities and the resulting international outrage: "The Neshoba lynchings . . . were decisive in persuading the state's white elite that continued violent resistance to federal law would lead to political anarchy and economic devastation." The prosecution and conviction of the killers signaled an official willingness to confront the worst manifestations of southern racism.

★

Veteran journalist William Bradford Huie, *Three Lives for Mississippi* (1965), investigates the Neshoba County murders. The definitive account of the case is in Seth Cagin and Philip Dray, *We Are Not Afraid: The Story of Goodman, Schwerner, and Chaney and the Civil Rights Campaign for Mississippi* (1988). The feature film *Mississippi Burning* (1988) is based on the FBI investigation of the Goodman, Chaney, and Schwerner murders. Although much of the film is fiction, its opening scene is a mostly accurate depiction of their execution. The impact of the murders on the summer project is examined in Doug McAdam, *Freedom Summer* (1988). John Dittmer, *Local People: The Struggle for Civil Rights in Mississippi* (1994), places the murders in the larger context of the Mississippi civil rights movement.

PAUL T. MURRAY

CHÁVEZ, César Estrada (*b.* 31 March 1927 near Yuma, Arizona; *d.* 23 April 1993 in San Luis, Arizona), founder of the United Farm Workers of America, who during the 1960s used boycotts and strikes to fight for human rights and labor concessions and who became the most important Mexican-American leader in the history of the United States.

Chávez was one of four children born to Librado Chávez and Juana Estrada, who lived near Yuma, a dusty town where the borders of Mexico, California, and Arizona converge. There they ran a farm and three small businesses, but in 1938, when Chávez was eleven, the family lost the farm to foreclosure and went to California, where they eked out a living by picking tomatoes, lettuce, and other crops. Chávez worked alongside his parents in the fields, attending school infrequently as the family moved from town to town in search of work. By the time he quit for good upon completing the eighth grade, Chávez had attended no fewer than thirty-six schools. Thereafter he continued his education on his own, reading the works of Gandhi and others in both Spanish and English.

After serving two years (1944–1945) in the Pacific with the U.S. Navy during World War II, Chávez married Helen Fabela in 1948. They had eight children. In 1952 Fred Ross, a labor organizer who would become a lifelong friend, recruited Chávez to help the Community Service Organization (CSO), a Mexican-American civil rights group, register voters. Soon Chávez had a full-time job as an organizer with CSO, and by 1959 he had become ex-

Cesar Chávez. AP/WORLD WIDE PHOTOS

ecutive director of the group. In 1962, when CSO rejected Chávez's suggestion to begin organizing farm workers, Chávez quit his post and formed his own union, the National Farm Workers Association (NFWA), later the United Farm Workers of America (UFW), in Delano, California, at the heart of the state's fertile central valley.

Chávez had grown up seeing his parents and other workers systematically mistreated by the growers who employed them; they toiled for next to nothing under conditions that were often horrific. When Chávez started the union, many farm workers had neither toilets nor running water in their homes, and most of their children did not receive vaccinations. The growers often promised one wage but paid another, and usually provided no toilet facilities or drinking water in the sun-baked fields. The workers earned an average of $2,400 per year, far below the poverty line. If they complained, they were fired, as an unlimited supply of immigrant labor was available through the Bracero Program, endorsed by the federal government.

Chávez logged hundreds of miles across California, convincing farm workers one by one to join his union. Soon the UFW was not only viable but had its own newspaper, *El Malcriado*, and a farm workers' credit union. In 1965 the union had its first small strike, wherein eighty-five rose growers won higher wages in a three-day walkout. In September of that year, after their wages were reduced from $1.40 to $1.00 per hour, 2,000 union grape pickers began an epic strike. The strikers were under strict instructions from Chávez to remain peaceful, even as the growers and their hired thugs brandished guns, sprayed pesticide on them, threatened them with dogs, and beat them with their fists while local law enforcement looked the other way. Chávez himself sustained bruised ribs from punches, but he remained steadfastly committed to the nonviolent philosophy he had absorbed from the writings of Gandhi. "We are engaged in another struggle for the freedom and dignity which poverty denies us," he said. "But it must not be a violent struggle, even if violence is used against us. Violence can only hurt us and our cause."

The strike made national news. Reporters flocked to the valley, students and clergymen arrived offering to help, and the Federal Bureau of Investigation (FBI) secretly began investigating Chávez and the UFW. On 19 October, forty-four picketers, including Chávez's wife, were arrested for shouting the word *huelga* (strike) in public. In December the union began a boycott of Schenley Industries, which produced wine with the grapes picked by the striking workers. Public opinion began to swing toward farm workers, and Chávez won the support of the labor leader Walter Reuther and of Senator Robert Kennedy, who marched on a picket line alongside the workers.

Finally, on 17 March 1966, after six months of striking, Chávez organized a march from Delano to the California state capitol in Sacramento, a 245-mile trek that was the longest protest march in United States history. By the end of the march Chávez had blistered feet and needed a cane to walk, but the protest resulted in new union contracts with several of the state's largest growers. Chávez's next target was the DiGiorgio Corporation, which had denied its workers the right to union representation. A UFW boycott of DiGiorgio grapes in grocery stores eventually forced the company to give in, a victory that prompted a congratulatory telegram to Chávez from the Reverend Martin Luther King, Jr.

In January 1968, with many grape growers still refusing to negotiate, Chávez launched an ambitious boycott of all California grapes; this became the most prolonged and successful boycott in American history. He began his first public fast the next month, consuming nothing but Diet Rite cola for twenty-five days. The fast brought publicity to the grape boycott, which succeeded in removing California grapes from grocery stores in most major cities. But what consumers would not buy, President Richard M. Nixon would. To combat the union, the new president ordered the Department of Defense to increase its consumption of California grapes from 6.9 million pounds to 11 million pounds per year.

On 29 July 1970 the grape growers agreed to a union contract. By this time Chávez was world-famous, having been the subject of several biographies and a *Time* maga-zine cover story. His movements were still monitored closely by the FBI, and frustrated fruit growers organized break-ins at UFW offices. Chávez survived two assassination plots, one allegedly masterminded by the grape growers and the other by the Teamsters Union, which wanted to take over the UFW's contracts.

In 1975, under intense pressure from Chávez, the California legislature passed the Agricultural Labor Relations Act, a state law that gave farmworkers the right to unionize even against their employers' wishes. Chávez continued to utilize fasts and boycotts throughout the 1970s and 1980s, and kept fighting against the growers' use of pesticides, which were believed to have caused illness in thousands of workers. In 1993 he traveled to Arizona to defend the union in a lawsuit filed by the lettuce conglomerate Bruce Church Incorporated, which claimed to have lost millions of dollars to union boycotts. (Ironically, Bruce Church was the current owner of the family homestead seized from Chávez's parents fifty-five years earlier.) After testifying in court on 22 April 1993, Chávez broke his final fast with a meal of rice and cabbage, retired for the evening, and died in his bed with a book in his hands. Chávez was buried at the UFW headquarters in Keene, California; at his request, he was interred in a plain pine coffin. Arturo Rodriguez, Chávez's son-in-law, succeeded him as president of the United Farm Workers.

A small, quiet man and a devout Catholic, Chávez was the antithesis of the stereotypical labor leader. He lacked fancy clothes and a formal education, never owned a house or a car, and never made more than $6,000 per year. But he was one of the most successful organizers in American history. At the time of his death the union he had started from scratch had 22,000 members. More importantly, he provided the moral compass for the Mexican-American civil rights movement that is in force to this day. Chávez had always envisioned the UFW not as a traditional labor union but rather as a social movement that could change the lives of Mexican-Americans in general. "Ninety-five percent of the strikers lost their homes and their cars," Chávez said after the 1970 grape strike. "But I think in losing those worldly possessions they found themselves."

★

Chávez collaborated with Jacques Levy on an autobiography, *César Chavez: Autobiography of La Causa* (1975). Dozens of other biographies have been published; among the most insightful are Fred Ross, *Conquering Goliath: César Chávez at the Beginning* (1989); Susan Ferriss and Ricardo Sandoval, *The Fight in the Fields: César Chávez and the Farmworkers Movement* (1997); and Ann McGregor and Cindy Wathen, *Remembering César: The Legacy of César Chávez* (2000). A cover article appears in *Time* (4 July 1969).

ERIC ENDERS

CHAYEFSKY, Sidney Aaron ("Paddy") (*b.* 29 January 1923 in New York City; *d.* 1 August 1981 in New York City), dramatist for television, stage, and screen, whose hour-long television plays, or teleplays, won acclaim in the 1950s. When the television industry abandoned this form of programming, Chayefsky turned his attention to writing for stage and film, efforts that won him three Academy Awards.

Chayefsky was the only child of Harry Chayefsky, an executive of a dairy company, and Gussie Stuchevsky, a homemaker. He grew up in the Bronx, attending DeWitt Clinton High School and the City College of New York, where he earned his B.S.S. in 1943. He then joined the U.S. Army, serving with the 104th Infantry Division in Germany. While recovering in a British hospital from a landmine explosion he wrote his first play, a musical, *No T.O. for Love* (1945). Produced by a service entertainment unit, the show proved so successful that it was mounted for the London stage. In the meantime, the writer had been jokingly dubbed "Paddy" for his attempts to be excused from duty to attend mass. Any Catholic so devout, his comrades had concluded, must surely be an Irishman.

Following his discharge from the army in 1945, Chayefsky worked in his uncle's printing shop, played semiprofessional football, took bit parts in plays, and wrote gags for radio personalities as he struggled to make a career as a

Paddy Chayefsky, 1972. © Bettmann/Corbis

writer. Television, which was in its infancy, had not drawn the attention of many established writers, and the young Chayefsky saw an opportunity and seized it. In 1952 he contributed scripts to two television anthology crime-drama series, *Danger,* on the Columbia Broadcasting System (CBS), and *Manhunt,* on the National Broadcasting Company (NBC). That same year, he met Fred Coe, production manager of NBC's *Goodyear-Philco Television Playhouse* and a key figure in creating the conditions for what is now remembered as "the golden age of television drama." Coe encouraged Chayefsky to write hour-long, commercially segmented "teleplays" for the series.

Marty, the third Chayefsky script produced for *Philco-Goodyear Television Playhouse* during the 1952–1953 season, catapulted the young writer to fame quite literally overnight, winning high ratings and enthusiastic attention from the New York press. It is the story of a depressed and pathetic unmarried butcher (Rod Steiger), who lives with his mother in a decaying house in the Bronx. Describing himself as "an ugly little man," he has given up on the possibilities of love or marriage for himself. One of the early scenes in the teleplay, during which Marty and a fellow bachelor discuss plans for the weekend, contains what 1960s activist Abbie Hoffman described as "the greatest vaudeville routine in all of existentialist philosophy."

The popular and critical acceptance of *Marty* put Chayefsky much in demand. Over the next two years he penned ten original teleplays for prime time television, including *The Bachelor Party, Sixth Year,* and *The Catered Affair.* Beckoned by Hollywood to adapt *Marty* into a motion picture, he won an Academy Award for his screenplay, while the film won the best picture award for 1955. Other adaptations of Chayefsky's teleplays followed. The theatrical premiere of *The Middle of the Night* in 1956 marked the first time that a television script had served as a source for a Broadway production. It was further adapted into a 1959 film starring Frederic March and Kim Novak. *The Bachelor Party* was also adapted for film in 1957.

Chayefsky's star had risen on the strength of his live television plays, but by the 1960s he found himself the master of a literary form that had become all but obsolete. As television expanded from its early base in large cities to national saturation, the networks dropped live drama in favor of filmed action series featuring outdoor shooting. Testifying at a congressional hearing concerning television programming, NBC president Robert Sarnoff dismissed the work of Chayefsky and other "golden age" writers as "depressing Beatnik stuff." Rejected by the medium that had "made" him—and that he had helped to make— Chayefsky turned his attention to writing new works for the theater. The results were less than spectacular. Two plays, *The Tenth Man* (1960), a retelling of a Yiddish folktale set in contemporary Long Island, and *Gideon* (1961), directed by Tyrone Guthrie, each ran in New York for about six months to mixed reviews. A third play, *The Passion of Josef D* (1964), was an outright flop.

Tied to the 1950s by a tendency to base motivation on Freud-meets-Sartre psychobabble, Chayefsky's work lacked political content, explicit sexuality, drug experimentation, or any of the other indicators of "relevance" that were finding cultural currency. Attempts to break away from type did little to help. Such attempts included screenplays for *The Americanization of Emily* (1964), a wartime romantic comedy starring Julie Andrews, and *Paint Your Wagon* (1969), one of the many attempts to revive the Hollywood musical that littered the decade.

In the late 1960s and 1970s, however, Chayefsky began to rebound. This phase culminated with his writing an extraordinary pair of screenplays, *The Hospital* (1971), and *Network* (1976), both of which won him Academy Awards. Directed by Arthur Hiller, *Hospital* is a blistering satirical attack on bureaucracy, demonstrating how even the most benevolent of institutions can be turned into an instrument of death by an uncaring power structure. Sharing the spirit and ideological bent of such 1960s novels as Ken Kesey's *One Flew Over the Cuckoo's Nest* and Richard Hooker's *M*A*S*H* (as well as the film adaptations they spawned), Chayefsky championed the capacity for love as the key to human survival by focusing on the way that the problems of illness, pain, and death have been handed over by society to institutions whose first duty is to mass production rather than to the alleviation of suffering.

In the film, George C. Scott plays Dr. Herbert Block, head of surgery at a large metropolitan teaching hospital. Although aware of the absurdities that surround him, he accedes to the political necessities of running a hospital out of sheer helplessness. Impotent, divorced, disowned by his children, and perplexed by a seemingly inexplicable juggernaut of daily blunders that have made the hospital as dangerous to patients as their illnesses, Block is at the brink of suicide as the film opens. Like Marty, however, Block falls in love (with Barbara Drummond, played by Diana Rigg) just when love seems to have passed him by. She wants to remove her comatose father from the hospital so she can take him back to the Sioux reservation in South Dakota, where he operated a clinic. The rebirth of eros in the doctor is accompanied by a rebirth of empathy, which turns his daily exercise in denial into an impossible nightmare. The prismatic quality of sudden shifts between tragic and comic circumstances is comparable to Joseph Heller's *Catch-22* and the film adaptation by Mike Nichols.

In *Network* (1976), Chayefsky takes revenge on the medium that declared him a genius and then sent him into enforced exile during the 1960s. Directed by Sidney Lumet, a fellow veteran of the "golden age" of television drama, the film critique of American commercial television is in some ways reminiscent of the sketches produced during the 1960s at the East Village theater in New York by the "underground television" collective known as Channel One. In one scene, a crazed network news anchor urges Americans to open their windows and shout, "I'm mad as hell and I'm not going to take it any more." This was Chayefsky's most memorable line of dialog since *Marty*. The writer's final project, a screen adaptation of his only novel, *Altered States* (1980), was a science-fiction drug adventure. Unhappy with changes imposed on the screenplay, Chayefsky took his writing credit as "Sidney Aaron."

Having disproved the adage that "there are no second acts in American life," Chayefsky died of cancer in New York City. The funeral was held at the Riverside Memorial Chapel in Manhattan. He is survived by his wife Susan Sackler, whom he married on 24 February 1949, and a son. Asked about his success in film after experiencing enforced departures from television and theater, Chayefsky said, "The simple truth is that Hollywood producers and executives are not the idiots they are frequently supposed to be."

★

Two critical biographies, John M. Clum, *Paddy Chayefsky* (1976), and Shaun Considine, *Mad as Hell: The Life and Word of Paddy Chayefsky* (1994), both offer detailed bibliographies. An obituary is in the *New York Times* (2 Aug. 1981).

DAVID MARC

CHECKER, Chubby (*b.* 3 October 1941 in Spring Gulley, near Andrews, South Carolina), singer and actor who popularized the dance craze "The Twist" in the early 1960s.

Checker, born Ernest O'Neil Evans, was one of three children of Raymond Evans, a tobacco farmer, and Eartie Evans, a homemaker. In 1950 the Evans family moved to south Philadelphia, where Checker attended South Philadelphia High School, graduating in 1960. While in high school, Checker worked at a poultry shop plucking chickens, and he gained a reputation as an offbeat entertainer who sang and told jokes. His boss introduced him to songwriter Kal Mann, who recommended Checker as a singer to Philadelphia television personality Dick Clark, the host of the popular teen dance show *American Bandstand*. Mann also helped Checker secure a recording contract with Philadelphia's Cameo-Parkway label. Checker, whose nickname was "Chubby" because of his large size, was signed by Cameo-Parkway in 1959; and Barbara Clark, then Dick Clark's wife, added "Checker" to his name, playing off the moniker of blues star Fats Domino. The newly rechristened Chubby Checker released his first single, "The Class," that same year.

The single reached the Top Forty, but the subsequent "Dancing Dinosaur" fared less well. With his third single, however, released in 1960, Checker became a star. Blues group *Hank Ballard and the Midnighters* originally recorded "The Twist" on 11 November 1958 as the flipside to the single "Teardrops on Your Letter," released in 1959. Checker's version toned down the raunchiness of the song, opting for a slicker pop sound that propelled the song to the top of the charts on its release in August 1960, thanks to its additional exposure on *American Bandstand*.

The dance itself was simple enough, as Checker helpfully explained: "Work your feet like you're putting out a cigarette and work your hands like you're drying your bottom with a towel." Another key element of the dance was the fact that it broke a dancing couple apart. Instead of touching each other, as a couple would in a traditional dance like a waltz, the Twist made each dancer an individual who did not necessarily even need a partner. Oddly enough, Checker lost a considerable amount of weight in just a few months time demonstrating the dance and was no longer "chubby"!

The success of "The Twist" ushered in a period of national dance crazes in the lull between the initial rock-and-roll explosion of the mid-1950s and the "British invasion" spearheaded by the Beatles in 1964. Songs popularized such dances as the Mashed Potato, the Swim, the Watusi, the Frug, the Fly, the Hully Gully, the Jerk, the Hucklebuck, and the Locomotion. Checker himself wasted little time in jumping on the dance bandwagon, hitting the Top Ten with "Pony Time" (a number-one pop hit accompanied by the Pony dance), "Let's Twist Again" (which reached number eight on the pop charts), and "The Fly" (a number-three pop hit), all in 1961, and "Slow Twistin'" (which reached number three on the charts) and "Limbo Rock" (which rose to number two), both in 1962. In October 1961 Checker appeared on *The Ed Sullivan Show*, and Checker merchandise such as chewing gum, T-shirts, ties, and dolls was being sold everywhere. In May 1962 Checker won a Grammy Award for best rock and roll recording of 1961 with "Let's Twist Again," even though it charted lower than his other records. He also appeared in films, singing and dancing in "jukebox musicals" including *Twist Around the Clock* and *The Teenage Millionaire* (both in 1961), and *Ring-a-Ding Rhythm* (released in England as *It's Trad, Dad!*) and *Don't Knock the Twist*, both in 1962.

In January 1962 "The Twist" made rock music history by becoming the first number-one song to top the charts again, over a year-and-a-half after its initial release. The trendsetters and celebrities that patronized the Peppermint Lounge in New York City discovered the dance and helped rekindle interest in Checker's version. The Lounge's house band, Joey Dee and the Starliters, had a hit with "Peppermint Twist." Although some religious and civic leaders ex-

Chubby Checker doing the dance that made him famous. ARCHIVE PHOTOS, INC.

pressed outrage over the perceived raciness of the dance, the report that first lady Jacqueline Kennedy was said to have twisted in the White House bestowed a healthy dose of respectability on the dance.

From 1959 to 1965 Checker had twenty-two hits in the Top Forty, but 1962 proved to be the peak year for "The Twist," as well as for Checker's career. Although he continued plowing the dance-song field, his singles met with less success. In 1963 his songs "Let's Limbo Some More" peaked at number twenty on the charts, "Loddy Lo" made it to number twelve, and "Twist It Up" only reached number twenty-five. His 1964 single "Hooka Tooka," reached number seventeen. By 1965 Checker had his last Top Forty hit for more than twenty years with yet another dance song, "Let's Do the Freddie" (named after Freddie Garrity, the zany lead singer of the English band Freddie and the Dreamers). His albums of the period followed a similar decline; while *Twist with Chubby Checker* (1960), *For Twisters Only*, and *Your Twist Party* (both 1961) all reached the Top Ten, 1963's *Let's Limbo Some More* peaked at number eighty-seven on the pop charts, and albums after that year did not chart at all.

Checker married Catharina Lodders, 1962's Miss World from the Netherlands, on 12 April 1964, and the couple have three children. His later records found little commercial success, but Checker remained a popular performer and eventually found a niche on the oldies revival circuit, singing at local fairs and corporate functions. He continued to champion his status as "King of the Twist" in films, turning up in the documentaries *Let the Good Times Roll* (1973) and *Twist* (1992). He also acted in *Purple People Eater* (1988) and *Calendar Girl* (1993), invariably cast as himself, just as he was in his television appearances in *Quantum Leap, Murphy Brown,* and *Ally McBeal.* Checker endorses a line of beef jerky and snack meat products, and in the 1990s he formed his own recording company, TEEC (The Ernest Evans Company), to release his own records.

A rap version of "The Twist" recorded by Checker and the rap group the Fat Boys returned Checker to the charts when it reached number sixteen on the pop charts in 1988. In 2001 Checker took the unprecedented step of taking out an advertisement in the music industry weekly *Billboard,* arguing that his contributions to rock music merited his inclusion in the Rock and Roll Hall of Fame and Museum in Cleveland. (Inductees are voted in by a select group of artists, record producers, and industry executives.) He further raised eyebrows by suggesting that a statue of himself, in mid-Twist, be erected in the hall's courtyard, insisting that if he was inducted, but not given a statue, he would turn down the award. His demands were met with a mixed reception.

★

Information about Checker is in Ed Ward, Geoffrey Stokes, and Ken Tucker, eds., *Rock of Ages: The Rolling Stone History of Rock & Roll* (1986); Irwin Stambler, *Encyclopedia of Pop, Rock, and Soul* (1989); Jim Dawson, *The Twist: The Story of the Song and Dance that Changed the World* (1995); and Joel Whitburn, *The Billboard Book of Top 40 Hits* (1996). Information on Checker's Rock and Roll Hall of Fame and Museum bid is in the *Philadelphia Inquirer* (4 Sept. 2001). The 1992 documentary *Twist* (directed by Ron Mann) is an excellent examination of the Twist phenomenon.

GILLIAN G. GAAR

CHER. *See* Sonny and Cher.

CHISHOLM, Shirley Anita (*b.* 30 November 1924 in New York City), educator, author, and member of Congress who was the first black and the first woman to seek the presidential nomination on the Democratic Party ticket, and who dedicated her life-long career to fighting for the disadvantaged.

Born Shirley Anita Saint Hill, Chisholm was the oldest of four children born to Charles Christopher Saint Hill, a factory worker, and Ruby Seale, a seamstress. Financial hardship forced the parents to send her, at age three, to Barbados to live with her maternal grandmother. Chisholm returned to Brooklyn in New York City at the age of eleven, after she had acquired her early education in the strict British school system, which she later credited for providing her with a strong academic background.

After receiving her secondary education from Girls' High School in Brooklyn, Chisholm entered Brooklyn College (1942), where she first gained a social consciousness concerning racial discrimination. After graduating cum laude with a B.A. in sociology, Chisholm taught in a nursery school and studied at Columbia University, where she earned an M.A. in elementary education (1952). She later became a director of a child care center in Harlem. On 8 October 1949 she married Conrad Chisholm, a social services investigator, who encouraged her to pursue her political career.

The 1960s marked an important stage in Chisholm's life. From 1959 to 1964 she was an education consultant in New York City's Bureau of Child Welfare. An advocate of the rights of disadvantaged blacks, Puerto Ricans, and women, she was prominent in the National Association for the Advancement of Colored People (NAACP). She participated in the Democratic League of Women Voters, Bedford-Stuyvesant Political League, and in 1960 helped form the Unity Democratic Club.

In 1964 the outspoken and independent-minded Chisholm ran for a New York State Assembly seat and won. She was an active legislator whose record of achievement reflected the needs of her constituency. Her achievements in Albany included legislation providing for publicly supported day care centers, unemployment insurance for domestic workers, and reversal of a law that caused female teachers in New York to lose their tenure while they were out on maternity leave. She was particularly responsible for the passage of a bill creating the program known as SEEK (Search for Elevation, Education, and Knowledge), which assisted black and Puerto Rican students in pursuing higher education. Chisholm served in the state assembly until 1968.

In 1968 Chisholm, under the slogan "Unbought and Unbossed," ran for Congress against James Farmer, a liberal Republican. As former chairman of the Congress of Racial Equality (CORE), Farmer had a nationwide reputation in civil rights activity, yet "Fighting Shirley" defeated him by a margin of 2.5 to 1. Her overwhelming victory made her the first black woman ever to be elected to Congress.

Assigned to the House Agriculture Committee in 1969, Chisholm demanded to be given an assignment that would benefit her constituency. She was later assigned to the Veterans' Affairs Committee, where she served for two years. Chisholm wrote her first book, *Unbought and Unbossed,* in 1970, and in 1971 she was appointed to the Education and Labor Committee. She remained in the House for seven terms, during which time she was a staunch advocate for civil rights and women's issues. She campaigned for the poor, pushed for equality for ethnic minorities, criticized

Shirley Chisholm. AP/WIDE WORLD PHOTOS

the Vietnam draft, and fought for minimum-wage increases and federal subsidies for day care centers.

On 25 January 1972 Chisholm rose to national prominence when she announced her candidacy for the Democratic presidential nomination. This ambitious congresswoman made history by becoming the first black and the first woman to seek the nomination, but lost her bid due in part to a poorly funded campaign and lack of support from the Congressional Black Caucus. Despite the opposition she encountered in her presidential race, Chisholm broke ground, made history, and inspired young black politicians to challenge the status quo. "If I can't be president I can be an instrument for change," she wrote in *The Good Fight* (1973).

In the wake of her campaign, Chisholm established and chaired the National Political Congress of Black Women and wrote *The Good Fight*. In 1977 she was appointed to the House Rules Committee and elected secretary of the Democratic Caucus. She also served as vice chairman of the Congressional Black Caucus. That same year she divorced her first husband and on 26 November married businessman Arthur Hardwick. Chisholm retired from public service in 1982, bringing an end to a political career that made her as well known nationally as she was in her home district.

Though petite, standing just five feet, four inches tall,

Chisholm earned a reputation as a powerful presence in Washington. A remarkable woman whose historic presidential campaign paved the way for others, she was a pioneer who refused to accept the status quo that society had set for women. Throughout her public life Chisholm was the voice of the poor, the disillusioned, and the powerless. She brought significant changes in the 1960s in both state and national laws regarding discrimination against minorities, and her involvement in politics greatly affected the consciousness of many Americans, making racial equality a national issue. Chisholm's refusal to cooperate with political machines at the local, state, or national level forced her to fight her way to victory the hard way, earning her the nickname "Fighting Shirley Chisholm."

★

Chisholm's speeches are printed in the *Congressional Record,* while recorded and videotaped speeches, lectures, campaign materials, press releases, clippings, and filmstrips are kept at the Schomburg Center for Research in Black Culture at the New York Public Library. Other correspondence can be found at the Presbyterian Historical Society, Philadelphia, while the Library of Congress houses her photographs and papers. Chisholm wrote two books, *Unbought and Unbossed* (1970), an autobiographical account depicting her life from her childhood to her election as New York congresswoman, and *The Good Fight* (1973), which discusses her unsuccessful run for the 1972 Democratic Party nomination. Other notable writings on Chisholm include Susan Brownmiller, *Shirley Chisholm: A Biography* (1971), and Susan Duffy, *Shirley Chisholm: A Bibliography of Writings By and About Her* (1988).

NJOKI-WA- KINYATTI

CHOMSKY, (Avram) Noam (*b.* 7 December 1928 in Philadelphia, Pennsylvania), linguist and outspoken critic of the Vietnam War.

Chomsky grew up in depression-era Philadelphia, the eldest son of Hebrew scholars William Chomsky and Elsie Simonofsky. His mother wrote children's books and his father, who had immigrated to the United States from the Ukraine in 1913 to avoid conscription in the tsar's army, taught at two local colleges. By age ten Chomsky's interest in both linguistics and politics became clear when he proved himself able to read proofs of his father's book on thirteenth-century Hebrew grammar and wrote an editorial for his school newspaper lamenting the rise of fascism in Spain.

After graduating from Philadelphia's Central High School in 1945, Chomsky matriculated at the University of Pennsylvania, where he found a mentor in Zellig Harris, a linguistics professor and political activist. He graduated with a B.A. degree in linguistics in 1949. That year he also married Carol Schatz, with whom he eventually had three children. In 1951 Chomsky earned his M.A. in linguistics from the University of Pennsylvania, and began his doctoral studies at the same institution with a three-year fellowship from the Society of Fellows at Harvard University. As he pursued his undergraduate and graduate degrees, Chomsky became intensely interested in the unfolding situation in the Middle East, hoping that a bi-national Arab-Jewish state could be negotiated. For six weeks in 1953 he and his wife lived on an Israeli kibbutz, but he was uncomfortable with the ideological rigidity of the experiment, he later said, and returned to the United States to complete his doctoral studies. In 1955 Chomsky earned his Ph.D. in linguistics from the University of Pennsylvania and accepted a position as assistant professor of modern languages at the Massachusetts Institute of Technology (MIT). By 1961 he had been promoted to full professor.

Chomsky's stature as one of the 1960s' most important philosophical and political theorists grew out of both his work at MIT in linguistics and his opposition to the Vietnam War. In 1957, at age twenty-nine, Chomsky published *Syntactic Structures,* thus revolutionizing the study of linguistics. The influence of his work not only in linguistics, but in psychology, philosophy, and other fields has been

likened to that of Galileo and Albert Einstein in their respective fields. Before Chomsky, most scholars saw language as a learned behavior, a system of habits acquired by imitation and training. Chomsky challenged the dominant behaviorist premise that the mind is a completely blank slate until it is molded, through the senses, by various experiences, and argued that despite the hundreds of languages spoken around the world, human beings share an innate faculty for language. While external stimuli trigger language acquisition, according to Chomsky, the human mind has a creative ability to reorder words into infinite variations of sentence structure and, therefore, meaning. He observed that very young children acquire language rapidly, without formal instruction, and with a minimum of external experiences beyond simply hearing others speak. Here he introduced the concept of generative transformational grammar as an essentially biological constant, suggesting that the meaning of a person's sentences originate in "deep structures" and are transformed within a finite set of rules that can be worked out like mathematical proofs. Although languages sound different to the human ear, the deep structures and the rules by which they are transformed remain the same from one person to another, and from one language to another. There is, in short, a kind of universal grammar innate to all humans. Equally important, the ability to manipulate language in infinite variations requires a level of innovation unique to humans.

Chomsky's theories were both exciting and controversial. In a 1959 review of the leading behavioral psychologist B. F. Skinner's book, *Verbal Behavior,* Chomsky attacked the premise that Skinner could control or anticipate "verbal behavior" through a series of experiments using various stimuli and responses. In *Current Issues in Linguistic Theory* (1964) and *Aspects of the Theory of Syntax* (1965), Chomsky further elaborated on his theories and continued his attack on the behaviorists. In addition to authoring dozens of papers and articles on linguistics, he also wrote a number of other books during the 1960s: *Topics in the Theory of Generative Grammar* (1966), *Cartesian Linguistics* (1966), *Language and the Mind* (1967), and, with Morris Halle, *Sound Patterns of English* (1968).

During this same period of tremendous scholarly output, Chomsky became a leading figure in the growing antiwar movement. As President Lyndon B. Johnson escalated the Vietnam War in 1964 and 1965, Chomsky quickly gained a reputation, first in the Boston area and then nationally, of being always available to speak at teach-ins and other antiwar demonstrations. He spoke at the First and Second International Days of Protest rallies in Boston (October 1965 and March 1966, respectively), and each time was relieved when police protected demonstrators from violent counter-protesters. Later in 1966 Chomsky called on Americans opposed to the war to withhold a portion of their income taxes until the administration ended the war. Meanwhile, at MIT, Chomsky and literature professor Louis Kampf began teaching a course outside their departments, and on their own time, called "Intellectuals and Social Change." The course covered both contemporary foreign policy and domestic issues and challenged students to consider the role of intellectuals in taking sides on the important questions of the day.

The theme of that course drove several of Chomsky's most influential essays of 1966–1967, in which he challenged other academicians to speak out against the war. In the fall 1966 issue of the *Harvard Educational Review,* he wrote, "One can only be appalled at the willingness of American intellectuals, who, after all, have access to the facts, to tolerate or even approve of the deceitfulness and hypocrisy [of the administration]." His most influential essay, "The Responsibility of Intellectuals," which appeared in the *New York Review of Books* in February 1967, moved scores of academicians to act in ensuing months. "It is the responsibility of intellectuals," he wrote, "to speak the truth and to expose lies." Regarding Vietnam, Chomsky implied, intellectuals had been content through the 1950s and 1960s to quietly accept the decisions of foreign policy and national security "experts" in successive administrations. In light of this inaction, Chomsky reminded his colleagues that "no body of theory or significant body of relevant information, beyond the comprehension of the layman . . . makes policy immune from criticism." He expected them to speak out against what he viewed as an obviously "savage American assault on a largely helpless rural population in Vietnam."

By the fall of 1967 Chomsky's ideas increasingly manifested themselves in the form of political action. In October, in anticipation of the first national draft card turn-in, Chomsky was among the high profile signers of the "Call to Resist Illegitimate Authority," published in the *New York Times* and other mainstream news organs. The "Call to Resist" cited examples of American war crimes and argued that the war was unconstitutional and violated the United Nations Charter and the Geneva Accords of 1954. As a result, it argued, "every free man has a legal right and a moral duty to exert every effort to end this war, to avoid collusion with it, and to encourage others to do the same."

Chomsky, Kampf, and others then announced the formation of Resist, an antiwar organization made up of older (in other words, beyond draft age) academicians, intellectuals, and others dedicated to supporting draft resisters. As Sandy Vogelgesang has written, Chomsky's strategy in forming Resist aimed to both stop the war and "resolve the larger dilemma of powerlessness which underlay the Vietnam experience." He hoped that the addition of older adults to the resistance movement would raise the economic and political stakes for the government and would make it "impossible for the government to ignore the pro-

Noam Chomsky. ARCHIVE PHOTOS, INC.

testers." For the duration of the war and long after, Chomsky served on the Resist steering committee, playing an active role in raising funds to support various antiwar and social justice organizations and determining which organizations got funded.

Throughout this period student antiwar activists joked that there must have been multiple Noam Chomskys, for he seemed able to appear in many places at once. In late October 1967 Chomsky was arrested with a number of other noted, older antiwar activists such as Dr. Benjamin Spock and the author Norman Mailer at the March on the Pentagon. As he continued to teach at MIT and publish in his field of linguistics, he traveled frequently between Boston and New York City to participate in Resist meetings. He also took part in later draft card turn-ins in Boston churches, and he wrote another influential essay, "On Resistance," that appeared in the *New York Review of Books.* In that essay he again noted that "by an overwhelming margin it is the young who are crying out in horror at what we all see happening," and the young who were resisting. "It is difficult for me to see how anyone can refuse to engage himself, in some way, in the plight of these young men," he wrote.

In early January 1968 the Justice Department indicted Spock and four others for conspiracy to aid and abet draft resisters. Chomsky was among those listed as an "unindicted co-conspirator," and many in the movement believed the government would soon move to repress even more draft resisters and their supporters. Chomsky's wife returned to school to get her degree, in fact, because the couple expected that he might soon find himself in prison.

Twenty years later *The Nation* magazine asserted that "if only for the role he played during the Vietnam War, Noam Chomsky should be honored as a national hero." By then the *New York Times* had famously declared him "arguably the most important intellectual alive today," but wondered "how can he write such terrible things about American foreign policy?" Indeed, the Vietnam War was merely the first chapter in close to forty years of Chomsky's dissent. Of the more than seventy books he has authored, more than half address issues of foreign policy and the media's influence in "manufacturing [the public's] consent" to immoral and unethical government policy.

★

Chomsky's mark on the 1960s can perhaps best be seen in the Resist papers, Trinity College, Hartford, Connecticut. In addition, the 1990s saw the publication of several books on Chomsky's life and work. The two that best cover the 1960s are Milan Rai, *Chomsky's Politics* (1995), and Robert Barsky, *Noam Chomsky: A Life of Dissent* (1998). Chomsky's own *American Power and the New Mandarins* (1969) is a compilation of his most important political writings of the 1960s, while his *Syntactic Structures* (1957), *Current Issues in Linguistic Theory* (1964), and *Aspects of the Theory of Syntax* (1965) remain the best sources for understanding his revolutionary contribution to the study of linguistics. Chomsky's most influential book since the 1960s is arguably *Manufacturing Consent: The Political Economy of the Mass Media* (1988), coauthored with Edward Herman. For an overview of the man and his work, see David Cogswell, *Chomsky for Beginners* (1996), and Peter R. Mitchell, *Understanding Power: The Indispensable Chomsky* (2002).

MICHAEL S. FOLEY

CLARK, Kenneth Bancroft (*b.* 24 July 1914 in the Panama Canal Zone), psychologist, educator, and civil rights leader best known for his influential research and writings on African Americans and institutionalized racism.

Clark grew up in the Harlem section of New York City, where he lived from the age of five. He had moved from the Panama Canal Zone with his mother, Miriam (Hanson) Clark, and his younger sister, while his father, Arthur Bancroft Clark, opted to remain alone in Panama, working

as an agent for the United Fruit Company. Clark was deeply influenced by his mother, who worked as a seamstress in a sweatshop, where she helped to form a unit of the International Ladies Garment Workers' Union. Clark graduated from George Washington High School in 1931, where he excelled in all subjects, especially economics. Clark matriculated at Howard University in Washington, D.C., and completed his B.A. in psychology in 1935 and his M.A. in 1936. He then joined the faculty at Howard and taught there for one year. Clark was the first black doctoral candidate in psychology at Columbia University, where he earned his Ph.D. in experimental psychology in 1940. From 1941 to 1942 Clark worked for the United States Office of War Information. He then joined the psychology faculty of the City College of New York (CCNY) and remained there from 1942 through his retirement in 1975 at the academic rank of Distinguished Professor. He was the first African American to be named a full professor at New York's city colleges. From its inception Clark's career was shaped by another woman—Howard undergraduate Mamie Phipps—who switched her major from mathematics to psychology after meeting the suave Clark. They wed on 14 April 1938 and had two children. Phipps completed her Ph.D. at Columbia in 1943, and the husband-and-wife team began collaborating on work concerning race relations.

In the 1960s Clark emerged as the outstanding black psychologist in the United States and became a cogent spokesperson for social justice inside and outside the American Psychological Association (APA). This role stemmed from his earlier work in 1938, when his wife worked in the Washington, D.C., office of the Legal Defense Fund of the National Association for the Advancement of Colored People (NAACP). She wrote her 1938 master's thesis at Howard on "The Development of Consciousness of Self in Negro Preschool Children," which the two then published in 1939 in the *Journal of Experimental Education*. This was the Clarks' famous "doll study," introducing a subtle projective method by which they questioned black preschoolers from the ages of three to seven using two black and two white dolls. From their observations of the children's reactions to the dolls, they concluded that these children unconsciously suffered from low self-image and "self-denigration" as a result of being in segregated schools. In 1951 Clark became a researcher with the NAACP Legal Defense Fund and the Society for the Psychological Study of Social Issues (SPSSI), a division of the APA. He also prepared a "Social Science Appendix" for a 1952 NAACP legal brief, which was then cosigned by thirty-two leading U.S. social scientists.

History was made on Monday morning, 17 May 1954, when the U.S. Supreme Court's desegregation decision in *Brown* v. *Topeka Board of Education* reversed 130 years of the court's rulings by decreeing that "separate but equal"

Kenneth B. Clark. ARCHIVE PHOTOS, INC.

education was unconstitutional. The unanimous decision was based in part on footnote eleven, citing the behavioral research findings by Clark and others. Oddly, except for jubilation within the SPSSI over the decision, the Court's citation of behavioral research and Clark's work went virtually unnoticed for years by the mass media, the APA, and the African-American community, much like the unspectacular reception of Clark's first book in 1955, *Prejudice and Your Child.*

Throughout this time, however, beginning in 1946, Clark quietly helped his wife in her dedicated if unglamorous mental hygiene work, serving Harlem's youth in their Northside Center for Child Development. (Mental hygiene work involves the maintenance of mental health and prevention of the development of psychosis, neurosis, or other mental disorders.)

In 1961 Clark received the NAACP's Spingarn Medal, which is awarded for work in advancing civil rights. Clark was also the founder of Harlem Youth Opportunities Unlimited (HARYOU) and worked with the organization from 1962 to 1964, producing research that provided much of the material for *Dark Ghetto.*

Clark was propelled to national prominence as the preeminent black psychologist and expert spokesperson on racial issues in America during the social ferment of the 1960s. He proved to be an articulate advocate and scientist who captivated the nation with the publication of his most riveting book, *Dark Ghetto,* in 1965. This graphic work went beyond his 1955 book to describe the pernicious effects of racism on whites as well as minority Americans and to call for national integration. For many observers, his

depiction of inner-city ghettos as neocolonial enclaves full of "institutionalized pathology" and "cultural deprivation" offered a penetrating diagnosis and prognosis for the race riots that were erupting in U.S. cities.

Through the 1960s Clark also had an enduring impact on his field of psychology, first in 1960 as president of the SPSSI, then as a member of the APA board of directors in 1965, and finally as the president of the APA in 1970—its only African-American president before or since. In 1967 Clark formed the MARC Corporation (Metropolitan Applied Research Center), a nonprofit organization, to help solve the problems of the urban poor. In 1970 the public school system of Washington, D.C., which was 90 percent black, had MARC design a new educational program for the city's schools. In 1971 Clark spearheaded the new APA Committee (later Board) for Social and Ethical Responsibility for Psychology (BSERP), which for the first time added "public advocacy" alongside science and practice as a third mission of organized psychology. Clark's 1971 APA presidential address, "The Pathos of Power," was a bold call to action later reprinted in *Pathos of Power* (1974). Perhaps no presidential address to the association ever sparked more controversy, as Clark went far beyond decrying the racism he saw embedded within scientific and professional circles to encourage lateral thinking in the application of social engineering. Clark, noting that political leaders are often emotionally stressed, asserted that in this new era of psycho-technology and drug therapy, society might well require that "all power-controlling leaders . . . [use] biochemical intervention which would assure their positive use of power and reduce or block the possibility of their using power destructively." In 1978 Clark was the recipient of the first annual APA Award for Distinguished Contribution to Psychology in the Public Interest, and in 1994 he received the APA Outstanding Lifetime Contribution Award, marking the fortieth anniversary of the 1954 Brown decision. This APA shift towards public advocacy marked a victory over some psychologists who might be termed scientific racists and others who felt that a scientific organization should remain aloof from social issues. Looking back on Clark's multiple contributions in the 1960s—as a scientist, author, administrator, and civil rights leader—some minimize his role as one of many actors in a partisan cause. Yet the much larger majority agrees with the 2002 assessment of historians Ludy Benjamin and Ellen Crouse that the Clarks' "research and work with the NAACP helped to change the course of American history." This accompanied his other enduring legacy within his field, to transform the APA by integrating public interest as one of U.S. psychology's basic goals.

★

Biographical information about Clark is in the article "The Integrationists," *New Yorker* (23 Aug. 1982) and in Gerald Markowitz and David Rosner, *Children, Race, and Power: Kenneth and Mamie Clark's Northside Center* (1996). The January 2002 issue of *American Psychologist* contains four articles on Clark as part of its "History of Psychology" series: Wade Pickren, "The Contributions of Kenneth B. and Mamie Phipps Clark"; Ben Keppel, "Kenneth B. Clark in the Patterns of American Culture"; Wade Pickren and Henry Tomes, "The Legacy of Kenneth B. Clark to the APA: The Board of Social and Ethical Responsibility for Psychology"; and Ludy T. Benjamin, Jr., and Ellen M. Crouse, "The American Psychological Association's Response to *Brown* v. *Board of Education:* The Case of Kenneth B. Clark." Clark's writings on psychology and social science include an article written with his wife, Mamie Clark, "Segregation as a Factor in Racial Identification in Negro Preschool Children, a Preliminary Report," *Journal of Experimental Education*, 8, (1939): 161–163; and five books, including *Prejudice and Your Child* (1955); *The Negro Student at Integrated Colleges* (1963), written with Lawrence Plotkin; *Dark Ghetto: Dilemmas of Social Power* (1965); *The Negro American* (1966), edited with Talcott Parsons; and *Pathos of Power* (1974).

HAROLD TAKOOSHIAN

CLARK, (William) Ramsey (*b.* 18 December 1927 in Dallas, Texas), United States Attorney General from 1967 to 1969, and an outspoken critic of U.S. participation in the Vietnam War.

Clark was one of three children born to Texas lawyer Tom Campbell Clark and Mary Jane Ramsey. He grew up in Dallas and Los Angeles, before his father's career in gov-

ernment necessitated a move to Washington, D.C. There, Tom Clark served as United States Attorney General from 1945 to 1949, when he was appointed to the United States Supreme Court by President Harry S Truman. After graduating from Woodrow Wilson High School in Washington in 1945, Ramsey Clark, then seventeen years old, joined the Marine Corps just before the end of World War II. He served at Parris Island and at Quantico, Virginia, before making several official trips to Europe. He received an honorable discharge with the rank of corporal in 1946. Years later, Clark commented that serving in the marines had been easy compared to facing the ostracism that some of his conscientious objector friends had had to endure.

An ambitious student, Clark earned his B.A. at the University of Texas in 1949 and then went on to the University of Chicago, where he earned both an M.A. in American history and his law degree in 1950. On 16 April 1949 he married Georgia Welch, with whom he later had two children. Clark was admitted to the Texas bar in 1951 and joined his grandfather and father's Dallas law firm, Clark, Coon, Holt and Fisher. Over the next ten years Clark established a reputation as both a successful trial attorney (by 1961, he had lost only one jury case) and an active booster of Democratic Party candidates. In February 1961 newly inaugurated President John F. Kennedy rewarded Clark for his support in the 1960 campaign with a Justice Department appointment as assistant attorney general in charge of the lands division.

Working under Attorney General Robert Kennedy, Clark gained a reputation as an efficient administrator, but more importantly, he demonstrated a commitment to civil rights. Kennedy tapped Clark to lead Justice Department officials in Mississippi and Alabama in 1962 and 1963, and Clark was one of the lead architects of the Civil Rights Act of 1964. In February 1965 President Lyndon B. Johnson, a longtime friend of Clark's father, appointed him deputy attorney general under Nicholas Katzenbach. Again, Clark's commitment to civil rights came through as he led federal officials to Alabama for the Selma-to-Montgomery march led by the Reverend Martin Luther King, Jr., and helped draft the Voting Rights Act of 1965. After Katzenbach accepted a position in the State Department, Clark succeeded him as attorney general on 28 February 1967. To avoid even the appearance of a conflict of interest, Tom Clark resigned his position on the Supreme Court.

Clark's tenure as attorney general coincided with major race riots, the rise of black nationalism, an antiwar movement committed to challenging federal law, and pressure from various sources to crack down on lawbreakers. One of those sources of pressure was Federal Bureau of Investigations (FBI) Director J. Edgar Hoover, who argued that the increasing number of race riots across the country reflected a conspiracy by black militants to create disorder in

Ramsey Clark, April 1968. © BETTMANN/CORBIS

America. Clark, for his part, viewed urban riots as symptoms of economic inequality and de facto segregation, and therefore tried to minimize the FBI's role in response to black militants and civil rights activists. For instance, he denied Hoover's persistent requests to authorize electronic wiretapping of civil rights leaders such as King and Elijah Muhammad. (Hoover ordered the wiretaps anyway.) At the same time Clark initiated programs to improve police-community relations, and improved intelligence-gathering to predict riot conditions. He also called for gun-control legislation and promoted a federal grants program to fund youth rehabilitation projects across the country.

Just as Clark faced pressure to crack down on black militants, by the fall of 1967 the president and Congress were regularly calling on him to prosecute antiwar protesters, especially draft resisters. Here again Clark hesitated. Although his father, as an assistant attorney general during World War II, had prosecuted some of the earliest draft violation cases, Clark recalled that his conscientious-objector friends had been "permanently hurt by the social ostracization" and "needlessly damaged" by their prosecution. Consequently, he instructed U.S. attorneys to suspend prosecutions against individual draft resisters. Instead, he indicted five draft resistance "ringleaders," including the noted pediatrician Dr. Benjamin Spock and Yale chaplain William Sloane Coffin, Jr., on charges of conspiring to aid and abet draft resisters. Years later, Clark claimed that his own opposition to the war also figured in his decision; sounding almost utopian, he argued that in any society "that wants to be democratic and free," important issues

like the war and the draft should be "vigorously debated" as early as possible. A draft resistance test case, therefore, would "ventilate the issues, escalate them where they can be seen, [and] provide vigorous defense" for the defendants. He did not count on the Boston judge ruling out all discussion of the war, and ultimately saw four of the defendants convicted (though the convictions were thrown out on appeal).

When antiwar activists announced plans for demonstrations at the Democratic National Convention in Chicago in August 1968, Clark sent representatives to meet with Mayor Richard Daley about providing the protesters with appropriate permits, but Daley refused to accommodate the demonstrators. After the convention—during which Chicago police, on Daley's instructions, attacked unarmed protesters in the city's parks and streets over several days and nights—the U.S. attorney convened a grand jury to investigate. While Republican presidential candidate Richard Nixon criticized him for his failure to ensure law and order in America, Clark urged that the Chicago grand jury should focus on police brutality violations. He was ignored, and when Nixon took office, his administration indicted eight men for conspiring to foment riots in Chicago.

After leaving office in 1969 Clark joined the New York City law firm of Paul, Weiss, Rifkind, Wharton and Garrison. He successfully defended the antiwar activist Philip Berrigan and others accused of conspiring to kidnap the government official Henry Kissinger, and led an investigation into the FBI killing of Black Panther Fred Hampton. In 1972 he traveled to Hanoi to condemn Nixon's escalated bombing of North Vietnam. After running un-successfully for the Senate from New York in 1974, Clark returned to private practice, often representing unpopular clients in political cases. He represented the Native American activist Leonard Peltier; Sheik Omar Abd el-Rahman, mastermind of the 1993 World Trade Center bombing; and the Bosnian Serb leader Radovan Karadzic. In 1991 he initiated a mock war crimes tribunal that found President George Bush and generals Colin Powell and Norman Schwarzkopf guilty for their roles in Operation Desert Storm, during which the United States thwarted Iraq's invasion of Kuwait.

During his tenure as attorney general, Clark distinguished himself with his fierce support of civil rights and his measured response to antiwar, student, and Black Power protests. Clark's willingness to consider the issues raised by protestors angered those who were fed up with the apparent lack of civil order, thus fueling Nixon's "law and order" presidential campaign of 1968 and a changing of the guard in the Justice Department.

★

Clark's Justice Department papers are deposited at the John F. Kennedy Presidential Library in Boston, Massachusetts, and at the Lyndon B. Johnson Presidential Library in Austin, Texas. His career as attorney general is recounted in Richard Harris, *Justice* (1970), and John Elliff, *Crime, Dissent, and the Attorney General* (1971). Joseph Califano, *The Triumph and Tragedy of Lyndon Johnson* (1991), and Michael Foley, "Confronting the Johnson Administration at War: The Trial of Dr. Spock and Use of the Courtroom to Effect Political Change," *Peace and Change* (Jan. 2003), detail Clark's role in White House debates over prosecuting antiwar protesters.

MICHAEL S. FOLEY

CLAY, Cassius. *See* Ali, Muhammad.

CLAY, Lucius Dubignon, Sr. (*b.* 23 April 1897 in Marietta, Georgia; *d.* 16 April 1978 in Chatham, Massachusetts), retired army officer and businessman who served as President John F. Kennedy's special representative to West Berlin during the Berlin crisis of 1961–1962.

The youngest of six children of Alexander Stephens Clay, a U.S. senator from Georgia, and Sarah Frances White, Clay graduated from the U.S. Military Academy at West Point, New York, in 1918, and was commissioned in the U.S. Army Corps of Engineers. On 21 September 1918 he married Marjorie McKeown, with whom he had two sons. During World War II Clay served in the Army Service Forces, helping to direct the procurement and production of war supplies and earning a reputation as a skilled administrator who could get things done.

In March 1945 Clay was appointed assistant military governor of the U.S. occupation zone in Germany, and two years later he became military governor and commander of U.S. forces in Europe. Committed to creating a viable German state, he promoted self-government, fostered economic self-sufficiency, played a key role in currency reform, and was a driving force behind the drafting of the constitution of the Federal Republic of Germany, or West Germany. When the Soviet Union in 1948 blockaded all land traffic between the western zone of Germany and Berlin in an attempt to drive the Western Allies out of the city, Clay ordered an airlift of supplies that ensured it would remain in Western hands, and led the Soviets to lift the blockade in 1949, just days before he retired from the army. Clay's efforts to create a new German nation and his steadfast determination to see that West Berlin did not come under Communist control made him a hero of towering stature in West Germany.

During the 1950s Clay was chief executive officer and chairman of the board of Continental Can Company, but he returned to government service on a temporary basis in 1961 as a result of a crisis over Berlin. Soviet premier Nikita S. Khrushchev had first tried in 1958 to 1959 to end the Western presence in West Berlin and force the Allies to recognize the German Democratic Republic (East Germany, or the GDR) by threatening to allow it to regulate traffic between West Germany and Berlin if German questions were not resolved within six months. In 1961, amid growing cold war tensions, he launched a new campaign. Tensions were further aggravated when Khrushchev supported East German president Walter Ulbricht's attempt to stem western influence in the GDR and staunch a massive outflow of East Germans to the West by erecting a wall separating West Berlin and East Berlin. At first the wall, which the East Germans began constructing on 13 August, consisted of little more than barbed wire. Before long, however, the wire was replaced with concrete blocks.

Kennedy had no intention of sparking a clash of the great powers by trying to knock down the wall; however, he knew he had to demonstrate Allied resolve to stay in the city and thereby shore up the confidence of West Berliners, who feared that the building of the wall was a precursor to a new blockade. Consequently, he sent a battle group through East Germany to Berlin to reinforce the U.S. garrison. He also dispatched Vice President Lyndon B. Johnson to West Berlin with a letter of support for Mayor Willy Brandt. At Kennedy's request, Clay accompanied Johnson, the idea being that his participation would reassure West Berliners about U.S. commitment to the city. Welcomed by enthusiastic crowds, the Johnson-Clay mission arrived in West Berlin in time to greet the battle group as it rolled into the city on 18 August. The additional U.S. troops and the Johnson-Clay mission had a calming effect on West

Berliners, and by the time the two men returned to the United States on 19 August, the city's morale had been stabilized.

During the next weeks the Soviets and East Germans interfered with Allied air access to the city, and placed restrictions on travel from West Berlin to East Berlin. When the Allies failed to take countermeasures, morale again plummeted in West Berlin, and neutralist sentiment in West Germany grew. Believing his leadership was being tested, Kennedy on 19 September sent Clay to Berlin as his personal representative to reaffirm his commitment to West Berliners. Immediately after his arrival, Clay flew to the isolated West German enclave of Steinstucken, a small village on the outskirts of the U.S. zone of Berlin that was separated from the city by GDR territory. Since the construction of the wall, the villagers had been virtually imprisoned, and by his visit, Clay took a dramatic first step in reversing the erosion of the West's position in Berlin.

Khrushchev, thinking he was pushing Kennedy too hard and worried about a U.S. military buildup, terminated his deadline in October 1961. But Ulbricht was still bent on eroding the Western position in Berlin, and GDR police began to challenge the right of Western personnel to move freely in and out of East Berlin. Determined to stand up to Soviet pressure and deny the GDR any legal authority over Berlin, Clay refused to permit U.S. officials to show their passports to East German border guards, and sent

Lucius D. Clay, Sr. North American Aerospace Command

military policemen to escort them into East Berlin. To give added weight to his hardline stance, he sent tanks to Checkpoint Charlie, the principal gateway between East and West Berlin, on 25 and 27 October. The Soviets responded by sending their own tanks to the checkpoint, and on 28 October they faced the U.S. tanks "nose to nose." Facing a no-win situation, both sides soon pulled back their forces, and the crisis passed. Clay claimed that by standing firm, he had discredited any notion of GDR sovereignty over East Berlin. In West Berlin, morale gradually recovered, and thereafter Kennedy and Khrushchev proceeded more cautiously in regard to Berlin. In 1962, Cuba replaced Berlin as the major hotspot in the cold war.

Clay returned to the United States in May 1962, and in 1963 was appointed a senior partner in the investment house of Lehman Brothers, remaining with the firm until his retirement in 1973. A tough, wiry man with a hawk-like nose and an autocratic temperament, he stands out in the 1960s as a living symbol of the continuing U.S. commitment to uphold the Allied position in West Berlin. Clay died of heart failure and was buried at West Point.

★

A collection of Clay's papers covering the period 1950 to 1978 is in the George C. Marshall Research Library, Lexington, Virginia. Collections of Clay's papers covering earlier aspects of his career are in the National Archives in Washington, D.C. Oral histories are in the Columbia Oral History Project at Columbia University in New York City, and the U.S. Army Military History Institute at Carlisle Barracks, Pennsylvania. The major biography of Clay is Jean Edward Smith, *Lucius D. Clay: An American Life* (1990). Clay's place in the Berlin crisis of 1961 is discussed in Jack M. Schick, *The Berlin Crisis, 1958–1962* (1971); Curtis Cate, *The Ides of August: The Berlin Crisis, 1961* (1978); and Lawrence Freedman, *Kennedy's Wars: Berlin, Cuba, Laos, and Vietnam* (2000). An obituary is in the *New York Times* (18 Apr. 1978).

John Kennedy Ohl

CLAYTON-THOMAS, David (*b.* 13 September 1941 in Surrey, England), musician, composer, and lead singer of the rock fusion group Blood, Sweat, and Tears.

Born in Great Britain during the most trying days of World War II, Clayton-Thomas was the son of Fred Thomsett, a Canadian serving in the British army, and his wife, Freda, a former music hall performer and native of England. (Originally called David Henry Thomsett, Clayton-Thomas purportedly changed his name in the mid-1960s to help escape a troubled past.) In 1944 Clayton-Thomas and his mother immigrated to Canada, where they took up residence in the remote Amich Lake region of Ontario. A year later, the father joined them. At the age of fourteen, Clayton-Thomas dropped out of school and subsequently moved out of his parents' home to find work and to escape a strained, and oftentimes violent, relationship with his father. For the next few years, he lived from hand to mouth, toiling in mining and logging camps; sleeping in parked cars; spending countless nights at blues clubs; singing at small venues in Quebec; and, finally, serving time at the Millbrook Reformatory in Peterborough, Ontario, for vagrancy, petty theft, and various other minor infractions.

After his release from Millbrook in the spring of 1962, Clayton-Thomas made his way to Toronto, where the vibrant nightlife and thriving music scene of Yonge Street beckoned the young man. He performed whenever and wherever the opportunity arose, sitting in with such established Yonge Street acts as Levon Helm, Robbie Robertson, and Ronnie Hawkins and the Hawks. Eventually, Clayton-Thomas formed his own band, the Shays (later the Bossmen) and began attracting wide attention across Canada. His deep, raspy vocals seemed perfectly suited for rhythm and blues and helped the group score several Canadian gold records over the next three years, including "Boom Boom" (1963), "Walk That Walk" (1964), "Take Me Back" and "Out of the Sunshine" (1965), and "Brainwashed" (1966). The latter song stayed at the top of the charts for sixteen weeks.

Clayton-Thomas's runaway success in his home country soon created opportunities abroad. After an appearance on the National Broadcasting Company program *Hullabaloo* in 1967, he decided to move the band to New York City and try his luck there. Settling in Greenwich Village, the young Canadian quickly became a mainstay on the coffeehouse circuit, attracting both the famous and the not so famous to his gigs. One evening, the folk singer Judy Collins attended a performance at the Scene and was impressed by the range and power of Clayton-Thomas's voice. Afterward, she contacted her friend Bobby Colomby, the drummer for the band Blood, Sweat, and Tears, and asked him to attend the next show. Colomby, who was trying to salvage what was left of his own band after the departure of its founding member, Al Kooper, and other key players, was deeply impressed by the white blues singer. After an audition in mid-1968, Clayton-Thomas became a full-fledged member of Blood, Sweat, and Tears, leaving the small stages of Greenwich Village and Ontario behind for good.

The group that now welcomed Clayton-Thomas into its fold was first formed in the summer of 1967 by Kooper, a former member of the Blues Project and a sessions musician who appeared on numerous recordings of the famed folksinger Bob Dylan. After cutting its first album, *Child Is Father to the Man,* which sold reasonably well, the band began to fall apart. Several members expressed dissatisfaction with Kooper's vocal ability and suggested that he move

over to the organ to make room for another front man. Kooper steadfastly refused and instead left Blood, Sweat, and Tears for a job as a producer at Columbia Records. Two other members, Randy Brecker and Jerry Weiss, quickly followed suit. The future of the band was in doubt until Colomby's fateful encounter with Clayton-Thomas in New York. Other vocalists, including Stephen Stills, had been considered, but Clayton-Thomas seemed a better fit for the group's unique style, which blended elements of rock, soul, and jazz. By the end of 1968 the new Blood, Sweat, and Tears, which included Clayton-Thomas on vocals, Colomby on drums, Steve Katz on guitar, Dick Halligan on keyboards, Chuck Winfield and Lew Soloff on trumpets, Jerry Hyman on trombone, Jim Fielder on bass, and Fred Lipsius on saxophone, had entered the studio to record a follow-up to *Child Is Father to the Man.*

Released in January 1969, the new album, aptly titled *Blood, Sweat, and Tears,* made a steady climb to the top of the charts. Powered by Clayton-Thomas's soulful voice and a beefy horn section, both of which seemed reminiscent of the big band era, the record produced a spate of hit singles, including "You've Made Me So Very Happy," "And When I Die," and "Spinning Wheel" (penned by Clayton-Thomas). The album stayed at the number-one chart position for seven straight weeks, eventually winning a Grammy Award for album of the year. Clayton-Thomas also took the Grammy for best performance by a male vocalist. The band followed up its success with *Blood, Sweat, and Tears 3* and *4* in 1970 and 1971, respectively. Although these albums did not measure up to their 1969 predecessor in terms of sales and critical acceptance, they did produce some minor hit singles, such as "Hi-De-Ho," "Lucretia MacEvil," and "Go Down Gambling," earning the band a place in the musical pantheon as daring innovators of jazz/rock.

Fueled by the success of three hit albums, Blood, Sweat, and Tears became a huge draw on the concert circuit, packing in audiences across the United States. They were among the featured performers at Woodstock in August 1969. In 1970 the band embarked on a goodwill tour of Eastern Europe on behalf of the U.S. State Department and gained legions of fans overseas. But by mid-1971 the band's days appeared numbered. Harsh reviews, creative differences, and declining record sales were slowly unraveling the group. In early 1972 Clayton-Thomas left the group to record his first solo album, *David Clayton-Thomas.* After another reorganization, the band carried on the best it could, but it clearly had been damaged by the loss of its star vocalist.

Clayton-Thomas followed up his solo debut with *Tequila Sunrise* in 1973 and *Harmony Junction* in 1974, but the commercial and critical success he had enjoyed with Blood, Sweat, and Tears failed to materialize. For a brief time in the late 1960s and early 1970s, he and his mates had risen above a field crowded with guitar-driven bands and delivered a refreshing mix of jazz, rock, and soul for a generation raised on the Beatles and Rolling Stones. By the mid-1970s the group's sound seemed a bit outdated. In 1974 Clayton-Thomas reunited with his former band for a series of ill-received albums, including *New City* (1975), *More Than Ever* (1976), *Brand New Day* (1977), and *Nuclear Blues* (1980). Clayton-Thomas continues to record and perform with Blood, Sweat, and Tears today, delighting audiences of aging baby boomers with his renditions of the group's classics. He has been married four times and lives in the Catskill Mountains in New York with his wife, Suzanne. Clayton-Thomas has one daughter from an earlier marriage.

★

Information on Clayton-Thomas can be found in Nicholas Jennings, "Blasts from the Past: Five Veteran Canadian Rockers Recall Their Glory Days," *Maclean's* (11 Mar. 1996). Clayton-Thomas's home page at <http://davidclaytonthomas.com> provides valuable biographical information, along with a discography, photo gallery, and reviews.

GARY SPRAYBERRY

CLEAVER, (Leroy) Eldridge (*b.* 31 August 1935 in Wabbaseka, Arkansas; *d.* 1 May 1998 in Los Angeles, California), writer and revolutionary, who was minister of information for the Black Panther Party (1967–1971) and author of the essay collection *Soul on Ice* (1968).

Cleaver was one of six children of Leroy Cleaver, a waiter and piano player, and Thelma Robinson Carver, an elementary school teacher and, later, a janitress. Cleaver spent 1954 to 1966—his entire youth—in penal institutions. In 1954, he was sent to prison for selling marijuana. After being paroled, he was charged with rape, convicted of assault and attempted murder in 1957, and sent to prison for those crimes and as a parole violator in 1958. He remained there until his release in November 1966. In prison Cleaver became exposed to the teachings of Elijah Muhammad of the Chicago-based Nation of Islam and became a Black Muslim. When Malcolm X split with Muhammad in 1964, Cleaver sided with the former and left the group. In an effort to deal with his grief over Malcolm X's assassination in February 1965, Cleaver began to write. It was this work that got him the promise of a job and a chance at parole after his lawyer, Beverly Axelrod, showed it to editors at *Ramparts* magazine. These writings, heavily edited, became *Soul on Ice*.

In February 1967 Cleaver attended a community meeting and was introduced to the leaders of the fledgling Black Panther Party for Self-Defense, Bobby Seale and Huey P.

Eldridge Cleaver, July 1969. ASSOCIATED PRESS AP

Newton. Cleaver joined the party and became the minister of information—that is, the major writer on the party newspaper, the *Black Panther*. *Soul on Ice* was published the following February, and Cleaver became an instant celebrity. The book was influential because of Cleaver's ability to articulate the feelings and opinions of activist youths, both black and white. What endeared him most to white liberals and radicals was his theme of interracial cooperation and future equality. At a time when Stokely Carmichael had taken the previously integrated Student Nonviolent Coordinating Committee (SNCC) in a separatist direction, Cleaver and the Black Panthers were stressing their dislike of "the oppressor," but they were not antiwhite. They followed Malcolm X's attitude toward whites following his visit to Mecca, where he realized that people of different races could pray together and get along, whereas Carmichael adhered to the antiwhite ideas of the Nation of Islam.

In a major essay, "Initial Reactions on the Assassination of Malcolm X," Cleaver expressed his admiration for Malcolm's honesty and explained why he had followed Malcolm out of the Nation of Islam in 1964. It was not the Black Muslim movement that had made Malcolm so important to African Americans, he wrote, but "the truth he uttered." Malcolm, Cleaver said, "articulated their aspirations better than any other man of our time." He, not the religion he had followed, had awakened "into self-consciousness . . . twenty million Negroes." Furthermore, Malcolm was a role model for those black militants who were now able to reject the "racist strait-jacket demonology of Elijah Muhammad," who taught that the white man is the "blue-eyed devil."

The essay "The White Race and Its Heroes" revealed Cleaver's understanding of young whites who wanted to break with the racist past and join with black radicals like him in creating what Cleaver sometimes referred to as "the Garden of Eden." It explores why the young whites of the day rejected past heroes of American history in favor of those who represented the exploited—"the wretched of the earth," in the phrase of the philosopher Frantz Fanon. The contradictions between the democratic principles of equality and freedom and the actual course of earlier American history, marked as it was by slavery, exploitation, and genocide, made unreflective patriotism impossible. Recognition of the need to repair this critical flaw drove students to the streets and into Freedom Rides and heroic sacrifice, as exemplified by the three civil rights workers killed in Mississippi in 1964. Just as Cleaver's hero, Malcolm X, had been able to walk away from his racism, so could Cleaver and the activist white youths of America, a generation "truly worthy of a black man's respect." He concluded, "The sins of the fathers are visited upon the heads of the children—but only if they continue in the evil deeds of the fathers." In "Convalescence" he wrote that the Supreme Court of the United States, "without benefit of any anesthetic except God and the Constitution," had performed lifesaving surgery on America in 1954 with its decision in *Brown* v. *Board of Education of Topeka*, which declared invalid the principle of "separate but equal." All that was needed, he continued, was a successful recovery from the stress of the operation.

Another major topic in *Soul on Ice* was the war in Vietnam. In "The Black Man's Stake in Vietnam," Cleaver stressed the importance of "intensifying the struggle" against the government while the army was busy elsewhere. In "Domestic Law and International Order," he drew a parallel between the role of the army in war and the role of the police in the ghetto, characterizing both as "muscles of control and enforcement." He stated that "the police do on the domestic level what the armed forces do on the international level: protect the way of life for those in power." Thus he created a sense of kinship with the Vietnamese, who were viewed by radicals primarily as people of color.

In its day, *Soul on Ice* was occasionally referred to as "the Red Book [after Chairman Mao's book on the Communist revolution in China] of the Second American Revolution," as the counterculture-antiwar-civil rights movement was sometimes labeled. In a new preface to the 1992 edition, the novelist and poet Ishmael Reed called Cleaver "a symbol of black manhood." He declared the book a "classic," because it is more than just *about* the 1960s: "Soul

on Ice is the sixties. The smell of protest, anger, tear gas, and the sound of skull-cracking billy clubs, helicopters, and revolution is present in its pages."

In April 1968, two days after the assassination of the civil rights leader the Reverend Martin Luther King, Jr., Cleaver and several other Black Panthers were involved in a shootout with the Oakland, California, police. Cleaver was imprisoned but released on a writ of habeas corpus. Accused of parole violation, he was ordered to return to prison on 27 November 1968, but instead he fled the country for Cuba. Between his June release from prison and his departure from the United States in late November, Cleaver was a guest lecturer in sociology at the University of California, Berkeley, and ran for president of the United States on the Peace and Freedom Party ticket. His running mate in some states was the Yippie Jerry Rubin and in others the Yippie Abbie Hoffman, author of *Woodstock Nation* and *Revolution for the Hell of It.* (Hoffman sometimes said that Yippie referred to a member of the Youth International Party; at other times he said that Yippie was just an extraverted variation of hippie.) Cleaver's stay in Cuba was short. Within six months he took refuge in Algeria. His pregnant wife joined him there, and both of their children were born in exile. (Cleaver had married Kathleen Neal, a law professor, in March 1967; they divorced in 1987.)

During the three-year period the family spent in Algeria, the Federal Bureau of Investigation was able to drive a wedge between Cleaver and Huey Newton. Newton had killed a police officer on 27 October 1967 and was imprisoned for this act. He was released in August 1970. In February 1971, during a radio interview with Newton in a San Francisco studio and Cleaver on the telephone from Algeria, Cleaver announced that he was leaving the party and would be running the international section of the Black Panthers by himself. He tried to do this for two years, but in 1973 he gave up, left Algeria, and moved his family to Paris. Two years later he returned to the United States to face the charges against him and became a "born again" Christian, to the derision of former leftist friends, who knew him to be an opportunist. (Cleaver used the claim to obtain new sources of money and support to begin a new crusade.)

Cleaver died of a heart attack in 1998 and is buried in Mountain View Cemetery, Altadena, California. He is of importance not only because of *Soul on Ice* but also because of his charismatic moment on the American political stage in 1968. His entire stateside public career lasted just nine months, from February 1968, when *Soul on Ice* was published, to November of that year, when he went into exile, but his name nonetheless is still recognized today.

★

The only full-length study of Cleaver is Kathleen Rout, *Eldridge Cleaver* (1991). Anthologies of his work that contain 1960s material are Louis Heath, *The Black Panther Leaders Speak* (1976) and *Off the Pigs!* (1976). Obituaries are in the *Washington Post* and the *New York Times* (both 2 May 1998).

KAY KINSELLA ROUT

CLEMENTE, Roberto Walker   (*b.* 18 August 1934 in Carolina, Puerto Rico; *d.* 31 December 1972 near San Juan, Puerto Rico), charismatic Hall of Fame baseball player, a graceful outfielder of exceptional talent with the Pittsburgh Pirates, who in the heyday of his career in the 1960s became a symbol of pride for Puerto Ricans and a humanitarian hero, dying in a plane crash while taking aid to earthquake victims in Nicaragua.

Clemente was the son of Melchor Clemente, who cut cane for the Rubert Brothers Sugar company, and Luisa (Walker) Clemente, who ran a grocery store for the plantation workers. The large family included seven children—the youngest, Roberto, his three brothers, a sister, a stepsister, and a stepbrother. A quiet, obedient boy, Roberto tossed a baseball against his bedroom ceiling at night and played on sandlots during the day. A milk delivery route and other manual labor helped him grow into a muscular, athletic young man, and he excelled at track and field, including the high jump and the javelin throw. On the Sello Rojo Rice Company team and at Julio Vizcarrondo High School he played shortstop but eventually was moved to right field. As a teenager Clemente played for the Juncos in the amateur Puerto Rican Double-A League and the Santurce Crabbers in the Puerto Rican Winter League. Legendary Brooklyn Dodgers scout Al Campanis called him "the greatest natural athlete I ever saw as a free agent." After two years with Santurce, Clemente signed with Brooklyn in 1953 for a $10,000 bonus—the largest ever given to a Hispanic player at that time.

The Dodgers had no room for Clemente in their All-Star outfield and sent him to their top farm club in Montreal, where they kept him on the bench to try to hide his talents from other teams. But Pittsburgh Pirates general manager Branch Rickey drafted him when the Dodgers didn't protect him. The Pirates chose Clemente in the first round of the minor league draft on 22 November 1954. Months before beginning his major-league career, Clemente suffered severe and permanent spinal damage when a drunk driver hit his car while Clemente was returning from a hospital visit with his dying brother. His early career with the perennially last-place Pirates was marred by injuries, including lower back problems stemming from the accident.

In the 1960s, however, Clemente became one of the top players in baseball. Had he been a marquee player in New York, Clemente would have become a household name.

Roberto Clemente. CORBIS CORPORATION (BELLEVUE)

Instead, he labored in relative obscurity in small-market Pittsburgh. During the 1960s Clemente batted over .300 nine out of ten seasons and four times led the National League in batting average (.351 in 1961, .339 in 1964, .329 in 1965, and .357 in 1967); he also led the league in hits in 1964 and 1967. He led his club to two World Series victories, in 1960 and in 1971, hitting safely in twelve consecutive World Series games and winning the series Most Valuable Player Award in 1971, when he hit .414. In 1966 he was named the National League's Most Valuable Player after years of complaining of being overlooked by the writers who voted for the award.

Sensitive to bigotry and to media portrayals that he thought denigrated his race—he was a Puerto Rican of African descent—Clemente distrusted reporters. His pride was easily offended, and he lacked the thick skin of other pioneers in baseball, such as Jackie Robinson, who broke Major League Baseball's longstanding color line. Early in his career, a few reporters labeled him a "hot dog" for his flashy style of play and frequent injuries, and he chafed at that description. He was a hypochondriac who suffered from insomnia, stomach disorders, headaches, and nagging back pain, but though he often complained, he didn't deserve his reputation as a malingerer.

Clemente's idiosyncratic, attention-getting style of play

was perfectly suited to the 1960s, and he embodied the way baseball, like society, was changing. Baseball was no longer America's pastime; with the help of Clemente and others it became the world's game, with a new flair, a transcendent energy, and expanded athletic dimensions. Clemente worked so hard at baseball and played with such joyful abandon and distinctive style that he rose above the game's limitations. At bat he engaged in constant psychological warfare with the pitcher. Huddling deep in a corner of the batter's box, he exploded with a slashing swing, his legs and torso twisting in opposite directions. His quick hands and fluid stroke could reach balls in and out of the strike zone, and there was no place a pitcher could safely throw the ball.

In the outfield Clemente was extraordinary, running into walls, making diving catches, and flinging the ball to the infield with incredible speed. He won twelve Gold Glove awards for fielding excellence. His powerful arm, which many experts consider the most potent in baseball history, changed his opponents' game. Clemente routinely threw out runners going from first to third on base hits—a difficult feat for a right fielder—and sometimes he nailed batters on clean hits before they reached first base or nipped them as they rounded a bag too wide.

For most of his career Clemente returned to Puerto Rico every winter to play in the league where he had begun his professional career. In 1964 he married Vera Cristina Zabala in Carolina. They had three sons. Though not directly involved in politics, Clemente was always interested in the welfare of poor Hispanics, and he was Puerto Rico's biggest hero in the 1960s, a symbol of Puerto Rican pride.

When a devastating earthquake ravaged Managua, Nicaragua, on 23 December 1972, Clemente became consumed with chairing the Nicaraguan Relief Committee in Puerto Rico, going door to door in wealthy San Juan neighborhoods to raise money and personally supervising the loading of relief items on a DC-7. On the last day of the year Clemente boarded the plane bound for Nicaragua; it crashed shortly after taking off from San Juan.

On the last day of the 1972 season Clemente had gotten his 3,000th hit, joining an exclusive club of baseball's greatest players. He became the first Hispanic in baseball's Hall of Fame. Clemente opened the door for many Hispanic stars who followed. In the ensuing decades Latin America became the world's most fertile area for recruiting U.S. Major League Baseball players. Baseball changed dramatically because of Clemente's dedication to the game he loved.

★

Clemente's papers and further information regarding his career are available at the Baseball Hall of Fame Library in Cooperstown, New York. Biographies of Clemente include Phil Musick, *Who Was Roberto? A Biography of Roberto Clemente* (1974); Peter C. Bjarkman, *Baseball Legends: Roberto Clemente* (1991); Thomas W. Gilbert, *Roberto Clemente* (1991); Bruce W. Conord, *Roberto Clemente* (1994); and Bruce Markusen, *Roberto Clemente: The Great One* (1998). An obituary is in the *New York Times* (2 Jan. 1973).

MICHAEL BETZOLD

CLIFFORD, Clark McAdams (*b.* 25 December 1906 in Fort Scott, Kansas; *d.* 10 October 1998 in Bethesda, Maryland), rich, successful lawyer who epitomized the Washington insider and power broker; adviser to four presidents; President Lyndon B. Johnson's Secretary of Defense (1968–1969); and a major influence on 1960s policy, particularly with respect to deescalating the Vietnam War.

Clifford was the son of Frank Andrew, a manager for the Missouri Pacific Railroad, and Georgia (McAdams) Clifford, a writer; he had an older sister. He attended Washington University in St. Louis, graduating with a law degree in 1928. On 3 October 1931 Clifford married Margery Pepperell Kimball. They had three daughters. Clifford served in the U.S. Naval Reserve from 1944 to 1946. As the tumultuous 1960s began, the fifty-three-year-old Clifford had already enjoyed a successful career, both privately and politically, since the administration of President Harry S Truman. But much more was to come.

Clifford conducted the unsuccessful 1960 campaign of Missouri Senator Stuart Symington for the Democratic Party's presidential nomination. The winner of the nomination, John F. Kennedy, was so impressed with Clifford's skill that he asked him to join his staff as an adviser. Clifford prepared an analysis of the difficulties Kennedy faced in the transfer of presidential power. Kennedy, again impressed with Clifford's work, asked him to head the transition team.

Kennedy continued to call on Clifford. After the disastrous Bay of Pigs invasion of Cuba in April 1961—an operation backed by the Central Intelligence Agency (CIA)—the president turned to Clifford, and on 16 May 1961 he became a member of the Foreign Intelligence Advisory Board; two years later, on 23 April 1963, Clifford became the board's chair. When in 1962 the country's top steel companies attempted to renege on an agreement not to raise prices, Kennedy used Clifford's good offices to convince the companies to retreat.

After Kennedy's assassination on 22 November 1963, the new president, Lyndon Johnson, almost immediately called on his friend Clifford to help with the transition of power. Clifford could have been rewarded with a high-level government position, but he preferred to remain an adviser and retain his remunerative private law practice. But Johnson needed Clifford's adroit touch in handling two potentially embarrassing scandals in 1964—one involving the presidential aide Walter Jenkins, who was arrested on a

Clark Clifford. AP/WIDE WORLD PHOTOS

morals charge, and the other arising from the shady business dealings of Robert G. (Bobby) Baker, who had been Johnson's secretary when he was the majority leader of the U.S. Senate.

Clifford's greatest service was given during the Vietnam War, one of America's longest and most unsettling wars. During the fall of 1965 Johnson sent Clifford to Southeast Asia in his capacity as chairman of the Foreign Intelligence Advisory Board. Clifford was convinced of the correctness of the war policy—to crush the Communist guerrillas and their North Vietnamese allies—by the upbeat attitude of the American and South Vietnamese military officials. He therefore opposed Johnson's thirty-seven-day halt in bombing North Vietnam and was generally regarded as in favor of the war. In October 1966 he joined Johnson at the Manila summit conference of Vietnam War allies and remained firm in his convictions. But, as he later revealed, Clifford changed his mind after yet another Southeast Asia trip in the summer of 1967, the purpose of which was to find out why America's Pacific allies—New Zealand, Australia, and the Philippines—had committed only token forces to the conflict. Clifford discovered these allies were not as fearful of Communist aggression as was the United States, even though they were closer to the war zone. He began to doubt America's appraisal of the danger to itself and others.

Despite his growing reservations about the war and his aversion to accepting government appointments, Clifford could not turn down Johnson's offer of the post of Secretary of Defense. Johnson appointed him on 19 January 1968; he was unanimously confirmed by the Senate on 30 January 1968 and sworn in on 1 March 1968.

On 28 February 1968 Clifford took the chair of the president's Ad Hoc Task Force on Vietnam, a group that was convened to decide how to provide over 200,000 more troops for Vietnam but, in fact, debated the reasons for the war. During these debates Clifford remained neutral and hoped he could clarify his own position. He soon found out no solid answers were available. No one could estimate with any accuracy how long the war would continue or whether the additional troops requested would be enough.

When submitting the recommendations of the task force to the president, Clifford made known his reservations about Vietnam policy. His warm friendship with Johnson suddenly turned cool. On 28 March 1968 Clifford met with other government leaders to compose a major presidential address to the nation. Clifford found the draft too warlike and urged "not a war speech but a peace speech." The speechwriting committee presented to the president Clifford's suggestion for a bombing halt, which Johnson, influenced by Clifford's wisdom and personality, included in his nationwide television address of 31 March 1968. Johnson, despite the differences that had developed between him and

Clifford, awarded him the Medal of Freedom with Distinction. After Clifford left office his feelings about the war continued to evolve. In July 1969 he called for the unilateral withdrawal of American troops, which was finally achieved in 1973.

Clifford died of pneumonia at age ninety-one at his home in Bethesda, Maryland. He is buried in Arlington National Cemetery in Arlington, Virginia.

Although his later career was marred by a banking scandal, Clifford will be remembered for his great service to his country during the 1960s, not only in business and political matters but, above all, for helping deescalate the Vietnam War.

★

Collections of Clifford's papers and related oral history material are in the Harry S Truman Presidential Library in Independence, Missouri, and the John Fitzgerald Kennedy Library in Boston, Massachusetts. Clifford's autobiography, *Counsel to the President: A Memoir* (1991), written with Richard Holbrooke, details his career as a government official. A biographical account of Clifford's life and career is Douglas Frantz and David McKean, *Friends in High Places: The Rise and Fall of Clark Clifford* (1995). A thorough overview of Clifford's life is provided by Allan L. Damon in volume 5 of *Scribner Encyclopedia of American Lives, 1997–1999*. Entries in *Current Biography* (1968) and *Political Profiles: The Johnson Years* (1976) are the sources for the 1960s. Townsend Hoopes, *The Limits of Intervention* (1969), concentrates on Clifford's involvement in the Vietnam War. An obituary is in the *New York Times* (11 Oct. 1998).

JOHN MORAN

CLINE, Patsy (*b.* 8 September 1932 in Winchester, Virginia; *d.* 5 March 1963 near Camden, Tennessee), first female country and western singer to earn success on the pop charts.

Born Virginia Patterson Hensley, Cline was the daughter of Samuel Hensley and Hilda Patterson. From an early age she showed talent as a performer, winning a dance contest at the age of four and learning to play piano by ear just a few years later. After the family moved to 608 South Kent Street in Winchester, Virginia, she began singing on a local radio show. In 1948 Cline auditioned (unsuccessfully) for the Grand Ole Opry in Nashville, Tennessee, and even sang on Roy Acuff's WSM radio program, but unable to secure a recording contract, she returned home. By 1942 she was lead singer for a Winchester act called the Melody Boys and Girls, whose bandleader Bill Peer suggested that Cline call herself "Patsy." On 7 March 1953 she married Gerald Cline, thus completing her stage name.

Cline returned to Nashville in 1954 and signed a highly disadvantageous contract with Four Star Records. Not only

Patsy Cline. ARCHIVE PHOTOS, INC.

did the contract provide her primarily with one-time fees rather than significant royalties, but Four Star owner William McCall stipulated that Cline would record only material owned or at least approved by McCall's company. There was, however, one bright spot in the deal with McCall. He paired her with the producer Owen Bradley, who, with his pop background, influenced Cline to expand her range beyond country.

Cline recorded "Walkin' After Midnight" on 8 November 1956, and on 8 January 1957 performed the song on the television show *Arthur Godfrey's Talent Scouts,* where she received a standing ovation. The single, released 11 February 1957, shot to number three on the country charts and, even more significantly, to number seventeen on the pop charts. After divorcing her first husband on 28 March of that year, Cline married Charlie Dick, a soldier, at what became their home on 720 South Kent Street in Winchester. They had two children.

Ramsey "Randy" Hughes became Cline's manager in the summer of 1959, and in January 1960 she joined the

Grand Ole Opry. She made her last recording with Four Star on 27 January 1960; then, taking advantage of the fact that McCall was embroiled in legal troubles, she signed a contract with Decca Records. The latter released the single "I Fall to Pieces" on 30 January 1961. Featuring back-up vocals by the Jordanaires (famous for their work with the singer Elvis Presley), "I Fall to Pieces" became Cline's first number-one country hit and, by mid-year, had reached number twelve on the pop charts. Next came "Crazy" (released 16 October 1961), which reached a top-ten position on the pop charts, and "She's Got You" (released 10 January 1962), a number-one pop hit. Other hits followed, including "When I Get Through with You, You'll Love Me," "Faded Love," and "Leavin' on Your Mind."

To promote these songs, Cline maintained an exhausting schedule that kept her almost constantly on the road, away from her husband and children. Among the milestones of her performing career were appearances on Dick Clark's *American Bandstand* (8 November 1961 and 22 February 1962); a spot on the first Grand Ole Opry show at New York City's Carnegie Hall on 29 November 1961; various tours with the country and western singer Johnny Cash, beginning in January 1962; and a number of shows in Las Vegas during November and December 1962. When she was at home, as she was for part of February 1962—a month in which she recorded fourteen songs—Cline arranged to record during the evenings so she could spend time with her children. Still, she spent so little time at her home in Nashville, where she and her family had moved on 16 November 1961, that she rarely bothered to unpack.

By early 1961 Cline had begun to experience foreboding with regard to the way that her fast-paced life might come to an end. On 22 April (ironically, while flying) she handwrote a will on a piece of Delta Airlines stationery. When tragedy first came on 14 June 1961, it was not in the form of a plane crash, however, but an automobile crash in Nashville. Cline's brother was driving, and Cline was in the front seat when another car, having pulled out to pass another vehicle on a blind curve, smashed into them head-on. Cline was thrown through the windshield and over the hood of the car. Badly scarred, with a dislocated hip and broken wrist, she spent a month in the hospital, but was playing shows within six weeks of the accident.

The real tragedy came almost two years later. On 2 March 1963 Cline left Birmingham, Alabama, via private plane for Kansas City, Missouri, where she had agreed to play a benefit for a local disc jockey before returning to Nashville for two weeks with her family. Returning from Kansas City on 5 March, the plane—carrying Cline, Hughes, Cowboy Copas, and Hawkshaw Hawkins—crashed outside Camden, Tennessee. Cline was buried at Shenandoah Memorial Park in Winchester on 10 March.

In addition to her burial place, there is a memorial at the crash site, several miles west of Camden.

In the world of 1960s country music, dominated as it was by men, Cline was an anomaly. Her brassy ways—it was said that she could drink and curse with the best of her male counterparts—helped her fit in, yet she also had a softer side, expressed in songs such as "Sweet Dreams," a top-ten hit released in April 1963, a month after her death. By the time her short career came to an end, she had proved not only that a woman could succeed in the world of country, but that a country singer could succeed in the mainstream market. Along the way, she helped many younger female artists such as Brenda Lee, on whom she made a deep impression when the two performed together in the summer of 1957. More famously, Cline befriended Loretta Lynn, whose version of "I Fall to Pieces" she heard in the hospital in 1961. Cline sent her husband, Charlie, to tell the young singer she wanted to meet her, and the two began a friendship that lasted until Cline's death. Years later, Lynn, by then famous in her own right, recorded a tribute album, *I Remember Patsy*.

★

Cline's letters to friend Treva Miller Steinbicker appear in Patsy Cline, Cindy Hazen, and Mike Freeman, *Love Always, Patsy: Patsy Cline's Letters to a Friend* (1999). Biographies include Ellis Nassour, *Honky Tonk Angel: The Intimate Story of Patsy Cline* (1993); Margaret Jones, *Patsy: The Life and Times of Patsy Cline* (1994); and Mark Bego, *I Fall to Pieces: The Music and the Life of Patsy Cline* (1995).

JUDSON KNIGHT

COFFIN, William Sloane, Jr. (*b.* 1 June 1924 in New York City), Presbyterian minister, Yale University chaplain, civil rights and antiwar activist, and defendant in the draft resistance conspiracy trial of the "Boston Five."

Coffin was the second of three children born to Catherine Butterfield and William Sloane Coffin, Sr., vice president of W and J Sloane, a prominent furniture store on New York's Fifth Avenue, and president of the Metropolitan Museum of Art's board of directors. His early boyhood was marked by wealth and privilege: the family spent summers on Long Island and in France and lived the rest of the year in a penthouse apartment in Manhattan. Following his father's death in 1933, however, finances tightened somewhat, and the family moved a number of times before Coffin completed his secondary education at Phillips Andover Academy in Andover, Massachusetts, in 1942.

In 1943 Coffin left Yale University after one year of study to join the army, and was soon stationed in Europe. There he demonstrated an uncommon facility for lan-

William S. Coffin addressing the opening session of "Washington Mobilization," a group of clergymen and laymen of various faiths opposed to the Vietman War, 1968. © BETTMANN/CORBIS

guages and, consequently, served as a liaison officer first with the French army and later with the Soviet army. Discharged with the rank of captain in 1947, Coffin returned to Yale and graduated with a B.A. in government in 1949. He matriculated at Union Theological Seminary (where his uncle, Henry Sloane Coffin, had once been president), but left after one year to work for the Central Intelligence Agency (CIA) during the Korean War. From 1950 to 1953 he put his Russian language skills to use training dissident Russians for espionage assignments in the Soviet Union. Upon returning to the United States, Coffin earned his bachelor of divinity degree at Yale University Divinity School in 1956, and he spent the following two years as chaplain at Phillips Andover Academy and Williams College. In 1956 he married Amy Anna Rubinstein, a ballet dancer and actress, with whom he had three children.

Appointed Yale chaplain in 1958, Coffin in 1960 led a group of fifteen students to Mamou, Guinea, to build a community center. The following year he participated in one of the early freedom rides from Atlanta to Montgomery, Alabama, where he and six others were arrested for "disturbing the peace." Their convictions were later overturned on appeal. In the meantime, Peace Corps director Sargent Shriver tapped him to go to Puerto Rico in the summer of

1961 to organize a capstone training program, modeled on the British Outward Bound, for the first Peace Corps volunteers.

After the U.S. war in Vietnam escalated in 1964 and 1965, Coffin became critical of American policy. By early 1967 he had begun speaking out openly against the intensifying war and, with several others, founded Clergy and Laity Concerned About Vietnam (CALCAV). The ecumenical organization presented a thirty-eight-page position paper and organized a two-day mobilization of clergy in Washington, D.C. There, ministers, priests, and rabbis lobbied congressmen and senators, and Coffin and several others met with Secretary of Defense Robert McNamara.

As the war raged on in 1967, however, Coffin concluded that working within the system had produced no change in the Johnson administration's prosecution of the war. Therefore, he moved more deliberately toward civil disobedience. He joined several others in pledging to "aid and abet" draft resisters, and in urging churches and synagogues to declare themselves "sanctuaries of conscience," or havens where draft resisters could await arrest. He also served as spokesperson for a group of older supporters of the draft-resistance movement at a press conference at which the "Call to Resist Illegitimate Authority" was unveiled. A petition written by several intellectuals, the "Call" argued that the war was unconstitutional and cited examples of American war crimes. As a result, it argued, "every free man has a legal right and a moral duty to exert every effort to end this war, to avoid collusion with it, and to encourage others to do the same." On 16 October 1967 Coffin gave the featured sermon at a nationally publicized draft card turn-in at the Arlington Street Church in Boston. The climactic event of the service included Coffin and several other clergy accepting the draft cards of 214 men who were openly defying selective service laws. Four days later Coffin again was the primary speaker at a rally outside the Justice Department in Washington, where he led a small group who delivered to a Justice Department representative nearly 1,000 draft cards that had been collected in cities across the country. He told the crowd outside that "to stand up in this fashion against the law and our fellow Americans is a difficult and even fearful thing, but in the face of what to us is insane and inhumane, we can fall neither silent nor servile."

For these acts the U.S. district court in Boston indicted Coffin with four others, including the noted pediatrician Dr. Benjamin Spock, for conspiracy to aid and abet draft resisters. Many within the antiwar movement were at once delighted and terrified. Some suggested that the trial of the "Boston Five" would provide a forum for dissenters to "put the war on trial," while others feared that the indictments signaled the beginning of widespread political repression. In the end the trial served only to disappoint. Judge Francis

Ford ruled out any discussion of the legality of the war, and the defendants adopted a First Amendment defense, denying that they had committed any overt acts in furtherance of a conspiracy. Rather, the defense argued that they had merely offered moral support to those young men who had already decided to resist the draft. The jury found Coffin and three others guilty, though the convictions were thrown out a year later.

Coffin continued to speak out against the Vietnam War, and in 1972 he was part of a delegation invited to North Vietnam to accept the release of three American prisoners of war. He resigned the chaplaincy at Yale in 1976, and the following year he was hired as pastor of the Riverside Church in New York City, where he continued to be active in a variety of social, political, and foreign policy issues until his retirement in 1987. In 1999 Coffin published *The Heart Is a Little to the Left: Essays on Public Morality*.

As a former CIA officer and a minister with a gift for oratory, Coffin brought an air of authority to the antiwar movement of the 1960s. Although many sympathizers were disappointed that his conspiracy trial failed to produce the promised fireworks, few have challenged his contribution in reaching a wider public with the movement's critique of the war.

★

Coffin emphasizes his 1960s activism in his memoir, *Once to Every Man* (1977). Mitchell Hall, *Because of Their Faith* (1990), gives a lucid history of CALCAV, and Michael Friedland, *Lift Up Your Voice Like a Trumpet* (1998), examines the role of white clergy in both the civil rights and antiwar movements. Jessica Mitford, *The Trial of Dr. Spock* (1969), and Michael Foley, "Confronting the Johnson Administration at War: The Trial of Dr. Spock and Use of the Courtroom to Effect Political Change," *Peace and Change* (Jan. 2003), provide the most thorough examinations of Coffin's conspiracy trial.

MICHAEL S. FOLEY

COLEMAN, James Samuel (*b.* 12 May 1926 in Bedford, Indiana; *d.* 25 March 1995 in Chicago, Illinois), sociologist best known for a report that concluded that a child's family background and a school's socioeconomic makeup are strong determinants of a student's academic success—ideas that would have a far-reaching impact on education policy.

Born the son of James Fox Coleman, a foreman, and Maurine Lappin, Coleman joined the U.S. Navy in 1944, soon after his high school graduation. He completed his navy service in 1946 and enrolled at Purdue University, where he earned a B.S. in chemical engineering in 1949. Coleman worked briefly at Eastman-Kodak in Rochester, New York, but soon realized that a purely scientific career was not

James S. Coleman. ARCHIVE PHOTOS, INC.

sufficient to his interests. He wanted a career that would combine the sciences with issues of moral and social importance, and therefore enrolled at Columbia University in New York City. There he worked as a research associate with the Bureau of Applied Social Research and earned his Ph.D. in sociology in 1955.

Coleman was assistant professor of sociology at the University of Chicago from 1956 to 1959 and then moved to Johns Hopkins University in Baltimore, Maryland, where he served as associate professor from 1959 to 1961. In 1959 he founded the Department of Social Relations (now the Department of Sociology) and in 1961 was promoted to full professor. Coleman became involved in the study of education in America in 1957, when he and his associates, supported by the United States Office of Education, embarked on a detailed analysis of academic and social aspects of ten high schools in Illinois. The result was a research monograph entitled *Social Climates in High Schools,* published in 1961, and two academic books hailed for their indepth research and objective analysis.

Following passage of the 1964 Civil Rights Act, the U.S. commissioner of education—under Title IV of the act—was to study "the lack of availability of equal educational opportunity by reason of race, color, religion, or national origin in public educational institutions at all levels." The commissioner selected Coleman and Ernest Q. Campbell of Vanderbilt University to conduct the study under a $1.5 million grant. Led by Coleman, their team surveyed sixty thousand teachers and more than 600,000 students at four thousand schools throughout the United States. Particular emphasis was placed on analyzing the type and quality of education to which underprivileged whites and members of minority groups had access. It was the second-largest social science research project in the history of the United States and considered by many to be the most important educational study of the twentieth century. Completed and published in 1966, the landmark study was entitled *Equality of Educational Opportunity* but became commonly known as *The Coleman Report.*

Barbara J. Kiviat, writing for *Johns Hopkins Magazine* many years later, noted that before Coleman's report, equal opportunity for students meant looking at the number and quality of a school's resources such as textbooks and other teaching tools. Indeed, Coleman began the study expecting to find a great disparity in funding between white and nonwhite schools that would prove to be the underpinning reason for the disparity in academic achievement between nonwhites and whites. However, noted Kiviat, "unlike his predecessors who focused on the equality of what was going into the school system, Coleman evaluated what was coming out." Coleman was the first to use students' test scores and overall performance to determine equality in education.

Surprisingly, the report found the standard of education offered by white and nonwhite schools to be relatively comparable. Teacher training and salaries, for example, as well as curriculum, were of similar quality. Also, while predominantly nonwhite classrooms were usually more crowded and teaching aids of somewhat lesser quality than those in white schools, neither factor was a major contributor to the dropout rate of black students (almost twice that of white students) or to the fact that only 4.6 percent of the nation's college students were black.

The report also pointed out that educational segregation occurred primarily by default, because most children attended school in the neighborhoods in which they lived, and those neighborhoods tended to develop according to income level and ethnicity. Another significant finding was that nonwhite students in primarily nonwhite schools lagged behind white students in primarily white schools by 1.6 years at grade six and by 3.3 years by grade twelve. On the other hand, students from lower-income families who attended schools in which the majority of students came from middle-income backgrounds improved in educational motivation. The basic deduction from these findings was that family background affected student academic achievement in the early years of education and that minority students attending minority schools suffered a continuing ac-

ademic disparity, because predominantly minority schools were unable to assist students in overcoming the negative effects fostered by their family backgrounds. Richard D. Kahlenberg, writing for *Education Week,* stated the situation simply: "Going to school with advantaged peers was an advantage, while going to school with disadvantaged peers was a disadvantage—above and beyond an individual's family circumstances."

Kiviat pointed out that the Coleman report was "full of subtleties and caveats, but the mass media and makers of policy focused on one prediction—that black children who attended integrated schools would have higher test scores if a *majority* of their classmates were white." The government soon enforced a radical affirmative action policy to overcome de facto segregation: students would be bused to schools outside their neighborhood to prevent nonwhite enrollment exceeding 60 percent of a school's student ratio. The report appeared during a time of enormous social and racial unrest—race relations and issues of equality and inequality were among the foremost topics of the day. The unexpected results of Coleman's report gave rise to public policy that added a new dimension to the unrest and caused volatile emotional reactions and societal upheaval.

In 1975 Coleman released the results of another study in which he concluded that busing failed "largely because it had promoted 'white flight.'" This mass movement of white families to suburbia, and the inevitable enrollment of their children in suburban schools, dashed the possibility for racially balanced schools. Many officials, sociologists, and policy makers were outraged that Coleman would abandon his earlier commitment to desegregation. In fact, Coleman was not committed, in his work as a social scientist, to any political position, but rather to discerning the results from his data—whether those results were popular or not. As Kiviat noted, his supporters "called him a true scientist who changed his opinion when empirical evidence required him to do so."

Coleman returned to the University of Chicago in 1973 as professor of sociology and served there until his death from prostate cancer. He had married Lucille Richey on 5 February 1949, but they were divorced in August 1973, after which he married Zdzislawa Walaszek. He had four sons, three of them by his first marriage. Coleman's third and final major report, following another pivotal study, was published in 1981. He concluded that even when family background was controlled for, students in Catholic schools achieved higher academic levels than did those in public schools. Each of Coleman's reports proved both groundbreaking and controversial, and each in its own way has been the forerunner for new and continuing studies into the disparity of academic achievement and the causes behind that disparity.

★

More information on Coleman and his work can be found in Jon Clark, *James S. Coleman* (1996), and Barbara J. Kiviat, "The Social Side of Schooling," *Johns Hopkins Magazine* (Apr. 2000). See also Coleman's own writings, most notably *Equality of Educational Opportunity* (1966).

MARIE L. THOMPSON

COLLINS, Judy (*b.* 1 May 1939 in Seattle, Washington), singer, composer, and activist, a key figure in the 1960s folk music revival, whose covers of songs by Joni Mitchell and Leonard Cohen, among others, gave a boost to their careers.

Collins was the first of five children of Charles Thomas Collins, a singer, composer, and radio broadcaster (whose career was not hampered by his blindness), and Marjorie (Byrd) Collins, a homemaker. Collins spent her early years in Seattle, then moved to Los Angeles and Denver with her family. She began studying classical piano as a child and by age ten was studying with orchestra conductor Dr. Antonia Brico (Collins later produced and codirected the 1974 documentary *Antonia: A Portrait of the Woman* about her mentor). Through her father, she also was exposed to popular music of the day ranging from Cole Porter to Irving Berlin to Broadway musicals. Hers was a diverse musical education that led to her singing standards like "My Funny Valentine" on her father's radio show one day and playing classical music with the Denver Businessmen's Orchestra the next.

Collins also performed with school and church groups and local bands, and it was assumed that she would pursue a career as a classical pianist. But when she discovered traditional folk music in her teens, she dropped piano lessons in favor of the acoustic guitar. She began her career as a folksinger in 1959 at Michael's Pub in Boulder, Colorado, and was soon playing clubs in Chicago, Illinois; Boston, Massachusetts; and New York City.

Collins quickly became a part of the growing folk scene developing in New York City's Greenwich Village, meeting up-and-coming songwriters like Bob Dylan, Arlo Guthrie, and the Journeymen (whose lineup included Scott McKenzie and the future founder of the Mamas and the Papas, John Phillips) at venues like the Gaslight, the Village Vanguard, and Gerde's Folk City. Her break came in 1961 while she was taping a television show at another Greenwich Village venue, the Village Gate. Jac Holzman, president of Elektra Records, impressed by Collins's crystal clear, soprano voice, offered her a recording contract; the next week she was in the studio recording her first album, *A Maid of Constant Sorrow* (1962), in a single day.

The album was largely composed of traditional songs, along with newer folk material like "Tim Evans," Ewan MacColl and Peggy Seeger's song about capital punishment. *The Golden Apples of the Sun*, released in 1962, adhered to a similar format. But by *Judy Collins #3*, released in 1964, Collins had begun to broaden her musical palette, moving beyond the realm of traditional folk to cover contemporary material, including Dylan's "Masters of War" and Pete Seeger's "Turn! Turn! Turn!" Jim (later Roger) McGuinn, who played guitar and banjo on the album, cowrote the arrangements of "Turn! Turn! Turn" and "The Bells of Rhymney" prior to recording the songs with his own group, the Byrds. The album received a Grammy nomination for best folk recording.

A live album, *The Judy Collins Concert*, was released in 1964, followed by *Judy Collins' Fifth Album* in 1965, in which Collins covered three more Dylan songs as well as numbers by Phil Ochs and Gordon Lightfoot. On *In My Life*, released in 1966, Collins began incorporating orchestral instrumentation and arrangements in her work. In addition to offering covers of the Beatles and Dylan and recording theater pieces from *The Threepenny Opera* and *Marat/Sade*, Collins became the first person to cover Leonard Cohen (who had not released an album of his own at the time) when she recorded "Dress Rehearsal Rag" and "Suzanne." She later brought Cohen on stage during a 1967 concert in Central Park. *In My Life* was also nominated for a Grammy for best folk performance.

Though Collins was a successful live performer, her records had yet to break into the Top Forty. That changed with the release of *Wildflowers* in 1967; both the album and its accompanying single, Joni Mitchell's bittersweet "Both Sides Now," hit the Top Ten. Collins first heard "Both Sides Now" when Mitchell played it for her over the telephone (like Cohen, Mitchell lacked a recording contract at the time she met Collins), and *Wildflowers* also featured Mitchell's song "Michael from Mountains." The album was Collins's first to feature her own songs. The entire album also featured orchestral arrangements.

Wildflowers and "Both Sides Now" were Collins's most commercially successful recordings ("Both Sides Now" won a Grammy for best folk performance), but she continued to have Top Forty hits in the 1960s and 1970s. *Who Knows Where the Time Goes*, released in 1968, was her last album of new material in that decade and featured highly acclaimed covers of Cohen's "Bird on the Wire" (which received a Grammy nomination for best folk performance) and "Story of Isaac," in addition to Ian Tyson's (of Ian and Sylvia) "Someday Soon," later one of Collins's signature songs, the wistful title track (by British folk singer Sandy Denny), and Collins's own tribute to her parent, "My Father." The album reached the Top Thirty, as did *Recollections: Judy Collins* (1969). In 1969 Collins also made her

Judy Collins, 1966. © BETTMANN/CORBIS

theatrical debut, playing Solveig in a New York production of Ibsen's *Peer Gynt* that starred Stacy Keach.

Collins's biggest hits after the 1960s include the singles "Amazing Grace" (1970) and "Send in the Clowns" (released in 1975 but not a hit until 1977), both of which hit the Top Twenty; "Clowns" was nominated for a Grammy for best female pop vocal performance and won a Song of the Year Grammy for its composer, Stephen Sondheim. Collins was also a political activist, campaigning against the Vietnam War in the 1960s and promoting women's rights in the 1970s; in 1995 she became a United Nations Children's Fund (UNICEF) Special Representative for the Performing Arts.

Collins married Peter Taylor in April 1958. They divorced in 1966. Their only son committed suicide in January 1992. Collins married Louis Nelson in February 1996. She continues to record, tour, and write.

★

Collins has written two autobiographies: *Trust Your Heart: An Autobiography* (1987) and *Singing Lessons: A Memoir of Love, Loss, Hope, and Healing* (1998). Her 1997 boxed set, *Forever: The Judy Collins Anthology,* also features substantial liner notes by Collins.

GILLIAN G. GAAR

COLTRANE, John William (*b.* 23 September 1926 in Hamlet, North Carolina; *d.* 17 July 1967 in Huntington, New York), tenor and soprano saxophonist, composer, and bandleader whose powerful tone, extensive technical and theoretical knowledge, and oblique, soul-searching improvisations made him the most influential jazz stylist of the 1960s.

Coltrane was the only child of John Robert Coltrane, a tailor and amateur musician, and Alice Blair Coltrane, a homemaker. Shortly after his birth, the family moved to High Point, North Carolina. Coltrane started playing an E-flat alto horn in 1939, the same year his father died of stomach cancer. He switched to the clarinet before settling on the alto saxophone around 1941. Following his graduation from high school in 1944 Coltrane moved to Philadelphia, Pennsylvania, where he found work in a sugar refinery and studied at the Ornstein School of Music and the Granoff Studios. In 1945 the navy drafted Coltrane, and he was stationed on the Hawaiian island of Oahu—where, in addition to fulfilling his seaman duties, he played in a dance band, the Melody Masters.

Following his discharge in 1946, Coltrane returned to Philadelphia and toured with Joe Webb and King Kolax from 1946 to 1947. After playing tenor saxophone with

John Coltrane. THE LIBRARY OF CONGRESS

Eddie "Cleanhead" Vinson in 1947 and 1948, he spent the next three years (1949 to 1951) with Dizzy Gillespie, with whom he made his first professional recordings, playing alto and tenor saxophone. He also worked locally in Philadelphia with Jimmy Heath and Howard McGhee, and in nameless rhythm-and-blues bands. After touring with saxophone masters Earl Bostic (from 1952 to 1953) and Johnny Hodges (from 1953 to 1954), Coltrane accelerated to fame as one-fifth of the legendary first Miles Davis quintet (1955 to 1957), of which the other members were pianist Red Garland, bassist Paul Chambers, and drummer Philly Joe Jones.

Coltrane's early style, although highly original, was conversant in the bop lingua franca of the day, having been strongly influenced by saxophonists Lester Young, Charlie Parker, Dexter Gordon, Sonny Rollins, Sonny Stitt, Stan Getz, and Coleman Hawkins. In the late 1950s and early 1960s Coltrane looked outside the boundaries of mainstream jazz for inspiration and became profoundly influenced by the free jazz saxophonist Ornette Coleman and the Indian classical sitarist Ravi Shankar.

Coltrane claimed to have had a spiritual awakening in early 1957, after which he kicked the addictions to heroin and alcohol that had plagued him while with Davis. From July to December of 1957, six nights a week, Coltrane

played in pianist and composer Thelonious Monk's quartet at the Five Spot in New York City. Coltrane's virtuosity grew rapidly through his apprenticeship with Monk, whom he saw as "a musical architect of the highest order." By 1958 Coltrane's powerful cascade of articulated eighth notes reached baroque perfection, inspiring critic Ira Gitler's "sheets of sound" description. Gitler also noted that "the amount of energy [Coltrane] was using could have powered a spaceship." Signing with Atlantic in early 1959, Coltrane recorded the album *Giant Steps,* an epochal work that set the high-water mark for harmonically complex, physically demanding hard bop. Coltrane rejoined Davis between 1958 and 1960, playing on Davis's comparatively subdued modal jazz masterpiece for Columbia, *Kind of Blue* (1959).

By all accounts Coltrane practiced constantly, regardless of his surroundings—stopping only to eat, sleep, or briefly acknowledge visitors to the Queens, New York, home he shared with his wife, Juanita ("Naima") Grubbs, whom he married in 1955, and her daughter, Sheila. In May 1960 he debuted his own quartet at the Jazz Gallery in New York City. Within a few months he settled on the lineup of pianist McCoy Tyner, bassist Steve Davis, and drummer Elvin Jones. The group recorded that fall for Atlantic, surprising everyone when Coltrane's soprano saxophone–led reworking of Rodgers and Hammerstein's "My Favorite Things" became a major hit. Coltrane singlehandedly established the soprano saxophone, which he began playing in 1959, as a modern jazz instrument.

Many of Coltrane's compositions from his eight Atlantic albums became jazz standards—for example, "Equinox," "Cousin Mary," and "Central Park West." In early 1961 he signed with Impulse Records. Shortly thereafter bassist Jimmy Garrison came on board and Coltrane's "classic" quartet lineup was complete. In 1963 Coltrane and his first wife separated, and he began living with Alice McLeod, a jazz pianist; they had three sons and were married after he and Naima divorced in 1966. Coltrane occasionally augmented his quartet with guest musicians, such as the alto saxophonist and bass clarinetist Eric Dolphy, who worked with the group off and on from 1961 to 1963 and was featured on the groundbreaking album *Live at the Village Vanguard* (1961), which spotlighted Coltrane's sixteen-minute, up-tempo blues workout, "Chasin' the Trane." Garrison's droning, driving bass, Jones's polyrhythms, and Tyner's crashing fourths could provoke a feverish intensity in Coltrane, resulting in lengthy solos some observers compared to a gospel sermon or speaking in tongues but others decried as boring or "anti-jazz." No stranger to adverse criticism, dating from his tenure with Davis, Coltrane mitigated its effects by occasionally recording more mainstream jazz fare, notably *Duke Ellington Meets John Coltrane* (1962) and his album of ballads with the singer Johnny Hartman

(1963). However, starting with the albums *Om* and *A Love Supreme* (both 1964), most if not all of Coltrane's subsequent music expressed overtly spiritual themes.

Coltrane continued to act as a mentor to younger musicians, recruiting saxophonists Archie Shepp and Pharoah Sanders for the 1965 recording of *Ascension*, a free jazz piece influenced by Ornette Coleman. That year, following a brief period in which Coltrane used Rashied Ali as a second drummer, Jones left the group, complaining of too much avant-garde noise. Tyner was the next to leave; he was replaced by Coltrane's wife, Alice. Garrison stayed, but eventually he too had a falling-out with Coltrane over the direction the music was taking and left following a tour of Japan in 1966.

Coltrane's most abstract and controversial period lasted from 1965 until his death from liver cancer in 1967. (After suffering abdominal pains, he was rushed to the hospital, where he died; those close to him suspected he had been aware of his illness but kept it a secret. Coltrane is buried at Pinelawn Memorial Park in Farmingdale, Long Island, New York.) He became engrossed in the ancient idea, fundamental to certain kinds of non-Western music, that various musical structures correspond to specific emotional states. His late music, which fitted his ingenious harmonic exertions into an abstract or free jazz template and used various vocal-sounding screeches and honks as well as multiphonics (the technique of playing two or three notes at one time), frequently had the effect of "clearing rooms," in Ali's words. Nevertheless, Coltrane attracted a new core of musical followers, among them the minimalist composers La Monte Young and Philip Glass, and rock musicians from the Byrds to Iggy Pop. In the African-American community Coltrane came to be viewed, even by some non-jazz listeners, as a sort of black saint—a living symbol of black accomplishment, spiritual unity, and strength.

For many listeners Coltrane's turbulent phrasing reflected the chaotic social and political atmosphere of the 1960s. He continued to be revered after his death for his profound devotion to music, his peaceful, thoughtful demeanor, and his religious convictions. Even when he stopped swinging in a conventional sense, Coltrane always told a story when he played.

★

Lewis Porter, *John Coltrane: His Life and Music* (1998), is the most thorough biography of Coltrane to date, consolidating previous works by J. C. Thomas, Bill Cole, Eric Nisenson, and others, while adding considerable historical research and musicological insight. Carl Woideck, *The John Coltrane Companion: Five Decades of Commentary* (1998), is an essential compendium based on journalistic and academic sources. Valerie Wilmer, *As Serious As Your Life: John Coltrane and Beyond* (1977), and Alyn Shipton, *A New History of Jazz* (2001), are helpful for understanding Coltrane's

impact in the 1960s and subsequent decades. An obituary is in the *New York Times* (18 July 1967). *The World According to John Coltrane* (1993) is a fascinating video documentary.

GREGORY K. ROBINSON

CONNELL, Evan S(helby), Jr. (*b*. 17 August 1924 in Kansas City, Missouri), author of fact and fiction who successfully experimented in documentary-style novels, building stories out of short vignettes in collage or mosaic style; his novels *Mrs. Bridge*, *Mr. Bridge*, and *Diary of a Rapist* are among his most acclaimed works.

Connell was born into a genteel and wealthy Kansas City family; his mother was the daughter of a judge, and his father was a prominent physician. He was a premedical student at Dartmouth College from 1941 to 1943, where he began writing short stories. In 1943 he joined the U.S. Navy and became a pilot and flight instructor. In 1947 he entered the University of Kansas on the GI Bill, attained his B.A. in English, and then enrolled in graduate studies in art and creative writing at Stanford and Columbia Universities. Connell, the author of twenty-one books by the year 2000, received a Guggenheim Fellowship, a Rockefeller Foundation grant, the California Literature silver medal, and the Lannan Foundation Lifetime Achievement award, among many other citations. Even so, he remains relatively obscure among the general public. "My own experience indicates that [writing] is mostly a career of rejection and lost illusions," Connell wrote in a letter to Gerald Shapiro, who published a profile of the author in *Ploughshares*.

In the early 1950s Connell traveled extensively throughout Europe, spending much time in Paris, where he associated with other young Americans pursuing interests in the arts. A relative loner, however, Connell found little satisfaction in mingling with this set, and in 1955 he settled in San Francisco, working various jobs to eke out a living. As the city became the hub of the underground Beat culture, Connell remained detached. "Never saw Kerouac. I've met Ginsberg two or three times since then, have been acquainted with Ferlinghetti for some years. But I'm not a part of any group," he commented to Shapiro. He committed his spare time to writing short stories and his first two novels, *Mrs. Bridge* (1958) and *The Patriot* (1960).

Mrs. Bridge became an immediate best-seller and is considered by many critics the benchmark against which his subsequent books are assessed. India Bridge, wife of a successful lawyer and mother of three in the post–World War II era, is bored, dominated by materialism, and hung up on the social graces. This documentary fiction depicts Mrs. Bridge's life through a series of 117 short vignettes, "each one carefully shaped into an epiphany—on the theme of Mrs. Bridge's existential imprisonment," commented Donovan Hohn in *Harper's Magazine*. He quoted Connell from an interview: "[F]or most of us, our lives do not reach a dramatic climax . . . . Most of us just go on . . . through major and minor trials and defeats. And finally time runs out."

That year Connell joined the staff, and ultimately became the editor, of *Contact,* a new San Francisco literary magazine and one of the most progressive in the country. He remained with the magazine for six years, the only major collaborative effort in his otherwise solitary career. The magazine permitted a forum for his new work, *Notes from a Bottle Found on the Beach at Carmel,* fictional prose that many called poetry. First published as a short piece in 1959, a much-expanded version published again in 1962 filled almost the entire magazine. Difficulty defining the work—fiction, as Connell claimed, or poetry, as others saw it—stalled its publication in book form until 1963. The book received scant but positive critical attention and sold poorly. *Notes* is a mosaic-style novel in which the protagonist is a mythic note-taker who, according to Hohn, accumulates "a jumble of textual fragments as . . . intricately patterned as the shards of a kaleidoscope . . . . Connell is at heart a deeply moral writer, a clear-eyed humanist grievously disappointed with his species."

By this time Connell was forty. His writing style, viewed as contrary and inaccessible, made publication of his works difficult. When they were published, they were neither widely reviewed nor read. *Contact* magazine failed financially in 1965, the year in which his second volume of short stories, *At the Crossroads,* was published. As with his previous works, it received few, albeit positive, reviews, and gained but a small readership. This was a period of isolation and discouragement for Connell, who still had to earn a living interviewing the unemployed at the California State Unemployment Office. He was also, however, working on his extraordinary novel, *Diary of a Rapist,* published in 1966. The novel documents the daily entries into a scrapbook by twenty-six-year-old Earl Summerfield who, like Connell, was an interviewer at the California State Unemployment Office. Discontented with his job and rejected by his ambitious ex-wife, Summerfield becomes obsessed with violence and clips sordid newspaper stories of violent crimes, daily writing his own feelings toward women and sex in his journal. Shapiro described the tension built by the accumulation of entries thus: "[E]ach day . . . becomes . . . more harrowing. . . . The effect is so powerful that when the rape actually occurs, the utter silence—there is no entry for that date—sounds like a scream." Shapiro also noted that because of the psychological decay experienced by the protagonist, *Diary of a Rapist* has been likened to Dostoevsky's *Notes from the Underground.*

Evan S. Connell, Jr. MR. JERRY BAUER

With the 1969 publication of *Mr. Bridge*, the companion novel to *Mrs. Bridge*, Connell again personified his perception of the idle rich. Shapiro called *Mr. Bridge* a "darker, more brooding novel. Here Connell's memory of his upbringing is informed more by bitterness than gentle irony." A critic for *Playboy* described it as "a brilliant dissection of the quintessential small-town WASP—performed under the light of high art, with irony, insight, and bleak pity." Hohn commented that the two *Bridge* books, which in 1990 were made into a movie starring Paul Newman and Joanne Woodward, express Connell's "desire, at once radical and old-fashioned, to represent human existence as accurately and as fully as possible."

While continuing to write fiction, Connell captured widespread notoriety and achieved financial success (paperback rights were sold for $200,000) with his 1984 nonfictional best-seller, *Son of the Morning Star: Custer and the Little Bighorn.* Called by Greg Bottoms "possibly the most unique historical essay ever published," the book was initially rejected by several publishers. Connell followed his 1991 novel, *The Alchymist's Journal,* considered particularly inaccessible, with *Deus Lo Volt!: A Chronicle of the Crusades,* published in 2000. Bottoms declared this historic work "like no other novel written . . . its remarkable and subtle intelligence is awe-inspiring."

In 2001, while conducting an interview for *Bookforum* with the reclusive Connell via letters, Bottoms commented to the author that several critics have called him "a bit of a liberal crank, someone out to debunk or subvert what we've come to view as our history, our origins." Connell replied: "'Liberal crank' isn't much of an epithet. Anyway, I've never decided to debunk or subvert, not unless that means pointing out lies and hypocrisy."

Hohn noted that "Connell aspires to see all, the most disturbing expressions of human nature as well as the beautiful and marvelous." In this respect, he compared Connell to Proust, noting that one of the final vignettes in *Mrs. Bridge* is called "Remembrance of Things Past." Hohn commented that while Proust explored deeply, Connell explores more widely. "It is humanity's past, and not merely his own, that Connell wishes to recover," wrote Hohn.

★

A critique of Connell's major works, along with his personal perspectives, can be found in his interviews with Gerald Shapiro for *Ploughshares* (fall 1987) and with Greg Bottoms for *Bookforum* (winter 2001). Donovan Hohn, in *Harper's Magazine* (Dec. 2001), wrote an insightful essay on Connell and his works.

MARIE L. THOMPSON

CONNOR, Theophilus Eugene ("Bull") (*b.* 11 July 1897 in Selma, Alabama; *d.* 10 March 1973 in Birmingham, Alabama), ardently segregationist commissioner of public safety for Birmingham, Alabama, whose tactics—most notably the use of fire hoses and police dogs against peaceful demonstrators—so shocked the nation that they ultimately aided the passage of civil rights legislation.

Connor was one of five children born to King Edward Connor, a railroad dispatcher, and Molly Godwin. The father's work forced a move in 1905 to Atlanta, where the mother died giving birth to her fifth child. Connor spent the remainder of his childhood with relatives in Birmingham, but traveled widely with his father. A boyhood accident rendered him sightless in one eye, and he never finished high school.

Connor learned the craft of telegraphy from his father, and went to work in that capacity after he married Beara Levens in 1920. In Dallas in 1921, he filled in for an ailing baseball announcer, and became popular for his booming voice, which earned him the nickname of "Bull." Returning to Birmingham in 1922, Connor announced games for that city's Barons baseball team. (Coincidentally, this team came to national attention in 1993 thanks to an African American, Michael Jordan, who played for them during his brief flirtation with a second career in minor-league baseball.)

In 1934 Connor was elected to the Alabama House of Representatives. From 1937 to 1954 and again from 1958 to 1963, he served as Birmingham's commissioner of public safety, which gave him administrative authority over the city's police and fire departments and made him part of a three-man team that ran the city. Over the years, Connor was an outspoken segregationist. In his inaugural remarks as commissioner in 1958, he stated that "These laws [segregation] are still constitutional and I promise you that until they are removed from the ordinance books of Birmingham and the statute books of Alabama, they will be enforced in Birmingham to the utmost of my ability and by all lawful means."

In Birmingham, a conservative stronghold of the South, Connor reacted violently when the policy of segregation was threatened. In 1961 the U.S. Supreme Court ruled that segregated interstate bus terminals were unconstitutional, and soon afterward a group of activists, calling themselves the Freedom Riders, rode into southern strongholds. They determined that if they were arrested, the Justice Department would be forced to act on their behalf, and Alabama's bus lines would be desegregated.

However, when the Freedom Riders reached Birmingham on 14 May, Connor gave full support to a group of Ku Klux Klansmen that set upon one of the buses, reportedly telling them to keep up their attack until the riders "looked like a bulldog got ahold of them." This was the first of the major standoffs over segregation involving Connor.

The 1960s was an era that increasingly called for compromise in race relations, but Connor stubbornly played the hard line, resisting integration as long as he remained in office. In December of 1961, rather than desegregate, Connor and his two fellow commissioners closed down Birmingham's sixty-seven parks, thirty-eight playgrounds, and four golf courses. Birmingham was given a choice to either integrate their minor-league baseball team, the Barons, or give it up. They gave it up.

Japanese newspapers in 1961 printed front-page photographs of the Birmingham mob attacking the Freedom Riders, and when these came to the attention of the city's chamber of commerce president Sidney Smyer, they caused him considerable embarrassment. From that point on, Smyer tried to find some way to get rid of Connor, but as the elected, independent chief commissioner, Connor was politically untouchable. The easiest way to expel him from government would therefore be to simply change the form of city government from a city commission (on which three commissioners ran the city government) to mayor-council (on which a mayor and city council ran the city government). This way Connor would be ousted from office by pulling the office out from under him.

In 1962 a majority of Alabama voters, in part tired of

Connor's reactionary politics, voted to change Birmingham's form of city government. Connor immediately announced his candidacy for city mayor, and a special election was scheduled for March 1963. Running on a prosegregationist platform, he pledged that if he were elected mayor, one of his first steps in office would be to buy 100 new police dogs to attack any Freedom Rider who ventured into Alabama. In a sign of the changing times, Connor lost the election.

Before he left office in May, Connor gained notoriety for ordering the use of police dogs and fire hoses to disperse civil rights demonstrators. In January 1963 Dr. Martin Luther King, Jr., had announced that the Southern Christian Leadership Conference, along with the Alabama Christian Movement for Human Rights, was going to Birmingham to integrate public facilities and department stores. On 9 April, Connor arrested King for violating an injunction against marching on Good Friday. It was during this period of incarceration that King wrote his famous "Letter from a Birmingham Jail," a reaction to city leaders' demands that African-American citizens slow down and wait for desegregation. Both King and local civil rights leader Fred L. Shuttlesworth were released from jail on 20 April. Throughout that month, small, peaceful movements occurred in Birmingham.

On 2 May, however, the intensity was raised a notch. King's plan was to have children from thirteen to eighteen years of age begin the march and fill up the city's jails, and thus, with the help of the media, embarrass city officials. Connor obliged by arresting 600 to 900 children, some as young as six years old. On 3 May, over 1,000 young people received their marching orders. Connor's jails, however, were quickly running out of room, so he ordered the police to bring high-pressured fire hoses and K-9 units in to repel the advancing tide of young marchers. All this was caught by television cameras and relayed to a stunned nation. Over a seven-day period, television viewers saw nonviolent demonstrators on one side and Connor's police with fire hoses on the other, attempting to enforce segregation.

Connor's resistance to desegregation set off a series of demonstrations around the country, and lit a fire under the administration of President John F. Kennedy. Pictures of one of Connor's police dogs attacking a black woman, said President Kennedy, made him sick. Determined to step up the federal role in civil rights, Kennedy promised major legislation. Indeed, the heavy-handed defense of segregation by Connor in 1963 hastened the passage of the Civil Rights Act of 1964. "The civil rights movement should thank Bull Connor," Kennedy stated. "He's helped it as much as Abraham Lincoln." In July the city of Birmingham repealed its segregation ordinances.

After Connor left his office of commissioner of public safety in 1963, he served two terms as president of Ala-

Eugene "Bull" Connor addressing the Alabama County White Citizens Council, 1963. ASSOCIATED PRESS AP

bama's public service commission, the state body responsible for regulating public utilities. He retired after failing to gain reelection to a third term in 1972 and died the following year.

★

Connor's papers are in the Birmingham Public Library, Birmingham, Alabama, and additional material can be found at the Alabama Department of Archives and History in Montgomery. A biography is William A. Nunnelley, *Bull Connor* (1991). See also Taylor Branch, *Parting the Waters: America in the King Years, 1954–1963* (1988).

KIM RICHARDSON

CONRAD, Paul (*b.* 27 June 1924 in Cedar Rapids, Iowa), political cartoonist who, in the 1960s, skewered right-wing politics and commented on civil rights, integration, and the Vietnam War.

Conrad is the son of Robert H. Conrad, a freight and passenger agent, and his wife, Florence G. (Lawler) Conrad. Conrad attended Saint Augustine's elementary school in Des Moines, Iowa, where he first started making social comments with his natural drawing talents. Spotting a remark written on the wall in the boys' room, he proceeded to draw a cartoon to go with it. After graduating from Roosevelt High School, Conrad went to Alaska in search of work in an economy that still had not completely rebounded from the Great Depression. He ended up in Valdez, Alaska, working in construction. He returned to Iowa within eight months, was drafted into the Army Corps of Engineers in 1942, and served in the Pacific theater of

Paul Conrad. SHELLEY GAZIN/CORBIS

operations during World War II. After his discharge in 1946 Conrad enrolled at the University of Iowa, where he started drawing editorial cartoons for the university's newspaper, the *Daily Iowan*. He graduated in 1950, although his academic average was only 1.79. Nevertheless, he impressed his art teachers, and one of them sent samples of his work to the *Denver Post,* which promptly hired him. Soon afterward he met Barbara Kay King, a society writer for the paper. The two were married on 27 February 1953 and had four children.

Conrad, who worked for the *Denver Post* from 1950 to 1964, won the 1964 Pulitzer Prize for editorial cartooning. He then joined the *Los Angeles Times.* Conrad's popularity and recognition continued to grow, and he became one the nation's hottest cartooning properties. Throughout the 1960s Conrad, a liberal Democrat, skewered some of the most prominent men and women of the day. A frequent target of his hard-hitting editorial cartoons was Ronald Reagan, who became the Republican governor of California in 1966 and was elected president in 1980. During his time as governor Reagan and his wife, Nancy, are reported to have called the newspaper regularly to complain about Conrad's cartoons.

Conrad also took special satisfaction in lampooning Re-

publican President Richard Nixon, who took office in 1969. Conrad's depictions of Nixon so enraged him that the cartoonist was placed on the president's infamous "enemies' list" a few years later. In addition, Conrad was audited four times during the Nixon administration, but the auditors failed to find anything wrong with his taxes. Conrad did not spare Democratic politicians, especially President Lyndon B. Johnson, who served from 1963, following the assassination of President John F. Kennedy on 22 November, until Nixon took office in 1969. "Even the White House wasn't big enough for that ego," Conrad would later comment in a 1994 article in *Editor & Publisher.*

Like most Americans in the 1960s, Conrad was deeply affected by the assassinations of John F. Kennedy, the civil rights leader Martin Luther King, Jr., and Senator Robert F. Kennedy. "I'll never forget those guys," Conrad said in the October 1999 issue of the *Information Bulletin*, published by the Library of Congress. "I often wonder what the country would have been like if those men had not been erased from the American political scene."

In addition to trenchant editorial content, Conrad's cartoons garnered attention because they reflected his extensive research and were characterized by technical accuracy. While he often focused on political pretension in his cartoons, Conrad also commented on the human condition in general, such as his 27 January 1967 cartoon about the Apollo 1 tragedy. The three men on the first planned flight to the Moon all died when their space capsule caught on fire on the launch pad. Conrad depicted the infallibility of humans and the dangers inherent in space flight with his drawing of the specter of death clothed in a space suit holding a Mercury mission spacecraft in one hand and a Gemini craft in the other, with the smoldering Apollo mission craft in the background. It was captioned, "I thought you knew, I've been aboard on every flight."

Despite his penchant for hard-hitting, gut-wrenching editorial cartoons, Conrad often displayed his sense of humor in his editorial comments. A 1969 cartoon commemorating the 20 July 1969 landing of Apollo 11 mission astronauts on the Moon and Neil Armstrong's historic Moon walk poked fun at the event with the now classic depiction of a mailbox for a Moon resident already sitting on the Moon's surface. Conrad also could poke fun at his own profession, as with his *Denver Post* cartoon of a reporter seated backward on a worn-out old burro, which represented the media getting everything "ass-backwards."

Nevertheless, politics and government in general were Conrad's primary focus throughout the decade. An opponent of the Vietnam War, Conrad published a cartoon on 15 June 1969 that commented on the war via the Vietnam Moratorium Day demonstrations. Thousands of antiwar demonstrators gathered in cities across the nation in protest of the war. Conrad's editorial cartoon depicted the ghosts of dead Vietnam soldiers with packs and weapons marching across the sky over Washington, D.C., and the Capitol Building while protesters demonstrated below. The caption read, "If only there'd been a Vietnam moratorium five years ago."

Conrad's cartoons have forced Americans to reflect on timely issues, often inspiring them and just as often enraging them. Throughout his career Conrad, who got his inspiration from reading, maintained his take-no-prisoners attitude. "I wake up angry every morning and start reading," he once said. "Then I'm furious." Conrad, who also won Pulitzer Prizes in 1971 and 1984, retired from the *Los Angeles Times* in 1994 but continued to draw editorial cartoons, which the *Los Angeles Times* syndicated throughout the United States. He began sculpting in the 1980s and is an avid golfer.

★

For insights into Conrad's work during the 1960s and 1970s, his own book, *Pro and Conrad* (1979), with an introduction by the journalist and humorist Art Buchwald, is a good place to start. Some of Conrad's 1960s work with the *Los Angeles Times* is available in *Conartist: 30 Years with the Los Angeles Times* (1993), which includes text by Norman Corwin and an introduction by Shelby Coffey III. Other sources of information about Conrad's early career include articles in *Newsweek* (12 Sept. 1977) and *Writer's Digest* (Dec. 1977).

DAVID PETECHUK

COOLEY, Denton Arthur (*b.* 22 August 1920 in Houston, Texas), cardiac surgeon, medical educator, and surgeon who performed one of the first American heart transplants and the first artificial heart implant.

Cooley, one of two sons of Ralph C. Cooley, a dentist, and Mary Augusta Fraley Cooley, graduated from San Jacinto High School in Houston and earned a B.A. from the University of Texas at Austin (UT) in 1941. He enrolled in UT's medical school but transferred to Johns Hopkins Hospital, earning an M.D. in 1944.

While at Johns Hopkins, Cooley became associated with Alfred Blalock, who had been experimenting with anastamosis, the tying of blood vessels, in dogs. At the suggestion of the cardiologist Helen B. Taussig, Blalock tried the procedure to repair a congenital heart condition known as *tetralogy of Fallot;* Cooley assisted on the very first one. Cooley left for brief stints in the army and with Lord Russell Brock, another noted surgeon in the rapidly growing field of pediatric heart surgery. In January of 1949 Cooley married Louise Goldsborough Thomas, the daughter of a surgeon and a nurse at Johns Hopkins; they had five daughters. In 1951 he returned to Houston.

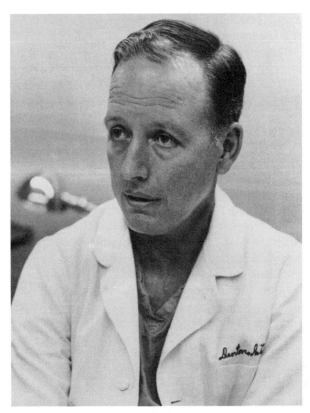

Denton Cooley. ARCHIVE PHOTOS, INC.

At Houston he teamed with the Baylor Medical School professor Michael DeBakey and in 1955 helped DeBakey design the heart-lung machine used at Houston's Methodist Hospital. In the early 1960s Cooley began to work with transplanting artificial valves in diseased hearts. By the start of 1967 he had become so skilled that he received the Rene Leriche Prize as "the most valuable surgeon of the heart and blood vessels anywhere in the world."

In December of that year, Dr. Christiaan Barnard of Cape Town, South Africa, transplanted the first human heart. Cooley watched this technique closely and performed transplant surgery himself in May 1968. Cooley implanted the heart from a fifteen-year-old female suicide victim into Everett Thomas, a forty-seven-year-old man. Previously, American surgeons had cooled the heart before implantation, but Cooley believed that he could suture a donated heart into place before damage to the heart could occur. Thomas lived 204 days. Cooley went on to transplant twenty-one human hearts and one ram's heart in the space of a year.

Controversy followed these operations, however. Shortly after the first transplant, Cooley had two patients in need of hearts and only one donor. Cooley installed the heart in the younger person; the older person was given a heart forty-eight hours later. The latter patient received the still beating heart of a brain-dead man. A grand jury indicted two hospital workers for the murder of the heart donor, but the charges later were dropped. Nevertheless, Cooley's transplants were raising questions that plagued medicine at this period: Who shall live, and what is the legal definition of death? Up to this point medical examiners always had been able to define death as cessation of a pulse. After the transplants brain death became the accepted criterion. As Cooley said in a *Life* magazine article, "the heart . . . is the servant of the brain."

On 4 April 1969 Cooley performed surgery on a patient named Haskell Karp, an Illinois printing estimator. Karp's heart muscle was so severely damaged by coronary artery disease that it could barely function, but a suitable heart for transplant could not be found. In what Cooley himself termed "an act of desperation," he inserted an artificial heart made of a type of silicon plastic in the patient at Saint Luke's Episcopal Hospital in Houston. A short-term measure, the pump was the same size as a natural heart. A large bedside pump sent out pulses of carbon dioxide into sacs on the artificial heart, which then forced Karp's own heart to expand and contract sufficiently to enable blood to oxygenate through Karp's own lungs. While he was on the artificial heart, Karp said a few words and survived long enough to receive Cooley's nineteenth heart transplant a few days later. DeBakey was furious. He charged that his former colleague had stolen the concept for the heart from him and had violated federal guidelines on the use of experimental devices. A Baylor committee recommended censuring Cooley. As a result of the controversy, Cooley terminated his eighteen-year relationship with Baylor and established the Texas Heart Institute. He also responded to DeBakey by insisting that he was obliged only to receive his patient's permission to perform the operation. A federal district court dismissed a suit by Karp's widow, and the United States Supreme Court denied review of the dismissal.

For his part Cooley argued that "we have demonstrated that a mechanical device will support the body. But we've got to get more experience." None of the transplant recipients, in Houston or elsewhere, survived long in that era of medicine. As a result Cooley turned his attention to perfecting the heart-bypass operation. By the end of the twentieth century he had performed 20,000 bypasses. All of these operations relied on perfecting the techniques of attaching and reattaching blood vessels that Cooley had learned in his initial contact with Blalock. Barnard observed Cooley at work and proclaimed, "Every movement had a purpose and achieved its aim. Where most surgeons would take three hours, he could do the same operation in one hour."

Cooley has been described as a man who speaks calmly. His secretary told Cooley's biographer that over the course of his career Cooley had dealt with "suicidal maniacs, religious fanatics, gypsies, cranks, reporters, politicians,

cracked inventors, and exhibitionists" in his practice. In 1972 he received an award for having performed the most bypass operations of any living surgeon. In 1984 he received the Presidential Medal of Freedom, the highest United States civilian honor.

Cooley and his associates have performed more than 100,000 open-heart operations. His patients have included the Hall of Fame baseball pitcher Whitey Ford. Cooley has published many technical works, including *Surgical Treatment of Congenital Heart Disease* (1966), written with Grady I. Hallman, a close associate at the Texas Heart Institute.

★

The most detailed biography of Cooley is Harry Minetree, *Cooley: The Career of a Great Heart Surgeon* (1973), written by a former patient who had access to Cooley and his staff. Other treatments are Thomas Thompson, *Hearts: Of Surgeons and Transplants, Miracles and Disasters Along the Cardiac Frontier* (1971), and Roger Rapoport, *The Super-Doctors* (1975), which view Cooley in the larger context of heart surgery of the time.

JOHN DAVID HEALY

COONEY, Joan Ganz (*b.* 30 November 1929 in Phoenix, Arizona), producer of children's television programs who co-founded and headed the Children's Television Workshop, the company responsible for creating and producing *Sesame Street*, *The Electric Company*, *3-2-1 Contact*, *Square One TV*, and other series aired on the Public Broadcasting System, and a pioneer in the licensing of products based on television characters.

Cooney was the youngest of three children born to Sylvan C. Ganz, a banker, and Pauline (Reardan) Ganz, a homemaker. Cooney's father was Jewish, but her mother was a practicing Roman Catholic who raised her children in that faith. Cooney attended both parochial and public schools, graduating from North Phoenix High School in 1947. She attended the Dominican College of San Rafael in California before transferring to and graduating from the University of Arizona in Tucson, cum laude, with a B.A. in education in 1951.

After briefly working as a reporter for the *Arizona Republic* in Phoenix, Cooney decided to work in the television industry, partly owing to the influence of Father James Keller, founder of the Christopher movement, whom she greatly admired. "Father Keller encouraged idealistic people—people who wanted to do good—to go into media . . . I . . . took that . . . seriously and came to New York in 1954 to get into . . . television." Using her family connections, Cooney was introduced to David Sarnoff, chair of the Radio Corporation of America, who arranged a job for her in the National Broadcasting Company's publicity department. A year later she became a publicist for

Joan Ganz Cooney speaking at a Senate subcommittee hearing on equal educational opportunities, 1970. © BETTMANN/CORBIS

the prestigious Columbia Broadcasting System drama series the *United States Steel Hour.*

By the early 1960s, however, most of the high-quality programs that are remembered as making up "the golden age of television" had been cancelled in favor of more profitable, formulaic dramas and situation comedies. Cooney concluded that there was little room in commercial television for the kind of work she hoped to do, and in 1962 she went to work for the nonprofit Educational Broadcasting Corporation, which had just been awarded the license to operate New York City's Channel Thirteen. Taking a 25 percent pay cut, she became the producer of *Court of Reason,* a weekly series that pitted teams of experts debating each other on the day's issues.

In 1964 she met Timothy J. Cooney, a civil rights activist, whom she married later that year; they were divorced in 1975 and had no children. At his urging she produced a documentary, "A Chance at the Beginning," concerning the pilot program being conducted at a Harlem school for what would eventually become Headstart. The film was later bought by Project Headstart and used for promotional and recruiting purposes. In 1966 Cooney produced a three-hour television documentary, *Poverty, Anti-Poverty, and the Poor,* for which she won her first Emmy Award. A bright career as a producer of public affairs documentaries beckoned.

In 1966, Cooney hosted a dinner party at her apartment that included Lloyd Morrisette, the head of the Carnegie Foundation. At this party a conversation took place that led to the creation of *Sesame Street.* "[We were] talking about

the great educational potential of television and how it was untapped. Something clicked in Lloyd's mind. Carnegie . . . was doing research on child development—cognitive acquisition in children." Impressed by Cooney's degree in education, the documentary on preschool education she had done, and her twelve years of experience in television, Morrisette hired her to conduct a study. Her report, "The Potential Uses of Television in Preschool Education," which was submitted later that year, was among the first to catalog basic facts about the influence that television had exerted on family life in America during its two decades of existence. More than 96 percent of American homes had television sets, and they were in operation for approximately sixty hours per week, thus, on a cumulative basis, stimulating children's cognitive abilities for an entire year before they entered school. The report expressed the hope that with the expert development of educational programs, television might function positively for preschoolers as a "classroom without walls."

The Children's Television Workshop (CTW) was founded in 1968 as a direct result of the report, with an $8 million budget that came from the Carnegie Foundation, other private foundations, and federal funds. Cooney, as head of CTW, initiated a series of seminars, bringing together experts in education and television to gather input for programming ideas. The result was a consensus on five curriculum goals for a program aimed at preschoolers. Three were simple: recognition of the letters of the alphabet, recognition of the numbers one through ten, and the introduction of new vocabulary words. Two goals were more complex: exercise of the child's early reasoning skills and, as Cooney put it, "increased awareness of self and world." Cooney served as president of CTW in 1970, chair and chief executive officer in 1988, and chair of the executive committee in 1990.

While content goals are basic for all educational television programs, Cooney and her team of collaborators departed from previous attempts by never losing sight of the medium in which they were working. Studies were conducted for CTW that involved observing children while they watched television in order to learn what attracted them. "[We] found that kids were fascinated by commercials with fast actions, catchy music, and cartoons. We wanted our show to jump and move," she told *Reader's Digest*.

Sesame Street, whose title was taken from the "Open Sesame" phrase in *Tales from the Arabian Nights*, premiered on 10 November 1969. It was indeed unlike any previous children's television program, with an accelerated pace that resembled *Rowan and Martin's Laugh-In,* then the most popular show on prime-time television. *Sesame Street* also made full use of children's familiarity with television convention, with letters and numbers "sponsoring" the program and presenting "commercials" for themselves. Most critics loved it, praising Cooney for her bold innovations and for the show's urban setting, racially integrated cast, and multicultural emphasis. (Mississippi Public Television dropped *Sesame Street* temporarily because of its racial integration.) Others criticized her for capitulating to the medium's fast-cutting format, which they thought was destroying the attention span of children and thus their ability to learn, regardless of content. Cooney underwent a radical double mastectomy for breast cancer in 1975. In 1980 she married Peter G. Peterson, chairman of the Bell and Howell Company, and together they established a foundation to support children's television programs.

Sesame Street is one of the most successful television programs of any type in terms of longevity and worldwide popularity, reaching an estimated 235 million viewers each week. Seventeen licensed foreign productions make the show available in more than 140 countries around the world. After the success of *Sesame Street*, CTW went on to expand programming to reach older children with *The Electric Company* (1971) and *Feelin' Good* (1974). More CTW shows focused on science, in *3-2-1 Contact* (1980); mathematics, in *Square One TV* (1987); and teenage writing, in *Ghostwriter* (1992).

Sesame Street survived to become an institution of American culture, something that few noncommercial television series have achieved. Cooney has won numerous honors as a television producer, including several Emmy, Peabody, and Christopher Awards, and she has emerged as a dominant figure in children's television. In 1989 she won an

Emmy Lifetime Achievement Award, and in 1995 she was awarded the Presidential Medal of Freedom, the highest national award given to a civilian. In 1999, after three decades on public television, Cooney brought CTW into a joint broadcasting venture with the commercial cable channel Nickelodeon, known as Noggin, a digital cable channel aimed at fast learners. She also initiated CTW's educational Web site and CTW's continuing production of magazines, software, toys, films, and community outreach programs for children.

★

There is no autobiography or biography of Cooney, but biographical information is in Cary O'Dell, *Women Pioneers in Television* (1996), and David Stewart, *The PBS Companion: A History of Public Television* (1999). Articles about Cooney include "The First Lady of Sesame Street," *Broadcasting* (7 June 1971); "Growing Up with Joan Ganz Cooney," *Public Telecommunications Review* (Nov.–Dec. 1978); "Cooney Casts Light on a Vision," *Variety* (13 Dec. 1989); and "Street Smart," *People Weekly* (2 Nov. 1998). Cooney also wrote the foreword for David Borgenicht, *Sesame Street Unpaved: Scripts, Stories, Secrets, and Songs* (1998), which is an insider's guide for adults that includes interviews and photographs of the *Sesame Street* family.

DAVID MARC

COUSINS, Norman (*b.* 24 June 1915 in Union Hill, New Jersey; *d.* 30 November 1990 in Westwood, California), journalist, editor, author, and lecturer; a vocal opponent of nuclear arms proliferation and a proponent of a nuclear test ban who, as special envoy between U.S. president John F. Kennedy and the Soviet Union leader Nikita Khrushchev, helped bring about a nuclear test ban treaty.

Cousins was the son of Samuel Cousins and Sara Barry Miller. He attended public school in New York City and Teachers College at Columbia University. Cousins served as the education editor for the *New York Evening Post* in the mid-1930s and then as literary editor and managing editor for *Current History*. He then became executive editor at the *Saturday Review of Literature* (renamed the *Saturday Review* after 1972) and served as editor until the mid-1970s.

Cousins also worked in the overseas bureau of the Office of War Information from 1943 until the end of World War II in 1945. In the 1950s he became involved in the world peace movement and various organizations focusing on altering what seemed to be an inevitable course toward nuclear war. Cousins also cofounded the committee for a Sane Nuclear Policy (SANE) in 1957. On 23 June 1939 he married Ellen Kopf; they had four children.

At the beginning of the 1960s Cousins published two books that reflected his commitment to exploring the implications of the "atomic age." In *The Last Defense in a Nuclear*

Age (1960), and *In Place of Folly* (1961), Cousins set forth his thoughts about nuclear arms proliferation and the need for a ban on nuclear testing. The books also delved into such issues as peace through world law administered through a democratic world federation, for example, a strengthened United Nations. In his book *In Place of Folly,* Cousins summed up his view concerning individual world governments and the ineffectiveness of the United Nations: "The nations have insisted on retaining for themselves ultimate authority in matters of security. They want the right to possess greater physical force than they are willing to invest in the organization chafed with the maintenance of world peace. They have provided no specific or adequate machinery to prevent aggression."

Cousins was the primary initiator behind the Dartmouth Conferences. Appalled by the growing tensions between the United States and the Soviet Union, Cousins had begun working in the 1950s on the idea of bringing together leading citizens from the two countries. When the Soviet Union agreed to the concept, Cousins and others organized the first meeting, to be held at Dartmouth College in 1960. The idea was to open up the lines of communication between the two countries. The Dartmouth Conference meetings were held throughout the decade in both the United States and the Soviet Union. They focused primarily on Soviet-American relations and included participants such as scientists, businesspeople, writers, and journalists.

Cousins's diplomatic success in bringing together the Dartmouth Conferences led to his becoming an unofficial ambassador who went on missions for President John F. Kennedy and his successor, Lyndon Baines Johnson. In 1963 Cousins was serving as an emissary on behalf of Pope John Paul XXIII to negotiate the release from the Soviet Union of two Catholic religious leaders who had been imprisoned at the end of World War II. President Kennedy requested that Cousins also talk with the Soviet prime minister Nikita Khrushchev about the U.S. government's sincere wish to pursue a nuclear test ban treaty. Cousins later said in an interview at the Institute of International Studies that "Kennedy felt that a dialog with the Soviet Union had to be based on mutual recognition, mutual respect for the security requirements of both countries." Cousins also began a massive public education campaign in the United States to sway public opinion in favor of a nuclear test ban. As a result, he played a pivotal role in the ratification of the test ban treaty by the U.S. Senate in 1963.

In the mid-1960s Cousins experienced a debilitating illness called ankylosing spondylitis, which results in the breakdown of the fibrous tissue (collagen) that binds cells of the body together. Cousins received the gloomy prognosis that he had only a few months to live. He decided to take matters into his own hands and had himself released from the hospital to a hotel room, where he treated himself

Norman Cousins. ARCHIVE PHOTOS, INC.

with massive doses of vitamin C. He also determined that he would keep up his spirits and boost his ability to fight off the disease by entertaining himself with Marx Brothers movies and humorous books by such authors as P. G. Wodehouse and James Thurber. Cousins recovered and used a similar approach in his fight against cancer more than a decade later.

Despite his illness, Cousins did not waver long from his duties. He continued to speak out on issues such as the Vietnam War, as in his 1967 *Saturday Review* piece titled "Public Opinion and Vietnam." He also published the first of his autobiographies, called *Present Tense: An American Editor's Odyssey* (1967). In the book, Cousins commented on the mood of Americans at the time: "In traveling around the United States, I have been made aware of a melancholy tension. The questions people ask are not related to their personal incomes or the need to find better ways to amuse themselves. They want to know how to overcome their sense of personal futility on the big issues."

Throughout the 1960s, Cousins used his talents as a writer and his position at the *Saturday Review* to pique the American public's conscience about issues concerning politics, government, and nuclear arms. He editorialized on many issues that later became popular, such as concern about cigarette advertising, the importance of controlling pollution, and the level of violence in entertainment. Cousins received numerous awards for his work in journalism and on the world stage, including the Eleanor Roosevelt Peace Award in 1963, an Overseas Press Club award in 1965, and the New York Academy of Public Education Award in 1966. In 1971 the United Nations honored Cousins with its Peace Medal.

By the time Cousins ended his tenure as the full-time editor of the *Saturday Review* in the 1970s, he had increased circulation from some 20,000 to 600,000. He became ill with cancer in the late 1970s but recovered, once again incorporating his belief in the physical healing power of positive thinking. He wrote about his views on health in *Anatomy of an Illness as Perceived by the Patient: Reflections on Healing and Regeneration* (1979). Cousins, who also later recovered from a heart attack, became more and more interested in the mind-body connection and health and wrote several books on the topic. He went on to become professor of medical humanities at the University of Los Angeles, where he also worked with the Brain Research Institute. Cousins died in 1990 of a heart attack.

★

Cousins's early autobiography is *Present Tense: An American Editor's Odyssey* (1967). An account of his work as a liaison between Kennedy, Khrushchev, and the pope is *The Improbable Triumvirate: John F. Kennedy, Pope John, Nikita Khrushchev* (1972). An obituary is in the *National Review* (31 Dec. 1990).

DAVID PETECHUK

COX, Harvey Gallagher, Jr. (*b*. 19 May 1929 in Phoenixville, Pennsylvania), Baptist clergyman, theologian, university professor, and best-selling author of *The Secular City*.

Cox was one of four children of Harvey Gallagher Cox, Sr., and Dorothy Dunwoody Cox. His father was a painter, decorator, and, later, a transport manager. His mother was a secretary and then a housemother at the Devereaux School in Devon, Pennsylvania. He attended Berwyn High School in Berwyn, Pennsylvania, and graduated in 1947. After attending the University of Pennsylvania from 1947 to 1951, where he graduated with a B.A. in history with honors, he entered Yale University Divinity School. Cox graduated from Yale with a B.D. degree cum laude in 1955 and then went on to Oberlin College in Ohio as director of the school's religious activities program. He was ordained a minister of the American Baptist Church in 1956. He served in the U.S. Merchant Marine in 1946–1947.

In June 1957 he married Nancy Lucille Nieburger, an actress. They divorced in 1986, and later that year Cox

married Nina Tumarkin, a professor of Russian history at Wellesley College. Cox had three children with his first wife and one child with his second wife.

Cox left Oberlin College in 1958 to become a program associate with the American Baptist Home Mission Society, a position he retained until 1963. His affiliation with Harvard began in December 1962, when he attended the New Delhi Conference of the World Council of Churches as an adviser to Harvard University Divinity School's department of church and society. Concurrent with his affiliation with Harvard, Cox also pursued his doctorate, which he received in history and the philosophy of religion in 1963. From 1963 to 1965 Cox was assistant professor of theology and culture at the Andover Theological School in Massachusetts, and then he joined the faculty of Harvard Divinity School in 1965.

A prolific writer, Cox first attracted wide attention with an article published in the 17 April 1961 issue of *Christianity and Crisis* titled "Playboy's Doctrine of Maleness." In the 21 February 1964 issue of *Commonweal* he published "Facing the Secular." Both articles later were rewritten and incorporated in his first book, *The Secular City: Secularization and Urbanization in Theological Perspective* (1965). Although Cox went on to author numerous other books, *The Secular City* earned him his reputation as one of the most influential theologians of the decade. The book sold nearly a million copies in eleven languages.

In *The Secular City*, Cox argued that unlike the premodern age, when "Christendom" could control culture and the political order, the age of secularization had placed "the responsibility for the forging of human values in man's own hands." Cox carefully distinguished between secularization and secularism, which he regarded as a restrictive ideology that was as oppressive as any constrictive theology. Cox called on Christians to welcome secularization and develop a theology to embrace it. In eschewing the traditional divide between the sacred and the profane, Cox argued that God was as present in the secular as in the religious realms of life. He decried those who would cramp the divine presence by confining it to a specially delineated spiritual or theological mode and contended that secularization is not everywhere and always an evil. Cox insisted that "if theology is to survive and make any sense to the contemporary world, it must neither cling to a metaphysical world-view nor collapse into a mystical mode, but must push on into the living lexicon of the urban-secular man." Thus, according to Cox, people of faith need not flee from the allegedly godless contemporary world.

Cox also challenged the so-called death of God theologians who were influential during the 1960s. He accused them of being obsessed with the classical God of metaphysical theism, whereas Cox contended that God was very much alive and could be found in unexpected quarters.

One of the places where God could be found, stated Cox, was among the poor. In the decade in which President Lyndon B. Johnson declared his War on Poverty and many idealistic Americans flocked to support the cause of civil rights as well as opposing the war in Vietnam, Cox's arguments resonated with a large segment of the public. Cox's ideas also were found compatible with the proponents of liberation theology in Latin America.

Cox contended that an act of engagement for justice in the world, and not a pause for theological reflection, should be the first "moment" of an appropriate response to God. As Cox wrote, "First hear the Voice, then get to work freeing the captives. . . . Theology is important, but it comes after, not before, the commitment to doing . . . discipleship." Cox agreed with a major tenet of liberation theology in its insistence that thought is embedded in the grittiness of real life. He also concurred with those who contended that accompanying the poor and the captives in their pilgrimage is not only an ethical responsibility but also the most promising context for theological reflection. Cox concluded with his contention that liberation theology "is the legitimate, though unanticipated, heir of *The Secular City*."

Cox also anticipated many of the issues that later would be raised by feminist theologians. In perhaps the most widely discussed chapter in *The Secular City*, "Sex and Secularization," Cox exposed the pseudo-sex of the *Playboy* centerfold. Cox argued that the "ideal woman," as portrayed in the centerfold, was preferred because she made no demands whatsoever. As Cox phrased it, the readers "can safely fold her up whenever they want to, which is not possible with the genuine article." He also lampooned the Miss America contest as a representation of the old fertility goddess cults, reworked in the interests of male fantasies and commodity marketing.

Following the publication of *The Secular City*, Cox became a strong force for innovation in the churches. He was in great demand as a speaker and became a proponent of religious creative expression. Writing at a time when "white flight" to the suburbs was becoming a major problem for the cities, Cox called on Christian ministers to pay more attention to the migration of middle-class whites from the cities and address the white racism that pervaded the growing suburbs. His message, however, was not confined to the lecture circuit. Cox was also an activist. He was a cofounder of the Boston chapter of the Southern Christian Leadership Conference, the organization then headed nationally by the Reverend Martin Luther King, Jr., and he actively supported Senator Robert F. Kennedy for president.

Following the publication of *The Secular City*, Cox wrote *On Not Leaving It to the Snake* (1967). The volume was not as popular as his best-seller, which probably had to do with the growing estrangement between the races as the Black

Harvey Cox. AP/WIDE WORLD PHOTOS

Power movement confronted a white backlash that complicated life in the secular city. In the next four decades Cox continued to publish important books about religion. None of his other books, however, was as influential and widely read as *The Secular City*. In 1970 he became Victor Thomas Professor of Divinity at Harvard University.

★

Cox's autobiography is *Just as I Am* (1983). There is no biography of him. The best sources, especially on his accomplishments during the 1960s, are *Current Biography* (1968) and Arvind Sharma, ed., *Religion in a Secular City: Essays in Honor of Harvey Cox* (2001). See also *Harvard Alumni Bulletin* (9 Dec. 1967): 9, and *Time* (15 Mar. 1968): 53.

JACK FISCHEL

CREMIN, Lawrence A(rthur) (*b.* 31 October 1925 in New York City; *d.* 4 September 1990 in New York City), Pulitzer Prize–winning historian, author, and popular educator and administrator who achieved distinction in the 1960s with a pioneering study breaking down the parochialism that for years had separated the fields of education and history.

Cremin was the elder of two children born to Arthur T. Cremin and Theresa Borowick, cofounders of the New York Schools of Music. Cremin spent his youth working with his parents at their music schools. He attended the Model School of Hunter College, and in 1941 graduated from Townsend Harris High School at the age of fifteen. He promptly enrolled at City College of New York (CCNY). His college studies were interrupted by military service during World War II, during which, beginning in 1944, he served nineteen months in the U.S. Army Air Corps, based in Milledgeville, Georgia. Discharged in November 1945, he returned to CCNY. Cremin was elected to Phi Beta Kappa and graduated with a B.S. in social science in 1946. He enrolled at Columbia University's Teachers College in the fall and planned to major in music education, but his exposure to the teachers in the department of social and philosophical foundations of education changed that plan. He received his M.A. in 1947, and his Ph.D. in the history of American education in 1949.

In 1949 Cremin joined the Teachers College faculty. His dissertation *The American Common School: An Historic Conception* was published in 1951, and initiated a prolific writing career; the dissertation was replete with relevant data and "exemplified an instrumental view of education history." From 1952 to 1959 he served as associate editor of the *Teachers College Record* and as editor of the *Classics in Education* series, which eventually numbered over fifty volumes. On 19 September 1956 Cremin married Charlotte Raup, the daughter of R. Bruce Raup, his former teacher and colleague. They had a son and a daughter.

The 1961 publication of *The Transformation of the School: Progressivism in American Education, 1876–1957* solidified Cremin's reputation as the foremost authority in the field of the history of education in America. The book won the 1962 Bancroft Prize in American history and was considered a model of the "new" historiography that championed the "thoughtful interpretation of the role of educational forces in certain great movements in American history." Anticipating the social forces altering U.S. society in the latter half of the 1960s, Cremin's work effectively "located the origins of educational reform in the progressive era and the two preceding decades of liberal dissent." The book showed how progressive education was an integral part of the liberal response to forces, such as industrialization, urbanization, scientific reasoning, and immigration, that were reshaping U.S. society. In 1966 Cremin was awarded an unusual joint appointment as a member of Columbia University's history department and the Teachers College department of philosophy and social sciences.

In many ways *The Transformation of the School* linked the progressive education movement to the humanitarian efforts facing the new urban-industrial civilization. Seeking to explain the social role of progressive education, Cremin

focused his work on four issues: (1) attempting to broaden school programs in health, vocation, and the quality of family and community life; (2) applying in the classroom the pedagogical principles derived from new scientific research in psychology and the social sciences; (3) tailoring instruction to the different types of children entering the public schools; and (4) believing in the radical faith that culture could be "democratized without being vulgarized."

Unlike previous efforts in the history of education, Cremin's work added significant areas of exploration in American intellectual, social, and political history. His theme was that "the exciting revolt against formalism at the turn of the century degenerated into a caricature of itself after 1960." The movement to improve the schools met with some initial success, reaching its height in the 1920s and 1930s, gradually declining in the 1940s, and ultimately dying in the 1950s. Cremin's books persuasively argued that the functions of the school should be broadened "to base teaching on the new science of psychology, to make learning relevant to the pupil, to extend culture to the many, and to look to education as an agency for social change."

Cremin's *Transformation* challenged the often uncritical and celebratory nature of works in American education history. At a time when "the topic of modernization was producing a rich body of historical literature," Cremin's work "showed how discourse on education and educational practice was a major element in one of the great watershed eras in American history." He effectively demonstrated that children and schooling were "central to the goals of those searching" for appropriate responses "to the ills and opportunities of the new urban industrial society." His work was considered pioneering in its efforts to develop "a usable past for educational policy." One reviewer in the *American Historical Review* summed up Cremin's achievement in these words: "He is the first historian to take the transformation of the school seriously enough to place it in the context of history and to give it the considerable attention it deserves." Fittingly, Cremin's book enabled other scholars to challenge the conventional histories of American education. Works like Michael B. Katz's *The Irony of Early American School Reform* and David Tyack's *The One Best System* utilized Cremin's historical approach to explore the social and political forces shaping the structures of American education.

In the 1960s, as social protests against the war in Vietnam and racial discrimination heated up, Cremin continued to explore the social structures of education. Although not a participant in the political and social struggles of the decade, he did explore how education in the United States acted as a fundamental lever of social change. Beginning in 1965 Cremin labored to produce his three-volume masterpiece. The first volume, *American Education: The Colonial Experience, 1607–1783*, appeared in 1970. Ten years later *American Education: The National Experience, 1783– 1876* garnered the Pulitzer Prize for Cremin. The trilogy was completed in 1988 with the publication of *American Education: The Metropolitan Experience, 1876–1980.* All three volumes reiterated Cremin's belief "in the generative significance of ideas, values, and purposeful actions in efforts to educate—hence, the attention given to religious institutions, to thinkers both great and popular, and to individual educational biographies." Beginning with *The Transformation of the School* and concluding with *The Metropolitan Experience,* Cremin's major works viewed schooling as an "adjunct to politics in realizing the promise of American life."

Throughout the 1960s and later, Cremin also managed to publish smaller, more general observations on the history of American education. These works focused on what he termed "configurations of education." In *The Wonderful World of Ellwood Patterson Cubberly* (1965), *The Genius of Education* (1965), *Public Education* (1976), *Traditions of American Education* (1977), and his final work, *Popular Education and Its Discontents* (1990), Cremin forcefully argued "the need to acknowledge in contemporary public policy the fact that 'many institutions educate' and to develop more and better knowledge that might help to ensure that those institutions were effective in educating all the people." The famed Columbia University philosopher and educator John Dewey, who developed the instrumentalist approach in philosophy, proclaimed that children learn best by doing. That idea became the engine driving the progressive education movement. In typical Deweyan fashion, Cremin looked beyond formal schooling to examine what constitutes education. Three of his favorite themes were popularization, "multitudinousness," and politicization. The question of how all three played pivotal roles in shaping public-policy debates in education was at the heart of his historical research.

Although Cremin "considered himself primarily a teacher, not an educational administrator or an author," he was all three. Cremin combined an energetic scholarly pace with involvement in public affairs. The general spirit of activism in the 1960s led to his greater involvement in organizational leadership roles. In 1965 he helped found the National Academy of Education and served as its president from 1969 to 1973. He chaired the Curriculum Improvement Panel of the United States Office of Education from 1963 to 1965, and served on the Carnegie Commission on the Education of Educators from 1966 to 1970. During Cremin's forty-four year association with Teachers College as a student, faculty member, and administrator, he channeled his energies into promoting educational programs that urged future teachers to view schools as a primary mechanism for social and political regeneration. From 1965 to 1974 he was director of the Teachers College Institute

of Philosophy and Politics of Education. He served as Frederick A. P. Barnard Professor of Education from 1974 to 1984, and as the seventh president and first Jewish president of Teachers College, also from 1974 to 1984. While serving as president, he continued to teach a popular course in public policy and education. In 1984 he decided to return to full-time teaching and research. A year later he accepted the presidency of the Spencer Foundation (a public policy and educational think tank) at the University of Chicago. He planned to retire from the foundation's presidency in 1995.

Among his many awards, Cremin received a Guggenheim Fellowship in 1957. In 1969 he received the American Educational Research Association Award and in 1971 New York University's Award for Creative Educational Leadership. In 1972 he was awarded Columbia University's Butler Medal for distinguished service. The sixty-four-year-old Cremin suffered a fatal heart attack on his way to work, and was pronounced dead at Saint Luke's-Roosevelt Hospital near the campus. Cremin is buried at the Beth Israel Memorial Park in Woodbridge, New Jersey.

In a fitting memorial tribute, friend and longtime colleague Harold J. Noah summed up Cremin's contributions to scholarship and learning: "[The] story of American education incorporated a peculiar genius for individual and collective action, so that what was wrong would be presently put right and a better future would surely emerge. He devoted himself . . . to the twin tasks of amelioration and reconstruction." Throughout Cremin's life, his spirit of practical optimism was reflected in his leadership, teaching, and publications.

★

Exhibits and publications in tribute to Cremin, as well as his personal papers, works, and manuscripts, are in the Milbank Library at Teachers College. Cremin did not write a memoir, nor is there a biography. Scholarly articles on Cremin's career and scholarship include Ellen Condliffe Lagemann and Patricia Albjerg Graham, "Lawrence Cremin: A Biographical Memoir," *Teachers College Record* 96, no. 1 (fall 1994): 102–113; Neil Sutherland, "Does Lawrence Cremin Belong in the Canon?" *Historical Studies in Education* 10, nos. 1 and 2 (1998); and Jurgen Herbst, "Cremin's American Paideia," *American Scholar* 61 (winter 1991). Sol Cohen, a former student of Cremin's, examines his contribution in "The History of the History of American Education, 1900–1976: The Uses of the Past," *Harvard Educational Review* 46 (Aug. 1976); and in "Lawrence A. Cremin: Hostage to History," *Historical Studies in Education* 10, nos. 1 and 2 (1998), which places Cremin's scholarship within the context of humanistic studies. Diane Ravitch wrote a moving tribute, "Lawrence Cremin," in *American Scholar* 61 (winter 1992): 83–89. Obituaries are in the *New York Times* and *Washington Post* (both 5 Sept. 1990), *Chicago Tribune* (6 Sept. 1990), *Los Angeles Times* (8 Sept.

1990), and the American Historical Association's newsletter, *Perspectives* 28, no. 8 (Nov. 1990).

CHARLES F. HOWLETT

CRONKITE, Walter Leland, Jr. (*b.* 4 November 1916 in Saint Joseph, Missouri), television anchorman who steered both the *CBS Evening News* and many Americans through rough waters in the 1960s, gaining a reputation as the "most trusted man in America."

Cronkite was the only child of Walter Leland Cronkite, Sr., a dentist, and Helen Lena Fritsche, a homemaker. He traced his early love of journalism to the inspiration of a high school teacher. While attending the University of Texas from 1933 to 1935, Cronkite worked on the college newspaper the *Daily Texan* and as a stringer (freelance journalist) for the *Houston Post,* in addition to holding a part-time job at a radio station. "I just fell in love with the darn business," he said later. He was so busy pursuing stories that he dropped out of college to take up journalism full-time. He returned to Missouri in 1936 to work at a Kansas City radio station, where he met a fellow journalist, Mary Elizabeth Simmons Maxwell, known as Betsy, whom he married on 30 March 1940.

In 1937 Cronkite joined United Press International (UPI); he worked for the press bureau throughout World War II, covering European action, including the D day invasion. He earned a reputation as a fast, ambitious, accurate journalist who could convey to the public both the intricacies and the ambiance of battle. He reported the Nuremberg war crimes trials and served as Moscow bureau chief for UPI from 1946 to 1948. When his wife became pregnant with the first of their three children, the pair returned to the United States, and Cronkite served as Washington, D.C., correspondent for several Midwest radio stations.

Cronkite joined the Columbia Broadcasting System (CBS) network news division in 1950, expecting to be sent to cover the Korean War. CBS had just purchased a Washington, D.C., television station, however, and instead put him on the air as an anchor there. They also assigned him to special network coverage, such as political conventions, and to other CBS news programs, including the mock-documentary program *You Are There,* which he hosted from 1953 to 1957. Cronkite later said of this work, "Those early days of television had to be about as exciting an assignment as anybody could ever have—any news person. We literally figured out how to do it as we went along."

In April 1962 CBS decided to replace Douglas Edwards, the anchor of its fifteen-minute evening newscast, with Cronkite. Cronkite took to the job, which he held for nineteen years. He immediately sought the title "managing editor" to indicate that he was not just reading the *CBS*

Evening News but also writing and shaping it. In September 1963 CBS expanded the newscast to half an hour; it was the first network to do so, although the National Broadcasting Company (NBC) quickly followed suit. In November 1963 Cronkite, who was already well known (having won a George Foster Peabody Award for his work in broadcasting the previous year), became a central figure in American life when he reported the shooting of President John F. Kennedy. Cronkite stayed on the air for much of the next four days, guiding Americans through the president's death, the swift transfer of power, and the funeral of the slain leader.

"The fact is that any news person, at a time like that, is not really aware of anything except getting the story out," Cronkite later said of the assassination. Nevertheless, his calm demeanor helped Americans get through those days. The NBC news anchor Tom Brokaw recalled almost four decades after the event, "When the world needed someone to turn to when John F. Kennedy was killed, [Walter Cronkite] became the father figure of this country." Cronkite went on to cover every major news story of that news-filled decade, including the murders of two more leaders, Robert F. Kennedy and Martin Luther King, Jr.

In 1964 Cronkite suffered his only major setback at CBS when the NBC news team of Chet Huntley and David Brinkley beat him severely in the ratings at the Republican National Convention and he was replaced by the newsmen Robert Trout and Roger Mudd in the CBS anchor booth at the Democratic convention. Cronkite weathered the storm, however, and when Trout and Mudd fared no better, he was assured that he would be in charge of covering future conventions. On a day-to-day basis, Cronkite ran neck and neck in the ratings with the regular evening newscast hosted by Huntley and Brinkley. As the decade progressed, he eventually emerged as the clear ratings leader.

One of Cronkite's great loves was the space program, which he covered extensively, beginning with Alan Shepard's first U.S. manned space flight in 1961. Cronkite later stated, "I think that our conquest of space will probably be the most important story of the whole 20th century." He studied the science behind space flight in order to explain its intricacies. He also shared his enthusiasm with his audience; his first words at the time of the *Apollo 11* lunar landing in 1969 were "Oh, boy! Whew! Oh, boy!"

In general, however, Cronkite appeared unflappable and objective onscreen—a trait that made his rare strayings into editorializing particularly potent. By early 1968 Cronkite, like many Americans, was beginning to doubt the validity of the nation's involvement in Vietnam. In February he journeyed to the battlefield to view the U.S. war effort. At the end of his CBS report on what he found there, he concluded that the United States was "mired in stalemate." He went on to suggest, "The only rational way out then

Walter Cronkite. AP/WIDE WORLD PHOTOS

will be to negotiate, not as victors but as an honorable people who lived up to their pledge to defend democracy and did the best they could."

Historians are divided in evaluating the influence of this broadcast on American public opinion and politics. Some argue that Cronkite only followed the will of the American people in advocating a negotiated end to the conflict. Others suggest that Cronkite's remarks and their effect on viewers helped persuade Lyndon B. Johnson not to run for another term as president. Tom Johnson, an LBJ aide, later recalled hearing Johnson say, "If I've lost Walter Cronkite, I've lost the war." Whether Cronkite's comments on Vietnam led or merely summed up the nation's opinion, his broadcast certainly constituted a key moment in public debate.

Another moment in which Cronkite let viewers know his opinion came during the Democratic National Convention in Chicago in 1968. After watching Mayor Richard Daley's minions throw the reporter Dan Rather onto the floor, Cronkite declared, "I think we've got a bunch of thugs here, Dan." Beginning in 1969 Cronkite defended journalists in speeches off camera when the Nixon administration, particularly Vice President Spiro Agnew, began to attack the press as a conspiratorial band of eastern left-leaning elitists. As Ron Powers pointed out in *Quill* in 1973, Cronkite also confounded charges of eastern elitism every night on the air just by being himself. Powers wrote that Cronkite "looked less like an Eastern intellectual than a

Tulsa general practitioner, and . . . had the extremely annoying habit of popping up in opinion polls everywhere as the most trusted man in America."

Cronkite went on to do Emmy Award–winning work on the Watergate scandal in 1972 and 1973 and to pioneer in international relations in 1977 by arranging a meeting between Egyptian president Anwar Sadat of Egypt and prime minister Menachem Begin of Israel. Despite rumored overtures from the Democratic Party, the popular avowed Independent never chose to attempt a career in politics. Cronkite was awarded the Presidential Medal of Freedom in 1981 by President Jimmy Carter. After his retirement from the anchor chair that same year, Cronkite worked on television specials and spent time aboard his beloved sailboat. In his seventies and eighties, the elder statesman served as an eloquent advocate for the unrestricted access of journalists to U.S. wars in the Persian Gulf and Afghanistan. Nevertheless, he often looked back on the 1960s as a challenging decade for journalists and for Americans overall. In a 1996 television special, he noted, "The '60s undoubtedly were the most turbulent decade of this century. There were the assassinations. The race riots. The Vietnam War. It was an incredible decade." He observed that the 1960s brought the "full flowering" of television news. Much of this flowering can be attributed directly to Cronkite, whom Tom Wicker in the *New York Times* called "a modest man who succeeded extravagantly by remaining mostly himself." When Cronkite uttered his trademark phrase, "And that's the way it is," Americans believed him.

★

Cronkite's autobiography, *A Reporter's Life* (1996), is the most complete recounting of his life, followed by the related CBS television special *Cronkite Remembers* (1996). A doting, but informative biography is Doug James, *Walter Cronkite: His Life and Times* (1991). Ron Powers interviewed Cronkite at length for *Playboy* (June 1973). See also Powers's article in *Quill* (June 1973), "The Essential Cronkite." A mid-1960s article that reveals Cronkite's feelings about the ratings war with NBC is Richard Schickel, "Walter Cronkite: He Must Be Doing Something Right," *TV Guide* (2 July 1966).

TINKY "DAKOTA" WEISBLAT

CROSBY, STILLS, AND NASH (Crosby, David Van Cortlandt, *b.* 14 August 1941 in Los Angeles, California; Stephen Arthur Stills, *b.* 3 January 1945 in Dallas, Texas; and Graham Nash, *b.* 2 February 1942 in Blackpool, Lancashire, England), folk-rock trio who came together at the end of the 1960s to form a massively successful "supergroup" after being prominent members of other popular groups.

Crosby was the youngest of two children born to Floyd Crosby, an Academy Award–winning cinematographer, and Aliph (Van Corlandt) Crosby, a homemaker. He showed an early interest in classical music as well as a natural aptitude for harmony singing when the family performed folk songs together in the living room. He also developed an interest in jazz, the music favored by his older brother, Floyd Crosby, Jr. (nicknamed Chip and later known as Ethan). He was not, however, interested in academics, and although his parents could afford to send him to private schools, he was expelled from a series of them. His brother taught him to play the guitar and, caught up in the folk boom of the late 1950s, he began performing publicly in 1958, at first in Los Angeles and later in New York City, San Francisco, and elsewhere. He returned to Los Angeles in the fall of 1962 and joined one of the editions of Les Baxter's Balladeers, a commercial folk group that appeared on the 1963 album *Jack Linkletter Presents a Folk Festival*, Crosby's first recording.

Leaving the Baxter group, Crosby returned to performing solo and caught the ear of the producer Jim Dickson, who recorded demos on him at World Pacific Studios in early 1964. Nothing came of that, but later Crosby hooked up with the duo of Jim (later Roger) McGuinn and Gene Clark to form a folk trio initially called the Jet Set, which made further demos that led to a contract with Elektra Records. Elektra changed the group's name to the Beefeaters for their sole single, "Please Let Me Love You"/"Don't Be

Long." The single was a failure, and Elektra dropped the group, but they stayed together, adding the drummer Michael Clarke and the bassist Chris Hillman, renaming themselves the Byrds, and getting a new contract with Columbia Records. Their first single in this configuration, a cover of Bob Dylan's "Mr. Tambourine Man," became a number-one hit in June 1965, and their third single, "Turn! Turn! Turn! (To Everything There Is a Season)," followed it to the top of the charts that December. The Byrds continued to score hits over the next two years as dissension rent the group, leading to the departures of Clark and Clarke. Crosby's strong personality led to conflict with the remaining members, McGuinn and Hillman, who bought out his share in the band and fired him in the fall of 1967.

Crosby married Jan Dance on 16 May 1987; they had one child. Another child, a daughter, was born in 1974 to his then-girlfriend, Debbie Donovan, and he also acknowledged fathering a son, James Raymond, by an unnamed woman. Crosby and his son would later perform in a band called CPR. In addition, he is the biological father of the two sons born to Julie Cypher and her former companion, the singer Melissa Etheridge, via artificial fertilization.

Stills was one of two children born to William Stills, an engineer who worked in various businesses, and Talitha Stills, a homemaker. The family moved frequently, and Stills grew up largely in Louisiana and Florida. An early interest in music, starting with the drums, was encouraged by his parents. While attending Admiral Farragut Military Academy in Saint Petersburg, Florida, he took up the guitar. By his teens he was playing in local bands. After his family moved to San José, Costa Rica, he finished high school there in 1963 and then briefly attended the University of Florida in Gainesville before turning to a career in music, at first in New Orleans and then in New York City. In 1964–1965 he was a member of a large commercial folk group, the Au Go-Go Singers, patterned after the New Christy Minstrels, releasing an album, *They Call Us the Au Go-Go Singers*. After that group broke up, he moved to Los Angeles, where he continued to struggle until March 1966, when he put together the folk-rock band Buffalo Springfield. Although the group never reached its full potential, it released three albums and scored a Top Ten hit with the Stills composition "For What It's Worth (Stop, Hey, What's That Sound?)" before breaking up in the spring of 1968.

Stills married the French singer Veronique Sanson on 14 March 1973; they had two children and divorced in 1981. He married Pamela Ann Jordan in December 1981. They had one child and later divorced. A third marriage, to Kristen Hathoway (27 May 1996), also produced a child, and Stills has acknowledged paternity of a son born to Harriet Tunis.

Nash was one of three children born to William and

Mary Nash. His father was in the army, and his mother had been evacuated from their home in Manchester when he was born. At the end of World War II, William Nash went to work in a foundry; Mary Nash later worked as an office administrator in a dairy. Nash met Allan Clarke during his first year of school, when he was five years old. Nash and Clarke became friends and sang together as children. By their teens they were performing publicly, by 1960 they were playing guitars and performing in bands, and in early 1962 they formed the Hollies. The group had the first of a long string of hits on the British charts in 1963, and in 1964 they followed the Beatles to America. But by 1968 Nash, looking for a greater outlet for his songwriting, quit.

Nash married and divorced Rose Eccles in the 1960s. He married Susan Sennett on 4 May 1977; they had three children.

Crosby, Stills and Nash came together in Los Angeles in 1968, working out three-part harmonies for their original songs and singing them for friends in the music business. Atlantic Records signed them and released their self-titled debut album in May 1969. It became a multimillion seller and spawned Top Forty hits in Nash's "Marrakesh Express" and Stills's "Suite: Judy Blue Eyes" (written for the singer Judy Collins, with whom he had a romantic relationship). In preparing to tour to promote the album, the trio decided to bring in a fourth member, Neil Young, a former member of Buffalo Springfield. Their appearance at the celebrated Woodstock Festival in August 1969 was only their second live performance. Their next single, a Top Twenty hit, was "Woodstock," written by the singer-songwriter Joni Mitchell. It prefaced their first album as a quartet, *Déjà Vu*, released in March 1970. This album topped the charts and spawned two other hits, Nash's "Teach Your Children" and "Our House." The group also reached the Top Twenty in 1970 with Young's "Ohio," a song written in protest against the killing of antiwar demonstrators at Kent State University.

By mid-1970, Crosby, Stills, Nash and Young were one of the most popular groups in the United States. They chose this moment to break up. A 1974 reunion tour was an enormous success, and in 1977 Crosby, Stills and Nash re-formed on a permanent basis. Although they were hampered by Crosby's drug and legal problems in the 1980s, they persevered and even reunited with Young on occasion, such as on the successful "CSNY2K" tour in early 2000.

Crosby, Stills and Nash represented a new phase in popular music at the end of the 1960s that reflected the influence of socially conscious folk music and rock 'n' roll but developed beyond it. The group was always a collective of songwriters presenting their individual compositions in a group context that showed the material off in its best light. Their work in the 1960s, both in their separate bands and together, proved to be only the start of a long, sometimes troubled career that remained vibrant at the end of the twentieth century.

★

The story of Crosby, Stills and Nash is told in their authorized biography, *Crosby, Stills and Nash* (1984), with text by Dave Zimmer and Henry Diltz, an excellent account updated with a new chapter for a 2000 reprint. The story is brought forward in Johnny Rogan, *Crosby, Stills, Nash and Young: The Visual Documentary* (1996), which is more of an illustrated chronology than a biography as such, and in David Crosby, *Long Time Gone: The Autobiography of David Crosby* (1988), written with Carl Gottlieb, a cautionary tale of not quite Augustinian proportions.

WILLIAM RUHLMANN

CRUMB, Robert (*b.* 30 August 1943 in Philadelphia, Pennsylvania), prominent "underground" cartoonist whose work was credited with revitalizing the comic book genre in the late 1960s.

The second child and second son of Charles Crumb, Sr., a career marine, and homemaker Bea Crumb, Crumb grew up on various military bases. His family's itinerant existence proved difficult for Crumb, who had trouble making new friends and fitting in. Life at home was not much better, as Robert and his siblings were targets of their father's physical and emotional abuse. As a boy, Crumb also watched his mother succumb to an amphetamine addiction. In an interview conducted in 1985, Crumb describes himself as a boy, saying, "I was very shy and scared of people and life, and I just retreated into drawing." But drawing was not entirely Crumb's idea. His older brother Charles, Jr., forced Crumb and his younger brother Max into creating their own comic books, an activity that Charles, Jr., knew his father abhorred, and for which the younger brothers would be punished.

Yet even at that early age, Crumb found solace in his art. He remembered that one day when he was sixteen he imagined that when he became "this great recognized artist, I wouldn't be alienated anymore." After graduating from high school in Milford, Delaware, in 1961, Crumb moved to Cleveland, where he took a job as a colorist for the American Greetings Corporation. His boss Tom Wilson, who later created the syndicated comic strip *Ziggy*, found Crumb's work so impressive that he allowed Crumb to design and draw all the humorous cards for the company. Still Crumb's work was not for everyone. Another of his superiors at the American Greetings Corporation found Crumb's work "too grotesque" and so had him "draw this cute stuff, which influenced my technique, and even now my work has this cuteness about it." During this period, Crumb also continued to work on his own cartoons.

In 1965 Crumb began experimenting with hallucinogenic drugs, an experience he credits with making him "stop taking cartooning so seriously." A year later, while visiting friends in Chicago, Crumb "took some weird acid. . . . and all this crazy stuff came out of my brain," which resulted in his conceiving some of the most memorable cartoon characters ever to grace a page. Soon afterward, Crumb quit his job at American Greetings and by 1967 had moved to the Haight-Ashbury district in San Francisco, then the center of the 1960s counterculture. While immersing himself in drugs, Crumb became part of a group of cartoonists whose work was deeply subversive toward what they regarded as the moralistic code of the comic book industry. Just a year later, in 1968, Crumb emerged as the most significant and influential figure of this "underground" movement when his first book *Zap* appeared in February. Because no mainstream distributor would take on underground comics, Crumb and his publisher sold copies of *Zap* on street corners throughout San Francisco.

A favorite target of Crumb's comics was middle-class America, and his cartoons were often sexually explicit and graphic in their depiction of violence. Among his most memorable characters were Flakey Foont, a suburban nebbish filled with doubts and hang-ups, Angelfood McSpade, a simple African-American girl exploited by greedy and lecherous white men, the small sex-fiend Mister Snoid, and Whiteman, a patriotic and moralistic businessman who is both sexually repressed and obsessed. Yet Crumb did not simply mock the middle class. He lampooned certain elements of the counterculture as well, depicting Mr. Natural, a sham guru, as exploiting his followers. Crumb's most famous character was Fritz the Cat, who first appeared in *Comics and Stories*, published in 1969. Fritz gained stardom as the first X-rated cartoon character in the film *Fritz the Cat* (1972), but Crumb hated the film so much that he killed his popular character with an ice pick through the forehead.

With *Zap* comics, Crumb also reintroduced the popular saying "Keep On Truckin'," a favorite among blues musicians of the 1930s. The phrase was often accompanied by a "series of screwball cartoon characters with tiny heads, funky old clothes and huge clodhoppers, strutting on down the street." The saying became one of the more enduring catch phrases of the 1960s, as a sign of perseverance and goodwill. According to one writer, "Crumb brought 'trash' art into the cultural mainstream and made it respectable."

In 1968 Crumb became the first underground cartoonist to have his work appear in what members of the counterculture referred to as a "straight" publication. A collection of Crumb's early comic strips and the original story "Fritz the Cat" were brought out in book form as *Head Comix* by the Viking Press. Despite the controversy surrounding his work, Crumb's comic books were soon selling between

Robert Crumb. ARCHIVE PHOTOS, INC.

8,000 and 10,000 copies per month. Although the numbers were small compared with popular mainstream comic books, Crumb developed a growing number of fans who clamored for his work, which was also gaining serious critical attention. Additional evidence of his influence comes from the increasing numbers who condemned his work as obscene. Whether praised or censured, Crumb's work clearly gave visual definition to the counterculture of the 1960s.

By the 1970s, however, Crumb's popularity had ebbed. Rebelling against his own success, Crumb ceased to draw some of his most popular characters and refused assignments from high-profile magazines. His first marriage, in 1964, to Dana Morgan collapsed in 1977, and he owed a considerable amount in back taxes. In 1978 Crumb married artist and cartoonist Aline Kominsky, and slowly began to make a comeback. By the 1980s, his work had evolved. Retaining his sharp and satirical edge, Crumb focused less on sexual themes and more on the greed and materialism that characterized the decade. He also branched out, illustrating cards and books and having a one-man show of his abstract paintings at a San Francisco gallery. Cartooning, though, remained his passion, and Crumb continued to produce comic books. He also stopped taking drugs, and instead began to sketch when he felt panicked or nervous.

Much of Crumb's work has been collected and published. Two such works include *Carload O' Comics* (1976), and *The Complete Crumb* (1998).

Throughout his career, critics have decried Crumb's racist and sexist stereotypes, which were particularly evident in the work he did during the 1960s. Crumb does not shy away from his critics and has admitted that "revealing the truth about myself is somehow helpful." One art critic, by contrast, has called Crumb the "Brueghel of the second half of the twentieth century," comparing him to the late-medieval Flemish painter whose work focused on ordinary people and everyday life, rather than religious subjects or the elite. As a chronicler of U.S. society during the 1960s, Crumb offered an idiosyncratic vision that made him a cultural icon, and his reputation as one of its most cogent observers of that decade has endured.

★

The closest thing to a biography of Crumb is Monte Beauchamp, *The Life and Times of R. Crumb: Comments from Contemporaries* (1998.) Assisted by Carl Richter, Crumb also compiled *Crumb-ology: The Works of R. Crumb* (1995). For Crumb's place in the history of comic books, see Donald M. Fiene, *R. Crumb Checklist of Work and Criticism: With a Biographical Supplement and a Full Set of Indexes* (1981), and Mark James Estren, *A History of Underground Comics* (1993).

MEG GREENE

CUNNINGHAM, Harry Blair (*b.* 23 July 1907 in Home Camp, Pennsylvania; *d.* 11 November 1992 in North Palm Beach, Florida), discount retail pioneer who opened the first Kmart store in 1962 and transformed the company into a retail giant during his tenure as president and chief executive officer of S. S. Kresge Company (later Kmart Corporation) from 1959 to 1970.

Cunningham was born on a Pennsylvania farm and graduated from Mifflintown High School in 1925. He left college after his sophomore year at Miami University in Oxford, Ohio, to work as a reporter at the *Harrisburg Patriot* newspaper from 1927 to 1928. That year, he entered the management training program of S. S. Kresge Company, a variety-store retailer founded in 1899 as a five-and-dime company. In 1935 he married Margaret Diefendorf, with whom he had three daughters. He worked his way up from the stockroom, becoming a store manager in 1940 and a district manager in 1947.

Cunningham's steep rise to success began in 1951, when he was promoted to assistant sales director at the company's Michigan headquarters. It was his idea to experiment with the same checkout system that had gained popularity in grocery stores, and the system helped the company expand into new suburban shopping centers throughout the 1950s. Company leaders recognized Cunningham's leadership potential, first inviting him to attend board meetings and then appointing him as a director in 1956.

In 1957 the company's board of directors created the new post of general vice president and appointed Cunningham, assigning him to the task of finding new, profitable endeavors for Kresge. He spent two years crisscrossing the country, racking up 100,000 miles in the air, to study a phenomenon just beginning to sweep the retail industry—discounting. "The retailers I visited walked their stores and shared their experiences with me," Cunningham said later. "At the end of two years I probably knew as much about discounting as anyone in America." At that time Kresge was made up of variety stores of about 6,000 square feet, which stocked mostly small items marked up as much as possible. Discounting, on the other hand, involved constructing larger stores and pricing with smaller markups, with the profits coming from faster turnover of merchandise. Cunningham saw that the concept fit with the emerging trend of more bargain-conscious consumers.

When Cunningham was appointed company president in 1959, he set Kresge on a path to becoming a discounter. Three years later he oversaw the opening of the first Kmart store in a Detroit suburb. It had about forty departments, ranging from an auto service and tire center to clothing, sporting goods, and a patio and garden shop. The store, the first of eighteen Kmarts to open that year, was what Cunningham later described as a "miniature one-stop shopping center." As cities nationwide saw retail development moving out of their cores and into the outskirts, Kmart stores ranging from 60,000 to 132,000 square feet sprouted up in suburbs, surrounded by parking lots with room for hundreds of cars. Kresge became the first variety store chain to jump into the discount business.

Some skeptics at the time thought discounting was a "flash in the pan that had run its course," according to a 1966 article in *Business Week*. But after years of lagging profits, the Kmart transformation caused the company's sales to zoom up more than 20 percent a year through the 1960s. As less-profitable Kresge stores closed, more than forty new Kmarts opened each year. In 1966 the company surpassed $1 billion in sales, up from $450 million in 1962. In 1967 Cunningham was elected chairman of the company's board. By 1970 Kresge was the nation's number-one discounter, with growth that outpaced rivals, including Sears, Roebuck and Company, J. C. Penney Company, and F. W. Woolworth Company, which had been much slower in opening its Woolco discount department stores. Sales for Kresge were $2.2 billion by 1970, and the company had 33.7 million square feet of retail space.

In 1970 Cunningham resigned as president, remaining as board chairman until 1972, when he relinquished duties to his chosen successor Robert E. Dewar. Cunningham was named honorary chairman in 1973, a post he held until 1992, when he died in his sleep at age eighty-five. The company changed its name to Kmart Corporation in 1977.

Even after Kmart's meteoric growth became overshadowed by the rise of rival Wal-Mart in the 1970s and 1980s, Kmart remained a powerful force in retailing, growing at one point to more than 4,000 stores. In the 1990s Kmart stumbled with consumers as it failed to keep up with the upgrading and modernizing of its competitors. The company closed waves of lower-performing stores, eventually filing for debt protection in bankruptcy court in 2002. It was the largest retail bankruptcy filing in history.

In spite of the demise of Kmart, Cunningham's legacy as a retail pioneer remained strong. Wal-Mart founder Sam Walton wrote in his autobiography that Cunningham's leadership helped spur Wal-Mart to its own success as the world's largest company. Cunningham, he wrote, "should be remembered as one of the leading retailers of all time." In 1993 David Pinto, editor of *Mass Market Retailers* magazine, wrote that Cunningham was "quite simply the single most important figure in the history of discount retailing in America."

★

Cunningham was profiled in *Business Week* magazine (29 Jan. 1966 and 24 Oct. 1970). David Pinto's column is in *Mass Market Retailers* (8 Feb. 1993). An obituary is in the *New York Times* (13 Nov. 1992).

LEIGH DYER

CUNNINGHAM, Mercier Philip ("Merce") (*b.* 16 April 1919 in Centralia, Washington), dancer and pioneering choreographer who in the 1960s began earning recognition for his dance events—collaborations with musicians and artists that relied on chance for their outcomes.

Cunningham was one of three children of Clifford Cunningham, a lawyer, and Marion Cunningham. He started taking dance lessons at the age of eight, a decision his parents fully supported. In high school Cunningham studied tap with Maud Barrett, who belonged to the same Catholic church as the Cunninghams. Barrett was an energetic, somewhat eccentric woman who inspired Cunningham to approach dance with a sense of adventure and fun.

Cunningham attended the University of Washington in Seattle for one year in 1937, then decided to go to New York City to pursue a career in theater. His parents refused, and referred him instead to Seattle's Cornish School for Performing and Visual Arts, which he attended in 1938 and 1939. It was here that he discovered the Graham technique (which he studied under Bonnie Bird) and met the composer John Cage, who became his lifelong partner. Cun-

Merce Cunningham. CUNNINGHAM DANCE FOUNDATION INC.

ningham spent his summers at Mills College in Oakland, California, where he took classes from the dancer and choreographer Martha Graham. Graham invited Cunningham to join her company in New York; he was a soloist with the Graham Company from 1939 to 1945.

Cunningham presented his first solo concert in New York in 1944, and began a lifelong collaboration with Cage, which continued until the composer's death in 1992. In 1947 the author and dance impresario Lincoln Kirstein commissioned Cunningham to create a work for the New City Ballet. Cunningham formed his first company of six dancers in 1953 at Black Mountain College in North Carolina; they gave their first New York performance in 1954. The musicians were Cage and David Tudor; Robert Rauschenberg, the company's artistic advisor, made the posters for the concert. The week of performances received not one printed word of review.

In 1954 Cunningham received his first Guggenheim Fellowship, which, he said, "saved my life," but the company continued to struggle financially and received little critical acclaim in the United States for the remainder of that decade. In 1964 Cunningham and his company prepared for a world tour, which proved a turning point. Rauschenberg and Cage sold art, and friends donated funds to help finance the tour. From 1965 to 1968 the company made numerous appearances in the United States and abroad, but it continued to be financed largely by the sale of works by such artists as Joan Miró, Jasper Johns, and Marcel Duchamp. Cunningham did not receive a salary until 1967.

Cunningham did not create works designed to make audience members think or feel a certain way. He relied entirely on chance in the construction of his performances. The choreography was done independently of sets and the music, which was usually performed live. These elements were not combined until the last possible moment.

For *Winterbranch* (1963), Cunningham derived the movement from the motion of falling. Rauschenberg, who designed the lighting, focused noncolored lights differently at each performance. Consequently, they lit the dancers directly only by happenstance. Often, more than half of *Winterbranch* would be performed in complete darkness. The musical score, by La Monte Young, consisted of two tape-recorded sounds played at near-deafening levels.

In *Story* (1963), Cunningham had his dancers select their costumes each evening from a pile of clothing and props on the stage, and then decide what to do with them. Rauschenberg was on stage during the performance, constructing the scenery using found objects.

Cunningham gave his dancers the freedom to choose from a menu of gestures and movements in *Field Dances* (1963), and to arrange their choices as they pleased, or not to perform at all. In *Variations V* (1965), the movement of the dancers interacting with sensors in the set triggered electronic signals that prompted the musicians to generate the sound. The set consisted of movies, television images, a bicycle, a gym mat, plastic plants, and furniture. *How to Pass, Kick, Fall, and Run* (1965), a piece inspired by images from sports and games, was performed to the sound of Cage reading aloud several of his stories.

In 1967 Johns replaced Rauschenberg as the company's artistic advisor, and an increasing number of artists collaborated with Cunningham in his works. Frank Stella designed the sets for *Scramble* (1967), Andy Warhol for *RainForest* (1968), Johns and Duchamp for *Walkaround Time* (1968), and Robert Morris for *Canfield* (1969). Cunningham continued to rely on chance for the outcomes of his pieces. For *RainForest,* Warhol designed helium-filled Mylar pillows that drifted around the stage buoyed by air currents generated by the dancers' movements; the lighting changed for each performance.

Cunningham based the choreography for *Canfield* on the game of solitaire, composing it in thirteen sections with interludes between each. The arrangement and inclusion of the sections was usually determined on the day of the performance, hence the length of the performance varied from 20 to 105 minutes. The "score" consisted of three pages of typewritten instructions, which only generally described the type of equipment the musicians were to obtain and the types and continuity of sounds they were to pro-

duce. Johns's set consisted of a backdrop coated with a highly reflective substance, and the dancers' costumes were to be made of the same material. Depending on chance had its risks; Johns said of *Canfield*'s premiere, "Nothing worked as intended."

Cunningham was also known for his "event performances" in the 1960s. These were uninterrupted, evening-long, nonrepertory works that he specifically choreographed for nonproscenium spaces such as gymnasiums or, in one instance, New York's Grand Central Station.

The 1960s were a time of experimentation, revolution, and freedom, and Cunningham embodied all of these forces. His followers at that time were largely other artists, but that began to change in the 1970s as his work gained exposure through regular video and television performances in New York. By the 1980s his company had an annual two-week season in New York City and regularly received respectful reviews and grant money. In 1988 they performed thirteen works over four weeks, with seven performances each week; Cunningham had become mainstream. He continued to perform with the company through the 1980s. In 1991 Cunningham performed in *Trackers,* partnering with a portable ballet barre.

Cunningham was "the key issue dividing the world of modern dance" in the 1960s, according to his biographer Richard Kostelanetz. At a time when people were questioning structures, Cunningham saw that dance could be done in another way, that anything, in fact, could be considered dance: performing a grand jeté, riding a bicycle, or simply standing still. For Cunningham, "Dance is a visible action of life." He revolutionized the way we think about and look at dance.

★

The partly autobiographical *Changes: Notes on Choreography* (1968), written by Cunningham and edited by Frances Starr, relates Cunningham's ideas on dance using his original working notebooks as source material. James Klosty, ed., *Merce Cunningham* (1975), includes an informative introduction followed by more than a dozen contributions by some of Cunningham's dancers and collaborators, including Carolyn Brown and John Cage; several striking photographs are also included. Elinor Rogosin, *The Dancemakers: Conversations with American Choreographers* (1980), offers a brief interview with Cunningham and the author's observations on his work. *The Dancer and the Dance: Merce Cunningham in Conversation with Jacqueline Lesschaeve* (1985) provides detailed descriptions and in-depth analyses of Cunningham's work by the choreographer himself. Richard Kostelanetz, ed., *Merce Cunningham: Dancing in Space and Time* (1992), is a compilation of essays by Cunningham's friends and colleagues from the 1950s to the early 1990s. David Vaughan, *Merce Cunningham: Fifty Years* (1997), also contains some biographical information.

KATHARINE FISHER BRITTON

D

DALEY, Richard Joseph (*b.* 15 May 1902 in Chicago, Illinois; *d.* 20 December 1976 in Chicago, Illinois), Democratic mayor of Chicago for six consecutive terms (1955–1976); he was thrust into the media spotlight after the assassination of Martin Luther King, Jr., in 1968.

Daley, an only child, was raised in an Irish neighborhood in Chicago. His father was Michael Daley, a sheet-metal worker, and his mother was Lillian Dunne. While growing up, Daley worked at a variety of part-time jobs and attended Catholic schools. He also attended De La Salle Institute, a vocational high school. In 1924 he was elected president of the Hamburg Council, a neighborhood organization with considerable influence; it was his first taste of politics. During the evenings Daley attended law school.

Daley graduated from DePaul University law school in 1934. On 23 June 1936 Daley married Eleanor Guilfoyle; they had seven children. Also in 1936 Daley began his political climb in the Democratic Party, enjoying his first big political win in a race for state representative. In 1955 Daley became Chicago's mayor, a post he held for the next two decades. His power base as the Cook County Democratic Central Committee chairman and city mayor gave him tight control over Chicago politics and put him into the central spotlight during the 1960s.

During the tumult that characterized the 1960s, Daley focused on moving ahead. He was on a mission to make his city great. He encouraged projects that would improve Chicago, including the construction of downtown skyscrapers, such as the Sears Tower, which was the world's tallest building at the time, and the enlargement of the O'Hare airport. Daley's improvements also included new public housing, expressway expansion, demolition of derelict areas, and urban renewal efforts. In his role as mayor, Daley was loved by some and loathed by others. During the 1960s he was praised for his effective municipal services initiatives and his downtown revitalization efforts, but he was criticized for his failure to address the concerns of Chicago's African-American poor and for his roughshod treatment of civil liberties.

Some might quibble about how Daley used his power, but during the turbulent 1960s he did keep the city running. Through giving municipal employees high wages and keeping layoffs at a minimum, Daley was able to bring labor peace to the city of Chicago during his tenure as mayor. He had many boyhood friends who held positions of power in the unions, and they helped him weather tumultuous labor uprisings. In 1960 Daley helped John F. Kennedy win the presidential election, and thereafter presidential candidates sought Daley's blessing. Daley was recognized as an important political force. Those who were seeking political office soon learned that Daley's support was crucial to their success. But Daley's reputation as a "president maker" did not survive the 1960s because of the crises he faced.

In 1968 Daley's star was eclipsed by disasters. In April,

when the civil rights leader Martin Luther King, Jr., was assassinated, riots ensued on the West Side of Chicago, along with arson and looting. As mayor, Daley was responsible for curbing the outbreak. He issued orders to "shoot to kill any arsonist," and this strict policy drew the censure of the outraged liberal news media. Daley was remembered by some for his response to the resultant civil disobedience, a response that many considered harsh.

As bad as the chaos that followed King's assassination was, more was to come. Daley had to face turmoil in August during the 1968 Democratic National Convention, when the actions of anti–Vietnam War demonstrators sparked retaliation by Chicago police. Although it is difficult to determine the exact sequence of events from accounts, one thing is clear: innocent people were caught up in the strife. Street violence between demonstrators and police lasted a week. Chicago was like a war zone, which the commentator Eric Sevareid compared to the Russian invasion of Czechoslovakia. The debacle made Daley notorious; his reputation was irreparably damaged.

Many predicted that the riots of the 1960s would mean the end of Daley's career. This was not exactly the case. It was true that Daley was no longer respected in some circles, but he continued to hold office as mayor. In December 1969 Daley shared the chagrin of the Democratic Party when the state's attorney Edward V. Hanrahan staged a police raid that ended in the deaths of two black members of the Black Panthers and stirred up racial unrest. In 1971 Daley's reputation was damaged further by the Chicago columnist Mike Royko, whose best-seller *Boss: Richard J. Daley of Chicago* exposed many of the scandals that plagued Daley's administration. Daley's own blunders contributed to the scorn and contempt some held for him. Among his famous misstatements are the following: "We must rise to high and higher platitudes" (instead of plateaus) and "The police are not here to create disorder; they are here to preserve disorder."

Still more disgrace was to come. U.S. attorney and later governor James R. Thompson exposed corruption among Chicago's police force during the 1970s, and members of the police force and a number of Daley's close friends and associates were put in jail. Although others were convicted of corruption, Daley himself was never charged, despite federal, state, and local investigations. He was known, however, to have given a profitable insurance contract to his son's company. In 1974 Daley suffered a stroke. To some it may have seemed that the Daley stronghold on Chicago was finished, but in 1975 he was elected to a sixth term of office. He was not to hold office much longer; he died of a heart attack in December 1976. Daley is buried in Holy Sepulchre Cemetery in Worth, Illinois.

To say that Daley's rule was unpopular would be untrue. During the 1960s he was able to keep political uprisings in check during a time full of strife. He modernized

Richard J. Daley. THE LIBRARY OF CONGRESS

public services and expertly managed Chicago's finances. Even though Daley's power was in decline by 1968, his successes were not entirely forgotten. Ten years after his death, a Gallup poll showed that Daley was still thought of as a good mayor. Never one to hesitate when it came to mixing business with politics, Daley repeatedly said, "Good politics makes for good government." The Daley legacy lived on after his death. His son Richard M. Daley was elected mayor of Chicago in 1989 and continued to hold the position for several terms.

★

Biographies of Daley include Mike Royko, *Boss: Richard J. Daley of Chicago* (1971), Len O'Connor, *Requiem: The Decline and Demise of Mayor Daley and His Era* (1977), and Eugene C. Kennedy, *Himself!: The Life and Times of Mayor Richard J. Daley* (1978).

A. E. SCHULTHIES

DAVIS, Angela Yvonne (*b.* 26 January 1944, in Birmingham, Alabama), activist within the Black Liberation Movement during the 1960s, and an establishment triple threat: a black woman espousing Communism.

Davis was the eldest of four children of B. Frank and Sally E. Davis, both of whom had been teachers. Her father also owned a service station. Both the era and the area in which Davis grew up were hotbeds in the civil rights movement; homes were being bombed and violence was commonplace. When Davis was offered a scholarship by the American Friends Service Committee to study at Elizabeth Irwin High School in New York City, she accepted. She joined Advance, a Communist youth group, while living there.

Davis attended the Sorbonne, University of Paris in her junior year of college. She graduated magna cum laude with a degree in French literature from Brandeis University in 1965. During her final year Davis studied with Herbert Marcuse, and the noted left-wing political philosopher became her mentor. She began graduate studies in philosophy in Germany between 1965 and 1967, but elected to return home to attempt to help in the growing Black Liberation Movement. By then Marcuse had moved to the University of California, San Diego, and Davis continued her doctoral studies there.

While attending UCSD Davis became active in various political organizations. She helped to found the Black Students Council on campus. She also worked with groups in Los Angeles. Davis became a member of the Communist Party of the United States of America (CPUSA) in July 1968. She allied with the Che-Lumumba Club, an African-American section of the Los Angeles party named for Che Guevara, the Marxist intellectual pivotal in the Cuban revolution, and Patrice Lumumba, the first prime minister of the Republic of Congo. Davis accepted a teaching position at the University of California, Los Angeles (UCLA), as assistant professor of philosophy, thinking it the perfect job to hold while she finished her dissertation. She was soon revealed as a Communist, generating calls for her dismissal.

Davis had become interested in the plight of a group of African-American prisoners known as the Soledad Brothers. George Jackson, John Clutchette, and Fleeta Drumgo were incarcerated in California's Soledad Prison, and had been charged with the murder of a white guard and were facing the death penalty. Supposedly framed for the killing because they were militants, they were considered emblematic of all that was wrong with treatment of African Americans in the justice system. Davis corresponded with Jackson and eventually became close to his family, but it was while working on behalf of the Soledad Brothers that she heard of the decision to dismiss her from her post at UCLA. Davis was finally dismissed from teaching in 1969. The board of regents pointed to Davis's political activities as "unbecoming" conduct. Then governor Ronald Reagan, well known for his hatred for Communists, instigated her firing. A court reinstated her briefly, but her contract expired and was not renewed in 1970. Davis had reportedly achieved an "excellent" rating as a teacher, and the Amer-

ican Association of University Professors censured the university.

While Davis was involved with the Soledad Brothers and busy with her research, her seventeen-year-old brother Jonathan decided to draw attention to the plight of African Americans in prison by attempting to take over a courtroom in Marin County on 7 August 1970, where a prisoner was being tried for the assault of a prison guard. Guns supposedly registered in Davis's name were used in a misguided attempt to free the man on trial and two of his inmate witnesses, and to draw attention to their cause. As the men attempted to flee with hostages, a San Quentin guard opened fire. Jonathan Jackson, Judge Harold Haley, and two prisoners were killed.

Davis was charged with kidnapping, conspiracy, and murder. She evaded arrest, and went underground. Davis was placed on the Federal Bureau of Investigation's (FBI) Ten Most Wanted Fugitives list. Davis was arrested in New York City on 13 October 1970. With these capital charges, there was a possibility that, if convicted, she might be given the death penalty. Her attorneys fought extradition, but Davis was moved to California in December 1970 to stand trial. After her arrest, Davis was incarcerated for about sixteen months. She told *Essence,* "there were many, many

Angela Davis, September 1969. © BETTMANN/CORBIS

times when I was scared to death. . . . When I first got arrested, they wouldn't let me see a lawyer, and I thought they were going to kill me."

A "Free Angela Davis" campaign was mounted with support from clergy prominent in the civil rights movement, such as the reverends Jesse Jackson and Ralph Abernathy, as well as political leaders such as Congressman Ronald Dellums, who represented California's Oakland Congressional District from 1970 to 1998. Singer Aretha Franklin also announced her support, saying she would provide bail for Davis. She was, however, out of the country at the time and unable to provide her signature in person. The support for Davis extended abroad. However, Davis was keen to use her notoriety to draw attention to other political prisoners. She spoke frequently about Black Panthers Bobby Seale and Ericka Huggins and others. By the time of her trial in San Jose, supporters from around the world were writing the judge and holding events in her behalf. Immediately before her trial, the California Supreme Court abolished the death penalty. Davis was acquitted on 4 June 1972.

"They were the most painful years of my life," Davis told *Essence* magazine of that turbulent period of her life. She said she was radicalized "mainly because of what was happening to other people. It seemed before we had the chance to mourn the death of one of us, another was killed." Davis said she had support from her entire family during this period, including from her mother. "She never thought about not supporting me. She started speaking out all over the country."

The UCLA philosophy department unsuccessfully attempted to bring Davis back on the faculty in 1972. At the time of her dismissal Ronald Reagan swore Davis would never again teach at a University of California campus, but Davis has taught at the University of California at Santa Cruz since 1992 and is a tenured professor within the history of consciousness department. She received an appointment as the University of California Presidential Chair in African American and Feminist Studies, an honor she held between 1994 and 1997. She lectures frequently and remains a vocal critic of racism in the criminal justice system. Among the books Davis has written are *If They Come in the Morning: Voices of Resistance* (1971), and *The Angela Y. Davis Reader,* a collection of her writings edited by Joy James (1998). Ralph Abernathy calls Davis "one intellectual who did not hide out in a library or behind a desk. She transformed her mental principles into an active commitment of struggle against injustice."

★

For information about Davis, see her autobiography, *Angela Davis: An Autobiography* (1974). Information about her trial is in Reginald Major, *Justice in the Round: The Trial of Angela Davis*

(1973). Articles that contain biographical information about Davis include: "Angela Davis' Firing: An Evil Act," *The Sun-Reporter* (27 July 1970); "Attack Against Angela: An Attack Against All," *The Sun-Reporter* (17 Oct. 1970); "Angela Free," *The Sun-Reporter* (10 June 1972); "The Case Of Angela," *Sacramento Observer* (26 Feb. 1975); "Angela Davis—Profiled by Maya Aneglou (sic)," *Sacramento Observer* (26 Feb. 1975); "Angela Davis Tells of Her Life," *Portland Skanner* (13 Nov. 1975); John Christopher Kim Fisher, "Angela Davis Today: Brutal Beginnings in the South," *The Sun-Reporter* (24 May 1979), and "Last of a Series: Angela Davis, The Person," *The Sun-Reporter* (7 June 1979); Paula Giddings, "Angela Davis," *Essence* (June 1989); and Kevin Chappell, "Where Are the Civil Rights Icons of the '60s?" *Ebony* (Aug. 1996).

LINDA DAILEY PAULSON

DAVIS, David Brion (*b.* 16 February 1927 in Denver, Colorado), cultural and intellectual historian best known for his studies of the changing idea of slavery in Western thought and the rise of the international antislavery movement.

The son of Clyde Brion Davis, a novelist and journalist, and Martha Wirt, a writer and painter, Davis graduated summa cum laude from Dartmouth College in 1950. He then attended Harvard University, earning a master's degree in history in 1953 and a doctorate in history in 1956. He received additional master's degrees from Oxford University in 1969 and Yale University in 1970. In his distinguished career Davis taught briefly at his alma mater Dartmouth and for longer periods at Cornell and Yale Universities. At Cornell he was Ernest I. White Professor of History between 1963 and 1969. He moved to Yale in 1969, where he was appointed Farnham Professor of History in 1972. In 1978 Davis became the Sterling Professor of History at Yale.

A prolific and accomplished scholar, Davis published his first book, *Homicide in American Fiction, 1798–1860: A Study in Social Values*, in 1957. This volume emerged from his interest in the effort to abolish capital punishment during the first half of the nineteenth century. As Seymour Drescher, another eminent historian of slavery, argued, Davis logically adjusted his focus to examine the movement to abolish slavery. In 1966 Davis published *The Problem of Slavery in Western Culture*. Awarded the Pulitzer Prize for nonfiction in 1967, as well as the Anisfield-Wolf Award for "an outstanding work in the field of race relations," and the National Mass Media Brotherhood Award from the National Conference of Christians and Jews, *The Problem of Slavery in Western Culture* garnered almost unalloyed praise. J. H. Plumb, for example, described the book as "one of the most scholarly and penetrating studies of slavery" and congratulated Davis for "his mastery not only of a vast source of material, but also of the highly complex, frequently contradictory factors that influenced opinion on slavery." Moses I. Finley echoed Plumb's assessment, characterizing *The Problem of Slavery in Western Culture* as an "immensely learned, readable, exiting, [and] disturbing . . . volume, one of the most important to have been published on the subject of slavery in modern times."

In his monumental study Davis not only sought to detail the religious, philosophical, and literary origins of antislavery thought but also to explain "the profound transformation in moral perception . . . that led a growing number of Europeans and Americans to see the full horror of a social evil to which mankind had been blind for centuries." Davis maintained that slavery had embodied a contradiction since antiquity. The "true" or "perfect" slave was the extension of the master's will. Yet, as Davis noted following Hegel's analysis, "the more perfect the slave . . . the more enslaved becomes the master." The identity of a master as master depends upon the slave's conscious recognition and acceptance of him as such. Hence, Davis concluded, in a profound and unsettling way, the master was psychologically dependent on the slave.

These tensions and contradictions in the nature of slavery had persisted for centuries. What historical circumstances had changed, Davis asked, to produce the transformation in moral consciousness that engendered a "widespread conviction that New World slavery symbolized all the forces that threatened the true destiny of man"? In looking beyond moral sentiments themselves for answers, Davis did not wish to diminish or discount the importance of moral outrage, arguing that "the emergence of an international antislavery opinion represented a momentous turning point in the evolution of man's moral perception." It was an evolution that at last required not merely opposition to slavery, but action taken to eradicate it

Researching and writing *The Problem of Slavery in Western Culture* during the turbulent 1960s, Davis never addressed himself directly to the ongoing civil rights crusade or the deepening racial animosity that was rending American society. But by showing that it had taken centuries to recognize and overcome the injustice of slavery, and that even after its abolition other forms of oppression remained, Davis offered an incisive, if oblique and subtle, commentary on his times. Of course American society remained troubled by the enduring legacy of slavery and the continued presence of racism and discrimination. Along with other historians of slavery, notably Eugene D. Genovese, Davis also affirmed rather more forthrightly that the advocates of justice and equality for blacks during the 1960s had benefited from the many heroic battles against slavery and racism that had taken place in the past.

To demonstrate how the moral aversion to slavery trans-

lated into political action against the practice, Davis wrote *The Problem of Slavery in the Age of Revolution, 1770–1823* (1975). His thesis was as provocative as it was controversial. Davis argued that, whatever their moral convictions, the political and economic elite of Great Britain had embraced the antislavery cause to deflect attention from the dislocation, misery, and tyranny attendant upon the rise of industrial capitalism. However, although he acknowledged these ulterior motives, Davis did not suggest that they compromised or discredited the indictment of slavery. Davis's objective was not to depreciate the accomplishments of the antislavery vanguard by admitting that their deeds originated in complex, contradictory, and often anguished human circumstances—that is, in history.

In *Slavery and Human Progress* (1984) Davis explored the connections between the reality of slavery and the idea of progress, revealing that thinkers frequently applied a belief in progress to justify slavery, or at least to challenge the moral and political urgency of antislavery rhetoric. Acclaimed for its astute judgments and encyclopedic range, *Slavery and Human Progress* was also criticized for being "superficial" and lacking "a straight-forward discussion of the ideas of progress and slavery."

Davis's first marriage, which produced three children, ended in divorce in 1971. That same year he married Toni Hahn, an attorney, and they have two sons. In 2002 Davis was at work on an investigation of *The Problem of Slavery in the Age of Emancipation, 1815–1890*, augmenting an already remarkable body of work. In a career spanning more than forty years, Davis has helped make the study of slavery one of the most intellectually dynamic and theoretically sophisticated areas of historical inquiry.

★

There is no biography of Davis. Thomas Bender, ed., *The Anti-Slavery Debate: Capitalism and Abolitionism as a Problem in Historical Interpretation* (1992), provides the best overview of the historical issues and scholarly debates that have engaged Davis throughout most of his career, and also enables readers to assess Davis's contributions to them. Seymour Drescher, "The Antislavery Debate," *History and Theory* 32 (1993), is also extremely useful.

MARK G. MALVASI

DAVIS, Miles Dewey, III (*b.* 26 May 1926 in Alton, Illinois; *d.* 28 September 1991 in Santa Monica, California), jazz trumpet player, composer, and bandleader instrumental in the development of hard bop, cool jazz, modal jazz, and fusion.

The second of three children born to Miles Dewey Davis II, a prosperous oral surgeon who once ran for a seat in the state legislature, and Cleota Henry, Davis grew up in East St. Louis, Illinois. His mother, a homemaker who was also a trained pianist, wanted him to play the violin. Davis, though, opted for the trumpet, which his father had given him for his birthday "because," as Davis said, "he loved my mother so much!"

At the age of thirteen, about the time his parents separated, Davis began learning to play under the tutelage of a local musician named Elwood Buchanan. By sixteen, while attending Lincoln High School, he had become a regular with Eddie Randle's Blue Devils at the Rhumboogie Club in downtown St. Louis. In 1944 he got the chance to substitute for the third trumpeter in Billy Eckstine's orchestra. "B's band changed my life," Davis recalled. "I decided right then and there to leave St. Louis and live in New York City where all these bad musicians were."

Acceptance at the Juilliard School of Music justified the move. Davis attended Juilliard but never graduated, instead receiving his musical education in the jazz clubs on Fifty-second Street. After serving his musical apprenticeship in the 1940s, Davis emerged as one of the preeminent figures in the jazz world of the 1950s. His work with trombonist J. J. Johnson, alto saxophonist Jackie McLean, and pianist Horace Silver heralded the arrival of hard bop. The fastidious but imaginative *Birth of the Cool* (1950) established the contours of cool jazz, which Davis cultivated during the late 1950s and early 1960s in collaboration with Gil Evans.

Despite his growing reputation, Davis's facility as a musician eroded conspicuously between 1949 and 1953 as the result of his debilitating heroin addiction. To combat his drug habit, Davis locked himself in a room at his father's 200-acre hog farm in Millstadt, Illinois, and overcame his dependence by utter force of will. With his drug problem under control, Davis began his collaboration with an extraordinary group of musicians, which included pianist Bill Evans and saxophonists John Coltrane and Julian "Cannonball" Adderley, to inaugurate modal jazz, producing the masterful *Kind of Blue* in 1959.

Between 1964 and 1968 Davis merged the innovations of hard bop with the harmonic structures of modal jazz to propel jazz more fully in the direction of melodic and rhythmic freedom. Yet Davis renounced the anarchy of free-form jazz. "You don't need to think to play weird," he said. "That ain't no freedom. You need controlled freedom." Although long overshadowed by the prestigious groups of the 1950s, the quintet that Davis formed in 1964, consisting of tenor saxophonist Wayne Shorter, pianist Herbie Hancock, bassist Ron Carter, and drummer Tony Williams, came in time to be classed among the finest ensembles in the history of jazz.

Exquisite, refined, inventive, and subtle, Davis's music during the early 1960s was less acclaimed than the more flamboyant and adventurous explorations of John Coltrane, Ornette Coleman, and Albert Ayler. Yet with such recordings as *Miles in Berlin* (1964), *E.S.P.* (1965), *Miles Smiles*

Miles Davis. MR. JACK VARTOOGIAN

(1966), *Sorcerer* (1967), *Nefertiti* (1967), and *Miles in the Sky* (1968), Davis fashioned a body of work that has not only stood the test of time but has grown in stature and importance as his career has come into sharper focus.

By the end of the 1960s Davis had begun experimenting with electric instruments on such recordings as *Filles de Kilimanjaro* (1968), and *In a Silent Way* (1969), a trend anticipated on *Miles in the Sky*. Then, in 1969, he astonished and perhaps dismayed jazz aficionados with the release of *Bitches Brew,* a combination of jazz, rock, and funk. Fusion, as Davis's new style became known, may have repelled some traditionalists, but the music enjoyed immediate commercial success. *Bitches Brew* remained Davis's best-selling recording for more than twenty years, establishing him as a pop star while simultaneously reinstating his sway over jazz. Not only fans but younger musicians, including Joe Zawinul, Miroslav Vitous, Chick Corea, and John McLaughlin, drew inspiration from it.

Davis's personal life during the 1960s was often turbulent. On 21 December 1960 he married dancer Frances Taylor. The couple moved into a renovated five-story brownstone on the upper West Side of Manhattan and brought the three children from Davis's previous relationship with Irene Birth to live with them. In 1968 Davis divorced Taylor to marry singer Betty Mabry, whom he divorced in 1969. Meanwhile, his intermittent romance with Marguerite Eskridge had, in 1970, resulted in the birth of a son Erin. Jailed in 1978 for nonpayment of child support, Davis brought Erin to live with him in California during the late 1980s and named him the principal beneficiary of his will.

Throughout the late 1960s and early 1970s Davis's health was in serious jeopardy. He suffered from sickle-cell anemia and arthritis, which led to hip replacement surgery. In 1972 he broke both ankles in an automobile accident. After 1975 he became reclusive, devoting himself, by his own admission, to a cocaine habit that cost $500 a day and to "kinky sex and other weird sick shit."

Davis's third wife, the actress Cicely Tyson, whom he married on Thanksgiving Day in 1981, helped restore his physical and mental health. He resumed his career and for the remaining decade of his life staged commercially successful but musically undistinguished international tours. During his last performances, however, he revived the elegant arrangements on which he had collaborated with Gil Evans.

Following an acrimonious divorce in 1989, Davis's health again declined. As well as sickle-cell anemia and arthritis, he had developed gallstones, heart palpitations, diabetes, bleeding ulcers, and a liver infection. Unsubstantiated rumors persist that he had also contracted HIV. When he died in St. John's Hospital and Health Center in Santa Monica, California, the official causes were listed as stroke, pneumonia, and respiratory failure. Davis is buried in Woodlawn Cemetery, Bronx, New York.

Despite a life marred by ill health, drug abuse, and domestic violence, Davis remains an icon in the history of jazz. Renowned neither for his technical prowess nor his association with a particular style, Davis four times altered the evolution of jazz. Since his death the popularity of his music has not waned, and he continues to exercise an influence on contemporary jazz unmatched by any musician of his generation.

★

Davis's autobiography, *Miles: The Autobiography* (1989), written with Quincy Troupe, offers an intimate portrait, revealing perhaps too much about his personal shortcomings and too little about his musical accomplishments. Troupe, *Miles and Me* (2000), details the complications he encountered while helping Davis write the autobiography. Bill Cole, *Miles Davis: A Musical Biography* (1974), is an uneven effort distinguished by Cole's admiration for Davis's music. The definitive study of Davis's life and career is Jack Chambers, *Milestones I: The Music and Times of Miles Davis to 1960* (1983) and *Milestones II: The Music and Times of Miles Davis Since 1960* (1985). Eric Nisenson, *'Round About Midnight: A Portrait of Miles Davis* (1996), focuses on Davis's image rather than his music, but is readable. Chambers, *Milestones: The Music and Times of Miles Davis* (1998), is a compilation of the previous two volumes with additional material on the last decade of Davis's life. More recent and also worthwhile is Ian Carr, *Miles Davis: The Definitive Biography* (1999). Ted Gioia, *The History of Jazz* (1997), contains informative and insightful analyses of Davis's contributions to jazz. Gary Carner, ed., *The Miles Davis Companion* (1996), and Bill Kirchner, ed., *A Miles Davis Reader* (1997), are collections of essays, and also include obituaries. Although brief, G. Pascal Zachary, "My Favorite Coltrane," *In These Times* (7 Jan. 2002) offers a thoughtful comparison of Davis's and Coltrane's music, personalities, and reputations.

MARK G. MALVASI

DAVIS, Raiford Chatman ("Ossie") (*b.* 18 December 1917 in Cogdell, Georgia), actor of stage, screen, and television; director, playwright, producer, novelist, and prominent figure in the civil rights movement of the 1960s.

Davis was the eldest of five children of Kince Charles Davis, a railroad construction engineer, and Laura Cooper Davis, a homemaker. He grew up in Waycross, Georgia. While attending Central High School in Waycross, he developed a love for the theater and wrote and produced his first play. After graduating from Central High in 1935 and receiving a National Youth Administration scholarship for

Ossie Davis. ESTATE OF MR. CARL VAN VECHTEN

college, Davis hitchhiked to Washington, D.C., to live with his aunts while attending Howard University. In 1938, influenced by Alain Locke, a leader of the Harlem Renaissance, Davis left Howard after his junior year to go to New York City, where he joined the Rose McClendon Players, a small theater group in Harlem. He was inducted into the U.S. Army in 1942 and spent most of his military service in Liberia, West Africa, as a surgical technician. He was then transferred to Special Services, where he produced several shows, including his own first play, *Goldbrickers of 1944.* Upon his discharge in 1945, he returned to Valdosta, Georgia, and in early 1946 again headed to New York City to pursue his acting career. He made his stage debut that year in the title role in *Jeb* and followed that success with significant roles on Broadway and in film and television throughout the 1950s. Davis married actress Ruby Dee (Ruby Ann Wallace), his *Jeb* costar, on 9 December 1948. They had two daughters and a son.

In the 1960s Davis achieved even broader success in the performing arts. In 1959 he replaced Sidney Poitier in the successful play *A Raisin in the Sun.* The following year he established himself as a playwright with *Purlie Victorious,* a satire on southern racism that combined folk-comedy with satire in portraying black and white southern stereotypes. Davis also wrote and starred in *Gone Are the Days,* the film version of the play. In 1970 the movie was transformed into the Broadway musical *Purlie.* The 1960s were also productive in film and television for Davis; he appeared in several other films during this decade, including *The Cardinal* (1963), *The Hill* (1965), *The Scalphunters* (1968), and *Slaves* (1969). He appeared in several television series, and in 1969 was nominated for an Emmy Award for his performance in the *Hallmark Hall of Fame* teleplay, *Teacher, Teacher.*

As a child in the Deep South, Davis encountered rampant racism but learned to keep quiet to avoid retaliation. Writing was his way of expressing the treatment he saw his father and others receive at the hands of white bigots. While a student at Howard University, and later as a young playwright and actor in New York City, Davis became vocal against civil rights abuses.

The civil rights era of the 1960s was one of the most important periods in the domestic history of the United States; the civil rights movement challenged the national conscience, and every facet of African-American life changed, including black performing arts. As Davis stated, "the civil rights movement made black people, women, and minorities free." Davis was a prominent figure in the movement and in political activities dating back to the 1950s, when he took a strong political stance on certain issues during the McCarthy era, a period when government officials led by Senator Joseph McCarthy sought to root out

Communism in the United States. He organized a fundraiser for the activist and writer Angela Davis, arranged a meeting between the activist Malcolm X and the main black leadership of the day, and spoke out at forums organized by the actor and singer Paul Robeson. Always a strong advocate of racial equality, Davis joined Dr. Martin Luther King, Jr., in his crusade for jobs and freedom by participating in King's Memorial March in Memphis, Tennessee. He helped raise money for the Freedom Riders arrested in the South and for the legal defense of the activist poet and playwright Le Roi Jones. Considering himself to be a cultural arm of the civil rights revolution, Davis's life and, to a larger extent, his work, were greatly influenced by the movement.

Davis has served on the advisory board of the Congress of Racial Equality (CORE) and supported the National Association for the Advancement of Colored People (NAACP), the Urban League, the Student Nonviolent Coordinating Committee (SNCC), and the Southern Christian Leadership Conference (SCLC).

In 1962 Davis testified at a congressional inquiry into racial discrimination in show business that "despite the success of a few blacks, discrimination in hiring is widespread in the theater" and proposed that black people use the boycott as a weapon in combating this discrimination. A year later he wrote a skit for the 1963 March on Washington and, with wife Ruby Dee, served as master of ceremonies for the historic occasion. In 1965 he delivered the eulogy at the funeral of his friend Malcolm X. He also served as one of the sixty sponsors for Robeson's sixty-fifth birthday salute, an event that many prominent black figures avoided because they were afraid that an association with Robeson would hurt their careers. In 1965 Davis's strong involvement in social and political issues earned him the first Mississippi Freedom Democratic Party Citation.

A distinguished actor, Davis has always been a forceful voice for human dignity and social justice, using his celebrity status while serving on the frontlines of the fight for social equality. His dedication to the cause of civil rights earned him a place in the NAACP Image Hall of Fame. Davis and Dee were the 1970 recipients of the Frederick Douglass Award from the Urban League for their civil rights activities.

The grand old man of black theater, who never intended to be an actor, but a writer, has been called one of the best African-American actors and directors of his era. From the period of the Great Depression, through the civil rights movement, to the present, Davis has been a strong, forceful advocate for human dignity, political freedom, and social justice, by telling the story of African-American people through song, through dance, through his writings, and through his storytelling.

★

An excellent biographical source is Ossie Davis and Ruby Dee, *With Ossie and Ruby: In This Life Together* (1998), a joint autobiography that covers their life and describes their involvement in the civil rights movement. Articles with information about Davis and his career are Lynn Norment, "Three Great Love Stories," *Ebony* 43 (Feb. 1988); W. Calvin Anderson, "One Minute at a Time: Ossie Davis and Ruby Dee Are Still Making Dreams Come True," *American Vision* 7 (Apr./May 1992): 20–24; and Dwight E. Greer, "Interview with Ossie Davis," *High Plains Literary Review* 9 (spring 1994): 74–80.

JOYCE K. THORNTON

DAVIS, Sammy, Jr. (*b.* 8 December 1925 in Harlem, New York; *d.* 16 May 1990 in Beverly Hills, California), variety artist known for his impressions, tap dancing, and singing, whose dynamic performances in nightclubs, films, television, recording studios, and on Broadway during the 1960s earned him the titles "Mr. Entertainment" and "Mr. Show Business."

Davis's mother, Elvera Sanchez, was a chorus girl, and his father, Sam Davis, Sr., a vaudeville dancer. His parents separated six months after his younger sister was born, and when Davis was two years old, the talented youngster joined his father in a traveling vaudeville revue, *The Will Mastin Trio.*

In 1943 Davis was drafted into the U.S. Army. In basic training at Fort Francis E. Warren in Cheyenne, Wyoming, he received inhuman treatment because of his race. Although five feet, six inches tall and never weighing more

Sammy Davis, Jr., 1967. THE KOBAL COLLECTION

than 130 pounds, Davis fought back, resulting in a broken nose and even more humiliation. Davis never attended a formal school but received occasional tutoring on the road. While in the Army he received remedial reading lessons and some high school–level education.

Discharged in 1945, Davis rejoined his father and Will Mastin. The trio played opening acts at Las Vegas, where Davis wowed nightclub crowds by being the first black impressionist to imitate white celebrities. A new friend, Frank Sinatra, helped the trio achieve its first major breakthrough at Ciro's, a Hollywood nightclub, in 1951. Davis's performance earned him instant stardom. In 1954 he recorded his first album, *Starring Sammy Davis, Jr.*

On 19 November 1954 Davis was involved in an automobile accident in which he lost his left eye. While convalescing, he was visited by the hospital rabbi, and soon thereafter he converted to Judaism. When he was released from the hospital he received tremendous media coverage. In succeeding years critics raved about Davis's dynamic talents, evidenced by recordings ("Black Magic," the number one radio song of 1955), Broadway performances (*Mr. Wonderful,* in 1956, Broadway's first integrated play), television work (*General Electric Theater,* in 1958; Davis was the first black actor to star in episodic television), and movie roles (*The Benny Goodman Story* in 1956, and *Porgy and Bess* in 1959).

In the early 1960s Davis became a permanent member of the infamous Rat Pack, the closely knit clique of fast-living entertainers that included Frank Sinatra, Dean Martin, Joey Bishop, and Peter Lawford. The Rat Pack made six movies together: *Ocean's Eleven* (1960), *Sergeants Three* (1962), *Johnny Cool* (1963), *Robin and the Seven Hoods* (1964), *Salt and Pepper* (1969), and *One More Time* (1970). When the Rat Pack went to Las Vegas to shoot scenes for *Ocean's Eleven* at the Sands Hotel and Casino while simultaneously performing together at the hotel's nightclub, they created a media sensation resulting in consecutive sold-out shows for their "Summit at the Sands."

Many African-American audiences felt that Davis's inclusion in the Rat Pack was nothing but tokenism, that he was the butt of Sinatra's and Martin's racist jokes. Davis, however, refused to leave the Rat Pack. He stated, "You can't please everybody. But you please the majority and don't ever let them say, 'Gee, I didn't like the performance.' That doesn't mean everybody is going to like what you're doing, but at least they can say, 'He performed for me, man. He gave his all.'"

Membership in the Rat Pack brought Davis new wealth and the publicity he had always desperately craved, but it wrought havoc on his personal life. His relationship with Loray White, an African-American dancer whom he had married on 1 January 1958, ended in divorce in 1959. On 13 November 1961 he married Mai (May) Britt, a Swedish actress he met at the Twentieth Century Fox commissary in Hollywood. Since in 1960 interracial marriage was illegal in thirty-one states, and Sinatra and Davis had campaigned actively for John F. Kennedy, the couple postponed their marriage until after the presidential election so as not to lose Kennedy any votes. Kennedy reciprocated for Sinatra's and Davis's support by inviting the couple to his inaugural gala, but he retracted the invitation at the last minute under pressure from advisers.

The newlyweds received so much hate mail and so many death threats that Davis had to hire personal bodyguards. To protect his wife from accusatory stares and racial epithets, he refused to take her out, remaining at home or in a hotel room while on the road. The couple had two children and adopted an infant son in 1966. The pressure of bringing up interracial children in an age of rampant segregation, plus Davis's frenzied marathon performances in pursuit of public adulation, led to their divorce in 1968.

Davis performed at a frenetic pace in 1966, when he was involved in three projects. He was nominated for a Tony Award for his performance in Clifford Odets's *Golden Boy*. He was also doing his own one-hour television variety show, *The Sammy Davis, Jr., Show*, which premiered on 7 January 1966. At the same time he made a movie, *A Man Called Adam*, the story of the rise and fall of a black jazz musician.

On 11 May 1970 Davis married Altovise Gore, an African-American dancer he met while doing *Golden Boy*. The couple later adopted a son. The 1970s were prolific for the indefatigable performer. He appeared on Rowan and Martin's *Laugh-In,* immortalizing the line, "Here come de judge." After his guest appearance on a 1972 episode of *All in the Family*, the show broke all previous ratings. In the same year he recorded "Candy Man," his all-time best-selling record, along with "I've Gotta Be Me," "Mr. Bojangles," and "What Kind of Fool Am I?" Davis was a lifelong donor to the United Negro College Fund and a life member of the National Association for the Advancement of Colored People.

Eventually, years of hard living and chronic drinking and smoking caught up with Davis. He developed liver and kidney problems, and in 1974 he suffered a mild heart attack. After a short recovery period he resumed his energetic schedule, performing on his television variety show, acting in the two highly successful *Cannonball Run* movies (1981 and 1984), and singing at concerts with friends Frank Sinatra and Liza Minelli.

In September 1989 Davis was diagnosed with cancer of the throat, and following a lingering illness, he died on 16 May 1990 at the age of sixty-four. At his funeral service on 18 May at Forest Lawn Memorial Park in Glendale (a suburb of Los Angeles), Frank Sinatra, Dean Martin, Michael Jackson, and Bill Cosby served as pallbearers; and the Reverend Jesse Jackson gave the eulogy.

★

Three autobiographies are Sammy Davis, Jr., and Jane and Burt Boyar, *Yes I Can: The Story of Sammy Davis, Jr.* (1965); Sammy Davis, Jr., *Hollywood in a Suitcase* (1980), a mixture of personal anecdotes and political observations; and Sammy Davis, Jr., and Jane and Burt Boyar, *Why Me? The Sammy Davis, Jr., Story* (1989), which condenses *Yes I Can* and adds details from the 1970s and 1980s. Biographies include "Sammy Davis, Jr.," *Current Biography Yearbook* (1978): 94–98; Lerone Bennett, Jr., "Sammy Davis, Jr., 1925–1990: The Legacy of the World's Greatest Entertainer," *Ebony* 45 (July 1990), a picture-filled bio of the celebrity's personal and professional life; and Tracey Davis with Dolores A. Barclay, *Sammy Davis, Jr., My Father* (1996), a somewhat sentimental look at the performer from his daughter's point of view. Obituaries are in the *New York Times* (17 May 1990), and *People Weekly* and *Time* (both 28 May 1990).

JOHN J. BYRNE

DAY, Doris (*b*. 3 April 1924 in Evanston, Ohio), prolific movie star from 1948 to her retirement in 1973 and best-selling recording artist.

Day was born Doris Mary von Kappelhoff, the daughter of William von Kappelhoff, a local music teacher, and Alma Sophia Welz, a housewife. She had two brothers. Day's parents separated in 1932, when she was eight, and her mother raised her. Day attended parochial schools in Cincinnati but did not graduate from high school. Initially, she was interested in dance, but both of her legs were badly broken in a train accident when she was thirteen. As she convalesced she discovered that she could sing and began performing on Cincinnati radio programs. She was just sixteen years old when she began working in 1940 as a singer for Barney Rapp, a regional bandleader. She changed her name to Doris Day, and through the 1940s she sang with both Bob Crosby and the Bobcats and Les Brown and his Band of Renown. In 1941 Day married Al Jorden, a trombone player, and they had a son in 1942. Jorden was a jealous and abusive husband, and the marriage ended in 1943.

Day's fame grew during the 1940s as she appeared on *Your Hit Parade,* sang with Les Brown's band, cut records of hit World War II vintage songs like "Sentimental Journey," and entertained the troops with the *Bob Hope Show*. Her second marriage, to the saxophone player George Weidler, lasted just eight months, and they divorced in 1946. In 1947 Day signed with Columbia Records, a relationship that lasted for two decades.

Now living in California, where she had moved with

Doris Day. ARCHIVE PHOTOS, INC.

Weidler, Day successfully auditioned for a role in the film *Romance on the High Seas* (1948). Warner Bros. signed her to a contract in 1948, and between then and 1955 she appeared in seventeen Warner Bros. pictures, fifteen of them musicals, playing opposite such leading men as Ronald Reagan, Gordon MacRae, Kirk Douglas, and Gene Nelson. In 1951 she married for the third time, to Marty Melcher, her agent, who adopted her son. Melcher and Day formed Arwin Productions, and after Day was released from her Warner Bros. contract in 1955, Arwin coproduced with major studios many of Day's films. Through most of the 1950s she was consistently a top-ten box office draw, had two-million-selling records, and was an internationally recognized celebrity. Her 1956 role in Alfred Hitchcock's *The Man Who Knew Too Much,* in which she reprised a song from the 1940s, "Que Sera, Sera," indelibly stamped her 1950s image.

Coming into the 1960s, however, Day's career was fading. The quaint musicals and her wholesome roles typecast her as America's virgin. The typical Day movie was a specific kind of sunny, nostalgic, and sexless film. Day knew that she needed to remake her image. Her career got a second wind in 1959 with her appearance opposite Rock Hudson in *Pillow Talk,* a sophisticated sex comedy in which she played a successful professional—an urbane New York career woman in a contemporary situation, fend-

ing off the illicit advances of a predatory male. The film changed Day's image from the girl next door to a chic, sexy-but-chaste career professional, although *Pillow Talk* may seem coy by contemporary standards. Day was nominated for an Oscar for the film. The moviegoing public came to expect an almost annual Doris Day romantic comedy. *Lover Come Back* (1962) and *Send Me No Flowers* (1964) reprised her appearances with Hudson and Tony Randall. *That Touch of Mink* (1962) teamed her with Cary Grant in a film about a struggling working girl who successfully defends her purity against Grant's advances. *The Thrill of It All* (1963) with James Garner and *Move Over, Darling* (1963) offered the public the same boy-chases-a-girl-until-she-catches-him fare. These films contained a hint of suggestiveness that Day said made her a new kind of symbol: sexy but pure, the woman with whom men wanted to go to bed, but not until they married her. The films changed her wholesome image so much that Oscar Levant caustically remarked, "I knew Doris Day before she was a virgin."

From 1959 to 1965 Day was number one at the box office. Hit tunes made from these films, as well as other recordings, sold briskly throughout the decade. All told, she acted in fourteen films during the 1960s. Her last film was *With Six You Get Egg Roll* (1968). Day had no formal training, but she had natural acting talent, and her colleagues admired her spontaneity and versatility. Jack Lemmon praised her intuition and her "impeccable comedic timing." Garner said that making a movie with her was "a sexy ride on her coattails all the way."

Melcher acted as Day's agent and investment adviser, and, with a Hollywood lawyer, Jerome B. Rosenthal, they invested her earnings in hotels, oil wells, and cattle ranches. When Melcher died in 1968 Day's son discovered that her investments were worthless and that she owed hundreds of thousands of dollars in back taxes. Just before his death Melcher had secretly committed Day to a television show. Although she disliked the medium, Day agreed to host *The Doris Day Show* because she was so in debt. The show was on the air from 1968 to 1973. Day subsequently appeared infrequently in TV specials and film anthologies. In 1969 she sued Rosenthal, and after a five-year court battle the judge rendered a scathing opinion against Rosenthal and awarded $22 million in damages to Day.

Day's son, Terry Melcher, became a successful record producer and had a brush with infamy arising out of a minor connection with the mass murderer Charles Manson, who in August 1969 killed the actress Sharon Tate and four others at Tate's residence in Los Angeles. Melcher had previously lived in the house, and police speculated that Manson and his cohorts may have targeted Melcher because he had rebuffed Manson's request for help with a musical career. In 1976 Day married a fourth time, to Barry Comden, whom she divorced in 1980.

Besides her 1959 Oscar nomination, five Day films received Oscar nominations in other categories. She is also the recipient of four Golden Globe Awards (1958, 1960, 1963, and 1989). She received the Columbia Gold Disc for "Que Sera, Sera" (1956) and a 1975 Hall of Fame nomination from the National Academy of Recording Arts and Sciences for "Sentimental Journey." She released almost fifty soundtracks and recorded albums. In 1989 the Hollywood Foreign Press Association awarded her a Golden Globe Lifetime Achievement Award. She received a Lifetime Achievement Comedy Award in 1991 from the American Comedy Awards. Day is installed in Hollywood's Star Walk of Fame. Since her retirement Day has become very active in Actors and Others for Animals and the Doris Day Animal League. The Doris Day Pet Foundation advocates on behalf of household pets. She and her son own the Cypress Inn in Carmel, a "pets welcomed" inn in California.

★

Two fine biographies of Day are A. E. Hotchner, *Doris Day: Her Own Story* (1976), which includes lists of her films, and Eric Braun, *Doris Day* (1991), which also contains a filmography as well as information about her recordings and television appearances. See also Alan Gelb, *The Doris Day Scrapbook* (1977); Christopher Young, *The Films of Doris Day* (1977); and Jane Clarke and Diana Simmons, *Move over Misconceptions: Doris Day Reappraised* (1980). Many of Day's records are widely available, and several of her films are on videotape.

WILLIAM J. MALONEY

DeBAKEY, Michael Ellis (*b.* 7 September 1908 in Lake Charles, Louisiana), surgeon, inventor, and medical statesman who, during the 1960s, developed the left ventricle assist devise (LVAD), performed heart transplants, demonstrated open-heart surgery for satellite transmission, and performed the first aortocoronary artery bypass.

DeBakey was the oldest of five children born to self-educated Lebanese immigrants Shaker Morris, a businessman, and Raheega Zorba. The valedictorian of his high school class, he attended Tulane University. There he acquired his B.S. degree in 1930 and attended medical school. He earned his medical degree in 1932 and an M.S. in 1935. In 1932, while he was still a student, he invented the roller pump used in the heart-lung machine.

Following graduation from medical school, DeBakey continued his education at Charity Hospital in New Orleans and in Europe. Upon his return to the United States in 1937, he joined the Tulane faculty, where he stayed until he volunteered for World War II. During the war he served in the Office of the Surgeon General, where he recommended the establishment of mobile army surgical

Michael DeBakey. AP/WIDE WORLD PHOTOS

hospital (MASH) units to serve wounded soldiers on the front line. He also helped to create the systems for treating soldiers returning from war, which became the Veterans Affairs (VA) Medical Center System, and for following veterans with specific medical problems, which became the VA Medical Research Program. When the war ended, DeBakey returned to Tulane. In 1948 he moved to Houston to join the faculty of Baylor University College of Medicine, where he has remained throughout his life.

By the 1950s DeBakey's energies were focused on the diagnosis and treatment of arteriosclerosis (hardening of the arteries). He pioneered revolutionary operation after revolutionary operation, many of which eventually became standard medical practice and saved countless lives. Between 1950 and 1953, using his wife's sewing machine, he created Dacron artificial arteries to replace damaged sections. Other procedures he pioneered were the removal and graft replacement of an aneurysm (swelling caused by weakness in an artery wall), the removal of blockage in a carotid artery (the artery of the neck carrying blood to the brain), the resection and grafting on the ascending aorta and on the section of the aorta that curves over the heart, and the patch-graft angioplasty to reverse narrowing of an artery.

Throughout the 1960s DeBakey continued his achievements in heart surgery. He and his team developed the then-controversial left ventricular assist device (LVAD). In 1966 the LVAD kept a patient alive until she could be weaned from the heart-lung machine. By the late 1960s DeBakey and his team had developed an artificial heart, which was tested in calves. The device was unsuccessful, so the team returned to researching LVAD. Later, two members of the team implanted a similar artificial heart without success, validating DeBakey's decision not to proceed.

In the early 1960s DeBakey developed coronary bypass surgery when he realized that the sections around diseased vessels were healthy, and that routing the flow of blood around the diseased vessels allowed normal blood flow to resume, preventing a heart attack. In 1964 he performed the first aortocoronary artery bypass surgery by using a vein from the patient's leg to bypass the damaged area. This, too, has become a standard surgical procedure. Other medical achievements in the 1960s included his involvement in interactive telemedicine and his performance of transplants. In 1963 DeBakey's demonstration of open-heart surgery was broadcast abroad. DeBakey performed the first twelve heart transplants in 1968 and supervised the first successful multiple-organ transplant the same year. A heart, two kidneys, and a lung were transplanted from one donor to four patients. Later, DeBakey stopped performing transplants until the drugs to combat rejection of transplanted organs improved.

DeBakey applied his prestige to influencing public medical policy—even if that policy went against the feelings of other physicians. He was appointed by President Lyndon Baines Johnson to head the Commission on Heart Disease, Cancer and Stroke in 1964. This commission recommended establishing intensive care centers for these diseases and community centers for diagnosis and emergency care. The commission also found that there were major differences in the quality of health care available in medical centers in major cities as opposed to smaller cities and rural areas, and that physicians delayed learning new life-saving techniques—a finding that angered the American Medical Association. Although many physicians were opposed to Medicare, DeBakey urged President Johnson to support it. He also helped Mary Lasker seek funding for medical research by helping her lobby Congress. In 1942 Lasker and her husband had founded the Albert and Mary Lasker Foundation to raise awareness of certain diseases and the need for more research funding. In 1944, the Laskers began honoring physicians and scientists for achievements in research. Many winners went on to receive Nobel prizes. The Laskers believed that only with government assistance could there be enough money for medical research. Lasker began lobbying Congress. She convinced Congress to fund research on cancer, heart disease, mental illness, blindness and other diseases. Lasker worked tirelessly to pass the National Cancer Act, which revamped the National Cancer Institute and increased its money for research. DeBakey was active in these efforts to secure government funding during the administrations of several presidents, from Harry S. Truman through Jimmy Carter.

In 1968, when the Baylor University College of Medicine faced a financial crisis, they turned to DeBakey. He suggested separating the medical school from the university and establishing a new board of trustees from Houston's business and civic leaders. The medical school received a charter from the State of Texas, and DeBakey became the president. The school's finances improved, DeBakey began recruiting new talent, and Baylor University College of Medicine evolved into a prestigious institution.

DeBakey married Diane Cooper on 15 October 1936. They had four sons. Cooper died of a massive heart attack in 1972, and DeBakey remarried two years later. He and his second wife, Katrin Fehlhaber, had one daughter. During the 1960s DeBakey earned numerous awards. He was corecipient of the Albert Lasker Award for Clinical Research (1963), and recipient of the Eleanor Roosevelt Humanities Award (1969), and the Presidential Medal of Freedom with Distinction (1969). In his nineties DeBakey still was considered the "Texas Tornado." He operated, wrote, and lectured around the world. He received a Lifetime Achievement Award from the United Nations in 1999 and was cited as a "Living Legend" by the Library of Congress in 2000. DeBakey's significance lies in his continued achievement into his nineties—he has never stopped inventing, researching, and lecturing.

★

Biographical information about DeBakey is in Denise Adams Arnold, "Michael Ellis DeBakey," *Notable Twentieth-Century Scientists* (1995), and Lawrence K. Altman, "Dr. DeBakey at 90: Stringent Standards and a Steady Hand," *New York Times* (1 Sept. 1998).

SHEILA BECK

DEE, Ruby (*b.* 27 October 1924 in Cleveland, Ohio), actress, writer, and social activist who was the first African-American woman to play major parts in theater and film during the 1960s and to receive critical acclaim for her performances and praise for her support of the civil rights movement in the United States.

Dee was born Ruby Ann Wallace, the third of four children of Marshall Edward, a railroad porter and waiter, and Emma Benson, a schoolteacher. The family relocated to Harlem in New York City, while Dee was an infant. Even though Dee grew up in the ghetto, her mother determined that she would study literature and music rather than watch movies and listen to the radio. The family read poetry by Longfellow, Wordsworth, and the African-American poet

Ruby Dee. THE LIBRARY OF CONGRESS

Paul Laurence Dunbar to one another. Dee's mother restricted her neighborhood interactions but allowed her to watch from a safe distance; thus she lived a somewhat sheltered existence. Dee eventually submitted her poetry to the *New York Amsterdam News,* a weekly newspaper catering to an African-American audience. Some of Dee's poems were published in the *News* and she later contributed to columns for the publication.

Dee enrolled at Hunter College to study Spanish and French, graduating in 1945 with a B.A. At the same time, from 1941 to 1944, she was an apprentice with the American Negro Theatre (ANT) and appeared in a variety of productions. During her tenure with ANT, Wallace adopted the stage name of "Ruby Dee." Her Broadway debut in December 1943 was as a native girl in *South Pacific.* Three years later she appeared in Robert Ardrey's *Jeb,* a drama about the troubles of a returning African-American war hero. The play starred Ossie Davis, whom she married two years later on 9 December 1948. They have three children. In 1944 and again in 1947, Dee starred in an adaptation of *Anna Lucasta,* first at ANT and then on Broadway, which drew attention to her acting abilities. Dee appeared in her first film, *Love in Syncopation,* in 1946. Between roles, she used her fluent French and Spanish to work as a translator

for an import business. She continued to garner wide acclaim with lead film appearances with Jackie Robinson in *The Jackie Robinson Story* (1950), Sidney Poitier in *No Way Out* (1950), and again with Poitier in *Edge of the City* (1957).

The 1950s were characterized by the specters of McCarthyism and red-baiting, as well as stereotypical imagery of African Americans. Dee received a role in *The World of Sholem Aleichem* (1953) through friends she made while protesting the treatment of Julius and Ethel Rosenberg. She campaigned for the return of Paul Robeson's passport, which had been confiscated due to his unpopular political beliefs. Despite the prevailing political climate, Dee managed to avoid damaging her career through hard work, determination, and a refusal to be boxed in as "the Negro June Allyson."

The 1960s were colored by the rise of social activism, protest against racial inequality, and the Vietnam War. In the 1950s, theater and film roles overwhelmingly portrayed African Americans as "mammie, jezebel, coon, and rascal" stereotypes. The 1960s saw the emergence of three-dimensional roles that humanized the black experience to reflect a heightened consciousness. Dee entered the 1960s with her strong portrayal of Ruth Younger in *A Raisin in the Sun* (1959), the prize-winning play by Lorraine Hansberry that depicted the struggles of a working-class family. Sidney Poitier costarred with Dee in the movie version two years later. Dee also appeared in *Purlie Victorious* (1961), a play by Ossie Davis that satirized southern black-white relationships, and later, the movie version, *Gone Are the Days* (1963). In 1965 Dee became the first African-American woman to appear in major roles at the American Shakespeare Festival at Stratford, Connecticut, playing Kate in *The Taming of the Shrew* and Cordelia in *King Lear.* Her work earned her an appearance on the cover of *Jet* magazine and continued acclaim and recognition. However, the persistent scarcity of challenging roles led Dee to join forces with other African-American performers to form the Coordinating Council for Negro Performers, which lobbied the entertainment industry for greater participation. This work led Dee to the front ranks of the civil rights movement.

Dee served on national committees and performed in benefit shows to raise money for the legal defense of civil rights workers arrested in demonstrations. She affiliated with the National Association for the Advancement of Colored People (NAACP), the Congress of Racial Equality (CORE), the Student Nonviolent Coordinating Committee (SNCC), and the Southern Christian Leadership Conference (SCLC). She also gave benefits for the Black Panthers, a youth organization formed to protect the African-American community against police brutality, and the Young Lords, a Puerto Rican youth organization patterned on the Black

Panthers for similar concerns of protecting their community. The murder of four girls at the Sixteenth Street Baptist Church in Birmingham, Alabama, in 1963, and the assassination of President John F. Kennedy the same year horrified an entire nation and prompted Dee to join with other prominent black writers, artists, and actors to form the Association of Artists for Freedom. This group organized a nationwide boycott of spending for Christmas in view of the atrocity in Birmingham. Many supporters of this effort instead used their Christmas money to support various civil rights groups.

Dee was friendly with prominent civil rights activists Dr. Martin Luther King, Jr., and Malcolm X. Although the two men held vastly different philosophies for achieving the goals of racial and economic equality, she had respect for both their public and private personas. She participated in the March on Washington with King. Malcolm X came to see *Purlie Victorious* and spent time in her home. Dee arranged meetings between Malcolm X and Paul Robeson as well as with members of King's civil rights organization. News of Malcolm X's death in 1965 caused her feelings of nausea, pain, and rage. The death of King in 1968 was completely "unutterable." She also spoke out against U.S. military involvement in Vietnam.

Against this backdrop of political and social turmoil, Dee continued to work steadily in theater, film, and television, making guest appearances on *The Fugitive* (ABC), *The Defenders* (CBS), and *The Nurses* (CBS). She toured with Ossie Davis to give recitals of dramatic scenes, poems, and stories. In 1964 Dee and Davis presented poetry readings against a jazz background at the Village Vanguard in New York and recorded *The Poetry of Langston Hughes* for Caedmon Records. Dee continued to break through racial barriers, winning roles as Julia Augustine in *The Wedding Band* (1966), Laurie in *Uptight* (1965), Joan Robinson in *The Incident* (1968), and Alma Miles, a surgeon's wife in ABC television's *Peyton Place* (1968 and 1969).

Dee received the Frederick Douglass Award from the New York Urban League in 1970. She starred in Spike Lee's *Do The Right Thing* (1989) and received numerous Emmy Award nominations for her television appearances, winning for outstanding supporting actress in a miniseries or special in 1991 for *Decoration Day* (NBC). The Ruby Dee Scholarship in Dramatic Art, which Dee endowed, helps young black women become established in acting, the profession Dee herself has used as a springboard for a lifetime of social activism.

★

An autobiography written by Dee with Ossie Davis is *With Ossie and Ruby: In This Life Together* (1998). Biographical accounts include Elton C. Fax, *Contemporary Black Leaders* (1970); Loften Mitchell, *Voices of the Black Theater* (1975); and Brian Lanker, *I Dream a World: Portraits of Black Women Who Changed America* (1989). Articles about Dee include Alan Ebert, "The Woman Ruby Dee," *Essence Magazine* (June 1976).

LEE MCQUEEN

DE KOONING, Willem (*b.* 24 April 1904 in Rotterdam, The Netherlands; *d.* 19 March 1997 in East Hampton, Long Island, New York), monumental figure of the abstract expressionist movement in art, which had worldwide influence and changed painting at the middle of the twentieth century.

Willem de Kooning was the youngest child of Leendert de Kooning, a wine and beverage distributor, and Cornelia Nobel, who owned a seaman's bar. When his parents divorced, his mother gained custody of his older sister, Maria; he was awarded to his father, but his mother appealed, and the young de Kooning went to live with her.

At the age of twelve de Kooning was apprenticed to a commercial art and decorating firm, where he worked for four years. Encouraged by its owners, he attended night

Willem de Kooning. ARCHIVE PHOTOS, INC.

classes at the Rotterdam Academy of Fine Art and Techniques for eight years. The academic training in the Dutch art school taught him a respect for tradition and craft that stayed with him his entire life. He learned designing, carpentry, portrait painting, and sign painting, skills that enabled him to find work wherever he went.

With a friend, in 1926 de Kooning stowed aboard the SS *Shelly*, working in the engine room and landing on the east coast of the United States, where he made his way to Hoboken, New Jersey. In 1927 he moved to New York City, where he did commercial art jobs and met other artists, including Stuart Davis, David Smith, Arshile Gorky, and Mark Rothko. Among the lofts and studios in and around Greenwich Village, the charismatic de Kooning became the leader whose abstract painting style the other artists strove to emulate.

In December 1943 de Kooning married Elaine Fried, an artist who was also a writer on art. They had an unconventional marriage but were together off and on until Elaine's death in 1989. They had no children, but in 1956 de Kooning fathered a daughter, Lisa, with Joan Ward, an artist with whom he was living at the time.

After his first one-man exhibit at the Charles Egan Gallery in 1948, de Kooning's reputation was established when the art critic Clement Greenberg called him one of the four or five most important painters in the country. He was invited to exhibit at the 1950 and 1954 Venice Biennales, among other major international shows.

His early paintings were essentially abstracted figurative works in shades of soft pink, gray, and green. The subject matter was the male figure. In the late 1940s he explored black-and-white motifs in mixed media and torn paper collage painted in a frenzy of shapes that covered the entire format.

During the 1950s de Kooning began his "Woman" series, perhaps the paintings for which he is most widely known. The visual onslaught of American advertising, which expressed the postwar economic boom in print, billboards, and television, was his springboard for these ferocious, slashing, grinning, big-breasted, sensual, bug-eyed monuments to abstract expressionism. This series is de Kooning's signature work, much as his friend Jackson Pollock's drip paintings and Franz Kline's black-and-white abstractions are theirs.

On 13 March 1961 de Kooning became a United States citizen, and soon after he purchased some land near East Hampton, Long Island, in a locale known as the Springs. He lived in a cottage while he worked on the plans for his new studio.

By 1963 de Kooning was living year-round in the Springs and working in his light-filled studio. He had found it difficult to accept his wealth and status before his move to Long Island. He commented, "I have no need to

be celebrated, to shake hands with a lot of people. In the end it's just your friends and your work that count." However, the media beyond the art magazines gave him and his work regular coverage.

Once established in the Springs in 1964 and comfortable with the lakes, marshes, and coastline of Long Island, de Kooning declared he was ready to start a new "Woman" series. In the works of this period he painted women in a softer light. As he declared in 1964, "I'm working on a water series. The figures are floating like reflections in the water. The color is influenced by the natural light. That's what's so good here."

Later in the 1960s de Kooning used the landscape of Long Island as a background for his softer, less ferocious women. He declared that images of nature were inside him, and his women lounged on the grass or in the water. He said, "They are brighter girls now, but they are all the same woman." These de Kooning women are playfully sexual, opened up, legs splayed and inviting voyeurism.

In 1967 de Kooning painted a series called "Women on a Sign." These yeasty, fleshy, erotic paintings carry an in-your-face sense of brutality and a life-affirming sense of iconography. He also painted a 1967 "Man" series. Pushing a squatting, comic, grotesque figure of a male around on the canvas, he painted his subject without the geometric structure of cubism or any recognizable features. A similar style appeared later in his sculptures of the 1970s.

The sexual revolution of the 1960s, with its relaxed social mores and laws regarding obscenity and pornography, affected all areas of pop culture and the arts. The viewer contemplating de Kooning's life-size fleshy figures is initiated into a deliberate erotic engagement. In his later series of 1967, "Women Singing," de Kooning painted women from the media—fashion models, young, thin, and long-legged.

By the end of the 1960s de Kooning was traveling in Europe and Japan and having exhibitions in major museums around the world. He continued to draw figures in various media and completed a number of small bronze sculptures. Honors and awards continued throughout the 1970s and 1980s; prices for his paintings escalated. In 1989 a record price, $20.8 million, was paid for a 1955 painting at a Sotheby's auction.

During the 1980s de Kooning moved away from painting figures and instead painted flat fields of white with ribbons of red, blue, and orange that danced and twisted across the canvas. Critics wondered whether his work was affected by his mental decline from Alzheimer's disease.

On 1 February 1989 Elaine de Kooning died. Ten days later de Kooning's daughter, Lisa de Kooning Villeneuve, and John Eastman filed for appointment as conservators of de Kooning's property on the grounds of his mental decline.

The last titan of the abstract expressionists died at his home at the age of ninety-three. He is buried in Green River Cemetery in East Hampton.

★

Biographies include three entitled *Willem de Kooning,* by Thomas B. Hess (1959), Harry F. Gaugh (1983), and Diane Waldman (1988); Judith Zilczer et al., *Willem de Kooning from the Hirshhorn Museum Collection* (1993); and Edvard Lieber, *Willem de Kooning: Reflections in the Studio* (2000). Obituaries are in the *New York Times* and *Times* (London) (both 20 Mar. 1997).

ROSEMARIE S. CARDOSO

DELBRÜCK, Max Ludwig Henning (*b.* 4 September 1906 in Berlin, Germany; *d.* 10 March 1981 in Pasadena, California), geneticist called the father of molecular biology who won the 1969 Nobel Prize in physiology or medicine for his cross-disciplinary approach to the study of viruses.

Delbrück was born to Hans Delbrück, a professor of history at the University of Berlin, and Lina Thiersch Delbrück, a granddaughter of the scientist Justus von Liebig, who is considered the originator of organic chemistry. The youngest of seven children, Delbrück grew up in a very active family and among members of the academic, professional, and merchant classes. As a youngster he developed a strong interest in astronomy, partly as a way to distinguish himself among so many strong personalities in his family and among their friends. However, Max Planck, a boy in the neighborhood who grew up to be a physical chemist of high distinction, became a mentor and a lifelong friend to Delbrück. Their relationship shifted Delbrück's focus from astrophysics to theoretical physics during the latter days of his graduate studies at the University of Göttingen, just after the breakthrough discoveries that opened the field of quantum mechanics. Delbrück received his Ph.D. in 1930.

Delbrück took three postdoctoral years (1929–1932) in England, Switzerland, and Denmark. He began a lifelong association with Wolfgang Pauli and Niels Bohr, and it was Bohr who first influenced Delbrück's final turn toward biology and cross-disciplinary studies in science. Delbrück moved to Berlin in 1932, where he wrote a very influential paper, *Über die Natur der Genmutation und der Genstruktur* ("On the Nature of Gene Mutation and Gene Structure"), with Nikolai Timoféeff-Ressovsky and K. G. Zimmer on mutagenesis that was published in 1935 and later reprinted in Erwin Schrödinger's essay, *What Is Life?* (1944). This association and the paper laid the foundation for the rapid development of molecular genetics in the 1940s, 1950s, and 1960s.

In 1937 Delbrück immigrated to the United States with the help of a Rockefeller Foundation fellowship, which provided him with greater freedom to pursue his research interests in biology. He went to the California Institute of

Max Delbrück *(left)*, receiving his Nobel Prize from King Gustaf Adolf of Norway, December 1969. ASSOCIATED PRESS AP

Technology because of its strength in fruit fly genetics and ended up working with Emory L. Ellis in phage research. Ellis introduced him to bacteriophages, or phages, viruses that affect bacteria, an area of study that appealed strongly to Delbrück's physics-trained mind. Like the hydrogen atom, the simplest form of matter, the bacteriophage was then considered the simplest form of life. When the fellowship ran out in 1939 and World War II started, Delbrück decided to stay in the United States, accepting an instructorship in the physics department at Vanderbilt University in Nashville, Tennessee. In 1941 Delbrück married Mary Adeline Bruce, and in later years they had four children.

During World War II, around 1941, Delbrück began his association with the Cold Spring Harbor Laboratory of Quantitative Biology on Long Island, New York, and with Salvador E. Luria and other well-known luminaries in the field of biology. This began what became known as the Phage Group, which eventually originated fluctuation theory. At this point, Delbrück and Luria began studying bacteria and viruses to determine their mode of transmission. Much to their surprise, they discovered that viruses and bacteria were capable of transferring their DNA in order to replicate rapidly. Research began into the mechanism of the transfer, and Luria came up with the idea of treating the bacteria as though they were slot machines. Exposure to viruses caused the bacteria to die, but those that survived would spring back with continued growth and take back the territory formerly possessed by the viruses. Thus the scientists could determine whether the survival was based on chance or if the bacteria were mutating in response to the challenge from the viruses. This discovery marked the beginning of phage research and began science's present-day insight into the nature of viruses. Among other discoveries and accomplishments from the Phage Group were the mutual exclusion principle, the fluctuation test, and the phage theory. Delbrück and Luria's students included James Watson, Renato Dulbecco, and other interested physicists and biochemists such as Leo Szilard, the father, with Enrico Fermi, of the nuclear chain reaction, and the atomic scientist Philip Morrison.

Delbrück became a U.S. citizen in 1945, and in the early 1950s his research interests shifted from molecular genetics to sensory physiology and phage research. One of the first grants the National Science Foundation ever awarded was to Delbrück for research. The study was called "Mechanisms Underlying Genetic Recombination in Bacteria." The results of Delbrück's work and teaching contributed to the rise of modern molecular genetics. Initially he began work on sporangiophores of *Phycomyces* to study stimulus transductions at the molecular level and to determine transducer processes of sense organs in general. In 1962 Delbrück was instrumental in setting up an institute of molecular genetics at the University of Cologne to demonstrate the possibilities behind modern interdisciplinary research within Germany and to promote the field of molecular genetics there. This institute was dedicated on 22 June 1962, with Niels Bohr the primary speaker, one of his last appearances.

Delbrück won the 1969 Nobel Prize in physiology or medicine using a cross-disciplinary approach to the study of viruses by fusing biochemistry, genetics, and physical principles to study replication mechanisms and the genetic structure of viruses. He shared the prize with Alfred Day Hershey and Luria, and a brief biography refers to him as "one of the founding fathers of modern genetics." Also in 1969 both Luria and Delbrück won the Louisa Gross Horowitz Prize for their contributions to the understanding of the genetics of bacteria and bacteriophages.

In 1978 Delbrück was diagnosed with multiple myeloma. Successful treatment prolonged his life for three years, and then a few months before his death in 1981, he also had a mild stroke that affected his vision.

Scientists writing about this era in genetics who worked closely with Delbrück refer often to his happy spirit, quick wit, and generosity of spirit. In 1966 Delbrück's colleagues honored his sixtieth birthday by publishing *Phage and the Origins of Molecular Biology,* a collection of essays by Phage Group members. It is remarkable to read the list of luminaries that Delbrück brought together at Cold Spring Harbor. He appears to have been a wonderful catalyst and mentor to many. His was a remarkable and intelligent influence on modern gene research, molecular biology, phage theory, and tumor virology. Perhaps his greatest strength was his broad, deep knowledge of several scientific fields and his ability to intermingle biochemistry, genetics, and physical principles in his research and thinking.

★

For more information, see Ernst P. Fischer and Carol Lipson, eds., *Thinking About Science: Max Delbrück and the Origins of Molecular Biology* (1988). See also Robert S. Edgar, "Max Delbrück," *Annual Review of Genetics* 16 (1982): 501–505, and William Hayes, "Max Ludwig Henning Delbrück," *National Academy of Sciences. Biographical Memoirs* 62 (1993): 67–117. An obituary is in the *New York Times* (13 Mar. 1981).

KIM LAIRD

DELLA FEMINA, Jerry (*b.* 22 July 1936 in New York City), irreverent copywriter, unconventional ad man, leading figure of advertising's creative revolution during the 1960s, and author of a brash, tell-all book on advertising.

Della Femina is the older of two sons born to Michael Louis Della Femina, a pressman for the *New York Times,* and Concetta (Corsaro) Della Femina, a homemaker. He grew up in a working-class neighborhood in the Gravesend section of Brooklyn. Della Femina went to a local school, graduated from Lafayette High School in 1954, and attended night school at Brooklyn College for one year. In 1957 he married his neighborhood sweetheart, Barbara Grizzi; they had three children and divorced in 1980. In February 1983 Della Femina married Judy Licht, a television reporter; they had two children.

Between 1954 and 1961 Della Femina held a succession of low-level jobs as a messenger boy, shipping-room clerk, and retail sales clerk. He later recalled that when he was a messenger for the *New York Times,* delivering ad proofs to Fifth Avenue department stores, he was impressed by seeing the ad writers "sitting around with their feet propped up on their desks," and he made up his mind to become one. He began freelancing for the Advertising Exchange, a retail agency, writing truss ads. His first ad-agency position was as a mailroom clerk with Ruthrauff and Ryan. When the company folded, he began writing spec ads and submitted them to a young, creative agency, Daniel and Charles. Daniel Karsch hired Della Femina in 1961 as a copywriter at $100 a week, writing ads for Kayser Roth apparel.

In 1963 Della Femina took a job at triple this earlier salary with a larger agency, Fuller and Smith and Ross, which specialized in industrial accounts. Within six months he quit to go to work for Ashe and Englemore as a writer and a copy chief, supervising other copywriters at the agency. In 1964 Della Femina's career received a major boost when he was hired as the creative director at Delehanty, Kurnit and Geller, an agency highly respected for its innovative work. In this job Della Femina supervised teams of writers and art directors and worked on many of the agency's high-profile accounts. His ads frequently won coveted copywriting awards. In 1966 Della Femina determined that he needed "big account" experience and accepted a position as creative director at Ted Bates, one of the largest old-line ad agencies populated with well-bred WASPs. Della Femina demanded and received an employment contract that paid him what was then an eye-popping $50,000 annual salary.

In 1967 Della Femina and Ron Travisano, an art director, along with two other partners, founded Jerry Della Femina, Travisano, and Partners with $80,000 that Travisano had raised. After three months and no business, two of the partners left, and Della Femina calculated that the agency had enough money left to operate for three more months. Facing the precipice of bankruptcy, Della Femina decided to gamble with their diminishing funds and invited more than a thousand people to a Christmas party. He spent $3,000 on food and liquor and knew that if the party did not generate immediate business, they were sunk. The event, however, gave them the aura of a highly successful

young agency, and the very next day, an insurance company ad manager placed their advertising business with Della Femina and partners. Within a year the agency was billing $8 million. Over time the agency garnered the advertising accounts of Blue Nun wines, Emory Air Freight, Teacher's Scotch, American Home Assurance Company, Geigy Chemical, Isuzu, Corum Watch, and a host of other high-profile accounts. In 1985 Travisano left to start a film production company.

As Della Femina's career developed, his reputation as an eccentric rebel grew. His feisty antics, like playing handball in the hallways at Fuller and Smith and Ross, frequently made the rounds of the ad industry rumor mills. Once he led a successful two-day strike against Delehanty, Kurnity and Geller over the placement of an ad. He told Ted Bates that he demanded a contract because he knew that "in four months you're going to hate me." At Bates, when he was called before the agency's creative review board, he felt that a group of "over-60 guys second guessing creative work was repugnant," so he insisted on recording the proceedings, which intimidated the board. One agency executive complained that Della Femina's "whole lifestyle is to be a provocateur."

Della Femina's most celebrated moment in advertising occurred shortly after he arrived at Ted Bates, when he was invited to a brainstorming session for the Panasonic account. Della Femina sat in a room full of people who were waiting to hear something brilliant from their trophy copywriter. Della Femina broke the silence with a joke: "I've got it! I see a whole campaign built around the headline 'From Those Wonderful Folks Who Gave You Pearl Harbor.' "

Della Femina had a wide impact on the ad industry through the 1960s. He transformed himself from a nameless writer behind a magazine or television advertisement into an ad industry guru, thanks to his unabashed self-promotion. He submitted a regular column in *Marketing/ Communications,* the leading advertising-agency publication, and he frequently contributed irreverent pieces to other advertising trade magazines. Journalists contacted him for a colorful quote on breaking news, his remarks on new ad campaigns, or saucy quips on the latest round of ad business rumors. Della Femina was constantly in the spotlight at the various ad-industry awards ceremonies, and he often spoke before ad-industry groups, especially those from outside the New York area. Comments he made during one speech, criticizing federal intervention in advertising, caused the chief executive officer of Bates, where Della Femina was employed at the time, to disavow his remarks publicly in a letter to the *New York Times.* His hilarious book, *From Those Wonderful Folks Who Gave You Pearl Harbor* (1970), became a nationwide best-seller.

Della Femina, a creative genius in advertising, is perhaps best known for the Talon Zipper ad campaign. Six panel illustrations show a youngster pitching in a sandlot baseball game, consumed with worry as the catcher slowly approaches the mound only to tell him, "Your fly is open." Other campaigns include a hard-hitting ad for McGraw-Hill publishers that ran under the headline "Before Hitler could kill 6 million Jews, he had to burn 6 million books." Della Femina wrote a headline for Ozone hair spray attempting to woo male users with a photo of Yogi Berra and the headline "Yogi Berra is one of those sissies who uses his wife's hair spray." For Feminique, a vaginal hygiene spray he wrote, "Five years ago most women would have been too embarrassed to read this page."

In 1986 Della Femina sold his agency, then billing $200 million a year, for $29 million to the London firm of Wight Collins Rutherford and Scott PLC, which renamed the firm Della Femina McNamee. He stayed on as a consultant until 1992. During a sabbatical from the ad business, Della Femina opened a trendy restaurant, Della Femina Restaurant, in Long Island's fashionable Hamptons and a second one in Manhattan in 1999. In 1998 Michael Jeary, an executive with Saachi and Saachi, accepted Della Femina's invitations to join him, and "Jeary" Della Femina appeared again on Madison Avenue. In 2000 the firm merged again and became Della Femina Rothschild Jeary and Partners.

At the beginning of the twenty-first century, Della Femina served on the boards of the Children's Aid Society and City Meals-on-Wheels, and he participated in an industrywide initiative named Ads Against AIDS. He was also philanthropically involved with the Make-a-Wish Foundation and Body Positive, an HIV/AIDS service organization.

★

Biographical information is in Della Femina's book, *From Those Wonderful Folks Who Gave You Pearl Harbor: Front Line Dispatches from the Advertising War* (1970), which has such catchy chapter titles as "Nazis Don't Take Away Accounts." Della Femina's second book, *An Italian Grows Up in Brooklyn* (1978), written with Charles Sopkin, is a description of his upbringing. Profiles of Della Femina are in *New York Times Magazine* (26 Jan. 1969) and *Fortune* (13 Apr. 1987). Articles about Della Femina are in *Time* (22 June 1970), *Advertising Age* (24 Apr. 1978), and *New York* (23 Oct. 1978).

WILLIAM J. MALONEY

DELLINGER, David (*b.* 22 August 1915 in Wakefield, Massachusetts), one of the leading organizers of the massive demonstrations against U.S. involvement in the conflict in Vietnam, the "old man" at the 1969 Chicago Eight conspiracy trial, and the publisher and editor of the influential 1960s leftist journal *Liberation*.

David Dellinger. ARCHIVE PHOTOS, INC.

Dellinger came from a well-connected New England family. His father, Raymond Dellinger, was an attorney and chairman of Boston's Republican Committee. His mother, Marie (Fiske) Dellinger, was a volunteer for charities and a social club organizer. Benjamin Franklin was David Dellinger's great-uncle, and President Calvin Coolidge was a friend of the family. Dellinger had two sisters and a brother.

Dellinger attended Yale University, first majoring in philosophy before graduating in 1936 with a degree in economics. He completed graduate work at Oxford University, in England, and while there became fascinated by the life of Saint Francis of Assisi. After serving as an ambulance driver with the resistance during the Spanish Civil War, he returned to the United States and entered Union Theological Seminary in New York City in 1939. While there he helped organize the Newark Commune, a multifaceted organization that established a cultural center for children, a communal farm, and the Essex County Equality League, which organized protests to desegregate local restaurants.

In 1940 Dellinger and seven other students at the seminary publicly announced their refusal to register for the draft, even though as divinity students they were exempt from military service. He later explained: "The exemption was a bribe to make sure that people who objected to killing their fellow humans would not speak out against war." After serving a year and a day at Lewisburg Penitentiary, he was reindicted and sentenced to a second term. In 1942 Dellinger met and married Elizabeth Peterson; they had three sons and two daughters. In 1943 Dellinger returned to prison after refusing to go to a camp for conscientious objectors. At Lewisburg he refused to stay in a segregated white portion of the jail and was sent to solitary confinement. After World War II ended Dellinger led demonstrations for amnesty for conscientious objectors.

In the 1950s Dellinger organized and participated in protests against nuclear weapons and the Korean War. As an official with the War Resisters League, he was frequently arrested during nonviolent demonstrations. In 1956 he founded *Liberation* magazine and served as its publisher and editor until 1975. The magazine was an incubator for influential radical political ideas of the 1960s and provided leading activists and scholars of the era with a solid intellectual forum.

By the time the United States entered the Vietnam War in 1961, Dellinger was a seasoned veteran of the nonviolence movement. He became one of the few respected elder statesmen of the organization against the war in Vietnam, a movement largely composed of young people in cities and on college campuses. Dellinger was an early and active opponent of the war and, as the cochair of the New Mobilization Committee to End the War in Vietnam, was one of the movement's most tireless organizers. In 1967 he played a major role in organizing the escalating protests against the war, including the Spring Mobilization, which brought 300,000 marchers into New York City and San Francisco, and the famous March on the Pentagon, which included 100,000 protestors.

Dellinger achieved his greatest fame as the "old man" of the Chicago Eight conspiracy trial. In 1968 Dellinger was one of the leading organizers of the protests in the streets outside the Democratic National Convention in Chicago. There, the Youth International Party, commonly known as the Yippies, and other groups joined Dellinger's antiwar protestors. Their demonstrations and street theater turned into a raging battle with police. After several days of increasingly tense confrontations, Dellinger, on 28 August, spoke to more than ten thousand protestors and then called for them to join him on a march to the convention hall. Police stopped the march and a melee ensued, which ended with looting and street fighting. Eight men were arrested and charged with conspiring to incite a riot.

The Chicago Eight trial, which began in September 1969, was the most memorable political theater piece of the 1960s, perfectly capturing the insolent spirit of the era's protestors. The defendants refused to acknowledge Judge Julius Hoffman's authority and alternated between comic antics and serious political speeches. The defendants would bring a North Vietnamese flag or a birthday cake to the courtroom or blow kisses to the jury. Hoffman ordered the Black Panther leader Bobby Seale bound and gagged after he refused to stop insulting the judge. Dellinger had more decorum than the other defendants, though he often hurled invectives at Hoffman, calling him a liar and a fascist. Dellinger stood out because he was by far the oldest of the group. He would appear every day in the same rumpled tweed sportscoat and flannel pants. In February 1970 the jury found Dellinger, Abbie Hoffman, and three others guilty of intent to incite a riot. Each was sentenced to five years in prison. The convictions were overturned by the Seventh Circuit Court of Appeals in 1972, after it was discovered that the Federal Bureau of Investigation had bugged the office of the defendants' attorneys.

Dellinger continued to write, speak, and organize on behalf of pacifism and social justice. In 1970 he wrote the manifesto *Revolutionary Nonviolence*. In 1975 he published *More Power Than We Know: The People's Movement Toward Democracy*. Also that year he became editor of the biweekly *Seven Days* magazine. A successor to *Liberation,* it lasted for five years. In the 1980s Dellinger moved to Vermont to write and teach at Goddard College and Vermont College. In 1986 he looked back on the Vietnam conflict and its resolution in the book *Vietnam Revisited: From Covert Action to Invasion to Reconstruction*. Even into his advanced years he continued to protest, and at age eighty-two he was arrested for demonstrating at a nuclear reactor site.

Dellinger was an influential figure in the 1960s antiwar movement. Though not as flashy or well known as other figures of the era, he was one of the few older activists who commanded the respect of the young protestors. His behind-the-scenes organizing was partially responsible for the success of many of the large demonstrations, which helped turn popular opinion against U.S. involvement in Vietnam. His work as a magazine publisher and editor helped promote and fertilize important progressive ideas throughout the 1960s.

★

By far the best source on Dellinger's life is his autobiography, *From Yale to Jail: The Life Story of a Moral Dissenter* (1993). Books on the Chicago conspiracy trial include J. Anthony Lukas, *The Barnyard Epithet and Other Obscenities: Notes on the Chicago Conspiracy Trial* (1970). Dellinger's work on the antinuclear movement is discussed in Michael Albert, *Beyond Survival: New Directions for the Disarmament Movement* (1983).

MICHAEL BETZOLD

DELORIA, Vine, Jr. (*b.* 26 March 1933 in Martin, South Dakota), historian, writer, lawyer, and activist known for speaking out against Native American conformity to U.S. culture.

Deloria's family heritage is the impetus for his writings. Born on the Pine Ridge Indian Reservation, Deloria is the son of the Reverend Vine Deloria and Barbara Eastburn. His grandfather was a Yankton chief, and his great-grandfather, Francois Des Laurias, was a medicine man who led the White Swan Band of the Yankton Sioux tribe.

Although Deloria's family converted to Christianity when his grandfather became an Episcopal priest, Deloria cherishes his Native American roots and the traditional teachings of the Hunkpapa Lakota tribe. His family has a history of leadership. For their prominent roles among their people, three members of the Deloria family were given achievement awards by Chicago's Indian Council Fire. One award went to Deloria's father, one to his aunt Ella (a prominent anthropologist), and one to Deloria himself.

After graduating from high school in Saint James Academy in Faribault, Minnesota, Deloria served in the U.S. Marine Corps from 1954 to 1956. He earned a B.A. degree from Iowa State University in 1958 and a B.D. degree in theology from Augustana Lutheran Seminary, Rock Island, Illinois, in 1963. In 1964 Deloria began developing a scholarship program for Native American students through the United Scholarship Service in Denver.

The 1960s was a pivotal decade for Deloria. His first book was published and his career was off to a promising start. From 1964 to 1967 Deloria was the executive director of the National Congress of American Indians (NCAI) in Washington, D.C. He found, however, that dishonest people stood in the way of bettering Native American lives. Indian tribes were often pitted against each other so that they became more involved in serving their own interests than in benefiting their people as a whole. Also, financial difficulties plagued the NCAI, limiting its ability to serve the Native American cause.

All of Deloria's work reflects a deep commitment to the well-being of the Native American people. His first book, *Custer Died for Your Sins: An Indian Manifesto* (1969), deals with the pain of generations of Native Americans trying to act as if their ancestors had not been murdered by white immigrants. The book advocates Native American self-rule and separateness. In his foreword to the book, Deloria explained his motivation for writing it. He felt he was giving voice to his people's silent suffering and loss: "One reason I wanted to write it was to raise some issues for younger Indians which they have not been raising for themselves. Another reason was to give some idea to white people of the unspoken but often felt antagonisms I have detected in Indian people toward them, and the reasons for such antagonisms."

Vine Deloria, Jr.

In Deloria's second book, *We Talk, You Listen: New Tribes, New Turf* (1970), he discusses the revival of tribalism and how living in harmony with the environment ensures the survival of the human race. Deloria's mixed religious feelings surfaced in his third book, *God Is Red: A Native View of Religion* (1973). In this book he compares Native American worship of the Great Spirit to Christianity. He considers the Native American religion to have the energy of creation and Christianity to have the energy of destruction. Although critics welcomed Deloria's views on Native American theology, some were offended by his treatment of Christian beliefs.

As an activist, Deloria sought to help Native Americans become educated so they could promote change peacefully rather than through violence. Deloria felt drawn to his Native American heritage and wanted to make certain his people did not forget their roots. His goal was to help Native Americans govern themselves rather than be governed by the United States.

Throughout the 1960s Deloria promoted Native American civil rights. By the end of the decade he was frustrated by his inability to make a difference in the lives of Native Americans and decided to try a different approach. He returned to school and earned a law degree from the University of Colorado in 1970. He knew that local tribes were not aware of their legal rights and that with a law degree he would be able to assist them. He believed that in order to preserve their identity as a unique people, Native Americans needed to pursue legal measures and renegotiate treaties with the United States. As an expert on U.S.–Indian treaties, Deloria sought to help Native Americans regain some of what they had lost.

As Native Americans agitated for more self-rule, incidents occurred such as the seizure of the village at Wounded Knee in 1973. Wounded Knee was in 1890 the site of the last major battle between U.S. federal troops and Native Americans; it is remembered because of the many Sioux who were massacred there. Inspired by the activism of the 1960s, the 1973 takeover began as an effort to secure a place where Native Americans could speak publicly of their grievances. But the takeover escalated into a clash between Native Americans and federal forces, and weapons were fired. As a Native American, Deloria sympathized with and helped defend Russell Means and Dennis Banks, two American Indian Movement participants who were put on trial for their actions at Wounded Knee.

Deloria was crushed when the Indian activist movement in the early 1970s failed. He blamed the failure on the views Americans held about Indians. "Americans simply refuse to give up their longstanding conceptions of what an Indian is," he wrote in *God Is Red.*

In the 1970s Deloria taught at Western Washington State College, the University of California at Los Angeles, and the University of Arizona. In 1991 he began teaching at the University of Colorado in Boulder. A prolific author, Deloria books include *Of Utmost Good Faith* (1971); *The Indian Affair* (1974); *Behind the Trail of Broken Treaties: An Indian Declaration of Independence* (1974); *Indians of the Pacific Northwest: From the Coming of the White Man to the Present Day* (1977); *The Metaphysics of Modern Existence* (1979); *American Indian Policy in the Twentieth Century* (1985); and *Red Earth, White Lies: Native Americans and the Myth of Scientific Fact* (1995).

Deloria cofounded the Institute for the Development of Indian Law in the 1970s, where he served as chairperson from 1970 to 1978. He and Barbara Nystrom married in 1958 and had three children. Deloria is six feet tall and wears his hair long, as did his forebears.

★

Articles on Deloria can be found in Gale Group's *Encyclopedia of World Biography* (2nd ed.), *Contemporary Authors Online,* *Contemporary Heroes and Heroines (Book I),* and *American Decades CD-ROM.* A book review by John C. Wittaker of Deloria's *Red Earth, White Lies* can be found in *Skeptical Inquirer* (Jan.–Feb. 1997). Deloria is mentioned in Jefferson Faye, "Revealing the Storyteller: The Ethical Publication of Inuit Stories," *American Review of Canadian Studies* (spring–summer 2001): 159.

A. E. SCHULTHIES

DE VARONA, Donna (*b.* 26 April 1947 in San Diego, California), two-time gold medalist in swimming at the 1964 Tokyo Olympics who set eighteen world swimming records before she retired from competition in 1964. She helped launch the Women's Sports Foundation and became a vocal and articulate champion of women's rights in the athletic domain.

de Varona was raised in Lafayette, California, near San Francisco. Her father, David de Varona, who sold insurance, was a Hall of Fame rower and an All-America football player at the University of California who served as de Varona's first swimming coach. Her mother, Martha (Smith) de Varona, was a retail sales associate. She had three siblings. Not surprisingly, being raised near the waters of the Pacific Ocean, de Varona was paddling by the age of three and diving at the age of seven. She especially enjoyed training with her elder brother in Olympic-size pools. During the 1950s and the 1960s athletic opportunities for women, much less young girls, were few and far between. While there were college athletic scholarships for superior female athletes, the vast number of girls were denied athletic and sports opportunities. Though she did not receive a scholarship, de Varona earned an undergraduate degree

Donna de Varona displaying the gold medal she won in the women's 400-meter individual medley event, 1964. ASSOCIATED PRESS AP

in political science from the University of California, Los Angeles.

Setback and loss have motivated de Varona all her life. As a ten-year-old she entered the Far Western American Athletic Union meet in San Francisco and finished dead last. This beating gave her the incentive to do what were then phenomenal training stints—five and six hours a day—at the Berkeley Young Men's Christian Association (YMCA) swim club and at the famous Santa Clara Swim Club. Then, at the age of thirteen, she first broke a world record in the 400-meter individual medley event at the Outdoor National Amateur Athletic Union Championship. To this day the medley is seen, arguably, as the most demanding of all swim events. It is like a quadrathlon, in that the four different strokes have to be performed in sequence, with the end race scenario being a frantic battle to retain stroke cadence as one drowns, "physiologically," in a sea of lactic acid. Indeed, the race was so much a cutting-edge event that it was not included in the program at the 1960 Rome Olympics. Nevertheless, the thirteen-year-old de Varona was a reserve for the U.S. swim team and the youngest American team member of the Olympics.

de Varona became a sensation. She later remarked on the fun and also the pressure of her early fame—being endlessly interviewed, photographed, and held up for scrutiny by a vast array of American magazines, ranging from the serious adult weekly to the glossy teenage comic. Celebrity status and her role as the quintessential Californian mermaid had both positive and negative consequences for her. In her life she has been featured on the cover of *Life, Time,* the *Saturday Evening Post,* and *Sports Illustrated* (twice).

At the 1964 Tokyo Olympics, the 400-meter individual relay was on the program. de Varona won the event, and she also swam on the 4 by 100–meter freestyle relay team that won a gold medal. For this tandem success she was recognized as the Associated Press Female Athlete of the Year for 1964. During her career she won thirty-seven individual national championship medals, including eighteen gold medals and three national high-point awards. She held world records in eight long-course events and American records in ten short-course events. In biography after biography her sobriquet is the "Queen of Swimming."

As a keynote speaker at the 1982 meeting of the International Olympic Academy in Olympia, Greece, de Varona reflected on the media attention she received as an Olympic athlete: "In 1964, there were many sponsors who wanted me to endorse their products, but because of ingrained Olympic ideals I felt my gold medals were not for sale." Instead, de Varona sought opportunities to create programs that would promote the sport. Following her retirement from competitive swimming in 1964, de Varona embarked on a multifaceted career. In 1965 she became the first woman to cover sports on network television for the American Broadcasting Company (ABC) program *Wide World of Sports.* A teenage American female's having the opportunity to appear on a major channel and present "sports" to a prime-time audience cannot be underestimated. Stories about the achievements of male athletes usually dominated such sports programs. The role of women and female accomplishments appeared, if at all, on the margins. The female athlete was treated as less than important, and repeatedly the sporting woman was trivialized.

Despite de Varona contributing color commentaries throughout the 1960s and at the 1968 Summer Olympics in Mexico City—and for that matter through the 1970s and the 1980s—the narrator and commentator Jim McKay remained the featured figure on the program. In hindsight, de Varona's media contributions have to be seen as minor, and she was never able to become an influential commentator on par with such broadcast news anchors as Peter Jennings, Tom Brokaw, and Dan Rather. Nevertheless, it is important to note her pioneering contributions to sports broadcasting and the fact that she provided color commentary at consecutive Summer Olympics from 1968 to 1996. She coanchored the late-night wrap-up at the Los Angeles Olympics (1984), and she joined the ABC *Eyewitness News* team in New York, following up with stints at *NBC Sports* and the *Today Show.* de Varona married John Pinto on 10 January 1987; they have two children. In 1991, when she received a Gold Medallion from the International Swimming Hall of Fame (ISHOF), a press release from the ISHOF listed her job as vice president of ABC Sports. de Varona worked for the National Broadcasting Company (NBC) at the 2000 Sydney Olympics, did weekly reports for Sporting News Radio, and in 2000 and 2001 received back-to-back Gracie Allen Awards for excellence in broadcasting.

de Varona, who was unable to get a college swimming scholarship after winning two Olympic gold medals, was a major advocate of the 1972 Title IX legislation, which prohibits sex discrimination in sports. In 1974 she and the tennis champion Billie Jean King cofounded the Women's Sports Foundation, and it continues to be an extraordinarily persuasive voice for encouraging women to participate in sports and to fight to achieve gender equality in sport. de Varona has served on special commissions for Presidents Gerald Ford, Jimmy Carter, and Ronald Reagan and is a tireless spokesperson at international Olympic congresses. She worked tirelessly with Eunice Kennedy Shriver in the late 1960s to create the Special Olympics movement, which embraces children and adults with developmental disabilities. de Varona was inducted into the International Swimming Hall of Fame in 1969. Janet Woolom nicely summarizes de Varona's lifelong contribution: "She had a profound impact on increasing opportunities for women in all levels of sports."

★

Biographical essays on de Varona include Shawn Ladda's entry in *Scribner Encyclopedia of American Lives, Sports Figures* (2002), and Janet Woolom's profile in *Outstanding Women Athletes* (1992). The *ABC Wide World of Sports* (highlights of 1960s, 1970s and 1980s) compilation is available from CBS/Fox Video Sports. The *Proceedings* of the twenty-second session of the International Olympic Academy (11–25 July 1982) contain a full version of de Varona's conference keynote speech, entitled "Partnership Between the Athletes and Organizations of the Olympic Movement."

SCOTT A. G. M. CRAWFORD

DEVOS, Richard Marvin (*b.* 4 March 1926 in Grand Rapids, Michigan), and **Jay VAN ANDEL**, (*b.* 3 June 1924 in Grand Rapids, Michigan), founders of the direct sales company Amway, who in the 1960s expanded their company from an out-of-a-basement operation into one of the largest network marketing companies in the world.

DeVos was born to Simon C. DeVos, an electrical contractor, and Ethel R. Dekker, a homemaker. Van Andel was born to James Van Andel, a car dealer, and Petronella ("Nellie") Van der Woude, also a homemaker. They share a Dutch immigrant background and membership in the conservative Christian Reformed Church, characteristics that often are cited as the basis of the high value they have placed on hard work, honesty, and religious faith. They have worked together since meeting in 1940 as students at Grand Rapids Christian High School, when they struck up a friendship and a business arrangement in which Van Andel drove DeVos to school in exchange for twenty-five cents per week. After serving in the U.S. Army Air Corps during World War II, they tried their hands at a number of businesses and traveled together in the Caribbean and South America. Both attended Calvin College in Grand Rapids.

In 1948 a cousin of Van Andel's brought them into Nutrilite food supplements as "distributors" in a multilevel marketing system in which they earned profits selling products and earned bonuses recruiting new distributors. DeVos and Van Andel worked hard as Nutrilite distributors throughout the 1950s, learning the marketing system they later made so astoundingly successful in Amway. As the Ja-Ri Corporation they built a profitable network by recruiting more than 5,000 new Nutrilite distributors with a "vision of a free and prosperous future." During this time they both married; DeVos to Helen June Van Wesep on 7 February 1953, and Van Andel to Betty J. Hoekstra on 16 August 1952; started families (both couples had four children); and settled down in Ada, Michigan, outside Grand Rapids.

When Nutrilite became unstable in the late 1950s, DeVos and Van Andel acted quickly to protect their distribution system and in early 1958 established the American Way Association (later Amway Distributors Association) to provide security and cohesion to their distributors. They

soon decided to develop their own products for distribution and in 1959 officially incorporated as Amway Sales and Amway Services. To build up the new business, DeVos and Van Andel developed a line of household and personal care products—commodities that were both inexpensive and used commonly. Among their first products were two biodegradable detergents: Frisk (later LOC, for "liquid organic compound") and the highly successful SA-8, which contributed to their reputation as a soap company. Amway's commitment to environmentally friendly products made for sales success in the 1960s, as support for ecology increased. As their product line expanded, Amway bought out suppliers and moved manufacturing processes to Ada.

The company grew quickly and in 1964 merged its sales, services, and manufacturing divisions to form the Amway Corporation. Amway's physical plant had been expanded forty-five times by 1966, and estimated retail sales grew from $500,000 dollars in 1960, to $35 million in 1965, and $85 million in 1969. Amway distributors increased to 65,000 by 1964, and to 100,000 by 1969. Amway's expansion into international markets began with Canada in 1962, and England in 1964. Within thirty years there were more than 3 million distributors in dozens of countries on every continent.

During the 1960s Amway's network of independent distributors selling household and personal products was established as more than just a manufacturing and distribution company. To its two founders and millions of distributors worldwide, Amway came to represent "the American way of private ownership and free enterprise." DeVos and Van Andel drew thousands and then millions of new distributors to Amway with a means to earn extra income, to achieve "dreams" of financial independence. The "be your own boss" opportunity provided by Amway also appealed to an "outside the system" sensibility—particularly in an era dominated by enormous corporations such as International Business Machines (IBM) and General Motors. Amway also provided new distributors with a means to participate as more than mere consumers in the expanding economy of the 1960s, seen in discount merchandising stores, such as Wal-Mart and Target, and other successful direct marketing ventures, notably Mary Kay Cosmetics (1963).

Yet while DeVos and Van Andel's dream of "financial independence and personal freedom" was attractive to many, for others the evangelistic recruitment and management style at Amway seemed like a cult that took advantage of unwitting "distributors" to make money for the company. In Amway's direct sales or multilevel marketing structure, distributors are self-employed sellers of Amway products who earn a small profit on product sales to individual consumers. Opportunities for significant income come when a distributor sponsors a new distributor into Amway, thereby earning a bonus from Amway based on the sales of sponsored, or "down-line," distributors. A single sponsor is entitled to a percentage on every sale made in her or his down-line network and all the networks descending from it. Success is measured in sales, and bonuses increase as one's network grows and earns.

Aggressive recruitment and motivation of distributors were a large part of Amway's "business." In the early 1960s, with DeVos as the "charismatic motivator," the two founders personally traveled the United States in their Showcase Bus to reach a larger audience with Amway products and employment opportunities. The company developed a mixed reputation as a determined recruiter, with huge conventions and smaller sales meetings that were compared to evangelical revival meetings. The importance of expanding the force of distributors in Amway cannot be overstated, for it is only through constantly increasing networks of distributors that real profits are made.

In fact, Amway is a pyramid organization, which led to legal and image problems in the 1960s. In 1969 the Federal Trade Commission (FTC) began investigating Amway, and formal charges were brought in the mid-1970s. A ruling by the full FTC in 1979 declared Amway's marketing scheme to be legal, primarily because Amway's bonuses are based on actual sales, and merchandise can be returned to the company for a full refund. In another legal problem, Canada brought a suit against Amway for underpayment of import duties in 1970. DeVos and Van Andel maintained that they had done nothing wrong, but they eventually paid fines of over $25 million.

Amway's success continued after the 1960s, and through adapting products and international expansion it has maintained an almost constant pattern of growth. Amway's insistent distributor recruitment efforts have led to accusations of cultlike behavior and made Amway a topic for jokes on late-night television. In fact, DeVos led a top-down "cleanup" of distributorships running as illegal pyramids in the 1980s. DeVos and Van Andel continued to lead Amway, and in the mid-1990s both were ranked by *Forbes* magazine as among the ten richest people in the United States. They have dedicated their influence and money to numerous causes, including business organizations, conservative politics, and the arts. The landscape of Grand Rapids reflects their munificence in the Amway Grand Plaza Hotel, DeVos Hall, and Van Andel Arena, among other projects.

★

Both DeVos and Van Andel have written books about their successes with Amway. DeVos, *Compassionate Capitalism: People Helping People Help Themselves* (1993), offers advice for living and doing well in a Christian tradition; Van Andel, *An Enterprising Life: An Autobiography* (1998), gives many details of the Amway story. For a closer look at network marketing, see Rodney K. Smith, *Multilevel Marketing: A Lawyer Looks at Amway, Shaklee,* *and Other Direct Sales Organizations* (1984). Stephen Butterfield, *Amway: The Cult of Free Enterprise* (1985), offers a critical view of Amway. Charles Paul Conn has written a number of books sympathetic to Amway and its founders, the most factual of which is *Promises to Keep: The Amway Phenomenon and How It Works* (1985). For the most complete and engaging book on DeVos, Van Andel, and Amway, see Wilbur Cross and Gordon Olson, *Commitment to Excellence: The Remarkable Amway Story* (1986).

MARIANA REGALADO

DICK, Philip K(indred) (*b.* 16 December 1928 in Chicago, Illinois; *d.* 2 March 1982 in Santa Ana, California), science fiction author best known for *The Man in the High Castle* (1968) and *Do Androids Dream of Electric Sheep?* (1968), which inspired the motion picture *Blade Runner* (1982). Dick was admired for his complex, thoughtful novels and is often ranked among the best of twentieth-century writers.

———

Dick was the son of Joseph Edgar and Dorothy (Kindred) Dick. Dick's father worked for the U.S. Department of Agriculture but deserted his family in 1931 to go to California to become a radio talk show host. Dick's twin sister died in infancy, and the family moved to Berkeley, California, in 1929. After his parents' divorce in 1933 Dick moved with his mother to Washington, D.C., where he attended boarding school. In 1939 they moved back to Berkeley. Dick graduated from Berkeley High School in 1945.

From 1948 to 1952 Dick worked at a Berkeley record store. One of the customers was Jeanette Marlin, whom he married on 14 May 1948. Dick's drug and alcohol addictions and mental instability made him almost unbearable to live with, and the stormy marriage officially ended on 30 November 1948.

In 1947 Dick began writing fiction with an eye toward publication, finally publishing a short story in 1951 in the *Magazine of Fantasy and Science Fiction*. He became a prolific writer and in 1952 decided to write full-time. In June 1950 he married Kleo Apostolides. When more than one of his stories would appear in a single issue of a magazine, Dick would sometimes use the pen names Richard Phillips and Jack Dowland to give the illusion that the stories were by different authors. In 1958 he divorced Kleon and married Anne Williams Rubenstein, with whom he had one daughter. They divorced in 1964.

Dick published nineteen novels and one collection of short stories during the 1960s. He tried to break out of science fiction by writing modernist, realistic novels, but these did not find publishers. In 1962 his most acclaimed novel, *The Man in the High Castle,* was published. It is a multilayered narrative with thematic depth, heralding the many complex novels to come. In this alternate history tale, Germany and Japan have won World War II and divided

North America between them. The main character, Mr. Tagomi, tries to find ways to relieve Americans from the horrors of Nazi brutality. The book is built around one of Dick's most important themes: distinguishing what is real from what is not real. For example, an underground novel, an alternate history in which Germany and Japan lose World War II, circulates in Japanese-held territory. *The Man in the High Castle* explores such issues as whether fiction can accurately convey reality and whether it is possible to separate wishful thinking from fact. Dick said that he spent seven years in the libraries at the University of California, Berkeley, researching the societies of Nazi Germany and Imperial Japan before writing the novel. Even though it was his most popular novel, with a market for sequels, he could not bear to revisit the evil of Nazi society. In 1963 *The Man in the High Castle* earned the Hugo Award for the best science fiction novel of the past year.

In his 1965 novel *The Three Stigmata of Palmer Eldritch*, Dick focuses on the issue of perceived reality versus actual reality by inventing a civilization in which a dope dealer poses as God. The inspiration for the novel came from a vision Dick had in 1963 while looking at the sky: a malevolent, steely face glared down at him, and he saw that it was God. Visions subsequently visited him ever more frequently, until he believed he was receiving divine revelations that he could translate into fiction. Thus the novel marks two important trends in Dick's writing: autobiographical details (drug addiction, in this case) and mysticism based on visions.

On 18 April 1967 Dick married Nancy Hackett. They had one daughter. In 1968 he published *Do Androids Dream of Electric Sheep?*, later released as *Blade Runner* (1982) after the motion picture title. In this tale Dick investigates what defines people as human beings. Androids that look and feel to the touch exactly like human beings are illegally loose in a grim future American society, but they lack emotions, setting them apart. It was Dick's conclusion that empathy is the defining aspect of humanity.

The year is 1992 in *Do Androids Dream of Electric Sheep?*—after World War Terminus, a nuclear war that poisoned the atmosphere, killing most living things. A living animal is a commodity, something of great value that serves as a status symbol as well as an investment. Even so, most "animals" are actually machines designed to look and behave like real animals. Protagonist Rick Deckard keeps an electric sheep on the roof of his home, where he cares for it as if it were alive—a wearisome process because it serves to remind him that he is wasting his time on a fake animal.

Deckard is an android hunter, and the novel tells of one day in his life in which he tracks down and kills six superbly designed androids that are pretending to be human in San Francisco. His encounters with the androids are unsettling; as he destroys each one, he becomes less certain that they are not living beings as well as machines. His day is counterpointed by the day of John Isidore, who works at a clinic for artificial animals. He is a member of a subclass called "specials," people who are not allowed to breed because of low intelligence or mutations caused by radiation. Isidore befriends three of the androids Deckard hunts and tries to show them how to empathize with other beings. Through Deckard and Isidore's experiences, Dick explores the problems people encounter respecting life and each other in an age when technology increasingly intrudes on the most intimate parts of life, and how people who rely on machines may become detached from both life and themselves.

Dick's health was deteriorating markedly by the 1970s, and he seemed to be nearing outright insanity. In 1972 he was committed to a hospital in Vancouver, British Columbia, where he was miserable because of the harsh treatment meted out to patients. Even so, he managed to cut back on his intake of pills and alcohol, replacing them with other obsessions, such as world peace, antiabortionism, and his visions. He was released from the hospital later in 1972.

He divorced Nancy and on 18 April 1973 married Tessa Busby, with whom he had one son. He left her in 1976 and again divorced. The prospect of a motion picture being made of *Do Androids Dream of Electric Sheep?* excited him. In 1982 he saw an advanced screening of *Blade Runner*, the tale's motion picture title, and he was happy with it. A few days later he died of heart failure. He is buried in Riverside Cemetery in Fort Morgan, Colorado.

Dick's reputation grew after his death. During the 1980s all of his writings came back into print. His story "We Can Remember It for You Wholesale" inspired the motion picture *Total Recall* (1990), which was a popular success, creating the prospect of more of Dick's fiction being made into movies. Some critics, perhaps extravagantly, regard Dick as one of the twentieth century's best novelists because of the depth and complexity of his best works.

★

The Selected Letters of Philip K. Dick (1992) offers insight into Dick's mysticism and work habits. In *Dream Makers: The Uncommon People Who Write Science Fiction* (1980), Charles Platt offers a portrait of Dick and a short interview with him. Alexander Star offers an outstanding introduction to the major issues of Dick's life and work in "The God in the Trash: The Fantastic Life and Oracular Work of Philip K. Dick," *New Republic* 209, no. 23 (6 Dec. 1993): 34–42. An obituary is in the *New York Times* (3 Mar. 1982).

KIRK H. BEETZ

DICKERSON, Nancy (*b.* 19 January 1927 in Milwaukee, Wisconsin; *d.* 18 October 1997 in New York City), pioneering female television news reporter.

Dickerson was born Nancy Hanschman to Frederick R. Hanschman, an architect, and Florence (Conners) Hanschman. She grew up in the small town of Wauwatosa, Wisconsin, and attended the local high school. Dickerson went to Clarke College, a Catholic girls' college in Dubuque, Iowa, and then transferred to the University of Wisconsin at Madison, where she received a B.A. in education in 1948. After traveling to Europe as a United Nations student delegate in 1948, she returned to Milwaukee to teach for two years, attending Harvard's graduate school during the summers. She graduated from Harvard with an M.A. in government in 1949.

In 1950 Dickerson moved to Washington, D.C., where she worked on the Senate Foreign Relations Committee. While she enjoyed her position, there were few opportunities for an ambitious young woman to advance her career. But her knowledge of Capitol Hill landed her a job with the Columbia Broadcasting System (CBS) in 1954, on the radio news programs *The Leading Question* and *Capitol Cloakroom*. During this time she formed valuable friendships with many people, including the young congressman John F. Kennedy, whom she briefly dated, and Senator Lyndon B. Johnson. Her charm and intelligence ensured her a leading position within Washington's elite social scene, which was to be crucial to her success as a journalist.

In the 1960s television rose to a position of cultural dominance. By 1963 more people received their news via the television than from the newspaper, a trend that would transform mainstream news forever. But at the start of the decade, the rapidly expanding world of television news was just finding its feet, and Dickerson was determined to be a part of it. Through her hard work, particularly her willingness to take on jobs that her male colleagues would not, she became CBS's first female television correspondent in 1960. This was the beginning of a successful decade in front of the camera. At the Democratic convention later that year, she became the first woman to report from the floor of a national political convention. Lyndon Johnson's decision to run with Kennedy as vice president was announced in an interview with Dickerson. She briefly interviewed Kennedy at his inauguration, just before he was sworn in as president, and directly after. She reported on the March on Washington in 1963, when the Reverend Martin Luther King, Jr., spoke to the nation of his dream of racial equality, and she covered the assassination and funeral of President Kennedy.

Dickerson's inside knowledge of the Washington social and political scenes enabled her to beat the competition. In particular, her friendship with Lyndon Johnson remained strong throughout the decade, and Johnson often spoke to her to the exclusion of any other reporters. The sight of Johnson stepping off a plane and heading over to drawl

Nancy Dickerson. © BETTMAN/CORBIS. Reproduced by permission.

"Hello, Nancy" into her microphone is one of the enduring images of Dickerson's career. Her connections undoubtedly helped her gain many exclusive scoops, such as at the 1964 Democratic convention, when Johnson announced Hubert Humphrey as his running mate. However, her intimate social ties also hindered her credibility as a serious journalist. Inevitably, there were rumors about her and Johnson as well as the accusation that her close relationships with many politicians brought her journalistic integrity into question.

On 24 February 1962 Dickerson married C. Wyatt Dickerson, a Washington businessman, with whom she had three children. By 1963 she had become dissatisfied with her position at CBS and felt that her stories were being sidelined, so she moved to the National Broadcasting Company (NBC). She had her first child later that year. She juggled her roles as mother, wife, and reporter at a time when there were few examples of working mothers to guide her. Her career continued to develop, and she was named one of the top ten television reporters by *Variety* in 1964, the only woman on the list. By this stage Dickerson had become a celebrity, and magazine articles with such titles as "Television's Princess of the Press Corps" and "Washington's Most Serious Butterfly" appeared. She was by then one of the most influential women within the Washington social scene and a feature at the most important parties and dinners, including the exclusive F Street Club.

Toward the end of the decade Dickerson again became dissatisfied with the progress of her career. She regarded herself as the victim of a backlash against women's liberation, as growing demands for equality between the sexes within the media industry began to cause tension and suspicion. In 1970 Dickerson decided to leave NBC to launch her own syndicated news program. This move was not successful, and the end of the 1960s was effectively the beginning of the twilight of her career. Dickerson shifted to producing independent documentaries, and in 1980 founded the Television Corporation of America. She divorced her husband in 1983 and married John C. Whitehead in 1989. She died in a New York City hospital in 1997 from complications related to a stroke that she had had earlier in the year. She is buried in Arlington National Cemetery.

On the news almost every day throughout the 1960s, Dickerson was one of the most visible examples of a professional working woman for many American women of the "baby boomer" generation that followed her. As a pioneer in her field, she was an important role model for other women seeking to establish a career in the media and in other fields. Dickerson epitomized the glamour and excitement that was associated with the fledgling world of television news and with Washington politics during the days of the Kennedy administration and beyond. But Dickerson's successful journalistic approach, which was based on close personal relationships and trust, became outmoded, particularly after the Watergate scandal, which brought down the presidency of Richard Nixon and forever changed the relationship between the news media and those in power.

★

Dickerson's autobiography, *Among Those Present* (1976), is an entertaining source of information on her career and on Washington politics during the 1960s. David H. Hosley and Gayle K. Yamada, *Hard News: Women in Broadcast Journalism* (1987), offers biographical information on Dickerson, as does Christine L. Ogan's entry on Dickerson in *Women in Communication: A Biographical Sourcebook* (1996). An article by Dickerson's son John F. Dickerson in *Time* (13 Nov. 2000) provides an interesting reflection on his mother's career. Obituaries are in the *Chicago Tribune, Los Angeles Times, New York Times,* and *Washington Post* (all 19 Oct. 1997).

KATRINA FORD

DILLER, Phyllis Ada (*b.* 17 July 1917 in Lima, Ohio), stand-up comic and television performer who gained fame in the 1960s for her outrageous appearance and skewed takes on marriage, child rearing, and suburbia.

The only child of Perry Marcus Driver, an insurance agency manager, and Frances Ada Romshe, a homemaker, Diller enjoyed a comfortable childhood in the northwestern Ohio city of Lima. Although she later recalled a shy and awkward adolescence, Diller engaged in tennis, dramatics, and journalism at Lima's Central High School. After graduating from high school in 1935 she left for Chicago and enrolled in the Sherwood Music Conservatory to study piano. Overcome by doubts about her chances to pursue a career as a concert pianist, Diller returned to Ohio after two years in Chicago and enrolled at Bluffton College. On 4 November 1939 she eloped with Sherwood Anderson Diller, whom she met at Bluffton during her senior year.

In 1940 the Dillers moved to the San Francisco Bay area. Over the next fifteen years, Sherwood Diller had a series of jobs ranging from factory inspector to salesman, and the Diller family grew to include five children. Diller also supported the family as a consumer columnist for the San Leandro *News-Observer* and as a copywriter for an Oakland department store. By the mid-1950s Diller worked full-time as a copy writer for KROW radio in Oakland and then as a press relations director at KSFO in San Francisco. Money remained tight in the household, a fact that Diller acknowledged in a 2000 interview with *Daily Variety*: "[M]y husband had a real objective point of view. His objective was, 'Hey, there's money to be made with this chick!' "

Phyllis Diller, 1969. ASSOCIATED PRESS AP

Diller served as an emcee at various civic functions around Alameda, California, and began writing routines for a stand-up comedy act, which debuted on 7 March 1955 at the Purple Onion nightclub in San Francisco. In its first incarnation, Diller's act relied on her musical training and a number of costume changes, as she spoofed Jeannette McDonald, Eartha Kitt, and novelty singer Yma Sumac in between her monologues. She immediately revised the act when she realized that the monologues were proving far more entertaining than her impressions, and her two-week engagement at the Purple Onion stretched to eighty-nine weeks. By the time the stint was over, Diller had refined the basic version of her act that would prove durable for the next forty years. Her hair in disarray, wearing outlandish, ill-fitting clothes, often with combat boots, Diller held a long cigarette holder as she reviewed her lackluster efforts at housekeeping, the crumbling state of her marriage, and the bumbling antics of her imaginary husband Fang. Punctuating her jokes with exaggerated expressions and a cackling laugh, Diller presented a version of domesticity far removed from its depiction on contemporary television shows such as *Leave It to Beaver*, *Father Knows Best*, and *The Donna Reed Show*.

Indeed, Diller presented a counterpoint to the images of femininity and domesticity that dominated the media in the 1960s. Although her stage persona and mannerisms were outlandish, she articulated the everyday frustrations that the so-called "average housewife" faced with her husband, children, and neighbors. Her commentary avoided the overtly political, but Diller's ultimate contribution to American culture in the 1960s was a decidedly subversive critique of domesticity and gender roles. Domestic squabbles were Diller's comedic stock-in-trade, as she demonstrated in her 1967 book *Phyllis Diller's Marriage Manual*. "My mother-in-law must be the probation officer I got for the crime I committed when I married my husband," she wrote, "I'm surprised she isn't nicer to me. With the kind of husband her son made, you'd think she'd be afraid I'd sue her." Diller published two other humor books, *Phyllis Diller Tells All About Fang* (1963), and *Phyllis Diller's Housekeeping Hints* (1966).

A regular cabaret and nightclub performer throughout the 1960s, Diller also made dozens of appearances on the *Tonight Show*, *The Ed Sullivan Show*, *The Andy Williams Show*, *The Hollywood Squares*, and *Laugh-In*. Diller also took on acting roles that usually stayed close to her comic persona. Her most successful film was 1966's *Boy, Did I Get a Wrong Number!* with Bob Hope. The same year she starred in the television series *The Pruitts of Southampton,* which was renamed *The Phyllis Diller Show* in its 1967–1968 season. Another series, *The Beautiful Phyllis Diller Show,* lasted just one year in 1968–1969. The title played upon Diller's deliberately bizarre appearance, as well as her

acknowledgment of undergoing plastic surgery. Making fun of her plastic surgery in her routine, Diller was one of the first celebrities to discuss the topic openly, albeit in a humorous fashion.

On 3 September 1965 Diller's real-life marriage to Sherwood Diller ended in divorce; she married actor Warde Donovan on 7 October the same year. Diller and Donovan divorced in 1975. From the 1970s through the 1990s Diller continued to appear as a guest star on numerous television shows while maintaining a constant touring schedule. Realizing her childhood dream, she also played as a guest pianist with dozens of symphony orchestras in the 1970s. After almost a half century of performing as one of America's favorite comics, the eighty-five-year-old Diller announced in 2002 that she was ending her career in stand-up, although she planned on continuing her television work.

★

Diller's life and career are discussed in Susan Horowitz, *Queens of Comedy: Lucille Ball, Phyllis Diller, Carol Burnett, Joan Rivers, and the New Generation of Funny Women* (1997). A profile of Diller, "Standup's First Lady," by Jason Smith appeared in *Daily Variety* (8 Sept. 2000). Tony Vellela interviewed Diller, "Pioneer Showed Women How to Stand Up and Be Funny," in the *Christian Science Monitor* (2 Mar. 2001).

TIMOTHY BORDEN

DINE, James ("Jim") (*b.* 16 June 1935 in Cincinnati, Ohio), painter, sculptor, printmaker, performance artist, set designer, and poet who, more than any other artist, captured and popularized the dynamic trends in American avant-garde art in the 1960s.

The eldest of two sons of Stanley Cohen, who owned a paint store, and Eunice Cohen, a homemaker, Dine grew up intrigued by the colors and texture of paint in his father's store. At fifteen, following his mother's death, he went to live with his maternal grandparents. Dine called his grandfather Morris Cohen one of the "real influences" on his art because he owned a hardware store, where Dine became fascinated with objects such as tools, lawn mowers, sinks, and plumbing supplies that would play a critical role in his art.

In 1952 Dine entered the University of Cincinnati, but stayed only one year. After briefly attending the art school of the Museum of Fine Arts in Boston, he enrolled in the art department of Ohio University, receiving a B.F.A. in 1957. That same year he married Nancy Minto, whom he had met at Ohio State; they had three sons. After receiving his degree, Dine moved to Long Island, New York, where he taught art in a high school. He moved to New York

Jim Dine. ARCHIVE PHOTOS, INC.

Greatly influenced by the work of Robert Rauschenberg and Jasper Johns, Dine's earliest paintings were designed to break the hold that abstract expressionism had on American art. Like Rauschenberg and Johns, Dine accomplished this by incorporating objects into his paintings. From his earliest exhibitions in 1958, objects took precedence in his work. By 1962 critics were calling his art "object paintings" because of the tools and articles of clothing that appeared in them. For example, *Black Garden Tools* (1962) featured real shovels and a rake hanging on a large painted canvas. As Dine later stated in an interview with Barbaralee Diamonstein in the late 1970s, he felt under "pressure to constantly be making something new, [to be] reacting against abstract expressionism."

The use of these domestic objects caused critics to label Dine a pop artist, since pop art also focused attention on everyday objects. Dine did share much with pop artists. One of his recurring themes was a series of "self-portraits" depicting a bathrobe shaped to his rather husky proportions. He got the idea from a newspaper advertisement, a source of many pop art paintings, but Dine denied that he was a pop artist. His concern with the texture and application of paint shared much with abstract expressionism. Also, pop artists used objects as objects; a soapbox was a box for soap, nothing more. But Dine's objects had autobiographical references; they meant something important to him. All Dine's work in the 1960s contained elements of this individuality. As he put it: "Pop is concerned with exteriors. I'm concerned with interiors. When I use objects I see them as a vocabulary of feelings." Thus there was a relationship between his art and the dominant existentialism of the period.

After 1962 Dine held a series of successful exhibitions in European cities—Milan (1962), Paris and Brussels (1963), and London (1965 and 1966). Although he continued to rework the same themes, he moved into other mediums. By the mid-1960s he was concentrating on sculpture, producing aluminum objects such as boots, hands, and axes, often in exaggerated forms. His *Long Boot* (1965), for instance, was almost ten feet high. Throughout the decade, Dine avoided depicting the human figure, although the London police confiscated some drawings from the 1966 exhibition on the ground that they were obscene. He also began to write poetry, and he designed sets and costumes for Shakespeare's *Midsummer Night's Dream* and Oscar Wilde's *Picture of Dorian Gray*.

A short, stocky, balding man who once described himself as looking like a "Tartar," Dine had a marked impact on the art world of the 1960s. An outgoing, social person, he seemed to enjoy collaborative efforts with other artists. He did a series of lithographs with the poet Ron Padgett and numerous collages with the artist Eduardo Paolozzi, for

City itself in 1959, where he taught at a private high school located near the Museum of Modern Art, which he visited almost daily. He also met a number of younger artists, among them Claes Oldenburg and Red Grooms, who introduced him to the avant-garde art world that was emerging in downtown New York as a challenge to the dominant school of abstract expressionism.

Dine immediately gained public attention as one of the originators of the "happenings" movement. Happenings, a series of shows held in art galleries, represented an effort to bridge the gap between the visual and performing arts. Produced and directed by artists, happenings were marked by a minimum of dialogue and by sudden bursts of action, often quite irrational, after long spells of inactivity. Although many spectators found these performances boring and inexplicable, they drew considerable attention. Dine produced four happenings in 1959 and 1960, *Car Crash* (1960) being the most successful. After 1960 he gave up happenings (except for one that he created in 1965), claiming that the effort took time away from his painting, but happenings had made him a recognizable force in the New York art scene.

example. In 1967 Dine moved to London, where he lived for four years. In this period he stopped painting for three years, devoting his energies to printmaking and poetry. In his interview with Diamonstein he admitted that he "was running out of these avant-garde ideas." When he resumed painting, he created his *Name Painting* (1969), a huge canvas on which he wrote out the names of everyone he ever knew, "except those I hated." He did so, he said, because "it would just be something no one had ever done."

In 1971 Dine returned to the United States, moving to Putney, Vermont, where he remained until 1985. Since then he has lived in New York and Connecticut. His influence faded in the post-1960s decades, in which he eschewed the use of objects and concentrated on refining his drawing and on making ceramics. As he candidly told Diamonstein, "I really did run out of gas. I could no longer face getting up in the morning and putting another object on a beautifully painted abstract ground."

Dine epitomized much of American art in the 1960s. In that decade his work contained elements of abstract expressionism, it reflected pop art's interest in the prosaic world of everyday objects, it was an expression of the existentialism so dominant among intellectuals in that period, and it symbolized the rebelliousness of young people challenging the status quo. Dine's popularity in the 1960s can be measured by the fact that he had thirty one-person shows and participated in almost fifty group exhibitions during the decade. In 1970 the Whitney Museum of American Art held a retrospective exhibition for him, although he was only thirty-five years old.

★

Lucy Lippard, *Pop Art* (1966), provides a contemporary view of the New York art world. Alan Solomon and Ugo Mulas, *New York: The New Art Scene* (1967), beautifully captures in text and photographs the avant-garde art world in which Dine played such a pivotal role. Barbaralee Diamonstein, *Inside New York's Art World* (1979), contains interviews with thirty leading figures in the 1960s art world, including Dine. Among the many exhibition catalogues of Dine's work, two of the most valuable are John Gordon, *Jim Dine* (1970), and Liesbeth Brandt Corstius, *Jim Dine* (1971).

ROBERT HENDRICK

DION (*b.* 18 July 1939 in New York City), rock-and-roll singer whose career first as lead singer of the doo-wop group the Belmonts and then as a solo act represented some of the best of early rock and roll, when it was rebellious and working class in sensibility, capturing the spirit of youth in the 1960s.

Dion was born Dion Francis DiMucci to a poor Italian-American family in the Bronx, New York. His father, Pasquale DiMucci, was a mostly out-of-work puppeteer,

and his mother, Frances DiMucci, was a hatmaker. He had two sisters and two brothers. At a young age Dion was drawn to music, at first influenced by his father's show business friends and then by the music of his favorite singer, the country artist Hank Williams. He also learned blues from an old black singer named Willie Green. Dion took up guitar and soon was entertaining friends and schoolmates as a would-be country singer.

As Dion entered into his teenage years at Theodore Roosevelt High School, he discovered rock and roll. He was especially drawn to vocal harmony groups, or doo-wop groups, so called because they performed in a vocal ensemble style that made use of nonsense syllables (notably "doo-wop"). Most of the early doo-wop groups were of African-American heritage, but as the style grew in popularity in the late 1950s, many Italian-American doo-wop groups were formed, largely in the New York area. In these years Dion picked up the heroin habit, with which he struggled throughout his early career.

Dion made his first record in 1957, "The Chosen Few," sung to a prerecorded vocal chorus and instrumental track. The record had limited success, and Dion felt that he needed a doo-wop supporting group. He recruited a group from his Bronx neighborhood—first tenor Angelo D'Aleo, second tenor Freddie Milano, and bass Carlo Mastrangelo—and adopted the name Dion and the Belmonts. The group's first hit for the newly formed Laurie label, "I Wonder Why" (number twenty-two on the *Billboard* pop chart in 1958), established the group as on the cutting edge of the Italian-American doo-wop renaissance in New York. They attained further success in 1959 with "A Teenager in Love" (a number-five pop hit) and "Where or When" (a number-three pop hit). *Presenting Dion and the Belmonts* (1959), which collected these hits, ranked as one of the best rock-and-roll albums issued that year.

In 1960 Dion left the Belmonts and began performing simply as Dion. His first hit was a mid-tempo ballad, "Lonely Teenager" (number twelve on the pop chart), which he sang with a yearning voice. Dion hit his stride in the fall of 1961 with a song he composed with Ernie Maresca, "Runaround Sue," a number-one pop hit, and quickly followed with a huge number-two pop hit, "The Wanderer," to close out the year. In 1962 Dion got a number-three pop hit with "Lovers Who Wander," which he cowrote with Maresca. During this period Laurie released two remarkable albums, the million-selling *Runaround Sue* (1961) and *Lovers Who Wander* (1962), which collected his hits and captured Dion at his rock-and-roll best. Aside from the exuberant music, these singles and albums presented Dion in the persona of a swaggering, confident teenage male, which appealed both to female fans, who adored his good looks and his bad boy persona, and to male fans, who wanted to be just like him. Dion

Dion. HULTON/ARCHIVE BY GETTY IMAGES

closed out 1962 with two more of his original compositions, "Little Diane" (number eight on the pop chart) and "Love Came to Me" (number ten on the pop chart).

Dion's extraordinary success at Laurie attracted a major record label, and in late 1962 he signed with Columbia Records, which continued his hit-making streak in January 1963 with a remake of an old Drifters song, "Ruby Baby" (a number-two pop hit), a song that fitted his style and persona. Other hits in 1963 included a Dion original, "Donna the Prima Donna" (number six on the pop chart), and a remake of another Drifters song, "Drip Drop" (number six on the pop chart). On 23 March 1963 Dion married his longtime sweetheart, Susan Butterfield. The union produced three daughters.

Dion's career went into a tailspin after 1963. He charted only one record in 1964, a remake of a Chuck Berry song, "Johnny B. Goode," but at lowly number seventy-one on *Billboard*. While he did not have any hits during the next several years, Dion began experimenting with new sounds, discovering folk music and blues, and recorded several sessions that reflected those interests. He dropped out of the rock-concert scene, took up acoustic guitar, and began performing in folk-music clubs. Dion left Columbia in 1966, and for ABC Records in 1967 he recorded an unsuccessful reunion album with the Belmonts. Lack of hit records was not Dion's only problem at this time, as his longtime use of heroin and alcohol had escalated until he was so mentally unfit that he was unable to tour or create music.

Dion had reached bottom and from the depths of despair in the spring of 1968 decided to turn his life around—he broke his drug and alcohol dependencies, moved to Miami with his family, and began working on his music again, adopting a folk-based contemplative style in the singer-songwriter mode. Returning to his old record company, Laurie, Dion came out with a folk-style number, "Abraham, Martin and John," about three assassinated leaders—Abraham Lincoln; Martin Luther King, Jr.; and John F. Kennedy. The song was a million seller, going to number four on the *Billboard* pop chart. Dion never had another hit, despite recording prolifically. In 1970 he signed with Warner Brothers and during the next six years recorded five solo albums, mostly in the singer-songwriter confessional style, plus a live reunion album with the Belmonts. In 1979 Dion became a born-again Christian and began recording Christian music. He returned to secular music in 1989 but failed to achieve a comeback.

Dion was elected to the Rock and Roll Hall of Fame in 1989. The award assuredly recognized his contribution to early rock and roll, but it also seemed to recognize his personal journey, which mirrored the extraordinary events of the 1960s. Leaving his blue-collar rock and roll in 1963, Dion entered into a period of musical experimentation, taking on other music traditions, as did much of the rock world during the 1960s. At the same time he was indulging his body in demon excesses. He reached his breaking point in 1968, as did America in that fateful year of marches, riots, and assassinations. Finally, Dion was there to present the coda to the musical yet turbulent decade, in the contemplative "Abraham, Martin and John."

★

Dion's autobiography, *The Wanderer: Dion's Story* (1988), with Davin Seay, takes his story up to 1987. Steve Dougherty, "Dion," *People Weekly* (21 Nov. 1988), provides a solid overview of Dion's life with the emphasis on his personal tribulations. A beautifully composed essay by Dave Marsh on Dion's career from his beginnings up to 2000 appears as part of the liner notes for the box set *Dion: King of the New York Streets* (2000). The most comprehensive article on Dion's recording career is Bill Dahl, "Dion: Forever King of the New York Streets," *Goldmine* (9 Mar. 2001).

ROBERT PRUTER

DIRKSEN, Everett McKinley (*b.* 4 January 1896 in Pekin, Illinois; *d.* 7 September 1969 in Washington, D.C.), member of the U.S. House of Representatives, U.S. senator, and recording artist famed for his public speaking, who was vital to the passage of the United Nations bond issue of 1962, the Nuclear Test Ban Treaty of 1963, the Civil Rights Act of 1964, and the financing of America's space program.

Dirksen's parents were German immigrants to the United States who settled in Pekin, Illinois. His father, Johann Frederick Dirksen, was a painter and home decorator who was paralyzed by a stroke when Dirksen was five years old; he lingered for four years and died on 15 April 1905. Dirksen's mother, Antje (Conrady) Dirksen, was a farmer, supporting Dirksen and his twin brother after their father's death. When he was eleven months old, Dirksen's parents gave him the middle name of McKinley in honor of America's president at the time.

Dirksen graduated from Pekin High School in 1913 and took a night job at a corn refining factory. In 1914 he entered the University of Minnesota, paying for school with various jobs. By the time of America's entry into World War I in 1917, Dirksen was studying in the university's law school, perhaps six months away from his undergraduate degree, but he enlisted in the U.S. Army in April 1917, and in January 1918 he was shipped to France. After training in artillery school in Saumer, he was commissioned a second lieutenant and assigned to balloon duty as a spotter. After the armistice he was first assigned to serve in Germany, but he ended up being shipped all over Europe for various duties.

After his discharge in 1919 Dirksen tried to run his own business, then worked from 1922 to 1925 for Cook Dredging Company. In 1927 he won election to the part-time post of finance commissioner for Pekin, serving into 1931. He married Louella Carver in 1927. They had one daughter, Danice Joy, who in 1951 married Howard H. Baker, Jr., eventual Republican majority leader of the U.S. Senate and then President Ronald Reagan's chief of staff. In April 1930 Dirksen lost a campaign to become a member of the House of Representatives, but he ran again, winning as a Republican in 1932. He became known as a conservative Republican serving a conservative district, and he opposed President Franklin D. Roosevelt's economic policies, but he surprised some by declaring his support for Roosevelt on foreign affairs, especially in the years just before America entered World War II. In 1936, while serving in the House, he completed his law degree.

In 1948 Dirksen retired from the House because of a serious eye disease, but he recovered in time to run for the U.S. Senate in 1950. He defeated the incumbent, Scott W. Lucas, and quickly gained a reputation as a fine orator for his speeches. He also won political friends by lending his powerful, Shakespearean voice to their campaigns. In 1957 Dirksen became the Senate's minority whip. He used his powers of persuasion and his skills at the give-and-take of political dealing to keep the Republican senators united. In 1959 he became the minority leader, a position he used with surprising power. He had a close relationship with President Eisenhower but also with the Democrats John F. Kennedy and Lyndon B. Johnson. When Kennedy, a fellow

Everett M. Dirksen. THE LIBRARY OF CONGRESS

senator, was elected president in 1960, Dirksen was the only senator who continued to call him "Jack" rather than "Mr. President"; Kennedy liked it that way and called Dirksen "Ev." The two men worked well together, and Dirksen's influence was critical to passing some of the most important legislation of the Kennedy administration. Though it was often difficult, he persuaded enough Republican senators to vote for legislation the White House wanted that the United Nations was saved from bankruptcy and Kennedy's aspirations for the American space program, including spy satellites, were passed.

Even so, not all was happy between Dirksen and Kennedy. The president had promised during his campaign that civil rights legislation would be a high priority of his administration. When no civil rights legislation came to Congress from the White House, Dirksen and his fellow Republicans introduced a bill of their own in 1961. Some observers thought Dirksen was trying to embarrass Kennedy, but during the 1950s Dirksen had supported civil rights bills. His efforts in 1961 were consistent with his views; the Democrats voted the bill down. Even as he was supporting Kennedy's foreign policy by helping find votes to implement the Peace Corps and support the Nuclear Test Ban Treaty negotiated by Kennedy, Dirksen opposed many of Kennedy's domestic policies, including anything that appeared to increase the size of the federal government's bureaucracy.

When Kennedy was assassinated and Johnson became president, Dirksen maintained his friendly relations with the White House. Linchpins to Johnson's vision of the Great Society in which no one went hungry or was poor were two bills, the Civil Rights Act and the Voting Rights Act. Both were opposed by Democrats from the American South ("Dixiecrats"), who saw the federal government trying to intrude on affairs best left to the individual states. Dirksen rounded up enough Republican votes to help pass the Civil Rights Act in 1964. Dirksen had, in the 1950s, supported a civil rights bill that would have outlawed abuses of citizens' right to vote. Again, even though some Republicans thought he was selling out to the Democrat Johnson, his support of the Voting Rights Act was in keeping with his long-held views. His speeches in favor of the legislation helped it pass.

During the mid-1960s Dirksen recorded four spoken-word albums in his fine voice; *Gallant Men: Stories of American Adventure* (1963) not only sold 500,000 copies but won a Grammy award. He did this while suffering from lung cancer. In the Senate he tried to cut down the cost of Johnson's Great Society programs, and he feared that the welfare program proposed by Johnson would make people permanently dependent on government money. On the other hand he supported Johnson's conduct of the war in Vietnam; Dirksen saw this as a moral issue, even though he risked losing votes in his 1968 reelection bid. He was reelected nevertheless, and in spite of being afflicted with several illnesses, he remained an effective leader until his September 1969 death in Walter Reed Hospital after an operation for lung cancer. He rested in state in the Capitol Dome and then was buried in the Garden of Devotion in Glendale Memorial Cemetery in Pekin.

Dirksen was one of the greatest speakers the U.S. Senate has known, and his ability to turn hostility into merriment with one of his rambling anecdotes helped save legislation. He was famous for changing his mind on issues; he explained that as he learned more about an issue, he might learn that his old views were in error, so he would change his mind. Critics, however, said that he changed his mind according to the political favors he might receive in return. In any case, his work in the 1960s helped change America.

★

Dirksen's papers are in the Everett McKinley Dirksen Congressional Leadership Center in Pekin, Illinois. About half of Neil MacNeil's *Dirksen: Portrait of a Public Man* (1970) is devoted to the 1960s, the decade in which Dirksen made his biggest mark on history. Another reference is Edward L. Schapsmeier and Frederick H. Schapsmeier, *Dirksen of Illinois* (1985). In *Current Biography Yearbook* (1957), the article on Dirksen provides details of his life before he went into politics and some of his achievements before the mid-1950s. Edward L. Schapsmeier, "Dirksen,

Everett McKinley" in *American National Biography* (1999), emphasizes Dirksen's career in the 1960s. His widow, Louella Dirksen, wrote a personal memoir, *The Honorable Mr. Marigold* (1972), with Norma Lee Browning. An obituary is in the *New York Times* (8 Sept. 1969).

KIRK H. BEETZ

DOHRN, Bernardine Rae (*b.* 12 January 1942 in Chicago, Illinois), prominent civil rights and anti–Vietnam War activist who went in the 1960s from serving as a national leader for Students for a Democratic Society to becoming the best-known member of the radical, violent Weather Underground.

The daughter of lower-middle-class Jewish parents, Dohrn grew up with one sister in Whitefish Bay, a suburb of Milwaukee, Wisconsin. Her father worked as an appliance-store credit manager, her mother as a secretary.

After graduating from Whitefish Bay High School in 1959, Dohrn entered Miami University of Ohio but left two years later because of rheumatic fever. Upon recovery Dohrn transferred to the University of Chicago, from which she received a B.A. in 1963. She subsequently spent a few months working in a Chicago ghetto for the Illinois Department of Public Aid and attempted to unionize her fellow caseworkers. Graduate work in history followed, as did advocacy for welfare families as a volunteer with the Welfare Rights Organization. Dohrn earned an M.A. from the University of Chicago in 1964, but disillusionment with academia led her to explore a legal career.

While at the University of Chicago Law School, Dohrn in 1965 joined Martin Luther King, Jr.'s Southern Christian Leadership Conference to organize rent strikes against slumlords and to promote the integration of Chicago's suburbs. At the end of summer in 1966 she joined Students for a Democratic Society (SDS) as an organizer in its community assistance program, Jobs or Income Now (JOIN). After receiving her law degree in 1967, Dohrn moved to New York City to work with the National Lawyer's Guild where, as national student director, she assisted the students involved in the 1968 Columbia University revolt. Dohrn also helped stage Draft Week, one of the first big antiwar demonstrations.

In the late 1960s Dohrn began to develop an awareness of women's issues. Angered when a group of women making a presentation at a 1967 SDS meeting were hooted down by men, she joined with fourteen other women to form a consciousness-raising group that met weekly to discuss their lives. In the next year Dohrn united with Naomi Jaffe to pen "You Got the Look" for the 18 March 1968 *New Left Notes,* in which they analyzed the impact of mass culture on women's lives and the view of women as sexual objects. But the SDS believed that women's struggles were secondary to the fight against capitalism and imperialism,

Bernardine Dohrn, 1969. ASSOCIATED PRESS AP

and Dohrn did not disagree with the New Left on this issue, as many other radical women did.

After Dohrn returned to Chicago in 1968, the SDS elected her national interorganizational secretary, one of the group's top three coequal offices. Standing five feet, five inches, with straight shoulder-length brown hair and brown eyes in a round face, the charismatic and self-assured Dohrn quickly became noted for her ability to command attention. With ten other SDS members, she authored a *New Left Notes* statement entitled "You Don't Need a Weatherman to Know Which Way the Wind Blows" (18 June 1969), which called for a white fighting force to support the black liberation movement. At a national SDS meeting a few days later, Dohrn asked if it was still possible to work with people who did not advocate violence. Supported by most of the delegates, she read an order expelling conservative members from the organization. The survivors became the group Weatherman (the name was later changed to the nonsexist Weather Underground).

Committing itself to armed revolution, Weatherman planned the "Days of Rage," an 8–11 October 1969 protest to coincide with the "Chicago Seven" trial. Days of Rage was expected to feature 25,000 radicals battling with Chicago police. When only a few protestors showed up, Dohrn rallied the Women's Militia to proceed with their plan to attack a draft board. About seventy women listened to

Dohrn declare, "A few buckshot wounds, a few pellets, mean we're doing the right thing here," adding that their fear "has to be put up against the hunger, fear, death, and suffering of black, brown, and yellow people all over the world." Dohrn and the others then charged toward the draft board, ran into a police blockade, and were attacked and arrested. She later said of the Chicago violence, "We were determined to carry out an action that would reveal how passionately we felt."

Sparked by rage at the murder of Black Panther Fred Hampton by Chicago police and by frustration at failing to draw large numbers to Chicago, Dohrn proposed at a December 1969 war council that Weatherman go underground and engage in armed struggle, including bombing government buildings, to liberate whites from capitalism. At this meeting Dohrn also made her notorious speech extolling the Tate-LaBianca murders by the Manson Family in Los Angeles. "Manson killed those pigs, then they ate dinner in the same room with them, then they shoved a fork into a victim's stomach! Parents are now gonna tell their kids to stay away from home vacation—they're afraid they'll get offed in their sleep." In later years an embarrassed Dohrn would disavow the remark.

Weatherman's romanticization of violence ended in March 1970, when three of its members blew themselves up with bombs intended for Fort Dix servicemen. Suspecting that she would be arrested at her next court appearance for her association with the dead revolutionaries, Dohrn went into hiding. On 17 March 1970 the first federal indictments for the Days of Rage were released, and Dohrn was among those charged with conspiracy to cross state lines with the intent to incite a riot. Following more indictments, the FBI placed Dohrn on its Most Wanted List. While on the run Dohrn lived in New York City, married fellow Weather leader Bill Ayers, and bore two sons and adopted another. She helped author 1974's *Prairie Fire*, a summary of Weather history and its plans for the future, then left Weather in 1977 and surfaced in 1980. For her crimes Dohrn received three years' probation and a $1,500 fine. By 2000 she had become a noted advocate for children's rights and a professor of law at Northwestern University.

By deciding that traditional political protest had done little to end the civil rights problems of American society and by advocating guerrilla combat as the solution, the articulate Dohrn became the best-known leader of the most radical of all white-dominated protest groups. Her career reflected the hope of the mid-1960s and the disillusionment of the latter part of the decade.

★

There is no biography of Dohrn, but she is covered in Kirkpatrick Sale, *SDS* (1970); Ron Chepesiuk, *Sixties Radicals, Then and Now: Candid Conversations with Those Who Shaped the Era* (1995); Ron Jacobs, *The Way the Wind Blew: A History of the*

Weather Underground (1997); and Bob Feldman, "Being Left: Years After the 1968 Columbia Revolt; Bob Feldman Interviews Bernardine Dohrn," *Zmag* (May 1998).

CARYN E. NEUMANN

DRUCKER, Peter Ferdinand (*b*. 19 November 1909 in Vienna, Austria), writer, teacher, and philosopher of business management principles and author of more than thirty well-received books, who is considered to be the founding father of modern management theory.

Drucker is the eldest son of Adolph Bertram, a lawyer and professor, and Caroline Drucker. The Drucker children were raised in a cultured environment in Vienna during World War I. Drucker detested the uninspired Austrian school system, and although he scored good grades, he was driven by curiosity and preferred to study on his own. At age seventeen he moved to Frankfurt, Germany, where he worked as a financial writer, studied toward his doctorate in law, and watched the rise of Hitler. His first book was a brief and admiring account of a nineteenth-century Jew, Friedrich Julius Stahl, which was banned and burned when the Nazis came to power. He later said that he had deliberately chosen to write a "book that would make it impossible for the Nazis to have anything to do with me." At age twenty-four he fled to England. He married his wife, Doris, and immigrated to the United States in 1937; the couple has four children. The rise of Nazism profoundly influenced Drucker. He determined that institutions that function "responsibly, autonomously, and on a high level of achievement" are the only safeguards of freedom.

More than fifty years after the publication of his first book, *The End of Economic Man: The Origins of Totalitarianism* (1939), Drucker declared that writing was the foundation for all of the diverse pursuits of his life. His body of work paints Drucker as an economist and historian as well as a political scientist and sociologist. Although he explored and understood many disciplines, he would not define himself by any one of them. He would come to describe himself as a social ecologist, that is, someone "concerned with man's man-made environment." With *The End of Economic Man*, Drucker established himself as an unorthodox thinker on economics, politics, and society. During the 1940s Drucker became deeply interested in the idea of the organization and its increasing influence on society. The responsibilities of business owners were being delegated from the business owner to a system of managers, each charged with bringing a team of people to work together effectively for a goal. Drucker became one of the first people to study business management when few noticed that it existed as a discipline. In the 1940s there were no business schools or management texts as they are known

in the twenty-first century. Drucker, who was at that time teaching, was warned by a colleague at Vermont's Bennington College that by pursuing this course, he would destroy his career in academia.

At first Drucker was not able to gain access to a business in order to study it. The companies he approached were suspicious of his motives, until he fell in with General Motors, which gave him total access. *Concept of the Corporation* (1946) was the revolutionary result and ultimately became one of the most popular management books in history. At the time, Drucker's idea that employees be given managerial responsibility in job structure was considered a challenge to managerial authority. He was ahead of the curve again in the early 1950s when he predicted that computers would change business and in 1961 when he was the first to see Japan's impending economic marvel. In 1954 Drucker essentially invented the concept of management with his book *The Practice of Management*.

By the 1960s Drucker's ideas on managers and management were widely accepted. He had so established himself as "the man who changed the face of industrial America" that President Richard M. Nixon presented him before a speech without a word of identification. Many of

Peter F. Drucker. CORBIS CORPORATION (BELLEVUE)

Drucker's writings of the 1960s were tomes of practical and mundane advice and instruction to managers. *Managing for Results: Economic Tasks and Risk-taking Decisions* (1964), was a drier and less exalted book than *The Practice of Management.* This work is rife with lists and is the only of his books to contain charts. *The Effective Executive* (1967), is Drucker's most enjoyable management book and is cleverly written and full of one-liners. He begins the book looking at the difference between doing the right thing and getting the right thing done. The difference between the two, he writes, is effectiveness—the effective executive gets the right things done.

Drucker published *The Age of Discontinuity: Guidelines to Our Changing Society*, a social and political analysis, in 1969. In it he describes societal changes of the decade that were resulting in business and social disharmonies, such as the revolutions in technology, specialization, and trade that were changing the face of business and society. *The Age of Discontinuity* calls for new theories and laws to help business achieve success in the face of these shifts. Drucker describes the development of a postindustrial society that emphasizes the qualitative problems of work and social organization "at a time when alienation and unrest characterize much of the world." While he discusses "very serious problems," Drucker writes about them as opportunities for new and more creative thinking and problem solving.

While many books of social analysis written in the 1960s have become nostalgic or even obsolete, *The Age of Discontinuity* reads as if it could have been written yesterday. In it Drucker predicts that knowledge would drive the economy of the twenty-first century. He also foresees the development of four new industries and patterns of economic activity: an increasing value for information, the rediscovery of the oceans as an economic resource, the rise of materials such as plastic, and the advent of knowledge workers working from home. He predicts the development of a new world economy and sees that people would soon become disenchanted with government. Drucker could not have been more accurate.

Well into his nineties, Drucker's ideas continued to be lively and viable. He wrote magazine articles and appeared on the cover of the investment magazine *Forbes,* which proclaimed him "Still the Youngest Mind." The hip technology magazine *Wired* featured an interview with Drucker asking not about the past but about the future. He continued for many years to teach management theory and consult to businesses and nonprofit organizations. His publisher, Harvard University Press, intends to keep his most popular books in print for seventeen years after his death.

★

Drucker's autobiography is *Adventures of a Bystander* (1979). Biographies include Jack Beatty, *The World According to Peter*

Drucker (1998), and John E. Flaherty, *Peter Drucker: Shaping the Managerial Mind* (1999). A useful article is Fritz F. Heimann's review of *The Age of Discontinuity* in *Commentary* (June 1969).

BRENNA SANCHEZ

DRYSDALE, Donald Scott ("Don") (*b.* 23 July 1936 in Van Nuys, California; *d.* 3 July 1993 in Montreal, Canada), dominant baseball pitcher for the Brooklyn and Los Angeles Dodgers during the 1950s and 1960s, who later became a sports broadcaster and was inducted into the National Baseball Hall of Fame.

Drysdale was one of two children born to Scott Sumner Drysdale, a one-time minor league baseball scout and a repair supervisor for the Pacific Telephone and Telegraphy Company, and Verna Ruth Ley, a homemaker. Drysdale graduated from Van Nuys (Calif.) High School in June 1954. After graduation, the right-handed pitcher signed with the Brooklyn Dodgers franchise. After spending two years in the minor leagues, Drysdale was called up to the majors in 1956, winning five games and losing five games. In 1957, the Dodgers' last season in Brooklyn, he led the team's pitchers with a record of 17–9.

Drysdale served in the U.S. Army from 1957 to 1958. On 27 September 1958 Drysdale married Eula Eugenia ("Ginger") Dubberly, the 1958 Miss Tournament of Roses. They had one child and divorced in 1970. The Los Angeles Dodgers captured the National League (NL) pennant in 1959, with Drysdale contributing by compiling a record of

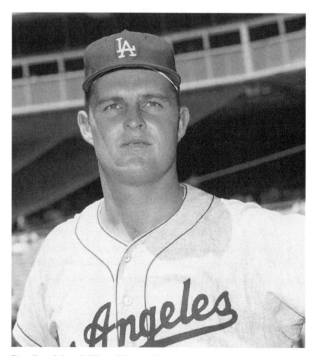

Don Drysdale. AP/WIDE WORLD PHOTOS

17–13 and leading the major leagues with 242 strikeouts. The Dodgers defeated the Chicago White Sox to win the World Series that year; Drysdale won game four. In 1960 he went 15–14 and again led the major leagues with 246 strikeouts. In 1961 he signed a contract with the Dodgers for $32,500, making him the highest-paid pitcher in baseball at the age of twenty-four.

Known as "Big D," Drysdale stood six feet, six inches tall, and weighed about 190 pounds (215 pounds later in his career). As a pitcher he threw three-quarter sidearm, a range of motion between overhand (throwing over the top) and sidearm (throwing when the arm is parallel to the ground). On the mound he was intimidating, not only for his size and pitching motion, but also for his tendency to pitch inside to hitters. In 1961 he hit twenty batters, the most in the National League since 1909. He led the league in this category five times and as of 2002 still held the NL career mark with 154 batters hit. Often accused of altering baseballs, Drysdale admitted in his 1990 autobiography that he used spit mixed with slippery elm. (Slippery elm derives from the inner bark of the slippery elm tree. Its application to a baseball produces the same effect as a knuckleball—the pitched ball has very little rotation, making its movement dependent upon air currents and therefore unpredictable. It finishes its trajectory with a sharp drop.)

Between 1962 and 1965 Drysdale was one of baseball's dominant hurlers, posting a record of 85–54. In each of these four years he started the most games of any pitcher in the National League, logging more than 300 innings in each of these seasons, and leading the league in innings pitched in 1962 and 1964. Drysdale's career season was 1962, when he led the major leagues with a record of 25–9. He led the National League with forty-one games started and topped both leagues with 314 and one-third innings pitched and 232 strikeouts, receiving the NL Cy Young Award in recognition of his achievements. He and his southpaw teammate Sandy Koufax dominated baseball's hitters and took the Dodgers to the World Series in 1963, 1965, and 1966.

Drysdale went 23–12 and Koufax notched a 26–8 record, as the Dodgers won the NL pennant in 1965. The Dodgers then defeated the Minnesota Twins in the World Series, with Drysdale going 1–1 and Koufax going 2–0. After the World Series, Drysdale and Koufax held out in an effort to become the first pitchers to make more than $100,000. After the pair missed most of spring training, the Dodgers signed them to one-year contracts. Koufax agreed to $125,000, and Drysdale signed for $110,000. The pitchers' holdout was a major challenge to the Dodgers management and to the baseball establishment, because Major League Baseball's reserve clause bound a player to a team in perpetuity. In the absence of collective bargaining or even legitimate negotiation, a player had two choices: accept the team's con-

tract offer or cease to play professional baseball. Drysdale and Koufax hired an attorney to negotiate, marking a significant step toward the abolition of the reserve clause and the establishment of collective bargaining and free agency.

During 1966 Drysdale's record declined to 13–6. This included two of the Dodgers four losses in the World Series, which they dropped to the Baltimore Orioles. In 1967 Drysdale again posted a discouraging 13–6 record. In 1968 he went 14–2, but, more importantly, from the period of 14 May through 8 June he threw 58 and two-thirds consecutive scoreless innings, eclipsing Walter Johnson's major league record of fifty-six scoreless innings. This led to 1968 being called the "year of the pitcher." As a result, the pitching mound was lowered in 1969 in an effort to lessen pitchers' domination of hitters. (Drysdale was a broadcaster for the Dodgers in 1988 when the Dodger pitcher Orel Hershiser broke his record.) Drysdale was selected for the NL All-Star team, pitching three scoreless innings to pick up the victory. After his twelfth start of the 1969 season, he retired with an injury to his right shoulder.

From 1969 until his death in 1993, Drysdale held a succession of broadcasting jobs with the Montreal Expos, Texas Rangers, Anaheim (California) Angels, American Broadcasting Company, and Los Angeles Dodgers. Drysdale was inducted into the National Baseball Hall of Fame on 12 August 1984. On 1 November 1986 he married Ann Elizabeth Meyers, a former All-America basketball star at the University of California at Los Angeles and a member of the Basketball Hall of Fame. They had three children. Drysdale died of a heart attack and is buried in Forest Lawn Cemetery in Glendale, California.

During his career with the Dodgers, Drysdale compiled 209 wins and 166 losses, posting a 2.95 earned run average. Also known as an excellent hitter for a pitcher, Drysdale hit twenty-nine career home runs, including two seasons with seven, and had a respectable batting average of .186. Only twice did he win more than twenty games in a season, but he was a dominant pitcher from 1962 to 1965. He played in five World Series, pitching in seven games, winning three and losing three. Drysdale was selected to eight All-Star teams, posting a 2–1 record. In a time when aggressive pitching dominated the game, "Big D" set the standard.

★

The National Baseball Hall of Fame Library in Cooperstown, New York, has a clippings file on Drysdale. His autobiography, written with Bob Verdi, is *Once a Bum, Always a Dodger: My Life in Baseball from Brooklyn to Los Angeles* (1990). See also Milton J. Shapiro, *The Don Drysdale Story* (1964). A chapter on Drysdale is in Bill Libby, *Star Pitchers of the Major Leagues* (1971). The 1966 holdout by Drysdale and Koufax is covered in William B. Mead, *World of Baseball: The Explosive Sixties* (1989). Drysdale's records are in John Thorn and Peter Palmer, eds., with Michael Gershman, *Total Baseball: The Official Encyclopedia of Major League Baseball,* 4th ed. (1995). From the many magazine articles written about Drysdale, three in particular give insights into the man and the baseball issues of his time: Don Drysdale, "You've Got to Be Mean to Pitch," *Sport* (30 June 1960), examines the role of intimidation in baseball; Huston Horn, "Ex-Bad Boy's Big Year," *Sports Illustrated* (20 Aug. 1962), provides background on Drysdale as he neared the completion of his best season; and Jack Mann, "The $100,000 Holdout," *Sports Illustrated* (4 Apr. 1966), offers a balanced appraisal of the situation faced by Drysdale and Koufax as they tried to improve their salaries. Obituaries are in the *Los Angeles Times* (4 July 1993), and the *New York Times* (5 July 1993).

PAUL A. FRISCH

DUKE, Anna Marie ("Patty") (*b.* 14 December 1946 in New York City), former child star who was the youngest actress ever to win an Academy Award and the youngest person to have a prime-time television series named after her. Her 1960s work is dominated by stunning dramatic work, including roles in the theatrical and film versions of *The Miracle Worker.*

Duke was the third child of John Patrick Duke, a navy veteran who held a succession of jobs from cabdriver to handyman, and Frances McMahon, a cashier. When Duke was six, her father, a chronic alcoholic, moved out. From that point until his death in 1963, his presence in his daughter's life was shadowy at best. Duke entered show business at age seven. Her brother Ray was an actor, and his managers, John and Ethel Ross, took an interest in the young girl. Their first order of business was to change her name to the perkier "Patty." She was allowed no input in the matter, she recalls in her autobiography, but was simply told, "Anna Marie is dead. You're Patty now." It was more than a name that she lost; she later realized that her identity had been taken from her.

The Rosses did more than manage Duke's career; they controlled every aspect of her life, eventually wresting her away from her family home. Her mother's emotional and financial troubles, combined with the Rosses' assurances that they alone could ensure Duke's success, led to an unusual living arrangement in which Patty moved in with her managers, seeing her mother sporadically. True to their word, the Rosses propelled Duke to stardom, but the arrangement took a profound personal and psychological toll. "I was stripped of my parents, I was stripped of my name, I was eventually stripped of my religion, and they had a blank slate to do with as they wished."

By the late 1950s Duke was working steadily, playing stereotypical cute kids in film and television productions, such as *Armstrong Circle Theatre* and *The U.S. Steel Hour.*

Patty Duke in a scene from *The Miracle Worker,* 1962. ARCHIVE PHOTOS, INC.

A 1959 appearance on *The $64,000 Question,* for which she and cowinner Eddie Hodges had been fed the answers that allowed them to split the top prize, led to her being called to testify before a congressional committee investigating the quiz show's fraudulent practices. The same year, she made her Broadway debut in *The Miracle Worker,* playing Helen Keller to Anne Bancroft's Annie Sullivan. Her name was raised above the title on the theater marquee in 1960, making her the youngest Broadway performer to be so honored. The 1962 film version, in which Duke and Bancroft recreated their stage roles, earned both actresses Academy Awards. At the time, Duke was the youngest person to win an individual Academy Award.

Curiously, on the heels of this achievement Duke's handlers decided to push her toward television, rather than pursue film roles. *The Patty Duke Show*'s unlikely premise had Duke playing Patty Lane, a typical boy-crazy American teenager, and her identical cousin, Cathy, a prim and proper Scottish lass. Ironically, the actress whose fame derived from playing television's "typical teen" had such an aberrant childhood that she later admitted she did not know the first thing about how kids of her generation talked, danced, or dressed.

Duke developed familial relationships with the cast and crew and enjoyed working, but she disliked her characters, particularly the scatterbrained Patty. She wrote, "I hated being less intelligent than I was, I hated pretending I was younger than I was, I hated not being consulted about anything, having no choice in how I looked or what I wore, I hated being trapped." *The Patty Duke Show* scored big with fans, spawning a board game, a twelve-inch Patty doll, and record albums. No doubt its success derived more from Duke's vivaciousness and likeability than from its kitschy theme song or wacky plotlines. Not surprisingly, Duke remained unfazed by the show's success. She was not allowed to watch the series and was never told about its ratings or her earnings (which she later learned were squandered by the Rosses).

While working on the series, Duke attended Quintano School for Young Professionals, a high school catering to children in show business. She turned eighteen during the series' run and broke away from her managers. Her bid for independence was largely prompted by her relationship with Harry Falk, Jr., an assistant director on her show. Her managers' attempts to end the union were what finally sent Duke packing. On 26 November 1965 she married Falk. Her series was cancelled in 1966. The late 1960s saw Duke desperate to reinvent herself. Her first adult role, in the film adaptation of Jacqueline Susann's novel *Valley of the Dolls* (1967), was a calculated effort to shed her bubblegum image. Duke played Neely O'Hara, a singer-dancer addicted to booze, pills, and sex. She continued to win accolades—a Golden Globe for her portrayal of a homely Jewish teen in *Me, Natalie* (1969), and an Emmy for the 1970 television movie *My Sweet Charlie*—but offscreen she was falling apart, her behavior becoming more and more erratic. Periods of deep depression led to multiple suicide attempts and brief stints in psychiatric hospitals. It was not until 1982, when the actress was in her thirties, that she was diagnosed as manic-depressive and began to understand the extreme highs and lows she had experienced since childhood.

Duke eventually became one of the reigning queens of television movies and miniseries, starring in more than fifty. Notable among them was a television remake of *The Miracle Worker*. This time, Patty enacted the Annie Sullivan role, and Melissa Gilbert played Helen. Duke's 1970 divorce from Falk was followed by a very brief marriage, from 24 June to July 1970, to the rock concert promoter Michael Tell, which was later annulled. She married actor John Astin on 5 August 1972. During her marriage to Astin, she was billed professionally as Patty Duke Astin. Duke and Astin divorced in 1985, and she married her fourth husband, the army drill sergeant Michael Pearce, on 15 March 1986. Duke had two sons with Astin and an adopted son with Pearce.

Duke's 1960s work is as dichotomous as her famous television counterparts. Her extraordinary stage and film characterizations of Helen Keller, still considered one of the most challenging roles ever written for a young actress, stand in stark contrast to those kooky sitcom cousins who looked alike but were different in every way. Perhaps her most extraordinary performance, however, was her public persona as Patty Duke, America's quintessential teenager, an image that masked a decade of private anguish.

★

Duke wrote her autobiography, *Call Me Anna* (1987), with Kenneth Turan. A follow-up book, *A Brilliant Madness: Living with Manic-Depressive Illness* (1992), written with Gloria Hochman, chronicles her battles with the disease. As Patty Duke Astin, she wrote *Surviving Sexual Assault,* with the Los Angeles Commission on Assaults Against Women (1983). Stephen L. Eberly, *Patty Duke: A Bio-Bibliography* (1988), includes Duke's professional credits, a brief biography, and a bibliography.

Brenda Scott Royce

DULLEA, Keir (*b.* 30 May 1936 in Cleveland, Ohio), actor who starred in the 1968 groundbreaking science-fiction film *2001: A Space Odyssey.*

Dullea is the son of Robert Dullea and Margaret Ruttan, who owned a Greenwich Village bookstore. He studied acting at San Francisco State College and first began to work professionally on the stage at the regional Neighborhood Playhouse. In 1959 he made his off-Broadway debut in New York City's Barbizon-Plaza Theatre, playing the role of Timmie Redwine in *Season of Choice,* a play that covers decades in the life of Redwine and focuses on his decision to marry a woman he gets pregnant but does not love. In 1960 Dullea married the actress Margo Bennett, whom he divorced in 1968. The following year Dullea married Susan Lessons, a fashion publicist, but the couple divorced a year later. His next marriage, to Susie Fuller in 1972, lasted until Fuller's death in 1998.

Throughout the early part of the 1960s, Dullea honed his craft on television in a variety of roles, including parts on such series as *Naked City* ("Murder Is a Face I Know," 1961, and "Apple Falls Not Far from the Tree," 1963), *The United States Steel Hour* ("The Big Splash," 1961; "Far from the Shade Tree," 1962; and "The Young Avengers," 1963), and *Empire* ("Stopover on the Way to the Moon," 1963). He also appeared in the made-for-television movies *Mrs. Miniver* (1960) and *Give Us Barabbas!* (1961).

Dullea made his feature film debut in 1961 playing the neurotic juvenile delinquent Billy Lee Jackson in the *Hoodlum Priest,* a film based on the true story of a St. Louis priest who devotes his life to helping criminals and pris-

Keir Dullea. THE KOBAL COLLECTION

oners turn their lives around. In 1962 Dullea received wide critical acclaim (including an award for best male performance at the 1962 San Francisco Film Festival) for his sensitive portrayal of David Clemens in *David and Lisa*. The classic drama focuses on two teenagers who fall in love in a mental institution. Dullea played the troubled David, a phobic who cannot stand to be touched, and Janet Margolin played the schizophrenic Lisa.

Dullea's work in *David and Lisa* established him as an accomplished actor. With his sensitivity and clean-cut good looks, he was in demand. He soon received roles as Private Doll in the war drama *The Thin Red Line* (1964), as Lee Carey in *Mail Order Bride* (1964), and as Aldo in *Le Ore nude* (also called *The Naked Hours*, 1964). In 1965 he starred as Stephen Lake in the movie *Bunny Lake Is Missing!* (1965). The role gave him the opportunity to work with one of the world's most respected actors, Laurence Olivier, and with the legendary director Otto Preminger. Although Dullea had become recognized in Hollywood as a proficient actor, the best was yet to come.

After two more projects, the film *Madame X* (1966), and the theater production *Dr. Cook's Garden* (1967), Dullea was offered a role that would forever secure his place in cinematic history. Stanley Kubrick was looking for two leads for a new film he had in mind. Based on Dullea's work in *David and Lisa, The Thin Red Line*, and *Bunny Lake Is Missing!*, Kubrick picked him for one of the roles, that of astronaut David Bowman in *2001: A Space Odyssey*. The film, based on the short story "The Sentinel," by Arthur C. Clarke, also starred the actor Gary Lockwood as coastronaut Frank Poole. "I was overwhelmed to have been cast in a Stanley Kubrick film," Dullea told Amy Reiter in a 1999 interview for *Salon* magazine. "A Stanley Kubrick film, even that long ago, was really something." In the film, Poole is murdered by the computer HAL, and Dullea's character Bowman is left to confront the paranoid computer. Eventually, Bowman ends up in another dimension as a very old man living in a bedroom where all his comforts are supplied.

Ironically, the landmark epic drama of space adventure and exploration initially received lukewarm critical reviews, and was often cited as being boring and lacking imagination. Part of the reason may have been that the film featured spectacular imagery and minimal dialogue. However, after repeated theater showings over the next several years, the film finally was recognized for its greatness and is included almost universally on greatest-films lists. Because of his role in *2001,* the Columbia Broadcasting System (CBS) television network asked Dullea to come to its new studios and comment on the first moon landing in the summer of 1969. Dullea found himself in the news control room, watching the historic landing with Arthur C. Clarke, who cowrote the screenplay for *2001.*

Although Dullea went on to appear in numerous films, he also worked extensively as a stage actor, including starring in the Broadway productions of *Dr. Cook's Garden* (1967), and *Butterflies Are Free* (1969 to 1970). In 1971 he went to London for three years to reprise his role in *Butterflies Are Free*, then returned to New York and Broadway in 1974 to star as Brick in Tennessee Williams's *Cat on a Hot Tin Roof.*

Despite a long career as an actor, Dullea has remained most widely recognized for his role in *2001: A Space Odyssey*. In a 1999 interview for *Biography* magazine, Dullea commented on his feelings about being associated with just one film, despite having starred in more than twenty. "I suppose it's like the model who posed for the Mona Lisa," he said. "She might have posed for a lot of good painters, but all we know now is the one hanging in the Louvre for hundreds of years. I think she would consider that pretty terrific."

Dullea, who married actress Mia Dillon in 1999 and has two stepdaughters, has continued as a "working" actor. He appeared in the sequel to *2001*, titled *2010: The Odyssey Continues* (1984), and as Audrey Hepburn's father Joseph Hepburn in the television movie *The Audrey Hepburn Story* (2000). Dullea has worked primarily as a stage actor on

Broadway, off-Broadway, and regional theater. He has said that he prefers stage work because of the opportunity to perform in front of a live audience and to explore a character's nuances through repeated performances.

★

A biography of Dullea can be found in *Contemporary Theatre, Film and Television* (2002), which includes a comprehensive listing of Dullea's stage, screen, and television credits. The actor was featured in *People* (28 Jan. 1985). Dullea's views on his career and the movie *2001: A Space Odyssey* can be found in *Salon* (29 May 1999), and the "Where Are They Now" section in a 1999 issue of *Biography* magazine, which is available at <http://www.biography.com>.

DAVID PETECHUK

DULLES, Allen Welsh (*b.* 7 April 1893 in Watertown, New York; *d.* 29 January 1969 in Washington, D.C.), lawyer, first civilian director of the CIA (1953–1961), and member of the Warren Commission (1963–1964), which investigated the assassination of President John F. Kennedy.

Dulles's father was Allen Macy Dulles, a Presbyterian minister, and his mother was Edith (Foster) Dulles, the daughter of Secretary of State John Watson Foster. Dulles, the youngest of three children, was born with a clubfoot and had difficulty walking for most of his life. His older brother, John Foster Dulles, was secretary of state under President Dwight D. Eisenhower. Their deeply religious parents encouraged their children to honor their obligation to serve all humanity. His parents hired tutors to homeschool their children, though they occasionally attended local schools as well. In fact, Dulles and his sister briefly attended the public Auburn Academic High School but found its curriculum unchallenging, so their parents took them out of school and to France. Dulles attended Princeton from 1910 to 1914, graduating with a B.A. in philosophy; after teaching in India for a year, he returned to Princeton, and in 1916 he received an M.A. in international law.

In 1916 Dulles joined the U.S. Foreign Service. On 16 October 1920 he married Clover Todd; they had three children. He was assigned to Constantinople (later Istanbul) from October 1920 to April 1922, and then went to Washington, D.C., to become the State Department's specialist on the Near East. While in Washington he studied law at George Washington University, receiving an LL.B. in 1926. That same year he resigned from the Foreign Service and joined the prestigious Wall Street law firm of Sullivan and Cromwell.

When the United States entered World War II, Dulles was tabbed to serve in the Office of Strategic Services (OSS). After Germany's surrender in 1945 he became a

leading advocate of rebuilding Western Europe and served as a congressional adviser on foreign aid and as part of the commission running the Marshall Plan. In 1953 Dulles was appointed director of the Central Intelligence Agency (CIA), the successor to the OSS, by President Dwight Eisenhower. He became legendary for his direction of America's espionage agents.

In early 1960 a summit of the leaders of the United States, the Soviet Union, the United Kingdom, and France was scheduled for mid-May. Eisenhower hoped to ease tensions between the United States and the Soviet Union in talks with Soviet leader Nikita Khrushchev. On 1 May 1960 a CIA U-2 spy plane was shot down over Soviet territory, putting the future of the talks at risk. Dulles offered to resign and take the blame, but Eisenhower insisted that no one working for him would take the blame for something the president had chosen to do. On 9 May Eisenhower took responsibility for the U-2 mission, and Khrushchev responded by taking an uncompromising stance against what the Soviet government called "aggression." The summit was a failure. In August 1960 the United States put a reconnaissance satellite in orbit that made U-2 overflights less necessary for tracking the Soviet Union's deployment of nuclear weapons.

Meanwhile, another problem was developing. In 1959 Dulles had expressed concern about Castro's Communism,

Allen W. Dulles. AP/WIDE WORLD PHOTOS

and the CIA station chief for Cuba, J. C. King, recommended subverting Castro. On 13 January 1960, when the matter was suggested to him, Dulles bluntly forbade any attempts to assassinate Castro. On 13 January 1960 Eisenhower authorized the subversion of Castro by the CIA. On 19 October 1960 the Latin American section of the CIA began training a brigade of Cuban exiles in Guatemala to wage a guerrilla war against Castro. When John F. Kennedy was elected president of the United States in November, Dulles told him about the plans to overthrow Castro, and Kennedy expressed his dislike of the idea.

Dulles and Kennedy had trouble communicating. When Kennedy learned of the plan to invade Cuba, two major mistakes were made. First, Kennedy changed the landing place for the Cuban exile brigade from a mountainous region, where the men could quickly disappear into the countryside, to a beach, Bahía de Cochinos (Bay of Pigs); he regarded the mountainous area as too spectacular and public. Second, to protect the brigade, warplanes flown by Cuban exiles were supposed to destroy Cuba's small air force before the landing took place; Dulles failed to tell Kennedy this, and Kennedy forbade the use of the warplanes. When the Bay of Pigs landing occurred, Cuba mustered three old aircraft that were enough to destroy the boats carrying supplies to the Cuban exiles. Further, the CIA leaders were under the impression that the U.S. military would come to the aid of the exiles if they ran into serious trouble, but Kennedy was unaware of this plan. After two days of fighting, on 19 April 1961, the exiles were defeated. Dulles was devastated by the botched operation and fell into a deep depression. Kennedy decided to fire Dulles but waited until August 1961 to do so.

On 22 November 1963 Kennedy was assassinated, and on 29 November 1963 President Lyndon B. Johnson appointed Dulles to the Warren Commission, which investigated the murder. Dulles tried to keep the commission from compromising American secret operations that had nothing to do with the killing of Kennedy, but he created suspicion that the CIA withheld knowledge of assassin Lee Harvey Oswald's relationship with the KGB, the Soviet Union's intelligence agency. Meanwhile, Dulles made a prolonged effort to sort out the ballistic evidence, trying to account for the three bullets known to have been fired, but did not do so to his own satisfaction. Eventually Dulles and two other commission members spent days in Dallas, Texas, retracing all of the evidence at the site of the assassination; all three became convinced that the FBI's theory of a lone gunman was the only one that fit the circumstances, and the rest of the commission agreed.

On 21 June 1964 three civil rights workers disappeared near Philadelphia, Mississippi, creating a national uproar. President Johnson asked Dulles to ascertain the facts, and on 24 June 1964 Dulles flew to Jackson, Mississippi, where he was alarmed by the conduct of the state government. He reported to Johnson that the civil rights workers needed protection and that the Mississippi leaders needed to accept that African Americans had a right to aspire to equality. He noted that Mississippi law enforcement actually cooperated with the Ku Klux Klan.

In late 1964 or early 1965 Dulles fell ill, perhaps from a stroke. He had more trouble walking than ever, was stooped, and the sparkle was gone from his speech. Even so, he and his wife enjoyed his retirement until he caught the flu, from which he died on 29 January 1969. He is buried in Green Mount Cemetery in Baltimore, Maryland.

Dulles's legacy included shaping the CIA into its modern form, developing rules of conduct for CIA officers, keeping presidents informed of the world's hidden events, contributing to a Warren Commission report that was soon deemed inadequate, and establishing the standard for statesmanship for the 1950s and 1960s.

★

Dulles's papers are scattered, but a large collection of personal papers is in the Seeley G. Mudd Manuscript Library of Princeton University. Dulles's *The Craft of Intelligence* (1963) is a not particularly revealing memoir of his career. Peter Grose, *Gentleman Spy: The Life of Allen Dulles* (1994) offers a brilliant account of even secret aspects of Dulles's career. Leonard Mosley, *Dulles: A Biography of Eleanor, Allen, and John Foster Dulles and Their Family Network* (1978) covers the lives of Dulles, his brother John Foster Dulles, and his sister Eleanor Dulles. An obituary is in the *New York Times* (31 Jan. 1969).

KIRK H. BEETZ

DUNAWAY, (Dorothy) Faye (*b.* 14 January 1941 in Bascom, Florida), actress, producer, and director, best known for her portrayals of intense, larger-than-life female characters, many based on such real-life personalities as Bonnie Parker, Joan Crawford, and Eva ("Evita") Peron.

Dunaway was one of two children born to John MacDowell Dunaway, a career army officer, and Grace April (Smith) Dunaway, a homemaker. Owing to her father's itinerant job in the military, Dunaway moved frequently as a child, living in Texas, Arkansas, Utah, and Mannheim, Germany. She graduated from Leon High School in Tallahassee, Florida, in 1958 and attended Florida State University and the University of Florida. In 1959 she was runner-up in the Miss University of Florida beauty contest. Dunaway graduated from the Boston University School of Fine and Applied Arts in 1962 with a B.F.A. in theater arts, and she immediately began to pursue an acting career.

Dunaway made her New York debut in September 1962

Faye Dunaway *(left)* with Warren Beatty on the set of *Bonnie and Clyde,* 1967. THE KOBAL COLLECTION

at the American National Theater and Academy (ANTA) when she replaced Olga Belin as Margaret More in *A Man for All Seasons.* Subsequent productions for ANTA include *After the Fall* and *But for Whom Charlie* (both in 1964), and *The Changeling* and *Tartuffe* (both in 1965). She also appeared in *Hogan's Goat* at the American Place Theater (1965), for which she won a Theater World Award in 1966, and she joined the Lincoln Center Repertory Company and worked for the Eileen Ford Agency as a model. By the mid-1960s Dunaway was beginning to move into film. She made guest appearances in the television shows *The Trials of O'Brien* (1966) and *The 34th Man* (1967) and made her film debut in *The Happening* (1967). The movie, set in Miami, featured Dunaway as one of a group of beach bums who kidnap a gangster, played by Anthony Quinn, only to find that no one is willing to pay his ransom. *Hurry Sundown,* also released in 1967 and set in post–World War II Georgia, concerned a land dispute between a white landowner and his poor tenants.

Neither film did much to enhance Dunaway's career. That changed with her third role, when she portrayed the bank robber Bonnie Parker in Arthur Penn's *Bonnie and Clyde* (1967). Like the 1969 film *Butch Cassidy and the Sundance Kid, Bonnie and Clyde* (which costarred Warren Beatty as Clyde Barrow) humanized and romanticized its protagonists, underscoring their bank-robbing exploits with a sizable dose of social commentary. Set during the Great Depression, the film portrays Bonnie and Clyde as modern-day Robin Hoods, who, if they do not always pass along their proceeds to the poor, at least refrain from stealing from the working-class patrons who are in the banks they are robbing. The ending, which shows in graphic detail the two outlaws being shot to death by authorities, was considered shockingly explicit for the time.

In preparation for the role, Dunaway lost thirty pounds by wearing sand weights and adhering to a strict diet. She felt that this sacrifice was necessary in order to create a lean and hungry look for her character. Her Bonnie exudes a smoldering but playful sexuality, making clear why she would leave her dreary, one-horse town to join Clyde Barrow for an exciting life on the road. The film became a major hit and was one of Warner Bros.' two top-grossing films of the decade (the other being the musical *My Fair Lady*); it made Dunaway a star. Her 1930s costumes also sparked a fashion craze for the retro look among women, who adopted the berets and maxiskirts that Dunaway wore in the film. She received an Oscar nomination for best actress for her performance.

Dunaway's other notable film role of the decade was in *The Thomas Crown Affair* (1968). Dunaway costarred with Steve McQueen, who played the film's title character, a suave, wealthy man who commits elaborate bank robberies mostly out of boredom. Dunaway is his perfect foil as the insurance investigator hired to catch him but who instead falls in love with him. Their romance is affecting and believable, and suspense over whether Dunaway will be able to capture her prey is maintained throughout. When the film was remade in 1999 with Pierce Brosnan and Rene Russo as the leads, Dunaway appeared in a small role as Brosnan's psychiatrist.

Dunaway's subsequent 1960s films illustrated a recurring problem in her career, following up noteworthy performances with ones that were less than memorable. *The Extraordinary Seaman* (1969) was a creaky, World War II comedy about three U.S. Navy men who are stranded on an island in the Philippines and meet a strange Royal Navy officer (played by David Niven) living aboard a beached ship. Dunaway joins this motley crew as they head out to sea. *Leonard Maltin's 2003 Movie & Video Guide* said of the film that its only high points were "clips from 1940s newsreels and Faye's eye makeup."

A Place for Lovers (released overseas as *Amanti,* the original name of the stage play) fared little better when it was released in 1969. Dunaway plays a fashion designer who has a passionate affair with a married engineer, played by Marcello Mastroianni, only to find that she is terminally ill. Many viewers found the location footage of Italy of more interest than the overwrought soap opera plot. Dunaway and Mastroianni embarked on a highly publicized offscreen romance as well, which did not last. *The Arrangement* (1969) marked a return to form. Dunaway was cast as the mistress of an advertising executive (played by Kirk Douglas) who becomes increasingly troubled over what he perceives as the meaninglessness of his own life. Elia Kazan directed the film and also wrote the screenplay, which was based on his own 1967 novel.

Dunaway has made numerous stage and film appearances since the 1960s. Some of her more notable films and characters include *Little Big Man* (1970); *The Three Musketeers* (1973) and its sequel, *The Four Musketeers* (1975); and the tantalizing femme fatale Evelyn Mulwray in *Chinatown* (1974), a role that garnered Dunaway another Oscar nomination as best actress. Dunaway won the best actress Oscar for playing the high-strung television executive Diane Christensen in *Network* (1976). She also appeared in a high-camp role as the actress Joan Crawford in *Mommie Dearest* (1981) and was the lead in the television film *Evita Peron* (1981), the first screen biography of the wife of Argentinian president Juan Peron. Dunaway was cast as Mickey Rourke's downtrodden girlfriend in *Barfly* (1987), based on the life of the writer Charles Bukowski. She appeared on stage in *Old Times* (1972), *A Streetcar Named Desire* (1973), and *The Curse of an Aching Heart* (1982).

In 1993 Dunaway starred in a short-lived situation comedy, *It Had to Be You,* which was cancelled after a few episodes. In 1994 she won an Emmy for best guest actress in a drama series for *Columbo: It's All in the Game.* She also crossed swords with the composer Andrew Lloyd Webber, who hired and then fired her as the lead in a Los Angeles production of his musical *Sunset Boulevard.* The dispute was settled out of court on 16 January 1995; no details of the settlement were made public. Dunaway has worked on the other side of the camera as well. She served as co-executive producer of the 1990 television film *Silhouette* (a murder mystery in which she also starred) and as writer and producer of *Yellow Bird* (2001), a short film in which she made her debut as a director. Dunaway's first marriage was to the rock star Peter Wolf, lead singer of the J. Geils Band, on 7 August 1974; the couple had no children and divorced in 1978. Her second marriage was to photographer Terry O'Neil in July 1983, with whom she had one son; the couple divorced in 1987.

★

Dunaway's autobiography is *Looking for Gatsby: My Life* (1995), co-written with Betsy Sharkey. A biography is Allan Hunter, *Faye Dunaway* (1986). Biographical information is also in Sandra Wake and Nicola Hayden, *The Bonnie and Clyde Book* (1967). Interviews with Dunaway are in *Newsweek* (4 Mar. 1968);

Photoplay (London) (Sept. 1983); *Films and Filming* (Sept. 1986); *New York Times* (11 Oct. 1992); and *Interview* (Feb. 1993). Articles about Dunaway include "Tough Act to Follow," *People Weekly* (8 May 1995), and "Faye Dunaway," *Entertainment Weekly* (22 Sept. 1996), in which she was voted one of the "Top 100 Greatest Movie Stars" of all time.

GILLIAN G. GAAR

DYLAN, Bob (*b.* 24 May 1941 in Duluth, Minnesota), songwriter, musician, and folksinger whose poetic songs, eclectic style, and creation of folk-rock music made him one of the most influential forces in the popular music of the 1960s.

Dylan, born Robert Allen Zimmerman, was one of two sons of Abram Zimmerman, a manager for the Standard Oil Company, and Beatrice Stone, a homemaker. When Dylan was five the family moved to Hibbing, northwest of Duluth. Young Dylan loved music and taught himself to play the piano without learning how to read music. He also tried the trumpet and saxophone, finally settling on the acoustic guitar as his main instrument.

Listening to music on the radio, he grew particularly fond of Johnny Ray and Hank Williams, Sr., who, he thought, was the greatest American songwriter. He also loved the blues and learned to play them himself. His fa-

Bob Dylan. AP/WIDE WORLD PHOTOS

vorite movie star was James Dean, but he also loved Elvis Presley and Little Richard.

In Hibbing High School, from which he graduated in June 1959, Dylan formed several bands with friends. He had been performing in high school bands as Bobby Zimmerman, a name he felt was too Jewish for success, and felt he needed a stage name. He took the common Hibbing surname Dillon, changing the spelling due to his fondness for the Welsh poet Dylan Thomas. His name was changed legally to Bob Dylan on 9 August 1962.

In September 1959 Dylan enrolled at the University of Minnesota in Minneapolis, majoring in music, which he was fonder of than attending classes. He frequented the Ten O'Clock Scholar, a coffeehouse hangout in Dinkytown, the bohemian neighborhood in downtown Minneapolis. He was fascinated by folk music, imitating the folk songs of the popular Kingston Trio, Pete Seeger, and his idol, Woody Guthrie, whose memoir, *Bound for Glory*, Dylan loved so much that he copied Guthrie's use of a wire harmonica rack worn around the neck while playing the guitar.

During his first year of college Dylan smoked marijuana and became sexually promiscuous. When he was not playing his acoustic guitar he was reading the Beat literature of the day, such as Jack Kerouac's *On the Road,* Allen Ginsberg's *Howl,* and Lawrence Ferlinghetti's *A Coney Island of the Mind.*

Leaving college to pursue his ambition of becoming a singing movie star like Elvis, Dylan hitchhiked from Minneapolis to New York City, arriving in Greenwich Village on 24 January 1961. After a visit to his hero, Woody Guthrie, in East Orange, New Jersey, Dylan wrote "Song to Woody," his first important composition. He sang for room and board at coffeehouses in Manhattan's Greenwich Village and, helped by new friends, including Tom Paxton and the Clancy Brothers, he got a regular gig at Gerde's Folk City on West Fourth Street.

In June 1961 he was spotted performing by Roy Silver, a show business manager, who signed Dylan with Columbia Records, the biggest record label in the United States. His first album, *Bob Dylan,* released in March 1962, sold only 5,000 copies at first. A year later, Albert B. Grossman, a successful Chicago businessman who was looking for talent to develop, became Dylan's personal manager.

The struggling artist had a banner year in 1962. He wrote "Blowin' in the Wind," the foundation stone of his career; the song became the anthem of the civil rights movement, sung by Peter, Paul, and Mary, a new group also managed by Grossman. This was followed by some of Dylan's most famous songs, including "Don't Think Twice, It's All Right," "Tomorrow Is a Long Time," and "A Hard Rain's a-Gonna Fall," which, because of the Cuban Missile Crisis, caught on and made Dylan famous. A

solo concert at New York City's Town Hall made him a star, as well as the high priest of protest singers for the new generation.

Dylan came along at just the right moment for these protesting idealists. His use of folk music created a connection with the common folk, the working class. Unlike his folk-singing predecessors, he was a true poet. His words dealt with the serious issues of the day. He was the resurrection of the troubadour singer who stuffed his possessions into a knapsack and traveled the road.

In May 1963 Dylan appeared at the Monterey Folk Festival in California with Joan Baez, a major folk star. This was the start of one of the most celebrated love affairs of the 1960s. Dylan's albums, including *The Freewheelin' Bob Dylan* (1963), *The Times They Are a-Changin'* (1964), and *Another Side of Bob Dylan* (1964), sold very well, and he played standing-room-only concerts. His fifth album, *Bringing It All Back Home* (1965), integrated the rock-and-roll sound of the Beatles with his own poetic lyrics, creating a new style of music, folk rock. In 1965 he recorded "Like a Rolling Stone," which rose to number two on the *Billboard* chart. However, when he traded in his acoustic guitar for an amplified electric guitar, often associated with rock-and-roll commercialism, Dylan lost many fans and was openly heckled and booed during concerts. This did not daunt the individualistic Dylan. He put together a rock-and-roll band, the Hawks, which later became The Band, led by Robbie Robertson. They toured the country playing rock music despite the boos. Other albums Dylan released in the 1960s include *Highway 61 Revisited* (1965), *Blonde on Blonde* (1966), *Bob Dylan's Greatest Hits* (1967), *John Wesley Harding* (1967), and *Nashville Skyline* (1969).

In spite of negative audience reactions, many singers recognized the timelessness of Dylan's words and recorded their own versions of his songs. Cher recorded "All I Really Want to Do" a month after the Byrds released their version. The Turtles had a version of "It Ain't Me, Babe," and Stevie Wonder did a rhythm-and-blues rendition of "Blowin' in the Wind." Imitators ground out what have been called Dylanesque singles, such as Barry McGuire's "Eve of Destruction" and Simon and Garfunkel's "Sounds of Silence."

In the mid-1960s Dylan was living in the Arts and Crafts Movement Colony of Byrdcliffe, a mile from Woodstock, New York, with Sara Lownds, whom he had met in Greenwich Village in 1964. Sara moved in with her daughter, whom Dylan later adopted. The couple married on 22 November 1965.

A few months after the birth of his first son, Dylan had a motorcycle accident on 29 July 1966 as he was leaving Grossman's house in upstate New York. After the accident, in which he broke his neck, Dylan became a recluse, leading a quiet, domestic life. He and Sara would have a daughter and two more sons. Because of the havoc wrought at the Woodstock Festival in the summer of 1969, a songfest at which he never appeared, Dylan moved his family to New York City and purchased a townhouse in Greenwich Village. Stalked by aggressive fans, Dylan bought a ranch house in Arizona.

The double album *Bob Dylan's Greatest Hits, Volume II* (1971) became the best-selling record of Dylan's career, with over five million sold in the United States. Following this success, Dylan went on Tour '74 with The Band, the first major stadium tour of the rock era. On tour, Dylan returned to drinking and womanizing. His wife left him and, in the summer of 1974, alone in Minnesota, he wrote songs about failed relationships for the album *Blood on the Tracks* (1975), which rose to number one on the charts. The following year he began the Rolling Thunder Revue, touring small towns by bus, inviting special appearances by celebrities like Joan Baez and Joni Mitchell.

In 1980 Dylan reassessed his career. He had gone through a bitter divorce and lost custody of his five children. His foray into Christian music earned terrible reviews and poor record sales. Mentally disturbed fans stalked him. Finally, he was involved in costly legal battles with Grossman. At the age of forty, Bob Dylan closed down his studios and took a sabbatical from music.

On 4 June 1986 Dylan married Carolyn Dennis, whom he had met during his 1978 world tour. They have one daughter. Dylan's career was at an all-time low. He was drinking more and more. In 1990 Dennis filed for dissolution of their four-year marriage; they divorced in 1992. As usual, whenever escaping domestic or financial problems, Dylan threw himself into touring and began to make a comeback.

Dylan was a huge hit at Woodstock '94. The same year he was nominated for the Nobel Prize for Literature. In September 1997 he sang "Knockin' on Heaven's Door" for Pope Paul II at the World Eucharistic Congress. Three months later he received the Kennedy Center Medal in Washington, D.C., from President William J. (Bill) Clinton. Dylan won three Grammy awards in February 1998 for *Time Out of Mind*, his first album of new songs in years. In 1998 *Time* magazine named him among the 100 most influential artists and entertainers of the twentieth century. In 2000 Dylan contributed the song "Things Have Changed" to the soundtrack for the film *Wonder Boys,* which netted him both a Golden Globe and an Oscar the following year for best original song. His album *Love and Theft* was awarded a Grammy for best contemporary folk album in February 2002. Dylan is credited with composing more than 500 songs, and he has twenty-nine gold albums and thirteen platinum albums.

Dylan helped define the rebellious 1960s. His antiestablishment, peace-loving songs of the early 1960s—"Blowin' in the Wind" and "The Times They Are a-Changin'"—influenced countless artists, including the Beatles. Always the individual, he withstood the booing of former fans and the scorn of critics when he entered his electric phase and whenever he changed his style. He continued to be innovative in the twenty-first century, continuing the Never Ending Tour. As Bruce Springsteen said at Dylan's induction into the Rock and Roll Hall of Fame on 20 January 1988, "Bob freed your mind the way Elvis freed your body."

★

Dylan's autobiography is *Bob Dylan: Self Portrait* (1970). Biographies of Dylan include Anthony Scaduto, *Bob Dylan* (1972); Michael Gross and Robert Alexander, *Bob Dylan: An Illustrated History* (1978); Bob Spitz, *Dylan: A Biography* (1989); Clinton Heylin, *Bob Dylan: Behind the Shades* (1991); William McKeen, *Bob Dylan: A Bio-Bibliography* (1993); Susan Richardson, *Bob Dylan* (1995); and Howard Sounes, *Down the Highway: The Life of Bob Dylan* (2001). Dylan's official web site is at <www.bobdylan.com>.

JOHN J. BYRNE

E

EASTWOOD, Clinton, Jr. ("Clint") (*b.* 31 May 1930 in San Francisco, California), actor and director whose films reshaped the western genre.

Eastwood was the oldest of two children born to Clinton and Ruth Eastwood. During the Great Depression the family moved frequently as Eastwood's father struggled to find employment, eventually landing an executive position with the Container Corporation of America in Oakland, California. Following his graduation from Oakland Technical High School in 1948, Eastwood worked as a lumberjack and forest firefighter in Oregon. In 1950 he was drafted into the army, although he did not see combat in the Korean War, primarily serving as a swimming instructor at Fort Ord in California. After his discharge in 1953 he briefly studied business administration at Los Angeles City College before securing a contract with Universal Studios, which brought him $75 a week.

Appearing in bit parts for such undistinguished films as the *Francis the Talking Mule* series (1950–1956), Eastwood was ready to abandon his pursuit of a film career when he was offered the part of Rowdy Yates in the television series *Rawhide,* which aired on the Columbia Broadcasting System (CBS) from 1959 to 1966. *Rawhide* was a realistic television western focusing on a group of cowboys herding cattle from Texas to Sedalia, Missouri. The series was initially quite successful, and as Yates, the assistant trail boss, Eastwood was a television star. When ratings for *Rawhide*

declined in 1965, the series lead, Eric Fleming, was fired by CBS, and the Eastwood character was elevated to the position of trail boss and first lead. This change, however, was unable to save *Rawhide,* which was canceled after the 1966 season.

Meanwhile, Eastwood planned for work on the big screen. During the summer of 1964, while taking a break from filming *Rawhide,* Eastwood traveled to Spain to make a low-budget film directed by the Italian filmmaker Sergio Leone. Although he acknowledged that he was initially attracted by the promise of a summer vacation in Spain, the actor also found promise in Leone's script, which transcended the mediocrity of most Italian "spaghetti westerns." Adapting his story from the Japanese director Akira Kurosawa's film *Yojimbo,* about the exploits of a fourteenth-century samurai, Leone created an antihero who would strike a chord with many young people during the turbulent 1960s.

After persuading Leone to pare what Eastwood perceived as the lead's overblown dialogue, the filmmakers created the persona of the "Man with No Name": a rootless, disheveled, ill-shaven, cheroot-smoking (although Eastwood was a nonsmoker), enigmatic gunfighter. Short on dialogue and plot, *A Fistful of Dollars* (1964) featured Eastwood as a gunman who hires himself out to two rival gangs who are fighting over a large sum of money. By the time the gun smoke clears, the Man with No Name has killed off both gangs and departs with the money. Made

269

Clint Eastwood. THE LIBRARY OF CONGRESS

for approximately $200,000, including Eastwood's salary of $15,000, *A Fistful of Dollars* was a box office hit in Europe, earning more than $7 million in its initial release.

This success gave birth to two sequels. In 1965 Eastwood agreed to return to Spain, reportedly for the sum of $50,000, and reprise his role in the even more violent *For a Few Dollars More* (1965), which proved to be more popular with European audiences than the original Leone-Eastwood collaboration. The final film in this trilogy was *The Good, the Bad, and the Ugly* (1966), for which Eastwood received $250,000 plus a percentage of the profits. Costarring Lee Van Cleef (who had appeared as a villain in *For a Few Dollars More*) and Eli Wallach, *The Good, the Bad, and the Ugly* was a more pretentious film, but it again featured the alienated Man with No Name hero and ample violence.

Release of the trilogy in the United States was delayed owing to legal questions regarding indebtedness to *Yojimbo*, but in February 1967 *A Fistful of Dollars* finally premiered. Audience reaction was positive, and United Artists released *For a Few Dollars More* later in the year, followed by *The Good, the Bad, and the Ugly* in early 1968.

The films were panned by such film critics as Judith Crist, Bosley Crowther, and Pauline Kael, who bemoaned the gratuitous violence and moral ambiguity. However, the spaghetti westerns made Eastwood an international film star who was especially popular among a young audience that perceived the Man with No Name as an antiestablish-

ment figure. Eastwood, a conservative Republican with libertarian leanings and a commitment to the environment, adorned many a college dorm room wall in a best-selling poster featuring the gun wielding, unshaven, and poncho-clad Man with No Name. Eastwood's youth appeal fit well with other cinematic antiheroes of the late 1960s, such as Paul Newman in *Cool Hand Luke* (1967) and Warren Beatty and Faye Dunaway in *Bonnie and Clyde* (1967). Amid political assassinations, urban and campus unrest, and the Vietnam War, Eastwood's spaghetti westerns reflected the moral ambiguity and growing violence of American life during the 1960s. Some also labeled the Eastwood westerns as misogynist, although as with *Bonnie and Clyde* and *Dr. Strangelove* (1964), the decision to deal openly with violence rather than sexuality might indicate that Americans were more comfortable with violence than sex. Nevertheless, the Man with No Name was certainly an alienated individual in an amoral and violent society where established authority offered no hope for salvation.

On the other hand, the Eastwood persona could appeal to an older audience, for he was modernizing one of Hollywood's most traditional and successful genres. He was a man of few words, like Gary Cooper, and appeared to play himself effortlessly on the screen, like John Wayne. In modernizing the western, however, Eastwood provided a sense of irony missing from the works of Cooper and Wayne.

Capitalizing on his fame and financial status, Eastwood in 1968 formed his own production company, Malpaso Productions, whose first film, *Hang 'Em High* (1968), was distributed by United Artists. Eastwood received $40,000 plus 25 percent of the profits for what proved to be a popular film. In *Hang 'Em High,* Eastwood plays Jed Cooper, who survives his own hanging and seeks revenge against the responsible parties. Again, the Eastwood character is the outsider who can find no solace within the system. In his next film, *Coogan's Bluff* (1968), however, Eastwood portrays an Arizona lawman who tracks a criminal to New York City. Eastwood is again the outsider, but the film, directed by Don Siegel, expresses misgivings regarding the moral decadence of countercultural types in the big city, foreshadowing the character of Dirty Harry, which Siegel and Eastwood would introduce in the 1970s.

By 1969 Eastwood was the world's top film box office draw, but he sought to expand his film image with roles in *Where Eagles Dare* (1969), a World War II action picture with Richard Burton; *Paint Your Wagon* (1969), a musical set on the American frontier; *Kelly's Heroes* (1970), a World War II farce; *Two Mules for Sister Sara* (1970), a western with Shirley MacLaine; and *The Beguiled* (1971), in which Eastwood portrays a wounded Union soldier victimized by residents of a southern girls school during the Civil War.

In 1971 Eastwood played the lead in and directed *Play Misty for Me,* in which a disc jockey is pursued by a psychopath. That same year, under the direction of Siegel, Eastwood introduced the character of the San Francisco police inspector Harry Callahan. *Dirty Harry* was a controversial film labeled as "fascist" by some critics. Frustrated by liberal judges who release a killer on a technicality, Callahan works outside the system to bring retribution. The popular Dirty Harry role was reprised five times by Eastwood in the 1970s and 1980s. Some observers felt that Callahan was the antithesis of the Man with No Name, but both characters were antiestablishment individuals who worked outside the system.

Eastwood's acting and directing career continued through the 1980s, 1990s, and into the twenty-first century. In 1992 his western *Unforgiven,* in which Eastwood also starred, earned the former *Rawhide* star Academy Awards for best picture and best director. His film career was honored with the Irving G. Thalberg Memorial Award (1995) and the American Film Institute Life Achievement Award (1996). Eastwood also served as mayor of Carmel, California, from 1986 to 1988.

On 19 December 1953 Eastwood married Maggie Johnson, and the marriage produced two children before the couple divorced in 1980. He also fathered a daughter with the dancer and actress Roxanne Tunis and another with the actress Frances Fisher, and he had two children with Jacelyn Reeves, a flight attendant. He had a lengthy relationship between 1975 and 1989 with the actress Sandra Locke, who costarred with Eastwood in such films as *The Gauntlet* (1977). On 31 March 1996 he married the television news anchor Dina Ruiz; they had a child that same year. Ever the outsider, Eastwood eschews the glamour of the Hollywood lifestyle, pursuing a passion for jazz and continuing to examine the human condition through his films.

★

For biographical information, see Douglas Thompson, *Clint Eastwood: Riding High* (1992), and Richard Schickel, *Clint Eastwood: A Biography* (1997). Eastwood's career and image in the 1960s are explored in David Downing with Gary Herman, *Clint Eastwood, All-American Anti-Hero: A Critical Appraisal of the World's Top Box Office Star and His Films* (1977), and Iain Johnstone, *The Man with No Name: Clint Eastwood* (1981).

RON BRILEY

EHRLICHMAN, John Daniel (*b.* 20 March 1925 in Tacoma, Washington; *d.* 14 February 1999 in Atlanta, Georgia), attorney, Republican campaign organizer, and domestic policy adviser to President Richard M. Nixon who went to prison for his role in the Watergate cover-up.

John D. Ehrlichman. AP/WIDE WORLD PHOTOS

Ehrlichman was the only child of Rudolph Ehrlichman, a World War I pilot who enlisted in the Royal Canadian Air Force early in World War II and died in a plane crash in 1941, and Lillian C. Danielson. Growing up in Washington State and California, Ehrlichman drove a milk truck and worked as a store clerk and a mailman. After his freshman year at the University of California at Los Angeles (UCLA), he enlisted in the U.S. Army Air Corps in 1943. As a lead navigator in a pathfinder squadron of the Eighth Air Force, he flew twenty-six bombing missions over Germany and was awarded the Air Medal with clusters and the Distinguished Flying Cross.

In 1945 Ehrlichman was discharged from the air corps and reenrolled under the GI Bill at UCLA. While a student there, he met H. R. ("Bob") Haldeman. He also met and courted Jeanne Fisher, whom he married on 21 August 1949. The couple had five children before divorcing in 1978. After receiving his B.A. in 1948, Ehrlichman entered Stanford University School of Law and earned his law degree in 1951. He was admitted to the bar in California and practiced for a few months, and then the family returned to Washington. Ehrlichman and a few colleagues established the firm of Hullin, Ehrlichman, Roberts, and Hodge in Seattle in 1952. Practicing in the area of land use and real estate law, he remained a partner in the firm until 1968.

While in New York City on business in late 1959, Ehrlichman visited Bob Haldeman at the latter's Connecticut residence. Haldeman was working part-time for Vice President Richard M. Nixon's presidential campaign, traveling to several states that had presidential primary elections to make arrangements for Nixon's campaign visits. He asked Ehrlichman to do similar advance work for the campaign. Ehrlichman was responsible primarily for logistics and public relations, but he occasionally engaged in "dirty tricks." For example, in his memoirs, *Witness to Power: The Nixon Years* (1982), he related how he was able to infiltrate the campaign of Nelson Rockefeller, Nixon's primary opponent in 1960. Ehrlichman signed on as a driver for the Rockefeller motorcade that traveled across North Dakota. In this position he was able to gather political intelligence about the Rockefeller campaign. Later in 1960 he was sent to the Democratic convention in Los Angeles to observe John F. Kennedy's campaign. Ehrlichman also worked on arrangements for the Nixon campaign at the Republican convention in Chicago. He later acknowledged that he knew more about Kennedy's campaign after observing the Democratic convention than he knew about the Nixon effort after the Republican convention. After Nixon was nominated, Ehrlichman continued doing advance work for the candidate, arranging rallies, public appearances, and visits with local Republican politicians. After Kennedy defeated Nixon in November 1960, Ehrlichman returned to Seattle.

Haldeman enlisted Ehrlichman to work as the scheduler for Nixon's 1962 gubernatorial campaign in California. In November the incumbent governor Edmund ("Pat") Brown soundly defeated Nixon. Ehrlichman was present the morning after the election, when Nixon informed the world that "the press wouldn't have Richard Nixon to kick around anymore." In 1964 Haldeman again called on Ehrlichman to assist with Nixon's appearance at the 1964 Republican convention in San Francisco. Although the former vice president's speech was well received, Ehrlichman left the convention convinced that Nixon's heavy drinking would cost him any return to public life.

In the fall of 1967 Nixon called Ehrlichman to New York to join another presidential campaign. Ehrlichman signed on to the campaign as national tour director, a position in which he managed Nixon's 50,000-mile travel schedule. He also oversaw most of the arrangements for the 1968 Republican convention in Miami. After winning the election, Nixon rewarded Ehrlichman by naming him White House counsel. He was promoted to assistant to the president for domestic affairs late in 1969. In this position Ehrlichman ranked second behind Chief of Staff Haldeman in the White House hierarchy.

Some in the Nixon administration viewed Ehrlichman as a closet liberal. As chief domestic policy adviser, he argued strongly in favor of increasing antipoverty programs, liberalized abortion laws, welfare reform, and school desegregation. He also advocated the development of a national energy policy. Over time, Ehrlichman and Haldeman, along with a few other trusted aides, became the primary sounding board for the president, filtering governmental activities for presentation to Nixon while protecting him from undue burdens on his time. To the public, Ehrlichman and Haldeman were interchangeable, and the two were criticized for being a "palace guard" in the White House. In an effort to protect the president, in 1969 Ehrlichman established a political intelligence operation to support the administration. This need for intelligence led him in 1971 to authorize a covert operation to uncover information on Daniel Ellsberg, the State Department and Defense Department employee who had leaked the so-called Pentagon Papers to the press. (The Pentagon Papers represented the fruits of a secret internal study examining the history of U.S. policy in Vietnam, the publication of which eroded public support for the war and for the Nixon administration.) The conspiracy in which Ehrlichman participated involved breaking into the office of Ellsberg's psychiatrist.

The White House aide John Dean implicated Ehrlichman and Haldeman in another conspiracy to cover up the 1972 break-in at the Democratic National Committee offices in the Watergate complex. Nixon asked them to resign on 30 April 1973, and he himself eventually resigned in August 1974 after Congress began impeachment proceedings. On 1 January 1975 Ehrlichman was convicted for his role in the cover-up and sentenced to thirty months to five years in prison. While appealing the conviction, he moved to Santa Fe, New Mexico, and wrote his first novel, *The Company* (1976). Although the book purportedly was a work of fiction, critics noted that the plot closely resembled the recent history of the Nixon administration. Ehrlichman served eighteen months at the federal minimum-security Swift Trail prison camp near Safford, Arizona.

After his release from prison in 1978, Ehrlichman married Christy McLaurine that November. They had one son. In 1991 his second marriage dissolved, and Ehrlichman moved to Atlanta, where he became senior vice president for Law Companies Group, an architectural and environmental engineering firm. He married Karen Hilliard in January 1995. At the end of his life, Ehrlichman was trying to redeem himself in the eyes of history when he died of complications from diabetes. His body was cremated.

★

The John Ehrlichman Papers are at the Hoover Institution Archives on the campus of Stanford University in California. Ehrlichman's gossipy memoir, *Witness to Power: The Nixon Years* (1982), provides a discussion of his role in Nixon's campaigns of the 1960s, as well as a view of his role in the Nixon administration.

William Safire, *Before the Fall: An Inside View of the Pre-Watergate White House* (1975), is another view of Ehrlichman's role at the White House. Dan Rather and Gary Paul Gates, *The Palace Guard* (1974), is an interesting look at the Nixon administration, which Ehrlichman claimed was an inaccurate account of events. Obituaries are in the *New York Times* and *Washington Post* (both 16 Feb. 1999).

JOHN DAVID RAUSCH, JR.

EPHRON, Nora Louise (*b.* 19 May 1941 in New York City), journalist, screenwriter, producer, and director, perhaps best known for her screenplay *When Harry Met Sally* (1989). She began her career as a reporter for the *New York Post* in 1963 and by the end of the 1960s had established herself as a social commentator on women, the feminist movement, and popular culture.

Ephron is the eldest daughter of Henry and Phoebe (Wolkind) Ephron, Hollywood writers who together and with others wrote plays for the stage and screen, most notably *Daddy Long Legs* (1955), *Carousel* (1956), and *Desk Set* (1957), in addition to producing films and directing stage plays. Along with her three sisters, Ephron was indoctrinated early by their mother, a Hunter College graduate and career woman, implicitly "that to be a housewife was to be nothing" and overtly to "take notes. Everything is copy." Ephron has stated that when "you grow up with your mother working . . . you pretty much know that you're going to." Ephron was student editor of the Beverly Hills High School newspaper and was filing sports and news items for publication in the *Los Angeles Times* during the late 1950s.

It is this early orientation to independence of thought and action that fostered Ephron's feminist sensibilities and the irreverence in her writing. As an adolescent her dream was to go to New York City and become another Dorothy Parker (a writer for the *New Yorker*), "the only woman at the table. The woman who made her living by her wit." Establishing her credentials as a journalist first and then as a writer on society, Ephron would say, "I care that there's a war in Indochina, and I demonstrate against it; that there's a women's liberation movement, and I demonstrate for it." In spite of these events, Ephron explained, she still went to the movies and had her hair done once a week. She observed, "Much of my life goes irreverently on, in spite of larger events." It is the irreverence of Ephron's chosen subject matter and commentary that makes her a quintessentially 1960s personality.

Ephron did her undergraduate work at Wellesley College (1958–1962). A political science major, she served as an intern in the office of the White House press secretary

Pierre Salinger during the Kennedy administration. In her senior year she was associate editor of the *Wellesley College News*. On summer vacations she worked in New York City as a copygirl for the Columbia Broadcasting System and later in a similar position for *Newsweek*, where she was promoted to article clipper. After graduating she worked as a reporter for the *New York Post* (1963–1968). Discussing the early progress of her career, Ephron noted, "I didn't sell a magazine piece until I had been a reporter for about four years. The point is I worked up very slowly." On 9 April 1967 she married Dan Greenburg, himself a writer. She quit her job at the *New York Post* and began freelancing. During this period (1968–1972) Ephron contributed articles to such national magazines as *Good Housekeeping, Cosmopolitan, Oui, McCall's, New York,* and *Esquire*.

From the articles published in 1968 and 1969 she selected twelve that would become her first book, *Wallflower at the Orgy* (1970). In it she addresses such subjects as the food establishment ("Food became, for dinner-party conversations in the sixties, what abstract expressionism had been in the fifties"), Helen Gurley Brown, the Arthur Frommer budget travel books, and her own professional makeover. Her signature use of humor and her own experience in her writings—which have been described as acerbic, iconoclastic, brazen, and malicious by some and witty, irresistible, perceptive, and original by others—enabled Ephron to infuse her material with her personal ambivalences and biases while diffusing some of the tensions inherent in her subject matter.

Revealing her "hopelessly midcult nature," in *Wallflower at the Orgy*, Ephron wrote about the menswear industry, the boon in publishing on the occult, and the merit of Jacqueline Susann's writing while the larger events of the decade played silently in the background. Ephron's interests, humanity, and critical intelligence were never overridden by politics. She would say of her approach to writing on the women's movement that "you could be very funny on the subject and be fundamentally serious about it." Giving weight to the lightness of her subjects, Ephron offered insight into then contemporary American culture, revealing its mores and biases by examining its mainstream.

In her interview with the fashion designer Bill Blass published in *Wallflower at the Orgy*, he stated that in the 1950s a menswear manufacturer told him that "there were two minority groups that doomed every fashion development—the homosexuals and the Negroes. Acceptance by these groups supposedly made fashion unacceptable to the rest of the population." It was the young, he pointed out, that began to set the trends in the 1960s. The boom and profit made on parapsychology in the publishing business, she speculated, were due to "people [being] unwilling to look within themselves for the source of their difficulties." In her assessment of Jacqueline Susann, she remarks on her own penchant for gossip columns and makes the impolitic statement there is a "streak of masochism in most women." Ephron's commentary is radical in a matter-of-fact way.

Wallflower at the Orgy was followed by *Crazy Salad* (1975), a selection of her writings from 1972 to 1974, during which time she progressed from freelance contributor to regular columnist and contributing editor for *New York* magazine and similarly progressed to senior editor at *Esquire*. Ephron would go on to change the focus of her columns in *Esquire* to the media, and from these columns she published *Scribble, Scribble: Notes on the Media* (1978). She divorced Greenburg in the early 1970s and married Carl Bernstein (14 April 1976), the *Washington Post* reporter of Watergate fame, with whom she had two sons. Their divorce in 1979 is the subject of her first novel, *Heartburn* (1983). In 1987 she married the writer Nicholas Pileggi; they had two sons. She wrote and collaborated on the screenplays *Silkwood* (1983), *When Harry Met Sally* (1989), and *Sleepless in Seattle* (1993). At the turn of the twentieth century she was at work on a film script based on Larry McMurtry's novel *Desert Rose* (1983), which she planned to direct.

During the 1960s Ephron established herself as a journalist and as an irreverent and witty cultural commentator. In her social criticism during the decade, she simultaneously articulated and bolstered the spirit of questioning and self-exploration that were emblematic of the period.

★

Biographical essays on Ephron are in *Current Biography Yearbook* (1990), *Women Filmmakers and Their Films* (1998), and *Authors and Artists for Young Adults* (2000). Ephron also was featured as Wellesley College Person of the Week (21 Aug. 2000).

ANNMARIE B. SINGH

EVERS, Medgar Wylie (*b.* 2 July 1925 near Decatur, Mississippi; *d.* 12 June 1963 in Jackson, Mississippi), civil rights leader and field secretary for the National Association for the Advancement of Colored People (NAACP), who organized African Americans to resist segregation and supported James Meredith's effort to enroll at the University of Mississippi; his assassination focused attention on Mississippi's resistance to the civil rights movement.

Evers was the third of four children born to James Evers, a farmer and sawmill worker, and Jessie (Wright) Evers, a homemaker. After serving in France with the U.S. Army during World War II, he attended Newton High School and used the GI Bill to enroll at Alcorn Agricultural and Mechanical College, where he participated on the football, track, and debate teams in addition to singing in the choir

Medgar Evers, 1963. ASSOCIATED PRESS AP

and editing the college newspaper and yearbook. During his senior year he married fellow student Myrlie Beasley. After graduating in 1952 with a bachelor's degree in business administration, Evers moved with his wife to Mound Bayou, Mississippi, where he became a salesman for the Magnolia Mutual Insurance Company. In December 1954 he became the first full-time Mississippi field secretary for the National Association for the Advancement of Colored People (NAACP). Described as "tall, low-key, intelligent, and dignified," Evers was an excellent choice for this demanding job. For the rest of the decade he traveled the state, building local branches of the organization and supporting school desegregation efforts, encouraging voter registration activities, and investigating racially motivated homicides.

The civil rights movement came later to Mississippi than to other southern states because of the frequent violence directed against civil rights advocates and because of the powerful opposition of well-organized segregationists. Evers was the most prominent leader of the movement in the state. He organized an unsuccessful boycott of white merchants in Jackson during the 1960 Christmas season and supported the first public demonstration against segregation by nine Tougaloo College students at the Jackson Public Library on 27 March 1961. When the students arrived at the courthouse for their trial on 1 April 1961, a group of African-American supporters began cheering. This provoked the Jackson police, who attacked the crowd. Evers was among those injured in the melee.

School desegregation absorbed much of Evers's energy. He was a key adviser to James Meredith in 1962 as he attempted to become the first African-American student to enroll at the University of Mississippi. Evers himself had been rebuffed when he applied to the law school in 1954. He was instrumental in bringing Meredith to the attention of the NAACP Legal Defense and Education Fund and convincing the fund's lawyers to take his case. As soon as his oldest son was of school age, Evers attempted to enroll him in an all-white Jackson school. At the time of Evers's death, two of the Evers children were lead plaintiffs in an NAACP lawsuit to desegregate Jackson schools. Evers advised representatives of other civil rights organizations, including Robert Moses of the Student Nonviolent Coordinating Committee and David Dennis of the Congress of Racial Equality. He also worked with John Doar of the Justice Department in bringing voting rights suits against recalcitrant county registrars.

Although the NAACP traditionally favored courtroom confrontation over mass demonstrations, Evers kept pressing his national office to adopt more militant tactics in the fight for civil rights. In December 1962 the North Jackson NAACP Youth Council, with the guidance of Evers and the Tougaloo College sociologist John Salter, launched another boycott of downtown businesses. They demanded an end to segregated lunch counters, restrooms, and drinking fountains; the hiring and promotion of black employees; and the use of courtesy titles for black customers. The boycott continued into the spring of 1963. When city officials refused to negotiate, the protest leaders increased their demands: the city should hire black police officers, desegregate parks and recreational facilities, and stop discriminating against black employees. When Mayor Allen Thompson went on television to condemn the boycott, Evers demanded and received equal time from station WLBT. On 20 May 1963 Evers delivered his rebuttal, articulating the grievances of Mississippi blacks, denouncing the denial of human rights, and calling for an end to segregation. This broadcast made Evers a marked man, transforming him from a faceless leader into the state's most visible advocate of racial equality. On 28 May 1963 Tougaloo College students escalated their protest by sitting in at Woolworth's lunch counter. The protesters were arrested after they were harassed and beaten by a crowd of angry whites. Two days later six hundred high school students were jailed as they paraded in support of the boycott. On 1 June Roy Wilkins, national head of the NAACP, joined the protest and was arrested with Evers for picketing in front of Woolworth's. Rallies and meetings continued but

not the mass demonstrations, as the national NAACP office called for a cooling-off period.

On 11 June 1963 Evers stayed late at his Jackson office to watch President John F. Kennedy deliver a television address to the nation. Earlier that day the federal government had forced Governor George Wallace to stand aside as two African-American students were enrolled at the University of Alabama. Kennedy described race relations as a "moral crisis" and outlined the landmark civil rights legislation he would soon introduce to Congress. Evers arrived at his home after midnight. As he left his Oldsmobile, carrying a bundle of NAACP T-shirts, a single bullet from a high-powered rifle tore into his back, just below the right shoulder blade. Myrlie Evers ran to the door to find her husband sprawled on the concrete carport, bleeding profusely from his wound. Neighbors rushed Evers to University Hospital, where he died a short time later. On 15 June a memorial service for the slain leader was held at Jackson's Masonic Temple. After the service a riot was narrowly averted when a crowd of several thousand angry young people confronted the police. Evers was buried at Arlington National Cemetery.

Ten days after the shooting Byron de la Beckwith, a fertilizer salesman and rabid racist from Greenwood, Mississippi, was arrested and charged with Evers's murder. Key evidence against Beckwith included his Enfield .30–06 rifle found at the crime scene, his fingerprint on the rifle's telescopic sight, and two witnesses who identified his white, 1962 Valiant parked near Evers's home on the night of the murder. Beckwith twice was tried for murder, and both times the all-white, all-male juries could not be persuaded to return a conviction. In 1989 the state of Mississippi reopened its investigation of Evers's murder. After discovering new evidence, Beckwith was tried a third time, this time before a jury of eight blacks and four whites. On 5 February 1994 Beckwith was convicted of killing Evers and was sentenced to life in prison, where he died on 21 January 2001.

While relatively unknown among civil rights leaders during his life, the assassinated Evers became a worldwide symbol of the movement following his death. Within days the NAACP published a poster bearing a photo of his grieving widow with the inscription, "Keep the idea of freedom alive—Join NAACP." Evers's older brother, Charles, returned to Mississippi from Chicago to take over as head of the state NAACP. His widow moved to California with their three children, Darrell Kenyatta, Reena Denise, and James Van Dyke. In 1995 she continued the family tradition of civil rights leadership when she was elected national chair of the NAACP. On 28 June 1992 the city of Jackson placed a life-size bronze statue of Evers in front of the public library named in his honor. A city street is named Medgar Evers Boulevard.

For most of his adult life Evers labored in obscurity,

against overwhelming odds, trying to win basic human rights for his fellow black Mississippians. In death he came to symbolize the courage, determination, and self-sacrifice that empowered the African-American freedom movement to demolish the legacy of discriminatory public policies.

★

For Us, the Living (1967), by Myrlie B. Evers with William Peters, is a personal account of Evers's work and their life together. Maryanne Vollers, *Ghosts of Mississippi: The Murder of Medgar Evers, the Trials of Byron de la Beckwith, and the Haunting of the New South* (1995), tells the story of Evers's life, murder, and the three trials of his killer. Bobby DeLaughter, *Never Too Late: A Prosecutor's Story of Justice in the Medgar Evers Case* (2001), is a detailed description of the third trial of Byron de la Beckwith by the attorney who obtained his conviction. In 1983 the Public Broadcasting System's American Playhouse series produced a television drama based on Evers's story. The 1996 feature film *Ghosts of Mississippi,* starring Alec Baldwin, Whoopi Goldberg, and James Woods, was based on the book by Vollers. Castle Rock Entertainment has produced an educational CD-ROM on *Ghosts of Mississippi* and on Evers. An obituary is in the *New York Times* (13 June 1963).

PAUL T. MURRAY

F

FALL, Bernard B. (*b.* 19 November 1926 in Vienna, Austria; *d.* 21 February 1967 near Hue, Vietnam), scholar, author, and journalist whose work on Vietnam challenged many of the assumptions underlying American policy in Southeast Asia during the Vietnam War.

Although Fall was born in Austria, he did not live there long. Fall's parents, Léon Fall, a businessman, and Anna Seligman, a housewife, fled with their son and daughter to France in 1938 following the *Anschluss* between Nazi Germany and Austria. After the fall of France, Fall's father was executed by the Germans for his resistance activities, and his mother was deported to Germany, where she disappeared. Following in his father's footsteps, Fall joined the French resistance, served in the French Army after liberation, was wounded twice, and was decorated for bravery.

From 1946 to 1948 Fall worked as a research assistant for the Nuremberg War Crimes Tribunal, and from 1949 to 1950 he was employed by the United Nations in the International Tracing Service. Meanwhile he completed his university studies at the Sorbonne in Paris (1948–1949) and the University of Munich (1949–1950). In 1951 Fall was awarded a Fulbright scholarship to pursue graduate studies at Syracuse University in Syracuse, New York, where in 1952 he earned an M.A. in political science. Searching for a dissertation topic, he was encouraged to take advantage of his French background to explore the neglected scholarly field of Indochina studies. Fall drew on his personal savings to make his first trip to Vietnam in 1953. While gathering information for his dissertation Fall traveled with French troops into the jungles of Vietnam, where the French colonial regime was struggling to quash a revolt by the Communist Viet Minh.

Upon his return from Vietnam, Fall married Dorothy Winer, an American citizen and graphic artist who often resided in Hong Kong, on 20 February 1954. They had three children. The following year he received his Ph.D. in political science from Syracuse. His three-volume dissertation on post–World War II Vietnam provided the basis for his first book, *The Viet-Minh Regime* (1954). In 1956 he secured a position teaching international relations at Howard University in Washington, D.C., where he taught until his death in 1967.

Fall was a scholar who relied on considerable field research. Accordingly, he continued his travels to Vietnam, making five more trips to Southeast Asia. Speaking fluent French and some Vietnamese (he also was fluent in German, Polish, and Hungarian), Fall used his French citizenship to gain access to areas of Vietnam that were often off-limits to Americans. Despite his long sojourn in the United States, Fall never applied to become a naturalized citizen, although his friends insisted he was exploring the naturalization process shortly before his death. Fall used his experiences with French troops during the First Indochina War to publish *Street Without Joy* (1961), named after the major Vietnamese coastal highway where the author observed fierce fighting between the French and Vietnamese.

In 1962 Fall was teaching at the Royal Institute of Administration in Phnom Penh, Cambodia, when he was invited to visit North Vietnam. While in Hanoi he was allowed exclusive audiences and interviews with Premier Pham Van Dong and President Ho Chi Minh. His research culminated in the influential book *The Two Viet-Nams* (1963), which became required reading for many U.S. politicians and military leaders, even though they often failed to implement Fall's suggestions. Fall's most scholarly volume was *Hell in a Very Small Place* (1966), an examination of the French defeat at Dien Bien Phu. Fall argued that air support from the Eisenhower administration might have saved the French garrison.

In addition to scholarly works, Fall wrote more than 250 articles for publications ranging from such mainstream titles as *U.S. News and World Report* and the *Saturday Evening Post* to the left-wing periodical *Ramparts.* Many of his articles discussing the origins of American intervention in Southeast Asia were compiled in *Viet-Nam Witness, 1953–66* (1966). Fall was in demand as a speaker as well as a writer, delivering lectures at the Foreign Service Institute, the National War College, and the military academies.

His critique of American foreign policy and military strategy in Southeast Asia antagonized many government officials, leading J. Edgar Hoover and the Federal Bureau of Investigation (FBI) to place Fall under surveillance as a "foreign agent." However, Fall's perceptions of Vietnam were complex and often misunderstood by thin-skinned policy makers because Fall did not fit easily into the Vietnam War dichotomy of "hawks" and "doves." While critical of French colonialism and American imperialism, Fall also denounced international Communism and Chinese expansionism. Perhaps his greatest complaint regarding American politicians was their ignorance regarding Indochina and their failure to consult expert advice. Of course, Fall perceived himself as one of these experts, remarking, "My ambition is to be the foremost military writer of my generation."

Fall did not oppose American aid to the regime in South Vietnam, but he insisted the failure to couple such assistance with land reform was undermining popular support for the South Vietnamese government. He also believed the U.S. military response in Vietnam was heavy-handed. For example, beginning in 1957 the Vietcong were gaining power in the countryside by murdering village chiefs and officials, many of whom were unpopular appointees of President Ngo Dinh Diem. Thus, with a fairly low level of violence the Vietcong gained the upper hand with the local population. The American military rejoinder to this Vietcong campaign of assassination was what Fall termed "weapons of mass destruction," such as napalm, rockets, artillery, and tanks, which killed indiscriminately and turned the population against the United States and its client state in South Vietnam. Fall concluded that if such massive retaliation were necessary to prevent a nation from

Bernard Fall. ASSOCIATED PRESS AP

falling to Communism, some people might accept Communist rule as the lesser of two evils.

Rather than a military solution Fall called for reform in South Vietnam along with diplomacy—carefully avoiding the word *negotiations*, which some American politicians associated with surrender. Fall argued that skillful diplomacy could exploit historical animosities between the North Vietnamese and the Chinese, driving a wedge between the Communist nations. As the war in Vietnam dragged on in the 1960s, Fall became increasingly critical of President Lyndon Johnson, asserting in a February 1967 piece for the *New York Review of Books* that the president was ignoring peace initiatives from Hanoi.

While disenchanted with political leaders, Fall had great respect for the common fighting men of France, Vietnam, and America, sharing their hardships on the field of battle. In his shorts, shirt open to the chest, and wearing tinted glasses, Fall often cut a dashing figure, but he remained a favorite of the common soldier, somewhat of a scholarly Ernie Pyle. He also expressed great admiration for the Vietnamese people, writing in the introduction to *The Two Viet-Nams* that his work was an "attempt to bring some understanding to the plight of a valiant people that happens to find itself, no doubt much against its will, at one of the focal points of world-wide struggle."

With no end in sight to the conflict in Vietnam, Fall planned on a return to Indochina in the autumn of 1966.

In an interview with Dick Hubert of American Broadcasting Company's (ABC) television news, Fall expressed misgivings about his upcoming journey to Vietnam, remarking, "It's just simply and purely for the first time I'm really apprehensive about what I'm going to find. You know, Viet-Nam to all accounts is really taking a horrible beating for a small country or for a country that size." He continued, "We've never really fought that intensive a war over that small a piece of real estate. . . . I'm just wondering what's going to be left of 'my old Viet-Nam.'"

His departure was delayed by the birth of his third daughter in September as well as concerns about his health; surgeries had removed one kidney and part of his colon, and Fall suffered from a rare and incurable fibrosis condition that affected his kidneys and bladder. In December 1966 Fall, with the support of a Guggenheim Fellowship, finally left for Vietnam. This proved his last journey to Southeast Asia, for on 21 February 1967, while on patrol with U.S. Marines about 14 miles northwest of Hue, along the stretch of seacoast Fall had popularized as the *Street Without Joy*, Fall was killed by a Vietcong mine. His final dispatches, along with a preface by Dorothy Fall, were published in *Last Reflections on a War* (1967). Fall is buried in Rock Creek Cemetery in Washington, D.C.

Fall's warning about America's approach to Southeast Asia went unheeded, and the Vietnam War continued to rage into the early 1970s. Closer attention to Fall's work might have spared both American and Vietnamese lives.

★

Fall's papers are available at the John F. Kennedy Library in Boston, Massachusetts. For Fall's writings see *The Viet-Minh Regime* (1956); *Street Without Joy: Indochina at War, 1946–54* (1961); *The Two Viet-Nams: A Political and Military Analysis* (1963); *Hell in a Very Small Place: The Siege of Dien Bien Phu* (1966); *Viet-Nam Witness, 1953–66* (1966); and *Last Reflections on a War* (1967). Obituaries are in the *New York Times* (22 Feb. 1967), *Newsweek* and *Publishers Weekly* (both 6 Mar. 1967), and *Commentary* (Mar. 1967).

RON BRILEY

FARIÑA, Richard George (*b.* 8 March 1937 in New York City; *d.* 30 April 1966 near Carmel, California), songwriter, singer, poet, and novelist who had a major influence on folk and protest music in the 1960s.

Fariña was born to an Irish mother, Theresa Crozier, and a Cuban father, Liborio Ricardo Fariñas, a toolmaker who later changed his name to Fariña. The younger Fariña attended Public School 181 and Holy Cross Catholic Elementary School before going on to Brooklyn Technical High School. There he was a member of the Aristas, a musical group comprising top students. Fariña majored in electrical engineering and graduated in February 1955, winning a Regents Scholarship to Cornell University, where he was a contemporary of the writer Thomas Pynchon. Although he began at Cornell studying electrical engineering, he was soon majoring in English literature, declaring that stories are more fun than statistics. Pynchon, who dedicated his novel *Gravity's Rainbow* (1973) to Fariña, recalls him as a charismatic presence on campus. Fariña eventually dropped out of college without finishing his senior year, in 1959.

Fariña's time at Cornell was interrupted by foreign travel. Proud of his Irish ancestry, he joined and fought with the Irish Republican Army and was forced to leave Ireland. He also fought on the side of the revolution in Cuba. When he returned to Cornell, Fariña was involved in protests to relax the curfews that prevented women students from being outside of their dormitories after eleven o'clock. In 1958 Fariña was one of four students suspended after eggs and rocks were thrown at the house of the university president, though he was reinstated when new demonstrations were threatened. After leaving college to work in advertising in New York City, Fariña married the folk singer Carolyn Hester on 17 June 1960. Besides working as Carolyn's agent, he began writing short stories and poems, some of which appeared in *Atlantic Monthly*. Carolyn taught Fariña to play the dulcimer, the instrument for which he later became famous, and the couple performed together at the Edinburgh Folk Festival in 1962. They divorced in 1963, and Fariña married Mimi Baez, sister of the singer Joan Baez, secretly in Paris, France, in spring of that year. They were married officially on 24 August 1963 in Carmel, California.

Almost immediately, Fariña and his new wife began a creative partnership that would make them among the most influential folk musicians of the time, boasting Bob Dylan and Pete Seeger as admirers. With Fariña writing the songs and accompanying on the dulcimer and Mimi singing, the pair debuted at the Big Sur Folk Festival in June 1964 as Mimi and Richard Fariña. They became regular performers at the famous Club 47 in Cambridge, Massachusetts, and released their first album, *Celebrations for a Grey Day*, in April 1965. With their mix of rock and idealistic folk music, they helped initiate the "folk rock" style, a powerful force in popular music until the mid-1970s. At the Newport Folk Festival in the summer of 1965 they were a huge success, appearing shortly before Dylan's performance, when he alienated his fans with his infamous electric set. In September they took part in the "Sing-In for Peace in Viet Nam" at Carnegie Hall. *Celebrations for a Grey Day* appeared in the *New York Times'* critics' choice top ten folk albums of the year in December 1965, at about the same time as they released their second recording on the Vanguard label, *Reflections in a Crystal Wind*.

Fariña's enthusiasm for new projects and people meant that he was often seen as unreliable or inconsistent. But he managed to produce hundreds of poems and song lyrics, even while he was touring the country as a singer. As his fame as a folk musician and songwriter grew, he was also working hard on other forms of writing. His first and best-known novel, *Been Down So Long It Looks Like Up to Me* (1966), is set at the end of the 1950s at Cornell and includes descriptions of protests similar to the ones in which Fariña had been involved. By the time it appeared student protests were taking place across the United States, ensuring an audience for a work described by a review in *Time* as "fashionably incoherent." Though reviews were mixed, the kindest have compared Fariña with Thomas Pynchon and Richard Brautigan. He shares with them a vision of an America peopled by lonely individuals pursuing happiness and fulfillment in a comically absurd cultural landscape. *Been Down So Long It Looks Like Up to Me* acquired a cult following in the mid-1960s. Its honest and personal voice spoke to the post-Beat generation. The novel's fame was further enhanced by the author's death just two days after publication. But Fariña's reputation as a novelist has fared less well than those of his postmodern contemporaries. By the end of the twentieth century he had all but disappeared from the map of American literature. His second book, a collection of shorter pieces titled *Long Time Coming and a Long Time Gone*, was published with a foreword by Joan Baez. It appeared posthumously in 1969 but did not have the impact of his first book.

Despite the success of Mimi and Richard Fariña as performers and recording artists, Fariña's long-term influence on folk music is difficult to judge. His blending of several folk styles and his effort to merge folk and rock were daring and dramatic in the early 1960s. Within a few years he became an accomplished dulcimer player, boosting the instrument's popularity. Fariña was at the heart of a folk music scene that has become synonymous with the turbulent politics of the 1960s. An energetic man, Fariña's restless style emerges in his music, his novel, and in his lifelong passion for travel. While his greatest success during his lifetime came as a musician, his ambitious but flawed novel demonstrates the breadth of his imaginative vision and creative drive. Fariña was killed in a motorcycle accident near Carmel, California, just a few hours after attending the launch party for his novel.

★

Very little information about Fariña is available, and there is no full-length biography. David Hadju, *Positively 4th Street: The Lives and Times of Joan Baez, Bob Dylan, Mimi Baez Fariña, and Richard Fariña* (2001), gives a useful overview of the period and

key personalities in the folk music scene. An article about Fariña is in *Time* (6 May 1966), and the problems of writing a biography about Fariña are outlined in William N. Flanagan, "Been Gone So Long: The Life of Richard Fariña," *Broadside* (Sept. 1986). An obituary is in the *New York Times* (9 May 1966).

CHRIS ROUTLEDGE

FARMER, James Leonard, Jr. (*b.* 12 January 1920 in Marshall, Texas; *d.* 9 July 1999 in Fredericksburg, Virginia), civil rights leader, union organizer, and social reformer who was a key leader in the 1960s civil rights movement and who organized the Freedom Riders.

Farmer was the middle of three children born to James Leonard, Sr., a preacher believed to be the first African American in Texas to earn a Ph.D., and Pearl Marion Houston, a teacher. Fluent in French, German, Aramaic, Hebrew, Greek, and Latin, Farmer's father taught theology and philosophy at southern black colleges. The young Farmer reportedly could read and write by the age of four. At age fourteen Farmer received a full scholarship to Wiley College, where his father taught. Farmer earned a B.S. in chemistry at Wiley and then attended Howard University, where he studied to become a minister and where he became aware of the Indian philosopher Mohandas K. Gandhi's concept of nonviolence.

After receiving his bachelor of divinity in 1941, Farmer refused to serve in the armed forces during World War II on the grounds that he was a conscientious objector who opposed violence. He had been a member of the Fellowship of Reconciliation while he was in school and began working with that organization to fight segregation in Chicago, Illinois, and New York City. In 1942 he helped establish the Committee of Racial Equality (CORE), an interracial organization that believed in nonviolent protest against racism. The organization later became known as the Congress of Racial Equality. In 1943 Farmer and CORE staged one of the first successful sit-ins, at a segregated restaurant in Chicago. Nevertheless, Farmer's association with CORE was sporadic over the next decade and a half, as he drifted from the group and worked as a union organizer. He married Winnie Christie in 1945, but the two divorced a year later. In 1959 Farmer became program director for the National Association for the Advancement of Colored People (NAACP).

Despite his differences with some of CORE's leadership, Farmer became national director of CORE on 1 February 1961, just days after the inauguration of John F. Kennedy as president of the United States. He soon began organizing the successful Freedom Rides. At the time, despite rulings to the contrary by the Supreme Court, the southern

James Farmer, December 1963. ASSOCIATED PRESS AP

states still required African Americans to sit in the back of interstate buses and to use separate facilities. Thirteen "Freedom Riders," including Farmer, left Washington, D.C., by bus on 4 May 1961. The riders were determined to disobey the "southern" rules concerning African Americans by having the black members ride in front of the bus while the white Freedom Riders rode in the back. Furthermore, they would refuse to move when asked.

The Freedom Riders split into two groups, riding different buses through Alabama. Both buses were greeted by mobs, and some riders were severely beaten. Although determined to continue, the Freedom Riders were fearful for their lives and gave up after unsuccessful negotiations with the bus companies, whose drivers were also afraid. However, student activists from Nashville, Tennessee, arranged to continue the Freedom Rides. The students also met with mob violence in Montgomery, Alabama, which forced U.S. Attorney General Robert Kennedy to call in the National Guard. The Freedom Riders continued on into Jackson, Mississippi, where they were jailed and sentenced to sixty days in the state penitentiary. However, the Freedom Rid-

ers were virtually unstoppable by this time, as they gained more and more sympathy from both African Americans and whites. The protest is largely credited with forcing President Kennedy's administration to take a stand on civil rights. The Interstate Commerce Commission outlawed segregation in interstate bus travel in September 1961.

Farmer went on to become one of the "Big Four" of the 1960s civil rights movement. The others were Dr. Martin Luther King, Jr., of the Southern Christian Leadership Conference, Roy Wilkins of the NAACP, and Whitney Young of the Urban League. As one of the movement's influential leaders, Farmer was integral in organizing a massive march on Washington, D.C., to dramatize the economic plight of blacks in the United States. However, Farmer was unable to attend the March on Washington for Jobs and Freedom. As 250,000 African Americans from around the country came to Washington to protest, Farmer sat in a Plaquemine, Louisiana, jail for protesting for civil rights.

Farmer, who once said that anyone who claimed not to be afraid during the civil rights movement was "either a liar or without imagination," did not let his own fear keep him from the front lines of the civil rights protests. During another protest trip to Plaquemine, Farmer was nearly lynched but escaped by hiding in a hearse and traveling on back roads to New Orleans. Some of Farmer's other associates were not so fortunate, including Dr. Martin Luther King, Jr., who was assassinated on 4 April 1968. However, four years earlier, three CORE workers—Andrew Goodman, Michael Schwerner, and James Chaney—disappeared in Philadelphia, Mississippi, while campaigning for black voter registration. Farmer had helped to recruit the activists, whose bodies were found three months after their disappearance. The brutality of their deaths and others associated with the civil rights movement helped lead to the Voting Rights Act of 1965.

In his 1965 book, *Freedom—When?*, Farmer outlined his views for nonviolent political action and proposed more active political participation and leadership by African Americans. Farmer had debated black radical leader Malcolm X several times during the early 1960s on the issue of separatism, which Farmer opposed. Nevertheless, the two eventually became friends, and Farmer greatly admired Malcolm X's message of self-pride.

Farmer is also credited with playing a vital role in influencing President Lyndon B. Johnson's push for passage of the Civil Rights Act of 1964. Although he had an adversarial relationship with President Kennedy, Farmer became friends with President Johnson. Johnson listened when Farmer talked about needing more than equal opportunity to help African Americans overcome racial barriers to access jobs. Farmer proposed a program of "preferential access" for African Americans qualified for certain jobs. Johnson, always the shrewd politician, disagreed with the use of the word "preferential" and coined the term "affirmative action."

Farmer had also developed a plan to fight functional illiteracy among poor and black Americans. He presented his plan to Johnson, who subsequently asked Farmer to submit a detailed proposal. The proposal was submitted to the Office of Economic Opportunity and approved by the office's director Sargent Shriver. However, its premature announcement in a 1965 *Washington Post* article led to Farmer's having to face the ire of CORE officials, who did not know of the plan and were upset at being kept in the dark. The opposition of the African-American representative from New York, Adam Clayton Powell, Jr., sounded the death knell for the plan.

Farmer left CORE in 1966 largely because of political infighting, which had become rampant in the civil rights movement. In fact, there had been an unsuccessful attempt to oust him during CORE's national convention in 1964. His legacy included dramatically increasing the organization's number of local branches, fostering numerous protests such as a 1964 demonstration at the New York World's Fair, and organizing voter-registration drives. Farmer was also troubled by the growing movement of young civil rights leaders to foster separatism between African Americans and whites. CORE eventually became an ineffective black nationalist group.

After leaving CORE, Farmer took posts teaching at Lincoln University and New York University and began to lecture to earn enough money to help support his young family and his ailing second wife, Lula A. Peterson, whom he had married in 1949 and who was now suffering from Hodgkin's disease. The couple had two daughters.

In 1968 Farmer lost a race for Congress to Shirley Chisholm, who became the first African-American woman to serve in that body. The following year, Farmer joined President Richard M. Nixon's administration as an assistant secretary in the Department of Health, Education, and Welfare, much to the shock of many of his civil rights colleagues. Nevertheless, Farmer believed the position provided a real opportunity to contribute within the "official" confines of government. Although he quickly became disillusioned and retired from the position in 1970, he was able to establish a fellowship program that would increase the number of women and minorities in the federal government. Farmer had pushed for this program because he found that one-fifth of the minorities working in the department had low-level jobs and that the intern program was nearly all white. Farmer also created the Office of Child Development, which raised the funding level and administrative status of the Head Start program.

Farmer went on to work for the Council on Minority Planning and Strategy, an African-American think tank, and to teach at several colleges, including teaching civil rights history at Mary Washington College, in Fredericks-

burg, Virginia, beginning in 1984. Although Dr. Martin Luther King, Jr., is thought of as the core leader and spiritual motivator of the 1960s civil rights movement, Farmer's commitment to civil rights and nonviolence predated King's efforts by nearly two decades. Farmer's keen intellect sometimes led others to view him as pompous, but his commitment to the movement and his leadership ultimately proved to be invaluable. Farmer was awarded the Presidential Medal of Freedom, the nation's highest civilian honor, by President William J. Clinton in 1998. By then Farmer was blind and a double amputee, largely due to complications from diabetes. He died in Mary Washington Hospital in 1999.

★

Farmer's autobiography, *Lay Bare the Heart: An Autobiography of the Civil Rights Movement,* was published in 1985 and reprinted in 1998. A detailed biography of Farmer is Jeff Sklansky, *James Farmer: Civil Rights Leader* (1992). August Meier and Elliott Rudwick, *CORE: A Study in the Civil Rights Movement, 1942–1968* (1975), includes information about Farmer's role in CORE. Obituaries are in the *New York Times* and *Washington Post* (both 10 July 1999).

DAVID PETECHUK

FARRELL, Suzanne (*b.* 16 August 1945 in Cincinnati, Ohio), principal ballerina of the New York City Ballet beginning in the early 1960s.

Born Roberta Sue Ficker, Farrell was one of three daughters of Robert and Donna Ficker. Donna, a nurse, prided herself on her daughter's athletic ability and grace. Farrell began studying ballet at the age of eight, about the time her parents divorced. In 1955 she received her first opportunity to perform onstage, as Clara in a touring presentation of *The Nutcracker* by the Ballet Russe. Two years later she formed the New York City Ballet Juniors.

Farrell, an admirer of Jacques d'Amboise and Diana Adams, never dreamed that she would one day have the opportunity to work with both dancers. While attending Ursuline Academy in Cincinnati, Farrell also attended the Cincinnati Conservatory of Music. In 1958 she auditioned for Diana Adams and the Ford Foundation scholarship program with the New York City Ballet, and although she did not initially receive the scholarship to study at the School of American Ballet (SAB), she did receive an invitation to meet with Adams at SAB.

In August 1960 she auditioned for SAB, although not for Adams but for noted choreographer George Balanchine. Her audition was a success, and on 19 August, at the age of fifteen, she was awarded a full scholarship for the 1960–1961 school year. By the end of the year, she had been offered a position in Balanchine's company despite the fact that her left foot had been injured several years before, leav-

Suzanne Farrell. THE LIBRARY OF CONGRESS

ing her without the arch necessary for a ballet dancer. At the age of sixteen, with the new name Suzanne Farrell, she danced her first solo in Balanchine's *Serenade.*

Farrell's rise to stardom occurred quickly; by the summer of 1965, at the age of nineteen, she had been promoted to the company's highest rank, that of principal dancer. At five feet, seven inches in height, Farrell was slightly tall for a dancer, but her quick and rhythmical allegro as well as her graceful leg extensions dominated the stage. She began immediately to work on the role of Dulcinea in Balanchine's *Don Quixote,* a performance that was a personal triumph. She later commented, "Even with the audience, dancing has always been a very private affair."

The role was more than just a stage persona, however. On the night of the premiere, Balanchine danced as Don Quixote, a move critics feel was highly symbolic, as the tale of a romantic artist in pursuit of perfection in the form of a virtuous woman seemed to mimic Farrell and Balanchine's offstage relationship. Although Farrell was flattered by the attention Balanchine paid to her, she was not enamored with him. She wrote in her autobiography, "It broke my heart not to be able to give him everything he wanted, but I couldn't. . . . Even if it had been bliss, I think we would have lost something on another level." During the next two years, Farrell danced with Arthur Mitchell in

Pithoprakta and in Balanchine's memorial to Dr. Martin Luther King, Jr., the *Requiem Canticles,* set to a 1966 score by Stravinsky. In the 1968 season alone Farrell was cast in the leading role of forty-one ballets.

It was at the height of her career that Farrell met Paul Mejia, a Peruvian-born New York City Ballet soloist, two years her junior. Their relationship was a friendship at first, but as their bond strengthened, so did their desire to keep their romance a secret, particularly from Balanchine. Farrell and Mejia married on 21 February 1969, the first Saturday of the layoff at the end of the ballet season, a day that they knew Balanchine would not be in town. Upon his return, Balanchine virtually ignored Farrell and excluded her and Mejia from performances. Farrell and Mejia never had children, and divorced in the mid-1990s.

The two resigned from the company in May 1969, and in September Farrell temporarily joined the National Ballet of Canada. By November 1970, Farrell and Mejia had joined the Ballet of the Twentieth Century, directed by Maurice Bejart and located in Brussels, Belgium. Somewhat more avant-garde and theatrical than Balanchine's style, the Bejart style did not initially appeal to Farrell, but the four years that she and Mejia spent with Bejart strengthened her dancing. In 1974 Farrell and Mejia returned to New York City. Farrell resumed partnering with Jacques d'Amboise and began dancing with Peter Martins, and Mejia assumed the direction of the Ballet Guatemala.

In April 1983 Balanchine died in his sleep, and Farrell danced *Ballet d'Isoline* in his honor. Farrell's hip soon began causing her pain, and in February 1987 she underwent a hip replacement operation. Farrell danced for the New York City Ballet for almost three more years, formally retiring on 26 November 1989 with a presentation of *Vienna Waltzes* and *Sophisticated Lady.* Since her retirement Farrell has remained active, dancing in the Masters of 20th Century Ballet, a ten-city road show that opened in Washington, D.C., and closed in New York City, in 1999. She is a much-sought-after dance instructor, and joined the Florida State University dance department in the fall of 2000.

★

Further information about Farrell's life and career can be found in her autobiography, *Holding on to the Air: An Autobiography* (1990, with Toni Bentley), and in Arlene Croce, *Sight Lines* (1987). Details about Balanchine's influence on Farrell are in Lynn Garafola, "Suzanne Farrell, Teacher: Holding on to Balanchine," *Dance Magazine* 71, no. 5 (1997): 56–63.

JENNIFER HARRISON

FARROW, Mia (*b.* 9 February 1945 in Los Angeles, California), actress who found fame in the television soap opera *Peyton Place* and whose big screen breakthrough came in the stylish horror movie *Rosemary's Baby* (1968).

Born Maria de Lourdes Villiers Farrow, Mia Farrow is the daughter of film director John Farrow and actress Maureen O'Sullivan, who starred as Jane in the popular *Tarzan* movie series of the 1930s. The third of seven children, Farrow attended convent schools in Madrid, Spain, as well as Marymount School in Los Angeles. At the age of nine she fought a battle with polio and in her teens took bit parts in several of her father's movies. Farrow's schooling finished at the Cygnet School, London, in 1962. From an early age, she craved fame, saying in a 1965 interview with Kitty Kelly, "I just couldn't stand being anonymous."

Aged just eighteen, Farrow made her off-Broadway debut as Cecily in *The Importance of Being Earnest* in 1963, and in 1964 she began her screen career as Allison Mackenzie on the hit television show *Peyton Place*. Farrow was known for roller-skating around the set and soon acquired a reputation for wild behavior. Despite the apparent intensity of her real-life ambition, Farrow's blonde hair, wide-eyed look, and gentle smile have led to numerous roles as sensitive, intelligent, but slightly misunderstood women. *Peyton Place* produced the first public outings for an acting persona Farrow would cultivate and refine over the next thirty years.

Although Farrow's role in *Peyton Place* was a supporting one, the show's success guaranteed national fame. Starting in 1964 with twice-weekly installments, the show, by the end of the first season, was airing three times a week. Between 1964 and 1966, Allison Mackenzie became one of

the show's most popular characters and won Farrow the 1965 Golden Globe for most promising newcomer. Farrow left *Peyton Place* just as the show's ratings were about to decline. She married fifty-one-year-old Frank Sinatra on 19 July 1966.

Aged just twenty-one and married to one of the greatest popular singers of all time, Farrow quickly became a household name, her photograph appearing in newspapers and magazines around the world. Her waiflike figure, short hair, and vulnerable appearance were much admired. She appeared on the cover of *Vogue* in 1967, helping to feed the 1960s fashion industry's obsession with thin, boyish women. This new look was a radical departure from the voluptuous figures of the previous generation of actresses, such as Marilyn Monroe and Jane Russell.

Although she was happy to be in the public eye, Farrow also wanted to work. After her marriage, her acting career stalled, and it was against Sinatra's wishes that she took the leading role in Roman Polanski's cult horror movie, *Rosemary's Baby* (1968). Farrow plays Rosemary Woodhouse, a young woman from the country who moves to New York with her new husband. The couple settle in an old apartment building called the Bramford, which is home to a strange group of neighbors. Rosemary becomes increasingly afraid of an occult presence in the building and is convinced that she has been raped and impregnated by Satan. *Rosemary's Baby* was perhaps the most influential horror

Mia Farrow *(right)*, with costar Dustin Hoffman in a production still from the movie *John and Mary, 1969.* © BETTMANN/CORBIS

movie of the decade, inspiring a whole subgenre of movies about possessed children, including *The Exorcist* (1973), and *The Omen* (1976). Unlike the Ira Levin novel on which it is based, Polanski's movie leaves it unclear whether or not Rosemary has been raped by Satan. The film is more about alienation, loneliness, superstition, and mental collapse than it is about supernatural evil. By the time of the film's release, Farrow was so well known that in an attempt to boost ratings, the writers of *Peyton Place* introduced a baby to coincide with the movie's opening weekend. The baby was introduced as the child of Allison Mackenzie, Farrow's character in the show.

A career high, *Rosemary's Baby* earned Farrow a nomination as best actress at the 1969 Golden Globes and won her a David at the 1969 David di Donatello Awards in Italy. However, although the finished movie was a success, the process of filming had been painful. Farrow's decision to continue working brought her marriage to Sinatra to an end, and he served her with divorce papers on the set. When filming was over in January 1968, Farrow went to India to recuperate. As if to confirm her place at the heart of 1960s popular culture, she spent her time in India with the Beatles at the ashram of Maharishi Mahesh Yogi. Farrow and Sinatra divorced on 16 August 1968.

After *Rosemary's Baby,* Farrow was much in demand in Hollywood. She was nominated for a second Golden Globe in 1970 for her role alongside Dustin Hoffman in the sex comedy *John and Mary* (1969), although the film was a commercial failure. The same year, she married the orchestral conductor André Previn, had twin boys, and adopted three other children. After their divorce in 1979, Farrow was linked with director Woody Allen for twelve years, although they never lived together. She had one child with Allen and adopted two more. By 1994, two years after her much-publicized split with Allen, Farrow had fourteen children, ten of whom were adopted.

Farrow was one of the most prominent young stars of the 1960s, with an attitude and "look" that have since come to embody the spirit of the decade. However, she failed to achieve the broad popular appeal of contemporaries such as Goldie Hawn and Jessica Lange, possibly because the "little girl lost" persona went out of favor as the decade ended. Yet despite this sense that she is stuck with a screen presence she can exploit but not escape, Farrow has in fact built on her achievements in the 1960s to show great technical breadth. This is especially true of her work for Woody Allen, who managed to draw performances from her that surprised many people. In performances between *The Purple Rose of Cairo* (1985), and *Husbands and Wives* (1992), Farrow augmented the vulnerable-yet-strong character she made her own in *Rosemary's Baby* to become one of the most admired actresses of her generation.

★

Farrow published her much-praised autobiography, *What Falls Away: A Memoir,* in 1997. Biographies include Sam Rubin and Richard Taylor, *Mia Farrow: Flowerchild, Madonna, Muse* (1989), and Edward Z. Epstein and Joe Morella, *Mia: The Life of Mia Farrow* (1991). Further information is available in Kitty Kelly, *My Way* (1965), Ivan Butler, *The Cinema of Roman Polanski* (1970), and David Shipman, *The Great Movie Stars: The International Years* (1972).

CHRIS ROUTLEDGE

FEYNMAN, Richard Phillips (*b.* 11 May 1918 in Queens, New York; *d.* 15 February 1988 in Los Angeles, California), charismatic Nobel Prize–winning theoretical physicist who made important contributions to all phases of modern nuclear physics and helped to popularize science in the 1960s.

Feynman was one of three children born to Melville Arthur Feynman, a sales manager for a uniform company, and Lucille (Phillips) Feynman, a homemaker. He was a precocious student, winning a citywide mathematics contest in 1936 during his senior year at Far Rockaway High School and publishing an article, "Forces in Molecules,"

Richard Feynman. CORBIS CORPORATION (BELLEVUE)

in the *Physical Review* while still an undergraduate at the Massachusetts Institute of Technology (MIT) in Cambridge. In 1939 he graduated from MIT with a B.Sc. (Honors) in physics.

Feynman earned his Ph.D. in theoretical physics in 1942 at Princeton University in New Jersey, writing a dissertation that examined the relationship of quantum mechanics to classical electrodynamics—the germ of his later Nobel Prize work. As a result of this research, he was drafted into working on the atomic bomb at Los Alamos, New Mexico, as part of the Manhattan Project. (Feynman was excused from compulsory military service during World War II because he failed the psychiatric part of the inductee's exam.) Working as a group leader at Los Alamos under Hans Bethe, he developed a formula to predict the yield of the untested weapon, and was present at the first detonation on 16 July 1945 at Alamogordo, New Mexico.

After the war ended, Feynman joined Bethe at Cornell University in Ithaca, New York, for five years. After what would prove to be a seminal year teaching in Rio de Janeiro, Brazil, Feynman in 1952 joined the faculty of the California Institute of Technology (Cal Tech) in Pasadena, where he spent the rest of his career as the Richard Chase Tolman Professor of Theoretical Physics. During these productive early years, Feynman developed the theory of quantum electrodynamics (QED). He was motivated by a series of conferences held in 1947 to 1949, and by a sense of competition between his own vision and that of Julian Schwinger, a Harvard physicist with whom he ultimately shared the Nobel Prize in 1965 (along with Shin-ichiro Tomonaga, who reached the same results independently just afterward). Feynman developed not only a method to "renormalize" (redefine) the competing models of classical and quantum physics, but also a method to diagram the resulting interactions of particles, known as "Feynman diagrams," and hence to compute their exact numerical value. There followed a string of triumphs: in 1957 he and Murray Gell-Mann published a brilliant paper on the "Fermi interaction," which resolved many outstanding issues concerning the so-called weak interaction of particles; his work on liquid helium the next year led directly to the successful development of superconductivity.

Feynman was not only a renowned theoretician, but also a superb lecturer. When he was asked to develop Cal Tech's new freshman physics course in 1960, he spent three years devising *The Feynman Lectures on Physics* (1963), which was still in print almost four decades later. Feynman's pedagogical persona—informal, humorous, as bedded in concrete experimental data as anything so theoretical could be—inspired three decades of students and set a new tone for physics instruction around the world. It also motivated Feynman to publish a series of books, including *Theory of Fundamental Processes* (1961) and *The Character of Physical Law* (1965), that were major factors in the popularization of science that began in the 1960s.

Feynman married his childhood sweetheart, Arline H. Greenbaum, in June 1942; she died of tuberculosis in July 1945. On 28 June 1952 he married Mary Louise Bell; the marriage was doomed from the start, since she wanted him to wear a suit and tie to work—this of a man whose father had raised him to distrust any kind of uniform. The marriage lasted less than four years, ending in divorce in 1956. Finally, while lecturing at CERN (the European Center for Nuclear Research) in Switzerland, Feynman met a young Englishwoman, Gweneth Howarth. He sponsored her immigration to the United States and married her on 24 September 1960; they had a son in 1962 and adopted a daughter in 1968. Thus the 1960s were marked for Feynman by his first true experience of domesticity. It is probably not coincidental that during this same period he took up art, becoming an accomplished sketch portraitist and a master of the samba drums.

Feynman's research work took a back seat to more pressing demands for much of the 1960s. This drought ended with a breakthrough in 1967, when Feynman read a book about the struggles of James Watson, a codiscoverer of DNA's structure, and wrote on a memo pad, "DISREGARD." He had been diligently reading all of the literature of modern physics, becoming caught up in the power struggles and theoretical battles, and had forgotten to trust his idiosyncratic instincts and methods. Now primed for another triumph, in 1968 Feynman developed a new model of proton collisions, based on theoretical entities called "partons"; his model allowed teams at the Stanford Linear Accelerator Center and at CERN to pursue research into quarks (key subatomic particles) that led them to two Nobel Prizes. This contribution to the theory of the strong interaction of particles made Feynman the only twentieth-century physicist to achieve breakthroughs in all three major areas of modern physics: electromagnetic forces, weak interactive forces, and strong interactions.

Eschewing retirement, Feynman continued working through the 1970s and 1980s. In February 1986 Feynman again earned public recognition when he was called in to help determine the cause of the *Challenger* space shuttle disaster of 28 January 1986. Using a dramatic demonstration that could have been drawn from his freshman course, Feynman showed the commission—and a huge television audience—exactly what happens when a rubber O-ring is subjected to freezing temperatures, and how this result led to the *Challenger* explosion. After suffering from recurring bouts of stomach cancer for ten years, Feynman finally succumbed to the disease in 1988. He is buried in Mountain View Cemetery in Altadena, California.

Feynman was one of the great theoretical physicists of the twentieth century. He worked on the development of the atomic bomb, made crucial contributions to the theory of superconductivity, created a method for diagraming the actions of subatomic particles, and won the Nobel Prize for his QED theory. As a professor, Feynman inspired students for three decades and wrote an enduring physics textbook. It is little wonder that one of his biographies is entitled, simply, "genius."

★

Feynman wrote two volumes of personal memoirs, *Surely You're Joking, Mr. Feynman!: Adventures of a Curious Character* (1985), and *What Do YOU Care What Other People Think?: Further Adventures of a Curious Character* (1988). His autobiography, with Christopher Sykes, is *No Ordinary Genius: The Illustrated Richard Feynman* (1994). Biographies include James Gleick, *Genius: The Life and Science of Richard Feynman* (1992); Jagdish Mehra, *The Beat of a Different Drum: The Life and Science of Richard Feynman* (1994); and John and Mary Gribbin, *Richard Feynman: A Life in Science* (1997). Obituaries are in the *New York Times* (17 Feb. 1988) and *Scientific American* (June 1988).

HARTLEY S. SPATT

FISCHER, Robert James ("Bobby") (*b.* 9 March 1943 in Chicago, Illinois), eight-time U.S. chess champion who dominated matches throughout the 1960s, hailed as the greatest chess player ever produced within the United States, known for his eccentricities and reclusive nature.

Fischer's father, Gerald Fischer, was a biophysicist, and his

Bobby Fischer playing against himself in a game of chess. THE LIBRARY OF CONGRESS

mother, Regina (Wender) Fischer, was a teacher and then a registered nurse. She is Jewish and was born in Switzerland. Fischer's parents divorced when he was two, and he was raised by his mother and his elder sister (his only sibling). Fischer's mother worked to support the family by teaching elementary school, and the family spent periods of time living in Los Angeles and Phoenix. Fischer's first schooling took place at Mobile in western Arizona. In 1948 the family moved to Brooklyn, New York.

As a teenager Fischer attended Erasmus Hall High School in Brooklyn. Not surprisingly, Fischer was at the head of his class in mathematics and science. However, he ended his formal education at age sixteen.

At the age of thirteen Fischer was the youngest player ever to win the national junior chess championship. His breakthrough performance was in August 1957 in Cleveland. In a field of 175 players, Fischer finished as first equal with Arthur B. Bisguier, the U.S. champion. Then on 7 January 1958 he defeated Bisguier at the U.S. Chess Federation's championship. As a result of being national champion, he represented the United States in international matches, and in the late summer of 1958 he visited Yugoslavia and Russia. At an international competition in Portoroz, Yugoslavia, Fischer finished in fifth place. Having become one of the top six chess players in the world, Fischer became a part of the complicated and convoluted matchmaking and selection process to find the one challenger to take on the world chess champion.

Throughout 1959 Fischer played chess internationally and visited places such as Mar del Plata, Argentina; Santiago, Chile; Zurich, Switzerland; and Bled, Zagreb. His game developed to such good effect that at the world championship challenges and tournament Fischer took fifth place. Clearly and consistently throughout 1959 Fischer demonstrated that he was one of the world's top chess players. However, it was not until April 1960 that Fischer showed himself as an heir apparent to the world crown. At Mar del Plata, Argentina, Fischer tied with Boris Spassky of the Soviet Union.

To look at Fischer's chess career over the decade of the 1960s is to cover a sporting and cultural landscape that could not divorce itself from a global stage dominated by the two superpowers, the United States and the Soviet Union. Chess has been, and continues to be, the most highly regarded sport in terms of status and recognition within the former republics of the old Soviet Union. Champions, especially in the 1960s, were seen as national icons and folk heroes. Spassky and then Anatoly Karpov had the appeal, name recognition, and celebrity clamor that a Joe DiMaggio (baseball) or a Muhammad Ali (boxing) or a Bart Starr (football) enjoyed in the United States during the years from 1960 to 1970. Furthermore, this was a time of heightened tension and hostility between America and the Soviet Union, and Fischer waged his own campaigns to wrest a world championship from a country grown used to being the Holy Grail of chess. Ruben Fine, a former international chess player, notes that following the conclusion of World War II, "the Soviets had the best [chess] team in the world," and "the leading contenders for the world title . . . consistently turned out to be Soviet grandmasters." Fischer, at the onset of 1960, was firmly confronted by a Soviet hegemony in chess.

At the 1960 Chess Olympics at Leipzig, East Germany, Fischer was a member of the U.S. team, which was a runner-up to the Soviet Union. In March of 1962 Fischer took part in a world tournament held in Stockholm, Sweden. His first place finish meant that he was automatically included in the play-offs to select a single challenger for the world chess championship.

At Willemstad, Curaçao, in May and June 1962, Fischer finished in fifth place in this play-off competition in a contest dominated by the Soviet Union. Soviet players filled the first four positions. This effectively meant that the selection process to pick a new challenger for the world title would come from the four Willemstad Soviets. Fischer railed against a system that he felt ensured continuing Soviet domination in chess. As far as he was concerned, the governing body of world chess, the Fédération Internationale des Échecs (FIDE), was "rigging" chess. Fischer announced that he would eschew any further FIDE competitions. *Sports Illustrated* (20 August 1962) published Fischer's allegations and, as with many of Fischer's outbursts, they contain much that is polemical. However, there is a strong thesis that merits support. Unequivocally, FIDE was a bulwark to the status quo and the retention of a Soviet monopoly on world chess. Fischer in his *Sports Illustrated* essay describes his Soviet competitors at Willemstad as being, to all intents and purposes, members of the same team. They socialized with one another, swam in the afternoons, and repeatedly settled for quick and early draws, which greatly restricted the intensity of their competition and created, for them, an almost recreational ethos. As Fischer recounts it, the Soviets successfully conspired to marginalize the Americans. Conspiracy theories aside, the evidence would support Fischer's claim that the challenge selection process, as supervised by FIDE, was "bad for chess" and "bad for any real standard of the world championship." There is little doubt that Fischer's vehement denunciation of the FIDE protocol played a role in that body changing its challenge selection formula.

In 1972 Fischer competed against Spassky, the Soviet world champion. Thanks to Fischer's feisty persona and his ability to bully and bluster, the title/challenger prize purse contained a quarter of a million dollars. Because of Fischer's presence, the matches were shown on television, and his success saw him receiving "Soviet-like" recognition in his homeland. He appeared on the cover of *Sports Illustrated, Time, Newsweek,* and *Life.*

Sadly, the glitz and glamour quickly faded. In 1975 Fischer refused to defend his world title against Anatoly Karpov. He retired to Pasadena, California, was stripped of his title, and gave generously to a new hobby, the Worldwide Church of God. In subsequent years he turned down chess exhibition tournament offers from Las Vegas and the Philippines.

In 1992 Fischer came out of retirement to play Spassky. The event was an ill-starred disaster. Chess experts called it "scandalous." In recent years Fischer has lived in Baguio City in the Philippines. He has been labeled a "mythical self-creation," and his political positions, coupled with his hysterical outbursts against Jews, has made the most celebrated world chess champion seem an unstable and unsavory maverick. He has written several chess books, and his *My 60 Memorable Games, Selected and Fully Annotated* (1969) is held up as a classic of chess literature.

★

Current Biography (1963) contains a rich narrative on Fischer's career in the early 1960s. Fischer's own thorough analysis of the 1962 Willemstad challenge tournament, "The Russians Have Fixed World Chess," *Sports Illustrated* (20 Aug. 1962), is a compelling read. Earl Blackwell, *Celebrity Register* (1990), provides a useful gestalt on the ups and downs of Fischer's life. The *Philippine Daily Inquirer* (20 and 26 Sept. 2000) gives some sense of the extent of Fischer's fractious disconnect with contemporary society, especially Western culture.

SCOTT A. G. M. CRAWFORD

FLEMING, Peggy Gale (*b.* 27 July 1948 in San Jose, California), winner of five U.S. National Figure Skating Championships between 1964 and 1968, three World Championships between 1966 and 1968, and an Olympic gold medal in 1968, who demonstrated the power and grace of female athleticism in competitive sports.

Fleming was the second of four daughters in the family of Albert Eugene and Doris Elizabeth Deal Fleming. Her father, who worked as a newspaper press operator, enjoyed skating as a hobby; when his second daughter was nine years old, a family trip to a San Francisco–area skating rink changed her life. "From that day on, I was a different girl," Fleming wrote in her 1999 memoir, *The Long Program.* "I had found the thing that made everything else fall into place." Her natural ability as a figure skater was encouraged by her parents, who signed Fleming up with her first coach during a six-month stay in Cleveland in 1958. By the time the family resettled in the San Francisco Bay area the following year, Fleming was practicing on the ice almost

Peggy Fleming. CORBIS CORPORATION (BELLEVUE)

every day. After the family moved to Pasadena, California, in 1960, Albert took his daughter to practice so early each morning that he ended up driving the rink's Zamboni machine to smooth the ice for her session.

While her father's encouragement was crucial in Fleming's early development as a skater, her mother became the dominant force in her competitive career, which began with a 1959 win in the Bay Area Juvenile Competition. The following year she won the juvenile division of the Pacific Coast Championships in Squaw Valley, California; in the two succeeding years, Fleming advanced to become the gold medalist in the novice and senior ranks of the Pacific Coast Championships as well. As her daughter moved through the ranks, Doris oversaw her development with a series of coaches specializing in figure skating choreography, technique, and interpretation.

Like the rest of the U.S. figure skating program, Fleming received a jolt when one of her first coaches, Bill Kipp, died along with thirty-three members of the U.S. delegation on its way to the 1961 World Championships in Prague. Seventy-three people perished when Sabena Flight 548 went down with a stalled engine just before landing at the Belgian National Airport near Brussels on 15 February 1961. In addition to Kipp, almost all of that year's U.S. medal winners died in the accident, including all three ladies champions. The World Championships were canceled in the wake of the tragedy, and the U.S. Figure Skating Association scrambled to rebuild its program after losing its top skaters. Fleming suddenly became a top prospect for the American team's future.

Just into her teens, Fleming won the Pacific Coast Novice Championship despite an illness that had her vomiting on the ice after her free skate. The win sent Fleming on her first trip to the U.S. National Championships in 1962, where she won a silver medal in the Novice Ladies competition. The next year she took a bronze medal in the Junior Ladies division of the Nationals, which qualified her for her first Senior National competition, scheduled for Cleveland in January 1964. Fleming astounded the figure skating world when she won the event and was awarded the gold medal as the U.S. ladies champion on 24 January 1964. The win also qualified her for the U.S. Olympic team for the 1964 Games in Innsbruck, Austria. That competition, where the fifteen-year-old finished an impressive sixth place, helped Fleming develop her sense of style on the ice in comparison to her European rivals, who dominated that year's event with performances that emphasized their athleticism. As Fleming later remembered in *The Long Program*, "I was very respectful of what the other women did athletically, but not aesthetically. . . . Seeing what I didn't want to be made me resolve to be both athletic *and* feminine. I could begin to see the skater I wanted to be." Indeed, the power that Fleming delivered in her subsequent skating performances belied her five-foot, four-inch frame.

At the U.S. Nationals in 1965, Fleming repeated her win of the prior year. Doris, who continued to sew all of her daughter's skating costumes and made the major decisions regarding her career, moved the family to Colorado Springs, Colorado, after the 1965 World Championships, where Fleming won her first world medal, a bronze. The move teamed Fleming with coach Carlo Fassi, who had a reputation for instilling technical superiority in his pupils, a major factor in competitions where compulsory figures counted heavily in the final score. Fassi also built up Fleming's strength and stamina by having her practice outdoors in the chilly, high-altitude climate of Colorado Springs. Fleming continued to work with coach Bob Paul on her choreography, and in the following three years, Fleming's competitive drive, coaching, and family support proved to be an unbeatable combination. At the 1966 World Championships in Davos, Switzerland, she pulled another upset victory by dethroning the previous year's champion, Petra Burka of Canada. The newly crowned seventeen-year-old champion made the cover of *Sports Illustrated* as "Our New World Champion" but suffered a devastating loss when her father died shortly thereafter of a heart attack at the age of forty-one.

Fleming repeated as U.S. and World champion in 1967. After winning the 1968 U.S. Nationals with a stunning performance in Philadelphia—which she considered the best free skate of her career—Fleming was considered the favorite for the gold medal at the 1968 Winter Olympic Games in Grenoble, France. While the scores on her compulsory figures put her far ahead of her competitors going into the final free skate, Fleming's nerves prevented her from doing her best. She was disappointed to miss some of her jumps—including her trademark move, a spread eagle into a double axel followed by another spread eagle—but her power and grace were sufficient throughout the rest of the routine to win the overall competition. As these games were the first Olympics televised in color, Fleming's appearance at the final free skate in a chartreuse dress made by her mother had an immediate impact on the American public. Featured on the cover of *Sports Illustrated* and *Life* magazine in February 1968, Fleming was the only U.S. gold medalist at the 1968 Winter Olympics. The following month Fleming won her third title at the 1968 World Championships in Geneva, Switzerland, and retired from amateur competition.

Through the 1970s Fleming starred in annual variety-show specials on ABC television that featured her in skits as well as on skates; she continues to star in ice reviews as well and remains in the public eye as a figure skating commentator for ABC Sports. Married to Greg Jenkins since 1970, Fleming has two sons and became a grandmother in 1999. She recovered from a 1998 bout with breast cancer to become a national spokesperson for early diagnosis and treatment of the disease. For her contribution to the development of figure skating's popularity and as an example of female athleticism, Fleming was honored in 1999 as one of only seven recipients of the *Sports Illustrated* Twentieth Century Sports Award: Athletes Who Changed the Game; she has also been inducted into the U.S. Olympic Hall of Fame, the International Women's Hall of Fame, and the World Figure Skating Hall of Fame. Few athletes have matched her combination of power and grace, let alone her competitive success.

★

Fleming wrote *The Long Program: Skating Toward Life's Victories* (1999) with Peter Kaminsky. She twice was the subject of a *Sports Illustrated* cover story. The first article, "A Paris Fling for a Teen Queen" (2 May 1966), celebrated her victory in the 1966 World Championship; the second, "The Perils of Peggy and a Great Silver Raid" (19 Feb. 1968), marked her Olympic victory. Background information on the 1968 Winter Olympics is covered in *Chronicle of the Olympics, 1896–1996* (1996), and Allen Guttman, *The Olympics: A History of the Modern Games* (1992). A series by Bob Duffy and John Powers on the 1961 plane crash that devastated the U.S. team appeared in the *Boston Globe*, "Remembering Flight 548: The Tragic Story of the 1961 U.S. Figure Skating Team" (29–31 Dec. 2000). Competition results for figure skating events are listed on the web site of the International Skating Union at <http://www.isu.org/historical/historical.html>.

TIMOTHY BORDEN

FOGARTY, Anne Whitney   (*b.* 2 February 1919 in Pittsburgh, Pennsylvania; *d.* 15 January 1980 in New York City), fashion designer who brought high fashion to middle- and low-income women and girls.

Fogarty, born Anne Whitney, was the youngest of four daughters of Robert Whitney, an artist, and Marion (Bosordnoff) Whitney. Fogarty received hand-me-down clothes, which she considered fun because no one cared what she did with them. She cut and sewed them to suit her own tastes, which at the time were extremely colorful, though not in fashion. She eventually would change that. She attended Pittsburgh public schools, graduating from high school in 1936. That year, she attended Allegheny College in Meadville, Pennsylvania. In 1937 Fogarty transferred to Pittsburgh's Carnegie Institute of Technology to study drama. The subject attracted her because it gave her the opportunity to wear elaborate historical costumes. In 1939 she attended the East Hartman School of Design to learn better how to make her own costumes.

She moved to New York City to live with her sister Poppy Cannon, who made a name for herself writing cookbooks. Fogarty had an eighteen-inch waist that she used to good effect working as a clothing model for junior misses. She modeled to support herself while looking for work as an actress. One of her employers was the designer Harvey Berin, who overheard Fogarty making astute comments about the cuts and colors of dresses to the fitters as they worked with her. When she was offered a job as an actress in a summer stock production, he suggested that she remain with him and learn the designer's trade. Her acting ambitions ended at that moment, and she devoted herself to modeling and learning how to design clothing.

In 1940 she met the artist Thomas E. Fogarty, Jr., at an art class, and on 10 August 1940 they married. They had two children and divorced in the mid-1960s. She learned the clothing trade by working as a model, stylist, and publicist for various fashion designers and manufacturers in the early 1940s. Her big break came in 1948, when Youth Guild, Inc., hired her to design dresses for teenagers. Throughout her career, Fogarty had a special understanding of what teenaged girls wanted. Her below-the-knee dresses with frills and lively colors influenced fashion, introducing the 1950s standards in petticoats and light, bouncy fabrics.

In 1951, while working for Margot Dresses, Fogarty's designs were influential enough for her to receive *Mademoiselle* magazine's Merit Award. She was also one of six recipients of the Coty American Fashion Critics Award, then the most coveted fashion award in America. Her use of light, comfortable fabrics in her designs garnered her an award from the International Silk Association (1955). She received the Cotton Fashion Award in 1957 and was hired by the Saks Fifth Avenue department store to design moderately priced dresses for young women. She put her years of experience in the design industry to work creating a full line of outfits that included purses, shoes, hats, lingerie, and jewelry. Her designs varied from the daring— low-necked chemises that emphasized bust lines—to the practical, including straight-cut dresses with short sleeves or no sleeves that were intended to give their wearers full freedom of movement. She also introduced Japanese patterns and colors (woody reds, pale seaweed greens, and ceramic blue) in her new line.

In 1959 Fogarty published *Wife-Dressing*, which offered tips on how a wife could dress to please her husband. Ironically, however, it was in the early 1960s that Fogarty and her own husband grew apart. He was a successful artist with paintings hanging in prominent museums, but he earned his living primarily at Rutgers University, far from New York City, where Fogarty worked. In 1960 Fogarty received the *Sports Illustrated* Designer of the Year Award for her sportswear designs for young women. She introduced bikinis that included frills and other touches that made them interesting, establishing a new, showier fashion for two-piece bathing suits. She expanded her Saks Fifth Avenue offerings from 1960 to 1962 by introducing a variety of fabrics, especially increasing her designs in silk and cotton. As young women's tastes changed, she kept up by introducing pants and jumpsuits to her line. All had her signature touches, such as paillettes (shiny spangles) and bright combinations of colors. In 1962, when she left Saks Fifth Avenue, she received the first American Express Fashion Award.

That year Fogarty and her partner Leonard Sunshine established Anne Fogarty, Inc., on Seventh Avenue in New York City. Being president of her own company allowed Fogarty to spread her wings as never before, and she busied herself in designing everything involving women's fashions, including accessories. She introduced polyester clothing by creating a division of her company, Collectors Items, which marketed practical designs, usually featuring vibrant colors, to low- and middle-income people. Another division, A. F. Boutique, offered inexpensive fabrics in coordinated ensembles of clothing, allowing purchasers to mix and match items, creating their own individual looks. Her bathing suits, which emphasized femininity, were very popular.

Fogarty married Richard Tomkins Kollmar on 22 June 1967. Theirs appears to have been a happy marriage until Kollmar's death in 1971; they had no children. In 1977 she married Wade O'Hara, but that marriage ended in divorce. In 1968 Anne Fogarty, Inc., had $7 million in sales, owing in large part to Fogarty's ability to identify trends in popular fashions and to translate them into attractive designs. By 1968 the bright colors she preferred were the rage among young people. Many young women preferred to wear casual clothing, and for them Fogarty established her Leisure-Pleasure line of sturdy but relaxed clothing.

In 1975 Fogarty sold her company and semiretired, but she would continue to take on independent projects for designers and manufacturers until her death. She thrived in the 1960s, a period in which the public's fashion preferences changed radically from one year to the next. She was not just reactive to the fads of the moment. Her use of oriental patterns started a long-term interest among Americans in Far Eastern designs, and her success with brightly colored fabrics and matching accessories inspired the fashion industry as a whole to offer similar designs. Her practical designs, such as short skirts, sleeveless straight dresses, pants, and jumpsuits, helped women feel good about their clothes while being able to participate in sports or to work at physically vigorous jobs.

★

Some of Fogarty's designs are in the collection of the Fashion Institute of Technology's National Museum of Fashion in New York City. Beryl Williams offers an early look at Fogarty in her *Young Faces in Fashion* (1956). Caroline Rennolds Milbank discusses Fogarty's fashions in her *New York Fashion: The Evolution of American Style* (1989). Valerie Steele examines Fogarty from a feminist perspective in her *Women of Fashion: Twentieth-Century Designers* (1991). An obituary is in the *New York Times* (16 Jan. 1980).

KIRK H. BEETZ

FOGERTY, John Cameron (b. 28 May 1945 in Berkeley, California), songwriter, lead singer, and driving force behind Creedence Clearwater Revival, the leading American rock band from 1969 to 1971.

Fogerty was the third of five sons born to Gayland Robert Fogerty, who worked in a newspaper print shop, and his wife, Lucile Fogerty, a store clerk and teacher. His father left the family in 1953. With Doug Clifford and Stu Cook, two junior high school friends in El Cerrito, California, where he grew up, Fogerty formed his first musical group, the Blue Velvets, in 1959. His older brother Tom soon joined them.

After graduating from high school in 1963, Fogerty worked as a clerk at Fantasy Records, an Oakland, California–based label. In 1964 the Blue Velvets signed a recording contract with Fantasy, which changed their name to The Golliwogs. After hours of practicing alone with a tape recorder, Fogerty began to sing in public for the first time, eventually sharing lead vocals with his brother. The Golliwogs released several singles in the mid-1960s, with little success.

Fogerty married Martha Piaz, his high school girlfriend,

John Fogerty performing at the Woodstock Music Festival, 1969. TUCKER RANSOM/GETTY IMAGES

on 4 September 1965. They had three children. He enrolled at Merritt College in Oakland but stayed only briefly. Fearing that he would be drafted, Fogerty enlisted in the U.S. Army Reserves in April 1966.

In 1967 Saul Zaentz, the new owner of Fantasy Records, encouraged the group to pick a new name. Their choice, Creedence Clearwater Revival (CCR), "was better than we were," Fogerty later observed. He produced the group's first album, *Creedence Clearwater Revival* (1968), on which he was lead singer and guitarist. While the Beatles were inspiring many rock artists to produce time-consuming and complex multi-track music, CCR recorded its first album essentially live in one week. Fogerty prepared meticulously for recording sessions but wasted little time once in the studio. While the album included some of his own songs, CCR's first two singles, "Suzie Q" and "I Put a Spell on You," were covers (songs originally performed by other artists). "Suzie Q," released in the fall of 1968, reached number eleven on the Billboard Pop Chart. Although the group had tasted its first national success, Fogerty was obsessed by the fear that they would be one-hit wonders. Confident of his own judgment, he insisted on producing the band's

subsequent albums, resisting the desire of other group members for greater creative input.

Creedence hit its commercial stride in January 1969 with the release of the album *Bayou Country,* which sold more than one million copies and gave CCR its first platinum record award. In cuts such as "Born on the Bayou," Fogerty found a musical idiom that seemed to evoke the Mississippi Delta, a place he had never visited. Some called his music "swamp rock," a label he shunned. Another song from *Bayou Country,* "Proud Mary," a song Fogerty composed and arranged, became the group's first gold single and their first number-one hit. Fogerty's high, urgent tenor and distinctive pronunciation ("boinin'" for "burning," for example) gave him one of the most recognizable voices in rock music.

A period of breathtaking productivity and success ensued. CCR released two more albums in 1969, *Green River* in August and *Willy and the Poorboys* in November. The albums brought CCR their second and third platinum record awards. *Cosmo's Factory* followed in 1970. The group had an unbroken string of Top Ten hits from 1969 to 1971, including "Bad Moon Rising," "Down on the Corner," and "Who'll Stop the Rain." Creedence was the first band to agree to play at the 1969 Woodstock Festival, but Fogerty was so disenchanted with the circumstances of the group's performance that he refused to allow its inclusion in the resulting movie and album. *Billboard* named Creedence Clearwater Revival the top singles artist for 1969. *Rolling Stone* proclaimed it to be the best American band.

In songs like "Fortunate Son" (1969) and "Don't Look Now" (1970), Fogerty expressed something rare in American rock music—a keen awareness of class differences. "Fortunate Son" was perhaps the only popular antiwar song of the 1960s to observe that the sons of the working class were more likely to be conscripted than the sons of the privileged.

Fogerty shunned the spotlight and was uncomfortable with the trappings of stardom. In numerous ways—his lyrics, his music, his aversion to hard drugs, his clothes (often flannel shirts and jeans)—he was a man of moderation in an era of frequent excess and flamboyance. That reticence was both integral to CCR's appeal and an obstacle to its superstardom.

When the Beatles broke up in 1970, CCR was considered by many to be the premier rock band in the world. But heightened expectations and festering discontent within the group over Fogerty's control tore them apart. CCR's sixth album, *Pendulum,* was released in December 1970 and had one million advance orders, guaranteeing it platinum status. The album marked the beginning of a more democratic band process, but it was not very successful after the initial surge of orders. Tom Fogerty left CCR in January 1971. The seventh CCR album, *Mardi Gras* (1972), featured equal contributions from the three remaining members. It was the group's least successful album. CCR disbanded in October 1972.

In later years Fogerty became bitterly estranged from the other band members and fought a series of legal battles with Zaentz and Fantasy Records. He released several solo albums, including *Blue Ridge Rangers* (1972), *John Fogerty* (1975), *Centerfield* (1985), and *Eye of the Zombie* (1986). *Blue Moon Swamp* (1997) won a Grammy as best rock album. The title cut from *Centerfield* became the unofficial anthem of Major League Baseball, and it reached number ten on the charts and sold more than two million copies in the United States. Fogerty and his wife divorced in 1985. He married Julie Kramer on 20 April 1991. CCR was inducted into the Rock and Roll Hall of Fame in 1993.

The creative force behind one of the most popular rock bands of the 1960s, Fogerty was nonetheless an anomalous figure. There was no place in his music for two of the era's favorite themes, idealism and love. Instead of imagining a world of peace and harmony, Fogerty's songs—"Bad Moon Rising" and "Tombstone Shadow" are two examples—were filled with apocalyptic images. At a time when some believed that all anyone needed was love, Fogerty dissented. Not a single song he wrote for CCR even contained the word. His music was obviously of the era, yet it transcended the times. Even at its commercial peak, CCR continued to cover old blues, country, and folk tunes, whose sound blended easily with Fogerty's original compositions. Few musicians kept their musical roots so close to the surface. A result, and one of Fogerty's goals, was to appeal to young and old, white and black. Another result was that his music aged well over the years. The "Age of Aquarius" belongs forever to a particular period in the late 1960s and cannot escape that time. Fogerty's bad moon is still rising.

★

Biographical information is in Ellen Willis, "Creedence Clearwater Revival," in *The Rolling Stone Illustrated History of Rock and Roll,* edited by Jim Miller (1980); Hank Bordowitz, *Bad Moon Rising: The Unofficial History of Creedence Clearwater Revival* (1998); and Craig Werner and Dave Marsh, eds., *Up and Around the Bend: The Oral History of Creedence Clearwater Revival* (1999). For Fogerty's view of his career, see his series of interviews in *Rolling Stone* (21 Feb. 1970; 5 Nov. 1987; 8 Sept. 1988; and 4 Feb. 1993).

FRED NIELSEN

FONDA, Henry Jaynes (*b.* 16 May 1905 in Grand Island, Nebraska; *d.* 12 August 1982 in Los Angeles, California), distinguished American actor of stage and screen who riveted film audiences with his roles in three political dramas, *Advise and Consent, The Best Man,* and *Fail-Safe,* during the 1960s.

Fonda was the eldest of three children of William Brace Fonda, a printer, and Herberta Jaynes. While he was still an infant, the family moved to Omaha, where Fonda's father opened a print shop. As a boy, Fonda enjoyed writing, and he won a short story contest when he was only ten. He began working in his father's print shop after school when he was twelve. After graduating from high school in 1923, Fonda enrolled in a journalism course at the University of Minnesota but dropped out after about two years. Returning to Omaha, he became involved in community theater, winning the role of Ricky, the juvenile lead, in a production of Philip Barry's *You and I.* Fonda was bitten by the acting bug. After three years of involvement in Omaha community theater, the tall, lanky Fonda headed for New York City to look for work in the theater.

Unable to land an acting job in New York, Fonda hired on as assistant stage manager with the Cape Playhouse in Dennis, Massachusetts. After playing one lead with the summer stock company, he joined the University Players in nearby Falmouth. Among his fellow players were such stars-to-be as Joshua Logan, Margaret Sullivan (whom Fonda married in 1931 and divorced in 1933), and James Stewart, with whom Fonda formed a close friendship. When the summer ended, Fonda headed back to New York, determined to find an acting job on the Broadway stage. His efforts were rewarded with a walk-on role in *The Game of Love and Death* (1929), his Broadway debut. A few years later, Fonda flew to the West Coast for an interview with Hollywood producer Walter Wanger, who signed him to a film contract paying $1,000 a week.

Because no film work was immediately available, Fonda returned to New York, where he landed the lead role in *The Farmer Takes a Wife,* which opened in the fall of 1934. Then, back in Hollywood, Fonda was signed to recreate his stage role in the film adaptation of the play. An instant hit with moviegoers, Fonda soon found his services in high demand. He married Frances Seymour Brokaw in 1936, a union that produced two children, Jane and Peter, both of whom attained movie stardom during the 1960s. Fonda and Brokaw divorced in April 1950.

Fonda's work was interrupted when he volunteered in 1942 to serve in the U.S. Navy during World War II. He was discharged in 1945, having attained the rank of lieutenant and earned a Bronze Star. In 1948 Fonda began a long run on Broadway in the title role of *Mr. Roberts,* which he recreated on film in 1955. Fonda worked extensively in the theater during the 1950s and also managed to make a number of important films. In December 1950 Fonda married his third wife, Susan Blanchard, and adopted her daughter from a previous relationship. Fonda and Blanchard divorced in 1956. The following year Fonda married again, this time to Afdera Franchetti. This fourth marriage ended in divorce in 1961. In 1965 he married for the fifth

Henry Fonda. AP/WIDE WORLD PHOTOS

and final time. His new wife was Shirlee Adams, a flight attendant and model.

Although Fonda made a number of motion pictures during the 1960s, he is perhaps best remembered for his roles in three political films during this tumultuous and intensely political decade. In the first of these films, *Advise and Consent* (1962), he played Robert Leffingwell, nominated by the U.S. president to be the country's next secretary of state. Leffingwell, however, harbors a secret that, if revealed, will almost certainly doom his quest for the position. Years earlier, Leffingwell had been briefly involved with a communist cell in Chicago. The film, based on the best-selling novel by Allen Drury, examines the process whereby the U.S. Senate investigates and ultimately approves or rejects presidential nominations.

Standing in the way of Leffingwell's confirmation as secretary of state is Senator Seabright Cooley (played by Charles Laughton), who holds a grudge against the candidate for an earlier incident and is armed with the knowledge of Leffingwell's past communist affiliation. Afraid that his past will be revealed and cause embarrassment to the president who nominated him, Leffingwell offers to withdraw his name from consideration. However, the president, convinced Leffingwell is the best man for the job, assures his nominee that together they can keep the wraps on Lef-

fingwell's questionable past. What follows is a study in political intrigue and behind-the-scenes horse trading that ultimately ends inconclusively, with the incumbent president dying in office and the nomination of Leffingwell left in limbo. After a tie vote in the Senate leaves the final decision to the vice president, who has suddenly been thrust into the presidency, he announces he will name a secretary of state of his own choosing.

The film was neither a critical nor a popular success in the United States, although Fonda received critical praise for his performance. The movie was warmly received abroad, particularly in France. Foreign audiences flocked to see a film critical of the political system in the United States.

The second of Fonda's politically themed films of the 1960s was *The Best Man* (1964), based on a play by Gore Vidal, who also wrote the screenplay. In this film Fonda played William Russell, a liberal pitted against right-wing populist Joe Cantwell (played by Cliff Robertson) in a pitched battle for the presidential nomination of their party. The film's action is set at a presidential convention in California. Both candidates have skeletons in their closets: Russell has suffered a nervous breakdown and is separated from his wife, who agrees to return for the duration of the campaign, and Cantwell is accused of a homosexual liaison while serving in the military. Russell and Cantwell each desperately need the endorsement of former president Art Hockstader (played by Lee Tracy). The film recounts each man's huddles with Hockstader and their struggles of conscience over whether or not to release to the press the dirt about their opponents.

Fonda's character William Russell, apparently modeled by Vidal on failed Democratic U.S. presidential candidate Adlai Stevenson, appears intellectual and indecisive. Joe Cantwell bears an uncanny resemblance to Richard M. Nixon. Ultimately Russell turns thumbs down on the proposal that he employ political blackmail to win the presidency. Critics praised Fonda's portrayal of Russell, as well as the performances of most of the film's stars. *Magill's Survey of Cinema* observed, "Fonda gives a performance full of regret and irony, a finely shaded portrayal of a detached yet sensitive human being which implies an intricate blend of rectitude and corruption."

Also released in 1964 was *Fail-Safe,* a film adaptation of the novel by Eugene Burdick and Harvey Wheeler. The film, a cautionary tale about the perils of nuclear confrontation, was released the same year as *Dr. Strangelove,* Stanley Kubrick's black comedy about nuclear warfare. Although some critics regarded the deadly serious *Fail-Safe* as a superior film in many respects, it was clearly overshadowed by the brilliantly satirical Kubrick film, which some have hailed as the director's finest work. Both deal with the deadly potential of cold war confrontation, but from very different points of view. In *Fail-Safe,* Fonda played a U.S. president faced with the ultimate cold war nightmare: the inability to abort a U.S. nuclear attack against the Soviet Union that had been launched in error because of a critical technical failure. The story recounts the deliberations and finally the steps taken by the president and his civilian and military advisers to head off a nuclear holocaust that would destroy the world. The president's solution to the crisis was to drop a nuclear bomb on New York City to demonstrate U.S. sincerity to the Soviets.

Another of Fonda's notable performances of the 1960s was in a film worlds apart from these political thrillers. In *Yours, Mine and Ours* (1968), Fonda, playing a widower, and Lucille Ball, playing a widow, meet, find love, and marry, thus forming a family with eighteen children. The endearing family comedy was a solid box-office success. Another success for Fonda was his role as a hired killer in Sergio Leone's *Once Upon a Time in the West* (1968).

Many of Fonda's other films of the 1960s were less successful artistically. In many he had little more than a cameo role; in others the characters he played were poorly drawn and largely undistinguished. Such films include *How the West Was Won* and *The Longest Day* (both 1962); *Spencer's Mountain* (1963); *Sex and the Single Girl* (1964); *The Rounders, In Harm's Way,* and *Battle of the Bulge* (all 1965); *A Big Hand for the Little Lady* (1966), *Welcome to Hard Times* (1967), and *Madigan* (1968). Fonda frankly admitted that he took most of these assignments for the money and for the opportunity to keep busy.

Fonda's adult children Jane and Peter generated a good deal of controversy during the 1960s, straining their relationship with their father. Jane received bad press for her outspoken stand against U.S. involvement in the Vietnam War, and Peter documented his fascination with renegade bikers and the drug culture in *Easy Rider*, a film he produced, cowrote, and starred in. As the Fonda children's rebelliousness moderated in the 1970s, relations within the family slowly returned to some semblance of normalcy, although Fonda was frank to admit his shortcomings as a parent. "I don't think I've been a particularly good father," Fonda said, "but I've been lucky."

Fonda continued to work steadily throughout most of the 1970s, but few of his films from the decade are memorable. The exceptions include *The Cheyenne Social Club* (1970), in which Fonda was reunited with his old friend Jimmy Stewart; together they recaptured some of their former magic. Fonda also turned in an impressive performance in the television film *The Red Pony* (1973).

Fonda's final film, *On Golden Pond* (1981), in which he costarred with daughter Jane and with Katharine Hepburn, won for him the Academy Award for best actor that had eluded him. Perhaps more importantly, the film, produced by his daughter, showcased Fonda's brilliance as an actor. He later said of his experience in making the film: "I'm

not a religious man, but I thank God every morning that I lived long enough to play that role." Fonda was too ill to attend the Oscar ceremony in March 1982, so Jane accepted his award on his behalf. Less than five months later Fonda died of chronic heart disease. He was cremated and his ashes scattered.

One of the most distinguished American actors of the twentieth century, Fonda will forever be remembered for his classic roles. During an acting career of almost half a century, Fonda appeared in more than 110 films, from historical drama and romance to war epics and slapstick comedy. Through them all, good and bad, Fonda's contribution was, above all, believable. It has been suggested that Fonda's many portrayals of a president or presidential contender had so endeared him to the American public that he probably could have been elected to national office handily.

However, one of Fonda's most striking qualities was his self-effacing nature. Perhaps his own words say it best: "I hope you won't be disappointed. You see I am not a very interesting person. I haven't ever done anything except be other people. I ain't really Henry Fonda! Nobody could be. Nobody could have that much integrity."

★

Fonda's autobiography, *Fonda: My Life* (1981), written with Howard Teichman, offers perhaps the most comprehensive and accurate review of the actor's life and career—"warts and all," according to Fonda. Interested readers also will find valuable insights in John Shipman, *The Fondas: The Films and Careers of Henry, Jane, and Peter Fonda* (1970); Michael Kerbel, *Henry Fonda* (1975); Norm Goldstein, *Henry Fonda* (1982); Allen Roberts and Max Goldstein, *Henry Fonda: A Biography* (1984); Gerald Cole and Wes Farrell, *The Fondas* (1987); and Tony Thomas, *The Complete Films of Henry Fonda* (1990). Obituaries are in the *New York Times* (13 Aug. 1982), and *Time* and *Newsweek* (both 23 Aug. 1982).

DON AMERMAN

FONDA, Jane Seymour (*b.* 21 December 1937 in New York City), the most celebrated and controversial American actress of the 1960s, whose own journey in art and politics was emblematic of her generation and gender. From pinup girl to political activist to feminist entrepreneur, she personified female emancipation and malleable identity in an era of sexual revolution and radical politics; even her successive choice of husbands—the softcore new wave auteur Roger Vadim, the hardcore New Left activist Tom Hayden, and the media mogul Ted Turner—kept pace with the prevailing zeitgeist.

Fonda was one of two children of the screen legend Henry Fonda, an icon of all-American decency, and the socialite Frances (Seymour) Brokaw Fonda. She inherited her fa-

Jane Fonda. ARCHIVE PHOTOS, INC.

ther's bone structure and natural ease before the camera. When Fonda was a young teenager, she was told that her mother had died of a heart attack; she did not find out until a year later that her mother, who had battled fits of depression, had committed suicide. Fonda graduated from the Emma Willard Preparatory School in Troy, New York, in 1954. She first acted on stage at a family fund-raiser at the Omaha (Nebraska) Community Playhouse in *The Country Girl* with her father in 1955. Fonda attended Vassar for two years, from 1956 to 1957, before leaving to travel to Paris. In 1958 Fonda returned to New York City and trained at the Actors Studio, where she parlayed her lithe five-foot, seven-inch form and regal pedigree onto the catwalk as a fashion model and then as an ingenue in a series of nondescript motion pictures in the early 1960s. Fonda made her film debut in *Tall Story* (1960) for Warner Bros. and her Broadway debut at the Cort Theatre in *There Was a Little Girl* (1960).

In 1963 Fonda returned to Paris to make films. Foreshadowing her later versatility, Fonda became a recognizable screen face by displaying flesh for Roger Vadim in *La Ronde* (1964), by exhibiting a comedic flair as the feisty outlaw in the western farce *Cat Ballou* (1965), and by playing the bubbly newlywed in the Neil Simon play *Barefoot in the Park* (1967). She also gave a hard edge to soft roles

in overwrought melodramas, such as Arthur Penn's *The Chase* (1966) and Otto Preminger's *Hurry Sundown* (1967). Often deemed cold and mechanical by critics, Fonda was indistinguishable at this stage from a bevy of shapely and big-haired motion picture actresses. On 14 August 1965 Fonda married Vadim; they had one daughter and divorced in 1973.

Fonda emerged as a bankable, above-the-title star by playing the compliant sex toy and wide-eyed bimbo in Vadim's *Barbarella* (1968), a kinky science fiction fantasy based on a French cartoon. *Variety* panned the film as "artless, tasteless, and misdirected vulgarity," but it was also profitable, popular, and (stylistically if not artistically) groundbreaking. Just a year earlier, with Hollywood operating under the censorious Production Code, such flaunting of promiscuity and nudity would have been unimaginable on American screens.

Fresh from the sexcapades of *Barbarella,* Fonda bid to be taken seriously not merely as an actress—a conventional enough goal for a Hollywood starlet—but as a political activist, an audacious and counterintuitive ambition. The cultural disconnect between "Fonda the sex kitten" so lately on-screen and "Fonda the firebrand" presently on television chat shows was too abrupt a persona shift even for the turbulent 1960s. The same actress who had cavorted in a reverse striptease over the opening credits of *Barbarella* and had ridden half-naked on horseback in *Spirits of the Dead* (1968) was now lecturing Americans on foreign policy, gender inequality, and racial prejudice. Dressed down in guerrilla streetwear and sporting a no-nonsense hairdo, passionately intense if not always persuasively well informed, she represented (depending on the ideological eye of the beholder) a woman transformed by heightened political consciousness or a Hollywood poseur undertaking a radical chic makeover. Nonetheless, as a titillating poster girl for charismatic 1960s radicalism, only the black activist Angela Davis competed with Fonda for the dormitory wall space of undergraduate males.

By the late 1960s the actress was a lightning rod for criticism, a kind of cross-generational Rorschach test. Fonda's filial rebellion, and the kindred rebellion of her brother, Peter, served as a celebrity synecdoche for the gulfs in sensibility and style opening up in homes across America: the pampered offspring of Hollywood royalty rejecting her birthright and turning apostate, the baby boomers bringing up a fifth column against the silent majority. "You don't mind if I turn on, do you?," she would ask interviewers as she lit up a marijuana cigarette.

Typical of Fonda's presentation of self during her avatar period was an appearance in 1970 on *The Virginia Graham Show,* a television talk show that showcased the controversial opinions of the young, the radical, and the photogenic. In tandem with the John F. Kennedy assassination conspiracy-monger Mark Lane, she spoke out for Native-American rights and against American military malfeasance. "With Miss Fonda, spouting the 'instant radical' line of dissent she's recently captured headlines with, coherence was at a minimum," sniffed a *Variety* critic unimpressed by her "strongly anti-establishment" views. When a Native-American activist from the studio audience rose to challenge Fonda's "whiteface" presumption of leadership, however, the seasoned performer's ability to mollify the heckler forced the critic to admit that Fonda had handled "the Indian slight in deft fashion." The activist might be an amateur, but the artist was always a professional.

Fonda often was labeled "strident," the adjective applied to feminists who refused to stifle opinions deemed unladylike. In truth, she spouted some of the ripest examples of 1960s revolution-speak on record. "We must oppose with everything we have those blue-eyed murderers—[President Richard M.] Nixon, [Defense Secretary Melvin] Laird, and all the rest of those ethnocentric American white male chauvinists," she declaimed from the stage during skits for a traveling antiwar theater group named FTA in 1971. The troupe toured in venues located off military bases to encourage soldiers to resist the war in Vietnam. The acronym stood for "Free the Army," though, as anyone under the age of thirty knew, "Free" was not the preferred F-word.

In 1972 Fonda journeyed to North Vietnam with a group of antiwar activists. In what in some ways would be her most indelible screen appearance, newsreel film captured the actress smiling in the turret of an anti-aircraft gun. To many Americans, the antics crossed the line between voicing legitimate protest and giving aid and comfort to the enemy. On 22 August 1972, in a propaganda broadcast over Radio Hanoi, Fonda charged the United States with "the systematic destruction of civilian targets—schools, hospitals, pagodas, the factories, houses, and the dike system" and compared the "sinister" language of President Nixon to that of "a true killer." Denounced by Congress and on the editorial pages, she earned the enduring enmity and loathing of many Vietnam War veterans. "Vietnam Vets Are Not Fonda Jane" read one of the less obscene bumper stickers. "Hanoi Jane," they dubbed her, and the label stuck.

The work was always a refuge and best retort. If her political opinions were derided or condemned, even the skeptics never denied her artistic talent. Utterly erasing the celluloid memory of *Barbarella,* the actress gained the upmarket respect she craved when she played the desperate marathon dancer Gloria Beatty in the director Sydney Pollack's grim, depression-set *They Shoot Horses, Don't They?* (1969). The melodrama chronicled the escalating torments of a melange of impoverished couples competing for the prize money in a marathon dance contest, a 1930s craze that served as a convenient 1960s metaphor for capitalist exploitation as popular entertainment, humanity as commodity. Reviewers commented on how Fonda intertextually evoked her father's touchstone performance as Tom Joad in another depression-era tale, *The Grapes of Wrath* (1940). Contrary to cultural expectations, however, *The Grapes of Wrath* ends on an upbeat note of defiance and endurance: "We're the people that live," says Tom Joad. "Can't wipe us out." *They Shoot Horses, Don't They?* ends on the most hopeless of notes, with the mercy killing of the defeated Gloria and the curtain line that gave the film its title.

Fonda's fiercely committed performance garnered the New York Film Critics Award for best actress of 1969 and an Academy Award nomination—though other critics said that Fonda's characteristically tight control and forceful personality conspired against the likelihood of her character's psychic breakdown. Like Fonda, Gloria seemed too much the born survivor to be beaten down by either a marathon dance or the interminable depression. Her failure to win an Oscar that year was attributed to her alienation of older Academy voters, who later recognized her as best actress for her role as the hard-bitten hooker in *Klute* (1971).

If Fonda gained critical respect the usual way pretty actresses accrued professional capital—through being unpretty—her follow-up film, the director Alan Pakula's *Klute*, had her again playing the sexy face card. As Bree Daniels, a high-priced call girl struggling to make it as a low-priced actress, she embodies erotic enticement and emotional emptiness: feigning orgasm for one customer as she checks her watch for her next appointment. Stylistically and thematically, the film prefigures the tropes that would dominate the next decade: psychotherapy, wiretap surveillance, casual sex, discotheques, and mind-deadening (as opposed to mind-expanding) drugs. Though Bree disrobed for her customers, and moviegoers, the real departure from Hollywood convention was the shocking level of verbal explicitness and the businesslike, nonjudgmental attitude toward the sex trade. Despite the clinical depiction of sex, however, by the end reel *Klute* devolved into a conventional Hollywood romance, with the heroic small-town male (played by Donald Sutherland, Fonda's offscreen collaborator in FTA) rescuing the messed-up female from the sordid dangers of the big city. "I'm in control," says Bree of her call girl calling. "I know what I'm doing. I know I'm good." The remark might also have expressed the sure sense of command of Fonda the actress, if not the stumbling uncertainties of Fonda the activist.

The 1970s extended her good fortune on screen and her mixed fortunes in romance and politics. In 1973 she divorced Vadim. "Jane wants to be Vanessa Redgrave," he said with a Gallic shrug, referring to the controversial British actress and celebrity radical. On 20 January 1973 Fonda married Tom Hayden, the politician and 1960s activist whose causes and candidacies she backed financially. They had one son and divorced in 1989. Among many screen roles, the most notable, appropriately, were the most politically charged—though only with conventional Hollywood liberalism, not with vanguard radical politics. In *Julia* (1977) she appeared as the hard-drinking left-wing playwright Lillian Hellman, co-starring with Vanessa Redgrave as a noble anti-Nazi resistance fighter, thereby impersonating one ideological kindred spirit while playing opposite another.

Fonda and the producer Bruce Gilbert formed the IPC production company, named after the Indochina Peace Campaign, to make movies that raise social awareness issues. The first IPC project was the sudsy Vietnam home-front melodrama *Coming Home* (1978), which was a telling cultural bellwether about retrospective American attitudes toward the war: the paraplegic antiwar veteran gets the girl, and the gung-ho warrior is driven to suicide. The film won Fonda her second Oscar as best actress. Finally, as the chirpy television anchor turned hard news reporter in IPC's *China Syndrome* (1979), a prescient warning about the dangers of nuclear power, Fonda enacted a transformation on screen that seemed to echo her own passage from eye candy to political activist. The next two IPC projects addressed such issues as women in the workplace in the satirical *Nine to Five* (1980) and the control of international economics in the thriller *Rollover* (1981).

Fonda's next screen landmark was *On Golden Pond* (1981), where she appeared with her father and Katharine Hepburn in a familial melodrama that acted out the generational squabbles of the 1960s. She played a rebellious daughter, and he played a crusty and remote patriarch. Ironically, however, it was another visible exposure of flesh that proved more epochal than any unveiling in *Barbarella*. Fresh from a flurry of magazine cover stories on "Jane Fonda Turns Forty," the actress removed her shirt to reveal a bikini-clad figure of stunning proportions. It was the best publicity possible for a high concept that entered the ground floor of the videotape revolution. In 1982 she released the first in a series of hugely profitable aerobic exercise tapes, *Jane Fonda's Workout*, and books, *Jane Fonda's Workout Book*. Students, housewives, and career women across the ideological spectrum all jumped, strained, and sweated to "Jane," the 1960s obsession with societal change evolving into the 1980s obsession with self-improvement: no longer "burn, baby, burn," but "feel the burn." As with her earlier incarnations, sarcastic remarks bubbled up from the gallery. "Who would ever have thought she'd embrace capitalism with such fervor?" wisecracked the singer Bette Midler.

Fonda embraced an actual capitalist by marrying Ted Turner, the colorful media mogul and founder of Cable News Network, on her birthday on 21 December 1991.

They had no children. In 1999 she appeared on a Barbara Walters *20/20* television special celebrating the great women of the twentieth century and apologized, after a fashion, for the hurt her trip to North Vietnam had caused Vietnam veterans. Excluding exercise videos, she retired from screen work after *Stanley and Iris* (1990), until, in 2002, she signed with the high-powered Creative Artists Agency in a bid to resume her acting career. On 22 May 2001 Turner and Fonda divorced, allegedly over Fonda's conversion to born-again Christianity, another unexpected role for the always mercurial, always fascinating Fonda.

★

Biographies of Fonda include Thomas Kiernan, *Jane: An Intimate Biography of Jane Fonda* (1973); Fred Lawrence Guiles, *Jane Fonda: The Actress in Her Time* (1981); James Spada, *Fonda: Her Life in Pictures* (1985); Michael Freedland, *Jane Fonda: A Biography* (1988); Tom Collins, *Jane Fonda: An American Original* (1990); Christopher P. Anderson, *Citizen Jane: The Turbulent Life of Jane Fonda* (1990); and Bill Davidson, *Jane Fonda: An Intimate Biography* (1990). Biographical information is also in Thomas Kiernan, *Jane Fonda: Heroine for Our Time* (1982); Jane Fonda, *Women Coming of Age* (1984); Peter Collier, *The Fondas: A Hollywood Dynasty* (1991); and Russell Shorto, *Jane Fonda: Political Activism* (1991).

THOMAS DOHERTY

FONDA, Peter Seymour (*b.* 23 February 1940 in New York City), actor, producer, and director who began the 1960s performing in traditional Hollywood studio films and transitioned to countercultural roles in independent B movies, then revolutionized U.S. film by producing and starring in the phenomenally successful *Easy Rider* (1969), a low-budget project that heralded the American New Wave and spawned a new generation of filmmakers.

Fonda was born into one of the premier acting dynasties in American film. His father, Henry Jaynes Fonda, was a theater actor and Hollywood movie star, professions also taken up by Fonda's older sister Jane. Fonda's childhood was filled with insecurity and constant uprooting between California and New England. He was frequently separated from his father due to Henry's active career and World War II military service. In addition, his mother Frances Ford Seymour, who before her first marriage had been a teller at the Guaranty Trust Company of New York, then bank president, suffered from a continuing mental illness and committed suicide in 1950. Henry Fonda quickly remarried, and Fonda continued to shuttle between the extreme lifestyles of the East and West Coasts. His family's physical and emotional instability led Fonda to be perceived as a troubled youth. He once shot himself while target practic-

Peter Fonda in a scene from *Easy Rider,* 1969. THE KOBAL COLLECTION

ing with a friend. He had borrowed the friend's .22 pistol, and the trigger was released by accident, causing a bullet to discharge into Fonda's intestines. The shot was almost fatal. Fonda states this incident was an accident, although others have reported it as an attempted suicide.

Fonda began the 1960s by dropping out of the University of Omaha in Nebraska after his third year. He joined the family business, learning the acting trade in a season of summer stock at the Ceilwood Theater in Fishkill, New York. At the end of the season in 1961, Fonda landed the lead in the premiere of *Amazing Grace,* a new play by the oral historian Studs Terkel. Fonda's lanky good looks and laid-back persona were perfect for the role and the times.

Fonda moved to New York City, where he hung out with the actor Robert Duvall and became attracted to the East Coast counterculture centered in Greenwich Village. Fonda auditioned for the Broadway play *Blood, Sweat, and Stanley Poole,* but he was rejected for not looking enough like the popular stage actor Robert Morse. After spending time in Omaha in deep psychotherapy to repair his broken psyche, Fonda was called back to Broadway. The producers of *Blood, Sweat, and Stanley Poole* changed their minds, and in 1961 Fonda won the part that began his professional acting career.

Fonda married Susan Jane Brewer on 8 October 1961. She gave birth to their daughter, Bridget, another future actor, in 1964. The couple also had one son in 1966. Still a struggling actor, Fonda did guest shots on anthology television shows including *Naked City* (1962), *The New Breed*

(1962), *The Alfred Hitchcock Hour* (1964), and *Twelve O'clock High* (1964).

Fonda's first role in a feature film was in *Tammy and the Doctor* (1963), where he gave Sandra Dee her first screen kiss in the goody-goody film series. He also appeared in the World War II drama *The Victors* (1963), and in *The Young Lovers* (1964). Screen roles were hard to find and Fonda began thinking about shaping his own cinematic destiny. He tried to purchase the rights to *Lilith*. When Fonda learned that the noted director Robert Rossen already owned them, he instead landed a role in the 1964 film. Fonda rebelled against the veteran film director, reacting in much the same way as he had to his father and to most authority figures, but he was given the opportunity to observe the editing process and the experience deepened his understanding of filmmaking.

By 1965 Fonda had begun his countercultural education. He met James Mitchum, another second-generation actor, was turned on to marijuana, and bought his first motorcycle, a BMW R27. Fonda befriended the musician Jim McGuinn of the band the Byrds, joined the Hollywood Sunset Boulevard psychedelic scene, and had his first LSD experience. Fonda also met the actor Dennis Hopper, another rebel who was interested in working outside the stifling Hollywood system. Together with Don Sherman they wrote the screenplay *The Yin and the Yang* (1966); Fonda began to accumulate funding, but was unable to get it into production.

The B-movie mogul Roger Corman directed Fonda in *The Wild Angels* (1966), the film that established the actor's persona as a hog-riding, drug-taking hippie. Fonda next starred in *The Trip* (1967), which connected him to the West Coast hippie scene and the spiritual quest energized by hallucinogenic drugs.

By the end of the 1960s, everything was in place for the production of Fonda and Hopper's joint effort. Fueled on psychedelics and the notion of a film about two men who go off in search of America, they began filming *Easy Rider,* which was released in 1969. Working independently of the industry, they brought in the screenwriter Terry Southern, who shaped the actors' endless, undisciplined raps into a shootable film. Fonda produced and cowrote the screenplay (which was nominated for an Academy Award in 1970), and Hopper directed. Fonda played the iconic character Wyatt, or "Captain America," who, after a cocaine score, bikes across the country with his friend Billy, played by Hopper. On the road, the Captain and Billy experience the commune phenomenon, the country's changing family structure, deep prejudices, the murder of a liberal idealistic lawyer (played by Jack Nicholson), the Mardi Gras, and an acid trip, before meeting their death on the two-lane blacktop. Fonda was responsible for the prophetic line, "We blew it," which predicted the dissolution of the hippie generation and its demise by the decade's end.

Easy Rider marked the end of classic Hollywood films and the beginning of a new era in U.S. filmmaking. The low-budget film changed the narrative and aesthetic methods of filmmaking and still managed to ring the box office bell. The audience was a new generation under thirty, who came of age during the 1960s and found themselves finally represented on the screen.

Fonda made his directorial debut in the 1970s with the mystical Western *The Hired Hand* (1971). Although he was instrumental in launching the American New Wave and led the way for young independent filmmakers, none of his films as a director received the success or acclaim of *Easy Rider*. In April 1974 Fonda and his first wife divorced, and he married Portia Rebecca Crockett McGuane on 11 November 1975. He continued to act during the 1970s and 1980s, but it was not until his performance as a remote beekeeper in *Ulee's Gold* (1997) that he finally earned respect as a mainstream actor with an Academy Award nomination and the Golden Globe award for best actor.

Fonda's lasting contributions to 1960s culture are his iconic roles as Heavenly Blues in *The Wild Angels* and Wyatt "Captain America" in *Easy Rider*. Both characters were maverick bikers steeped in the myth, legend, and symbolism of the road—the American rebel with the wisdom and spirituality of a Zen master. As one of the creators of *Easy Rider,* Peter Fonda seeded the American New Wave of the 1970s, a legacy that continues to resonate with the now middle-aged baby boomers and their creative offspring of cutting edge filmmakers of the 1980s, 1990s, and beyond.

★

Fonda's autobiography is *Don't Tell Dad: A Memoir* (1998). Biographies of the Fonda family include John Springer, *The Fondas: The Films and Careers of Henry, Jane, and Peter Fonda* (1970); Gerald Cole and Wes Farrell, *The Fondas: Portrait of a Dynasty* (1984, rev. ed. 1985); and Peter Collier, *The Fondas: A Hollywood Dynasty* (1991).

VINCENT LOBRUTTO

FOOTE, Shelby Dade, Jr. (*b.* 17 November 1916 in Greenville, Mississippi), novelist and historian best known for his three-volume narrative of the Civil War.

The only child of Shelby Dade Foote and Lillian Rosenstock, Foote spent an itinerant childhood in Jackson and Vicksburg, Mississippi; Mobile, Alabama; and Pensacola, Florida. When Foote's father, an executive with the Armour Meat Packing Company, died of septicemia in 1922, Foote and his mother returned to Greenville. There Foote came under the informal tutelage of poet and memorialist William Alexander Percy and began a friendship with Percy's nephew and ward, the future novelist Walker Percy, that lasted until Percy's death in 1990.

Between 1935 and 1937 Foote attended the University of North Carolina, but he left without earning a degree. He returned to Greenville, took a job writing for Hodding Carter's *Delta Star*, and completed a draft of his first novel, *Tournament*. At the outbreak of World War II in Europe, Foote joined the Mississippi National Guard. Promoted to the rank of captain, Foote was attached to Battery A of the 50th Field Artillery, 5th Infantry Division, stationed in Northern Ireland. He was court-martialed and dishonorably discharged in 1944 when he took an unauthorized leave of absence to visit Tess Lavery, whom he married later that year.

During the fall and winter of 1944 Foote worked at the New York offices of the Associated Press before enlisting in the Marine Corps in January 1945. Released from the service the following November, Foote came home to Greenville, where he resumed writing fiction. Between 1949 and 1954 he published five novels—*Tournament* (1949), *Follow Me Down* (1950), *Love in a Dry Season* (1951), *Shiloh* (1952), and *Jordan County* (1954)—all of which he wrote in a garage behind his mother's house.

Foote divorced Lavery in 1946 and married his second wife in 1948, divorcing her in 1952. He moved to Memphis, Tennessee, in 1953 and began work on his masterpiece, *The Civil War: A Narrative*, an endeavor that consumed the next twenty years. Writing eight hours a day, seven days a week, Foote completed the first volume of the trilogy, *Fort Sumter to Perryville*, in 1958. He published the second volume, *Fredericksburg to Meridian*, in 1963.

On 5 September 1956 Foote married Gwyn Rainer; they had two children. Following publication of the second volume of *The Civil War*, Foote accepted a series of temporary appointments at various foundations, colleges, and universities. He was a Ford Foundation fellow in 1963 and 1964 while serving as lecturer at the University of Virginia during the 1963 academic year. At the same time Foote was playwright-in-residence at the Arena Theater in Washington, D.C., adapting his novel *Jordan County* for the stage. Throughout 1966 and 1967 he was writer-in-residence at the University of Memphis, a position he next held at Hollins College in Virginia in 1968.

Despite the critical acclaim and professional recognition he received, Foote found the 1960s an often wearisome and vexing decade. He and his family moved to the gulf coast of Alabama in 1964, but his opposition to racial discrimination angered local Klansmen and made life there uncongenial. Foote left Alabama and returned to Memphis in July 1965. Although he ran afoul of the Ku Klux Klan, Foote also incurred the wrath of African Americans. His alleged glorification of the South during the Civil War and his

Shelby Foote. CORBIS CORPORATION (BELLEVUE)

continued support for the display of Confederate symbols brought charges of white supremacy. Foote's views on race relations, however, were far more progressive than his critics allowed. In 1955 Foote told the literary scholar Louis D. Rubin, Jr. that he thought the South "ought to just go ahead and integrate all the way." Continued outrage at segregation prompted him to write to Walker Percy in 1963 that "I'm beginning to hate the one thing I really ever loved—the South. No thats [sic] wrong: not hate—despise. Mostly I despise the leaders, the pussy-faced politicians, soft-talking instruments of real evil."

His condemnation of southern racism notwithstanding, Foote dismissed as "rabble" many advocates of civil rights, especially northern white activists and agitators who knew nothing of southern history or the intricate balance of southern race relations. It came as no surprise to him, therefore, that the "decent people of the South" preferred to have nothing to do with these activists, but instead allowed those whom Foote referred to as "southern rabble" to confront them. These confrontations were explosive, and almost invariably led to violence. Regrettably, the "southern rabble," those whites who hated the idea of racial equality and the demagogues who urged them on, caused at least as many problems as they solved. Their inveterate and vicious racism further infuriated and sickened Foote, for it represented the sort of moral degeneracy that he loathed in southern politicians. More serious from Foote's point of view, once those southerners who had sympathy for blacks abdicated their responsibilities and refused to help in modifying southern race relations, most Americans came mistakenly to identify racist whites as being representative of

the entire South. These skewed perceptions, Foote thought, eroded what remained of the influence the "upstanding men and women of the South" exercised over the political and social life of their region.

Amid the deepening racial tumult of the 1960s, Foote toiled to complete the final volume of *The Civil War*, which took longer to write than the previous two installments combined. After a hiatus of eleven years, *Red River to Appomattox* at last appeared in 1974. Foote did not write a partisan history of the war calculated to reassure, gratify, or exonerate southerners distressed about the civil rights struggles of the 1960s. Whatever his personal allegiances, Foote was dispassionate in his approach to the subject. Rubin noted that Foote "could separate himself and what he thought was right from the passions and attitudes and beliefs of the southern community, and not be caught between truth and community loyalty. . . . [His] cast of mind was such that in undertaking to interpret the military events of the Civil War he was not likely to be influenced in his assessment of the campaigns of 1861–1865 by the community's emotional needs during 1961–1965." Foote composed his history in the grand narrative style of the historians Thucydides, Tacitus, and Gibbon, drawing on what he had learned about human nature from experience and reflection, as well as from such writers of fiction as Mark Twain and Marcel Proust. The result is not only an extraordinarily detailed and astute military history, but also an account of the war that conveys the heroism and humanity of the participants along with the barbarism and tragedy of events.

In 1978 Foote published a sixth novel, entitled *Septem-*

ber, September. Set in Memphis, the book tells the story of a young African-American boy kidnapped by whites. He also wrote *The Novelist's View of History*, which appeared in 1981. A member of the American Academy of Arts and Letters, Foote continues to live and work in Memphis. Since 1990 he has profited from, if not always welcomed or enjoyed, the public attention he gained as the result of his appearance in Ken Burns's documentary film *The Civil War*.

★

In addition to Foote's books mentioned in the text, see William C. Carter, ed., *Conversations with Shelby Foote* (1989), and Jay Tolson, ed., *The Correspondence of Shelby Foote and Walker Percy* (1997), for a discussion of Foote's work from his point of view. Louis D. Rubin, Jr., "Shelby Foote's Civil War," in *A Gallery of Southerners* (1982), offers an insightful discussion of Foote's trilogy, as do these articles: William Wirt, "Shelby Foote's *Civil War*: The Novelist as Humanistic Historian," in *Mississippi Quarterly* 24 (fall 1971); George Garret, "Foote's *The Civil War:* The Version of Posterity?," in *Mississippi Quarterly* 28 (winter 1974–1975); and James M. Cox, "Shelby Foote's Civil War," in *Southern Review* 21 (Apr. 1985). For a general overview and analysis of Foote's fictional and historical writing, see Helen White and Redding S. Sugg, Jr., *Shelby Foote* (1982), and Robert L. Phillips, Jr., *Shelby Foote: Novelist and Historian* (1992).

MARK G. MALVASI

FORTAS, Abraham ("Abe") (*b.* 19 June 1910 in Memphis, Tennessee; *d.* 5 April 1982 in Washington, D.C.), leading civil libertarian who served as an associate justice on the U.S. Supreme Court from 1965 to 1969, until charges of misdeeds forced him to resign.

Fortas, the youngest of five children of William Fortas, a cabinetmaker, and Ray Berson, was raised in Memphis. His parents, Orthodox Jews, had emigrated from England and operated a small shop in one of the city's poorer sections. At the age of fifteen, Fortas graduated second in his class from a Memphis high school, earning an academic scholarship to Southwestern College (now Rhodes College), a Presbyterian-sponsored institution in his hometown. Graduating at the top of his class with a bachelor's degree in 1930, he was offered scholarships from both Harvard and Yale law schools. Fortas opted for Yale because its monthly stipend was more generous than that of Harvard. Named editor of the prestigious *Yale Law Journal* in his final year of law school, Fortas graduated second in his class with a law degree in 1933.

Fortas remained at Yale for the next four years as a teacher. During this period he also worked part-time for the Securities and Exchange Commission (SEC), where he

Abe Fortas. ARCHIVE PHOTOS, INC.

established a close relationship with William O. Douglas, another future justice of the U.S. Supreme Court. In July 1935 Fortas married Carolyn Eugenia Agger, whom he had met while he was a student at Yale. He left Yale in 1937 and joined the SEC full-time. He later took a position with the Public Works Administration and then served as undersecretary in the U.S. Department of the Interior from 1942 to 1946.

Having developed a network of valuable New Deal (social and economic reforms introduced in the 1930s by Franklin D. Roosevelt) contacts, Fortas left government service in 1946 to join his former Yale law professor Thurman Arnold as a partner in the new firm of Arnold, Fortas and Porter. Although his specialty was corporate law, Fortas also was interested in criminal law, particularly in the rights of criminals. In this arena, one of his more high-profile cases was *Gideon* v. *Wainwright* (1963), in which he argued successfully before the U.S. Supreme Court for the right to counsel of criminal defendants in felony cases, even at public cost. In 1948 Fortas defended the Texas congressman Lyndon B. Johnson in a challenge to his eighty-four-vote victory in the Democratic senatorial primary, winning a victory for the Texan before the Supreme Court. This marked the beginning of a close friendship between Fortas and Johnson.

When Johnson won the presidency in 1964, he offered Fortas the office of attorney general, but Fortas declined. The following year, however, Johnson created a vacancy on the Supreme Court by appointing associate justice Arthur J. Goldberg as U.S. ambassador to the United Nations. In late July 1965 the president nominated Fortas as Goldberg's replacement on the Court. In his memoirs, Johnson reflected on his reasons for naming Fortas: "I was confident that the man would be a brilliant and able jurist . . . . He had the strength of character to stand up for his own convictions, and he was a humanitarian." Another factor in Johnson's choice of Fortas was his desire to continue the tradition of the Court's so-called Jewish seat, which had begun with the appointment of Justice Louis Brandeis in 1916 and most recently had been occupied by Goldberg. Despite the fact that he had not yet fully agreed to the appointment, Fortas was confirmed by a voice vote in the Senate on 11 August 1965.

Fortas was well established as a civil libertarian long before his appointment to the Supreme Court, his reputation having been forever secured by his involvement in *Gideon* v. *Wainwright*. In fact, the Supreme Court had appointed him as counsel for the indigent Clarence Early Gideon in the case that set the precedent for the right to counsel in almost all criminal cases. Given his background, Fortas fit in exceptionally well with the prevailing liberal temperament of the Warren Court. A number of the decisions that Fortas supported on the Court involved the expansion of individual and civil rights. In *Miranda* v. *Arizona* (1996), which led to the requirement that law enforcement officers inform suspects of their constitutional rights before they could be questioned, Fortas cast the fifth and deciding vote.

Fortas wrote the majority opinion for the Supreme Court decision in *In re Gault* (1967), which guaranteed juveniles the right to counsel and protection against self-incrimination. In his opinion, Fortas observed: "There are rights granted to adults which are withheld from juveniles. Under our Constitution, the condition of being a boy does not justify a kangaroo court." In *Tinker* v. *Des Moines Independent School District* (1969), the Court found that a prohibition against passive protest by high school students (namely the wearing of black arm bands in protest of the Vietnam War) violated the students' constitutional right to freedom of expression. According to the majority opinion, written by Fortas, "free speech is not a right that is given only to be so circumscribed that it exists in principle but not in fact." Freedom of expression, Fortas observed, would not really exist if it were a right that could be exercised only in an area "that a benevolent government has provided as a safe haven for crackpots."

Fortas did break with his liberal brethren on the Court in questions involving antitrust law. Although his views generally were very much in line with those of Goldberg, his predecessor on the bench, Fortas expressed far less skepticism about the machinations of big business, particularly in the realm of mergers and acquisitions. In 1968 Fortas released *Concerning Dissent and Civil Disobedience,* which provides perhaps the clearest insight into the jurist's views of American justice.

The beginning of the end for Fortas came with his June 1968 nomination by President Johnson to replace retiring Chief Justice Earl Warren. Conservative Republicans and Democrats alike opposed the nomination, charging that Johnson, a "lame duck" who already had announced that he would not run for reelection, was trying to pack the court with liberals before he left office. During the opening round of hearings on the Fortas nomination, it was revealed that the associate justice had accepted $15,000 for teaching a nine-week course at American University Law School during the summer of 1968. Reportedly, a former law partner of Fortas's had raised the fee from five wealthy business executives. Further imperiling his nomination was the revelation that Fortas had counseled Johnson on national policy after he had taken his position on the Court. Critics of the nomination argued that Fortas lacked the "sense of propriety" to be expected of a chief justice. Opponents began a filibuster in the Senate to block the confirmation of Fortas as chief justice. On 1 October 1968, shortly after the Senate was unable to close the debate (and thus end the filibuster by asking for a vote), Fortas asked that his name be withdrawn from consideration.

Seven months later, in May 1969, a report in *Life* magazine charged that Fortas in 1966 had received a payment of $20,000 from the family foundation of Louis Wolfson, who later was indicted and imprisoned for selling unregistered securities. The payment, which eventually was returned, was to be the first in a series of annual payments to Fortas for services rendered to the Wolfson Foundation. Amid talk of possible impeachment proceedings, Fortas resigned on 14 May 1969, "for the good of the Court," although he admitted no wrongdoing. Fortas returned to private practice in Washington. He and wife continued to live in their Georgetown town house, spending summers at their vacation home in Connecticut. Fortas died in Washington of a ruptured aorta.

Looking back on Fortas's short tenure on the high court, author Henry J. Abraham, one of the country's foremost experts on constitutional law, wrote: "Not even Fortas's most advanced detractors would deny his uncanny ability, towering intellect, indeed brilliance. It is a pity [that] by his ill-conceived, arrogantly thoughtless, downright stupid, off-the-bench actions" it became necessary for him to resign after only a few short years on the high court. According to Abraham, Fortas had shown himself to be a dedicated libertarian in the arena of fundamental human rights.

Abraham likened Fortas, at least in that respect, to Goldberg. "But Fortas's promising career was to be cut short by a combination of political power plays and personal greed," Abraham concluded.

Although it has been to some degree overshadowed by the circumstances of his fall from grace, the lasting contribution of Fortas remains his steadfast defense of individual rights. From his inspired defense of Clarence Earl Gideon in the landmark case of *Gideon* v. *Wainwright,* through his votes in such Supreme Court cases as *Miranda* v. *Arizona,* *In re Gault,* and *Tinker* v. *Des Moines Independent Community School District,* Fortas worked tirelessly to expand the civil rights of all Americans.

★

A biography of Fortas is Laura Kalman, *Abe Fortas: A Biography* (1992). Readers may find greater insight into the life of Fortas and his years on the Supreme Court in Robert Shogan, *A Question of Judgment: The Fortas Case and the Struggle for the Supreme Court* (1972), and Bruce Allen Murphy, *Fortas: The Rise and Ruin of a Supreme Court Justice* (1988). Articles on Fortas include Fred P. Graham, "The Many-Sided Justice Fortas" (4 June 1967), and Fred Rodell, "The Complexities of Mr. Justice Fortas" (28 July 1968), both from the *New York Times Magazine.* An obituary is in the *New York Times* (7 Apr. 1982).

DON AMERMAN

FOSSEY, Dian (*b.* 16 January 1932 in Fairfax, California; *d.* 24 December 1985 in Ruhengeri, Rwanda), primatologist and conservationist who greatly advanced knowledge of the mountain gorilla.

Fossey was the only child of George Fossey III and Kitty Fossey. George, a frustrated insurance salesman, left when Fossey was a child. After a divorce Kitty married Richard Price, a contractor. By all accounts Fossey seems to have had a relatively unhappy childhood and never completely reconciled with her mother or her stepfather. After graduating from high school she enrolled at the University of California, Davis, in 1950 to study veterinary medicine. Doing poorly in the science courses, she dropped out in her second year. Returning to college to study occupational therapy, she graduated with a B.A. from San Jose State University in 1954.

Eager to put space between her and her tense family life, Fossey took a position at Kosair Crippled Children's Hospital, in Louisville, Kentucky. There she became friends with Mary White Henry, secretary to the hospital director. The Henry family provided her with inroads into Louisville society, although she seemed happiest with her patients and around animals. Through the Henrys she met some young African planters and became fascinated with

that continent. George Schaller's book *The Mountain Gorilla: Ecology and Behavior* (1963) introduced her to the mountain gorilla.

Determined to visit Africa, Fossey mortgaged her future salary to the hospital. In 1963, in Kenya, she met the famed anthropologist Louis Leakey. When Fossey expressed an interest in gorillas, he suggested she consider a long-term study of those little-known primates (the British ethologist Jane Goodall was then working with chimpanzees).

Fossey tried to get stories of her trip published in popular magazines, and finally the Louisville *Courier-Journal* accepted three articles. In 1966 she met Leakey again when he gave a lecture in Louisville. Leakey remembered their previous meeting (possibly because, ill from the pain of a sprained ankle, she had vomited on one of his fossils) and again raised the possibility of a long-term study, promising to find financial support.

After support was arranged from the Wilkie Foundation (and later from the National Geographic Society), Fossey quit her job and arrived at Kababa, in Zaire, in January 1967. She made her first sighting of gorillas later that month. Although her work progressed well, she had some difficulties with camp workers and with herders and poachers in the area. By July the political situation in Zaire had deteriorated so badly that she was detained on more than one occasion, ultimately fleeing to Rwanda. Later stories of her mistreatment and possible rape seem to have been exaggerations.

With Leakey's approval, Fossey transferred her work to Karisoke, just across the mountains from Kababa. By September the new center was established and her work progressed rapidly throughout the next year. From the start she was determined to end herding and poaching in the park. For about five months, early in 1968, she did little active research as she nursed two baby gorillas that had been injured in being captured for a German zoo.

After a year at Karisoke, Fossey returned to the United States, stopping on the way in Cambridge, England, to arrange for doctoral studies under the primate specialist Robert Hinde. Returning to Africa after three months at Cambridge, she made international headlines, including a cover story in *National Geographic.*

At the same time her personal life grew increasingly complicated. By December 1971 she had had an abortion to terminate a pregnancy that resulted from an affair with a research student. When that relationship began to sour Fossey increasingly turned to alcohol. In addition, her interaction with most of the students who worked at Karisoke was strained. She also began to develop less-than-friendly relations with the park directors and much of the local population (the African camp workers seem to have been an exception). On one occasion, determined to keep herders

Dian Fossey points out Rwanda on a globe. AP/WIDE WORLD PHOTOS

out of the park, she kidnapped a cow. In 1973 she began shooting cattle.

In the early years of the 1970s, she made occasional lecture trips and worked on her doctorate. In 1976 she earned her Ph.D. in primatology from Cambridge and also participated in a primate symposium with Goodall and Birute Galdikas, a Canadian primatologist who had been chosen by Leakey to conduct a study of orangutans in Borneo.

By this time Fossey's work in Africa as a scientist seems to have declined considerably. Part of the decline was due to her health; she suffered from various allergies, asthma (although she continued to smoke), broken bones because of calcium loss, an irregular heartbeat, and eye problems. At times she had to use an oxygen inhaler. Nevertheless, she increased her battles against poachers. On one foray she burned the possessions of a poacher and kidnapped a child. As a result she was spending less time in the field. Her notoriety increased when poachers killed Digit, one of her study gorillas. She used his death to raise funds for antipoaching patrols, though most of the funds were channeled to organizations for which she had little sympathy.

In 1980 Fossey left Africa to take a year-long position at Cornell University in Ithaca, New York. While there she worked on her book, *Gorillas in the Mist,* which was ultimately published in 1983. Her year in the United States was punctuated by a pair of symposiums with the other two "primate ladies" (Goodall and Galdikas) and the publication of some scientific papers. All this while, though, she

was in torment about Karisoke, which was under the direction of a former student with whom she had strong disagreements.

Her final years saw little scientific advancement. By now she was persona non grata with park authorities, many conservation groups, and most of her former students. Her health continued to decline, and research seemed far less important than her antipoaching patrols. Because gorilla tourism had brought money to impoverished Rwanda, there were moves to keep her out of the country. When at Karisoke she was seldom able to visit the gorillas.

On Christmas Eve of 1985 Fossey was murdered in her cabin at the Karisoke Research Center. Eventually, Wayne McGuire (her latest student) and Emmanuel Rwelekana (a tracker she had fired) were charged with the murder. McGuire had returned to the United States but was convicted of her killing in absentia. Rwelekana committed suicide while awaiting trial. Many observers were dissatisfied with the result of the investigation and trial, believing that she was killed by poachers, herders, or Rwandan officials who wanted her out of the country. On 31 December 1985 Fossey was buried next to the gorilla graveyard she had established at Karisoke.

Fossey's career as a scientist was relatively short, yet in that time she greatly increased the world's knowledge of the largest primate and eradicated their false reputation for fierceness. She triggered international sympathy for endangered animals in Africa and spurred conservation efforts. The strategy of ecotourism as a source of national wealth developed from her popular writings. Yet her personal life remains shrouded in mist, much like her favorite study subjects.

★

Fossey's own account of her life with mountain gorillas is in *Gorillas in the Mist* (1983), which was the basis of a 1988 film. Though mawkish and sentimental, the biography by Farley Mowat, *Woman in the Mists* (1987), is quite usable. Less critical is the section on Fossey in Bettyann Kevles, *Watching the Wild Apes* (1976). Although also sympathetic, Harold T. P. Hayes, *The Dark Romance of Dian Fossey* (1990), is more aware of some of the more controversial aspects of her life. There is a section on Fossey's work and death in Alex Shoumatoff, *African Madness* (1988). *National Geographic* published accounts of her work in "More Years with Mountain Gorillas" (Oct. 1971) and "The Imperiled Mountain Gorilla" (Apr. 1981). Obituaries are in the *Los Angeles Times* and *New York Times* (both 29 Dec. 1985) and in the *Chicago Tribune* (30 Dec. 1985).

ART BARBEAU

FRANKENHEIMER, John Michael   (*b.* 19 February 1930 in Malba, New York; *d.* 6 July 2002 in Los Angeles, California), film director who brought techniques learned in live television to Hollywood, revolutionizing American filmmaking in the process.

Frankenheimer's parents were Walter Martin, a stockbroker, and Helen Mary (Sheedy) Frankenheimer, a homemaker. He grew up in New York and was educated at La Salle Military Academy, graduating in 1947. He went on to Williams College and obtained a B.A. in 1951, before serving for two years in the U.S. Air Force, where he attained the rank of first lieutenant in the USAF Film Squadron. Upon leaving the military Frankenheimer found work as an assistant director at the television division of the Columbia Broadcasting System (CBS). He was soon winning awards and nominations, including the Grand Prize at the Locarno Film Festival in 1955, an Emmy Award nomination for best direction in a live series in 1955, for his work on the *Climax* series, and critics' awards for best direction in 1956 and 1959. He married Carolyn Diane Miller on 22 September 1954, and they had two daughters before divorcing in 1961. He married for the second time to Evans Evans in 1964.

Frankenheimer spent most of the 1950s working in television, directing twelve episodes of the *Playhouse 90* series and working on the CBS series *Climax*. These feature-length dramas were broadcast live and were a good proving ground for moviemaking. He made his first movie, *The Young Stranger,* in 1957, cashing in on the success of *Rebel Without a Cause* (1955) and the fashion for films about

John Frankenheimer, 1962. © BETTMANN/CORBIS

troubled teenagers and their violent behavior. The experience was not a happy one. Frankenheimer himself said that he didn't understand films and didn't like working with only one camera. He returned to making live television shows for the next three years.

Yet in 1961 Frankenheimer became one of the first directors to make a successful move from television to the big screen, and he did so to huge critical acclaim. Starring Burt Lancaster, *The Young Savages* (1961) is a courtroom drama about the prosecution of three teenage delinquents and the judge's misgivings about punishing them. Frankenheimer's clever direction of closeups creates huge tension in courtroom scenes and makes a forceful point about the problem of juvenile delinquency and its causes. But while *The Young Savages* convinced him that his future was in feature films, it was *The Manchurian Candidate* (1962) that established Frankenheimer as one of the most innovative, flamboyant, and exciting directors in Hollywood.

Perhaps because of his training in the rapidly changing world of television, Frankenheimer was quick to embrace new technologies such as Panavision and to use new cameras, fast film stocks, and technologically advanced editing techniques. *The Manchurian Candidate* tells the story of a Korean War veteran who has been brainwashed and returns home programmed to assassinate a presidential candidate. Thanks to Frankenheimer's direction, *The Manchu-*

rian Candidate was one of the hardest-hitting thrillers of the 1960s. He was widely praised for the daring camera work and choice of shots, in particular an out-of-focus shot of Frank Sinatra, who played one of the lead roles. But according to Frankenheimer, the shot was simply the best of a lot of bad takes. Sinatra had the film withdrawn after the assassination of President John F. Kennedy in 1963. When it reappeared in 1987 many critics listed it among the best releases of the year.

After *The Manchurian Candidate,* Frankenheimer found his brand of solid, socially aware filmmaking much in demand. Returning to the interior-based drama of *The Young Savages,* and again drawing on his experience in television, Frankenheimer made *All Fall Down* (1962), a family drama that helped launch the career of the actor Warren Beatty. The film again makes excellent use of close camera work. He was also hired to take over from the director Charles Crichton on *The Birdman of Alcatraz* (1962), a true story about an inmate of the famous prison who becomes an acknowledged expert on birds but cannot win release. Filmed, like *The Young Savages, The Manchurian Candidate,* and *All Fall Down* in Frankenheimer's trademark black and white, *The Birdman of Alcatraz* is also his second feature starring Lancaster, who was nominated for an Oscar for his performance. Lancaster seemed to benefit from Frankenheimer's approach and starred in two more films for him: *Seven Days in May* (1963) and *The Gypsy Moths* (1969).

Seven Days in May allowed Frankenheimer even more freedom to indulge his passion for new technology. The appearance of advanced surveillance technology in the film, including hidden cameras and bugging devices, opened up new possibilities for thrillers of the type and pointed the way toward the paranoia of such films as Francis Ford Coppola's *The Conversation* (1974). *Seven Days in May* also marks the end of Frankenheimer's most successful period as a director. By 1964 he had made at least two of the most influential thrillers of the decade, but his interest in technological trickery was beginning to outweigh attention to genuine dramatic impact. Perhaps the best example of this flaw is *Grand Prix* (1966). Filmed in color in Cinerama-SuperPanavision, the film employs split screens and other technical tricks, and does so with great skill. But although it is one of the few films ever to capture the noise, grime, and extreme speed of motor racing, it lacks real human drama.

From the late 1960s, with a few exceptions such as *The Gypsy Moths* (1969) and *French Connection II* (1975), Frankenheimer made poor decisions in choosing projects. In the 1990s he returned to television with some success, winning Emmy awards for the miniseries *Against the Wall* in 1994, for *The Burning Season* and *Andersonville* in 1996, and for *George Wallace* in 1998. Frankenheimer's talent for tense,

thought-provoking thrillers peaked in the early 1960s, and by the 1990s he was recognized as a major influence on the look of the Hollywood thriller. He challenged accepted visual styles and in doing so helped redefine the thriller genre for a new age of paranoia and technological threat. Frankenheimer's dedication to using new technology was undimmed even at the age of seventy-one, when he won an award for Best Internet Video Premiere for *Ambush* (2001).

Frankenheimer died at Cedars-Sinai Medical Center in Los Angeles from complications arising from spinal surgery.

★

The most comprehensive book on Frankenheimer and his work in the 1960s is Gerald Pratley, *The Cinema of John Frankenheimer* (1969). Frankenheimer has been the subject of many articles. Among the best are John Thomas, "John Frankenheimer, The Smile on the Face of the Tiger," *Film Quarterly* (winter 1965–1966), Alan Casty, "Realism and Beyond: The Films of John Frankenheimer," *Film Heritage* (winter 1966–1967), and Michael Scheinfeld's review of the re-released *The Manchurian Candidate,* in *Films in Review* 39, no. 11 (1988). A short article demonstrating Frankenheimer's influence on moviemaking is Matt Zoller Seitz, "Those High-tech Shoot-em-ups Got the Formula from *The Train,*" *New York Times* (30 Apr. 1995). An obituary is in the *New York Times* (8 July 2002).

CHRIS ROUTLEDGE

FRANKLIN, Aretha Louise (*b.* 25 March 1942 in Memphis, Tennessee), singer who established herself in the 1960s as the "Queen of Soul."

From a young age Franklin was steeped in the tradition of black gospel music. Her father, the Reverend C. L. Franklin, was a well-known evangelical preacher and a nationally known gospel singer. Her mother, Barbara, was also a gospel singer. Franklin spent most of her childhood with her five brothers and sisters in Detroit, where her father was the pastor of the New Bethel Baptist Church. Both at church and at home, Franklin's father introduced her to great black secular and gospel singers, among them Dinah Washington, Lou Rawls, Mahalia Jackson, and Sam Cooke. Her father's friendship with the jazz pianist Art Tatum and the blues singers Bobby Bland and Clara Ward exposed her to varied musical styles and traditions.

Franklin began singing in the choir of her father's church and eventually became a featured soloist. During the summer, she traveled the country with her father's gospel revival tour. Franklin, who had had one child out of wedlock at the age of fifteen, quit school after the birth of her second child, when she was seventeen. In the early 1960s, at age eighteen, Franklin left Detroit and headed to

Aretha Franklin. AP/WIDE WORLD PHOTOS

In the 1960s Franklin established herself in the United States and in Europe as the undisputed "Queen of Soul."

Through her recordings and her concert and television appearances, Franklin displayed the sense of black pride that her father had preached, and that pride became the rallying cry of the U.S. civil rights movement during the turbulent decade of the 1960s. In particular, Franklin's "Respect" captured the essence of the times, the need for all people—white or black—to respect each other as human beings regardless of color. To many people, her recordings gave voice to the confidence and will of black Americans who had been struggling for equality for hundreds of years. As a black woman whose music was applauded and embraced by black people and white people alike, Franklin's enormous success reflected not only her huge talent but also the social, political, and cultural changes that had begun to take place in the 1960s. Franklin performed at various fund-raising events in support of the civil rights movement. The civil rights leader the Reverend Martin Luther King, Jr., was a close family friend and an inspiration to Franklin. In 1968 she was honored to receive a special award from King's Southern Christian Leadership Council, which King personally presented to her. Later that year, Franklin would sing at King's funeral, after his assassination in Memphis.

Although Franklin is truly an artist of the 1960s, she continued to record through the 1970s, 1980s, and 1990s and is still active today. Moving closer to mainstream pop music by the mid-1970s, Franklin had won by that time six gold albums, fourteen gold singles, and eight Grammy Awards. Eventually, she would win a total of seventeen Grammy Awards. In 1980 Franklin left Atlantic to move to Arista Records. At Arista she recorded in a wide variety of musical styles, from gospel to dance to pop, including the hits "Freeway of Love," "Who's Zoomin' Who," and "I Knew You Were Waiting (for Me)." Although she was not as consistently commercially popular as she had been in the 1960s, she did enjoy considerable success. In 1998 Aretha released her fortieth album, *A Rose Is Still a Rose,* collaborating with younger stars and with the producers Lauryn Hill, Sean Combs, and Jermaine Dupri. The album reached the Top Forty in the rhythm and blues (R&B) music charts and was nominated for two Grammys, best female R&B vocal, and best R&B album.

Although her personal life has been marred by unsuccessful marriages and reports of financial and drinking problems, Franklin is recognized as a national treasure. (Franklin and White, who had married in 1961, had one child and were divorced in 1969. She had another child with Ken Cunningham before marrying Glynn Turman in 1978. They were divorced in 1984.) *Time* named her "one of the most influential people of the last century," and the popular television channel VH-1 ranked her number one

New York City, where she signed her first major recording contract, with Columbia Records. Columbia marketed her primarily as a pop and jazz singer despite her roots in gospel music and her admiration for blues music, but Franklin brought the label no major hits. Success came quickly, however, when Franklin signed in 1966 with Atlantic Records, where the producer Jerry Wexler had a successful track record in building the careers of black musicians. More important, unlike Columbia Records' decision to market Franklin as a jazz and pop singer, Wexler decided to develop Franklin as a rhythm and blues artist rising out of gospel roots. His vision was more in sync with Franklin's natural musicality and instincts.

Franklin believed in music's universality. Although blues and soul music may have arisen out of the cotton fields of southern slavery, she felt and believed in its ability to speak to and reach people of all colors. The overwhelming success of her recordings for Atlantic proved that her belief was correct. Franklin's recording "I Never Loved a Man (the Way I Loved You)" marked the first of a long list of hits for Atlantic in the late 1960s. Her recordings "Respect," "Baby, I Love You," "You Make Me Feel Like a Natural Woman," "I Say a Little Prayer," and "Chain of Fools," among others, were all commercial and artistic hits that remain classics today. She also recorded many of her own songs, such as "Think" and "Save Me," some cowritten with her first husband, Ted White, or with her sister.

on its list of the 100 greatest women in rock and roll. In 1987 Franklin was the first woman inducted into the Rock and Roll Hall of Fame. She was awarded a Grammy Legends Award in 1991 and a Grammy Lifetime Achievement Award in 1994. She also received a Kennedy Center Honors Award for Lifetime Achievement in the Performing Arts in 1994, the youngest person ever to be so honored. At the dawn of the twenty-first century, the White House Millennium Council selected Franklin's "Respect" to be included in the time capsule that would preserve important cultural symbols of the twentieth century for future generations to learn about and enjoy.

All the many honors and awards that Franklin earned during her long career acknowledge her astounding achievement as an extraordinarily gifted singer and performer and an important symbol of the American civil rights movement. She has broken down traditional musical boundaries by melding the traditions of gospel, pop, jazz, rock, soul, and R&B music; by spreading gospel and blues beyond the black church; and by appealing to diverse audiences of these different musical genres. The fact that Franklin, who made her name in the 1960s, is still treasured today as one of the icons of American music is a testament to her contributions to American music, society, and civil rights.

★

Franklin's autobiography is *Aretha: From These Roots* (1999), with David Ritz. Other discussions of Franklin's life and career include David Nathan, *The Soulful Divas* (1999), and Mark Bego, *Aretha Franklin: The Queen of Soul* (2001). Additional biographical information can be found in Patricia Romanowski and Holly George-Warren, eds., *The Rolling Stone Encyclopedia of Rock & Roll* (2001).

MATTHEW J. PIERCE

FRANKLIN, John Hope (*b.* 2 January 1915 in Rentiesville, Oklahoma), historian, professor, and activist whose writings helped create the intellectual foundations of the fight by African Americans for civil rights.

Franklin was the youngest of four children of Buck Colbert Franklin, a lawyer, and Mollie Parker, a teacher. He started college at Fisk University with the intention of following his father into the legal profession, but a history course inspired him to change his career plans. After earning a doctorate from Harvard in 1941, he taught at Fisk University, Saint Augustine's College, North Carolina College, and Howard University. While at Howard, Thurgood Marshall, then director-counsel of the National Association for the Advancement of Colored People (NAACP) Legal Defense and Education Fund, recruited him to work on the

John Hope Franklin. AP/WIDE WORLD PHOTOS

historical background for the 1954 *Brown* v. *Board of Education* case.

In 1956 the *New York Times* ran a front-page article on Franklin's appointment as the chair of the history department at Brooklyn College, reporting that as far as was known he was the first African-American chair of any academic department in the New York State college system. Franklin taught at Brooklyn from 1956 to 1964, a watershed experience for him because, for the first time, he was not part of an African-American community but in a predominantly white environment. While at Brooklyn he published his revised second edition of *From Slavery to Freedom* (first published in 1947), and three new seminal works: *The Militant South* (1956), *Reconstruction After the Civil War* (1961), and *The Emancipation Proclamation* (1963). Franklin also edited two books and published over twenty articles in newspapers, books, and scholarly journals.

Reconstruction After the Civil War has been instrumental in overturning the dogma on Reconstruction propounded by the "Columbian school" of historians, and the distorted images that filmmaker D. W. Griffith in his *Intolerance* (1916) and *Birth of a Nation* (1915) burned into the popular mind. Franklin's new paradigm was crucial in creating a more positive image of African Americans. He showed that the promise that was held out to the newly freed slaves had been most unjustly denied them.

The Militant South, 1800–1861 was a pioneering study that traced the region's antebellum tendency toward violence, a predilection that increased as abolitionist pressure grew and militant whites saw themselves and their institutions, primarily slavery, threatened. Its publication in a popular paperback format in 1964 came at a time when white southerners' aggressive "massive resistance" to desegregation in education, and violence directed against the Freedom Riders and voter registration activists, seemed an echo of the previous century.

In the academic year 1962–1963 Franklin was honored with the Pitt Professorship of American History and Institutions at Cambridge University. While in England he also served as a commentator for the British Broadcasting Corporation (BBC), providing an American perspective on events. Two major incidents on which he commented were the 1962 attempt by James Meredith to enter the University of Mississippi, and the 1963 March on Washington, D.C., led by the Reverend Martin Luther King, Jr.

In 1963 Franklin was elected the first African-American member of the Cosmos Club, an elite Washington, D.C., institution of intellectuals in science, literature, and the arts. President John F. Kennedy appointed Franklin to the Board of Foreign Scholarships, the first of many governmental assignments, capped in 1997 when he was named chair of the advisory board for President William J. Clinton's initiative on race and reconciliation.

In 1964 Franklin was appointed professor of American history at the University of Chicago, one of the most renowned history departments in the United States. He served as chair of the department from 1967 to 1970 and was awarded the prestigious John Manly Distinguished Service Professorship in 1969. The University of Chicago held a strong attraction for Franklin, not only because of the outstanding reputation of its history program, but also because he had graduate students to assist him in his research. Although Franklin's intellectual contributions to the cause of the civil rights movement were paramount, he did walk with a group of historians in the historic Selma to Montgomery march in Alabama in March 1965, but as he said, "I doubt that Martin [Luther King, Jr.] ever knew that I was there, far back in the ranks as I was."

Franklin's scholarship and publishing did not diminish during his eighteen years at Chicago, with three revisions of *From Slavery to Freedom,* and its translation into several languages. Major new books were *A Southern Odyssey: Travelers in the Ante-Bellum North* (1976), and *Racial Equality in America* (1976); he also wrote scores of journal and newspaper articles and book chapters.

Overall, however, Franklin's highly respected *From Slavery to Freedom* has been his most influential publication, selling over two million copies. By 2002 it was in its eighth edition and had become the definitive textbook on African-American history. Its scope is broad, covering the African beginnings and touching on the Canadian and South American experiences. Although it did not sell well at first, the book's reputation grew as colleges and universities began to implement courses and programs in black studies in the 1960s and later. This is somewhat ironic, because when he was at the University of Chicago, Franklin opposed the establishment of a black studies program, a stance for which younger activists accused him of being an ivory-tower academic.

Franklin always considered himself a part of the mainstream, a believer in integration, and saw his scholarship as enlightening the nation as to the integral nature of the contributions of black Americans to the American story. He opposed black studies programs because he believed standard courses should increase their coverage of the accomplishments of black Americans and feared that separate programs would lead to intellectual segregation. It is due to the work of Franklin and others that the achievements of African Americans are no longer seen as a minor tributary of the nation's history. He has changed the way U.S. history is studied and taught.

Franklin left Chicago and returned to the South in 1982, when he was named the James B. Duke Professor of History at Duke University, a position he holds in an emeritus status since his retirement in 1985. From 1985 to 1992 he was professor of legal history in the Duke University Law School. Franklin has served as president of the three major historical associations, and is the first African American to head both the Southern Historical Association and the Organization of American Historians. He has also served as the president of Phi Beta Kappa. He is recognized as the dean of black historians, the nation's leading scholar of African-American history, and is one of the most celebrated American historians with well over one hundred honorary degrees.

Throughout his career Franklin found that the things that made his life worthwhile were his love for teaching, lecturing, doing research, and helping his students. He also grows orchids. His greenhouse contains over 700 specimens, and has he one variety named after him. He was married to Aurelia Whittington Franklin from 1940 until she died in 1999. He has one son.

★

Franklin's papers are held at the John Hope Franklin Research Center for African and African-American Documentation at Duke University, Durham, North Carolina. He is currently working on his autobiography, to be titled *The Vintage Years.* The Web site of the John Hope Franklin Center for Interdisciplinary and International Studies at http://www.duke.edu/web/jhfcenter/main.

html includes a bibliography and news about Franklin. The one-hour Public Broadcasting System (PBS) video directed by Dick Young, *First Person Singular: John Hope Franklin* (1997), provides insight into the character of the soft-spoken historian.

SEAN P. MALONEY

FRAZIER, Joseph William ("Joe") (*b.* 12 January 1944 in Beaufort, South Carolina), Olympic gold medalist in boxing in 1964, New York world heavyweight champion from 1968 to 1969, and unified world heavyweight champion between 1970 and 1973.

One of thirteen children and the youngest of seven sons born to Rubin and Dolly Frazier, Frazier grew up in poverty in rural South Carolina. A sharecropper, woodcutter, and junk dealer, Rubin Frazier lost an arm in an automobile accident shortly before Joe was born. In part as a consequence of their father's disability, all the Frazier children contributed to the household income by picking vegetables for fifteen cents a crate. An indifferent student, Frazier dropped out of high school in the tenth grade and, in 1959, married his childhood sweetheart, Florence Smith.

Frazier went north in search of work. He stayed briefly with relatives in New York City and worked for a short time in the garment district before settling in Philadelphia, where he found a job as a butcher's apprentice in a kosher slaughterhouse. Living frugally, he sent most of the $75 he earned each week to Florence, who had, by that time, given

Joe Frazier. CORBIS CORPORATION (BELLEVUE)

birth to the first of the couple's seven children. The couple eventually divorced in 1985.

A weight problem drove Frazier to the Police Athletic League gymnasium in 1961. There he attracted the attention of veteran fight trainer Yancey "Yank" Durham, who, impressed with the speed and power of Frazier's punches, encouraged him to try boxing as a career.

Frazier enjoyed immediate success as an amateur. In 1962 he won the Philadelphia Golden Gloves novice heavyweight title, and he took the Middle Atlantic Golden Gloves heavyweight championships in 1962, 1963, and 1964. Named an alternate to the 1964 U.S. Olympic boxing team, Frazier replaced Buster Mathis after Mathis broke his thumb. Frazier made the most of his opportunity, winning the gold medal in the heavyweight competition.

In his professional debut on 16 August 1965, Frazier posted a first-round technical knockout of Woody Goss. He defeated former contenders Billy Daniels, Oscar Bonavena, and Eddie Machen in 1966, and by the end of the year was ranked sixth among heavyweights. After knocking out Doug Jones in the fifth round on 21 February 1967 and scoring a fourth-round technical knockout of George Chuvalo on 19 July, Frazier stood atop the division. Only three years after launching his professional career, Frazier was poised to claim the most coveted prize in all of boxing: the heavyweight crown.

When in 1967 Muhammad Ali was convicted in federal court of violating the Selective Service Act by refusing induction into the armed services during the Vietnam War, various boxing associations divested him of his titles and revoked his license to box in the United States. (The government had already invalidated his passport so he could not fight abroad.) To fill the vacated New York World Heavyweight Championship, the New York State Athletic Commission matched Frazier against his former nemesis, Buster Mathis, who had administered Frazier's only amateur defeat in the 1964 Olympic trials. At Madison Square Garden on 4 March 1968, Frazier stopped Mathis with an eleventh-round knockout. Between 1968 and 1969, Frazier successfully defended the title four times, besting Manuel Ramos, Bonavena, Dave Zyglewicz, and Jerry Quarry. He unified the heavyweight championship on 16 February 1970 with a fifth-round technical knockout of Jimmy Ellis, who held the World Boxing Association (WBA) crown.

Yet the three most celebrated bouts of Frazier's career took place not in the 1960s during his rise to preeminence but in the 1970s against Ali. Frazier and Ali met for the first time at Madison Square Garden on 8 March 1971 in an epic brawl that pundits christened the "Fight of the Century." In the months leading up to the contest a genuine animosity ripened between the two men. Ali denigrated Frazier as "too ugly to be the champ" and mocked him as an "Uncle Tom" who was the white man's plaything. Frazier retorted that "the fists are stronger than the mouth" and vowed to do his talking in the ring. Although Ali battered Frazier in the early rounds, Frazier's tenacity eventually wore Ali out. By the late rounds Ali was spent and Frazier went on the offensive. Midway through the fifteenth, Frazier connected with a mammoth left to the jaw that sent Ali sprawling onto the canvas. He struggled to his feet and finished the fight, but the judges awarded Frazier a unanimous decision.

Frazier defended the heavyweight crown against Terry Daniels and Ron Stander in 1972 before losing it in 1973 to George Foreman, who knocked him down six times in two rounds. Although Foreman had the title, 20,748 fans paid a then-record sum of $1,053,688 to watch Ali avenge his earlier defeat to Frazier, winning a twelve-round unanimous decision at Madison Square Garden on 28 January 1974.

Frazier and Ali fought for the last time on 1 October 1975 in Quezon City, Philippines, with the World Heavyweight Title, which Ali had wrested from Foreman the year before, at stake. Boxing savants consider the "Thrilla in Manila," as Ali dubbed the fight, among the greatest heavyweight confrontations in history. Frazier punished Ali, but in the late rounds Ali unleashed a pitiless onslaught that bloodied Frazier's mouth and swelled shut his left eye. At the end of the fourteenth round, Frazier's trainer, Eddie Futch, stopped the fight.

Frazier lost a rematch with Foreman in 1976 and did not fight again for five years, battling journeyman Floyd "Jumbo" Cummings to a draw in 1981 before permanently retiring. After leaving the ring, Frazier trained fighters at his gym in Philadelphia and became a singer, performing and recording with his band, Smokin' Joe and the Knockouts.

Elected to the International Boxing Hall of Fame in 1990, Frazier compiled a record of 32 victories, 4 defeats, 1 draw, and 27 knockouts in 37 professional fights. In a career that spanned eleven years, he lost only to Ali and Foreman, and despite Ali's towering presence, it was Frazier who commanded the heavyweight division during the 1960s. Fighting him, Ali later confessed, "was the closest I've come to death."

★

Frazier, in collaboration with Phil Berger, wrote an informative autobiography, *Smokin' Joe: The Autobiography of a Heavyweight Champion* (1996). See also the interview with Frazier in *Playboy* (Mar. 1973). Although dated, John D. McCallum, *The World Heavyweight Boxing Championship: A History* (1974), contains a useful chapter on Frazier. Bert Randolph Sugar, ed., *The Great Fights* (1981), offers a detailed account of Frazier's most important bouts, especially those with Ali. Jeffrey Sammons, *Beyond the Ring: The Role of Boxing in American Society* (1988), presents a cultural history of boxing in which Frazier is discussed, and Mark Kram, *The Ghosts of Manila: The Fateful Blood Feud*

Between Muhammad Ali and Joe Frazier (2001), reassesses the significance of their memorable confrontations in and out of the ring. In *King of the World: Muhammad Ali and the Rise of the American Hero* (1998), David Remnick explores the professional and personal relationship between Frazier and Ali. Thoughtful essays on Frazier include Dave Anderson, "Beaufort, S.C. Loves Frazier," *New York Times* (10 Apr. 1971) and Richard Sandomir, "No More Floating, No More Stinging: Ali Extends a Hand to Frazier," *New York Times* (15 Mar. 2001). James B. Roberts and Alexander G. Skutt, *The Boxing Register: International Boxing Hall of Fame Official Record Book*, provides a brief but intelligent assessment of Frazier's life and career, including a useful summary of all his professional fights.

MARK G. MALVASI

FRIEDAN, Betty Naomi (*b.* 4 February 1921 in Peoria, Illinois), prominent writer and political activist who helped start the feminist movement that began in the 1960s and flowered in the 1970s by publishing *The Feminine Mystique* (1963) and founding the National Organization for Women (NOW).

Friedan was born Bettye Goldstein, the first child of prosperous Russian-born Jewish jeweler Harry M. Friedan and his American-born second wife, Miriam Horowitz. Another daughter and a son followed Bettye (who dropped the "e" from her name in 1942). Short, with a chunky body, full face, and long nose, she received admiration for her high intelligence but not for her looks in an era when beauty mattered most in girls. A formidable character, even as a child, Friedan was earthy, strongly opinionated, easily frustrated, and had a notoriously bad temper.

A lover of debate, Friedan wrote for the school newspaper while attending Peoria's Central High School from 1934 to 1938. Excelling as a psychology major at Smith College from 1938 to 1942, she served as the editor of its newspaper. Already described as a radical, Friedan wanted to remedy her lack of knowledge concerning labor unions with the aim of perhaps using the information as a journalist or union organizer. Accordingly, in the summer of 1941, she went to Highlander Folk School in Monteagle, Tennessee. Unorthodox and controversial, Highlander trained people to fight for social justice on behalf of African Americans and women.

After graduating summa cum laude with a B.A. in psychology from Smith, Friedan gathered fellowships and a scholarship to pursue graduate study in psychology under Erik Erikson at the University of California, Berkeley. In March 1943 she won the prestigious Abraham Rosenberg Research Fellowship, the largest grant available at Berkeley, and one sufficient enough to last her through the end of doctoral studies. Rather than being overjoyed, Friedan ap-

Betty Friedan, November 1966. ASSOCIATED PRESS AP

proached the award with conflicted emotions. She observed that women who obtained doctorates rarely married, and she did not want to be an "old maid college teacher." Adding to the pressure, Friedan's boyfriend at the time reminded her that he would never win such an award, pushing her to sublimate her wishes to his by refusing the fellowship. Friedan later used this episode in *The Feminine Mystique* as an example of the hostile forces weighing down women who were struggling to reach their full potential.

Moving to New York City in 1943, Friedan found work as a labor journalist with the left-wing Federated Press. In 1946 the United Electrical, Radio, and Machine Workers hired her away as a reporter for their official organ the *UE News*. In June of the next year, Betty embarked on a tumultuous marriage to Carl Friedan (formerly Friedman), an entrepreneur and advertising executive. When she became pregnant with her second child in 1952, the union fired Friedan from her job. She later cited this event as an example of society forcing women to abandon work in favor of family.

The Friedans produced three children—Daniel in 1948, Jonathan in 1952, and Emily in 1956—while exchanging physical and verbal blows. Later, when she became prominent as a leader in the feminist movement, Friedan came to fear that her abusive marriage would become a matter of public knowledge, and that the movement would be hurt by her inability to maintain a happy home. Therefore, she always avoided the issue of violence against women, even after divorcing in 1969.

Friedan spent the 1950s as a freelance author for mass-circulation women's and family magazines, writing articles

that contained muted critiques of the stereotyping and conformity of suburban life. Then in 1957 her Smith College class held its fifteenth reunion and, with the aid of two other women, Friedan prepared and distributed a detailed questionnaire for classmates. The idea for the survey grew out of the 1952 reunion, when many of the women had small children and had stopped focusing on intellectual matters. Friedan herself felt guilty that she had not lived up to the glorious future forecast for her in college, and she sought the reason why so many of the best and brightest women of her generation felt dissatisfied. Many of the survey questions were open-ended: *What do you wish you had done differently? How do you feel about getting older? Do you put the milk bottle on the table?* Most of the women professed to be happy with their lives, but 60 percent did not find fulfillment in their role as homemaker.

Friedan tried to turn the survey into an article, "Are Women Wasting Their Time in College?," which would add to a debate currently raging in the press on the appropriateness of advanced education for women. Editor after editor rejected the article, and with each rejection, Friedan interviewed more housewives, sociologists, and psychologists to add to and refine the article. She gathered masses of information, and eventually realized that she had been taking the wrong approach. Rather than disprove the popular notion that education had failed to train women for lives as wives and mothers, Friedan now began to argue that domesticity did not suit all women. She had discovered what she would term "The Problem That Has No Name," the deep-seated and confused dissatisfaction her classmates felt but could not fully articulate. Friedan found a publisher, W. W. Norton, and spent the next five years producing her masterpiece.

February 1963 saw the publication of *The Feminine Mystique,* so-named because it challenged the widespread myth that women could only find true fulfillment in the home as wives and mothers. Excerpted in the major women's magazines of the day, including *McCall's, Ladies' Home Journal, Good Housekeeping,* and *Mademoiselle,* the book combined the seriousness and rigor of the social and behavioral sciences with a lively and accessible style that grew out of Friedan's decades as journalist. Focusing on white, middle-class suburban women, Friedan provided a coherent explanation for the routine belittlement that women had experienced all their lives. In chapters on psychology, sociology, anthropology, economics, and the mass media, she argued that the feminine mystique required women to renounce their brains and deny their senses, retreat to a childlike state, and immolate themselves on the altar of their family's needs to find satisfaction in life. A distinctive aspect of the book was Friedan's use and gendering of contemporary psychology, particularly the theories of Abraham Maslow. She took what psychologists had written about men and turned it to feminist purposes by arguing that people developed a healthy identity not through housework but through commitment to purposeful and sustained effort.

Although critics noted that Friedan seemed indifferent to women outside of her race and class, the book clearly struck a nerve and became a huge best-seller. Demand for it soon surpassed supply. The book became the number-one-selling paperback of 1964, with 1.3 million copies of the hardback first edition sold. By 1970, 1.5 million copies of the paperback edition had also been sold.

In the meantime, an author tour turned Friedan into a national celebrity. A combative and not always likeable personality, she proved an enormously entertaining guest on television and radio shows. One of the more notable moments of the tour came on *Girl Talk,* a television show hosted by Virginia Graham, when Friedan found herself competing with other guests for time until she declared, "If you don't let me speak, I'm going to say 'orgasm' ten times." An intimidated Graham gave Friedan the floor, but then made the mistake of dismissing *The Feminine Mystique* by saying to her audience, "Girls, what better thing can we do with our lives than to do the dishes for those we love?" Friedan quickly pointed out on air that Graham would have no viewers or career if housewives went off to work.

In *The Feminine Mystique,* Friedan had argued that cultural attitudes were ephemeral and that women could be a force for change. Partly as a result of the book, the Equal Employment Opportunity Commission (EEOC) received a flood of job-discrimination complaints from women. However, the EEOC simply ignored women's problems,

continuing to permit such practices as categorizing help-wanted advertisements by the gender of the worker sought. Activists planning a civil rights organization for women invited Friedan to the 1966 conference of state women's commissions. Famous and fearless, she looked like the perfect choice for president of the new group, particularly when she described the goals of the organization as "to take the actions needed to bring women into the mainstream of American society—now, equality for women, in fully equal partnership with men."

Membership in the National Organization for Women (NOW) reached 1,200 by the end of 1966. In 1969, NOW held a protest at the Plaza Hotel in New York that received media coverage as far away as Hong Kong. The week of 9–15 February had been designated Public Accommodations Week to protest the common practice among upscale restaurants of barring women during certain hours, and the Plaza became the focus because it had embarrassed a number of women, including Friedan, by refusing to seat them at business lunches. The protest helped bring down barriers. Friedan served as NOW president until 1970. None of the women who followed her had such an enormous impact.

The founding mother of modern feminism, Friedan also played a significant part in other groups. In 1969 Friedan helped found the National Abortion Rights Action League (NARAL). The first Congress to Unite Women, called by Friedan, took place in New York in 1969. The 500 women who attended approved resolutions for the repeal of all abortion laws and passage of the Equal Rights Amendment. Friedan and NOW also came out in support of complete reproductive choice in 1969. To celebrate the fiftieth anniversary of women's suffrage on 26 August 1970, Friedan called for a strike that would paralyze the workplace by denying women's labor to all businesses. Scaled down, the strike became a march in which Friedan led 50,000 women down New York's Fifth Avenue at the height of the evening rush hour. She hoped that the mass display of unity would impress men in power with the seriousness of the movement, as well as bring together the many disparate women's groups.

When the women's movement turned more radical, Friedan objected. Never comfortable scorning femininity and men, she feared that radicals, especially lesbians, would destroy the credibility of the movement, since the media habitually disparaged feminists as man-haters or lesbians. Friedan's prejudice against homosexuals had been lifelong, perhaps a reflection of her Middle American background. In her book, she had warned that for an increasing number of sons, the consequence of the feminine mystique was that "parasitical" mothers would cause homosexuality to spread. Well before gay rights became a national issue, Friedan coined the term "lavender menace," a play on the Red menace of the 1950s, to describe the women that she regarded as a potential public-relations disaster.

Friedan continued to attack lesbians long after other feminists had accepted them. As the dispute with radicals in NOW illustrated, Friedan tried to expel from the movement everyone who disagreed with and everything that deviated from her original vision. She made peace with lesbians in 1977, but by then she had collaborated in her own decline.

Unable to work well with others, Friedan found herself shunted aside as women such as Gloria Steinem rose to the forefront of the feminist movement. In 1970 she cofounded an independent pressure group for women of both political parties, the National Women's Political Caucus. By 1977, however, so much of her power base had disappeared that she participated in the 1977 National Women's Conference in Houston as a delegate-at-large.

By the 1980s Friedan had virtually disappeared as a factor in organized feminism, although she continued to publish successfully. Both *The Second Stage* (1981), and *The Fountain of Age* (1993), became best-sellers. Living in Sag Harbor, New York, at the end of the twentieth century, Friedan has spent her later years enjoying the company of her children and grandchildren.

The publication of *The Feminine Mystique* marked the end of the days of doldrums for feminism. A turning point in the postwar period, the book raised the nation's awareness of the challenges faced by white middle-class women. By helping women comprehend the direction of their lives and encouraging them to make changes to reach their full potential, Friedan made an enormous contribution with her writing and extended this contribution through her political activities. A giant of the women's movement, Friedan helped women gain full rights as citizens.

★

Friedan's papers, including an oral history (1970) marking the Smith Centennial of 1971, are housed at the Schlesinger Library, Radcliffe College. Her autobiography is *Life So Far* (2000), and many of her writings and the works that influenced her are reprinted in her book *It Changed My Life: Writings on the Women's Movement* (1976). Biographies of Friedan include Daniel Horowitz, *Betty Friedan and the Making of The Feminine Mystique: The American Left, the Cold War, and Modern Feminism* (1998), and Judith Hennessee, *Betty Friedan: Her Life* (1999). A number of books address aspects of Friedan's life in the 1960s, with the most coverage found in Marcia Cohen, *The Sisterhood: The Inside Story of the Women's Movement and the Leaders Who Made It Happen* (1988), and Ruth Rosen, *The World Split Open: How the Modern Women's Movement Changed America* (2000). Cohen's papers at the Schlesinger Library include interviews that she conducted with Friedan.

CARYN E. NEUMANN

FRIEDMAN, Milton (*b.* 31 July 1912 in New York City), Nobel Prize–winning American economist and one of the twentieth century's most prominent advocates of free markets, perhaps best known for his advocacy of "monetarist" theory, which considers money supply (and changes to it) to be the primary determinant of economic activity.

The only son of Jeno Saul and Sarah Ethel Landau, Jewish immigrants from Austria-Hungary, Friedman was born in Brooklyn, but the family moved to Rahway, New Jersey, when he was only one year old. In Rahway his mother ran a small dry goods store. His father died when Friedman was fifteen years old. Friedman earned his B.A. degree in mathematics and economics from New Jersey's Rutgers University in 1932, his studies financed by a partial scholarship and a series of part-time jobs. The following year Friedman received his M.A. degree from the University of Chicago. During his year of studies at Chicago, he met fellow economics student Rose Director; they married on 25 June 1938. The couple has two children. After earning his M.A. degree, Friedman was offered a fellowship at Columbia University, where he spent the next year.

Friedman returned to Chicago after his year at Columbia and began working as a research assistant in the field of demand analysis. In the fall of 1937 he went to work for the National Bureau of Economic Research, the beginning of an association that would continue for more than four decades. During the years of World War II, Friedman worked on wartime tax policy at the U.S. Treasury Department in Washington, D.C., from 1941 to 1943, after which he went back to Columbia to work as a mathematical statistician on problems of weapon design, military tactics, and metallurgical experiments.

After receiving his Ph.D. degree from Columbia in 1946, Friedman became associate professor of economics at the University of Chicago. He was made a full professor two years later. In the early 1950s he began writing prolifically. His *Essays in Positive Economics*, published in 1953, contained a controversial essay entitled "Methodology of Positive Economics" in which he argued that economic theories should be proved only by the correspondence of predictions and facts. Even more controversial was Friedman's *Theory of the Consumption Function* (1957), in which he pointed out flaws in the Keynesian theory on the regularity and predictability of the consumption function.

During the late 1950s and early 1960s Friedman's monetarism began to come to the forefront. In his *Studies in the Quantity Theory of Money* (1956), he presented ideas to resurrect the quantity theory of money; that is, the idea that the level of prices is dependent upon the money supply. In his landmark work on money theory, he suggested that although increased monetary growth boosts prices but has little effect on output in the long run, in the short run such

Milton Friedman. ARCHIVE PHOTOS, INC.

ism, he began to be drawn increasingly into the public arena. Although he consistently refused offers of full-time positions in Washington, he served as an economic adviser to a number of Republican candidates and officeholders. In 1964 he offered his economic counsel to Arizona's Senator Barry Goldwater in his unsuccessful bid for the presidency. Four years later, Friedman served on a panel of economic advisers to Richard M. Nixon during Nixon's successful 1968 presidential campaign. He also began writing a column on current affairs for *Newsweek,* alternating with his fellow economists Paul Samuelson and Henry Wallich.

Despite his occasional excursions into the political arena and current affairs, the dominant theme of Friedman's work throughout the 1960s and beyond was an examination of the impact of variations in money supply on prices, output, and nominal income. In *Monetary History of the United States,* Friedman and his coauthor Schwartz lay the blame for the Great Depression on the ill-conceived monetary policies of the Federal Reserve. After having received a copy of the manuscript in advance of publication, the Fed's governors abruptly discontinued their policy of releasing minutes from their meetings to the public. The Fed also sought to counter the effect of *Monetary History* by publishing its own version of monetary history, written by Elmus R. Wicker.

Although many of his fellow economists scoffed at Friedman's wholehearted embrace of monetarism, his influence on economic thinking during this period is undeniable. One measure of that influence can be seen in the changes his fellow economist Samuelson made in his treatment of monetary policy in various editions of his well-known *Economics* textbook. For example, in the book's 1948 edition, Samuelson wrote: "Few economists regard Federal Reserve monetary policy as a panacea for controlling the business cycle." In the 1967 edition, the Massachusetts Institute of Technology economist allowed that monetary policy had "an important influence" on total spending. In its 1985 edition, co-written with William Nordhaus of Yale, he observed: "Money is the most powerful and useful tool that macroeconomic policymakers have."

During the late 1960s Friedman also challenged the prevailing view of most mainstream economists that government policy makers faced a trade-off between unemployment and inflation—the so-called Phillips curve. According to this view, regulators could reduce unemployment by increasing the demand for goods and services, thus ratcheting up prices. Friedman, with strong support from Edmund Phelps of Columbia University, argued that once the public adjusted to the higher inflation rate, joblessness would begin to creep back up as well. Thus, to keep unemployment permanently lower would require a permanently accelerating inflation rate. The stagflation of the

increased monetary growth brings higher output and employment growth. Money supply decreases have the opposite effect.

Friedman suggested that the vexing economic problems of inflation and short-term fluctuations in real gross national product (GNP) and employment might best be addressed by applying a simple money supply rule. Inflation would all but disappear, he argued, if the Federal Reserve Board ("the Fed") was required to increase the money supply at the same rate as growth in real GNP. In *A Monetary History of United States, 1867–1960*, co-written with Anna Schwartz and published in 1963, Friedman further elaborated on his previously enunciated call for floating exchange rates, a natural extension of his belief in the efficacy of free markets. He argued that it would be impossible to ensure stable growth in the money supply as long as fixed exchange rates were in force. Friedman's revival of monetarist theory and his development of the theory on the natural rate of unemployment added significantly to the prestige of the "Chicago school" of economics, named for the University of Chicago where Friedman taught.

Beginning in the early 1960s, just as Friedman was becoming established as the leading proponent of monetar-

1970s—a lengthy period of rising inflation accompanied by increasing unemployment—provided strong support for the views of Friedman and Phelps, forcing many economists, notably Keynesians, to reconsider their thinking. Writing in the *New York Times* in 1970, the economist H. Erich Heinemann contended that "one of the most profound intellectual changes in the last decade has been the emergence of the monetarist school [the Chicago school] of economics, led by Professor Milton Friedman."

For Friedman, the high point of the 1970s came with the award of a Nobel Prize in economic sciences in 1976. The official citation accompanying the award said Friedman was being recognized "for his achievements in the fields of consumption analysis, monetary history and theory, and for his demonstration of the complexity of stabilization theory." The year after receiving the Nobel Prize, Friedman retired from active teaching at the University of Chicago, although he retained a link with the university's department of economics and its research activities. In 1982, working again with his coauthor Anna Schwartz, Friedman published another of his studies in monetary analysis. This work, the product of more than two decades of research, was entitled *Monetary Trends in the United States and the United Kingdom, Their Relation to Income, Prices, and Interest Rates, 1867–1975*.

One of the most influential economists of the twentieth century, Friedman profoundly transformed the way in which the public thinks about and uses economics. In terms of the breadth and scope of his influence, his only rival among the economists of the past century was John Maynard Keynes, author of an economic theory that Friedman himself believed was flawed. Writing in the *Times Literary Supplement*, the economist Ezra J. Mishan observed: "Friedman masterminded a counter-revolution in macroeconomics which eventually succeeded in rolling back the once-triumphant Keynesian revolution and, through the lucidity of his writings and teaching, created countless disciples to spread the gospel." Perhaps best known for his advocacy of monetarism, Friedman also was one of the most outspoken and efficient proponents of free markets during the second half of the twentieth century. The economist's belief that "economic freedom is an essential requisite for political freedom" has won wide support in countries around the world.

★

For more about Friedman's personal life, read his autobiography, *Two Lucky People: Memoirs* (1998), written with his wife, Rose. Assessments of Friedman's economic theories can be found in William J. Frazer, *Power and Ideas: Milton Friedman and the Big U-turn* (1988), and John Cunningham, ed., *Milton Friedman: Critical Assessments* (1990).

DON AMERMAN

FROWICK, Roy Halston. *See* Halston.

FULBRIGHT, J(ames) William (*b.* 9 April 1905 in Sumner, Missouri; *d.* 9 February 1995 in Washington, D.C.), U.S. senator from 1945 to 1974, chairman of the Senate Committee on Foreign Relations for fifteen years, author of the Fulbright scholarship program, and an outspoken critic of U.S. involvement in Vietnam.

Fulbright was raised in Fayetteville, Arkansas, the fourth of six children of Jay Fulbright, a banker and entrepreneur, and Roberta Waugh, a journalist and businesswoman. He was educated in experimental secondary education programs at the University of Arkansas and then entered the university proper at the age of fifteen, receiving a B.A. in 1925. As a Rhodes Scholar at Oxford University, he received a B.A. in 1928 and an M.A. in 1931; he attained a law degree from George Washington University in Washington, D.C., in 1934. In 1932 he married Elizabeth Kremer Williams, a Washington debutante, who died in 1986. They had two daughters. In 1990 Fulbright married Harriet Mayor, director of the Fulbright Association.

In 1941 Fulbright was elected as a representative to Congress. He served as a representative until 1944, when he defeated Homer Adkins to win election to the Senate. (As a result, Fulbright did not serve in the military.) During his thirty-two years in Congress, Fulbright reflected Wilsonian principles he had learned at Oxford, promoting understanding of other cultural and political systems. In 1942 his "Fulbright resolution" helped shape the United Nations. President Harry Truman signed Fulbright's student-exchange program for international studies into law in 1946. More than 150,000 Fulbright scholars remain his legacy.

Long before the war in Vietnam, Fulbright's name suggested controversy. In June 1941 he was dismissed from his post as president of the University of Arkansas by a new board of trustees, directed by the newly elected governor, Homer Adkins (who would later be his nemesis in the Senate race). Fulbright's newspaper (one of many family enterprises) had opposed Adkins's election. He jarred the Democratic Party in 1946 by suggesting the resignation of President Truman. In the 1950s he was one of the first Washington insiders to criticize McCarthyism, the wide-ranging investigation of Communists in various branches of government, which took its name from Senator Joseph McCarthy. During the early 1960s Fulbright denounced several organizations and people exhibiting radical right-wing persuasions, including the John Birch Society and Senator Strom Thurmond. He questioned the Vietnam policy of the John F. Kennedy administration, and, as a believer in containment, countered President Kennedy's

J. William Fulbright. THE LIBRARY OF CONGRESS

decision on 22 October 1962 to "quarantine" Cuba from Soviet ships during the Cuban Missile Crisis, recommending instead a land invasion and bombing.

In two areas Fulbright remained principled but inconsistent. The first area was civil rights legislation. He voted as a southern segregationist whose racism was rooted in class rather than race, but he toned down racial provocation in the "Southern Manifesto" written and signed in 1956 by one hundred southern senators and representatives in protest against the Supreme Court's ruling in favor of school integration. Likewise, Fulbright was disgusted by Governor Orval Faubus's action in Little Rock, Arkansas, when he dispatched the National Guard to block black students' entry to Arkansas Central High School in September 1957. Fulbright was distraught over the 1963 Birmingham, Alabama, church bombing that killed four African-American girls.

The second area of Fulbright's ambiguity involved the powers of the executive branch. Fulbright reversed his position on presidential foreign policy power. A trend for consensus followed World War II, with Congress deferring to the executive branch. Fulbright defended this view until he became disillusioned over the continuation of the Vietnam War. On 14 March 1964 Fulbright's U.S. Senate speech "Old Myths and New Realities" bid senators "to cut loose from established myths." His message angered conservatives and annoyed President Lyndon B. Johnson, but his speech backed the ongoing Vietnam policy. On 27 March, Fulbright and the former vice president Richard Nixon appeared on the "Town Meeting of the World." Fulbright, still Johnson's advocate, agreed with Nixon's goal to win

the war. On 30 July, Fulbright discussed his book *Old Myths and New Realities* on the National Broadcasting Company's *Today Show,* with emphasis on diplomatic settlement rather than an "all victory route." He also pressed for détente with the Soviet Union.

On 30 July 1964 the United States was conducting a secret operation, "Oplan 34-A," which sent South Vietnamese commando patrols on raiding forays along the North Vietnamese coast. On 31 July the USS *Maddox,* an American destroyer, was also conducting a covert intelligence operation, described as "De Soto" patrol. On 2 August three North Vietnamese torpedo boats attacked the *Maddox,* which repelled the attack with assistance from planes on the aircraft carrier *Ticonderoga.* On 3 August another 34-A raid occurred. On 4 August commander John J. Herrick on the *Maddox* radioed that the North Vietnamese were preparing to attack both the *Maddox* and the *C. Turner Joy.* The Pentagon received additional radio messages from Admiral Ulysses S. Grant Sharp, Jr., in Honolulu that the destroyers were under continuous torpedo attack. Later investigations cast doubt about the reliability of the second attack in the Gulf of Tonkin. The destroyers showed no damage from the second attack. Nevertheless, following Johnson's request, Fulbright called for a resolution to show Hanoi and, by inference, Peking that the United States stood "in support of freedom and in defense of peace in southeast Asia." The Gulf of Tonkin Resolution passed the Senate with a vote of eighty-eight to two and became the instrument behind the escalation of war against North Vietnam.

Despite his early support of U.S. actions in Vietnam, by

1966 Fulbright was the war's most important critic. No legislator had ever voted to withhold support for American troops without suffering political reprisal. In March, Fulbright reluctantly voted to authorize $4.8 billion in additional military funds. There were Senate Foreign Relations Committee meetings with Secretary of State Dean Rusk in 1966 to discuss the government's position in Vietnam. Fulbright reported that from the January to the October meetings, no peace developments emerged, since the government remained firmly opposed to peace negotiations with the Communist National Liberation Front (NLF). Fulbright recommended a peace plan in his book *The Arrogance of Power,* released by Random House on 23 January 1967. It immediately became a best-seller both in America and abroad. In 1967, as bombing continued, more opposition arose from the American public. Fulbright's tactical, rather than strategic, recommendation included an end to the bombing of North Vietnam, recognition of the NLF, assurance that United States troops would be withdrawn, and consolidation of American military forces into defensible areas should negotiations fail. Max Frankel of the *New York Times* reported that the book "gropes for a doctrine of dissent that transforms mere criticism into bitter condemnation." Ronald Steel's review in the *Washington Post* was more forthcoming: "There may be arrogance in our attitude toward power, but there is also deep anguish through the nation over the use of power." Steel's review accentuated the courage of Fulbright's dissent.

By 1968 Fulbright and the Senate Foreign Relations Committee had collected enough evidence to support the rebel journalist I. F. Stone's proclamation that the administration had lied to Congress. The committee was shocked over war atrocities, particularly the My Lai incident, the massacre by U.S. troops of several hundred unarmed inhabitants of a village in South Vietnam in 1968. After the election that year Fulbright told reporters, "The majority support my stand on Viet Nam." At first he believed the new Nixon administration would quickly end the war. Fulbright soon realized Nixon's policies of "Vietnamization" and "peace with honor" represented delays. As the 1960s came to a close, Fulbright continued as leader of the Senate Foreign Relations Committee, admitting that he should have been more skeptical about the Gulf of Tonkin Resolution. He reflected, "The biggest lesson I learned from Vietnam is not to trust government statements." Fulbright died following a stroke and was buried in Evergreen Cemetery in Fayetteville, Arkansas.

When Senator Everett McKinley Dirksen learned of Fulbright's inquiry into U.S. conduct in Vietnam, he said, "You know, Bill Fulbright has a lot of guts to do a thing like this." His doubting of "outright victory" in Vietnam and his investigation of it prompted Senator Frank Church of Idaho to say, "When all of us are dead, the only one they'll remember is Bill Fulbright."

★

The Fulbright papers are located in Special Collections, Mullins Library, the University of Arkansas. Fulbright's books and articles include "The Legislator," *Vital Speeches* (15 May 1946); "American Foreign Policy in the 20th Century Under an 18th Century Constitution," *Cornell Law Quarterly* (fall 1961); *Prospects for the West* (1963); *Old Myths and New Realities, and Other Commentaries* (1964); *The Arrogance of Power* (1966); *The Pentagon Propaganda Machine* (1970); "Reflections: In Thrall to Fear," *The New Yorker* (8 Jan. 1972); and *The Crippled Giant: American Foreign Policy and Its Domestic Consequences* (1972). Randall Bennett Woods, *Fulbright: A Biography* (1995), is the definitive biography of Fulbright. William C. Berman, *William Fulbright and the Vietnam War* (1988), provides insight on Fulbright as a foreign policy maker.

Some of the best periodical articles on Fulbright during the 1960s include "Fulbright: The Wedding of Arkansas and the World," *New Republic* (14 May 1962); "The Ultimate Self-Interest," *Time* (22 Jan. 1965); "The Speechmaker: Senator Fulbright as the Arkansas de Tocqueville," *New Republic* (2 Oct. 1965); "Advice and Dissent," *Newsweek* (21 Feb. 1966); "People of the Week: A Controversial Senator Surrounded by Controversy," *U.S. News and World Report* (14 Mar. 1966); "The Apprenticeship of J. William Fulbright," *Virginia Quarterly Review* (summer 1967); "Just Plain Bill," *Time* (26 July 1968); "Out of the Woods," *Time* (9 Aug. 1968); "Just Plain Bill," *Newsweek* (12 Aug. 1968); "The Senate: Season on Doves," *Newsweek* (7 Oct. 1968). Two of many tributes to Fulbright that were published following his death were "Crippled Giant," *New Republic* (6 Mar. 1995) and "A Politician of Principle," *Newsweek* (20 Feb. 1995). An obituary is in the *New York Times* (10 Feb. 1995).

SANDRA REDMOND PETERS

FUNICELLO, Annette. *See* Avalon, Frankie, and Annette Joanne Funicello.

G

GALBRAITH, John Kenneth (*b.* 15 October 1908 in Iona Station, Ontario, Canada), world-famous economist and critic of materialism who served as U.S. ambassador to India and was an economic adviser to the administration of President John F. Kennedy.

Galbraith was the second of four children born to William Archibald Galbraith and Catherine Kendall in the farming community of Iona Station near Lake Erie in Canada. His parents were farmers, and it seemed natural that Galbraith should study agriculture. With this in mind, Galbraith attended Ontario Agricultural College, then part of the University of Toronto and since known as the University of Guelph, graduating with a B.S. in agricultural economics in 1931. He then attended the University of California, Berkeley, where he earned an M.S. in 1933, and a Ph.D. in 1934. Galbraith's doctoral dissertation concerned public expenditure and agriculture in California, a topic indicative of a future career in public service. Galbraith began his Harvard teaching career immediately after graduating in 1934. He married Catherine Atwater on 17 September 1937, the same year he became a U.S. citizen. The couple had four sons.

Galbraith's early career included both university teaching and public service as a government adviser. His keen intelligence and ability to explain complex problems in concise terms made him invaluable in both roles. During the 1930s, working for President Franklin D. Roosevelt, Galbraith became the most influential economic adviser in the United States, implementing New Deal policies intended to halt the collapse in farm incomes begun in the 1920s and regulating the supply of goods during World War II. The ideas for which he became famous, chiefly that governments should intervene to protect citizens from large corporations, were cemented in this period. In 1952 Galbraith published *The Theory of Price Control,* a book based on his wartime experience, which sealed his reputation as one of the great economists of his generation. Galbraith later worked as adviser and speechwriter to Democratic presidential hopeful Adlai Stevenson and for John F. Kennedy. Kennedy rewarded him in 1961 by making him U.S. ambassador to India, a post he held for two years.

Yet despite his deep involvement in government and education, Galbraith's major influence on the economics and culture of the 1960s came through his books *The Affluent Society* (1958), *The New Industrial State* (1967), and *Economics and the Public Purpose* (1973). From the time of his early work on agricultural economics in the 1930s, Galbraith had been interested in the balance between sectors of the economy and ways of maintaining it. In *American Capitalism: The Concept of Countervailing Power* (1952), Galbraith outlined his belief that power relations are the single most important factor in managing the economy. It was an argument that would become central to the politics of the 1960s.

John Kenneth Galbraith. THE LIBRARY OF CONGRESS

Unlike the so-called neoclassical economists of the political right, Galbraith was not convinced that market forces could achieve a stable and fair society. As an institutionalist economist he was convinced not only that governments should intervene to influence economic factors such as wages and prices, but also that they should do so to maintain the balance of power between, for example, employers and employees. In *The Affluent Society* Galbraith attacked the conventional view that the economic boom of the 1950s was necessarily a good thing. He pointed out that market forces had created an economy that wasted its wealth on goods and services that did little to improve the quality of life. The artificially high demand created by advertising and social expectations did not benefit those with limited incomes or those who lacked access to decent schools; rather, it enriched the political, cultural, and economic elite who benefited from the neglect of public services.

Written in a clear, easy style, *The Affluent Society* soon became a best-seller. Galbraith emphasized culture, history, and education as crucial for the economic well-being of nations, and he was suspect among the conservatives who dominated the economics profession. But Galbraith's influence went far beyond economics. With its focus on the role of power and vested interests, *The Affluent Society* was in step with dissenting movements of the 1960s counterculture, including antiwar protests, civil rights campaigns, and the nascent feminist movement. These ideas were expanded in *The New Industrial State* (1967), in which Galbraith developed his concept of the "revised sequence." Conventional economics saw the sequence of production

as being governed by the demands of informed consumers; firms would change their products and modes of production according to decisions made by their customers in competitive markets. Galbraith took an opposite view. In his revised sequence, which applies only to industrial economies, a small number of corporations strive to exercise and expand their power over consumers. Detached from price fluctuations because of their size, such corporations influence politics, culture, and social attitudes. This, Galbraith argued, was undemocratic, and prevented industrial societies from achieving the quality of life their affluence should make possible.

The New Industrial State also became a best-seller. The institutionalist school of economics, to which Galbraith belongs, was at the time obscure, but Galbraith's views on the structure of the economy and society gained popular appeal, especially among readers who were concerned about the relationship between corporations and government and about the rise of large monopolies. Galbraith's book gave expression to long-held suspicions that the people were being manipulated and controlled. The third book in the trilogy, *Economics and the Public Purpose,* was published in 1973 and expanded on the range of the previous two to describe the whole capitalist system, not just industrial capitalism.

By then Galbraith was acclaimed as one of the foremost economists of the post–World War II period and as a writer who brought wit and clarity to complex ideas. He was Paul M. Warburg Professor of Economics at Harvard University from 1959 to 1975, and over the course of his long career has taught at universities around the world. Galbraith holds many honorary degrees, and in 2000 was honored by President William J. Clinton with the Presidential Medal of Freedom, the highest civilian honor in the United States.

★

Galbraith's memoir, *A Life in Our Times* (1981), is a highly readable account of his experience in government and public life, and his *Letters to Kennedy* (1998), provides insight into his time in the Kennedy administration. James Ronald Stanfield, *John Kenneth Galbraith* (1996), is an affectionate biography, and Allan G. Grunchy, *Contemporary Economic Thought* (1972), is a useful contemporary view of Galbraith's thought and influence. David Reisman, *Galbraith and Market Capitalism* (1980), provides a longer view of the period.

CHRIS ROUTLEDGE

GANZ COONEY, Joan. *See* Cooney, Joan Ganz.

GARCIA, Jerome John ("Jerry") (*b.* 1 August 1942 in San Francisco, California; *d.* 9 August 1995 in Forest Knolls, California), musician, artist, and founding member of the seminal 1960s-era rock and roll band the Grateful Dead.

Garcia was the son of Jose Ramon Garcia, a musician, bandleader, and businessman of Spanish descent, and Ruth Marie Clifford, a registered nurse. Raised in a musical family, Garcia began playing piano as a child. As a teenager he was first given an accordion, which he disliked; he was later given a guitar and taught the basics of playing by his uncle. In 1947, at the age of five, two incidents occurred that would affect Garcia's life. While cutting wood together, Garcia's older brother, Tiff, accidentally chopped off the tip of Garcia's right middle finger. Later the same year, while fishing on the Trinity River in northern California, Garcia's father slipped on a rock and was carried under the rapids and drowned, reportedly while Garcia stood on the bank watching. Garcia said the death of his father left him emotionally crippled for years. Garcia and his brother went to live at the home of their grandparents, Pop and Tillie Clifford, while their mother assumed the operation of her husband's bar in downtown San Francisco to support the family.

Garcia was a quick-witted student who attended various middle and high schools in the San Francisco area but often skipped class to hang out with his friends. In 1957, at the age of fifteen, in what was a defining moment in his life, Garcia's mother bought him his first guitar from a pawnshop. Garcia was thrilled with the guitar and with the idea of playing rock and roll music, which he had heard on the radio, collected on records, and seen played in movies by early rock musicians such as Elvis Presley, Bill Haley, and

Jerry Garcia. AP/WIDE WORLD PHOTOS

Chuck Berry. Garcia also developed a deep interest in folk and bluegrass music. In addition, other popular musical acts of the early 1960s, especially the Beatles and Bob Dylan, inspired Garcia to want to be a musician.

In 1959, at the age of seventeen, tired of school and of being idle, Garcia joined the army. He did his basic training at Fort Ord near Monterey, California. After basic training he was stationed at Fort Winfield Scott in San Francisco's Presidio. However, by the middle of October 1960, Garcia was honorably discharged from the army because of his inability to adapt to military life.

Out of the army and free to pursue his artistic interests full-time, Garcia moved to Palo Alto, California, and began to practice the guitar and banjo seriously and to play in public with his friends whenever he could, especially with Robert Hunter, who became Garcia's lifelong songwriting collaborator. Garcia was fascinated with the burgeoning musical and cultural activities taking place in San Francisco in the early 1960s, particularly the poetry and experimental jazz of the Beats, as well as with the social, political, and artistic ideas circulating around the campuses of Stanford University and the University of California, Berkeley.

In 1963 Garcia married Sara Ruppenthal, whom he met in the Palo Alto arts and music scene. A daughter was born in 1964, but the couple divorced three years later. Garcia married three more times in his life and fathered three more daughters: two with Carolyn "Mountain Girl" Adams and one with Manasha Matheson. Garcia married Deborah Koons, a filmmaker, in 1994.

While living in the Palo Alto area between 1961 and 1964, Garcia played mostly folk, blues, and bluegrass styles in small clubs and coffeehouses, appearing in a number of groups including Bob and Jerry (with Hunter), the Asphalt Jungle Boys, the Sleepy Hollow Hog Stompers, the Wildwood Boys, and Mother McCree's Uptown Jug Champions. This final band was an acoustic jug combo; the group later gave birth to the Warlocks, the predecessor band to the Grateful Dead.

In 1965 the Warlocks formed, and were the first band to feature Garcia and all of the members of the Grateful Dead playing together. The Warlocks were more interested in playing electric music than the acoustic music favored by Mother McCree's Uptown Jug Champions. The Warlocks' first performances were in standard nightclubs and bars, but soon they were invited to play their trademark loud improvisational sets at local gatherings known as the "Acid Tests." The Acid Tests were primarily multimedia events sponsored by the Merry Pranksters, an antiauthoritarian group of artists and rogues headed by the novelist Ken Kesey, who organized the gatherings, the history of which is chronicled in Tom Wolfe's *The Electric Kool-Aid Acid Test* (1968). The Acid Tests typically involved the attendees taking the psychotropic drug LSD and participating in free-form dancing, film and light shows, and other activities while the Grateful Dead provided the musical soundtrack.

Although other influential 1960s San Francisco bands, such as Jefferson Airplane and the Lovin' Spoonful, preceded the Grateful Dead in popularity and record sales, the Dead became the band most identified with the colorful 1960s San Francisco youth movement, which eventually evolved into the larger nationwide hippie movement. The band members lived communally in the Haight-Ashbury district of San Francisco from 1965 to 1969, played many free concerts on the streets and in the parks, and were known for their magical and mesmerizing live performances.

The Grateful Dead recorded their first record, *The Grateful Dead*, in 1967, but sales outside of California were slow. However, by 1970 they had recorded five extraordinary albums—*Anthem in the Sun* (1968), *Aoxomoxoa* (1969), and *Live Dead, Workingman's Dead,* and *American Beauty* (all 1970)—and in 1971 had their first million-seller with the live album *Grateful Dead*. The band continued to grow in national popularity and reputation, at the center of which was Garcia's original guitar playing, songwriting, and distinctive voice. Throughout the 1960s the band toured ceaselessly and played to larger and larger audiences, especially at music festivals such as the Newport Pop Festival and Woodstock. The Grateful Dead's loyal fans,

known as Deadheads, often followed the band from concert to concert in carnival fashion.

Garcia, who had problems throughout his life with various addictions, died in his sleep at a drug treatment center at the age of fifty-three. His body was cremated and the ashes scattered both in the Ganges River and beneath the Golden Gate Bridge. Garcia's musical career with the Grateful Dead, who were inducted into the Rock and Roll Hall of Fame in 1994, defined and illuminated the 1960s ideals held by young people growing up in that era. Garcia is a major figure in the history of rock and roll music not only because of his fluid guitar playing, soulful voice, and songwriting abilities with the Grateful Dead, but, more importantly, because he embodied for the 1960s generation, as well as for later generations, the spirit of openness, experimentation, and authenticity that characterized the 1960s.

★

Biographies of Garcia include Sandy Troy, *Captain Trips: A Biography of Jerry Garcia* (1994); Robert Greenfield, *Dark Star: An Oral Biography of Jerry Garcia* (1996); and Blair Jackson, *Garcia: An American Life* (1999). Collections of interviews include Charles Reich and Jann Wenner, *Garcia: A Signpost to New Space* (1972); and David Gans, *Conversations with the Dead: The Grateful Dead Interview Book* (1991), and *Not Fade Away: The Online World Remembers Jerry Garcia* (1996). An obituary is in the *New York Times* (10 Aug. 1995).

RICHARD STRINGER-HYE

GARDNER, Edward George (*b.* 25 February 1925 in Chicago, Illinois), entrepreneur and founder of Soft Sheen Products, which became the largest African-American–owned beauty products company in the United States.

Gardner grew up in Chicago, which became his base throughout his life. He served in World War II as a staff sergeant, then returned to his hometown, where he married Bettiann, with whom he had four children. All but one of the Gardner children would eventually become involved in the company their parents founded.

After earning a B.A. at Chicago Teachers College, Gardner enrolled at the University of Chicago, where he earned a masters degree in education. In 1950 Gardner went to work in the Chicago public school system, where he would serve for the next fourteen years as an elementary-school principal. In addition to his work in education, Gardner had a part-time job as a sales representative for a black hair-care company.

For African Americans, hair care is a matter both of functionality and of something much deeper—something that has no analogue in the lives of most Americans descended from northern Europeans. On a practical level, the hair of African Americans is quite different from that of whites, and therefore the materials that work for whites are not likely to work for blacks. In the years since the Civil War, however, and especially during the 1960s, black hair-care came to have actual political and even spiritual significance. Because the texture and quality of their hair set African Americans apart from the mainstream, hair became a matter of pride, and hair care for African Americans became a special area of interest. Just as the clergyman was most likely the sole educated professional in a typical African-American community during Reconstruction, sellers of hair-care products were usually the entrepreneurs.

In 1954, just ten years before Gardner began the enterprise for which he would become noted, George E. Johnson borrowed $250 from a finance company and established Johnson Products. With the assistance of his wife, Joan, Johnson began manufacturing Ultra Wave, a hair straightener for men. That this would be the first item sold by Johnson Products says a great deal about the political implications of hair products for African Americans. Eager to fit in with the white community, many were willing to surrender the wiry, tight curls typical of African hair and undergo chemical treatments. This, however, would change in the course of the 1960s.

Recognizing that most hair-care companies created products solely for whites, Gardner saw great potential in the black hair-care market and decided to establish his own company. In 1964 he left his job with the school system and founded Soft Sheen Products Company, Inc., with Bettiann as his partner. Their first factory was in the basement of their Chicago home, where they began developing a line of straighteners, shampoos, and other products. The first two Soft Sheen products, which the Gardners tested on their children before marketing them, were Soft Sheen Hair and Scalp Conditioner and Miss Cool Five Minute Fast Set. The latter allowed users to set their hair without having to wear rollers while they slept.

Soft Sheen's inaugural product line established the company on the conservative side of the central black hair-care dilemma. By contrast, the late 1960s saw a more radical development in African-American hairstyles, the Afro. The Afro was radical in the truest sense of the word, indicating a return to roots, since the style—also called a "natural"—was the most basic and effortless coiffure for persons of African heritage. Yet it was also radical by association with the many figures who sported Afros in the late 1960s and early 1970s, including Stokely Carmichael, Huey Newton, Angela Davis, and others.

Soon the Afro spread to the world of sports and entertainment, becoming associated with stars from Jim Brown to Jimi Hendrix to the Jackson Five. Johnson Products responded by developing a whole line associated with the

natural hairstyle, including Afro Sheen, Sta-Sof-Fro, and Bantu. Gardner and Soft Sheen, however, continued to market products for African Americans who desired straight hair. For this reason, growth was fairly slow for the first fifteen years of the company's existence; only in the late 1970s, when the Afro was on its way out, did Soft Sheen begin to emerge as the market leader.

In 1979 Soft Sheen introduced a hair relaxer called Care Free Curl, which, in contrast to other such products on the market, took two hours, rather than eight, to take effect. The product was an instant success, and with sales topping $500,000, Soft Sheen had a banner year in 1979. Greater success, however, awaited the company in the years that followed. In 1980 Soft Sheen began developing a vast array of shampoos, conditioners, gels, and sprays, and by 1982 sales were at $55 million.

In 1985 Gardner turned over the leadership of the company to his son Gary, who assumed the titles of president and chief executive officer. By 1989 the popularity of the "Jheri-curl" hairstyle worn by Michael Jackson and others had helped push Soft Sheen sales above $87.2 million. During the early 1990s, however, the company fell on hard times, thanks to the growing popularity of more natural-looking hairstyles. Leadership passed to Gardner's daughter Terri in January 1996, and in July 1998 Soft Sheen was sold to L'Oreal for $160 million.

Some African-American critics have derided Gardner and his company for their association with attempts by blacks to "look white." This, however, is an unfair appraisal of a man who became one of America's most noted black entrepreneurs at a time when such figures were rare. Furthermore, throughout his years with Soft Sheen, both in the leadership and later as a powerful voice on the board, Gardner saw his purpose as one of service to the community. The company, he once said, is simply "a tool to make life better for people."

★

A profile of the Gardner family is in *USA Today* (28 Feb. 1991); otherwise, information on Gardner is scarce and consists primarily of articles on Soft Sheen. Examples include company profiles in *Black Enterprise* (Sept. 1995), *Crain's Chicago Business* (6 Jan. 1997), and *Chain Drug Review* (19 June 2000). An analysis of the ethnic hair-care industry is in *Black Enterprise* (Nov. 2000).

JUDSON KNIGHT

GARDNER, John William (*b.* 8 October 1912 in Los Angeles, California; *d.* 16 February 2002 in Stanford, California), noted educator and public official during the 1960s who served as the secretary of the U.S. Department of Health, Education, and Welfare and was best known as the founder of the public interest group Common Cause.

Gardner was the younger of two sons of William Frederick and Marie Flora (Glover) Gardner. Both of his parents were real-estate brokers. His father died when he was one, and Gardner was raised by his mother, who became his intellectual and moral compass and who taught him the value of literature and travel. Gardner married Aida Marroquin on 18 August 1934; they had two daughters. He attended Stanford University in California, receiving a B.A. in psychology in 1935 and an M.A. in psychology in 1936. While at Stanford, Gardner competed on the school's swim team, breaking several Pacific Coast Conference records. He completed his doctoral studies in psychology at the University of California at Berkeley, where he received his Ph.D. in 1938. He began his academic career at Connecticut College for Women in New London as an instructor in psychology from 1938 to 1940. Gardner continued his teaching at Mount Holyoke College in South Hadley, Massachusetts, as an assistant professor of psychology from 1940 to 1942.

Gardner left academia in 1942 to serve in World War II, during which he monitored Axis radio propaganda and then moved to the Office of Strategic Services (the forerunner of the Central Intelligence Agency), where he contributed to the development of personnel assessment tests. He was discharged in 1946 with the rank of captain. World

John Gardner. THE LIBRARY OF CONGRESS

War II shaped Gardner's interest in world affairs and his desire to live a life of action. In 1946 he joined the Carnegie Corporation of New York City, where he later served as an executive associate (1947–1949), vice president (1949–1955), and president of the Carnegie Foundation for the Advancement of Teaching (1955–1965). Gardner played a decisive role in awarding Carnegie grants to support the development of the Russian Research Center and the Cognitive Studies Center at Harvard University. He was also a frequent consultant to federal agencies.

Gardner produced his best-known book in 1961; *Excellence: Can We Be Equal and Excellent Too?* discusses the dilemma of encouraging merit in a democracy and urges commitment to higher standards in education. Gardner observed, "We don't even know what skills may be needed in the years ahead. That is why we must train our young people in the fundamental fields of knowledge, and equip them to understand and cope with change. That is why we must give them the critical qualities of mind and durable qualities of character that will serve them in circumstances we cannot now even predict." The book's message caught the attention of President John F. Kennedy, and in 1961 Gardner edited a collection of the president's speeches and position papers, *To Turn the Tide* (1962).

In 1964 Gardner published *Self-Renewal: The Individual and the Innovative Society,* which argues that both personal and societal changes are great sources of renewal and should be embraced. That same year Gardner was appointed by President Lyndon B. Johnson to chair a White House task force on education. The panel concluded that the federal government should equalize education by funding public schools and encourage qualitative improvements and innovations in local communities. Many of the panel's recommendations were enacted in the Elementary and Secondary Education Act of 1965. As a result of this work, Gardner received the Presidential Medal of Freedom in 1964.

Gardner served as the secretary of the U.S. Department of Health, Education, and Welfare (HEW) from 1965 to 1968. As the leader of a federal agency with a multibillion-dollar budget and more than 100,000 employees, he consolidated several of HEW's social rehabilitation agencies and administered many of Johnson's newly enacted Great Society programs, which were meant to end poverty, promote equality, improve education, rejuvenate cities, and protect the environment. Gardner played a large role in enforcing the Civil Rights Act of 1964, making sure that federal funds were not distributed in a discriminatory way. He undertook the giant task of launching the Medicare program, which brought quality health care to senior citizens. According to one estimate, 195 million Americans were affected by the programs supervised by Gardner. He resigned as the secretary of HEW in 1968, in opposition to Johnson's policies regarding the Vietnam War.

A few weeks after leaving this position, Gardner became the chair and chief executive officer of the Urban Coalition, positions he held from 1968 to 1970. The coalition lobbied to halt the deterioration of inner cities by tackling the problems of race and poverty that underlay the nationwide riots of 1968. New York Governor Nelson Rockefeller asked Gardner to fill Robert Kennedy's seat in Congress after the New York senator was assassinated in 1968, but Gardner turned down the job. In 1970 he launched Common Cause, a public interest group concerned with a wide range of issues, including the Vietnam War, social welfare, and environmentalism. As the chair of Common Cause he was known for supporting election-law reform and the public financing of presidential elections. Due to his great leadership in education during the 1960s, Gardner was later selected to serve on many government, academic, and private boards and commissions. He died at age eighty-nine of complications from prostate cancer and is buried in Palo Alto, California.

Gardner was prominent as an educator and social activist who exerted tremendous influence on American education, urban development, and civil rights during the 1960s. His leadership in the Carnegie Corporation led to the funding of many seminal projects in education.

★

No biography of Gardner exists. His own books provide a perspective on his beliefs and approach to public service. They include *Excellence: Can We Be Equal and Excellent Too?* (1961); *Self-Renewal: The Individual and the Innovative Society* (1964); *No Easy Victories* (1968); *The Recovery of Confidence* (1970); *In Common Cause* (1972); *Morale* (1978); with Andrew McFarland, *Common Cause: Lobbying in the Public Interest* (1984); and *On Leadership* (1990). Obituaries are in the *New York Times* (18 Feb. 2002), and the *Stanford Business School News* (Mar. 2002).

REED B. MARKHAM

GARFUNKEL, Art. *See* Simon and Garfunkel.

GARLAND, Judy (*b.* 10 June 1922 in Grand Rapids, Minnesota; *d.* 22 June 1969 in London, England), teenage star and singing sensation during Hollywood's Golden Age who began the 1960s thrilling audiences at London's Palladium and New York City's Carnegie Hall and ended the decade the victim of a drug overdose.

Garland, born Frances Ethel Gumm, was the youngest of the three singing Gumm Sisters and debuted at the age of two and a half years on the vaudeville stage owned by her father, Frank Avent Gumm, and accompanied on the piano by her mother, Ethel Marian Milne Gumm. Allegations of

Judy Garland. THE LIBRARY OF CONGRESS

sexual misconduct involving Garland's father and a minor forced the family to flee Grand Rapids in 1926 for southern California. Ethel nurtured her daughters' careers in Los Angeles, while Frank managed the Valley Theater in Lancaster. In 1931 the Gumm Sisters appeared at the Ebell Theater in the show *Stars of Tomorrow,* and the nine-year-old Garland stole the show. Her rich, commanding voice and stage savvy impressed the comedian George Jessel at Chicago's Oriental Theater in 1934, where he first introduced the act as the Garland Sisters. Garland chose her first name after the title of a popular Hoagy Carmichael song.

The sisters were signed by Metro-Goldwyn-Mayer (MGM) to appear briefly in a star-studded Technicolor short film, *La Fiesta de Santa Barbara* (1935). Roger Edens, a studio musician, persuaded the studio chief Louis B. Mayer to sign Garland to a seven-year contract on 27 September 1935. The starting salary was $100 a week. The excitement of this event was shattered by the news of the sudden death of Garland's doting father. The fourteen-year-old Garland dazzled audiences opposite the musical hopeful Deanna Durbin in the MGM short film *Every Sunday* (1936) but was disappointing in a supporting role in Twentieth Century–Fox's *Pigskin Parade* (1936), her first feature. A bit part in which she sang Edens's tune "Dear Mr. Gable" was a showstopper in MGM's *Broadway Melody of 1938* (1937) and led to a recording contract at Decca

Records. In 1937 Garland graduated from Bancroft Junior High School and enrolled in University High School in Los Angeles.

MGM had difficulty casting the plump, plain-looking teenager. *Thoroughbreds Don't Cry* (1937), *Everybody Sing* (1938), *Love Finds Andy Hardy* (1938), and *Listen, Darling* (1938) were unremarkable movies. Garland, however, caught the break of her career when Fox would not release the child star Shirley Temple to appear as Dorothy in MGM's long-awaited *Wizard of Oz* (1939), and Garland was cast instead. The result was a consummate classic that catapulted Garland and her wistfully hopeful rendition of "Over the Rainbow" into box-office heaven. Garland received a special miniature Oscar in 1940 for her role in the film.

Garland's remaining decade at MGM enlarged her star power while covering her descent into drugs and depression. She was taking amphetamines to help regulate her weight and energize her through a grueling schedule and barbiturates to help her sleep. She teamed with Mickey Rooney in *Babes in Arms* (1939), *Strike Up the Band* (1940), *Babes on Broadway* (1941), and *Girl Crazy* (1943), all fan favorites. By the time she was twenty-one she had married (on 28 July 1941) and divorced composer-arranger David Rose, had an abortion, begun using barbiturates and amphetamines, and started seeing a psychiatrist. The studio kept Garland's troubles private. *For Me and My Gal* (1942) introduced Garland's friend Gene Kelly to movie audiences, and the moneymaker *Meet Me in St. Louis* (1944) introduced Garland to her second husband, the film's director, Vincente Minnelli. They married on 15 June 1945. Their daughter Liza, who became a singer and a star on stage and screen, was born 12 March 1946.

MGM reluctantly tolerated Garland's chronic absences from work, because films like *The Harvey Girls* (1946) and *Easter Parade* (1948) made the studio millions. By 1950 the cash-strapped studio suspended Garland when her behavior pushed *Annie Get Your Gun* well over budget. A well-publicized suicide attempt followed. Her triumph at the London Palladium in April 1951 launched a series of successful comebacks. Garland divorced Minnelli in March 1951 and married her business manager, Sid Luft, on 8 June 1952. They had two children. Garland was nominated for an Academy Award for her bravura performance in *A Star Is Born* (1954), whose plot paralleled her stormy life. Her failure to win an Oscar only increased the devotion of her adoring fans.

The 1960s opened hopefully for the thirty-eight-year-old star. She had recovered from health problems that had virtually turned her into a recluse. Knockout performances at the Palladium in London in the fall of 1960 and at New York City's Carnegie Hall in April 1961 followed. The double album, *Judy at Carnegie Hall*, sold two million copies

and won her five Grammys, including one for album of the year. An Oscar-nominated dramatic role as a supporting actress in *Judgment at Nuremberg* (1961) led to leads in *A Child Is Waiting* (1963) and her final film, *I Could Go On Singing* (1963). *The Judy Garland Show*, airing in twenty-six episodes from 29 September 1963 to 30 March 1964 opposite the western hit *Bonanza*, was a critical success and had good ratings but was not renewed for a second season. Guest appearances by Gene Kelly, Lena Horne, Mickey Rooney, Jane Powell, Peter Lawford, Donald O'Connor, and others fondly recalled Garland's days in Hollywood. Her work on the show with the singers Tony Bennett, Barbra Streisand, Nat ("King") Cole, Peggy Lee, Vic Damone, and Ethel Merman showed that she was without peer as a vocalist. Most memorable were her one-woman shows, where she would sing "Born in a Trunk," "The Man That Got Away," "Rock-a-Bye Your Baby," "The Trolley Song," the inevitable "Over the Rainbow," and her personal favorite, "Get Happy."

Garland hoped that the television series would provide her with financial security. She had made more than $8 million in thirty years in show business, but she had entrusted it to business managers who had placed her $1 million in debt. Throughout the 1960s headlines chronicled Garland's cyclical dramas of despair and redemption. Australians jeered her off a Melbourne stage in May 1964 after she arrived an hour late. Days later she was reported to be near death, suffering from pleurisy and chronic hepatitis. In July of that year she was admitted to a psychiatric clinic in London after cutting her wrists. Three hours after her release "against doctors' orders," she followed the Beatles onto the stage of the Palladium at a charity show, where she "brought down the house" by softly singing "Over the Rainbow" before belting out "Swanee." She had the audience "on its feet, cheering, stamping, shouting and crying." Her 8 November 1964 appearance with her daughter Liza at the Palladium was a triumph for both singers.

Garland's divorce proceedings against Luft, finalized on 20 May 1965, were protracted, public, and acrimonious. In a July 1965 concert ten thousand fans packed the Forest Hills Tennis Stadium in New York City, an assembly that the *New York Times* described as "one of the most unusual cults in show business." Even though Garland's voice was "just a memory" and was often off pitch, her fans were unbridled in their devotion. Garland might forget the lyrics, but her fans knew the old, familiar songs better than she did. When her once vivid voice displayed signs of weakness, the vulnerability made the performance all the more endearing.

On 14 November 1965 Garland married her traveling companion, Mark Herron, in Las Vegas. They divorced on 11 April 1967, when Garland told a judge she had been beaten repeatedly in Herron's drunken brawls. She was to have appeared in the 1967 potboiler *Valley of the Dolls* but was fired when she failed to appear on the set. Garland was in court again in April 1968 charging that her twenty-nine-year-old boyfriend, Thomas Green, had pawned two of her diamond rings while she was hospitalized. Charges were dismissed. Two months later she had to be hospitalized again after falling off a stage at the Garden State Arts Center in suburban New Jersey. In November she was hospitalized with blood poisoning. For much of this time Garland was virtually homeless, living with friends or admirers and trying to find club work at $5,000 a night while fending off creditors.

On 9 January 1969 Garland married for a fifth and final time. Mickey Deans, a discotheque manager, was with her that June in their London flat when Garland succumbed to what police and a coroner later ruled was an accidental overdose of sleeping pills. She was forty-seven years old and $4 million in debt. More than twenty thousand people waited hours to view the body when it was flown back to New York City. On Madison Avenue crowds surged through barricades for a last glimpse of what little remained of their idol. Several hundred more had to be escorted away by police when the casket was placed in a crypt at Ferncliff Cemetery in Hartsdale, New York. Obituary writers carefully chronicled the enormous talent and painful vulnerability of Garland's life but could hardly have anticipated the widening affection of her many fans in the years after her death.

★

Materials on Garland's career are in the Performing Arts Research Center at the New York City Public Library. Biographies include Al DiOrio, Jr., *Little Girl Lost: The Life and Hard Times of Judy Garland* (1974); Anne Edwards, *Judy Garland: A Biography* (1975); Christopher Finch, *Rainbow: The Stormy Life of Judy Garland* (1975); Gerold Frank, *Judy* (1975); Lorna Smith, *Judy, with Love: The Story of Miss Show Business* (1975); Thomas J. Watson and Bill Chapman, *Judy: Portrait of an American Legend* (1986); John Fricke, *Judy Garland, World's Greatest Entertainer* (1992); David Shipman, *Judy Garland: The Secret Life of an American Legend* (1993); Sheridan Morley and Ruth Leon, *Judy Garland: Beyond the Rainbow* (1999); Lorna Luft, *Me and My Shadows: A Family Memoir* (1999); and Gerald Clarke, *Get Happy: The Life of Judy Garland* (2000). Joe Morella and Edward Z. Epstein, *Judy: The Films and Career of Judy Garland* (1969), and James Juneau, *Judy Garland* (1974), are two filmographies of Garland's screen work. Emily R. Coleman, *The Complete Judy Garland: The Ultimate Guide to Her Career in Films, Records, Concerts, Radio and Television, 1935–1969* (1990), and Scott Schechter, *Judy Garland: The Day-by-Day Chronicle of a Legend* (2002), summarize Garland's career in show business. Mickey Deans and Ann Pinchot, *Weep No More, My Lady* (1972), self-indulgently summarizes Garland's brief marriage to her fifth husband. Vincente Minnelli

frankly recounts his troubled marriage to Garland in *I Remember It Well* (1974). Garland's relationship to her daughter Liza Minnelli is the subject of James Spada, *Judy and Liza* (1983). Garland's childhood and early career is chronicled in David Dahl and Barry Kehoe, *Young Judy* (1975). Aljean Harmetz remembers Garland's classic work in *The Making of the Wizard of Oz* (1977). Coyne Steve Sanders analyzes Garland on 1960s television with *Rainbow's End: The Judy Garland Show* (1990). Mel Torme's troubled telling of his work on that show appears in *The Other Side of the Rainbow: With Judy Garland on the Dawn Patrol* (1970). Edward R. Pardella has produced *The Judy Garland Collector's Guide* (1999) for Garland fans. Articles include life and career profiles in *Current Biography* (1941) and (1952); James Robert Parish and Ronald L. Bowers, "Judy Garland," in *The MGM Stock Company: The Golden Era* (1973); Ernest A. McKay, "Judy Garland," *Dictionary of American Biography*, supplement 8 (1988); Wade Jennings, "The Star as Cultural Icon," in J. P. Telotte, ed., *The Cultural Film Experience: Beyond All Reason* (1991); and Geoffrey Nowell-Smith, "On Kiri Te Kanawa, Judy Garland, and the Cultural Industry," in James Naremore and Patrick Brantlinger, eds., *Modernity and Mass Culture* (1991). An obituary is in the *New York Times* (23 June 1969).

BRUCE J. EVENSEN

GARRISON, Earling Carothers ("Jim") (*b.* 20 November 1921 in Dennison, Iowa; *d.* 21 October 1992 in New Orleans, Louisiana), New Orleans district attorney who claimed that he had solved the assassination of President John F. Kennedy and who unsuccessfully prosecuted the only man ever charged with the murder.

Garrison was born to Earling R. Garrison and Jane Ann Robinson, a schoolteacher. Garrison's parents divorced when he was three years old, and his mother raised him in Chicago and New Orleans. He enlisted in the U.S. Army in 1940 and served in Europe during World War II from 1941 to 1946 as the pilot of an unarmed observation plane, earning the Decorated Air Medal. Following the war Garrison enrolled at Tulane University in New Orleans to study law and graduated with an LL.B. in 1949. He found employment as a special agent with the Federal Bureau of Investigation (FBI) in Seattle and Tacoma, Washington, but he soon became bored with his duties and returned to New Orleans. He received an LL.M. from Tulane in 1951.

Garrison then attempted to return to active duty in the armed forces, but army doctors rejected him as suffering from a "severe and disabling psychoneurosis" that "interfered with his social and professional judgment to a marked degree." Critics of Garrison's later behavior would point to this diagnosis as evidence of his incapacity for public office. After briefly working for the New Orleans law firm

Jim Garrison during a December 1967 press conference. © BETTMANN/CORBIS

Deutsch, Ketrigan and Stiles, Garrison was appointed an assistant district attorney in 1953. He married Leah Elizabeth ("Liz") Ziegler on 20 September 1957; the stormy marriage produced five children. After losing an election for criminal court judge in 1960, Garrison officially changed his first name to "Jim."

In 1961 Garrison ran as a reformer against incumbent District Attorney (DA) Richard Dowling and won. The new DA then proceeded to strap a pistol to his hip and accompany his men on nightly vice raids on Bourbon Street, in New Orleans's famous nightclub district. The press coverage of the raids gave Garrison a reputation as a crusader as well as a publicity-seeker. An enormously charismatic man, with a sharp sense of humor and immense self-confidence, Garrison stood six feet, six inches tall, was usually immaculately dressed, and spoke in a deep, well-modulated voice. A popular DA, Garrison easily won re-election in 1965.

In Garrison's world coincidences did not exist. He developed a system, called the "application of models," in which he matched suspects against a list of categories such as military service, residences, sexual orientation (although the only orientation that interested Garrison was homosexuality), and ethnic origin. When President John F. Kennedy was assassinated in Dallas, Garrison used his system to develop a conspiracy theory behind the killing. As he explained in 1977, the typical investigating methods employed by law enforcement would not work when applied

to assassinations because ordinary evidence (footprints, fingerprints, confessions) was unavailable due to the covert nature of the crime.

Two days after Kennedy's murder, Garrison received a telephone call from a former police officer who accused David Ferrie, a New Orleans pilot, of teaching Kennedy's assassin, Lee Harvey Oswald, how to shoot. Garrison's investigation of the pilot eventually led him to Clay Shaw, a prominent businessman who had served on the welcoming committee for Kennedy's visit to New Orleans in 1962. Garrison developed a theory of the killing, then found the evidence to support it, as he made clear in this oft-quoted remark, "We know what cities were involved, we know how it was done, . . . we know the key individuals involved and we are in the process of developing evidence now." Garrison believed that Kennedy was killed because anti-Castro Cubans, training in a military camp just outside New Orleans for an invasion of Cuba, felt betrayed by Kennedy's peaceful overtures to the Communist leader. Furious with Kennedy, they decided to kill him, with the cooperation of Shaw and Oswald. According to Garrison, the guerrilla team that purportedly murdered the president with shots from three different directions did not include Oswald, contrary to the findings of the Warren Commission investigation. "I have no reason to believe at this point that Lee Harvey Oswald killed anybody in Dallas on that day," Garrison stated.

When news of his investigation leaked to the press, Garrison arrested Shaw on 1 March 1967 and charged him with conspiracy to murder Kennedy. He also subpoenaed two men in New Orleans because they shared the last name of Oswald, leading the *Washington Post* to comment, "The field for Mr. Garrison is unlimited. After he finishes with all the Oswalds in New Orleans he can move his show elsewhere." Garrison shared none of his evidence with federal agencies; he asserted, "the Federal Government has as much jurisdiction over a murder conspiracy in New Orleans as has the SPCA" (Society for the Prevention of Cruelty to Animals). He believed that the FBI and the Central Intelligence Agency (CIA) had conspired to "obstruct the discovery of the truth," forcing him to conduct the investigation that they should have undertaken. It took a jury just fifty-four minutes to acquit Shaw. The *New York Times* characterized his prosecution as "one of the most disgraceful chapters in the history of American jurisprudence." Garrison blamed the verdict on the poor testimony of a prosecution witness and his own inability to link Shaw with the Central Intelligence Agency (CIA), a link that was later proven to be true.

In the next years Garrison continued to talk obsessively about the Kennedy killing and the new leads that he was investigating. He won reelection in 1969 but lost his office in 1973 after being acquitted of accepting bribes from organized crime figures. His wife divorced him, and he entered into a brief second marriage that also failed; he then remarried his first wife. Garrison returned to public office as an appeals court judge in New Orleans in the mid-1980s. The Oliver Stone–directed film *JFK,* a glorified account of Garrison's investigation, brought Garrison both renewed fame and a good deal of money, as did his memoirs that were published in 1988. Garrison retired in November 1991 and died a year later, and is buried at Metairie Cemetery in New Orleans.

While not the first person to question the official government account of the Kennedy assassination, Garrison had the power to act on his theory of a vast conspiracy to murder the popular president. His attacks on the credibility of federal officials appealed to Americans who had lost all faith in government in the wake of the Vietnam War and who wanted to believe that Kennedy would not have allowed the country to sink into such a morass.

★

Garrison's son Lyon donated 16,000 pages of Garrison's papers, files, photographs, interviews, newspaper clippings, and the transcripts of the grand jury testimony to the John F. Kennedy Collection of the U.S. National Archives and Records Administration at College Park, Maryland. Garrison also is covered extensively in Clay Shaw's papers in the same collection. Garrison's memoirs are recorded in *On the Trail of the Assassins: My Investigation of the Murder of President Kennedy* (1988). Most accounts of Garrison are sharply partisan, with the best being Patricia Lam-

bert's exhaustively researched and uncomplimentary *False Witness: The Real Story of Jim Garrison's Investigation and Oliver Stone's Film, "JFK"* (1998). Biographical information also appears in other accounts of the investigation in Joachim Joesten, *The Garrison Enquiry: Truth and Consequences* (1967); Milton E. Brener, *The Garrison Case: A Study in the Abuse of Power* (1969); Paris Flammonde, *The Kennedy Conspiracy: An Uncommissioned Report on the Jim Garrison Investigation* (1969); Edward Jay Epstein, *Counterplot* (1969); James Kirkwood, *American Grotesque: An Account of the Clay Shaw–Jim Garrison Affair in the City of New Orleans* (1970); James D. Eugenio, *Destiny Betrayed: JFK, Cuba, and the Garrison Case* (1992); and Oliver Stone and Zachary Sklar, *"JFK": The Book of the Film* (1992). Obituaries are in the *New York Times, Los Angeles Times,* and *Detroit Free Press* (all 22 Oct. 1992), the (London) *Times* (23 Oct. 1992), and *The New Yorker* (30 Nov. 1992).

CARYN E. NEUMANN

GARSON, Barbara (*b.* 1942, in New York City), 1960s radical who gained notoriety as the playwright of the 1960s black comedy *MacBird!*

Garson seems to have emerged into the world in the 1960s as a fully formed radical and a sophomore at the University of California, Berkeley, since little information exists about her youth and personal life. Garson was an active campus radical, as was her husband, Marvin. (They had one daugh-

Barbara Garson. ASSOCIATED PRESS AP

ter.) She was a member of the Young Socialist Alliance, Campus CORE (Council on Racial Equality), and United Front. She was also a key member of the Free Speech Movement (FSM) at Berkeley, whose purpose was to protect free speech on the campus, and the editor of that organization's newsletter. Garson also contributed to other publications related to the groups' campus organizing activities and espousing their issues, including the *CORE-lator* and *The Wooden Shoe.* One article in the January 1965 *CORE-lator,* "Oakland: Crisis Next Door," demonstrates her journalistic interest in labor issues.

The semester after the FSM had overturned the university's ban prohibiting leafleting for off-campus political events to support free speech on the Berkeley campus, another problem arose. This time a nonstudent, passing through Berkeley, sat down on campus with a homemade sign on which there was a single vulgarity. University president Clark Kerr had the man arrested and made quips to the press about the start of the "Filthy" Speech Movement. Members of the FSM, including its leader, Mario Savio, were understandably confused and upset about taking on this latest assault on free speech. "If the FSM couldn't afford to lose, perhaps the larger movement couldn't afford the FSM," wrote Garson in reflection. "We must disband, we decided, and let younger people (most of us were over twenty) launch future battles unfettered. I agreed." There was a second, perhaps more compelling rationale for disbanding. "We were tired; we had lived totally public lives for ten months; the private was so alluring. . . . So for high-minded, low-minded, and just pure lazy reasons, we officially disbanded the Free Speech Movement."

It was also during this time that Garson wrote *MacBird!* The play, which drew from the Shakespearean drama *Macbeth,* suggests that Lyndon Baines Johnson killed President John F. Kennedy. Johnson was vice president at the time of Kennedy's assassination in Dallas, on 22 November 1963. Kennedy was a popular political figure who especially appealed to young Americans, who enthusiastically embraced his ideals of a better world through individual action. The genesis of the script came in August 1965, when Garson accidentally referred to Lady Bird Johnson, the first lady, as "Lady MacBird Johnson" while speaking at an antiwar rally. According to the foreword to one edition of the play, "Since it was just a few weeks after the Watts insurrection and the Berkeley troop-train demonstration, the opening lines of a play suggested themselves immediately: 'When shall we three meet again / In riot, strike, or stopping train?'"

Originally conceiving of the play as a skit, Garson opted instead to create a full-length work. The Independent Socialist Club of Berkeley printed the first copies of her early draft in spring 1966. Those 2,000 copies sold in six weeks. While the play was still being rehearsed in New York, the

manuscript was circulating among the literary scene's noted figures. It received much adulation, but no publisher was willing to print it, and the Garsons created Grassy Knoll Press to publish the play themselves. The 105,000 copies of the first five printings (the first in 1966) sold out. Grove Press published subsequent editions in the United States, and Penguin published *MacBird!* in the United Kingdom. The script ultimately sold more than half a million copies. These later editions were double the length of the original.

Garson took the first draft of *MacBird!* with her to New York and showed the script to her longtime friend, stage designer Roy Levine, who championed the idea of staging the play. *MacBird!* was produced by Julia Curtis, then a secretary at the book publisher Random House, and Levine directed. Garson had continued to work on the play between December 1965 and the spring of 1966, adding dialogue and scenes under Levine's direction. The drama originally was staged off-Broadway, opening in January 1967 at New York's Village Gate. Numerous original cast members would go on to noted careers in film, television, and stage. Among them were Cleavon Little, Rue McClanahan, William Devane, and Stacy Keach. Keach won the 1966–1967 Obie award (off-Broadway theater awards sponsored by *The Village Voice*) for his portrayal of the title role, MacBird.

Several publications, including *City Lights Journal, Ramparts,* and *New York Review of Books,* featured excerpts from the script. It was later published in translation in France, Brazil, and Uruguay. Most people, especially reviewers, seemed incredulous at the play's conspiracy theory, especially because the assassination of Kennedy was still fresh in the collective American psyche. Assassinations of other progressive leaders, such as Senator Robert Kennedy and Dr. Martin Luther King, Jr., kept that event in sharp focus throughout the decade.

Although Garson used this alternate view of the Kennedy assassination in the service of her comic satire, she claims never to have agreed with conspiracy buffs. "It's quite true that I said Johnson killed Kennedy because of the plot. I have no proof and no reason to believe it. . . . but it was fun to play with it anyway." Garson later called the play "as much a product of the movement as it was of me." At the end of the 1960s Garson moved from Berkeley to Tacoma, Washington, where she worked at an antiwar coffeehouse for soldiers, strategically located near Fort Lewis, an army base. She says a compelling factor in her decision to move was to escape the continuing notoriety and attention that trapped her as the author of *MacBird!*

Since the 1960s Garson has continued her career as a playwright and journalist. As a freelance writer, she contributes to various newspapers and magazines, including the *New York Times, Ms., Mother Jones,* the *Progressive,* and *In These Times.* She has written three books: *All The Live-*

long Day (1975), *The Electronic Sweatshop* (1988), and *Money Makes the World Go Round: One Investor Tracks Her Cash Through the Global Economy, from Brooklyn to Bangkok and Back* (2001).

★

Garson recounts her days in the Free Speech Movement in "Me and Mario Down by the Schoolyard: Recollections of the Berkeley Free-Speech Movement," *Progressive* 61, no. 1 (Jan. 1997): 24–25. Additional information about the Free Speech Movement is in Hal Draper, *Berkeley: The New Student Revolt* (1965); Bettina Aptheker, Robert Kaufman, and Michael Folsom, *FSM: The Free Speech Movement at Berkeley* (1965); W. J. Rorabaugh, *Berkeley at War: The 1960s* (1989); and David Lance Goines, *The Free Speech Movement: Coming of Age in the 1960s* (1993).

LINDA DAILEY PAULSON

GAVIN, James Maurice (*b.* 22 March 1907 in New York City; *d.* 23 February 1990 in Baltimore, Maryland), airborne general, business executive, ambassador to France, critic of the military (especially with respect to the Vietnam War), and author.

Orphaned at birth, Gavin became a ward of New York State. It is believed that his mother was Katherine Ryan, but the identity of his father is unknown. Martin and Mary (Terrel) Gavin adopted him when he was two and took him to Mount Carmel, Pennsylvania, an anthracite coal–mining town where his adoptive father worked as a miner. His early life was unhappy. He experienced no compassion from his passive father and his mother, who was an abusive alcoholic. Gavin worked odd jobs and did not finish high school. At the age of seventeen, determined not to be a miner, Gavin ran away from home and went back to New York, where he joined the army without parental consent, declaring himself an orphan. He graduated from West Point in 1929 but was humiliated when he washed out of flight training. He married Irma Baulsir on 5 September 1929. They had one daughter and divorced in 1943. In the army Gavin was made first lieutenant in 1934 and captain in 1939, following which he taught tactics at West Point until 1941. On 31 July 1948 he married Jean Emert Duncan. They had three daughters.

Gavin's military career blossomed in World War II. He rose from paratrooper through various command positions and eventually leadership of the forces that invaded Sicily and, then, Italy. Though Gavin became famous for his command brilliance in World War II, it was following the war that he became a creative examiner of American military and foreign policy. A lieutenant general at the age of thirty-seven, he was on the fast track to becoming Army Chief of Staff. In 1958, however, he abruptly resigned from the army following disputes over the development of ballistic missiles. The Arthur D. Little research company in Massachusetts offered him a lucrative salary and a vice presidency, a job that gave him access to a new group of political leaders, such as those surrounding Senator John F. Kennedy, who was running for U.S. president in 1960. Gavin became an adviser to Kennedy's campaign—contributing, significantly, the suggestion for development of a "peace corps" that would allow Americans to use their education and skills throughout the world.

After Kennedy's election, Gavin was asked to serve as ambassador to France, the idea being that a soldier with his credentials would be able to work with Charles de Gaulle, the venerable military commander and then president of France. Relations with France were prickly. The United States was concerned that France would not be amenable to Western cooperation in international affairs. There was considerable evidence that the Central Intelligence Agency was involved in operations that ran counter to French interests; therefore, Gavin's task was difficult. He also had trouble financing his stay in France. He had been made president of Arthur D. Little, and the company graciously offered to pay his salary and finance an eighteen-month leave. Kennedy assured Gavin that appropriations were forthcoming to sustain him and his family.

Gavin's relations with de Gaulle were stiff at first but grew more cordial as a general trust developed. The U.S. State Department, headed by Dean Rusk, was alarmed by Gavin's brash estimates of the French view toward granting Algerian independence and exclusion of Great Britain from the common market. Gavin gained a coup of sorts, however, by helping manage the triumphant visit of President Kennedy and his wife, Jacqueline, to France. He also gained assurances from the president that he had no fear for his job. After eighteen months, however, he knew the State Department had gained the upper hand.

Civil rights demonstrations ripped the nation during the Kennedy administration as black leaders and sympathetic northerners marched on southern states to force access to public institutions. Gavin, who had served in Arizona with black regiments, was not oblivious to the segregation issue. He had insisted that the all-black 555th Regiment, which had not been committed to combat in World War II, march with the Eighty-second Airborne Division in the New York victory parade. He became increasingly engaged in cultural politics and in formulating ideas for foreign aid. He also promoted using the United Nations, creating schools for training of Foreign Service personnel, developing free-trade zones with Latin America, and pushing the Peace Corps as the means of changing international perceptions of the United States.

Gavin saw the Kennedy administration as a vehicle for

James Gavin testifying before the Senate Foreign Relations Committee, February 1966. Arnold Sachs/ CNP/Getty Images

dramatic change and, personally, as a vehicle for his ideas. Kennedy's assassination was a tragic blow. The rise of Lyndon Johnson was a double blow to Gavin's hopes for change. The escalation of America's role in the Asian war whetted Gavin's appetite for dealing with the issue of keeping "limited" wars contained. He saw immediately that the policies of Johnson and his advisers would enlarge the war until it became unmanageable. He spoke out against saturation bombing, which he felt simply hardened resistance. He suggested the creation of secure enclaves of U.S. troops in strategic areas to support the South Vietnamese, whom, he thought, had to be trained to fight their own war. Withdrawal of U.S. forces was always a consideration to Gavin, and he rejected the notion of domino Communist expansion as a naive perception of Asian politics. He was joined in some of his ideas by the redoubtable General Matthew Ridgway, who had commanded forces during the invasion of Normandy in World War II and later served as Army Chief of Staff.

A new cadre of officers, men bloodied by the Korean experience and by the cold war conflict, were caught up in making their mark in Vietnam. General William Westmoreland, once a young friend of the Gavins, was now commanding the military in Vietnam and was an adherent of Washington's policy. Gavin wrote an open letter published in *Harper's* magazine in November 1966 that called

for the end of bombing and consideration of withdrawal from a war that could not be won. The piece caused a sensation, but it did not alter policy. Gavin, spelling out his thinking, testified against the war before the Senate Foreign Relations Committee, chaired by J. William Fulbright.

Gavin turned to writing a book, an omnibus of ideas written with the *Newsweek* feature writer Arthur T. Hadley and published in 1968. Called *Crisis Now: Crisis in the Cities; Crisis in Vietnam; and Commitment to Change,* it may have been designed as a political campaign vehicle as well, for Gavin was interested in offering himself as a presidential candidate for the Democratic Party nomination. Senator Robert Kennedy's end run on Eugene McCarthy thwarted that idea, but soon Kennedy was assassinated. Gavin was dismayed. He gave little thought to the notion that he was regarded as a gadfly critic determined to keep his face and name before the public. He gave up his own plans and became a sometime adviser to Nelson Rockefeller's campaign for the presidency.

Gavin always clung to the military training and experiences that had given him fame and now fortune. His connection with Arthur D. Little was, despite rationalization, a use of his military connection for private gain. He stayed close to the airborne legend, attending reunions and making appearances at veterans gatherings. His outside activities concerned the Little company, which began to question his leadership and to seek a successor to Gavin. He agreed to a successor and continued writing his World War II memoir as well as collaborating on a biography.

Gavin searched for his natural parents without success through the Catholic Church in New York and Ireland. He found a Katherine Ryan on paper but not in the flesh. Just as with his large efforts to effect change, his attempts to find his heritage were unsuccessful. His health began to fail. He had severe back pain as a result of a parachute jump in Holland during the war, and then Parkinson's disease bent and eventually broke him. Though his home was in Cambridge, Massachusetts, the location of some of the finest medical facilities in the world, ever the soldier, Gavin turned to Walter Reed Hospital in Washington, D.C., for care and treatment. He published his memoir, *On to Berlin*, in 1978, following his retirement from Arthur D. Little in 1977. He had a second home in Florida, but he passed his final years in Washington and eventually the Keswick Home in Baltimore, Maryland. He was buried with full military honors at West Point.

Gavin challenged conventional government and military thinking in the 1960s and sacrificed his career in defense of his beliefs regarding the direction of defense spending and military intervention in Southeast Asia. Despite his limited early education, he was a creative military and social thinker who used his corporate status to prevail upon government to listen to his ideas concerning effective use of American influence on Europe and on undeveloped nations.

★

Gavin's *Crisis Now* (1968) presents a synopsis of his thinking about domestic and world problems, and his *War and Peace in the Space Age* (1958) displays his early thinking on foreign policy. Gavin's war memoir, *On to Berlin: Battles of an Airborne Commander, 1943–1946* (1978), provides a useful foundation for understanding his creativity as a commander. His article entitled "A Communication on Vietnam," in *Harper's* (Feb. 1966), is worth reading. See also his testimony to the Fulbright Committee, "Conflicts Between United States Capabilities and Foreign Commitments" (1967). The final chapters of T. Michael Booth and Duncan Spencer, *Paratrooper: The Life of Gen. James M. Gavin* (1994), are also useful. An extensive obituary is in the *New York Times* (25 Feb. 1990).

JACK J. CARDOSO

GAY, Peter ("Jack") (*b.* 20 June 1923 in Berlin, Germany), author, historian, and political scientist, whose studies of the Enlightenment and the Victorian era changed how historians viewed the people of those times.

Born Peter Joachim Fröhlich, Gay changed his name when he came to the United States, with "gay" being the English

translation for *fröhlich*. His father Morris Peter Fröhlich was a Jewish businessman, and his mother Helga Kohnke, a homemaker. Gay was their only child. Gay's father was a decorated veteran of World War I and a Social Democrat. The takeover of Germany by the Nazis seemed unbelievable to the Fröhlichs, but by 1936 they were alienated enough from the German government to cheer for the Americans during the Olympics held in Berlin. In 1938 the gentile partner of Morris Fröhlich confiscated Fröhlich's share of their company.

In 1939 the Fröhlichs fled to Cuba, among the last Jews to escape from Germany before the Nazis attempted to annihilate all Jews as part of the so-called Final Solution. They managed to immigrate to the United States in 1941, settling in Denver, Colorado, a location they chose because Helga Fröhlich had tuberculosis and required treatment in a sanatorium. Gay's father had trouble finding work at more than the minimum wage, and Gay had to drop out of East High School in his senior year to find full-time work to help support his family. Gay was determinedly shedding all vestiges of his German heritage, and he later remembered, "The . . . feeling of relief to have escaped . . . was overshadowed . . . by the fact that there were others who had not . . . and a frantic concern with what we could do about them."

Gay entered the University of Denver in 1943, working full time during the day and studying at night. In 1946 he not only graduated from college with a bachelor's degree, but he also became a naturalized citizen of the United States. Gay then went to graduate school at Columbia University, earning a master's degree in political science in 1947. In 1948 he became an instructor at Columbia, and in 1951, he received his doctorate in political science. In his scholarly career, he was interested in what had gone wrong in Germany, and his dissertation concerned the work of a turn-of-the-century political theorist, Eduard Bernstein. He published his dissertation as *The Dilemma of Democratic Socialism: Eduard Bernstein's Challenge to Marx* in 1952.

On 30 May 1959 Gay married Ruth Slotkin, a writer who had three children from a previous marriage; the couple had no children of their own. During the 1950s Gay became interested in the Enlightenment and wrote *Voltaire's Politics: The Poet as Realist* (1959). He followed this with a translation of Voltaire's *Candide* (1963). Although Gay was successful in his literary career, he was losing his hopes of tenure in the political science department at Columbia; however, the history department provided him with a tenure-track position, and he was promoted to professor in 1962. His next book was a collection of articles he had written for scholarly magazines, *The Party of Humanity: Essays in the French Enlightenment* (1964).

In 1966 Gay published three books. The first was a

Time-Life book, *Age of Enlightenment*. Another was *The Loss of Mastery: Puritan Historians in Colonial America,* a collection of the Jefferson Memorial lectures he had delivered that year at the University of California, Berkeley. The third book was *The Rise of Modern Paganism,* which was volume one of the two-volume set, *The Enlightenment: An Interpretation.* Its thesis was that the intellectuals of the Age of Enlightenment had rejected Christianity and adapted classical philosophy to create deism. An atheist himself, Gay seems to have been especially interested in how modern atheism originated.

The Rise of Modern Paganism became a landmark in historical writings because of its synthesis of divergent views of the people of the Enlightenment. Gay argued that the Enlightenment philosophers were not "responsible for the evil of the modern age," as some critics had charged. Further, the Enlightenment was not marked by "superficial rationalism, foolish optimism, and irresponsible Utopianism," as it was sometimes depicted in history books. On the other hand, the admirers of the Enlightenment were also superficial in their writings; thus, Gay rejected the "malice" of one view and the "naïveté" of the other.

The volume was greeted by praise from historians. It was regarded as sensible and rational, and it was expected to change how people regarded the Enlightenment. Among historians, the volume was considered revolutionary, as it applied common sense in understanding the figures of the Enlightenment as well-rounded human beings with strengths and weaknesses. Gay had developed a friendly, relaxed literary style that made *The Rise of Modern Paganism* accessible to the general reader. In 1967 Gay received the National Book Award for the volume.

Gay also was honored with the position of William R. Shepherd Professor of History at Columbia, a post he held from 1967 to 1969. The political and cultural failure of Germany continued to puzzle and interest Gay, and he expanded four lectures into *Weimar Culture: The Outsider as Insider* (1968). This book focused on Germany from 1918 to 1933, examining the arts of the period and trying to decipher how a humane culture could succumb to the Nazis.

Gay left Columbia in 1969 to take a position at Yale University as professor of comparative European history. Gay served as the Durfee Professor of History from 1970 to 1984, and as the Sterling Professor of History from 1984 to 1993, when he was named professor emeritus. That year the second volume of *The Enlightenment—An Interpretation: The Science of Freedom*—was published. *The Science of Freedom* was a social history in which Gay put the philosophers of the Enlightenment into the context of their own cultures. He contended that the societies of the era provided an environment in which reason could thrive. In addition, he contended that one of the strengths of the era was atheism, which, he argued, enabled people of the age to gain true, objective views of their lives and of their world. Gay posited that the American Revolution was the embodiment of atheistic rationality and proof to the philosophers that human beings had the capacity for self-rule.

Gay went on to write many other books, the most notable of which were the four volumes of *The Bourgeois Experience: Victoria to Freud* (1984, 1986, 1993, and 1995). Gay had trained in psychoanalysis from 1976 to 1983 at Western New England Institute for Psychoanalysis, and he applied what he learned to the people of the Victorian period, arguing that the Victorians were not sexually repressed and that historians had failed to consider how much ordinary people, especially the middle class, contributed to the arts and culture of the era.

Gay's books usually generated more interest among academics than the public, but his witty style sometimes won him an audience among general readers, especially history buffs. His two-volume *The Enlightenment: An Interpretation,* increased in reputation during the succeeding decades, becoming very influential among teachers.

★

Gay long felt estranged from his home country and even refused to speak or write in German for many years after fleeing Germany; his autobiography, *My German Question: Growing Up in Nazi Berlin* (1998), helps to explain his mixed feelings towards the land of his birth. Additionally, Linda Metzger and Deborah A. Straub, eds., *Contemporary Authors: New Revision Series* 18 (1986), features a biographical sketch, astute criticism by Bryan Ryan, and an interview by Walter W. Ross.

Kirk H. Beetz

GAYE, Marvin Pentz, Jr. (*b.* 2 April 1939 in Washington, D.C.; *d.* 1 April 1984 in Los Angeles, California), singer and songwriter whose career, particularly his stint with Motown Records, paralleled the development of rhythm and blues music.

The son of Marvin P. Gay, a Pentecostal minister, and Alberta Gay, a domestic worker, Gaye was the oldest of four children. He grew up in Washington, D.C., and was raised in his father's church, located near the East Capitol Projects in southwest Washington. His early family life centered on religion. His exposure to music began when he started playing piano, organ, and drums in church groups. From early childhood Gaye clashed with his father, who was stern and quick to punish for any behavior that he deemed inappropriate.

Gaye attended Cardozo High School in Washington, where he played piano for a doo-wop group called the D.C. Tones. He dropped out of school after the eleventh grade and enlisted in the U.S. Air Force but was discharged in 1957 after only one year.

Marvin Gaye. CORBIS CORPORATION (BELLEVUE)

Gaye returned to Washington and formed another doo-wop group called the Marquees. He now considered himself a professional and added the letter *e* to the end of his name. He sang a tenor part with the group. The Marquees had a following among rhythm and blues (R&B) fans, but although the group recorded "Wyatt Earp" and "Hey Little School Girl" in 1957, it was considered a commercial failure.

In 1958 Harvey Fuqua, an R&B singer, hired the Marquees to sing backup for him and changed the group's name to the Moonglows. In 1960 Gaye and Fuqua left the group and moved to Detroit. Coincidentally, an upstart record label named Motown, founded by Berry Gordy and located in Detroit, was slowly becoming a force in popular music. A 1961 performance by Gaye and Fuqua impressed Gordy so much he signed Gaye on the Motown label as a solo artist.

Motown's formula for success was to repackage the work of emerging black artists to create music that would be popular with everyone, especially to white youths. Gordy transformed what were formerly known as "race records" into a genre of popular music.

Gaye's early Motown work was limited to playing drums in the studio for recordings by Smokey Robinson and the Miracles, Stevie Wonder, and the Marvelettes (on the hit album *Please Mr. Postman*). Gaye also coauthored the song

"Dancing in the Streets," recorded by Martha and the Vandellas. His first Motown singing efforts were heard on jazz and standards recordings, but unfortunately those works were commercial failures. "Stubborn Kind of Fellow" (1962), his fourth single, became his first hit on the R&B charts. In 1963 he recorded "Hitch Hike" and "Can I Get a Witness," which were both hits. The records *How Sweet It Is to Be Loved by You* and *M.P.G.* (including the song "Too Busy Thinking About My Baby") soon followed. Also in 1963 he recorded "Pride and Joy." Later that year Gaye married Berry Gordy's sister Anna, the subject of "Pride and Joy."

In the 1960s Gaye worked with all of the major Motown producers and writers, especially the songwriting and production duo Nick Ashford and Valerie Simpson. He released many hit records, and his songs, both solo recordings and duets with Mary Wells, Kim Weston, Diana Ross, and Tammi Terrell, reached the Top Forty about forty times during this period. They included "Ain't That Peculiar" (1966), written by Smokey Robinson, and his biggest hit of the decade, "I Heard It Through the Grapevine" (1968), which was number one on the pop music charts for over seven weeks. The album of the same title sold more than four million copies and was Motown's best-selling record of the decade.

In 1967 Gaye recorded a number of duets with Tammi Terrell, including "Your Precious Love," "Ain't Nothing Like the Real Thing," "Ain't No Mountain High Enough," and "You're All I Need to Get By." They generated three albums and nine singles that reached the top of both the R&B and pop music charts during the latter years of the decade. Tragically, during a 1967 performance in Virginia, Terrell collapsed on stage in Gaye's arms, the result of a brain tumor that eventually took her life in 1970.

Gaye ceased working for more than a year after Terrell's death. He became depressed, attempting to join the Detroit Lions football team and producing and writing for a struggling R&B group named the Originals. Nevertheless, Gaye's contributions to pop and R&B music after the 1960s are virtually unparalleled in the music industry. His most influential album, *What's Going On*, which he composed, arranged, and produced, was released in 1971. It served as a political statement about the conflicts in the United States and the world in the late 1960s. It spoke against the Vietnam War, poverty, police brutality, and drug addiction while supporting ecology, peace, and nonviolence. It was the first concept and protest recording in the soul music spectrum.

Gaye's 1960s recordings remain popular. Some songs were later recorded by a variety of artists, including Mick Jagger, James Taylor, Diana Ross, and Elton John, during the 1970s and 1980s. They have also been heard in movie soundtracks and television advertisements.

Gaye's personal life following 1970 was mired in controversy, inner struggle, and conflict. Later recordings, although successful, made him a reluctant sex symbol. He fought the Internal Revenue Service, bankruptcy, and drug addiction, left Motown records, and lived in self-imposed exile in London and Belgium. He divorced Anna Gordy, with whom he adopted one child, in 1976. A year later he married Janis Hunter, with whom he had two children, including a daughter, Nona, who also became a singer. Gaye and Hunter also divorced.

Gaye enjoyed a successful comeback with the album *Midnight Lane* (1982), whose song "Sexual Healing" won two Grammy Awards. Gaye died after his own father shot him during an argument at their home in Los Angeles on 1 April 1984. His body was cremated and the ashes scattered in the Pacific Ocean.

★

Biographies of Gaye include David Ritz, *Divided Soul: The Life of Marvin Gaye* (1985); Sharon Davis, *I Heard It Through the Grapevine: Marvin Gaye, A Biography* (1991); and Steve Turner, *Trouble Man: The Life and Death of Marvin Gaye* (2000). Obituaries are in the *Washington Post* and *New York Times* (both 2 Apr. 1984).

ANTHONY TODMAN

GELL-MANN, Murray (*b.* 15 September 1929 in New York City), distinguished theoretical physicist whose influential research at the California Institute of Technology (Caltech), proposing the existence of quarks, advanced the study of particle physics and led to his being awarded the 1969 Nobel Prize in physics.

The younger of two sons born to Austrian immigrants Arthur Gell-Mann, a teacher and bank guard, and Pauline Reichstein, a homemaker, Gell-Mann exhibited a precocious intellect, which included the ability to multiply large numbers in his head by the age of three. Often bored with school, Gell-Mann nevertheless excelled in his studies. In 1944 he graduated at the age of fourteen from Columbia Grammar School. He was class valedictorian, and his graduation speech was the subject of a cartoon for *The New Yorker*. Following his father's wishes, Gell-Mann majored in physics and graduated from Yale in 1948 with a B.S. degree. In 1951 he received a Ph.D. in physics from the Massachusetts Institute of Technology.

In 1951 Robert Oppenheimer invited Gell-Mann to the Institute for Advanced Study in Princeton, New Jersey. While at the institute, Gell-Mann met Albert Einstein and collaborated on subatomic work with Francis Low. A year later Gell-Mann began researching "strange particles" at the University of Chicago. Gell-Mann developed the "strangeness" theory of quantum numbers, which ex-

plained the longevity of these subatomic particles. Gell-Mann then left Chicago to teach at Columbia University. In 1955 he married J. Margaret Dow; they had two children. The couple moved to southern California, where Gell-Mann had accepted a position at the California Institute of Technology.

At Caltech, Gell-Mann's work in subatomic physics quickly established his reputation as a brilliant, cautious, and competitive physicist whose eclectic interests included conservation, linguistics, and ornithology. Working alongside another well-regarded Caltech physicist, Richard Feynman, Gell-Mann's public popularity grew, and he was profiled in the *New York Times, Newsweek,* and *Time.*

In 1961 Gell-Mann introduced the eightfold way, a taxonomic system that organized the subatomic particles baryons and mesons into familial groups called multiplets. In 1964 scientists working with an accelerator in Brookhaven were able to prove the validity of the eightfold way model. That same year, Gell-Mann further extended this model when he published a concise yet radical paper titled "A Schematic Model of Baryons and Mesons." This paper introduced the concept of quarks, a term he borrowed from James Joyce's novel *Finnegans Wake*. According to Gell-Mann, quarks came in three varieties, which he later termed "up," "down," and "strange"; these varieties could be combined to create variously charged protons or neutrons.

Although Gell-Mann proposed the theoretical existence of quarks, he initially was hesitant to believe in their physical existence. In the mid-1960s Gell-Mann gave numerous lectures in which he dismissed the reality of these subatomic particles. Yet many physicists, including Gell-Mann, believed that even if quarks did not physically exist, they remained a useful theoretical tool. However, Gell-Mann's initial caution about the existence of quarks did not prevent other physicists from carrying out experiments designed to locate individual quarks.

In addition to his physics research, Gell-Mann played an active role in policy and politics. He was a member of the European Center for Nuclear Research, and in the late 1950s he was recruited to join a group of physicists who sought to influence federal governmental policy. This group, which was called Jason, and whose other members included Edward Teller and Francis Low, met once a year during the 1960s to advise the Pentagon on a variety of cold war military matters, including antiballistic missile systems, and on the Vietnam War. In addition, Gell-Mann frequently was asked by both United States and international groups to consult on issues such as science education and arms control. In 1968 President Richard M. Nixon named Gell-Mann to his science advisory committee.

In 1969, at the age of forty, Gell-Mann was awarded the Nobel Prize in physics. Citing Gell-Mann's "contributions and discoveries concerning the classification of elementary

Murray Gell-Mann. AP/WIDE WORLD PHOTOS

particles and their interactions," which advanced the study of subatomic particles, the Nobel Committee for Physics named Gell-Mann as the lone recipient of that year's prize.

Several years after Gell-Mann was awarded the Nobel Prize, the existence of quarks was confirmed by data gathered with the Stanford Linear Accelerator (SLAC). By the mid-1970s, quarks were considered the foundation of the Standard Model, which has been used in physics to account for all subatomic particles and nongravitational forces.

In the years following the Nobel Prize award, Gell-Mann remained active at Caltech and continued to serve as an advisory member on numerous committees. His later work included research into supergravity, and he also served as an advocate for environmental issues and public literacy in the sciences. Gell-Mann's wife died of cancer in 1981, and in 1992 he married Marcia Southwick. During the mid-1980s Gell-Mann applied his interest and skill in multidisciplinary research to establishing the Santa Fe Institute, where he worked throughout the 1990s. He retired from teaching at Caltech in 1993 and in the next year published a best-selling book, *The Quark and the Jaguar: Adventures in the Simple and the Complex.*

Gell-Mann entered the particle physics field when it was a nascent science, and his insights, especially during the 1960s, revolutionized the understanding of particles. This work significantly contributed to the growth of the field. His insistence on simplicity and elegance in constructing theories and models of the subatomic world helped intro-

duce coherence and organization to an originally chaotic system of unpredictable and little-understood particles. Gell-Mann's seminal work sharply influenced the subsequent direction of particle research. In addition, his analogies of subatomic particle behavior often were embedded with whimsical, creative, and simplified imagery, which helped to capture public interest in subatomic physics.

★

A detailed biography of Gell-Mann is George Johnson, *Strange Beauty: Murray Gell-Mann and the Revolution in Twentieth-Century Physics* (1999). Histories of particle physics include Laurie Brown and Lillian Hoddesson, eds., *The Birth of Particle Physics* (1983); and Leon M. Lederman and David N. Schramm, *From Quarks to the Cosmos* (1989).

JULIA GOODFOX

GENEEN, Harold Sydney (*b.* 22 January 1910 in Bournemouth, England; *d.* 21 November 1997 in New York City), corporate executive who, during his tenure as the president and chief executive officer of International Telephone and Telegraph (ITT), transformed it from a minor telecommunications firm into one of the most powerful multinational corporations of the late 1960s and early 1970s.

Geneen was the only child of a Russian Jewish father and an Italian mother. When not quite one year old, he emigrated to the United States with his father, Alexander Geneen, a concert manager, and his mother, Aida DeGruciani. Geneen became a naturalized citizen in 1918. Soon after the family's arrival in the United States, Geneen's parents separated, and he later looked back on his childhood as a lonely time spent at boarding schools and summer camps.

Geneen worked his way through college by serving as a runner at the New York Stock Exchange, and earned a B.S. in accounting and finance from New York University in 1934. After graduation he went to work as a senior accountant at the prestigious firm of Lybrand, Ross Brothers, and Montgomery. Geneen spent eight years at Lybrand, and then served as the chief accountant at the American Can Company (1942–1946); controller for Bell and Howell Company in Chicago (1946–1950), and Jones and Laughlin Steel Corporation in Pittsburgh (1950–1956); and executive vice president and director of Raytheon Manufacturing Company in Waltham, Massachusetts (1956–1959).

Geneen's first marriage came to an end in 1946, and in December 1949 he married June Elizabeth Hjelm, his secretary at Bell and Howell. He never had any children, a fact that may have been closely tied to work habits that gave him little time for a personal life. Prone to working weeks of seventy hours or more, Geneen, who was noted for his aphorisms, once said, "Some people accuse me of being a workaholic. I plead guilty."

In 1959 the board of directors of International Telephone and Telegraph (ITT) named Geneen as the company's president, chief executive officer (CEO), and director of the board. He held the first position until 1973, the second until 1977, and the third until 1983, but he performed most of his most important work in the 1960s. During that decade, Geneen not only transformed ITT, but established a reputation as a management innovator. He also helped to create the blueprint for the U.S. multinational corporation.

When Geneen took the helm of ITT, it had annual sales of about $700 million; by the time he left the company, he had turned it into the eleventh largest corporation in the United States, with sales of $17 billion. Profits soared from $29 million to $550 million. Along the way, ITT acquired some 250 companies in more than eighty countries. Among these were the Sheraton hotel chain; Continental Baking, the makers of Wonder bread; the Hartford, an insurance company; Avis Rent-a-Car; and scores of smaller companies that manufactured or sold products ranging from cosmetics to automobile parts. The philosophy guiding this rampant diversification and expansion was Geneen's belief that competent management and leadership could make a success of any business. His principles of business leadership focused on setting targets, making decisions based on numerical data, receiving frequent reports from subordinates, and taking judicious risks.

Harold S. Geneen. ASSOCIATED PRESS/ITT CORP.

With regard to goal setting in business, Geneen was quoted as saying, "You read a book from beginning to end. You run a business the opposite way. You start with the end, and then you do everything you must to reach it." His accounting background gave him a strong faith in the power of numbers to provide an accurate picture of economic performance, and he devoted much of his time to meeting with various leaders in the company, attempting to discern what he called the "unshakable facts" regarding each division. Management meetings, held in Brussels, Belgium, on the last Monday of each month, ran for four days and took place in a room with the curtains drawn. Top managers representing ITT's various holdings around the world would present progress reports, and then would be subjected to a withering series of questions by the CEO.

According to Geneen, "Will Rogers said he never met a man he didn't like. Well, I never met a business that I didn't find interesting." Nevertheless, he refused to invest in computers, airlines, or films, all of which he maintained were too risky. Not all of his attempted acquisitions ended in success. In 1966 ITT tried to purchase the American Broadcasting Company (ABC) television network for $700 million. The fact that this amount was equal to the company's annual sales when Geneen took over just seven years earlier says a great deal regarding his abilities as a leader; however, the ABC deal came to an unsuccessful conclusion when federal antitrust regulators put a stop to it.

During the early 1970s ITT ran into difficulties springing from charges of corruption both at home and abroad. First there were allegations that the company had subsidized the 1972 Republican National Convention in San Diego to gain a favorable antitrust ruling. Given that ITT had its hand in a wide range of businesses, antitrust scrutiny such as that arising from the ABC deal seemed almost inevitable. ITT became the target of investigations by the U.S. Securities and Exchange Commission, the Watergate special prosecutor, a Senate subcommittee on multinational corporations, and a federal grand jury. Additionally, rumors circulated that ITT had been involved in a plot by the Central Intelligence Agency (CIA) to destabilize the democratically elected government of the Chilean president Salvador Allende in 1973. ITT's subsidiary in Chile had been seized by the Allende regime, and the company later admitted that it had provided the CIA with $350,000 for "political" purposes.

Geneen served as the ITT board chairman from 1964 to 1979, and as the chairman of its executive committee from 1974 to 1980. As soon as he departed, the dismantling of ITT, which by then had come to be seen as bloated and vulnerable, began. ITT sold off most of its holdings, including its core telecommunications divisions. After his so-called retirement, Geneen continued to work ten hours a day, creating small companies and further building his investment portfolio. He wrote *Managing* (1984), with Alvin Moscow, as well as *The Synergy Myth and Other Ailments of Business Today* (1997). In the latter, he critiqued modern business trends, including the merger mania of the 1990s. Despite his own penchant for acquisitions in the 1960s, Geneen maintained that joining businesses with different management styles was an exercise in futility: "If you mix beef broth, lemon juice, and flour, you don't get magic, you get a mess." Geneen also commented on ITT's fate following his departure: "After I left, the company veered on to a new course, emphasizing consolidation rather than growth. Often I have felt the stab of frustration and regret, wondering what might have been."

In late 1997 the eighty-seven-year-old Geneen was admitted to a local Manhattan hospital after complaining of pain. He soon suffered a heart attack and died in the hospital. His secretary, Marie Serio, who disclosed information regarding his death to news organizations, did not disclose to reporters where he would be buried.

Geneen's management style and his grueling monthly meetings earned him a reputation as a harsh, plain-speaking CEO. Yet he was also widely regarded as a visionary and one of the few true innovators in twentieth-century American business. ITT under Geneen was a prototype for the international conglomerate at a time when such an en-

tity had yet to be comprehended by the leadership of even the largest corporations. As such, it possessed both the strengths and the shortcomings embodied in the phrase "multinational corporation." In the 1960s and early 1970s the company was a powerful player on the national and international stages; but, as symbols of international capitalist influence, Geneen and ITT were targets of scorn among left-wing political activists of the era.

Under Geneen's leadership, ITT diversified and expanded, yet in so doing, it became unwieldy. In hindsight, his attitude of resistance toward the computer industry seems positively quixotic. However, he managed to produce fifty-eight straight quarters of earnings growth, an impressive record by any standard. Although he claimed that numbers and "unshakable facts" governed the growth of ITT, later events suggest that the company's success owed much to Geneen's visionary leadership.

★

For a full-length biography of Geneen, see Robert J. Schoenberg, *Geneen* (1985). An overview of his business philosophy can be found in Stuart Crainer, *The Ultimate Book of Business Gurus: 110 Thinkers Who Really Made a Difference* (1998). Anthony Sampson, *The Sovereign State: The Secret History of ITT* (1973), contains an analysis of Geneen's contribution to the corporation. For a critique of his role in the history of telecommunications, see Robert Teitelman, "How ITT Blew It: How the Greatest Businessman of the 1960s Turned His Back on the 1990s," *Financial World* (1989). Obituaries are in the *Wall Street Journal* (23 Nov. 1997), *The Economist* (6 Dec. 1997), and the London *Times* (22 Dec. 1997).

JUDSON KNIGHT

GENOVESE, Catherine ("Kitty") (*b.* 7 July 1935 in New York City; *d.* 13 March 1964 in New York City), New York City woman whose murder in front of thirty-eight witnesses became an international symbol of urban crime and bystanders who "did not want to get involved."

Genovese was the first of five children born to Vincent Genovese, Sr., owner of the Bay Ridge Coat and Apron Supply Company, and Rachel Genovese, a homemaker. Genovese was a vivacious woman, an admired role model for her siblings, and remembered by her family as a "real high-energy person." In 1954 the Genovese family moved to the suburb of New Canaan, Connecticut, after Genovese's mother witnessed a murder in front of their Brooklyn home, but Genovese chose to stay in New York City, a bold decision for a single nineteen-year-old Italian-American woman.

On Friday, 13 March 1964, the petite five-foot, one-inch, 105-pound Genovese was returning home at 3:00 A.M. from

Ev's Eleventh Hour Tavern in Hollis, Queens, where she worked as a manager who kept customers in line. As usual, she parked her red Fiat 100 feet from her apartment at 82-70 Austin Street in quiet Kew Gardens, Queens. When a man stepped from the shadows and slashed her, she screamed, "Oh my God, he stabbed me! Please help me!" Some house lights came on, and the attacker left when he saw a few of the neighbors shout or quietly watch from their windows. But over the next thirty-five minutes the attacker returned twice to rape, mutilate, and fatally stab Genovese. She screamed for her life in front of the watching neighbors, but no one intervened or so much as telephoned for the police or an ambulance. Only after her death did one neighbor, at 3:55 A.M., finally notify the police at the 102nd precinct. The police officers arrived in 120 seconds and clearly could have saved Genovese and captured her attacker if they had been contacted sooner.

By 7:00 A.M. forty detectives and technicians were scouring the murder scene for clues. Even hardened detectives were surprised to hear that at least thirty-eight neighbors admitted witnessing the attack. The neighbors offered several explanations for not doing more to help, including the now infamous refrain, "I just didn't want to get involved."

News of this murder nearly passed unnoticed on 14 March 1964, when the *New York Times* printed a small police blotter item, "Queens Woman Stabbed." But over lunch eight days later, police commissioner Michael Murphy casually mentioned to the *New York Times* metropolitan editor A. M. Rosenthal his puzzlement over a murder in front of so many inactive witnesses. Rosenthal's inquiry led to a front-page story on 27 March 1964 and a book, *Thirty-eight Witnesses*, published later that year. By then the police had in custody a serial killer who had slain two women before Genovese; he was stopped by two alert neighbors during a brazen daylight burglary when they removed the distributor cap from his car and called the police. In chilling detail, Winston Moseley described slashing Genovese's larynx to silence her screams and his lack of fear of the witnesses: "I knew they wouldn't do anything. People never do."

The facts of the Genovese murder struck a chord that resonated throughout America. Immediately Genovese's name and her published photograph were internationally known, symbolizing different things to different people and becoming the subject of countless articles, essays, even songs, plays, and movies. Some simply saw Genovese as the unfortunate victim of New York City and its crime-ridden streets. Others placed her murder in the broader context of the brutality of the urban condition in all U.S. cities during the era. For yet others, the event was indicative of America in the 1960s, with its do-your-own-thing, don't-get-involved, "Me Generation" ethos. Some saw evidence

of a worldwide twentieth-century malaise in which anonymity spreads as communities break down.

More than any other of the century, this crime became a haunting symbol of the senselessness of urban street violence and of the individual's inability to rely on other people for protection. It led to national soul-searching and to changes in U.S. law. For example, most states enacted Good Samaritan laws that encouraged witnesses to intervene to stop a crime, and a few states even enacted duty-to-aid laws that obliged citizens to help victims of certain crimes. Genovese's name has been associated with many other post-1964 social reforms: victim/witness assistance programs, crime victim compensation, neighborhood watch programs, the Guardian Angels, and other grassroots anti-crime efforts.

The behavioral sciences were also heavily affected, particularly after Rosenthal's book found that the "experts" he interviewed realized they had little or no idea why people do or do not help each other. The Genovese tragedy was cited in well over 1,000 scholarly articles—more than any other incident—and literally created a new social psychology specialty termed *helping behavior* or *prosocial behavior*. Through experimentation, scientists found that, more than simple apathy, social phenomena including diffusion of responsibility, pluralistic ignorance, concerned confusion, Bad Samaritanism, and social loafing caused witnesses in groups to be less helpful to strangers in need than single individuals might be. It seemed Genovese-type incidents were all too common due to what has been called the secret of street crime—that criminals often commit crimes in public and rely on witnesses not to challenge them.

On the twentieth anniversary of Genovese's murder (10–13 March 1984), the heads of three federal agencies—Justice, Mental Health, and Public Service—met at Fordham University in New York City with one hundred behavioral scientists and lawyers. U.S. Surgeon General C. Everett Koop's voice quivered as he spoke: "I am not pleased to be here at all. I wish there were no event to commemorate. . . . I wish Catherine Genovese were still alive. She would be forty-eight years old now, maybe married, maybe a mother. Or maybe she'd still be single, a working woman, one of the twelve million single women in the work force today."

The Genovese family was devastated by their loss. They did not get involved in the trial of the killer, who was speedily convicted in Queens on 11 June 1964. His death sentence was later reduced to life in prison as convict 64A0102 at the Great Meadow State Prison in Comstock, New York. In 1995 the Genovese family stepped forward for the first time to speak with media and authorities in response to Moseley's nearly successful legal maneuvers to petition for a new trial.

Sadly, Genovese is known more for her death than her

life. She appears in this book because of that final hour of her twenty-eight years, which has been microscopically studied by criminal investigators, journalists, and psychologists. It was an hour not of her own choosing, when she suddenly found herself excruciatingly alone in an unhelpful crowd. A 1999 survey of college students found that almost all of them were familiar with the Genovese tragedy, though virtually none of them were alive in 1964. Her screams may have been ignored by her thirty-eight neighbors at the time, but they have been heard around the world and touched millions of people since then.

★

Information on the Genovese murder is in A. M. Rosenthal, *Thirty-eight Witnesses: The Kitty Genovese Case* (1964); Bibb Latane and John M. Darley, *The Unresponsive Bystander: Why Doesn't He Help?* (1970); Albert A. Seedman and Peter Hellman, *Chief! Classic Cases from the Files of the Chief of Detectives* (1974); and Carl Sifakis, *The Encyclopedia of American Crime* (1982). Articles about the crime include A. Weinberger, "What the Street Thieves Know," *New York Magazine* (23 Nov. 1981); M. Dowd, "20 Years After Kitty Genovese Murder, Experts Study Bad Samaritanism," *New York Times* (12 Mar. 1984); P. Rogers and M. Eftimiades, "Bearing Witness," *People Weekly* (24 July 1995); and Michael Dorman, "The Killing of Kitty Genovese," *Newsday* (10 June 1998).

HAROLD TAKOOSHIAN

GENOVESE, Eugene Dominick (*b.* 19 May 1930 in New York City), marxist historian who wrote extensively about the slave economy in antebellum America and gained national attention as an outspoken critic of the U.S. policy on Vietnam, testing the limits of academic freedom.

The son of Italian immigrant parents Dominick F. Genovese, a dockworker, and Lena Chimenti, a homemaker, Genovese grew up in the working-class Brooklyn neighborhood of Bensonhurst, where he befriended children of left-wing families, joined the Communist Party at seventeen, and organized for the American Youth for Democracy, a communist front group. He was expelled after three years for his refusal to follow party orthodoxy.

After receiving a B.A. from Brooklyn College in 1953, Genovese served ten months in the U.S. Army before being discharged for his former membership in the Communist Party. He earned an M.A. in history from Columbia University in 1955, and a Ph.D. in 1959. He taught at Brooklyn Polytechnic Institute of Brooklyn (1958 to 1963) and at Rutgers University (1963 to 1967).

In March 1965 President Lyndon B. Johnson, fearing the imminent collapse of the South Vietnam government, sent U.S. Marines to South Vietnam, a significant change in the direction of U.S. military presence in the country,

Eugene Genovese. ASSOCIATED PRESS AP

which up to this time consisted of military advisors. This military escalation touched off protests, including those on college campuses that took the form of "teach-ins." On 23 April 1965 the Rutgers University chapter of the Students for a Democratic Society in New Jersey sponsored a teach-in at which Genovese spoke. The transcript of his remarks is nearly ten pages long, and reveals that he told the audience of his marxist and socialist views, welcomed the opportunity to discuss matters clearly outside the scope of his classes, and generally took U.S. imperialism to task. *Targum,* the Rutgers student newspaper, condensed Genovese's remarks to "I am a Marxist and a Socialist, and I would welcome a victory by the Vietcong." This statement was picked up by the press, creating controversy far beyond the university setting.

In response to complaints from citizens and organizations, the General Assembly of the state of New Jersey ordered an investigation. The ensuing report, issued on 28 June, recommended that the General Assembly request Rutgers's Board of Governors and administration to reappraise university regulations pertaining to academic freedom and employment practices and procedures. On 6 August the board sent a report on the Genovese case to New Jersey governor Richard J. Hughes, noting that all board members were out of sympathy with Genovese's views, and that five of the nine members believed the expression of some of his views demonstrated a lack of good judgment. The board, however, stood behind its 9 April decision to promote Genovese to associate professor and grant him tenure, effective 1 July 1965, and saw no reason to revise regulations on academic freedom. The board also denied that Genovese had violated the loyalty oath.

The controversy intensified during the fall 1965 New Jersey state elections, especially when Senator Wayne Dumont, Jr., the Republican candidate for governor, demanded that Governor Richard J. Hughes, the Democratic candidate, dismiss Genovese. Former vice president Richard M. Nixon campaigned for Dumont and called for Genovese's termination, arguing that academic freedom did not apply to anyone advocating the enemy's victory in wartime. It should be noted that Genovese wanted the Vietcong to prevail in the political arena, and did not wish any U.S. battlefield casualties. Hughes won reelection. Genovese left Rutgers in 1967 for a professorship at Sir George Williams University in Montreal.

Although Genovese continued to oppose the Vietnam War, he organized opposition that foiled the radical leftist historian Staughton Lynd's 1969 bid for the presidency of the American Historical Association (AHA). Lynd wanted the AHA to go on record as opposing U.S. involvement in Vietnam, while Genovese wanted universities and professional organizations to promote intellectual freedom and avoid political entanglements. In 1969 Genovese returned to the United States as chair of the history department at the University of Rochester. On 6 July he married Elizabeth Fox, a graduate student at Harvard University; this was his third marriage.

As well as gaining attention for the controversy ignited by his criticism of the Vietnam War, Genovese also garnered attention for his scholarship, which applied a marxist analysis to the slave-era South. In his first book, *The Political Economy of Slavery* (1965), Genovese received both widespread acclaim and criticism for his analysis of the economy, culture, and ideals of the southern slaveholders. He argued that slavery ruined the economy of the antebellum South, while creating a patriarchal and aristocratic social system and society very different from and hostile to the bourgeois capitalism of the North. Genovese believed that the antagonistic worldviews of the premodern, agricultural South and the modern, capitalist North, rather than purely economic factors, prevented the southern ruling class from eliminating slavery and made the Civil War inevitable. *The World the Slaveholders Made* (1969) continued his research into the ideology and hegemony of the Southern planters.

Genovese, who relied heavily on the ideas of Ulrich B. Philips's classic *American Negro Slavery* (1918), wrote a foreword to a 1968 reprint edition that praised Philips for his insightful views on the economic failure of slavery and planter paternalism, with its concomitant lack of slave rebellion, while condemning Philips's racism. Radical and

liberal historians of the 1960s, who viewed Philips as a racist, Southern apologist for slavery, were outraged by what they perceived as Genovese's attempt to give scholarly respectability to Philips.

The rise of black nationalism during the mid-1960s stimulated the search for the roots of African-American culture and resistance. In 1968 Genovese published an essay in defense of William Styron's *Confessions of Nat Turner,* which came under sharp criticism from African-American writers for its fictional account of an actual nineteenth-century slave revolt. While Genovese rejected what he viewed as the exaggerated historical claims made by black nationalist supporters, his views evolved as he engaged in extended dialogues with some prominent African-American historians, eventually contributing to his acceptance of the importance of studying African-American culture.

During the following decades, Genovese remained steadfast in his determination to protect academic freedom and to keep politics, especially political correctness, out of academia. During the mid-1990s Genovese embraced social conservatism, receiving support from his former critics on the right.

★

World Authors, 1950–1975 offers a biographical sketch of Genovese, and his intellectual development is discussed in August Meier and Elliot Rudwick, *Black History and the Historical Profession, 1915–1980* (1986). *Twentieth-Century American Historians* (*Dictionary of Literary Biography,* vol. 17) examines Genovese's major works. Two interviews shed light on Genovese's political struggles during the 1960s: Christopher Hitchens, "Radical Pique," *Vanity Fair* (Feb. 1994); and James Surowiecki, "Genovese's March," *Lingua Franca* (Dec.–Jan. 1997).

PAUL A. FRISCH

GERNREICH, Rudolph ("Rudi") (*b.* 9 August 1922 in Vienna, Austria; *d.* 21 April 1985 in Los Angeles, California), avant-garde fashion and costume designer, style setter, and creator of the monokini and no-bra bra.

Gernreich was the only child of Elizabeth Mueller and Siegmund Gernreich, a middle-class hosiery manufacturer in Vienna, Austria, who killed himself when Gernreich was eight years old. As a young boy, Gernreich spent his spare time in his aunt's upscale dress shop, where he sketched the elegant women's fashions and learned firsthand about fabric basics, French fashion, and good clothing design. Then in 1938, when he was sixteen, Gernreich's mother joined a stream of Jewish refugees who escaped to the United States and settled in California. Gernreich attended Los Angeles City College and Los Angeles Art Center School. After college (he never earned a degree), he joined the Lester Horton Company, a regional California dance

Rudi Gernreich *(left)*, shown with models wearing clothes from his fall 1961 collection. © BETTMANN/
CORBIS

troupe, where he danced and designed costumes. Gernreich felt that he lacked sufficient talent to become a first-rank dancer and began concentrating on designing costumes for the company. He became a naturalized U.S. citizen in 1943.

His early experience as a dance costume designer had a decided effect on Gernreich's career as a fashion designer: "I became less interested in the static details, the decorations of clothes and more concerned with how they looked in motion," he said in an interview with the *New York Times Magazine*. He continued, "Dancers made me aware of what clothes did to the rest of the body, to the hands and feet and head." Between 1949 and 1951, Gernreich spent time in New York in an unsuccessful attempt to make a name as a designer. He moved back to California and started a business with Walter Bass called Jax, a store that featured simple, youthful clothes. Throughout the 1950s, he caught the eye of several fashion critics who praised his designs for their strong silhouettes and uncluttered surfaces. During the 1950s Gernreich designed shoes for the Ted Saval division of General Shoe Company, and from 1951 to 1959, swimsuits for Westwood Knitting Mills. His swimsuits were constructed without the bones and structure that were then commonly used, and he often featured sleek maillot tubes that fitted his aim to create clothing for active women. He also designed some costumes for theater. In 1959, ending his association with Bass and Westwood Knitting Mills, he opened a New York City showroom, G.R. Designs.

In 1960 Gernreich received his first fashion industry award, an honorable mention for swimwear design in the Coty American Fashion Critics competition. By 1962 fashion columnists in European fashion capitals such as Paris and London were referring to him as a major designer. His lines were now being carried in Henri Bendel and other high-end stores. In 1962 he took a Winnie award, the top honor in the Coty competition.

In the 1960s Gernreich became known as the United States' most radical designer. He showed jackets with one lapel notched, the other lapel rounded. He created boyish looks for women, faux horsehide garments, and safari suits. His designs could change drastically, showing models in girlish smocked dresses one season, and then in camouflage outfits accessorized with dog tags the next. He created the unisex look of interchangeable clothes such as caftans and bell-bottom trousers for men and women. Gernreich's collections often did not even present a single "look" for each season. In a 1966 show, one model wore a belted shirtwaist dress covering the knees, with padded bra, nylon stockings, and spiked heel pumps with gloves and a bag to match. The very next model appeared on the runway in a thigh-high mini of the same print with little heeled shoes.

Throughout his design career, Gernreich strove to free clothing from the restraints of haute couture Paris-style fashion and to give women nonrestrictive garments. Wool jersey and knits were favorite materials. Shift dresses, cut-back shoulders, and halter necklines marked his less restrictive designs. He eliminated unnecessary linings and structures like shoulder pads, lightened the fabrics, and incorporated vibrant colors such as shocking pinks with orange, red, and purple, along with other nontraditional pairings. Hemlines inched above the knee, and a *New York*

Times review in 1961 noted that "kneecaps show . . . skirts swirl and ripple, clothes fall freely, touching the body only at the bosom." Style setters such as Jacqueline Kennedy were often seen wearing his garments.

Gernreich's two most notable 1960s designs were the monokini and the no-bra bra. Early in the decade the fashion world predicted that women would soon wear topless bathing suits. Gernreich wanted to be first, and brought out the monokini at his 1964 show. The monokini was a high-waisted, boy-leg black trunk with suspender straps that went over the shoulder, leaving the breasts exposed. Voices as diverse as *L'Osservatore Romano* in Italy and *Izvestia* in the Soviet Union condemned the monokini for its decadence and immorality. Most stores refused to carry it, and many of those that did were picketed or received bomb threats. Mayors and police chiefs of seaside communities warned that women wearing the suit would be arrested. Gernreich himself said that the monokini was an exaggerated social statement that had to do with setting women free and was surprised that his firm actually sold three thousand suits.

In 1965 Gernreich designed the no-bra bra for Exquisite Form, a lingerie company. The bra consisted of two cups of soft, transparent nylon attached to shoulder straps, with a narrow band of stretch fabric encircling the rib cage. The bra allowed breasts to look natural, freeing them from the highly constructed padding, boning, and topstitching that characterized bras of the era. In following years, he extended the line to include the no-front bra to accommodate slit-to-the-wait necklines, a no-side version worn with dresses with deep armholes, and the no-back bra, anchored around the waist rather than the rib cage. The no-bra bra became as well known as the monokini, a retail success that sold well in the United States and throughout Europe.

Not everyone was taken with Gernreich. When he received his Coty award in 1963, the designer Norman Norell returned his own award in protest. Norell later regretted his action, saying he was wrong and that Gernreich had grown in talent. John Fairchild, publisher of the influential *Womens Wear Daily*, criticized Gernreich's clothing as being badly constructed. Gernreich entered an agreement to produce a line for the department-store chain Montgomery Ward, thereby violating an unwritten fashion industry rule that real designers do not sell to chain stores.

Gernreich himself noted that his greatest contribution was designing clothes for young American women. "For three hundred years, the French woman dictated fashion. Now at last, the American woman is coming into fashion maturity," he said. Many of his original fashion concepts, such as the mini skirt and patterned stockings, are now commonplace fashions.

In 1968 Gernreich announced that he was taking a year off to relax. In fact, he confided to friends, he was growing disenchanted with the pressures of running a design business. Also, the dawning of an era of antiwar demonstrations, War on Hunger, and an antiestablishment social mood made outrageously expensive clothes seem out of place. Even so, Gernreich returned to work a year later and did continue to design clothing. Through the 1970s he also began working outside the clothing industry, designed furniture, quilts, and costumes for a dance troupe, as well as launching a fragrance and a line of gourmet soups. Gernreich died of cancer. His homosexuality was not widely known, but he was survived by Oreste Pucciani, his partner since 1954.

Gernreich was widely celebrated during his lifetime. The museum at the New York State University Fashion Institute of Technology had a show of his work in 1967, and the Coty American Fashion Critics awarded him four times in 1960, 1963, 1966, and 1967. He was admitted to the Coty American Fashion Critics' Hall of Fame in 1967. He received industry awards from the Wool Knit Association (1960), and the Knitted Textile Association (1975). Gernreich was singled out for awards from retailers Neiman Marcus (1961) and Filene's (1966). He received a Special Tribute from the Council of Fashion Designers of America in 1985.

★

The Rudi Gernreich Book (1991) is a fashion biography of Gernreich written by his favorite model and close friend, Peggy Moffitt, with photography by William Claxton. There are lengthy sections about Gernreich in Joel Lobenthal, *Radical Rags: Fashions of the Sixties* (1990). For information about Gernreich at the height of his career, see Gloria Steinem, "Gernreich's Progress; or, Eve Unbound," *New York Times Magazine* (31 Jan. 1965). An obituary is in the *New York Times* (22 Apr. 1985).

WILLIAM J. MALONEY

GETTY, J(ean) Paul (*b.* 15 December 1892 in Minneapolis, Minnesota; *d.* 6 June 1976 in London, England), billionaire oil producer and founder of the Getty Oil Company who had amassed a great fortune by the 1960s.

Getty was the son of George Franklin Getty, an insurance lawyer and an oilman, and Sarah McPherson Risher. The Gettys lost their ten-year-old daughter to typhoid fever in 1890. Sarah had her second child, Getty, at the age of forty. Sarah never gave her son any physical affection. Getty's unemotional style characterized his approach to business and was the reason family members were kept at a distance his entire life. He decided early on that he needed little else than money. Getty attended the University of Southern California and the University of California, Berkeley, from 1909 to 1911. In 1913 he transferred to Oxford University

J. Paul Getty, October 1966. ASSOCIATED PRESS AP

as one of the wealthiest men in the world, but most of his money was tied up in corporate structures and oil in the ground. Getty admitted that he seldom carried more than $25 with him.

Getty moved to Europe in 1960 to escape U.S. taxes. Sutton Place, his home and office, was a 700-acre manor outside London. He bought the estate at a bargain price, because its owner, the duke of Sutherland, was in financial trouble. Getty made worldwide headlines when he had a pay phone installed for his guests and numerous workers. "My friends will understand, and, as for spongers, well, I just don't care," he commented. He prized the large and elegant mansion for the bargain price he paid for it. He was also thrifty in other ways—for example, he washed his own socks and wore rumpled suits and sweaters worn at the elbow.

Although Getty was admired by many Americans for his great wealth, he did not give to philanthropic organizations or to individuals. He received over three thousand letters a month from individuals asking for money. Getty told the media, "I never give money to individuals because it's unrewarding and wrong. If . . . I could make a real contribution toward solving the problems of world poverty, I'd give away 99.5% of all I have immediately." Getty always kept personal control of his financial empire, often working sixteen to eighteen hours a day. He told the media in 1965, "I can't remember a single day of vacation in the last 45 years that was not somehow interrupted by a cable, telegram or telephone call" related to business. In contrast to his corporate counterparts, Getty continued micromanaging his holdings during the 1960s and into the early 1970s. He lamented that none of his sons was in the oil business. "I suppose I would have liked to keep the Getty name, but the name isn't enough. You have to be qualified too. There is nobody to step into my shoes." George F. Getty II was expected to take over until he developed sharp differences with his father over the future direction of the company. Jean Ronald proved incapable, and Gordon Peter wanted to pursue a career in the opera.

Getty spent a great deal of time in the early and mid-1960s reflecting on his career and writing about it. He wrote about everything, including the history of the oil business, art collecting, and how to succeed in business. His best-known book, *My Life and Fortunes*, was published in 1963. *How to Be Rich* was published by Playboy Press in 1965. The book included a series of articles written for "young executives and college students" who read *Playboy*. Getty wrote about his hobby of art collecting in a book titled *The Joys of Collecting* (1965). He published *The Golden Age* in 1968 and *How to Be a Successful Executive* in 1971.

In a complicated rearrangement in 1967 Getty merged the Tidewater Oil Company and the Mission Development Company into the Getty Oil Company. The surviving com-

in England, where he took a degree in political science and economics in 1914. Although he is on record for having received a diploma, there is no record that he completed the requirements.

Getty married and divorced five times. His first wife was Jeanette Dumont; they married in 1923 and had one son. In 1926 he married Allene Ashby; they divorced a year later. He then married Adolphine Helmle in 1928, which whom he had one son. In 1932 he married Ann Rourk, with whom he had two sons. His last marriage, in 1939, was to Louise Lynch; they had one son.

In 1914 Getty began a partnership with his father, buying and selling oil leases in Tulsa, Oklahoma. Getty became the president and general manager of George F. Getty, Inc., in 1930. In the largest business coup of his career, Getty acquired half the interest rights to Saudi Arabia's Neutral Zone in 1949 and hit oil in 1953, an investment of $30 million that produced more than sixteen million barrels of oil a year. He won numerical control of renamed Tidewater Oil Company in 1951 and obtained control of Mission Development Corporation and its holdings in Tidewater Oil Company and Skelly Oil in 1953. In 1956 he made Pacific Western into Getty Oil Company, the master link in the Getty holdings and world's largest personally controlled oil company. Getty entered the 1960s pany had assets of more than $3 billion, a figure that multiplied after oil price increases in the early 1970s. Getty was asked what satisfaction he derived from making so much money. He replied, "It is just to prove that you can keep step with the regiment," alluding to Exxon, Gulf, and Texaco, his rivals.

At Sutton Place, Getty began collecting important artwork. In 1969 he began construction of the Getty Museum, a replica of an ancient Roman villa, on his Malibu, California, property. He made art purchases to avoid paying taxes and sheltered the largest part of his income by donating art objects to museums, especially his own. The museum began as a small collection of Greek and Roman antiquities, eighteenth-century French furniture, and European paintings. Later it included works by Tintoretto, Titian, Thomas Gainsborough, George Romney, Peter Paul Rubens, Jean Renoir, Edgar Degas, and Claude Monet. By the time the museum opened in 1974, Getty's empire consisted of two hundred companies, twelve thousand employees, and annual profits of $142 million. The museum building cost $17 million to construct and housed a collection with an estimated worth of $200 million. In addition to a large endowment, Getty made a promise (later fulfilled) to leave the major part of his holdings to the J. Paul Getty Museum.

Aside from his tremendous wealth and frugality, Getty was most famous in the 1960s for his shortcomings as a family man. All his wives were eighteen or younger at the time he married them. Getty was twice a bigamist in the 1930s and clearly lacked the ability to maintain relationships with his wives or his children. In 1962 his son Gordon asked for an increase in the payments he received from the Sarah Getty Trust, and in 1966 filed a lawsuit against his father, claiming $7.4 million in unpaid dividends from the trust. Getty had resisted making payments, in large part to avoid tax penalties. In 1973 Getty's grandson, J. Paul Getty III, was kidnapped, and the ransom demanded was $16 million. Getty refused to pay. After part of an ear was sent to a newspaper in Rome and was confirmed as his grandson's, Getty reluctantly agreed to loan Eugene Paul, his son, $850,000 at interest to complete a reduced ransom offer, which the kidnappers accepted.

Getty died at Sutton Place of heart failure. He is buried on his Malibu estate. His fortune remains a phenomenon to observers worldwide. He took such risks as buying oil stock during the depression and succeeded, thus making his name known. His wealth influenced government, politics, and Wall Street. Getty was an oil producer who defined the way the oil business operates. He credited his fortune to his father's foresight, his strong work ethic, and his own luck and ingenuity. The Getty Oil Company became one of the largest oil producers and distributors in the world.

★

Getty's autobiographies are *My Life and Fortunes* (1963), *How to Be Rich* (1965), and *As I See It: The Autobiography of J. Paul Getty* (1976). Biographies include Ralph Hewins, *The Richest American* (1960); Russell Miller, *The House of Getty* (1985); Robert Lenzner, *The Great Getty: The Life and Loves of J. Paul Getty, The Richest Man in the World* (1986); and John Pearson, *Painfully Rich: The Outrageous Fortune and Misfortunes of the Heirs of J. Paul Getty* (1995).

REED B. MARKHAM

GIANCANA, Salvatore ("Sam") (*b.* 15 June 1908 in Chicago, Illinois; *d.* 19 June 1975 in Oak Park, Chicago), crime syndicate boss who began his career as a "soldier" for Al Capone, controlled organized crime in Chicago between 1956 and 1966, and was an ally and later enemy of the Kennedy family.

The son of Antonino Giancana, a fruit seller who had emigrated from Sicily, and Antonia DiSimone, Giancana began life in poverty in an area of Chicago's near west side known as the Patch. With a reputation for violence, Giancana dropped out of elementary school and began a life of crime with a gang, the 42s. In 1925 he was jailed for auto theft and in 1927 was imprisoned for burglary. By his early twenties Giancana was working as an enforcer and "wheelman," or driver, for Al Capone under the direction of Paul Ricca and Tony Accardo. One of the most violent criminals in U.S. history, Giancana acquired the nickname "Momo," from the slang term "mooner," meaning "madman." During the draft for WWII, when he was declared 4F (unfit for active service), army doctors labeled him a "constitutional psychopath." On 26 September 1933 he married Angeline DeTolve; they had three daughters. His eldest daughter, Antoinette, wrote a *New York Times* best-seller, *Mafia Princess* (1984), and a television movie was made based on the book (1986).

After a spell in prison in the early 1940s, Giancana began to take over the numbers racket from black mobsters in Chicago, and by 1952 he controlled illegal gambling in the city for his boss Tony Accardo. In the 1950s, as FBI investigations into organized crime intensified, Giancana took over from Accardo. After the death of his wife in 1954, Giancana began the most successful period of his career, which would last until the mid-1960s. Giancana's influence spread to the highest levels of government, as he was part of a new generation of organized criminals, a generation that relied on political influence as much as violence. With many of the Mafia old guard either imprisoned, elderly, or dead, Giancana's empire grew quickly. After the fall of Cuba to Fidel Castro in 1959, crime syndicates had to find new outlets for their gambling and prostitution businesses.

Sam Giancana. ASSOCIATED PRESS AP

Giancana bought controlling stakes in hotels and casinos in Las Vegas, a move that brought him into contact with celebrities and politicians.

Giancana had many affairs with famous women, including the singers Keeley Smith and Phyllis McGuire. He was a close associate of the entertainer Peter Lawford, brother-in-law of President John F. Kennedy, and a friend of Frank Sinatra. With McGuire he was a frequent guest at Sinatra's retreat at Lake Tahoe, Nevada. Giancana and President Kennedy even shared a mistress, Judith Katherine Exner, though Kennedy ended the affair in 1962 when he learned of her connection with the gangster.

Giancana had strong political ambitions. He controlled local police chiefs and mayors as well as labor unions, and sought favors from the federal government. Between them, Giancana and Sinatra have been credited with helping to deliver votes in Chicago and Illinois to Kennedy in the 1960 presidential election, a victory crucial to Kennedy's win.

In 1957 Senator Robert Kennedy set up the McClellan Committee to look into organized crime. However, although the government was outwardly hostile to the Mob, in the early 1960s the two groups shared a desire to end Castro's grip on Cuba. Giancana worked with fellow mobster John Roselli and the Central Intelligence Agency (CIA) in a plot to kill Castro after the disastrous Bay of Pigs in-

vasion in 1961. News of this involvement broke in May 1962, after Robert Kennedy, by then attorney general, stepped up his investigations into Mob activity. Giancana became the subject of intense surveillance by the Federal Bureau of Investigation (FBI) in 1963. He tried to sue the FBI and the U.S. Justice Department for harassment, but the courts ruled against him. To make matters worse, the publicity turned his flamboyant Oak Park home into a popular tourist attraction. Giancana's anger at what he saw as a betrayal has led to speculation that he was involved in the assassination of President John F. Kennedy in November 1963. He faced prosecution in the months leading up to the assassination, and the FBI recorded death threats and other vows of revenge against John and Robert Kennedy. Giancana also tried and failed to blackmail the Kennedys over affairs with Exner, Marilyn Monroe, and many other women.

All this time Giancana was a prominent figure, well known to the news media. By the early 1960s his numbers rackets were generating millions of dollars, and his interests in Las Vegas, Miami, and elsewhere made him a wealthy and influential figure. After Kennedy's assassination, and in the wake of the trial of the teamster Jimmy Hoffa for jury tampering, Giancana again came under FBI scrutiny. After refusing to testify before a Chicago grand jury in 1965, he was sentenced to a year in jail. By the time of his release, his involvement in the Castro plot and the dubious legality of his business dealings were starting to catch up with him. In 1966 he went to live in Mexico, where he had business interests, and remained there until he was extradited in 1974 to appear before a Chicago grand jury investigating Mob activity. His testimony, given on four separate occasions, was less than helpful.

The role of the Mafia in public life in the United States in the 1960s was the subject of many government investigations and media speculation. As one of the most powerful and ruthless Mafia bosses of all time, Giancana was formidable. Although he undoubtedly exaggerated his influence, in the early 1960s he certainly had access to influential figures at the heart of U.S. government. In 1974 Giancana was subpoenaed to appear before a Senate investigation of the plot to assassinate Castro. But he never made it to Washington. While making supper at his Oak Park home on the night of 19 June 1975, he was shot in the back of the head. His killer has never been identified, and he had so many enemies among local mobsters and in government that it seems unlikely his murder will ever be solved. He is buried at Mount Carmel Cemetery in Chicago.

★

A biography of Giancana is William Brashler, *The Don: The Life and Death of Sam Giancana* (1977). Interesting insights into life with Giancana are offered by his daughter Antoinette and Thomas C. Renner in *Mafia Princess: Growing Up in Sam Giancana's Family*

(1984), and by Judith Exner and Ovid Demaris in *My Story* (1977). Articles about Giancana published after his death include "The Demise of a Don," *Time* (30 June 1975), and "Giancana, Gangster, Slain," *New York Times* (21 June 1975).

CHRIS ROUTLEDGE

GINSBERG, (Irwin) Allen   (*b.* 3 June 1926 in Newark, New Jersey; *d.* 5 April 1997 in New York City), one of the most influential of the Beat Generation poets, whose poem "Howl" became an anthem of the countercultural, antiwar, and pro-drug movements of the 1960s.

Ginsberg was the second of two children born to Louis Ginsberg, a teacher and poet, and Naomi Levy, a Russian émigré who supported the Communist Party and struggled with mental illness. Although his mother's illness made his childhood difficult, Ginsberg excelled in academics and entered Columbia University as a pre-law major at the age of seventeen. Suspended from the university in 1945 for writing vulgarities on a window, Ginsberg avoided the draft for World War II by declaring his homosexuality and joined the U.S. Merchant Marine. He returned to Columbia the following year and received a B.A. degree in 1949.

During and after his years at Columbia, Ginsberg met many of the characters who formed the countercultural Beat Generation, including Jack Kerouac, William S. Burroughs, and Carl Solomon. (The Beat Generation comprised a group of American writers in the 1950s and 1960s who rebelled against the establishment values of American culture.) Ginsberg allowed his drug-dealing friends to store stolen property in his Manhattan apartment, and was arrested as an accessory to burglary in 1949. With the help of a Columbia dean, Ginsberg was able to receive eight months of treatment at the New York State Psychiatric Institute of Columbia Presbyterian Hospital rather than serving jail time. After his release he held a number of jobs, but his focus was on writing poetry, some of which he sent to his neighbor William Carlos Williams, a poet who strongly influenced his work. Ginsberg's poetry was first published in 1953, in the annual anthology *New Directions*. In 1954 Ginsberg moved to San Francisco, where the Beat Movement was taking hold. There he met Peter Orlovsky, another poet, with whom he immediately fell in love and subsequently entered a committed and lifelong, although at times intermittent, relationship.

Ginsberg's career as a poet was launched on 7 October 1955 when he read his poem "Howl" at the Six Gallery in San Francisco. With the opening lamentation that became a rallying cry for the disenfranchised, "I saw the best minds of my generation destroyed by madness, starving hysterical naked, / dragging themselves through the negro streets at dawn looking for an angry fix," his reputation was estab-

Allen Ginsberg. AP/WIDE WORLD PHOTOS

lished. Lawrence Ferlinghetti, founder of City Lights Books, had attended the reading and quickly published Ginsberg's *Howl and Other Poems* in 1956. The graphic sexual imagery of the poems prompted the San Francisco Police Department to declare the book obscene. However, in the ensuing trial Judge Clayton Horn deemed the poems not obscene, and "Howl" quickly assumed the status of a manifesto of the countercultural movements.

Drug use contributed greatly to Ginsberg's poetry during the early 1960s, particularly the collection *Kaddish and Other Poems* (1961), an elegy for his mother, who had died in 1956. With Dr. Timothy Leary, the Harvard scientist and hallucinogen advocate, Ginsberg planned a "psychedelic revolution" to encourage individuals to explore their minds through drug use. However, Ginsberg's advocacy of drugs as a catalyst for creativity was short-lived; a trip to India in 1962 convinced him of the superiority of meditation and yoga to expand the mind.

Ginsberg traveled to many other parts of the world in the 1960s, including Europe and Israel, and encountered much of the same controversy that he had faced at home. In 1965 he was expelled from Cuba and Czechoslovakia for his homosexuality and dissident politics. Prior to his expulsion from Czechoslovakia, however, he was elected "King of May" by thousands of Czech citizens for the annual celebration. In 1967 the Arts Council of Great Britain invited Ginsberg to their international festival. In addition to international travel, Ginsberg ceaselessly toured the United States to read poetry and to participate in political protests. In 1964 he joined the author Susan Sontag in defense of the director Jonas Mekas, who was accused of obscenity for screening Jean Genet's *Chant d'Amour*; he also fought zoning ordinances designed to prohibit coffeehouses from holding poetry readings. In 1967 Ginsberg helped to organize the "happening," A Gathering of the Tribes for a Human Be-In, in San Francisco's Golden Gate Park, at which Leary uttered the sound bite of the decade: "Turn On, Tune In, Drop Out." Later that year, Ginsberg and Dr. Benjamin Spock were arrested for antiwar protests in New York City. At the riots surrounding the 1968 Democratic National Convention in Chicago, Ginsberg joined Abbie Hoffman and the Yippies (the anarchist Youth International Party) to protest U.S. involvement in the war in Vietnam. The tumultuous decade of the 1960s ended for Ginsberg on his farm in Cherry Valley, New York. He was injured in an auto accident in November 1968 and suffered an attack of Bell's palsy, a condition that causes the facial muscles to weaken or become paralyzed, in April 1969.

Despite the drugs, the travel, and the war protests, Ginsberg remained an incredibly prolific poet during the 1960s. In addition to *Kaddish,* he published such poems and collections as *Empty Mirror* (1961), *A Strange New Cottage in Berkeley* (1963), *Reality Sandwiches* (1963), *The Change*

(1963), *Kral Majales* (1965), *Wichita Vortex Sutra* (1966), *TV Baby Poems* (1967), *Wales—A Visitation, July 29, 1967* (1968), *Scrap Leaves, Hasty Scribbles* (1968), *Messages II* (1968), *Planet News, 1961–1967* (1968), *Airplane Dreams: Compositions from Journals* (1968), and *Ankor-Wat* (1969). The steady stream of vital, exuberant, and raw poetry ensured Ginsberg's reputation as an eloquent spokesperson for his generation. His awards during the decade included a Guggenheim Fellowship and a grant from the National Endowment for the Arts.

After the upheavals of the 1960s, the remaining decades of Ginsberg's life were marked by critical acclaim, enormous productivity, and relative calm. He cofounded the Jack Kerouac School of Disembodied Politics as a branch of the Naropa Institute, a Buddhist center of learning, in 1974; toured with Bob Dylan's Rolling Thunder Review in 1975; was awarded the National Arts Club Gold Medal for lifetime achievement in 1979, and was named distinguished professor at Brooklyn College in 1986. He continued to publish throughout his life, including such collections as *First Blues* (1975), *Selected Gay Poems and Correspondence* (1979), *Mostly Sitting Haiku* (1979), *White Shroud* (1986), and *Cosmopolitan Greetings* (1994). Ginsberg died of a heart attack in New York City while battling liver cancer, and was cremated.

Although Ginsberg was one of the most influential American poets of the twentieth century, his life almost overshadowed his work, as many fans of the Beat Generation idolized the poets more than their poetry. Ginsberg's "Howl," however, gave voice to the disaffected of the 1950s, as this group rose to prominence in the 1960s. Having refused to countenance injustices wherever he saw them, Ginsberg served as a model of the power of passion in literature and life. As time has passed, many of his viewpoints that were once seen as extremist have become increasingly mainstream.

★

Ginsberg's archives are at Stanford University, Palo Alto, California; subsidiary holdings belong to the University of Texas at Austin and Columbia University, New York City. Ginsberg's autobiographical writings include *The Yage Letters* (1963), cowritten with William S. Burroughs; *Indian Journals* (1970); *To Eberhart from Ginsberg* (1976); *As Ever* (1977); *Journals: Early Fifties, Early Sixties* (1977); *Straight Hearts' Delight* (1980); *Journals: Mid-Fifties* (1995); and *Family Business* (2001). Biographies include Jane Kramer, *Allen Ginsberg in America* (1969); Barry Miles, *Ginsberg: A Biography* (1989; rev. ed. 2000); Michael Schumacher, *Dharma Lion* (1992); Graham Caveney, *Screaming with Joy* (1998); and Ed Sanders, *The Poetry and Life of Allen Ginsberg* (2000). Obituaries are in the *Washington Post* (6 Apr. 1997) and *New York Times* (8 Apr. 1997).

TISON PUGH

GIOVANNI, Nikki (*b.* 7 June 1943 in Knoxville, Tennessee), African-American poet who first emerged in the 1960s as a voice in the Black Power and Black Arts movements, and later earned widespread popularity and respect for her work.

Giovanni was born as Yolande Cornelia Giovanni, Jr., to Gus Jones Giovanni, a probation officer, and Yolande Cornelia Watson Giovanni, a social worker. She grew up in Cincinnati in a happy, relatively poor home with her older sister. Her father had difficulty supporting the family; frustrated with the limited number of jobs available for a black man (despite his degree from Fisk University in Nashville, Tennessee), he became abusive. Giovanni escaped by returning to Knoxville, her birthplace and the home of her beloved grandmother Louvenia Terrell Watson.

Watson greatly influenced Giovanni. An outspoken woman, she instilled a sense of activism in her granddaughter, even volunteering Giovanni to participate in antisegregation rallies. Watson provided Giovanni with a lasting appreciation for her African-American heritage. In 1960 Giovanni's academic achievements allowed her to enter Fisk University a year early. Giovanni was asked to leave before the end of her first semester because she had returned to her grandmother's home for Thanksgiving without first asking permission, a public display of individuality that would soon mark her art.

Giovanni returned to Fisk in 1964, where she edited the university literary journal *Elan,* participated in the Fisk writer's workshop, and reestablished the campus chapter of the Student Nonviolent Coordinating Committee (SNCC). Giovanni found herself working with members of the Black Power movement and the Black Arts movement as both gained momentum. These connections led her to create and direct Cincinnati's Black Arts Festival in 1967. The festival showcased the wealth of talented African-American writers and actors who had gone unnoticed in the predominantly white community. The festival was a success and led to the formation of the New Theatre, which remained a respected member of the Cincinnati arts scene for more than three decades. Later in 1967 Giovanni graduated from Fisk with a B.A. (honors) in history. She subsequently studied at the University of Pennsylvania's School of Social Work in Philadelphia and took classes at Columbia University's School of Fine Arts in New York City.

The assassinations of Martin Luther King, Jr., Robert Kennedy, and Malcolm X prompted Giovanni to focus her attentions on writing poetry. In 1968 she released *Black Feeling/Black Talk.* Originally a self-published book, it sold more than 10,000 copies in the first year—unheard of for self-published poetry. The book's success attracted the attention of major presses, such as William Morris. The book was later republished by Broadside Press, a company established and run by African Americans. Critics who read the work focused on the revolutionary overtones present in about half of the collection's poems. They praised Giovanni's call for black unity and militaristic action, increasing her currency as a charismatic speaker and popular figure at poetry readings. By 1969 to 1970 she was drawing sizable crowds and had attained mainstream success, an extremely rare accomplishment for African-American poets of the time.

Giovanni continued to explore revolutionary ideas in *Black Judgment* (1968). Once again, only about half the poems echoed messages of the Black Power movement; nevertheless, her reputation as a voice of the revolution was cemented. Other poems in *Black Judgment* suggest she had already begun to distance herself from the Black Power movement, which she increasingly felt was becoming too rigid. Giovanni was put off by most of the comments made about her and her work. She felt that no one needed to define her writing or her life for her.

Giovanni believed African Americans should support individuality and resist the single, collective face the Black Power movement had constructed, a face similar to the homogeneous view proffered by whites. She argued that the Black Power movement was more concerned with evincing power from whites, which she felt perpetuated racial prejudices, than it was in developing individual voices within the black community.

This realization, coupled with the birth of her son in 1969, helped to propel Giovanni's poetry from revolution to exploration as she shifted into children's poetry. *Spin a Soft Black Song: Poems for Children* (1971), was another immediate success. Giovanni's increasing popularity among all races, and the turn of her attention to children led members of the Black Power and Black Arts movement, such as LeRoi Jones and Don Lee, to claim she was "ego-tripping." They argued that Giovanni was too caught up in her own success to lend her voice to the now-fractured movement, yet Giovanni believed acting as an individual was more important than becoming a poster child for a cause. To a small, vocal group, *Spin a Soft Black Song* represented Giovanni's rejection of the Black Power movement. However, the biographer Virginia C. Fowler argues that Giovanni never intended to join the movement and simply placed the "rhetoric of black power" within the context of her interest in individuality.

Giovanni paid little attention to her critics. She wrote about what she felt was important. As she grew as a writer and a mother, her themes expanded to include family and racial pride. Her style changed as well, as she added prose and spoken word to her art form. Giovanni intended her poetry to be spoken, a fact that critics acknowledge even as they comment that her words do not translate well when

Nikki Giovanni. AP/WIDE WORLD PHOTOS

left on the page. Throughout the 1970s she accepted more than 100 speaking engagements per year and released the first of five spoken word albums, *Truth Is on Its Way* (1971), which won the National Association of Radio and TV Announcers award for best spoken word album.

For the remainder of the twentieth century, Giovanni continued to write, releasing more than twenty books of poetry and prose, and to speak around theUnited States. Her reputation as a writer grew, and several of her poems, including "Knoxville, Tennessee" and "Nikki-Rosa," both from *Black Judgment,* are frequently anthologized. She received many honorary degrees, awards, and citations, gave numerous poetry readings and lectures worldwide, and became a poet of the collective people.

The 1960s civil rights movement altered the American perception of racial difference and became fertile ground for African-American artists longing to give voice to the struggle for black identity and to provide black audiences with genuine reflections of African-American culture. Giovanni's poetry during the 1960s sings of this struggle. Her unprecedented popularity eased the way for the African-American women poets who followed.

★

Giovanni's autobiography, which earned a nomination for the National Book Award, is *Gemini: An Extended Autobiographical Statement on My First Twenty-five Years of Being a Black Poet* (1971). Additional information can be found in Don L. Lee, *Dy-*

namite Voices I: Black Poets of the 1960's (1971), and Virginia C. Fowler, *Nikki Giovanni* (1992). See also Jennifer Walter, "Nikki Giovanni and Rita Dove: Poets Redefining," *The Journal of Negro History*, 85, no. 3 (summer 2000): 210–217.

LESLIE BOON

GLASER, Donald Arthur (*b.* 21 September 1926 in Cleveland, Ohio), physicist who received the 1960 Nobel Prize in physics for his invention of the bubble chamber, a scientific instrument that opened up a new world for nuclear physics.

The son of William J. Glaser, a businessman, and Lena, both Russian immigrants, Glaser went through the Cleveland Heights, Ohio, public schools, graduating at the age of sixteen. At age twenty he earned a B.S. in physics from Case Institute of Technology (later Case Western Reserve University) in Cleveland. Glaser then entered the California Institute of Technology in Pasadena, where he finished his Ph.D. work in 1949, although he officially received the degree in physics and mathematics in 1950. A year before he received his Ph.D., he joined the faculty at the University of Michigan in Ann Arbor. During summers in the 1950s, Glaser served as a consultant at the Lawrence Radiation Laboratory in Berkeley, California. In September 1959 he joined the faculty at the University of California, Berkeley, and was named a professor of physics and molecular bi-

Donald Glaser. THE LIBRARY OF CONGRESS

ology in 1964; he remained at Berkeley for the rest of his career. On 28 November 1960 Glaser married Ruth Thompson; the couple had two children.

Glaser had an interest in elementary particle physics, especially in the behavior of high-energy particles. The world of particle physics research had opened up with C. T. R. Wilson's invention of the cloud chamber at the beginning of the twentieth century. However, the cloud chamber's detection capabilities were limited to low-energy particles. By the 1960s newly developed particle accelerators ("atom smashers") were producing high-energy particles of up to twenty-five billion volts—energies 1,000 times larger than the voltages observable with the cloud chamber.

At Michigan, Glaser began experimenting with methods for studying the high-energy particles that could be produced with the new accelerators. In a cloud chamber, a stream of liquid droplets condensing from a subcooled vapor provided jet-stream images of the charged particles. Glaser instead looked at using a denser medium—superheated liquid in which high-energy charged particles could produce tracks of gas bubbles. The principle sounded simple, but developing it was challenging. Glaser worked for several years to perfect the first radiation-sensitive bubble chamber. He succeeded by applying the physics of bubble formation, developing a pressurized container of superheated liquid that he described as "a pressure cooker with windows."

One month after his thirty-fourth birthday, in 1960, Glaser became the second-youngest recipient of the Nobel Prize for his development of the bubble chamber. In presenting the prize to Glaser, the physicist Kai M. Siegbahn recalled the 1959 discovery of "anti-particles" using the bubble chamber, explaining, "One could say that Glaser's

bubble chamber is an anti-Wilson chamber. Particle tracks in Glaser's chamber are composed of small gas bubbles in a liquid," as opposed to small liquid droplets in a gas chamber. Siegbahn added, "Glaser's idea was that an atomic particle passing through the liquid would be able to provoke boiling by means of the ions which the atomic particle produces along its path and which act as bubble development centers." By placing a camera at the "window" to take flash pictures immediately after a particle passes through the chamber, scientists could get a record of the bubble track. From the trails, they could then study atomic nuclei and the forces that hold them together.

During the 1960s there was a particle discovery explosion in nuclear physics, which was made possible by Glaser's invention of the bubble chamber. His first bubble chamber, constructed in 1952, had been about one inch long by one-half inch in diameter; by the 1960s bubble chambers were the size of buildings and required a magnet the size of a locomotive. The same year Glaser made his first successful bubble chamber, the Brookhaven Cosmotron, a 1.3 GeV (giga electron volts) accelerator, started operation. Glaser carried out experiments on elementary particles at the Cosmotron and also at the Bevatron accelerator in the Lawrence Radiation Laboratory.

After moving to the University of California, Berkeley, Glaser changed his field of study to research the internal control systems of the simplest bacterial cells. Again he developed the tools he needed, this time building large-scale automated equipment to study how the cells functioned, including how they reproduced, overcame threats from the environment, and optimized growth opportunities. The equipment Glaser developed was later used in medicine, pollution monitoring, the genetic studies of cells of higher organisms, and the study of the effects of carcinogenic and growth-inhibiting agents.

Glaser's next research focus concerned psychophysics and the sensory physiology of human perception. In particular, he worked to construct computational models of the human visual system that would explain its performance in terms of its physiology and anatomy. In addition to the 1960 Nobel Prize in physics, Glaser received numerous awards, among them the Gold Medal award from the Case Institute of Technology (1967), the distinguished fellow designation from the Smith-Kettlewell Institute for Vision Research (1983–1984), and the American Academy of Achievement's Golden Plate award (1989).

From the first publication of Glaser's ideas, his experiments were recognized by other scientists as having the potential to make an important contribution to the study of particle physics. Others helped to develop bubble chambers, but the Nobel Prize committee saw Glaser as "the one who made the really fundamental contributions." In the 1960 Nobel Prize citation, the presenter noted, "It is unusual for a development of modern physics to be due to such a large extent to one single man." Glaser's bubble chambers have been described as the "factories of physics," because they enabled a wealth of high-energy physics information to be collected during the 1960s and 1970s.

★

Biographies of Glaser include information in the Nobel archives, *Donald Arthur Glaser—Biography* (1960); Harriet Zuckerman, *Scientific Elites: Nobel Laureates in the United States* (1977); and Russell Schoch, *The Nobel Tradition at Berkeley: University of California, Berkeley* (1984).

M. C. NAGEL

GLENN, John Herschel, Jr. (*b.* 18 July 1921 in Cambridge, Ohio), astronaut who piloted the first manned U.S. orbital mission, politician, successful businessman, and oldest human sent into space.

Glenn was born to John Herschel Glenn, Sr., an owner of a successful plumbing supply business, and Clara Sproat, an educator. Glenn, along with his adopted sister, Jean, was raised in New Concord, Ohio. After graduating from New Concord High School (which has since been renamed after him), Glenn pursued a degree in chemistry at Muskingum College, in New Concord. During his years at Muskingum, Glenn earned his private pilot license through a U.S. Navy program. He dropped out of school and joined the military after the Japanese attacked Pearl Harbor on 7 December 1941. While serving in the U.S. Marine Corps, Glenn earned a B.A. degree in engineering from Muskingum in

John Glenn.

the early 1960s. In early 1942 Glenn entered the Naval Aviation Cadet Program. In March 1943, following his graduation, he was commissioned a second lieutenant in the U.S. Marine Corps. In April the same year, Glenn married Anna Margaret Castor, his childhood sweetheart; they had two children.

Shortly after his marriage, Glenn was sent to the Pacific theater, where he flew fifty-nine missions and earned various awards. In the early 1950s Glenn would once again find himself flying combat missions, this time in the skies over Korea. After the Korean conflict ended, Glenn served as a military test pilot and flew some of the most sophisticated and fastest jet planes of the day. On 16 July 1957 he piloted an F8U-1 Crusader from Los Angeles to New York, reaching speeds of 726 miles per hour and setting a new transcontinental flight record of just over three hours and twenty-three minutes.

The space race between the United States and the Soviet Union officially began on 4 October 1957, when the Soviets successfully launched the world's first artificial satellite, *Sputnik,* into orbit. In a scramble to avoid falling farther behind in the quest to dominate the sky, the U.S. government initiated an ambitious space program—the National Aeronautics and Space Administration (NASA). The first phase of the program, known as Project Mercury, was to put a man in orbit around Earth. While this program was still in its organizational stages, Glenn and other volunteers subjected themselves to a selection process of strenuous physical and psychological testing, with the hope of filling one of the seven astronaut positions available with Project Mercury.

In 1959 Glenn and six other military pilots were selected as the first astronauts. The next months were filled with extensive physical training at the Langley Research Center in Hampton, Virginia, and at the Missile Test Center in Cape Canaveral, Florida. The astronauts studied astronomy, astronautics, astrophysics, meteorology, geography, and aviation biology, and spent numerous hours in simulation machines, in which they were exposed to various training exercises preparing them for space flight. Additionally, each astronaut specialized in one particular aspect of the Mercury Project. Glenn was responsible for designing the layout of the cockpit, the location of control panels, and the development of necessary instrumentation needed for orbital flight.

Prior to his own flight in space, Glenn suffered two major disappointments regarding his involvement in the space program. First, he was not chosen for the first two U.S. suborbital flights into space. This distinction went to Alan Shepard (5 May 1961) and Virgil Grissom (21 July 1961). Next, Glenn shared in the frustrations of all those involved in the Mercury Project when they learned that the Soviets had already placed a man in orbit. On 12 April 1961 Soviet cosmonaut Yuri Gagarin became the first person to successfully orbit Earth. However, Glenn was pleased to learn that NASA had decided to launch its own manned orbital flight in December of the same year and that he was scheduled as pilot.

After nearly a dozen delays due to weather conditions and technical problems, Glenn finally blasted off into space on 20 February 1962 at 9:47 A.M. Eastern Standard Time. The cramped capsule *Friendship 7* orbited Earth three times in just over four hours and fifty-five minutes. There were two problems during the flight, both of which were perceived as potentially life threatening. The first problem was that the thrusters that kept the capsule from drifting off its orbital course malfunctioned. Glenn solved this problem by manually adjusting the position of *Friendship 7*. However, piloting the ship manually was tricky because pilot errors could leave the capsule without enough fuel to safely reenter Earth's atmosphere. The second problem resulted from faulty warning signals emitted from a sensor, showing that the capsule's heat shield was loose. Later investigations confirmed that the shield was firmly attached to the ship; however, ground control had no way of knowing whether or not the warning sensor was working properly. Ground control did know that without the heat shield in place, the spacecraft would inevitably burn up in Earth's atmosphere on reentry. To counter this problem, Glenn was ordered not to jettison the retro-rocket pack that was strapped to the bottom of the capsule beside the heat shield, in an effort

356

to keep the shield stabilized. In the end the mission was a success, and Glenn's ship splashed down in the Atlantic Ocean intact. Instantly, Glenn became an American hero, and the U.S. public's confidence in the space program was renewed.

Following his successful mission, Glenn was eager to return to space and participate in NASA's Apollo program, the effort to send a man to the Moon. However, unknowingly to Glenn at the time, President John F. Kennedy had sent word to top NASA officials that he did not want Glenn to go back to space. Apparently, Kennedy felt Glenn was too important a hero to the American people to risk being killed in another space flight. Frustrated by not getting the opportunity to return to space, Glenn resigned from the space program in January 1964 and initiated the paperwork for retiring from the marines. His retirement became official in January 1965.

In the same year he retired from NASA, Glenn became interested in pursuing a political career. He entered the Ohio Democratic primary against the incumbent senator Stephen M. Young. However, Glenn had to withdraw from the race after he fell in his bathroom and severely injured his inner ear. After several months of recovery, Glenn entered the private sector, becoming a top executive with the soft-drink company Royal Crown Cola. He also sat on the board of directors of the Questor Corporation, invested in Holiday Inn franchises, and hosted a television documentary series.

Glenn continued to prosper in the decades following the 1960s. He became the first four-term senator from Ohio, winning his first election in 1974, and subsequent elections in 1980, 1986, and 1992. Glenn did not limit his aspirations to the U.S. Senate. He unsuccessfully attempted to earn the Democratic Party's presidential nomination in 1984, but was defeated by Walter Mondale. His most crowning achievement, however, came in October 1998, when Glenn went back to space on shuttle flight STS-95 *Discovery*, making him the oldest human ever to be sent to space.

★

Numerous works have been written about Glenn's life and accomplishments. For the best single-volume account of Glenn's public and private life, see his autobiography, *John Glenn: A Memoir* (1999), written with Nick Taylor. Also see Frank Van Riper, *Glenn: The Astronaut Who Would Be President* (1983), and Peter N. Carroll, *Famous in America: The Passion to Succeed* (1985). For a closer examination of the Mercury Project and Glenn's involvement in it, see *We Seven, by the Astronauts Themselves: M. Scott Carpenter, L. Gordon Cooper, John H. Glenn, Virgil I. Grissom, Walter M. Schirra, Alan B. Shepard, Donald K. Slayton* (1962), and Tom Wolfe, *The Right Stuff* (1979). For the U.S. response to Glenn's Mercury-Atlas 6 orbital flight, see Glenn, *Letters to John Glenn: With Comments by J. H. Glenn, Jr.* (1964).

KENNETH WAYNE HOWELL

GOEPPERT-MAYER, Maria (*b.* 28 June 1906 in Kattaivitz, Germany [now Katowice, Poland]; *d.* 20 February 1972 in San Diego, California), physicist and cowinner of the 1963 Nobel Prize in physics for her discoveries concerning the structure of the atomic nucleus.

Goeppert-Mayer was the only child of Dr. Friedrich Göppert, a pediatrician and university professor, and Maria Wolff Göppert, a piano and French teacher. She entered the University of Göttingen in 1924 at a time when many well-known physicists visited or taught there, including Niels Bohr and Max Born, whose classes ultimately led Goeppert-Mayer to study physics. She learned English during a semester in Cambridge, England, and on 19 January 1930 married Joseph E. Mayer, an American student studying in Göttingen who was a boarder in the family house. They had two children.

After Goeppert-Mayer received her doctorate in physics in 1930 and her husband finished his studies, the couple moved to the United States, where she changed the spelling of her name to the anglicized "Goeppert" and became a U.S. citizen in 1933. As a woman working in a male-dominated field, Goeppert-Mayer was unable to secure a full-time appointment at Johns Hopkins University, where her husband worked. After the beginning of World War II Goeppert-Mayer and her husband went to Columbia University in New York City, where they wrote the book *Statistical Mechanics* (1940), which became a standard text in the field. As the war progressed Goeppert-Mayer joined a team of researchers working on a nuclear bomb. After the war Goeppert-Mayer became a senior physicist at the Argonne National Laboratory in 1946, where a nuclear reactor was under construction. She also joined the faculty at the University of Chicago, but once again, primarily because of her gender, she first had to work as a volunteer associate professor until she was appointed a full professor in 1959.

In 1960 Goeppert-Mayer and her husband joined the University of California at its new San Diego campus. Two years later she received the 1963 Nobel Prize in physics, only the second woman to be so honored in the category, and the first woman to receive the prize for research into theoretical physics. (Marie Curie had won the prize in 1903 for her research into radiation.) Goeppert-Mayer was honored for her contribution to the understanding of the structure of the atomic nucleus through her work on the nuclear shell model and spin-orbit coupling.

Goeppert-Mayer shared the prize with Eugene Paul Wigner and J. Hans D. Jensen for their collective work concerning theories of atomic nuclei and elementary particles. Goeppert-Mayer's research focused on the nuclear shell model. This theoretical model examines the energy levels of individual protons and neutrons and is used to explain the stability of nuclei. In its simplest form a shell model is a model of a system that is believed to consist of individual particles moving in bound orbits in response to the entire system.

Through her studies of the nuclear shell model, Goeppert-Mayer became the first physicist to provide convincing evidence for the existence of the higher numbers in the so-called "magic numbers." These seven numbers—2, 8, 20, 28, 50, 82, and 126—are the atomic numbers "N" or atomic mass number "Z" of the atomic nucleus that occur again and again in nature. At the time only the first three magic numbers had been explained as corresponding to the shells for light nuclei, but there was no evidence for the existence of such correspondence for the higher numbers. Goeppert-Mayer's work essentially rediscovered the magic numbers, especially the higher numbers, in a more convincing manner, providing evidence for their existence and the existence of closed shells.

Goeppert-Mayer had observed that any element that had any of the magic numbers of protons or neutrons was extremely stable. She believed the existence of magic numbers indicated that protons and neutrons in the nucleus might be arranged in specific energy levels, like those available to electrons in the atom. She theorized that the shell model for the nucleus would be similar to an onion in that layers of protons and neutrons would revolve around each other. The magic numbers represented the points at which the various shells (layers) would be complete. This theory

Maria Goeppert Mayer. AP/WIDE WORLD PHOTOS

led Goeppert-Mayer to become known as the "Madonna of the Onion." The theory helped to explain why protons and neutrons in a nucleus did not continuously collide with each other.

After this discovery she immediately began to work out the consequences for nuclear properties, such as ground state and angular momenta. Her research suggested that the spin-orbit coupling, which is an interaction between the orbital angular momentum and the spin angular momentum of individual particles, is particularly strong in nuclei. In essence, the particles have different energies as they spin and revolve around the nucleus. Goeppert-Mayer used the analogy of spinning dancers that move clockwise and counterclockwise on their axes as they orbit a central point. In April 1949 Goeppert-Mayer published her hypothesis in *Physical Review*. With Jensen, one of her Nobel Prize co-winners, who independently had discovered similar findings, she wrote *Elementary Theory of Nuclear Shell Structure* (1955). The book provided further evidence to the scientific community that their theories were valid.

Although Goeppert-Mayer would later say that conducting the research was more exciting than winning the Nobel Prize, the prize did validate her as an important scientist to the wider scientific community. Such recognition was a just reward after years of working for little or no pay and being treated with much less respect than her male counterparts despite being an accomplished physicist. The American Physical Society annually awards the Maria Goeppert-Mayer Award to an outstanding woman physicist.

Goeppert-Mayer, who smoked throughout her life, suffered a series of health problems throughout the 1960s but continued to teach and conduct research. In 1960 she suffered a stroke that paralyzed one of her arms. She had a pacemaker surgically implanted in 1968. In 1971 she went into a coma after suffering a heart attack, and she died from heart disease the following year.

★

Goeppert-Mayer's papers, correspondence, photographs, and lecture notes are collected at the Central University Library, University of California, San Diego. A discussion of Goeppert-Mayer's contributions to physics is in Robert G. Sach, "Maria Goeppert-Mayer, A Biographical Memoir," *Biographical Memoirs* (1979): 302–328. Biographical information is also in Olga S. Opfell, *The Lady Laureates: Women Who Have Won the Nobel Prize* (1978): 194–208; and Joan Dash, *The Triumph of Discovery: Women Scientists Who Won the Nobel Prize* (1991). An article on her scientific work is "Maria Goeppert-Mayer," *Physics Today* (1986). An obituary is in the *New York Times* (22 Feb. 1972).

DAVID PETECHUK

GOLDWATER, Barry Morris (*b.* 1 January 1909 in Phoenix, Arizona; *d.* 29 May 1998 in Phoenix, Arizona), U.S. senator, Republican presidential candidate, and leader of the U.S. conservative movement.

Goldwater was born in Arizona when it was still a territory, and was the grandson of an immigrant Jewish peddler. His parents were Baron Goldwater, a department store merchant, and Josephine Williams, a homemaker. The eldest of three children, Goldwater was raised as an Episcopalian. Goldwater attended Union High School in Phoenix, and then Staunton Military Academy in Virginia. He then enrolled at the University of Arizona. Following his father's death in 1929, he left college after only a year to manage the family's Phoenix department store. He married Peggy Johnson, an heiress to the Borg-Warner automobile fortune, on 22 September 1934. They had four children. In addition to his business activities, Goldwater obtained an extensive collection of Native American art, published several volumes of photographs of Arizona people and places, and helped establish the Arizona Historical Foundation.

During World War II Goldwater served with the U.S. Army Air Corps, airlifting war supplies over the hazardous 500-mile route from India over the Himalayas to China.

Barry Goldwater. ARCHIVE PHOTOS, INC.

Returning to Phoenix after the war, he was elected to the city council in 1949, then rode General Dwight Eisenhower's coattails to a victory in the U.S. Senate race in 1952. In Washington, D.C., he joined the conservative Republican bloc in the Senate and sought to reduce federal spending and curb labor union power while bolstering military defense. In 1958 he claimed leadership of the Republican right wing when he was reelected despite a national Democratic sweep that defeated more experienced party conservatives.

Goldwater cemented his authority by publishing *The Conscience of a Conservative* (1960), which quickly became a best-seller and eventually sold 3.5 million copies. The 123-page primer was a call to battle for conservatives. Goldwater declared that the federal government had become "a Leviathan, a vast national authority out of touch with the people, and out of their control." Government must be restrained, he wrote, limited only to establishing order, maintaining the defense, and administering justice. Powers beyond those delegated were illegitimate and unconstitutional. Goldwater's agenda was clear: the federal government must "withdraw promptly and totally from every jurisdiction reserved to the states." Specifically, he called for an end to the income tax, farm subsidies, public housing, urban renewal, and aid to education. Southerners were particularly interested in Goldwater's views on civil rights. He offered a defense of states' rights and a narrow interpretation of federal responsibilities. The Constitution, he argued, protected African Americans only in voting, contractual relations, and property holding. He denied the legitimacy of federal efforts to integrate schools or to desegregate public accommodations.

In the last chapter of *The Conscience of a Conservative,* which constituted a third of the book, Goldwater turned to foreign affairs. He condemned American weakness that had resulted in Communist advances in Europe, Asia, and Central America. To turn the tide Goldwater insisted that the United States confront the Communists militarily and economically at every opportunity and pursue total victory. He rebuffed negotiations, advocated the resumption of nuclear weapons testing, and called for rolling back Communist advances in Asia and Eastern Europe. However, even though Goldwater was prepared to go to the "brink," he considered the possibility of war "unlikely," for "the mere threat of American action" to save a people hostile to Soviet ambitions "would probably result in the communists' acceptance of the ultimatum." *Why Not Victory?,* which Goldwater published in 1962, further detailed his conservative critique of U.S. foreign policy and called for victory through strength.

In the Senate, acting on his conservative ideology, Goldwater supported a strong military, with heavy reliance on air power to counter the communist threat. He opposed the Nuclear Test Ban Treaty (1963) for fear that it would weaken U.S. defense. He rejected President John F. Kennedy's New Frontier initiatives and the Great Society of President Lyndon B. Johnson. He voted against aid for education and the Civil Rights Act of 1964 as unconstitutional extensions of federal power.

In response to Goldwater's call to conservatives at the 1960 Republican convention to "grow up" and "take this party back," a movement arose to draft him for president. Goldwater had prepared the ground for its advance. He had served two terms as the chair of the Senate Republican Campaign Committee. In this position he became a prime source for news reporters and the point man for rallying the faithful and for raising money for Republican senatorial candidates. Those who listened to his speeches detected a greater mission than the election of Republicans. He preached the cause of modern conservatism—individualism, the sanctity of private property, militant anticommunism, and the dangers of federally centralized power. During his tenure he traveled hundreds of thousands of miles and visited nearly every state in the Union. This yeoman service enabled him to capture the loyalty of Republican partisans down to the district and county levels. Charismatic and evoking the image of the western hero, the tanned, square-jawed Goldwater appealed to Americans as a man of action, a rugged individualist standing against all odds and refusing to compromise his beliefs or country. He was candid and quotable, ready to voice his convictions regardless of consequences. The senator's staff nurtured the mystique by distributing publicity photographs of the Arizonan clad in jeans and a cowboy hat, astride a horse, or entering, dressed in his flight suit, a U.S. Air Force jet fighter.

The draft-Goldwater movement focused on capturing the party machinery and winning a majority of delegates to the 1964 convention. The conservatives' strategy bypassed liberal organizations in the eastern industrial states to forge a coalition of white, middle-class voters in the South and West. This effort alone would ensure the Arizona senator sufficient support to win a first-ballot victory. Looking forward to running against President Kennedy, Goldwater nearly left the race after his friend's assassination in November 1963. However, believing he owed a debt to the conservative movement, he reconsidered and announced his bid in January 1964.

The primary election campaign pitted him against opponents Henry Cabot Lodge, the U.S. ambassador to South Vietnam, and New York governor Nelson Rockefeller. Primaries in New Hampshire and Oregon stigmatized the Arizonan as an extremist eager to trigger nuclear war, a foe of social security, and a racist. In June 1964 Goldwater clinched the nomination by narrowly winning the bitter California primary. But the victory was a Pyrrhic one because Republican moderates and liberals balked at supporting him in the general election. Widening the breach, Goldwater made no overtures to his opponents and even provoked them by declaring in his acceptance speech, "Extremism in the defense of liberty is no vice. Moderation in the pursuit of justice is no virtue."

In the general election Goldwater faced President Lyndon Johnson, a man he detested. The campaign was certain to focus on Goldwater-the-man because he met with the president and both agreed to desist from raising the central issues of civil rights and Vietnam. Goldwater acted from a sense of patriotism and fear of exacerbating racial tensions in the wake of urban rioting during the summer of 1964. To maintain a united front before the Communist enemy in Vietnam, he avoided direct and specific mention of U.S. involvement in the war. Although the press praised both candidates for their wisdom, Goldwater's initiative on Vietnam denied a public examination of the administration's emerging policy and robbed Americans of a last opportunity to debate the war before the beginnings of a large-scale military buildup.

With opinion polls heavily in his favor, President Johnson boasted of peace and prosperity and raised the specter of Goldwater as a warmonger eager to press the nuclear button and as a pawn of right-wing extremists. Democrats exploited his gaffes in order to scare voters with the image of a politically inept and irresponsible candidate eager to destroy the world and social security. Goldwater countered by raising "the social issue"—decrying pornography, racial quotas, busing, immorality, and crime in the streets. These tactics had little effect, and Johnson slaughtered Goldwater at the polls in November 1964, winning 61 percent of the forty-three million votes cast. Only five states in the Deep South and Arizona fell into the conservative's column, yet the results masked crucial changes at the grassroots level. Republicans had made significant inroads in the Democratic South, and Johnson received a clear majority of the white vote only in Texas. In the northeastern cities Irish and Italian voters continued to drift from the Democratic to the Republican Party. Most important, conservatives had captured the Republican machinery. Future Republican candidates took notice and pursued Goldwater's electoral strategy and issues to eventual national power.

After the election Goldwater returned to Arizona and for the first time in fifteen years found himself a private citizen. National and international events ensured that his retirement was brief. Growing popular dissatisfaction with the Vietnam War gave the conservative's words new meaning and urgency. Goldwater lashed President Johnson for ignoring the advice of military commanders and demanded the quick defeat of North Vietnam through massive air bombardment and naval blockade. He also insisted that air sorties be launched against Vietcong sanctuaries in Cambodia and Laos. Similarly, as racial violence engulfed U.S.

cities after 1964, people reappraised Goldwater's views about crime in the streets and the breakdown of authority and traditional values. Goldwater campaigned hard for conservatives in the 1966 congressional elections and helped spark a Republican resurgence. In 1968 he ran for reelection to the U.S. Senate and won handily.

Goldwater strongly endorsed President Richard M. Nixon. Not only was Nixon one of the few Republican leaders who had campaigned for Goldwater in 1964, but the new administration recruited key Goldwater loyalists. Goldwater cheered Nixon's escalation of the air war against Vietnam and the invasions of Laos and Cambodia. Still, Goldwater chafed at Nixon's decisions to institute wage and price controls, withdraw from Vietnam, and pursue diplomatic overtures to the People's Republic of China. As the Watergate scandal evolved into a national crisis, Goldwater kept his doubts to himself and vigorously supported the president. Only in August 1974, when White House tapes revealed the extent of Nixon's participation in the cover-up, did the Arizona senator desert the cause. Part of a three-man delegation sent to the Oval Office by fellow Republicans, Goldwater informed the president that his support in the Senate had collapsed, and he pressed Nixon to resign. Reelected again in 1974 and 1980, Goldwater retired from the U.S. Senate in 1987. He died of natural causes, and his ashes were scattered over the Colorado River in the Grand Canyon.

Goldwater was a businessman, artist, historian, philanthropist, and politician. In spite of his overwhelming defeat in the 1964 presidential election, the five-term U.S. senator from Arizona profoundly affected U.S. history. He led a conservative movement that captured control of the Republican Party, developing a campaign strategy that linked whites living in the South and West. Goldwater also introduced "the social issue" to national politics, an element that became a staple of Republican campaigning. Goldwater's challenge to liberalism began the shift of the U.S. mainstream to the right.

★

Goldwater's papers are housed in the Arizona Historical Foundation, Arizona State University. His autobiographies are *With No Apologies* (1979), and *Goldwater* (1988), with Jack Casserly. Recent biographies include Robert Alan Goldberg, *Barry Goldwater* (1995), Lee Edwards, *Goldwater: The Man Who Made a Revolution* (1995), and Peter Iverson, *Barry Goldwater: Native Arizonan* (1997). See also Mary Brennan, *Turning Right in the Sixties: The Conservative Capture of the GOP* (1995), and Rick Perlstein, *Before the Storm: Barry Goldwater and the Unmaking of the American Consensus* (2001). Obituaries are in the *New York Times, Los Angeles Times,* and *Washington Post* (all 30 May 1998).

ROBERT ALAN GOLDBERG

GOODE, Malvin Russell ("Mal") (*b.* 13 February 1908 in White Plains, Virginia; *d.* 12 September 1995 in Pittsburgh, Pennsylvania), newspaper reporter and radio commentator who became the first black correspondent hired by an American television network during the rise of the civil rights movement, and who was known as the "Dean of Black Journalism."

Goode was raised in Homestead, Pennsylvania, a steel mill town near Pittsburgh. His father, William Goode, the son of slaves, married a schoolteacher, Mary Ellen Hunter. They had six children. Although Homestead had a sizable black population, all of Goode's schoolteachers were white and often made him sit in the back of the classroom. After graduating in 1927 from high school, Goode went to work at U.S. Steel's Homestead Works to support himself while enrolled in the pre-law program at the University of Pittsburgh.

Goode earned his bachelor's degree in 1931, but the only job he could find was as a clothing store janitor. Later jobs included working as a counselor at a Pittsburgh YMCA, a probation officer, and a manager for the Pittsburgh Housing Authority. Goode and Mary Louise Lavelle were married in 1936. They raised six children.

In 1948 Goode began his career in journalism as an assistant to the circulation manager of the *Pittsburgh Courier,* the nation's largest newspaper serving the black community. Goode also worked in public relations for the *Courier.* The next year Pittsburgh's KQV radio offered the newspaper

Mal Goode. AMERICAN BROADCASTING COMPANY

fifteen minutes of airtime two days each week. Goode was selected as the host of "The *Courier* Speaks," a program dealing with issues affecting the black community. In 1950 the program moved to radio station WHOD. Goode eventually became the news director of WHOD and also the first African-American member of the National Association of Radio and TV News Directors.

Goode's friendship with the baseball great Jackie Robinson, who broke the color barrier in Major League Baseball, led to Goode being hired by the ABC television news division in 1962. Robinson was critical of network television's lack of black reporters. Jim Hagerty, vice president of ABC News, asked the well-known athlete to recommend suitable candidates for an on-air position. Among those Robinson suggested was Goode. The fifty-four-year-old reporter auditioned for fourteen ABC executives and signed a contract on 10 September that year.

The novice television reporter, who now made his home in Teaneck, New Jersey, was assigned to the usually slow United Nations beat to get acquainted with the new medium. He was thrust into the vortex of international events, though, with the outbreak in October 1962 of the Cuban Missile Crisis. On the first day, Goode delivered seven special bulletins on network television and nine on network radio, all without the assistance of a producer. His light-colored skin and wavy hair confused some viewers regarding Goode's race. A South Carolina woman wrote to the network: "I think that was a colored man I saw reporting all day long on the Cuban Missile Crisis. And although I am white, and although he is a colored man, I want to thank him and I want to thank ABC because this is America, and that's the way it ought to be."

One of the assets Goode brought to his United Nations beat was his familiarity with African diplomats, who were routinely ignored by white reporters. Goode's insight was critical during the 1960s, when African nations were declaring their independence from European powers. In 1963, through the auspices of the State Department and the African American Institute, Goode taught advanced journalism courses in Ethiopia, Nigeria, and Tanzania.

In America, however, Goode often endured racism on the job. Occasionally, a white cameraman assigned to Goode's stories would twist the film in the camera to sabotage the report. But Goode persevered. Throughout the 1960s he covered many of the decade's critical stories, including the Democratic and Republican National Conventions of 1964 and 1968. He interviewed Malcolm X and Martin Luther King, Jr., and was the sole African-American network correspondent assigned to cover King's funeral in April 1968. Goode also covered the 1968 funeral of Robert Kennedy. His reports from the Poor People's March on Washington, D.C., that same year were passionate in calling attention to the hunger and poverty in black America.

Goode also narrated the ABC documentary *It Can Be Done* (1969), which chronicled the resignation of a Ku Klux Klan grand dragon in Atlanta and his eventual support of black voter registration and increased minority employment.

By 1968, when the famous Kerner Commission report called for white media organizations to hire more black reporters, Goode had already been mentoring young black journalists for several years. Throughout his tenure at ABC News, Goode prodded network executives to reverse their discriminatory hiring practices.

Goode retired in 1973 but remained a consultant to ABC News for fifteen years. As former president of the United Nations Correspondents Association, he maintained an office at the UN building until he was nearly eighty. Goode was also active on the lecture circuit. One of his favorite themes, particularly for young black audiences, was "I did it. You can do it, too." The Minorities in Broadcast Training Program—a nonprofit organization that selects, trains, and places minority college graduates in news reporting and management jobs—presents an annual Mal Goode Lifetime Achievement Award.

Goode was both a reporter and an advocate for civil rights throughout his professional life. As a reporter, he was an impartial observer of events. But when fighting for the cause of African Americans, he was single-minded. Goode died from the complications of a stroke. In a little over three decades he had witnessed dramatic progress in American broadcasting. Prominent African Americans in television news, such as Carole Simpson, the Emmy Award-winning senior correspondent for ABC News, and the Cable News Network anchor Bernard Shaw, have acknowledged the pioneering role of Goode in the 1960s as an inspiration for their own success. He is buried in East Liberty, Pennsylvania, in Saint Peter's Cemetery.

★

Goode is included among the subjects in Joan Potter and Constance Claytor, *African Americans Who Were First* (1997). When Goode was honored with the Racial Justice Award from the YWCA of Greater Pittsburgh, the *New Pittsburgh Courier* carried a synopsis of his accomplishments in an article by Sandy Hamm, "Former Courier Editor Mal Goode Set for Honors" (9 Nov. 1994). Several obituaries profiled the significance of Goode in the history of American journalism, including the *New York Times* (15 Sept. 1995), *New York Amsterdam News* (23 Sept. 1995), and *National Association of Black Journalists Journal* (30 Sept. 1995). The most complete story of Mal Goode's life and career is found in the PBS documentary *Pioneer of Color: A Conversation with Mal Goode* (1991).

MARY ANN WATSON

GOODMAN, Andrew. *See* Chaney, James Earl, Andrew Goodman, and Michael Henry Schwerner.

GOODMAN, Paul (*b.* 9 September 1911 in New York City; *d.* 3 August 1972 in North Stratford, New Hampshire), writer and activist whose essays in *Growing Up Absurd* (1960) helped to set the tone for the prevailing attitude of discontent among American youth in the 1960s.

Goodman was one of three children born to Barnett and Augusta Goodman. After experiencing a business failure, his father, a German-Jewish immigrant, deserted the family. Their sudden impoverishment forced a move from New York City's Greenwich Village to a cheap apartment on the Upper East Side, and Goodman's mother later took a job in sales that required her to travel. As a result, he was largely raised by maternal aunts and his older sister.

In addition to studying at a Hebrew school, Goodman attended Townsend Harris High School, a public institution for gifted students. He graduated at the top of his class in 1927. At the City College of New York, he studied under the liberal philosopher Morris Raphael Cohen and absorbed the writings of the nineteenth-century Russian anarchist Peter Kropotkin. After graduating with honors with

Paul Goodman. ARCHIVE PHOTOS, INC.

a degree in philosophy in 1931, Goodman attended classes at both Columbia University in New York City and Harvard University in Cambridge, Massachusetts, without officially enrolling. Later, he entered the graduate program at the University of Chicago, where he earned his Ph.D. in 1940. However, due to lack of funds, a problem that would plague Goodman throughout the first five decades of his life, he could not afford to meet all the requirements for receiving his degree until 1954.

In 1938 Goodman entered into a common-law marriage with Virginia Miller. The two, who remained together until 1943, had a daughter in 1939. In 1945 Goodman married his occasional secretary, Sally Duchsten, with whom he had a son in 1946 and a daughter in 1963. They remained together for the rest of Goodman's life, but this, too, was a marriage under common law. Goodman refused on principle to obtain a marriage license: "I don't believe that people's sexual lives are any business of the state," he explained. "To license sex is absurd."

During the 1940s and 1950s Goodman published seven novels (one of these, *The Empire City* in 1959, was actually a tetralogy), four volumes of poetry, and seven works of nonfiction. Each of these, and particularly the nonfiction, constituted a building block in Goodman's emerging vision of society. For example, *Communitas* (1947, revised 1960), which he cowrote with his younger brother, an architect, presented a utopian vision of community and urban planning.

Goodman's radicalism, which had not been far from the intellectual mainstream in the 1930s, became decidedly unfashionable with the coming of World War II and the subsequent cold war. This philosophy, along with Goodman's unconventional lifestyle (he was openly bisexual), condemned him to a series of dismissals from jobs and forced his family to live at or below the poverty line. Following the bombing of Pearl Harbor in 1941, he lost a job as an occasional film critic for the *Partisan Review* because of his bisexuality and his opposition to the draft. His outspokenness regarding his lifestyle also led to dismissals from teaching positions at the Manumit School of Progressive Education in New York City in 1942, and from the experimental Black Mountain College in North Carolina in 1950. During those troubled years, he earned a part-time income as a lay therapist at the New York Institute of Gestalt Therapy; this work, combined with occasional teaching at New York University, helped to support his family. More often than not, however, his wife's secretarial income kept them fed and housed.

The characteristics that made Goodman an outcast in the 1940s and 1950s, ironically, placed him at the cultural forefront during the 1960s. The decade also brought him the fame and even commercial success that had eluded the forty-nine-year-old Goodman prior to 1960. Instrumental

to this turnaround was *Growing Up Absurd,* a loose collection of essays that had been rejected by a dozen publishers (including the one that commissioned it) before *Commentary* agreed to serialize it. Random House picked it up, and Goodman suddenly found himself with a nationwide audience.

It is hard to imagine a book more suited to its time than *Growing Up Absurd,* a work that epitomizes the discontent with 1950s normality then on the rise among certain American youths. Goodman assailed what he called "the organized system": capitalism, bureaucracy, and especially educational institutions. Setting the tone for the distrust of "the system" that would become rampant in the decade that followed, Goodman argued such bastions of repression served to stifle the basically generous and creative impulses in the human spirit.

With the success of *Growing Up Absurd,* Goodman suddenly found himself bombarded with publishing offers, and his record of publications from the 1960s reflects the change. In 1960, before crossing the watershed of his career, Goodman's *Day, and Other Poems* was privately printed. By contrast, Macmillan and Random House respectively issued *The Lordly Hudson: Collected Poems* (1962), and *Hawkweed* (1967). The same pattern occurred with his fiction: Horizon Press released a story collection called *Our Visit to Niagara* in 1960, but Macmillan took on the novel *Making Do* in 1963, and Random House issued the story collection *Adam and His Works* in 1968.

Yet Goodman's greatest strength, and his most prolific output, lay in his nonfiction. In addition to his breakthrough essay collection and the revised *Communitas,* Goodman published ten other nonfiction works during the decade. With a great deal of unpublished material to draw from, and with his writing suddenly in great demand, he availed himself of the opportunities the moment afforded, and in 1962 alone published three nonfiction books: *The Community of Scholars, Utopian Essays and Practical Proposals,* and *Drawing the Line.*

The tone of *Compulsory Mis-Education* (1964) is typical of Goodman's confrontational style in assessing the woes of Western society in general, and education in particular. "[I]n the tender grades," he wrote, "the schools are a babysitting service. . . . In the junior and senior grades, they are an arm of the police, providing cops and concentration camps." He went on to argue that the purpose of schools is actually "to provide apprentice training for corporations, government, and the teaching profession itself, and to train the young to adjust to authority."

The year 1964 also saw the rise of the Free Speech Movement at the University of California, Berkeley. Heavily influenced by Goodman, leaders of the movement regularly quoted his writings. For his part, Goodman praised the Berkeley environment as a laboratory for radicalism and anarchism. He lectured there occasionally, and in 1966 he taught at the Experimental College of San Francisco State College. In 1963 he served as the first visiting fellow of the Institute for Policy Studies, a radical think tank founded that year.

Goodman edited the pacifist journal *Liberation* from 1962 to 1969, and, with the writer Grace Paley and the photojournalist Karl Bissinger, helped to form a New York City branch of the anti–Vietnam War organization Resist. His involvement in the antiwar movement became deeply personal in 1967 when his son turned twenty-one, the age at which federal law required that he register for the draft. Instead of complying, Goodman's son participated in the first mass burning of draft cards in New York. His case was under investigation by the Federal Bureau of Investigation when he was killed during a mountain-climbing accident on 8 August 1967. Understandably devastated by the loss of his son, Goodman became much more deeply involved in the antiwar movement, often participating in demonstrations and being arrested.

His successes as a writer in the 1960s provided Goodman with an unaccustomed measure of economic freedom that made it possible for him to purchase a farm in North Stratford, where, aside from a stint at the University of Hawaii (1971 to 1972), he spent much of his remaining life. During that time, he continued to write, publish, and lecture widely. His other nonfiction works from the 1960s include *The Society I Live in Is Mine* (1963); *People or Personnel: Decentralizing and the Mixed System* (1965); *Five Years: Thoughts During a Useless Time* (1967), a partial autobiography; *Like a Conquered Province: The Moral Ambiguity of America* (1967); *The Individual and Culture* (1969); and *The Open Look* (1969). Goodman suffered a heart attack and died at his home. He is buried in Stratford Center Cemetery in Stratford, New Hampshire.

Although he is remembered as a radical, Goodman is not easily classified politically. He once said that in his libertarianism, his views sometimes veered close to those held by the radical right. He also refused to let his antipathy toward aspects of U.S. society and government sour him on what he once praised as "our beautiful, pluralist, and populist experiment" in democracy. During the latter part of his career, Goodman became increasingly disillusioned at some of the excesses taking place partly in the name of ideas he had helped to pioneer. His *The New Reformation: Notes of a Neolithic Conservative* (1970), a critique of the anti-intellectualism growing within the student movement, serves to illustrate his political independence. By the mid-1960s some student radicals had reacted by dismissing him as a "bourgeois individualist," yet many years later Todd Gitlin, the former president of the radical Students for a Democratic Society, remembered him warmly: "We loved

him for his bad manners," Gitlin wrote. "He was the insider's outsider, enormously learned yet economically and socially a man of the margins."

★

For a full-length biography of Goodman, see Kingsley Widmer, *Paul Goodman* (1980). Biographical insights may be found in Richard Kostelanetz, *Master Minds* (1969), and Todd Gitlin, *The Sixties: Years of Hope, Days of Rage* (1987). *Artist of the Actual: Essays on Paul Goodman* (1986), Peter Parisi, ed., deals with Goodman's ideas as a whole, and his psychology is addressed in Taylor Stoehr, *Here Now Next: Paul Goodman and the Origins of Gestalt Therapy* (1994). See also Tom Nicely, *Adam and His Work: A Bibliography of Sources by and About Paul Goodman* (1979). An obituary is in the *New York Times* (4 Aug. 1972).

JUDSON KNIGHT

GORDONE, Charles (*b.* 12 October 1925 in Cleveland, Ohio; *d.* 13 November 1995 in College Station, Texas), first African-American playwright to receive a Pulitzer Prize for drama.

One of seven children of William Gordone and Camille Morgan, Gordone left his boyhood home in Elkhart, Indiana, to earn a B.A. degree in drama from Los Angeles State College in 1952. After graduating, he moved to New York to pursue a singing career, abandoning that soon after to become an actor. He found work waiting tables at a Greenwich Village bar called Johnny Romero's, where he found material that would later resurface in *No Place to Be Somebody*. By 1953 Gordone had risen in the ranks of New York's struggling actors to win an Obie Award for his performance in an off-Broadway production of *Of Mice and Men*. He appeared in the original production of Jean Genet's *The Blacks* and toured with the show for four years.

Gordone spent most of the 1950s and 1960s directing stage productions of plays such as *Rebels and Bugs, Peer Gynt, Tobacco Road,* and *Detective Story*. His first play, *Little More Light Around the Place,* was cowritten with Sidney Easton and performed at the Sheridan Square Playhouse in New York in 1964. He married Jeanne Warner in 1959. The two had four children and nine grandchildren but eventually separated. He later married Susan Kouyomijan. His activism began in the 1960s when, as chair of the civil rights organization Congress of Racial Equality's (CORE) committee for employment of Negro performers, he fought for the inclusion of African Americans in the performing arts. Gordone himself claimed his ethnicity as "part Indian, part Irish, part French, and part nigger." He donned eccentric hats and rainbow love beads.

The years 1969 and 1970 were dense with success for Gordone. His play *No Place to Be Somebody* opened off-

Broadway in 1969 to rave reviews, and comparisons of Gordone to Eugene O'Neill abounded. He was called "the most astonishing new American playwright to come along since Albee." The play's lead characters are Johnny Williams, an African-American bar owner, and Gabe Gabriel, a struggling actor-playwright and the play's narrator. In the play, with his business struggling, Johnny survives off the earnings of the white prostitute who loves him, while anticipating the release of Sweets Crane from prison so the two can launch a black Mafia. Sweets returns reformed, however, and Johnny is left to scheme on his own. He ends up getting involved with the white Mafia and is shot.

The title *No Place to Be Somebody* implies alienation, and the characters cling desperately to their dreams in an attempt to fill the void. The action in the play is harsh and raw; feelings of love and hate fuel the passionate confrontations among the characters. The work was praised for the development of its colorful cast of characters and for its dialogue, which is lyrical and convincing, filled with pathos and insults. Gordone was generally praised for the sense of compassion, excitement, and intimacy he achieved between the characters. Some critics cited the influence of the tradition of Greek, Elizabethan, and Jacobean drama, although Gordone denies the influence of other writers on his work.

Given Gordone's ethnicity, many critics took the work to be an exploration of the African-American experience—he was, in fact, hailed as the new voice for blacks. But Gordone believed that his themes did not apply solely to blacks, and thus some African-American critics faulted the play. They cited "evidence" of self-hate in the work, a hint of contempt for his race. Other critics gave him kudos for tackling the complete human experience. Among black revolutionary dramatists, Gordone would be considered conservative. But he believed that not being categorized is an advantage for any playwright, and that lack of definition gave him the freedom to create diverse characters. For these efforts Gordone was sometimes criticized for trying to cover too much dramatic ground.

When he won the Pulitzer Prize for drama in 1970, Gordone was the first African American to do so, and *No Place to Be Somebody* was the first Pulitzer-winning drama to win before being staged on Broadway. Gordone also earned the New York and Los Angeles Critics' Circle Awards and the Drama Desk Award. *No Place to Be Somebody* went on to a two-year run on Broadway and a three-year national tour. The play has been widely translated and produced abroad, as well as on many community and college stages in the United States.

The acclaim Gordone garnered for *No Place to Be Somebody* set him up for a letdown of sorts; none of his later works would ever match that play's critical or popular success. The prize also broke his momentum as a writer; he

neglected his typewriter for several years during the 1970s to direct national tours of *No Place to Be Somebody*. In 1975 he worked with a group of inmates in a New Jersey youth correctional facility on Clifford Odets's play *Golden Boy*. But Gordone managed to churn out a handful of plays, including *Willy Bignigga* (1970), *Chimpanzee* (1970), *Baba-Chops* (1975), *The Last Chord* (1977), and *A Qualification of Anabiosis* (1978).

Gordone spent the last two decades of his life directing plays and lecturing. As a director, he continued his activism by casting minority actors in nontraditional roles that did not acknowledge ethnicity. He cast Hispanics as migrant laborers in *Of Mice and Men* in a production at the American Stage in Berkeley, California, and a Creole actor as Stanley in *A Streetcar Named Desire*. Over the course of his career, Gordone directed more than thirty-four productions, including *The Colored Museum, The Glass Menagerie, Death of a Salesman, Book of the Dead,* and *Faust.* In 1987 he took a faculty position at Texas A&M University in College Station, Texas, where he taught English and theater until his death from cancer at his home.

★

Further information on Gordone is in *Speaking on Stage: Interviews with Contemporary American Playwrights* (1996), Philip C. Kolin and Colby H. Kullman, eds. See also Jeanne-Marie A. Miller, "A Drama of the Black Experience," *Journal of Negro Education* (spring 1971); Dorothy Lee, "Three Black Plays: Alienation and Paths to Recovery," *Modern Drama* (Dec. 1976); and Richard H. Costa, "The Short, Happy Afterlife of Charles Gordone," *Touchstone* (Feb./Mar. 1996). An obituary is in the *New York Times* (19 Nov. 1995).

BRENNA SANCHEZ

GORDY, Berry, Jr. (*b.* 28 November 1929 in Detroit, Michigan), songwriter and founder of Motown Records, the most successful African-American–owned and operated business of the 1960s.

Gordy was the seventh of eight children born to Berry Gordy and Bertha Ida Fuller. The Gordy family had a history of entrepreneurship as farmers and small business owners in rural Georgia. Migrating to Detroit in 1922, Gordy's father worked as a plasterer before opening up a grocery store in the city's east side Black Bottom neighborhood and running his own contracting business. Bertha Gordy taught elementary school in Georgia and subsequently founded the Friendship Mutual Life Insurance Company. In addition to running a family-owned print shop, the Gordys established a cooperative fund to help family members open their own businesses.

Throughout his young adulthood Gordy seemed to depart from his family's model of success. Dropping out of

Berry Gordy, Jr. (*left*), 1964. HULTON ARCHIVE

Detroit's Northeastern High School, he pursued a short-lived career in boxing in the late 1940s. After a tour of duty in the Korean War from 1951 to 1952, he returned to Detroit and took out a loan from his family to open up a record store specializing in jazz music. The store failed, but it provided Gordy with insight about the shifting tastes in popular music of the mid-1950s. To make ends meet, Gordy took a job on the assembly line of a Lincoln-Mercury plant. He hated the work, but later cited the assembly line at the factory as an inspiration for the operation of Motown Records. Compounding his business failures was the breakup in 1959 of his marriage to Thelma Coleman, whom he had married in 1953, and with whom he had three children. Gordy later had a brief marriage, from 1960 to 1962, to Motown executive Raynoma Liles, which produced a son; he also fathered four children during other relationships, including a daughter with Diana Ross.

Through his older sisters Gwen and Anna, who operated the photo concession at Detroit's renowned Flame Show Bar, Gordy met singer Jackie Wilson around 1957. By the end of the year Wilson had a minor hit with "Reet Petite," a song composed by Gwen and Gordy and produced by Gordy in a Detroit recording studio. Wilson followed it with a string of hits that Gordy cowrote and produced, including the Top Ten pop hit "Lonely Teardrops." Although the records gave Gordy the chance to gain ex-

perience as a producer, the difficulties he had getting record distributors to pay him led him to start his own publishing company, Jobete Music. On 12 January 1959 Gordy took out an $800 loan from the Gordy family cooperative to buy a bungalow at 2648 West Grand Boulevard, in Detroit, and establish Motown Records.

Under Gordy's supervision, Motown Records focused on three primary tasks: creating popular music, controlling its distribution, and selling it to the broadest possible audience. As he told *Rolling Stone* in 1990, "I worked in the Ford factory before I came in the business, and I saw how each person did a different thing. And I said, 'Why can't we do that with the creative process?' . . . It was just that assembly-line approach to things."

He would later be criticized for restricting Motown artists to less generous contracts than those offered by major labels, but Gordy's system allowed for a creative freedom that resulted in some of the best pop and rhythm and blues (R&B) records of the 1960s. Motown's first million-selling single, the Miracles' "Shop Around," was released at the end of 1960, and the company had its first number-one single on the pop chart the following year with the Marvelettes' "Please Mr. Postman." Motown also scored Top Ten hits in 1962 and 1963 with Mary Wells and with Martha and the Vandellas. Both Wells and Martha Reeves would later claim that Motown paid insufficient royalties to its artists, a claim that Gordy dismissed as unjustified in light of the company's success in turning the singers into household names.

By 1964 Gordy's stable of producers included Smokey Robinson (also lead singer of the Miracles), Norman Whitfield, and the team of Eddie Holland, Lamont Dozier, and Brian Holland (H-D-H). The Supremes scored ten of their twelve number-one singles between 1964 and 1969 with songs written and produced by H-D-H, including "Where Did Our Love Go?," "You Can't Hurry Love," and the group's biggest hit, "Baby Love." The Supremes were Motown's most successful group of the decade, followed by the Temptations, the Miracles, and the Four Tops. Among solo artists, Marvin Gaye, who had Motown's biggest single of the decade with "I Heard It Through the Grapevine," and Stevie Wonder were the most consistent hit-makers.

Although some civil rights and Black Power activists criticized Motown artists for not taking an overt political stand on contemporary social issues, Berry took a different view, as he reflected in a 1990 *Rolling Stone* interview: "Both sides were playing Motown music. . . . We were just trying to create the type of music that would move us into a wider audience." Motown's commercial success symbolized the economic progress that African Americans hoped to achieve during the civil rights era; in similar fashion, the widespread recognition that Motown artists achieved on radio and television airwaves represented a cultural breakthrough for African-American artists during the decade.

By the mid-1960s "the Motown sound"—up-tempo bass and drum beats, clear vocal arrangements, and romantic lyrics—made the company the most successful independent record label in the United States, with revenues of $8 million in 1965. With Motown's "assembly line" consistently producing hits, Gordy only grudgingly allowed social commentary to creep into the lyrics of Motown releases such as "Cloud Nine," by the Temptations, "Love Child," by Diana Ross and the Supremes in 1968, and Marvin Gaye's 1971 album *What's Going On?* In 1973—the year after Gordy announced that Motown was relocating to Los Angeles—the company was the largest African-American–owned corporation in the United States, with revenues of over $40 million. In 1988 Gordy announced the sale of Motown Records to media giant MCA Records. In 1997 he sold half of Jobete, which held the copyrights to over 15,000 songs, to EMI Music Publishing for $132 million. To those who equated Motown's success with the advances made by the civil rights movement, the sales represented the end of an era in African-American history. Gordy was inducted into the Rock and Roll Hall of Fame in 1990.

★

Gordy's autobiography is *To Be Loved: The Music, the Magic, the Memories of Motown* (1994). Histories of Motown Records include Nelson George, *Where Did Our Love Go?: The Rise and Fall of the Motown Sound* (1985); Suzanne E. Smith, *Dancing in the Street: Motown and the Cultural Politics of Detroit* (1999); and Kingsley Abbott, ed., *Calling Out Around the World: A Motown Reader* (2001). Berry's former wife Raynoma (Liles) Singleton published an account of Motown's history in *Berry, Me, and Motown: The Untold Story* (1989). Berry conducted lengthy interviews in *Rolling Stone* (23 Aug. 1990), and with Adam White and Terry Barnes in *Billboard* (5 Nov. 1994). Profiles of Gordy and Motown have appeared in *Crain's Detroit Business* (1 Nov. 1999), and on National Public Radio's *Morning Edition* (4 June 2000). A list of Motown's chart singles appears in Joel Whitburn, ed., *The Billboard Book of Top Forty Hits,* 6th ed. (1996).

TIMOTHY BORDEN

GREGORY, Richard Claxton ("Dick") (*b.* 12 October 1932 in St. Louis, Missouri), African-American stand-up comic and political activist who exploited his fame to promote social causes.

Gregory was the second of six children born to Presley Gregory and Lucille Franklin. The Gregory siblings were raised by their mother in dire poverty in an African-American ghetto. A track star at Sumner High School, Gregory graduated as class president in 1952. He enrolled at Southern Illinois University in Carbondale on an athletic scholarship, but was drafted into the U.S. Army in 1954. He reenrolled at Southern Illinois after his discharge in 1956, but did not earn a degree.

Gregory despised both poverty and racism. He often masked his pain with humorous ad-libs, a talent that would develop into a full-blown comedy career in adulthood. In the mid-1950s he moved to Chicago, where he worked assorted day jobs and performed as a comedian in nightclubs, eventually operating his own club, the Apex, in Robbins, Illinois, in 1958. On 2 February 1959 he married Lillian Smith; they had ten children.

On stage Gregory transcended racial barriers and attracted diverse audiences through sarcasm and ridicule of bigotry. His career as a stand-up comic was in full swing by the mid-1960s, and he had earned a reputation as a civil rights activist even while appearing as a comedian at popular venues nationwide. In 1963 he was involved with a black voter-registration drive in Greenwood, Mississippi, and during the Christmas holiday that year he took part in a protest to integrate restaurants in Atlanta. His wife, then pregnant with twins, accompanied him and was arrested for sitting at a public eatery; she spent Christmas day in the local jail. Gregory's name recognition was instrumental in bringing the cause to national attention.

In 1964 Gregory threw his influence behind a grassroots

civil rights organization called ACT; he attended a school boycott rally in New York City and worked also to initiate a boycott by 200,000 students in Chicago. At the request of Gloria (Richardson) Dandridge, he made several appearances in Cambridge, Maryland. Also that year he touted the cause of human rights internationally, visiting Europe and the Soviet Union. While in Moscow he learned of the suspicious disappearance of three civil rights workers in Jackson, Mississippi, and hurried back to the United States to assess the situation. Almost immediately he raised $25,000 toward a reward fund for information concerning the perpetrators of the incident.

Gregory's agenda as an entertainer brought him to San Francisco during the Republican National Convention of 1964, where he found no dearth of material for his comedy routine. He made arrangements to appear in the tri-state (New York, New Jersey, Pennsylvania) area the following month for the Democratic National Convention in Atlantic City, then celebrated the Christmas holiday in Jackson, assisting with the delivery and distribution of thousands of turkeys to LeFlore County families who had lost their food subsidies when local officials retaliated against the black voter-registration program.

While working on a feature film in Philadelphia in 1965, Gregory abandoned the movie set and traveled to Selma, Alabama, to march with Dr. Martin Luther King, Jr., in the historic crossing of the Pettus Bridge. He rejoined the film crew in Pennsylvania but returned to the marchers four days later for the triumphant entry into Montgomery, Alabama. When asked whether his political involvements affected his career, Gregory indicated that the reverse was true: his career, he said, hampered his political agenda. When the film *Sweet Love, Bitter* premiered on 30 January 1966, it received excellent reviews.

In the summer of 1965 Gregory demonstrated again, to halt illegal school segregation in Chicago; he was arrested and beaten in the presence of his family outside the city hall in June. He refused to abandon the protest, and in July, despite a performance engagement in San Francisco, he commuted daily between California and Chicago. A march on Mayor Richard Daley's house in Chicago in August led to his arrest and conviction for provoking violence by his very presence; on appeal, the U.S. Supreme Court reversed the judgment as unconstitutional.

When Gregory learned of the outbreak of rioting in the Watts district of Los Angeles in 1965, he flew to the scene, where he received a superficial gunshot wound while attempting to quell rioters. In January 1966 he backed the successful mayoral campaign of John Lindsay in New York City, and in March, while performing in Seattle, Gregory took up the cause of the Nisqually Indians against Washington State over fishing rights. He was arrested, tried, and convicted of illegal fishing during a protest.

Dick Gregory. THE LIBRARY OF CONGRESS

On a break from touring the college lecture circuit during the 1966–1967 academic year, Gregory joined Father James Groppi in support of fair housing for Milwaukee, Wisconsin, residents. After campaigning as an independent write-in candidate for mayor of Chicago that fall, he endured a self-imposed forty-day fast, from Thanksgiving to New Year's Day 1968, in protest of the Vietnam War. His facetious run for the U.S. presidency that year lost its thunder in the spring when King and Robert F. Kennedy were assassinated within weeks of each other. The gloom was exacerbated by a Washington State appeals court, which upheld Gregory's earlier conviction for illegal fishing. He began serving a ninety-day sentence at the Thurston County Jail on 7 June, fasting the entire time; after forty days he was released because of health problems. He resumed fasting in Chicago's Cook County Jail in the spring of 1969 after being sentenced to five months on charges stemming back to 1965 for assaulting an officer. After forty-five days of fasting, Gregory's sentence was commuted. He attended the World Assembly for Peace in June and the first Vietnam War moratorium in Washington, D.C., in October of that year.

After a decade of change and upheaval, Gregory resumed his performance career with greater intensity in 1970. According to a report in *Variety* that year: "Dick Gregory . . . [took] a break from his civil rights activities and related college speaking dates to play a rare . . . gig." *Newsweek* called this resurgence of the comic "Return of the Native Son." Gregory appeared in the Mario Van Peebles film *Panther* in 1995.

★

Gregory chronicles his 1960s escapades in *Up from Nigger* (1976), with James R. McGraw. He recaps his life in the twentieth century in *Callus on My Soul: The Autobiography of Dick Gregory* (2000), with Shelia P. Moses. For more information on Gregory see Thonnia Lee, "Fasting for Life," *Health Quest: The Publication of Black Wellness* (31 Mar. 1994); and Juan Williams, "Interview: Author, Activist and Comedian Dick Gregory Discusses His Life and His Views on Social Consciousness," *Talk of the Nation* (NPR) (25 Dec. 2000).

GLORIA COOKSEY

GRISSOM, Virgil Ivan ("Gus") (*b.* 3 April 1926 in Mitchell, Indiana; *d.* 27 January 1967 in Cape Kennedy [now Cape Canaveral], Florida), U.S. Air Force pilot who in the 1960s became one of the first seven U.S. astronauts; the second American to fly in space and the first to maneuver his spacecraft; the first American to fly into space twice; and the commander of *Apollo 1,* the prototype vessel for those used to fly astronauts to the Moon.

Grissom was the first of four children of Dennis Grissom, an employee of the Baltimore and Ohio Railroad, and Cecile (King) Grissom, a homemaker. Almost as soon as he could read, Grissom was studying airplanes, and for much of his youth he made wooden models of planes, fascinated by their mechanical complexity as well as by their ability to fly. He wanted to become a pilot.

Grissom graduated from Mitchell High School in 1944 and enlisted in flight school for the U.S. Army Air Corps with an eye to flying in World War II. He married Betty Moore, his high-school sweetheart, on 6 July 1945; they had two sons. With the end of the war, instead of flying, Grissom was assigned a desk job, much to his dismay. He soon left the air corps in November 1945 to take a job maintaining buses.

Grissom wanted to be more than a bus mechanic and enrolled at Purdue University in West Lafayette, Indiana, to pursue a degree in mechanical engineering. He graduated with a B.S. in 1950, enlisted in the air force, and received his wings in 1951. He was assigned to the 334th Fighter Interceptor Squadron in Korea, where he flew one hundred combat missions as a wing man. Grissom won the Air Medal with an oak-leaf cluster and the Distinguished Flying Cross for his service in Korea.

After completing his combat missions, Lieutenant Colonel Grissom was assigned to Bryan, Texas, to train raw pilots; he half-jokingly said that training those pilots was much more dangerous than flying in combat. He wanted to become a test pilot and therefore put in many extra hours of flying and training, earning a reputation as a dedicated worker and as one of the air force's best pilots. In 1955 he was sent to Edwards Air Force Base in California to attend test pilot school, and in 1957 he began test flying cutting-edge jet aircraft at Wright-Patterson Air Force Base in Ohio.

In 1958 the U.S. Congress created the National Aeronautics and Space Administration (NASA), and Grissom received a mysterious order from the air force to report to Washington, D.C., in civilian clothes for a top-secret mission. It turned out he was one of the 110 pilots selected as candidates for a NASA program to launch people into space. Grissom felt honored and excited and agreed to undergo lengthy, unpleasant tests in order to qualify to become an astronaut.

On 13 April 1959 Grissom was named as one of the Mercury Seven, the seven pilots chosen to become the first U.S. astronauts. The Grissoms moved to Langley Air Force Base in Virginia to be near the training site for his spaceflight. On 12 April 1961 Yuri Gagarin of the Soviet Union became the first person to travel in space. Alan Shepard was selected to be the first American in space, taking a short flight on 5 May 1961. Grissom was chosen for the next flight, and he named his craft *Liberty Bell* 7 because the capsule was bell shaped. His craft was an improvement over Shepard's, with a bigger window and better controls. Grissom's mission was to test how the spacecraft maneuvered (he found the controls sluggish) and to confirm some of what was learned from Shepard's flight.

Fifteen minutes after his launch on 21 July 1961, Grissom splashed down in the Atlantic Ocean. He went through all of his splashdown procedures, then relaxed and waited for helicopters to hoist the capsule out of the water so he could safely exit the craft. According to Grissom, the hatch to the craft abruptly boomed and popped off. The door had explosive bolts on it, so that it could be blown open by the astronaut inside or a rescuer from the outside. Only days earlier a test had been scrubbed because one of the bolts was misaligned. There are many theories about what happened on 21 July. One is that Grissom panicked and blew the door open prematurely, although the engineers involved said this was not possible without Grissom's leaving evidence of his actions.

When NASA opened its new headquarters in Houston, Texas, the Grissoms moved to nearby Seabrook, where they had a house built with no windows facing the street; Gris-

Virgil "Gus" Grissom before the Gemini flight, 1961. Associated Press, NASA

som disliked the news media prying into his private life. At the Manned Space Center in Houston, Grissom joined the Gemini space program, which involved having two astronauts, not just one, inside spacecraft. He was made the backup for Shepard for a 23 March 1965 spaceflight. When Shepard became seriously ill, Grissom was named as the commander of the flight. He had worked on the Gemini designs from the beginning of the program. The craft he flew showed his influence, especially in the layout of the controls, which his fellow astronauts admired for their good sense. After the launch at Cape Kennedy, Grissom became the first person to fly in space twice.

Grissom was next assigned to the Apollo program, which was intended to send people to the Moon and back. He was named as the commander of *Apollo 1,* a test craft meant only to orbit Earth. Grissom was dismayed by the spacecraft's design flaws, and many parts had to be replaced, redesigned, or eliminated. On 27 January 1967 Grissom and his fellow astronauts Roger Chaffee and Edward White were sealed inside the *Apollo 1* capsule, testing its systems, when a spark ignited the oxygen in the chamber. Although the Soviets had been using ordinary air successfully, the U.S. program was using only pure oxygen for the astronauts to breathe. The oxygen exploded. The door required ninety seconds to open, by which time all three astronauts had died of suffocation.

Grissom was buried on 10 February 1967 in Arlington National Cemetery in Virginia.

Grissom's most lasting accomplishment may have been his development of a system of controls that put astronauts in charge of their craft. This was important for the first Moon landing in 1969, during which the landing craft had to be manually maneuvered to a safe landing place, and in 1970, when the *Apollo 13* crew members still were able to maneuver their craft after most of the automatic controls had ceased functioning. Grissom's design influence continued in the space shuttles of the 1980s and 1990s, in which the controls allowed pilots to take the initiative.

★

Grissom, *Gemini: A Personal Account of Man's Venture into Space* (1968), offers a firsthand account of his experiences. Another good resource is Betty Grissom and Henry Still, *Starfall* (1974). See also M. Scott Carpenter, *We Seven, by the Astronauts Themselves* (1962) and Carl L. Chappell, *Seven Minus One: The Story of Gus Grissom* (1962). An obituary is in the *New York Times* (28 Jan. 1967).

Kirk H. Beetz

GROOMS, Charles Rogers ("Red") (*b.* 2 June 1937 in Nashville, Tennessee), multimedia artist famous since the 1960s for environmental walk-in sculptures that are boldly colored and comic-book naive in style.

The older of two sons born to Charles Grooms, a highway equipment engineer, and his wife, Martha, a homemaker, Grooms was known from his youth by the nickname "Red" because of his carrot-colored hair and his preference for wearing bright red clothes. What Grooms would become famous for, beginning in the 1960s, was the creation of walk-in environments for the public. When they were children, he and his brother, Spencer, filled their backyard with an elaborately constructed toy circus so that they could live in their own Ringling Brothers environment. Grooms avidly attended movies, and Saturday afternoon cliffhanger serials especially absorbed him. During the 1940s into the 1950s, such matinee experiences included cartoons, a feature, and a weekly serial. Serial heroes such as Captain America or Dick Tracy would face dastardly villains who, in elaborate and campy plots, would almost vanquish them. In those days before television, these serials constituted the principal form of episodic entertainment, leaving audiences to wait until the next week to see how the hero escaped. Grooms was disappointed, however, in the filmed versions of his favorite comics: "I expected," he later said, "to see Dick Tracy with the same hook nose and famous profile I saw on the comic pages." His later artworks would retain the cartoonish quality of his comic-book sources, and those

Red Grooms. THE LIBRARY OF CONGRESS

sources would provide the content of the later walk-in art environments.

Classmates at Nashville's Hillsboro High School, which Grooms attended from 1951 to 1955, considered him witty and fun loving, yet it was in his high school art class that he first decided to become an artist. During his senior year he enrolled in the Famous Artists Correspondence School, but he discontinued it because the correspondence school gave him low grades for his shading in illustrations. In 1955 he briefly attended Nashville's George Peabody School for Teachers and then enrolled at the Art Institute of Chicago. In 1958 he moved to Provincetown, Massachusetts, to take a summer course in painting with the painter Hans Hoffmann. Grooms, however, did not appreciate Hoffmann's abstract style and rigorous teaching methods.

Later that year, he permanently settled in New York City, where he supported himself as a dishwasher, a sandwich maker, and as the head usher at the Roxy Theater while living in various cold-water lofts in New York's Greenwich Village and Chelsea areas. During this time, Grooms attended uptown painting shows and downtown avant-garde theater. He was fascinated, in particular, by "happenings" or "painter's theater," in which a visual artist animated an environment with nonactors performing assigned tasks. In the late 1950s a group of artists—Allan

Kaprow, Jim Dine, and Claes Oldenberg, among others— formed a cooperative loft space called the Reuben Gallery, which became the locale for their exhibitions and happenings. In 1958 and 1959 Grooms participated as a performer and then as a director of happenings, including *The Burning Building* (1959), which comically evoked flames devouring a cardboard construction, with Grooms playing both a pyromaniac and a fireman. In addition to happenings, Grooms made small sculptures from cast-off materials.

In 1960–1961 Grooms lived in Europe, where he spent time studying painting and sculpture with the expressionist painter Oskar Kokoschka. A fellow student was Mimi Gross, daughter of the sculptor Chaim Gross; after they finished their course, they toured northern Italy in a horse-drawn gypsy wagon, vividly decorated by Gross. "Ruckus" was the name of the horse, and that name would be attached to Grooms's later projects when he founded the "Ruckus Construction Company." Grooms and Gross were married in 1964. Like his brother, his wife would become a part of the troupe of collaborators who assisted Grooms in his later productions.

When Grooms returned to New York in 1962, he collaborated in making films with Rudi Burckhardt and, in 1963, with George and Mike Kuchar. These animated and action films suggest the antics of his earlier happenings and exude the childlike wonder of his experiences watching Saturday matinees. *Shoot the Moon* (1962) celebrates the poetry and magic of Georges Melies, a very early French film director who blended sculptural design and science fiction. Later Grooms films spoof the elaborate Hollywood musicals he had enjoyed as a child.

In 1963 Grooms constructed *The Banquet of Douanier Rousseau,* the first of his elaborate signature art tableau environments, which he called "picot-sculptoramas," affectionate and joke-filled allusions to art history and culture. This particular piece alludes to a famous 1908 dinner by the Parisian avant-garde to honor the "primitive" artist Henri Rousseau. (Grooms himself was associated with a particularly American primitive tradition: the 9 April 1965 issue of *Time* nicknamed him "Grand Pop Moses," likening him to Grandma Moses with his "quaint, cozy, whimsical realism.")

Another Ruckus construction was *An Installation: The City of Chicago* (1967) in which an arch with caricatures of that city's notables hovers over tilted skyscrapers and the Chicago River. In 1968 this work would be the sensation of the Venice Biennale, an international art-world showcase held every two years. Later "picot-sculptoramas" comically send up a discount store, a rodeo, the Moon landing, and Manhattan. They are all walk-through environments that teem with brightly colored and sometimes mechanically animated allusions to characters, events, and places of a particular locale or event. The gaudy colors, exaggerated features, and inventive satire of his Ruckus environments are characteristic also of the hundreds of drawings, prints, and small sculptures he has produced since the 1960s.

Grooms would research a theme or a subject thoroughly. "I like to make sort of documentaries," he explained to *Time* in 1965. "Something you can see as it happens— what people wear and do." His observations of a theme were transformed by his art into detailed and colorful entertainments. Since the early 1960s Grooms has specialized in highly engaging and comically naive style works in all media. They are crammed with amusing detail and chaotic incident. His sprawling mixed media constructions are deranged comic-book environments that hark back to his original backyard circus as a child. They also anticipated and enormously influenced many emerging artists since the 1970s, who have combined Grooms's loony and boldly painted style with a more urbane sophistication. Critics associate Grooms with the pop art that transformed American commercial and pop culture into works of art in their own right. For his part, Grooms has always seen himself as both an entertainer and a comic artist. His work, even when it deals with potentially satirical or lurid material, is that of showman who creates joyous and exhilarating toys and shows for art-world adults.

★

An overview of Grooms's work is Carter Ratcliff, *Red Grooms* (1984), and a comprehensive exhibition catalogue is J. E. Stein, John Ashbery, and J. K. Cutler, *Red Grooms: A Retrospective*. Also see "Grand Pop Moses," *Time* (9 Apr. 1965).

PATRICK S. SMITH

GROPPI, James Edmund (*b.* 16 November 1930 in Milwaukee, Wisconsin; *d.* 4 November 1985 in Milwaukee, Wisconsin), Catholic priest who led members of the Milwaukee National Association for the Advancement of Colored People (NAACP) Youth Council on a series of marches into white neighborhoods in 1967 and 1968, marches that forced the city council to pass a strong open-housing ordinance.

Groppi grew up in a largely Italian working-class neighborhood in Milwaukee, the eleventh of twelve children born to Giocondo and Giorgina (Magri) Groppi. Giocondo ran a grocery store. As a student at Bay View High School, Groppi wrote an essay on brotherhood and racial justice after an incident with a black player on an opposing basketball team. In 1953 he began studying for the Roman Catholic priesthood at Mount Calvary Seminary, transferring to Saint Francis Seminary after two years. During three of his summers as a seminarian, he directed a day camp at Blessed Martin de Porres parish in Milwaukee's inner city. He received a B.A. in theology in 1959 and was

ordained and assigned to Saint Veronica's parish that same year. In 1963 he was appointed assistant pastor at Saint Boniface, a predominantly black parish on Milwaukee's north side.

The slight, intense young priest soon became engrossed in the civil rights movement. In 1963 he participated in the March on Washington. In March 1965 he traveled to Selma, Alabama, with three other priests to join voting rights demonstrations led by the Reverend Martin Luther King, Jr. Returning to Milwaukee, he confronted the pervasive de facto segregation existing in northern cities. He joined the Milwaukee United School Integration Committee to press for the racial integration of public schools. The first of his more than one dozen arrests occurred on 4 June 1965, when he protested the segregation of black children within a white Milwaukee school. Groppi embraced a radical social gospel that held that justice required clergymen to confront established authority when working for the poor and disenfranchised. "Agitate, agitate, agitate is my motto," he once told a reporter. His militant stance attracted an enthusiastic following among young blacks, who asked him to be their adviser in the Milwaukee National Association for the Advancement of Colored People (NAACP) Youth Council.

The Youth Council's first target under Groppi's leadership was the Fraternal Order of Eagles and its whites-only membership policy. When picketing the Eagles' club building in February and March 1966 produced little attention, the group switched its protests to the homes of elected officials who were members. In August picketers appeared in front of the suburban home of Judge Robert C. Cannon. Their presence attracted a crowd of white bigots, who showered the demonstrators with eggs, bottles, and firecrackers. After nine nights of increasing violence, the mayor requested that National Guard troops be called out to protect the young picketers. Although many officials resigned from the organization, the Youth Council was unable to force a change in the Eagles' policy.

Groppi gained national notoriety in August 1967 when he led the Youth Council and other supporters on a series of marches into predominantly white south side neighborhoods. Their objective was to gain passage of a citywide open-housing ordinance. The protestors were met by white mobs that threw bottles, hurled obscenities, and hanged the priest in effigy. Security for the marches was provided by the Youth Council's direct action committee, better known as the "commandos," who dressed in distinctive black berets. On 31 August 1967 Groppi was among 137 people arrested for defying a ban on nighttime demonstrations. The marches, which continued for 200 consecutive days, have been described as "the most extensive campaign in the U.S. against housing bias." They finally ceased in April 1968, when the city council passed a strong open-housing

James E. Groppi speaking at the American Society of Newspaper Editors convention, 1968. © Bettmann/ Corbis

law. More than fifty other Wisconsin communities subsequently adopted statutes modeled on the Milwaukee ordinance.

In later years Groppi championed the causes of welfare recipients and Native Americans as well as protesting against the Vietnam War. On 29 September 1969 he and one thousand followers shut down the Wisconsin state assembly in Madison with a sit-in to protest cuts in welfare payments. The U.S. Supreme Court eventually overturned Groppi's conviction for contempt in this demonstration.

In 1970 Groppi left Saint Boniface's parish, turning over that ministry to a black priest. He served as part of the pastoral team at Saint Michael's parish until 1972, when he entered Antioch Law School in Washington, D.C. On 22 April 1976 he married Margaret Rozga, a fellow activist, and was excommunicated from the Catholic Church. He always considered himself a priest and continued to celebrate mass in private homes and perform weddings and baptisms for friends. The father of three children, he worked as a cabdriver and later as a bus driver for the Milwaukee County Transit System. In 1983 he was elected president of the transit workers' union. He died of brain cancer at the age of fifty-four.

Groppi epitomized the radical Catholic activism that flourished during the late 1960s. Drawing their inspiration from the Gospels and from Martin Luther King, Jr.'s nonviolent tactics, these militants disrupted the status quo in the name of social justice. None was more dedicated or persistent than Groppi. He suffered criticism from his ec-

clesiastical superiors and from lay Catholics who felt uncomfortable seeing a priest leading a demonstration or going to jail. Groppi maintained that his agitation was a legitimate expression of his religious calling—ministering to the needs of society's most underprivileged members. His legacy may be found in the open-housing legislation he championed and in the commandos, who reorganized as an inner city social service agency.

★

Groppi's papers are housed in the State Historical Society of Wisconsin collection at the University of Wisconsin-Milwaukee. Frank A. Aukofer, *City with a Chance* (1968), contains a journalistic account of his early activism. Obituaries are in the *Milwaukee Journal* (4 Nov. 1985) and *New York Times* (5 Nov. 1985).

Paul T. Murray

GRUENING, Ernest (*b.* 6 February 1887 in New York City; *d.* 26 June 1974 in Washington, D.C.), U.S. senator from Alaska (1959–1969) and ardent opponent of U.S. policies in Vietnam.

The son of Emil Gruening, a German-born eye and ear surgeon, and Phebe Fridenberg, Gruening was educated in various New York City schools, and at the Hotchkiss School in Connecticut. He graduated from Harvard College in 1907 and Harvard Medical School in 1912, but gave up medicine in order to become a newspaper journalist. He reported for *Boston American* in 1912, and for several other Boston newspapers, before moving on to become managing editor of the *New York Tribune* (later the *New York Herald Tribune*) in 1917. In 1918 Gruening entered the U.S. Army, and briefly served in the field artillery corps, but was discharged after World War I ended later that year. Gruening married Dorothy Elisabeth Smith on 19 November 1914; they had two sons.

Throughout the 1920s Gruening worked as a journalist, and opposed what he saw as U.S. imperialism. Writing for *The Nation* from 1920 to 1923, he criticized U.S. intervention in Haiti and Central America. This opposition to U.S. adventurism abroad was a central theme to which he would frequently return throughout his life.

From 1934 to 1939 Gruening directed the territories and island possessions division of the U.S. Department of the Interior and from 1935 to 1937 headed the Puerto Rico Reconstruction Administration. In 1939 President Franklin D. Roosevelt appointed him governor of the territory of Alaska. Reappointed twice, Gruening served until 1953.

Known as "the father of Alaska statehood," Gruening earned this title by arguing that in a country claiming to be a democracy, Alaska should become a state simply because the majority of its inhabitants wished it. Furthermore, Alaska as a state would serve to strengthen the Union, and in a post–World War II era in which U.S. foreign policy focused on preventing the spread of Communism around the globe, Alaska would serve as a bulwark of defense, especially considering its location directly opposite Soviet Russia.

In 1959 Alaska became a state, and Gruening, a Democrat, went to the U.S. Senate as one of its first two senators. He served as senator until 1969. Gruening was notable for his passionate stance against the Vietnam War, which began in October 1963 when he launched his first wave of attacks, criticizing President John F. Kennedy for sending so-called advisers to support the army of South Vietnam. His dissent joined with that of Senator Wayne Morse of Oregon, who also criticized the administration, claiming that U.S. intervention had violated international law and defied the constitution. According to Gruening and Morse, the United Nations, not the United States, should serve to arbitrate this dispute in Southeast Asia.

On 10 March 1964 Gruening delivered his first full-length speech in the Senate, "The United States Should Get Out of Vietnam." Urging the withdrawal of U.S. forces in South Vietnam, he called it absurd to "persist in seeking to prevent what is ultimately inevitable, in impossible terrain, for people who care not." To his dismay, his speech was largely ignored.

On 7 August 1964 the Senate voted 88 to 2 to approve a resolution granting President Lyndon B. Johnson blanket authority to respond to two North Vietnamese attacks against U.S. patrol vessels in the Gulf of Tonkin. In opposing this Gulf of Tonkin Resolution, Gruening stated that he did so because "That means sending our boys into combat in a war in which we have no business, which is not our war, into which we have been misguidedly drawn, which is steadily being escalated." In short, he said, "I am opposed to sacrificing a single American boy in this venture." However, the only other senator to agree with Gruening was Morse. Although Gruening and Morse displayed outspoken opposition to the escalating U.S. involvement in Vietnam, a direct result of the Gulf of Tonkin Resolution, administration officials considered the two to be too weak in the Senate to threaten the executive branch's freedom of action. They became the first of a long list of opponents to U.S. involvement in Vietnam.

In later years Gruening claimed that he had not been a pacifist; rather, "I just think that this war was so completely without justification that we should never have been in it." After all, he stated, Gruening had fought in World War I. In addition, Gruening and some of his colleagues believed that anticommunism had too frequently justified aid to dictatorial right-wing regimes. Throughout his life, Gruening constantly argued that the United States, founded by revolution and the ideals of democracy and a participatory system of government, must adopt a foreign policy friendly to reformers overseas. Thus he proposed in the early 1960s to restore democracy in the Dominican Republic, where the Johnson administration had supported a dictatorship with troops, by "whatever steps are necessary"—including the use of the U.S. military. It was in Latin America, Gruening said in the mid-1960s, that the United States could return to a foreign policy faithful to the country's traditional ideals. By the same token, Gruening proposed to decrease U.S. military aid to Europe and other areas, thus reverting to his anti-U.S. imperialist stance of the 1920s.

Gruening, though less famous for domestic issues once he entered the U.S. Senate, was also concerned with clean air, water pollution, overpopulation, and the need for birth control, and visited numerous times with President Johnson to discuss these issues.

Nevertheless, Gruening would always revert to the issue of Vietnam. In an interview given in 1974 shortly before his death, he called the Vietnam War an "inexcusable and unjustified war." He went on to say, "It wasn't our war; we had no business there . . . the vital interest of the United States wasn't in jeopardy; we hadn't been attacked as we had been by the Japanese at Pearl Harbor."

Gruening left the Senate in 1969, after a defeat in the 1968 primary. Before his death of cancer in 1974, he wrote his autobiography, gave lectures, and worked as a political consultant in Washington, D.C. Throughout the 1960s and into the 1970s, Gruening never let up in his outspoken fight against U.S. military involvement in Vietnam. Declaring all acts of resistance against the Vietnam War justifiable, he advocated clemency to all who had resisted.

★

Gruening's autobiography is *Many Battles: The Autobiography of Ernest Gruening* (1973). Works on Gruening include Robert David Johnson, *Ernest Gruening and the American Dissenting Tradition* (1998). An obituary is in the *New York Times* (27 June 1974). The transcript of the 1974 interview with Gruening by Joe B. Frantz is in the Lyndon Baines Johnson Library at the University of Texas at Austin.

KIM RICHARDSON

GUTHRIE, Arlo Davy (*b.* 10 July 1947 in New York City), singer-songwriter and actor who recorded *Alice's Restaurant,* one of the most popular antiwar songs of the 1960s, and was a featured performer at the original Woodstock Festival.

Guthrie was the second-oldest child of Woodrow Wilson ("Woody") Guthrie and Marjorie Greenblatt Mazia's four children. Woody Guthrie was an Oklahoma-born singer and celebrated composer of neotraditional folk songs such as "This Land Is Your Land" and "Pastures of Plenty." Marjorie Guthrie, of Russian-Jewish descent, was a Martha Graham dancer who operated her own studio. The couple's eldest child, Cathy, died in a fire before Guthrie's birth.

Arlo Guthrie, 1968. © BETTMANN/CORBIS

They had another son, Joady, born in 1948, and another daughter, Nora Lee, born in 1950.

Marjorie became the family's primary breadwinner as Woody's behavior grew increasingly irrational. In 1954 he was diagnosed with Huntington's Disease, a hereditary degenerative neurological disorder that caused him to be institutionalized until his death in 1967. Thanks to the generosity of Woody's friends, the folksingers Pete Seeger and Lee Hays, and his manager, Harold Leventhal, the Guthrie Children's Fund was founded to provide for Guthrie's education.

Guthrie graduated from high school in Stockbridge, Massachusetts, in 1965. Deciding that his retiring personality was best suited for the outdoor life, he enrolled at Rocky Mountain College in Billings, Montana, that fall to study forestry. He dropped out after six weeks, however, and returned to Massachusetts. There he renewed his friendship with Ray and Alice Brock, former faculty members at the Stockbridge School, who were living at the deconsecrated Trinity Church in Great Barrington. Alice ran a restaurant nearby.

By this time Guthrie had decided to follow in Woody's footsteps. He hired Leventhal as his manager and began to play folk dates, accompanying himself on guitar and harmonica. Guthrie's commercial breakthrough came with *Alice's Restaurant Massacree,* an eighteen-minute talking blues piece that originated as an advertising jingle for the Brocks's eatery. The song told the story of Guthrie's arrest for littering following a Thanksgiving Day dinner at Alice and Ray's church in 1965 and how his "prison record" eventually saved him from being drafted into the army and going to Vietnam. The song, a droll, ironic commentary on war and the mindless officialdom that supported it ("I was inspected . . . injected . . . and selected"), struck a chord with America's disaffected middle-class youth.

The song also appealed to an older generation of folkies and social activists, as attested by Guthrie's warm reception at the Newport Folk Festival on 16 July 1967. The album *Alice's Restaurant,* released in late September (two weeks before Woody's death on 3 October), sold 700,000 copies. In January 1968 Guthrie performed at a tribute to Woody Guthrie at Carnegie Hall along with Bob Seeger, Bob Dylan, and Joan Baez. The proceeds went to the Committee to Combat Huntington's Disease.

Established as a countercultural figure, Guthrie was a featured performer at the Woodstock Festival on 15 August 1969. The movie *Woodstock* (1970) shows him singing one of his best-known songs, "Coming into Los Angeles," with his patented nasal twang. His drug-inflected millennial rap to the audience ("There'll be 500,000 people here by tonight . . . can you dig it?) remains the most memorable portion of his performance.

Two weeks after Woodstock, the movie version of *Alice's*

Restaurant was released, with Guthrie in the lead role. Directed by Arthur Penn, the film, like another 1969 countercultural hit, *Easy Rider,* is basically an elegy to the doomed hippie dream. The sense of loss is underscored by a secondary story line involving Woody's impending death (Seeger and Hays appear in cameo roles). Guthrie was no actor, but with his curly brown locks, beatific smile, and earnest passivity, he managed to convey both the rebelliousness and idealism characteristic of the times. The film was a surprise hit and received generally favorable reviews. Meanwhile, Guthrie's appearance on the cover of *Newsweek* on 29 September 1969 affirmed his status as America's best-known hippie.

Guthrie's post-1960s career never scaled the commercial heights of *Alice's Restaurant.* In 1972 he had a hit single, "City of New Orleans," but his albums, although well received by critics, have sold poorly. Fame and adulation, however, have never been particularly important for the publicity-shy Guthrie. He maintains a dedicated cult following and tours extensively, both as a solo act and, until recently, with Seeger. The now white-maned Guthrie remains an engaging performer, frequently stopping mid-song to regale the audience with a story or joke. The highlight of his concert tour is the annual Thanksgiving Day appearance at Carnegie Hall.

In 1992 Guthrie bought the Trinity Church featured in *Alice's Restaurant.* It houses the Guthrie Center, a nonprofit community-service organization. He is also active in the Committee to Combat Huntington's Disease. (Guthrie and his siblings, all of whom have a fifty-fifty chance of contracting the disease, have yet to show symptoms.) His own spiritual search has led him from his Protestant-Judaic roots to Catholicism to the interfaith teachings of Jaya Sati Bhagavati Ma. Guthrie and Alice Hyde Guthrie, whom he married in 1969, live on a farm in Washington, Massachusetts. They have four children.

The record and film *Alice's Restaurant* and his performance at Woodstock established Guthrie as one of the era's most recognizable countercultural figures. Neither as musically prolific as Dylan nor as politically polarizing as Baez, he was nevertheless for many the embodiment of 1960s idealism. Shadowed by both his father's fame and disease, he has managed both burdens with admirable equanimity, and forged a long career as a singer, humorist, social critic, and community activist.

★

There are no biographies of Guthrie. For information about Guthrie's life and career, see articles in *Newsweek* (29 Sept. 1969) and *Rolling Stone* (3 Mar. 1977 and 6 Sept. 1979), as well as Guthrie's commentary on the DVD version of *Alice's Restaurant* (2001), and in his "Official Autobiography" at <www.arlo.net>.

RUBIL MORALES VÁZQUEZ

H

HAAS, Peter E., Sr. (*b*. 20 December 1918 in San Francisco, California), and **Walter A. HAAS, Jr.** (*b*. 24 January 1916 in San Francisco, California; *d*. 20 September 1995), members of the Levi Strauss family clothing business that propelled the blue-jean fashion revolution of the 1960s.

Levi Strauss and Company was founded as a San Francisco dry-goods store in 1853 by a young Jewish-Bavarian immigrant merchant named Levi Strauss. Strauss and tailor Jacob Davis came up with a denim pant using rivets to strengthen stress points; they patented their "waist overalls" in 1873. Sales of lot number 501 of the design, produced in 1881, were fueled by the booming mining business. Strauss had no children when he died, so he left the company to the children of his brother-in-law, David Stern. Walter A. Haas, Sr., married Stern's daughter Elise and ran the business from 1928 to 1955. Haas eliminated the dry-goods business when he took over and focused the company on clothing, doubling revenue from $3 million to $6 million per year. The sons of Walter A. Haas and Elise Stern, Peter E. Haas, Sr., and Walter A. Haas, Jr., were born into the Levi-Strauss family business.

Both Walter and Peter earned B.A. degrees from the University of California at Berkeley and received M.B.A.s from Harvard. Walter joined the family business in 1939, after his graduation from Harvard, whereas Peter began at Levi Strauss in 1945. Walter served fifty-two months of active duty in World War II, and married Evelyn Danzig in 1940; they had three children.

Although Walter and Peter's relationship with their parents had been somewhat formal and distant while they were growing up, the sons grew closer to their father when they began working for him. Walter became president of Levi Strauss in 1958. Segregation had not yet been declared a violation of federal law when Levi Strauss and Company opened its first manufacturing plant in the South, in Blackstone, Virginia. Despite pressures to do otherwise, Walter insisted that the plant be integrated from the start.

The Hollywood screen cowboys of the 1930s wore Levi's blue jeans in western movies, and western wear and the cowboy image were Levi Strauss's mainstay until the company launched a women's line and began selling it in department stores. As the Levi's line grew to include clothes beyond basic blue jeans, the brand's profile also expanded. Blue jeans were no longer thought of as clothing worn only for work. When Levi Strauss brought out a line of pants in citrus colors they called orange, lemon, and lime, Americans took notice. *Life* magazine featured a story on Levi's, and although the fruit-colored line was a flop, it grabbed people's attention. Major department stores took on the Levi Strauss line, and the company had to adapt its advertising and marketing schemes to accommodate the boom. Smoldering 1950s movie stars like James Dean and Marlon Brando, sporting Levi's jeans in films like *Rebel Without a Cause* and *On the Waterfront*, did not hurt the Levi's image, either. The brand grew to represent independence and became such a symbol of youthful disaffection that blue jeans were banned in many schools.

Walter led the Levi Strauss blue-jean revolution of the 1960s, and he started by going global. The company's French distributor exhibited the clothing in Paris in 1961, and the Levi Strauss Europe arm of the company followed soon after. Levi Strauss was awarded President John F. Kennedy's "E" Award for contributions to the United States export program in 1962. Levi Strauss International and Levi Strauss Far East followed in 1965 and the brand appeared in Russia, Czechoslovakia, and Poland soon afterward. Levi's jeans became part of the permanent collections of the Smithsonian Institution in 1964. The company aired its first television commercial in 1965. Levi's jeans became forever associated with rock and roll in 1967, when such rock groups as Jefferson Airplane and Paul Revere and the Raiders recorded radio commercials for the brand. Walter came up with the slogan "Levi's is people" in 1968, and by that time, it was true—Levi's blue jeans were being worn the world over.

In 1969 a writer for *American Fabrics* magazine declared denim "eternally young." Over the course of the decade, Levi's competitors came and went. A particular brand, such as Haggar or the television star Farah Fawcett's line of jeans, would spark interest and become popular for a few years, but Levi's outlasted and outsold them all. Just before the turn of the decade, the Levi's line introduced the bell-bottom design, which then became the fashion statement of the 1970s.

In 1970 Walter turned the company over to Peter, who remained president until 1981; Walter became chairman of the board and chief executive officer. Although Walter made the company public in 1971, his son Robert D. Haas returned it to privately held status in 1985, after he became president. Employees such as Rita Guiney, a forty-five-year veteran of Levi Strauss and Company, thrived in the environment that Walter and Peter created. "They had a lovely manner and tremendous respect for the people who were here," she said. "They felt strongly about providing us with a good environment and the opportunity to move ahead."

★

Historical and biographical information on Levi Strauss and Company and the Haas family is included in David Bollier, *Aiming Higher: 25 Stories of How Companies Prosper by Combining Sound Management and Social Vision* (1996). An obituary for Walter Haas is in the *San Francisco Chronicle* (21 Sept. 1995). An oral history of Walter A. Haas, Jr., *Levi Strauss & Co. Executive, Bay Area Philanthropist, and Owner of the Oakland Athletics* (1995), is available at the Bancroft Library at the University of California, Berkeley.

BRENNA SANCHEZ

HACKMAN, Eugene Alden ("Gene") (*b.* 30 January 1931 in San Bernardino, California), leading Hollywood character actor who shot to stardom at age thirty-six in a supporting role in the groundbreaking movie *Bonnie and Clyde* (1967).

Hackman was born in the depths of the Great Depression, and his childhood was disrupted when the family moved from California to Illinois, where his father had the promise of work as a newspaper press operator. Hackman's father, Eugene Ezra Hackman, walked out on Hackman and his mother, Lynda, in 1944, and Hackman himself left home three years later to join the armed services. Just sixteen years old, he lied about his age but was allowed to join the U.S. Marine Corps, where he finished his high school education and served from 1947 to 1952.

While he was a marine, Hackman worked as a newscaster and disc jockey for his unit's radio station, a job that would lead him to study journalism at the University of Illinois at Urbana-Champaign after his discharge. After six months at Urbana, he moved to the School of Radio Technique in New York City and then took jobs as a broadcaster in Florida and Illinois. Hackman eventually enrolled at the Pasadena Playhouse in California, where he studied along-

Gene Hackman in a scene from *Bonnie and Clyde,* 1967. THE KOBAL COLLECTION/WARNER BROS.

side Dustin Hoffman. The pair were voted "least likely to succeed" by their fellow students. Hackman married Faye Maltese on 1 January 1956. The couple had three children, and divorced in 1985. Hackman married Betsy Arakawa in December 1991.

Hackman's first professional acting roles came soon after his marriage, with an off-Broadway debut in *Chaparral* in 1958, and a television debut in 1959 in an episode of *The United States Steel Hour* called "Little Tin God." He did not appear in a movie until *Mad Dog Coll* in 1961, just short of his thirtieth birthday. Hackman's career since then has been one of extremes. From the high points of *Bonnie and Clyde* (1967), and *I Never Sang for My Father* (1969), his career sank to such lows as *The Split* (1968), and *Narrow Margin* (1990). Hackman has stated that he is uncomfortable when he is not working, and this may be the reason for the variable quality of the films he has chosen. Nevertheless, he is rarely less than a magnetic presence on-screen. His performance in *Lilith* (1964), so impressed the film's star Warren Beatty that Beatty had him cast as Buck Barrow in *Bonnie and Clyde* (1967). Hackman's performance in the groundbreaking gangster movie showed he was capable of outstanding character performances and earned him an Academy Award nomination for best supporting actor.

Five years into his movie acting career, age thirty-six and still relatively unknown, Hackman suddenly became a star. His edgy, wild performance as Buck Barrow, the brother of the notorious outlaw Clyde Barrow, is impressive in itself, but *Bonnie and Clyde* also turned out to be one of the most important Hollywood movies of the decade. Arthur Penn's masterpiece won two Academy Awards and helped revive the financially struggling movie studio Warner Bros. Although it is primarily a retelling of the story of a real-life spree of bank robbing and killing that enthralled Americans in the 1930s, the movie is also at the beginning of a tradition of films that take a new look at American history. The characters are quite different in other respects, but the ignorant, often comically malicious Barrow is a worthy precursor to the bigoted Popeye Doyle, Hackman's Oscar-winning role in *The French Connection* (1971).

Hackman's work often has connected with the mood of the times, and this is especially true of the films he made in the 1960s and early 1970s. In *Bonnie and Clyde,* the gang members are presented at times almost as young heroes persecuted by ruthless authorities, an attitude resonant of youth culture in 1960s America. Hackman's long and gory death scene encourages sympathy more than a sense of justice having been done. The 1960s theme of rebellious youth reappears in *I Never Sang for My Father* (1969), in which Hackman plays Gene Garrison, a young man unable to communicate with his father. This role brought him his second Academy Award nomination, but by then he was a regular figure on-screen. *Bonnie and Clyde* was his fourth

movie of 1967, and he appeared in seven more (including the television movie *Shadow on the Land*) between 1967 and 1970. Some of these performances, such as in *Downhill Racer* (1969), in which he plays a ski coach, show off his skills to impressive effect.

In the 1960s Hackman carved out a niche for himself as an actor capable of playing bullies, bad guys, as well as troubled, ordinary men. The characters he played fit with the atmosphere of change and disturbance in American life. By the early 1970s, with seventeen movies behind him, Hackman took on the role of Popeye Doyle, the troubled narcotics cop in *The French Connection* (1971). In many ways the realistically shot, hard-hitting thriller built on the work he had done in the 1960s. Hackman finally won the Academy Award for best actor and became a major star. Since then he has managed to avoid typecasting and too many obvious star vehicles. In *The Poseidon Adventure* (1972), he cashed in on his status, playing a heroic priest leading passengers to safety while retaining a sense of troubled humanity. In *The Conversation* (1974), his character Harry Caul faces moral confusion in a timely film about surveillance and paranoia. Hackman also showed a capacity for comic acting in *Young Frankenstein* (1974), in *Superman II* (1980), and as the idiotic movie producer Harry Zimm in *Get Shorty* (1995).

Movies such as *Bonnie and Clyde* helped revive Hollywood in the 1960s. Hackman's specialty—men whose ambition, unorthodoxy, or outright viciousness get the better of them—became a staple of thrillers in the 1970s and 1980s. Although Hackman may not have been as discriminating with projects as perhaps he should have been, he is one of the finest character actors to have emerged from Hollywood since the 1950s. His performance as Buck Barrow in *Bonnie and Clyde* helped redefine the movie bad guy for the late twentieth century as someone with ambition and drive but no conventional way of achieving his goals. Hackman's impressive career covers more than forty years and seventy screen appearances, and includes two Academy Awards.

★

Biographies of Hackman include Allan Hunter, *Gene Hackman* (1987), and Michael Munn, *Gene Hackman* (1997). Articles about his career in the 1960s and early 1970s include H. G. Luft, "Gene Hackman: An American of Strength and Doubts," *Films in Review* (Jan. 1975). Hackman was interviewed by Paul Fischer for *Film Monthly* (Nov. 2001).

Chris Routledge

HAGGARD, Merle Ronald   (*b.* 6 April 1937 in Bakersfield, California), singer, songwriter, guitarist, and fiddle player who overcame adversity to achieve country music stardom.

Haggard was the youngest of three children of James Frances Haggard, a railroad worker, and Flossie Mae (Harp) Haggard, a homemaker who later took up bookkeeping. He was raised in a converted boxcar in Oildale, near Bakersfield. Haggard took violin lessons as a child, later adding singing and guitar playing to his talents. His father died of a cerebral hemorrhage in 1946, when Haggard was nine. When he was a teenager, his dislike of school led to frequent stays in reformatories; he also ran away from home on several occasions, living as a hobo and doing manual labor. As early as 1951, when he was thirteen, he found work singing in bars, and he developed a minor career as a performer over the next several years. In 1956 he married Leona Hobbs, with whom he had four children. The couple divorced in 1965.

Haggard became involved in petty crime that gradually grew more serious, leading to several brief jail terms. In December 1957 he attempted to rob a bar, was quickly apprehended, and was sentenced to a prison term in San Quentin. There he reformed and decided to make a career in country music. He was paroled in November 1960 after serving two years and nine months of a five-year sentence. (In 1972 he was pardoned by California's governor, Ronald Reagan.) Returning to Bakersfield, Haggard worked as a ditchdigger for his brother's electrical firm, but he also began playing in bands. Over the next few years he attracted

the attention of such established performers as Wynn Stewart, who hired him to play bass in his backup band. In 1963 he was signed to the tiny Tally Records label and earned his first country chart entry, Stewart's "Sing Me a Sad Song," which peaked in the *Billboard* country singles Top Twenty chart in early 1964. That song was followed by "Sam Hill" and "Just Between the Two of Us," the latter a duet with Bonnie Owens, who became Haggard's second wife, in 1965. (They divorced in 1976.) Haggard married the singer Leona Williams in 1978, but that marriage also ended in divorce, as did a fourth marriage. He was married for the fifth time to Theresa Lane in 1993; they have had two children.

Following the 1965 Top Ten hit "(My Friends Are Gonna Be) Strangers," Haggard switched to the much larger Capitol Records label and formed a permanent backup band, the Strangers. The twelve singles he released on Capitol between 1966 and 1969 all reached the country Top Ten; in fact, Haggard saw thirty-seven consecutive Top Ten country hits, most of which he wrote himself, between 1966 and 1977. The string began with the self-penned "Swinging Doors," which peaked in July 1966. It was followed by "The Bottle Let Me Down," and in March 1967 Haggard topped the country charts for the first time with "The Fugitive," written by Casey and Liz Anderson. Haggard's albums *Swinging Doors* and *Bottle Let Me Down* topped the record charts in December 1966. His own "I Threw Away the Rose" just missed topping the charts in June 1967, and his composition "Branded Man" began a string of four consecutive number-one hits and eight of his next nine singles. The *Branded Man* LP, meanwhile, was a chart topper in December 1967.

Increasingly, Haggard began to acknowledge his background in his songs. "Sing Me Back Home," which topped the charts in January 1968, concerned a death-row prisoner and was sung in the voice of a fellow inmate. "The Legend of Bonnie and Clyde," which became number one in April, was about the famous criminal couple. (The *Sing Me Back Home* LP went to number one in March 1969.) Near autobiographical details were heard on Haggard's next single, "Mama Tried," written for the film *Killers Three* (1968), in which the singer appeared. The song's narrator tells of youthful malfeasance culminating in a life sentence in prison by the time he is twenty-one, but concludes that he alone is to blame, because "Mama tried."

Having thus unburdened himself, Haggard turned toward a style of belligerent patriotism in some of his songs of the late 1960s and early 1970s, starting with his early 1969 Top Five country hit "I Take a Lot of Pride in What I Am." He also delved into country music history, reaching number one on the record charts in July 1969 with the Jimmie Rodgers tribute album *Same Train, a Different Time*. He identified himself increasingly with blue-collar

Merle Haggard, 1975. HENRY DILTZ/CORBIS

workers, notably in the 1969 number-one hits "Hungry Eyes" and "Workin' Man Blues." These themes also appear in his controversial song "Okie from Muskogee," co-written with Eddie Burris and topping the country charts in November 1969. The song would become his first single to cross over to the pop charts. It contrasts the straight-living residents of Muskogee, Oklahoma, with the dope-smoking hippies presented in the media of the late 1960s. "Okie from Muskogee" became a conservative anthem, and Haggard quickly followed it up with the even more explicit "The Fightin' Side of Me," a country number-one hit in March 1970, which criticized anti–Vietnam War protesters. Both songs lent their titles to chart-topping country LPs in 1970.

Such songs gave Haggard an image as a right-wing crank to many people outside the country music world, even though the songs constituted only a small part of his repertoire. He continued to be a major force in country music for the next two decades. According to the *Billboard* chart researcher Joel Whitburn's *Top Country Singles, 1944 to 1997* (1998), Haggard ranked as the second most successful country singles artist of the 1970s, behind Conway Twitty, and third for the 1980s, behind Twitty and Willie Nelson. Haggard's record sales subsided in the 1990s, but he continued to tour and record regularly.

By confronting his personal history unflinchingly and responding to the political turmoil of the 1960s in song, Haggard effectively expanded the kinds of subject matter that could be addressed in country music. In this sense he was akin to Bob Dylan in the popular music realm, and he was a tremendous influence on other writers such as Kris Kristofferson, whose success would be practically unthinkable without him.

★

Haggard is the author of two autobiographies: *Sing Me Back Home: My Life Story* (1981), with Peggy Russell; and *Merle Haggard's My House of Memories: For the Record* (1999), with Tom Carter. Also useful are Paul Hempill's profile of Haggard in Bill C. Malone and Judith McCuloh, eds., *Stars of Country Music* (1975), and Alanna Nash, *Behind Closed Doors: Talking with the Legends of Country Music* (1988).

WILLIAM RUHLMANN

HALBERSTAM, David (*b.* 10 April 1934 in New York City), respected journalist and historian who won a Pulitzer Prize for international reporting in 1964 for his coverage of the Vietnam War and went on to write an impressive string of best-selling books on Vietnam, civil rights, politics, the U.S. media, and sports.

Halberstam was the son of Charles A. Halberstam, a surgeon, and Blanche Levy, a teacher. The family moved fre-

quently as Charles Halberstam's military assignments dictated, and his son grew up in cities such as El Paso, Texas; Rochester, Minnesota; and Winsted, Connecticut. The Halberstams settled in Westchester County, New York, where Halberstam attended high school, after his father's return from Europe at the end of World War II. Halberstam wrote for his Yonkers high school newspaper and ran track before graduating in 1951 and entering Harvard University. Though he did not excel as an undergraduate, he was named managing editor of the prestigious *Harvard Crimson*, the school's daily newspaper. The assignment was both a challenge and a high-profile proving ground for the journalism student.

After graduating from Harvard in 1955, Halberstam took a job reporting for the West Point, Mississippi, *Daily Times Leader*. He soon moved on to the *Nashville Tennessean*, covering civil rights issues during increasingly tense times. The threats and violence he faced as a reporter failed to faze Halberstam, and the controversy of the issues he covered only attracted him to journalism that much more. When he left the *Tennessean* in 1960, he was a solid reporter with well-honed writing and interviewing skills. He then took a job with the prestigious *New York Times*, first on assignment to cover Washington, D.C., and shortly thereafter to cover the war in the Congo. When he accepted an assignment to South Vietnam in 1962, Halberstam supported U.S. involvement there. But as he saw more of the chaos, misinformation, misjudgment, and resulting loss of life, his position shifted. He won his first journalism honor that year, the Page One award from the Newspaper Guild of New York.

Like many front-line reporters in Vietnam, Halberstam foraged constantly for the contacts and leads that furnished the material for his daily stories for the *Times*. His Vietnam experience was very unlike that of many big-name journalists, who avoided chilling exposure to the realities of the war—they had their interviews lined up for them, were given four-star treatment, and did their reporting from the air-conditioned comfort of the Caravelle Hotel. Halberstam's coverage of the Vietnam War and the 1963 overthrow of South Vietnamese president Ngo Dinh Diem earned him the 1964 Pulitzer Prize for reporting of international affairs, which he shared with Malcolm W. Browne of the Associated Press. The two also received the first Louis M. Lyons award the same year for conscience and integrity in journalism for reporting "the truth as they saw it [in the Vietnam conflict] . . . without yielding to unrelenting pressures," according to the Pulitzer advisory board.

When his assignment in Vietnam ended in 1963, Halberstam went on to Warsaw and Paris for the *New York Times*. He is noted for his books written after this period, which all are the result of exhaustive research and reporting. Journalists and authors alike marvel at his ability to produce such extensive works while they are still current and topical. His 1965 book, *The Making of a Quagmire: America and Vietnam During the Kennedy Era*, explored what had gone wrong in South Vietnam since 1961. Halberstam focused on accurate reporting and presentation of his facts—without offering a solution—while evoking a sense of regret at the blood needlessly shed in the war as a result of missed opportunities and misjudged events. Halberstam left the *Times* in 1967 to devote more time to writing books. He worked as a contributing editor to *Harper's* magazine until 1971. Halberstam had married actress Elzbieta Tchizevska in 1965; they divorced in 1977. In 1979 he married Jean Sandness Butler; they had one daughter.

One Very Hot Day, Halberstam's 1968 novel, was described as "the right kind of book about Vietnam." Unlike many war novels, it evoked not a sense of grandeur but one of irony and absurdity. Halberstam studied the intricacies of small incidents—many of which he had to leave out of his daily copy for the *Times*—that were as telling as any study of the war as a whole. Anecdotes and fascinating tidbits pepper the book, such as the observation that the Vietcong were poor snipers because of poor vision resulting from a protein deficiency. The war was still escalating when *One Very Hot Day* was published, and the book served an immediate educational function—it encapsulated the texture of an incredibly complex conflict.

Halberstam's final book published in the 1960s, *The Unfinished Odyssey of Robert Kennedy* (1969), further explored the profiles of Robert F. Kennedy and New York Democratic senator Allard Lowenstein that Halberstam wrote for *Harper's*. The book was ambitious and experimental compared to other Kennedy studies of the era. Halberstam abandoned the common chronological approach for a story line that roughly follows Kennedy's final campaign trail, but jumps back and forth to his life before his presidential candidacy. The book ends abruptly, as did Kennedy's life. The final sentence reads: "Then he descended to acknowledge his victory, to talk about the violence and the divisiveness, and to let a nation discover in his death what it had never understood or believed about him during his life." The ending was so abrupt that *New York Times* reviewer Victor Navasky initially thought his copy of the book was printed without a final chapter.

After the 1960s, Halberstam continued to explore the Vietnam War. He wrote *The Best and The Brightest* (1972), a best-seller that remains one of the foremost chronicles of the Vietnam War era. He also pursued his love for sports in the books *The Breaks of the Game* (1981), *The Amateurs* (1985), *The Summer of '49* (1989), *October 1964* (1994), and *Playing for Keeps: Michael Jordan and the World He Made* (1999). His other works include *The Powers That Be* (1979), *The Reckoning* (1986), and *War in a Time of Peace: Bush, Clinton, and the Generals* (2001). His eighteenth book, *Fire-*

house, about Engine 40 Ladder 35 of the New York City Fire Department (which lost twelve men in the 2001 World Trade Center attacks), was published in 2002.

★

Books on Halberstam include Leonard Downie, Jr., *The New Muckrakers: An Inside Look at America's Investigative Reporters* (1976), and William W. Prochnau, *Once Upon a Distant War* (1995). Reviews of his work include Peter Kihss, "Pulitzer Prizes Omitted in Drama, Fiction, Music," *New York Times* (5 May 1964); Bernard B. Fall, "Errors Escalated Too," *New York Times* (16 May 1965); Wilfrid Sheed, "En Route to Nowhere," *New York Times* (7 Jan. 1968); Victor S. Navasky, "The Unfinished Odyssey of Robert Kennedy," *New York Times* (2 Feb. 1969); and Victor S. Navasky, "How We Got Into the Messiest War in Our History," *New York Times* (12 Nov. 1972).

Brenna Sanchez

HALDEMAN, H(arry) R(obbins) ("Bob") (*b.* 27 October 1926 in Los Angeles, California; *d.* 12 November 1993 in Santa Barbara, California), advertising executive, advance man during Richard M. Nixon's 1956 and 1960 campaigns, manager of Nixon's 1962 gubernatorial bid and his victorious 1968 and 1972 presidential campaigns, and White House chief of staff (1969–1973).

Haldeman was the son of Henry Francis and Katherine (Robbins) Haldeman. He was raised in Southern California, where his father was a successful plumbing, heating, and air conditioning purveyor and supporter of the Republican Party. An Eagle Scout, Haldeman displayed his discipline, devotion to duty, and organizational skills at a young age; at fourteen he created and ran a summer camp for neighborhood children at his family's Toluca Lake, California, home. He spent time at the University of Redlands, at the University of Southern California, and in the U.S. Naval Reserve during World War II before attending the University of California, Los Angeles, with the future White House domestic affairs aide John Ehrlichman. Haldeman earned a B.S. degree in business administration in 1948 and began a nearly twenty-year career as an advertising executive with the J. Walter Thompson advertising agency in 1949. Haldeman married Jo Horton on 19 February 1949. They had four children.

Haldeman became an admirer of Richard Nixon in 1947 during the Alger Hiss hearings of the House Un-American Activities Committee. (Hiss, a U.S. State Department official, was accused and later convicted of passing secret documents to an agent for an international Communist spy ring.) Haldeman was one of Nixon's advance men in his 1956 vice presidential reelection campaign and became Nixon's chief of advance in his 1960 presidential bid against

John F. Kennedy. Although he advised Nixon not to run for governor of California in 1962, Haldeman became his campaign manager. His advertising and management background was the perfect foundation for promoting his candidate. Previous campaign managers had allowed Nixon to become overwhelmed with tactical details and accessibility to the press. Although Nixon lost the race, Haldeman maximized Nixon's poise and improved his image by limiting his campaign appearances and exposure to the media. It was during Nixon's 1968 presidential campaign that Haldeman became known as "the man closest to the candidate's elbow," a role that he would continue to expand and develop in his new position as chief of staff.

Following Nixon's victory in the 1968 election, Haldeman began to build a White House staff to meet Nixon's requirements. After studying the varied staff structures of previous presidents, he created a new staff structure that was influenced by past administrations but tailored to Nixon's desire for order and efficiency. Haldeman became the head of the largest White House staff since the time of Franklin D. Roosevelt. His immediate staff was made up primarily of inexperienced but dedicated young men from his former advertising firm, including his own assistant, Lawrence Higby; the press spokesman Ron Ziegler; and Nixon's appointments secretary, Dwight Chapin.

Haldeman was responsible for maintaining Nixon's paramount requirement of privacy, and he became known as the gatekeeper of the Oval Office. This became one of the most demanding aspects of his job, and one that attracted much criticism and resentment from Washington veterans and the press. Nixon also demanded, as Haldeman put it, large "chunks of time" alone to ponder big questions. Nixon wanted to be kept prepared at all times and briefed on important people, situations, and proposals in advance, and Haldeman provided Nixon with dossiers on each day's scheduled visitors. He supervised the scheduling of Nixon's appointments; managed memos, telephone calls, and Nixon's moods; made recommendations and presented contrary views; attended private meetings; and served as Nixon's sounding board for political matters and public relations issues, including civil rights and the conflict in Vietnam.

Above all else, Haldeman was the one person whom Nixon knew he could reach in order to get something done. He devoted himself to his responsibilities, operating at Nixon's beck and call, traveling with him on all trips, and answering his telephone calls and requests at any hour of the day or night. He was the only member of the White House staff without his own schedule; his was completely determined by Nixon's. Although their relationship was entirely professional, Haldeman's intelligence, objectivity, and loyalty made him indispensable.

It was a combination of these things—his access, his

H. R. Haldeman. AP/WIDE WORLD PHOTOS

control, his loyalty—that made it difficult to imagine that he could have escaped a role in, or at least intimate knowledge of, the Watergate scandal. During the presidential campaign of 1972 a team of burglars was caught inside the Democratic Party headquarters at the Watergate hotel and office complex. Their connections were traced to the White House. Haldeman, along with Domestic Council Chief John Ehrlichman, was forced to resign on 30 April 1973. In March 1974 Haldeman, Ehrlichman, Attorney General John Mitchell, and four other former administration officials and members of Nixon's reelection committee were indicted on charges of conspiracy in covering up the Watergate break-in. Haldeman, Ehrlichman, and Mitchell were each convicted of obstruction of justice, conspiracy, and perjury. Facing almost certain impeachment, Nixon himself resigned in August of 1974.

Haldeman served eighteen months in the federal minimum-security facility at Lompoc, California. Following his release on 20 December 1978, Haldeman became vice president of the David H. Murdoch real estate development company and managed his own investments in several restaurants and hotels. As he had during his political career, Haldeman continued to serve his community and the Church of Christ, Scientist. Most of all, he was devoted to his family up until his death of abdominal cancer at his Santa Barbara home.

A study of Haldeman's contributions to the Nixon campaigns and administration, particularly those made during the 1960s, reveals that there was much more to his tenure than Watergate. Haldeman restructured the modern White House. He was also an active participant in the opening of China, the attainment of détente with the Soviet Union, and the end of American involvement in Vietnam. Despite the criticism he endured as chief of staff, it is clear that Haldeman's focus was on his president's success, not his own. Haldeman reflected in 1978 that he gained satisfaction "not from any personal power or glory but from my secure knowledge of the vital part I played in the day-to-day development and exercise of the Presidential powers by Richard Nixon." In his memoir, Haldeman referred to his political journey as the "mountain-top experience" of his life.

★

Haldeman's memoir, *The Ends of Power* (1978), focuses primarily on the Watergate affair, but it also details his role in the Nixon White House. *The Haldeman Diaries: Inside the Nixon White House* (1994) is a condensed volume of the daily entries he made as chief of staff and is an invaluable resource. Stephen E. Ambrose, *Nixon: The Triumph of a Politician 1962–1972* (1987), is a comprehensive study of Nixon's first presidential term; this work benefited from Haldeman's own critique. An obituary is in the *New York Times* (13 Nov. 1993).

TRACY L. EDDY

HALEY, Alexander Murray Palmer ("Alex") (*b.* 11 August 1921 in Ithaca, New York; *d.* 10 February 1992 in Seattle, Washington), author who during the 1960s instituted the standard format for the *Playboy* magazine interview; his *Playboy* interview with the civil rights activist Malcolm X led to the publication of *The Autobiography of Malcolm X* (1965).

Haley was the oldest of three sons born to Simon Haley, a college professor, and Bertha (Palmer) Haley, a teacher. Six weeks after his birth his parents took him to Henning, Tennessee, to live with Bertha's parents, Will and Cynthia Palmer. Haley and his mother remained with the Palmers while Simon returned to Cornell University to complete his graduate studies in agriculture. Haley graduated from high school at the age of fifteen. He attended Elizabeth City Teachers College in North Carolina for two years (1937–1939). Instead of pursuing a career in education, however, he joined the U.S. Coast Guard in 1939. Approximately thirteen years after entering the Coast Guard he became the chief journalist of the service, editing the official Coast Guard publication, *The Outpost*. Haley developed his

Alex Haley, 1966. HULTON-DEUTSCH COLLECTION/CORBIS

writing skills by writing love letters on behalf of fellow servicemen and creating adventure stories.

In 1941 Haley married Nannie Branch, with whom he had two children. They divorced in 1964. He married Juliette Collins later that year. They had one child and divorced in 1977. Haley married his third wife, Myra Lewis, in 1977. They were separated at the time of his death.

In 1959 Haley retired from the military after twenty years of service. He became a freelance writer for *Reader's Digest*, *New York Times Magazine*, *Harper's*, and *Atlantic*. At *Playboy* he created and inaugurated the critically acclaimed *Playboy* interview, interviewing such notables as the Reverend Martin Luther King, Jr.; Melvin Belli; Johnny Carson; Miles Davis; George Lincoln Rockwell, the leader of the American Nazi Party; and a minister of the Nation of Islam, Malcolm X. Haley's Miles Davis interview established the now-standard format used for *Playboy* interviews.

The Malcolm X interview was published in 1963 and was a success. The extensive notes gathered in preparation for the interview and Malcolm's desire to tell his own story proved the right ingredients for a full-length autobiography. While others had requested to write Malcolm's biography, he agreed to collaborate with Haley. But cooperation was not easily developed. Both men had to work at finding a level of trust and move past their skepticism of one another. Haley eventually gained Malcolm's confidence but not without stipulation. Malcolm told Haley, "I don't completely trust anyone. . . . You I trust about twenty-five percent." Haley worked two years, in daily sessions, sometimes in New York and, on numerous occasions, while accompanying Malcolm on trips.

The Autobiography of Malcolm X (1965) depicts the life of one of the most controversial leaders of the 1960s. At one point Malcolm spoke venomously about his hatred of white people, yet later, after his trip to Mecca, he was strong enough to reconsider his position when he met white people who treated him as an equal. Haley states that Malcolm summarized his pilgrimage to Mecca as "eye-opening" and "mind-changing." Malcolm found it necessary to toss aside much of the religious dogma he had been taught by the Nation of Islam leader Elijah Muhammad.

Haley's vibrant yet sensitive writing style made it possible for readers to recognize Malcolm as an astute and courageous leader. Haley successfully captured Malcolm's tone and the sharpness of his intellect and wit. He was able to illuminate the many facets of Malcolm's character and yet maintain the dignity of his story. He wrote in the epilogue how Malcolm insisted "that nothing could be in the book's manuscript that he did not say, and nothing could be left out that he wanted to have in it." Haley assures us that the story is Malcolm's very own. He respectfully asked Malcolm for permission to write his own comments at the end of the book, and his request was granted.

The autobiography candidly describes Malcolm's life experiences of growing up in racist small towns. Born Malcolm Little, Malcolm saw his father killed by the Ku Klux Klan. The book also shares Malcolm's experiences as a criminal and discusses his life transformation when he joined the Nation of Islam in the 1950s.

During the writing of the autobiography Malcolm was disenchanted with Muhammad, his leader and father figure, who had silenced Malcolm. Living under the constant threat of death, Malcolm told Haley he felt he would not live to see the publication of his story. His premonition was all too well founded, for he was assassinated at the Audubon Ballroom in Harlem, New York City, in 1965, but he had been able to read and approve the manuscript form. Haley describes the assassination of Malcolm, noting that the lives of both Malcolm and his father "were fundamentally shaped to their violent ends by the fact that they were born black in America and tried to combat the inferiority to which their color condemned them."

The Autobiography of Malcolm X was translated into eight languages and sold over six million copies. Its publication gave Haley international recognition and proved he was a writer with great potential and promise. As a result of its success, in the early 1970s Haley received honorary doctorates from Simpson College, Howard University, Williams College, and Capitol University. During the late 1990s a movie was produced based on the autobiography. The book has since experienced renewed popularity and is required reading in many schools. The work is invaluable

due to the lack of primary literature collected and archived, even though Malcolm made hundreds of speeches.

In 1976 Haley received the National Book Award for *Roots*, the multigenerational saga of a black family whose forebear, Kunta Kinte, was brought to the United States as a slave. In 1977 he received the Pulitzer Prize and the Spingarn Medal from the National Association for the Advancement of Colored People (NAACP). *Roots* was made into an enormously successful television miniseries. Haley was nominated to the Black Filmmakers Hall of Fame in 1981. In 1989 he became the first person to receive an honorary degree from the Coast Guard Academy, in addition to numerous other honorary degrees.

Haley died of a heart attack en route to a speaking engagement in Seattle on 10 February 1992. On 15 February, after funeral services in Memphis, Tennessee, Haley's body was conveyed to Henning and interred in the front yard of his boyhood home, which was purchased and restored by the state of Tennessee. In 1994 the Children's Defense Fund purchased the farm. It is now the home of the Langston Hughes Library and serves as a conference and training center for people who work with children.

The impact of Haley's literary contributions has extended beyond the decade of the 1960s. His influence can be felt in the study of genealogy and family life, how television audiences view multicultural programming, and, more importantly, the depth of consciousness-raising and respect for African Americans and their contributions to the United States.

★

Biographies of Haley include David Shirley, *Alex Haley* (1994), and Sylvia Williams, *Alex Haley* (1996). Other biographical resources on Haley include *Black Literature Criticism,* vol. 1 (1992); *Contemporary Black Biography,* vol. 4 (1992); and *Contemporary Literary Criticism,* vol. 12 (1984). An obituary is in the *New York Times* (11 Feb. 1992).

JOHNNIEQUE B. (JOHNNIE) LOVE

HALSTON (*b.* 23 April 1932 in Des Moines, Iowa; *d.* 26 March 1990 in San Francisco, California), millinery and fashion designer who became internationally famous for designing hats for First Lady Jacqueline Kennedy as well as introducing a revolutionary minimalism into women's fashions in the late 1960s.

Born Roy Halston Frowick, Halston grew up attending local public schools in Des Moines until his father, James Edward Frowick, a bookkeeper, moved the family to Carbondale, Illinois, in 1940. His mother, Hallie May (Holmes) Frowick, was a homemaker and mother of four children, of whom Halston was the second son. He showed

Halston *(left)*, with actress Virna Lisi, May 1964. © BETTMANN/CORBIS

an early interest in sewing, keeping his mother company when she retreated from his father's temper tantrums to busy herself with crocheting afghans. An interest in making hats was apparent when Halston made a braided wreath of flowers for his mother's hair and a hat decorated with chicken feathers for his sister when she was two years old. In December 1943 the family moved to Evansville, Indiana. For Easter 1945 Halston created a red cloche hat for his mother with a pom-pom made from a scouring pad. She wore it proudly.

Halston attended Indiana University in Bloomington for two years before moving to Chicago, where he attended fashion illustration classes at the School of the Art Institute. He worked as a window dresser and made hats in his spare time. Then, in 1957 the hairdresser Andre Basil and Halston opened the Boulevard Salon on Michigan Avenue. There Halston's hats drew the attention of *Women's Wear Daily*. In 1958 Halston was lured to New York City to work for the famous milliner Lilly Daché. He was fired because he allowed models to "borrow" hats to wear on dates. Halston then went to work in the custom millinery salon of the exclusive Bergdorf Goodman department store in midtown Manhattan. The store's young, tall, handsome, and affable milliner became known for the custom designs that he quickly and expertly executed for the individual needs of wealthy customers. His first hat, a brown organdy sunbonnet, appeared on the cover of *Harper's Bazaar* in 1960.

Jacqueline Kennedy, the nation's fashion-plate First Lady, supported American designers and selected Oleg Cassini to design her dresses and Halston to design her hats. The beige pillbox hat that she wore to her husband's

presidential inauguration in 1961 was one of the most widely copied of Halston's designs. In 1962 Halston won his first of many Coty Fashion Critics awards, for millinery. By 1966 Halston sensed that newly liberated women were beginning to eschew wearing hats, so he began designing clothing. In June of that year Halston held his first fashion show of women's ready-to-wear clothing for Bergdorf Goodman. The success of the fashion collection led to the opening of the Halston boutique at Bergdorf's.

On 12 January 1968 Halston resigned from Bergdorf Goodman, and in April of that year he set up his own incorporated business, Halston, Ltd. With financial backing from Estelle Marsh Watlington, Halston, Ltd., launched made-to-order and ready-to-wear divisions by September 1968. Halston showed his first solo clothing collection in his new showroom at 33 East Sixty-eighth Street on 2 December 1968. In March 1969 he opened a boutique on the third floor of Bloomingdale's department store. His garments for women were a stark departure from the hippie-inspired romantic and exotic looks that prevailed in the fashions of the late 1960s. Paring away excess collars, cuffs, and even zippers, Halston introduced a new sleek and modern way of dressing for women who, although wealthy enough to afford his clothes, led active lives of work and travel. For day, classic sportswear looks were presented in luxurious cashmere knits that packed well. For evening, figure-flattering caftans were interpreted in glittery sequins and beads, or fluid dresses of silk satin or chiffon were draped and tied on the body. A special Coty Award for the total look of his first solo collection was given to Halston on 13 October 1969.

In 1969 Halston staged a benefit retrospective fashion show of the designs of the famed couturier Charles James, whom Halston admired so much that he employed him as a consultant the next year. "Ease and Elegance Designed by Halston" was the headline of a *Newsweek* cover story (21 August 1972). Norton-Simon, Inc., bought Halston Originals and Halston, Ltd., the Halston trademark and design services, in November 1973. Halston Enterprises now owned the Halston name. "I want to design for all of America," Halston stated. Internationally known, Halston held a phenomenally popular fashion show in Paris at the Palais de Versailles in 1973. American designs were showcased alongside those of such renowned French couturiers as Yves St. Laurent. In June 1974 Halston was inducted into the Fashion Hall of Fame.

One of the most popular fragrances ever, "Halston" was launched in 1975. This perfume won the Fragrance of the Year award from the Fragrance Foundation in 1976. In 1977 Halston received a Tony Award nomination for costume designs for the musical *The Act*. During the 1970s and 1980s he designed costumes for the modern dancer Martha Graham and her dance troupe, for the Dance Theatre of Harlem, and for stage shows. His talents extended to designing the uniforms for Braniff Airlines' flight attendants and the Girl Scouts of America.

As a gay man, Halston never married and never had children. In the late 1980s he began to experience the symptoms of AIDS. He succumbed to the disease in a San Francisco hospital at the age of fifty-seven. Funeral services were held at the Calvary Presbyterian Church in San Francisco, and Halston's body was cremated. In June 1990 the actress Liza Minnelli held a memorial show in honor of Halston in Lincoln Center in New York City.

Halston is remembered not only as a designer of hats in the 1960s but also as a giant figure in American fashion whose legacy of minimal fuss in practical yet elegant wearable clothing for working women has been carried on by many famous American designers since the late 1960s. His story also remains a cautionary tale against selling one's name and losing control of one's own creative product in the process.

★

The Fashion Institute of Technology in New York City houses thousands of Halston sketches and patterns in the Halston Archives and Study Room. Elaine Gross and Fred Rottman, *Halston: An American Original* (1999), is a well-illustrated and comprehensive chronicle of Halston's career. Steven Bluttal, ed., *Halston* (2001), is "a visual anthology of Halston's life and legacy." The seamier side of Halston's glamorous life is explored in Steven Gaines, *Simply Halston: The Untold Story* (1991). Obituaries are in the *New York Times* and *Los Angeles Times* (both 28 Mar. 1990).

THERESE DUZINKIEWICZ BAKER

HAMMER, Armand (*b.* 21 May 1898 in New York City; *d.* 10 December 1990 in Los Angeles, California), controversial twentieth-century industrialist, art collector, and philanthropist with business and family ties to Soviet Russia, who, during the 1960s, rescued Occidental Petroleum Company from the brink of financial ruin.

Hammer was one of two sons of the Russian immigrants Julius Hammer, a physician and the owner of a pharmaceutical outlet, and Rose Lipschitz. (Rose Lipschitz also had a son from a previous marriage.) An interesting legend that circulated about Hammer's name is that Hammer's father, leader of the U.S. Communist Party, named him for the Communist Party arm-and-hammer symbol. Hammer operated the family pharmaceutical firm while earning his medical degree from Columbia University Medical School and developed the company into a million-dollar venture.

After graduating in 1921, Hammer went to Soviet Russia, where he developed a unique rapport with Vladimir Lenin, the first premier of the USSR, and secured the rights to export grain to Russia. In 1925 Hammer built a successful pencil factory in the Soviet Union, which he sold back to the Soviet government before returning to the United States in 1928. Over the next few years, Hammer continued to travel back and forth between the two countries, nurturing a variety of business interests. Hammer married Olga van Root, a singer he met in the Soviet Union, in 1927; they had a son, Hammer's only legitimate child, and divorced in 1943. He married his second wife, Angela Carey Zevely, an opera singer, the same year; they divorced in January of 1956. Hammer had a daughter out of wedlock in 1956 with Bettye Murphy, his mistress of many years.

During the Great Depression, Hammer sponsored a series of retail art sales at prominent department stores in New York City and elsewhere. The first of these sales featured pieces of the treasure of the Romanovs, the last Russian royal family, assassinated in 1918 when the Bolsheviks came to power; the treasure had been secured by Hammer while he was in Russia. In 1941 he used a similar method of retailing fine art to liquidate the art treasures of the millionaire American publisher William Randolph Hearst. At that time Hammer was also a breeder of prize Angus cattle and a manufacturer of whisky.

In the late 1950s Hammer acquired Occidental Petroleum, a faltering oil firm dating back to the 1920s. He invested $50,000 to purchase a 50 percent interest in the development of two new wells for the company in 1956, when Occidental stock was valued at $100,000. Hammer anticipated a loss and subsequent tax write-off from the exploration venture; instead he realized a profitable oil find, which launched Occidental stock into a growth pattern. Company shares increased from a low of eighteen cents to $1 per share, inspiring Hammer to speculate on a field of nine existing wells, which he acquired for $1 million. By 1960 Occidental's red ink ledger was reduced to a small loss of only $127,000, and by 1961 Occidental stock had appreciated to $10 million—although some critics maintained that Hammer buoyed stock prices to his advantage by exaggerating unsubstantiated rumors of lucrative geological discoveries on the part of Occidental.

In the wake of this early success, Hammer diversified and embarked on an aggressive acquisition strategy, buying and selling other companies and utilizing Occidental stock like a form of private currency to purchase each new enterprise. In December 1961 Occidental acquired an exploration site in Lathrup, California. One high-volume well discovered in that field was estimated to contain $200 million worth of crude oil and an unprecedented reserve of natural gas. It was the largest petroleum find in the history of California. The rising value of Occidental Petroleum stock reflected Hammer's fortuitous risk taking, and the

Armand Hammer. © BETTMANN/CORBIS

shares increased in value to $15 per share, up from $4 in a matter of months.

Hammer in 1963 set off a boom in the sulfur market when Occidental purchased Best Fertilizer Company. In need of sulfur to manufacture the fertilizer, Hammer mined sites in northern Florida. The Florida mines realized sufficient product to supply another Occidental acquisition, Jefferson Lake Sulfur Company of Texas, which Hammer had acquired in a deal to purchase 70 percent of Jefferson Lake Petro Chemicals of Canada. The stabilization of Hammer's fertilizer empire generated a spike in the price of sulfur, causing it to quadruple. Hammer then built a concentrating plant in Florida and arranged an $8-billion deal with the USSR for the export of sulfur. After completing a stock-based purchase by Occidental to acquire International Ore and Fertilizer Company (Intercore), Hammer began exportation to fifty-nine nations. The fertilizer export operation by then accounted for 90 percent of Occidental's earnings.

In February 1961 Hammer visited the Soviet Union, marking his first visit to his family's homeland in more than twenty-five years. Before his departure he attempted unsuccessfully to secure an endorsement from President John F. Kennedy in support of any anticipated industrial venture that might transpire. When he failed in this effort, he made an arrangement instead to represent Kennedy's secretary of commerce, Luther Hodges. Traveling as a private citizen, Hammer departed for the Soviet Union on 11 February.

Through personal influence with the deputy prime minister, Anastas Mikoyan, Hammer secured a meeting with Soviet Premier Nikita Khrushchev to discuss trade. Hammer returned to the Soviet Union in June 1964, and at that time he developed a plan with Khrushchev to build ten sulfur-processing plants in Siberia. The facilities were slated to provide $1 billion of concentrate for use in the production of fifty million tons of fertilizer annually by the Soviet Union.

Hammer solidified the deal by sending two Angus heifers and two bulls to Khrushchev, but just weeks after finalizing the agreement, Khrushchev was deposed, and the fertilizer project was shelved during the transition to a new administration. The following year Hammer established Occidental International, a government relations firm, which made successful inroads in influencing the administration of President Lyndon B. Johnson, always with the goal of entrenching Hammer's position as a primary conduit for commerce with the Soviet Union, a function he accomplished admirably throughout his lifetime.

In 1961 Hammer also had established a wholly owned subsidiary of Occidental in Libya. The Arabian oil industry at that time was the bastion of the so-called Seven Sisters cartel, consisting of Standard Oil of New York, Standard Oil of California, Standard Oil of New Jersey, Rockefeller Holding, Gulf Oil, Texaco, and Anglo-Persian Oil. These companies controlled all of the Arabian oil wealth with the exception of those in Libya, a new state organized by the

United Nations in December 1951. With only one million people, an impoverished economy, and a vast desert wasteland, Libya was a no-man's-land among petroleum speculators. In 1955 the Libyan government had allotted the first of eighty-five oil-drilling concessions to private developers, but in 1965 the concessions automatically reverted to the Libyan monarchy of King Idris. As the head of the government, Idris reopened the bidding on the newly apportioned concessions, and Hammer returned to Libya in 1966 for the purpose of finalizing the acquisition by Occidental of some of these oil fields once operated by Mobil Oil.

With characteristic persistence and shrewd bartering, and as a result of clandestine deal making, Hammer successfully upstaged the Seven Sisters and secured the drilling rights to two rich inland oil fields. When Occidental made its original bid on 26 July 1965, it offered Libya a water-drilling project, to be located in al-Kufrah, which would provide desert irrigation at no charge to the Libyan government in return for the oil concession. When the oil fields were awarded in February 1967, Occidental received two rich sites. The company struck oil in December, with the strike estimated at three billion barrels in the two fields combined. Oil at that time was selling for $1 per barrel; the discovery caused Occidental stock to jump to $100 per share.

Hammer then contracted with Bechtel Corporation in San Francisco to finance and build a forty-inch-diameter pipeline across the desert to bring oil from the exploration site to the Mediterranean coast. Also contracted was the construction of floating docks at Ez Zueitina, from August 1967 through February 1968. Following a strike in December 1967, Occidental Petroleum started shipping by the spring of 1968. As Occidental stock peaked, Hammer traded company shares in return for new industrial acquisitions, including Island Creek Coal. The Libyan oil fields, meanwhile, were pumped to a capacity of 600,000 barrels per day and increased to 800,000 barrels by 1969.

That same year Colonel Muammar al-Gadhafi (a Libyan revolutionary) accomplished a bloodless coup over the Libyan monarchy, leaving Occidental dramatically disadvantaged in bargaining for oil rights. The new Libyan government coerced Hammer to slow the output from Occidental's wells by threatening to expose the illicit deal making, which had clinched Hammer's oil contract with Libya in 1967. Hammer attempted, but failed, to procure additional oil from the Seven Sisters cartel, a situation that left him with few options but further dealings with the new Libyan government. Before the end of the summer of 1970, Hammer had agreed to a deal that gave Libya virtual control over the output from the national oil fields, regardless of which concessionaire might be mining the sites at any given time. The agreement between Occidental and Libya set a precedent, and it was not long before the Seven Sisters cartel fell prey to similar strategies imposed by other Arab governments. By means of such agreements, Libya and a growing consortium, called the Organization of Petroleum Exporting Countries (OPEC), took control of Middle Eastern oil and acquired the power to effect future pricing and supply. Hammer was criticized roundly for his dealings with Libya, which were considered to have had a huge impact on the increase in oil prices worldwide due to the strengthening of OPEC.

Hammer entered into an impressive round of philanthropic ventures during the 1960s, influenced by his third wife, the socialite Francis Tolman, whom he had married in 1956. (The couple had no children.) Among these charitable projects was a sizable grant to the Jonas Salk Institute to fund the establishment of the Armand Hammer Cancer Center. The Hammers also donated the twenty-acre family retreat of President Franklin Delano Roosevelt at Campobello—including the original furnishings—as a joint gift to the U.S. and Canadian governments. The estate was opened to the public officially on 20 August 1964; it is known as the Roosevelt Campobello International Park. Hammer died of bone cancer at the age of ninety-two and is buried at Westwood Village Cemetery in Los Angeles.

★

Armand Hammer wrote his autobiography, *Hammer,* with Neil Lyndon (1987). Bob Considine chronicles the life of Hammer in *The Remarkable Life of Armand Hammer* (1975). Edward Jay Epstein paints a dubious picture of Hammer in *Dossier: The Secret History of Armand Hammer* (1996). An obituary is in the *New York Times* (12 Dec. 1990).

GLORIA COOKSEY

HANSBERRY, Lorraine Vivian (*b.* 19 May 1930 in Chicago, Illinois; *d.* 12 January 1965 in New York City), award-winning playwright, essayist, and activist whose writings, most notably the play *A Raisin in the Sun* (1959), were characterized by astute observations on racial and social inequalities in the United States.

Hansberry was born into a middle-class African-American family. Her grandfather, Elden H. Hansberry, taught history at Alcorn College, Mississippi's first black college. Her uncle, William Leo Hansberry (1894–1965), was a pioneer in the study of African antiquity and developed Howard University's African studies curriculum. Hansberry's parents, Carl Augustus and Nannie Perry, migrated north to Chicago, where Carl established one of the city's first black banks and proved himself a successful real estate broker; Nannie was a school teacher. Hansberry, the youngest of four children, was only six when her politically active par-

Lorraine Hansberry. AP/WIDE WORLD PHOTOS

ents decided to defy the covenants that restricted Chicago's African-American population to residence in a small, overcrowded area. On 6 October 1936 the Hansberrys moved to 549 East Sixtieth Street, in an all-white neighborhood. This move began what would be a four-year struggle to undermine legalized segregation in Chicago housing, culminating in the landmark U.S. Supreme Court ruling *Hansberry* v. *Lee* on 12 November 1940, which effectively outlawed racially restrictive covenants in housing. That same year Hansberry's father ran unsuccessfully for U.S. Congress.

Hansberry's parents also combated racism in other ways. They opted to enroll their children in segregated south side public schools and fight for integration rather than accept the ease of sending them to private schools, which they would have well been able to afford. Her high-profile family also developed friendships with a variety of prominent African Americans, including the scholar W. E. B. DuBois, the entertainer and composer Duke Ellington, the writer Langston Hughes, the athlete Jesse Owens, and the singer and activist Paul Robeson. These connections would later prove useful to Hansberry. The concrete and gritty model of dedication to civil rights and political activism that her parents provided Hansberry would prove seminal in her later work.

In 1946, embittered by the lack of visible social change

despite the Supreme Court's decision, Hansberry's father died in the midst of planning to relocate the family to Mexico. Two years later Hansberry graduated from the segregated Englewood High School in Chicago and enrolled in the University of Wisconsin, studying theater and stage design. During her two years in Wisconsin she was politically active, joining the Labor Youth League and chairing the Young Progressives of America. Ultimately dissatisfied, she left the university in 1950 to study painting at the Art Institute of Chicago, Roosevelt University in Chicago, and in Guadalajara, Mexico. In August of the same year she moved to Harlem in New York City. Within a short time she was enrolled in classes at the New School for Social Research and was working as a reporter for *Freedom*, Robeson's monthly magazine. By 1952 she was working full-time at *Freedom*, teaching at the Frederick Douglass School and attending the Intercontinental Peace Congress in Montevideo, Uruguay, as Robeson's representative. On 20 June 1953 Hansberry married Robert Nemiroff, who was Jewish and white; the couple had no children.

From 1953 to 1957 Hansberry focused on drama. In 1957 she presented the first draft of *A Raisin in the Sun* to publisher Philip Rose. In 1959, after successful runs in New Haven, Connecticut, Philadelphia, and Chicago, the play opened on Broadway at the Ethel Barrymore Theater. An instant success, the play ran for 538 performances, signaling its acceptance by a predominantly white Broadway audience. Hansberry became the first African-American woman ever to have a play on Broadway and, in 1959, the first African-American woman and the youngest person ever to receive the New York Drama Critics Circle Award. In 1961 a film version, featuring Sidney Poitier and Ruby Dee, was nominated for best screenplay by the Screenwriters Guild and received a special prize from the Cannes Film Festival. These successes raised the profiles of African Americans in the theater world, enabling the increased production of black theatrical endeavors throughout the 1960s. The success of *A Raisin in the Sun* is attributable to its compelling depiction of an African-American family attempting to succeed in an often hostile world. Hansberry drew on her parents' own attempts to integrate a white neighborhood in her depiction of the Younger family. Evident in the play is Hansberry's commitment to political activism, which resonated with a nation in the midst of the civil rights movement. The frustration and anger expressed by Walter Lee Younger foreshadowed the black militancy that emerged in the 1960s. Also prescient was Hansberry's inclusion of a Nigerian character (no doubt a result of her uncle's early influence) who urges the family's daughter to discover her African roots and stop extolling white values that continue to "mutilate" African Americans. As a result of *Raisin*'s success, in 1960 Hansberry received a landmark commission from the National Broadcasting Company

(NBC) to write a television drama about slavery to commemorate the anniversary of the Civil War. *The Drinking Gourd* was deemed too controversial to be aired and was not published until 1972. Despite this disappointment, Hansberry continued to integrate her activism and writing: in 1963 along with the writer James Baldwin and others, she used her public profile to meet with Attorney General Robert Kennedy in the hope of convincing him to become more active in protecting those working toward civil rights in the South. In 1964 she assisted the Student Nonviolent Coordinating Committee (SNCC) and provided the text for *The Movement: Documentary of a Struggle for Racial Equality in America*. She also argued in favor of militancy in advancing black rights but denounced racial hatred.

Hansberry's next play, *The Sign in Sidney Brustein's Window* (1964), opened on Broadway at the Longacre Theatre to mixed reviews. The play again incorporated both her political beliefs and her sympathetic observations on humanity. It was to be the last play she would complete; in 1963 Hansberry had been diagnosed with cancer. Private donations kept *The Sign in Sidney Brustein's Window* afloat until 12 January 1965, the day of Hansberry's death. Her significance was evident at her funeral at the Church of the Master in Harlem. Among the hundreds of mourners were such important personages as the actor Ossie Davis, Robeson, and the activist Malcolm X. She is buried in Beth-El Cemetery in Croton-on-Hudson, New York.

After Hansberry's death it was revealed that she had divorced her husband the previous year but retained him as her literary executor. Nemiroff arranged for the posthumous completion, publication, and production of her unfinished works, including *To Be Young, Gifted, and Black* (an assortment of her personal writings), *Les Blancs* (a play of African liberation), *What Use Are Flowers?*, and *The Drinking Gourd*. Popular productions and adaptations, both stage and screen, followed.

In the 1980s it emerged that Hansberry had been a member of the Daughters of Bilitis (a lesbian organization) and had written to the lesbian periodical *The Ladder*, identifying herself as a "heterosexually married lesbian." Her tombstone features an excerpt from *The Sign in Sidney Brustein's Window*: "I care. I care about it all. It takes too much energy not to care. . . . The why of why we are here is an intrigue for adolescents; the how is what must command the living. Which is why I have lately become an insurgent again." The way in which Hansberry utilized her passion for writing to forward her belief in "insurgency," her civil rights activism, and her success as a playwright established her as an important artistic and political figure of the 1960s.

★

Hansberry's autobiography is *To Be Young, Gifted, and Black: A Portrait of Lorraine Hansberry in Her Own Words* (1970), adapted by Robert Nemiroff. For brief biographical information, see Anne Cheney, "Lorraine Hansberry," *Twayne's United States Authors Series*, 430 (1984). An obituary is in the *New York Herald Tribune* (13 Jan. 1965). Additional information can be found on the audio recording *Lorraine Hansberry Collection*, James Earl Jones and Ruby Dee, eds., which includes two interviews with, and five speeches by, Hansberry (2001).

JENNIFER HARRIS

HARGIS, Billy James (*b.* 3 August 1925 in Texarkana, Texas), fundamentalist Christian minister and evangelist and founder of the Christian Crusade Ministries, known for his fervent anti-Communist crusades during the 1960s.

Hargis was the only child of Jimmie Earsel Hargis, a railroad worker, and Laura Lucille Fowler, a homemaker. He grew up in a deeply poor but deeply religious household where daily Bible readings were a form of entertainment, and his church ministry began when he was ten years old. Hargis made a promise to God in a cow pasture while his mother underwent major surgery: If his mother survived, he "would do anything that [God] asked." Because his prayer was answered, Hargis "became very interested in church work of any kind." At seventeen he was ordained by the Christian Church (Disciples of Christ) at the Rose Hill Christian Church in Texarkana. Hargis attended Ozark Bible College from 1943 to 1945, but a lack of money forced him to leave without a degree. Years later, in 1957, he obtained a B.A. degree from Pikes Peak Bible Seminary and a Th.B. degree from Burton College in 1958. On 21 December 1951 he married Betty Jane Secrest; they had four children.

Hargis served as a Christian Church evangelist before becoming a full-time minister at churches in Oklahoma and Missouri. In 1947 Hargis organized the Christian Crusade as a ministry "to fight 'for Christ' and against godless Communism," after a fellow evangelist alerted him to the "threat of Communism internally." He first attracted national attention in 1953, when he and Dr. Carl McIntire floated "Bible balloons" (Bible scriptures attached to helium balloons) from Western Europe over the Iron Curtain as a way to introduce Christianity to Communist countries.

In 1961 Bob Jones University awarded Hargis an honorary doctorate in recognition of his fight against Communism. Moreover, his anticommunist sentiments echoed those of many everyday Americans, who held bomb drills in their schools, built bomb shelters in their backyards, and watched the spy thriller television show *The Man from U.N.C.L.E.*, in which two secret agents battle the forces of evil. For the burgeoning fundamentalist religious right, Hargis's ultraconservative message was an anchor to which they clung in a stormy decade marked by rapidly changing

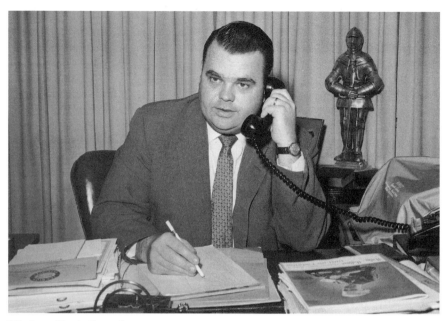

Billy James Hargis. GETTY IMAGES

religious, political, and moral institutions, coupled with un-stable political situations in Vietnam and the Soviet Union. Thus, Hargis built a consensus among fundamentalists through a shared set of beliefs—and fears. For example, he attacked American popular culture in his 1964 pamphlet entitled *Communism, Hypnotism and the Beatles.* He ma-ligned the Beatles and rock-and-roll music as a Communist plot to overthrow America's youth. And during the civil rights movement, he stated that God had ordained segre-gation. As for the hippies, yippies, and radicals of the antiwar movement, Hargis blamed "the Playboy philosophy of per-missiveness," Communism, liberal clergy, and the media.

In the early 1960s Hargis's Christian Crusade made na-tional headlines when the press reported that a U.S. Air Force manual alleging Communist infiltration in the Na-tional Council of Churches used one of Hargis's pamphlets as its source. During this period Hargis wrote five widely circulated books: *Communist America—Must It Be?* (1960), *Communism: The Total Lie* (1961), *The Facts About Com-munism and Our Churches* (1962), *The Real Extremists—The Far Left* (1964), and *Distortion by Design* (1965). His fourth book, *The Real Extremists—The Far Left,* touted the idea that President John F. Kennedy's assassination was the result of a Communist conspiracy. Next Hargis became overtly involved in national politics. At a 1962 meeting of his Anti-Communist Leadership School in Tulsa, Okla-homa, he endorsed national conservative political candi-dates and rallied for the defeat of liberal politicians in Washington.

Because of his political activities, Hargis's ministry lost its tax-exempt status, (although it was reinstated several

392

years later). Hargis claimed, however, that the Internal Revenue Service (IRS) blocked his tax-exempt status be-cause he supported the Bricker Amendment, which would return school prayer to the public schools. Hargis's 1964 radio broadcast attack against Fred Cook, the author of *Goldwater—Extremist on the Right* (1964), resulted in *Red Lion Broadcasting Co.* v. *FCC* (1969). In this case, the Federal Communications Commission (FCC) ruled that, under the Fairness Doctrine, the victim of an on-air personal attack such as Cook could demand free airtime to answer that at-tack. In 1965, boosted by his rising success, Hargis founded the Church of the Christian Crusade in Tulsa and built a $750,000 cathedral. His ministry went international with the formation of the David Livingston Missionary Foundation. At the height of Hargis's ministry, his broadcasts appeared on 140 television stations and 500 radio stations.

The hallmark of Hargis's 1960s war against Commu-nism was his numerous anticommunist rallies, which in-corporated political and military leaders as speakers (for youth he ran a summer Anti-Communist Youth University in Colorado). He attacked liberal political leaders of the time such as John F. Kennedy and Robert Kennedy, Lyndon Johnson, and the Reverend Martin Luther King, Jr. In 1969, at the eleventh national convention of the Christian Crusade, the speakers included retired Brigadier General Clyde G. Watts, retired Major General Edward A. Walker, and for-mer Alabama governor (and 1968 presidential candidate) George C. Wallace. Hargis's notoriety even led to guest appearances with national television talk-show hosts, in-cluding Phil Donahue, Tom Snyder, and Mike Wallace.

In 1970 Hargis established the American Christian College in Tulsa. He envisioned this as a Christian educational institution of higher learning that taught "God, government, and Christian action." This feat was ultimately his downfall. Hargis's ministry and leadership came to an abrupt halt when students of both sexes accused him of sexual misconduct. He was forced to resign his presidency in 1974, and the college closed in 1977 owing to financial insolvency. Hargis was not defeated entirely. He remained active in the Church of the Christian Crusade and the David Livingston Foundation and returned to the evangelical circuit, founding the Billy James Hargis Evangelistic Association. Nevertheless, his heyday was over, and he never regained his former status. In 1992 Hargis left Tulsa to run his international Christian Crusade Ministries from his Rose of Sharon Farm in Neosho, Missouri. He has written more than 100 books.

During the 1960s Hargis, a fundamentalist religious broadcaster whose efforts were chronicled and abetted by the new medium of television, qualified as an achiever of Andy Warhol's "fifteen minutes of fame." The endurance of the religious right, the Moral Majority, and the Christian Coalition in U.S. politics, however, remains as a testament to the power of his original anticommunist message, which joined together fundamentalist Christians in the "flyover states" of the United States into a right-wing coalition.

★

Hargis's autobiography is *My Great Mistake* (1968). John Harold Redekop, *The American Far Right: A Case Study of Billy James Hargis and the Christian Crusade* (1968), provides an overview of Hargis's organization in the 1960s.

LAURA BARFIELD

HARKNESS, Rebekah West (*b.* 17 April 1915 in St. Louis, Missouri; *d.* 17 June 1982 in New York City), capricious and exceptionally wealthy philanthropist and patron of the arts who backed the Joffrey Ballet before founding the Harkness Ballet, Harkness Youth Dancers, and Harkness House for Ballet Arts.

Harkness, born Rebekah Semple West, grew up amidst splendor in St. Louis as the third and youngest child of Allen Tarwater West, heir to a banking fortune, and Rebekah Semple, daughter of a wealthy merchant. She attended finishing school at Fermata in Aiken, South Carolina, from 1929 to 1932, before pursuing advanced instruction in harmonic structure and composition while studying piano and dance.

After a very brief career as a model, Harkness married the photographer Charles Dickson Pierce on 10 June 1939; they had two children and then divorced in 1945. Two years later on 1 October 1947, Harkness wed the philanthropist William Hale Harkness; they had one child before her hus-

Rebekah Harkness, June 1966. ASSOCIATED PRESS AP

band died in 1954. After her husband's death, Harkness resumed her interest in the arts, aided by an inheritance of about $27 million. Ambitious, possessing a campy sense of humor, and with a weakness for sycophants, Harkness would eventually squander most of the fortune. She made three semiclassical records in the 1950s, which were self-financed vanity pressings that received good reviews only from society columnists. Harkness had better luck with dance, and her composition *Journey to Love* had its premiere as a ballet with the Marquis de Cuevas's company at the Brussels World's Fair in 1958.

Enthralled with the reception accorded *Journey to Love,* Harkness focused on dance. Founding the Rebekah Harkness Foundation in 1959, she chose Jerome Robbins's Ballets: USA as the first beneficiary of her largess and sponsored its three-month European tour of major cities and festivals beginning in June 1961. When Robbins moved to other pursuits, Harkness sponsored a 1962 ethnological dance tour of Africa by Pearl Primus, then became the patron of the Robert Joffrey Ballet. Harkness pushed the Joffrey to use her ballet compositions. Accordingly, it scheduled one of her scores, *Dreams of Glory,* as the opening number of its 1962 European tour. Attacked by the dancers for being inane, this story of a teenage boy and girl who visit a museum, fall asleep, and dream that they become the president and first lady was yet another vanity production. Looking for any excuse to cancel the piece, Joffrey informed *Dance* magazine that there were too many problems with the costumes. The ballet was presented only once, in Teheran that year, as a special performance for Harkness and the Shah of Iran.

In 1963, at the invitation of President John F. Kennedy, the Joffrey performed at the White House and included Harkness's medley of vaudeville tunes among its pieces. Set to ballet, the one-act production cost $135,000 (more than the annual budget of the Joffrey before Harkness joined) and received mixed reviews in the United States but raves from the head of the Kirov Ballet when it was performed in Russia. It would be the last Harkness composition used by the company. Determined to assert his artistic integrity, Joffrey refused to return Harkness's phone calls. Her millions had bought new compositions, costumes, scenery, a masseuse, swimming facilities, and medical care for the company, but not control of it. In 1964 Harkness decided to form her own company. Left without prospects, many of the Joffrey dancers joined her. The international dance world, once friendly, now castigated Harkness for building her company upon the bones of the Joffrey.

The Harkness Ballet, a blend of modern dance and classical ballet, began its performing career with a European tour in 1965. Harkness insisted on playing an active role, but the only constant was her changeability, perhaps worsened by an increasing reliance on alcohol and amphetamines. Artistic directors came and went, with major decisions made by Harkness. As it became abundantly clear, she believed that she was the star. Rather than showcase the company's world-renowned dancers (among them, Larry Rhodes, Marjorie Tallchief, Helgi Tomasson, Lone Isaksen, and Erik Bruhn), photos in *Paris Match* and *Time* magazine featured Harkness doing lifts. To add further to the embarrassment of the dancers, she had them do her ballet *Macumba* (1965), in which she performed onstage with the choreographer Alvin Ailey in Barcelona. Demanding better leadership, the Harkness dancers threatened to leave after the 1968 season unless Harkness stepped aside and appointed Rhodes as artistic director. She agreed, and the 1969 season brought excellent reviews.

Having lost control of her company, Harkness founded another one. The Harkness Youth Dancers formed in the summer of 1968 under the direction of the choreographer Ben Stevenson. The company became an outlet for students trained at the Harkness House for Ballet Arts, which had opened in New York City in November 1965. Typically, Harkness spent lavishly upon the school. Each of the house's four dance studios was outfitted with special "springy" floors and eight-foot-high mirrors. The building also contained a music classroom, costume room, locker rooms, a masseur's room, bathing facilities, a laundry, record-listening rooms, a canteen, administrative offices, an

art gallery, a reception hall, and a library decorated with some of Harkness's sculptures. The school, with thirty-five dancers, fifty trainees, and a staff of ten, became a serious force in the New York dance world, and the opportunity to study there was coveted by young dancers. By 1970 Harkness had become so involved with the Harkness Youth Dancers that she did not attend the main company's New York premiere. While playing at Monte Carlo on 26 March 1970, the Harkness Ballet's general manager received a telegram. On a whim, Harkness was canceling the remaining engagements and ordering the troupe home. At the same time, the Youth Company, mostly consisting of sixteen- and seventeen-year-old pupils, was granted senior status and accepted the name of the former company. The dancers asked if they could borrow costumes and continue the tour without pay, but were refused.

In subsequent years, Harkness continued her involvement with the arts, opening the Harkness Theater on Broadway 1974. Designed especially for dance, the facility never made a profit. Harkness also provided $2 million for the construction of the William Hale Harkness Medical Research building at New York Hospital. Following a brief marriage to Dr. Benjamin Harrison Kean from 1961 to January 1965, Harkness made her fourth match to Dr. Niels Lauersen, which lasted from 12 October 1974 to 1977. Her final years were plagued by family problems and health woes, and she succumbed to cancer at the age of sixty-seven. Her funeral was held at Saint James Episcopal Church in Manhatten. Harkness was cremated, and her ashes are interred in the Harkness family mausoleum in Woodlawn Cemetery in the Bronx, New York City.

★

Harkness's personal papers, including a short interview, are held at the New York Public Library Lincoln Center Branch for the Performing Arts. The gossipy biography *Blue Blood* (1988), by Carl Unger, paints an unflattering portrait of her. Biographical information is also in Fernaul Hall and Mike Davis, *The World of Ballet and Dance* (1970). The demise of the Harkness Ballet is discussed in Maria B. Siegel, "The Harkness Ballet in Decline," *Los Angeles Times* (29 June 1970). An obituary is in the *New York Times* (19 June 1982).

CARYN E. NEUMANN

HARRIMAN, W(illiam) Averell (*b.* 15 November 1891 in New York City; *d.* 26 July 1986 in Yorktown Heights, New York), financier, sportsman, diplomat, governor of New York, and elder statesman of the Kennedy and Johnson administrations of the 1960s.

Harriman was one of six children born to the railroad titan Edward Henry Harriman and Mary Williamson Averell

W. Averell Harriman (left), with President John F. Kennedy, July 1963.
© BETTMANN/CORBIS

Harriman, daughter of an upstate New York railroad and banking family. He and his siblings were reared in an atmosphere of extraordinary privilege, the family dividing its time between an East Fifty-first Street mansion in Manhattan and a twenty-thousand-acre Arden estate in the Ramapo Mountains of Orange County, New York. Educated at Groton School in Massachusetts and Yale University (B.A., 1913), Harriman was just weeks from high school graduation when his father died in the spring of 1909. His inheritance included not only fabulous wealth, judiciously passed on to him by his mother, but parental expectations for great achievement.

Although he once seemed destined to follow in his father's footsteps as a capitalist, Harriman broke with his family's Republican traditions and became an ardent New Dealer and, eventually, one of America's most durable government officials and political figures, serving five Democratic presidents. Although he was then in his seventies, he was a globe-trotting ambassador and troubleshooter for presidents John F. Kennedy and Lyndon B. Johnson in the 1960s. In 1963 he led U.S. negotiations concluding the first nuclear weapons agreement with the Soviet Union, and in 1968 he headed the U.S. delegation in the first peace negotiations with the government of North Vietnam.

Before beginning his government and political career as

one of the Wall Street figures referred to as Franklin Roosevelt's "tame millionaires," Harriman was known widely as a sportsman and a businessman whose career was notable for both spectacular initiatives and conspicuous setbacks. In 1915, after a two-year apprenticeship, he was named vice president for purchasing of Union Pacific Railroad, the legendary line his father had rescued from bankruptcy and turned into the centerpiece of a huge railroad empire. Two years later, opting out of military service, he set out to make his own mark as an industrialist and financier while also making a contribution to the United States' effort in World War I. He opened two shipyards and built oceangoing freighters for the government until the end of the war. Thereafter, he operated passenger and merchant ships and financed such highly publicized ventures as manganese mining in the Soviet Republic of Georgia and the creation of a giant aviation conglomerate called the Aviation Corporation of America. In December 1930, as the Great Depression deepened, he and his brother Roland merged their banking and financing operations, W. A. Harriman and Company and Harriman Brothers and Company, with Wall Street's venerable Brown Brothers Bank. Brown Brothers Harriman and Company, the investment bank thus created, remained a stalwart of the New York financial district into the twenty-first century. In 1932, twenty-three years after his father's death, Harriman was named chairman of the board of the Union Pacific and led a highly publicized modernization of the railroad, including the introduction of streamline passenger trains.

Although his business and financial activities frequently put him in the news, Harriman was equally well known as a sportsman and socialite. He bred and trained both Labrador retrievers and thoroughbred horses, played polo with a passion, and mastered croquet, then a favored weekend diversion on the lawns of Long Island, New York, estates. In 1928 he starred in the U.S. defeat of Argentina's national polo team for America's Cup and the sport's unofficial world championship. He also became a major figure in popularizing downhill skiing in the United States, creating the Sun Valley resort in Idaho, which became a favorite getaway for Hollywood film stars after its opening in 1936. During the mid-1920s gossip and press accounts linked Harriman romantically with Teddy Gerard, an actress and cabaret singer. In the spring of 1929 his fourteen-year marriage to Kitty Lanier Lawrence, which produced two daughters, ended with a Parisian divorce. The following February he married Marie Norton Whitney, the recently divorced wife of Cornelius Vanderbilt (Sonny) Whitney.

By the time John F. Kennedy was inaugurated president in 1961, Harriman had become an icon of the Democratic Party. After a number of New Deal jobs, he had risen to prominence as America's special emissary in London, overseeing the flow of lend-lease supplies and equipment to

Great Britain in the days leading up to World War II. From 1943 until 1946 he was the U.S. ambassador to the Soviet Union. A participant in nearly all of the wartime Allied summits, he became an important channel of communication between President Roosevelt, British Prime Minister Winston Churchill, and the Soviet dictator Josef Stalin. Later a favorite of President Harry S Truman, Harriman served, briefly, as U.S. ambassador to Great Britain, secretary of commerce, director of mutual security, and, on occasions, as a special envoy for the White House. Twice, in 1952 and again in 1956, he made his own bid for the Democratic Party's presidential nomination, but he was a hopelessly inept campaigner and was never in serious contention. Despite his political awkwardness, he was elected governor of New York in 1954 and led a progressive and modestly successful administration. But in his 1958 campaign for reelection, he was portrayed as an instrument of Tammany Hall (the most powerful of the Democratic Party committees in New York City) and lost to Nelson A. Rockefeller in a landslide.

Because of his age, increasing deafness, and only modest success as a politician in his own right, Harriman seemed an unlikely candidate for a significant role in the Kennedy administration, given its emphasis on youth. But he aggressively lobbied for an appointment, and Kennedy rewarded him with an honorific and ambiguous assignment as ambassador-at-large. Beginning in April 1961 Harriman's dogged efforts to create a neutral government and prevent Laos from falling to the Communists established his bona fides with the new president. Thus, when Kennedy initiated a major shakeup of the State Department in November 1961, Harriman was named assistant secretary of state for Far Eastern affairs. The job was one ordinarily filled by young diplomats on the way up, but Harriman eagerly accepted it, because it gave him his own turf and involved him in issues far beyond the quixotic struggle to form a coalition government from the disparate political and family factions in Laos. Just as he became assistant secretary, Vietnam emerged as a first-order foreign policy problem for the Kennedy administration. As the U.S. stake in the conflict was raised, Harriman supported the implicit decision to make Vietnam, not Laos, the place for the U.S. stand against communist insurgency in Southeast Asia. But, along with other liberals in the administration, he soon became a sharp critic of the U.S.–supported regime of Ngo Dinh Diem in South Vietnam, urging the president to give more attention to the political situation in Saigon. At the State Department, he became de facto leader of a group that considered political and civic action as important as military intervention in confronting the threat from the north.

Because he was assigned to the Far East, Harriman was generally excluded from the foreign policy area that inter-

ested him most, the complex and crucial relations with the Soviet Union. He was not among the advisers Kennedy summoned to address the Cuban Missile Crisis in October 1962, and he was devastated. The Soviet Union had been his passion since his ill-fated manganese-mining venture, which had taken him to Moscow for business talks with Leon Trotsky in 1926. Since leaving Moscow as U.S. ambassador at the end of World War II, he had returned as a private citizen. He had met with Premier Nikita Khrushchev in Moscow and had been one of Khrushchev's hosts during the Soviet leader's visit to the United States in 1959. Left off the president's missile crisis team, Harriman sent unsolicited memos and advice to the attorney general, Robert F. Kennedy, with whom he had assiduously cultivated a close personal relationship. Like his brother the president, Robert Kennedy increasingly valued Harriman's long experience. In the wake of the missile crisis, as the attorney general became deeply involved in foreign policy, Harriman's stock continued to rise in the administration. In March 1963 he was named undersecretary of state for political affairs, putting him in the upper echelon of the country's foreign policy apparatus, where he had yearned to be.

Shaken by the missile crisis and the specter of nuclear war, Washington and Moscow moved dramatically to break a long diplomatic impasse over nuclear weapons testing. On 10 June 1963, after an exchange of messages with Khrushchev, Kennedy announced that direct negotiations on limitation of nuclear weapons testing would take place in Moscow. The following day Harriman was named to lead the U.S. delegation in deliberations with the Soviets and Great Britain. Although the parties had signaled a clear willingness to restrict testing, the issue of verification, specifically the number and type of permitted inspections, remained contentious.

With Khrushchev himself joining the first day of talks, negotiations got under way on 15 July. The possibility of a comprehensive test ban was given up early in the twelve days of talks that followed, and the delegations focused on a pact to ban nuclear weapons tests everywhere except underground. Each day Harriman cabled detailed reports to the White House, giving specifics of private informal conversations with Khrushchev as well as the progress of the negotiating sessions. Late on July 25, following a telephone call to the Situation Room at the White House, Harriman joined the Soviet foreign minister, Andrei Gromyko, and the British delegation leader, Lord Hailsham, in initialing the Limited Test Ban Treaty.

Although Harriman remained eager to serve, his importance faded after Lyndon Johnson became president in November 1963. He was given responsibility for African affairs, turning his attention principally to new strife in the Congo, where Kennedy had faced one of his first foreign policy crises. At the same time he tried to establish himself with the new president by energetically campaigning for Johnson in 1964, but in 1965 he found himself back where he had been in the first days of the Kennedy administration, as a roving ambassador. For more than a year he traveled the world continually, to meetings, on troubleshooting assignments, and on goodwill ventures. In 1966 Johnson made Harriman his unofficial "Ambassador for Peace," giving him authority to pursue any potential opening to a diplomatic resolution. Harriman took his mandate seriously, but his "peace shop" was spoken of derisively at the State Department, and some of his closest allies believed that his assignment was merely a way to keep him occupied.

Not until after Johnson's announcement on 31 March 1968 that he would not seek reelection did the government of North Vietnam agree to peace talks. There followed a month of jockeying over a location. On 10 May the president announced that negotiators would meet in Paris and Harriman would lead the U.S. delegation. Opening in a circus-like media atmosphere and with the U.S. presidential campaign under way, the talks proved to be a farce, with prolonged haggling over such procedural issues as the shape of the negotiating table and, eventually, recalcitrance by the government of South Vietnam. Harriman remained engaged as delegation leader until Johnson's last day in the White House. On 19 January 1969, the evening before Richard Nixon's inauguration as president, he arrived back in Washington and left government once again.

On 21 September 1971, a year after the death of his wife, Marie, Harriman married for the third time, to Pamela Digby Churchill Hayward, with whom he had carried on a secret wartime liaison while she was the wife of Winston Churchill's son, Randolph. During the administration of President Jimmy Carter, Harriman and his wife worked for arms control and for ratification of treaties ceding ownership of the Panama Canal to the government of Panama. In retirement, Harriman made six more trips to Moscow, the last in 1983. Half a century had passed between his first job in the New Deal and his last trip to the State Department to report on his final visit to the Kremlin. In the end his career had become a symbol of stability and continuity in U.S. government and foreign policy across the American century. Harriman died of respiratory arrest and other afflictions of age four months shy of his ninety-fifth birthday. He is buried at the family's Arden estate near Harriman, New York.

★

See Papers of W. Averell Harriman, Manuscript Division, Library of Congress, Washington, D.C. W. Averell Harriman and Elie Abel, *Special Envoy to Churchill and Stalin, 1941–1946* (1975), is the first of what might have been a multivolume autobiography. Rudy Abramson, *Spanning the Century: The Life of W. Averell Harriman* (1992), the only Harriman biography to date, was writ-

ten with Harriman's cooperation. Harriman, *America and Russia in a Changing World: A Half Century of Personal Observation* (1971), is drawn from a series of lectures in which Harriman considered the past and future of U.S.–Soviet relations. Chester L. Cooper, *The Lost Crusade: America in Vietnam* (1970), is an insider account by a longtime Harriman aide. Roger Hilsman, *To Move a Nation: The Politics of Foreign Policy in the Administration of John F. Kennedy* (1967), is a State Department official's view of Vietnam mistakes. David Halberstam, *The Best and the Brightest* (1972), views an aging Harriman as one of the wiser architects of American policy. Murray Klein, *Union Pacific: The Rebirth* (1990), is the second volume of a railroad history that chronicles the Harriman years. Two articles about Harriman are Douglass Cater, "Averell Harriman: Portrait of a Public Servant," *Reporter* (19 Feb. 1952), and E. J. Kahn, Jr., "Plenipotentiary," *New Yorker* (3 May 1952). Obituaries are in the *Los Angeles Times, New York Times,* and *Washington Post* (all 27 July 1986).

RUDY ABRAMSON

HARRINGTON, (Edward) Michael (*b.* 24 February 1928 in St. Louis, Missouri; *d.* 31 July 1989 in Larchmont, New York), author, educator, and political activist involved in a number of socialist movements, whose most famous work, *The Other America: Poverty in the United States* (1962), was an inspiration for President Lyndon B. Johnson's War on Poverty.

Harrington was the son of Edward M. Harrington, Sr., a patent attorney, and Catherine Fitzgibbon, a former schoolteacher, and grew up in a well-to-do, middle-class suburb of St. Louis, Missouri. His family has been described as enlightened Roman Catholic with the typical loyalty to the Democratic Party common among the Irish in St. Louis at that time. He was strongly influenced by his mother, who was active in community causes. Harrington went through parochial schools and then attended Holy Cross College, a Jesuit institution. He graduated second in his class at the age of nineteen. Harrington briefly attended Yale University Law School, but left when he discovered he really did not want to be a lawyer. Harrington transferred to the University of Chicago and earned an M.A. in English literature in 1949.

Harrington had adopted socialist thinking when he had a summer job in 1948 working with a St. Louis project for Arkansas sharecroppers. Following graduation from the University of Chicago, he went to New York City, where he worked as an associate editor at Dorothy Day's *Catholic Worker,* a radical periodical that advocated social reorganization and pacifism. Harrington also worked at Saint Joseph's House of Hospitality, a settlement house in the Battery. For about ten years Harrington was a regular at the White Horse Tavern, famous in Greenwich Village,

Michael Harrington *(right)*, shown with Ira S. Robbins *(left)* and Alvin E. Rose *(center)*, October 1962. ©
BETTMANN/CORBIS

where he lived, for the poets and writers who frequented it. Early in that period he considered himself a bohemian poet and participated in nightly discussions on politics and literature. In 1963 Harrington married Stephanie Gervis, a writer for the *Village Voice*. The couple had two sons.

By the mid-1950s Harrington had left organized religion and was an active member of the Young Socialist League. He declared conscientious objector status during the Korean War. Throughout this period he wrote articles for a number of activist publications, and in 1959 he co-edited *Labor in a Free Society*. That year the editor of *Commentary* commissioned Harrington to write an article on poverty as a social and political issue. He based the article, "Our Fifty Million Poor," on information he gathered from the U.S. Department of Labor.

In the 1960s, Harrington was over thirty and belonged to the old Left Socialist party called the League for Industrial Democracy (LID), but he still had the respect of the New Left college student organization known as Students for a Democratic Society (SDS), until an unfortunate mix-up regarding the manifesto drafted by SDS at their annual 1962 meeting. Harrington attended part of that meeting, suggesting to the group that the first draft of their manifesto did not adequately condemn Soviet totalitarianism, nor did it support liberal trade unions. He recommended these changes, then had to leave the meeting. When he was later misinformed that his suggestions were not included, he criticized the group who had, in fact, incorporated his recommendations. This misunderstanding ultimately led to a split between the old and new groups, a result he long

regretted. Harrington wrote frequently about this incident with regret for his "rude insensitivity to young people struggling to define a new identity."

After the article in *Commentary,* Harrington then wrote a more detailed work, *The Other America: Poverty in the United States,* published in 1962. He expanded the statistics with first-hand experiences he had from his travels among the poor in New York, Appalachia, and among migrant workers in California and other states. It was his first book and became his best-known work. He subsequently wrote fourteen books that included *The Accidental Century* (1965) and *Toward a Democratic Left: A Radical Program for a New Majority* (1968), in which he examined social and political problems in the United States. Included were the extensive inequities left unresolved by the War on Poverty, which had been seriously reduced in funding because of the demands of the Vietnam War. In the book he promoted a coalition of the groups on the left to solve the problems.

The Accidental Century was written to defend democratic socialism in the context of a philosophical review of the crises in values Harrington saw as being caused by the technological revolution. It was not, as expected by some, a sequel to *The Other America*. However, Harrington did continue the theme of *The Other America* in *The Next America: The Decline and Rise of the United States* (1981) and in *The Politics at God's Funeral: The Spiritual Crisis of Western Civilization* (1983).

The prevailing theme of most of Harrington's work was democratic socialism. Harrington won the George Polk Award and the Sidney Hillman Award for *The Other*

America. However, nothing he wrote after his first book had the same political and social impact. Harrington sometimes said that he could envision his epitaph: "Wrote *Other America,* downhill after that."

The senior labor columnist of the *New York Times* described *The Other America* as "a scream of rage and a call to conscience." An even more influential review was published in the *New Yorker.* In a forty-page feature on the book, Dwight Macdonald, a tough critic and staff writer for the magazine, described the book as "excellent and important" for its analysis of the reasons for the persistence and vast poverty that existed in the United States in the midst of general prosperity. Macdonald knew Harrington from the days when they were both members of a small socialist group. Discussing the impact of Macdonald's review, Harrington said that it had "made poverty a topic of conversation in the intellectual-political world of the Northeast." Soon it became even more influential.

In *The Other America,* Harrington pointed out that there were between 40 and 50 million poor. "The millions who are poor in the United States tend to become increasingly invisible. [I]t takes an effort of the intellect and will even to see them." Harrington described how these people lived. "Here are unskilled workers, the migrant farm workers, the aged, the minorities, and all the others who live in the economic underworld of American life." Harrington says, "These people . . . are hungry, and sometimes fat with hunger for that is what cheap foods do. They are without adequate housing and education and medical care." President John F. Kennedy was said to have read the reviews and then the book, and he was working on addressing the issues of the poor when he was assassinated.

President Lyndon B. Johnson picked up the theme with his War on Poverty, and during his term as president, the Economic Opportunity Act of 1964, the Appalachian Redevelopment Act of 1965, and the Medicare Act of 1965 were enacted. In 1964 Harrington briefly worked with Johnson's cabinet to draft antipoverty programs, but he preferred to keep to his role as critic. He continued his efforts lecturing in the United States and in Europe on his ideals for a democratic socialist society. In Europe he was better known for his socialist beliefs, whereas in the United States he was best known for *The Other America.*

Harrington was chairman of the League for Industrial Democracy in 1964 and a member of the executive board of the Socialist Party from 1960 to 1968. He became chairman of the Democratic Socialists of America in 1982 when it was formed out of two other Socialist groups. By the late 1980s the Democratic Socialists of America had become the largest socialist organization in the United States. Harrington said that the organization supports "incremental changes that create a welfare state that modulates and humanizes capitalist society."

The *New York Times* said of Harrington that he was probably the most visible spokesman for socialist ideals in the United States after Norman Thomas, the Socialist Party leader and frequent candidate for president. In his first autobiography, *Fragments of the Century* (1973), Harrington said, "To be socialist . . . is to make an act of faith, of love . . . toward this land. . . . To be radical is, in the best and only decent sense of the word, patriotic." Harrington was diagnosed with cancer of the esophagus in 1987; in spite of the disease, he published another autobiography, *The Long Distance Runner,* in 1988. Harrington died of cancer in 1989.

Just one year before his death, Harrington founded the Next America Foundation to support research on poverty. At a fund-raiser in Manhattan for the foundation, 600 people came to support him and to celebrate his life. In speaking to the group, Harrington summed up his political philosophy: "The democratic socialists envision a humane social order based on popular control of resources and production, economic planning, equitable distribution, feminism, and racial equality."

Harrington was appointed professor of political science at Queens College of the City University of New York in 1972, and was named a distinguished professor in 1988. The Michael Harrington Center was formed at Queens College of the City University of New York to honor his "life-long commitment to social justice and democracy." Harrington's ideals live on in the center, which exists to "promote public, democratic discussion of social issues, to advocate for social change and to work in partnerships with others to build a more just, equitable and democratic society."

★

Information on Harrington can be found in his autobiographies, *Fragments of the Century* (1973) and *The Long Distance Runner: An Autobiography* (1988). Further information about Harrington and his political beliefs is in Loren J. Okroi, *Galbraith, Harrington, Heilbroner: Economics and Dissent in an Age of Optimism* (1988). An obituary is in the *New York Times* (2 Aug. 1989).

M. C. NAGEL

HARTLINE, Haldan Keffer (*b.* 22 December 1903 in Bloomsburg, Pennsylvania; *d.* 17 March 1983 in Fallston, Maryland), neurophysiologist who shared the 1967 Nobel Prize in physiology or medicine for "discoveries concerning the physiological and chemical visual processes," with Hartline's work being cited for its contribution to the understanding of the physiological mechanisms of vision.

The son of Daniel Schollenberger Hartline and Harriet Franklin (Keffer) Hartline, Hartline was known to family

Haldan K. Hartline, 1967. © BETTMANN/CORBIS

and colleagues as "Keffer." Hartline's father taught science and his mother taught English at the Bloomsburg State Normal School (later Bloomsburg State College). His parents shared their strong interest in the natural sciences with their only child.

Hartline attended Lafayette College in Easton, Pennsylvania, where he became interested in research on phototropism from reading about work done by the biophysiologist Jacques Loeb. His first scientific paper was on the visual responses of land isopods. During his college years, Hartline spent his summers at the Woods Hole Marine Biological Laboratory in Cape Cod, Massachusetts. There he met Loeb, who introduced him to Selig Hecht, a biophysicist recognized for vision research. He also met the American biologist George Wald, with whom he would share the Nobel Prize in physiology or medicine. Hartline's scientific future was enormously influenced by these early experiences.

After graduating from Lafayette with a B.Sc. in 1923, Hartline went to Johns Hopkins University in Baltimore, where he earned an M.D. in 1927. He was more interested in studying mathematics and physics than medicine, and often said facetiously that he was awarded the M.D. on the condition that he never practice medicine. At Johns Hopkins, Hartline used a sensitive galvanometer to conduct pioneering research on retinal action potential that contributed to the groundwork for electroretinography.

After receiving his medical degree, Hartline briefly studied mathematics and physics at Johns Hopkins and at the universities of Leipzig and Munich in Germany. In 1931, at the invitation of Detlev W. Bronk, the director of the Eldridge Reeves Johnson Foundation Laboratory at the University of Pennsylvania in Philadelphia, Hartline took a position in medical physics at the foundation. On 11 April 1936 Hartline married Elizabeth Kraus, the daughter of a well-respected chemist. They settled into a country home in Hydes, Maryland, and raised their three sons there.

Hartline met the Swedish neurophysiologist Ragnar Granit, his other Nobel cowinner, while at the Johnson Foundation. When Bronk became the president of Johns Hopkins in 1949, he appointed Hartline as the first professor of biophysics and chair of the new laboratory. Four years later Bronk became the president of the Rockefeller Institute of Medical Research (later Rockefeller University) in New York City and again appointed Hartline as the head of biophysics. When he took the position at Rockefeller, Hartline moved into a small apartment in the city that he dubbed a "winter camp"; his family stayed at the "summer camp" in Maryland, and he returned there for weekends and holidays.

During the 1960s Hartline continued conducting research at the Rockefeller Institute and frequently returned to Woods Hole. In 1967 he was awarded the Nobel Prize in physiology or medicine, along with Wald and Granit. Although he never collaborated with either of them, Hartline was aware of, and admired, the research of both of his cowinners. Throughout his career, Hartline conducted all of his research in collaboration with colleagues and generously acknowledged all who influenced his work.

At the 1967 Nobel award ceremony, C. G. Bernhard noted that Hartline was given the prize for his elegant analysis of impulse generation in sensory cells and the code they transmit in response to illumination of different intensity and duration, research that provided the basic understanding of how sensory cells evaluate light stimuli. In his Nobel lecture, on 12 December 1967, Hartline described his work: "C. H. Graham and I sought to apply to an optic nerve the technique developed by Adrian and Bronk for isolating a single fiber; we made a fortunate choice of animal. The xiphosuran arachnid, *Limulus polyphemus,* commonly called 'horseshoe crab,' abounds on the eastern coast of North America. These 'living fossils' have lateral compound eyes that are coarsely faceted and connected to the brain by long optic nerves." The horseshoe crab is sometimes also described as a contemporary of the dinosaurs. Its eye has roughly 1,000 clusters of photoreceptors, where the human retina has more than 100 million photoreceptors.

Among the discoveries Hartline and his colleagues made from their work with the eyes of horseshoe crabs was lateral inhibition, which in the horseshoe crab's eye was shown to be mediated by simple neural connections. As Bernhard explained in his 1967 Nobel presentation speech, "After having shown the interconnections of adjacent visual cells, Hartline employed his discovery in a most imaginative way in order to obtain a quantitative description [of] how a nerve-net processes the data from sensory cells by means of inhibition. His discoveries have in a unique manner contributed to our understanding of the physiological mechanism whereby heightened contrast sharpens the visual impression of form and movement."

Commenting on Hartline's modus operandi, Bernhard said, "Your laboratory has been described as a slightly disorganized but extremely fertile chaos," adding that Hartline's work was best characterized for its elegance in design, expertise in manipulation, and clarity of exposition. Although the horseshoe crab has large photoreceptors and a long optic nerve compared to other species Hartline might have studied, the work still required demanding microdissection skills.

Ironically, in 1967 when Hartline was awarded the Nobel Prize for his intricate research into the visual processes of the eye, his vision was slowly failing as a result of senile macular degeneration. Hartline commented to friends, "The loss of central vision is bad enough in itself, but to be prematurely labeled senile only adds insult to injury." In 1974 Hartline retired from Rockefeller University. He died from a heart attack at the age of seventy-nine.

Hartline's research in the 1960s culminated with the successful development of theoretical predictions of sensory cell responses to a wide variety of stimuli. This work provided the foundation for major advances in the neurophysiology of vision.

★

A collection of Hartline's writings is Floyd Ratliff, ed., *Studies on Excitation and Inhibition in the Retina: A Collection of Papers from the Laboratory of H. Keffer Hartline* (1974). Biographies of Hartline include information in the Nobel archives, *Haldan Keffer Hartline—Biography* (1967); Harriet Zuckerman, *Scientific Elites: Nobel Laureates in the United States* (1977); and Floyd Ratliff, *Haldan Keffer Hartline: December 22, 1903 to March 18, 1983* (1990). An obituary is in the *New York Times* (19 Mar. 1983).

M. C. NAGEL

HASSENFELD, Merrill Lloyd (*b.* 19 February 1918 in Providence, Rhode Island; *d.* 21 March 1979 in Providence, Rhode Island), president and chairman of the board of Hasbro, Inc., the toy manufacturing giant that during the 1960s launched G. I. Joe, the first male action figure with accessories.

The oldest of three children of Henry Hassenfeld, a pencil and toy manufacturer, and Marion Frank, a homemaker, Hassenfeld was born one year after his father and uncles Herman and Hillel founded Hassenfeld Brothers, Inc. As Hassenfeld grew up in comfortable surroundings in Providence, the family's company first manufactured cloth-covered pencil boxes, using remnants from local textile mills.

After graduating as a business major from the University of Pennsylvania in 1938, Hassenfeld joined the family's firm, which by then had bought a pencil company. Just before World War II, Hassenfeld married Sylvia Kay; they had three children. At that time the company began including in its pencil boxes play stethoscopes and other toy medical equipment, sewing kits, and school supplies. In 1943 Hassenfeld's father placed his sons to lead the company's divisions. Merrill was put in charge of toys, while his brother Harold, headed pencils. Later, his brother's division split from Hassenfeld Brothers and became the Empire Pencil Corporation.

The first best-seller made by Hassenfeld Brothers (the name was changed to Hasbro Industries in 1968) was Mr. Potato Head, invented by George Lerner. Introduced in 1952, it was the first toy advertised on national television. At first these toys were only plastic facial parts applied to an actual potato; by 1964 they came complete with a hard plastic body. Mr. Potato Head has sold over 50 million units since its development.

In 1962 the company's original doctor and nurse kits were tied in with the phenomenally popular *Dr. Kildare* television show. The same year of the *Dr. Kildare* kits, Hasbro sold a puttylike product called Flubber as a tie-in with the Disney film *Son of Flubber* (1963). Unfortunately, the product was recalled when pretesting indicated that it caused a mild skin rash. By 1963 the company's future was in doubt, and Hassenfeld knew that toys were fashionable and that consumers were fickle and faddish. He needed another toy that would become, and hopefully remain, a best-seller.

In spring 1953 Hassenfeld had just returned from a philanthropic trip to Israel. (He would later become the honorary national chairman of the United Jewish Appeal.) Back in his office, he called Don Levine, his product development chief and a veteran of the Korean War. Hassenfeld wanted to know how the next year's product line was developing. Levine then presented him with an articulated toy soldier inspired by the television series *The Lieutenant.* Levine had passed by an art supply store and had seen a sculptor's model figure in the window. Out of that concept grew a plastic figure with twenty-one moving parts. Levine made four brawny models of eleven and one-half inches, each dressed in the uniform of the army, navy, marines, or air force. The face of each was a composite of the faces of Congressional Medal of Honor winners, and a small scar was cut into the chin to add distinction.

"How the hell are we going to sell a boy a doll?" Hassenfeld asked. After all, dolls were for girls. Yet boys had played with tiny cast-metal soldiers since at least the Middle Ages, and youngsters did play with Raggedy Andy dolls. The company wanted to broaden its boys' offerings beyond doctor kits. Moreover, a toy soldier was an "open-end concept." In the toy field, an open-end concept is a product that is multifunctional and has separately sold accessories. Arch-rival Mattel's Barbie doll had become the toy world's most famous gold digger, with boyfriend Ken, outfits for every occasion, and seemingly countless accessories to go with the outfits. Hassenfeld bet that the muscular soldier concept would sell, but it was a major risk that could easily backfire. He decided not to tie it in with any specific television show or movie.

G. I. Joe was not a "doll," but an "action figure." The toy's name was chosen from the war film *The Story of G. I. Joe* (1945), with Burgess Meredith and Robert Mitchum. Levine's four service models, each initially selling for $4, included separately sold outfits and accessories, for a total outlay of $330. Among the toy weapons were a bazooka that launched plastic projectiles, and a flamethrower that shot a stream of water. There were jeeps and tanks to carry the figures, and tents for rest. War dramas with stiff cast-metal soldiers of the past now were fully articulated and accessorized fighters of the present.

Hassenfeld created a total mystique for G. I. Joe. "I have always been a firm believer," he told a reporter, "that there can be no civilization without the soldier. He represents a civilizing rather than a destructive force." The advertising budget was doubled to $1.5 million for print and television. Bruns Advertising Agency created for "America's Movable Fighting Man" squads of toys who were not "at war," but in "action adventures." "G. I. Joe . . . G. I. Joe," intoned the advertising jingle, "fighting man from head to toe." Within one week after G. I. Joe toys appeared on shelves,

they were sold out. For boys the action figure was decidedly "cool." A fan club and newsletter soon followed.

Within two years other models appeared, including an African-American G. I. Joe. Other models evoked World War II, including toy soldiers with special features and uniforms of Nazi Germany, Imperial Japan, and Soviet Russia. In 1967 male action figures made up an astonishing 15 percent of all toys sold that year. G. I. Joe's fans were decidedly hawkish. One fast-selling competitor was a Green Beret doll that had a grenade for one hand and an M-16 rifle for the other. By 1965 a backlash began, spearheaded by dovish parental groups who protested against the new action-adventure culture. With anti–Vietnam War sentiment rising in the later 1960s, G. I. Joe's profits dropped, beginning in 1967, and plummeted in 1968 following the assassinations of Dr. Martin Luther King, Jr., and Senator Robert Kennedy. In 1969 Sears, Roebuck and Company pulled all war toys out of its mail-order catalogue.

Hassenfeld's response to the antiwar sentiment was to retain the drama of action figures, but to relaunch them as the Adventure Team in 1969. Now action figures searched for sunken treasure and hunted wild animals, and they were fully accessorized. Hasbro continued to reinvent other variants, from kung fu warriors to ecofighters. In 1974 Hassenfeld retired and his son Stephen became president. When Stephen died in 1989, his brother Alan became head of Hasbro. The third generation of the family expanded their product lines and bought out competitors Knickerbocker, Milton Bradley, and Tonka. As the largest toy-and-game manufacturing corporation, Hasbro offers products ranging from Play-Doh modeling compound to Easy-Bake ovens to board games like Trivial Pursuit. Licensed brands include Pokemon, Furby, Harry Potter, and Monsters, Inc. Hassenfeld died of a heart attack, and is buried at the Lincoln Park Cemetery in Warwick, Rhode Island.

Hassenfeld parlayed a modestly successful family business into a Fortune 500 corporation. By using aggressive and saturating print advertising and the first national television commercials for a toy, he launched and perpetuated the Mr. Potato brand. During the 1960s, Hassenfeld tied in toys with Hollywood and applied the open-end concept of endless accessories to a new toy category, the male action figure embodied as G. I. Joe.

★

There is no biography of Hassenfeld. For a profile of Hasbro, Inc., that emphasizes the third generation of ownership, see G. Wayne Miller, *Toy Wars: The Epic Struggle Between G. I. Joe, Barbie, and the Companies That Make Them* (1998). See also Vincent Santelmo, *The Complete Encyclopedia to G. I. Joe* (1993). Important newspaper articles are Joan Cook, "G. I. Joe Doll Is Capturing New Market," *New York Times* (24 July 1965), with a quote from Hassenfeld; and Harry F. Waters, "Dolls at War,"

New York Times Magazine (4 June 1967). An obituary is in the *New York Times* (22 Mar. 1979).

PATRICK S. SMITH

HATCHER, Richard Gordon   (*b.* 10 July 1933 in Michigan City, Indiana), civil rights activist, lawyer, and five-term mayor of Gary, Indiana, who in 1967 (along with Carl Stokes of Cleveland) became the first African-American mayor of a large American city.

Hatcher, a Baptist of African-American descent, grew up in poverty. He was the youngest of thirteen children in a family that had witnessed the deaths of six of its offspring. His father, Carlton, was a semiskilled laborer for Pullman Standard and his mother, Katherine, worked in a factory. Hatcher was an introverted youth who suffered from a stuttering problem as well as blindness in one eye. Despite these physical limitations, he blossomed into a high-school track and football star.

With an athletic scholarship and financial assistance from churches and siblings, Hatcher enrolled at Indiana University in the fall of 1951. Once on campus, however, Hatcher, like most of his African-American peers, was unprepared for college work. While many of the African-American students flunked out, Hatcher successfully juggled academic pursuits, track practice, and part-time work. During his sophomore year Hatcher joined with the National Association for the Advancement of Colored People (NAACP) chapter to picket Nick's, a segregated restaurant

located on campus. Significantly, he and other activists picketed this segregated restaurant in Indiana seven years before North Carolina A&T students decided to launch their renowned sit-in campaign in Greensboro. When Hatcher graduated with a B.S. in 1956, he was a campus activist and a regular member of the dean's list.

In the fall of 1956 Hatcher started law school at Valparaiso (Indiana) University. He went to classes during the day, worked full time as a psychiatric aide in the evening, and still had time to participate in politics. In 1958 he and some friends completed a successful sit-in at Brownie's Griddle in Michigan City. During the same year Hatcher lost his first election when he came in fourth place as a Democratic primary candidate for Michigan Township justice of the peace. In 1959 he completed his law degree, was admitted to the bar, and headed to Gary, Indiana, where he worked in private practice. After winning a high-profile extradition case involving a black youth from Mississippi, he became a deputy county prosecutor.

As a member of the informal group "Muigwithania," Hatcher sought to loosen the stranglehold of Gary's Democratic machine. Muigwithania took its inspiration from the emerging African nations that had thrown off the shackles of colonial government, and in fact, the organization's name was the Swahili term meaning "We are together." In 1962 Hatcher became president of Muigwithania, resigned from his duties as deputy prosecutor, and threw himself into such issues as school integration, police brutality, and the open housing movement.

In 1963 Hatcher, as city councilman-at-large and then

Richard Hatcher, 1967. © BETTMANN/CORBIS

as council president, continued to champion civil rights, but white intransigence sent an omnibus civil-rights bill to defeat, and his own low-cost housing campaign produced no additional housing units. In 1966 Hatcher received much acclaim when a group of Gary citizens recruited him to run for mayor, and Vice President Hubert Humphrey invited him and several other leaders to discuss African Americans' frustration with the limited progress the administration of President Lyndon B. Johnson was making on civil rights.

In January 1967 Hatcher agreed to run for mayor of Gary under the slogan "New Freedom." In his campaign, Hatcher attacked what he termed Gary's "plantation politics" and defended the term "Black Power." He also critiqued the Democratic machine for a legacy of racism, corruption, and poverty, and condemned the steel companies for polluting the environment and refusing to pay their share of taxes. The incumbent mayor, A. Martin Katz, was favored in the Democratic primary, because while African Americans composed a majority of Gary's population, more whites were registered to vote. Hatcher upset Katz, however, because a third candidate, Bernard W. Konrady, divided the white vote. Traditionally, when candidates won a Democratic primary in Gary, they were guaranteed victory in the general election. However, Democratic county chairman John Krupa, after an ill-fated effort to turn Hatcher into his puppet, tried to throw the election to Republican challenger Joseph Radigan by tampering with the voter rolls. Nevertheless, Hatcher won a close election with 95 percent of the black vote and 12 percent of the white vote and shared a historic milestone with Carl Stokes of Cleveland when they became the first African-American mayors of large American cities.

After Hatcher was sworn in as mayor in January 1968, he began a first term that left a mixed legacy. His greatest success was turning Gary into an "urban laboratory" that attracted millions of dollars from private foundations and the Model City Programs in Johnson's "Great Society." With those funds, Hatcher's administration was able to establish antipoverty programs that improved housing and health care and gave disadvantaged youngsters an opportunity with "Head Start" programs. Hatcher also unflaggingly supported civil rights, fought crime and poverty, tried to revitalize the business district, and broke the power of the Democratic Party machine. Hatcher's detractors, however, could point to labor disputes with city employees, a school boycott, a threat of disannexation by the white Glen Park neighborhood, unmet expectations among African Americans, and hostile relationships with council members, county and state governments, and the local newspaper.

By the time Hatcher lost the mayoral election of 1987, he had been in office for five terms and twenty years. Over that time he had gained a reputation as a powerful advocate of civil rights and low-income residents, but as federal

funding rapidly decreased in the 1970s and 1980s, he never was able to turn Gary from its path of decline. In the final analysis, Hatcher led his city at a time when "white flight," disinvestment, and increasing crime rates were ravaging cities across the United States. Though many critics demonized the African-American Hatcher for Gary's depleted economy and infrastructure, nearby cities such as Hammond and East Chicago suffered similar fates with white mayors. In 1991, when Hatcher made an ill-fated bid for a sixth mayoral term, he could find solace in the fact that at that time more than 300 African-American mayors held office.

In addition to his tenure as mayor, Hatcher had an impact on national politics when he helped organize the first National Black Political Convention in 1972 and chaired Jesse Jackson's campaigns for the presidency in 1984 and 1988. Since leaving office he has worked as a lawyer and a professor and has embarked on a campaign to build a National Civil Rights Museum and Hall of Fame in Gary. Hatcher married Ruthellyn Marie Rowles in 1976, and they have three daughters.

★

Alex Poinsett, *Black Power Gary Style: The Making of Mayor Richard Gordon Hatcher* (1970), though dated, offers the most biographical information about Hatcher's early life. David R. Colburn and Jeffrey S. Adler, eds., *African-American Mayors: Race, Politics, and the American City* (2001), includes an informative introduction to the emergence of the black mayor as well as a fine essay on Hatcher by James B. Lane. Robert A. Catlin, *Racial Politics and Urban Planning: Gary, Indiana 1980–1989* (1993), emphasizes Hatcher's later terms. William E. Nelson, *Black Politics in Gary: Problems and Prospects* (1972), and James B. Lane, *"City of the Century": A History of Gary, Indiana* (1978), both place Hatcher in the broader context of Gary's history.

ALAN BLOOM

HAYAKAWA, S(amuel) I(chiye) (*b.* 18 July 1906 in Vancouver, British Columbia, Canada; *d.* 27 February 1992 in Greenbrae, California), professor of semantics and acting president of San Francisco State College in the 1960s who brought the school through a time of civil unrest during a strike by students and faculty in 1968 and 1969.

Hayakawa was one of four children of Ichiro, a Japanese import-export businessman, and Tora Isono Hayakawa, who worked in the family business. The Hayakawas, who had immigrated to Canada at the turn of the century, named their first son Samuel, in honor of the British lexicographer and poet Samuel Johnson. Highly educated and liberal in his political views, Hayakawa earned a B.A. in English from the University of Manitoba in 1927, an M.A. from McGill University in Montreal the following year, and a Ph.D. in English and American literature from the Uni-

S. I. Hayakawa. CORBIS CORPORATION (BELLEVUE)

versity of Wisconsin in 1935. In 1937 he entered into a racially mixed marriage with Margedant Peters; the couple was married for more than fifty years, until Hayakawa's death in 1992; they had three children.

For a variety of reasons, including his race and his mixed marriage, Hayakawa was shunned in the social order, an action reflective of the conservative culture of the early twentieth century. Because of his ancestry, he was threatened with detention in a Japanese internment camp during World War II, but because he was a Canadian citizen at the time, he retained his freedom. Oddly, the U.S. government alternately listed him as an enemy alien and as fully eligible for the draft (classification 1A) during the war years. Although he never served in the U.S. military, Hayakawa was able to convince the draft board of their error in listing him as an enemy when he pointed out that the United States was not at war with Canada.

Hayakawa distinguished himself as a writer and lecturer and was the author of one of the most influential books in the field of semantics, *Language in Thought and Action,* which went through successive editions from 1949 through 1990. (The book was an expanded version of an early work, *Language in Action.*) As a result of his background, he remained outspoken on many issues and was at first considered a liberal, although he later adopted conservative politics, changing his political affiliation from Democrat to Republican in 1973.

Hayakawa became a U.S. citizen in 1955. He began his affiliation with California's San Francisco State College (now University) at about the same time, initially as a lecturer. He was hired later as an English professor to teach

semantics. After more than a decade of relative obscurity at the San Francisco campus, Hayakawa was called upon by the state's Board of Regents to serve as acting president of the college. His appointment followed the resignation of the school's president, Robert Smith, on 28 November 1968 after three weeks of student unrest and violence instigated by striking students, members of the Black Student Union (BSU). The strike had been launched on 6 November following a public endorsement from Stokely Carmichael, the prominent 1960s black civil rights activist, with strikers demanding, among other issues, that the college establish a black studies department. The controversy was aggravated by the suspension of an outspoken African-American instructor, George Murray, on 1 November.

Hayakawa's ascension to the acting presidency of the school generated campus-wide controversy. Two weeks before his appointment, with the college under threat of the escalating strike, he had delivered a memorable speech to his peers at the school, expressing displeasure with those faculty members who supported the chaos. At that time Hayakawa publicly accused some faculty members of patronizing the strikers. Additionally, he called on the staff of the college to help quell the crisis, at the same time that a group of faculty members—aligned with the liberal American Federation of Teachers (AFT)—huddled in deliberation over whether to engage in a sympathy strike. The AFT also called for the resignation of the state's chancellor, Glenn S. Dumke, who had dictated Murray's suspension.

Despite the increased threat of violence, Hayakawa resolved to keep the campus open for business during the strike and called upon the San Francisco Police Department to increase its presence on campus. He advised BSU representatives that their demands were not unreasonable but urged them to reconsider their tactics, which were unnecessarily extreme and therefore self-defeating. Hayakawa also issued orders and guidelines for all on-campus protests. He specifically prohibited the students from setting up public address systems on campus for the purpose of instigating a demonstration.

The BSU rejected Hayakawa in his position as acting president, labeling him an Uncle Tom and a puppet of the school's all-white Board of Regents. On 2 December a group of student leaders attempted to use a public address system to heighten the mood of the strikers, leaving Hayakawa affronted over the challenge to his authority. In an incident he later described as "the most exciting day of my life," the paunchy, sixty-two-year-old acting president scaled the speaker's platform to the strikers' podium and disconnected the electrical cord, disabling the loudspeakers. It was an iconic moment: Hayakawa by his actions dramatized the emotions of many middle-class Americans who were confounded and disgruntled by the mindset of the militant college students and the civil unrest of the 1960s. The protesters shoved Hayakawa as he descended the platform; they grabbed at the colorful tam-o'-shanter that he wore and tossed it around spitefully. "Don't shove me! I'm the president," he asserted, adding to the melee. The incident was caught on videotape and was televised widely; California's governor, Ronald Reagan, applauded Hayakawa for his assertive action, however symbolic.

The atmosphere at San Francisco State, in fact, deteriorated, prompting Hayakawa to close the college one week early for the winter holiday, in part to avert the looming strike by the AFT. Regardless, the BSU strike resumed with the reopening of school in January; likewise, the AFT was granted strike sanction by the San Francisco Labor Council. The striking parties signed an agreement on 20 March 1969, including guidelines for the admission of third world students and rules for the administration of financial aid. In the aftermath, Hayakawa was officially named president of the college, a post he held until 1973.

As president emeritus of San Francisco State College, in 1976 Hayakawa was elected to the U.S. Senate, representing the state of California as a Republican. He served until 1982, and in 1983 he became an adviser to the secretary of state under President Ronald Reagan. Hayakawa also is remembered for spearheading a movement to establish English as the official language of the United States. He died of a stroke at the age of eighty-five.

★

Papers from Hayakawa's federal government service from 1977 to 1988 are held by the Hoover Institution Library and Archives of Stanford University. Dikran Karagueuzian, a journalism student at San Francisco State during the 1968 and 1969 uprisings, chronicled Hayakawa's role in the struggle in *Blow It Up: The Black Student Revolt at San Francisco State College and the Emergence of Dr. Hayakawa* (1971). Interviews with Hayakawa appeared in *U.S. News & World Report* (3 Oct. 1983) and *Forbes* (11 June 1990). Additional insight on the times can be found in Kenneth J. Heineman, *Campus Wars* (1993), and in Gerard De Groot, "Reagan's Rise: Ronald Reagan in California During the 1960s," *History Today* (1 Sept. 1995.) An obituary is in the *New York Times* (28 Feb. 1992).

GLORIA COOKSEY

HAYDEN, Thomas Emmett ("Tom") (*b.* 11 December 1939 in Royal Oak, Michigan), civil rights activist, founder and first president of Students for a Democratic Society, primary author of the Port Huron Statement, antiwar activist, and defendant in the conspiracy trial of the "Chicago Eight."

Hayden is the only child of John Francis Hayden, an accountant and World War II veteran, and Genevieve Isabelle (Garity) Hayden, a librarian. His parents divorced soon after the war, and Hayden's mother supported herself and her son. Hayden attended the Shrine of the Little Flower Church and parish school. Although the church's pastor

Tom Hayden testifying before the President's Commission on Violence, October 1968. ASSOCIATED PRESS AP

was Father Charles Coughlin, the prominent "radio priest" and depression-era critic of President Franklin D. Roosevelt, Hayden remembered nothing overtly political in his weekly sermons to his parish.

In 1957 Hayden graduated from Royal Oak High School, where he had been editor of the school newspaper; enrolled at the University of Michigan in Ann Arbor; and soon began reporting for the campus newspaper, the *Michigan Daily*. Although he had been exposed to campus politics at Michigan, he gradually became more committed to activism following a trip to California in 1960. There he met students from the University of California, Berkeley, who had protested against the House Un-American Activities Committee, and he attended a meeting of the National Student Association, where he interviewed Dr. Martin Luther King, Jr. "Ultimately, you have to take a stand with your life," King told Hayden.

During his senior year (1960–1961) Hayden used his position as editor of the *Daily* to promote the work of student civil rights activists in the South; he also made a trip to Tennessee to deliver food to black sharecroppers evicted from their land for registering to vote. Hayden graduated with a B.A. from the University of Michigan in 1961. Following graduation he married the civil rights activist Sandra ("Casey") Cason, and the two worked full-time for the Student Nonviolent Coordinating Committee (SNCC) in Atlanta. Hayden and Cason would divorce in 1963. As racist violence increased in Mississippi in response to SNCC's voter-registration drive, Hayden went to McComb, Mississippi, where he was attacked by segregationists and arrested. Later, he and Casey took part in a Freedom Ride by train from Atlanta to Albany, Georgia, where both were arrested for attempting to integrate the public train station in Albany.

By 1961 Hayden was one of a handful of people making up Students for a Democratic Society (SDS), an organization formed by some Michigan friends out of the Old Left Student League for Industrial Democracy. Inspired by the courage of the SNCC students in the face of southern hostility and believing that an entire generation could be aroused over issues of race, war and peace, and political apathy, Hayden called on his colleagues to make SDS a national organization and a counterpart to SNCC. In June 1962 students from across the country met in Port Huron, Michigan, where Hayden produced the first draft of the "Port Huron Statement," the defining document of the New Left. It began, "We are people of this generation, bred in at least modest comfort, housed in universities, looking uncomfortably to the world we inherit." It assailed the racism in American society and the peril of atomic weapons and suggested that, contrary to appearances, most Americans experienced "deeply-felt anxieties about their role in the new world." Even so, Hayden's optimism came

through: "We regard men as infinitely precious and possessed of unfulfilled capacities for reason, freedom, and love. . . . We oppose the depersonalization that reduces human beings to things . . . . We see little reason why men cannot meet with increasing skill the complexities and responsibilities of their situation." In addressing social problems, the Port Huron Statement included a lengthy section on "participatory democracy." This was a central New Left tenet that called for "the individual [to] share in those social decisions determining the quality and direction of his life" and demanded "that society be organized to encourage independence in men and provide the media for their common participation." At the end of nearly seventy-five pages, the statement indicated that SDS planned to spread its vision to communities and campuses across the country. "If we appear to seek the unattainable, then let it be known that we do so to avoid the unimaginable."

In 1962 and 1963 Hayden served as SDS's first president, operating from a home office in Ann Arbor (where he also completed an M.A. degree in sociology in 1963). Eventually it became clear to him and the SDS leadership that a "participatory democracy" would not begin by itself. The organization, therefore, set up the Economic Research and Action Project (ERAP), intended as a northern equivalent to SNCC, sending students to organize the poor in urban slums. From September 1963 to July 1967 Hayden led the ERAP in Newark, New Jersey. Hayden and the other volunteers went door to door, inquiring about residents' grievances and arranging meetings to organize citizens into effective community groups. They helped organize rent strikes, elected poor people to the city's Anti-Poverty Board, held welfare demonstrations, and demanded that new playgrounds be built in poor neighborhoods. When the Newark riots erupted in 1967, Hayden, already under surveillance by the Federal Bureau of Investigation, challenged the official claims of a conspiracy in his book, *Rebellion in Newark*. As he put it, "Americans have to turn their attention from the law-breaking violence of the rioters to the original and greater violence of racism, which is supported indirectly by the white community as a whole."

In the meantime the 1965 escalation of the American war in Vietnam also captured Hayden's attention. That year, with the radical historians Staughton Lynd and Herbert Aptheker, he made the first of several trips to North Vietnam, and with Lynd he wrote *The Other Side* (1967), in which the authors attempted to explain the nationalist motives and goals of North Vietnam. In 1967, during a meeting between North Vietnamese officials and American peace activists in Bratislava, Czechoslovakia, he was invited to Cambodia to convey three American prisoners of war back to the United States.

At the beginning of 1968, however, with the war still escalating, Hayden moved from Newark to Chicago to serve as codirector of projected protests at the August Democratic National Convention. In his memoir Hayden said that he felt as though he were "living on the knife edge of history." That winter and spring saw the unfolding of the Tet offensive, a series of battles launched by the Vietnamese Communists to capture cities in South Vietnam. The short-term success of the campaign served as a psychological victory and undermined the claim of the U.S. government that the war in Vietnam was almost won. At the same time the senators Eugene McCarthy and Robert Kennedy challenged Lyndon B. Johnson for the Democratic presidential nomination. Hayden, who had grown fond of Kennedy, hoped that Johnson would be defeated. His aspirations for peace in the wake of Johnson's announcement that he would not run for reelection were quickly erased by the assassinations of Martin Luther King, Jr., and Kennedy. In May 1968 Hayden also participated in the student strike and seizure of buildings at Columbia University by chairing the "commune" in charge of the mathematics building.

Meanwhile, the mayor of Chicago, Richard Daley, "in order to discourage the hippies from coming," refused to grant marching permits or overnight camping permits to Hayden's National Mobilization Committee to End the War in Vietnam, or "Mobe," as it was often called. Attorney General Ramsey Clark sent Justice Department representatives to negotiate with the mayor and the demonstrators, but Daley would not budge. With thousands expected to descend on the city to demonstrate against the war, this virtually guaranteed that there would be street violence during the convention.

The protest plan for the convention involved four days of picketing, rallies, and concerts culminating in a ten-mile march from Grant Park to the convention headquarters at the International Amphitheatre. Most of the ten thousand people who came to Chicago had supported either McCarthy or Kennedy. Daley and the police, however, assumed that the few outspoken leaders, such as Abbie Hoffman and Jerry Rubin of the Youth International Party, or "Yippies," who were threatening to kidnap delegates and dump LSD in the city's water supply, were representative of the whole. When the 11:00 P.M. curfew arrived in Lincoln Park on the eve of the convention's opening, Chicago police invaded the park and used tear gas and police batons to disperse the crowd.

Hayden was arrested twice the next day, once in Lincoln Park and again, around midnight, outside the Conrad Hilton hotel. The next day Hayden wore a disguise to avoid harassment. On 28 August, the day of the planned march to the convention center and after three days and nights of police attacks, the police once again moved in on Hayden and other Mobe leaders in Grant Park. When Mobe's codirector Rennie Davis was knocked unconscious, Hayden, furious, told the crowd that since the city would not allow

them to march, they should move in small groups out of the park. "Let us make sure that if blood is going to flow, let it flow all over this city . . . . If we are going to be disrupted and violated, let this whole stinking city be disrupted and violated." The crowd scattered. The Illinois National Guard stopped some protesters, but a few thousand made it to the Conrad Hilton hotel, where again they were clubbed, gassed, and arrested by police. News crews filmed the chaos as the demonstrators shouted, "The whole world is watching!"

Hayden and seven others, known as the "Chicago Eight," were indicted for crossing state lines to incite a riot. In February 1970, following a sensational trial in which the defendants openly sparred with the judge, Hayden and four others were found guilty and sentenced to five years in prison. The convictions were overturned on appeal in 1972. On 20 January 1973 Hayden married the actress Jane Fonda, with whom he continued to work on the Indochina Peace Campaign. They divorced in 1990. Hayden lost an election bid for the U.S. Senate on the Democratic ticket in California in 1976 but was elected to the California State Assembly in 1982 and served until 1992. He also served Los Angeles as a state senator from 1992 to 1999. On 8 August 1993 Hayden married Barbara Williams; they have one son.

Few Americans personify the tumultuous decade of the 1960s like Hayden. From his 1962 authorship of the Port Huron Statement, which inspired thousands of young people in the 1960s and beyond, to his civil rights, ERAP, and antiwar activism, Hayden participated in many of the defining events of his generation and left an enduring mark.

★

Hayden has published eleven books, including his memoir, *Reunion: A Memoir* (1988). Biographical information about Hayden is in Kirkpatrick Sale, *SDS: Ten Years Toward a Revolution* (1973); David DeLeon, *Leaders from the 1960s: A Biographical Sourcebook of American Activism* (1994); and Hayden's personal website at http://www.tomhayden.com. Information about Hayden's activities in the SDS and the Chicago protests and trial is in Todd Gitlin, *The Sixties: Years of Hope, Days of Rage* (1987); Maurice Isserman, *If I Had a Hammer: The Death of the Old Left and the Birth of the New Left* (1987); James E. Miller, *Democracy Is in the Streets: From Port Huron to the Siege of Chicago* (1987); David Farber, *Chicago '68* (1988); and Terry H. Anderson, *The Movement and the Sixties: Protest in America from Greensboro to Wounded Knee* (1995). SDS's papers are available on microfilm and are deposited at the University of Wisconsin.

MICHAEL S. FOLEY

HAYNSWORTH, Clement Furman, Jr. (*b.* 30 October 1912 in Greenville, South Carolina; *d.* 22 November 1989 in Greenville, South Carolina), federal appellate judge who was rejected for appointment to the U.S. Supreme Court.

Haynsworth was the son of Clement Furman Haynsworth and his wife, Elsie Hall Haynsworth. One of three children, Haynsworth was of the fourth generation in his family to enter the law. He attended the private Darlington School in Rome, Georgia, and then, like his father, graduated from Furman University and received his LL.B. from Harvard University in 1936. He then joined the family law firm, which his father had founded in 1910. During World War II he served as a lieutenant with naval intelligence, stationed in the United States. On 25 November 1946 he married Dorothy Merry Barkley, who had two sons by a previous marriage. After the war he returned to the family law practice and remained there until 1957, when President Dwight D. Eisenhower appointed him to the U.S. Court of Appeals for the Fourth Circuit, which serves Virginia, West Virginia, Maryland, and the Carolinas. At the time of his appointment Haynsworth was the youngest judge on the court.

As a member of the court of appeals in the 1960s, Haynsworth was involved in many important cases focusing on issues such as civil rights and the rights of workers. In one notable instance, *Griffin* v. *the Board of Supervisors* (1963), Haynsworth (as part of the majority ruling) appeared to support segregation in a Virginia case that involved a decision by the Prince Edward County board of supervisors to close the public schools rather than integrate them. The court maintained that closing the county's schools did not deny black children equal protection of the laws guaranteed by the U.S. Constitution. In a 1964 decision the U.S. Supreme Court nullified the circuit court's

Clement Haynsworth, October 1969. © BETTMANN/CORBIS

decision, stating unequivocally that "the closing of the county schools denied the plaintiffs the equal protection of the laws."

Haynsworth was promoted to the chief judge of the U.S. Court of Appeals for the Fourth Circuit in 1964. He might have remained in relative anonymity if not for his nomination to the U.S. Supreme Court by President Richard M. Nixon in 1969. Supreme Court Justice Abe Fortas had resigned after a 1969 *Life* magazine exposé revealed that he had improperly accepted money while serving on the court. In his nomination of Haynsworth, Nixon had several goals in mind. He wanted to appoint a judge from the South to repay the southern politicians who had helped him to garner substantial votes during the 1968 presidential election. Haynsworth's appointment also was designed to help Nixon retain southern votes in the 1972 election. Finally, Nixon was looking for a conservative judge who was a "constructionist" and would, according to theory, interpret the Constitution rather than seek to amend it by judicial decisions. Haynsworth seemed to fit the bill. He was a fourth-generation southerner and appeared to be a strict constructionist.

On 18 August 1969 Nixon announced Haynsworth's nomination, even though Haynsworth had told Nixon that he was concerned about a prior conflict of interest charge against him. Nixon and his advisers also ignored the fact that Haynsworth's record would undoubtedly draw the opposition of labor and civil rights groups and politicians aligned with these causes. Almost immediately, an outraged Senator Birch Bayh, a Democrat from Indiana, vociferously opposed Haynsworth's appointment, focusing on the allegation that Haynsworth had adjudicated cases in which he had a financial interest.

Although there were several instances of an "appearance of impropriety," one stood out in particular. It involved a court case whose origins dated back to 1956 when, six days after workers voted to be represented by a union, the Deering-Milliken plant in Darlington, South Carolina, announced that it was closing. Roger Milliken, the plant's owner, made the decision to shut down the operation. The textile magnate refused to change his mind even after 400 workers capitulated and said they would withdraw their votes for the union. The court case charged the business with unfair labor practices, which were prohibited under national labor laws. The court of appeal's 1963 ruling cleared the textile company of all wrongdoing. However, the Textile Workers' Union shortly thereafter accused Haynsworth of a conflict of interest because he held stock in a company owned by Milliken.

The chief judge of the circuit court at the time investigated the case and cleared Haynsworth. The matter also had been referred to Attorney General Robert F. Kennedy for further investigation, but the attorney general's office determined that Haynsworth had not acted improperly. Nevertheless, the die was cast. Based on this case and vocal opposition by civil rights and labor groups, the Senate voted down Haynsworth's nomination fifty-five to forty-five, with seventeen Republicans voting for rejection, including some in the Republican leadership.

In a 16 January 2001 article in the *Wall Street Journal,* Robert H. Bork, a conservative U.S. Court of Appeals judge who in the 1980s also was rejected for nomination to the Supreme Court, said that Haynsworth once told him that the charges against him were so rancorous that, upon reading the papers, Haynsworth said to himself, "This man won't do!" The vote against Haynsworth's nomination to the Supreme Court marked Nixon's first major legislative defeat of the congressional session and also caused a huge rift in the Republican Party. In the long term, Haynsworth's rejection by the Senate, the first such rejection in thirty years, appears to have paved the way for more political infighting concerning appointments of Supreme Court justices.

Haynsworth continued to serve as the chief judge of the U.S. Court of Appeals for the Fourth Circuit until he retired to senior judge status in 1981. Interestingly, almost immediately after his failed nomination and return to the court of appeals, Haynsworth signed an order to enforce the integration of five southern school districts by 1970. Although his most publicly defined moment was an apparent failure, Haynsworth went on to serve in the judiciary with distinction and dignity. Eventually he was totally vindicated, and his reputation as an outstanding jurist and person of high moral character grew. In fact, the Clement F. Haynsworth, Jr., Award in Federal Practice and Procedure is awarded by the Emory Law School to a member of its graduating class for outstanding performance in federal courts courses. Haynsworth died of a heart attack in his Greenville, South Carolina, home and is buried in the city's Springwood Cemetery.

★

For an overall view of Haynsworth's career, see a letter to the editor by Leonard I. Garth, "Clement Haynsworth's Invaluable Contributions," *New York Times* (29 July 1986). For analyses of Haynsworth's nomination to the U.S. Supreme Court, see Joel B. Grossman and Stephen L. Wasby, "Haynsworth and Parker: History Does Live Again," *South Carolina Law Review* 23 (1971): 345–359, and John Anthony Maltese, "The Selling of Clement Haynsworth: Politics and the Confirmation of Supreme Court Justices," *Judicature* 72 (Apr. to May 1989): 338–347. The most exhaustive analysis is John P. Frank, *Clement Haynsworth, the Senate, and the Supreme Court* (1991). Obituaries are in the *New York Times* (23 Nov. 1989) and *Time* (4 Dec. 1989).

DAVID PETECHUK

HEFNER, Hugh Marston (*b.* 9 April 1926 in Chicago, Illinois), publisher of *Playboy* magazine, who supported individual liberties and created a new image for the successful urban bachelor.

Hefner was the older of two sons of Glenn Hefner, an accountant, and Grace Swanson Hefner. After serving in the U.S. Army from 1944 to 1946, he attended the University of Illinois and earned a B.A. in psychology in 1949, the same year he married Mildred Williams. They had two children.

In 1953 Hefner published the first issue of *Playboy,* featuring a nude photograph of Marilyn Monroe, then one of the most popular actresses in America. She was the first "Playmate of the Month," the woman whose nude picture was printed on a three-page full-color foldout in the middle of the issue. Sexual permissiveness in America had reached the stage where it was legal to publish photos including bare breasts (or, more precisely, bare white breasts, because *National Geographic* had been publishing such pictures of African, Asian, and Polynesian women for many years). Hefner took advantage of this social change, but the real key to the success of *Playboy* was that it treated sex as only one aspect of the good life, also talking about cars, clothing, and fine wines and offering writing good enough to make plausible the claim that readers purchased the magazine

Hugh Hefner. ARCHIVE PHOTOS, INC.

for that. By the 1960s the magazine was well known for its articles, its interviews with important artists and public figures, and its fiction, by such writers as Graham Greene, Vladimir Nabokov, and Kurt Vonnegut.

Hefner himself began to exemplify the image that his magazine was promoting. In 1959 he and his wife divorced, and he purchased a seventy-room mansion in Chicago, where the parties soon became legendary. (One famous feature of this *Playboy* mansion was a round revolving bed, eight feet in diameter, in the master bedroom.) In the same year he opened the first of his Playboy Clubs, where the customers could eat, drink, and be merry, served by waitresses called "Playboy Bunnies": attractive young women in outfits that resembled one-piece bathing suits, with fake-fur rabbit ears on their heads. The clubs eventually spread throughout the country and then to Great Britain and Japan. Hefner further publicized his approach with two television shows: *Playboy's Penthouse* (1959–1961) and *Playboy After Dark* (1969–1971).

Hefner's approach was not all hedonism, however. In 1962 his magazine began publishing "The *Playboy* Philosophy," a series of editorial columns in which Hefner advocated a libertarian approach to sex and lifestyle issues: repeal of laws against consensual sex acts, an end to police attempts to entrap gays, the abolition of censorship, and the legalization of abortion. The series ran to twenty-five installments and 150,000 words before concluding in 1966, and it branched out into the "*Playboy* Forum," featuring news reports and reader letters and discussions, which continued for many years after. The *Playboy* philosophy was by no means restricted to sexual freedom. Hefner strongly supported civil rights, and his clubs and television shows were significantly ahead of the curve in hiring African-American performers (such as Dick Gregory and Nancy Wilson). As part of its support for individual freedom, the magazine spoke out strongly against draconian drug laws. Hefner also created the Playboy Foundation to support civil liberties and civil rights.

When the Democratic National Convention came to Chicago in 1968, Hefner had no intention of taking part in the demonstrations it inspired. During the convention, however, Hefner went out for a walk one evening several blocks from where the convention was being held. Rampaging police officers came up to him, and one struck him a glancing blow with his baton. It was far more a matter of indignity than pain or damage, but this direct experience of illegitimate government power strengthened Hefner's libertarianism and helped him question such other excesses as the Vietnam War.

Hefner and *Playboy* had always faced opposition, not all of it from reactionaries. There were those who were offended that the magazine published pictures of bare breasts and those who thought it should also show pubic hair. (Such an act would have led to arrests in 1960; Hefner did not feel safe enough to depict that part of the human anatomy in *Playboy* until 1970.) There were those who assumed that the Playboy Clubs were brothels and those who objected to the club rules against bunnies' fraternizing with customers, a rule that was intended to ensure that the clubs did not become brothels. In the late 1960s the rising feminist movement joined the opposition, pointing out that the *Playboy* image could be seen as treating women as objects for pleasure and display like the commercial products it encouraged, rather than as people in their own right.

Playboy fell from the heights of fame and fortune it had enjoyed in the 1960s. On the one hand, *Penthouse* and *Hustler* stole much of the audience by being more sexually graphic; on the other, conservative groups attacked the magazine, sponsoring secondary boycotts of stores that sold it. The original Chicago Playboy Club closed in 1986, and the last of the clubs did so in 1988. Hefner himself, after moving to Los Angeles, suffered a mild stroke in 1985. At that point he turned the operation of the *Playboy* empire over to his daughter, Christie, whom he named chair and chief executive officer of Playboy Enterprises, Inc. He even settled down, marrying Kimberley Conrad, a former Playmate of the Year, in 1989; they had two sons. Hefner was not through with the playboy lifestyle, however. In 1998 he separated from his wife and soon was seen squiring beautiful young women around town. He expressed gratitude to the inventors of Viagra, a drug for men that enhances sexual performance.

Playboys, like hippies, now seem to many people like some ancient and excessive artifact of the long-gone 1960s. Still, Hefner represents progress from what went before. When *Playboy* began publishing, the social consensus was that everyone was supposed to refrain from premarital sex, any deviation from monogamous heterosexuality was criminal and perverted, and sex was so shameful that pictures of even seminaked women were consigned to a category separate from "proper" magazines and books. By challenging these taboos, particularly the last, Hefner helped change society, and the pendulum has not swung back to anything near its original position.

★

The several biographies of Hefner include Joe Goldberg, *Big Bunny* (1966); former *Playboy* editor Stephen Byer's *Hefner's Gonna Kill Me When He Reads This* (1972); Frank Brady, *Hefner* (1974); and Russell Miller, *Bunny: The Real Story of Playboy* (1987).

ARTHUR D. HLAVATY

HELLER, Joseph (*b.* 1 May 1923 in New York City; *d.* 12 December 1999 in East Hampton, New York), author whose 1961 novel, *Catch-22,* based on his own World War II experiences, reached the peak of its popularity during the Vietnam War, exposing the insanity of war and bureaucratic institutions.

Heller was born in the Coney Island section of Brooklyn. He was the son of Isaac Donald Heller, a delivery truck driver for a wholesale baker, and Lena Heller. Heller's father had two older children from a previous marriage. When Heller was five years old his father died of complications from a bleeding ulcer, and his stepbrother Lee served as a surrogate father. His mother struggled financially and took boarders into the family home. Mischievous as a youth, Heller was hardly a model student. He primarily enjoyed reading adventure stories such as the Rover Boys and Tom Swift, until about the age of ten, when a cousin introduced him to a children's version of Homer's *Iliad.* After reading Homer, Heller decided that he wanted to be a writer. He attended Public School 188 in Brooklyn and graduated from Abraham Lincoln High School in 1941.

Following graduation Heller got a job as a blacksmith's helper at the Norfolk Navy Yard in Virginia, but he continued to pursue writing in his spare time. In October 1942 Heller enlisted in the U.S. Army Air Force. He was sent to armorer's school and was content there until he heard a rumor that armorers were being turned into gunners, whose wartime life expectancy was extremely short. Accordingly, Heller volunteered for cadet school and became a wing bombardier in the Twelfth Air Force. He was commissioned a second lieutenant and stationed on the island of Corsica in the Mediterranean, from which he flew bombing missions over France and Italy. Heller experienced little anxiety until his thirty-seventh mission, when he witnessed several planes flown by his friends destroyed and the top turret gunner on his B-25 injured by flak. Henceforth, Heller related that he was terrified on all of his bombing runs. In June 1945 he was discharged at the rank of first lieutenant after having flown sixty missions.

Taking advantage of his GI Bill benefits, Heller studied briefly at the University of Southern California before enrolling at New York University, where he earned a Phi Beta Kappa key and graduated in 1948 with a B.A. in English. The following year he secured an M.A. in English from Columbia University. On 3 September 1945 Heller married Shirley Held; they had two children. During the 1949–1950 academic year Heller studied at Oxford University in England under a Fulbright Scholarship. After returning to the United States he accepted a position as an instructor of freshman English composition at Pennsylvania State University. For the remainder of the decade Heller left acade-

Joseph Heller. MR. JERRY BAUER

mia and worked in the magazine business, serving as an advertising writer for *Time* and *Look* and a promotion manager at *McCall's.*

Meanwhile, Heller continued to pursue his passion for writing, publishing short stories in *Esquire, Atlantic Monthly,* and *Cosmopolitan.* Becoming disenchanted with the short story format, Heller turned his attention to the preparation of a novel. After eight years of work Simon and Schuster published *Catch-22* in 1961.

Heller originally planned to use the number 18 in his title but was dissuaded after Leon Uris published *Mila 18.* Based loosely upon Heller's experiences during World War II, *Catch-22* tells the story of bombardier John Yossarin, who is stationed on the imaginary island of Pianosa off the Italian coast in the Tyrrhenian Sea. On a mission to Ferrera, Yossarin tries to save the life of a fatally wounded gunner, Snowden, bandaging the wrong wound as Snowden dies. In protest, Yossarin strips and sits naked in a tree, but he is still awarded a medal. Yossarin fears for his own life, recognizing that the only way to escape from further dangerous missions is to be declared crazy and therefore not be assigned to any additional missions. However, the very act of requesting to be excused from potentially deadly flights indicates a rational mind, and the individual making such a plea could not be insane. Therefore, to be excused one only has to ask, but the very request denotes sanity, and one has to keep flying. As Doc Daneeka says, "It's some catch; that catch-22."

Yossarin becomes convinced that his own officers, such as Colonel Cathcart and General Dreedle, are a greater danger to his life than the enemy Germans. To save himself Yossarin makes a deal with colonels Cathcart and Korn that he will lie for them to their superior officers. With this agreement Yossarin will be excused from flying, but his compliance will increase the number of missions for his comrades. Yossarin recognizes that he has made a pact with the devil when he is attacked and stabbed by Nately's whore, who holds Yossarin responsible when Nately is killed in action. He admires Nately's whore as someone willing to break the chain of compliance. Accordingly, Yossarin reneges on his deal with Colonels Cathcart and Korn, and, following Orr's example, he deserts, steals a lifeboat, and begins rowing for neutral Sweden.

Catch-22 was more than an antiwar novel; it questioned the conventional wisdom and assumptions of post–World War II America. Some scholars have used the "consensus" concept to describe the United States in the period from the late 1940s to the mid-1960s. According to consensus values, the twin pillars of American society were anticommunism and capitalistic economic expansion. The system was sound, and sustained economic growth would extend the benefits of the system to any disadvantaged groups. There was no reason to protest actively against society, and the only real threat to the promise of American life was encroaching Communism. But Catch-22 challenged these assumptions, poking fun at the U.S. government, bureaucracy, World War II, the cold war, McCarthyism, anticommunism, suburban conformity, and capitalism. In fact, as the supreme capitalist entrepreneur, Milo Minderbender creates an international syndicate for war profiteering with the slogan "What's good for M & M Enterprises is good for the country." The ultimate irony comes when Milo bombs his own camp for the Germans because they pay their bills promptly. Scores of Americans are killed, but the mission was profitable.

In 1961 Heller was ahead of his time. Initial sales of Catch-22 were slow, and some reviewers did not know what to make of the book. For example, R. C. Stern, writing in the New York Times Book Review, termed Catch-22 an "emotional hodgepodge," and Whitney Balliett of the New Yorker complained that Heller "wallows in his own laughter, and finally drowns in it." Nevertheless, most reviews were positive. Writing in The Nation, Nelson Algren argued, "Below its hilarity, so wild that it hurts, Catch-22 is the strongest repudiation of our civilization in fiction to come out of World War II." In a review for the New Re-

public, Robert Brustein concluded, "Through the agency of grotesque comedy, Heller has found a way to confront the humbug, hypocrisy, cruelty, and sheer stupidity of our mass society."

Although reviews were somewhat mixed, sales of the book grew through word of mouth, and it became an underground classic with the youth counterculture. With the expansion of the Vietnam War and the growing protest of that conflict, Heller's novel became increasingly relevant, and by the early 1970s over seven million copies had been sold. In an interview with the New York Times, Heller acknowledged the role that Vietnam played in the growing popularity of his novel, proclaiming, "Because this is the war I had in mind; a war fought without military provocation, a war in which the real enemy is no longer the other side but someone allegedly on your side. The ridiculous war I felt lurking in the future when I wrote the book." Heller's sentiments were echoed by Josh Greenfield in a 1968 piece for the New York Times Book Review in which the critic asserted, "There seems no denying that though Heller's macabre farce was written about a rarefied part of the raging war of the forties during the silent fifties, it has all but become the chapbook of the sixties." In a 1999 eulogy to Heller, the novelist E. L. Doctorow observed, "When Catch-22 came out, people were saying, 'Well, World War II wasn't like this.' But when we got tangled up in Vietnam, it became a sort of text for the consciousness of that time." In 1970 the director Mike Nichols completed a film adaptation of Catch-22 with Alan Arkin in the role of Yossarian. Heller announced that he was pleased with the film, although some critics insisted that Nichols downplayed the novel's satire of capitalism.

Before Catch-22 became a best-seller, Heller had to engage in script writing and teaching to sustain himself economically. Under the pen name of Max Orange, he contributed to the television comedy series McHale's Navy, and he worked on the screenplays for Sex and the Single Girl (1965), Casino Royale (1967), and Dirty Dingus Magee (1970). In the late 1960s Heller taught fiction and dramatic writing at Yale University, while in the early 1970s he served as the distinguished visiting writer on the English department faculty at the City College of the City University of New York.

Heller's opposition to the war in Vietnam was most apparent in his two-act play, We Bombed in New Haven, which he wrote at Yale in 1968. The absurdist play was an indictment of war and a denouncement of the military's adherence to following orders. Directed by Larry Arrick and starring Stacy Keach, it was first presented by the Yale School of Drama Repertory Theatre on 4 December 1967. The play also enjoyed a brief eighty-six performance run on Broadway in 1968, under the direction of John Hersch and with Jason Robards in the lead. Heller also adapted *Catch-22* into a play. It was first produced at the John Drew Theater in East Hampton, New York, in 1971.

Heller did not produce another novel until *Something Happened* (1974), which tells the story of disillusioned businessman James Slocum. In 1979 Heller's third novel, *Good as Gold,* was published. The protagonist in the novel is English professor Bruce Gold, who wants to become the first real Jewish Secretary of State, an obvious statement regarding Henry Kissinger's role as Secretary of State during the Vietnam War. *God Knows,* published in 1984, was an irreverent look at religion through the eyes of King David, who laments that God doesn't talk to him anymore.

In 1980, while dealing with the collapse of his marriage to Held, Heller was diagnosed with Guillain-Barre syndrome, a life-threatening neurological disease. He survived this brush with death after a partial and temporary paralysis, writing a book about his experience, *No Laughing Matter* (1986), which he coauthored with his friend Speed Vogel. During his rehabilitation Heller worked with nurse Valerie Humphries, whom he married in 1987.

Returning to writing in 1988, Heller published *Picture This,* using art as an entry vehicle through which to address his criticism of power, war, and mass society. In 1994 Heller surprised his readers with *Closing Time,* a sequel to *Catch-22.* An ambitious undertaking, *Closing Time* enjoyed decent sales and a favorable critical reaction. Even when critics complained that the author had never written another book as good as *Catch-22,* in reply Heller often quipped, "Who has?"

In 1999 Heller suffered a fatal heart attack at his home in East Hampton. While ignored following its publication, Heller's novel *Catch-22* found resonance among those in the 1960s questioning American society and the Vietnam War. The term "Catch-22" has entered the English language, and the book has sold approximately twelve million copies.

★

Heller provided autobiographical information in *No Laughing Matter* (1986) and *Now and Then: From Coney Island to Here* (1998), both cowritten with Speed Vogel. For literary criticism of Heller and his work, see: Frederick Kiley and Walter McDonald, eds., *A Catch-22 Casebook* (1973); Brenda M. Keegan, *Heller: A Reference Guide* (1978); Stephen W. Potts, *From Here to Absurdity: The Moral Battlefields of Joseph Heller* (1982); James Nagel, ed., *Critical Essays on Joseph Heller* (1984); Robert Merrill, *Joseph Heller* (1987); and Sanford Pinsker, *Understanding Joseph Heller* (1991). Obituaries are in the *New York Times, Washington Post, Los Angeles Times, Chicago Tribune,* and (London) *Times* (all 14 Dec. 1999).

RON BRILEY

HELLER, Walter Wolfgang (*b.* 27 August 1915 in Buffalo, New York; *d.* 15 June 1987 near Seattle, Washington), economist who, as adviser to President John F. Kennedy, served as the architect of the 1964 federal tax cut that stimulated economic growth and national prosperity.

Heller, the son of German immigrants Ernst Heller, a civil engineer, and Gertrude Warmburg, graduated from Oberlin College with a B.A. in 1935. He received his M.A. in 1938 and Ph.D. in 1941 from the University of Wisconsin–Madison, where he served as an instructor from 1941 to 1942. He married Emily Karen Johnson on 16 September 1938; they had three children.

During and after World War II, Heller served as a fiscal economist at the U.S. Department of the Treasury in Washington, D.C., from 1942 to 1946. In 1947 he was chief of finance for the U.S. military government in Germany, a role that gave him a particularly unique opportunity to study the building of national economies. In order to take that position, he obtained a leave of absence from the University of Minnesota, where he had gone to work as an associate professor in 1946. Heller remained at the university for the rest of his career, becoming a full professor in 1950 and regent's professor of economics in 1967. He held the latter position until 1986, a year before his death. He also chaired the economics department from 1957 to 1960. From 1955 to 1960 he served as an economic adviser to Minnesota governor Orville Freeman, and in 1960 he provided tax advice to King Hussein and the Royal Commission of Jordan.

In the course of his education and practical experience as an economist, Heller had embraced the theories of British economist John Maynard Keynes, who advocated interventionist government policies. With the December 1960 announcement by President-elect John F. Kennedy that Heller had been chosen to chair the Council of Economic Advisers in the new administration, the opportunity arose for putting his ideas into action on a national scale. Events would show that Heller, although remaining a staunch Keynesian throughout the 1960s, favored a policy of low taxation not commonly associated with Keynesian economics.

The first test of these principles occurred in 1961, when the new administration was only a few months old. During the electoral campaign, Kennedy had promised to raise military spending above $40 billion a year, that ceiling having been placed on the defense budget by his predecessor Dwight D. Eisenhower. Following a tempestuous Vienna summit with Soviet premier Nikita Khrushchev in June, Kennedy vowed to make good on his promise. By August tensions were rising, as the Soviets and East Germans launched the construction of the Berlin Wall, at which point Kennedy announced to his economic council that he intended to raise taxes by $3 billion.

Walter Heller. AP/WIDE WORLD PHOTOS

Judging such a move a disaster at a time when the unemployment rate was nearly 7 percent, Heller implored Kennedy not to go through with his plan. In an effort to sway the president's opinion, he brought Paul A. Samuelson, a prominent economist and council member, to the Kennedy home at Hyannis Port on Cape Cod in Massachusetts. Between them, they helped change Kennedy's mind.

Early in his administration, Kennedy sent his Council of Economic Advisers to Paris to study the secrets behind the rapid post–World War II growth of western European economies. From observing the economic strengths of Europe, Heller developed the idea of measuring economic performance against the point an economy would reach if it were functioning at full potential, rather than comparing present figures with those of the past. He therefore produced a study to determine the size of the federal budget under conditions of 4 percent unemployment, which he defined as virtual full employment. This "high employment budget," as Heller dubbed it, would contain a substantial budget surplus, indicating a "fiscal drag"—taxes were too high, thus producing a government budget out of phase with the economy. As a result, he called for tax cuts as a stimulus for investment and consumption, and he convinced an initially wary Kennedy that planning for a balanced budget was not a necessity under conditions of a weak economy.

With the adoption in 1962 of an investment tax credit to encourage private investment, Kennedy put in place another building block of Heller's economic plan for lowered taxes and a growing economy. The president also introduced plans for a 10 percent cut in personal income taxes for all brackets, but Congress blocked this plan, passing it only after Kennedy's assassination in 1963.

In the meantime, Heller, concerned that rising wages might spur inflation by raising the costs of goods and services, convinced Kennedy to enact wage and price guidelines in early 1962. The guidelines, a classic piece of Keynesian economic theory in action, made wage increases contingent on gains in productivity. Although they were voluntary, as demonstrated when the steel industry increased its prices in an open act of defiance, such guidelines emphasized the policy-making power of a centralized government. Wage and price guidelines, implemented with even greater vigor under the administration of Richard M. Nixon, would ultimately prove unpopular across a wide ideological spectrum. Conservatives opposed the expansion of government influence they embodied; labor unions, although they traditionally supported the Democratic Party, tended to bristle at measures that they perceived as taking a greater toll on wages than on other types of income.

Heller remained in office for almost exactly a year after Kennedy's death, during which time Congress passed the 1964 tax cuts. He resigned from his position in the administration of President Lyndon B. Johnson on 16 November 1964, not because of ideological differences, but rather for economic considerations of his own. With three children in college, he needed to raise his own earnings, which he did by providing economic consulting services to government agencies, businesses, and other institutions. At various times in his career, Heller served as adviser to the United Nations, several agencies of the Minnesota state government, the Brookings Institution, and the U.S. Census Bureau.

With the economy strengthened by the mid-1960s and with the costs of the Vietnam War mounting, Heller had advised Johnson to raise taxes as a means of paying for the war and hedging against inflation. His successor as council chair, Gardner Ackley, took up the same position, and on 1 July 1968 Johnson approved the tax increase. By then, however, inflation had begun to climb. At the same time, wage and price guidelines had begun to unravel, thanks in large part to the opposition of organized labor. Yet the Nixon administration took up the idea again, along with a concept Heller had advocated since his days with the Treasury Department in the 1940s, the federal sharing of revenue with the states.

A prolific writer, Heller authored or coauthored numerous books, including *New Dimensions of Political Economy* (1966), *Perspectives on Economic Growth* (1968), *Revenue-*

Sharing and the City (with Harvey S. Perloff, 1968), *Monetary vs. Fiscal Policy: A Dialogue* (with Milton Friedman, 1969), and *The Economy: Old Myths and New Realities* (1976). During the 1970s, in addition to his work as a teacher and consultant, he gained wide exposure as an economic pundit, both on television talk shows and in the *Wall Street Journal.*

In addition to his other work, Heller served as visiting professor at the University of Washington–Seattle and at Harvard University. He sat on the boards of numerous corporations, among them International Multifoods, Inc., and Northwestern National Life Insurance Company. Additionally, he presided over the American Economic Association in 1974 and chaired the National Bureau of Economic Research from 1971 to 1974. He was affiliated with a number of other professional organizations, including the American Finance Association and the National Tax Association.

Heller initially criticized the supply-side economics advocated by Friedman and others, a philosophy that gained political muscle with the inauguration of President Ronald W. Reagan in 1981. Yet Heller himself had advocated an early version of supply-side theory, which is based on a correlation between economic growth and low taxes. Recognizing his own affinity for views embodied in the new administration, he eventually became involved in economic decision making alongside Friedman and key Reagan adviser Martin Anderson.

A case of rheumatic fever in the 1950s had given Heller lasting health problems, and these contributed to heart problems. He died of a heart attack at his vacation home near Seattle.

Along with Samuelson, James Tobin, Arthur Okun, and Otto Eckstein, Heller is widely regarded as a seminal figure in the formation of the New Economics, which incorporated Keynesian theory into the realities of Kennedy's New Frontier and Johnson's Great Society. Given his predilection for interventionist government policies on the one hand, and for the use of tax reduction to stimulate the economy on the other, Heller is not easily placed into either the liberal or conservative economic camps. Indeed, he has had admirers on both sides. Among the outstanding economists who have cited Heller as an influence is Alan Greenspan, who called him "a major contributor if not the father of modern economic policymaking." Commenting on his abilities as an educator and public speaker, journalist George J. Church praised Heller's "genius for putting economic analysis into simple terms."

★

Heller's papers from his term as chair of the Council of Economic Advisers are at the John F. Kennedy Presidential Library in Boston. For more information on Heller's career in the Kennedy-Johnson years see J. Ronnie Davis, *The New Economics and the Old Economists* (1971). Joseph A. Pechman and Norman J. Simler, eds., *Economics in the Public Service: Papers in Honor of Walter W. Heller* (1989), is a tribute to Heller's thinking. A more critical approach can be found in Martin F. J. Prachowny, *The Kennedy-Johnson Tax Cut: A Revisionist History* (2000). Information on Heller's invitation to join the Reagan administration appears in Martin Anderson, *Revolution* (1988). An obituary is in the *New York Times* (17 June 1987).

JUDSON KNIGHT

HENDRIX, James Marshall ("Jimi"; "Jimmy"; "Maurice James") (*b.* 27 November 1942 in Seattle, Washington; *d.* 18 September 1970 in London, England), musician, singer, and songwriter, whose experimentation and innovations in guitar performance and design have been much admired and imitated by fellow musicians and have given him a faithful audience decades after his death.

Hendrix was one of two sons of James Allen ("Al") Ross Hendrix and Lucille (Jetter) Hendrix. Al, a gardener, met

Jimi Hendrix. ARCHIVE PHOTOS, INC.

Hendrix's mother by chance while visiting a friend and found in her a perfect dance partner. Their romance was shortened by her pregnancy and by his being drafted in 1942 during World War II. They were quickly married, and Hendrix's mother named their son Johnny Allen Hendrix at birth. Hendrix's father later changed his son's name to James Marshall Hendrix. His nickname for most of his life was "Jimmy," even during the period that he called himself "Maurice James."

Although racial discrimination hurt his family and kept his father from securing good jobs, Hendrix seemed relatively unaffected in his own dealings with people of other ethnic groups. On the other hand, his mother's waywardness and the resulting poverty that once left him, his father, and his brother eating horse meat hurt enough to be carried inside him all his life. Even at the age of three, he had become quiet, introspective, and lost in his own world. Young Hendrix was shuffled among family members and neighbors because of his father's intermittent employment and his mother's alcoholism. Hendrix's mother left the family and eventually died on 2 February 1958 of cirrhosis of the liver and a ruptured spleen.

Hendrix was musically inclined, but he had to learn to play with right-handed guitars even though he was left-handed. Throughout his career, he played right-handed guitars upside down, one of the factors that encouraged his innovations in guitar design and allowed him to make his electric guitars "wah-wah," whoop, and thunder like a storm. In 1961 Hendrix left Seattle's Garfield High School at the age of sixteen to enlist in the army. On 31 May 1961 he was sent to Fort Ord in California for basic training. On 8 November 1961 he went to Fort Campbell, Kentucky, where he joined the Screamin' Eagles 101st Airborne Division, a matter of considerable pride for him. Hendrix loved jumping out of airplanes, remarking that it was especially fun if he kept his eyes open. He and his fellow serviceman and bassist Billy Cox formed a group called King Kasuals that played rhythm and blues in local music houses.

Hendrix, who remained a private during his military service, received a medical discharge from the army because of a back injury in 1962, and he went to Nashville to work in the music industry. His ability to learn songs in an instant and to master even difficult styles quickly became well known in Nashville, and he was in demand as a sideman. Hendrix was slightly irritated by this, because he yearned to improvise while playing in a band; instead, he was expected to follow the routine set for him and never upstage the band's leader.

Audiences, especially other musicians, began seeking Hendrix out in 1963. Through word of mouth they learned which band he would be playing with on a given night. His technique was esteemed and emulated. By then Hen-

drix was experimenting with the designs of his guitars, seeking out innovative manufacturers, and making additional adjustments himself. His signature "wah-wah" sound developed out of these innovations, a sound that later musicians have imitated but never quite captured.

In 1964 Hendrix joined the Isley Brothers' band as a backing guitarist, calling himself "Maurice James." This led to a brief stint with Little Richard, who was attempting a comeback. Many writers place this period in 1963, but Little Richard and others in the band, as well as the Isley Brothers, all recall it as January 1965. When Little Richard fell five-and-a-half weeks behind on Hendrix's pay, Hendrix left the band, saying that a musician cannot live without money while on the road. In Greenwich Village, New York, he formed Jimmy James and the Blue Flames in late 1965, a group that performed in clubs. There, his performances included electronic feedback and electronic experimentation that overlaid a solid blues guitar rhythm.

Chas Chandler, the bass guitarist for the rock group the Animals, urged Hendrix to go with him to England, where Hendrix quickly found a following in small nightclubs. Other musicians, including the Beatle Paul McCartney, soon sought out the places where Hendrix was playing, to hear for themselves the revolutionary sounds he had added to songs. On 15 October 1965 the producer Ed Chalpin signed Hendrix to a three-year contract for PPX Enterprises.

From 1965 to 1966 Hendrix played with the Squires, and his reputation in England as a blues player grew. In 1966 Chalpin wanted to form a band around Hendrix, who was still calling himself Maurice James. Chalpin wanted a harder, edgier name, so he brought back the last name "Hendrix" and shortened the first name of "James" or "Jimmy" to "Jimi." The new band featured the esteemed bassist Noel Redding and the drummer Mitch Mitchell, and it was called the Jimi Hendrix Experience. The band debuted at the Olympia in Paris in 1966. They were marketed mostly to preteen and young teenage girls, and they released their first single, "Hey, Joe," in December 1966. The song went to number six on the charts in the United Kingdom. By that time Hendrix was abusing drugs, especially the hallucinogen LSD, marijuana, and alcohol. Hendrix often finished a day's performance by becoming stupefyingly drunk.

On 17 March 1967 the Jimi Hendrix Experience released the song "Purple Haze." Its downbeat became instantly recognizable, breaking cheers from audiences the moment they heard it. On his guitar, Hendrix used a "Fuzz Face" distortion pedal for creating warm mixtures of tones, and an Octavia, the invention of the Royal Navy electronics expert Roger Mayer, that enabled Hendrix to move notes by entire chords up and down the scale. His guitar seemed to be rhythm, bass, and singer all at once. In September 1967 his first album, *Are You Experienced?*, was released, and it established him in England as a leader of psychedelic music.

Hendrix returned briefly to the United States in June 1967, and he signed with staid, upscale Warner Bros., which released *Are You Experienced?*. On 18 June 1967 the Experience made its U.S. debut at the Monterey Pop Festival, and Hendrix capped off a mesmerizing performance by indulging in his oft-repeated ritual of burning his guitar onstage. American audiences had never seen anything like it. Worry from Warner Bros. that the quiet, shy, bushy-haired, chain-smoking, eccentric Hendrix was too big a risk turned to delight as Hendrix's album sold 2.2 million copies, outselling all other Warner Bros. stars, including Frank Sinatra. Hendrix also added the "wah-wah" pedal to his guitars, accentuating his unique sound.

In January 1968 the Jimi Hendrix Experience released its second album, *Axis: Bold as Love,* with such tracks as "Little Wing," "If 6 Was 9," and "EXP." Hendrix combined his visionary lyrics with multitrack rhythms and further experimentation, perhaps influenced by the Beatles but still leaving its mark on popular music for decades thereafter. Hendrix was unhappy with the album, because he believed his sound was not accurately reproduced on vinyl. At the same time that he was producing musical innovations, he was also experimenting with various concoctions of drugs, mostly involving LSD, and the deleterious effect on his creativity was becoming apparent to those close to him.

The third album of the Jimi Hendrix Experience, the double set *Electric Ladyland,* was released in September 1968. Although all three of the band's albums went gold, this album went to number one in the charts, the only number-one album that Hendrix had in America. In it he makes blues music into a complex, richly textured sound, classic in its depth, stretching the genre by mixing in jazz riffs and hard chords. Even so, the hit single from the album, "All along the Watchtower," the group's first and only Top Twenty single, was direct and forthright. Other memorable cuts from the album included "Voodoo Child" and "Crosstown Traffic." In 1968 Hendrix was named artist of the year by *Billboard* and *Rolling Stone.* Hendrix wanted to expand beyond his reputation as a psychedelic musician, and he disbanded the Jimi Hendrix Experience in 1969. On 29 June 1969 the band played their final show at the Denver Pop Festival, the same month that their *Smash Hits* album was released. In August 1969 Hendrix appeared at the Woodstock Festival, giving the performance of a lifetime. His jazzy, metallic version of the "Star Spangled Banner" was the harbinger of a new era of experimentation in traditional music within the idioms of modern popular music, and it electrified young audiences. More than thirty years later, that single performance speaks

volumes for where music had been and where it was going to go—and Hendrix was the stationmaster.

At least since 1968, when he went violently insane in a German hotel, destroying a room, Hendrix had been subject to terrible periods of madness in which his eyes went glassy and he could be a danger to himself and others. To avert these periods, which often occurred at night, he took sleeping pills. In 1970, under pressure from black militants to form an all-black band, he brought his old friend the bassist Billy Cox and the drummer Billy Miles together to record *The Band of Gypsys,* a "live" album recording from New York's Fillmore East. Still unhappy with how recordings conveyed his music, he created his own studio, Electric Lady Studios, which he designed to meet the needs of his electronics. Hendrix logged more than 600 hours of studio tapes performing with a variety of jazz and rock musicians.

On 6 September 1970 Hendrix, Cox, and Mitchell performed at the Isle of Fehmarn in West Germany; it was Hendrix's final performance. While visiting London and staying in the Cumberland Hotel, Hendrix's girlfriend, Monica Dannemann, discovered him immobile in his bed. He seemed to have overdosed on sleeping pills. He was taken to a hospital but was pronounced dead on arrival due to asphyxiation caused by a drug overdose. His repeated abuse of drugs was common knowledge, and many people assumed that he either had committed suicide in a drugged despair or had overdosed accidentally on a cocktail of drugs. The generally accepted assumption is that his prescription for sleeping pills was too weak to help him sleep and that he took too many in order to help himself rest. He was buried in Greenwood Memorial Park in Renton, Washington. Hendrix's studio archives produced numerous posthumous albums, such as *Crash Landing* (1975), *Midnight Lightning* (1975), *Nine to the Universe* (1980), *Kiss the Sky* (1985), *Live at Winterland* (1987), and *Radio One* (1988).

At the age of twenty-seven Hendrix was only beginning to mature as a musician, singer, and composer. His successive recordings showed him mastering a variety of styles, with his mastery reaching its apex in *Electric Ladyland,* promising a truly mature style that Hendrix died too early to achieve. For his fans in the 1960s he became a symbol of what creativity could achieve, and his performances were memorable. In 1992 Hendrix was inducted into the Rock and Roll Hall of Fame in Cleveland, Ohio, and in 1993 he received a Grammy Lifetime Achievement Award. On 23 June 2000 the Experience Music Project, a gallery of Hendrix memorabilia funded by Microsoft's cofounder Paul Allen, opened in Seattle near the Space Needle. Hendrix influenced nearly every metallic band, either directly or indirectly, after his time, and he expanded the horizons of blues music with his innovative style. Often lost in the glamorous accounts of his life are his honest humanity, his graceful handling of racial issues, and his love of making music for the sake of finding a beautiful sound.

★

Biographies of Hendrix include Chris Welch, *Hendrix: A Biography* (1972), and Curtis Knight, *Jimi: An Intimate Biography* (1974), which are both anecdotal accounts. See also Dave Henderson, *'Scuse Me While I Kiss the Sky: The Life of Jimi Hendrix* (1980); Jerry Hopkins, *Hit and Run: The Jimi Hendrix Story* (1983); Victor Sampson, *Hendrix* (1984); Harry Shapiro and Caesar Glebbeck, *Jimi Hendrix: Electric Gypsy* (1991), which is thorough and detailed about Hendrix's years in Europe and America; and James A. Hendrix and Jas Obrecht, *My Son Jimi* (1999), an account of Hendrix's life by his father. Biographical information also is found in Gary Carey, *Lenny, Janis, and Jimi* (1975); Charles Shaar Murray, *Crosstown Traffic: Jimi Hendrix and the Post-War Rock 'n' Roll Revolution* (1989); Mitch Mitchell and John Platt, *Jimi Hendrix: Inside the Experience* (1990); and Jerry Hopkins, *The Jimi Hendrix Experience* (1995). An obituary is in the *New York Times* (19 Sept. 1970).

KIRK H. BEETZ

HENTOFF, Nathan Irving ("Nat") (*b.* 10 June 1925 in Boston, Massachusetts), social critic, civil libertarian, and journalist who wrote about civil rights, education, and First Amendment rights for the *Village Voice* and *New Yorker* during the 1960s, and who authored fiction and nonfiction books for adults and children about jazz and social issues.

Nat Hentoff. BILL SPILKA/GETTY IMAGES

Hentoff was the oldest son of Simon Hentoff, a haberdasher, and Lena Katzenburg. His parents were Russian-Jewish immigrants, and his father operated Hentoff's Men's Shop until the Great Depression forced him out of business. Hentoff lived in a Jewish ghetto in the Roxbury section of Boston, where his experience of anti-Semitism taught him to empathize with other excluded groups. For six years he attended Boston Latin School, a prestigious institution that served as a melting pot for divergent ethnic groups. Hentoff read voraciously, and became interested in how language worked after reading *Alice In Wonderland*. He also began his long love affair with jazz, often hiding copies of *Down Beat* inside his geography book.

Hentoff was classified as 4F, or physically unfit, for military service during World War II. He attended Northeastern and wrote for the *Northeastern News,* the student newspaper. He became the editor of the paper as a junior and served in that position until the college threatened to remove him if he published a story concerning administrative corruption. Hentoff, along with the entire staff, quit. After earning his B.A. in English in 1946, he worked as a disc jockey for WMEX in Boston, where he interviewed several of his jazz heroes, including Charlie Parker and Duke

Ellington. Hentoff also wrote a review column for *Downbeat,* and moved to New York City in 1953 to edit the magazine. He lost the position in 1957, however, and believed he was fired because he advocated the employment of an African-American writer. The magazine, he maintained, made its income writing primarily about African-American musicians; therefore, it was only fair to hire an African American.

Hentoff had a difficult time securing other writing jobs. "The years working for *Down Beat* and the books on jazz I'd written," he noted in *Speaking Freely* (1997), "had pigeonholed me as a specialist in jazz." In 1958 he began writing for free for the *Village Voice* on the condition that he could discuss social issues rather than jazz.

In 1960 Hentoff began writing a column a year for the *New Yorker,* and in 1961 published his first book, *The Jazz Life.* Although he remained interested in jazz, he began writing a series of books about social justice during the 1960s. "By this point," Hentoff recalled in *Speaking Freely,* "I had spent several years writing about some of the leading adherents of nonviolence in the United States—especially A. J. Muste, who was an advisor to Martin Luther King." In 1963 Macmillan published his biography of Muste, *Peace*

Agitator, and in 1964 Viking published *The New Equality,* a book analyzing civil rights issues. Hentoff believed that white liberal guilt, disconnected from action, would never resolve social inequality, and advocated cooperation between the poor of all colors.

Hentoff soon discovered another outlet for writing about social issues when he was approached by Ursula Nordstrom of Harper and Row and invited to write a children's novel. At first he refused, believing that writing for young adults would limit his style and substance. When Nordstrom convinced him otherwise, he agreed and wrote *Jazz Country.* Relying on his background in the jazz world, Hentoff's novel tells the story of Tom, an eighteen-year-old white trumpeter who dreams of success in the jazz world, and of the older African-American players he befriends. In 1967 Hentoff followed *Jazz Country* with *I'm Really Dragged but Nothing Gets Me Down*, a book about a high school student's response to being drafted during the Vietnam War.

Hentoff also became involved, directly as an activist and indirectly as a writer, in the civil rights and the antiwar movements during the 1960s. He befriended Malcolm X and attended the 1963 March on Washington. In June 1965 he was a member of an anti–Vietnam War delegation that met with U.S. Ambassador Adlai Stevenson at the United Nations and asked him to resign his post in protest of the war. (Stevenson remained in the position.) Hentoff also wrote frequently about the war in the *Village Voice.* "It was senseless for Americans to kill Vietnamese, children included, and to die themselves in this obscure civil war," he recalled in *Speaking Freely.* These activities, along with a 1968 *Playboy* article entitled "The War on Dissent," which offered an unfavorable assessment of Federal Bureau of Investigation (FBI) director J. Edgar Hoover, led to the FBI maintaining a file on Hentoff.

Hentoff wrote two novels for adults, both dealing with issues of race, in the mid-1960s. In *Call the Keeper* (1966), a white liberal detective searches for the murderer of a black policeman, while *Onwards!* (1967) relates the story of an intellectual in mid-life crisis, caught between the old and new left. Hentoff also continued to write nonfiction books, including *A Doctor Among the Addicts* (1967), about a successful methadone clinic in Harlem, and *A Political Life* (1969), a biography of New York City mayor John V. Lindsay.

Hentoff continued to be a feisty social critic in the decades after the 1960s. Although generally considered a political liberal, his opinions, such as his pro-life position on abortion, occasionally placed him at odds with his traditional allies. Hentoff, however, never backed away from the conflict his opinions have generated. "I've become accustomed to it over the years, and also I enjoy argument," he noted to *Contemporary Authors.* "I enjoy showing that ideas are for debating." In 1995 he received the National Press Foundation Award for distinguished contributions to journalism, and in 2000 received a Lifetime Achievement Award from the National Society of Newspaper Editors.

★

Hentoff's autobiography has been published in two volumes, *Boston Boy* (1986) and *Speaking Freely: A Memoir* (1997). For a review of *Boston Boy,* see Kenneth C. Davis, *Publishers Weekly* (11 Apr. 1986): 29; and for a review of *Speaking Freely: A Memoir,* see the *New York Times Book Review* (19 Oct. 1997).

RONNIE D. LANKFORD, JR.

HEPBURN, Audrey   (*b.* 4 May 1929 in Brussels, Belgium; *d.* 20 January 1993 in Tolochenaz, Switzerland), award-winning screen and stage star whose graceful beauty and Givenchy-inspired elegance created a distinctive 1960s style that made her one of the most admired and imitated women of her generation.

Hepburn, born Audrey Kathleen Ruston and baptized Edda Van Heemstra Hepburn-Ruston, was the only child of Joseph Victor Anthony Ruston, an Anglo-Irish banker and importer, and Ella van Heemstra, a baroness whose family had long-standing ties to the Dutch throne. She was born in the third year of their brief and volatile marriage. Van Heemstra's two sons from a previous marriage became Hepburn's playmates. Her parents became active fascists in Belgium and England, where the family spent its time. When her parents separated in 1935, Hepburn was sent to a boarding school in Kent, where she suffered from migraine headaches and a feeling of abandonment.

When World War II broke out in Europe, Hepburn was evacuated into Arnhem, in what was then neutral Holland, where she lived with her mother and half-brothers. One day after her eleventh birthday, the German army occupied Arnhem and the rest of Holland. One brother was sent to a forced labor camp, and the other went into the German army. During the war Hepburn took dancing lessons at the Arnhem Conservatory of Music and gave performances in people's basements to raise money for the Dutch resistance. She also carried messages in her shoes to resistance leaders. Hepburn's home was reduced to rubble on 17 September 1944, when the Nazis beat back an Allied offensive, forcing evacuation of the entire town. That winter Hepburn and her mother survived on tulip bulbs and grass pies. Hepburn suffered from jaundice and edema and became anemic and asthmatic. One day after her sixteenth birthday, the Germans surrendered, and food and emergency supplies sent by the United Nations reached the Rustons and other refugees.

After the war Hepburn studied dance with Sonia Gaskell in Amsterdam. Hepburn's first film work was as a KLM flight attendant in a thirty-nine-minute travelogue called

Audrey Hepburn. ARCHIVE PHOTOS, INC.

Nederlands in 7 Lessen (1948). A bigger break was a scholarship to Marie Rambert's ballet school in London.

"Audrey Hepburn," as she was now billed, proved to be "a good worker and wonderful learner," but "too tall" at five feet, seven inches, and years behind in her training. Hepburn was devastated. She took modeling jobs and appeared in the chorus line of several West End productions, including *High Button Shoes* (1949), for eight pounds a week. Her almond eyes and long-legged good looks impressed impresario Cecil Landeau, who cast her in the musical-comedy revue *Sauce Tartare* in 1949 and *Sauce Piquante* in the spring of 1950.

Hepburn had bit and supporting roles in several British film comedies in 1951, including *One Wild Oat, Young Wives Tale, Laughter in Paradise,* and *The Lavender Hill Mob*. She was also given the second lead in *The Secret People* and, during its filming, was briefly engaged to the trucking magnate James Hanson. Hepburn traveled to the French Riviera in the summer of 1951 to film the forgettable *Monte Carlo Baby*. There she met the French novelist Colette, who gave her the lead role of the French courtesan in *Gigi*. The play opened in New York City's Fulton Theater on 24 November 1951, and Hepburn's reviews were even better than those of the play. One week later Hepburn's name went up on the theater marquee.

Hepburn played a princess opposite Gregory Peck in William Wyler's *Roman Holiday* in 1953, beguiling costars, critics, and audiences alike with her cinematic innocence and sophistication. Her slender elegance and graceful charm celebrated "the spirit of youth" and seemed an antidote to the pessimism of the postwar world. The film was a huge hit, and Hepburn received an Academy Award for best actress for her first major dramatic role.

Days after winning her Oscar, Hepburn received a Tony Award for her performance as a water sprite opposite Mel Ferrer's knight in the play *Ondine*. The couple married in Burgenstock, Switzerland, on 25 September 1954. By that time Hepburn had completed shooting *Sabrina,* opposite Humphrey Bogart and William Holden, a film that would win her another Oscar nomination and confirm her superstar status. The usually irascible director Billy Wilder thought Hepburn had "a special quality that every star needs." She made the Cinderella story of a chauffeur's daughter "look so unforced, so simple, so easy." The metamorphosis was greatly aided by the Paris couturier Hubert de Givenchy's bare-shouldered ball gown of white organdy that delicately feminized Hepburn's spare figure. The look served as an antidote to the lush sexuality of the "blonde bombshell" look then being popularized by Marilyn Monroe.

Wilder and Hepburn would collaborate again with *Love in the Afternoon* (1957). By then Hepburn had appeared in *War and Peace* (1956), opposite Ferrer, and in Stanley Donen's *Funny Face* (1957), with Fred Astaire. The latter was warmly received and allowed Hepburn to show her skill as a dancer. Richard Avedon's photography and Givenchy's gorgeous outfits made a lasting impression. The scene of Hepburn in a strapless red evening gown unfurling a red shawl behind her as she runs down a white marble staircase best captured the image of Hepburn as a fantasy nymph.

Hepburn entered the 1960s as the screen's most popular actress. *Green Mansions* (1959), directed by Ferrer, had done little to advance the career of either, but *The Nun's Story* (1959), directed by Fred Zinnemann on location in the Belgian Congo, became a personal favorite and made more money than any previous Warner Brothers release. The film reflected a new realism in Hepburn's movie roles. Critics found her performance of Sister Luke so subtly rich and suggestive that it required a second and third viewing to capture completely. The performance merited her third Oscar nomination in six films and won best actress honors from New York film critics and the British Film Academy.

The 1960s started with Hepburn's happiest role. After three miscarriages, her son Sean was born on 17 September 1960 in Lucerne, Switzerland. For nine months she staunchly turned aside all offers, including the part of Maria in *West Side Story*. John Huston's critically acclaimed *The Unforgiven* (1959) was released during this interval, with Hepburn playing the part of the foundling daughter of a frontier family. Few films better capture big city chic than *Breakfast at Tiffany's* (1961), based on Truman Capote's sardonic summary of life among New York's glitterati. Hepburn's character, Holly Golightly, is in on the self-deception. Her swinging parties where sex mixes easily with sophistication are really a pretense, as she chases after South American millionaires and makes most of her money as a call girl. Later in the film, viewers learn she is really an acutely vulnerable backwoods girl named Lulamae Barnes with a much older husband. George Peppard plays a struggling writer suffering from a long dry spell who is fascinated and repelled by his intriguing neighbor. The outcome is a thoroughly modern romantic comedy of characters who struggle over uncertainty and personal identity. The performance is one of the most memorable of Hepburn's career and the decade and won her a fourth Academy Award nomination.

The film's award-winning score by Henry Mancini had Hepburn singing Johnny Mercer's lyrics to "Moon River." Its evocation of lost innocence and dreamlike hope made it the most recorded song of the decade. Long lasting too was the look Givenchy gave Hepburn for the film. Holly's oversized dark glasses and black evening gown, with long gloves topped by a rhinestone tiara in her upswept hair, became a 1960s standard of sophistication. Director Blake Edwards quickly discovered "the camera loved her." Hepburn said the excitement had to be generated "from the inside out." That was why "understanding" a character was her way of "re-creating" her. In Holly's case this meant "looking back to my days in London as I was starting out, hoping someone would notice me."

It was now impossible for Hepburn to go unnoticed. She was a reluctant interviewee, making her all the more attractive to fans starved for celebrity. The reclusive star was stalked by tabloid photographers and often retreated to her Burgenstock chalet to tend her gardens and raise her son. *The Children's Hour* (1961) reunited her with William Wyler, and *Paris When It Sizzles* (1962) returned her to the arms of William Holden. Her following film, *Charade* (1963), directed by Stanley Donen and costarring Cary Grant, became a huge hit. This homage to Alfred Hitchcock, set in Paris to a Henry Mancini score, has the two stars chased by a trio of sinister crooks in a polished piece of implausibility that delighted audiences and entertained the critics. Hepburn's salary was now $750,000 and a percentage of the picture's profits.

The role of Eliza Doolittle in *My Fair Lady* (1964) was one of the few parts Hepburn actually campaigned for. She loved the story of a cockney flower girl who is transformed into a gentlewoman by Professor Henry Higgins because of the character's "attractive vulnerability" and "beautiful inner strength." With $17 million staked on the film's success, Jack L. Warner snubbed Julie Andrews, who originated the part on Broadway, and sought a bankable leading lady to play opposite Rex Harrison. Hepburn was signed for a salary of $1.1 million.

The long-awaited film, directed by George Cukor, was a critical and box-office triumph, even though Hepburn's notices were uncharacteristically mixed. She had spent five weeks in rehearsal, planning to sing the songs Andrews had made so famous—"Wouldn't It Be Loverly," "Just You Wait," "The Rain in Spain," and "I Could Have Danced All Night," but at the last minute studio officials insisted the songs be dubbed by vocal understudy Marni Nixon. Hepburn, whose voice was pleasant if unspectacular, proceeded professionally. Trade papers made much of the film's eight Academy Awards and Hepburn's failure to even be nominated in the year that Andrews won an Oscar in her screen debut in *Mary Poppins*.

The Ferrers settled far away from Hollywood in an old country farmhouse in Tolochenaz, Switzerland, above Lake Geneva, which Hepburn christened "La Paisible" (the Peaceful). She worked only when she wanted to—with Wyler again in *How to Steal a Million* (1966), costarring Peter O'Toole, and *Two for the Road* (1967), directed by Donen and costarring Albert Finney. Hepburn and Finney portrayed a couple on the eve of divorce, paralleling the breakup of Hepburn's own marriage. Ferrer produced the highly successful *Wait Until Dark* (1967), in which Hepburn plays a blind woman terrorized by narcotic smugglers. The star's fifth Oscar nomination only deepened the impression that the proud Ferrer lived in his wife's considerable shadow. Hepburn wanted to work less, but Ferrer was filled with ambition for himself and his wife. Their separation was amicable and their divorce final on 5 December 1968. One month later, on 18 January 1969, Hepburn abruptly married Andrea Dotti, an outgoing Italian psychiatrist she had first met while filming *Roman Holiday*. Their son Luca was born on 8 February 1970.

Hepburn "withdrew from pictures to take care of my boys." For nine years she stayed off the screen, turning down offers to star in *Forty Carats, Nicholas and Alexandra, The Turning Point,* and other projects. She later admitted, "I would have liked to have made a few more movies, but I hate to think what I would have felt if I hadn't known my children." Hepburn came out of retirement to make *Robin and Marian* (1976) for her family. Hepburn's return to the screen created a good deal more excitement than the film. Even that, however, diminished with successive films—*Bloodline* (1979) and *They All Laughed* (1981)—pale imitations of Hepburn's previous work.

Hepburn had long been separated from Dotti, and in 1982 their divorce was finalized. She hosted a cable series "Gardens of the World," and appeared in only two features—*Love Among Thieves,* a 1987 television movie for the American Broadcasting Company, and Steven Spielberg's *Always* (1989), in which she had two brief scenes as a guardian angel. Hepburn, often accompanied by Dutch companion Robert Wolders, began traveling the world on behalf of the United Nations Children's Fund (UNICEF), speaking out for needy children and drawing attention to the plight of Third World families wracked by war, famine, and disease. As a goodwill ambassador she made hundreds of speeches, raising millions of relief dollars. Her last trip to drought-stricken Somalia in September 1992 publicized international famine relief efforts. Her impassioned plea for "collective responsibility" earned her the Presidential Medal of Freedom in 1992 from President George H. W. Bush, and the Jean Hersholt Humanitarian Award, posthumously presented in 1993 by the Academy of Motion Picture Arts and Sciences.

Hepburn died at the age of sixty-three from colon cancer. She is buried in Tolochenaz. The American Film Institute listed Hepburn behind only Katharine Hepburn and Bette Davis among significant actresses during the first century of filmmaking. At the height of her career she had made only sixteen films in thirteen years, but their impact was so stunning that she set a standard for substance and style that women have imitated ever since.

★

A summary of the literature on Hepburn is in David Hofstede, *Audrey Hepburn: A Bio-Bibliography* (1994). Major biographies include Charles Higham, *Audrey: The Life of Audrey Hepburn* (1984); Ian Woodward, *Audrey Hepburn* (1984); Robyn Karney, *Audrey Hepburn: A Star Danced* (1993); Diana Maychick, *Audrey Hepburn: An Intimate Portrait* (1993); Warren G. Harris, *Audrey Hepburn: A Biography* (1994); Alexander Walker, *Audrey: Her Real Story* (1995); and Barry Paris, *Audrey Hepburn* (1996). Hepburn's screen career is carefully chronicled in Caroline Latham, *Audrey Hepburn* (1984); and Jerry Vermilye, *The Complete Films of Audrey Hepburn* (1995). Hepburn's impact on the fashion of the 1960s is in Pamela Clarke Keogh, *Audrey Style: The Subtle Art of Elegance* (1999). A pictured presentation of her life is in Carol Krenz, *Audrey: A Life in Pictures* (1997). Also see Gene Ringgold, "Audrey Hepburn," *Films in Review* (Dec. 1971): 585–601. Obituaries are in the *New York Times, Chicago Tribune, Detroit Free-Press,* and *Los Angeles Times* (all 21 Jan. 1993); *People, Time,* and *Maclean's,* (all 1 Feb. 1993); *Entertainment Weekly* (5 Feb. 1993); and *Film Comment* (Mar.–Apr. 1993). An appreciation by Sheridan Morley appears in the (London) *Sunday Times* (24 Jan. 1993). "Audrey Hepburn Remembered," produced for the Public Broadcasting System in 1993, is a compilation of her infrequent broadcast and film interviews. Hepburn recounted her life and career in a Library of Congress series, "Reflections on the Silver Screen" (1990).

BRUCE J. EVENSEN

HERLIHY, James Leo (*b.* 27 February 1927 in Detroit, Michigan; *d.* 21 October 1993 in Los Angeles, California), author and playwright whose stories, novels, and plays, including *Blue Denim* (1958) and *Midnight Cowboy* (1965), were populated with derelicts, grotesques, and unfortunates.

Herlihy was one of five children of William Francis Herlihy, a city engineer, and Grace Elizabeth Oberer, a homemaker. Herlihy became interested in writing at the age of seven. While attending John J. Pershing High School in Detroit, he began writing short stories. After graduating in 1945, he enlisted in the U.S. Navy, receiving his overseas orders just two days before the end of World War II. From 1947 to 1948 he studied sculpture, painting, music, and literature at Black Mountain College, a small, experimental institution in North Carolina whose faculty included the dancer Merce Cunningham, the artist William De Kooning, and other innovative figures in the arts. From 1948 to 1950 he attended the Pasadena Playhouse College of Theatre Arts in Pasadena, California, where he wrote and acted.

As an actor, Herlihy appeared in approximately fifty roles in West Coast theaters between 1948 and 1953. He made a striking actor—six feet tall, 162 pounds with brown hair, blue eyes, and regular features. He was an avid swimmer. His friends, including writers Anaïs Nin and William Goyen, called him Jamie.

Herlihy's early plays include *Streetlight Sonata* (1950), *Moon in Capricorn* (1953), *Crazy October* (1958), *A Breeze from China* (1958), and with William Noble, *Blue Denim* (1958). As its title indicates, the latter concerns youths and rebellion—blue jeans and sweatshirts being the school uniform of the day. The play concerns a dysfunctional family in Detroit—an ex-military father who drinks and does not attempt to understand his son; the son, who prefers to spend his time in the basement; a rebellious daughter; and an ineffectual mother. The son Arthur falls in love with a girl, Janet, who convinces him he is someone special. The crux of the play is when Janet gets pregnant and has an abortion. The play featured the film actor Chester Morris as the father, and was made into a film in 1959.

Between 1953 and 1958 Herlihy wrote television scripts. He published his first collection of short stories, *The Sleep of Baby Filbertson and Other Stories,* in 1959. But it was as a novelist that he most distinguished himself. His first novel, *All Fall Down* (1960), was about another dysfunctional family, this time located in Cleveland. The novel bore an epigraph from the American novelist and short-story writer Sherwood Anderson, and Herlihy's characters resembled Anderson's grotesques as well as reflecting Anderson's feeling for place. *All Fall Down* was stylistically distinctive, shifting from narration and dialog to sample pages

423

taken from the younger brother's notebook, a compendium of everything he hears, most of what he thinks, and copies of his mother's correspondence. In 1962 the novel was made into a film, starring Warren Beatty as the older brother and Eva Marie Saint as the mother. In 1963 Herlihy returned to acting, appearing in the role of Jerry in the Boston and Paris productions of Edward Albee's *Zoo Story*.

Herlihy's second novel, published in 1965, firmly established his place as a novelist. *Midnight Cowboy* was a departure from his concentration on the American Midwest and the Andersonian style. This time Herlihy explored the neon nightmare world of the big city and the lives of two street people who become friends, Joe Buck from Houston and a physically handicapped swindler, Ratso Rizzo from the Bronx. One source of the novel's interest is the way it moves between Joe Buck's thoughts and expectations and the actual situation. Eventually Joe Buck comes to an insight almost too momentous to acknowledge: "He was a nothing person, a person of no time and no place and no worth to anyone at all." This self-awareness parallels the son Arthur's feelings in *Blue Denim*. But just as Arthur is redeemed by Janet's belief in him, Joe Buck finds redemption and self-esteem in his attempt to save Ratso's health and life.

Midnight Cowboy was made into a film in 1969, featuring Jon Voight as Joe and Dustin Hoffman as Ratso, with a stellar supporting role played by Sylvia Miles. Directed by John Schlesinger, the movie won the Academy Award for best picture of the year—the first X-rated film to do so. Herlihy had reservations about the film. Voight and Hoffman in no way physically resembled his novel's characters, and Herlihy objected to a popcorn explosion sequence in a movie house that was supposed to parallel Joe Buck's orgasm in the balcony. The scene was not in the novel; indeed, the orgasm took place on a city rooftop. But both book and film portray the poverty and desperation of street people and deal with male prostitution in a way not possible before the 1960s.

Herlihy had published his second collection of short fiction in 1967, *A Story That Ends with a Scream and Eight Others*. In 1970 *Stop, You're Killing Me,* a production of three plays—*Laughs, Etc., Terrible Jim Fitch,* and *Bad Bad Jo-Jo*—had a run in New York. His last novel, *The Season of the Witch*, was published in 1971. Herlihy claimed it was written after a seven-year immersion in the so-called "youth culture." It involved draft evasion, homosexuality, the mores of the love generation, and American Diaspora. According to one critic, it was "the first reliable rendering of the New Consciousness," which, "with all its in-group fads, nonce words, and distractions, is still an essentially human and attractive one."

Herlihy taught playwriting at City College of the City

University of New York from 1967 to 1968, and was a distinguished visiting professor at the University of Arkansas (1983). He also taught at other schools, including Colorado College and the University of Southern California. In 1981 he appeared in the film *Four Friends,* directed by Arthur Penn.

In 1980 Herlihy's partner Bill Lord died, an early victim of acquired immunodeficiency syndrome (AIDS). In the following years Herlihy gave hospice to many close friends who had the same disease. In the early 1990s he found he himself had AIDS. He died of a deliberate overdose of sleeping pills at his home in the Silverlake neighborhood of Los Angeles, just one year before the drug treatment known as the AIDS cocktail became available. Herlihy's greatest contribution to the 1960s was his depiction of the alienation of young Americans.

★

The James Leo Herlihy Papers (1959–1986) are in the Special Collections Department, University of Delaware Library. The collection contains manuscripts, correspondence, notes, and theater memorabilia. Obituaries are in the *New York Times* (22 Oct. 1993) and the *San Francisco Chronicle* (23 Oct. 1993).

ROBERT PHILLIPS

HERSH, Seymour M. (*b.* 8 April 1937 in Chicago, Illinois), Pulitzer Prize–winning investigative reporter whose stories in the late 1960s uncovered the My Lai massacre by U.S. troops in South Vietnam.

Hersh, the son of Isadore Hersh and Dorothy Margolis, grew up in Chicago. After graduating from high school he enrolled at the University of Chicago, from which he received his bachelor's degree in history in 1958. Planning a career in law, Hersh enrolled in the university's law school but soon found his interest in the subject waning. Casting about for something else to do, he heard from a friend that the City News Bureau was hiring anyone with a college degree. Although he had neither experience nor any particular interest in journalism, he applied for a job and was soon working as a copyboy for the news agency that had been the model for Ben Hecht's celebrated play, *The Front Page*.

Before long Hersh had graduated from copyboy to police reporter. In a 1998 interview with Saul Landau of *The Progressive,* he recalled, "Chicago's a hell of a town to be a reporter in. For a while I worked the midnight shift, midnight to eight, at the main police headquarters." He said that he learned in ways that he did not understand until much later. From the City News Bureau, Hersh in 1960 went into the U.S. Army and after basic training found himself working on the base newspaper in Fort Riley, Kansas, and writing speeches for a general. After his release from military service in the early 1960s he took a reporting job with a suburban Chicago newspaper. He was next hired by United Press International (UPI) to cover the news from Pierre, South Dakota, where he wrote stories about taxes and the Ogalala Sioux. He returned to Chicago to work for Associated Press (AP), which in 1964 moved him into its Washington, D.C., bureau. It was in Washington that Hersh became obsessed with the growing war in Vietnam. He was eventually named AP's Pentagon correspondent, giving him access to a wide range of military personnel and broadening his understanding of the war. Hersh married Elizabeth Sarah Klein, a physician, on 31 May 1964. They had three children.

His increasingly critical articles about the war created a strain between Hersh and his editors at AP. In 1967 he left the news agency to write a book, *Chemical and Biological Warfare: America's Hidden Arsenal* (1968), in which he charged that the United States was spending $235 million annually on such weapons. In 1968 he went to work as press secretary and speechwriter for the antiwar presidential candidate Eugene McCarthy. The experience left Hersh with a distaste for the world of politics, and he returned to journalism as a freelance reporter.

Hersh first came to national prominence in 1969 when he broke the story of the massacre of Vietnamese villagers by U.S. troops at My Lai, South Vietnam. He learned of the incident from Geoffrey Cowan, a lawyer working with military deserters, who later became director of the Voice of America early in the Clinton administration. Cowan tipped off Hersh that an army officer was about to be court-martialed for the massacre of civilians in Vietnam.

Armed with this information, Hersh sought out the U.S. soldiers alleged to have participated in the massacre of about 500 unarmed civilians, including Lieutenant William L. Calley, Jr., the officer facing charges, who shared with Hersh details of the incident. Hersh's articles were rejected by the magazines to which he offered them. However, a friend who ran a small newspaper syndicate offered to distribute the exposé. The articles, which appeared in the *Boston Globe,* the *London Times,* the *San Francisco Chronicle,* and the *Washington Post,* revealed that in March 1968 a division of U.S. troops called Charley Company, led by Calley, had killed every man, woman, and child in the village of Son My (My Lai Four on military maps). Hersh's articles on the My Lai massacre won him the 1970 Pulitzer Prize for international reporting.

Hersh further explored the My Lai massacre in two books, *My Lai 4: A Report on the Massacre and Its Aftermath* (1970), and *Cover-Up: The Army's Secret Investigation of the Massacre of My Lai 4* (1972). Of the latter, he told Landau: "It's the most interesting book I ever wrote because it's about how the Army as an institution couldn't deal with what happened, this horrific murder of 500 people." Despite its controversial and somewhat sensational content, *Cover-Up* was a commercial failure. "I've never had a book sell less in my life," Hersh told Landau. "I never made a cent on it, and as far as I know not many people have read it. Nobody wanted to hear about Vietnam in 1972. We were losing the war."

Hersh worked at the Washington bureau of the *New York Times* from 1972 until 1975, when he transferred to New York. After three years he returned to the Washington bureau. In 1992 he became a correspondent for *The New Yorker* magazine.

Hersh's fascination with the 1960s and the early 1970s is clearly reflected in his more controversial books. Published in 1983, *The Price of Power: Kissinger in the Nixon White House* explores the relationship of Henry Kissinger and President Richard M. Nixon during the latter's administration. "Nixon had a consuming need for flattery and Kissinger a consuming need to provide it," Hersh wrote. The strange relationship between the two, Hersh suggested, may have brought the world dangerously close to nuclear war. Even more controversial was Hersh's take on the Kennedy years, *The Dark Side of Camelot* (1997), which covered such topics as the late president's liaisons with mistresses and prostitutes and his administration's ties to organized crime.

One of America's premier investigative reporters, Hersh's impressive legacy is headed by his breaking the story of the My Lai massacre and his insightful examinations of the Kennedy and Nixon administrations. Although he has covered current events from the 1960s into the new millennium, Hersh shows a special fascination for the 1960s and the early 1970s.

A longtime reporter for the *New York Times,* Hersh became the newspaper's "ace investigative reporter," according to Richard Lee, a contributor to the *Washington Post.* At the *Times,* Hersh became "virtually a world unto himself . . . , breaking important stories about the CIA's domestic intelligence activities, the secret bombing of North Vietnam, and Kissinger's wiretapping of his closest aides at the State Department."

★

For insight into Hersh's career as an investigative reporter, see his *My Lai 4: A Report on the Massacre and Its Aftermath* (1970); *Cover-Up: The Army's Secret Investigation of the Massacre of My Lai 4* (1972); *The Price of Power: Kissinger in the Nixon White House* (1983); *The Samson Option: Israel's Nuclear Arsenal and American Foreign Policy* (1991); and *The Dark Side of Camelot* (1997). Further biographical information about Hersh is in W. J. Burke and Will D. Howe, *American Authors and Books* (1972); *Contemporary Authors, New Revision Series* (1985); William H. Taft, *Encyclopedia of Twentieth-Century Journalists* (1986); and

Robert B. Downs and Jane B. Downs, *Journalists of the United States* (1991).

Don Amerman

HERSHEY, Alfred Day   (*b.* 4 December 1908 in Owosso, Michigan; *d.* 22 May 1997 in Syosset, New York), Nobel Prize–winning bacteriologist, biochemist, and molecular geneticist whose work with bacteriophages helped prove that DNA is the source of heredity, thus paving the way to an understanding of viral infections.

Hershey was the son of Robert Day Hershey, an auto manufacturer, and Alma Wilbur, a homemaker. He attended public schools in Owosso and Lansing, Michigan, and Michigan State College, from which he received a B.S. degree in bacteriology in 1930 and a Ph.D. in chemistry in 1934. He then took a research assistant position at the Washington University School of Medicine in St. Louis, where he became an associate professor in 1942 and taught until 1950. On 15 Nov. 1945 Hershey married Harriet Davidson, a former research assistant who later became editor of a biological review; they had one son.

Hershey focused his research on bacteriophages (com-

Alfred D. Hershey. Archive Photos, Inc.

monly known as phages), small particles made of a protein shell and a DNA molecule that are found in the nucleus of cells. Phages are viruses that can infect bacteria, turning the latter into virus manufacturers and subsequently killing them. While working in St. Louis, Hershey met the physicist Max Delbrück and the biologist and physician Salvador E. Luria, and the three researchers formed the basis of what would later be known as the "phage group," scientists who shared their phage research results to advance science.

In 1950 Hershey moved to the department of genetics of the Carnegie Institution of Washington (now the Carnegie Institute) in Cold Spring Harbor, New York. It was there that he carried out one of modern biology's most famous experiments, in 1952. Together with his assistant Martha Chase, Hershey tagged the DNA of phage T2 with radioactive phosphorous (DNA contains a lot of phosphorous, proteins have very little), and the protein shell of another batch of the same phage was labeled with radioactive sulfur (DNA contains no sulfur). Using a kitchen blender to separate the infected bacteria from phage particles clinging to the outside walls of the bacteria, Hershey and Chase found the radioactive DNA inside the bacteria, while the radioactive protein shell stayed outside. This provided the answer to a question that scientists had been asking for several decades: Which is the hereditary material, protein or DNA? Most researchers had assumed that proteins, owing to their greater complexity, were the hereditary molecules. The results of the blender experiment surprised even Hershey. His proof heralded the explosion of genetics that has changed life as we know it today. According to James Watson, the blender experiment was the final push that he and his research partner Francis Crick needed to determine the structure of DNA.

Following the blender experiment, Hershey continued to work with phages and supplied other molecular biologists with valuable tools and insights. To characterize phage DNA further, he needed to be able to extract and purify it from a phage. In the 1950s and early 1960s there were no techniques to achieve this end, so Hershey and his colleagues set out to develop them. As Hershey would say in his Nobel lecture on 12 December 1969, "Without knowing it, we were entering one of those happy periods during which each technical advance yields new information." By 1961 Hershey had discovered a way to extract both intact and fractured DNA. His method, with further refinements, continues to be used by researchers today.

Once he found the way to purify DNA and obtained controlled fractures of the molecule, Hershey went on to prove that T2 DNA was a single linear molecule. Because this conclusion seemed at odds with observations of another phage, T4, efforts to reconcile the seeming contradictions led to the discovery that phage DNA can be circular. Hershey's final 1965 proof of circular viral DNA was, in James

Watson's words, "a bombshell result, because circular molecules had 2 years before been hypothesized as an intermediate in the integration of I [phage λ I] DNA molecules into bacterial chromosomes." Hershey helped show how viruses infect bacteria, and his finding has been instrumental in the later development of the recombinant DNA technique. Recombinant DNA has saved countless lives around the world by enabling the production of needed compounds, such as insulin, cheaply and in large quantities. Phage λ I has been widely used in recombinant DNA techniques.

In 1962 Hershey was appointed director of the genetics research unit at Cold Springs Harbor, where he remained until his retirement in 1973. He continued to characterize phage DNA along with colleagues in his lab. Experiments by Gisela Mosig in 1964 helped create a map of genetic markers of phage T4. Mosig credited Hershey's pioneering work when she said: "Everything we do now is really based on that knowledge [that DNA is the hereditary molecule]." In 1963 and 1968, respectively, his colleagues Fred Frankel and Rudy Werner investigated the intracellular structure of certain T phages and thus helped researchers gain insight into how phage recombination works.

Along with giving researchers insights into the structure and characteristics of phage DNA, Hershey developed laboratory methods for handling and measuring DNA. These methods were adopted by molecular biology and genetics researchers all over the world. In 1969 Hershey, Delbrück, and Luria were awarded the Nobel Prize in physiology or medicine for their contributions to molecular biology, an honor that many thought they should have received earlier. Hershey died of heart failure.

Although Hershey's work in the 1960s may not have been as earth shattering as his blender experiment in 1952, the swift pace of developments in the field of genetics, beginning with Watson and Crick's discovery of the double helix and continuing through recombinant DNA and beyond, started with this single experiment. Although Hershey is typically remembered for that one achievement, his continuing work and collaboration with others on the mechanisms of phage infection, both before and after 1952, were instrumental in laying the basis for vaccines for such diseases as polio and mumps and expanded our understanding of viral infections. Hershey was one of the founders of molecular biology, and during the 1960s he continued to advance this new discipline. His influence on the burgeoning sciences of genetics and molecular biology went beyond the lab. In addition to his own papers, he wrote review articles that educated others.

★

Biographies of Hershey include Franklin Stahl, *We Can Sleep Later: Alfred D. Hershey and the Origins of Molecular Biology*

(2000). Articles on Hershey's life include John Cairns, "Alfred Hershey (1908–1997): One of the Founding Fathers of Molecular Biology," *Nature* 388 (1997), and A. Campbell and F. W. Stahl, "Alfred D. Hershey," *Annual Review of Genetics* 32 (1998): 1–6. Obituaries are in the *New York Times* (24 May 1997), *Times* (London) (2 June 1997), and *Independent* (London) (7 June 1997).

ADI R. FERRARA

HESBURGH, Theodore Martin (*b.* 25 May 1917 in Syracuse, New York), civil rights advocate and president of the University of Notre Dame who, during the 1960s, confronted student unrest, influenced federal legislation, and increased the national prominence of his institution.

Hesburgh was the second of five children born to Theodore Bernard Hesburgh, a salesman for the Pittsburgh Plate Glass Company, and Anne Murphy. Raised in a devout Roman Catholic household, at the age of seventeen he entered the seminary of the Congregation of Holy Cross at the University of Notre Dame du Lac (Notre Dame) in South Bend, Indiana. In 1939 he finished his bachelor of philosophy (Ph.B.) degree at Gregorian University in Rome, and in 1941 he began graduate studies at Holy Cross College in Washington, D.C. Ordained as a priest on 24

Theodore Hesburgh. THE LIBRARY OF CONGRESS

June 1943, Hesburgh hoped to serve as a military chaplain; however, in obedience to his superior, he instead pursued a doctorate in theology at Catholic University of America in Washington, from which he graduated in 1945 with an S.T.D. (doctor of sacred theology) degree. Returning to Notre Dame, Hesburgh initially taught theology and served as chaplain to the university's war veterans. In 1948 he became head of the theology department, and in 1949 he was appointed executive vice president of the university. In 1952 the Holy Cross religious community elected him as Notre Dame's president.

Throughout his thirty-five-year tenure, Hesburgh sought to expand the university's faculty, facilities, and academic programs while maintaining its Roman Catholic character. Beginning in 1960 with a Ford Foundation grant of $6 million, the fundraising efforts of Hesburgh and executive vice president Edward P. Joyce increased the university's endowment from $9 million to $35 million. The operating budget grew from $9.7 million to $176.6 million and research funding from $735,000 to $15 million. Enrollment also rose from approximately 5,000 to 9,700 students, and campus facilities increased by forty buildings, including a fourteen-story library constructed in 1963.

In addition to his role as president of Notre Dame, Hesburgh influenced federal policies on civil rights beginning in 1957, when President Dwight D. Eisenhower appointed him to the newly created U.S. Commission on Civil Rights. Throughout the late 1950s and 1960s the civil rights commission collected evidence of abrogated voting rights and discrimination in employment, housing, justice, education, and public facilities; reported this evidence to the U.S. Congress and the public; and recommended civil rights legislation based on the commission's findings. Reports of the Civil Rights Commission resulted in the Omnibus Civil Rights Act of 1964 and subsequent bills in 1965 and 1968. Hesburgh in particular viewed the Civil Rights Commission as "a kind of national conscience" on racial concerns and encouraged individuals to respond to racial inequalities with "moral indignation" and love for their neighbors. In 1964 President Lyndon Johnson awarded Hesburgh the Medal of Freedom in recognition of his contributions to civil rights.

Responding to the Second Vatican Council's call for greater lay involvement in church institutions, as well as to concerns of academic freedom and the increasing complexity of university management, Hesburgh in 1967 facilitated a shift in the university's governing power from the Congregation of Holy Cross to two boards, one of lay trustees and another of lay and clerical fellows. Hesburgh also presided over the establishment of coeducation at Notre Dame in 1972. As president of the International Federation of Catholic Universities, in 1963 he developed an ecumenical institute of Christian theologians in Jerusalem and, from 1963 to 1973, worked with church authorities to modernize Catholic higher education's identity and mission.

However, Hesburgh's administration is best known for its firm handling of student antiwar demonstrations and discouragement of federal intervention in campus discipline. During the late 1960s Notre Dame student protestors threatened to burn the Reserve Officer Training Corps (ROTC) facility and obstructed on-campus recruiters from the Central Intelligence Agency (CIA) and Dow Chemical Company, a manufacturer of napalm.

Arguing that legal rights and boundaries were essential to free academic inquiry, on 17 February 1969 Hesburgh, in an open letter to the university community, announced that if student protesters who impeded university operations or violated others' rights did not "cease and desist" their activity within fifteen minutes, the offending students would be punished by suspension from the university and confiscation of their student identification cards. If, after five additional minutes, suspended students did not end their disruption, they would be expelled and, if necessary, forcibly removed from campus. Throughout this process, students who refused to surrender their identification cards to university authorities would be reported as trespassers to the local police.

While Hesburgh's "cease and desist" edict provoked some strong student criticism and gave Hesburgh a nationwide reputation as a Vietnam War proponent—an inaccurate image he tried in vain to dispel—in general Notre Dame students and faculty accepted his policy. In February 1969 Hesburgh also persuaded a conference of state governors to vote against requesting federal legislation to control demonstrations on academic campuses, an action for which the American Association of University Professors honored him in 1970.

In March 1969 Hesburgh and a group of concerned students also developed an academic program to study nonviolent political action. Perhaps the first university president to take a decisive position on student demonstrations during the 1960s, Hesburgh worked to protect university operations from inside and outside interference while encouraging students to express their idealism peacefully.

Also in 1969, President Richard M. Nixon promoted Hesburgh to chair of the Civil Rights Commission. However, Hesburgh's subsequent criticism of White House policies on civil rights and racial integration prompted Nixon to request Hesburgh's resignation from the commission in November 1972. Hesburgh later founded the Center for Civil Rights at Notre Dame.

In June 1987 Hesburgh resigned the presidency of Notre Dame and retired to offices in the university's main library. In the course of his ongoing career in public service and education he has served in over fifty private and federal organizations, including the National Science Board; the

International Atomic Energy Agency; the Overseas Development Council; the Select Committee on Immigration and Refugee Policy; the Rockefeller Foundation's board of trustees; the Presidential Clemency Board, which recommended draft evaders and deserters for amnesty; the Knight Commission on Intercollegiate Athletics; the Pontifical Council for Culture; and Notre Dame's Kellogg Institute for International Studies and Kroc Institute for International Peace Studies. Hesburgh also has received several prestigious awards, including the Franklin D. Roosevelt Freedoms Medal, the Distinguished Peace Leader Award, the Elizabeth Seton Award, the National Lifetime Achievement Award, and the Congressional Gold Medal. As of 2002 he held more honorary degrees (135) than any other American.

★

Works on Hesburgh include an autobiography written with John Reedy, *God, Country, Notre Dame: The Autobiography of Theodore M. Hesburgh* (1990), and John C. Lungren, Jr., *Hesburgh of Notre Dame: Priest, Educator, Public Servant* (1987). Notre Dame's Office of Public Relations provides information on Hesburgh's career from 1990 until 2002. For a general history of the University of Notre Dame, see Robert E. Burns, *Being Catholic, Being American: The Notre Dame Story* (1999).

RAE SIKULA BIELAKOWSKI

HESTON, Charlton (*b.* 4 October 1923 in Evanston, Illinois), Academy Award–winning screen and stage actor and narrator who starred as unforgettable historical figures or fictional heroes in numerous epic films and who, during the 1960s, was president of the Screen Actors Guild, a civil rights supporter, and an appointee on national arts programs.

Heston, the second of three children, was born John Charlton Carter to Russell Whitford Carter, a sawmill operator, and Lilla Charlton, a homemaker. Shortly after his birth, his family relocated from Chicago to Saint Helen, Michigan; about ten years later, his parents separated. After her divorce, Heston's mother married Chet Heston. Heston graduated from New Trier High School in Chicago in 1941 and then attended Northwestern University in Evanston from 1941 to 1943. (He did not graduate.) He served in the U.S. Army Air Force from 1943 to 1946. While stationed at Greensboro, North Carolina, he married Lydia Marie Clarke, a classmate from Northwestern, on 17 March 1944. They had two children. In 1946 they moved east, where in 1948 Heston debuted on Broadway as Praculeius in Shakespeare's *Antony and Cleopatra* and on television in *Studio One* plays. His first Hollywood film, *Dark City* (1950), initiated a decade of appearances in nearly twenty films, including two Cecil B. De Mille blockbusters, *The Greatest Show on Earth* (1952) and *The Ten Commandments* (1956).

Charlton Heston, 1965. THE KOBAL COLLECTION

During the 1960s, Heston's handsome physique and classical profile assisted in elevating him as an epic American actor. He performed in *The Tumbler*, directed by Laurence Olivier, on Broadway in March 1960. Heston received the Academy Award in 1960 for best actor for the title role in William Wyler's *Ben-Hur* (1959). The Academy Awards ceremony had been preceded by a strike called by the president of the Screen Actors Guild (SAG), Ronald Reagan; Reagan soon asked Heston to join SAG's negotiating committee. Heston next began researching his role as Spain's great hero in *El Cid* (1961) and soon left for location filming abroad. In late May 1961 Heston joined a three-person civil rights demonstration outside an Oklahoma City, Oklahoma, restaurant. The group was picketing for desegregation of restaurants. As Heston said in *The Actor's Life,* he had come to a time and place in his life when he believed that it was time to act rather than simply deploring injustices at cocktail parties.

Overseas he viewed the "horrifying" contrasts between East and West Berlin when the U.S. Department of State Cultural Presentation Program sent him to the Berlin Film Festival in June and July that year. Near the end of July, Heston began shooting the World War II comedy *The Pigeon That Took Rome* (1962) in Italy, where he received the David di Donatello Award in July 1961. On 13 November 1961 he was elected a vice president of SAG and testified on its behalf before Congress the next month. Heston made hand imprints in the cement outside Grauman's Chinese Theatre in Hollywood on 18 January 1962 and throughout the year worked on two 1962 film releases: *Diamond Head* and *55 Days at Peking*. In January 1963 and again that July, Heston was busy as SAG's negotiating committee chairman. His acting projects that year included the roles of John the Baptist in George Stevens's *Greatest Story Ever Told* (1965) and Thomas Jefferson in *The Patriots* for *Hallmark Hall of Fame* and scenes from *Mister Roberts* (9 December) upon the twentieth anniversary of the New York City Center Theatre.

Heston played roles in two monumental events of 1963. The civil rights leader the Reverend Martin Luther King, Jr., whom Heston considered "a twentieth-century Moses for his people," had upon occasion conferred with Heston about the need for integrating certain Hollywood technical unions. Heston helped form the Arts Group, along with fellow actors Marlon Brando, Burt Lancaster, Paul Newman, James Garner, Harry Belafonte, and Sidney Poitier, to support King's civil rights march on Washington, D.C., on 28 August 1963. On Sunday 24 November, the eve of the funeral for President John F. Kennedy, Heston joined a handful of performers selected by the American Broadcasting Company to pay tribute to the assassinated president. Heston chose to recite parts of psalms from the Bible and poems by Robert Frost. Heston worked during 1964 on several films released the following year: a western, *Major Dundee*; Carol Reed's *The Agony and the Ecstasy* (as Michelangelo); and *The War Lord* (as a medieval warrior).

Politically independent, Heston wrote that up until the 1964 presidential election, he had cast 80 percent of his state and national votes for Democrats and had campaigned for Kennedy. But the 1964 slogan ("In your heart, you know he's right") for the Republican presidential candidate, Arizona senator Barry Goldwater, convinced Heston that the Democratic Party had changed so much that it could no longer nominate a John F. Kennedy. He became a Republican. In March 1965 Heston participated in a Department of State cultural visit to Nigeria and in July achieved acclaim as Sir Thomas More in a Chicago production of his favorite non-Shakespeare play, Robert Bolt's *A Man for All Seasons*. On the screen he played Charles Gordon in *Khartoum* (1966). Near the end of the year Heston was elected to his first of six terms as SAG's president (1965–1971). He remained proud of his negotiation work, frequent congressional testimony, public "ambassador" role in the U.S. and abroad, and his efforts in securing superior pension, welfare, and medical plans for SAG members.

Heston made his first of two United Service Organizations tours to Vietnam in January 1966 (the second was in September 1967). His special interaction with U.S. troops, particularly the wounded, was his promise to tele-

phone their loved ones upon his return to the United States. During a limited 1966 U.S. tour, he repeated the role of Thomas More. His film project through early 1967 was playing a wartime conductor in *Counterpoint* (1968). On 12 December 1966 President Lyndon B. Johnson appointed Heston to a six-year term on the National Council on the Arts. Heston's 1967 film projects were a western, *Will Penny* (1967), and the box-office hit *Planet of the Apes* (1967). He performed opposite Judith Anderson in Maxwell Anderson's *Elizabeth and Essex* on the Columbia Broadcasting System's *Hallmark Hall of Fame* in October 1967. During 1968 he worked on two films released the following year, reprising his role as the futuristic astronaut George Taylor in *Beneath the Planet of the Apes* and playing an aging quarterback in *Number One*.

In tribute to the assassinated Martin Luther King, Jr., Heston narrated *King—A Filmed Record . . . Montgomery to Memphis* (1970). In 1969 Heston worked on two films released in 1970: Shakespeare's *Julius Caesar* (as Marc Antony) and *The Hawaiians,* based on James A. Michener's novel *Hawaii*. In April he attended the weeklong tribute to his screen work at the British Film Institute. Certain California Democrats probed Heston about running for the U.S. Senate (as would Republicans in the early 1970s and in 1984), but he rejected the idea. Heston's resonant speaking voice provided the commentary for many shorts and commercial or federal promotional and documentary films during the 1960s, including *The American Film* (1967), directed by George Stevens, Jr., for the American Film Institute, and *Rowan and Martin at the Movies* (1969) for U.S. Treasury Bonds. Heston, an avid tennis player, narrated *Rod Laver's Wimbledon* in 1969.

Heston received the Jean Hersholt Humanitarian Award in 1978. In 1981 President Ronald W. Reagan appointed Heston cochairman of the Presidential Task Force on the Arts and Humanities. He was chairman of the American Film Institute from 1972 to 1982 and took on the presidency of the National Rifle Association in 1998. On 9 August 2002, Heston announced publicly that his doctors had confirmed that he had the early symptoms of Alzheimer's disease, adding that he felt that it was important not to exclude his fans from this stage in his life. "I've lived my whole life on the stage and screen before you," he said. "For an actor, there is no greater loss than the loss of his audience."

The 1960s highlighted a sustained peak for Heston, particularly as a star of film epics, and the resulting renown made him a readily identifiable and crowd-attracting American celebrity at home and abroad. His acting versatility enabled him to embody both the American spirit of Robert Frost's best poems and the internationalized hero of biblical proportions.

★

The Charlton Heston Room at the Theater Arts Library of the University of California at Los Angeles contains memorabilia and other items donated since 1983 by Heston. Heston's autobiographical works are *The Actor's Life: Journals, 1956–1976* (1978), with Hollis Alpert, ed.; *In the Arena: An Autobiography* (1995); and *To Be a Man: Letters to My Grandson* (1997). *Beijing Diary* (1990) refers to his directing for the Chinese Cultural Ministry, through the U.S. Department of State, an all-Chinese production in Beijing of Herman Wouk's *Caine Mutiny*. *Courage to Be Free* (2000) relates to his responsibilities for the National Rifle Association. See also Jeff Rovin, *The Films of Charlton Heston* (1977); Bruce Crowther, *Charlton Heston: The Epic Presence* (1986); Michael Munn, *Charlton Heston* (1986); and Heston, with Jean-Pierre Isbouts, *Charlton Heston's Hollywood: 50 Years of American Film* (1998). Articles in the *New York Times* relating to Heston's activities during the 1960s include "Charlton Heston Heads U.S. Delegation to West Berlin International Film Festival" (23 June 1961); "Unionist Decries TV Music Imports" (3 Dec. 1961); Murray Schumach, "Heston Refunds Salary to Studio" (9 May 1964); and Robert E. Dallos, "City and State Rights Agencies Will Act on Bias" (27 Aug. 1968).

MADELINE SAPIENZA

HEWITT, Don S. (*b.* 14 December 1922 in New York City), news executive involved in some of the most memorable television programs of the 1960s, including the Kennedy-Nixon presidential debates, who implemented enduring innovations to evening news broadcasts and created *60 Minutes,* the venerable investigative news program.

Hewitt is one of two sons of Ely S. Hewitt, who worked in advertising sales, and Frieda (Pike) Hewitt. He was raised in New Rochelle, New York, where he enjoyed going to the movies. One of his favorites was *The Front Page* (1931), a film about the newspaper business. Hewitt graduated from New Rochelle High School in 1940 and then briefly attended New York University on a track scholarship but withdrew from the school during his sophomore year, before he could "flunk out." He chose instead to work as a copyboy at the *New York Herald Tribune.* A year after the United States entered World War II, Hewitt enrolled at the U.S. Merchant Marine Academy in Kings Point, New York. He was stationed in London, where he was a correspondent for *Stars and Stripes,* the U.S. military newspaper; he was discharged from the service at the end of the war.

In 1948 Hewitt was hired by the news division of the Columbia Broadcasting System (CBS), where he first worked as associate director of the network's evening news broadcast. Throughout the 1950s he produced and directed *Douglas Edwards with the News,* and he remained with the

program when it became *CBS Evening News with Walter Cronkite* in the early 1960s. During these early days of television, Hewitt was instrumental in pushing such innovations as the addition of film clips and graphics into newscasts. He also implemented the use of cue cards to force anchors to look directly into the camera. Hewitt directed the 1960 presidential campaign debates between John F. Kennedy and Richard Nixon. This first ever televised debate between presidential candidates took place on 26 September 1960 and is often cited as a watershed event in that election, in which Kennedy narrowly won the presidency. Despite Hewitt's advice, Nixon chose to wear minimal makeup for the broadcast. The vice president had been ill days earlier and appeared pale and sweaty compared with the vital-looking, young Senator Kennedy. According to Hewitt, "Nixon never recovered from that disastrous first round and the lousy makeup job that did him in."

Evening newscasts were extended from fifteen minutes to half an hour in 1963. CBS and its news anchor, Walter Cronkite, were competing head to head with the National Broadcasting Company (NBC) and its anchors, David Brinkley and Chet Huntley. Politics behind the scenes at CBS ultimately resulted in Hewitt's firing in 1965. "[G]etting canned . . . turned out to be the best thing that ever happened to me. But at that moment, I was filled with despair," remembers Hewitt. "It was devastating, the end of my short, happy career." He went on to say, "I figured my life was over. I'd had this great run, and now what?" Hewitt was reassigned to work on news documentaries as a director and producer. In those days, documentary television suffered from shifting time slots and little commercial sponsorship. In 1966 and 1967 Hewitt started mulling over how he could make a personal, long-form, journalistic news show entertaining.

In developing *60 Minutes,* Hewitt sought to make events of the day both provocative and entertaining for viewers, while creating an inexpensive show for the network to produce. The first pilot did little to impress the network executives. Instead of selecting a single anchor, two presenters, Harry Reasoner and Mike Wallace, were chosen. At 10 P.M., Tuesday, 24 September 1968, *60 Minutes* premiered. The program included interviews with the presidential candidates Nixon and Hubert Humphrey filmed on the nights of their respective parties' nominations; a segment about the turbulent events of the 1968 Democratic National Convention in Chicago; a commentary from the humorist Art Buchwald; and excerpts from a film about Kaiser Aluminum.

Initially, *60 Minutes* was never seen at the same time for four consecutive weeks. It was shown every other Tuesday night from 10 P.M. to 11 P.M. Other programs continually preempted it. The network even bumped the news show to position the hour-long drama *Cannon* to compete against *Marcus Welby, M.D.,* which was airing on the American

Don Hewitt *(right)*, with Senator John F. Kennedy *(center)* and J. Leonard Reinsch, September 1960. ©
BETTMANN/CORBIS

Broadcasting Company (ABC). Slowly, *60 Minutes* developed a reputation for its blend of investigative muckraking with lighter news features. Topics that reporters tackled in its early days included European student unrest and drug addiction. It also featured in-depth interviews with notable people of the day from the varied fields of politics, business, and entertainment.

The 1970s brought changes to Hewitt's program. Reasoner defected to ABC in 1970 and Morley Safer, who had been CBS's bureau chief in London and the main correspondent in South Vietnam, signed on. His only condition was that he be allowed to return to his London post when the program folded. In 1972 the network moved the program from Tuesday to Sunday nights at 6 P.M. Now professional football would be the only cause for *60 Minutes* to be bumped. The 1960s and 1970s also saw transitions in Hewitt's personal life. His first marriage, to Mary Weaver, with whom he had two sons, ended in divorce in 1962. Weaver died in 1963. Hewitt then married Frankie Lea Teague Childers; they had two daughters and were divorced in the 1970s. Hewitt has been married to Marilyn Berger, a news correspondent for the *Washington Post* and then for NBC, since 14 April 1979.

Hewitt and *60 Minutes* have won numerous awards. Since its creation, the program has consistently been on Nielsen's top-ten list and after more than thirty years on the air it reportedly has earned more than $1 billion for CBS. Hewitt has said that he does not understand the news show's enduring popularity. In 1990 Hewitt was named to the Television Hall of Fame by the Academy of Television

Arts and Sciences. From 1968 to 2002 *60 Minutes* accumulated seventy-three Emmy Awards, ten Alfred I. du-Pont–Columbia University Journalism Awards, and nine University of Georgia George Foster Peabody Awards. Hewitt has continued to work on *60 Minutes,* saying in 2001, "I'm never gonna retire. I can't think of my life without *60 Minutes.* We're so intertwined that I don't know where I end and where the show begins." Hewitt created some of the decade's most memorable television programs and implemented innovations that became standards in evening television news.

★

Hewitt's autobiography, *Tell Me a Story: Fifty Years and 60 Minutes in Television* (2001), chronicles his life in journalism from World War II through the years with *60 Minutes.* For an overview of the program, see Axel Madsen, *60 Minutes: The Power and the Politics of America's Most Popular TV News Show* (1984), and Don Hewitt, *Minute by Minute* (1985).

LINDA DAILEY PAULSON

HEWLETT, William Redington ("Bill") (*b.* 20 May 1913 in Ann Arbor, Michigan; *d.* 12 January 2001 in Palo Alto, California), and **David PACKARD** (*b.* 7 September 1912 in Pueblo, Colorado; *d.* 26 March 1996 in Stanford, California), electronics engineers, inventors, and businessmen who helped build Hewlett-Packard into one of the world's largest electronics manufacturing companies.

Hewlett was one of two children of Albion Walter Hewlett, a university medical professor, and Louise (Redington) Hewlett, a homemaker. Hewlett was thought to be a poor student, but he had undiagnosed dyslexia and had such difficulty taking notes that he learned to listen intently instead and memorize what he heard. At the age of twelve Hewlett lost his father to a brain tumor. He then traveled in Europe with his mother and grandmother, who tutored him while his sister attended a school in Paris. When the family returned to California, they settled in San Francisco, and Hewlett attended Lowell High School, the city's outstanding college preparatory school. Although Hewlett initially wanted to become a physician like his father, he was mostly interested in mathematics and chemistry as well as in building electrical devices. It was at Stanford University that he met Packard.

Packard was one of two children of Sperry Sidney Packard, a lawyer, and Ella Lorna (Grabor) Packard, a high school teacher. Packard grew up with a love of the outdoors. In 1930 he graduated from Centennial High School in Pueblo and entered Stanford University. As a freshman, the six-foot, five-inch Packard became a star in track and field. He also lettered in basketball and football. Packard and Hewlett became fast friends and shared many wilderness adventures together; they would later incorporate hunting and fishing into activities their employees could share.

By 1933 Packard and Hewlett had agreed to start a company after they graduated, but it was the middle of the Great Depression, and jobs were scarce. In 1934 Packard received a job offer from General Electric (GE) in Schenectady, New York, and Hewlett urged him to take it, thus delaying their plans. The job did not start until 1935, so between graduating from Stanford with a bachelor of arts degree in 1934 and moving to New York, Packard took graduate courses at the University of Colorado in Boulder. Meanwhile, Hewlett began developing an audio oscillator as a school project.

At General Electric, newly hired engineers were expected to perform the most repetitive chores. In Packard's case, he worked on vacuum tubes, using a process involving mercury and liquid air to create vacuums. Whenever there was an accident, the engineer had to evacuate the area until the mercury vapor dissipated; when Packard took on the job, his predecessor had just had twenty such accidents in a row. Packard improved the success rate considerably and then was allowed to move on to other projects. His experiences at GE showed him not only the importance of the process itself to manufacturing but also the importance of communication. Packard helped improve products by taking the time to work with the laborers to show them, rather than just tell them, what they needed to do.

After graduating with a B.A. in engineering from Stanford, Hewlett attended the Massachusetts Institute of Tech-

nology in Cambridge, Massachusetts, where in 1936 he earned a master's degree in electrical engineering. In 1938 Packard left GE to return to Stanford for further study in electronics, receiving the bachelor of science degree in 1939. By then he and Hewlett were working in his garage, making devices for medical and other scientific fields. Their first important success was a resistance-stabilized audio oscillator, based on Hewlett's research at Stanford. An audio oscillator improves sound quality and is used in musical recordings and sonar. The only audio oscillator available before 1939 was produced by General Radio, for $400 apiece; the Hewlett-Packard audio oscillator was more efficient and sold for only $71.50. Their first of many sales was seven audio oscillators to Disney's chief sound engineer, Bud Hawkins, for use in the recording of the movie *Fantasia* (1940). By the end of 1939 they had made profits of $1,500.

In 1938 Packard married Lucile Laura Salter; they had four children. On 10 August 1939 Hewlett married Flora Lamsen; they had five children. Lamsen died in 1977, and Hewlett married Rosemary Bradford on 24 May 1978. Also in 1939 they named their new company, consisting of a garage and some machine tools, the Hewlett-Packard Company.

Hewlett served a stint in the U.S. Army reserves and had just finished his service when Japan bombed Pearl Harbor. He was called up for the remainder of World War II, serving first on the staff of the army chief signal officer and then as the head of the electronics department of the New Development Division of the War Department. In the meantime, Packard applied what he had learned about production processes at GE to his growing company. He tried to diversify his company's products, finding the War Department to be a big customer of his special vacuum technology that used fine oil instead of mercury to create devices for radar and other electronic equipment. When Hewlett returned in 1946, he and Packard decided to focus the company on manufacturing measuring devices, and in 1947 they incorporated Hewlett-Packard as a $1 million enterprise with 111 employees. In the 1950s their radiation measuring devices were so accurate that they sold very well, despite being prone to damage, and Hewlett-Packard began its tradition of quick, close technical support of its products by having people ready to fix broken radiometers.

Also during the 1950s Packard and Hewlett developed the "HP Way." Their business expanded into warehouses and machine shops, and in 1957 they moved into the Stanford Industrial Park. They would walk the shop floors inspecting the work and showing employees how the work should be done; this was referred to as "management by walking around." Even as their business expanded into locations in other states and overseas, Hewlett occasionally would appear and walk the floors; this led to a company-wide network of employees reporting to each other on the whereabouts of Hewlett. Even so, Hewlett's emphasis was on the invention aspect of the company's business, while Packard emphasized the implementation of the business. Key to Hewlett's vision of the company and of the HP Way was his emphasis on personnel—he wanted the best people doing their best work, which to him meant not only training them but also giving them independence. Therefore, employees were free to develop their individual work habits to best improve the manufacturing process.

In 1967 Packard introduced flexible hours. Employees were allowed to show up for work as late as 9:00 A.M. and still work a full eight-hour day. During an economic downturn, when he was faced with laying off 10 percent of his workforce in order to stay profitable, Packard initiated a five-day work week followed by a four-day work week. This spread the hardship among all of his employees and enabled Packard to retain all of his well-trained workers. By the mid-1990s Packard estimated that Hewlett-Packard spent $200 million a year on employee training.

In 1960 Hewlett-Packard began using computers to enhance the precision of their oscilloscopes. At the time, Packard was certain that computers were not a significant part of Hewlett-Packard's future, because International Business Machines (IBM) provided the business model for computer manufacturers. Also, IBM used a vertical top-down command structure, whereas Hewlett-Packard spread out responsibilities for making manufacturing decisions horizontally among the employees of each of the corporation's "groups." In 1963 Packard and Hewlett established a circuit board manufacturing plant in Japan, Yokogawa-Hewlett-Packard, with an American manager. When a Japanese employee, Kenzo Sasaoka, asked that the plant be run by the Japanese, Packard put him in charge; not only did productivity go up, but failure rates on the circuit boards also dropped to a sensational ten per million.

In 1966 Hewlett-Packard manufactured a computer the HP Way for helping to control the company's programmable measuring devices, laying the foundation for Hewlett-Packard's future leadership in calculating devices. From 1964 to 1967 Hewlett-Packard developed portable atomic clocks using cesium; they became standard timing devices throughout the world and were used to synchronize international times. They also were used on the Apollo space missions. In 1966 Hewlett and Packard created the HP Laboratories for research into innovative technologies.

In December 1968 Packard was asked to become the U.S. deputy secretary of defense, under Melvin Laird. He accepted the job but had to divest himself of his holdings in Hewlett-Packard to avoid conflicts of interest, because the corporation did business with the federal government. He placed his holdings in a trust that gave all of his Hewlett-Packard earnings to charity. He surrendered more than

$20 million in salary while working his $30,000 job in Washington, D.C. Packard worked to remake the military chain of command so that the armed services were clearly under civilian control, with the chairman of the Joint Chiefs of Staff having the principal responsibility of reporting to the president. He championed the development of the F-16 and F-18 fighter aircraft, worked on the anti-ballistic missile program, and tried to streamline the Pentagon bureaucracy.

In 1971 Packard left his government post, although he remained in government service into the 1980s by serving on oversight commissions for federal economic and military programs. In 1972 he returned to Hewlett-Packard and became the chairman of the board. In the early 1970s Hewlett challenged his engineers to produce a portable calculator, and in 1972 the first pocket calculator, the HP-35, was developed. Hewlett served as the president and chief executive officer (CEO) for the corporation until he retired as the president in 1977 and as the CEO in 1978. Hewlett continued as a management adviser until 1987. Packard helped oversee Hewlett-Packard's development as a major computer manufacturer during the 1980s.

Both men were philanthropists who gave away tens of millions of dollars to charities. Packard, who was active in the California Nature Conservancy, contributed $55 million for the establishment of the Monterey Bay Aquarium project. Packard and his wife began the David and Lucile Packard Foundation in 1964 and the Packard Center for the Future of Children. Packard received the Presidential Medal of Freedom in 1988. Hewlett and his wife began the William and Flora Hewlett Foundation, and Hewlett established the Public Policy Institute of California with a $70 million endowment. Hewlett received the National Medal of Science in 1985.

Packard died of complications from pneumonia at Stanford University Hospital, and Hewlett died in his sleep of the effects of heart disease. In 2000 the company the two men had built conducted $60 billion in business. Hewlett-Packard is a world leader in the manufacture of personal computers, computer peripherals, pocket calculators, and such medical devices as the fetal heart rate monitor, which was developed in 1967 to indicate whether a fetus is in difficulty during labor. Other medical measuring devices developed during the 1960s helped physicians diagnose illnesses and keep track of a patient's status during surgery. In 1968 Hewlett-Packard introduced the first desktop scientific calculator, the progenitor of the personal computer. The corporation also introduced the first electronic diode during the 1960s, an invention used to illuminate countless household devices, such as electric glow-in-the-dark clocks and illuminating buttons on printers, and lamps on street lights, all for less energy usage than incandescent bulbs.

★

Biographical information about Hewlett is in Rosabeth Moss Kanter, *The Change Masters* (1983); John N. Ingham and Lynne B. Feldman, *Contemporary American Business Leaders* (1990); and Frederick E. Allen, "Present at the Creation," *American Heritage* (May–June 2001). Obituaries for Hewlett are in the *New York Times* and *Los Angeles Times* (both 13 Jan. 2001). Packard's autobiography, *The HP Way: How Bill Hewlett and I Built Our Company* (1995), is a sprightly account of the public and private lives of Hewlett and Packard that also offers advice on how to build a manufacturing company. For biographical information about Packard see also *Current Biography Yearbook* (1969), and for both Packard and Hewlett see Michael S. Malone, *The Big Score: The Billion Dollar Story of Silicon Valley* (1985). Obituaries for Packard are in the *Los Angeles Times* (27 Mar. 1996), *Computerworld* (1 Apr. 1996), and *Business Week* (8 Apr. 1996).

KIRK H. BEETZ

HILSMAN, Roger (*b.* 23 November 1919 in Waco, Texas), State Department official and adviser on Vietnam policy during the Kennedy administration.

The only son of Roger Hilsman, a career U.S. Army officer, and Emma Prendergast, Hilsman attended schools in Minnesota, the Philippines, California, and Washington, D.C., before entering the U.S. Military Academy in 1939. He graduated in 1943 and was commissioned a second lieutenant in the infantry. During World War II, Hilsman served in the China-Burma-India theater. Initially assigned as a platoon leader in the famed Merrill's Marauders, he

Roger Hilsman, March 1963. ASSOCIATED PRESS AP

was wounded in the battle for Myitkyina, Burma, in May 1944. Later he was part of Detachment 101 of the Office of Strategic Services (OSS), leading a guerrilla battalion in operations behind Japanese lines.

After the war Hilsman served for two years at OSS headquarters in Washington, using his Burmese experiences to promote the development of a guerrilla war capability in the agency. On 22 June 1946 he married Eleanor Willis Hoyt; they had four children. In 1947 the army sent Hilsman to Yale University to study international relations. He was awarded a master's degree in 1950 and a doctorate in 1951. From 1950 to 1953 Hilsman was stationed in Europe, working on strategy for the North Atlantic Treaty Organization, first with the Joint American Military Advisory Group in London, England, and then at the headquarters of the United States European Command in Frankfurt, Germany.

Hilsman resigned his commission in 1953 and for the next three years was associated with the Center of International Affairs at Princeton University. In 1956 he was appointed chief of the Foreign Affairs and Defense Division of the Legislative Reference Service of the Library of Congress, and two years later he was named deputy director. While working with the service, Hilsman became acquainted with Senator John F. Kennedy, for whom he prepared memoranda for Kennedy's 1960 presidential campaign. Kennedy was impressed with Hilsman's intellect and readiness to express his opinions, and, as president, he appointed him director of the Bureau of Intelligence and Research in the State Department in February 1961.

In this post Hilsman was concerned with most of the foreign policy issues of the Kennedy era. Ultimately, however, he would play his most significant role in matters relating to South Vietnam, which was beset by a Communist insurgency that was gaining control over much of the rural population. American military advisers believed the most effective way to defeat the Communists, or Vietcong (VC), was to have regular Army of the Republic of Vietnam (ARVN) forces, utilizing infantry, armor, artillery, and air power, clear an area of VC and then turn it over to local self-defense forces. Hilsman, in contrast, thought the VC could best be countered by a combination of civic action, intelligence, police work, and constabulary-like small units aimed at protecting the population from the VC and securing government control.

Kennedy, who was increasingly frustrated by the deteriorating situation in Vietnam, sent Hilsman to Saigon in early 1962 to assess the progress of the war. During his visit Hilsman met with President Ngo Dinh Diem and Robert Thompson, head of a British advisory mission and the architect of the British victory over an insurgency in Malaya in the 1950s, and observed an operation against the VC near Bien Hoa. In his report he defined the war as a political rather than a military struggle and argued that conventional military tactics were of little value in defeating guerrillas. Instead, he said the South Vietnamese should emphasize aggressive patrolling and ambushes by small units and, drawing upon Thompson's experiences in Malaya, create "strategic hamlets" in densely populated rural areas to protect villagers against the VC.

Kennedy endorsed many of Hilsman's ideas, and in the spring of 1962 Diem adopted the strategic hamlet plan. Hilsman's prescription, however, did not sit well with many American military men. Already repelled by his aggressiveness in presenting his views in other policy matters, they did not relish a second-level State Department official telling them how to fight a war and continued to favor offensive strikes against the VC in their lairs. The strategic hamlet program, meanwhile, was soon floundering because of poor administration, corruption, and the efforts of Ngo Dinh Nhu, Diem's brother, to use it to strengthen the political power of the Ngo family.

In April 1963 Hilsman was named assistant secretary of state for Far Eastern affairs. Now the department's principal official for Vietnam, he was increasingly convinced that Diem's narrow political base, ARVN's incompetency, and Nhu's repressive actions towards Buddhists protesting government policies made it unlikely that Diem could lead South Vietnam to victory. Along with Michael Forrestal of the National Security Council and W. Averell Harriman, undersecretary of state for political affairs, Hilsman sent a cable to U.S. Ambassador Henry Cabot Lodge, Jr., on 24 August 1963 recommending that he let dissident ARVN generals know that the United States was ready to abandon Diem if he did not rid himself of Nhu.

While the cable did not actually call for a coup, it implicitly encouraged the generals to act against Diem. In sending it, however, the Hilsman group had assumed too much about the readiness of the generals to unseat Diem and, despite having cleared the cable with Kennedy, the willingness of many senior American officials to have the United States engineer his removal. Nothing immediately materialized in Saigon, but the cable was never revoked, and over the next weeks the administration fiercely debated its options in the face of Diem's refusal to dismiss Nhu. Finally, at the beginning of November 1963, a group of ARVN generals, with tacit American approval, staged a coup and murdered Diem and Nhu. A major turning point in the Vietnam conflict, the coup ushered in a period of political instability in Saigon and, ultimately, the Americanization of the war in 1965.

Kennedy's assassination on 22 November 1963 foreshadowed the end of Hilsman's tenure at the State Department. President Lyndon Johnson, who had favored continued support for Diem, did not like Hilsman for his encouragement of the coup and his brash style. Secretary of State Dean Rusk did not like him because of his pen-

chant for going outside channels, and the military did not like him because of his criticism of its strategy in Vietnam. Rather than wait to be fired, Hilsman resigned from the State Department in February 1964 and joined the government faculty at Columbia University. He was named professor emeritus in 1990. Hilsman is remembered for his advocacy of a counterinsurgency strategy in the Vietnam War and his place in the downfall of Diem.

★

Hilsman's papers are in the John F. Kennedy Library in Boston, Massachusetts. For Hilsman's views on Vietnam see Roger Hilsman, *To Move a Nation: The Politics of Foreign Policy in the Administration of John F. Kennedy* (1967), the first book by a policy maker to question Johnson's escalation of the war, and Hilsman, *American Guerrilla: My War Behind Japanese Lines* (1990). Hilsman's place in Vietnam policy making is also discussed in Lawrence Freedman, *Kennedy's Wars: Berlin, Cuba, Laos and Vietnam* (2000), and David Kaiser, *American Tragedy: Kennedy, Johnson and the Origins of the Vietnam War* (2000). Oral histories are located in the Kennedy Library, the Lyndon B. Johnson Library, the Columbia University Oral History Project, the Congressional Research Service of the Library of Congress, and the historical office of the State Department.

JOHN KENNEDY OHL

HIRSCH, Eric Donald, Jr. (*b.* 22 March 1928 in Memphis, Tennessee), educational reformer and author whose book *Cultural Literacy: What Every American Needs to Know* (1987) brought him into the public eye, although he had been an independent thinker on K–12 education long before that.

Hirsch is the son of Eric Donald, a businessman, and Leah Aschaffenburg. Growing up in Memphis, Hirsch noticed distressing inequalities—in particular that disadvantaged children often received an inferior education. Then Hirsch read Gunnar Myrdal's *American Dilemma: The Negro Problem and Modern Democracy* (1944) and became concerned about how racism affects education.

As he pursued his own education, Hirsch continued to think about education issues. In 1950 Hirsch graduated from Cornell University with a B.A. in English, and he earned his M.A. from Yale University three years later. During this time he was a member of the U.S. Naval Reserve and on active duty from 1950 to 1952. In 1957 Hirsch earned his Ph.D. from Yale University. He married Mary Monteith Pope on 15 June 1958, and the couple eventually had three children.

Hirsch began his teaching career in 1956 as an English instructor at Yale University. During the 1960s he advanced in academia, becoming an assistant professor in 1960 and an associate professor in 1963. He began teaching at the University of Virginia in Charlottesville in 1966, where he also served as chair of the English department; he continued to teach at the University of Virginia while he became a noted author.

As he continued to build his career, Hirsch thought about the learning process. His experiences teaching in the 1960s brought him insights that were to shape the rest of his career. He was a Morse fellow (1960–1961) and a Guggenheim fellow (1964–1965), both distinguished positions in the field of education. During his experiences as an instructor in the classroom, Hirsch noticed that teaching styles had evolved, but not necessarily for the better. Education shifted from making sure students had background knowledge to helping them develop learning skills.

Hirsch began to form many of his own ideas on education. He believed literacy is more than just understanding how to read. Instead, it requires enough education to understand references that belong in a literate person's world, such as who Dante was and what he wrote, what a flapper is, and why Sherlock Holmes is synonymous with solving crime.

Hirsch believed that taking facts and figures out of the schools affects learning, especially the learning of poor children whose parents do not fill in the gaps. To improve early childhood education, Hirsch helped start the Cultural Literacy Foundation, which promotes teaching a shared core curriculum in U.S. schools.

Hirsch told *Contemporary Authors Online* that early education is essential because language is not as simple as it may appear. "One theme is consistent: language is saying more than appears on the page, or in the sounds we make," Hirsch said. "The actual words are able to convey meaning only because of all sorts of implications that are *not* said. The reader must bring those meanings to the words by virtue of background knowledge."

Hirsch's views departed from the mainstream and were contested by those who believed the process of learning is more important than the content. But Hirsch insisted that background knowledge, not just methods of learning, must be provided in schools. For example, whereas some teachers would instruct first graders how to identify the values of certain cultures, Hirsch would teach them about ancient civilizations and world religions before covering values. In this way the students would have specific information—including historical, geographical, and philosophical details—on which to base their identifications.

Hirsch began publishing his views in the 1960s, beginning with practical analyses of literature. His first book, *Wordsworth and Schelling: A Typological Study of Romanticism* (1960), looked at the similarities of these two authors and claimed they shared the same psychology, or Weltanschauung. Hirsch concluded that his two subjects shared a pattern of experience he called "enthusiasm," or a "constant and sober way of confronting reality."

The next book, *Innocence and Experience: An Introduction to Blake* (1964), was again primarily a literary study. Hirsch chose a systematic approach that looked at William Blake's works both contextually and thematically. With this book, Hirsch won the *Explicator* magazine prize. In 1965 he contributed to *From Sensibility to Romanticism: Essays Presented to Frederick A. Pottle*.

Gradually Hirsch built the foundation for his next book, which addressed the academic trend of accepting imaginative conjectures in lieu of fact. In *Validity in Interpretation* (1967), Hirsch took to task the notion that there are no correct standards in interpreting human knowledge. Instead of approaching learning as if everyone's interpretation has validity, Hirsch advocated weighing evidence and reaching a consensus. He took a firm theoretical stance that did not allow for discounting facts, however bothersome they might be to those who would ignore them. "Severe discipline in interpretation would seem to require just this irritable reaching after fact and reason," Hirsch wrote in his preface.

Hirsch's work showed a determined effort to fight the tide that was washing away discipline and reason in academic circles. After the 1960s he went on to write many books expressing his views on education. His publications include *The Aims of Interpretation* (1976), *The Philosophy of Composition* (1977), *Cultural Literacy: What Every American Needs to Know* (1987), *The Dictionary of Cultural Literacy* (with Joseph Kett and James Trefil [1988]), *A First Dictionary of Cultural Literacy: What Our Children Need to Know* (1991), *The Schools We Need and Why We Don't Have Them* (1996), and *Books to Build On: A Grade-by-Grade Resource Guide for Parents and Teachers* (edited with Holdren [1996]). He has also written books for the "Core Knowledge" series, resource books for K–6 instruction.

During the 1960s and afterward many schools focused on "tool skills," or the ability to use critical thinking and problem solving. According to Hirsch, these teaching methods actually cheat children out of a solid education. He believes that taking facts and figures out of school harms reading comprehension. Hirsch was a contributor to *History as a Tool in Critical Interpretation: A Symposium* (1978) and *What Is Literature?* (1978). He has also written essays and articles for *American Educator, American Scholar, College English, Critical Inquiry,* and the *Times Literary Supplement*. Hirsch's theories have been put into practice by the Core Knowledge Foundation, which publishes core curriculum materials for elementary schools. Schools that have implemented core curriculum plans have reported improved test scores, better attendance, and more involved students.

★

Information about Hirsch can be found in *Contemporary Authors Online*. Articles about Hirsch appear in *Scholastic Update* (6 Nov. 1987), *The Economist* (18 Feb. 1989), *Phi Delta Kappan*

(Sept. 1997), *The New Republic* (10 Aug. 1998), and *Forbes* (16 Nov. 1998). Hirsch's article "Why Traditional Education Is More Progressive" can be found at <http://www.theamericanenterprise.org/taema97e.htm>.

A. E. SCHULTHIES

HITCHCOCK, Alfred Joseph (*b.* 13 August 1899 in Leytonstone, England; *d.* 29 April 1980 in Bel Air, California), filmmaker and master of suspense whose sixty-year odyssey into fright peaked in the 1960s with popular classics *Psycho* (1960) and *The Birds* (1963).

Hitchcock was the youngest of three children born to William Hitchcock, a greengrocer and fruit wholesaler, and his wife, Emma Jane Whelan, cockney Catholics who lived in a working-class section of London's East End. The unsurpassed master of bringing primal fears to the screen recalled being regularly frightened as a child. He remembered the day his father had him give a note to a local policeman, who took him down a long corridor and locked him in a jail cell for several minutes. When he was released the constable abjured, "That's what we do with naughty boys." As

Alfred Hitchcock. ARCHIVE PHOTOS, INC.

an adult, Hitchcock would tell interviewers, the experience deepened his sense of alienation and gave him a lifelong fear of police and authority figures.

When he was eleven Hitchcock was enrolled in Saint Ignatius College, a Jesuit day school for boys. He later painfully recalled priests beating students into obedience with a black leather strap, an experience that intensified his sense of imminent peril. He began night classes in navigation at the University of London when he was fourteen, and after his father's death in December 1914, he found office work at the Henley Telegraph and Cable Company. Eventually he became an illustrator in their advertising department.

In the summer of 1920 Hitchcock was hired as a part-time title illustrator by Famous Players-Lasky, a film company, and by November was designing their title cards full-time. During a three-year apprenticeship Hitchcock saved the studio money by designing sets, supervising props, preparing costumes and casts, and even writing scripts. Hitchcock's debut as assistant director came in 1923 with *Woman to Woman.* Encouraged by its success, the studio used him as assistant director on its next two features—*The White Shadow* and *The Prude's Fall.*

Hitchcock's editor in his early work was Alma Reville, a Nottingham native who shared his passion for film. They married on 2 December 1926, just weeks before the release of *The Pleasure Garden,* Hitchcock's first film as director. Their collaboration continued in more than fifty films with Hitchcock trusting his wife's judgment on scripts, continuity, and casting. *The Lodger,* released in 1927, made Hitchcock Britain's hottest young director. Hitchcock's existential hero, wrongly accused of a monstrous crime, is terrorized by forces seeking his destruction.

At Gainsborough and British International, Hitchcock directed nine silent and six sound films by the end of 1932, including *The Lodger* as well as *Blackmail* (1929), Britain's first talking picture. Their success confirmed Hitchcock's growing reputation as Britain's leading director. Beginning in 1934 at Gaumont-British Films, Hitchcock directed a series of suspense classics that brought him to Hollywood's attention. *The Man Who Knew Too Much* (1934), *The 39 Steps* (1935), and *The Lady Vanishes* (1938) were generally considered the masterpieces of this period.

The Hitchcocks and their ten-year-old daughter, Patricia, arrived in America in March 1939, with the director now under contract to David O. Selznick, America's foremost film producer. Their first collaboration, *Rebecca,* starring Laurence Olivier and Joan Fontaine, was voted best picture of 1940, and Hitchcock received the first of five Academy Award nominations for best director. The much-in-demand director continued his winning streak with *Foreign Correspondent* (1940); *Suspicion* (1941), his first teaming with Cary Grant; *Saboteur* (1942); and *Shadow of a Doubt* (1943), Hitchcock's personal favorite of the period.

However, *Rope* (1948), his first teaming with James Stewart, was a flop, and *Under Capricorn* (1949), his third and final film with Ingrid Bergman, did even worse. The drought finally ended with *Strangers on a Train* (1951), the study of a psychopath that would anticipate Hitchcock's success with *Psycho*. The middle and late 1950s were a period of unparalleled success for Hitchcock. *Dial "M" for Murder* (1954), *Rear Window* (1954), and *To Catch a Thief* (1955), three successive films with Grace Kelly, were artistic and box- office bonanzas. *Vertigo* (1958) and *North by Northwest* (1959), his fourth and final films with James Stewart and Cary Grant, respectively, showed Hitchcock at the peak of his powers.

At the start of the 1960s Hitchcock was as rich and famous as any of the stars he had directed. Audiences waited to catch his cameo appearances in his films. That unique profile was weekly on display when Hitchcock signed with the Columbia Broadcasting System (CBS) in 1955 to occasionally direct and serve as weekly host of *Alfred Hitchcock Presents*. Hitchcock's amusing on-camera introductions became immediate fan favorites. The successful series of offbeat melodramas moved to the National Broadcasting Company (NBC) in 1960, and after 250 episodes expanded to *The Alfred Hitchcock Hour* in 1962, running three more seasons. Hitchcock also lent his name as "editor" to popular suspense anthologies, published through Random House. *Stories for Late at Night* (1961); *Ghostly Gallery* (1962); *Stories My Mother Never Told Me* (1963); *Stories Not for the Nervous* (1965); *Sinister Spies* (1966); *Spellbinders in Suspense* (1967); *Stories That Scared Even Me* (1967); and *A Month of Mystery* (1969) were among the titles selling to a wide readership.

Paramount had hoped that Hitchcock would start the 1960s with a wide-screen successor to *North by Northwest*. They were not, however, interested in Hitchcock's first attempt at a "shocker," so Hitchcock, financing the film himself with a little less than $1 million, used his television team to shoot a small picture on Universal's back. He aimed at making "a horror film which comes to you when you are at home alone in the dark" for the younger audience that he had won over with his television series. *Psycho* (1960) was Hitchcock's conscious effort at achieving "pure cinema." He hoped it would "evoke fear by the way in which the film was assembled." He planned on "transferring the menace of the screen to the mind of the audience, increasing it to the point where it becomes unendurable."

In the film Hitchcock encourages his audience to follow the trail of a woman, played by Janet Leigh, who has stolen $40,000 from her employer. Halfway through the film she stops off at a harmless looking hotel, where she meets a shy, boyish-looking proprietor, played by Anthony Perkins. Hitchcock has taken "scenes of complete order" that he will soon "throw into complete disorder." He is out to undermine the viewer's sense of security by showing how fragile and illusory order and safety are in the face of madness. The realization comes in one of cinema's most shattering moments. A forty-five-second shower scene that took a week to shoot and seventy-eight separate shots to edit starts with the camera uncomfortably close to the unsuspecting heroine. Bernard Herrmann's piercing score signals the arrival of a shadowy intruder silhouetted just outside the shower curtain. Each slice of the knife is an exercise in pure terror against the victim and an audience unable to come to her rescue even as she reaches out for help. Her hopeless fight for life seems interminable. Hitchcock finally pulls back to reveal blood swirling down a drain, and dissolves to the uncomprehending eye of his victim.

Some critics chaffed at the film's relentless savagery and absence of a moral center, but audiences, particularly members of the drive-in generation, waited in long lines to see it. "A lot of people think I'm a monster," Hitchcock told interviewers. "What they don't know is that I'm more scared of the movies I make than they are." Hitchcock's psychopath is "an attractive and charming man. That's how he gets near his victims." What is particularly unsettling for the viewer is how "evil and good are getting closer and closer together" where "you can barely tell one from the other." That is what finally fills the audience with "unbearable apprehensions."

The Birds (1963), Hitchcock's ultimate apocalyptic film, was first conceived by screenwriter Evan Hunter as a screwball comedy, loosely based on several bird attacks reported on the West Coast. What appealed to Hitchcock was the idea of nature in revolt. "Everyone takes nature for granted," he later explained, "and one day the birds turned on them." Hitchcock saw the film as a commentary on mankind's "disruption of the natural order" through his flirtation with the atomic bomb.

The film's 1,500 shots and twenty-week shooting schedule showed Hitchcock's supreme confidence in "managing an audience's anxiety" by giving and withholding information. The "McGuffin" was his playful word for the object that appears to be of most importance in a film that is least important of all. The audience follows the teasing relationship of a San Francisco socialite and a man who lives in Bodega Bay, sixty miles up the coast. The woman is played by Tippi Hedren, a model Hitchcock discovered in a television commercial. Her cocky self-assurance is shattered by a sudden, unexpected bird attack. Later, as she waits in a playground, only the audience is aware of the gathering menace behind her. Finally, five days of filming produced an unforgettable bird attack in an attic that thrilled moviegoers. Hedren, however, was reduced to trembling exhaustion by the experience.

Pre-production planning on *The Birds* involved the creation of 300 trick shots, some of them including bird animations. Afterward, Hitchcock admitted his visual sense had been put to its severest test. He knew "every shot by heart" before the first day of shooting. He likened the art of "pure cinema" to a score that is directed by "a musical conductor." That is what made the elaborately staged film such a satisfying experience for Hitchcock as well as its huge fan following. "I'm not interested in content anymore than an artist worries if the apples he's painting are sweet or sour," he later said. "The cinema appeals to the widest possible audience" because of its ability to dramatize what audiences most felt and feared. It made the cinema of Alfred Hitchcock a dangerous place. "My idea of happiness," he often said, "is a clear horizon."

When *The Birds* premiered in March of 1963 at the Museum of Modern Art in New York City, it was accompanied by a retrospective of Hitchcock's work. Later that year the Cannes Film Festival continued the celebration. Five films followed in the final fourteen years of Hitchcock's creative output. Over time, *Marnie* (1964), *Topaz* (1969), and *Frenzy* (1972) grew in critical stature as the man who made them was honored for his career in film. An Oscar for lifetime achievement came in the spring of 1968 followed by the D.W. Griffith Award from the Directors Guild of America. Cinema schools began teaching his technique in storytelling, and in March of 1979, a year before his death, Hitchcock made one of his last public appearances to accept the Lifetime Achievement Award from the American Film Institute.

Hitchcock became an American citizen on 20 April 1955, yet on 3 January 1980 he was knighted by Queen Elizabeth II. Hitchcock, wracked by arthritis, then stricken with heart disease and kidney failure, briefly retired to the Bel Air bungalow he had shared with Alma since arriving in Hollywood more than forty years before. Recognition of his lasting contribution to the vocabulary of the cinema has only expanded in the generation since his passing.

★

Hitchcock donated his private papers, including scripts, production notes, and publicity files, to the Academy of Motion Picture Arts and Sciences in Beverly Hills, California. Among the most notable writings on him is Francois Truffaut, *Hitchcock* (1967), the result of fifty hours' worth of interviews involving the two directors. More recent works include Robert E. Kapsis, *Hitchcock: The Making of a Reputation* (1992); Jane E. Sloan, *Alfred Hitchcock: A Guide to Reference and Resources* (1993); Sidney Gottlieb, ed., *Hitchcock on Hitchcock: Selected Writings and Interviews* (1995); and Dan Auiler, *Hitchcock's Notebooks: An Authorized and Illustrated Look Inside the Creative Mind of Alfred Hitchcock* (1999). Hitchcock has been the subject of many biographies. The most widely quoted include John Russell Taylor, *Hitch: The Life and Times of Alfred Hitchcock* (1978), and Donald Spoto, *The Dark Side of Genius: The Life of Alfred Hitchcock* (1983). Obituaries and appreciations of his work are in the *New York Times* and *Los Angeles Times* (both 30 Apr. 1980) and *Time* (12 May 1980).

BRUCE J. EVENSEN

HOFFA, James Riddle ("Jimmy") (*b.* 14 February 1913 in Brazil, Indiana; *d.* c. 30 July 1975), powerful and effective trade union leader with gangster connections; after a scheduled meeting with the Mafia, he disappeared in 1975 and was declared "presumed dead" in 1982.

Before his name became associated with organized crime, Hoffa started out life in an ordinary way. In fact, he had fairly humble beginnings. His father, John Cleveland Hoffa, was a coal driller; his mother, Viola Riddle, supported her four children after her husband's death in 1920 by working as a radiator cap polisher.

All that changed when the Hoffa family moved from Indiana to Detroit. After his father's death, Hoffa had to help support the family. He stopped going to school after reaching the ninth grade and started working as a department store stock boy. In 1930 he became a freight handler for the Kroger grocery chain. That job was pivotal because it set Hoffa on the path that put him in the center of controversy for the rest of his life. He organized a successful warehouseman strike against Kroger just as a shipment of

James "Jimmy" Hoffa. ARCHIVE PHOTOS, INC.

strawberries was arriving. Soon he was inextricably tied to the labor movement.

In 1934 Hoffa brought his four coworkers, the "Strawberry Boys," into the International Brotherhood of Teamsters, the largest union in the United States. In 1935 he became president of the local Teamsters chapter. While helping nonunion workers, Hoffa met Josephine Poszywak in a laundry workers' picket line and married her in 1936. The couple had two children. By 1937 Hoffa was entrenched in Teamsters affairs and under the tutelage of Farrell Dobbs, who had helped the Teamsters more than triple their membership in just five years.

Union activities were dangerous in those days, and Hoffa quickly learned how to play for high stakes. Soon Hoffa was attacking those who threatened his power base. He used goon squads, or armed troops of gangsters, to enforce his will. As time went on, Hoffa expanded his power by moving further from the realm of labor representation and into the world of racketeering.

On his way to the position of power he enjoyed in the 1960s, Hoffa developed a habit of using violence to further his ends. John McClellan unwittingly helped Hoffa reach his pinnacle of power when he summoned Dave Beck, then the Teamsters' president, to his U.S. Senate committee. Beck, unable to say much without incriminating himself, was convicted of grand larceny in 1957, and Hoffa's way was clear to secure the Teamsters' top spot.

Hoffa's activities did not stop short of the law, but somehow he always managed to skirt the consequences. During the hearings that ruined Beck, Hoffa was indicted for trying to bribe someone to spy on the McClellan committee staff, but the indictment did not lead to a conviction. Hoffa was acquitted and continued to secure his power base.

As the Teamsters' president, Hoffa was quick to edge out the competition from nonunion drivers. Teamster members enjoyed higher wages than ever before. In 1964 Hoffa achieved his longtime goal of securing for the Teamsters the first national contract in the trucking industry. During the early 1960s he reached the heights of success, but he was about to fall.

The problem was that Hoffa had led the Teamsters to greatness through strong-arm tactics. An economics professor who saw the Teamsters up close in the 1960s wrote, "As recently as 1962, I heard him order the beating of a man 3,000 miles away, and on another occasion, I heard him instruct his cadre on precisely how to ambush nonunion truck drivers with gunfire . . . to frighten them, not to kill."

All these activities attracted attention. Attorney General Robert Kennedy was certain that Hoffa was involved in organized crime, and he investigated Hoffa relentlessly. Kennedy believed Hoffa was engaged in criminal activities because the mob was working closely with the Teamsters;

organized crime figures even held positions of union leadership. Reportedly, a Teamsters' local in Detroit was not involved in union activities but was actually a headquarters for drug dealing. These illegal practices kept Kennedy in pursuit of Hoffa, and Hoffa was said to have murder contracts out on Kennedy as well as on his brother John, the president of the United States. Hoffa is said to have been delighted at each Kennedy assassination.

Hoffa also attracted the enmity of the Federal Bureau of Investigation (FBI). It was obvious that FBI director J. Edgar Hoover wanted Hoffa behind bars, but Hoover so disliked Kennedy and vice versa that the two never joined forces against Hoffa. This may have helped Hoffa stay out of jail; in any case, Hoffa was an expert at avoiding the consequences of his actions. In 1962 Hoffa was tried for taking a million-dollar bribe to ensure labor peace, but he eluded sentencing. Then, in 1964, the same year Hoffa realized the Teamsters' national contract, his luck changed and he was convicted of conspiracy, fraud, and jury tampering and sent to jail.

Even so, Hoffa remained president of the Teamsters. He appealed his case and managed to stay out of jail for a few years, but in 1967 he was sent to the federal penitentiary in Lewisburg, Pennsylvania. He was sentenced to serve thirteen years, but President Richard Nixon pardoned him in 1971. According to the terms of Hoffa's pardon, he was not supposed to participate in union leadership until 1980, but he secretly continued to exercise power with the Teamsters. Meanwhile, Hoffa went to court in an effort to invalidate the restrictions set on his pardon; but even though he did not win in court, he continued his involvement with the union. He also wrote an autobiography, *Hoffa: The Real Story* (1975).

On 30 July 1975, after last being seen in a restaurant in Bloomfield Hills, Michigan, Hoffa disappeared. He was legally declared dead on 8 December 1982. Most people were convinced that his untimely disappearance and probable death were related to his ties with organized crime. His family wanted answers. In 1987 Hoffa's daughter, Barbara Crancer, a court judge in St. Louis, sued the government unsuccessfully for access to the Hoffa investigation files. In 2001 the FBI found DNA evidence that Hoffa had been in the vehicle of his friend Charles (Chuckie O'Brien), indicating that possibly O'Brien knew something about Hoffa's disappearance. Hoffa's son, James P. Hoffa, who also became a Teamsters president, was convinced that O'Brien was involved in his father's probable death. Still looking for justice twenty-six years after his father's disappearance, James P. Hoffa pleaded for anyone with information to come forward.

As notorious in death as he was in life, Hoffa lives in American memory as a tough bargainer with gangster connections who kept organized labor alive.

★

Numerous books have been written about Hoffa, including James Clay, *Hoffa! Ten Angels Swearing* (1965); Ralph C. James and Estelle Dinerstein James, *Hoffa and the Teamsters: A Study of Union Power* (1965); Walter Sheridan, *The Fall and Rise of Jimmy Hoffa* (1972); Dan E. Moldea, *The Hoffa Wars: Teamsters, Rebels, Politicians, and the Mob* (1978); and Arthur A. Sloane, *Hoffa* (1991). An article on Hoffa is in *American National Biography*, vol. 10 (1999). An obituary is in *Time* (11 Aug. 1975). The furor over Hoffa's disappearance had not died down when *Editor and Publisher* (24 Sept. 2001) reported that the *Detroit Free Press* had sued the FBI for refusing access to the files from the Hoffa investigation.

A. E. SCHULTHIES

HOFFMAN, Abbott Howard ("Abbie"; "Barry Freed")

(*b.* 30 November 1936 in Worcester, Massachusetts; *d.* 12 April 1989 in Solebury, Pennsylvania), writer and political activist who throughout the 1960s led flamboyant demonstrations and in 1968 cofounded the Youth International Party ("Yippies").

The oldest of three children of John Hoffman, owner of a pharmaceutical supply store, and Florence Schanberg Hoffman, a homemaker, Hoffman grew up in Worcester, Massachusetts, in a middle-class, apolitical Jewish household. Always clamoring for attention, Hoffman frequently clashed with his physically abusive father, establishing a lifelong pattern of hostility toward authority figures. Expelled from Classical High School in his sophomore year following a disagreement with a teacher, Hoffman graduated from Worcester Academy in 1955. At Brandeis University (1955–1959) Hoffman earned a B.A. in psychology, captained the tennis team, and, characteristically, battled with his coach. Always an intellectual, although he chose not to emphasize this aspect of himself, Hoffman began graduate studies in psychology at the University of California at Berkley. When his girlfriend, Sheila Karklin, became pregnant, Hoffman dropped out to marry her on 14 July 1960. They had a son in December 1960 and a daughter in 1962.

Hoffman tried to live the life of a traditional husband and father, but his marriage disintegrated at the same time as his career as a psychologist at Worcester State Hospital floundered. A frequent writer and speaker around town, he soon became known for fabricating stories to further his liberal political objectives. Hoffman once said, "One of the greatest mistakes any revolution can make is to become boring." Attacking the conservatism of the local chapter of the National Association for the Advancement of Colored People (NAACP), Hoffman argued in the spring of 1964

that civil rights activists should use weapons against racist vigilantes. Although he later claimed to have participated in Freedom Summer (a drive organized in Mississippi in the early 1960s to register black voters) that year, its organizers found Hoffman to be emotionally unstable and banned him from participating. Hoffman traveled to McComb, Mississippi, in August 1965 to teach black children for three weeks at a Student Nonviolent Coordinating Committee Freedom School. He had also begun to use marijuana and hallucinogenic drugs, especially LSD, much to the disgust of his wife, who divorced him in 1966.

In the summer of 1966 Hoffman became the national sales director for the Poor People's Corporation and began to manage a New York City store, Liberty House, where Mississippi-produced crafts were sold, as well as pop-culture posters and left-wing magazines. With its determinedly noncommercial, low-key atmosphere, the store was significant as an early example of the counterculture. Hoffman saw styles of dress, music, and drugs as elements of rebellion needing political focus. In 1967 Hoffman became a Digger, a group of politicized hippies who believed that everything should be without charge; he later explained his philosophy in *Steal This Book!*, a guide to living for free in New York. Liberty House fired him and banned him from the premises for giving away its products. Hoffman and his fellow radical Jerry Rubin organized the March on the Pentagon on 21 October 1967, mobilizing thousands of people to protest the Vietnam War. On 8 June 1967 Hoffman married Anita Kushner in a hippie wedding ceremony covered by *Time* magazine.

Categorized 4-F (ineligible for military service) because of bronchial asthma, Hoffman was not personally threatened by the Vietnam War, but he objected on principle to wars being fought for economic gains. Determined to advance the anti-Vietnam movement, Hoffman concluded that the cause could develop only through media coverage and that the media would respond only to highly visual events. On 24 August 1967 Hoffman and a few friends entered the gallery of the New York Stock Exchange and protested the military-industrial complex by dropping dollar bills to the traders below while photographers snapped photos. At this point Hoffman was devoting most of his energies to street theater and cofounded the Youth International Party, popularly known as the Yippies, with Rubin in 1968.

The Yippies, more of a joke that the media took seriously than a full-fledged movement, sought a society based on humanitarian cooperation. The Grand Central Station Yip-in in New York, to celebrate the spring equinox and to encourage "spring mating," reflected typical Yippie humor. Riot police stopped the celebration by clubbing demonstrators and beating Hoffman into unconsciousness. De-

Abbie Hoffman holding a toy bomb, September 1969. ASSOCIATED PRESS AP

spite his injuries, Hoffman was thrilled about the national publicity. When the Democrats headed to Chicago to nominate a presidential candidate in 1968, Hoffman and the Yippies joined them. Despite warnings from Chicago Yippies, Hoffman baited the police with a steady barrage of threats, such as plans to lace the reservoir with LSD and to kidnap delegates. The Chicago police, fearing the Yippies as drug-crazed, bomb-throwing sex maniacs, attacked the protesters on 25 August 1968. Hoffman, who had been arrested earlier in the day for a four-letter obscenity scrawled on his forehead, missed the bloodshed.

Charged with conspiracy, Hoffman joined other members of the Chicago Eight (later known as the Chicago Seven, after the Black Panther leader Bobby Seale's case was handled separately) on trial in September 1969. During much of the government's presentation of its case, the defendants disrupted the trial. "We have contempt for this court and for you and for this whole rotten system," Hoffman declared before an obviously biased judge Julius Hoffman (no relation) in a sentence that earned him eight

months in jail for contempt. Hoffman was found not guilty of conspiracy but guilty of crossing state lines with the intention of creating a riot, a charge that brought a maximum of five years in prison and $5,000 in fines. Later revelations confirmed that agents of the Federal Bureau of Investigation had tapped the defendants' phones, opened their mail, and conducted secret meetings with the judge. Hoffman appealed until November 1972, when the U.S. Court of Appeals reversed the conviction, stating that the defendants had not received a fair trial. The contempt conviction was overturned in early 1973.

After 1970 Hoffman appeared to lose his sense of direction. His wife, Anita, gave birth to a son, America, and the family moved to Saint Thomas in the Virgin Islands in 1971. Hoffman began smuggling and dealing cocaine, and on 28 August 1973 he was arrested in New York City for selling three pounds of cocaine, a felony. Afraid of jail, Hoffman transformed himself into New York environmental activist "Barry Freed" and entered a bigamous marriage to Johanna Lawrenson. As Freed, he was commended by the governor of New York for his work as a conservationist, appeared before a U.S. Senate subcommittee to testify on the environment, was a guest on local radio and television stations, and even served on a federal water resources commission. His second wife, Anita, quietly divorced the fugitive in 1980. Surrendering on 4 September 1980, Hoffman served three years in prison. He then embarked on the lucrative college lecture circuit but, continually plagued by bipolar disorder, he overdosed on phenobarbital at the age of fifty-two.

The preeminent political prankster of the 1960s, responsible for the dictum "Don't trust anyone over thirty," Hoffman challenged the manner in which the Left had traditionally communicated with a mass constituency by introducing humor, theatricality, and studied irreverence into the repertoire of protest. A colorful and exuberant man, his actions reflected the optimism and the sheer joy of the counterculture.

★

Because of Hoffman's habit of fabricating facts, his autobiography, *Soon to Be a Major Motion Picture* (1980), is of limited value. Marty Jezer, *Abbie Hoffman: American Rebel* (1992), relies too heavily on Hoffman's unreliable autobiography, while *Run, Run, Run: The Lives of Abbie Hoffman* (1994) is a gossipy account by his younger brother, Jack Hoffman, and Daniel Simon. Jonah Raskin, *For the Hell of It: The Life and Times of Abbie Hoffman* (1996), is a solid biography. Much of Hoffman's writing appeared in radical newspapers and has not yet been anthologized. His first book, *Revolution for the Hell of It* (1968), is essential for understanding the counterculture. *Woodstock Nation* (1971) describes Hoffman's feelings about the music festival and the counterculture movement. The Chicago Eight trial is covered in Mark Levine, George McNamee, and Daniel Greenberg, eds., *The Tales of Hoffman* (1970), as well as in John Schultz, *The Chicago Conspiracy Trial* (1993). Obituaries are in the *New York Times* and the *Washington Post* (both 14 Apr. 1989).

CARYN E. NEUMANN

HOFFMAN, Dustin Lee (*b*. 8 August 1937 in Los Angeles, California), two-time Academy Award winner and a 1960s acting sensation who captured the decade's preoccupation with alienated youth in his first starring film, *The Graduate*.

Hoffman is the second of two sons born to Ukrainian Jews who first settled in Chicago and then in Los Angeles shortly before his birth. Harry Hoffman was a furniture salesman who had worked as a set designer and prop man for Columbia Pictures before losing his job during the Great Depression. His mother, Lillian Gold, loved show business and managed to get Hoffman's older brother Ron a walk-on in Frank Capra's *Mr. Smith Goes to Washington* (1939).

Hoffman's development in childhood was slow. He rode his first scooter when he was two-and-a-half and did not speak until he was three. Arguments over money meant "we lived in a great state of friction in our house." Those struggles forced the family to move from one working-class neighborhood to another, contributing to the shy child's sense of alienation and uncertainty. From his earliest days he saw himself as an undersized "outsider and observer."

He remembers being "a kid who was always too short, wore braces on his teeth, and had one of the worst cases of acne in California." Hoffman's brother Ron received "straight As," but his own grades were poor. "I lacked concentration and discipline," he later admitted.

Hoffman found that comedy routines at the expense of his teachers won attention and approval from other students. His height won him the part of Tiny Tim in the John Burroughs Junior High School production of *A Christmas Carol*. At Los Angeles High School he turned to tennis, lifted weights, ran track, and began studying classical piano. Beginning in 1955 he half-heartedly pursued piano studies at Santa Monica City College. He then attended the Los Angeles Conservatory of Music. In early 1957 Hoffman enrolled at the Pasadena Playhouse, where he "picked certain acting classes because of the girls in them."

Hoffman had enough success at the playhouse to try acting in New York City. He reasoned "it would be easier to fail at a distance" than closer to home. For seven years Hoffman lived the life of a struggling New York actor with an increasingly intense commitment to his developing craft. Five times he auditioned for Lee Strasberg's Actors Studio, a famous method acting school prominent in the 1960s, and failed to get in, before he was finally admitted. He shared an $80-a-month cold-water flat on New York's Lower East Side with classmates Gene Hackman and Robert Duvall. Around odd acting jobs Hoffman found work as a psychiatric attendant, dishwasher, waiter, typist, and

A movie still of Dustin Hoffman in a scene from *The Graduate*, 1967. © BETTMANN/CORBIS

for three consecutive Christmases, a toy demonstrator at Macy's department store. He studied acting at Lonnie Chapman's Manhattan studio, taught acting at a Harlem boys' club, and directed community theater productions.

Hoffman's first stage appearance in New York was unpaid. On the evening of 20 May 1959 he opened in the Sarah Lawrence College production of Gertrude Stein's *Yes Is for a Very Young Man*. His Broadway debut was a one-word walk-on in *A Cook for Mr. General*, which ran twenty-eight performances in 1961. He joined the Theater Company of Boston and performed in ten plays in nine months as a character actor making $65 a week. This led to a one-evening stand at the Circle in the Square in the off-Broadway production of *Waiting for Godot*, in which he played Pozzo the slave driver. He got bit parts on two television series—*Naked City* and *The Defenders*—and then assisted Ulu Grosbard in directing Duvall in *A View from the Bridge*, which opened at the Sheridan Square Playhouse in New York on 28 January 1965 and ran for 780 performances.

Hoffman might have given up acting for directing if it weren't for the rave reviews he received for the part of Immanuel, a crippled German homosexual, in Ron Ribman's *Harry, Noon and Night*, which opened in lower Manhattan at the American Place Theater in the spring of 1965. The play's director, George Morrison, remembered that Hoffman had already learned "to annihilate his own ego and become the character," leading to "the most memorable performance I have ever witnessed." Hoffman appeared poised for his first major role on Broadway when he was set to replace Martin Sheen in Frank Gilroy's Pulitzer Prize–winning *The Subject Was Roses*, but he was dropped from the cast after his first rehearsal when a cooking accident at home left his hands badly burned.

Hoffman's disappointment didn't last long. On 21 April 1966 he opened in Ribman's *The Journey of the Fifth Horse*, in a role that won him the Obie Award as the best actor in an off-Broadway production. On the eve of its opening the part of Zoditch, a bitterly ingrown Russian clerk, had Hoffman perplexed. He was desperately looking for "the key to the character." The more he thought about the part, the less certain he seemed about how to play it. On opening night, instinctively, he "let go," delivering his first line in a nasal, high-pitched voice that unlocked the character for him. The *New York Times* critic Stanley Kauffmann was captivated. Hoffman's ironic portrayal of a paranoid, he wrote, "has the vitality of a born actor and the fine control of the skillful one." Hoffman had succeeded "in making this unattractive man both funny and pathetic." Kauffmann seemed certain that those who had seen the performance were "watching an extraordinary career develop." Years later Hoffman considered his evocation of "an impotent bird" the best work he had ever done.

In August 1966 Hoffman continued experimenting as an actor, appearing as a schizophrenic in Murray Schisgal's play *Fragments* at the Berkshire Theater Festival in Stockbridge, Massachusetts. He began to develop a reputation for being difficult. Two directors quit the off-Broadway production of Henry Living's play *Eh?* before its 16 October 1966 premier. Hoffman had the lead role of Valentine Brose, a deliberately inefficient cockney machine operator, and he was clearly struggling with the character on the eve of his opening. He clashed with Broadway veteran Alan Arkin's directing advice as well. Eventually there was a truce. Arkin found Hoffman "difficult because he's passionate about his work." In Hoffman's view, "The director's job should be to open the actor up and . . . leave him alone! There are a . . . lot of good actors around, and not even a handful of good directors." The play's four-month run was a huge success. Critics compared his work to Charlie Chaplin's and Buster Keaton's. The *Times* of London celebrated "the finest new American actor." Hoffman won the Theater World, Drama Desk, and Vernon Rice awards for off-Broadway excellence. More importantly, he won an audition to play the lead in *The Graduate*.

The film's director, Mike Nichols, and its producer, Lawrence Turman, had been seeking someone to play the part of Benjamin Braddock, an irresolute college grad who is seduced by a bored, middle-aged friend of the family before he falls in love with her daughter. The audition did not go well. The pale and pimply actor, only five feet, five-and-a-half inches in height, "seemed three feet tall" to female lead Katharine Ross as they rehearsed a love scene. Hoffman was painfully aware that Charles Webb's book called for a tall, blonde, athletic leading man and that Nichols had first sought "a walking surfboard" for the part. Nichols, however, liked Hoffman's nervous energy and ability to project bewildered, youthful vulnerability. Hoffman was not so sure. At thirty he felt he was ten years too old for the part and still thought of himself as "a character actor on Broadway." He flubbed his lines and struggled to make sense of the character. Nichols told him, "He's Jewish on the inside." Hoffman later called it the "key" he'd been looking for.

Greatly aided by Paul Simon's score, *The Graduate* soared to revenues of $80 million within a year of its December 1967 release, establishing a youth market in movies and making Hoffman, who had earned $17,000 for the title role, an "overnight" success. Writing in the *Nation*, Robert Hatch found Hoffman's performance "disconcertingly direct and well armed by incredulity." Bosley Crowther of the *New York Times* appreciated his "wonderfully compassionate sense of the ironic and the pathetic." *Newsweek* considered the performance "unforgettable." To the *Time* magazine critic, Hoffman was a symbol of disillusioned youth. Hollis Alpert of the *Saturday Review* agreed, calling

Hoffman the most unexpected "film hero of our generation." Nichols won the Oscar as best director, and Hoffman was nominated as best actor. It was now official. He had finally "plummeted to stardom"—a phrase he used to signal his ambivalence about becoming a celebrity.

In April 1968 Hoffman signed a contract for $250,000 to appear in the role of Enrico "Ratso" Rizzo in the film *Midnight Cowboy* for United Artists. The gimpy, tubercular con man who hustles the underside of New York City helped make James Herlihy's novel a best-seller. The part appealed to Hoffman as a vast departure from the "Andy Hardy" roles he was being offered. Jon Voight was signed as the male prostitute who shares his loneliness and friendship. Under the direction of John Schlesinger, Hoffman "got inside one of those people" society regards "as the scum of the earth." His discovery was that Rizzo "is really no different from us. Only his circumstances are different."

Hoffman appreciated Schlesinger's patience during filming. He liked "coming at the character from the inside," and that meant "going down to the basement and starting to explore" before "getting the character locked in." Hoffman told interviewers, "I don't know how to act . . . . [But] certain things . . . I've learned. The biggest thing is when it doesn't feel right, . . . you go until it does feel right." Critics and fans seemed certain he'd gotten Rizzo right. *Midnight Cowboy* was released to selected theaters on 26 May 1969 after receiving an "X" rating for its frank sexuality. It became a smash hit, winning Hoffman his second Oscar nomination in two years. The movie won the Academy Award for best picture of the year, and Schlesinger was honored as best director.

Before the distribution of *Midnight Cowboy,* Hoffman returned to the Broadway theater in Schisgal's *Jimmy Shine,* playing the role of a teen who turns on to drugs, art, and the hippie culture of the 1960s. The play was panned, but on the strength of Hoffman's deft performance and large fan following, it ran 161 performances, closing 26 April 1969. Hoffman was proving as good a businessman as he was an actor. He received $4,500 a week for creating the role plus 10 percent of the show's receipts. In addition, he was guaranteed half the profits from every souvenir program sold. Hoffman earned $450,000 for his next screen role, the part of a Manhattan swinger who tours singles bars and sleeps with a woman he barely knows. *John and Mary,* costarring Mia Farrow, was released on 25 November 1969 but generated indifferent box office receipts and mediocre critical reviews.

Firmly entrenched financially, Hoffman married his longtime love, the ballet dancer Anne Byrne, on 4 May 1969 and helped raise her daughter, Karina, a child from a previous marriage. They joined him on location during the shooting of *Little Big Man* (1970), Arthur Penn's well-received, revisionist Western in which Hoffman plays the part of 121-year-old Jack Crabb, the sole survivor of Custer's Last Stand. The Hoffmans' daughter was born on 15 October 1970, shortly after the film's release.

Hoffman remained a major film star throughout the 1970s, drawn to controversial projects. In Sam Peckinpah's violent *Straw Dogs* (1971), he is a meek mathematician forced to defend his wife and home from predatory English hooligans. In the graphically realistic *Papillon* (1973), Hoffman and costar Steve McQueen escape from Devil's Island, a famously draconian prison off the coast of French Guiana. Hoffman received an Oscar nomination for his portrayal of legendary nightclub comic Lenny Bruce in the profane *Lenny* (1974), directed by Bob Fosse. He teamed again with Schlesinger and costarred with Laurence Olivier in the Nazi-hunting thriller *Marathon Man* (1976). Hoffman played *Washington Post* reporter Carl Bernstein investigating the Watergate cover-up, costarring with Robert Redford as Woodward, in *All the President's Men* (1976). He starred in and codirected *Straight Time* (1978) for Warner Brothers before winning an Oscar for his performance as a divorced father trying to cope with his young son in *Kramer vs. Kramer,* the Academy Award's best picture of 1979 and a $100 million success at the box office.

Hoffman split his time between Hollywood and the stage in the 1980s and started a new family. His first marriage ended in divorce in 1980. On 21 October 1980 he married Lisa Gottsegen, a twenty-five-year-old law school graduate; they have four children. Hoffman appeared as an out-of-work actor who disguises himself as a woman in *Tootsie* (1982), a Sydney Pollack farce that made $177 million at the box office and earned its star another Oscar nomination. He received a second Oscar for his portrayal of an autistic savant in *Rain Man,* the Academy Award–winning, $172-million megahit of 1988. Hoffman also achieved stage success in a 1984 revival of Arthur Miller's *Death of a Salesman.*

By the end of the 1990s Hoffman's twenty-seven starring vehicles had grossed $1.1 billion, with *Dick Tracy* (1990) and *Hook* (1991) contributing $224 million to the total. *Outbreak* (1995) and *Sphere* (1998) were commercial successes but critical busts. His sardonic look at moviemaking and politics in *Wag the Dog* (1997) won Hoffman his seventh Oscar nomination. In 1999 Hoffman received the Lifetime Achievement Award from the American Film Institute in recognition of his artistic and commercial success. "Above all else," he told interviewers, he had done all he could "to find the proper note" in each performance. For an actor, there was "nothing like realizing that moment." Film historians duly noted that at their best, those moments captured as well as any actor's his generation's painfully uncertain encounter with postmodern America in the second half of the twentieth century.

★

English-language biographies of Hoffman include Jeff Lenburg, *Dustin Hoffman: Hollywood's Anti-Hero* (1983), and Patrick Agan, *Hoffman vs. Hoffman: The Actor and the Man* (1986). Major articles include those in *Current Biography* (1969): 215–217 and (1996): 213–217. An early filmography is Douglas Brode, *The Films of Dustin Hoffman* (1983). Hoffman was interviewed on his filmmaking technique by Susan Dworkin for *Making Tootsie: A Film Study with Dustin Hoffman and Sydney Pollack* (1983).

BRUCE J. EVENSEN

HOFFMAN, Julius Jennings (*b.* 7 July 1895 in Chicago, Illinois; *d.* 1 July 1983 in Chicago, Illinois), former law partner of the mayor of Chicago, Richard J. Daley, and controversial federal judge for the U.S. District Court for the Northern District of Illinois who presided over the trial of the Chicago Seven, the radical activists who were charged with conspiracy to incite riots during the 1968 Democratic National Convention.

Hoffman received his Ph.B. in 1912 and his LL.B. in 1915, both from Northwestern University in Evanston, Illinois. He served in private practice from 1915 to 1947 and then as a judge of the Superior Court of Cook County, Illinois, from 1947 to 1953. Thereafter, Hoffman was nominated to the federal bench by President Dwight D. Eisenhower and

Julius Hoffman, September 1969. ASSOCIATED PRESS AP

received his commission on 14 May 1953. He took senior status on 3 February 1972 and served until his death on 1 July 1983.

Hoffman perhaps is most famous for presiding over one of the most well-known legal cases of the 1960s, the trial of the Chicago Seven. In the eyes of many, this trial came to symbolize the wide cultural divide that had split the nation over such issues as the ongoing war in Vietnam, civil rights, free speech, feminism, and the use of psychedelic drugs. Originally dubbed the "Chicago Eight," the group was made up of the activists Rennie Davis, David Dellinger, John Froines, Tom Hayden, Abbie Hoffman (no relation to Judge Hoffman), Jerry Rubin, Bobby Seale, and Lee Weiner. The Chicago Eight case arose out of the activities of the defendants prior to and during the August 1968 Democratic National Convention in Chicago. Many groups from across the nation had descended on the convention site to protest the various issues confronting their generation, not the least of which was the conflict in Vietnam. From Sunday, 25 August through Thursday, 29 August, the defendants gathered in Grant Park in proximity to the Conrad Hilton Hotel, which housed important members and groups of the Democratic National Committee. There, protestors organized a rock concert and engaged in various antigovernment speeches and activities, including teach-ins and other nonviolent demonstrations.

Fearing that the thousands of youths rallied there would disrupt the convention, the administration of Chicago's mayor, Richard J. Daley, refused to grant the demonstrators permits to sleep in the city parks and imposed an 11:00 P.M. curfew. In addition, Daley placed the city's twelve thousand police officers on twelve-hour shifts and requested that the state and federal governments supply him with thousands of additional army troops and national guardsmen to supplement his police force. Not surprisingly, clashes, some of which were quite violent and involved clubs and tear gas, occurred between the demonstrators and the police, troops, and guardsmen sent in to try to keep order.

One after another of the Chicago Eight was arrested during the course of convention week for various acts of defiance. Hoffman encouraged demonstrators to hold the park and engage in violence against the police. Hayden let the air out of the tires of a police car and, along with Dellinger, Seale, and Davis, told a crowd of fifteen thousand to "make sure that if blood is going to flow, let it flow all over the city." Davis encouraged demonstrators to "fight the pigs." Seale made a speech advocating violence against the police. Rubin incited a crowd to "Kill the pigs! Kill the cops!" And Weiner and Froines attempted to organize the use of Molotov cocktails against the police. In light of their activities, the government contended that the Chicago Eight's antics were designed to incite the thousands who had gathered there to riot.

Five of the codefendants were charged under a newly enacted law—the Anti-Riot Act of 1968—"with making certain speeches for the purposes of inciting, organizing, promoting, and encouraging a riot." Two of the codefendants "were charged with teaching the use of an incendiary device," and all eight were charged with conspiracy to commit these offenses. On 20 March 1969 a grand jury returned indictments as charged against all of them. The trial commenced in Chicago on 24 September 1969 in the federal courtroom of the seventy-four-year-old Hoffman. From the beginning of the case, it was clear that Hoffman did not hold either the defendants or their attorneys in high regard. For example, of the defendants' fifty-four proposed questions for the potential jurors—a process known as voir dire, wherein parties are able to ascertain whether a potential juror should be excluded for bias—Hoffman allowed only one: "Are you or do you have any close friends or relatives who are employed by any law enforcement agencies?" The defendants had sought to ask the jurors, in an effort to ascertain their "cultural biases," such questions as "Do you know who Janis Joplin and Jimi Hendrix are?" and "If your children are female, do they wear brassieres all the time?" The U.S. Court of Appeals for the Seventh Circuit would later cite Hoffman's decision limiting defendants' voir dire questions as reversible error.

Eventually, two white men, two black women, and eight white women were empanelled as jurors. As indicated by their post-verdict remarks, the jurors clearly were biased against the defendants. One female juror stated that the defendants "should be convicted for their appearance, their language and their lifestyle," while another juror stated that the defendants "should have been shot down by the police."

Another example of Hoffman's lack of tolerance for the defendants was exemplified by his ordering that the defendant Bobby Seale be bound and gagged because of his repeated outbursts during the course of the trial, demanding representation by a lawyer of his own choosing. This action ultimately led to the severance of Seale's case from the other seven on 5 November 1969. Seale was tried separately for contempt of court, but his trial also took place before Judge Hoffman, who sentenced Seale to four years in prison for contempt. This sentence and conviction, however, were overturned by the Court of Appeals.

Thereafter the Chicago Eight became known as the Chicago Seven. The trial, of course, was unusual, but not just because of its political nature and the demeanor of the defendants, who at times would make faces to the jurors, blow them kisses, and even, on at least one occasion, bring a bag of marijuana to court. The witnesses for the defendants were some of the best-known names of the American counterculture scene. They included the Harvard LSD advocate Timothy Leary; the poet Allen Ginsberg; the folksingers Phil Ochs, Arlo Guthrie, "Country Joe" McDonald, Pete Seeger, Judy Collins; and even the author Norman Mailer.

As the trial came to a close, Hoffman became increasingly intolerant of the defendants' courtroom demeanor, issuing forty-eight contempt citations to them and their attorneys in one two-week period alone. Hoffman ultimately would issue 159 criminal contempt citations for such acts as failing to stand when he entered the courtroom, blowing kisses to the jury, and calling Hoffman a "liar," "hypocrite," and "fascist dog." The Court of Appeals later reversed all the contempt citations, stating that the defendants (which now included the defendants' attorneys) were entitled to a jury trial on the contempt citations. Finally, on 14 February 1970 the jury began its deliberations, and four days later, on 18 February 1970, they found five of the defendants—Davis, Dellinger, Hayden, Hoffman, and Rubin—guilty of violating the Anti-Riot Act. Sentencing took place on 20 February 1970. Froines and Weiner were acquitted of the charge of teaching the use of an incendiary device.

In the era before federal sentencing guidelines, judges had virtually unbridled discretion to sentence defendants to any term of imprisonment they felt was just, up to the maximum provided by law. Not surprisingly, given his contempt for the defendants and finding "that the defendants are clearly dangerous persons to be at large," Hoffman sentenced each of them to the maximum term: five years' imprisonment plus a $5,000 fine. The defendants, of course, appealed. On 21 November 1972, in a lengthy opinion, a three-judge panel of the U.S. Circuit Court of Appeals for the Seventh Circuit reversed all of the Chicago Seven's convictions. (On 5 March 1973 the U.S. Supreme Court declined to hear the government's appeal of the reversal.) Among the reasons cited by the appellate court for reversing the defendants' convictions was Hoffman's "deprecatory and often antagonistic attitude toward the defense." The appellate court stated that "there are high standards for the conduct of judges and prosecutors, and impropriety by persons before the court does not give license to depart from those standards."

The appellate court found that Hoffman had departed from these standards "from the very beginning" and "in the presence and absence of the jury." According to the appellate court, the most significant problem with Hoffman's courtroom demeanor was his "remarks in the presence of the jury, [which were] deprecatory of defense counsel and their case." The appellate court argued that cumulatively, Hoffman's comments "must have telegraphed to the jury the judge's contempt for the defense." Ironically, then, the trial of the Chicago Seven served not to limit the speech and protestations of a generation but to reassess the standards of courtroom decorum.

For information on the Chicago Seven trial, see Anthony J. Lukas, *The Barnyard Epithet and Other Obscenities: Notes on the Chicago Conspiracy Trial* (1970). An obituary is in the *New York Times* (2 July 1983).

MARK ALLENBAUGH

HOFSTADTER, Richard (*b.* 6 August 1916 in Buffalo, New York; *d.* 24 October 1970 in New York City), cultural intellectual historian whose work in the 1960s explored conflicts both within the United States and within its historiography, and preserved the concept of free inquiry against the turmoil of the period.

One of two children of a Polish-born secular Jewish father, Emil A. Hofstadter, a furrier, and a Protestant German-American mother, Katherine Hill, he was baptized a Lutheran. His mother died when he was ten, and his maternal grandmother brought him up as an Episcopalian. Hofstadter was educated at the University of Buffalo, where he was mentored by the historian Julius Pratt. He graduated in 1937. He briefly attended the New York School of Law and then transferred as a history major to Columbia University, where he earned an M.A. degree in 1938 and a Ph.D. in 1942. His dissertation, *Social Darwinism in Amer-*

Richard Hofstadter. AP/WIDE WORLD PHOTOS

ican Thought, 1860–1915 (1944), was published and won the American Historical Association's Albert J. Beveridge Award.

Hofstadter went to New York City with Felice Swados, a bright fellow University of Buffalo student who later graduated from Smith College. She was from a prominent Buffalo Jewish family and was the sister of the poet Harvey Swados. Hofstadter and Felice married in 1936 and had a son. Felice worked for *Time* magazine and was immersed in the vibrant political life of the Communist Party. Hofstadter also joined a Communist group at Columbia but grew disenchanted with its regimented beliefs and drifted away from the party by 1940. Hofstadter and his wife became part of the community of Jewish intellectuals. Alfred Kazin called Hofstadter "the most charming fellow he had ever met."

Following teaching positions at Brooklyn College of the City University of New York and at the University of Maryland, Hofstadter came back to New York City in 1945. The Alfred A. Knopf publishing house gave him a fellowship to work on a new book. This allowed him to devote attention to his wife, who was stricken with cancer and died in that year. He worked sporadically on his book, which was published in 1948 as *The American Political Tradition and the Men Who Made It*. The book was a great success, both critically and financially. It is rated by Modern Library as one of the one hundred most influential nonfiction books of the twentieth century. Hofstadter married again on 13 January 1947, this time to Beatrice Kevitt of Buffalo. They had a daughter.

In 1946 Hofstadter began teaching at Columbia University, where he would remain for rest of his life. Hofstadter's career blossomed, as did his writing. His new wife devoted herself to editing his material, and he was immensely pleased with the result. He prided himself as a writer who melded the other social sciences with historical study and was able to do so without the semantics of other disciplines. Ideas and interpretation took precedence over facts for their own sake. Hofstadter was more interested in developing broad concepts. His work became provocative and dominant as he reexamined the work of historians who had founded the base of professional thought on American development. He attacked the agrarian/frontier concepts of Frederick Jackson Turner, the capitalistic monolithic politics of Charles Beard, and the notions of Vernon Louis Parrington that American progressivism was a product of the Midwest. By the 1960s Hofstadter was an established giant in the field of history. *The Age of Reform: From Bryan to F.D.R.* (1955) won a Pulitzer Prize and charged ideas of agrarian nostalgia and stilted nineteenth-century morality as being unable to understand the urban and industrial society that followed 1890. His work was designed to attract a public as well as an academic audience.

The life of the mind and the freedom of ideas were compelling concerns of Hofstadter. He reacted to the assaults on academia during the 1950s, when Senator Joseph McCarthy led a government effort to rid American society of Communists, by collaborating on education histories of the growth of academic freedom in 1952 and 1955, and in *American Higher Education: A Documentary History,* a two-volume work published in 1961. His controversial *Anti-Intellectualism in American Life* followed in 1963, and again he won the Pulitzer Prize. This provocative work offered the trenchant view that intellectuals were not appreciated in the course of American political history. Hofstadter argued that democratic and egalitarian foundations of the United States actually contributed to the alienation and the distrust of intellectuals. He declared that mass education and emphasis on technical education came at the expense of the mind and eroded the values of the old patrician elite. Hofstadter can be seen here as the intellectual mentor to the American historian and social critic Christopher Lasch, whose intellectual breadth and depth are perhaps most derivative of Hofstadter.

The 1960s were Hofstadter's most prolific years. He wrote *The Progressive Historians: Turner, Beard, Parrington* (1968); *The Idea of a Party System: The Rise of Legitimate Opposition in the United States, 1780–1840* (1969); and a book of controversial essays entitled *The Paranoid Style in American Politics and Other Essays* (1965). In this work, which was part of a lecture in 1962, he examined conspiracy theories. He saw them as related to a crusading mentality that held the notion that all ills could be traced to single evil sources that could be eliminated. Failure to heed the warnings soon enough meant society was finished. The world confronts an apocalypse akin to that mentioned in the Book of Revelation. Hofstadter called this "the rhetoric of the dispossessed." Characteristic of this element was not the absence of facts but rather what he termed "the curious leap of imagination that is made at some critical point in the recital of events."

Hofstadter's thinking was keyed to conflict in history. The clash of ideas and forces excited his writing, and in the 1960s he became more daring as he suggested that the negative impulses in American development—agrarian hostility to the city, racism, anti-Semitism, antiliberalism, parochial anti-intellectualism, and cultural ethnocentrism—were the products of the very environment that produced the idea of democracy. This contradiction engaged him while it often enraged his critics. Hofstadter created an urban view and understanding of American history in which the culture of the city was made both directly and inferentially significant in the making of national life. He suggested that the same environment that produced the American politician Robert La Follette and admirable progressive politics also produced Senator Joseph McCarthy and his assault on the life of the mind.

Hofstadter's histories are beholden to Charles Beard. He inherited that great historian's place in the profession and in the university that had the temerity to dismiss Beard, who refused to compromise academic freedom by recanting his political opinions. Here lay an irony that Hofstadter must have relished, given his championship of the freedom of thought in the university. His work on Beard represented something of historical patricide, for he sought both to demolish and to venerate Beard. Like Beard, he saw history as though under a glass rather than as a physical reality.

Hofstadter's insular view of events was never more exposed than in 1968, when civil rights, free speech, and antiwar issues swept college campuses. Columbia became a sorry example of the weakness of academic institutions; its faculty and administrators meekly surrendered both their offices and their integrity and trooped off the campus to the chorus of taunts and jibes of the raging students who took over the buildings. To save something of themselves, the school, and the community of the mind, Columbia's administration turned to Hofstadter to give the 1968 commencement address. He was the only faculty member ever to be given this task. For Hofstadter, who was shy and retiring when it came to public addresses, it was not a welcome assignment.

Perhaps Hofstadter guessed he was selected to bridge his assessment of radical ideas and conflict of the past with the reality of the radical action of the present. The most raucous and rebellious students marched from the auditorium before he gave his address. Their actions did not distract him from his ivory tower discourse on the university as a peculiar and unique institution dedicated to serve as the "citadel of intellectual individualism." He was, in effect, speaking of himself in his declaration that the university encouraged an independence of the intellect that served society as "an intellectual and spiritual balance wheel." The university was a retreat, a sanctuary of the mind where ideas would always be respected.

In the same year Hofstader wrote a piece on violence for the *New York Times* in which he posed the argument of America as a violent society and one that decried violence but could not bring itself to control the use of its instruments. He cited D. H. Lawrence's comment on the American soul as being "hard, isolate, stoic, and a killer." The deaths by assassination of Senator Robert F. Kennedy and the Reverend Martin Luther King, Jr., left society with a cry against violence but a paralysis in action. This fatalistic view of description over prescription of historical events encouraged the American historian Arthur Schlesinger, Jr.'s succinct statement that the permanence of Hofstadter's "historical writing will rest rather in the grace, subtlety, and elegance of his literary style. History, to Hofstadter, was always a part of literature."

Toward the close of his life, while suffering from leukemia, Hofstadter continued working. He collaborated on *American Violence: A Documentary History* (1970) and negotiated a contract for a three-volume history of the United States, the first volume of which was published as he left it: *America at 1750: A Social Portrait* (1971). The disruptive events of the 1960s were discouraging to Hofstadter, who in an interview with *Newsweek* (6 July 1970) declared his time to be the "age of rubbish." This was a denouement that did not discourage fellow historians from declaring his to be "the finest . . . most humane historical intelligence of our generation."

Hofstadter died of leukemia. His obituary in the *New York Times,* although generally complimentary, described him as a man of regular habits, scrupulous discipline, and insulated temperament who "went through life with a contained methodicalness that might dull a less lively intelligence." It characterized him as "a blue-eyed, graying, almost nondescript man who wore clip-on bow ties and was constantly hitching up his trousers." Further, it described Hofstadter as having limited social flair but a decided talent for mimicry. A protest was voiced by Hofstadter's colleague Lionel Trilling, who in an unusual letter to the *Times* insisted that Hofstadter was anything but nondescript or limited in social flair. Speaking for his colleagues, Trilling declared Hofstadter "one of the most clearly defined persons I have ever known. . . . An enchanting companion, often memorably funny . . . open not only to ideas but to people of all kinds." He argued that the obituary possessed a "grudging quality" that should be ignored and attention paid instead to the photograph accompanying it. He declared the photograph an accurate representation of "this remarkable man's grace and charm and luminosity of spirit." The photograph shows Hofstadter with full dark hair and obviously much younger than his fifty-four years.

★

Biographical works include Lawrence A. Cremin, *Richard Hofstadter (1916-1970): A Biographical Memoir* (1972); Stanley Elkins and Eric McKitrick, eds., *The Hofstadter Aegis: A Memorial* (1974); and Susan Stout Baker, *Radical Beginnings: Richard Hofstadter and the 1930s* (1985). See also Christopher Lasch, "On Richard Hofstadter," *New York Review of Books* (8 Mar. 1972), as well as Lasch's introduction to the fiftieth-anniversary edition of *The American Political Tradition and the Men Who Made It* (1998). Essays on Hofstadter include Arthur M. Schlesinger, Jr., "Richard Hofstadter," in *Pastmasters: Some Essays on American Historians,* edited by Marcus Cunliffe and Robin Winks (1969); and Daniel Joseph Singal, "Beyond Consensus: Richard Hofstadter and American Historiography," *American Historical Review* 89 (1984). See also Alfred Kazin, *Starting Out in the Thirties* (1965), and also Kazin on Hofstadter in *American Scholar* 40 (1970–1971). See Richard Hofstadter, "Spontaneous, Sporadic, and Disorganized," *New York Times* (28 Apr. 1968). An obituary is in the *New York Times* (25 Oct. 1970). Lionel Trilling's letter of response is in the *New York Times* (5 Nov. 1970).

JACK J. CARDOSO

HOFSTADTER, Robert (*b.* 5 February 1915 in New York City; *d.* 17 November 1990 in Stanford, California), Stanford University physics professor who successfully applied atom-smashing technology to study the structure and size of nuclear particles.

Hofstadter was the third of four children of Louis Hofstadter, a salesman, and Henrietta Koenigsberg. After attending elementary and secondary schools in New York City, Hofstadter attended the College of the City of New York (now City University of New York). Despite an early interest in philosophy, he elected to major in physics and earned a B.S. from City College in 1935.

Hofstadter distinguished himself early in his academic career. He graduated magna cum laude and was honored further with the Kenyon Prize for mathematics and physics. He then completed a postgraduate program at Princeton University, focusing his doctoral research on the infrared spectra of organic molecules. After earning an M.A. and a Ph.D. in 1938, he remained at Princeton through 1939, funded by a Proctor Fellowship. Hofstadter's postdoctoral research was an investigation of the photoconductivity of crystals. He was awarded a Harrison Fellowship to continue his work at the University of Pennsylvania and also served as an instructor there. Hofstadter later taught at the College of the City of New York. He married Nancy Givan on 9 May 1942. They had three children, including a son Douglas, a physicist who won a Pulitzer Prize for nonfiction in 1980.

During World War II Hofstadter worked at the National Bureau of Standards in Washington, D.C., developing a proximity fuse for bomb detonation. He also worked at Norden Laboratory Corporation but returned to Princeton as an associate professor after the war. There, in 1948, he built the first sodium iodide thallium scintillator.

In 1950 Hofstadter accepted a position at Stanford University in California, where a version of W. W. Hansen's linear accelerator (atom smasher) was under construction. Hofstadter, through his experiments with the Stanford atom smasher, achieved a new level of understanding in his study of the structure of the highly dense neutrons and protons at the atomic core of all matter. By 1957 he had successfully measured and recorded the diameter of neutron and proton particles. In these tests he used gold, lead, tantalum, and beryllium atoms.

Hofstadter's ongoing research was funded in 1958 and 1959 by a Guggenheim Fellowship. Additionally, he was elected to the National Academy of Sciences in 1958 and was named California scientist of the year in 1959. His many contributions to scientific journalism included a sojourn as associate editor of the *Physical Review* in the early 1950s and his work on the editorial board of the *Review of Scientific Instruments*. He served on the board of *Reviews of Modern Physics* from 1958 to 1961, and beginning with the publication of "High-Energy Electron Energy Scattering Tables" in 1960, published numerous writings in which he discussed his experimental findings.

In April 1961 Hofstadter formally presented his conclusions on nuclear structures in a speech before the American Physical Society. At that time he described the size and structure of neutrons and protons. Each of these particle types, he revealed, consists of a highly dense and positively charged core. The core, with a density that is 130 trillion times that of water, is surrounded by a soft, cloudlike layer of particles called mesons. In the case of protons, the cloudy meson layer is positively charged, augmenting the charge on the dense inner core of the particle and resulting in a net positive charge. The outer meson layer of the neutron particle is negatively charged, a characteristic that serves to cancel the positive charge of the dense core of the neutron, resulting in a net charge of zero for this type of particle. Hofstadter further reported that both types of nuclear particles are similar in size, with neutrons and protons alike measuring 3×10^{-14} inches in diameter (.00000000000003 in.). He likened the dense core and cloudlike outer layer of the nuclear particles to a peach pit surrounded by pulpy fruit.

These particles, because they are smaller than light waves and therefore too small to reflect light rays, are therefore too small to see, even under magnification. Hofstadter surmounted this problem by using the atom smasher to scatter the nuclear particles. By bombarding the scattered particles with electrons and measuring the angle of deflection of the electrons, he calculated the size and density of the smaller particles. Thus, Hofstadter's discoveries are significant not only because of the data he collected, but also because he explained this method for measuring the subatomic neutrons and protons. Furthermore, as the accuracy and power of the atom-smashing machines improved with time, Hofstadter's nuclear measurements became more precise.

On 10 December 1961 he was awarded a Nobel Prize for physics with Dr. Rudolf Ludwig Mossbauer of the California Institute of Technology, who successfully created recoil-free gamma rays. The two scientists shared a prize of $48,300. Hofstadter's Nobel lecture, in which he described the substance of his research, was delivered 11 December 1961, and was titled "The Electron-Scattering Method and Its Application to the Structure of Nuclei and Nucleons."

In 1962 Hofstadter's alma mater, the City College of New York, honored him with the Townsend Harris Medal. His book, *Electron Scattering and Nuclear and Nucleon Structure*, was published by Stanford University in 1963. This volume is made up of a collection of articles pertinent to Hofstadter's prize-winning research, including several of his own papers, among them "Scattering of High-Energy Electrons and the Method of Nuclear Recoil" and "High Energy Electron Scattering and Nuclear Structure Determinations."

Esteemed as a researcher and a scientist, Hofstadter was likeable and personable and also earned respect for his skills as a teacher and academic. Among the many courses that he taught during his career was a class geared toward liberal arts students called "Physics for Poets."

Hofstadter, who became a full professor at Stanford in 1954, was named director of the Stanford High Energy Physics Laboratory in 1967, a position he held until 1974. He continued at Stanford until his retirement in 1985. Hofstadter died of heart disease.

★

There is no full-length biography of Hofstadter. In-depth profiles appear in H. W. Wilson Co., *Current Biography Yearbook* (1962), and Gale Group, *Notable Scientists* (2001). For more information on his work, see Hofstadter's Nobel lecture, "The Electron-Scattering Method and Its Application to the Structure of Nuclei and Nucleons" (11 Dec. 1961).

GLORIA COOKSEY

HOLLEY, Robert William (*b.* 28 January 1922 in Urbana, Illinois; *d.* 11 February 1993 in Los Gatos, California), biochemist who in 1965 completed the sequencing of the first transfer RNA molecule and in 1968 was a co-winner of the Nobel Prize in physiology or medicine.

Holley was one of four sons born to Charles Elmer and Viola Esther (Wolfe) Holley. Both of his parents were teachers. In 1942 Holley received a B.A. in chemistry from the University of Illinois in Urbana. Five years later he earned a Ph.D. in organic chemistry from Cornell University in Ithaca, New York. During World War II, Holley participated as a civilian in war research conducted at the United States Office of Research and Development. Between 1944 and 1946 he was part of the research team at Cornell that was the first to produce synthetic penicillin. Holley married Ann Lenore Dworkin, a math teacher, on 3 March 1945; they had one son.

In 1948, after a year of postdoctoral work at Washington State College (later Washington State University) in Pullman, Holley returned to Cornell and became an assistant professor at the New York State Agricultural Experiment Station in Geneva. From 1950 to 1957 Holley was an associate professor at the same facility. In 1955 he took a sabbatical as a Guggenheim Memorial Fellow at the California Institute of Technology in Pasadena. While there, Holley began studying protein synthesis and became interested in how the information in nucleic acids is translated into proteins.

The scientific community's interest in nucleic acids intensified in the 1950s following Alfred Hershey's 1952 experiment confirming deoxyribonucleic acid (DNA) as the hereditary material. The following year, James Watson and Francis Crick solved the mystery of the DNA molecule's structure, and the era of genetics truly began. At the end of his sabbatical, Holley began researching receptors for amino acids, the building blocks of proteins. He discovered that the amino acid alanine binds to what at the time was known as low-molecular-weight soluble ribonucleic acid (RNA). This molecule was later called transfer RNA (tRNA).

Intrigued by this discovery, Holley continued his research upon his return to Cornell in 1957; at that time he worked for the U.S. Plant, Soil, and Nutrition Laboratory, a U.S. Department of Agriculture laboratory at Cornell. The first challenge for Holley and his colleagues was to try to isolate pure tRNA that was amino acid specific. Proteins are a combination of any of twenty amino acids, and there are twenty different tRNA molecules, each specific to one of these amino acids. Holley used yeast RNA, because it was easy to obtain in large quantities. Four years after they started, Holley and his colleagues were satisfied that they had a method good enough to isolate individual tRNAs for alanine, tyrosine, and valine. Of these, the alanine tRNA was the purest, and the decision was made to use it for structural analysis. Interestingly, with so little knowledge of the molecule, Holley and his team could not be sure that the material was indeed as pure as they thought. In his 1968 Nobel lecture, Holley recounted, "There seemed no alternative but to gamble a few years of work on the problem hoping that the material was sufficiently pure for structural analysis." Fortunately, Holley's gamble paid off.

Since both molecular biology and genetics were in their infancy in the early 1960s, Holley's task was momentous. The technique he perfected in his lab for obtaining pure alanine tRNA gave very low yields of the material. Over the next three years, Holley and his team used 140 kilograms (308.65 pounds) of commercial baker's yeast to obtain 1 gram (0.0035 ounce) of pure alanine tRNA. The experiments they carried out to sequence the molecule were described by Holley as being "equivalent to breaking a sentence into words, identifying the words, and reconstructing the sequence of the letters in the sentence by de-

Robert William Holley. THE LIBRARY OF CONGRESS

termining the order of the words." By the end of 1964 Holley's team had completed the sequencing of alanine tRNA, having dedicated roughly nine years to this project from start to finish. Through the sequencing analysis, Holley also was able to show how alanine attached to its tRNA molecule.

After the confirmation that DNA was the hereditary material, scientists struggled to understand how the information coded in DNA was translated into proteins—the complex molecules that make up all living things and differentiate between various living organisms. Crick suggested that "adaptor molecules" were responsible for translating DNA into proteins. In 1961 Sydney Brenner, François Jacob, and Matthew Meselson discovered that messenger RNA (mRNA) is the molecule that takes DNA's code outside the cell nucleus into the cytoplasm, where protein synthesis can occur.

Holley's discovery of tRNA's specificity and its sequence was the next step in a rapid deciphering of the genetics of protein synthesis. Holley's colleague Elizabeth Keller used the sequence to figure out the cloverleaf structure of tRNA, a model she sent to Holley in a Christmas card, according to Cornell legend. For this contribution to his efforts Holley shared his Nobel Prize money with her. By 1968, when Holley received his Nobel Prize in physiology or medicine with Marshall Warren Nirenberg, and Har Gobind Khorana, the genetic code had been deciphered completely. Scientists knew which amino acids were coded by which three-base combination on the DNA molecule. They knew how the DNA was translated to RNA and how RNA facilitated the assembly of proteins. Holley's contribution was a large piece of that puzzle, made all the more impressive because he tackled the problem from scratch, creating the tools for his discovery as he went along.

In 1966 Holley spent another sabbatical in California, this time at the Salk Institute for Biological Studies and the Scripps Clinic and Research Foundation in La Jolla. While there, he moved on to the next phase of his career and began looking into mechanisms that control cell growth and division. Holley sequenced several compounds that controlled or inhibited cell growth. His work provided insights that proved useful in the understanding of cancer, and pharmaceutical companies were able to use his results to create better cancer treatments. In 1968 Holley joined the Salk Institute as a resident fellow, also becoming an adjunct professor at the University of California, San Diego. He remained at the Salk Institute until his death in 1993. Holley was the recipient of many awards, including the prestigious Albert Lasker Award in basic medical research, which he won in 1965. He died of lung cancer at his home in Los Gatos.

The 1960s saw an explosion of knowledge and discovery in genetics. In an amazingly short time scientists moved to learning not only how the DNA code was translated into actual proteins but also how to read the code. Holley's discovery was a huge contribution to our ever increasing knowledge of genetics in the 1960s. That alone would have been enough, but not satisfied, Holley moved on (in the late 1960s) to studying cell growth and increased our understanding and knowledge in the area of cancer medicine and pharmacology. In both areas Holley's influence extended from the 1960s to the present day.

★

Biographical essays on Holley are in *Encyclopedia Britannica* (1997) and *Notable Scientists: From 1900 to the Present* (2001). Obituaries are in the *New York Times* (14 Feb. 1993) and the *Times* (London) (16 Feb. 1993).

ADI R. FERRARA

HOLT, John Caldwell (*b.* 14 April 1923 in New York City; *d.* 14 September 1985 in Boston, Massachusetts), critic and reformer of the U.S. educational system, whose books *How Children Fail* (1964) and *How Children Learn* (1967) won him a national audience.

The only son of Henry Holt, an insurance executive, and Elizabeth Crocker, Holt grew up amidst wealth. His education took place in exclusive private schools: Le Rosey in Switzerland, Phillips Exeter Academy in New Hampshire (1936–1938), and, later, Yale College (1939–1943), from which he graduated with a B.S. in industrial engineering. During World War II, Holt served as a junior officer on a U.S. Navy submarine in the Pacific and won a combat ribbon.

After returning to civilian life in 1946, Holt moved to New York City. Soon afterward, he went to work for the United World Federalists, a group devoted to establishing one world government. He quit abruptly in 1952, however, due to the fear that the group might become a target of rising anticommunist sentiment. Holt traveled in Europe for about a year, then worked as a teacher in a succession of schools.

At Colorado Rocky Mountain School in Carbondale, Colorado (1953–1957), Holt taught high school English, French, and mathematics, and coached soccer and baseball. He soon grew weary of what he later described as the school's neglect of students who performed poorly, so in 1957 he took a job as a fifth-grade teacher at Shady Hill School in Cambridge, Massachusetts. Holt's style of teaching, which emphasized understanding over rote memorization, earned him a dismissal in 1959, whereupon he went to work at Lesley Ellis School in Cambridge. Once again, he taught fifth grade, but he also concerned himself with redesigning the entire elementary mathematics curriculum in line with his idea that students should not merely memorize but truly learn. He also began to teach reading to students in the first and second grades.

Holt gained national prominence with the publication of *How Children Fail* in 1964. The book, on one level a chronicle of his experiences at Shady Hill and Lesley Ellis, is in fact a withering critique of the entire U.S. educational system. Teachers and school administrators, Holt maintained, cared more for the appearance of learning rather than for actual learning. Thus, they were content to force students to commit abstract facts and figures to memory, then regurgitate these on tests—a system that, in Holt's view, was quite literally mind-numbing. "It is a rare child," according to one passage in *How Children Fail,* "who can come through his schooling with much left of his curiosity, his independence, or his sense of his own dignity, competence, and worth."

The book won acclaim from many educators for its brutally honest appraisal of education in the United States, and Holt found himself in demand as a lecturer, and even as a consultant to school systems. At the same time, he continued to teach, taking a position as a high school English teacher at Commonwealth School in Boston.

How Children Learn (1967), as its title suggests, is something of a companion piece to Holt's earlier work, this one focusing on hopes for the future rather than condemnation of past abuses. In the book, Holt called for smaller classes, for individualized instruction, and for greater student control over the learning process.

His fame and influence now at its peak, Holt in 1968 served as visiting lecturer at the Harvard University Graduate School of Education, and in 1969 as visiting lecturer at the University of California, Berkeley. Also in 1969, he founded an educational consulting firm, Holt Associates, and published *The Underachieving School* (1969).

Even as he became more established and influential, Holt's views on education became more radical. By the early 1970s, schools had attempted some measure of reform, but for Holt the pace was too slow, and he began calling for what he described as a "de-schooled society in which learning is not separated from but is integrated with the rest of life." What this meant, in sum, was the complete eradication of the existing educational system.

After 1969, Holt's success permitted him to quit teaching, but for the remaining sixteen years of his life he stayed very busy, as he described it, "writing, reading, lecturing, playing the cello, working on large issues confronting society." He also wrote a number of books: *What Do I Do Monday?* (1970), *Freedom and Beyond* (1972), *Escape from Childhood* (1974), *Instead of Education: Ways to Help People Do Things Better* (1976), *Never Too Late: A Musical Autobiography* (1978), *Teach Your Own: A Hopeful Path for Education* (1981), and *Learning All the Time* (1989).

From 1977 to the time of his death in 1985, Holt published a newsletter, *Growing Without Schooling,* which had more than 5,000 readers. He also contributed regularly to magazines on education and home schooling. True to his beliefs about personal education, he continued to teach himself new skills: French and Italian at the age of thirty, skiing a year later, cello at age forty, water skiing at forty-seven, horseback riding a year after that, and violin at age sixty. He never married. Holt died of cancer and is buried in Boston.

In evaluating Holt's contribution, it is necessary to do so with the awareness that much of what changed in U.S. education during the 1960s was not an improvement. At the beginning of that decade, the average American student could easily discuss, or at least recognize or identify, topics from classical antiquity, whereas by the end of the 1970s, few students even had a grasp of twentieth-century history and culture. How much of this regression was a result of radical theories such as Holt's, or perhaps the misapplication of those theories, is open to question.

On the other hand, Holt's critique of education was unmistakably a blast of fresh air at the time, and one might well argue that the greatest problem with education in the United States is that schools have not applied his ideas thoroughly enough. Certainly Holt, in the latter part of his career, found himself with a new and growing group of supporters who, like him, challenged the very legitimacy of the U.S. educational system. These new rebels were not teachers but parents, and their politics was not leftist but conservative; like Holt, however, members of the home schooling movement sought to flee what they perceived as the sinking ship of U.S. education.

★

Holt's own works—most notably the autobiographical *How Children Fail* (1964; rev. ed. 1982), and *Never Too Late: A Musical Autobiography* (1978)—provide the best possible starting place for a study of the man and his ideas. Also extremely useful is Susannah Sheffer, ed., *Selected Letters of John Holt* (1990). Analyses of Holt's effect on U.S. education can be found in Diane Ravitch, *The Troubled Crusade: American Education, 1945–1980* (1983); *Urban Education* 19 (Oct. 1984): 227–244; and *Mothering* 61 (22 Sept. 1991). An obituary is in the *New York Times* (16 Sept. 1985).

JUDSON KNIGHT

HOOVER, J(ohn) Edgar (*b.* 1 January 1895 in Washington, D.C.; *d.* 2 May 1972 in Washington, D.C.), first director of the Federal Bureau of Investigation (FBI) who in the 1960s presided over aggressive counterintelligence operations targeting civil rights leaders, high-ranking government officials, and members of the Mafia.

The youngest of four children, Hoover was the son of Dickerson Naylor Hoover, the head of the printing division of the U.S. Coast and Geodetic Survey, and Annie Marie Scheitlinr, a homemaker. At an early age Hoover attended the Church of the Reformation and, as a teenager, the Old First Presbyterian Church, where he acquired strong religious convictions. The single greatest influence in his life, however, was his mother, with whom he lived until her death in 1929.

At Washington's Central High School, Hoover overcame a speech impediment so he could perform on the debate team. He also commanded a squad of Reserve Officers Training Corps (ROTC) cadets and graduated as the valedictorian of his class in 1913. That autumn he enrolled at George Washington University, earning an LL.B. in 1916 and an LL.M. in 1917 in legal jurisprudence, while working as a librarian at the Library of Congress. After dating in high school and later socializing with celebrities at New York City's Stork Club, Hoover spent most of his free time with his confidant Clyde A. Tolson, the associate director of the FBI. During Hoover's lifetime, he had no serious relationships with the opposite sex, giving rise to innuendo and rumor that he was a homosexual.

Hoover began his government career as a clerk with the Alien Enemy Bureau in the U.S. Justice Department on 26 July 1917. Putting his experience at the Library of Congress into practice, Hoover and his administrative skills caught the eye of the assistant attorney general, who recommended that Hoover be promoted. As the chief of the General Intelligence Division, Hoover compiled files on suspected radicals. Those suspects, mostly European immigrants, were the targets of a nationwide Justice Department dragnet on 19 November 1919, the climatic culmination of a phenomenon in U.S. history known as the Red Scare.

Hoover served as the assistant director of the Bureau of Investigation (the agency was renamed the Federal Bureau of Investigation [FBI] in 1935) from 1921 to 1924. On 10 May 1924 the attorney general appointed Hoover as the bureau's director, a post he held for forty-eight years. Hoover and his law enforcement officers gained notoriety when G-men (government men), as his agents came to be known, gunned down the notorious killers John Dillinger and Charles "Pretty Boy" Floyd in 1934. The bureau also received sensational publicity with the arrests of Bruno Richard Hauptmann for kidnapping the son of Charles Lindbergh in 1935, and of Ethel and Julius Rosenberg for espionage in 1950.

The FBI's improprieties during the 1960s can be traced largely to intensified national security concerns in the aftermath of World War II and the cold war, which broadened the bureau's jurisdiction and greatly increased Hoover's authority. A staunch anticommunist, Hoover detested demonstrations and deplored civil disobedience; he believed student activism and the civil rights movement constituted part of a worldwide Communist conspiracy to incite revolution and dominate the United States politically and militarily.

Racial unrest in America's cities, student protests against the Vietnam War, and the militant, antiestablishment rhetoric of the New Left only reinforced Hoover's beliefs. To infiltrate and neutralize the Communist Party in the United States, Hoover launched a counterintelligence program (COINTELPRO) beginning in 1957. During the 1960s the FBI sponsored a counterintelligence campaign of Orwellian proportions that included wiretappings, burglaries, mail tampering, propaganda, and electronic surveillance, all with Hoover's approval.

The bureau chief's relationship with the administration of President John F. Kennedy in the early 1960s was a troubled one. Convinced that the civil rights leader Dr. Martin Luther King, Jr., was a Communist puppet, Hoover attempted to persuade the president to distance himself from King and deny him access to the White House. Within months after Kennedy was sworn into office in January 1961, a power struggle ensued between the aging Hoover and Attorney General Robert Kennedy, the president's brother, over the decision to wiretap King's conversations.

After voicing his concerns to the president regarding

J. Edgar Hoover. ARCHIVE PHOTOS, INC.

King, Hoover placed the president and the attorney general under surveillance. From Hoover, Kennedy learned that his lover Judith Campbell Exner was also the mistress of the reputed Chicago crime boss Sam Giancana. Prior to the ominous newspaper headlines in November 1957 of the Apalachin Conference, a nationwide conclave of Mafia figures, Hoover refused to acknowledge the Mafia's existence in the United States. By 1961, however, under the leadership of Robert Kennedy, the FBI began pursuing and disrupting the sordid business interests of the crime syndicate, resulting in numerous indictments, deportations, and convictions, the most noteworthy of which was the arrest of the teamster boss Jimmy Hoffa in 1964.

After Lyndon B. Johnson ordered an investigation of the FBI, Hoover's obsession with protecting the agency's image led to a cover-up of crucial evidence exposing Kennedy's assassin Lee Harvey Oswald as a security risk prior to the president's visit to Dallas on 22 November 1963. With Johnson's presidency came a period of accommodation and mutual understanding, even though Hoover believed the Texan to be politically naive. When Johnson ordered the FBI to investigate the Ku Klux Klan in the aftermath of the murder of three civil rights workers near Philadelphia, Mississippi, in June 1964, Hoover virtually declared war on America's hate groups in the Deep South. So pernicious was the FBI's diabolical plan of misinformation aimed at the Black Panther Party that the militant leadership's induced paranoia caused a lethal power struggle to erupt within the organization. Carefully planted informants, constant surveillance, and harassment drove the Students for a Democratic Society, the radical Weathermen, and the New Left in general underground. Befriending Johnson, Hoover even loaned the president tape recordings that Johnson used to entertain White House guests of King partying with female guests in a motel room.

Hoover's most flagrant violation of the law occurred when President Richard M. Nixon ordered him to blackmail liberal members of the U.S. Supreme Court in an attempt to tilt the high court in the conservative direction. One casualty of the FBI investigation was Justice Abe Fortas, who resigned in May 1969 in the midst of a congressional inquiry. According to Nixon, Hoover's refusal to authorize a full-scale investigation of the reporter Daniel Ellsberg and the *New York Times* after the newspaper published the Pentagon Papers persuaded White House aides to secretly create their own counterintelligence squad.

Hoover amassed a secret file of highly classified, cryptic documents he labeled "official and confidential." He wielded the sensitive information like a scalpel, exploiting human weaknesses and intimidating all who opposed his will. There is little doubt that heavy-handed FBI policies during the 1960s contributed to the utter contempt for the law felt in some quarters of society. The blatant disregard for civil liberties in the Nixon White House led to the Watergate crisis, multiple congressional investigations, and Nixon's eventual resignation. To promote the bureau and improve public relations, Hoover authorized the American Broadcasting Company's production of *The FBI,* a television series starring Efrem Zimbalist, Jr., that ran for most of the decade.

In 1972 Hoover died suddenly from undiagnosed heart disease. He was given a state funeral and was the first civil servant to have his body lie in state in the Capitol rotunda. Nixon gave the eulogy at Hoover's funeral, and Hoover is buried in the Washington Congressional Cemetery in Washington, D.C.

Upon hearing of Hoover's death, the Reverend Ralph Abernathy of the Southern Christian Leadership Conference, a victim of FBI voyeurism, remarked sarcastically, "With the passing of J. Edgar Hoover, I am reminded that Almighty God conducts the ultimate surveillance." Paradoxically, even though the bureau could boast of bringing infamous hoods, bank robbers, and kidnappers to justice, the white supremacists responsible for the bombing of the Sixteenth Street Baptist Church, which killed four young African-American girls on 15 September 1963, never had their day in court in Hoover's lifetime.

★

Volumes of documentation dealing with Hoover and the FBI in the 1960s are a matter of public record as the result of numerous lawsuits filed under the Freedom of Information Act. The historian Athan G. Theoharis has authored and edited several books on Hoover, the best of which is *From the Secret Files of J. Edgar Hoover* (1991), written with Ivan R. Dee. Hoover's life and the early history of the FBI are inseparable. The most thorough synthesis of the two is Curt Gentry, *J. Edgar Hoover: The Man and the Secrets* (1991). Obituaries are in the *New York Times* and *Washington Post* (both 3 May 1972).

JEAN W. GRIFFITH

HOPE, Leslie Townes ("Bob") (*b.* 29 May 1903 in Eltham, England), stand-up comedian, comic actor, philanthropist, beloved entertainer, successful television performer, noted traveling entertainer of American servicemen and servicewomen in times of war and times of peace, and recipient of the Congressional Gold Medal (1962) and the Presidential Medal of Freedom (1969).

Hope was the fifth of seven sons of William Henry Hope, a stonemason, and Avis (Townes) Hope, a singer. In 1907 the family moved to Cleveland. Hope disliked school and left Fairmont High School when he was in the eleventh grade. In 1920 he became a naturalized American citizen.

When film star Fatty Arbuckle was looking for talent for a 1924 road show, Hope and a buddy, Lloyd Durbin, dreamed up a comic dancing routine that Arbuckle loved. Durbin contracted tuberculosis and died before he and Hope were to appear in a Broadway show in New York. Hope's manager found him a new partner, George Byrne; after unpleasant years in New York, Hope went solo.

Hope married the aspiring actress Dolores Reade on 19 February 1934. They would adopt four children. During the early 1930s Hope honed his act in vaudeville, but he was always ambitious, and by 1935 he had made his way into the *Ziegfeld Follies,* working with Fanny Brice. He made his first appearance on radio in 1935 in the show *Atlantic Family.* His rapid-fire delivery of jokes made him a hit, and in 1938 he had his own show on NBC. That year he appeared in the motion picture *The Big Broadcast of 1938,* and instead of doing comedy, he sang "Thanks for the Memories," which became his signature song for radio and television specials. By the time he made his first road picture, he had been in seven movies, but the *Road to Singapore* (1940), with Bing Crosby and Dorothy Lamour, was a huge success; this was followed by *Road to Zanzibar* (1941), and Hope became an established movie star with significant drawing power.

The United States entered World War II after the bombing of Pearl Harbor by Japan on 7 December 1941, and in

Bob Hope. CORBIS CORPORATION (BELLEVUE)

1942 Hope tried to enlist in the army. He was denied enlistment on the grounds that he would do more good in the United Service Organization (USO), entertaining and raising the morale of troops engaged in the war. He was often in danger, nearly killed now and again, and he became a folk hero. His 1944 book *I Never Left Home* was a funny and endearing best-seller that added to the public's love for him.

By 1960 times were happy, and Hope's humor was becoming deeper and more probing into attitudes of the public and current events. In September 1962 President John F. Kennedy presented Hope with the Congressional Gold Medal, the highest expression of national appreciation for distinguished contributions. Hope would later receive the Presidential Medal of Freedom from President Lyndon B. Johnson. On 8 November 1962 Hope's manager, Mack Millar, died. Hope himself had a serious ailment that almost stopped his career; vascular blockages in his left eye were making him dizzy and blinding him. Just standing up was difficult. Even so, Hope made arrangements to do a USO tour of military bases in the Pacific, including South Vietnam, which by then had several thousand U.S. advisers. The Pentagon canceled the South Vietnam appearance because of the danger it posed to Hope, but while performing at Iwakuni Air Base in Japan on 22 December 1962, he received a petition that seemed to have been signed by nearly every troop in South Vietnam, asking him to come; the Pentagon still said no. The television documentary of the Christmas 1962 trip was broadcast in January 1963 and received a Golden Globe Award.

Each Christmas season thereafter, Hope managed to entertain in South Vietnam, bringing with him a host of volunteers from stagehands to movie stars. In 1963 he became a spokesman for Chrysler and hosted specials on NBC sponsored by Chrysler. The most popular of these were the January shows of his Christmas season tours to military bases, performing to audiences of anywhere from twenty-five to tens of thousands, often putting himself at risk. At least once the North Vietnamese tried to blow up Hope and his entire crew, missing by about ten minutes. To Hope's horror, a man he deeply liked, President Kennedy, was assassinated on 22 November 1963. Hope wanted to attend services for the president, but his left eye had suffered ruptures, and he had trouble standing and walking. On 6 December 1963 he underwent an experimental operation in San Francisco in which veins behind the eye were cauterized by laser beams. The procedure was repeated several times before surgeons declared that there were no more veins to work with.

During engagements at colleges Hope would end his show with a few words urging his audience to support the soldiers in South Vietnam. He seemed haunted by what he had seen and never really revealed all. When Hope was on the *Tonight Show,* host Johnny Carson asked him about the accuracy of incidents shown in the motion picture *Apocalypse Now* (1979)—Hope pointedly and repeatedly changed the subject.

Hope had been in remote encampments where snipers were killing Americans. He had toured hospitals and clinics, shaking hands with men whose intestines were hanging out; he remembered a man who had been injured in the explosion intended for Hope, smiling with blood streaming down his face as shards of glass were pulled out of his head and wishing Hope a hearty "Merry Christmas." By 1968 he wanted America to pull out of South Vietnam in an honorable manner that would not encourage Communist aggression elsewhere. Even though popular sentiment in the United States had turned heavily against American involvement in South Vietnam, Hope's television shows drew ever higher ratings. His January 1970 special about his Christmas 1969 tour of South Vietnam set a new record for an entertainment show's viewership; almost 65 percent of all televisions in America tuned in.

After the 1960s Hope's motion picture career slowly waned, with the chance of making one more road picture ending when Bing Crosby unexpectedly died in 1977. Hope loved to dance, but walking upright became increasingly difficult. He managed to continue shooting stand-up routines for television specials into the late 1980s. By the early 1990s Hope's wife began to take over much of the on-screen workload while Hope remained seated.

Even in the twenty-first century, Hope is remembered fondly. In 2002 a chapel at the Los Angeles National Cemetery was named after him. During the twentieth century public opinion polls always rated him America's favorite comedian, and often he was named America's favorite person. His legacy is one of compassion and of selfless giving, some fine motion pictures, and some of the best television shows ever made. He was almost certainly twentieth-century America's comedian of choice.

★

Hope wrote or cowrote ten books, nine of which are memoirs or autobiographies. *I Never Left Home* (1944), about his work for the USO during World War II, was a best-seller and was his most loved book well into the 1960s; *So This Is Peace* (1946) continued in the same vein as its predecessor; *Have Tux, Will Travel* (1954), with Pete Martin, describes Hope's busy, frenetic life; *I Owe Russia $1,200* (1963) tells of Hope's tour of the Soviet Union; *Five Women I Love: Bob Hope's Vietnam Story* (1966) is a memoir in the style of *I Never Left Home; The Last Christmas Show* (1974), with Martin, refers to Hope's trips to Vietnam; *The Road to Hollywood: My Forty-Year Love Affair with the Movies* (1977), with Bob Thomas, is an excellent account of Hope's motion picture career; *Confessions of a Hooker: My Lifelong Love Affair with Golf* (1985), with Dwayne Netland, is funnier than it is informative; *Don't Shoot, It's Only Me: Bob Hope's Comedy History of the United States* (1990), with Melville Shavelson, is an account of Hope's career in the context of historical events. William Robert Faith, *Bob Hope: A Life in Comedy* (1982), offers a good account of the most active years of Hope's very active life.

KIRK H. BEETZ

HOPPER, Dennis (*b.* 17 May 1936 in Dodge City, Kansas), iconoclastic actor and director who rejected Hollywood filmmaking and developed an underground and independent American cinema that culminated in the landmark counterculture film *Easy Rider* (1969).

Hopper was one of two boys born to Jay Hopper, who usually worked as a traveling postal worker on the railroad, and Marjorie Hopper, who managed a swimming pool and gave swimming lessons. Hopper's childhood was chaotic. When he was five years old, his mother told him his father had been killed during military basic training. Hopper later learned that his father was alive and working on an intelligence assignment in China related to Mao Zedong (Jay Hopper resumed his railway job after this assignment). Amidst this parental confusion, Hopper found love with his maternal grandparents and was raised on their farm, where at age six he showed an interest in drama, especially westerns and war movies.

Hopper's predilection for altered mental states began early when he discovered that sniffing gasoline fumes induced hallucinations. He hung out with older boys in pool halls, smoking cigarettes and drinking beer. Hopper attended Grossmont High School and Helix High School in California, graduating in 1954. A disinterested student, Hopper's artistic spirit was aroused, and he began taking art classes at the Nelson Art Gallery in Kansas City, Missouri.

In 1950 the family moved to California, where Hopper studied theater and won three contests reciting poems and soliloquies. He made his acting debut at the Old Globe Theatre in San Diego, playing an urchin in Charles Dickens's *A Christmas Carol*. He performed at the San Diego Community Players Theater and the Pasadena Playhouse when he was sixteen. In 1953, at the La Jolla Playhouse, he was coached by actress Dorothy McGuire.

Hopper won a scholarship to the National Shakespeare Festival at the Globe Theatre. He arrived in Hollywood in 1954 armed with contacts from McGuire, and a casting director at Hal Roach Studios gave him a walk-on for the American Broadcasting Company's (ABC) *Cavalcade of America*. He also won a role as an epileptic in an episode of the popular dramatic series *Medic* on the National Broadcasting Company (NBC). Hopper delivered phone books to support himself, but when the *Medic* episode aired on 5 January 1955, his performance set off a firestorm, and no less than seven studios offered to sign him to a contract. Columbia pictures was anxious to sign him but when tyrannical studio chief Harry Cohn told Hopper they would get the Shakespeare out of him, the rebellious Hopper shot back, "Go fuck yourself!"

During a seven-year contract at Warner Brothers, Hopper was cast in *Rebel Without a Cause* (1955) and *Giant* (1956). Both films featured James Dean, who would have a lifelong impact on Hopper's attitudes toward acting and lifestyle. During a loan-out to Twentieth Century–Fox for the western *From Hell to Texas* (1958), directed by martinet Henry Hathaway, Hopper refused to play a scene as Hathaway insisted. After eighty-seven takes, Hopper broke down and Hathaway pledged to blackball the difficult actor. Hopper could not get work.

By 1959 Hopper had moved to New York, grown his hair long, and immersed himself in the museum, gallery, and studio scene. He mingled with cultural icons such as Andy Warhol and Miles Davis, hung out in after-hour clubs, and indulged in sex and drugs. He studied Method acting for two years with Actor's Studio guru Lee Strasberg.

Hopper's idol James Dean had recommended that Hopper learn still photography as a means of artistic expression. Hopper took up Dean's suggestion and photographed artists, painters, poets, musicians, actors, and the "Happenings" that blossomed in the New York artistic community. His distinctive work was published in *Vogue* magazine and *Harper's Bazaar.*

Hopper began the 1960s portraying a gang leader in Phil Karlson's *Key Witness* (1960). He was still difficult on the set; his inner angst and desire to direct compounded his personal and artistic conflicts and generated quirky, maverick results.

In New York, Hopper met socialite Brooke Hayward, a *Vogue* model who studied acting and the daughter of actress Margaret Sullavan and Broadway impresario Leland Hayward. They married on 9 August 1961; the reception was held in the New York apartment of Brooke's childhood friend Jane Fonda. Hopper and Hayward had one child.

After his marriage Hopper returned to California, where from 1961 to 1967 he developed a reputation as a painter and photographer, working out of a studio in his Bel Air Canyon home. Because of Brooke's society connections, Hopper was invited to all the right Hollywood parties, but he was often out of control and lashed out at the guests, ranting that he would one day run the town. Hopper's involvement with LSD drew him into the Aquarian hippie lifestyle at the expense of his acting career. Although he appeared in *Night Tide* (1963), and *Cool Hand Luke* (1967), he also acted in duds like *Queen of Blood* (1966). Hopper found vehicles that reflected the growing youth culture through B-movie mogul Roger Corman, playing roles in *The Glory Stompers* (1967), and *The Trip* (1967), that merged his screen profile with his persona. He began collecting guns, studying karate, and experiencing drug delusions and paranoia. His marriage was deteriorating, and his wife's revulsion for the material in the screenplay for

Easy Rider, based on ideas from Hopper and Peter Fonda and written by Terry Southern, finally ended his marriage in 1967. In the divorce settlement, Brooke gave Hopper all the profits from *Easy Rider*, making him a millionaire after the film's spectacular reception in 1969.

Easy Rider is the quintessential road-trip movie—the story of two men looking for America—and its aesthetic approach was a seismic split from the studio system. Fonda played Captain America and produced; Hopper played the role of his sidekick, Billy. Hopper boldly announced he would break every cinematic rule and delivered by reinventing the American movie under the influences of LSD and European and underground cinema. In the film, Hopper, Hungarian cameraman Laszlo Kovacs, and editor Donn Cambern combined images and music a decade before MTV. Traditional editing and camera grammars, as well as Hollywood narrative strategies, were violated. *Easy Rider* was aimed at youth, not their "greatest generation" parents.

This low-budget movie that grossed millions caused the studios to open the gates to any young director with long hair. The film's soundtrack provided new markets. The baby boomers wanted to see themselves on screen, and Hopper and Fonda created a paradigm that heralded the New American Cinema of the 1970s.

Hopper proceeded to destroy his career in an orgy of excess. After *Easy Rider,* he returned to Hollywood from three years of self-destruction in Taos, New Mexico, directing *The Last Movie* (1971). The title almost became reality; its reception was abysmal. For Hopper, the 1970s were lost in drugs, self-abuse, and a trip into the dark side that few were willing to take with him.

In 1970, during the period that he was making *The Last Movie,* Hopper was married to actress and singer Michelle Phillips for eight days. In 1972 he married Daria Halprin; they had one daughter. In 1989, after his divorce from Halprin, Hopper married Katherine La Nasa. The couple had one son, but divorced in 1992. Hopper is currently married to Victoria Cane Duffy, whom he married on 4 December 1995.

During the 1980s, rehab and Hopper's genuine acting talent delivered one of the great movie comebacks. Performances in *Hoosiers* and *Blue Velvet* (both 1986) introduced him to a new generation. Hopper, a true 1960s survivor full of conflicts and contradictions, continues to act incessantly and direct on occasion.

★

Hopper's biography is Elena Rodriguez, *Dennis Hopper, A Madness to His Method* (1988). Critical studies of his career include *Dennis Hopper: Movie Top Tens Series* (1988), Jack Hunter, ed.; and Jay Hoberman, *Dennis Hopper: From Method to Madness*

(1988). Volumes of Hopper's work as artist and photographer include Rudi Fuchs, *Dennis Hopper: Out of the 60s* (1986), and *Dennis Hopper: Paintings, Photographs, Films* (2001).

VINCENT LoBRUTTO

HOPPER, Edward (*b.* 22 July 1882 in Nyack, New York; *d.* 15 May 1967 in New York City), premier realist artist of the twentieth century known for his haunting images of rural desolation and urban alienation; he strongly influenced the pop artists of the 1960s and represented the United States in the São Paulo Bienal exposition of 1967.

The second of two children born to Garret Henry Hopper, a dry goods store owner, and Elizabeth Griffiths Smith, a homemaker, Hopper grew up in a comfortably middle-class household and attended Nyack Baptist Church. After graduating from Nyack High School in 1899 he studied painting at the New York School of Art (1900–1906). Hopper visited Europe three times between 1906 and 1910 but studiously avoided the trappings of the avant-garde. He returned to New York in 1910, and in December 1913 he settled into a studio on the top floor of 3 Washington Square North in Greenwich Village, where he lived for the

Edward Hopper. ASSOCIATED PRESS AP

rest of his life. He worked as a freelance illustrator as he struggled for recognition as a painter. He sold his first painting, *Sailing* (1911), in the famous Armory Show of 1913, but did not sell another work for the next ten years. On 9 July 1924 Hopper married the painter Josephine ("Jo") Verstille Nivison; they had no children. In October of that year Hopper had a one-man show at the Frank K. M. Rehn Gallery, his first critical and financial success. Rehn remained as Hopper's dealer for the rest of his career.

House by the Railroad (1925), a desolate view of a Victorian house in a bare landscape, marked the crystallization of Hopper's mature style, and was the first painting acquired for the permanent collection of the Museum of Modern Art in New York City. A stark realism, architectural solidity, and the dramatic contrast of light and shadow combined to create a mood of loneliness, isolation, and deadening melancholy. So foreboding was the image of the dilapidated dwelling that it gave the film director Alfred Hitchcock the idea for the eerie house in *Psycho* (1960), a fact that delighted Hopper, an avid film fan whose compositions often owed much to the movies. Hopper's style remained consistent throughout his career as he pursued his unique perception of the American scene and produced some of the most enduring images in American art: the dreary facade of small shops on an empty street in *Early Sunday Morning* (1930); the noirish late-night diner of *Nighthawks* (1942); and the surreal doorway opening onto an expanse of sea and sky in *Rooms by the Sea* (1951).

Although Hopper's fame was partially eclipsed by the abstract expressionists of the 1950s, his reputation as the dean of American realists was firmly established by the 1960s. Some critics, however, still derided his style as outdated and merely "illustrative." Hopper in turn remained convinced that abstraction was a "temporary phase in art," and in 1960 he met with a group of like-minded artists to protest the growing influence of the abstractionists in American museums. At the age of seventy-eight Hopper, a tall and rangy man with an imposingly bald head, piercing blue eyes, and a well-weathered face, produced only one or two canvases a year.

In 1960 he completed *People in the Sun,* a mysterious depiction of a group of people in street clothes seated with faces raised to the sun as if trying to absorb its restorative powers, and *Second Story Sunlight,* in which two women—one young and voluptuous, the other aged—sit on the top-floor porch of a white house. Although such works lend themselves to psychological interpretations, the famously reticent Hopper discouraged such pursuits. "Maybe I am not very human," he once observed, but "what I wanted to do was paint sunlight on the side of a house." Both canvases evidence the preoccupation with the transfiguring power of sunlight that characterizes Hopper's later work. In some instances sunlight seems to have represented life itself to the aging Hopper. *Sun in an Empty Room* (1963), for example, is simply the stark play of sunlight on the bare walls of an empty room. When asked by his friend the writer Brian O'Doherty what he was after in this painting, Hopper replied, "I'm after me."

Invited to John F. Kennedy's presidential inauguration, the curmudgeonly Hopper, a lifelong Republican, declined, but was pleased when First Lady Jacqueline Kennedy chose a watercolor of his, *Houses of Squam Light* (1923), from the Boston Museum of Fine Arts to exhibit in the White House in 1961. In December 1960 Hopper received *Art in America*'s annual award for his contribution to American art and was praised for having brought "eloquence to silent desolation and a sunlit, poignant beauty to the commonplace." *A Woman in the Sun* (1961) exemplifies such poignancy: a haggard nude in a shabby room stands transfigured in the glare of morning sun from an unseen window. In 1962 Hopper completed *New York Office* and *Road and Trees*, which won the 1964 M. V. Khonstamn Prize for painting from the Art Institute of Chicago, and at year's end his complete graphic work was exhibited by the Philadelphia Museum of Art.

In September 1964 the Whitney Museum of American Art honored Hopper with his third major retrospective, which opened to lavish critical praise and popular success. The exhibition refocused attention on Hopper, especially among a new generation of pop artists and photo-realists seeking to break away from abstractionism. They greatly admired Hopper's representational style and the incorporation of the commonplace into his art. Indeed, such advertising motifs as the Phillies cigar sign in *Nighthawks* and the Mobil logo in *Gas* (1940) anticipated the mass-market imagery of much of pop art, as epitomized by Andy Warhol's famous Campbell's soup cans.

Illness prevented Hopper from painting in 1964, but in 1965 he completed his final painting. *Two Comedians* depicts the artist and his wife as Pierrot-like clowns bowing together from the edge of a darkened stage. It is Hopper's strangely moving farewell. He died of a heart attack in his studio at the age of eighty-four and was buried in the family plot in Oak Hill Cemetery in Nyack. In September 1967 Hopper was chosen as the key figure to represent the United States in Brazil's São Paulo Bienal, along with younger artists including Jasper Johns, Robert Rauschenberg, and many pop artists.

Hopper is generally considered the greatest realist of the twentieth century. His haunting images are engrained in the American imagination, and "Hopperesque" is immediately suggestive of desolation and estrangement. His work provides a continuum from the ash can school of the 1920s to the pop art of the 1960s, and his choice as the key American artist in the São Paulo Bienal underscores his importance to the latter decade. Hopper's tradition of realism offered an alternative to the pop artists and photo-realist painters who adopted him as an ancestral figure and embraced both the commonplace of his subject matter—gas stations, diners, empty streets—as well as his use of imagery drawn from popular culture and advertising media. They also found Hopper's impassive and unsentimental vision of America appropriately "cool" for their era. Moreover, Hopper's essential themes of loneliness and alienation reverberated strongly not only with these younger artists but with the entire generation that came of age during the troubled 1960s.

★

More than 2,500 works by Hopper, and other visual and written archival material, were deposited as a bequest to the Whitney Museum of American Art in New York City. The oversized monograph by Lloyd Goodrich, *Edward Hopper* (1976), is a lavishly illustrated classic study. See also Gail Levin, *Edward Hopper: The Art and the Artist* (1980), which contains color plates of all of Hopper's important works and a selected bibliography. The most comprehensive assessment of Hopper is Gail Levin, *Edward Hopper: A Catalogue Raisonne* (1994), a four-volume catalog of all of the artist's oils, watercolors, and illustrations that includes a complete exhibition history, biographical sketch, and exhaustive bibliography. The definitive biography is Gail Levin, *Edward Hopper: An Intimate Biography* (1995); also useful is Justin Spring, *The Essential Edward Hopper* (1998). An intriguing profile of Hopper during the 1960s is in Brian O'Doherty, *American Masters: The Voice and the Myth* (1973). An obituary is in the *New York Times* (17 May 1967).

MICHAEL MCLEAN

HOWE, Irving (*b.* 11 June 1920 in New York City; *d.* 5 May 1993 in New York City), literary critic, author, and social activist who played a significant role in both the world of New York City intellectual circles and in the democratic socialist arena for much of his life.

Howe was born Irving Horenstein, the son of the immigrants David and Nettie Goldman Horenstein. His parents led a hard life, first as owners of a failed grocery and then as garment workers. Howe, who recalled becoming involved in left-wing, anti-Stalinist politics at age fourteen, graduated from DeWitt Clinton High School in 1936 and from the City College of New York in 1940. Although he graduated from college as Horenstein, he began using the name Howe and legally changed his name in 1946.

Howe worked politically for a branch of the Trotskyites as a speaker and editor, becoming known for his "polemical ferocity," and continued with this work even after he was drafted into the U.S. Army in 1942, during World War II. (Trotskyism was a form of Marxist thought, developed by the Russian revolutionary Leon Trotsky, that emphasized the internationalism of socialism and the need for permanent revolution.) Among the pseudonyms Howe used was R. Fahan. He served in the army until 1946, mostly in Alaska, reaching the rank of sergeant. The isolation caused him to lose his singular focus; after returning to civilian life he became more passive politically. In 1941 he married Anna Bader and subsequently Thalia Filias (the mother of his two children), Arien Hausknecht, and Ilana Wiener.

Howe began study for an M.A. at Brooklyn College in 1946. While continuing his political activities, he began publishing essays in the literary/political journals *Commentary* and *Partisan Review*. He held various literary jobs, including stints as a book reviewer at *Time* (he estimates half his reviews were never published) and as an editorial assistant at Schocken Books, and he performed various editorial chores at the radical magazine *Politics* (often using the name Theodore Dryden). Despite never obtaining an advanced degree, Howe had a first-rate academic career. After teaching at the University of Washington summer session in 1952, he joined the Brandeis University faculty in 1953 and subsequently taught two years (1961 to 1963) at Stanford University. Homesick for New York City, he began teaching at Hunter College of the City University of New York in 1963 and subsequently became a distinguished professor of English in 1970, renowned for his passionate lectures on literature. He retired in 1986.

As one obituary said of Howe, "He lived in three worlds, literary, political, and Jewish." In 1954 Howe and some colleagues founded *Dissent,* a cerebral political literary quarterly (somewhat confusingly dedicated to a form of "democratic socialism") for which he served as editor until his death. Over the years Howe produced a large, steady output of essays, articles, and books dealing with cultural influences on literature, advocating democratic socialism, and depicting the Jewish experience in the United States. The *New Republic* found him "excessively sane about literature. . . . He likes individualism, humanism, and a modest brand of socialism." Among the notable books he wrote or edited are *The UAW and Walter Reuther,* with B. J. Widick (1949); *The American Communist Party: A Critical History 1919–1957,* with Lewis Coser (1957); *Politics and the Novel* (1957); *Jewish-American Stories* (1977); and *The American Newness: Culture and Politics in the Age of Emerson* (1986). He wrote critical studies of the writers Sherwood Anderson (1951), William Faulkner (1952), and Thomas Hardy (1967). His "intellectual biography," *A Margin of Hope,* appeared in 1982, and *World of Our Fathers* (1976), a history of Eastern European Jewish immigrant life in the United States, was a best-seller and won a Na-

tional Book Award. Among Howe's other honors were awards from the Bollingen Foundation (1959–1960) and the National Institute of Arts and Letters (1960). He was awarded a Guggenheim Fellowship in 1964–1965 and again in 1971, and appointed a MacArthur Fellow in 1987.

The 1960s have been called "the middle period" in Howe's life, a time when he evolved a more apolitical approach to literature while simultaneously becoming more at odds with some of the chief issues of the day. Serious controversy arose over Hannah Arendt's book *Eichmann in Jerusalem: A Report on the Banality of Evil* (1963), which first appeared as a series of articles in *The New Yorker.* In this work Arendt espoused the view ("perverse and torturous," according to the critic Julian Symons) that during the Holocaust the Jews had collaborated in their own destruction and that its perpetrators were ordinary men. (She called it the "banality of evil.") Troubled by the magazine's unwillingness to publish correspondence challenging articles that it published as well as by the range of Arendt's arguments, Howe presided over an emotional forum between defenders of Arendt's theses and her primary critics. The forum was organized by *Dissent* and held at a Manhattan hotel in the early fall of 1963.

The "confrontation politics" that characterized much New Left activity during the 1960s had no attraction for Howe. A meeting in 1962 between leaders of the Students for a Democratic Society (a 1960s radical antiwar group) and *Dissent*'s editorial board ended sourly. Over the next several years Howe criticized what he considered the New Left's "tendencies towards violence, irrationalism, petulance, and intolerance." He did not completely condemn the New Left, hoping that it might yet find a proper way to voice protest, but *Dissent* did not adopt the apocalyptic view of revolution at a time when many others did. *Dissent* and Howe kept what has been called "democratic sanity," continuing to argue for the achievement of a more equitable democratic society without resorting to violence.

The escalation of the Vietnam War created enormous turmoil in the United States and provided Howe with his "first chance for wholehearted electoral work since . . . the undistinguished soap boxing" of his youth. He campaigned hard for the antiwar Senator Eugene McCarthy in his effort to win the Democratic presidential nomination in 1968. Howe strenuously attacked the war but refused to support any policy that was pro-Communist and, given the limited choices at the time, felt himself to be "politically beleaguered."

After retiring from Hunter College Howe continued to be culturally and politically engaged. In 1987, along with two colleagues, he edited *The Penguin Book of Modern Yiddish Verse.* In 1990 he published a volume of his selected writings. As his health deteriorated, he was forced to cut back on his activities. Howe died of cardiovascular disease.

Until his death he remained, in the words of one colleague, "a counter-puncher who tended to dissent from the prevailing orthodoxy of the moment, whether left or right."

★

Howe's *Margin of Hope* (1982) contains little personal information. A first-rate biography is Edward Alexander, *Irving Howe: Socialist, Critic, Jew* (1998). Useful for Howe's milieu are Alexander Bloom, *Prodigal Sons: The New York Intellectuals and Their World* (1986), and Alan Wald, *The New York Intellectuals: The Rise and Decline of the Anti-Stalinist Left from the 1930s to the 1980s* (1987). See also a special issue of *Dissent* (fall 1993), "Remembering Irving Howe." Also available on video is Joseph Dorman, *Arguing the World* (1997), which traces the views and life of Howe and three of his peers (Daniel Bell, Nathan Glazer, and Irving Kristol). An obituary is in the *New York Times* (6 May 1993).

DANIEL J. LEAB

HUDSON, Rock   (*b.* 17 November 1925 in Winnetka, Illinois; *d.* 2 October 1985 in Beverly Hills, California), Academy Award–nominated actor who dominated the box-office charts in the 1960s, gaining particular popularity for a string of risqué romantic comedies that earned him the title "king of the sex comedy."

Rock Hudson. CORBIS CORPORATION (BELLEVUE)

Hudson was born Roy Harold Scherer, Jr., the only child of Roy Harold Scherer, Sr., an auto mechanic, and Katherine ("Kay") Wood, a homemaker and, later, a telephone operator. Hudson's parents divorced when he was four years old, and his mother was remarried to Wallace Fitzgerald, a former Marine Corps officer, in 1932. Fitzgerald adopted Hudson, whose legal name became Roy Fitzgerald. That marriage also ended in divorce. Hudson had no siblings.

After graduating from New Trier High School (Winnetka, Illinois) in 1943, Hudson served in the navy from 1944 to 1946 and after his discharge moved to Los Angeles, where he worked a string of odd jobs while trying to break into the film industry. The talent agent Henry Willson is credited with discovering the blandly named Roy Fitzgerald and giving him the more macho sobriquet of Rock Hudson—a name the actor never liked. Willson introduced Hudson to the film director Raoul Walsh, who signed Hudson to a personal contract. Walsh gave the actor his first film role, a bit part in *Fighter Squadron* (1948).

In 1949 Walsh sold Hudson's contract to Universal Pictures, where the actor remained for the next sixteen years. During the 1950s Hudson gradually rose through the ranks of Universal's stable of contract players, starting out with minor parts in "B" movies and working his way up to lead roles in melodramas. He earned his only Academy Award

nomination for the big-screen adaptation of Edna Ferber's novel *Giant* in 1956. Hudson's last film of the 1950s remade his image and set the tone for the remainder of his career. *Pillow Talk* (1959) was Hudson's first screen comedy and the first of three films to pair him with Doris Day. The film earned rave reviews and several Oscar nominations. More important to Hudson, it widened his box-office appeal. Moviegoers learned that the stalwart hero of melodramas and adventure films also had a flair for comedy.

In *Pillow Talk*, Hudson played a charming womanizer who employs duplicitous tactics to win the heart of Day, a chaste career girl. The fast-paced script was filled with witty banter and sexual innuendo. The term "sex comedy" was coined to describe this type of film, and before long Hudson was the genre's reigning king. He tried to replicate *Pillow Talk*'s winning formula in a string of similar comedies, including two follow-up vehicles with Day—*Lover Come Back* (1961) and *Send Me No Flowers* (1964). He frolicked with Gina Lollobrigida in *Come September* (1961) and *Strange Bedfellows* (1965), Paula Prentiss in *Man's Favorite Sport?* (1964), and Leslie Caron in *A Very Special Favor* (1965).

Hudson's popularity skyrocketed during the 1960s, his face adorning countless movie magazines. He reportedly received ten thousand fan letters a month, and Universal subsidized the actor's fan club at a cost of $10,000 a year.

He won numerous popularity polls and motion picture exhibitor awards (given by theater owners to stars who command the biggest box-office receipts), including United Theatre Owners' Star of the Year (1961), Theatre Owners of America's Actor of the Year (1961), three Golden Globe Awards, and five Bambi Awards as Germany's most popular male star. The *Motion Picture Herald* and *Independent Film Journal* both named Hudson the top moneymaking actor of 1960. That same year he was one of the first actors to be immortalized with a star on Hollywood Boulevard's Walk of Fame.

Though his screen comedies had propelled him to the top of his profession, Hudson continued to do dramatic roles—a sheriff standing down the gunfighter Kirk Douglas in *The Last Sunset* (1961) and an atheist who finds God in *The Spiral Road* (1964). These vehicles proved less popular with moviegoers and reviewers alike. As one critic of *The Spiral Road* noted, "His devotees are apt to wish he was back romping with Doris Day." By the mid-1960s Hudson had grown tired of romantic comedy and told reporters that he would rather leave that type of role to Cary Grant.

In 1965 Hudson's contract with Universal expired, and he decided to become a free agent. The same year he formed his own production company, Gibraltar Productions. Feeling pigeonholed in comedy, he sought out dramatic roles once again, beginning with *Seconds* (1966), the grim cautionary tale of a banker (John Randolph) who trades his aging body for a younger model (Hudson). Though praised by critics, the film was a commercial failure, a fact that hurt Hudson, who considered it one of his best. Hudson's efforts to break out of the comedy mold continued with *Ice Station Zebra* (1968), a spy thriller that cast him as a submarine commander desperate to beat the Russians to the North Pole to retrieve a film capsule containing satellite photos of missile locations. In the Civil War drama *The Undefeated* (1969), Hudson took second billing to John Wayne. Wayne played a Yankee colonel, Hudson a Confederate colonel. The war has just ended and both are headed for Mexico. Circumstances along the way force the former enemies into an unlikely alliance.

By the 1970s Hudson's film career was on the decline, and he turned to television, starring in the mystery series *McMillan and Wife* (renamed *McMillan* when "wife" Susan Saint James left the series) from 1971 to 1977. He also starred in several made-for-television movies and miniseries, most notably Ray Bradbury's *Martian Chronicles* (1980). In his last years Hudson's career was eclipsed by the media furor surrounding the revelation that the actor, who had labored to keep his homosexuality a secret, had AIDS. Hudson succumbed to the disease at his Beverly Hills home in Los Angeles. He was cremated, and his ashes were scattered at sea.

Hudson had been married briefly, from 1955 to 1958, to Phyllis Gates, who had been his agent's secretary. The marriage likely was arranged to squelch rumors of Hudson's homosexuality. The actor had no children. Though Hudson achieved critical acclaim—as well as an Oscar nomination—for his dramatic roles, it was his metamorphosis into a comedic farceur that made him one of the most bankable actors of the 1960s. Considered classics, his comedies with Doris Day have been much emulated by younger generations of filmmakers. Ironically, Hudson never felt fully comfortable in these roles and avoided them completely once he became a free agent, a choice that coincided with the decline of his film career.

★

Rock Hudson and Sara Davidson, *Rock Hudson: His Story* (1986), was written by Davidson with Hudson's cooperation, although the star was already dying and reportedly was incoherent for much of the six weeks that Davidson worked with him. Other full-length biographies of Hudson include Mark Bego, *Rock Hudson, Public and Private* (1986); Phyllis Gates (Hudson's wife of three years), *My Husband, Rock Hudson* (1987); and Tom Clark, *Rock Hudson, Friend of Mine* (1990). Brenda Scott Royce, *Rock Hudson: A Bio-Bibliography* (1995), provides a comprehensive analysis of Hudson's career.

BRENDA SCOTT ROYCE

HUGGINS, Charles Brenton (*b.* 22 September 1901 in Halifax, Nova Scotia; *d.* 12 January 1997 in Chicago, Illinois), oncologist, surgeon, educator, and author who was awarded the Nobel Prize in physiology or medicine in 1966 for his work using hormones in cancer treatment.

Huggins was the elder of two sons of Charles Edward Huggins, a pharmacist, and Bessie Marie Spencer, a homemaker. In 1920 Huggins earned a B.A. from Acadia University in Wolfville, Nova Scotia, and then went to Cambridge, Massachusetts, to attend Harvard Medical School. In 1924 Huggins earned an M.A. and an M.D. from Harvard. He completed an internship at the University of Michigan Hospital in Ann Arbor, where he became a surgery instructor in 1926. The following year Huggins became an instructor of surgery at the University of Chicago Medical School and married Margaret Wellman on 29 July 1927. The couple had one son and one daughter. In 1933 Huggins became a U.S. citizen and achieved the rank of full professor.

When Huggins began his cancer research, little was known about the connection between hormones and cancer, but he was determined to unlock these mysteries. In 1939, using dogs as test subjects, Huggins and his colleagues found a way to separate the prostate gland from

Charles B. Huggins. THE LIBRARY OF CONGRESS

the urethra and urinary tract. A stumbling block soon presented itself—some of the dogs developed prostate tumors. Despite this apparent setback, Huggins believed he might be on the track of what caused tumors and discovered that the male sex hormone testosterone seemed to be present in high amounts in cancerous prostates.

In 1943 the National Academy of Sciences gave Huggins the first Charles L. Mayer Award in cancer research. The following year he performed the first procedure to remove both adrenal glands, or a bilateral adrenalectomy. In 1946 Huggins served briefly as a professor of urological surgery and the director of the department of urology at Johns Hopkins University in Baltimore, Maryland. He was about to embark on the cancer research that would lead to revolutionary treatments in the 1960s.

From 1936 to 1962 Huggins was a professor of surgery at the University of Chicago, where from 1951 to 1969 he was the director of the Ben May Laboratory for Cancer Research. During this time Huggins focused on studying breast cancer, which had the highest incidence rate of any neoplastic disease in both men and women. Together with two students, D. M. Bergenstal and Thomas Dao, he developed a treatment involving the removal of both ovaries and both adrenal glands that improved prospects for patients with advanced breast cancer. In about 30 to 40 percent of the cases, patients in his studies experienced definite, long-lasting improvement.

Surgery was not the only cancer treatment Huggins developed during the 1960s. While at the Ben May Laboratory, he experimented with cancer in female rats. He found that one dose of 7, 12-dimethylbens(a)anthracene (DMBA) quickly caused mammary tumors to develop, and that the cancer responded to hormonal activity. His work was the basis for the development of drugs that block estrogen production in order to treat breast cancer.

Because of Huggins's work in the 1960s, doctors began to view cancers differently. His research on cancers in the prostate and breast changed the widely held belief in the medical field that cancers were self-perpetuating. As the decade progressed, doctors began to understand that hormones played a large role in the formation and growth of cancerous tissues. Radical surgery was not always necessary to treat cancer; hormone treatments were often very effective.

Also in the 1960s scientists began questioning whether birth control pills increased the chances of developing cancer in the breasts and reproductive organs. As the controversy grew, Huggins decided to investigate the problem. With more than thirty years of experience studying how hormones affect cancer, he was prepared to interpret the evidence. After studying data collected from thousands of women who were taking birth control pills, Huggins concluded that the pills had no cancer-causing effects. He also suggested that in some cases they might even keep tumors small.

It was not until the 1960s that all of the research Huggins had conducted in prior decades was recognized. In 1962, the year he became the William B. Ogden Distinguished Service Professor at Ben May Laboratory, he earned the Valentine Prize from the New York Academy of Medicine and the Hunter Award from the American Therapeutic Society. For his contributions to science, in 1963 he received the Lasker Clinical Research Award, a high honor in the medical field. The following year Huggins was given the honor of laurea from the University of Bologna and an award from the Rudolf Virchow Society. In 1966 he shared the Nobel Prize in physiology or medicine with Peyton Rous, who had researched the viral causes of cancer fifty-five years earlier.

The Nobel Prize recognized Huggins for discovering the connections between hormones and cancer. The Nobel committee cited his "fundamental discoveries concerning the hormone dependence of normal and neoplastic cells in experimental animals and their immediate practical application to the treatment of human prostatic and breast cancer." The committee praised Huggins for giving so many patients with advanced cancer a chance to improve their lives by offering them new treatment options.

Huggins never forgot the source of his scientific achievements—unearthing scientific truths. "Discovery is for the single mind, perhaps in company with a few students," he told colleagues. "Don't write books. Don't teach hundreds of students. Discovery is our business." After the 1960s Huggins changed his career direction. From 1972 to 1979 he was the chancellor of Acadia University. He also resumed his earlier bone research and helped to find substances that cause bone formation. This research was helpful in orthopedic, periodontal, and reconstructive surgery.

Huggins wrote almost 300 medical articles and scientific books, including *Frontiers of Mammary Cancer* (1961), *The Scientific Contributions of the Ben May Laboratory for Cancer Research* (1961), and *Experimental Leukemia and Mammary Cancer: Induction, Prevention, and Cure* (1979). He received two gold medals for research from the American Medical Association, the Order of Merit from Germany, and the Order of the Sun from Peru. Huggins was an honorary fellow of the Royal College of Surgeons in Edinburgh and London and received many honorary degrees. He died at his home in Chicago at the age of ninety-five.

Because of his work during the 1960s, Huggins led the medical community to develop treatments for cancer based on the chemical signals the body sends out. Distinguished by his 1966 Nobel Prize in physiology or medicine, Huggins changed the direction of cancer research forever and extended the lives of many cancer patients.

★

Huggins's biography may be found in *Current Biography* (1965). An updated biography appears in Tyler Wasson, ed., *Nobel Prize Winners: An H. W. Wilson Biographical Dictionary* (1987), and Frank N. Magill, ed., *The Nobel Prize Winners: Physiology or Medicine* (1991). See also Paul Talalay and Guy Williams-Ashman, "1966 Nobel Laureates in Medicine or Physiology," *Science* (21 Oct. 1966). Obituaries are in the *New York Times* and *Chicago Tribune* (both 15 Jan. 1997).

A. E. SCHULTHIES

HUMPHREY, Hubert Horatio, Jr. (*b.* 27 May 1911 in Wallace, South Dakota; *d.* 13 January 1978 in Waverly, Minnesota), U.S. senator and vice president who became identified with activist social legislation and aggressive policies during the Vietnam War, prior to narrowly losing the presidency to Richard M. Nixon in 1968.

The son of Hubert Humphrey, Sr., a pharmacist, and Christine (Sannes) Humphrey, a housewife, Humphrey was raised in Doland, a small town in South Dakota, along with his older brother and two younger sisters. He gained a childhood interest in politics from his father, a Democrat who served as Doland's mayor in the 1920s. After earning a B.A. in political science at the University of Minnesota at Minneapolis–Saint Paul in 1939, Humphrey pursued graduate studies at Louisiana State University in Baton

An official portrait of Hubert H. Humphrey. THE LIBRARY OF CONGRESS

Rouge, completing an M.A. in 1940 before taking a job as the director of a Works Progress Administration (WPA) program training teachers in Duluth, Minnesota. On 3 September 1936 he married Muriel Fay Buck, who became his lifelong partner (and, briefly, his successor in the U.S. Senate following his death). They had four children.

In 1940 Humphrey joined the faculty of Macalester College in Saint Paul and edged toward a political career. From 1941 to 1945 he served as the state director of war production training and reemployment and as the assistant director of the War Manpower Commission. In 1943 he made an unsuccessful bid to become the mayor of Minneapolis; two years later, he won. Humphrey gained national attention in 1948 for his passionate speech on behalf of civil rights at the Democratic National Convention. That same year, he became the first Democrat ever elected to the U.S. Senate from Minnesota.

At first Humphrey was seen as a brash, confrontational liberal by his fellow senators. When his legislative battles for civil rights and labor law reform failed, he adopted a more conciliatory approach. He became a protégé of Senate Majority Leader Lyndon Johnson, who sharpened his skills at compromise. In 1956 he was considered as a running mate by the Democratic presidential nominee, Adlai Stevenson, although Stevenson chose Senator Estes Kefauver of Tennessee instead. Humphrey had reason to harbor national ambitions—he was well-regarded in Washington, D.C., for his expertise in labor, farm, and civil rights issues. His foreign policy credentials were enhanced by a highly publicized meeting with the Soviet premier Nikita Khrushchev in late 1958.

Humphrey's chances of winning the 1960 Democratic presidential nomination rested on a strong showing in the primaries. His chief rival was Senator John F. Kennedy, who enjoyed the advantages of personal wealth and a glamorous image. The first primary between the two was on 5 April in Wisconsin, where Humphrey was a well-known campaigner who enjoyed support among union members and farmers. Although he tried to engage Kennedy on the issues, the senator from Massachusetts avoided debating Humphrey and emphasized his greater national appeal in a contest against the likely Republican nominee, Richard M. Nixon. Outspent and out-organized, Humphrey said he felt like "an independent merchant competing against a chain store." Kennedy won in Wisconsin, but his victory margin was small enough to encourage Humphrey to continue the fight into West Virginia. By this point, voters' misgivings about Kennedy's Catholic faith had become an issue, making the primary a referendum on intolerance. Dipping into his personal savings, Humphrey struggled against his opponent's increasing momentum. On 10 May, West Virginia's Democrats gave Kennedy 61 percent of the vote, effectively knocking Humphrey out of the race. He went on to campaign for Kennedy in the autumn and ran successfully for reelection to the Senate.

After Kennedy's narrow victory over Nixon, Humphrey was elected as the majority whip in the Senate and began his most fruitful period as a legislator. His warm personality and tireless energy helped him to turn into law such groundbreaking proposals as the establishment of the Peace Corps, Medicare, Food for Peace, and the first nuclear test ban treaty. His most impressive accomplishment was the passage of the 1964 Civil Rights Act. Forging an alliance with key Republicans such as Everett Dirksen, Humphrey defeated a determined filibuster by southern senators to pass the first meaningful antiracial discrimination statute since Reconstruction. He was at the height of his influence when President Johnson tapped him to be his running mate in 1964. Humphrey took on the role with typical gusto, lambasting the Republican nominee, Barry Goldwater, in campaign stops across the country. The Johnson-Humphrey ticket won by a landslide.

Humphrey's term as the thirty-eighth U.S. vice president proved frustrating and often humiliating. At the start, he hoped to help shape the Johnson administration's domestic policy agenda. Instead, he watched his influence steadily diminish as he was given the role of cheerleader

for the president. Johnson demanded absolute loyalty from his vice president and became enraged at any sign of independence on Humphrey's part. America's growing military presence in Vietnam became an early friction point. In February 1965 Humphrey sent Johnson a memo arguing against escalating the war. Johnson reacted angrily and shut Humphrey out of Vietnam strategy meetings. Rather than suffer further estrangement, the vice president put aside his doubts and defended Johnson's war policies in the United States and abroad. As time went on, Humphrey became a fervent champion of U.S. involvement in Southeast Asia, comparing it to the struggle against the Nazis during World War II. His stance was tough and uncompromising—in 1966 he likened the inclusion of the Vietcong guerrilla forces in the South Vietnamese government to "putting a fox in the chicken coop." During a visit to Saigon in November 1967, he hailed the Vietnam War as "our great adventure—and what a wonderful adventure it is!"

Such remarks earned Humphrey the disdain of the U.S. antiwar movement. Many liberals saw him as a pathetic, even tragic figure, forsaking his own better judgment in order to curry Johnson's favor. Once criticized as too radical, he became identified with the Democratic Party's more conservative factions. When Johnson announced his decision not to seek reelection in March 1968, the Democratic old guard urged Humphrey to enter the presidential contest. He did so on 27 April in typically upbeat fashion, claiming to represent "the politics of joy." Rather than face his Democratic opponents Eugene McCarthy and Robert F. Kennedy in the primaries, Humphrey methodically gathered delegates at party caucuses; by early summer, he was all but certain of nomination. Antiwar Democrats remained bitterly opposed to him, ensuring that the party's late August convention in Chicago would be rancorous. Supporters of McCarthy and George McGovern (who, like McCarthy, was a former Humphrey ally turned opponent) failed in an attempt to insert a peace plank into the Democratic platform. As police beat demonstrators in the Chicago streets and tear gas burned the eyes of delegates in their hotels, Humphrey won his party's nomination on the first ballot. He decried the violence outside the convention in an emotional acceptance speech. It was evident, though, that the wounds inflicted on the Democrats in Chicago would not be easily healed.

September voter surveys found Humphrey and his running mate, Senator Edmund S. Muskie of Maine, badly trailing Nixon, the Republican nominee. Polls also indicated that former Alabama Governor George Wallace, running as a conservative third-party candidate, was cutting into the Democratic vote among southern whites and northern union workers. Disorganized and underfunded, Humphrey struggled to establish himself as his own man without breaking ties with Johnson. Taunted by hecklers at campaign rallies and abandoned by the left wing of his party, he seemed headed for defeat. Retrenching, Humphrey began to turn his fortunes around on 30 September, when he advocated a bombing halt in Vietnam during a televised appearance in Salt Lake City, Utah. The move was bold enough to sway undecided voters and help raise needed campaign funds. Humphrey's poll numbers began to improve as he barnstormed the country with renewed vigor. The AFL-CIO and other labor unions mounted a massive effort on his behalf in key industrial states.

Still, many antiwar Democrats remained reluctant to support the Democratic ticket. Among the notable holdouts was McCarthy, who waited until late October to offer Humphrey a lukewarm endorsement. Straining to pull his party together, Humphrey campaigned furiously against Nixon and Wallace, offering a theme of national unity against his opponents' divisive "law and order" appeals. Miraculously, he had pulled even or taken a small lead in the polls by election day. When the voting was over, Humphrey had lost the presidency to Nixon by one of the narrowest margins in history, winning 191 electoral votes against Nixon's 301. In the popular vote, a mere 514,947 votes separated the two candidates. Humphrey's remarkable comeback had come agonizingly close to success. After his narrow defeat, Humphrey returned to Minneapolis to serve as a professor of public affairs at the University of Minnesota from 1968 to 1970.

Restless in private life, Humphrey returned to the U.S. Senate in 1970. Two years later, he tried for the Democratic presidential nomination once more, losing to McGovern after a hard-fought primary season. In 1976 he was again spoken of as a White House contender, but decided against running. Diagnosed with bladder cancer that same year, he won reelection to the Senate shortly before his health declined. On 5 January 1977 Humphrey's fellow Democrats elected him as the deputy president pro tem of the Senate. After a gallant struggle, he died in January 1978, mourned by old friends and foes alike. Humphrey's body lay in state in the rotunda of the U.S. Capitol for public viewing before being interred in Lakewood Cemetery in Minneapolis.

In hindsight, Humphrey's accomplishments on behalf of civil rights, arms control, affordable health care, and other progressive policies have balanced the negative assessments of his vice presidential years. Ridiculed at times, his contributions to American life were undeniably substantial. "He was, it is true, the easiest politician in recent times to deride and make fun of," wrote the *Baltimore Sun* reporter Ernest Ferguson after his death. "He was also the easiest to love, for the simple reason that he himself was full of love. You might say he based his whole career on it."

★

Humphrey's papers are held by the Minnesota Historical So-

ciety in Saint Paul, Minnesota. Hubert H. Humphrey, *The Education of a Public Man: My Life and Politics* (1976), is an engaging though somewhat spotty memoir. Edgar Berman, *Hubert: The Triumph and Tragedy of the Humphrey I Knew* (1979), offers the perspective of a close friend. Carl Solberg, *Hubert Humphrey: A Biography* (1984), remains the best biography. Theodore H. White, *The Making of the President, 1960* (1961), and Lewis Chester, Geoffrey Hodgson, and Bruce Page, *An American Melodrama: The Presidential Campaign of 1968* (1969), provide detailed accounts of Humphrey's bids for the White House. Obituaries are in the *New York Times* (14 Jan. 1978), and *Washington Post* (15 Jan. 1978).

BARRY ALFONSO

HUNT, H(aroldson) L(afayette), Jr. (*b.* 17 February 1889 in Vandalia, Illinois; *d.* 29 November 1974 in Dallas, Texas), businessman and oil tycoon, a right-wing conservative who focused on influencing the political and social consciousness of America throughout the 1960s.

Hunt was the youngest of eight children of Haroldson Lafayette Hunt, a farmer, commodity dealer, and owner of a local bank, and Ella Rose Myers. He was educated at home. By the time he was fifteen, Hunt had begun his travels throughout the West, including Colorado, California, and Texas. After working at various jobs, he joined the oil boom in Arkansas, became an oil lease broker, and developed his first oil well. By 1925 he is believed to have had a personal worth of $600,000, a considerable fortune at that time. By 1930, however, Hunt was nearly bankrupt because of bad business operations. Nonetheless, he continued in the oil business and by 1932 he owned approximately 900 wells in East Texas.

Over the next decade, Hunt became the largest independent operator during the East Texas oil-field boom and amassed a huge fortune. A 5 April 1948 article in *Fortune* magazine named him as the richest man in the United States. By the 1950s Hunt was becoming more and more interested in politics, and he financed Facts Forum in 1951 as an "educational" foundation. Through Facts Forum, Hunt produced a series of radio and television programs featuring right-wing conservative and anticommunist messages. Hunt and Facts Forum came out in strong support of Senator Joseph McCarthy and McCarthyism, which essentially became a witch-hunt for communists in the United States.

By 1960 Hunt's sons were primarily running his business enterprises. Hunt was more interested in promoting his political agenda by espousing his views on society and politics. In 1960 he self-published *Alpaca,* a utopian novel about a small nation under a dictatorship. The book was a

H. L. Hunt shown in front of his mansion in Dallas, Texas. ASSOCIATED PRESS AP

thinly disguised platform for Hunt's message about what he believed to be a perfect society, including his view that the oldest, wealthiest, and most ambitious citizens, especially those among the top 25 percent of the taxpayers, should have more votes than the common man or woman. Hunt also addressed his pet peeves: big government and high taxation. He wrote, "Big taxes encourage overbearing and despoiling government, and government has been and always will be destructive to human liberty." Nevertheless, Hunt failed to acknowledge that he benefited from government regulations bolstering the oil business, including President Franklin D. Roosevelt's 1934 federal order blocking interstate shipment of "hot oil" and a federal regulation in place in 1936 that maintained oil field pressure and price.

In its appendix *Alpaca* included an example of what Hunt considered to be the "perfect constitution." Reportedly, Hunt sent copies of the book to leaders of numerous countries. Despite his immense wealth, Hunt was noted for his frugality; he even brought brown-bag lunches to the office. Thus the book, which sold for fifty cents a copy, was printed on inferior paper with cheap glue and often literally fell apart in the reader's hands. An often repeated anecdote about the book is the instance when Hunt brought his two daughters to a book signing and had them sing—to the tune of "How Much Is That Doggy in the Window?"—the lyrics "How much is that book in the window? The one that says all the smart things."

During the 1960 presidential primaries, Hunt strongly supported the nomination of Lyndon B. Johnson as the Democratic Party candidate, primarily because Johnson had supported oil-depletion allowances when he served in Congress and the Senate. When John F. Kennedy was nominated instead and chose Johnson as his vice presiden-

tial running mate, Hunt made a large donation to the Kennedy campaign. But Hunt soon came to dislike Kennedy, especially after Kennedy showed little inclination to provide tax breaks for the oil business. Specifically, Hunt was upset over Kennedy's growing efforts to get rid of the oil-depletion allowance. Dating back to 1926 the allowance represented a significant tax break by allowing certain companies to deduct a sizable percentage of the gross income derived from oil and gas wells for as long as those wells were still producing. As a result, Hunt used his fifteen-minute *LIFE LINE* radio broadcasts, which had replaced Facts Forum, to regularly attack the Kennedy presidency. The *LIFE LINE* broadcasts were carried by more than 400 stations throughout the United States and cost Hunt, through his companies, an estimated $2 million a year. Overall, the radio shows were essentially a form of propaganda to promote conservative viewpoints and habitually used scare tactics, such as warnings that Communist infiltrators had plans to enslave America.

Hunt's efforts to influence public opinion backfired when his *LIFE LINE* radio show criticized Kennedy on 22 November 1963, the very day the president was assassinated in Dallas, where Hunt lived. In addition, Hunt's son Nelson Bunker Hunter was one of the contributors to a full-page advertisement in that day's issue of the *Dallas Morning News* that asked the president questions such as "Why has the foreign policy of the U.S. degenerated to the point that the CIA is arranging coups and having staunch anti-Communist allies to the U.S. bloodily exterminated?" A citizen group boycotted HLH Products, a division of the Hunt Oil Company and leading sponsor of the radio broadcasts.

Hunt and members of his family, including his sons,

were also questioned by the Federal Bureau of Investigation (FBI) after the assassination because of their many public and sometimes vitriolic attacks on Kennedy and his administration. In an interview conducted with Hunt's son Lamar Hunt, the FBI questioned Lamar about the fact that his name and address appeared in the address book of Jack Ruby. Ruby had shot and killed Kennedy's alleged assassin, Lee Harvey Oswald, on 24 November 1963—just two days after Kennedy's assassination. Although no evidence was found that any of the Hunts were involved in an assassination plot, Hunt did receive death threats. In addition, conspiracy theorists continued to publish reports describing Hunt as one of the financial backers and manipulators in the assassination. Nevertheless, after Kennedy's death, the *Houston Chronicle* quoted Hunt as deploring the assassination, saying, "Freedom is in fearful danger when a president dies by violence."

Hunt also wrote the newspaper column *Hunt for Truth,* which was syndicated throughout the United States. Much like the *LIFE LINE* radio programs, the column was a format for Hunt's ultraconservative viewpoints. Hunt eventually gathered these columns and self-published them in book form in 1965 under the same title. Hunt's outlook was strongly antigovernment in the sense that he thought government-run organizations and programs were inherently wasteful and misguided. James Hepburn, in his 1968 book *Farewell America,* quoted Hunt as saying, "All services to the public should be abolished in favor of personal enterprise." As for his old political ally Johnson, who assumed the presidency after Kennedy's assassination, Hunt openly supported Johnson's Republican rival Senator Barry Goldwater in the 1964 presidential campaign.

Hunt's name continued to pop up in relation to various anticommunist efforts throughout the 1960s. The 12 November 1968 edition of the *Miami Herald* reported on the federal trial of the Cuban Power organization and several Cuban exiles accused of plotting to bomb foreign ships. A tape that was played during the trial revealed one of the defendants saying that Hunt had given $15,000 to help with the bombing. Interviewed by telephone, Hunt denied any involvement and said that he had only "helped in the political campaign" of a Cuban running for a Florida office. In a 27 February 1969 article in the British *Guardian Weekly,* Hunt also said that he had once been approached by the Catholic Church to help support the Vatican's anticommunist movement in South America.

In the 1960s Hunt began practicing what at the time were considered avant-garde dietary habits. His interest in promoting health continued, and in 1968 he began to sell aloe vera cosmetics. Throughout his life Hunt was an eccentric; he built a modest home in Dallas that imitated George Washington's famous home at Mount Vernon. He also kept three families. He married Lyda Bunker in 1914, with whom he had six children. In 1925, while still married

to Bunker, Hunt married Frania Tye, and the couple had four children together. Two years after Bunker died in 1955, Hunt married Ruth Ray and adopted her children, who were born between 1943 and 1950. Ray later said that the children were actually Hunt's biological offspring. Ray is credited with persuading Hunt to become a Baptist and to give up gambling, especially high-stakes poker, a game that helped to finance his first forays into the oil business.

Regardless of whether one agrees with Hunt's political and social philosophies, he was undoubtedly one of the shrewdest businessmen and financiers of the twentieth century. His strong will and dedication to his businesses and causes is reflected in his often repeated quote: "Decide what you want, decide what you are willing to exchange for it. Establish your priorities and go to work." Hunt is buried at Sparkman-Hillcrest Memorial Park in Dallas. At the time of his death, his estate was estimated to exceed $2 billion, and its settlement was bitterly contested for several years in the courts, largely because of disagreements among Hunt's three different families.

★

An overview of Hunt's life can be found in the *Encyclopedia of World Biography,* 2nd ed. (1998). Books about the Hunt family dynasty include Harry Hurt, *Texas Rich: The Hunt Dynasty, from the Early Oil Days Through the Silver Crash* (1981), and Jerome Tuccille, *Kingdom: The Story of the Hunt Family of Texas* (1984). For more information on Hunt in the 1960s, see Tom Buckley, "Just Plain H. L. Hunt," *Esquire* (Jan. 1967). A look back at Hunt's novel *Alpaca* is in Rusty Crawley, "How H. L. Hunt Viewed Utopia," *Dallas Business Journal* (22 Sept. 2000). An obituary is in the *New York Times* (30 Nov. 1974).

DAVID PETECHUK

HUNTLEY, Chester Robert ("Chet") (*b.* 10 December 1911 in Caldwell, Montana; *d.* 10 March 1974 in Bozeman, Montana), and **David McClure BRINKLEY** (*b.* 10 July 1920 in Wilmington, North Carolina), much-admired broadcast journalists who changed television news in the 1960s.

Huntley was the son of Percy ("Pat") Adams Huntley and Blanche Wadine Tatham, a former schoolteacher; he had three sisters. His father, a failed rancher, returned to being a railroad telegrapher, working much of the time as a replacement, and the young Huntley grew up in a succession of Montana towns. In 1926 the family settled in Whitehall, where he graduated from high school in 1929. Scholarships enabled Huntley to obtain a college education; he first attended Montana State College from 1929 to 1932 and then won a national oratory contest that allowed him to attend the Cornish School of Arts in Seattle (1932–1933). He graduated in 1934 with a B.A. from the University of Washington and married Ingrid Rolin on 23 February 1936.

They had two daughters and divorced in 1959. On 7 March 1959 Huntley married the television weathercaster Tipton Stringer.

Huntley's broadcast career began at a small Seattle radio station following his graduation. After a succession of broadcast jobs he became a commentator, news analyst, and reporter for a Los Angeles station affiliated with the Columbia Broadcasting System (CBS). Huntley joined the American Broadcasting Company's Los Angeles operation in 1951, conducting three daily radio shows and one on television. He moved to New York City in 1955 to work for National Broadcasting Company (NBC) Radio, and the next year conducted a television news show.

During his West Coast years, according to the media historian Barbara Matusow, Huntley had gained a reputation as a "fighting liberal," known for "siding with the underdog and embracing the cause of individual liberty." His radio series combating prejudice against Mexican Americans in California won a Peabody Award in 1942, a special citation from Ohio State's Institute for Education by Radio, and an award from New York University. Huntley left CBS after refusing to sign a loyalty oath. (In the early 1950s Senator Joseph McCarthy led a wide-ranging investigation into the alleged presence of Communists in the government and society at large, charging countless Americans with "disloyalty" to the United States.) He spoke out against anti-Communist excesses and won a slander suit in 1954 against a woman who had called him a Communist; he was granted damages and a public apology. He received a second Peabody Award in 1954 for his "talent for mature commentary."

Brinkley was the youngest of five children born to William Graham Brinkley, a railroad worker, and Mary MacDonald West. He attended New Hanover High School but dropped out during his senior year to take a full-time job as a reporter for the *Wilmington Star-News*. From 1940 to 1941 he served in the U.S. Army as a supply sergeant based at Fort Jackson, South Carolina. For the next two years he worked as a reporter for United Press International. NBC hired him as a news writer in 1943 but quickly put him in front of the camera as an announcer. For the next decade he honed his craft at NBC, providing reports for such programs as *Camel News Caravan* and *Comment*.

In 1956 NBC teamed Huntley with Brinkley to cover the presidential nominating conventions. The combination made such a favorable impression that NBC assigned them to the nightly network news show. They worked together for fourteen years at a time when television journalism was rapidly replacing the print media. (In 1963 the pollster Elmo Roper found that for the first time a majority of the American people queried said their "chief source of news was television rather than newspapers.") Huntley, the rangy, straightforward Westerner, and Brinkley, the

David Brinkley *(left)* and Chet Huntley *(right)*. ARCHIVE PHOTOS, INC.

smooth, clever East Coast sophisticate, complemented one another, but their news program was not an overnight success, even though their convention coverage trounced CBS's. (They did better in 1960 and 1964, garnering more than 50 percent of the viewing audience.) Their program did not pull even in the ratings with CBS until 1958, but then, with only brief lapses, they stayed number one until 1967.

In alternating between Huntley in New York City and Brinkley in the nation's capital, the program introduced an innovative, energetic, fast-paced style very different from the "rip and read" newscasters who had preceded the team. They revolutionized television news reporting by writing their own copy. Their sign-off phrases—"Goodnight, Chet"; "Goodnight, David"—became such a cliché that at John F. Kennedy's 1961 inaugural gala the entertainers Frank Sinatra and Milton Berle sang (to the tune of "Love and Marriage") a parody: "Huntley, Brinkley. Huntley, Brinkley. One is glum. The other twinkly."

Huntley and Brinkley were at the forefront of the transformation of network news. The 1960s was a decade of great and continuing breaking news (for example, the assassination of President Kennedy, the space race, civil rights agitation, the youth culture, and the Vietnam War). In 1963, as it became clear that news could be profitable, the networks expanded their nightly news programs from fifteen minutes to half an hour. The producers of the Huntley-Brinkley program tailored it to showcase their stars, and it has been estimated that the more sober Huntley got at least 60 percent more airtime than the individualistic Brinkley and had a broader audience appeal. (Not every viewer found Brinkley's light touch attractive.) In 1965 a polling company found that the Huntley-Brinkley team was even better known than the rock group the Beatles. Huntley did not personally write as much of his material as Brinkley did, but he did compose his "think pieces." He also spent considerable time preparing his daily radio commentary, *Chet Huntley Reporting*. Brinkley, on the other hand, devoted some of his energies to *David Brinkley's Journal,* which NBC aired from 1961 to 1963 and which earned Brinkley a Peabody Award as well as an Emmy.

Huntley spoke out against the attacks on reporters by the Nixon administration during the Vietnam War, defending free speech as a hallmark of a free society. It was later revealed that his name had been placed on the White House enemies list during the early 1970s. Although the team worked together for fourteen years, Huntley and Brinkley were not close. They collaborated in relative harmony but did not socialize; in addition, the two had ideological differences. Huntley did not become disenchanted with the Vietnam War as did Brinkley, and in 1967, when the American Federation of Television and Radio Artists struck the networks, Huntley—unlike Brinkley—crossed their picket lines, arguing that it was "inappropriate" for newsmen to belong to a union of performers. His actions resulted in considerable ill feeling among the team's writers. Huntley later explained his position: "The majority membership of the union . . . are fine people, but journalists have no business associating with them in a union and otherwise handing so much of their collective destiny to entertainers."

Toward the end of the 1960s critics felt that the team had lost its sparkle. Huntley's last broadcast as part of the team was on 31 July 1970; he continued as a syndicated commentator. Over the next few years he joined a New York City advertising agency, worked as a spokesperson for American Airlines, and headed Big Sky, Inc., a multimillion-dollar Montana resort complex opposed by environmentalists. He died following abdominal surgery for cancer days before the complex opened. He is buried in the Sunset Hills Cemetery in Bozeman.

After Huntley left the show in 1970, NBC renamed it *NBC Nightly News* and experimented with different hosts before settling on John Chancellor as sole host beginning in 1971. Brinkley returned as coanchor from 1976 to 1979. In 1981 he joined the American Broadcasting Company (ABC), where he enjoyed success with his Sunday morning news program *This Week with David Brinkley*. He retired from ABC in 1998.

Huntley and Brinkley altered the landscape of television news with their influential program during the 1960s.

Their differing personalities and styles, combined with innovative programming techniques, created a landmark in broadcast journalism. Noted *McCall's* magazine of their partnership: "it was part of a fresh new way of treating the news—lively, personal and impressively literate."

★

Recordings and other biographical material are in the NBC archives at the State Historical Society of Wisconsin. Huntley's book *The Generous Years: Remembrances of a Frontier Boyhood* (1968) is a memoir of his youth. Brinkley's autobiography is *Eleven Presidents, Four Wars, Twenty-two Political Conventions, One Moon Landing, Three Assassinations, Two Thousand Weeks of News and Other Stuff on Television, and Eighteen Years of Growing Up in North Carolina* (1995). See also *McCall's* (Oct. 1966), and Barbara Matusow, *The Evening Stars: The Making of the Network News Anchor* (1983). Obituaries of Huntley are in the *New York Times* and *Washington Post* (both 21 Mar. 1974).

Daniel J. Leab

HUSTON, John Marcellus (*b.* 5 August 1906 in Nevada, Missouri; *d.* 28 August 1987 in Middletown, Rhode Island), film director, screenwriter, and actor whose influential career spanned six decades and whose films in the 1960s included several commercial flops as well as successes such as *The Night of the Iguana* (1964) and *The Bible . . . in the Beginning* (1966).

Huston was the only child born to Walter Huston, an actor, and Rhea (Gore) Huston, a journalist. The couple divorced when Huston was six, and he lived primarily with his mother. He attended Lincoln Heights High School in Los Angeles but dropped out at the age of fifteen. Although Huston was one of the best amateur lightweight boxers in California, he opted not to pursue a career in prizefighting. During the 1920s Huston studied art in Los Angeles, lived in Mexico for two years, appeared in several off-Broadway productions, published a short story in *American Mercury,* and did some reporting for the (New York) *Daily Telegraph.*

Through his father's connections Huston secured a writing position at Universal Studios. However, he left Hollywood in 1933 when a car he was driving struck and killed a young woman. Huston was absolved by a coroner's jury, but the traumatized young man drifted around London, Paris, Chicago, and New York City. In 1937 he returned to Hollywood, preparing scripts for *Jezebel* (1938), *Juarez* (1939), and *High Sierra* (1941). *The Maltese Falcon* (1941) was Huston's directorial debut; the film adaptation of Dashiell Hammett's 1930 novel was a financial success and became a cinema classic. In 1942 Huston joined the U.S. Army Signal Corps. He made three documentaries for the army while working under the director Frank Capra: *Report from the Aleutians* (1943), *The Battle of San Pietro*

John Huston, March 1966. HULTON-DEUTSCH COLLECTION/CORBIS

(1944), and *Let There Be Light* (1945). At the end of World War II Huston was discharged from the army with the rank of major.

Huston returned to work in Hollywood, winning Academy Awards for writing and directing *The Treasure of the Sierra Madre* (1948), a film in which his father received an Oscar for best supporting actor. His other major films during this period were *Key Largo* (1948), *The Asphalt Jungle* (1950), *The Red Badge of Courage* (1951), and *The African Queen* (1952). Huston found the anticommunist hysteria in Hollywood to be intolerable. He helped to form the Committee for the First Amendment and, complaining of "moral rot" in the film capital, moved to Ireland in 1952, becoming an Irish citizen in 1964.

Huston's career declined in the late 1950s, as his *Barbarian and the Geisha* (1958) and *The Roots of Heaven* (1958) failed to find audiences. Huston described *The Unforgiven* (1960), featuring Audrey Hepburn, as the worst of his films. His productions of the 1960s tended to be financial and artistic flops. He blamed the films' lack of success on improper editing by studio executives; however, it is possible that Huston was simply out of step with the times. He was an establishment figure whose films often focused on group quests that failed or individuals who lacked self-understanding, the antithesis of the rebellious spirit of the 1960s.

Huston's identification with an older Hollywood was evident in his 1961 film *The Misfits*. Written by Arthur Miller as a starring vehicle for Miller's wife, Marilyn Monroe, *The Misfits* also features Clark Gable and Montgomery Clift in a story about a group of cowboys who round up wild horses to be slaughtered for dog food. The film was besieged with production problems, many of them resulting from Monroe and Miller's unraveling marriage. Filmgoers avoided *The Misfits,* while some critics found Huston's direction pretentious.

On the eve of the sexual revolution, Huston's next film, *Freud* (1962), appeared to be a marketable project. For the film's lead Huston selected Clift, a 1950s matinee idol. The director used his own powerful voice for the movie's omnipresent narrator. Huston began the film, "This is the story of Freud's descent into a region as black as hell, man's unconscious, and how he let in the light." Freud is presented as a Christ figure who brings a message of salvation for humanity, but he is rejected and betrayed by his disciple Breuer. Huston was proud of the film, but he insisted that clumsy post-production editing deleted "vital links" from the picture's intricate plot. Accordingly, it was not well received by filmgoers. *Freud* was followed by *The List of Adrian Messenger* (1963), which featured Huston and such established stars as Kirk Douglas, George C. Scott, Robert Mitchum, Burt Lancaster, and Frank Sinatra in well-disguised cameo appearances. Huston himself received an Academy Award nomination for best supporting actor in 1963 for his role as a church official in Otto Preminger's *The Cardinal.*

In his autobiography Huston defined a film's failure purely in commercial terms, observing, "The industry operates for profit, and a failure is a film that doesn't make money." This measure is certainly not accurate for all of Huston's work in the decade. In 1964 he adapted Tennessee Williams's play *The Night of the Iguana* (1961) for the screen. Filmed on location in Puerto Vallarta, Mexico (where Huston would take up residence in 1975), the movie features Richard Burton as an alcoholic former minister who is a tour guide in Mexico and becomes involved with Deborah Kerr and Ava Gardner. The film earned four Academy Award nominations, reviving Huston's reputation as a bankable commodity.

In 1966 Huston teamed with the producer Dino De Laurentiis to make *The Bible . . . in the Beginning,* based on the first twenty-two chapters of Genesis. The film, one of the most lucrative in Huston's long career, also featured the director as Noah and the voice of God. As Hollywood was responding to the growing youth culture and market of the mid-1960s, Huston's film harkd back to the biblical epics of the 1950s and an older generation of moviegoers. Huston's string of hits continued with his direction of the opening segment in the James Bond parody *Casino Royale* (1967).

Seeking more serious fare for his talents, Huston signed on with Warner Bros. to film *Reflections in a Golden Eye* (1967), based upon the 1941 novel by Carson McCullers. The story focuses on repressed homosexuality, madness, and murder at a southern army base in 1948. Again using film stars of the 1950s, Huston cast Marlon Brando and Elizabeth Taylor in the leads. Although Huston was proud of the movie, it failed at the box office. Huston concluded that the film's treatment of homosexuality was ahead of its time. He also criticized Warner Bros. for altering his use of color in the film. Huston ended the 1960s with three commercial flops: *Sinful Davey* (1969), *A Walk with Love and Death* (1969), and *The Kremlin Letter* (1970). He increasingly was perceived as a filmmaker out of touch with the changing times.

However, Huston resurrected his career and reputation in the 1970s with critically acclaimed cinematic adaptations of *Fat City* (1972), *The Man Who Would Be King* (1975), and *Wise Blood* (1979). In the 1980s he enjoyed his greatest commercial success with *Annie* (1982), and he was nominated for an Academy Award as best director for *Prizzi's Honor* (1985), a film about the Mafia for which his daughter, Anjelica, was honored with an Oscar for best supporting actress. In 1983 Huston received the American Film Institute Lifetime Achievement Award. Huston's final film, *The Dead* (1987), based upon a 1914 story by James Joyce, also featured an outstanding performance by Anjelica Huston.

Huston was married five times, divorced four times, and widowed once. His wives were Dorothy Jeane Harvey (1926–1933), Lesley H. Black (1937–1944), Evelyn Keyes (1946–1950), Enrica ("Ricki") Soma (1950–1969), who was killed in a car accident and with whom Huston had a son and a daughter (Anjelica), and Celeste ("Cici") Shane (1972–1977). Huston also had a son with his longtime lover Zoe Sallis. While in Rhode Island filming *Mr. North* in 1987, Huston died in his sleep at the age of eighty-one from complications from emphysema. He is buried in Hollywood Memorial Cemetery in California.

Huston directed forty-one films during his career. He worked steadily during the 1960s, attaining commercial success with *The Night of the Iguana* and *The Bible . . . In the Beginning,* but his films appeared somewhat out of step with the antiestablishment themes of the period. While his reputation suffered in the 1960s, by his death Huston's claim to being one of America's finest filmmakers had been reestablished.

★

Huston's papers are held by the Margaret Herrick Library of the Academy of Motion Pictures Arts and Sciences in Los Angeles. Huston's autobiography, *An Open Book* (1980), is less forthcoming than the title suggests. Biographical information and discussion of Huston's films may be found in Robert Benayoun, *John Huston* (1966); Axel Madsen, *John Huston: A Biography* (1978); Stuart Kaminsky, *John Huston: Maker of Magic* (1978); Scott Hammen, *John Huston* (1985); and Lawrence Grobel, *The Hustons* (1989). Obituaries are in the *New York Times* and *Los Angeles Times* (both 29 Aug. 1987).

RON BRILEY

I-J

ILLICH, Ivan (*b.* 4 September 1926 in Vienna, Austria), theologian, social activist, and Roman Catholic priest who in the 1960s challenged his church's policies on Latin America and birth control and left the priesthood, and who subsequently became a radical humanist critic of modern education, medical care, and technology.

Illich was the son of Ivan Peter Illich, a landowner and civil engineer, and Ellen (Regenstreif-Ortlieb) Illich, a homemaker. He attended the universities of Florence, Rome, and Munich and came under the influence of the Catholic philosopher Jacques Maritain. In 1951 he earned a licentiate in theology from Gregorian University in Rome and was ordained as a Roman Catholic priest. He earned a Ph.D. in history at the University of Salzburg that same year and immigrated to the United States; he became a U.S. citizen in 1953.

For five years he served as an assistant pastor at the Incarnation Church, a Puerto Rican parish in New York City. In 1956 he was named a monsignor and became the vice rector of Catholic University of Puerto Rico in Ponce. While there, he began promoting humanist views and agitating for Puerto Rican independence. He was a vocal defender of education for children, saying no public money should go to universities until elementary schools were properly funded. After being recalled briefly to the United States, Illich was assigned to Cuernavaca, a small town fifty miles outside Mexico City. There, he was instrumental in founding the Intercultural Center for Documentation (1961), which offered Spanish-language classes and cultural training for priests and lay people coming to Latin America to work among the poor.

By the mid-1960s Illich came to believe that government agencies like the U.S. Peace Corps, as well as Catholic Church projects, should stay out of Latin America. He believed that outside assistance, even from well-meaning people, kept the peoples of the region dependent and inferior. His center began promoting cultural independence for the indigenous peoples of Mexico and Latin America. Instead of continuing to train priests for work in the missions, Illich inculcated radical ideas about the immorality of intervention in local cultures. Illich and his center became a thorn in the side of the church. His goal, he told one reporter, was to "corrupt" his students so they would return home rather than carry out their missions.

Illich also was a vocal critic of the Catholic Church's policies in Latin America and the Third World, arguing that the church's stance on birth control kept poor people subjugated. Catholic peasants in the Third World could never be expected to rise out of poverty if church laws doomed them to having large families, he suggested. In 1968 papal authorities, hearing more about Illich's ideas, called him to Rome for an inquiry. Illich refused to answer questions about his beliefs or to cooperate with the church's investigation. Breaking entirely with his upbringing, he left the priesthood in 1969.

Illich played a quiet but important role in the radical progressive movement within the Roman Catholic Church in the 1960s. After the reforms of the Second Vatican Council (1962–1965) under Pope John XXVII, many Catholics pushed for even bolder changes in the liturgy and moral teachings, especially in the areas of birth control, clerical marriage, and social outreach to the world's poor. Within the priesthood and the church as well as the burgeoning popular progressive movements in Latin America, Illich was a prominent figure of dissent. Within society at large, however, he was little known until the publication of his important books of the 1970s.

In 1970 Illich published *Celebration of Awareness: A Call for Institutional Revolution,* a collection of his radical humanist essays on topics such as education and the role of priests in modern society. In 1971 he published *Deschooling Society,* a scathing critique of mandatory public education. Staking out a position independent of most leftist scholars, Illich argued that public schools were a mechanism of indoctrination and subjugation, stifling initiative and obliterating traditional cultures and independent thought. His strong and controversial arguments, written in a challenging yet straightforward style, caused a stir in education circles and beyond. This book was followed by *After Deschooling, What?* (1973).

In 1973 Illich also published *Tools for Conviviality,* which expanded his unique views on the dangers of modern technology. He argued that technology is not neutral and that the automobile culture and other "advancements" reduced people's independence and robbed them of social connectedness, intellectual vigor, and well-being. Many critics reviled Illich as a modern Luddite, but he continued to attract interest among nonsectarian thinkers.

In his next and most famous book, *Medical Nemesis: The Expropriation of Health* (1975), Illich railed against modern health care. Using a similar argument to those he had advanced to skewer public education and technology, Illich contended that medical services robbed people of their natural healing abilities. He noted the increasing incidence of iatrogenic disorders and diseases (those maladies inadvertently caused by doctors and medical care), and argued that people needed to take charge of their own health. The book dovetailed with the increasing popular interest in health foods and alternative therapies and treatments, and it became his most widely read work.

Illich remained the director of the center in Cuernavaca until its closing in 1976. Many young people from the United States and elsewhere—stimulated by the humanist values of the 1960s—flocked there to participate in political discussions led by Illich. After closing the center in Cuernavaca, he continued to live in Mexico and to write and lecture. His later books included *Toward a History of Needs* (1978), *The Right to Useful Unemployment, and Its Profes-*

Ivan Illich. THE LIBRARY OF CONGRESS

sional Enemies (1978), *Energy and Equity* (1979), *Shadow Work* (1981), *Gender* (1982), *H2O and the Waters of Forgetfulness* (1986), *ABC: The Alphabetization of the Popular Mind* (1988), and *In the Mirror of the Past: Lectures and Addresses, 1978-1990* (1992). In his later years he took on the mass media and the computer culture, arguing in the essay "Silence Is a Commons" (1983), "Computers are doing to communication what fences did to pastures and cars did to streets." Illich is a polymath who speaks six languages fluently and writes in three languages, so it is fitting that his books have been published in twenty-six languages. His teaching career has included stints at the University of Kessel (1979–1982), the University of California, Berkeley (1982), the University of Marburg (1983–1984), and Pennsylvania State University (1986–1987).

Illich embodied the questioning spirit of the 1960s and the counterculture's belief that power should reside in people and that governments and corporations were agents of oppression. He gave a unique voice and solid intellectual backing to these sentiments, laying out a consistent theory of antimodernism and upholding the values of nature, spirit, and individual and collective initiative. Illich did not look kindly on the 1960s, however, noting in a 1988 article in *Whole Earth Review* that the decade "added terms like 'needs test,' 'needs analysis,' 'need pattern'—neologisms indicating lacks operationally verified and managed by the many social experts in needs recognition. And since 1960, needing has become a social learning goal." In celebrating autonomy and berating the increasing authority of experts and corporate power, Illich kept alive the philosophy of the 1960s during the following decades.

★

An anthology of critical essays is in Lee Hoinacki and Carl Mitcham, eds., *The Challenges of Ivan Illich: A Collective Reflection* (2002). Three interviews in the *Whole Earth Review* (summer 1997, winter 1988, fall 1989) are among the best sources on Illich's thinking. Information about Illich is also in Francine du Plessix Gray, *Divine Disobedience: Profiles in Roman Catholic Radicalism* (1970), and David Gabbard, *Silencing Ivan Illich: A Foucauldian Analysis of an Intellectual Repression* (1993). An article in the *National Catholic Reporter* (28 Oct. 1994) discusses his views on medical care.

MICHAEL BETZOLD

INDIANA, Robert (*b.* 13 September 1928 in New Castle, Indiana), painter, sculptor, poet, and set designer best known for his *LOVE* image, one of the most recognizable symbols of the 1960s, who, as a major adjunct to the pop art movement, helped to lead the art world away from abstract expressionism.

Nothing is known about Indiana's biological parents; he was adopted at birth by Earl Clark, a low-level manager at various petroleum companies, and Carmen Watters, a homemaker. In 1958 he unofficially changed his surname to the name of his native state, and since all of his important work was done after that date, commentators have always referred to him as Robert Indiana. According to Indiana himself, "Robert Clark didn't really exist artistically."

An only child, he was raised in and around Indianapolis. However, after his parents divorced when he was eleven, Indiana acquired a stepsister when his father remarried. Indiana graduated from Arsenal Technical High School, and in 1948 attended night classes at the Munson-Williams-Proctor Institute and the Utica branch of Syracuse University (to study Russian). He served in the U.S. Army Air Corps from 1946 to 1949. In 1949 Indiana entered the Art Institute of Chicago under the GI Bill, graduating with a B.F.A. in 1953. In autumn 1954 he moved to New York City. Indiana has never married nor had children.

Claiming he "wanted to be original and contribute something fresh," Indiana rejected the dominant movement of abstract expressionism: "Everybody was jumping into the canvas with buckets of paint; . . . my own disposition [was] to turn around and go the other way." Under

the influence of Ellsworth Kelly, Indiana developed a hard-edged, realistic style of painting that emphasized the use of primary colors, a style he retained throughout the 1960s. However, he first attracted notice in 1959, not with paintings, but with "assemblages" that he constructed from old beams scavenged from his neighborhood.

These unpainted objects, which Indiana called "herms," were decorated with wheels, pieces of iron, and pegs he had found. (The name "herms" derives from the quadrangular stone stelae guardian figures that were used as guardian figures in ancient Greco-Roman cultures.) Indiana attracted attention by stenciling short words on his decorated herms. By 1962, Indiana had exhibited assemblages in gallery shows and at the Museum of Modern Art's "Art of Assemblage" exhibition (1961). Success with the herms led Indiana to stencil words on large canvases, which were meticulously painted in a hard-edged manner with brightly colored paint. He called his style "verbal-visual" because he felt the words and numbers on the paintings were as important as their color and painted shapes, which were usually circles or polygons. In 1961 the Museum of Modern Art purchased his picture *The American Dream #1* (1960), launching his career. Indiana had his first one-man show at the Stable Gallery in New York City in 1962.

Indiana's pre-1967 paintings have remained the best known of his career. He profited from the fact that the pop art movement was gaining in popularity in this same period. Although his paintings shared much with pop art, Indiana's pictures occasionally expressed concern over social issues, something pop art studiously avoided. His painting *Yield Brother* (1962) featured the international peace movement symbol, while his Confederacy series (1965–1966) attacked racism in four southern states. In addition, in pop art the object portrayed often referred to commercialism, whereas Indiana insisted his work was always self-referential. For instance his *EAT/DIE* diptych (1962) was, he said, based on his memory of his adoptive mother's death in 1949, when the last word she spoke to him was "eat." Indiana also collaborated with Andy Warhol on the short film *EAT* (1964) and, in his first public commission, made a twenty-foot *EAT* sign for the New York State pavilion at the 1964 World's Fair. A soft-spoken individual, Indiana expressed an interest in various art forms throughout the 1960s, writing poetry and designing the sets and costumes for the Virgil Thomson–Gertrude Stein opera about female suffrage, *The Mother of Us All* (1967).

In 1964 Indiana was commissioned to do a painting for a new museum located in a former church. He created a painting bearing the words *Love Is God* (1964). As he refined the theme, the stenciled word "love" on his paintings clearly referred to the nonphysical: "The *LOVE* I am talking about is spiritual." In 1966 Indiana exhibited a series of "love" paintings, including what proved to be a definitive

Robert Indiana reflects on his work. CORBIS CORPORATION (BELLEVUE)

version. This was a seventy-two-inch-square painting with the four red block letters completely filling the canvas against a blue and green background. Each letter filled a quarter of the picture, the *L* and a tilted *O* in the top two quadrants, the *V* and *E* in the bottom two quadrants.

The image had an unintended, immediate social impact, particularly among young people, who were already radicalized by the civil rights and free speech movements then erupting on college campuses. Although Indiana's message was intended to be metaphysical, the adoption of the image by the youth movement quickly changed the public's perception of it. The *LOVE* image was soon appearing on hippies' clothing and body paintings. Love-ins, love beads, love children, and so forth were endemic in the late 1960s, and Indiana's *LOVE* painting was co-opted as a countercultural, erotic icon.

Although Indiana pursued other themes in the late 1960s, he continued to produce more *LOVE* images. In addition to painting variations of the image, Indiana created, with Herbert Feuerlicht, sculptured versions of carved aluminum, ranging from twelve inches to twelve feet in height and up to three tons in weight. He also authorized the manufacture of the image on rings and silk screens. Since Indiana held no copyright to the image, pirated versions appeared everywhere. Paperweights, coffee cups, and posters bearing the *LOVE* image inundated the country, but Indiana received no remuneration for these products. Even when the U.S. Postal Service issued a *LOVE* stamp in 1973 that sold 330 million copies, Indiana received only a token $1,000 designer fee.

The appearance of the *LOVE* image marked the major

turning point in Indiana's career, as museums and collectors stopped pursuing his new work. Some in the art world resented the identification of *LOVE* with the youth culture. To others, the image confirmed the supposition that Indiana was a graphic designer rather than a fine arts painter. For whatever reason, Indiana's popularity faded. In 1978 he left New York City and moved to Vinalhaven, Maine, an island in Penobscot Bay, where he has resided ever since. Although he continues to receive some important commissions, he is no longer a force in the art world.

Nevertheless, in the early and mid-1960s Indiana was such a force. Never had an artist so successfully merged words and color, numbers and form into works of art. In the process he gave great impetus to the pop art movement, and his *LOVE* image became *the* left-wing icon of the 1960s and early 1970s, along with the peace symbol.

★

Indiana has written several versions of an "autochronology," two of which appear in exhibition catalogs: John W. McCoubrey, *Robert Indiana* (1968), and Donald B. Goodall, *Robert Indiana* (1977), which also contains an interview with the artist. An excellent monograph is Susan Elizabeth Ryan, *Robert Indiana: Figures of Speech* (2000). Biographical information is also in Nicola and Elena Calas, *Icons and Images of the Sixties* (1971); and Carl Weinhardt, *Robert Indiana* (1990). See also Barbaralee Diamonstein, *Inside New York's Art World* (1979): 151–166; and "Indiana on Indiana," *Indianapolis Monthly* (Apr. 2002): 122–127. There is an exhaustive four-part interview with Richard Baker in *Smithsonian Archives of American Art/Oral History Interview with Robert Indiana* (1963).

ROBERT HENDRICK

JACKSON, Henry Martin ("Scoop") (*b.* 31 May 1912 in Everett, Washington; *d.* 1 September 1983 in Everett, Washington), U.S. Democratic senator who was an expert on environmental affairs, military matters, and national security over a time span that ranged from Roosevelt to Reagan; he became influential during his nearly forty-three years in Congress and was considered a cold war liberal.

Jackson was the son of two immigrants from Norway: Peter Jackson, a building contractor, and Marine Anderson, a homemaker. Along with his four siblings, Jackson grew up emulating the strong work ethic of his parents. When he was a teenager he set a record for delivering 74,880 copies of the *Everett Herald*—all without any complaints from newspaper subscribers. His oldest sister gave him the nickname "Scoop" because he reminded her of a comic-strip character of that name. The sobriquet followed Jackson throughout his congressional career.

After graduating from Everett High School, Jackson attended the University of Washington during the Depression. He earned his law degree there in 1935 and practiced law before he became a prosecutor in his native Snohomish County. Known as a serious and deliberate man, he was the youngest prosecutor the county had ever had, and a tenacious one. When he came to Washington, D.C., in 1940 Jackson was just twenty-eight and the youngest member of the House. Soon he gained a reputation as a proponent of national security. Jackson served in the army as an

enlisted man during World War II until President Roosevelt recalled him to the House.

In 1952 Jackson began his long career as a senator when he defeated Republican incumbent Harry P. Cain. Over thirty-one years, Jackson became influential in foreign affairs. Ever watchful when it came to the security of the United States, Jackson hated Soviet communism and did his best to fight it.

The 1960s brought Jackson recognition as an ardent advocate of national defense. He was a proponent of the nuclear submarine program and always pressed for public acceptance and endorsement of the arms race. A strong and vocal supporter of civil and labor rights legislation, Jackson worked tirelessly. He chaired hearings on foreign and defense policy in 1959. As chairman of the Democratic Party in the 1960 campaign, Jackson was greatly responsible for getting the public to accept the idea of a defense missile gap, which became part of John F. Kennedy's successful presidential campaign. Jackson was Kennedy's first choice as running mate, but because of Jackson's focus on military defense, Lyndon Johnson was deemed more politically advantageous.

Unceasing in his pursuit of national readiness, Jackson spent most of his efforts on the job and did not take much time for a personal life. When he married Helen Hardin on 16 December 1961, he was nearly fifty. The couple had two children.

Jackson's reputation for opposing all efforts to improve relations between the USSR and the United States grew to colossal proportions in the 1960s. He was firmly against all nuclear arms controls. In 1963 he supported the Nuclear Test Ban Treaty, but he was not really in favor of it and hoped it would be withdrawn because he thought it put the United States at a disadvantage.

Also in 1963 Jackson became chair of the Interior Committee and began setting energy and environmental policies. In 1969 he wrote the National Environmental Policy Act, which required federal agencies to examine and report on environmental impact before beginning projects. He was also on the alert for conservation and warned of the impending energy crisis before it became a reality in the 1970s. For his support of conservationist efforts, including expanding wilderness areas and national parks, Jackson was the first politician to receive the Sierra Club's John Muir Award for Conservation in 1969. He was given the National Wildlife Federation's legislator of the year award in 1970.

Jackson's skill in foreign policy and defense attracted conservative Republicans. In 1968 he turned down an offer from Richard Nixon to serve as secretary of either state or defense because Jackson believed he could have more impact on policies from within the Senate. He was always interested in setting public policy, especially national security policy, rather than securing large personal wealth. Those who admired him said he was patriotic; certainly

Henry M. Jackson. ARCHIVE PHOTOS, INC.

Jackson tried to act in ways he thought would benefit the country. But Jackson's detractors considered his attitude far too militant and criticized his approach as combative. He was not an advocate of making peace with the Russians; instead, he concentrated on being prepared to meet any foreign attack. It might be fair to say that Jackson did not want to trust any enemy who held a bigger gun, so he did not seek to stop the arms race but to keep the United States ahead of Russia.

Not just an expert on national security, Jackson was also a skilled orator who gave detailed speeches that were frequently printed and circulated. His book *Fact, Fiction, and National Security* (1964) gives insight into military policy.

After the 1960s Jackson continued his vigilance on behalf of national interests. In 1972 and 1976 he ran for the Democratic presidential nomination and lost. But he kept his seat in the Senate and continued to influence policy.

Even after his death, signs of Jackson's reputation as a proponent of national defense continued. In 1984 the Trident submarine was named after him. The same year the Kissinger Commission on Central America dedicated its report to him. In the years that followed, Jackson was remembered for his support of the Vietnam War, his endorsement of big military budgets, and his unending efforts to keep the United States on the alert for foreign enemies.

Jackson died of a ruptured aorta at home in Everett. He is buried in Evergreen Cemetery in Everett. He received the Presidential Medal of Freedom posthumously.

★

An article on Jackson is in *American National Biography,* vol. 11 (1999). Also see Peter Ognibene, *Scoop: The Life and Politics of Henry M. Jackson* (1975). Another source of biographical information is William Prochnau and Richard Larsen, *A Certain Democrat: Senator Henry M. Jackson, A Political Biography* (1972). The most complete biography of Jackson is Robert G. Kaufman, *The Quiet Giant: Henry M. Jackson and the Transformation of American Liberalism from the New Deal to the Present* (1999). An article of interest is Jonathan Alter, "The Myth of Scoop Jackson: Big Spender, Big Hawk, and Big Loser," *The New Republic* (12 May 1986). Worth reading is "Holding the Bridge," Andrew Marshall's book review in *The National Interest* (22 Dec. 2000) of Robert G. Kaufman, *Henry M. Jackson: A Life in Politics* (2000). Obituaries are in the *New York Times* and *Washington Post* (both 3 Sept. 1983) and the *National Review* (30 Sept. 1983).

A. E. SCHULTHIES

JACKSON, Jesse Louis (*b.* 8 October 1941 in Greenville, South Carolina), civil rights and political activist, Baptist minister, and orator who became an influential member of the Southern Christian Leadership Conference during the 1960s.

Jesse Louis Burns was home-birthed to a gifted eighteen-year-old singer, Helen Burns. His father was Noah Louis Robinson, a married man living next door. Noah Robinson made a comfortable living as a cotton grader, while Helen Burns and her single mother, Matilda, had far less financial stability. Soon after Jackson's birth, his mother became a cosmetologist. In 1944 she married Charles Henry Jackson, a shoeshine attendant at a local barbershop, shortly before he entered the U.S. Army. After serving in the Army, Charles Jackson became a janitor and was soon employed in the post office building in Greenville. In 1957, when Jesse was a teenager, Charles Jackson formally adopted him.

As a child, Jackson delivered stove wood with an older relative, caddied at the Greenville Country Club, and waited tables at the airport restaurant. He was a good student and lettered in three sports at the all-black Sterling High School in Greenville. Jackson received a football scholarship at the University of Illinois but had difficulty making the team, became discouraged by racism, and lacked academic focus. He voluntarily left the University of Illinois at the end of his freshman year, transferring to North Carolina Agricultural and Technical State University (North Carolina A & T) in Greensboro in 1960.

Jackson thrived at North Carolina A & T. He quarterbacked the football team, was elected student body president, joined the Omega Psi Phi fraternity, and was elected president of the North Carolina Intercollegiate Council on Human Rights. By 1963 Jackson was deeply involved in the civil rights movement. He participated in marches, sit-ins, and boycotts designed to break down racial barriers.

During his senior year in college, on 31 December 1962, Jackson married Jacqueline Lavinia Brown, who shared his background and many of his interests. They have five children. In 1964 Jackson completed his bachelor's degree in sociology and took a job as field representative for the southeast region of the Congress on Racial Equality (CORE). In the fall of 1964 he accepted a Rockefeller grant to attend the Chicago Theological Seminary at the University of Chicago. Jackson arrived in Chicago with a letter of introduction from the governor of North Carolina to Mayor Richard J. Daley. When Jackson asked Daley for a job, he was told that he must see his ward committeeman and do some precinct work to earn a city job. Jackson, who did not understand Chicago politics, was insulted. Instead, he supplemented his scholarship with part-time work for John Johnson, founder and publisher of *Jet* and *Ebony* magazines.

Chicago already had a host of strong African-American leaders when Jackson arrived in the city. William Dawson and his protégé, Ralph Metcalfe, were powerful "political-machine" politicians, and a bevy of ambitious African Americans, including Erwin France, Wilson Frost, August "Gus" Savage, and Richard Newhouse, were poised to climb the ladder of political power. Nor was there a short-age of independent African-American spokespeople. Bobby Rush of the Black Panthers and comedian Dick Gregory were among those already agitating for change.

African-American unemployment rates in Chicago, which hovered around 17 percent, and the rough-and-tumble of the city's politics complicated Jackson's rise to power. The crime syndicate had a strong presence through-out the city, particularly on the south side. "Fast Eddie" Vrdolyak and Vito Marzullo, among others, were under-stood to have close ties to syndicate boss Tony Accardo. Police officers "fished" for five dollars in cash in lieu of a traffic ticket, and the County Clerk of Courts, Les Beck, openly fixed court cases.

In March 1965, after six months of graduate studies, Jackson spent five days in Selma, Alabama, where he met Dr. Martin Luther King. Upon his return to Chicago, Jackson failed to submit required papers and attended classes irregularly. He did, however, participate in the activities of the Chicago Coordinating Council of Community Orga-nizations and allied himself with the Reverend Clay Evans, pastor of the Fellowship Missionary Baptist Church. Rev-erend Evans had one of the largest congregations on Chi-cago's south side and was one of the few black ministers not allied with the Daley political machine.

Jackson registered for fall classes at Chicago Theological Seminary, but he was not devoted to his studies. After meet-ing King, Jackson focused his efforts on becoming a staff member of the Southern Christian Leadership Conference (SCLC) and bringing King's crusade to Chicago. Jackson worked with Evans to invite King to preach from the Fel-lowship Missionary Baptist Church pulpit in the spring of 1966. On 6 June 1966, after visiting Chicago, King offered Jackson a $3,000-per-year job with the SCLC to organize Operation Breadbasket. The project was based on a model developed by Reverend Leon Sullivan in Philadelphia in the early 1960s, and King hoped to expand the program to cities across the nation.

On 10 July 1966 King held a nonviolent rally at Soldier Field in Chicago that attracted 40,000 people. King de-manded that Mayor Daley end "plantation politics" and housing discrimination. The rally was designed to be the start of a nonviolent crusade against de facto segregation in northern cities. But four days of rioting, arson, and looting broke out in the Lawndale neighborhood, and it was nec-essary to bring in the National Guard to stop the violence. On 5 August a march through Gage Park, a blue-collar suburb on Chicago's south side, turned violent. King was forced to leave Chicago with little to show for his effort.

Streetwise blacks felt that King had stirred up trouble but had done little to solve problems. In 1967 Daley won reelection with overwhelming support from African Amer-icans. Dawson produced a 61,522 plurality for Daley in the

Jesse Jackson at the funeral of Dr. Martin Luther King, Jr., April 1968. FLIP SCHULKE/CORBIS

five wards he controlled. Eighty-seven percent of black votes cast went to Daley.

When King left Chicago, Jackson vigorously undertook the task of organizing Operation Breadbasket. Just before Easter weekend 1967, Jackson announced that Operation Breadbasket would boycott Country Delight, a large local white-owned dairy that had no black employees. He en-listed more than 100 African-American ministers to instruct members of their congregations to boycott Country Delight products. After losing more than a half-million dollars, Country Delight hired forty-four African-American work-ers. Subsequently, Jackson won similar quick victories against the city's major soft drink suppliers.

Jackson then turned to the grocery industry. The Hi-Lo grocery stores soon agreed to provide 184 new entry-level jobs for black workers and to make more shelf space avail-able for products made by minority-owned businesses. However, when Operation Breadbasket attempted to target the A & P chain and the strongly entrenched Red Rooster food stores, Jackson experienced problems. Despite four months of picketing, he made no progress. It was not until he enlisted the help of the Black Stone Rangers, a notorious youth gang known for engaging in extortion, that things changed.

Under the auspices of Jackson, members of the ruling body of the Black Stone Rangers were placed on Red Rooster's payroll as "no-show" security workers—a kind of protection racket scheme. Jackson also introduced his half-brother, Noah Robinson, Jr., to Black Stone Rangers' leader Jeff Fort. Robinson soon became closely linked with the Rangers, and along with Fort became a kingpin in drug-dealing. In 1983 both were arrested, convicted, and sent to prison.

When King was assassinated on 4 April 1968, the twenty-six-year-old Jackson was in Memphis with King supporting the sanitation workers strike. Jackson immediately returned to Chicago, where he marched into a City Council meeting wearing a blood-spattered sweater. As riots on the west side of Chicago burned dozens of blocks of stores and houses, Jackson addressed the council with a pledge to uphold King's nonviolent goals and practices.

On 30 June 1968 Evans and the singer Aretha Franklin's father, the Reverend C. L. Franklin, held an ordination service for Jackson at the Fellowship Missionary Baptist Church in Chicago. Jackson then took the position of associate minister at that church. In 1969 Jackson received an honorary doctorate from Lincoln University in Pennsylvania. In 1970 he received honorary doctorates from Oberlin College, Howard University, and North Carolina A & T.

As a result of agitation against prejudice and injustice at regular SCLC Saturday morning rallies at the Capital Theater on Chicago's South Halsted Street, Jackson became a familiar spokesperson for African-American causes.

In the fall of 1968 Republicans paid the Black Stone Rangers, who also called themselves the Black P. Stone Nation, to discourage African-American voting by holding a gang war in the Chicago neighborhood of Woodlawn. Nixon was elected president in part because low voter turnout in black neighborhoods tipped the election to Republicans in Illinois. The number of votes cast in Chicago fell nearly 25 percent below 1964 levels. The number of blacks voting in Illinois that year was particularly low; unregistered potential black voters in Chicago exceeded the entire black population of Mississippi.

Under the auspices of Operation Breadbasket, in 1970 Jackson inaugurated Black Expo, a trade fair that featured the leaders, products, and services of African-American–owned businesses. While several thousand people attended the exhibits, entertainment, and presentations at Black Expo, Ralph Abernathy, president of the SCLC, became concerned about the poor accounting for the proceeds from the event. His concerns increased in 1971 when it was rumored that the Black Stone Rangers were paid a share of the profits for providing "security services." As a result of unpaid bills, Jackson was sued. In court he was unable to provide a plausible explanation for the shortage of funds.

In September 1971 Jackson incorporated the Expo independent of the SCLC, and that December resigned from the SCLC and formed Operation People United to Save Humanity (PUSH). Jackson soon expanded PUSH to the fourteen metropolitan areas of the United States with the largest African-American populations.

Following the 1968 Democratic National Convention, the party was pressured to revise its rules to broaden participation of minorities, women, and young people. In 1972 Jackson was part of the slate of Illinois delegates that successfully challenged the Richard J. Daley delegation to the Democratic convention on the grounds that Daley had violated the party's reformed rules in selecting his delegation.

Subsequently Jackson became one of the nation's most visible African-American spokespersons, frequently exhibiting his oratory skills before conventions and other large crowds. Although he failed to win many policy concessions, he kept issues of racial equality alive at a time when it was unpopular to speak up for the underrepresented. Jackson ran for the Democratic presidential nomination in 1984 and 1988. In 1989 Jackson moved to Washington, D.C. The following year the D.C. city council created two unpaid offices of "statehood senator"—popularly called "shadow senators"—to lobby the U.S. Congress for statehood for the District of Columbia. Jackson was elected to one of those positions. He was appointed U.S. special envoy for the promotion of democracy in Africa in 1997. His son, Jesse Jackson, Jr., was elected to the U.S. Congress in 1998.

★

Jackson, with Roger D. Hatch and Frank E. Watkins, eds., published *Straight from the Heart* (1987). He also wrote *A Time to Speak: The Autobiography of the Reverend Jesse Jackson* (1988). Biographies include Barbara Reynolds, *Jesse Jackson: America's David* (1985); Dorothy Chaplik, *Up with Hope: A Biography of Jesse Jackson* (1986); Elizabeth Colton, *The Jackson Phenomenon: The Man, the Power, the Message* (1989); Marshall Frady, *Jesse: The Life and Pilgrimage of Jesse Jackson* (1996); and Kenneth R. Timmerman, *Shakedown: Exposing the Real Jesse Jackson* (2002). Also of interest is Len O'Connor, *Clout: Major Daley and His City* (1975). Articles of interest include Gaylord Shaw, "A Clash Within: The Mixed Blessing of Rev. Jackson," *Los Angeles Times* (16 Dec. 1987); and Tom Brune and James Ylisela, Jr., "The Making of Jeff Fort," *Chicago Magazine* (Nov. 1988).

KEITH MCCLELLAN

JACOBS, Jane (*b.* 4 May 1916 in Scranton, Pennsylvania), award-winning writer and urban theorist whose *Death and Life of Great American Cities* (1961) has been credited with changing the way in which many Americans view cities and their future.

Jacobs was born Jane Butzner, daughter of John Decker Butzner, a physician, and Bess Robison, a schoolteacher.

She was raised in the heart of Pennsylvania's anthracite coal region. Although large-scale underground coal mining in the area continued until the end of the 1950s, the industry had already begun its decline when she was a child. This gradual decline forced hundreds of local residents to move in search of work. After graduating from high school, Jacobs worked briefly as a reporter for the *Scranton Tribune* before joining the exodus. She headed to New York City in 1934, settling eventually in Manhattan's Greenwich Village. While in New York, she studied briefly at Columbia University. To make ends meet, she worked as a freelance writer until landing an associate editor's job in 1952 with *Architectural Forum*. She was working on a freelance assignment for the Office of War Information when she met her future husband, architect Robert Hyde Jacobs. The couple had three children.

From her vantage point in the largest city in the United States, Jacobs was an eyewitness to the foibles and failures of post–World War II urban renewal, which planted the seed for her seminal book, *The Death and Life of Great American Cities,* published in 1961. The book, one of the most influential works in the history of city planning, took to task the much-vaunted urban renewal and garden city movements of the period. Jacobs minced no words. The opening sentence of her classic: "This book is an attack on current city planning."

The initial reaction of urban planners to Jacobs's attack was much as might be expected. Of *Death and Life,* Dennis O'Harrow, director of the American Society of Planning Officials, wrote in the society's newsletter: "The Jane Jacobs book is going to do a lot of harm . . . but we are going to have to live with it. So batten down the hatches." In the more than four decades since the book appeared, however, the attitude of city planners toward Jacobs's views changed significantly. Most planners refer to the book positively, and many cite it as a source of inspiration that drew them into the urban planning profession.

Interviewed by Jim Kunstler for *Metropolis* magazine in 2001, Jacobs discussed the factors that motivated her to write *Death and Life:* "Well, what was getting immediately under my skin was this mad spree of deceptions and vandalism and waste that was called urban renewal." She also expressed her anger at the dishonesty about what was being done.

Jacobs was also motivated to write her classic frontal assault on urban planning by a very real threat to her neighborhood of Greenwich Village. When the city's master planner Robert Moses proposed running a highway through the neighborhood's Washington Square Park and building a parking lot in Central Park, Jacobs felt compelled to speak out. In 2002 she told *Maclean's,* "I didn't inherit a great wish to be an activist. I was pushed into it by things that were just so outrageous."

What comes through loud and clear in Jacobs's book is her deep affection for New York City and, more specifically, the scores of neighborhoods scattered throughout it. In one of the book's best-known passages, she writes of her own neighborhood, calling it "an intricate sidewalk ballet." She explains, "I make my own entrance into it a little after eight when I put out the garbage can, as the droves of junior high school students walk by the center of the stage."

In the late 1960s Jacobs actively disagreed with the growing U.S. involvement in the Vietnam War. After one antiwar demonstration she was arrested, and both her sons declared publicly they would go to jail before serving in the overseas campaign. As her sons neared draft age in 1968, the Jacobs family decided to leave the United States and move to Canada. They settled in Toronto, where Jacobs eventually became a naturalized Canadian citizen. The change in residence did nothing to dampen her enthusiasm for writing. In 1969 she published *The Economy of Cities,* and wrote another four books over the next few decades, including *Cities and the Wealth of Nations: Principles of Economic Life* (1984), and *The Nature of Economies* (2000).

Although she has no formal training in urban design or urban history, Jacobs for more than four decades has been a powerful force in the field of urban planning. In her writings, beginning with the classic *The Death and Life of Great American Cities,* Jacobs is fiercely critical of a planning style that has destroyed existing communities, separated land uses, and rebuilt sterile areas. With equal passion she advocates a fresh approach to planning in which greater attention is paid to the protection of neighborhoods and design details that truly matter to people.

The genius of Jacobs's vision is perhaps best summed up in Marcus Cunliffe's comments on *Death and Life* in *Spectator:* "No one who reads her arguments closely can avoid being exhilarated by her rare combination of good plain prose and good plain common sense."

★

Further information about Jacobs's life and career is in Roger Montgomery, "Is There Still Life in 'The Death and Life'?" *Journal of the American Planning Association* (22 June 1998); Jim Kunstler, "Jane Jacobs Interviewed by Jim Kunstler," *Metropolis* (Mar. 2001); Bill Steigerwald, "City Views," *Reason* (June 2001); and Robert Sheppard, "Jane Jacobs," *Maclean's* (1 July 2002).

DON AMERMAN

JENSEN, Arthur Robert (*b.* 24 August 1923 in San Diego, California), psychologist and educator, best known since the 1960s for his prolific writings and research on intelligence testing and on racial and ethnic differences in cognitive abilities.

Jensen and one sister were born to Linda Mary (Schachtmayer) and Arthur Alfred Jensen, the owner-operator of a local lumber company. A lifelong lover of music, Jensen

Arthur R. Jensen. AP/WIDE WORLD PHOTOS

played clarinet as a teen in the San Diego Symphony but put aside his interest in the symphony orchestra to enter the University of California, Berkeley, where he earned his B.A. degree in psychology in 1945. He taught high school while completing his M.A. degree in psychology at San Diego State College in 1952, then his Ph.D. in psychology at Teacher's College of Columbia University in 1956. During his two-year postdoctorate study in London from 1956 to 1958, Jensen was heavily influenced by his mentor Hans Eysenck's methods of experimental research on personality. In 1958 Jensen joined the faculty of the University of California, Berkeley, where he has remained a teacher and researcher, except for a few leaves, including a Guggenheim Fellowship to London (1964–1965) and a fellowship with the Center for Advanced Study in the Behavioral Sciences (1967–1968). Jensen married Barbara Jane DeLarme on 6 May 1960. They had one daughter.

Long before President Lyndon B. Johnson envisioned the Great Society in 1964, some psychologists were involved in activism on many fronts—education, social welfare, civil rights, and health care. For example, the Society for Psychological Study of Social Issues (SPSSI), formed in 1936, played a key role in the U.S. Supreme Court's 1954 desegregation decision in *Brown* v. *Board of Education*. The SPSSI also sponsored a series of books, including a 1968 volume on social class, race, and psychological development

in which coeditors Martin Deutsch, Irwin Katz, and Jensen extolled the value of educational reform on children's school performance.

By invitation, Jensen soon published an electrifying article in the winter 1969 issue of *Harvard Educational Review*, "How Much Can We Boost IQ and Scholastic Achievement?" This 123-page opus began with a provocative sentence ("Compensatory education has been tried and it apparently has failed"), then went on to marshal data documenting four points: (1) one's intelligence is best seen as a single general ability, or g; (2) among individuals, variations in g are due more to one's genetic inheritance than environmental experiences; (3) among groups, there are large differences in g based on race and social class, which are also due primarily to inheritance; and (4) because of this, past and future compensatory education programs likely have limited impact in equalizing achievement for low-performance groups.

Criticism was swift and heated. The spring 1969 issue of *Harvard Educational Review* devoted 118 pages to lengthy critiques by seven prominent psychologists, along with Jensen's rejoinder. Jensen's article was a surprise, quickly assailed by activist psychologists as ill-timed scientific racism that could undermine society's evolution towards greater racial equality. These critics attacked "Jensenism" on many levels—that its conclusions were premature, inaccurate, misleading, ill-willed, and pandering to reactionary forces in society. Supporters acknowledged Jensen's expertise, his right to publish his views, and even his courage to express unpopular conclusions on a taboo topic. Controversy quickly escalated, as Jensen threatened to sue SPSSI president Martin Deutsch (his former coeditor) for defamation, and rare editorials in *Psychology Today* and the *Wall Street Journal* in 1973 chastened SPSSI for overdoing its caustic attacks. Leftist death threats moved Cal-Berkeley administrators to assign plainclothes police officers to accompany Jensen around campus. His classes were disrupted, and there were unsuccessful calls for his censure by Cal-Berkeley and the American Psychological Association (APA).

After 1969 Jensen continued undaunted through the next three decades, publishing a dozen books and over 200 research articles on differential psychology, as well as group differences in personality and ability. Jensen's writing is aimed at the public as well as colleagues and is known for its clarity, statistical prowess, and attention to detail. Jensen avers that the recognition of group differences is not the same as racism, which is a political philosophy of differential treatment that he does not espouse. Jensen regards himself as an early target of scientific intolerance and political correctness (even before the term *PC* was coined), one who was attacked simply for trying to report his scientific findings without bias or compromise. At the time the controversial book *The Bell Curve,* written by Charles Murray and Richard J. Herrnstein, appeared in 1994, Jensen was recognized as one of a small cadre of top scientists also known for their outspoken hereditarian views, along with Herrnstein at Harvard, Hans Eysenck in London, and J. Philippe Rushton in Canada. While attempts to marginalize him and his work have had some success, Jensen has remained by all measures a prolific researcher whose books and presentations draw large and interested audiences, and his work has partially segued into the emerging field of evolutionary psychology.

The nature–nurture issue had a tragic history earlier in the twentieth century. At one extreme, National Socialist (Nazi) scientists in Germany during the 1930s and 1940s held a radical genetic view of behavior consistent with their ideas of Aryan supremacy and "inferior human stocks." At the other extreme, the Communist Party of the Soviet Union (CPSU) under Joseph Stalin and scientist Trofim Lysenko developed an equally radical environmentalist view trying to "outlaw" the notion of any fixed genetic tendencies. The very mixed views of American behavioral scientists prior to World War II veered sharply from genes toward environment in the wake of Nazi horrors (sterilization, genocide, eugenics, breeding camps, and slavery), and then even more so during the accelerating environmental optimism of the Great Society of the 1960s. The dual impact of Jensen's work since the 1960s has been to retain the hereditarian view within behavioral science discussions and to clarify the interplay between science and politics on a sensitive issue such as race—clearly, some see behavioral science more as a valuable engine for social change, while others see it more as a search for truth and open dialogue not to be compromised by policy concerns or stifled by political correctness.

★

No full-length biography of Jensen has been written. Several scientists have written books in response to Jensen's theories. See Arthur Stanley Goldberger, *Jensen's Twin Fantasies* (1976), and Sonja C. Grover, *The Cognitive Basis of the Intellect: A Response to Jensen's "Bias in Mental Testing"* (1981). A biographical profile is in *Contemporary Authors Online* (2002).

HAROLD TAKOOSHIAN

JOFFREY, Robert (*b.* 24 December 1928 in Seattle, Washington; *d.* 25 March 1988 in New York City), American dancer, choreographer, and director who founded the Joffrey Ballet.

Born Anver Bey Abdullah Jaffa Khan, Joffrey was the only child of Dollha Anver Bey Jaffa Khan and Marie Gallette. (Although born in 1928, Joffrey widely circulated his date of his birth as 1930, and it appears incorrectly in many references.) Joffrey's father came to the United States from

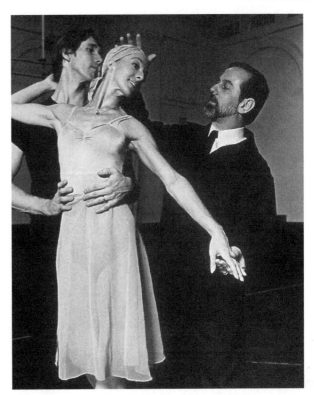

Robert Joffrey *(right)*. AP/WIDE WORLD PHOTOS

Afghanistan in 1916. He moved to Seattle, where he opened the Rainbow Chili Parlor and changed his name to Joseph Joffrey. Joffrey's mother was an amateur concert violinist from northern Italy, who worked as a cashier at her husband's tavern upon their arrival in Seattle. Joffrey's childhood was marked by physical deformities and illness, and much of it was spent undergoing medical treatment and rehabilitation.

In 1938 Joffrey persuaded his parents to let him study ballroom and tap dance at the dance school above the family restaurant. The following year he took his first classical ballet lesson, and he was soon performing minor roles with Diaghilev's Ballet Russe de Monte Carlo during their regular appearances in Seattle. These early experiences made a deep impression on Joffrey, who expressed the desire to someday have his own dance company.

Joffrey moved to New York City in 1948, accompanied by his lifelong companion, dancer Gerald Arpino. By 1953 the two had established the American Ballet Center in Greenwich Village. But that same year the unthinkable happened—Joffrey tore a ligament during a performance, ending his career. Unable to dance, he turned to choreography and pursued his dream to found a dance company. On 2 October 1956 the Joffrey Ballet debuted with six dancers, who toured the country in a station wagon. Joffrey was taking an incredible chance in launching a new company.

Many in the dance world believed there was little hope for an American from the West Coast to succeed in the elite ballet community, which was centered in New York and dominated by Russian and European dancers and choreographers.

For Joffrey, the 1960s were marked by a series of glorious triumphs and bitter disappointments. In 1962 Rebekah Harkness Kean, a noted patron of the arts, sponsored his company on a series of international tours, but in 1964 Joffrey lost the company to Harkness during a dispute over its name. He and Arpino formed another company in 1965 known as the City Center Joffrey Ballet.

In 1967 Joffrey staged two groundbreaking performances. The first, *The Green Table,* a 1930s ballet with a strong antiwar message, emerged as his comment on the social and political upheaval of the Vietnam War. The war had hit the company particularly hard, as Joffrey lost one of his dancers to the service. *The Green Table* was the first full-scale restaging of a historic ballet under Joffrey's direction. Its success opened up the world of ballet to a whole new generation of dancers and enthusiasts. At the same time Joffrey realized it would be to his benefit to stage productions that were more closely linked with modern art, rather than trying to compete continually with the classical repertoire of the other New York companies.

During the summer of 1967 Joffrey began staging a new production, *Astarte*. He created a multimedia spectacle, combining film imagery by Gardner Compton with rock music, and using themes from the 1960s counterculture such as the use of psychedelic drugs, the expression of free love, and the embrace of Eastern philosophy. Through his innovative choreography, Joffrey broke with age-old dance conventions.

Astarte emerged as the foundation for Joffrey's pop dance repertoire, and showcased his company as a "tuned-in, turned-on Ballet troupe that excited young people." The ballet marked the first time a classical ballet company had successfully appropriated pop culture, adapting dance theater to the mood of the period. *Astarte* also became the first ballet ever to grace the cover of *Time* magazine, as well as the covers of *Life* and *Saturday Review,* and was the subject of an illustrated story in *Playboy*. Despite harsh critical reaction it became one of the most popular and fashionable dance events of the season, and many of its performances were standing room only. Although some in the ballet world dismissed Joffrey's work as nothing more than a gimmick, for others it was a realization of the choreographer's claim that "there was an audience for dance that was bigger than the dance audience."

Joffrey closed out the decade by staging *Le Tricorne* in 1969, the first of the four masterworks from the Ballet Russe repertory that he produced. Its success led to productions of *Le Beau Danube* in 1972, *Parade* in 1973, and *Le Sacre*

du printemps in 1987. These revivals were superior to the original productions in every sense and yet paid homage to the works that had inspired them.

During the 1970s and 1980s Joffrey struggled to keep his company afloat while continuing to acquaint millions of Americans with dance. On 21 January 1976 he realized another milestone with the filming of *The City* by the Public Broadcasting System. The program reached an estimated television audience of four million.

Joffrey died from AIDS on 25 March 1988. He was cremated, and one-third of his ashes went to Arpino, one-third was scattered in the Puget Sound, and the final third was buried in the Cathedral of Saint John the Divine in New York City. Arpino took charge of the company and in 1996 moved it to Chicago, reestablishing the troupe as Joffrey Ballet of Chicago.

Joffrey believed that ballet ought not to be reserved for the elite but should become a form of popular entertainment. In his productions he always tried to combine mass appeal with artistic eloquence, staging everything from rock-'n'-roll ballets to the lost repertoire of the Ballet Russe. Joffre's accomplishments forever altered the perception of ballet and affirmed his reputation as one of the great figures in the history of dance theater.

★

Although most of Joffrey's records and personal papers are owned by Gerald Arpino, some are stored at the Joffrey School of Ballet in New York City, Harvard University, the Newberry Library in Chicago, and the Dance Collection of the New York Public Library. The only biography of Joffrey is Sasha Anawalt, *The Joffrey Ballet: Robert Joffrey and the Making of an American Dance Company* (1996). An interview with Joffrey is in John Gruen, *The Private World of Ballet* (1975). Obituaries are in the *Chicago Tribune, Los Angeles Times*, and *New York Times* (all 26 Mar. 1988).

MEG GREENE

JOHNS, Jasper (*b.* 15 May 1930 in Augusta, Georgia), painter and sculptor who presented the first viable challenge to the authority of abstract expressionist painting and to formalist criticism in American art after World War II.

Johns was the only child of William Jasper Johns, a farmer who had practiced law, and Jean Riley, and was raised in Allendale, South Carolina, near the Georgia border. His early artistic training came from occasional art classes in high school and from three semesters at the University of South Carolina, in Columbia. In 1948, a year after dropping out of the university, Johns moved to New York City. There he took courses at Parsons School of Design and viewed work by Picasso, Pollock, Cézanne, Munch, and others who would provide inspiration and motifs throughout his career. In 1951 he was drafted and stationed in

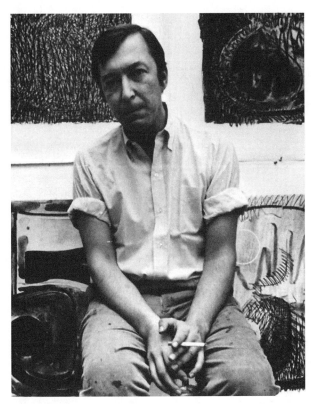

Jasper Johns. CORBIS CORPORATION (BELLEVUE)

Sendai, Japan, where he achieved the rank of private first class. Honorably discharged two years later, Johns returned to Manhattan, burned all his existing work, and decided that he was now an artist.

Johns received his first one-person show in January 1958 at the gallery of young Hungarian émigré Leo Castelli. Castelli remained Johns's representative until the dealer's death in 1999. The debut was a critical and financial success. *Target with Four Faces* (1955) appeared on the cover of *Art News,* and three paintings sold to the Museum of Modern Art. The show introduced Johns's controlled technique and what would become his signature motifs: flags, numbers, targets, and letters. His work during the early sixties was singled out by critics, including formalist Clement Greenberg and minimalist Donald Judd, for its curious combination of abstract handling and representational content. As critic Robert Rosenblum noted, Johns made "loved, handmade transcriptions of unloved, machine-made images." These quiet and meticulously painted objects posed the first significant challenge to the emotional catharsis and psychological exploration of abstract expressionism. Johns produced self-conscious analyses of the means of picture making that would be elaborated on for the rest of the century.

Johns's challenge to the 1950s New York School was fundamentally one of inversion. He confused abstract

means and representational ends and avoided the surrealist influences of the abstract expressionists to address the dadaist projects of Marcel Duchamp. In works like *Painted Bronze* (*Ale Cans,* 1960), Johns turned the tables on Duchamp's ready-mades (ordinary objects elevated to the status of art through the artist's declarations). Reintroducing technique to Duchamp's antiaesthetic, Johns presented ready-made subjects, "things the mind already knows," as he described them, crafted through laboriously handmade processes. In works that replicated everything from styles of painting to beer cans and paintbrushes, Johns created art that, like the music and dance of his close colleagues John Cage and Merce Cunningham, did not appear inventive in conventional terms. The search for alternative indications of artistry provides a link from Johns's work to the projects of Pop, minimalism, and Conceptual Art of the 1960s. Even identity-oriented art of the 1970s and 1980s returned to the stylistic analyses carried out by Johns in the 1960s.

Though Johns's work asserted the right to address content, his messages came veiled in their own coded structures. Like the work of many of his peers, from Robert Rauschenberg to Frank Stella, Johns's art proclaimed the importance of content while taking pains to obfuscate its specific meaning. Paintings like *In Memory of My Feelings—Frank O'Hara* (1961), or *Periscope (Hart Crane)* (1963), refer through their titles to love poems and, like the flags, suggest serious content without explaining it. The interpretative strategies Johns's work has inspired have included formal examinations of his motifs, attempts at cracking his codes, and queries into the meaning of coding itself. These studies have made Johns relevant to discussions of communicative strategies that rely on coded behavior, of which modern art is but one.

The early sixties were tumultuous for Johns. He saw his career and influence rise, found and visited audiences from New York to Tokyo, moved his studio from cosmopolitan Manhattan to the isolated Edisto Beach, South Carolina, and ended an intense romantic and professional relationship with Rauschenberg. During the latter part of the decade Johns ruminated over his early work, expanding compositions, repositioning elements, and changing media. With the encouragement of Tatyana Grosman at Universal Limited Art Editions, a small publishing company, he become one of the premier artists working in print media in the second half of the century. His editions include the most developed explorations into lithography to date, as well as screen prints, etchings, aquatints, and even lead reliefs. Print technology appeared in his works on canvas as well, further developing his interest in mixing media.

Since the 1960s Johns has become one of the most influential American artists of the century, arguably second only to Jackson Pollock. His methodical combination of expression and reserve in both content and form has been a touchstone for a variety of artists and critics. His strategy of combining intellectual and highly abstract stylistic devices with emotionally loaded objects has been a mainstay in his art, from the target or poetry paintings of the 1960s to fragmentary citations of Picasso, Mathias Grünewald, and the artist's own home and studio in the 1980s and 1990s. Since his debut in the 1960s, when the existence of universal certainties was being disputed, Johns has created a workable model for addressing both form and content in art. An inspiration to those of his own generation sorting out the legacy of abstract expressionism, Johns has been no less important to artists struggling to prioritize analysis and doubt over catharsis and purity.

★

Biographies of Johns include Leo Steinberg, *Jasper Johns* (1963); Alan R. Solomon, *Jasper Johns* (1964); Richard Francis, *Jasper Johns* (1984); Michael Crichton, *Jasper Johns* (1994); and Kirk Varnedoe, *Jasper Johns* (1996). Discussions and illustrations of Johns's work are in Roberta Bernstein, *Jasper Johns Paintings and Sculpture 1954-1974* (1985); Nan Rosenthal and Ruth E. Fine, *The Drawings of Jasper Johns: 1954–1984* (1990); Fred Orton, *Figuring Jasper Johns* (1994); and Gary Garrels, *Jasper Johns: New Paintings and Works on Paper* (1999). *Jasper Johns: Writings Sketchbook Notes, Interviews,* Kirk Varnedoe, ed., (1996) contains the same.

PETER R. KALB

JOHNSON, Claudia Alta Taylor ("Lady Bird") (*b.* 22 December 1912 in Karnack, Texas), wife of president Lyndon B. Johnson, environmental activist and businesswoman who is best remembered for her campaign to help beautify the United States while serving as first lady.

Johnson was the third child and only daughter of Thomas Jefferson Taylor, a merchant landowner, and Minnie Lee Pattilo, a homemaker. A petite, dark-haired woman with a prominent, slightly hooked nose, Johnson attended Marshall High School in Marshall, Texas, graduating at the age of fifteen. She completed two years at Saint Mary's Episcopal School for Girls in Dallas before enrolling at the University of Texas at Austin, where she obtained a B.A. degree in education in 1933, and a B.J. degree in journalism in 1934. Her career plans were derailed, however, when she went on a date with Lyndon Baines Johnson in August 1934. A case of "love at first sight," Lyndon Johnson proposed immediately, and on 17 November they were on a road trip when they stopped in San Antonio and decided to get married on the spur of the moment.

Although she had expressed her disdain for her husband's political aspirations, Johnson quickly proved to be a loyal and dedicated spouse. In 1937, with money inherited from her mother, she bankrolled Lyndon Johnson's run for U.S. Congress. During 1941 and 1942, while her husband was serving in the U.S. Navy, she oversaw the day-to-day operations of his congressional office. The following year she proved her mettle as a businesswoman, buying a struggling Austin, Texas, radio station, KTBC, and turning it into the cornerstone of a media empire that was worth more than $3 million by 1960. She also found time to raise two daughters.

In 1960, a pivotal year in U.S. politics, Lyndon Johnson ran for president. As she had in all his previous campaigns, Johnson served as both critic and adviser, and she founded an organization of women to boost his candidacy. Although John F. Kennedy won the Democratic nomination, he selected Lyndon Johnson as his running mate, a position Johnson initially attempted to dissuade her spouse from accepting. However, once he had accepted the offer she went into her public mode, fully supporting her husband's ambitions. Indeed, thanks to Jacqueline Kennedy's pregnancy, which kept her confined to Massachusetts, Johnson became the most visible female in the Democratic Party. Although there was a marked contrast between the two women in the eyes of the American public—Jacqueline Kennedy was the epitome of youth and glamour, while Johnson was the down-to-earth, efficient, yet accessible next-door neighbor—they developed a cordial working relationship.

Once on the campaign trail, Johnson proved tireless. With female members of the Kennedy family, she hosted six Texas tea parties in an attempt to assuage the concerns over Kennedy's Catholicism. With her husband, Johnson made sixteen appearances in eleven states and over 150 solo campaign stops. On 4 November, just days before the election, the Johnsons were involved in what some felt was the turning point for the Kennedy/Johnson ticket in Texas. On their way to a speech in Dallas, the Johnsons were accosted by a group of some 400 Republican women (dubbed "the mink coat mob"). During the melee, Johnson was spat upon and struck with a sign. Newspaper coverage of the incident, complete with photographs, shifted public support, and the Democrats narrowly carried Texas in the national election.

As the wife of the vice president, Johnson set up a series of informal luncheons with congressional wives and willingly participated in any ceremonial duties that Jacqueline Kennedy opted not to do. Johnson earned significant praise for her dedication to public service.

Following Kennedy's assassination on 22 November 1963, Johnson immediately concentrated on selling their Washington, D.C., home, putting her media empire into a blind trust, and seeking advice on how best to serve as first lady. Instead of her predecessor's press conferences, she instituted a series of informal luncheons spotlighting "Women Doers," which allowed her and her staff some

Claudia "Lady Bird" Johnson (*right*). THE LIBRARY OF CONGRESS

control over the agenda. Johnson also began to keep a formal daily record, a small portion of which was published in 1970 as *A White House Diary*.

In early 1964 Johnson began to develop her unique style as first lady, when she made a trip to the coalfield regions of Pennsylvania to publicize her husband's War on Poverty. Over the course of the next few years, she made numerous visits around the United States as an ambassador for her husband's Great Society programs. Additionally, she continued the efforts spearheaded by Jacqueline Kennedy to restore and preserve the White House, and she made the initial forays into the areas that would later come to define her tenure: public beautification programs and environmental conservation. Working closely with U.S. Secretary of the Interior Stewart Udall, Johnson toured national parks and Native American reservations and was a primary consultant with the president on the Task Force on Natural Beauty.

During Lyndon Johnson's 1964 bid for reelection, Mrs. Johnson made a 1,700-mile train trip through the American South. The "Lady Bird Special" was a throwback to old-fashioned politicking. At each whistle stop, the first lady made a speech tailored to the local community. Despite the occasional hecklers, whom she handled with aplomb and tact, the trip was considered a triumph for the campaign and for Johnson personally. She had fully emerged as a public figure.

After the 1964 election, Johnson promoted the National Head Start Program for preschool children, raising awareness of the program and lobbying for funding for its expansion. The first lady also organized committees to oversee the planting of trees and flowers throughout the Washington, D.C., area, including more than 2 million daffodil bulbs and thousands of dollars worth of dogwoods, cherry trees, and evergreens. Johnson was the founder of the Committee for a More Beautiful Capital in 1965. Under the oversight of this committee, statues of prominent figures that dotted the city were cleaned and repaired. Local parks were restored, and playgrounds and public school grounds were landscaped and improved. Under her auspices, "Project Pride" was launched, an initiative that encouraged inner city residents to clean up litter and make home repairs. On a wider scale, Johnson was involved, as a trustee of the Washington Gallery of Modern Art, in the negotiations with Joseph Hirschorn to bequeath his extensive art collection to the nation's capital. She also worked closely with Nathaniel Owings, who revitalized the Mall and the area around Pennsylvania Avenue.

The first lady's efforts to beautify the United States were not limited to Washington, D.C. She expressed concern over litter and the unsightly junkyards and billboards that proliferated along the roadways. Behind the scenes she lobbied for the passage of the Highway Beautification Act of 1965, a tribute to her tenacity and a first step in the battle to improve the roadsides of the United States. She served as an active spokesperson for this cause into the 1970s and 1980s.

Although the Johnsons were beset by Vietnam War protesters, Johnson did her best to concentrate on the good she was achieving on the home front. At a 1968 Women Doers lunch, she was confronted by singer-actress Eartha Kitt, who spoke out in support of the counterculture and against the war in Vietnam. Although Johnson received a sympathetic portrayal in the press, Kitt's outburst was indicative of the growing public sentiment against the military escalation in Vietnam. When Lyndon Johnson barely won the New Hampshire primary, and Robert F. Kennedy declared his candidacy for president, Lyndon Johnson chose not to seek another term. The Johnsons began to spend more time at their ranch in Texas, and on her final day in the White House, Johnson told her husband she had no regrets and looked forward to going home and spending the next twenty years with him.

That was not what fate had in store, however; Lyndon Johnson died in January 1973. Until she was beset with health problems in the 1990s, Johnson continued to guard her husband's legacy and remained active in conservation and environmental affairs. She helped raise money to rebuild a hike and bike trail in Austin, Texas, and in 1983 opened the Wildlife Research Center near Austin. She also served on the national committee of the Helen Keller World Crusade for the Blind. Johnson suffered a mild stroke on 3 May 2002, which has left her unable to speak. On 6 August 2002 the United States National Arboretum awarded Johnson its inaugural gold medal of excellence for sustained contributions to national landscaping and beautification.

★

Material documenting Johnson's role as first lady from 1963 to 1969 is at the Lyndon Baines Johnson Library and Museum in Austin, Texas. Johnson's own thoughts about her time as first lady are in her book, *A White House Diary* (1970). Biographical information about Mrs. Johnson is in Bill Adler, *The Common Sense Wisdom of Three First Ladies* (1966); Gordon L. Hall, *Lady Bird*

and Her Daughters (1967); Jan Jarboe Russell, *Lady Bird: A Biography of Mrs. Johnson* (1999); and Kati Marton, *Hidden Power: Presidential Marriages That Shaped Our Recent History* (2001). Lewis Gould examines Johnson's environmental work in two books, *Lady Bird Johnson and the Environment* (1988) and *Lady Bird Johnson: Our Environmental First Lady* (1999). Books about the Lyndon B. Johnson administration with information about Johnson include Vaughn Davis Burnet, *The Presidency of Lyndon B. Johnson* (1983); and Robert A. Divine, ed., *The Johnson Years: Volume Two: Vietnam, the Environment and Science* (1987). A three-volume set, Robert A. Caro, *The Path to Power: The Years of Lyndon Johnson* (1983); *Means of Ascent: The Years of Lyndon Johnson* (1990); and *Master of the Senate: The Years of Lyndon Johnson* (2001), is also informative. Articles about Johnson include "Reflections on Life in a Fishbowl," *U.S. News & World Report* (28 Sept. 1987); "Lady Bird Looks Back," *Texas Monthly* (1 Dec. 1994); "Lady Bird's Legacy," *Architecture* (1 July 1995); "Hits and Mrs.," *Texas Monthly* (1 Sept. 1999); and "Rare Bird," *People Weekly* (1 Jan. 2000).

TED MURPHY

JOHNSON, Haynes Bonner (*b.* 9 July 1931 in New York City), noted journalist and writer on national politics and affairs who established a reputation in the 1960s as a political writer who goes beyond the facts of the news to include opinion and commentary.

Johnson was born to Malcolm (Mike) Malone Johnson, a Pulitzer Prize–winning reporter for the *New York Sun,* and Ludie Adams Johnson, a homemaker. He received a bachelor's degree from the University of Missouri in 1952 and then served in the U.S. Army from 1952 to 1955. Johnson married Julia Ann Erwin in 1954 (they were later divorced), with whom he had three daughters and two sons.

Johnson's career in journalism began in 1956, when he joined the *Wilmington News-Journal* after completing a master's degree in American history at the University of Wisconsin, Madison. In 1957 he moved to the *Washington Evening Star,* where he worked for the following twelve years successively as city reporter, copy editor, night city editor, and national and special assignment reporter. During his tenure at the *Star,* Johnson earned a number of awards, including the Grand Award for reporting and public service from the Washington Newspaper Guild (1962 and 1968), the Front Page Award for political reporting by the American Newspaper Guild (1964), and the Headliners Award for national reporting (1968). In 1966 he was awarded the Pulitzer Prize, making Johnson and his father one of only two pairs of father and son to win it.

Johnson's Pulitzer Prize for national reporting was awarded for "Selma Revisited," published in the *Star* on the article serves as a measure of the civil rights movement through contrasting bitter realities with dearly held hopes and dreams.

Throughout the 1960s Johnson wrote about race and politics in America in the *Star,* as well as in several books. *Dusk at the Mountain—The Negro, the Nation, and the Capital: A Report on Problems and Progress* (1963) was based on a series of articles, entitled "The Negro in Washington," published in the *Star.* In it, Johnson looks critically at the social, political, and economic situation of African Americans living in the nation's capital and their struggles for equality and a better life. The book was generally well received, with several reviewers commenting on it as a thorough and serious analysis.

Johnson co-wrote *The Bay of Pigs: The Leaders' Story of Brigade 2506* (1964) with Cuban exiles who had participated in the attempted overthrow of Fidel Castro in 1961. The book is based primarily on interviews with the invasion leaders and creates a human narrative out of a story about which the American public had little information. Though not all reviewers agree with Johnson's conclusion that the Central Intelligence Agency had ultimate responsibility for the failed invasion, journalists and historians concur that the book is "detailed and well written." In the *New York Times Book Review,* Tad Szulc called it "unquestionably the most coherent, detailed and complete account of the brigade's adventures." In 1967 Johnson provided the historical background on the Ku Klux Klan for David Lowe's documentary of the Klan after Selma, *Ku Klux Klan: The Invisible Empire.* In a somewhat different vein, in 1968 he published *Fulbright: The Dissenter,* co-written with Bernard M. Gwertzman, a critical view of the Arkansas senator that was praised for its fairness and sharp criticism.

In 1969 Johnson was hired by the *Washington Post,* where he served as a national correspondent (1969–1973), assistant managing editor (1973–1977), and columnist (1977–1994). He has taught as the Ferris Professor of Journalism and Public Affairs at Princeton University (1975 and 1978), as the Professional in Residence at the Annenberg School of Journalism at Northwestern University (1993), and as Political Commentary and Journalism Professor at George Washington University (1994–1995). He is still well known as a commentator on such television programs as *Today, Washington Week in Review,* and *The NewsHour with Jim Lehrer.*

Among the books Johnson wrote or collaborated on since the 1960s, the most noted are *In the Absence of Power: Governing America* (1980), an examination of President Jimmy Carter's first thirty months in office, and *Sleepwalking Through History: America in the Reagan Years* (1991). As with his other writings, while not all reviewers agree with Johnson's opinions and conclusions, most praise him for

Haynes Johnson. ASSOCIATED PRESS AP

26 July 1965. In this front-page article Johnson wrote about his visit to Selma, Alabama, four months after the nation's attention had been riveted there during the civil rights march to the capitol in Montgomery. The events of the march—or more accurately, marches—of the previous February and March had drawn much attention to the civil rights movement and had speeded President Lyndon Johnson to deliver his voting rights legislation to the U.S. Congress. What the journalist found in Selma four months later was the civil rights forces "in disarray" and the African-American community divided. In the article, Johnson chronicled the lack of material or economic change in the lives of African Americans in Selma since the march and scandals within the civil rights movement as well as the continued success of voter registration drives. He ended the article by quoting a local African-American man "respected throughout Selma," who expresses his continued hopes for a better future, in which Selma would be "a tremendous place to live." More than just a curious glimpse at the city,

his thorough research and willingness to include opinion and judgment in his work.

A political independent, Johnson's knowledgeable, perceptive, and opinionated approach to news and events has been his greatest strength as a political reporter. While tackling the thorny issues and events of the day, he managed to impress even his critics with his thoroughness and evenness. The *Encyclopedia of Twentieth Century Journalists* quotes Johnson as having once written that newspapers have "two functions, both vital: to report what is the news of the day, fully and fairly, and also to go beyond these events and draw a larger portrait," something he has done throughout his career.

★

A useful overview of Johnson's career and a thorough bibliography of writings by and about Johnson can be found in *Contemporary Authors, New Revision Series,* vol. 48 (1995). Excerpts from his Pulitzer Prize–winning article are in John Hohenberg, *The Pulitzer Prize Story II* (1980). Reviews of Johnson's books are in many publications, including the *New Republic* (27 June 1964) and the *Times Literary Supplement* (7 Aug. 1969).

MARIANA REGALADO

JOHNSON, Lyndon Baines (*b.* 27 August 1908 near Stonewall, Texas; *d.* 22 January 1973 near Johnson City, Texas), premier American politician who became the thirty-sixth president of the United States (1963–1969).

Some people said that Johnson was like a colossus looming over the land. Others said that he was an "elemental force" in twentieth-century American politics. Indeed, he was a legendary titan who strode onto the pages of American history determined to fashion a political career that would have meaning long after his death. South Koreans once called him the "King of Kings," and they called his wife "Blue Bird." The television commentator Bill Moyers once suggested that he could walk on water. Society women in Dallas called him a Communist, spat on him, and hit him and his wife on their heads with placards, while pundits in Washington, D.C., called him a conservative. He stood six feet, four inches tall, and his legacy is equally huge. For good or ill, he changed America forever. With his massive reform program, he challenged Americans to be better than they were; he challenged them to care about the lowly, the dispossessed, and the downtrodden. While he strove for a Great Society, his administration was ruined by the Vietnam War.

Johnson was the eldest of five children of Sam Ealy Johnson, Jr., a politician, farmer, cotton speculator, and newspaper owner, and Rebekah (Baines) Johnson, a homemaker and sometime newspaper editor. Until the age of

President Lyndon B. Johnson. AP/WIDE WORLD PHOTOS

five, he grew up on the family farm in the hill country of Texas, but in 1913 the family shut down the farm and moved to Johnson City, a town of about 350 residents that was named after one of Johnson's ancestors. After attending the town's public schools, Johnson graduated in 1924 from Johnson City High School, one of a class of six.

Believing that he could find fame and fortune in California, Johnson, along with four friends, headed west. He ended up working as a clerk for an attorney who was one of his relatives. Without the fame and fortune that he sought, young Johnson decided to return home a year later. Back home, he worked on a highway construction crew for a time but eventually listened to his mother's advice that he attend college. In 1927 he enrolled in Southwest Texas State Teacher's College (SWTSTC) in San Marcos, Texas, a town just south of Austin and not far from Johnson City. Johnson worked his way through school and eventually came to the attention of Cecil Evans, president of SWTSTC. Johnson worked his way up from building janitor to Evans's student assistant.

After his junior year, when he was almost totally without funds, he took a temporary nine-month teaching job at Cotulla in southern Texas, a place about midway between San Antonio and Laredo. When he arrived in Cotulla, he was surprised and shocked by what he observed. The town had a population of about three thousand; Mexican Americans numbered 2,250. In fact, the place was a slave-labor camp, where the majority of Hispanics labored long to produce wealth for the white community of the region. The

Tejanos received in return poverty, segregated slum housing, and a segregated school, the one that hired young Johnson as a teacher-principal. Hispanics lived in one-room shacks, amid open sewers and incredible filth. The white community largely viewed the Hispanics with derision, and some even denied them their humanity by treating them like inferiors and insulting, humiliating, and abusing them day in and day out. Although Johnson had about two hundred Tejano children in his school, the majority of underage youth labored long in the fields rather than attending school. Many times Johnson observed even tiny Mexican-American children digging in garbage cans for food.

At his school, Johnson saw hopeless children every day. The school did not even schedule a lunch hour, for most students had no food to bring from home. His school did not have playground equipment; indeed, the playground was just an empty dirt lot. Johnson spent part of his first paycheck buying recreation equipment for the children. He also found enough money in the Hispanic community to begin a lunch program in which all children received hot food. Johnson hated how the area Anglos treated the Tejanos. Reflecting later, Johnson said that the biggest problems for a free nation were ignorance and poverty and that both were simply bad habits that could be stopped.

After his nine months in Cotulla, young Johnson returned to college and finished his B.S. degree in 1930, with majors in government and history. After teaching in Houston for a year, he received the proverbial chance of a lifetime when Congressman Richard Kleberg hired him as congressional secretary. They arrived together in Washington, D.C., in 1931, and Johnson quickly learned that Kleberg, a rich southern Texas rancher, had no intention of doing the work of a congressman. He excelled as a golfer and also loved high-stakes poker games. Kleberg was an all-around playboy who found many diversions, and he wanted only the prestige that came with the job of congressman. Consequently, Johnson soon became a de facto congressman, doing all the work that Kleberg would not. That Kleberg cared not at all was probably for the best. An archconservative, Kleberg criticized the Herbert Hoover administration as an overly activist organization that was going to drive western civilization into permanent decline. As for the depression, Kleberg knew what really had precipitated it: the gangster Al Capone and other bootleggers had caused it by "draining billions of dollars from legitimate trade."

When President Franklin D. Roosevelt and his New Dealers arrived in Washington in 1933, Johnson quickly became known as one of "Roosevelt's boys." He was like many a young New Deal optimist who was ready to devise social programs that would help the people cope with the depression. Johnson supported all the programs of the First

New Deal (1933), while his boss, Kleberg, opposed most of them. The congressman believed that the New Deal agenda was only barely veiled socialism or Communism. Still, the congressman did not hamper the New Deal: Johnson always told him how to vote. When Kleberg rebelled, Johnson threatened to resign. He also told Kleberg that he would never win reelection if Kleberg did not help the Hispanics in his Texas district. The fellow who thought that Al Capone had started the depression ended up voting for most of the major reforms of the New Deal.

In 1934, while on a trip home to visit his family, Johnson met Claudia Alta ("Lady Bird") Taylor, a beautiful twenty-one-year-old woman who recently had graduated from the University of Texas. Only a day after he met her, Johnson proposed to her. Although Lady Bird took some time to consider Johnson's proposal, she finally agreed. They married in San Antonio, Texas, on 17 November 1934 and had two daughters.

Helped by Sam Rayburn, a longtime friend of the Johnson family and an influential Texas congressman, Johnson escaped Kleberg in 1935 when Aubrey Williams, with Roosevelt's approval, named young Johnson as the Texas state director of the National Youth Administration (NYA), a program that Williams was tapped to administer nationally. The son of Alabama sharecroppers, Williams never lost his reforming zeal. He became an ardent New Dealer, and like Johnson, he believed that the power of the federal government could be used to help the people cope with the depression. The young Texan quickly went to work and became recognized as the best state director in the nation. In proportion to the population, Hispanics and blacks received more aid than whites, as Johnson focused on the lower class, not the middle class as did many state directors. Daily, Johnson held the fate of the poor in his hands, and he offered help. He was evolving as a neopopulist-nationalist who believed that government must work to improve the lives of its citizens, especially those living in harsh circumstances. Breaking with many southerners, he believed that flaws in the capitalistic socioeconomic system caused poverty, that the state governments cared not a bit, and that the federal government had to take control to get the country out of the depression.

Johnson left the NYA in 1937 to run in a special election to replace the congressman from his home district, the Tenth Congressional District, who had died suddenly. Running as a Roosevelt supporter, Johnson won the election for the house seat and headed back to Washington, where he continued to support all New Deal initiatives, including the Judicial Branch Reorganization Plan of 1937 that Congress refused to pass. Shortly after taking office, he faced a tough political task, one that helped define his career. The Fair Labor Standards Act was bottled up in a House committee. Many Republicans and southern "Dixiecrats" (conservative

Democrats from the South who often sided with Republicans to slow the pace of change, politically, socially, and economically) opposed the bill. They argued that a minimum wage and maximum work-hour law would wreck capitalism and would steer the country toward Communism, in addition to destroying all that was good in human life and western civilization. Opponents threatened Johnson, telling him that he would be tossed out of office if he supported the bill. Following his neopopulist leanings, the freshman congressman became one of only twenty-two southerners who voted to force the bill out of committee. Subsequently, the measure became law. A new day was coming for the lowly; now there would be a wages floor below which they could not fall. Some southerners, including several Texans, who supported the bill were indeed defeated for reelection, but Johnson survived.

As America's entry into World War II approached, Johnson supported Roosevelt's foreign policies, including his massive war-preparedness campaign. But Johnson did more. With various associates helping him, he began Operation Texas—an illegal plan to rescue Jews in Germany and Poland. In 1938 an Austin friend asked Johnson to help get a noted Jewish musician out of Europe. In complex maneuvers that involved several Latin American countries, false passports, and false visas, Johnson smuggled the man into Texas and hid him in an NYA work project for a time. The success encouraged Johnson to continue Operation Texas, even though the project continued to bend a few laws. By the end of 1938 he had imported forty-one more Jews, and between 1939 and 1941 he smuggled scores more Jews into Texas.

In addition to helping the Jews, once the United States entered World War II, Johnson volunteered to serve in the navy. He served briefly as a lieutenant commander, receiving a Silver Star for service on a hazardous aircraft mission before Roosevelt called him home to continue his term in Congress. After returning to Washington, D.C., Johnson continued to work for his district. Washington insiders said that he secured more federal programs than any congressman in the nation during the war years. Although Roosevelt's death shook Johnson, he gave Roosevelt's successor, Harry Truman, the same loyalty that he had given Roosevelt. In 1948, when Dixiecrats bolted the party, Johnson spurned their appeals, instead helping hold Texas for the president and thus playing a prominent role in Truman's miracle win.

When Johnson moved into the Senate in 1949, political winds in Texas forced him to move to the right; yet he supported almost all of Truman's Fair Deal, especially when programs for the poor were involved. He continued that course through the years of President Dwight D. Eisenhower, working with the president and the Republicans to secure additional programs once he realized that

Eisenhower accepted most of the programs of both the New Deal and the Fair Deal. Becoming majority leader in 1954, he continued to cooperate with Eisenhower's agenda, especially if the poor, the elderly, or the lowly had a chance to benefit. In 1957 and 1960 he also pushed through the Senate the first civil rights acts since Reconstruction. He did what he thought was right while knowing that he would take political heat in Texas and the larger South.

In 1960 John F. Kennedy secured the Democratic nomination for president even though Johnson wanted and halfheartedly campaigned for the nomination. Kennedy surprised many people when he offered Johnson the second spot on the ticket. Johnson accepted and began working immediately to hold the South for Kennedy, the urban Catholic northeasterner. Johnson held a number of states, including the much-needed Texas, and the Democratic ticket won by a very narrow margin. After inauguration day, Johnson was not buried in the vice presidency. Instead, he participated actively in the administration's decisions. Most important, he continued to work in the area of civil rights. He also became a goodwill ambassador, visiting thirty-three countries to represent the United States.

Johnson became president on 22 November 1963, when Lee Harvey Oswald assassinated Kennedy while he and Johnson were on a goodwill trip to Dallas. At first Johnson was deeply shocked, but he recovered in time to present a calm demeanor to the American public and to assure them that the business of government would continue even as people tried to understand and deal with the tragedy. To ensure continuity, Johnson (in what may have been a mistake) retained most of the Kennedy people in his new administration, although several gave him only lukewarm support. Some, in fact, worked against him. Johnson publicly committed himself to reforms that Kennedy espoused while adding new goals for his own administration.

The new president was not a perfect man. He had his weaknesses and flaws, defects that the presidency seemed to magnify. He could be crude and vulgar, and he sometimes offended even his closest advisers and friends. His personality was such that in any situation he wanted to be in complete command. The presidency gave him a grand stage to act upon, and he sometimes exploited his power on a personal level. Many of his aides had to take a severe tongue-lashing at one time or another. During his days with the NYA in the 1930s, he drove one such aide to a nervous breakdown. Johnson was also such a hard worker that he logged eighteen- to twenty-hour days. He demanded as much from others in his administration, often driving them to exhaustion.

Despite his flaws, Johnson also had positive traits. He remained loyal to his personal and political friends and on numerous occasions extended many kindnesses to people in his circle who suffered personal or political problems.

He never forgot the old New Dealers and did what he could to help them. For example, the Alabamians Clifford and Virginia Durr lobbied in the 1930s and 1940s for repeal of poll taxes that effectively disfranchised many poor whites and blacks in the South. Into the 1950s and 1960s the Durrs continued to work, often arguing with their friend even after he became president. Johnson always said that he must wait until "we have the votes." And when he got the votes, he made the Durrs happy, for he initiated the drive that led to the Twenty-Fourth Amendment to the Constitution, which banned the poll tax in federal elections. As president, Johnson also campaigned for what became the Twenty-Sixth Amendment, which lowered the voting age from twenty-one to eighteen.

Johnson brought skills to the presidency that many previous presidents, including Kennedy, had not mastered. First, Johnson was the consummate politician. Even in his student days at SWTSTC, he lived and breathed politics. Then, beginning with his stint as a congressional secretary, he studied politics until he learned how Washington worked. He learned how to get things done—what to do, whom to see, and what to say. Once he had a goal, he never gave up. As a congressman, and especially as Senate majority leader, he studied his colleagues—what they wanted and what they did not want, what they would do and what they would not do. He was an excellent negotiator, especially in small groups, and he learned how to "count the house"; that is, any time a bill came up for a vote, he already knew how the senators would vote. As president, he used his political skills learned over the years to push programs through Congress. Most important, he led the forces that brought about a partial revolution in race relations in the United States.

In 1960 Kennedy had promised the black community a civil rights law that would make African Americans "first-class" citizens. Because he needed to mollify white southern Dixiecrats, he took no action—not even after such developments as the sit-in movement, the freedom rides, and the Birmingham crisis of 1962–1963, which horrified people nationwide when their televisions showed them scenes of policemen assaulting little children with batons, attack dogs, tear gas, and high-pressure water hoses. After they witnessed the brutal attacks, many more people, both black and white, began supporting the civil rights crusade.

Next came the protests in Jackson, Mississippi, that cost the civil rights leader Medgar Evers his life. Evers had been leading demonstrations in Jackson, but many whites had no intention of giving blacks even a modicum of equality. Acting for that group, Byron de la Beckwith shot Evers in the back, killing him instantly. In the ten weeks after Evers's assassination, there were 750 racial demonstrations in the United States. Finally, the turmoil convinced Kennedy that he could no longer delay introducing a civil rights bill. His staff, with heavy input from Vice President Johnson, hammered out a bill.

To generate support for the bill and to lobby Congress, A. Philip Randolph and other black leaders organized the March on Washington. In August 1963 between 200,000 and 250,000 people, including about 50,000 whites, assembled near the Washington Monument. Led by such blacks as Randolph and the Reverend Martin Luther King, Jr., and such whites as Johnson and Senator Edward ("Ted") Kennedy, the group made the short march to the Lincoln Memorial. Notably, King gave his now famous "I Have a Dream" speech, which riveted the throng. Others, including Johnson, also made remarks. Afterward, many black and white leaders went to the White House, where the president welcomed them and again announced his support for civil rights. Originally billed as a protest, the march turned into a great rally that one reporter characterized as an "exercise in mass decency."

Kennedy's untimely death not only put Johnson in the White House, but it also placed Johnson in the leadership role to make the civil rights bill law. The measure easily passed the House of Representatives, where southern racists did not have the numbers to defeat it, but the measure stalled in the Senate when, as expected, a group of seventeen southern senators began a filibuster. Never in American history had a filibuster against civil rights legislation been broken. Johnson put Minnesota senator Hubert Humphrey in charge of the floor fight to vote cloture and thus allow the bill to come to the floor for a vote. Meanwhile, the president used all his powers of persuasion and promises of favors to help Humphrey corral votes. After long negotiations, Johnson made a breakthough. Republican minority leader Everett Dirksen of Illinois threw his political weight behind the bill, and he brought over enough Republicans to end debate and bring up the bill for a vote.

By an overwhelming majority, the Senate passed the historic Civil Rights Act of 1964, a law that began a virtual political and social revolution in the United States. The new law forbade discrimination in all places of public accommodations, prohibited discrimination in employment, protected everyone's voting rights, outlawed discrimination in schools, and called for stiff penalties for anyone who violated the civil rights of another person. Furthermore, a southern senator who hoped to defeat the bill had inserted the word "women" in the appropriate place in the bill. Therefore, the same law that protected racial and ethnic minorities also protected the gender minority. When Johnson signed the new law amid much public fanfare, he turned to an aide and predicted ominously, "I think that I've delivered the South to the Republican Party for a long time to come." And, indeed, as the future unfolded, the Republicans gained much more support in the South.

Although Johnson must have congratulated himself for the civil rights victory, the struggle was far from over. Martin Luther King, Jr., and his Southern Christian Leadership Conference (SCLC) began a massive voter registration drive in the South. Opposition was widespread, and some of the drive's opponents used violence, including murder, to stop the movement. Ultimately, King entered the fray personally, targeting Selma, Alabama, the seat of a county where no blacks had voted since Reconstruction, although they made up a majority in the county. Selma's sheriff, Jim Clark, and his men went to war against the protesters, a war that was televised nationally. What was happening shocked the country. Then, unknown assailants murdered a Detroit housewife who had been a volunteer in the Selma voter registration campaign. That last act inflamed Johnson, who, on national television, could not disguise his anger. His staff already had prepared a voter bill, and now the president demanded that Congress pass the measure. The lawmakers responded, and the Voting Rights Act of 1965 provided federal protection to blacks (and members of any other group) who attempted to claim, but were denied, their right to register and to vote.

As much as Johnson tried, he could not keep up with the black community's rising expectations as the focus of the civil rights movement shifted from political, civic, and social rights to economic improvement. After his 1964 landslide election victory over the archconservative senator Barry Goldwater, Johnson launched his "War on Poverty," and new programs came fast as the president strove to outdo his mentor, Franklin D. Roosevelt. As Johnson said to an aide, he wanted to "finish the revolution that FDR started." Nonetheless, elements of the African-American community remained unsatisfied. Martin Luther King's nonviolence gave way to "Black Power" and to new leaders who shouted, "Burn, baby, burn"; flaunted the law; and openly carried weapons. From 1965 to 1968 some 150 major urban riots occurred, mostly in the inner cities, where many African Americans were mired in poverty with, seemingly, no way out. As the cities burned, many whites began to desert the civil rights movement, out of either fear or disgust. Johnson had no choice but to call out troops to quell the violence. Almost immediately after its greatest victories, the civil rights movement began to unravel.

King continued to try to hold the movement together, but in April 1968 he was assassinated in Memphis, Tennessee, while trying to direct another peaceful protest. Johnson used King's death and the sympathy it engendered to push one more piece of civil rights legislation: the Fair Housing Act of 1968, which banned discrimination in renting or purchasing homes. During his brief presidency, then, Johnson did all he could to help minorities, but he became a lighting rod for a vast horde of reform movements engendered partly by idealism and partly by various groups simply demanding what they considered their rights. An environmental movement gathered steam as the decade of the 1960s passed, as did the Native American movement, the gay movement, the free speech movement, the women's movement, the "gray panther" movement for the elderly, and the Hispanic movement. Almost all reformers held Johnson personally responsible when they could not achieve all that they wanted, even though they had in the White House the greatest "establishment" liberal that the country had ever produced.

Johnson's inability to satisfy all demands led to the "New Left" revolution. Spearheaded by such groups as the Students for a Democratic Society (SDS) and by such individuals as the SDS president Tom Hayden, the New Left lambasted political leaders and political institutions for not doing more for the racial, ethnic, and gender minorities or for the elderly and the infirm. In a related development, the country witnessed the rise of the "counterculture." Thousands of Americans, mostly of the younger set and the middle class, rejected the values of the generation that had sired them. Called "hippies," the young people demanded "liberation" from traditional values; espoused spiritual exploration, new forms of music, and experimentation with drugs and sex; and rejected the consumer society and the corporate state that America had become. Establishment politicians—Johnson included—had no hope of reaching the people in the counterculture.

Even Johnson's Great Society could not please everyone, despite such reforms as Medicare, the Job Corps, Medicaid, Volunteers in Service to America (a domestic peace corps), increased federal aid to education, extended benefits for social security, and raises in the minimum wage. Johnson also sponsored national programs related to housing, employment, and other economic measures, most managed by the Office of Economic Opportunity. Many conservatives opposed Johnson's reforms as misguided and expensive. For example, the American Medical Association (AMA) resisted health reform, fearing that such reform might lead to socialized medicine, while many businessmen objected to raises in the minimum wage, arguing that such raises would drain them of profits and lead to the downfall of American civilization. Furthermore, some programs of the Great Society bypassed traditional local and state authorities, which complained bitterly and tried to undercut the reform efforts.

Despite such opposition, to a degree, the programs worked. When Johnson became president, almost 25 percent of Americans lived below the poverty line in what was the richest country in the world. When Johnson left office in 1969, the poverty rate had fallen to 11 or 12 percent. Other figures showed that 56 percent of blacks had lived in poverty in 1959, but only 32 percent continued to do so in 1969; 18 percent of whites had been poor in 1959, but a decade later only 10 percent were poor. For his domestic reform programs, Johnson has been called alternately the "Education President," and the "Civil Rights President." Such titles were consistent with two of Johnson's core beliefs: Let very adult vote, and allow everyone to be educated to the level of his or her intellectual capacity, so that people can live meaningful lives and make America a better place as well.

Johnson also threw his support behind America's space program. Kennedy had promised that America would put a man on the moon by decade's end. Johnson accelerated support, and Kennedy's promise came true in 1969 when the astronaut Neil Armstrong became the first person to set foot on the moon.

Despite fashioning a domestic record as a reformer, Johnson left office as one of America's most disliked presidents, and the Vietnam War helped explain why. U.S. involvement in Vietnam had a long history. In the immediate post–World War II years, President Truman used American manpower to help the French retake their colonial possessions. Even as a war for independence raged in Vietnam, Truman continued to give material support to the French effort. Truman saw Vietnam as being in danger of falling to the Communists, something that all cold warriors abhorred. By 1953 the United States was paying for about 50 percent of the French costs to fight the revolutionary Ho Chi Minh and his Viet Minh forces. Eisenhower further involved the United States, after the French withdrew from Vietnam, by supporting a pro-French government that the French left behind. While continuing to give material aid to South Vietnam, Eisenhower also sent in American personnel—five hundred "military advisers" to help train the South Vietnamese army. With the ebb and flow of war, South Vietnam became weaker and weaker and was on the verge of collapse when Kennedy took office. He escalated the war by sending in the first American combat troops, approximately twenty-seven thousand men. The enemy seemed only to grow stronger.

When Johnson became president, he faced the same quandary that had bedeviled Kennedy. Again, more American aid was necessary to "save" South Vietnam. At first, Johnson was most hesitant to become more involved. Indeed, he originally questioned whether the United States should be in Vietnam at all. White House tapes that have now been released verify that Johnson's first "gut" feeling was that America should exit the war. Nonetheless, various military and civilian advisers lobbied Johnson to remain steadfast behind South Vietnam, for the war was being fought against the backdrop of the larger, global cold war. America could not afford to let another region go Communist, said most of Johnson's advisers. After securing the Gulf of Tonkin Resolution that gave him sweeping authority to pursue the war from an almost unanimous Con-

gress in the summer of 1964, Johnson, like the other presidents before him, escalated the war. By mid-1965, more than 100,000 American troops had been sent to Vietnam, the number rising to about 180,000 by the end of the year. By the end of 1967 between 500,000 and 550,000 had been sent.

Even as Johnson escalated the war, he was getting bad military advice. Always told that just a few thousand more men would spell victory, the president eventually found himself in a quagmire that offered no escape. Indeed, he once said of the Vietnam involvement that he felt like a west Texas rancher caught in his pasture during a hail storm: "I can't run, I can't hide, and I can't make it stop." As the war dragged into 1968, the American public, including many political leaders, proved to be fickle in their support for the war. Originally, Johnson had public and congressional opinion solidly behind him, but he soon began to lose the support of both groups. Then came the Tet offensive on 31 January 1968, which was the first day of the Vietnamese New Year.

During the Tet offensive, the North Vietnamese coordinated attacks on many American positions in South Vietnam. Some cities, including Hue, fell. Others suffered pandemonium. In Saigon, the headquarters of American forces, the enemy even briefly held the grounds of the U.S. Embassy. At home, Americans saw the shocking details, all carried by television networks. They saw bombs exploding and people killing other people. They viewed all the brutality of total war. One scene remained particularly memorable: a South Vietnamese officer executing a captive Vietcong by shooting him in the head while his hands were tied. What the networks did not report was that shortly before this incident, the Vietcong had murdered one of the officer's close relatives.

After the initial assaults, U.S. forces regrouped, attacked the enemy, and inflicted heavy casualties on their foes—so many casualties that the enemy did not recover for many months. Still, the public relations damage had been done. Americans who watched their televisions during the initial assaults perceived the Tet offensive as a major victory for the opposition. Now many more people turned against American involvement in the region and blamed Johnson for getting their country into a war that, in fact, he had not begun. The development amounted to a political defeat for Johnson, even though American forces counterattacked and won a military victory. More and more young protesters joined the chant "Hey, hey, LBJ. How many kids did you kill today?"

Within a few weeks after Tet, Johnson's popularity rating fell to 35 percent. It was the lowest rating for an American president since the days of Harry Truman when the country was suffering from high inflation, the Red Scare, and accusations of government corruption. Now dissident Democrats were emboldened to challenge Johnson's leadership. They began to look for an antiwar candidate who could challenge Johnson in the 1968 primaries. Senator Robert Kennedy (the brother of the slain president John F. Kennedy) declined, but Minnesota's senator Eugene McCarthy ("Clean Gene") stepped into the fray. After McCarthy recorded 42 percent of the popular vote in the New Hampshire primary against an incumbent president, Robert Kennedy sensed weakness and declared for the presidency. He brought money and a strong political network with him. After New Hampshire, Wisconsin loomed as the next primary, and polls showed Johnson hopelessly behind.

Consequently, in a nationally televised statement on 31 March 1968, Johnson surprised the nation by withdrawing from the presidential race, citing his desire to concentrate on peace negotiations to end the war. He also announced a halt in the bombing of North Vietnam. What he did not add was that he was shaken by the now tremendous opposition to his policies and that he was also a sick man with serious heart problems. All his adult life he had feared losing, and now the possibility of defeat loomed larger than ever. As a new political race began, Johnson threw his support to his loyal vice president, Hubert Humphrey, who was destined to lose to Richard Nixon in the 1968 election. Upon Nixon's inauguration in January 1969, Johnson and Lady Bird retired to their ranch. The former president spent his last years overseeing the development of the Lyndon Baines Johnson Library in Austin and in the founding and early management of the new Lyndon B. Johnson School of Public Affairs, which is attached to the University of Texas at Austin.

Near the end of his life, Johnson expressed bitterness about his political decline. He could not understand why the American voters had forsaken him after he had tried to do so much for the lowly, the downtrodden, and the racial, ethnic, and gender minorities. Johnson remained to the end an American populist-nationalist who was but a New Dealer writ large. He had tried to use federal power as an instrument of good. As he disappointedly told Lady Bird shortly before he died, "Well, at least they know we tried." Johnson died of a massive heart attack at his ranch on 22 January 1973. He is buried on the ranch, only a few hundred yards from his childhood home.

★

Johnson's voluminous papers, both state and personal, are located at the Lyndon Baines Johnson Library in Austin, Texas. The Library of Congress also has a collection of Johnson material. His memoir of his presidency is *The Vantage Point: Perspectives of the Presidency, 1963–1969* (1971). Doris Kearns relies heavily on scores of interviews with Johnson in *Lyndon Johnson and the American Dream* (1976). In his *Lyndon: An Oral Biography* (1980),

Merle Miller relies heavily on interviews of people who knew Johnson. The most exhaustive, objective biography is Robert Dalleck's two-volume study *Lone Star Rising: Lyndon Johnson and His Times, 1908–1960* (1991) and *Flawed Giant: Lyndon Johnson and His Times, 1961–1973* (1998). A good one-volume biography that is objective and generally favorable to Johnson is Paul K. Conkin, *Big Daddy from the Pedernales: Lyndon Baines Johnson* (1986). More critical of Johnson are Ronnie Dugger, *The Politician: The Life and Times of Lyndon Johnson—The Drive for Power, from the Frontier to Master of the Senate* (1982), and Robert Caro, *The Years of Lyndon Johnson: The Path to Power* (1982) and *The Years of Lyndon Johnson: Means of Ascent* (1990). Fairly balanced is Vaughn Davis Bornet, *The Presidency of Lyndon B. Johnson* (1983). Also see Alfred Steinberg, *Sam Johnson's Boy: A Close-up of the President from Texas* (1968). For the 1960s in general, the classic volume is William L. O'Neill, *Coming Apart: An Informal History of America in the 1960s* (1971), which captures the essence of the decade.

A number of Johnson's associates have left memoirs about the thirty-sixth president. They include Hugh Sidey, *A Very Personal Presidency: Lyndon Johnson in the White House* (1968); Eric Goldman, *The Tragedy of Lyndon Johnson* (1969); Sam Johnson, *My Brother, Lyndon* (1970); Liz Carpenter, *Ruffles and Flourishes: The Warm and Tender Story of a Simple Girl Who Found Adventure in the White House* (1970); Jack Valenti, *A Very Human President* (1975); Joseph A. Califano, Jr., *Governing America: An Insider's Report from the White House and the Cabinet* (1981) and *The Triumph and Tragedy of Lyndon Johnson: The White House Years* (1991); and Clark M. Clifford, *Counsel to the President: A Memoir* (1991).

In addition, various accounts of Johnson and U.S. foreign policy include Chester Cooper, *The Lost Crusade: America in Vietnam* (1970); Brian VanDeMark, *Into the Quagmire: Lyndon Johnson and the Escalation of the Vietnam War* (1991); Tom Wells, *The War Within: America's Battle over Vietnam* (1994); George C. Herring, *LBJ and Vietnam: A Different Kind of War* (1994); Robert S. McNamara, *In Retrospect: The Tragedy and Lessons of Vietnam* (1995); H. W. Brands, *The Wages of Globalism: Lyndon Johnson and the Limits of American Power* (1995); and Lloyd C. Gardner, *Pay Any Price: Lyndon Johnson and the Wars for Vietnam* (1995).

JAMES M. SMALLWOOD

JOHNSON, Philip Cortelyou (*b.* 8 July 1906 in Cleveland, Ohio), architect who coined the term "International Style" to describe European architecture of the 1920s, and who reached the height of his fame in the 1960s when he worked to make American architecture more "monumental."

Johnson grew up in Cleveland, the son of Homer M. Johnson, a lawyer, and Louise Pope, a homemaker. Although Johnson would later become famous for designing buildings, his early interest was in architectural history. It was

Philip Johnson standing with the final model of the New York State Theater at Lincoln Center, 1961. ©
BETTMANN/CORBIS

an interest that informed his most important buildings of the 1950s and 1960s, during which time he attempted to imbue buildings as diverse as nuclear reactors and churches with classical elegance. Johnson attended Harvard University in 1923 to study classics and graduated with a B.A. degree in philosophy in 1930. The following year, while touring Europe, he met the celebrated German architect Ludwig Mies van der Rohe. Johnson's enthusiasm for the new European architecture was fired by his meeting with Mies van der Rohe, and on his return to the United States he became the founding director of the Department of Architecture at the Museum of Modern Art, New York City. Working with Henry-Russell Hitchcock, in 1932 Johnson published *The International Style: Architecture Since 1922,* the book that gave the name "International Style" to European architecture of the time.

In 1937, with the Nazis in power in Germany, Johnson arranged the arrival from Europe of Mies van der Rohe, who took up the post of director at the Armour Institute School of Architecture in Chicago. Johnson would later collaborate with Mies van der Rohe on the Seagram Building in New York City (1958), one of the most important high-rise buildings in the United States and a project that

launched Johnson's career as an architect of major public buildings. Johnson graduated from Harvard with a B.Arch. degree in 1943, but it was not until the 1960s that he directly influenced American public architecture with his "monumental" designs. After serving briefly in the U.S. Army, he returned to the Museum of Modern Art as its director of architecture in 1946. For the next decade Johnson concentrated on domestic dwellings, developing his trademark "glass box" style. This style is expressed most dramatically in the house he built for himself, known as the "Glass House," in New Canaan, Connecticut (1949).

In the 1960s Johnson was instrumental in popularizing glass walls on a much larger scale. By the late 1950s he had begun to concentrate on large public buildings rather than small domestic dwellings. He took commissions for university campuses, science centers, and museums. Johnson hoped to express the wealth and power of the United States through buildings that recaptured the relative scale and authority of early American civic architecture. In the 1960s his buildings tried to emphasize the importance of American civic life through grand street frontages and impressive public spaces. In a 1964 *New York Times* article, Johnson described architecture as the "art of how to waste space."

Many of his buildings at the time, such as the Museum of Art Building (1960), for the Munson-Williams-Proctor Arts Institute at Utica, New York, are consistent with this philosophy. The museum's central stairwell, around which runs a gallery, forms a void that would certainly be considered wasteful, or at least flamboyant, in a commercial setting. Yet the museum offers open, well-lit galleries with plenty of room for visitors to move around.

Johnson's designs at this time reflected a renewed confidence in U.S. institutions, but the expression of authority and importance through architecture required building on a huge scale. In 1965 Johnson wrote that "architecture is surely not the design of space . . . [but] the organization of procession. Architecture exists only in time." What he meant was that the best buildings are those that cannot be seen all at once; instead, users experience them by walking around, connecting up different spaces over time. Perhaps the finest example of this is the New York State Theater (1964), in Lincoln Center in New York City. Designed in collaboration with Richard Foster, the building includes a colossal forecourt and main entrance, complete with columns that refer back to American architecture's neoclassical past. It was the first in a series of collaborations with Foster that include the New York State Pavilion for the 1964 World's Fair at Flushing, New York, and the Kline Science Center at Yale University (1965). The Kline Science Center, in particular, includes hallmark Johnson glass walls and a spacious entrance lobby, but the weight of the supporting columns also reflects the solemnity of the work being carried out there.

That solemnity is the problem at the heart of Johnson's work in the 1960s. Critics have accused him of reducing architectural history to the addition of classical columns. And while his museums and university campus buildings were expressing the dominance of the American academy, student protests were challenging the authority of those who controlled higher education. In a sense, despite his commitment to public open spaces, Johnson's work was on the side of an establishment that was increasingly seen as bullying and corrupt. By the 1970s American "monumental" architecture was overburdened with arches and "megastructure" in the form of concrete pillars and marble cladding. It was a far cry from the sleek glass-and-aluminum structures of the International Style. Johnson's own work went in a similar direction, leading to criticism that he was more interested in style than real design. The Crystal Cathedral (1980) at Garden Grove, California, is perhaps the best example of this postmodern excess. Known as the first "megachurch," the huge building is clad in mirrored glass, and parts of the walls open out to allow members of the congregation to observe services from their cars.

After Johnson's partnership with Foster ended in 1967, he began working with John Burgee. Johnson and Burgee were one of the most prolific architectural partnerships of the 1970s and 1980s. Critics have argued that Johnson's later buildings are overly elaborate; nevertheless, his work in the 1960s was a major influence on civic and corporate architecture in the 1970s and 1980s. Working with Burgee, Johnson built museums, corporate buildings, theaters, churches, and libraries until his retirement in 1987. Since then Johnson has continued to work on projects of his own. He was awarded the American Institute of Architecture Gold Medal in 1978 and the Pritzker Architecture Prize in 1979.

★

There are several books about Johnson and his work, including John M. Jacobus, *Philip Johnson* (1962); Johnson's *Architecture 1949–1965* (1966), with an introduction by Henry-Russell Hitchcock, Jr.; and David Mohney and Stover Jenkins, *The Houses of Philip Johnson* (2001). Dennis Sharpe, ed., *The Illustrated Encyclopedia of Architects and Architecture* (1991), gives a useful summary of Johnson's career. Johnson outlined his ideas about 1960s architecture in an article for the *New York Times* (27 Dec. 1964).

CHRIS ROUTLEDGE

JOHNSON, Rafer Lewis (*b*. 18 August 1935 in Hillsboro, Texas), decathlete who won the Gold Medal at the 1960 Olympic Games and who later became a successful business executive and public service leader.

The eldest of Lewis and Alma Gibson Johnson's five living children, Johnson was named for his father's childhood friend. During Johnson's early years the family moved to Oklahoma, then to Dallas and on to Houston. Johnson's father picked cotton and sugarcane and worked at odd jobs, including being a handyman and chauffeur. His mother was a domestic worker. In 1944 Johnson's father moved to Oakland, California, to work in the booming shipyards, and in 1945 the family followed. Later the family moved to California's San Joaquin Valley to do farm work near Chowchilla, Madera, and Fresno, and, for the first time, Johnson attended integrated schools. He also worked alongside his father and mother in the fields as a cotton and crop picker. In 1946 Johnson's father was hired as a section hand for the Southern Pacific Railroad, and the family moved to Kingsburg, California, where they took up residence in a "section house," approximately the size of a boxcar, adjacent to the Del Monte cannery. They were the only African-American family in a town of about 2,500 people, most of whom were of Swedish decent. Johnson and his siblings were assimilated into the community with little prejudice, and his father and mother were soon employed locally.

Johnson was an outstanding student and athlete at

Rafer L. Johnson competing in the shotput, 1960. AP/WIDE WORLD PHOTOS

Kingsburg Joint Union High School. He excelled in four sports, became team captain in three, earned eleven varsity letters, and was inducted into the honor society. His coach also introduced him to the decathlon and fueled his desire to become an Olympic athlete.

In the fall of 1954 Johnson entered the University of California, Los Angeles (UCLA), on an academic scholarship, where he was strongly influenced by the track coach Elvin "Ducky" Drake. At UCLA, Johnson joined the Air Force Reserve Officers Training Corps, participated in varsity track and basketball, was active in Pi Lambda Phi, served as president of the student body, headed three honor societies, carried a B average, and received a bachelors degree in 1959.

While in college Johnson set the world record in the decathlon, won the national decathlon Amateur Athletic Union (AAU) championship, won that event at the Pan American Games in Mexico City (1955), and overcame injuries to win an Olympic silver medal in the decathlon in Melbourne, Australia, in 1956. He also participated in track meets against the USSR and was named *Sports Illustrated* Sportsman of the Year on 5 January 1959.

Despite sustaining serious injuries in a 1959 automobile accident, Johnson became the first African American to carry the U.S. flag in the opening ceremonies for the Olympic Games. In Rome in 1960 he won an Olympic gold medal in the decathlon with a record-breaking 8,392 points. Subsequently he was named Associated Press Athlete of the Year and California Athlete of the Year, and won the coveted Sullivan Award, given to the outstanding amateur athlete of the year. B'nai B'rith, the National Conference of Christians and Jews, and the George Washington Carver Memorial Institute also honored him. He was inducted into the national Track and Field Hall of Fame in 1974 and the U.S. Olympic Hall of Fame in 1983.

Johnson turned down opportunities in professional sports to undertake a multifaceted career that involved acting in motion pictures, sports broadcasting, and promotional activities for People to People International, the Peace Corps, and Special Olympics. In 1961, while working with People to People International, Johnson met Robert F. Kennedy, and they struck up a friendship that lasted until Kennedy's death in 1968.

Johnson was a frequent visitor at the Kennedy home, and he came to admire Kennedy's strong support for the United Farm Workers, his opposition to the Vietnam War, and his committed, steady support for civil rights. In the spring of 1968 Johnson left his job as sports broadcaster for KNBC in Los Angeles to work full time on Kennedy's presidential campaign. Johnson was part of the Kennedy entourage the night Kennedy was assassinated at the Ambassador Hotel in Los Angeles. Johnson helped subdue the assassin, Sirhan Sirhan, and wrestled the gun from his hand. Johnson was a pallbearer at Kennedy's funeral and a Kennedy delegate to the 1968 Democratic National Convention in Chicago.

Throughout the decade of the 1960s Johnson was an important black leader, but not a leader of blacks. His friends were drawn from several racial and ethnic groups. He was active in a Jewish fraternity. He maintained close ties with the decathlon competitors C. K. Yang of Taiwan and Vasily Kuznetsov of the USSR. He was a good friend of Tom Brokaw, who wrote the introduction to Johnson's autobiography, long before Brokaw became the national news anchor for the National Broadcasting Company (NBC). Johnson was the first of several black men to date the journalist and activist Gloria Steinem, several years before she started *Ms.* magazine (1972). On 18 December 1971 Johnson married Elizabeth Ann Thorsen, an elementary school teacher; they have two children.

Johnson's interests also transcended racial and ethnic boundaries. He acted in several television programs, including *Mission: Impossible, Daniel Boone, Dragnet,* and *The Dating Game,* and in several movies, including *The Last Grenade, None but the Brave, The Game,* and *Soul Soldier.*

Moreover, in the late 1960s Johnson became active in the Special Olympics program; in 1969 he helped establish the California chapter of this competition. He also became a member of the National Advisory Committee on Physical Education and Recreation for Handicapped Children.

In 1971 Johnson joined the executive staff of Continental Telephone Company (Con Tel), and served with that corporation until 1986. Johnson had two public school buildings named for him and was active in the Reebok Human Rights Award program and the Hershey Track and Field Youth Program.

★

Johnson's autobiography, written with Philip Goldberg, is *The Best That I Can Be: An Autobiography* (1998). See also "Johnson Top Decathlon Man," *St. Louis Argus* (27 July 1956); *Sports Illustrated* (5 Jan. 1959); "Big Man on Campus," *Ebony* (14 May 1959); "To Do a Little Better," *Time* (29 Aug. 1960); and *Newsweek* (27 Dec. 1971).

KEITH MCCLELLAN

JOHNSON, Virginia. *See* Masters, William Howell, and Virginia Eshelman Johnson.

JONES, Everett LeRoy (Amiri Baraka, "LeRoi") (*b.* 7 October 1934 in Newark, New Jersey), African-American poet, playwright, novelist, essayist, orator, and activist whose confrontational style strove to awaken audiences to the political concerns of black Americans during the 1960s and beyond.

The son of Coyette Leroy Jones, a postal worker, and Anna Lois Russ Jones, a social worker, Jones and his younger sister grew up in an integrated neighborhood of Newark. Jones graduated with honors at the age of sixteen from Barringer High School in Newark. Having earned a scholarship, he attended Rutgers University in Newark from 1951 to 1952, though he later transferred to Howard University. Failing at Howard, Jones entered the U.S. Air Force and rose to the rank of sergeant; in 1957 he was discharged from military service and began an artistic life in New York City's Greenwich Village.

In 1958 Jones married Hettie Cohen. The two were coeditors of *Yugen,* an avant-garde literary magazine founded by Jones that often featured the works of Beat writers, such as Jack Kerouac and Allen Ginsberg. The couple had two children. With Diane di Prima, Jones also coedited *Floating Bear,* a mimeographed magazine delivered by mail, whose rapid production process permitted immediate exposure of new works to fellow artists. In 1965 Jones divorced Hettie and left the Beat milieu, and in 1966 he married Sylvia Robinson (now known as Bibi Amina Baraka), with whom he had five children. Gifted as both a writer and an orator, Jones became well known for his chal-

LeRoi Jones (Amiri Baraka) with his family, 1968. © BETTMANN/CORBIS

lenging, confrontational style. His writing lashes out at academics, established authorities, Jews, gays, whites, and middle-class blacks, with ridicule and contempt for what he sees as their hypocrisy, ignorance, or oppressive conduct. These attacks dramatize issues; if the object of ridicule becomes upset, Jones asserts, then his or her guilt is evident; if the object of ridicule remains undisturbed and secure, then the attack only affirms the person's intrinsic worth. Jones stings his targets with humor and clever insight, often winning the enthusiasm of an audience that may also be the object of his derision.

Jones's first collection of poems, *Preface to a Twenty Volume Suicide Note* (1961), reveals his early connection to the Beats. Some of the poems are dedicated to fellow poets John Wieners, Michael McClure, Gary Snyder, or Ginsberg. In the collection Jones experiments with the projectivist approach of the American poet Charles Olson, refers to comic book heroes and pop culture figures with the playfulness of Kerouac, and creates surrealistic imagery in the manner of the French poet Arthur Rimbaud. The work's title suggests the agonizing urgency of suicide, but the suicide is absurdly deferred because twenty volumes of work must be completed before it can be carried out. The poems free themselves from standard stanza patterns and rhyme schemes and discover their own form in the process of creation. Their style includes wordplay; variations on normal patterns of spelling, capitalization, and punctuation; and startling images. While some poems relate to Jones's wife and daughter, others turn to the literary, social, and political worlds that surround the marginalized poet.

Jones's essay collection *Blues People: Negro Music in White America* (1963) effectively combines his knowledge of musical history with his perspectives on cultural history. The blues are tied to the traditions of West African music, including a special musical scale, call-and-response arrangements, and invention of lyrics during performance. Functionality, another African characteristic, is part of the blues because the music accompanies work, family traditions, and courtship. The music of the white culture, Jones argues, comes from a contrasting tradition that separates art from the functions of daily life. *Blues People* traces the transformation of African music into American music by following the changes in the lives of black people and artists. The roles of Louis Armstrong, Duke Ellington, and many others are cited. In Jones's view African music becomes American when white people discover that the African musical influences can be understood and adopted.

The play *Dutchman* (1964) is perhaps Jones's best-known work for the stage and is clearly the one that marks the key transition he underwent in the 1960s. First produced at the Cherry Lane Theater in New York City on 24 March 1964, the play pits Lula, "a thirty-year-old white woman," against Clay, a "twenty-year-old Negro." The scene is a subway car on a hot summer night; the underground environment is "the flying underbelly of the city." Lula taunts Clay, who is uncertain about her intentions yet inescapably interested in her. Lula blends suggestive provocations and racial insults until Clay finally explodes in anger. He scorns her ignorance and insincerity, paying her back for her taunts with an angry revelation that black musicians have always had a special code in their music, a code that lets white listeners perceive a plain message while the music secretly curses and belittles them. Clay's triumph is brief, however, because Lula suddenly stabs him. In the surreal subway scene, Clay's body is jettisoned. Lula records her victory, and in moments another young black man appears, obviously Lula's next intended victim. The play dramatizes the tension and hypocrisy behind interracial relations, but it is also partly autobiographical, marking Jones's abandonment of the "Negro" that Clay represents in favor of a new black cultural identity, which is still to be discovered, explored, and empowered.

Other works completed by Jones during the 1960s include the poetry collection *The Dead Lecturer* (1964); the experimental novel *The System of Dante's Hell* (1965); the collection of essays *Home: Social Essays* (1966); the short story collection *Tales* (1967); the study *Black Music* (1968); an anthology (coedited with Larry Neal) of black writers,

Black Fire (1968); and a collection reflecting his participation in Black Nationalism, *Black Magic* (1969).

In 1967 Jones changed his name to Imamu ("spiritual leader" in Swahili) Amiri Baraka ("blessed prince") to reflect his African heritage; he later dropped "Imamu." In addition to his writing he has had a lengthy teaching career since 1962. In the 1970s he intensified his political activities, including his work for the election of Kenneth Gibson as mayor of Newark, and in 1984 he published his autobiography. Baraka has received numerous awards, including a Poetry Award from the National Endowment for the Arts in 1982, an American Book Award in 1984, a PEN-Faulkner Award in 1989, and a Langston Hughes Medal in 1989 for outstanding contribution to literature. In 2001 he was inducted into the National Academy of Arts and Letters, and in July 2002 he became poet laureate of New Jersey.

★

A revised edition of Jones's autobiography, *The Autobiography of LeRoi Jones* (1984), was published in 1997. Studies of Jones/Baraka include Kimberly Benston, *Baraka: The Renegade and the Mask* (1976), Werner Sollors, *Amiri Baraka/LeRoi Jones: The Quest for a "Populist Modernism"* (1978), and Jerry Gafio Watts, *Amiri Baraka: The Politics and Art of a Black Intellectual* (2001).

WILLIAM T. LAWLOR

JONES, James Earl (*b.* 17 January 1931 in Arkabutla, Mississippi), dynamic actor of stage and screen, and only the third African-American actor to star in a major stage production of Shakespeare's *Othello*.

Jones is the son of Robert Earl and Ruth (Connolly) Jones, who parted before his birth. His mother later left him in the custody of her parents, John Henry and Maggie (Anderson) Connolly, in Arkabutla near the Mississippi delta. An only child, Jones was raised as a sibling to his aunts and uncles and to a younger cousin; he called his grandparents "mama" and "papa." When the Connollys moved from Mississippi to Michigan in the mid-1930s, John Connolly took Jones to Memphis to live with his paternal grandmother, Elnora Jones Jackson. Sensing rejection by the only family he knew, Jones refused to stay with her and moved instead to Michigan with the Connollys. He remained traumatized by the incident, began to stutter uncontrollably, and plunged into silence for many years.

After eight years at a one-room schoolhouse in Dublin, Michigan, Jones enrolled at Dickson High School in Brethren, where an English teacher named Donald Crouch noticed the boy's writing talent and took a special interest in him. With Crouch's encouragement, Jones not only conquered his stutter but also joined the school's debating team, played varsity basketball, and served as a class officer

James Earl Jones. THE LIBRARY OF CONGRESS

and on the student council. By the time he graduated in 1949 he had won a public speaking championship and a Regents Alumni Scholarship to the University of Michigan in Ann Arbor. That summer he visited his father in New York City. It was his first contact with the elder Jones, who had been working as an actor for some years, and the experience stimulated the son's interest in the theater. Although he had intended initially to become a doctor, Jones graduated from the University of Michigan in 1953 with a degree in drama.

While he was in college, Jones joined the Reserve Officers Training Corps and served a mandatory hitch from 1953 to 1955. Following his tour of duty in the armed forces, he used GI Bill funding to finance an apprenticeship with the American Theatre Wing in New York in 1957 and became affiliated with the New York Shakespeare Festival in Central Park in 1960. In 1961 Jones accepted a part in Jean Genet's controversial farce, *The Blacks*. The project, directed by Gene Frankel, opened off-Broadway at Saint Mark's Playhouse on 4 May 1961 and brought a number of rising young African-American stars together. Among them, Maya Angelou, Cicely Tyson, and Lou Gossett, Jr., all went on to rewarding careers on stage and in film. An offbeat play within a play, *The Blacks* was an ethereal tale

of white colonialism and racially motivated murder. The all-black cast of actors donned eerie white masks to symbolize the colonialists, thus providing a macabre and provocative commentary on the morbid blackface theater of the post-slavery era. Jones, who appeared as Deodatus Village, recalled in his memoir that in the context of the 1960s, the play roiled a troubling reality inherent to a racially prejudiced social order; it was, he said, evocative of "pure conscience."

While continuing an affiliation with Shakespeare in the Park during the summer of 1961, Jones appeared in other live theater productions and in minor television roles. That year he won an Obie Award for best actor in the off-Broadway theater. An appearance with his father in *Moon on a Rainbow Shawl* further heightened Jones's stature on stage, and he received the 1962 Daniel Blum Theatre World Award for Most Promising Personality. Jones added the cinematic dimension to his career in 1962, when Stanley Kubrick cast him as Lieutenant Lothar Zogg in *Dr. Strangelove*. He appeared with George C. Scott in *The Merchant of Venice* that year, and in 1963 a reunion of the original cast of *The Blacks* led Jones to reprise his Village role for a landmark 1,000th performance, marking the longest off-Broadway run of a play in New York history.

Among his signature roles, Jones earned notoriety as Shakespeare's Othello on many occasions, beginning with a summer stock production at the Ramsdell Opera House in 1956. In March 1964 Joseph Papp cast Jones in the role for Shakespeare in the Park opposite Julienne Marie as Desdemona. Before Jones's Othellos, Paul Robeson was the only African-American actor to appear as the Moor in any major U.S. production in the twentieth century. The Papp production, directed by Gladys Vaughan, ran for nineteen performances in the park and went off-Broadway in October for 224 performances at the Martinique Theatre. Jones, who won a Drama Desk Award in 1964 and a Vernon Rice Award in 1965 for his performance, prompted Tom Prideaux's timely commentary in *Life*, "[Jones's] Othello, for better or worse, is affected by our own contemporary state of history. The ancient story of a dark-skinned Moor married to a fair Venetian noblewoman has special meaning to us in 1964." Jones later as dynamic in his personal life as in his career and, despite the conservative social mores of the 1960s, entered into a short-lived marriage in real life with his white costar, Marie, in 1968. The couple had no children and divorced in 1971. He went on to marry Cecilia Hart in 1982; they have one child.

Beginning in 1965 Jones appeared off-Broadway as Ekhart in Bertholt Brecht's *Baal*, spent the summer as Ajax in a Central Park production of *Troilus and Cressida*, and appeared on a daytime television series, *As the World Turns*. In 1967, while filming *The Comedians* with Richard Burton and Elizabeth Taylor, Jones reviewed a script for *The Great*

White Hope from the director Edwin Sherin. A fictional drama by Howard Sackler, the play is based on the true-life story of an African-American fighter, Jack Johnson, who won the world boxing championship title in 1908. Jones accepted the role of the fictional boxer Jack Jefferson, and the play opened to critical acclaim in Washington, D.C., in 1967. The production moved to Broadway's Alvin Theater in 1968, and Jones earned an Antoinette Perry Award (the Tony) as best actor and a second Drama Desk Award, both in 1969. Jones later appeared in the film version of the play and was nominated for an Academy Award.

In later years Jones was recognized for the deep, broad sound of his bass voice as much as for his dramatic presence. In 1977 he gave voice to the intergalactic villain Darth Vader in the George Lucas *Star Wars* films, and in 1994 he was heard as King Mufasa in Disney's animated feature *The Lion King*. His booming bass voice makes him a popular choice for narrator for films and television, and in the twenty-first century he is heard around the clock as the voice of Time-Warner's Cable News Network.

★

Jones penned an autobiography, *James Earl Jones: Voices and Silences*, with Penelope Niven (1993). He is featured in *James Earl Jones*, in a series of books for juveniles by Judy L. Hasday (1998). See also Christine Arnold, "James Earl Jones: A New Standard for Othello," *Philadelphia Inquirer* (30 Dec. 1981), and Tom Prideaux's review of *Othello* in *Life* (11 Dec. 1964).

GLORIA COOKSEY

JONES, Quincy Delight, Jr. (*b.* 14 March 1933 in Chicago, Illinois), prolific composer, arranger, musician, producer, businessman, and winner of twenty-five Grammy Awards for his motion picture soundtracks and recordings.

Jones's father, Quincy Delight Jones, Sr., was a carpenter. At the time Jones was born, his father worked as a carpenter for the Jones Boys, an African-American gang that controlled much of South Chicago. His mother, Sarah, was mentally ill and prone to violent outbursts; in 1941 she was sent to Mantina State Hospital in Kankakee, Illinois, from which she often escaped. Jones and his younger brother, Lloyd, were sent to live with their maternal grandmother in Kentucky, whose home had no electricity and where meals often consisted of fried rats caught on the banks of a nearby river.

In 1943 their father gathered the boys up and settled with them in Bremerton, Washington, a suburb of Seattle; he had landed a job as a carpenter in the Puget Sound naval-shipyard. After divorcing their mother, Jones's father married Elvera Miller, who already had three children of her own, and they had three more children. Miller was

Quincy Jones. THE LIBRARY OF CONGRESS

cruel to Jones and his brother, often humiliating them. It was in 1943 that Jones took an interest in music and began to play the trumpet. When he was fourteen years old, Jones met the "soul" musician Ray Charles, who was two years older than Jones and already living on his own, supporting himself mainly by playing jazz. Jones peppered him with questions about composing and arranging music, which Charles answered patiently. They became lifelong friends.

Jones attended Garfield High School, where he met his first wife, Jeri Caldwell. They tried to get married when she was eighteen and he was nineteen, but their marriage papers were deemed improper when government clerks discovered that Caldwell, who was white, was marrying a black man. They lived together as man and wife and had the first of their two children, until they were able to make their marriage official in 1956. When Jones graduated from high school, he received a music scholarship to Seattle University's music program, but he did not find the school challenging enough and applied to a better school, Schillinger House (later renamed Berklee College of Music) in Boston, on a scholarship.

At the prestigious Berklee, he learned classical music composition, helping him make music for large bands and orchestras. In 1957 he went on a U.S. government—

sponsored goodwill overseas circuit with the jazz trumpeter Dizzy Gillespie, and in 1957 he toured Europe with the legendary vibraphone player Lionel Hampton's band, in both cases serving as a trumpet player and music arranger. From 1959 to 1960, Jones arranged the music for Harold Arlen's blues opera *Free and Easy,* which died for lack of funding in France. Jones had put together a fine orchestra, so when the show closed in February 1960, he persuaded the band to stay in Europe and barnstorm. He took on the responsibilities of finding gigs for the band and keeping track of their money. Traveling with the band were the families of the musicians and singers, making the job of keeping track of everyone, especially while traveling by train, very difficult. The stress Jones endured was severe, but from 1960 to 1961, he learned about the business end of music—how to negotiate deals and how to lead. Even though the band was admired by critics and jazz fans, it did not make enough money to cover expenses.

In 1961 Jones accepted a job offer from Irving Green, the president of Mercury Records, becoming a music director for Mercury's studio. In 1963 he received his first Grammy (an annual award given by the National Academy of Recording Arts and Sciences) for best instrumental arrangement for "I Can't Stop Loving You," performed by the jazz pianist Count Basie. In 1964 Green made Jones the vice president of Mercury Records, with responsibilities in all aspects of the recording business. He became the first African-American executive in a recording company owned by whites. That year he and Jeri separated; they divorced in 1966. In 1963 Jones wrote his first motion picture soundtrack for the Swedish film *Pojken i Trader* (The Boy in the Tree). The producer Sidney Lumet was impressed by Jones's work and invited him to write the soundtrack for *The Pawnbroker* (1965), an opportunity that greatly enhanced his reputation among moviemakers. He remembered writing the musical score in two months and then recording it in two days.

In 1964 Jones formed a friendship with the singer Frank Sinatra, with whom he had worked on arrangements for Sinatra's albums. Jones also helped arrange the music for Sinatra's appearances in Las Vegas. Sinatra hired bodyguards for each band member; Jones's bodyguard was from Yugoslavia and taught Jones to speak Serbo-Croatian. He wrote the score for the 1966 motion picture *The Slender Thread,* and then work began pouring in. Soon Jones was constantly writing, not only motion picture scores but also music for television shows. In 1968 he was offered a contract for $50,000 per year for twenty years to remain with Mercury Records, but Jones turned the offer down and resigned from the company to strike out on his own. In the late 1960s, he married his second wife, Ulla Anderson, with whom he had two children. They soon divorced.

Jones wrote musical scores for the motion pictures *In the Heat of the Night* and *In Cold Blood,* both released in 1967. He received an Academy Award for best original music score for *In Cold Blood,* and he received a nomination for best original song for the motion picture *Banning.* It was his score for *In Cold Blood* that made him famous; people outside the entertainment business began remembering his name. In 1967 he agreed to write the music for the television series *Ironside;* he labored to write original music for each episode. In 1968 he fell ill with appendicitis, narrowly receiving treatment in time.

In 1969 Jones won a Grammy for best instrumental jazz performance, large group or soloist with large group, for his tune "Walking in Space." By then he had found that constantly writing motion picture scores, television scores, and music for bands was too much of a strain on him, so he eased away from writing scores, focusing more on the recording business. He continued to write television scores and motion picture scores on occasion; for instance, for the 1977 miniseries *Roots* and for the 1985 motion picture *The Color Purple.*

In 1974 Jones married again, to the actress Peggy Lipton; they had two children and divorced in 1990. The same year that he married Lipton, Jones suffered two brain aneurysms (burst blood vessels in the brain) and underwent surgery that left him with metal plates in his skull; six months after lifesaving surgery, he returned to work. After his divorce from Lipton, he went on to have a live-in relationship in the mid-1990s with the actress Nastassja Kinski, with whom he had his seventh child. His interests turned toward business, and he founded Qwest, his own record label, and invested in cable television and television stations, becoming very wealthy.

★

The Autobiography of Quincy Jones (2001), an entertaining narrative, is frankly told and includes chapters about Jones by people who knew him. The best complete biography is Raymond Horricks, *Quincy Jones* (1985). Lee Hill Kavanaugh, *Quincy Jones: Musician, Composer, Producer* (1998), leans toward a teenage audience.

KIRK H. BEETZ

JOPLIN, Janis Lyn (*b.* 19 January 1943 in Port Arthur, Texas; *d.* 4 October 1970 in Hollywood, California), blues-influenced vocalist whose powerful voice and excessive lifestyle made her a legend even before her untimely death.

Joplin was the daughter of Seth Joplin, an engineer, and Dorothy East Joplin, the registrar of a business college. Encouraged from an early age to take an interest in the arts and literature, she became fascinated with the writing of F. Scott Fitzgerald and with the reckless, tragic life he shared

Janis Joplin. ARCHIVE PHOTOS, INC.

with his wife Zelda. Though she had no musical training except a stint singing in glee club at Thomas Jefferson High School, she developed an early appreciation for blues and jazz artists, including Billie Holiday, Bessie Smith, Lead-belly, and Odetta.

Located close to the Louisiana state line, on the Gulf of Mexico about an hour due east of Houston, Port Arthur is noted for its oil refineries and its shipbuilding facilities but is not an obvious breeding ground for artists and poets. By the standards of the South in the 1950s, it was unusual for a white girl to take an interest in "black music," and although Joplin's parents were liberal, she probably exceeded their expectations for nonconformity.

Some biographers have suggested that she later exaggerated tales of her troubled experiences in school, but it is clear that Joplin's offbeat interests and shy personality tended to make her something of an outcast. On the other hand, her claim that she was never close to her family—an assertion made, no doubt, to emphasize the contrast between her lonely childhood and her wildly successful adulthood—seems to have been a fabrication.

As a teenager Joplin learned to sing the blues and to

play guitar, piano, and autoharp. At that point, however, her ambition was to become a visual artist, not a singer. She drew and painted, and after graduating from high school in 1960 began taking arts classes, first at Lamar State College of Technology (now Lamar University) in nearby Beaumont and then at Port Arthur State College.

Joplin first sang professionally at the Halfway House in Beaumont in 1961. Soon thereafter she embarked on her first sojourn in a state where the most pivotal events of her later life were destined to take place: California. During that summer she lived with an aunt in Los Angeles, where she worked briefly as a keypunch operator for the Los Angeles Telephone Company. A fan of Beat poetry from her high school days, she soon gravitated to Venice Beach, home to communities of beatniks and other rebels.

Back in Texas, Joplin returned to college in Port Arthur and began making regular forays into Houston. There she discovered a small but growing beatnik scene and soon found work singing in country and western clubs such as the Purple Onion. Playing her autoharp as accompaniment, with a bluegrass band called the Waller Creek Boys backing her up, she sang a repertoire that included Lead-belly, Bessie Smith, and Jean Ritchie. Around this time she began drinking heavily and using drugs.

By 1962 Joplin had enrolled as a fine arts major at the University of Texas at Austin. Instead of living in the dormitory, she took up residence in a ramshackle apartment house nicknamed "the ghetto," which served as a nerve center for Austin's emerging counterculture scene. She also performed at Threadgills, a local bar.

Joplin, who was nearsighted and had frizzy, mouse-brown hair, a wide nose, and occasional problems with acne, was not conventionally pretty. Later, wealth and stardom would bolster her confidence immensely, and she became widely recognized as a sex symbol. As a shy and off-beat college student, however, she was an easy target for callous treatment. Thus it was that her classmates voted her "the ugliest man on campus," an incident that led to her leaving the university in 1963.

It had long been Joplin's intention to return to California, and she had saved money from her gigs in Texas for this purpose. With a friend named Chet Helms she hitch-hiked to San Francisco, where she attended several different colleges while singing folk songs at local coffeehouses. Pay was low, but she also sold a few paintings and managed to find money to feed a growing amphetamine addiction. Her work as an artist brought her into contact with cartoonist Robert Crumb and others.

After a summer visit to New York's Lower East Side, during which time she began shooting up amphetamines, Joplin spent the rest of 1964 in San Francisco. Concerned about her drug habit, she contemplated the prospect of marrying and settling down and enrolled as a sociology major at Lamar State College in June 1965. Events, however, conspired to send her on a trajectory toward fame and, ultimately, tragedy.

Helms, who had become successful as a rock promoter in San Francisco, asked Joplin to take on the role of lead singer for a newly formed group called Big Brother and the Holding Company. Joplin returned to California, and in June 1966 she and the group made their debut at San Francisco's Avalon Ballroom. The band had a hard-driving rock sound, but what truly made them a local success was the singer's distinctive voice, by turns brassy and tender.

Big Brother and the Holding Company emerged on the national scene with its performances at the Monterey International Pop Festival on the weekend of 16 to 18 June 1967. Monterey was the first of the great outdoor festivals of the 1960s, a trend that culminated in 1969 with Woodstock, where Joplin also performed. Despite a distinguished lineup that included the Who, Simon and Garfunkel, and the Byrds, the Monterey festival is best remembered for the performances of Joplin and Jimi Hendrix.

On the heels of Monterey, Big Brother secured a recording contract with a small label called Mainstream, which released their debut album, *Big Brother and the Holding Company, Featuring Janis Joplin* (1967). Composed primarily of singles the group had already released independently in San Francisco, the album is an uneven mix of folk, psychedelia, and pop, but the band began to find its sound during extensive tours of the United States and Canada. That sound emerged on *Cheap Thrills* (1968), which features Joplin's sizzling "Piece of My Heart" and a sultry cover of the George Gershwin standard "Summertime."

Joplin had emerged as by far the most notable aspect of the group, and soon after the release of *Cheap Thrills* she opted to leave the band and sign a contract with Columbia Records. She brought together a group called the Kozmic Blues Band, which backed her on *I Got Dem Ol' Kozmic Blues Again Mama* (1969). Although the album contains no hit singles, it was certified a gold record, an impressive achievement in an era when platinum albums were rare. Joplin had reached the apex of her career, but her life began to spiral out of control even as her restless talent explored new creative territory. Turning to heroin, she sought to recreate in life the excesses of her stage shows, and thus began the final chapter of her career.

Disdaining the horn-laden Kozmic Blues Band's sound,

Joplin formed yet another group, the Full-Tilt Boogie Band, to back her on *Pearl* (1970). The album's title refers to the nickname by which she was known to her closest friends, and critics widely regard it as Joplin's finest work. It contains her greatest hit, "Me and Bobby McGee," written by her sometime lover Kris Kristofferson, as well as "Get It While You Can" and "Cry Baby." Also notable is "Mercedes Benz," one of the few songs Joplin wrote herself; the song's engaging mix of humor and pathos is heightened by Joplin's a cappella performance. By contrast, the prophetically titled "Buried Alive in Blues" is an instrumental, because Joplin did not live long enough to record the vocals. After completing a recording session, she overdosed on heroin in a room at the Landmark Motor Lodge in Hollywood in October 1970. Her remains were cremated, and the ashes were scattered off the coast of California.

Joplin has often been compared with Hendrix and Jim Morrison: all emerged from the West Coast in 1967; all were creative geniuses who turned to drugs and alcohol for release; and all succumbed to the effects of their lifestyles over a ten-month period between September 1970 and July 1971. Yet Joplin's story is remarkably different in that she was a woman in a world still dominated by men. Though the 1960s produced numerous great female vocalists, none had a voice as bold and brassy as Joplin's, nor a performing style as frenzied and orgiastic.

As with Hendrix and Morrison, one cannot help wondering what Joplin might have achieved had she not wasted her talent on drugs, but Joplin herself (again like Hendrix and Morrison) maintained that the excess and artistry were intertwined. When her friends warned her that her full-on, shrieking vocal style would ruin her voice, she replied that she would rather burn out young than have a long, mediocre career. For better or worse, she got her wish; certainly nothing about Janis Joplin was mediocre.

★

Biographies of Joplin abound. Notable examples include books by Joplin's publicist Myra Friedman, *Buried Alive: The Biography of Janis Joplin* (1973), and younger sister Laura Joplin, *Love, Janis* (1992). Other important Joplin biographies include David Dalton, *Piece of My Heart: A Portrait of Janis Joplin* (1985); Ellis Amburn, *Pearl: The Obsessions and Passions of Janis Joplin* (1992); and Alice Echols, *Scars of Sweet Paradise: The Life and Times of Janis Joplin* (1999). An obituary is in the *New York Times* (5 Oct. 1970).

JUDSON KNIGHT

K

KAHANE, Meir (*b*. 1 August 1932 in New York City; *d*. 5 November 1990 in New York City), rabbi, militant political organizer, and founder of the Jewish Defense League and the Israeli political party Kach.

Kahane was born Martin David Kahane to Rabbi Charles Kahane, who immigrated to the United States from Palestine, and Sonia Trainin Kahane, who emigrated from Latvia. The elder Kahane became a congregational rabbi in Brooklyn and head of the rabbinical board of Flatbush, a neighborhood in Brooklyn. The couple's younger son, Nachman, also became a rabbi and an official in the Israeli Ministry of Religion.

Kahane received his primary and secondary education at the Yeshiva of Flatbush. He continued his religious education at the Mirrer Yeshiva in Brooklyn while enrolled at Brooklyn College, from which he graduated with a bachelor's degree in 1954. He earned a degree from New York Law School in 1956 and a master's degree in international affairs from New York University in 1957, the same year he was ordained as a rabbi and began using the first name Meir.

However, the political education that most profoundly shaped Kahane's life began during his childhood. Through his father he absorbed the philosophy of Ze'ev Jabotinsky, the founder of Revisionist Zionism. Deeply affected by the destruction of European Jewry during the Holocaust, in 1946 Kahane joined Betar, a paramilitary Jewish youth

movement of the Israeli right-wing Herut Party led by Menachem Begin, which had roots in the Jabotinsky Revisionist movement. At age fifteen he was arrested for smashing the car windows of British Foreign Secretary Ernest Bevin as a protest against the British Mandate over Palestine.

In 1955 Kahane married Libby Blum, with whom he had two sons and two daughters. He served for two years as a congregational rabbi in Howard Beach, Queens, but left because the Conservative synagogue members found him too Orthodox in his beliefs and practices. In 1963 Kahane made his first trip to Israel, where he briefly served as a rabbi on a kibbutz. Soon after returning to the United States he began writing for the *Jewish Press,* an English-language weekly published in Brooklyn with a primarily Orthodox Jewish readership, using the byline Michael King.

As Michael King, Kahane frequently traveled to Washington, D.C., working as a consultant for government agencies and congressional committees along with a childhood friend, Joseph Churba. Kahane's activities included infiltrating the John Birch Society for the Federal Bureau of Investigation (FBI). He also used his position in the Jewish community to inform the House Un-American Affairs Committee about Jewish groups that were critical of Israel. As an operative of the Central Intelligence Agency (CIA), Kahane promoted the U.S. position on Vietnam.

In 1965 Kahane and Churba founded Consultants Research Associates, with the U.S. government as their client. They also organized the July Fourth Movement to build support for the war in Vietnam on college campuses and wrote a book, *The Jewish Stake in Vietnam*, advocating Jewish support of the war. During this time Kahane, using the Michael King alias, formed a self-proscribed relationship with a Christian woman, a model named Gloria Jean D'Argenio. When he eventually confessed that he was married and severed the relationship, she threw herself off the Queensboro Bridge to her death.

In 1967 Kahane left Consultants Research and again became a congregational rabbi, this time at an Orthodox congregation in Queens more in agreement with his views. He continued to write for the *Jewish Press*, soon becoming its editor. Through correspondence from his readers he learned of increasing crime and anti-Semitism perpetrated against poor and often elderly Jews in New York and other cities. To address these problems, which were not being dealt with by any other Jewish organization, Kahane founded the Jewish Defense League (JDL) in 1968 with the help of two members of his congregation, Bertram Zweibon and Mort Dolinsky. They adopted the slogan "Never Again," a reference to the Holocaust, and used the Black Panthers' organization as their model. The JDL provided members with classes in self-defense and weapons training and formed patrols to protect Jews in high-crime neighborhoods.

Soon the JDL branched out to embrace the plight of the Jews in the Soviet Union. To inaugurate its campaign on behalf of Soviet Jewry, the JDL in a single day, 29 December 1969, took over the New York offices of Tass, Intourist, and Aeroflot and boarded a Soviet passenger plane at Kennedy International Airport to spray paint the cabin with the Hebrew phrase "Am Yisrael Chai" ("The Jewish Nation Lives"). Despite furious Soviet protests the JDL kept up the attack, bombing Soviet and Arab property in the United States and harassing, even beating, Soviet and Arab diplomats.

To his followers Kahane was the bulwark of the defense of Jewish rights. But to many others, including the Jewish establishment, he was an embarrassment to the liberal traditions of Judaism. Some saw him as a terrorist. Indeed, in 1971 Kahane was convicted in a New York court of conspiring to make firebombs; he was fined $5,000 and given a five-year suspended sentence. Two months later he moved to Israel, where he was embraced by the political right as a hero. He opened a JDL office in Jerusalem, adapting the tactics he had used against the Soviets to confront Israeli Arabs and even Christians.

Shortly after moving to Israel, Kahane founded a political party, Kach ("Thus"). The Kach platform included removal of the entire Arab population from Israel, annexation of all territories liberated in the 1967 war, and the

right of unlimited Jewish settlement there. Kahane was concerned with the high Arab birthrate, which made an Arab majority in Israel likely in the future. He was known to assert, "Every Arab is a cancer in our state."

Kahane was elected to the Knesset, the Israeli parliament, in 1984. But in 1988, as Kach was expected to win eight to twelve seats in the legislature, the Israeli Central Election Committee banned the party, citing its "Nazi-like," "racist," and "undemocratic" positions.

On 5 November 1990 Kahane was shot and killed in a New York hotel where he was giving a speech. The alleged assassin, El Sayyid A. Nosair, was an Egyptian-born American Muslim who apparently acted alone.

Kahane, who is buried in Israel, was remarkably deft at harnessing the fears and resentments of the less affluent members of the Jewish community and manipulating the mass media. These two skills made him the most controversial American Jew of his time.

★

Books on Kahane include Robert I. Friedman, *The False Prophet, Rabbi Meir Kahane: From FBI Informant to Knesset Member* (1990). Kahane's own views are perhaps best summarized in his books *Never Again!* (1971) and *The Jewish Idea* (1974). An obituary is in the *New York Times* (7 Nov. 1990).

NATALIE B. JALENAK

KAHN, Herman Bernard (*b.* 15 February 1922 in Bayonne, New Jersey; *d.* 7 July 1983 in Chappaqua, New York), brilliant military strategist, lecturer, author, and founder of the Hudson Institute (a conservative think tank), whose pioneering futuristic views in the 1960s made him the most prominent, as well as the most controversial, strategist of that decade.

Kahn was the son of Jewish immigrants Abraham Kahn, a clothing manufacturer, and Yetta Koslowsky, a homemaker, who divorced when Kahn was very young. Kahn, along with his mother, two brothers, and a sister, lived in New York City and at times had to depend on public assistance to survive. In 1935 Kahn and his family moved to Los Angeles. Kahn worked long hours to help support the family. He graduated from Fairfax High School in 1940 and entered the University of Southern California prior to serving in Burma with the U.S. Army Signal Corps from 1943 to 1945. After his discharge in 1945, he resumed his studies at the University of California, Los Angeles (UCLA), graduating with a B.A. in physics later that year.

Kahn's first jobs were in the aviation industry and as a teaching assistant at UCLA. During this time he also attended the California Institute of Technology in Pasadena, earning a M.S. in 1948. Kahn was a physicist with the RAND Institute, a think tank for the U.S. Air Force, from 1948 to 1960. There he developed expertise in military strat-

Herman Kahn. CORBIS CORPORATION (BELLEVUE)

egy by studying the critical relations between weapons and tactics, and conducting lectures for military and civilian leaders. Early in his career at RAND, Kahn stated, "They were doing what I always wanted—making integrated studies of important questions and pontificating on a range of issues." Kahn also pursued his interests in economic and political issues by participating as a roving consultant in special-interest projects. As a child Kahn loved science fiction, and at RAND he enjoyed using his skills in applied mathematics to solve game theories of strategic warfare. While at RAND, Kahn met mathematician Rosalie Jane Heilner. They married on 31 March 1953; the couple had two children.

As an expert on the problems of weapons design and a proponent of applying games theory to strategic warfare, Kahn urged the United States to accept a strong civil defense program, both for protection and as a deterrent to war. He expressed his views in *On Thermonuclear War* (1961), which was based on a series of lectures given at Princeton. In the early 1960s, nuclear war was not a topic of discussion, and heated controversy and debate surrounded the book because it was the first to describe openly the likely effects of nuclear war. Kahn emphatically insisted, "nuclear war is not only a possibility, but a probability." He claimed arms control and military preparation

were necessary to survive the arms race. The book received praise for being "instructive and absorbing" and became a landmark in literature on military strategy. It also suffered criticism for "minimizing the dangers of nuclear war" and as a "moral tract on mass murder." The book stimulated public interest in its scenarios concerning survival, thus earning Kahn the title "father of deterrence theory" in the United States. Some critics viewed the 1964 film *Dr. Strangelove, Or: How I Learned to Stop Worrying and Love the Bomb* as a satire of Kahn and *On Thermonuclear War.*

In September 1961, the controversial Kahn resigned from RAND and founded the Hudson Institute in White Plains, New York, which later moved to Croton-on-Hudson. Kahn served as its chairman and director of research. The institute's mission was to bridge the gap between politicians and academicians about nuclear strategy and other public policy issues and thus possibly influence policy decisions involving national security and international order. Kahn began speaking nationwide about the dangers of war and his political revulsion about participating in wars. In 1962, with the publication of his second book on nuclear war, *Thinking About the Unthinkable,* Kahn speculated about nuclear disaster and tried to dismiss any concerns that he was advocating the use of nuclear weapons. His views on wars were that "to act intelligently we must learn as much as we can about the risks. We may thereby be able better to avoid nuclear war."

A strong supporter of the Kennedy administration's civil defense measures, Kahn's third book, *On Escalation: Metaphors and Scenarios* (1965), focused on a broader framework within which to understand and manage conflict situations. Kahn showed the many distinct steps to the escalation of war, and explained what the United States must look for to determine our position on the "escalation ladder" and how we can act to prevent thermonuclear war. He also emphasized that maintaining a strong bargaining position is the central factor in a nuclear strategy.

Although many are controversial, his numerous lectures, articles, and classified documents (some still not available to the public) gained Kahn fame as a brilliant military strategist. His three books made this self-described "free-thinking intellectual" not only a figure of national prominence, but also a misunderstood intellectual outcast.

Later in the 1960s, Kahn turned his attention from thermonuclear war to economics and politics. His *Year 2000* (1967), although making some outlandish predictions, discussed future developments relevant to business and international economics. Kahn was the first futurist to predict a boom in the Japanese economy and its emergence as the model for economic and business development.

Labeled as a curious and very outgoing man, Kahn's commanding presence, three hundred pounds, florid face, and tailored white beard often mesmerized those to whom he lectured for hours without notes, interspersing his comments with anecdotes and jokes. His presentations were often entertaining and always informative. It is said that Kahn briefed every president from Harry S. Truman to Ronald W. Reagan. Kahn died of a heart attack at his home in Chappaqua and is buried in Fair Ridge Cemetery there.

Kahn was an important figure in the development of futurology in the 1960s. He explored realms of thought on defense strategy into which few others dared to enter during that decade. A misunderstood futurist, lover of life, personable genius, achiever of the impossible, by openly expressing and presenting his thoughts in a convincing manner, Kahn's futuristic thinking clearly has come to influence how we view what is "impossible" and what is "certain."

★

An early biographical sketch on Kahn is in *Current Biography 1962* (1963), Charles Moritz, ed. Biographical information and a listing of his publications and summary of his major publications appear in Susan M. Trosky, ed., *Contemporary Authors,* vol. 83, New Revision Series (2000). *The Cold War, 1945–1991* (1992), Benjamin Frankel, ed., gives a brief biographical sketch and contains summaries of Kahn's first three books. Other sources offering critiques and appraisals of his works include Richard Kostelanetz, *Master Minds: Portraits of Contemporary American Artists and Intellectuals* (1969), and Robert Holmes, *On War and Morality* (1989). W. Basil McDermott, "Thinking About Herman Kahn," *Conflict Resolution* 15, no. 1 (Mar. 1971), offers an excellent analysis of Kahn's works and his views on a variety of subjects. Obituaries are in the *New York Times* (8 July 1983), and the *Futurist* 17 (Oct. 1983): 61–65.

JOYCE K. THORNTON

KAHN, Louis Isidore (*b.* 20 February 1901 in Saaremaa [now Oesel], Estonia; *d.* 17 March 1974 in New York City), architect who transformed the governing principles of design and influenced a shift away from modernism and toward postmodernism in architecture.

Kahn's parents, Leopold Kahn and Bertha Mendelsohn, immigrated to the United States in 1905 and settled in Philadelphia. He was naturalized as a U.S. citizen in 1915. Kahn's childhood was marked by poverty and the misfortune of an accident that left him with a permanently scarred face; as a result, Kahn was always shy in public, even when he came to a position of national prominence. While attending Central High School and Public Industrial Art School in Philadelphia, Kahn displayed a talent as a draftsman. In his senior year of high school, after taking a course in architectural history, he decided that he would become an architect, and he enrolled in the design program at the University of Pennsylvania in 1920. There Kahn came un-

Louis Kahn. AP/WIDE WORLD PHOTOS

der the influence of Paul Philippe Cret, himself a graduate of the Ecole des Beaux-Arts in Paris. Cret instilled in him a respect for the classical tradition, later reflected in Kahn's designs, which hearken back to ancient Greece and Rome and to even older styles of the Near East.

Upon receiving his B.A. degree in 1924, Kahn went to work for the Philadelphia architect John Molitor. Perhaps recognizing Kahn's abilities, Molitor gave the young architect a substantial role in large public projects; in fact, Kahn served as chief designer for the 1926 Sesquicentennial Exposition. (Half a century later in the early 1970s, Kahn—by then nationally and internationally famous—developed the design for the Bicentennial Exposition of 1976.) He left the firm in early 1928, studied for nearly two years in Europe, and in 1929 returned to Philadelphia. Also in 1930, Kahn married Esther Virginia Israeli, with whom he had one daughter.

With the Great Depression raging, Kahn found few opportunities for commissions, and he joined with other architects in 1931 to form the Architectural Research Group as a means of finding work. Nevertheless, Kahn's career prior to 1947 was confined primarily to consultancies. Then in 1947 George Howe (with whom Kahn had entered into a business partnership in 1941, and who later became chair of the Yale University department of architecture) recommended him as a visiting critic at the Yale School of Architecture.

In the quarter century that followed, Kahn, from his influential pulpit at one of the nation's most distinguished universities, transformed the way that American architects regarded their profession, its materials, and its purposes. Striking a tone that called to mind the notions of perfect form first articulated by Plato twenty-three centuries earlier, Kahn urged architects to seek out "what the building wants to be." His was not an architecture of functionality, although there was nothing whimsical or capricious in his designs. However, he maintained that the architect's role is not to give the client what he or she demands, but rather to seek out the essential quality of the building's own character.

Invigorated by a year spent as architect in residence at the American Academy in Rome between 1950 and 1951, during which time he had an opportunity to drink once again from the wellspring of Western architecture's guiding influence, Kahn began a series of designs that during the next two decades would quite literally give form to his ideas. First among these was the Yale Art Gallery (1951–1953), in which he became the first architect to leave ductwork and other mechanical features exposed in the ceiling. That this is commonplace today is a hallmark of Kahn's influence; in the early 1950s it was a daring move.

Kahn's work in the 1950s and 1960s showed an amazing versatility with regard to the varying scales of interaction that his designs addressed. He could work on large, potentially impersonal public spaces or on small, deeply intimate ones. His ability in the latter respect is displayed prominently with his plan for the Jewish Community Center Bath House in Trenton, New Jersey (1954–1959). A small, but highly influential project, the bath house gave the first physical expression to Kahn's emerging idea that the built environment could be divided into "served" and "servant" spaces. The first is the space for which the building is designed, whereas the second is the supporting space of mechanical rooms, heating and cooling systems, and other purely functional aspects of the building. In the bath house, composed of four small buildings, "servant space" was hidden in square blocks at the corner of each building.

The A. N. Richards Medical Research Building at the University of Pennsylvania (1957–1964) takes the idea of "servant" and "served" even further. Among the building's most striking features is a row of towers inspired by those built in Italian towns during the Renaissance, yet these towers actually hold mechanical and ventilating equipment.

The late 1950s and early 1960s saw the design and construction of Kahn's most important works, none perhaps more notable than the laboratory buildings at the Salk Institute for Biological Studies in La Jolla, California (1960–1965). The famed virologist Jonas Salk himself discussed

with Kahn his ideas regarding his vision for the buildings as a place he "could invite Picasso to" but otherwise left the architect with a free hand. The resulting design at once pays tribute to and transcends a quintessential idiom of public space in American life—the New England town common.

By choosing the common as his template, Kahn seems to have made a deliberate statement regarding his attempt to rewrite the codes by which Americans view the built environment. Whereas the New England common symbolized an earlier America that still looked eastward toward Europe, the Salk Institute buildings gazed upon a western shore that points not so much to Asia as to a culmination of deeply felt aspirations in the American spirit. Kahn's design makes this purpose clear in its substitution of the key component in the New England common, the church. In place of its spire, anchoring the western fringes of the complex, he left open space, thus offering a view toward something even more majestic—the waves of the Pacific Ocean and the sun setting above it.

The La Jolla complex also reflects a continuing fascination with light, its qualities, and the creative approach to the practical needs of enhancing light in certain places and occluding it in others. Kahn's Yale Art Gallery, for instance, features a wide glass curtain wall to channel in the sunlight, whereas the Salk Institute Laboratory is designed in such a way as to diminish the brightness of excess light. Kahn later applied the same principles in his National Assembly Building in Dacca, Bangladesh.

Begun in 1962 as a building for the chief legislative body of the country that was then known as East Pakistan, the project was fraught with challenges, not least those brought about by the 1971 war that gave the country independence from the Pakistani government in Islamabad. For this reason, the Dacca project did not reach completion until 1974, the year of Kahn's death. Yet the design itself—although it clearly pays tribute to the region's ancient past—is so revolutionary that it would have looked contemporary if it had been completed a decade later. In designing it, Kahn as always applied creative solutions to practical problems, fashioning massive walls that provide a sheltering curtain against the relentless sunlight of the region.

Other notable designs by Kahn in the 1960s and thereafter include the Institute of Management in Ahmedabad, India (1962–1974); the Kimbell Art Museum in Fort Worth, Texas (1966–1972); the library and dining hall at Phillips Exeter Academy in Exeter, New Hampshire (1967–1972); and the Center for British Art and Studies at Yale. The latter project brought his career full circle, inasmuch as it stood directly across the street from his Yale Art Gallery.

Throughout his life, Kahn had a sometimes unfulfilled longing to create and transform large public spaces. His career ended with several proposals still on the drawing board for the renaissance of his beloved Philadelphia. He did not live to see the completion of the Dacca or Ahmedabad project, and a large-scale design for Teheran, Iran, never came to fruition. On 17 March 1974, on his way home from a trip to Bangladesh and India, Kahn succumbed to a heart attack in a New York train station. He is buried at Montefiore Cemetery in Philadelphia. Despite his status as the most influential American architect since Frank Lloyd Wright, his firm was in grave economic trouble and was saved from bankruptcy only when a grateful State of Pennsylvania purchased his drawings and sketches.

Changes in architecture, the most practical of all arts, take longer to manifest than do those in other artistic fields, a function of the costs involved and the permanence of the creations themselves. A famous example of this is the magnificent vice-regal residence in New Delhi, widely regarded as representing the zenith of colonial architecture. When the British architect Edwin Lutyens designed it, Britain firmly controlled India, but by the time of its completion in 1931, British power had eroded, and thus the world that had created it was long gone.

This historical lag between conception and completion only served to heighten the impact of Kahn's work. Many of his designs from the early 1950s on belong to the world of the 1960s and much later. Even in the 1960s and early 1970s, most of the major buildings under construction reflected an earlier influence—that of Wright, though usually without many traces of Wright's genius. Only in the 1980s did postmodernism begin to take firm hold in American architecture, thus extending Kahn's influence far beyond his lifetime.

★

Kahn's papers, as well as his architectural drawings, models, and other materials, are housed at the University of Pennsylvania in Philadelphia. His collected writings appear in Alessandra Latour, ed., *Louis I. Kahn: Writings, Lectures, Interviews* (1991). For his designs and other works, see Eugene Feldman and Richard Wurman, eds., *The Notebooks and Drawings of Louis I. Kahn* (1973); Heinz Ronner, Sharad Jhaveri, and Alessandro Vasella, eds., *Louis I. Kahn: The Complete Works, 1935–1974* (1977); and Jan Hochstim, ed., *The Paintings and Sketches of Louis I. Kahn* (1991). Two good introductions to Kahn's work are Romaldo Giurgola and Jaimini Mehta, *Louis I. Kahn* (1975), and John Lobell, *Between Silence and Light: Spirit in the Architecture of Louis I. Kahn* (1979). An obituary is in the *New York Times* (2 Mar. 1974).

JUDSON KNIGHT

KARNOW, Stanley (*b.* 4 February 1925 in New York City), journalist, Pulitzer Prize–winning author, Far East correspondent, and historian who brought the Vietnam War and East Asian history to life through his writings.

Karnow, born to Harry, a businessman, and Henriette (Koeppel) Karnow, a homemaker, began his writing career in high school, covering sports for his school's newspaper. With a brief interruption to serve in the U.S. Army Air Corps from 1943 to 1946, he continued writing at Harvard University for the student daily, *Crimson,* until he graduated with a B.A. in 1947. Following graduation Karnow took a summer job in Paris and ended up staying ten years. His GI Bill benefits paid for his study at the Sorbonne from 1947 to 1948 and the Ecole des Sciences Politiques from 1948 to 1949. While he was in Paris, he married Claude Sarraute on 15 July 1948; they divorced in 1955. Karnow also learned to speak French, which helped him secure a job at *Time* magazine in 1949. He spent the next nine years as a correspondent in Paris. In 1958 he moved to North Africa as *Time*'s bureau head and then became the Hong Kong bureau chief in 1959. He married Annette Klein on 21 April 1959; they had three children.

When Karnow moved to Hong Kong, he began a career that served to define him as an Asia expert not only for the 1960s but for future decades as well. He worked out of Hong Kong for the next twelve years, from 1959 to 1971, serving with *Time* until 1962 and as a Far East correspondent with the *Saturday Evening Post* from 1963 to 1965 and the *Washington Post* from 1965 to 1971. His first cover story for *Time,* in the March 1960 issue, was an in-depth analysis of Australia's flourishing economy under the leadership of its prime minister, Robert Gordon Menzies. Karnow's coverage of Australia set the tone for his journalistic style—provocative, comprehensive, and sometimes controversial. He was more renowned, however, for his coverage of the two Asian countries at the forefront of American foreign affairs, Vietnam and China.

Karnow reported on the Vietnam War continuously for sixteen years. While most American journalists scrambled to understand the country as U.S. involvement intensified, Karnow was already knowledgeable about the region as a result of his visits there in the 1950s. He had covered the French Indochina War while he was in Paris and had already learned the names of people and places through his study of Vietnamese culture. Karnow's coverage of the war began with the first American casualties. On 9 July 1959 he arrived at Bienhoa, the future site of a major American base, to gather information on two American advisers killed there. The landscape, still largely untouched by war, offered a glimpse of the gravity of the future devastation, with the small military camp an eyesore in the serene countryside. Karnow admitted later that he never imagined the destruction that would follow over the next sixteen years, but he had a feeling that the war would soon dominate American foreign policy.

Journalists in the 1960s did not just report the war, they analyzed policy and strategy and attempted to influence public opinion and, through it, government decision making. Early in the war, Karnow believed that Vietnam was the most pressing concern for the United States when many others did not. During a brief trip to Washington, D.C., in 1961, he interviewed Robert Kennedy about the war. Kennedy responded, "Vietnam? We [President John F. Kennedy's administration] face twenty Vietnams a day." In 1963 Karnow wrote against continued U.S. support of South Vietnam's President Ngo Dinh Diem, calling Diem the greatest ally the North Vietnamese ever had. Every policy and military operation that Diem implemented resulted in more South Vietnamese becoming sympathetic to the Vietcong. Karnow also understood the importance of learning the culture and history of the region and wrote *Southeast Asia* (1963), published by Time-Life Books as part of the "Life World Library" series. In his reporting he commented that few Westerners, particularly those in government, attempted to learn about this region. The book offers general information about the culture, geography, history, and economics of the area.

Stationed in Hong Kong, Karnow also covered events in China, a country that grew increasingly important to the United States, particularly as President Richard Nixon attempted to take advantage of Sino-Soviet tensions. In 1964 Karnow published *Bitter Seeds: A Farmer's Story of the Revolution in China*. From 1966 to 1969 the dominant news event in China was the Cultural Revolution, which Karnow described as the first legitimate attempt at creating a free press in the country. Numerous newsletters, documents, handbills, and radio broadcasts emanated from China during this time with little or no interference from the ruling Communist Party. This information formed the basis for most reports about China in the Western media, but Karnow saw a larger story emerging from the individual pieces. With this larger story in mind, he returned to Harvard in 1970 to work as a research fellow at the East Asia Research Center. In 1972 he published *Mao and China: From Revolution to Revolution,* a comprehensive look at China's Cultural Revolution. Karnow's writings on China secured a rare invitation for him to accompany Nixon on his historic visit to China in 1972.

Karnow's reporting on Asia in the 1960s earned him several awards, including the Overseas Press Club Citation in 1966 and the 1967 and 1968 annual award for the best newspaper interpretation of foreign affairs, also from the Overseas Press Club. Karnow considered himself a journalist rather than a writer—"journalists are writers, not all writers are journalists"—even when he wrote books. At the time he wrote *Mao and China,* journalistic histories were becoming more accepted as authoritative, and his work was no exception. Even his few critics, who considered his work shallow because he did not utilize primary source material, applauded his ability to provide a clear look at a complex world event.

Karnow worked as a journalist and syndicated colum-

nist throughout the 1970s and 1980s. In the early 1980s Karnow began to see himself as a full-time historian, calling journalism the "first rough, vivid draft of history." Relying on his experiences in Asia, he produced a series of highly regarded histories and documentaries. His works include *Vietnam: A Television History* (1983), a documentary for the Public Broadcasting Service (PBS), which won an Emmy award in 1984, and *Vietnam: A History* (1983). His documentary *In Our Image: America's Empire in the Philippines* (1989) won the 1990 Pulitzer Prize in history. Later, Karnow produced *Asian Americans in Transition* (1992) and *Paris in the Fifties* (1997). On 17 January 2002 Karnow was named as the first recipient of the Shorenstein Award for lifetime work in journalism.

★

Much about Karnow's life is found in his own writings, especially *Mao and China: From Revolution to Revolution* (1972), *Vietnam: A History* (1983), and *Paris in the Fifties* (1997). An autobiographical essay is in Brian Lamb, *Booknotes: America's Finest Authors on Reading, Writing and the Power of Ideas* (1997). A thorough overview of his life and career is in *Contemporary Authors* (2001).

MICHAEL C. MILLER

KATZ, Lillian. *See* Vernon, Lillian.

KATZENBACH, Nicholas de Belleville (*b.* 17 January 1922 in Philadelphia, Pennsylvania), attorney and U.S. Justice Department official in the 1960s who helped draft civil and voting rights legislation and who was involved in the desegregation of southern universities, the blockade of Cuba, and the President's Crime Commission.

Katzenbach was the son of Edward Lawrence, a corporate lawyer who died when Katzenbach was twelve, and Marie Louise (Hilson) Katzenbach, who was on the New Jersey State Board of Education for forty years. Katzenbach attended Phillips Exeter Academy and then enrolled at Princeton University. After the Japanese attacked Pearl Harbor in December 1941, Katzenbach joined the U.S. Army Air Force, was eventually shot down, and spent two years in a prisoner of war camp, escaping twice. When he returned to the United States, he completed his undergraduate requirements at Princeton via a special examination and received his B.A. degree cum laude in 1945. He then obtained an LL.B. cum laude in 1947 from Yale Law School. He married Lydia King Phelps Stokes on 8 June 1946. From 1947 to 1949 he was a Rhodes scholar at Oxford University, Oxford, England. He became an associate in the law firm of Katzenbach, Gildea, and Rudner in 1950. From 1950 to 1952 he was attorney-adviser to the secretary of the Air Force. Katzenbach taught law at Yale from 1952 to 1956 and at the University of Chicago from 1956 to 1960.

Nicholas Katzenbach. AP/WIDE WORLD PHOTOS

Katzenbach was appointed to the U.S. Department of Justice as assistant attorney general of the Office of Legal Counsel in 1961. He immediately began working on many of the initiatives set forth by President John F. Kennedy and his administration, including wiretapping and conflict-of-interest legislation and the administration's foreign-trade program. Katzenbach, who was appointed deputy attorney general in 1962, was a key participant in an international crisis involving Cuba. The 1962 Cuban Missile Crisis resulted from the U.S. government's discovery that Cuba had allowed the Soviet Union to place long-range missiles on its soil. The Kennedy administration decided to form a blockade. On the evening of 18 October 1962, Attorney General Robert Kennedy called Katzenbach and requested that he prepare a brief establishing the legal basis for the blockade. Katzenbach, who co-wrote with Morton A. Kaplan the 1961 book *The Political Foundations of International Law,* presented a case based on this area of his expertise and stated that U.S. action was justified on the principle of self-defense.

In December 1962 the crisis was resolved when the Soviet Union agreed to remove its missiles from Cuba. Katzenbach became part of a group that negotiated the release of prisoners captured during the Bay of Pigs invasion, which had taken place on 17 April 1961. The invasion

was part of a plan to overthrow the Communist regime in Cuba headed by Fidel Castro. It included approximately 1,300 members of a Central Intelligence Agency-supported counterrevolutionary Cuban exile force, which stormed the beaches of Cuba but were quickly defeated. Katzenbach and others gained the captured invaders' release in exchange for medical supplies and baby food.

In the early 1960s the civil rights movement was rapidly gaining momentum. Katzenbach became a prominent figure in the movement as the federal government's chief representative in civil rights cases in Mississippi and Alabama. One of the key initial issues was the integration of college campuses. In the fall of 1962 many whites in Mississippi were outraged when the African-American James Meredith tried to enroll at the University of Mississippi. After Meredith was prevented from registering on two different occasions, President Kennedy ordered federal marshals and other federal authorities to take up positions on the campus on 30 September. Katzenbach and Meredith rode together in a convoy to the campus, where Meredith spent the night alone in a dormitory. Mob violence erupted again the next day, but the troops and marshals made sure that Meredith was able to register.

A nearly identical crisis occurred on 11 June 1963, when Alabama's governor George Wallace stood in the doorway at the University of Alabama to keep two black students from registering. Finally, Katzenbach, who was sent to enforce a federal court's decision to integrate the university, approached with the two students—James Hood and Vivian Malone. Although tensions were high when Katzenbach and Wallace confronted each other, Wallace stepped aside and let Katzenbach and the students enter.

President Kennedy was assassinated in Dallas shortly afterward, on 22 November. Katzenbach worked closely with the Warren Commission in its investigation of the assassination. Although the commission ultimately determined that the assassin Lee Harvey Oswald had worked alone, many came to believe that the assassination was really part of a conspiracy that the commission had helped cover up. A memo from Katzenbach to the presidential assistant Bill Moyers at the White House on 25 November 1963, the day of President Kennedy's funeral, was pointed to by later conspiracy theorists as being suspicious in its quick determination of who assassinated the president. In it Katzenbach wrote that it was important for the public to "be satisfied that Oswald was the assassin; that he had no confederates who are still at large; and that evidence was such that he would have been convicted at trial."

Katzenbach remained deputy attorney general and was instrumental in drafting the Civil Rights Act of 1964. On 11 February 1965 President Lyndon B. Johnson appointed him attorney general of the United States, an office he held until 2 October 1966, when he became undersecretary of state. During this time Katzenbach also chaired the President's Commission on Law Enforcement and the Administration of Justice, which produced an extensive 1967 report called "The Challenge of Crime in a Free Society." The report focused on the increasing rate of crime in the late 1960s and concluded that law enforcement was ineffective in its approach to both organized and street crime. The report also included more than two hundred specific recommendations to overhaul the criminal justice system.

After leaving government service in 1969, Katzenbach worked for the IBM Corporation until 1986. He then returned to private law practice. In 1991 he was named chairman of the failing First American Bank of Washington, D.C., with the assignment of clearing up the scandal surrounding the bank and its ties to the Bank of Credit and Commerce International. This appointment reflected the respect Katzenbach commanded as a man of integrity throughout his career in both government and the private sector. Katzenbach and his wife have four children. Their son John, a novelist, wrote *Hart's War* (1999), based partly on his father's experiences as a World War II prisoner. Katzenbach and his wife live in Princeton, New Jersey.

★

Biographies of Katzenbach are in the 1965 edition of *Current Biography,* which covers Katzenbach's career until the mid-1960s, and *The Cambridge Dictionary of American Biography* (1995). For an overview of Katzenbach's role in the early years of the civil rights movement, see Taylor Branch, *Parting the Waters: American in the King Years 1954–63* (1988). Oral history interviews with Katzenbach concerning the civil rights legislation in the 1960s are in the Lyndon Baines Johnson Library and Museum in Austin, Texas.

DAVID PETECHUK

KAUFMAN, Bel (*b.* c. 1911 in Berlin, Germany), teacher and writer noted for her 1964 novel *Up the Down Staircase,* which depicts a year in the life of a young teacher in an inner-city school.

Kaufman, the daughter of Michael J. Kaufman, a physician, and Lola Rabinowitz Kaufman, a writer, was born in Berlin, Germany, but grew up in Russia. Because they were Jewish in an anti-Semitic culture, Kaufman, her parents, and her younger brother were threatened with execution by Russian revolutionary forces. Kaufman's grandfather, Sholom Aleichem, was a noted Yiddish writer, respected even by Russian authorities, and through his influence with the minister of culture, Kaufman's family was allowed to immigrate to the United States in 1923. They traveled on a private train from Moscow, accompanied by a bodyguard.

Arriving in the Bronx, a borough of New York City,

Kaufman, then twelve years old, was placed in the first grade because she did not know any English. She learned the language quickly, however, and her experiences with a kind and understanding teacher inspired her to become a teacher, too. Kaufman was educated in New York City, earning a bachelor's degree from Hunter College and a master's degree from Columbia University. She then taught in New York City schools for more than twenty years.

The novel *Up the Down Staircase,* published in 1964, is based on Kaufman's own teaching experiences in New York City public schools. Its main character is Sylvia Barrett, an energetic and idealistic first-year teacher who arrives at an inner-city school beset by administrative incompetence, financial woes, and troubled students. Barrett battles red tape and tries to encourage students to learn and grow despite their disadvantages.

In the novel, students are portrayed with sympathy and insight despite their sometimes overwhelming problems, including homelessness, drug addiction, poverty, and crime; one student even threatens to rape a teacher. As Lenore Skenazy wrote in the *New York Daily News,* "Any warm, fuzzy feelings you might have harbored about public education . . . get tossed out the window in *Staircase.* The kids in it are snotty, cynical, and scary." Barrett, however, manages to reach most of them through her own honesty and humor. The novel was the first popular work to portray the realities of inner-city schools, with their escalating racial tensions, drug and crime problems, overcrowded classrooms, and limited resources, and it immediately fascinated the American public.

The book's title is derived from a characteristically inane note that a student arriving late to class hands to his teacher. Written by the school's discipline-obsessed vice principal, the note explains that the student is late because he was "detained by me for going up the down staircase and subsequent insolence." In *Commonweal,* the critic David Lodge noted that the title provides "a sense of both the anarchic world the heroine inhabits and of the bureaucratic interference which makes it well-nigh impossible for her to cultivate any true educational order." Kaufman did not use traditional narrative techniques in her book; instead, the story is told through a montage of letters, notes written by students, administrative memos, student compositions and workbooks, lesson plans, pieces from the school paper, and blackboard writings.

Up the Down Staircase became a Book-of-the-Month Club selection and sold more than 1.5 million copies during its first month in print; the book also spent sixty-four weeks on the *New York Times* bestseller list. In 1966 the novel received the Paperback of the Year Award from the National Bestsellers Institute, and in 1967 it was made into a Warner Bros. movie starring Sandy Dennis. A *Time* magazine article called *Up the Down Staircase* "easily the most popular novel about U.S. public schools in history." In *America,* C. D. Gause commented that the novel was "a must for teachers and a revelation for the outside world . . . who do not know that this profession . . . is a 24-hour job all 365 days a year." By 2002 it had been translated into sixteen languages and had sold 6.5 million copies worldwide.

In 1979 Kaufman published a second novel, *Love, Etc.* Herself the divorced mother of a son and daughter, Kaufman describes a difficult divorce that precipitates the main character's journey of self-exploration and new love. Like *Up the Down Staircase,* the book treats serious subject matter with humor. Kaufman told Herbert Mitgang in a *New York Times Book Review* interview that the long delay between her novels was because, in writing her second novel, she "could not find the right form to fit the content. What I needed was a way of combining seriousness and humor— laughter behind tears, tears behind laughter." Kaufman is married to Sidney J. Gluck, a photographer, textile consultant, and designer.

Kaufman was named to the Hunter College Hall of Fame in 1973 and won a National Human Resource Award in 1974, among other honors. She has published several short stories and magazine articles in addition to her novels and won the National Education Association/P.E.N. Short Story Contest in 1983 for her story "Sunday in the Park." In 2001 she delivered the commencement address at Hunter College and received an honorary Doctor of Letters degree. She has taught fiction workshops at the University of Rochester in New York and lectures at educational conferences for Jewish organizations. Kaufman told *New York Daily News* reporter Skenazy, "I seize my audience and speak more or less impromptu. And with no false modesty, I must say I'm very good."

In *Fiction 100: An Anthology of Short Stories,* Kaufman wrote in her introduction, "I do not like writing . . . and would rather do anything else. But the joy comes when, almost in spite of myself, I come close to what I want to say." Of the phenomenal success of *Up the Down Staircase,* she told Skenazy, "My book was a straw in the wind that has become a hurricane."

★

Fiction 100: An Anthology of Short Fiction (2001), edited by James H. Pickering, contains a short profile of Kaufman. A longer profile appears in Gale Group's *Contemporary Authors Online* (2001). Articles about Kaufman and reviews of her work appear in *America* (6 Feb. 1965), *Time* (12 Feb. 1965), the *New York Times Book Review* (14 Feb. 1965; 29 June 1979; and 21 Oct. 1979), *Commonweal* (14 May 1965), and the *New York Daily News* (24 Jan. 2001).

KELLY WINTERS

KELSEY, Frances Kathleen Oldham (*b.* 24 July 1914 in Cobble Hill, Vancouver Island, British Columbia, Canada), pharmacologist, physician, and U.S. government employee who gained national fame in 1962 for single-handedly preventing the sedative drug thalidomide from being marketed (and thus prescribed for patients) in the United States.

Kelsey was born Frances Oldham, the daughter of Frank Trevor Oldham, a retired British army officer, and Katherine Stuart. She had two brothers. After completing her early education in Victoria on Vancouver Island, she entered McGill University in Montreal, where she received a B.S. in 1934 and an M.S. in 1935. In 1936 Kelsey moved to the United States to attend the University of Chicago. She earned a Ph.D. in pharmacology in 1938 and joined the faculty of the department of pharmacology at the university that same year.

Kelsey had influential colleagues at Chicago. E. M. K. Geiling, a pioneer in the field of pharmacology, instilled in Kelsey the importance of studying the effects of drugs on the body and the need for scrupulously high standards of research. Kelsey, Geiling, and another pharmacologist, Freemont Ellis Kelsey, performed experiments that demonstrated the antimalarial drug quinine was lethal to rabbit fetuses although harmless to adult rabbits. Their studies were

Frances O. Kelsey. THE LIBRARY OF CONGRESS

among the first to show that the effects of drugs on the unborn could be very different from the effects on adults. Kelsey maintained her interest in this phenomenon all her life, as well as maintaining her interest in Freemont Kelsey. The two were married on 6 December 1943. After marrying, Kelsey left her job and entered medical school. She received an M.D. from the University of Chicago in 1950 and had two daughters while in school. She worked as an editorial associate for the American Medical Association in Chicago from 1950 to 1952, after which the Kelseys moved to South Dakota. Both taught pharmacology at the University of South Dakota Medical School, Frances Kelsey from 1954 to 1957. She completed an internship and was in private practice from 1957 to 1960. Kelsey became a naturalized U.S. citizen in 1956.

In 1960 Freemont Kelsey's work brought the family to Washington, D.C. That August, Kelsey accepted a position as a medical officer with the Food and Drug Administration (FDA). Her responsibility was to evaluate license applications from pharmaceutical firms seeking to market new drugs in the United States. It was an unglamorous job in an agency fraught with problems. The Antitrust and Monopoly Subcommittee of the Senate Judiciary Committee, chaired by Senator Estes Kefauver of Tennessee, was conducting a major investigation of the drug industry at the time, and the FDA was suspected of having a less than ethical relationship with the industry.

Kelsey's first major assignment was to review an application submitted in September 1960 by the William S. Merrell Company of Cincinnati. The company was requesting permission to market the sedative drug thalidomide under the brand name Kevadon. Thalidomide was already widely used in Europe, mainly as a sleeping pill, but it was also prescribed for other conditions, including morning sickness during pregnancy. The firm Chemie Grunenthal had developed the drug in West Germany, and it had been on the market there since 1957.

Kelsey was not satisfied with the research presented in Merrell's application, indicating it did not provide enough information about how thalidomide worked. She was particularly concerned about the possible toxicity of thalidomide in certain populations, including unborn babies. Kelsey withheld approval of the application, asking Merrell to provide more complete data. The company complied, but Kelsey was still not satisfied. When she rejected the application for a second time in January 1961, Dr. Joseph Murray, a representative from Merrell, began applying pressure by repeatedly contacting both Kelsey and her superiors with complaints about the delay. Murray referred to Kelsey as "nitpicking" and "unreasonable," but her resolve only became stronger after reading a report in the December 1960 *British Medical Journal* that suggested thalidomide might be causing numbness in the arms and legs of some patients. She rejected Merrell's application for a third time in March 1961, asking once more for better evidence of the drug's safety.

The battle between Kelsey and Merrell continued over the next several months, as disturbing reports began to emanate from Europe, where large numbers of women were giving birth to severely deformed babies. Many of the babies exhibited phocomelia, a previously rare condition that results in abnormally short and malformed limbs. By November 1961 German doctors were associating the birth defects with women who had taken thalidomide during their first three months of pregnancy. The drug was quickly pulled from the German market, and countries worldwide followed suit. In late November 1961 Merrell withdrew its application to market thalidomide in the United States.

Over ten thousand babies in forty-six countries had been exposed to the devastating effects of thalidomide. As stories and images of horrible deformities reached the United States, people slowly began to realize that Kelsey had virtually single-handedly prevented a national tragedy. On 15 July 1962 the *Washington Post* ran a front-page story with the headline "Heroine of FDA Keeps Bad Drug Off of Market." It began, "This is a story of how the skepticism and stubbornness of a government physician prevented what could have been an appalling American tragedy, the birth of hundreds, or indeed thousands, of armless and legless children."

On 7 August 1962 President John F. Kennedy presented Kelsey with the Distinguished Federal Civilian Service Award, which stated, "Her exceptional judgment in evaluating a new drug for safety for human use has prevented a major tragedy of birth deformities in the United States. Through high ability and steadfast confidence in her professional decision she has made an outstanding contribution to the protection of the health of the American people." In October 1962, with Kelsey present at the ceremony, Kennedy signed the landmark Kefauver-Harris Amendments to the federal Food, Drug, and Cosmetic Act of 1938. The amendments required a drug to be proven both safe and effective before it is approved for the U.S. market. They also gave the FDA greater control over drug experimentation on human subjects.

In December 1962 Kelsey became head of the new Investigational Drugs Branch of the FDA, whose function it was to regulate the testing of new drugs. She continued to work in various capacities at the FDA for the rest of her career, which lasted until she was well into her eighties. On 7 October 2000 Kelsey was inducted into the National Women's Hall of Fame in Seneca Falls, New York.

★

Kelsey's collected papers, primarily from the 1960s, are located at the Library of Congress in Washington, D.C. Chapter-length biographies include "The Doctor Who Said No," in Margaret Truman, *Women of Courage* (1976); and "Francis Oldham Kelsey and Thalidomide," in William Hoffman and Jerry A. Shields, *Doctors on the New Frontier: Breaking Through the Barriers of Modern Medicine* (1981). An article entitled "Drug Market Guardian: Frances Oldham Kelsey" appeared in the *New York Times* (2 Aug. 1962). Other biographical sources include *Notable Women in the Life Sciences: A Biographical Dictionary* (1996).

VICTORIA TAMBORRINO

KENNAN, George Frost (*b.* 16 February 1904 in Milwaukee, Wisconsin), Foreign Service officer, historian, and political commentator who mapped out the U.S. cold war "containment" strategy and was ambassador to Yugoslavia under President John F. Kennedy (1961–1963).

Kennan was the son of Kossuth "Kent" Kennan, a prosperous lawyer of Scotch-Irish descent, and his German-American wife, Florence James, who died two months after Kennan's birth. He had three older sisters. He attended Saint John's Military Academy in Delafield, Wisconsin, and Princeton University, graduating in 1925 with a B.A. degree. In 1926 Kennan joined the U.S. Foreign Service, undergoing intensive specialized Russian training at Berlin University and in Riga, Latvia. In 1931 he married the Norwegian Annelise Sorensen, with whom he had four children.

After the United States resumed diplomatic relations with Russia in 1933, Kennan spent five years in the U.S. embassy in Moscow (1933–1937), returning in 1944 as minister-counselor. His influential February 1946 "Long Telegram," sent from Moscow to the State Department in response to a request for elucidation of the reasons for the rapid postwar deterioration of Soviet relations with the West, argued that the internal dynamics of Russian communism made genuine Soviet-Western understanding unattainable. From 1947 to 1950 Kennan headed the State Department's Policy Planning Staff, exercising his greatest immediate impact upon U.S. foreign policy by enunciating the "containment" doctrine, which stated that the United States and other Western powers must firmly and resolutely oppose any further expansion of Soviet influence or territorial domination. This doctrine became the basis of U.S. cold war strategy toward the Soviet Union. In 1952 Kennan was briefly ambassador to the Soviet Union, but his outspoken criticism of Stalin's regime quickly brought his expulsion. His opposition to the creation of the North Atlantic Treaty Organization (NATO) and support for German reunification and neutralization led Secretary of State John Foster Dulles in 1953 to dispense with his services, whereupon Kennan began a lengthy career as a historian and influential political commentator. Eager to return to public life, in 1960 Kennan advised and supported John F. Kennedy, the Democratic presidential candidate, lobbying discreetly for a diplomatic position. Keen to encourage polycentrism, the development of rival groupings within the communist world, Kennan welcomed his appointment as ambassador to Yugoslavia, where he remained until his resignation in 1963. Kennan enjoyed a good relationship with Yugoslavia's leader, Marshal Josip Broz Tito, and loved the country's spectacular and historic scenery, but Tito's support for the Soviet Union during the Bay of Pigs invasion (1961) and Cuban Missile Crisis (1962) disappointed him. Kennan resigned when, retaliating against

George Kennan *(left)*, with Yugoslav president Josip Tito, May 1961. ASSOCIATED PRESS AP

human-rights offenses, the U.S. Congress temporarily rescinded Yugoslavia's most-favored-nation trading status. He resumed academic writing and lecturing, based at Princeton's Institute for Advanced Study.

While in Yugoslavia, Kennan had shown little interest in Vietnam. In 1950 he had urged U.S. attempts to encourage non-Communist, nationalist "third forces" in Indochina, but by 1955 he had grown pessimistic that such endeavors would succeed. Despite some misgivings, he endorsed President Lyndon B. Johnson's 1964 Tonkin Gulf Resolution. Johnson's subsequent escalation of the war convinced Kennan that the United States was too heavily involved militarily in a country of relatively slight strategic significance to its fundamental interests. He did not recommend immediate withdrawal, but underestimating North Vietnamese resolve, he suggested from 1965 to 1967 that the United States restrict itself to fortifying and defending strategic enclaves such as Saigon and supporting the South Vietnamese government; such policies would, he hoped, force North Vietnam into negotiating. During widely publicized congressional hearings in 1967, Kennan further argued that employing the force levels needed to ensure victory would likely trigger Chinese intervention and a full-scale, probably nuclear, Sino-American war. Tall, bald, elegantly dressed, and imposing, Kennan had considerable personal presence. In 1968 he endorsed the presidential candidacy of Senator Eugene McCarthy, who sought a negotiated settlement to the war in Vietnam. In November 1969 he finally publicly advocated unilateral U.S. military withdrawal, notwithstanding the probability that Communists would then take over South Vietnam. Paradoxically, as he stated in *Democracy and the Student Left* (1968), Kennan was frequently repelled by radical critics of the war, particularly student protesters whose often violent tactics, intolerance, and lack of civility he deplored, regarding them as symptoms of a broader malaise afflicting U.S. society. He ascribed this malaise to an overdependence on technology and a consequent rampant materialism, industrialism, and consumerism, and he consequently questioned the capability and moral authority of the United States to conduct an activist foreign policy. This may have been one reason why Kennan later suggested, in *The Cloud of Danger* (1977), that the United States eliminate its overseas commitments to Greece, Turkey, South Korea, the Philippines, Taiwan, and South Africa, retaining only those to Western Europe, Japan, and Israel. Far from convinced of the value of one-man, one-vote democratic systems, Kennan also regretted the civil rights movement, thinking segregation more desirable, and he tended to oppose black majority rule in Africa.

Kennan applauded the manner in which President Kennedy and the Soviet leader Nikita Khrushchev handled the Cuban Missile Crisis of 1962 and then negotiated a limited test-ban treaty, and he greatly regretted the subsequent disappearance of both men from the political scene. A long-term supporter of negotiations with the Soviet Union, Kennan believed that the Vietnam War distracted U.S. officials from pursuing détente, which he felt should have been a far higher priority. He applauded the initiatives of French president Charles de Gaulle in this direction and called for the Western recognition of East Germany. Outraged by the 1968 Soviet invasion of Czechoslovakia, Kennan initially demanded massive U.S. troop reinforcements in Western Europe but soon overcame his anger and endorsed West German Chancellor Willy Brandt's *Ostpolitik* (the "Eastern Policy" taken in 1969 to ease diplomatic tension with East Germany).

Kennan opposed the 1969 congressional Mansfield Amendment, which would have withdrawn U.S. forces from Europe, but he welcomed President Richard M. Nixon's efforts to promote disarmament and cooperation with the Soviet Union, even though he felt these were too modest. In the early 1970s Kennan nonetheless minimized the potential impact of resuming Sino-American relations, warning against overly optimistic expectations of the likely consequences for Soviet-American policy. Kennan published two volumes of best-selling confessional memoirs, *Memoirs, 1925–1950* (1967), and *Memoirs, 1950–1963* (1972). He continued to write prolifically well into his nineties, producing several magisterial historical tomes, further autobiographical works, and numerous articles on current political issues. He frequently warned against the tendency of the United States to intervene in nations and issues of little direct interest to U.S. citizens, suggesting that wider concerns, particularly the environment, resources, population growth, and arms control, were of far more crucial significance, both to the United States and to other countries. In 1982, alarmed by the Reagan administration's infatuation with nuclear weapons, Kennan campaigned for a U.S. "no first use" nuclear policy with three other former officials, McGeorge Bundy, Robert S. McNamara, and Gerard Smith.

Kennan was always an intellectual maverick. Except as ambassador to Yugoslavia, after 1950 he exercised little direct influence upon policy. His reputation, buttressed by the rather intimidating breadth of learning that characterized all his writings and the elegant prose style he consciously cultivated, nonetheless greatly enhanced the ability of his prolific writings to win a broader general audience, and assured his views wide currency and publicity and a respectful hearing.

★

Kennan's personal papers are in the Seeley G. Mudd Manuscript Library of Princeton University. Some of his official papers are included in the records of the Department of State in National

Archives II, College Park, Maryland, and the holdings of the John Fitzgerald Kennedy Library in Boston, for which Kennan also recorded an oral history. Some of his dispatches from Yugoslavia are included in the series *Foreign Relations of the United States*. Kennan wrote several autobiographical volumes, including *Memoirs, 1925–1950* (1967); *Memoirs, 1950–1963* (1972); *Sketches from a Life* (1989); *Around the Cragged Hill: A Personal and Political Philosophy* (1993); and *At a Century's Ending: Reflections, 1982–1995* (1996). The fullest biography is Walter L. Hixson, *George F. Kennan: Cold War Iconoclast* (1989). Valuable personal insights are included in Walter Isaacson and Evan Thomas, *The Wise Men: Six Friends and the World They Made: Acheson, Bohlen, Harriman, Kennan, Lovett, McCloy* (1986). Among the most significant studies of Kennan's thinking on foreign policy are David Mayers, *George Kennan and the Dilemmas of U.S. Foreign Policy* (1988); Anders Stephanson, *Kennan and the Art of Foreign Policy* (1989); and Richard L. Russell, *George F. Kennan's Strategic Thought: The Making of an American Political Realist* (1999).

PRISCILLA ROBERTS

KENNEDY, Edward Moore ("Ted") (*b.* 22 February 1932 in Brookline, Massachusetts), U.S. senator who opposed the Vietnam War and fought for civil rights and other liberal causes of the 1960s.

Senator Edward M. Kennedy. THE LIBRARY OF CONGRESS

Kennedy, a liberal Democrat and Roman Catholic, was the fourth son and last of nine children of Joseph Patrick and Rose (Fitzgerald) Kennedy. A successful entrepreneur in shipbuilding, investment banking, motion picture distribution, and real estate, Kennedy's father also served briefly in the 1930s as chairman of the Securities and Exchange Commission, head of the U.S. Maritime Commission, and ambassador to Great Britain. Kennedy served in the U.S. Army from 1951 to 1953. He received his undergraduate degree from Harvard University in 1956 and his law degree from the University of Virginia in 1959. On 29 November 1958 he married Virginia Joan Bennet.

Kennedy became actively involved in politics at a relatively young age when, at the age of twenty-six, he served as the manager of his brother John F. Kennedy's 1958 senatorial campaign. Two years later he became the western states manager for his brother's successful 1960 presidential campaign, which was managed overall by Kennedy's other older brother, Robert Kennedy. Kennedy went on to serve as the assistant district attorney of Suffolk County, Massachusetts, from 1961 to 1962. Then, at the age of thirty, he won the U.S. Senate seat from Massachusetts to complete the term of the seat's previous holder, his brother John, who had vacated the office to assume the presidency. Although his brother was president, Kennedy behaved like the junior senator that he was, often deferring to more senior members of the Senate as he learned the ropes.

After President John Kennedy's assassination on 22 November 1963, Kennedy was reelected to a full six-year Senate term with nearly 75 percent of the vote. During the latter part of the 1964 campaign for his reelection, Kennedy was hobbled by a severe back injury that he had suffered in a small plane crash earlier in June that took the life of his aide Edward Moss. By then, Kennedy was becoming more assertive as a senator and led the fight for the Immigration and Nationality Act of 1965, which was first proposed by President Kennedy in 1963. The bill's passage effectively ended the quota system based on nationality for immigration into the United States.

By 1967 the Vietnam War had become the preeminent issue in the United States. Rapid buildup of troops over the previous two years had led to growing unrest among both politicians and the public about U.S. involvement in the war. Expressions of antiwar sentiment on college campuses and other public dissent expanded rapidly from university sit-ins in 1965 to massive demonstrations and antiwar parades by 1967. Kennedy and his brother Robert, also at that time a U.S. senator, both spoke out against the war, especially criticizing the draft and America's neglect of civilian war victims. In early 1968 Kennedy's visit to South Vietnam only served to solidify his opposition. Although his resistance never reached the vehement protests of the Congress's leading dove, Senator J. William Fulbright of Arkansas,

Kennedy became increasingly vocal as the 1960s neared an end and the war continued.

Kennedy and his extended family, however, soon faced another more personal tragedy when Robert Kennedy was assassinated in June 1968. Kennedy delivered the eulogy at his brother's funeral at Saint Patrick's Cathedral in New York City. During the eulogy, he said that his brother should be "remembered simply as a good and decent man, who saw wrong and tried to right it, saw suffering and tried to heal it, saw war and tried to stop it." In an interview conducted decades later with Terrence Samuel for *U.S. News and World Report,* Kennedy reflected on his brothers' deaths. "They were my heroes and my best friends," he said. "The happiest time for me in the Senate was when my brother Bobby was here, and we were working together."

Although devastated by the loss of two brothers by assassins' bullets within five years, Kennedy pushed forward. After Robert Kennedy's death, he became the acknowledged leader of Senate liberals, and he was elected the youngest Senate majority whip in American history in January 1969. The stage seemed to be set for another Kennedy to run for the presidency, but his chances for nomination suffered an irreparable blow when, on 19 July 1969, he drove off a bridge in Chappaquiddick, Massachusetts. Mary Jo Kopechne, a twenty-eight-year-old secretary, was also in the car and drowned. Although Kennedy denied any romance with Kopechne, he did plead guilty to leaving the scene of an accident and received the standard two-month suspended sentence. At the time, Kennedy was viewed as the heir apparent to "Camelot," the name by which his brother John's presidential administration had come to be known through a 6 December 1963 article in *Life* magazine in which the author, Theodore H. White, pronounced, "Don't let it be forgot, that once there was a spot, for one brief shining moment that was known as Camelot." The Chappaquiddick incident, however, led Kennedy to withdraw from seeking the Democratic nomination for the 1972 presidential race.

Many political observers point to Chappaquiddick as ending, for all intents and purposes, any chance of Kennedy's ever being elected president. Nevertheless, Kennedy continued his work in the Senate as a major advocate for liberal programs targeting the sick, the poor, and the disenfranchised, including issues such as national health insurance, minimum wage increases, tax reform, and civil rights. During his four decades in the Senate, Kennedy matured from being seen as the "kid brother" of two accomplished politicians who were idolized by the public to one of the most influential and powerful lawmakers of the times. Even his political foes have acknowledged his political savvy, his talent for debate, and his personal kindness. Kennedy and his first wife divorced in 1982, and Kennedy married Victoria Reggie in 1992. He has three children

from his first marriage. Kennedy lives in Hyannis Port, Massachusetts, with his second wife.

★

Comprehensive biographies of Kennedy include William H. Honan, *Ted Kennedy: Profile of a Survivor: Edward M. Kennedy After Bobby, After Chappaquiddick, and After Three Years of Nixon* (1972), and Adam Clymer, *Edward M. Kennedy: A Biography* (1999). Other informative books about Kennedy and his political life include Burton Hersh, *The Education of Edward Kennedy: A Family Biography* (1972) and *The Shadow President: Ted Kennedy in Opposition* (1997). A more recent brief, but informative, discussion of Kennedy's stature in politics is Terrence Samuel, "A Liberal in Winter," *U.S. News and World Report* (11 Mar. 2002).

DAVID PETECHUK

KENNEDY, John Fitzgerald (*b.* 29 May 1917 in Brookline, Massachusetts; *d.* 22 November 1963 in Dallas, Texas), decorated World War II veteran, congressman (1947–1953), U.S. senator (1953–1961), and thirty-fifth president of the United States (1961–1963), whose rhetoric inspired political and social activism through the end of the 1960s.

Kennedy was the second of nine children born to parents of Irish descent, Joseph Patrick Kennedy, a wealthy businessman, and Rose Fitzgerald, a devout Roman Catholic

President John F. Kennedy. THE LIBRARY OF CONGRESS

and the daughter of John Francis ("Honey Fitz") Fitzgerald, a prominent Boston politician. Known as "Jack" to family and close friends, Kennedy lived a privileged childhood, but his father's wealth could not shield him from a lifetime of ill health. Kennedy turned to books for companionship during his long periods of illness, fostering a love for reading that carried into adulthood.

Despite his reading habits and natural intelligence, Kennedy was an average student. He was rebellious, disorganized, and often sloppy in appearance. In 1931 he entered the Choate School, an elite preparatory academy in Connecticut, but was absent for long periods due to illness. After briefly attending Princeton University in 1935, Kennedy entered Harvard, the alma mater of his father and eldest brother, in 1936.

Kennedy's father, Joseph, Sr., was named ambassador to Great Britain during Kennedy's sophomore year at Harvard. Kennedy joined his father and the rest of the family in England for a long stay between his sophomore and junior years at Harvard. He returned to assist his father during the second semester of his junior year. Kennedy's experiences in Europe during the years leading up to the outbreak of World War II made a lasting impression. Upon returning to the United States in the fall of 1939, Kennedy researched and wrote his senior thesis on the subject of England's failure to respond to the threat posed by Nazi Germany. The work earned only mediocre marks from Kennedy's professors, but the journalist and family friend Arthur Krock revised the text, and the book *Why England Slept* became a best-seller in the summer of 1940. Kennedy graduated from Harvard cum laude with a B.S. degree in political science in June 1940.

Kennedy secured a commission in the U.S. Naval Reserve in October 1941 and was later cleared for service at sea despite earlier concerns over his checkered medical history. He reported for duty commanding motor torpedo boats in the South Pacific in April 1943. While patrolling in the Solomon Islands chain on the evening of 2 August 1943, Kennedy's boat *PT-109* was rammed by the Japanese destroyer *Amagiri*. The collision sliced Kennedy's craft in two pieces, killing two crewmen. Kennedy rallied the remaining crew, which included two badly wounded men, and the group swam to a tiny, uninhabited island in the midst of Japanese-controlled waters. Allied forces rescued the skipper and his crew after several anxious days.

Word of Kennedy's heroism quickly reached the United States and became a factor when Kennedy embarked on his political career. Unlike his eldest brother, Joseph Kennedy, Jr., who had been preparing for a life in politics but who was killed in action during World War II, Kennedy was not a natural politician. He had made friends easily throughout his lifetime, but he was shy in public. Yet despite his skinny, often sickly, appearance, Kennedy possessed a certain charisma that many voters found endearing. He enjoyed some other tangible advantages as well. Beyond the notoriety associated with being the son of the former ambassador to Great Britain, he was well known for his book *Why England Slept* and for his wartime heroism.

In late 1945 Kennedy decided to run for the open seat for the U.S. Congress in the Massachusetts eleventh congressional district. He campaigned aggressively, easily defeating ten rivals in the Democratic primary in June 1946. This victory ensured his place in Congress, where he represented a heavily Democratic district that included parts of Boston, Cambridge, and Somerville. Kennedy easily won reelection in 1948 and 1950.

Kennedy challenged and defeated Henry Cabot Lodge, Jr., for a seat in the U.S. Senate in 1952. Despite his relative youth and a lackluster congressional career, Kennedy drew on his father's considerable fortune and a well-organized campaign to outpoll the complacent Lodge by 70,000 votes.

More senior senators doubted Kennedy's seriousness of purpose, however, and the young senator embarked on a concerted campaign to improve his image. The handsome Kennedy had a reputation as a playboy, and this reputation was not dispelled by his well-publicized marriage to Jacqueline Lee Bouvier on 12 September 1953. Meanwhile, serious medical problems forced Kennedy to miss many important votes. In addition to his ongoing battle with Addison's disease, an adrenal condition that weakened his body's immunity to infection, Kennedy underwent surgery in 1954 to repair his ailing back. The operation nearly killed him and also failed to relieve him of his back pain.

Undaunted, doctors operated on Kennedy's back again in 1955. During his lengthy convalescence, Kennedy conceived of another book that would help him to further his political ambitions while also communicating his attitudes towards public service. The result was *Profiles in Courage* (1956), a book celebrating the efforts of politicians who bucked the popular will to make principled decisions. The book reflected Kennedy's deeply felt belief that political leaders must motivate citizens to make sacrifices for the greater good of the society. Although Kennedy's trusted assistant Theodore ("Ted") Sorensen admitted years later that he had prepared the materials for the book, Kennedy won the Pulitzer Prize for *Profiles* in 1957.

Kennedy gained still more national notoriety from his surprise bid to win the Democratic nomination for vice president at the party convention in 1956; he was edged out by Senator Estes Kefauver of Tennessee. After easily winning reelection to the Senate in 1958, Kennedy immediately began preparations to run for the presidency. During this period, Kennedy seized upon the issue of the missile gap—a presumed strategic disparity between the United States and the Soviet Union believed to have been created by Soviet technological advances in missiles and rockets—to criticize President Dwight D. Eisenhower's military policies and economic philosophy. Eisenhower had sought to restrain defense spending out of concern that an overly burdensome military budget would threaten the foundations of American democracy, but Kennedy thought otherwise. Accusing Eisenhower of complacency in the face of the Soviet threat, Kennedy argued that the nation could afford to take the measures necessary to close the missile gap.

Kennedy declared his candidacy for the presidency on 2 January 1960. He chose to run in the primaries to prove to his detractors that a Roman Catholic could win popular support. His strategy worked. Primary victories over Minnesota senator Hubert Humphrey in Wisconsin and West Virginia gave Kennedy momentum as he moved on to the Democratic convention. He secured his party's nomination on the first ballot by convincing the delegates that the nation was ready to elect a Catholic president. Later, during the general election campaign, Kennedy confronted concerns over his Catholicism head-on during a televised speech before the Greater Houston Ministerial Association on 12 September 1960. Although anti-Catholic bigotry continued to be a factor during the campaign, many voters respected Kennedy's eloquent and reasoned defense of his right to hold the office.

Kennedy's first major decision as his party's nominee—selecting Senate Majority Leader Lyndon B. Johnson of Texas as his vice presidential running mate—was crucial to Kennedy's eventual victory in November. The choice angered liberals, including his brother and putative campaign manager Robert Kennedy, but made sense for political reasons because Johnson solidified the ticket's credentials in the South.

In his speech accepting his party's nomination on 15 July 1960, Kennedy framed his discussion of domestic problems within the context of the global challenge of the cold war. The threat of Communism called for bold action. "We stand today on the edge of a New Frontier," Kennedy declared, "the frontier of the 1960s—a frontier of unknown opportunities and perils—a frontier of unfulfilled hopes and threats." This New Frontier could be conquered only by collective action; therefore, Kennedy stressed that his campaign would offer "not a set of promises, but . . . rather a set of challenges."

Kennedy established his viability as a leader by besting Republican nominee Vice President Richard M. Nixon in a series of televised debates. Looking poised and mature, Kennedy combined his handsome appearance with a well-crafted message that Nixon could not match. Ultimately, the vice president did not differentiate his positions from those of his challenger, and he completely failed to counter Kennedy's image. Many observers point to Kennedy's de-

cisive advantage over Nixon—particularly during the first of the four debates—as the turning point of the campaign.

The presidential contest between Nixon and Kennedy was decided by one of the smallest popular vote margins in U.S. history. Scholars later determined that Kennedy's religion helped him in the big electoral vote states that he most needed to win, contributing to his substantial margin of victory in the electoral college, but that his religion hurt him in the popular vote by dragging down his margin of victory in otherwise "safe" states for the Democratic Party. Whatever the reason for the narrowness of Kennedy's victory, his uncertain political mandate heavily influenced his conduct as president as he struggled to strike a balance between liberals and conservatives of both political parties.

These political pressures, in part, encouraged Kennedy to increase defense spending in the spring and summer of 1961. Much of this new spending was used to implement a "flexible response" military strategy that included both conventional forces and nuclear weapons. Meanwhile, Kennedy also opted to expand the nuclear deterrent force inherited from his predecessor by calling for the building of 1,000 Minuteman Intercontinental Ballistic Missiles (ICBMs). This buildup proved unnecessary, given that Kennedy was told in early February 1961 that the United States possessed a clear advantage over the Soviet Union and was, in fact, on the favorable end of the missile gap.

Leaders within the Soviet Union interpreted these spending increases as evidence of Kennedy's intention to carry through on his campaign rhetoric, rhetoric that Kennedy repeated during his inaugural address. The youngest man ever elected to the presidency, Kennedy declared that "the torch" of leadership had been "passed to a new generation of Americans—born in this century, tempered by war, disciplined by a hard and bitter peace." He pledged to "pay any price" and "bear any burden" to "assure the survival and the success of liberty." And as he had during his address to the Democratic National Convention in July 1960, Kennedy placed the burden of this contest on the citizens of the United States. "In the long history of the world, only a few generations have been granted the role of defending freedom in its hour of maximum danger." It was time for action. "And so, my fellow Americans," he continued, "ask not what your country can do for you—ask what you can do for your country."

Several of the most urgent foreign policy crises of the cold war quickly tested Kennedy's resolve and the resolve of his generation. In April 1961 Cuban exiles trained in U.S.-run camps in Guatemala landed at Bahía de Cochinos (Bay of Pigs) on the Cuban coastline with the intention of overthrowing the government of Cuban leader Fidel Castro. Alerted to the possibility of an invasion from news stories within the United States and from his own intelligence, Castro swiftly mobilized his armed forces, rounded up political dissidents, and crushed the nascent revolt. Among the Cuban exiles who landed at the Bay of Pigs, nearly 1,200 were taken prisoner and another 200 were killed in three days of fighting.

Critics on both sides of the political spectrum assailed Kennedy. Those who approved of the use of force to remove Castro from power criticized the president for providing only halfhearted support for the invasion. On the other hand, although Kennedy had explicitly criticized the Eisenhower administration during the presidential campaign for failing to take action against Castro, liberals were dismayed by Kennedy's willingness to employ military force to attempt to change the regime.

The disaster at the Bay of Pigs reflected an administrative weakness within the Kennedy White House characteristic of a new administration, but exacerbated by Kennedy's penchant for ad hoc decision making. Kennedy had ridiculed the Eisenhower administration for being too hierarchical and bureaucratic. In place of formal bodies such as the Cabinet and the National Security Council, Kennedy consulted with dozens of advisers prior to his decision to go ahead with the operation, but he excluded or ignored those who might have counseled against the invasion. Kennedy took responsibility for the debacle, but privately felt betrayed by senior military leaders and the Central Intelligence Agency (CIA), which had planned the invasion. Relations between the president and the military worsened during the remainder of Kennedy's presidency, as he asserted his authority to direct military strategy.

Kennedy met with Soviet leader Nikita Khrushchev in early June 1961 in Vienna, Austria, less than two months after the failed Cuban invasion. The Soviet leader bullied Kennedy, whom Khrushchev had once dismissed as no more than a boy, and the experience shook Kennedy's confidence still further. When he appeared on national television on 6 June 1961 on his return from Vienna, Kennedy called on Americans to make sacrifices to meet the challenges posed by the Soviets. In the ensuing weeks, he asked for still further increases in military spending. He placed U.S. military forces on a heightened state of alert, and he increased the size of the standing army, resulting in an increase in draft calls. He also advocated renewed civil defense measures to protect Americans in the event of a nuclear attack.

But such actions did not dissuade the Soviets from addressing their greatest foreign policy priority. Determined to halt the crippling emigration of the most talented and ambitious individuals from their country, East German military police began building a wall between East and West Berlin on 13 August 1961. The Berlin Wall became a symbol of the tension and hostility between the two superpowers during the remainder of the cold war. Although Kennedy delivered one of the most memorable speeches of

his presidency while standing before the wall in June 1963, condemning the Communists for stifling freedom in Eastern Europe, the building of the wall in the late summer of 1961 served to ease tensions between the two superpowers.

The tensions did not abate, however. In October 1962 U.S. aerial surveillance discovered Soviet offensive nuclear missiles in Cuba. Khrushchev may have opted for this dramatic action in an effort to obtain nuclear parity with the United States, or he might have believed that the weapons would deter the U.S. from trying to topple Cuban leader Fidel Castro's government. These efforts had been ongoing following the failed Bay of Pigs invasion and included covert operations conducted under the codename Operation Mongoose, as well as plans for more overt forms of military force, such as a U.S. invasion of the island.

Whatever the reasons for Khrushchev's actions, the Soviet missiles posed a direct threat to many of the major cities in the Western Hemisphere, including Washington, D.C. After being shown the aerial photographs on the morning of 16 October 1962, Kennedy assembled a team of advisers to recommend a course of action to counter the Soviet gambit. This Executive Committee, or ExComm as it came to be known, was chaired by Kennedy's brother Attorney General Robert F. Kennedy, and included most of the president's senior foreign policy and military advisers.

After several contentious days of deliberations, ExComm recommended a blockade of Cuba. Kennedy hoped that the blockade would buy him additional time to negotiate with the Soviets for the removal of the existing weapons. He also hoped that the blockade would prevent the existing weapons already on the island from becoming operational.

The administration had kept the crisis concealed while ExComm deliberated, adding further drama to Kennedy's announcement in an address to the nation on the evening of 22 October 1962. In his televised eighteen-minute speech, Kennedy revealed that the Soviets were installing offensive nuclear weapons in Cuba. He announced that he would halt further shipments of these weapons to Cuba, and that he had instructed the U.S. military to "prepare for any eventualities" should the building continue. In announcing the blockade (the administration called it a quarantine), Kennedy also made clear to the Soviets—and to the world—that the stakes were very high. "[A]ny nuclear missile launched from Cuba against any nation in the Western Hemisphere," Kennedy explained, would be interpreted "as an attack by the Soviet Union on the United States, requiring a full retaliatory response upon the Soviet Union." Kennedy knew that such a response might result in the deaths of hundreds of millions of people. For the next seven days, he and the rest of the world waited anxiously to see how the Soviets would respond.

Contemporary accounts of Kennedy's handling of the

missile crisis boosted the president's popularity, helping the Democratic Party in the midterm elections of 1962. According to these early accounts, the crisis eased when several Soviet vessels halted at the blockade line on Wednesday, 24 October. But historians later learned that Khrushchev did not simply back down in the face of the naval blockade. The crisis continued over the next five days, as several ships continued toward Cuba, and as Soviet technicians accelerated their construction activities. On Saturday, 27 October, a Soviet-made surface-to-air missile (SAM) shot down a U-2 reconnaissance plane over Cuba, killing the pilot instantly. On that same day Soviet fighter planes scrambled to intercept another U-2 that had inadvertently strayed into Soviet airspace.

Fearing further incidents, President Kennedy offered a compromise to Khrushchev. In a letter sent on the evening of 27 October, Kennedy promised to end the blockade, and he also pledged not to invade Cuba, in exchange for Khrushchev's promise to remove the missiles from Cuba. That same evening, Robert Kennedy told Soviet ambassador Anatoly Dobrynin that President Kennedy would also agree to remove U.S. intermediate-range missiles based in Turkey at a later date. The attorney general insisted, however, that the trade be kept secret. President Kennedy and his top advisers had ridiculed others for proposing such a trade in the early days of the crisis, but his public deception protected Kennedy politically against those who would accuse him of selling out to the Soviets. Most importantly, the compromise helped to defuse a crisis that had threatened to spiral into World War III.

Kennedy's overblown rhetoric, which emphasized the need to confront and defeat Communism, got the young president in trouble in the first two years of his presidency. However, his inherent pragmatism and his acute political instincts brought him back from the brink of conflict with the Soviet Union. In addition to the peaceful resolution of the Cuban crisis, Kennedy also negotiated a limited nuclear test ban treaty with the Soviets in 1963. Although tensions remained, communications between the two countries improved during Kennedy's last year in office.

Not all the foreign policy crises during Kennedy's presidency involved the threat of nuclear annihilation. For example, he presided over a substantial increase in military assistance to South Vietnam. This conventional military buildup would serve as the precursor to full-fledged U.S. involvement during the latter half of the 1960s under Kennedy's successor, Lyndon Johnson. But while this limited war did not directly threaten Soviet interests and therefore did not threaten to escalate into nuclear war (Kennedy's greatest fear), the war in Vietnam ultimately resulted in the loss of over 58,000 American lives, caused untold suffering for the people of Southeast Asia, and imposed an economic and political burden on Kennedy's successors.

Kennedy contended with other crises in Latin America and in the Third World in Laos and Congo. Sympathetic to nationalist impulses as a senator, Kennedy often operated within the cold war paradigm as president. In general, he sought to balance the aspirations of the native populations against the wishes of former imperialist powers who were allies in the fight against Communism. Kennedy was also willing to provide nonmilitary economic aid to poorer nations, as was envisioned by the Alliance for Progress in Latin America, and he invoked the message of self-sacrifice in the service of improved international relations by calling on young Americans to volunteer for the Peace Corps.

Although foreign-policy crises dominated Kennedy's attention during his presidency, he also had to contend with a number of domestic challenges, including a brief but contentious battle with major steelmakers in April 1962. When industry leaders announced price increases not in keeping with the voluntary wage and price guideposts that had been put in place to control inflation, Kennedy mobilized all of the resources of government to force the steelmakers to reverse themselves. The public rallied to the president's cause, but Kennedy's tactics troubled many within the business community.

Less than two months later, the stock market suffered its worst one-day drop since 1929, erasing over $20 billion worth of paper assets. The business community grew restless, and the Kennedy administration engaged in a concerted public relations campaign to resurrect the president's image with industry leaders. The most effective means for cementing business support proved to be tax reform.

Kennedy's support for a major tax cut reflected the influence of both conservative and liberal voices in his administration. Although Kennedy had campaigned on a Democratic Party platform that pledged government action to help the economy achieve 5 percent growth, he was privately skeptical of such claims. With the notable exception of military spending, which Kennedy deemed essential in the face of the Soviet threat, he was inclined toward balanced budgets and limited federal government spending. More conservative advisers, such as Secretary of the Treasury C. Douglas Dillon, reinforced Kennedy's inclination towards fiscal conservatism, frustrating the president's more liberal advisers such as Walter Heller, chairman of the Council of Economic Advisers, and Paul Samuelson, a prominent economist from the Massachusetts Institute of Technology (MIT).

Kennedy turned aside early calls for a tax cut, fearful of the backlash from Republicans and conservative Southern Democrats. The president was also skeptical of the mixed message such a tax cut would send to the men and women on whom he had called to sacrifice for the good of the country. Kennedy's attitudes towards deficit spending softened over time, however, as he became progressively convinced of the economic benefits of a tax cut. Accordingly, Kennedy proposed a dramatic reduction in income tax rates in early 1963. Overcoming stiff opposition in Congress, these tax cuts were enacted into law in early 1964 after Kennedy's death.

The question of civil rights for African Americans represented one of Kennedy's greatest domestic challenges. His lukewarm support for the civil rights movement reflected his desire to strike a balance between what was politically safe and what was morally right. As a senator, Kennedy had not always supported the cause of racial justice, at times siding with southern Democrats who blocked civil rights legislation. Kennedy did, however, telephone the wife of civil rights leader Rev. Martin Luther King, Jr., in October 1960, consoling Coretta Scott King after her husband's arrest and pledging his support for King's cause. This largely symbolic act solidified Kennedy's support among African Americans, a majority of whom voted for Kennedy in the November election.

As president, Kennedy feared that civil rights activism would undermine the shaky political coalition that made up the Democratic Party, divided as it was between liberal northerners who favored civil rights legislation, and reactionary southerners who bitterly opposed all forms of racial integration. But while the president hoped to postpone the issue of racial equality, events largely overtook the new administration. An early test for Kennedy came in May 1961, when Freedom Riders attempting to end segregation in bus terminals were attacked in South Carolina and Alabama. In September 1962 violence again erupted, as mobs of angry whites attempted to block James Meredith from becoming the first African American to enroll at the University of Mississippi. Supporters praised Kennedy for calling on the National Guard to restore order, but many southerners harbored resentment towards the president's use of power.

By 1963 Kennedy was more willing to advance the cause of civil rights. This shift coincided with a change in popular opinion, as many northerners were outraged by graphic footage of peaceful black activists being attacked by police dogs and fire hoses in Montgomery, Alabama. When Alabama governor George Wallace threatened to prevent African Americans from attending the University of Alabama in June 1963, Kennedy federalized the Alabama National Guard, signaling his willingness to use the military to enforce the law. Wallace retreated. Following this confrontation, Kennedy issued one of his most eloquent and heartfelt defenses of the morality of the civil rights crusade when he announced his support for comprehensive civil rights legislation in a televised address to the nation on 11 June. This legislation moved slowly through Congress in the late summer of 1963, but was enacted after Kennedy's death in 1964.

The Moon landing, one of the most memorable events of the 1960s, was the most tangible expression of Kennedy's campaign promise to embark on a crusade to conquer the New Frontier. As with so many Kennedy initiatives, the race to the moon was a function of the cold war contest between the United States and the Soviet Union, and it reflected Kennedy's desire to regain the technological and cultural initiative from the Soviets. On the positive side, the space race represented all of the promise of the New Frontier, and it inspired a generation of Americans to pursue dreams that had once seemed unattainable. However, critics questioned whether the intangible benefits of an increase in American pride and prestige were worth the more than $30 billion that was spent on the space program during the 1960s.

Kennedy's political success was at least partially attributable to a carefully projected image. Jacqueline Kennedy gave this image a name when she likened the Kennedy White House to the mythical kingdom of Camelot. Scholars later learned, however, that the Kennedy image was largely a myth.

For example, Kennedy appeared to enjoy a happy family life. Photographers captured many memorable pictures of him with his young children, daughter Caroline, born in 1957, and son John, Jr., born in 1960. And as with any family, there was also grief and sadness: Jacqueline became pregnant with a third child in 1963, but the infant Patrick Bouvier was born prematurely on 7 August 1963 and died less than two days later on 9 August.

Kennedy's love for Caroline and John, Jr., was genuine, and his grief over the loss of Patrick was deep; his marriage, however, was more show than substance. Kennedy was known to have had a number of extramarital affairs throughout his lifetime. He was rumored to have had sex with several high-profile beauties, including Marilyn Monroe and Angie Dickinson. He also had illicit romances with less-well-known women, including Judith Campbell, a young woman who was also romantically involved with Sam Giancana, the reputed leader of the Chicago mafia. It was also alleged that Kennedy was involved with Ellen Rometsch, a high-priced call girl under surveillance by the Federal Bureau of Investigation (FBI) as a suspected Communist spy. These affairs posed a threat to Kennedy's presidency because they subjected him to the possibility of blackmail and intimidation by individuals who might threaten to make them public.

Another distortion inherent in Kennedy's public image was his supposed good health; in fact, Kennedy suffered from numerous health problems. Although medical treatments brought his Addison's disease under control, these treatments could have troubling side effects. Further, Kennedy was persistently bothered by his weak back. As president, Kennedy often wore a back brace, he occasionally was forced to walk with crutches, and he frequently sat in a rocking chair in the Oval Office for hours at a time. Kennedy sought relief for his pain through a number of questionable medications, including amphetamines and other addictive drugs.

Kennedy's assassination on 22 November 1963 was a defining event of the 1960s. It was also one of the most emotionally jarring. That fateful day is seared in the memory of an entire generation of Americans, as well as millions of overseas admirers.

Although many doubt the official version of events surrounding Kennedy's death, the general timeline is clear. In Texas to heal a rift within the Democratic Party, Kennedy traveled to Dallas on the morning of 22 November 1963. Shortly after 12:30 P.M., as his motorcade proceeded through Dealey Plaza in downtown Dallas, gunshots rang out. One bullet struck the president in the neck; a second bullet struck him in the head. Texas governor John Connolly, who was riding in Kennedy's automobile, was also wounded. Kennedy was rushed to Parkland Memorial Hospital in Dallas, where doctors pronounced him dead at 1:00 P.M. CST. The body of the slain president was transported to Washington, D.C., that day. He was buried on 25 November 1963 in Arlington National Cemetery, beneath an eternal flame lighted by his widow, Jacqueline.

Lyndon Johnson, who immediately succeeded to the presidency after Kennedy's death, appointed a commission to investigate the murder. The commission, headed by Supreme Court Chief Justice Earl Warren, determined that Lee Harvey Oswald was the sole assassin. The Warren Commission reported that the shots that killed John Kennedy were fired from Oswald's rifle from a window overlooking Dealey Plaza in the Texas School Book Depository building where Oswald worked. Oswald had professed his innocence, but Dallas nightclub owner Jack Ruby murdered him before investigators could question Oswald about his role in Kennedy's killing. Since that time a number of theorists have contended that other shots were fired at the presidential motorcade from other locations within Dealey Plaza, fueling a spirited historical controversy.

Much of the interest associated with Kennedy's assassination is related to speculation about what Kennedy might have accomplished had he lived. Kennedy left an ambiguous legacy on the United States for the balance of the 1960s and beyond. By advocating an increase in military spending combined with a partial relaxation of the economic conservatism of the Eisenhower years, Kennedy provided political and philosophical cover for his successors who aimed to buy both "guns and butter" with America's growing economic wealth. Kennedy especially criticized his predecessor for refusing to spend more money on conventional military forces. However, by the end of the 1960s the harmful economic effects of heavy spending for a conventional army waging a "limited" war in Southeast Asia fu-

eled rapid inflation, impinged upon domestic spending, and forced higher taxes. Meanwhile, beyond these economic considerations, U.S. military adventures in the Third World that were facilitated by Kennedy's embrace of a military strategy of "flexible response" ultimately harmed U.S. prestige, as indigenous peoples equated U.S. intervention with the worst forms of imperialism.

On the other hand, Kennedy admirers celebrate the energy and vitality of his presidency. Drawing on his popular appeal, an appeal that grew during his presidency, Kennedy convinced his fellow Americans to make personal sacrifices to serve common ends. As the youngest man ever elected president, at the age of forty-three Kennedy was particularly effective at inspiring a generation of young Americans to serve their country. Thousands heeded Kennedy's call to service by volunteering for the Peace Corps. Millions more who were too young to participate directly in Kennedy's initiatives during his brief presidency were inspired to social and political activism in the late 1960s.

★

Kennedy's professional and personal papers are in the John Fitzgerald Kennedy Library in Boston, Massachusetts. For accounts of Kennedy's early life, see Joan Blair and Clay Blair, Jr., *The Search for JFK* (1976); Herbert S. Parmet, *Jack: The Struggles of John F. Kennedy* (1980); and Nigel Hamilton, *JFK: Reckless Youth* (1992). The sections of John Hellman's *The Kennedy Obsession: The American Myth of JFK* (1997) that explore Kennedy's life before the presidency are thought-provoking. There are also a number of highly critical works, including Victor Lasky, *J.F.K.: The Man and the Myth* (1963); Thomas C. Reeves, *A Question of Character: A Life of John F. Kennedy* (1991); and Seymour M. Hersh, *The Dark Side of Camelot* (1997). The best works on Kennedy's presidency are Herbert S. Parmet, *JFK: The Presidency of John F. Kennedy* (1983); James N. Giglio, *The Presidency of John F. Kennedy* (1991); and Richard Reeves, *President Kennedy: Profile of Power* (1993). Harris Wofford, *Of Kennedys and Kings: Making Sense of the Sixties* (1980), and Richard N. Goodwin, *Remembering America: A Voice from the Sixties* (1988), both cast a reflective glance on Kennedy's legacy in the context of the 1960s. See also Garry Wills, *The Kennedy Imprisonment: A Meditation on Power* (1982); Montague Kern, Patricia W. Levering, and Ralph B. Levering, *The Kennedy Crises: The Press, the Presidency, and Foreign Policy* (1983); and Thomas G. Paterson, ed., *Kennedy's Quest for Victory: American Foreign Policy, 1961–1963* (1989). Published collections of primary sources include *The Kennedy Presidential Press Conferences* (1978), with an Introduction by David Halberstam; and Theodore Sorenson, ed., *"Let The Word Go Forth": The Speeches, Statements, and Writings of John F. Kennedy* (1988). The first comprehensive account of the presidential campaign of 1960, Theodore H. White, *The Making of the President, 1960* (1961), is masterful but dated. See also Sidney Kraus, ed., *The Great Debates: Background, Perspective, Effects* (1962), which includes the full transcript of all four televised debates, and the relevant chapters in Robert A. Divine, *Foreign Policy and U.S. Presidential Elections, 1952–1960* (1974). An extensive oral history collection is in the John Fitzgerald Kennedy Library. Gerald S. and Deborah H. Strober, *Let Us Begin Anew: An Oral History of the Kennedy Presidency* (1993), is a published collection of oral history interviews conducted from 1989 to 1992 that provide perspective on Kennedy's influence during the 1960s.

CHRISTOPHER A. PREBLE

KENNEDY, Robert Francis (*b.* 20 November 1925 in Brookline, Massachusetts; *d.* 6 June 1968 in Los Angeles, California), prominent political figure who served as attorney general in the administration of his brother, President John F. Kennedy, and as a senator from New York, and who was involved in many of the key issues and events of the 1960s, including U.S. relations with Cuba and Russia, civil rights, the Vietnam War, antipoverty, and the fight against organized crime.

Kennedy was the seventh child and third son born to Joseph Patrick Kennedy and Rose (Fitzgerald) Kennedy. Having made a fortune through a variety of activities, the father turned to politics, which led to involvement in Franklin D. Roosevelt's campaign and ultimately to ap-

pointment in 1938 as ambassador to England. But his strong isolationist views put him at odds with the president's concern over the growing menace of Adolf Hitler and Nazi Germany, and after Roosevelt won his third term, Joseph Kennedy resigned his post.

During Kennedy's childhood, his father focused greater attention on his two eldest sons, Joseph, Jr., and John. Some observers believe that Kennedy's quest for paternal approval had a formative effect on his behavior for years to come. Often reserved and awkward (but with a dry sense of humor), Kennedy was a mediocre student, though not for lack of determination or intelligence. He was well-versed in public affairs as a result of the family's mealtime discussions about politics, which Joseph, Sr., and the two older boys dominated. More religious than his siblings, he seemed to find refuge in identification with the Catholic Church.

Despite his father's reluctance, since his eldest sons were already enlisted, Kennedy joined the V-12 naval officer training program in March 1944 after graduating from Milton Academy. In August, Joseph, Jr., died in a plane explosion while on a bombing mission. His family shattered by grief, Kennedy nonetheless continued his training but ultimately did not pass the aptitude test for flight school. In July 1945 Kennedy resigned from officer training and enlisted as a sailor on a ship named after his brother. By the

Robert F. Kennedy speaking on the television program *Face the Nation.* NATIONAL ARCHIVES AND RECORDS ADMINISTRATION

time he shipped out, the war was over. He was discharged in May 1946.

With Joseph, Jr., gone, his father's ambitions shifted to John, and the family undertook to elect him congressman for the Eleventh District of Massachusetts. Robert Kennedy helped in the campaign and then returned to Harvard to finish his remaining three semesters. Still aiming to earn his father's attention and respect, he continued to receive mediocre grades but played football with a furious intensity. On graduation in 1948 he enrolled at the University of Virginia School of Law and continued seeing Ethel Skakel, whom he had met during his work on his brother's campaign. They were married on 17 June 1950, when Robert was twenty-four and Ethel twenty-two. They had eleven children. For Kennedy, Ethel provided an essential complement, accentuating his passion and humor and helping him work through his insecurities. He graduated in the middle of his law school class in 1951.

Kennedy began working at the Justice Department but quickly left to work in his brother's successful 1952 U.S. Senate campaign, in which he played an important role in mediating the interventions of his overbearing father. Kennedy was determined and driven, and his performance finally began to earn him his father's respect and his brother's confidence. In January 1953 Joseph, Sr., asked Senator Joseph McCarthy to hire Kennedy as a lawyer on the staff of the Senate Permanent Subcommittee on Investigations. After just five months Kennedy resigned, disagreeing with the committee's increasing emphasis on rooting out Communists inside the American government and its methods in pursuing that goal. He returned shortly thereafter as counsel to the Senate Democratic minority, who were increasingly at odds with McCarthy, and then became chief counsel to the Permanent Subcommittee on Investigations after the Democrats regained control of the Senate.

Two years later Kennedy convinced Senator John McClellan of Arkansas to create a Select Committee on labor racketeering, which became known as the Rackets Committee, and for which Kennedy became chief counsel. He focused the committee's investigations on the Teamsters Union, which had organized the trucking industry, and especially on its president, Dave Beck, and Beck's chief rival, Jimmy Hoffa (who took over when Beck fell from power). Kennedy wrote a book about the investigations, entitled *The Enemy Within* (1960).

At the end of 1959 family duty called him to manage his brother John's presidential campaign. Kennedy, putting his own ambitions on hold, was tough and effective. The campaign was not easy. A Catholic had never been elected president, and the party apparatus was not instinctively enthusiastic about John Kennedy, who had never been a Senate insider. Nonetheless, with important assistance from Kennedy, John prevailed in a very close election.

Campaigning exposed and awakened Kennedy to the most important issues of the day, including race and poverty. When John Kennedy was elected, Joseph, Sr., wanted Robert Kennedy to be named attorney general. Robert was initially reluctant to sacrifice his desire for an independent identity, but President Kennedy decided that he needed someone he could trust absolutely and that his brother was that person, so Robert agreed. He recruited an exceptionally strong staff and began his tenure by redeclaring his war on organized crime. But his quest ran into considerable resistance from J. Edgar Hoover, the longtime director of the Federal Bureau of Investigation (FBI), whose people would have to conduct the investigations necessary for prosecutions to occur. Hoover had always been more interested in rooting out Communism than in addressing organized crime and above all was unwilling to be accountable to anyone for his stewardship of the FBI. Nonetheless, Kennedy persisted, placing special emphasis on pursuing Hoffa.

In April 1961 the Kennedy administration faced its first crisis. The Central Intelligence Agency (CIA) convinced the president to sign off on a plan (developed during the Eisenhower administration) to send a covert force into Cuba, predicting that with the help of the invading force the Cuban people would revolt and overthrow the communist dictator Fidel Castro. The mission failed spectacularly. Most of the invaders were killed or captured. The Bay of Pigs crisis taught both brothers a hard lesson and solidified Kennedy's position as the president's most important and trusted adviser. It also hardened his resolve to find a way to remove Castro and free the Cuban exiles captured at the Bay of Pigs. In addition, the cold war context in which the Kennedy administration came to power led them to see a positive American presence in the Third World as a critical strategic stance in the struggle to defeat Communism. Accordingly, Kennedy made trips to Africa, India, Japan, and Indonesia to promote the ideals of democracy. His 1962 visit to Japan was especially successful, as he interacted with students, workers, intellectuals, and others, winning them over with his frankness, understanding, and demonstrated knowledge of their concerns.

At the same time, the civil rights movement was gaining momentum, with the Reverend Martin Luther King, Jr., as its most visible leader. At first civil rights were not at the forefront of Kennedy's concerns, consumed as he was by the aftermath of the Bay of Pigs and the war on organized crime. But on 4 May 1961 thirteen young protesters known as the Freedom Riders boarded a bus to test a Supreme Court decision that prohibited segregation in interstate transportation. They were dragged from the bus and beaten by mobs in Anniston, Alabama, and again in Montgomery, Alabama, a few days later. Kennedy, shocked by the violence, worked to get protection for the riders. But he also preferred to keep the clamor down, fearing that news of racial unrest would harm the country's cold war activities. He believed that racial problems could eventually be solved without the need for confrontation, so his commitment was to the pursuit of voter registration, focusing on gradual change rather than the more dramatic demonstrations led by King.

Both Kennedys were jolted out of their underestimation of the civil rights issue by the crisis surrounding the enrollment of James Meredith at the University of Mississippi. In September 1962 Meredith won a court order enforcing his acceptance to the university and forbidding any interference by the governor of the state, Ross Barnett. Barnett disobeyed the order and stopped Meredith from registering. Kennedy entered into secret negotiations with Barnett, securing an agreement that federal marshals would escort Meredith to the university so the governor could save face by seeming to succumb to overpowering federal force. But the crowd that had gathered was too threatening, and the attempt was called off. Four days later, after Barnett proposed a similar deal and then canceled, Kennedy told Barnett that the president was going to federalize the National Guard because Barnett had broken his word. This time Barnett agreed to cooperate, and Meredith, accompanied by U.S. marshals, registered at the university. But as it grew dark, a mob came together, shouting racial epithets, and the situation quickly deteriorated. The marshals protected themselves with tear gas, but the riot continued and gunfire began to ring out. A total of 160 marshals were injured. It was remarkable that none of them was killed. (There were two deaths, one a photographer and the other a bystander.) Eventually, there was no choice but to send in troops. Although Kennedy had failed to accomplish Meredith's enrollment peacefully, to the country and the world the show of force demonstrated the Kennedys' commitment to civil rights.

In October 1962 confirmation came that the Soviets were installing medium-range ballistic missiles in Cuba. Kennedy and CIA director John McCone had been the only senior officials concerned in the preceding months that Soviet ships then entering Cuban harbors were delivering such weapons. To everyone else it seemed too unlikely that the Soviet leader Nikita Khrushchev would dare to put nuclear missiles so close to American soil. Kennedy had pushed for more action, but the senior national security apparatus outvoted him in September and in fact canceled U-2 spy plane flights over Cuba to prevent an incident should one of the planes be shot down. Thus, the United States was unaware that the Soviets were indeed unloading ballistic missiles and nuclear warheads in Cuba. The Soviets claimed that they were only defensive weapons, but in truth, half of the cities in the United States were within the range of the missiles.

The United States discovered the sites in aerial reconnaissance photographs on Tuesday, 16 October 1962. At first, like his brother and the other advisers involved, Kennedy was furious about the Soviets' deception and wanted to retaliate. But within a day he saw things differently, and his measured judgment and discerning advice were invaluable throughout the thirteen days of the Cuban Missile Crisis. He was against bombing the missile sites, resisting the urgings of the hawks on the Executive Committee, or ExComm, the name given to the group put together to advise the president. Instead, he agreed with those who wanted to put a naval blockade around the island as a way to buy time and avoid the escalation of reprisals that could follow an outright attack. On Friday morning Kennedy managed to convince most of the members of ExComm that a blockade was the best response, and the president later endorsed the decision. On Monday night President Kennedy addressed the nation and announced the blockade. The threat of an impending nuclear war sent a wave of fear across the country.

Kennedy worked his diplomatic back channels, attempting to discover whether the Soviets would accept a trade of U.S. missile bases in Turkey for the Soviet bases in Cuba. On Wednesday morning, 24 October, tensions rose further as two Soviet ships and a submarine approached the blockade line. The United States went to Defense Condition (DEFCON) 2, one step away from war. Anxious moments passed until word came that the ships had stopped. The quest for a diplomatic solution continued, and on Friday, Khrushchev sent a letter suggesting that he would remove the missiles from Cuba in exchange for a lifting of the blockade and a U.S. promise not to invade Cuba. But Saturday morning brought a harsher letter from Khrushchev, in which he also demanded the removal of the missiles the Americans had in Turkey. Working with Ted Sorensen, the president's speechwriter, Kennedy drafted a letter back to Khrushchev, accepting the demands of the first letter but deftly setting aside those of the second for later negotiations. Then word came that a U-2 plane had been shot down, and President Kennedy had to resist demands by the military to launch air strikes in response. Instead, he sent Kennedy to meet with the Soviet ambassador with two messages: one, if the Soviets would withdraw the missiles, the United States would not invade; and two, the United States would remove its missiles from Turkey after the crisis was resolved, but only if the Soviets did not try to depict it as a response to Soviet pressure. On Sunday morning Khrushchev announced the withdrawal of nuclear missiles from Cuba.

Kennedy's continued focus on Cuba led to the successful release of the Bay of Pigs prisoners in December 1962, in exchange for donated cash and medical supplies. Kennedy never gave up on his desire to oust Castro, but as 1963 unfolded, the country became consumed by the continuing struggle over equal rights for African Americans. Not satisfied with the administration's efforts, including a proposed civil rights bill that dealt only with voting rights, Martin Luther King, Jr., continued staging demonstrations and marches, especially in Birmingham, Alabama, where covered by national television, Sheriff Eugene "Bull" Connor turned fire hoses and police dogs on marching children. More than any other single set of events, this galvanized national concern. In early June, amid the growing national pressure for action, Kennedy, now more deeply committed, deftly negotiated Alabama governor George Wallace's capitulation to the enrollment of black students at the University of Alabama. On the same day, after continuing advocacy by Kennedy, President Kennedy delivered a nationally televised speech and sent a comprehensive civil rights bill to Congress.

In October 1963 worries about growing difficulties in Vietnam pushed their way into Kennedy's field of concerns. The Kennedys were not interested in waging a ground war against Communism in Vietnam and instead looked to their longstanding belief in counterinsurgency. Distrustful of the CIA's bleak assessment of the chances of success, President Kennedy asked the Pentagon to begin secret operations to undermine the Ho Chi Minh regime in the North. At the same time Washington had authorized a coup against its one-time ally, South Vietnamese President Ngo Dinh Diem and his increasingly troubled regime. Kennedy opposed the coup, fearing that if it failed the United States would be blamed. But on 1 November, the generals in charge of the coup attacked the presidential palace in Saigon and assassinated Diem, and the problems in Vietnam began to escalate.

Kennedy was at home at 1:45 P.M. on 22 November 1963 when J. Edgar Hoover called to tell him that the president had been shot. At 2:30 P.M. word came that the president was dead. Stunned, Kennedy stayed with friends and family and comforted his children until it was time to go meet his brother's body. He attended to the details of the funeral, preserving an outward reserve and composure, but inwardly he was in agony at the loss of the brother with whom his career and ambitions had been so intimately connected. He appeared to have no interest in the investigation of the murder. It seemed he felt that taking an interest would only prolong his unbearable grief.

Eventually, at the beginning of 1964, he began to take up work at the Justice Department again. In March 1964 Jimmy Hoffa was found guilty of jury tampering and sentenced to eight years. In July he was found guilty of stealing a million dollars from Teamster funds and sentenced to five more years. Kennedy, though, showed little interest. Meanwhile, his personal relationship with Lyndon B. Johnson, his brother's successor, degenerated from mutual dis-

like and resentment to outright enmity. In the spring of 1964 it spurred Kennedy to reenter the public arena. He did nothing to discourage speculation that he would accept designation as President Johnson's running mate. He offered to be President Johnson's ambassador to South Vietnam. Then his younger brother, Senator Edward Kennedy of Massachusetts, suffered a broken back in a plane crash, and Kennedy questioned his own reemergence once again. But he went as scheduled, nonetheless, to Germany to dedicate a memorial to his brother, and to Poland, where the Communist government tried, without success, to keep his visit a secret. Kennedy seemed to feed off the energy of the crowds that gathered to hear him speak, and this seemed to revive his confidence and passions. When he returned, the pressure on Johnson to select Kennedy as his running mate dissipated when the conservative Barry Goldwater won the Republican nomination. Kennedy made up his mind to run for the Senate in New York. He announced his candidacy on 22 August 1964 and resigned as attorney general on 2 September.

The campaign began slowly, with Kennedy falling behind in the polls. He was initially tentative as a candidate and acted as though he did not want to trade on his brother's memory, but at the same time he seemed to lack confidence that there was any independent reason to elect him in his own right. The accusation that he was a carpetbagger—running for office to represent a region where he had never lived—resonated with some voters. In October, Kennedy's opponent, the incumbent Kenneth Keating, pushing for the Jewish vote, hinted that Kennedy, as attorney general, had made an overly generous settlement deal with a company that had produced goods for the German war effort in World War II. The charge inflamed Kennedy, animating his spirit and competitive instinct. His speeches acquired life and energy, and he pulled ahead in the polls. In November he won by over 700,000 votes.

Kennedy was an unusual senator. As the brother of the murdered president, having been so deeply involved in so many issues both foreign and domestic, and so obviously a future candidate for president himself, he had an immediate celebrity status. He defined his role in ways that departed from the norm. He performed his Senate work—introducing and voting on legislation, participating in hearings, attending to the people and the problems of New York State. But he also traveled the globe, meeting with heads of state and especially seeing and connecting with the people, particularly the poor and the oppressed, of each place he visited. His visits to Latin America and South Africa would stir millions of people who had never seen an American leader up close and projecting concern. And he would also burrow deeply into the neighborhoods and communities of his adopted state, spending countless hours in particular on a project in the Bedford-Stuyvesant (Bed-

Stuy) section of Brooklyn, New York, to demonstrate that a low-income, run-down, black neighborhood could revitalize itself in a civic partnership with outside public and private leaders.

He began conventionally enough, adding an amendment to the pending Appalachian regional development legislation to add thirteen low-income New York counties situated along the Pennsylvania border. His work the first year included proposing funding for drug treatment and reform in the financing of social security. He succeeded in amending the Voting Rights Act of 1965 to protect U.S.-educated non-English speakers (mainly Puerto Ricans in New York State) from unfair imposition of English-language literacy tests and added an evaluation requirement to the new federal program to help educationally disadvantaged children.

But events both foreign and domestic brought him into confrontation with the Johnson administration. The president began escalating the war in Vietnam and sent troops to the Dominican Republic to undo a coup against the military regime there. Simmering unrest in inner cities boiled up in the Watts section of Los Angeles. Kennedy was critical of the administration's actions on these fronts. Largely muted in 1965, his criticism intensified through the following two years.

Throughout, he offered new ideas and new departures: his maiden speech in the Senate on nuclear proliferation, a call for rejuvenation of the Alliance for Progress in Latin America, his often-quoted speech that thrilled many but infuriated those in power in South Africa, a trilogy of speeches about urban race and poverty issues, a call for engagement with Communist China, critiques of administration policy in Vietnam and in the American inner city.

He traveled to learn, not only abroad but all over America. He met the labor leader Cesar Chavez and members of the farmworkers union in California, people in Mississippi who were struggling with hunger bordering on starvation, unemployed former coal miners in eastern Kentucky, Native Americans on reservations, and the largely black urban poor in New York, Chicago, and Los Angeles. In every case he came away determined to help and offered legislation to respond to the problems he had seen.

Two powerful themes animated Kennedy's activities through 1966 and 1967: his concern about race and poverty in the United States and his growing opposition to the war in Vietnam.

In early 1966, having given a speech calling for community-driven revitalization efforts in low-income neighborhoods (but with outside financing and other assistance)—a speech that was part of Kennedy's response to the violence in Watts a few months earlier—he met with a group of African-American community leaders in the Bed-Stuy section of Brooklyn. Each side challenged the

other to act. The result was a yearlong planning process in which Kennedy involved himself intensively. The entity that emerged, the Bedford-Stuyvesant Restoration Corporation, was a model for the ensuing wave of community development corporations around the country. Kennedy enlisted the participation of powerful business and political leaders to assist and succeeded in amending the federal antipoverty program to provide funding for programs like the Bed-Stuy initiative (of which Bed-Stuy was the main beneficiary for some years).

In February 1966 Kennedy, increasingly troubled over the American escalation of the war in Vietnam, delivered a major speech on the floor of the Senate, calling for negotiations, with the formation of a coalition government as the major aim of the talks. The speech elicited a storm of criticism (largely organized by the White House), as well as some important support. In its wake Kennedy worried that, in view of Johnson's enmity toward him, his criticism of the president's policies would have the perverse effect of stimulating accelerated escalation of the war. He was largely silent on the subject for the next year.

When he traveled to a new place or gave a speech about a new subject, Kennedy's modus operandi was to follow up. His trip to Latin America in late 1965, which included meetings with students and visits to see the conditions faced by low-wage workers, brought a campaign to reform U.S. aid to Latin America. His meeting with Chavez when he went to California for a Senate hearing on farmworker labor organizing led him to become the leading advocate for the farmworkers in Washington. His shocking discovery of near-starvation in Mississippi in 1967 made him the prime force behind getting food to feed hungry Americans. His June 1966 trip to South Africa brought him to the forefront of the antiapartheid cause. The surprising media attention given a speech criticizing the welfare system in May 1967 impelled him to play a major role in trying to improve regressive welfare legislation wending its way through Congress at the time. Kennedy was a reader, but his learning style was multisensory as well. He learned by seeing, listening, touching—by using all of his senses—and then, always, the result was a determination to act.

By 1967 Kennedy was more overt in his criticisms of President Johnson's handling of the war and what he and many others thought was the inadequate response to the increasing racial strife at home. In the fall a "dump Johnson" movement began to emerge. Its chief organizer, the New York activist Allard Lowenstein, visited Kennedy and urged him to challenge Johnson for the Democratic nomination. Kennedy equivocated, and Lowenstein recruited Senator Eugene McCarthy of Minnesota to make the effort. The weakness of the American position in Vietnam was further revealed at the end of January 1968, when the North Vietnamese and Vietcong mounted a strikingly successful, multipronged offensive. McCarthy very nearly defeated President Johnson in the New Hampshire Democratic primary on 12 March 1968. Four days later Kennedy entered the race.

Why did Kennedy equivocate? One reason was surely his continuing worry that his actions would evoke counterproductive policy steps from President Johnson, who had such a personal animus toward him. Another was his remaining fealty to politics as taught to him by his father— that one does not undertake an effort in which he believes he cannot succeed. Another part of him, perhaps more recent in its prominence, was more cause-oriented, and this part took hold as matters deteriorated further in Vietnam in early 1968. Nonetheless, polling data from New Hampshire that foretold Senator McCarthy's showing cannot be ignored in analyzing Robert Kennedy's decision-making process. He had to have realized the task was not as impossible as he had thought.

Kennedy's entrance into the race was electrifying. He drew crowds of 15,000 and more at such unlikely places as the University of Kansas. Finally unleashed, his initial speeches were especially passionate and strong. Fifteen days after Kennedy's announcement, President Johnson dropped out of the race, leaving his mantle to his vice president, Hubert H. Humphrey. Humphrey's entry seemed to throw Kennedy off balance because so much of his passion came from his disagreement with and disapproval of President Johnson. In addition, if Kennedy was attractive to many, there were disaffection and anger from many others—people who had joined the McCarthy campaign but would have supported Kennedy had he gotten into the fray three or four months earlier. The crosscurrents were difficult to handle.

The campaign was tumultuous. King was murdered in early April, less than a week after President Johnson's withdrawal. One momentous event followed another at a dizzying pace. Kennedy won his first ballot test in the Indiana primary on 7 May and won the Nebraska primary a week later. As politics were then, the nomination would depend on the decisions of political leaders as well as the outcome of primaries, but Kennedy's electoral showing would certainly influence the professionals as they decided what to do. Kennedy suffered a setback in losing the Oregon primary at the end of May but recouped to win the California primary on 4 June. He seemed to have found his footing.

As Kennedy left the podium shortly after midnight on 5 June after finishing his speech at the victory celebration in the Ambassador Hotel in Los Angeles, he was shot by Sirhan Sirhan, a deranged man who resented Kennedy's pro-Israeli sympathies. Kennedy lay unconscious through the next day and was pronounced dead at 1:44 A.M. on 6 June 1968. He is buried in Arlington National Cemetery in Arlington, Virginia.

Although it is impossible to say for sure, many believe Kennedy would have been nominated and elected. If so, it is likely that he would have sought to end the Vietnam War far more quickly than President Richard M. Nixon did and undertaken a major effort at racial reconciliation at home. Regardless, Kennedy was an important figure in the 1960s. He played a vital role in his brother's administration, especially on civil rights issues and in the Cuban Missile Crisis, and his leadership as a U.S. senator constituted a rallying point for the mounting concerns about President Johnson's policies. His decision to run for president, belated as it was, had a catalytic effect in bringing about President Johnson's decision not to seek reelection. More than any other important elected official of his time, Kennedy was seen by low-income and minority people in the United States and to some extent around the world as someone who cared about them and spoke for them. This is perhaps his most lasting legacy.

★

Robert F. Kennedy's speeches are collected in Edwin O. Guthman and C. Richard Allen, eds., *RFK: Collected Speeches* (1993). Works by Robert F. Kennedy include *The Enemy Within* (1960) and *Thirteen Days: A Memoir of the Cuban Missile Crisis* (1969). Biographies of Robert F. Kennedy include David Halberstam, *The Unfinished Odyssey of Robert Kennedy* (1968); Jack Newfield, *Robert Kennedy: A Memoir* (1969); Jules Witcover, *85 Days: The Last Campaign of Robert Kennedy* (1969); William Vanden Heuvel and Milton Gwirtzman, *On His Own: Robert F. Kennedy, 1964–1968* (1970); Arthur M. Schlesinger, Jr., *Robert Kennedy and His Times* (1978); Jeff Shesol, *Mutual Contempt: Lyndon Johnson, Robert Kennedy, and the Feud that Defined a Decade* (1997); and Evan Thomas, *Robert Kennedy: His Life* (2000).

PETER EDELMAN

KERNER, Otto, Jr. (*b.* 15 August 1908 in Chicago, Illinois; *d.* 9 May 1976 in Chicago, Illinois), governor of Illinois and statesman who headed the National Advisory Commission on Civil Disorders that issued the Kerner Report in 1968 (concerning racial divisions in America) and who in 1974 became the first sitting federal appeals court judge to be convicted of a felony.

Kerner's father, Otto Kerner, Sr., was a prominent Illinois politician who served as the attorney general of Illinois, as Cook County Circuit Court judge, and as a U.S. Appeals Court judge. Kerner's mother was Rose Barbara Chmelik. After graduating from high school in 1926, Kerner attended Brown University in Providence, Rhode Island, receiving his B.A. degree in 1930. From 1930 to 1931 he attended Trinity College, Cambridge University, in England and then Northwestern University School of Law in Evanston, Illinois, graduating in 1934. On 20 October 1934 Kerner married Helena Cermak Kenlay. His wife's daughter from a previous marriage died in an automobile accident in 1954, and the Kerners adopted the daughter's two children; they had no other children. In 1934 Kerner went to work for the law firm of Cooke, Sullivan, and Ricks, but in 1935 he left to join his father's law firm, Kerner, Jaros, and Tittle, where he became a partner. Also in 1934 Kerner joined the Black Horse Troop of the Illinois National Guard, rising to the rank of captain by 1941. In March 1941 President Franklin D. Roosevelt called up the National Guard, and Kerner was transferred to the Thirty-third Infantry Division of the U.S. Army. In 1942, after the United States entered World War II, he was transferred to the Ninth Infantry Division and was promoted to major; he underwent training for field artillery and returned to action. Kerner saw action in North Africa and Sicily; he was decorated with the Bronze Star. Promoted to lieutenant colonel, he served in the Philippines and Japan from July to December 1945. Although he was discharged from active service, he remained in the National Guard until 1954, retiring as a major general.

In 1947 Kerner was appointed the U.S. attorney for the Northern District of Illinois. In 1954 he was elected Cook County judge and was reelected in 1958. In 1960 he resigned from his judgeship to run for governor of Illinois. He defeated the sitting two-term Republican governor, William G. Stratton, by more than 500,000 votes, an impressive landslide, especially considering that his fellow Democrat John F. Kennedy defeated Richard Nixon in the presidential race by fewer than nine thousand votes in Illinois. Kerner proved to be a dynamic leader. In April 1961 he requested increases in corporate taxes and the state sales tax, meeting opposition from both Republicans and Democrats, but he used his considerable powers of persuasion to gain enough votes to pass his new sales tax and $3 billion budget through the state legislature on 29 June 1961, with his corporate tax plan passing on 18 July 1961.

The 1960s seemed to be a period of untarnished success for Kerner, but by 1962 he was sowing his own seeds of destruction. Through the state revenue director, Theodore Isaacs, Kerner became involved in illicit deals with gambling interests, especially the owners of horseracing tracks. In 1964 he was reelected governor in a closer contest than the one in 1960. There were race riots in Chicago in 1965, 1966, and 1967, and in each instance Kerner called out the National Guard to bring peace to the city. During 1966 Kerner purchased stock in a racetrack, paying $70,158 for stock that was worth $356,000. He then quickly sold the stock for its true value. In return for the favor, he helped push legislation desired by racetrack owners. In 1967 he falsified his tax returns by claiming the money he had earned as a long-term capital gain, which at that time meant that he could pay at a lower tax rate than if the income were a short-term gain (which it actually had been).

Otto Kerner speaking outside the White House, 1967. © BETTMANN/CORBIS

In July 1967 President Lyndon B. Johnson appointed Kerner head of the National Advisory Commission on Civil Disorders (sometimes called the Kerner Commission). In March 1968 the commission issued what became known as the Kerner Report, an important document in the history of civil rights in America and very controversial. It would be debated for at least two decades, as America tried to achieve racial equality in its society. In sum, the report declared that America was becoming "two societies, one black and one white—separate and unequal." The phrase "separate and unequal" became part of the American lexicon when describing issues of discrimination on the basis of race. At the root of America's racial division, the report said, were bigotry and injustice caused by racism.

In May 1968 Kerner's wife was seriously ill, and he resigned from his governorship to be able to stay close to home. President Johnson nominated him to a position that would not require much travel, judge on the U.S. Court of Appeals for the Seventh Circuit. It was, he said, the job he had always wanted. As the decade of the 1960s closed, he was respected for his honesty and fairness, but soon thereafter his career came apart. In December 1971 a federal grand jury handed down nineteen indictments of corruption against Kerner. He denied the charges and insisted on remaining a judge, although he took a leave of absence from work while continuing to draw his salary. On 19 February 1973 he was convicted on seventeen of the charges, including tax evasion, fraud, perjury, and conspiracy to commit crimes, becoming the first sitting federal appeals court judge to be convicted of a felony. He faced eighty-three years in prison and a $93,000 fine but was sentenced to three years in prison and fined $50,000. In 1973 his wife died. In 1974 he entered the federal prison at Lexington, Kentucky, but was released early—6 March 1975—so that he could be treated for lung cancer. The last year of his life was devoted to advocating prison reform and to trying to prove that his "indiscretion," as he put it, was not particularly bad. He died in Chicago, still very well liked. His guidance of the Kerner Commission had a powerful effect on the writing and passage of civil rights laws and won him permanent admirers among civil rights groups.

★

The Illinois State Historical Library holds Kerner's personal papers and most of his official papers; the Illinois State Archives hold many of his official gubernatorial papers. Hank Messick, *The Politics of Prosecution: Jim Thompson, Marje Everett, Richard Nixon, and the Trial of Otto Kerner* (1978), offers a partisan account of Kerner's criminal convictions. Robert P. Howard, *Mostly Good and Competent Men: Illinois Governors 1818–1988* (1988), includes an outline of Kerner's political activities. *Quiet Riots: Race and Poverty in the United States* (1988), edited by Fred R. Harris and Roy W. Wilkins, analyzes the Kerner Report. The best obituary is in the *Chicago Tribune* (10 May 1976).

KIRK H. BEETZ

KERR, Clark (*b.* 17 May 1911 in Stony Creek, Pennsylvania), labor and management expert, economist, and university president who led the 1960s expansion of the University of California and wrestled with growing campus unrest including the Free Speech Movement.

Kerr is the son of Samuel William Kerr, a teacher and apple farmer, and Caroline Clark, a homemaker. His father, the first member of his family to go to college, held a master's degree from the University of Berlin and spoke four languages. He instilled in Kerr the importance of independent thought. Kerr received his B.A. from Swarthmore College in 1932. While at Swarthmore, he was captain of the debating team and president of the student body.

Kerr received his M.A. degree in economics from Stanford University in 1933. He completed additional studies at the Institute of International Relations in Geneva, Switzerland. In 1936 and 1939 Kerr studied at the London School of Economics and Political Science. He married Catherine Spaulding on 25 December 1934; they have three children. Kerr began his teaching career in 1936 at Antioch College in Yellow Springs, Ohio. From 1937 to 1939 he was a teaching fellow at the University of California, Berkeley. He received his Ph.D. in economics from Berkeley in 1939. From 1939 to 1940 Kerr was acting assistant professor of labor economics at Stanford.

In 1940 Kerr began teaching at the University of Washington in Seattle as an assistant and then as an associate professor. In 1942, in addition to teaching, Kerr undertook his first labor arbitration assignment when the Pacific Coast Coal Company and its operating engineers were unable to agree on wage increases. He continued to solve hundreds of labor/management disputes in several industries including public utilities, newspapers, aircraft, canning, oil, and local transport. Known as the busiest arbitrator on the West Coast, Kerr became renowned for his toughness, his sense of fairness, and his expensive fees. Kerr tried to find what he called the "inner logic" of every situation. He was skilled in the arts of persuasion. With his mild expression, his unostentatious suits, and rimless glasses, he at first would strike the observer as a typical organization man who melts into the background. The resemblance disappeared once Kerr began to dispense his own brand of inner logic. He chose the most difficult disputes, worked tirelessly, and tried to reach settlements as quickly as possible. Kerr was soon the highest paid negotiator (he charged $200 a day) on the West Coast.

Kerr served on many federal fact-finding boards in labor controversies. During World War II he was a member of the National War Labor Board. As a public member, appointed by President Harry S. Truman, Kerr served in 1950 and 1951 on the National Wage Stabilization Board, which recommended wage policies and administered any pay controls imposed on labor. In 1960 President Dwight D. Eisenhower appointed Kerr to the Commission on National Goals. Kerr reported to the commission several months later on "the effective and democratic organization of the economy."

After five years at the University of Washington, Kerr returned to Berkeley, where he developed and directed the Institute of Industrial Relations. When the statewide University of California (UC) system was reorganized in 1952, he was appointed the first chancellor of the Berkeley campus. He initiated the modernization of the residence halls, student union, and intramural and recreational facilities. During the period of his leadership, the American Council on Education designated the Berkeley campus as "the best balanced distinguished university in the country."

In 1958 Kerr succeeded Robert Gordon Sproul as the twelfth president of the multicampus University of California, one of the largest university systems in the world.

Clark Kerr. ARCHIVE PHOTOS, INC.

As president, Kerr had to coordinate the operations of all UC campuses and establish their role in a state educational system that also supported four-year and junior colleges. In so doing, he was often called on to resolve conflicts of interest similar to those involved in sensitive labor disputes. Kerr was already familiar with the art of mediation, having over twenty years of experience resolving hundreds of industrial controversies as a private and federal mediator.

Because of the postwar baby boom, U.S. colleges and universities were growing rapidly. During Kerr's tenure as president, the university doubled its enrollment to more than 50,000 students. The previous president had restricted political activism on campus, not even allowing the presidential candidate Adlai Stevenson to speak. In 1949 Kerr had voiced his disapproval of mandatory faculty loyalty oaths, thus earning him the label of liberal. When he became president, he opened the campus to even controversial communist speakers and relaxed some other campus rules. The American Association of University Presidents gave Kerr the Meiklejohn Award in 1964 for his contributions to academic freedom.

Kerr believed the role of a university administrator was mostly that of a mediator among students, faculty, regents, alumni, and public groups. Civil rights activist groups in

1963 and 1964 put Kerr's free speech policies to the test. Students were actively pressuring the administration to find remedies to racial discrimination in the university community. The activist students confronted local businesses, which led to protests and arrests. Kerr responded to the activists by banning on-campus recruiting and solicitation of funds for off-campus groups. Student activists denounced Kerr's action, and the Free Speech Movement (FSM) was founded. This movement's activities at UC Berkeley ushered in the age of student activism in the United States.

In 1964 the police tried to arrest a nonstudent who was promoting the Congress of Racial Equality (CORE) at Berkeley. The police action led to a thirty-hour sit-in in which student activists denied access to campus buildings. Kerr met with Marco Savio, the FSM leader, and negotiated an apparent solution to the crisis. But Governor Edmund Brown intervened the next day, ordering the arrest of the students. The Berkeley faculty responded by voting overwhelmingly to meet FSM demands. From 1964 to 1967 the Kerr administration attempted to mediate between the university and various interest groups. When Ronald W. Reagan became governor of California in 1967, a conflict arose over cuts to the university's operating budget and a proposal to end free education by imposing tuition and other fees. An impasse developed, and Kerr was fired by the California State Board of Regents on 20 June 1967 for his failure (in their opinion) to deal effectively with the unrest at Berkeley.

Kerr's major accomplishment during his tenure as president was the evolution of the University of California into what he called a "multiversity." Kerr believed the university was a "prime instrument of national purpose." He assumed the leadership of statewide efforts to develop a master plan for higher education in California. He also held that a university must cater to the elite, but at the same time meet the need of several constituencies including government, industry, and the general public. Kerr developed a plan to coordinate programs in the state's colleges and universities. His hierarchy would give the top twelve percent of high school graduates admission to the University of California. The rest of the top third would be admitted to a California state university, and the remainder would be admitted to junior colleges.

Following his dismissal, Kerr returned to teaching at Berkeley's School of Business Administration. He assumed a leadership role in the development of the Carnegie Commission on Higher Education from 1967 to 1973. In 1968 Kerr was appointed to head a Carnegie Commission study on the structure and finance of higher education. The commission called for the development of a federal civilian "bill of educational rights" to guarantee a college education to any qualified student regardless of his or her ability to pay.

Kerr led the Carnegie Council on Policy Issues in Higher Education until 1979. The commission and the council together produced over 150 seminal reports and books on the condition and future of higher education. Kerr's final commission report, *Three Thousand Futures: The Next Twenty Years in Higher Education* (1980), became the benchmark for reform in higher education.

★

Information about Kerr can be found in Clark Kerr, *The Gold and the Blue: A Personal Memoir of the University of California 1949–1967* (2001). Key publications by Kerr include *Unions, Management, and the Public* (1948); *Industrialism and Industrial Man* (1960); *The Uses of the University* (1964); *Labor and Management in Industrial Society* (1964); and *Marshall, Marx, and Modern Times* (1969).

REED MARKHAM

KESEY, Kenneth Elton ("Ken")   (*b.* 17 September 1935 in La Junta, Colorado; *d.* 10 November 2001 in Eugene, Oregon), writer, farmer, filmmaker, and teacher whose primary novels, *One Flew over the Cuckoo's Nest* (1962) and *Sometimes a Great Notion* (1964), both of which championed the power of the individual over authoritarian repression, captured and reflected the counterculture spirit of the 1960s.

Kesey was the son of Fred A. Kesey and Geneve (Smith) Kesey, who were dairy farmers; he had one brother. In 1946, after Kesey's father was discharged from the navy, the family moved to Springfield, Oregon, where Fred Kesey established the Eugene Farmers Cooperative; it became the biggest dairy operation in the area, selling under the retail name Darigold. Kesey was an avid reader and was active in sports (particularly wrestling) and theater in high school; he was voted "most likely to succeed" by his graduating class at Springfield High School in 1953. Kesey attended the University of Oregon in Eugene, continuing his involvement in wrestling and acting. In 1956 he married his high school sweetheart, Faye Haxby; they had three children. After graduating with a B.A. in speech and communications in 1957, Kesey moved to Hollywood, where he pursued a career as an actor. He also wrote his first (unpublished) novel, *End of Autumn*.

In 1959 Kesey entered a graduate writing program at Stanford University in Palo Alto, California, on a Woodrow Wilson scholarship. At the suggestion of the psychology student Vik Lovell, he signed up for government-sponsored drug experiments at the Veterans Administration hospital in Menlo Park, where he was given LSD, among other psychedelics. He later took a job as a night attendant at the hospital's psychiatric ward, planning to use downtime on the job to complete a second unpublished novel, *Zoo*. In-

Ken Kesey. © BETTMANN/CORBIS

stead, his experiences with drugs and hospital work inspired the novel *One Flew over the Cuckoo's Nest* (dedicated to Lovell). Set in a mental hospital, the novel is narrated by a Native-American inmate, "Chief Broom" Bromden, who plays at being deaf and dumb to escape the horrors of his surroundings. He recounts the arrival of a new inmate, the free-spirited former marine Randle P. McMurphy, who gradually inspires the inmates—most of whom have committed themselves to the hospital voluntarily—to rediscover their inner strength. This naturally flies in the face of the hospital's and, by extension, society's so-called proper social order, symbolized by McMurphy's chief adversary, the head nurse Ratched. In retaliation for McMurphy's attempts to reawaken the inmates' sense of individuality, Ratched arranges for McMurphy to have a lobotomy. Sickened at the sight of seeing his friend turned into a vegetable, Bromden smothers McMurphy and escapes from the hospital.

Cuckoo's Nest was highly acclaimed on its publication in 1962; the *New York Times Book Review* called it "a glittering parable of good and evil," while the *New York Herald* hailed it as "a first novel of special worth." Not every critic was so impressed; some felt that the writing style was uneven and too laden with symbolism, while others attacked what they saw as racist and sexist overtones. Overall, the reception to the book was positive. The theme of the individual (McMurphy) versus the state (the hospital/Nurse Ratched) resonated strongly with a burgeoning counterculture, a new generation that saw itself as the successors to the beat generation of the 1950s (one of whose leading writers, Jack Kerouac, was a key influence on Kesey's work). In 1963 a theatrical version of *Cuckoo's Nest* debuted on Broadway, starring Kirk Douglas, but the play closed after a short run.

Before the publication of *Cuckoo's Nest,* Kesey had returned to Springfield to work on his brother's farm. He then moved to the logging town of Florence, Oregon, to gather material for his second book, *Sometimes a Great Notion.* After four months, he returned to Palo Alto and in 1963 moved to La Honda, California, where he finished the novel. The book, whose title was taken from the folk song refrain "Sometimes it seems a great notion / to jump in the river and drown," was published in 1964. Set in Oregon, the story concerns the conflict between a logging family, the Stampers, and their local union. Atypically, the union (and its national agent, Jonathan Draeger) is presented as the repressive force, ultimately brought down by Hank Stamper's stubborn stance as a strikebreaker. Another source of conflict is the struggle between Hank and his Yale-educated younger half brother, Lee; Kesey later explained that he viewed the brothers as representing two sides of himself. The novel was written in an elaborate and complex fashion, utilizing flashbacks and a constantly shifting point of view. This made it challenging to read, and as a result it was not as well received as *Cuckoo's Nest.* But Kesey was still regarded as a writer of great merit, and there was keen anticipation of what he would do next.

What he did was to sidestep writing in favor of the immediate life experience. He had maintained his interest in psychedelic drugs, "tripping" with his friends in La Honda. This loose-knit group, eventually dubbed the "Merry Pranksters," began hosting what they called "acid tests." These were large parties that featured light shows (events that featured all manner of colored lights projected onto the ceilings and walls), rock music by local bands like the Warlocks (soon to become the Grateful Dead), and LSD (which was not yet illegal) in abundance, frequently distributed in vats of Kool-Aid. The Pranksters then decided to take the acid tests on the road, and Kesey bought a 1939 International Harvester school bus for $1,500, which the Pranksters decorated in suitably psychedelic style. The destination sign on the front read "Furthur" (sic), and a sign on the back warned, "Caution: Weird Load."

The Pranksters traveled across the country, inadvertently wreaking havoc with their outrageous dress and copious drug use. Kerouac's sidekick Neil Cassady (immortalized as "Dean Moriarity" in Kerouac's 1957 novel *On the Road*) was taken on as the Pranksters' bus driver. During his escapades with the Pranksters, Kesey had a child with Carolyn Adams, a Prankster also known as "Mountain Girl," but he remained married to his wife. The trip, which was filmed for posterity, was chronicled in Thomas Wolfe's *Electric Kool-Aid Acid Test,* published in 1968. By that time Kesey's immersion in the counterculture had led to considerable trouble with the authorities. He was arrested for marijuana possession in April 1965 and January 1966, and he fled to Mexico after the second arrest. He returned to the United States in October 1966 and was promptly arrested, eventually serving five months in the San Mateo County Jail and the San Mateo County Sheriff's Honor Camp. He wrote about his jail experiences in *Cut the Motherfuckers Loose,* which was published in *The Last Whole Earth Catalogue* (1971).

Kesey was released in November 1967, and the following year he sought refuge in Pleasant Hill, Oregon, where he bought a cattle farm. The move was intended to distance him as much from the Prankster tribe as from the authorities. Although he continued writing short stories and essays, he did not write another novel until 1992's *Sailor Song.* In 1969 Kesey went to London to work for Zapple Records, a short-lived label that was part of the Beatles' company, Apple Corporation, but the project ultimately fell apart. Back in the United States, Kesey declined the opportunity to accompany the remaining Pranksters to the last gasp for the 1960s counterculture, the Woodstock (New York) music festival in August 1969.

In 1971 the film version of *Sometimes a Great Notion* was released, directed by and starring the acclaimed actor Paul Newman; it received mixed reviews. Conversely, the film version of *One Flew over the Cuckoo's Nest,* released in 1975, was a critical and commercial success, winning the top five Oscars for best picture, director, actor, actress, and screenplay. Ironically, the one person who did not like it was Kesey; he refused to see the film and filed suit against the filmmakers for breach of contract. The suit was settled the following year.

Kesey's notable post-1960s work includes *Kesey's Garage Sale* (1973), a collection of previously published articles and the autobiographical screenplay *Over the Border; Demon Box* (1986), a collection of articles about the successes and failures of the counterculture; *Caverns* (1990), a novel written collaboratively with students from his creative writing class, credited to the pseudonym O. U. Levon (an anagram for "University of Oregon novel"); *The Further Inquiry* (1990), an autobiographical screenplay about Kesey's Merry Prankster days; the novel *Sailor Song* (1992); and the novel

Last Go Round (1994), co-written with Ken Babbs. Another novel, *Seven Prayers by Grandma Whittier,* was serialized in Kesey's magazine *Spit in the Ocean* (published in 1974). He also wrote two children's books, *Little Tricker the Squirrel Meets Big Double the Bear* (1990) and *The Sea Lion: A Story of the Cliff People* (1991).

Kesey was diagnosed with liver cancer in October 2001 and underwent surgery in Eugene, Oregon, that same month. Complications arose, and he died at age sixty-six; he was buried at his Pleasant Hill farm. During his lifetime Kesey received a Distinguished Service Award from the State of Oregon in 1978, the Western Literature Association Award for distinguished achievement in writing in 1988, and the *Los Angeles Times* Robert Kirsh Award in 1991.

A leading figure of the 1960s counterculture, Kesey's work served as a bridge between the beat movement of the 1950s and the hippies of the 1960s. The humor and love of the human spirit expressed in his writings gave his work a universal appeal, even to those not involved in (or born too late to experience) the counterculture.

★

A general biography is Stephen L. Tanner, *Ken Kesey* (1983). A chronology of Kesey's life through 1989 is available in M. Gilbert Porter, *One Flew over the Cuckoo's Nest: Rising to Heroism* (1989). Books on Kesey's Merry Prankster exploits include Tom Wolfe, *The Electric Kool-Aid Acid Test* (1968) and Paul Perry, *On the Bus: The Complete Guide to the Legendary Trip of Ken Kesey and the Merry Pranksters and the Birth of the Counterculture* (1990). Obituaries are in the *New York Times* (11 Nov. 2001) and *People* (26 Nov. 2001).

GILLIAN G. GAAR

KHORANA, Har Gobind (*b.* 9 January 1922 in Raipur, India), biochemist who received the 1968 Nobel Prize in physiology or medicine for his work in deciphering the genetic code and who was also the first scientist to create an artificial gene.

Khorana was the youngest of five children of Ganpat Rai Khorana, a tax collector for the British colonial government, and a Krishna Devi Khorana, a homemaker. He was brought up in the portion of India that later became part of Pakistan. Although the literacy level was low in his home village and his family was poor, Khorana's parents valued education, and he attended Punjab University in Lahore on a government scholarship. He completed a bachelor's degree in chemistry there in 1943 and stayed on to gain a master's degree in 1945. Receiving a fellowship from the Indian government, he earned a doctorate in biochemistry from the University of Liverpool in England in 1948. Khorana did postdoctoral work at the Federal Institute of Technology in Zurich, Switzerland, and then at Cambridge

University in England, where he developed an interest in the chemistry of nucleic acids, including deoxyribonucleic acid (DNA), the molecule that carries genetic information, and its adjunct, ribonucleic acid (RNA).

In 1952 Khorana married Esther Elizabeth Sibler, who was born in Switzerland. They had three children. In the same year he was appointed director of the organic chemistry section of the British Columbia Research Council at the University of British Columbia in Vancouver, Canada. In 1959 Khorana and his associate, John Moffatt, synthesized coenzyme A, a complex molecule and one that is important in cell chemistry. This achievement brought Khorana international recognition, and in 1960 he moved to the University of Wisconsin at Madison, where he was named codirector of the Institute for Enzyme Research.

Khorana performed the research on the genetic code for which he won the Nobel Prize at Wisconsin in the 1960s. It had been established previously that DNA is a long, double-stranded molecule composed of four different building blocks, or nucleotides. The sequence of nucleotides forms a code that contains the information to make proteins, also linear molecules made up of twenty different building blocks called amino acids. The go-between in the synthesis by which the information in the DNA is used to make protein is RNA. In 1961 Marshall Nirenberg showed that a specific sequence of three nucleotides contains the code for one amino acid. Mathematically, by taking four nucleotides in groups of three, with the order within each triplet taken into account, there are sixty-four different nucleotide triplet codes. Since there are only twenty different amino acids, it was not surprising to discover that there is more than one triplet coding for most amino acids. Also, two of the triplets do not code for any amino acid; instead, they are "stop" messages that signal the end of the sequence.

After Nirenberg's initial work, several laboratories, including Khorana's, sought to discover the code for all twenty amino acids. Khorana did this by synthesizing strings of DNA with specific nucleotide sequences and then using them to make strings of RNA nucleotides, called ribopolynucleotides. He synthesized molecules with all sixty-four possible sequences, confirming that the information in the DNA is indeed used to make RNA, which in turn is used to make protein.

By 1966, the year in which Khorana became a naturalized U.S. citizen, the entire genetic code had been worked out, and this research was of such significance that Khorana and Nirenberg were awarded the Nobel Prize just two years later. They shared the prize with Robert W. Holley, who had discovered the role of a molecule called transfer RNA in protein synthesis. After winning the Nobel Prize, Khorana continued his work on synthesizing nucleic acids through the end of the decade. In 1970 he published the results of his research on creating a synthetic gene, a piece

Har Gobind Khorana. AP/WIDE WORLD PHOTOS

of DNA that he had made in a test tube. While he had been able to synthesize short lengths of DNA in the past, this was the first time anyone had fabricated a DNA molecule long enough to contain all the information needed to make a gene product, in this case a transfer RNA molecule. This DNA molecule was seventy-seven nucleotides long. Khorana later synthesized a second gene, one that coded for a protein. Both these genes functioned normally, producing normal products. This work received a great deal of attention, in some cases being heralded as a first step in the creation of life in a test tube. A modest man, Khorana shied away from such claims and saw his work as just another step in understanding the machinery of the cell.

In 1970 Khorana moved to the Massachusetts Institute of Technology (MIT), where he became the Alfred P. Sloan Professor of Biology and Chemistry. In the early twenty-first century, he remained at MIT as a professor emeritus. Like many other researchers who made contributions to molecular biology in the 1960s working on the biochemistry of such simple organisms as bacteria and yeast, Khorana moved on in the 1970s and 1980s to study the more biochemically complex systems of animals. For many years his research focused on photoreceptor cells. He studied the structure and function of rhodopsin, a complex protein found in the rods, the cells of the eye's retina that are sensitive to dim light.

Khorana's work in the 1960s was crucial to the development of the field of molecular biology. Until the genetic code was worked out, it was impossible even to consider the manipulation of genes. After the code was broken, mo-lecular biologists went on to discover how to remove genes from one organism and insert them into the DNA of another, opening up the field of genetic engineering. Khorana's synthesis of a gene was crucial to this research, because it showed that nucleic acids could be manipulated in a test tube and still work when reinserted into a cellular environment.

★

Biographical articles on Khorana include "Har Gobind Khorana" in *Current Biography* (1970); "Har Gobind Khorana" in *Modern Scientists and Engineers* (1980); and Donna Olshansky, "Har Gobind Khorana," in *Notable Twentieth-Century Scientists* (1995). Khorana wrote a biographical article, "A Life in Science," in *Science* (2000).

MAURA C. FLANNERY

KILLEBREW, Harmon Clayton, Jr. (*b.* 29 June 1936 in Payette, Idaho), one of the most prolific sluggers in baseball history, a small but potent batter who hit more home runs than anyone in the 1960s, shattering seats with his legendary blasts and bringing the Minnesota Twins franchise into prominence.

Killebrew was the youngest of four children born to Harmon Clayton Killebrew and Katherine Pearl May Culver, a homemaker. He had two older brothers and a sister. Killebrew's father was a local sheriff and a house painter, and young Killebrew often took painting jobs after school. At Payette High School, Killebrew became a varsity baseball, basketball, and football player as a freshman, and the school honored him by retiring his number twelve uniform after he graduated.

Killebrew planned to accept a football scholarship to the University of Oregon, but major-league scouts came to watch him play baseball in a local semiprofessional league the summer he graduated from high school. Idaho senator Herman Walker, a native of Payette, told Clark Griffith, president of the Washington Senators team, to sign Killebrew before some other club did. A week before he turned eighteen, Killebrew signed a $30,000 three-year contract, including a $12,000 bonus.

Killebrew, a poor fielder at first base, third base, and left field, needed to go to the minor leagues for more seasoning, but the Senators had to keep him on their roster for two seasons or risk losing him. He batted less than 100 times in 1954 and 1955, and then spent the next three years shuttling between Washington and its farm clubs. Most team officials gave up on him, but Calvin Griffith, Jr., the new club president (and nephew of the former club president), ordered third baseman Eddie Yost traded and had Killebrew installed as the regular third baseman in 1959. Killebrew rewarded Griffith with a league-leading 42 home runs, despite a second-half slump and 30 fielding errors in 100 games.

Killebrew was an instant sensation in Washington, but in 1961 Griffith packed up his team and moved to Minnesota, where the team was renamed the Twins. There, during the 1960s, Killebrew led the American League (AL) in home runs five more times, peaking at forty-nine home runs in 1964 and again in 1969. Despite his subpar fielding and low batting averages (he finished with a career mark of .256), Killebrew was named to the AL All-Star team thirteen times during his career.

Soft-spoken and reserved, Killebrew shunned the spotlight. A Mormon, he never drank, and he was never thrown out of a major-league game for arguing with an umpire. At six feet tall and weighing two hundred pounds, Killebrew was small compared to sluggers of later days, but he was a fearsome figure in the batter's box, with massive, menacing forearms and a compact, powerful swing. Killebrew married Elaine Roberts on 1 October 1955; the couple had five children.

During the 1960s he hit home runs at a rate not seen since the New York Yankees' player Babe Ruth, and many of his clouts were almost as legendary. In 1962 Killebrew became one of the few players ever to hit a ball over the left-field roof at Tiger Stadium in Detroit. On 3 June 1967 Killebrew hit a home run into the upper deck in left field at Metropolitan Stadium in Minnesota, shattering two seats with a ball estimated to have gone 530 feet. The splintered seats were painted orange and never sold again.

Perhaps Killebrew's most memorable home run came

Harmon Killebrew. AP/WIDE WORLD PHOTOS

in July 1965, a game-winning blast against the Yankees that cemented the Twins' lead over the perennial New York powerhouse. The Washington-Minnesota franchise had long been an AL doormat, but Killebrew, Tony Oliva, and other stars put the club into a dominant position. After another losing record in 1964, the so-called Impossible Twins reached the World Series in 1965. In his only World Series, Killebrew hit one home run and batted .286, and the Twins lost to the Los Angeles Dodgers.

In the mid-1960s Killebrew, not better-known stars such as Hank Aaron, Willie Mays, or Mickey Mantle, seemed to have the best chance of breaking Ruth's career home run record of 714. By the end of 1967, Killebrew was thirty-one, and had 380 home runs, twenty-four more than Ruth at the same age. "It was mostly the press talking about [catching Ruth]. I wasn't thinking about that," Killebrew said later. "I thought more about [Roger Maris's season record of] sixty-one. A couple of times, I had opportunities. I got hurt. Sometimes you put more pressure on yourself than pitchers put on you. I wasn't trying to hit sixty-one, but I probably had opportunities."

In 1968 Killebrew tore a hamstring during the All-Star game, the first of a series of debilitating injuries. The next year he bounced back and led the AL in home runs, runs batted in, walks, and on-base percentage, and was named Most Valuable Player. After that, however, his production declined rapidly.

During the 1960s Killebrew hit 403 home runs, more than any of his rival sluggers. But in 1973 he hit only five homers. After 1974 the Twins released him, and he played one more season for Kansas City before retiring with 573 career home runs, the fifth-highest total recorded at the time, behind Aaron, Ruth, Mays, and Frank Robinson.

Killebrew was elected to the National Baseball Hall of Fame in 1984. He stayed in baseball as a broadcaster for the Twins, the Oakland Athletics, and the California Angels, and later in life became a spokesman for hospice care after almost dying of an infection in 1991.

As a player Killebrew was a one-dimensional force. He lacked speed and defensive skills and was not much of a hitter. But his power has rarely been equaled. As a home run hitter he dominated the 1960s just as Ruth dominated the 1920s and Mark McGwire the 1990s.

★

Biographies of Killebrew include Hal Butler, *The Harmon Killebrew Story* (1966), and Wayne J. Anderson, *Harmon Killebrew: Baseball's Superstar* (1971). Entries on Killebrew are in Jim Ison, *Mormons in the Major Leagues* (1991), and in Bob Allen and Bill Gilbert, *The 500 Home Run Club: Baseball's 16 Greatest Home Run Hitters from Babe Ruth to Mark McGwire* (2000).

MICHAEL BETZOLD

KING, B. B. (*b.* 16 September 1925 near Itta Bene, Mississippi), blues singer and guitarist whose career blossomed in the mid-1960s during the blues and folk revival.

King, the first of two sons, was born Riley B. King to Albert Lee King and Nora Ella (Pully) King, who worked as sharecroppers on a cotton plantation. (His younger brother died in infancy.) King's parents separated when he was just four, and his mother took him to live in Kilmichael, Mississippi, to be closer to her family. Between chores King attended the one-room Elkhorn Schoolhouse. After his mother's death, when King was nine, his grandmother, Elnora Farr, who sharecropped in Kilmichael, took over child rearing until her death shortly later. For five years King lived alone in a cabin and worked as a tenant farmer. Then, at age fifteen, he moved to Indianola, Mississippi, to live with his father and stepmother. King briefly attended Ambrose Vocational High School but soon returned to his mother's family and work on a cotton plantation.

On 26 November 1944 King married Martha Denton. Although he enlisted in the army in 1943, he was released after basic training because he could drive a tractor; he was thus obligated to remain in sharecropping until the end of World War II. After the war an accident, in which a tractor was damaged, sent him running to Memphis, Tennessee, ahead of the plantation owner's wrath and in search of his cousin, the legendary blues singer Booker ("Bukka")

White. In Memphis, King first became a popular disc jockey and then moved into singing, recording, and touring. From White he learned exceptional vocal phrasing and a crowd-pleasing, storytelling style that White had perfected in rural Texas in the 1930s. King became a major bandleader and significant guitarist during this period. Eschewing chords, he sought the right note on his guitar, nicknamed "Lucille," which he lovingly played with an uncluttered style. He also made liberal use of his note-bending, signature tremolo and jazzy-sounding blues runs. Influential figures in his development included Charlie Christian and T-Bone Walker. King first became known through an appearance on Sonny Boy Williamson's radio show in Memphis and by his association with Pepticon, a health tonic. At the same time he adopted the nickname "B. B." for "Blues Boy."

In 1951 his recording of Lowell Fulson's tune "Three O'Clock Blues" became his first hit. Signed to the Los Angeles–based Kent Records, King became a staple of the blues circuits. At the beginning of the 1960s King was a veteran of many years of touring on the exhausting "chitlin' circuit." In 1956 alone he and his band performed 342 one-night stands. He developed an immense repertoire of songs and led a powerful blues combo, but over the years touring cost him his first and second marriages. He divorced Denton in 1952 and married Sue Carol Hall on 4 June 1958; they divorced in 1966. He fathered approximately eight children with other women during this period.

In 1962 King moved to ABC Records, which was in the process of enlarging the fame of the legendary "soul" singer Ray Charles. King had to wait, because many young urban blacks were disenchanted with his blues style, and the mainstream white audience could barely understand his talent. He owned hard-won but limited stardom in a pop world that was open to such black rhythm-and-blues artists as Chuck Berry and Little Richard but closed to authentic blues singers like King. The way to bigger stardom did not arrive until the blues and folk revival of 1965. The popularity of the integrated Paul Butterfield Blues Band led the promoter Jim Rooney at Club 47 in Cambridge, Massachusetts, to book the blues men Muddy Waters, Howlin' Wolf, and Junior Wells and to pave the way for King's popularity among Harvard intellectuals.

Added to this, the prestige of Charles Keil's influential book *The Urban Blues* (1966), which devoted an entire chapter to the praise of King, began to open doors. Keil prophesized that eventually King would be more popular with whites than with blacks. King benefited from new, more intellectual disc jockeys oriented to the college and professional markets. As white Britons and Americans sought greater authenticity, King was ready to provide it. Another factor was the rise of the guitar maestro in the British rock music invasion. English rockers had studied blues men like King for years and used their lessons to

B. B. King, 1969. HULTON-DEUTSCH COLLECTION/CORBIS

popularize hard, driving guitar music, which began to eclipse saxophone and vocal songs. King's signature style of complex single-string runs punctuated by loud blues notes and sublime vibratos set the terms white rockers had to follow.

King's first break came in 1968. Armed with a new hit, "The Thrill Is Gone," King began making inroads into the lucrative world of young white blues enthusiasts. Appearing at the Fillmore West in San Francisco that year, he was amazed at their devotion and knowledge of his career. Although he was hampered by a change in management from the older black team that had brought him through the 1950s to an exploitative white entrepreneur, who took most of his money, King was ready for a move. He took on a new, honest promoter, who obtained dates for him on college campuses and at new, hip nightclubs across urban America. He gained further popularity on a ten-day tour with the Rolling Stones in 1969. His climb to the peak of this new world came on 8 October 1970, when he and his band performed a medley for six uninterrupted minutes on *The Ed Sullivan Show*, which was watched by fifty million Americans. From *The Ed Sullivan Show*, King parlayed his name recognition to immensely profitable appearances in Las Vegas and abroad.

King was able to extend his fame by careful management of durability and political contacts to become one of the best-known musicians of the late twentieth century. Scholars recognized innumerable other figures to be as talented as King, but with the possible exception of the legendary, but long-dead Robert Johnson, no other singer had as much popular appeal as did King. He recognized that "as long as you are out there, people don't forget you." As

the blues became part of American folklore, King was the key interpreter. His name became so widely accepted that in the late 1990s, when political leaders in New York City sought to "sanitize" Times Square and Forty-second Street, King obtained a lucrative franchise to open a nightclub bearing his name. He has received innumerable honors, including doctorates from Yale and Tougaloo College in Mississippi, a 1990 Presidential Medal of Freedom, Grammy Awards in eleven different years, four hall of fame memberships, and hosts of awards from publications including *Downbeat, Ebony, Living Blues, Guitar, Melody Maker, Jazz,* and *Pop.* His talents may not be as legitimate as blues purists would like, but he is now among the major American musical legends, ranking with such legends as Tony Bennett and Ray Charles.

★

King's autobiography, with David Ritz, is *Blues All Around Me: The Autobiography of B. B. King* (1993). Biographical works include a chapter devoted to King in Charles Keil, *The Urban Blues* (1966), and Charles Sawyer, *The Arrival of B. B. King: The Authorized Biography* (1980).

GRAHAM RUSSELL HODGES

KING, Billie Jean Moffitt (*b.* 22 November 1943 in Long Beach, California), prominent tennis player and leading advocate of equality for women within sport who won sixteen Grand Slam tournaments during the 1960s.

The older of two children born to Willis B. Moffitt, a fireman, and Betty Jerman, a housewife, King first began ten-

Billie Jean King. ARCHIVE PHOTOS, INC.

nis lessons at the age of eleven. (Her brother, Randy, would become a Major League Baseball player.) A natural at the sport, the following year (1955) she won the Class D women's singles of the Long Beach Closed tournament and in 1959, at age sixteen, she earned the number-nineteen spot in the U.S. women's national rankings. In 1960 King won her first national women's title, teaming with Darlene Hard to capture the doubles crown at the National Clay Courts. Despite her relatively small size (five feet, four and one-half inches and 130 pounds), King possessed the quickness and athleticism that enabled her to play the serve-and-volley style of game, and in 1960 she began to capitalize on this ability on the faster playing surfaces. King proceeded to win the Philadelphia District Grass Court singles title and then reached the semifinals of the prestigious Eastern Grass Court and Pennsylvania Lawn tournaments. After reaching the third round of the U.S. Nationals at Forest Hills, New York, she was rewarded with a number-four ranking in U.S. women's tennis.

After graduating from Long Beach Poly High School in 1961, that summer, at age seventeen, King made her first trip to England, where she teamed with Karen Hantze to win the doubles title at London's Queen's Club tournament. The unseeded American teenagers then shocked everyone by sweeping to the doubles championship at Wimbledon without losing a set—King's first Grand Slam title. After playing for the U.S. Wightman Cup team for the first time, King returned to America, where she reached the

singles semifinals at the National Clay Courts and the Eastern Grass event. She then won singles and doubles titles at the Philadelphia District Grass Court tournament and a week later won the singles crown at the important Philadelphia Lawn tournament. At the end of the season King was elevated to the number-three U.S. ranking, and in the fall she entered Los Angeles State College.

In the summer of 1962 King signaled her readiness to become a serious challenger on the international tennis scene as she advanced to the quarterfinals at Wimbledon, after registering a stunning second-round singles victory over number-one-seeded Margaret Smith of Australia (1–6, 6–3, 7–5). This match began a long rivalry between the two players. King and Karen Hantze-Susman repeated their doubles championship at Wimbledon before losing in the final of the U.S. Doubles tournament later in the summer. The American duo would be ranked number one among U.S. women's teams at the end of the year—the first of thirteen such doubles rankings King achieved with various partners during her career.

King was still attending Los Angeles State in 1963 and early 1964, but increasingly her interests were focused on tennis. Her place as one of the top women players in the world was solidified in singles play at Wimbledon with a second-place finish in 1963 and a semifinal berth in 1964—losing to Smith on both occasions. King also notched her first national singles crown at the Irish Championships of 1963, while in 1964 she captured the Eastern Grass singles title and, with Hantze-Susman, won the U.S. Doubles title that summer. Despite disappointing singles performances at the U.S. Nationals, King was ranked number two among U.S. women at the end of both years.

In the fall of 1964 King decided to leave college and concentrate on tennis, playing the Australian tournaments in January 1965. There she reached the semifinal or final of three tournaments, before returning home to win the singles titles of the California State and Southern California tournaments. That summer King reached the semifinals at Wimbledon, and she came home with another Grand Slam doubles crown after teaming with Maria Bueno of Brazil. In America she won the singles titles of the Eastern Grass and Pennsylvania Lawn tournaments before advancing to the final of the U.S. Nationals, where she lost to Margaret Smith. On 17 September 1965 she married Larry King, a law student, and at the end of the year she was ranked as the number-one player in U.S. women's tennis.

The seasons of 1966 through 1968 represent the peak of King's play during the decade, as she notched the number-one ranking in the world for all three years. In 1966 she demonstrated her versatility on different surfaces as she won singles titles at the U.S. National Indoors, the U.S. National Hard Courts, the South African Nationals (beating Smith), and, at last, Wimbledon. In 1967, along with winning the singles at the California State and Eastern Grass tournaments, King repeated her triumph at Wimbledon (also sharing in the doubles and mixed doubles titles). She capped off her year with the long-sought singles championship at the U.S. Nationals and the South American singles crown, and she was named the Associated Press Female Athlete of the Year.

By 1967 the landscape of world tennis was changing, and King was one of the major advocates of open tennis play between professionals and amateurs and an outspoken critic of the sport's hypocritical pose of so-called amateurism—stances that brought her into conflict with U.S. tennis officials. After open tennis was approved in early 1968, she signed a professional contract and joined the National Tennis League tour; that year she also won the singles title at the Australian Nationals and repeated her championship at Wimbledon. In 1969 she won titles at the South African and Irish National Opens and lost in the final at Wimbledon.

Always a vigorous campaigner for equal tournament prestige and prize money for women's tennis, in 1970 King played a significant role in organizing and promoting the Virginia Slims women's tour, while in 1973 she founded and was the first president of the Women's Tennis Association players' union. During the 1970s, while working to popularize women's tennis, she continued to play at the top level of the game, although most people primarily recall her famous 1973 nationally televised exhibition match against Bobby Riggs. King ended her competitive tennis career in 1984 with a total of thirty-nine singles, doubles, and mixed doubles championships in Grand Slam tournaments, and in 1990 *Life* magazine named her one of the 100 Most Important Americans of the Twentieth Century.

★

There are a wide variety of writings on King's tennis career—both in books and sport periodicals during her playing days. She coauthored an autobiography with Kim Chapin entitled *Billie Jean* (1974) and then advanced the story with another version coauthored with Frank Deford, also entitled *Billie Jean* (1982). There were several short books issued during her career, including Marshall and Sue Burchard, *Sports Hero, Billie Jean King* (1975). King herself, with Cynthia Starr, authored a work on the development of women's professional tennis, *We Have Come a Long Way: The Story of Women's Tennis* (1988).

RAYMOND SCHMIDT

KING, Martin Luther, Jr. (*b.* 15 January 1929 in Atlanta, Georgia; *d.* 4 April 1968 in Memphis, Tennessee), religious and civil rights leader who, as president of the Southern Christian Leadership Conference, spearheaded the struggle for racial equality throughout the 1960s.

King was the second of three children of Martin Luther King, Sr., pastor of the Ebenezer Baptist Church and one of the principal leaders of the black community, and Alberta Christine (Williams) King, a teacher. King enrolled at Morehouse College at age fifteen. He continued his studies at Crozer Theological Seminary in Chester, Pennsylvania, graduating with a bachelor of divinity degree in 1951, and at Boston University, from which he earned his doctorate in systematic theology in 1955. By that time he had married Coretta Scott (18 June 1953), with whom he would have four children, and become pastor of the Dexter Avenue Baptist Church in Montgomery, Alabama.

In a political career that spanned little more than twelve years, King helped revolutionize American race relations. He first came to international attention during the Montgomery bus boycott of 1955–1956. On 1 December 1955 Rosa Parks was arrested for refusing to surrender her seat to a white passenger on a segregated bus. Her arrest led to the organization of the Montgomery Improvement Association (MIA), which launched a boycott of the city's bus system. As president of the MIA, King communicated the aspirations of the protesters not only to the nation but to the world as well. Inspired by the teachings of Jesus Christ and the Indian nationalist leader Mohandas Gandhi, he placed a resolute emphasis upon nonviolence, which sustained African Americans in the face of constant intimidation and violence. When terrorists bombed his home on 30 January 1956, King restored calm to a potentially riotous black community. His determined appeal to meet "violence with nonviolence" also enhanced his stature as a moral leader.

King was not the first African-American leader to espouse the philosophy of nonviolence. In 1941 the black union leader A. Philip Randolph proposed leading a mass march on Washington in protest against racial discrimination in the armed forces and defense industries. The threat of civil disorder forced President Franklin D. Roosevelt to establish the Fair Employment Practices Commission. It was nonetheless under the leadership of King that African Americans implemented nonviolent direct action on a mass scale, with revolutionary consequences. King adhered to the concept of nonviolence throughout his political career, even when surrounded by the chaos and urban disorder that characterized the late 1960s. He was particularly influenced by Gandhi's concept of *Satyagraha*, or "soul force," which taught him that love was the instrument to overthrow the violent hatred of white racists.

Following the success of the 381-day boycott, in February 1957, King founded the Southern Christian Leadership Conference (SCLC). The organization initially floundered. Much of its efforts were concentrated on the Crusade for Citizenship, a voter registration drive that, as King conceded in the late 1950s, had "not really scratched the surface." These years were nonetheless of great signif-

Martin Luther King, Jr. THE NEW YORK AMSTERDAM NEWS

icance in terms of King's intellectual growth. In particular, the civil rights leader deepened his philosophical understanding of nonviolent direct action. His visit to India in 1959 as a special guest of Prime Minister Jawaharlal Nehru allowed him an opportunity to discuss Gandhian principles with some of the late Indian leader's disciples. (Gandhi himself had been assassinated in 1948.)

On 1 February 1960 four black students from North Carolina Agricultural and Technical College entered a Woolworth store in Greensboro, sat at the lunch counter reserved for whites, and demanded service. This incident stirred a wave of similar protests across the South. The student sit-ins were fuelled by a sense of increasing frustration at the retarded pace of civil rights reform. Although he was reluctant, King was persuaded to participate in the Atlanta sit-in movement. On 19 October 1960 he and fifty-one other activists were arrested at a downtown demonstration. King was sentenced to four months' hard labor at Reidsville State Prison. Within only two days, however, he was a free man. His release had been negotiated by Robert Kennedy in a calculated attempt to increase black votes for

his brother John F. Kennedy, who was running a closely contested presidential race against Richard Nixon. The plan proved decisive: African-American voters helped secure Kennedy's narrow electoral victory in November.

The newly elected president nonetheless did little to promote civil rights, instead prioritizing an aggressive foreign policy against the Soviet Union. Black activists understood that more direct action was needed to force the hand of the federal government. In May 1961 the Congress of Racial Equality launched the Freedom Rides in an attempt to desegregate interstate transportation facilities. Although King served as chairman of the Freedom Ride Coordinating Committee, he refused to take a seat aboard one of the buses. While King was immediately identifiable as the intellectual and spiritual leader of the civil rights movement, it was others who implemented the tactics of nonviolent direct action. The pioneering protests of the early 1960s therefore raised expectations that King would lead his own campaign of mass civil disobedience.

In December 1961 King received a telegram inviting him to lend his support to the black protest movement in

Albany, Georgia. Inspired by the enthusiasm of local blacks, King swiftly assumed leadership of the movement. Albany was the first significant civil rights campaign in which King had participated since Montgomery, and it was to end in ignominious failure. Numerous forces conspired to frustrate the Albany Movement. King's arrival complicated the already fractious relations between local activists. Members of the Student Nonviolent Coordinating Committee particularly resented King's assumption of authority. King also had to contend with Chief of Police Laurie Pritchett. Pritchett had read King's memoir of the Montgomery bus boycott, *Stride Toward Freedom,* which enabled him to anticipate his opponent's tactics. King attempted to dramatize the plight of local blacks by precipitating a conflict between the protesters and the police. By ordering his men to use the utmost restraint in arresting black activists, Pritchett succeeded in preserving community order and removing the threat of federal intervention. King abandoned Albany in August 1962.

The SCLC leader was to learn from the lesson of defeat. In April 1963 he launched an audacious campaign in Birmingham, Alabama. Among local blacks the violently repressive political climate had earned the city the bleak sobriquet "Bombingham." Under the control of Commissioner of Public Safety Eugene ("Bull") Connor, the police used intimidation and violence to suppress incipient black protests. Connor, for instance, had failed to protect the Freedom Riders from a brutal assault by the Ku Klux Klan. Nonetheless, it was precisely because of the appalling reputation of Birmingham that it was chosen as the target of an SCLC campaign. As the SCLC's executive director Wyatt T. Walker asserted, "We knew that as Birmingham went, so went the South. And we felt that if we could crack that city, then we could crack any city."

Unlike in Albany, King started the Birmingham campaign with several advantages. King was not properly prepared for the Albany campaign and, as a result, could not impose complete control over a divided local movement. The SCLC leader established a clearer line of authority in Birmingham. He benefited in particular from close strategic planning with the Reverend Fred Shuttlesworth, head of the Alabama Christian Movement for Human Rights, a local SCLC affiliate. In Albany, King had fought against the unified front of the white power structure. By contrast, with an imminent mayoral election, the white community in Birmingham was split between those who supported the extremist Bull Connor and others who backed the moderate Albert Boutwell. The Albany Movement also had suffered from a failure to define its objectives clearly. King now understood that a broad-based assault on segregation could result in a lack of strategic focus. In Birmingham he therefore directed his efforts toward a more clearly defined goal: the desegregation of downtown stores.

Despite its elaborate planning, the SCLC campaign experienced a less than auspicious start. The SCLC was forced to postpone the campaign to allow for the election of Albert Boutwell as mayor. When the protests eventually commenced on 3 April, King was taken aback by the strength of local black opposition. Many African Americans believed that the new administration should be given an opportunity to introduce reforms. The SCLC campaign could prove counterproductive, as it would arouse renewed racial hostilities. Although Connor continued to hold his position as Commissioner of Public Safety, he, too, confounded King. The SCLC anticipated that Connor would play into their hands by ordering a violent crackdown on civil rights protests. By exposing the brutal realities of white racism, the activists would create public pressure for federal government intervention. However, Connor exercised uncharacteristic self-control.

In an effort to improve the faltering momentum of the campaign, King was arrested during a march on Good Friday (12 April). The timing of the arrest imbued King's actions with the symbolism of Christian martyrdom. In his prison cell King read a letter published in the local newspaper, written by eight white clergymen. The letter castigated the SCLC leader for creating renewed racial tensions at a time when real change had seemed imminent. An angry and embittered King responded by penning his passionately worded "Letter from Birmingham City Jail." A scathing indictment of white liberals who urged greater caution, this document stands as the most thorough articulation of King's philosophy of nonviolent direct action. Throughout his career King was accused of cynically inciting violence as a way to advance his political objectives. King adamantly asserted that he did not create the violent disorder that accompanied SCLC campaigns: "We merely bring to the surface the tension that is already alive." It also should be emphasized that King did not expose black protesters to the serious risk of murderous retribution by white racists. SCLC campaigns were carefully stage-managed morality plays. The presence of the media constrained the actions of the police, enabling the SCLC to control the levels of violence. In comparison with civil rights protests in such countries as South Africa, police brutality created a dramatic effect but without a deadly impact.

Upon his release from prison, King was confronted by the problem of how to crack the resolve of Connor. The SCLC activist James Bevel offered the solution. On 2 May hundreds of black schoolchildren marched from the Sixteenth Street Baptist Church into the arms of arresting officers. Within a week more than two thousand children were in police custody. Connor could not control his anger any longer. Under his command, the police turned German Shepherd dogs on the protesters. Those activists who failed to disperse then were assaulted with high-pressure water hoses. The scenes of racial brutality on the streets of Birmingham drew international condemnation. In particular, the violence provided enormous political capital to the Soviet Union, which ridiculed the failure of the federal government to fulfill the ideals of American democracy. King therefore proved astute in his ability to manipulate cold war tensions toward advancement of the black cause. An embarrassed Kennedy administration immediately ordered Justice Department officials to negotiate a settlement. With the desegregation of the downtown department stores accomplished, King turned his sights upon the nation's capital.

On 11 June, President Kennedy announced his intention to present Congress with a comprehensive civil rights bill. The bill was intended to ban segregation in all public facilities, to promote black employment, and to abolish black disfranchisement. In a dramatic expression of public support for the bill, King led the March on Washington. On 28 August the SCLC leader addressed an audience of 250,000 from the steps of the Lincoln Memorial. His "I Have a Dream" speech was the most powerful and important address delivered by an American in the twentieth century. King cloaked his language in the traditional symbols of American identity: patriotism, religious conviction, the Declaration of Independence, and the Constitution. The speech resonated all the more powerfully because of the way King portrayed the black freedom struggle as part of the broader moral redemption of the entire American people: "I have a dream that one day this nation will rise up and live out the true meaning of its creed, 'We hold these truths to be self-evident, that all men are created equal.'"

The Birmingham campaign and the March on Washington sealed King's reputation as the outstanding moral and political leader of his generation. In January 1964 *Time* magazine named him "Man of the Year," the first African American to receive this accolade. The civil rights bill, however, continued to face entrenched opposition from politicians in the South. King sustained the political pressure on Congress through a series of demonstrations in Saint Augustine, Florida, in May and June 1964. A series of violent assaults on black protesters maintained the political focus on civil rights. The defeat of a southern filibuster in the Senate finally led President Lyndon B. Johnson to sign the Civil Rights Act into law on 2 July 1964. One of several such laws enacted during the late 1950s and 1960s, this one outlawed segregation in public places. The persistent public protests of King and the SCLC had proved instrumental, stirring the conscience of the nation and creating a relentless political pressure in support of racial reform. In October 1964 King became the youngest-ever recipient of the Nobel Peace Prize.

In 1965 King launched a new campaign of nonviolent direct action in Selma, Alabama. His purpose was to press for the enactment of a federal voting rights law. Selma provided an ideal stage upon which to dramatize the plight of black disfranchisement. Although African Americans made up more than half the population, fewer than 2 percent of them were registered to vote. The SCLC also anticipated that it could provoke the local sheriff, Jim Clark, into a confrontation as violent as the one it had instigated with Bull Connor in Birmingham. A series of almost daily marches to the county courthouse culminated with the arrest of King on 1 February. The SCLC used the occasion to publicize the black community's lack of political rights. In his "Letter from a Selma Jail," King proclaimed, "THIS IS SELMA, ALABAMA. THERE ARE MORE NEGROES IN JAIL THAN THERE ARE ON THE VOTING ROLLS." Even so, the Selma movement was slow to gather momentum. On 18 February, Jimmie Lee Jackson was shot dead as he sought to protect his mother from state troopers during a protest in the nearby community of Marion. Despite this incident, the movement still had not stirred national awareness.

On 5 March, King announced his intention to lead a fifty-four-mile march from Selma to Montgomery to petition Alabama's governor, George Wallace, for the enforcement of black voting rights. Two days later six hundred demonstrators marched to the Edmund Pettus Bridge, where they were met by state troopers and members of the sheriff's posse. The troopers charged the marchers with tear gas, billy clubs, and bullwhips. According to one newspaper report, "The Negroes cried out as they crowded together for protection, and the whites on the sideline whooped and cheered." An estimated one hundred protesters were injured on what became known as "Bloody Sunday."

King was not actually among the marchers, having returned to Atlanta. His absence aroused intense criticism from younger radicals, who accused him of cowardice. King responded by issuing a call to clergymen across the country to join him in a second march. Still, the SCLC leader stirred further controversy when he ordered the marchers to turn around once they had crossed the Edmund Pettus Bridge. Confronted by a federal court injunction against the march, King feared that the protesters would be unprotected against a further outbreak of violence. His decision nonetheless intensified criticisms of his leadership.

Despite criticisms, the campaign had succeeded in arousing national indignation. On 15 March, Lyndon Johnson addressed a joint session of Congress. As he concluded his emotional appeal for passage of a voting rights law, the president invoked the anthem of the civil rights movement: "And We Shall Overcome." Never before had the U.S. government so completely embraced the cause of black civil rights. On 19 March a federal court lifted the injunction against marching. Two days later King set out for the state capital. On 25 March, twenty-five thousand demonstrators gathered outside the Alabama statehouse. "We are on the move now," declared King, "and no wave of racism can stop us." On 6 August 1965 President Johnson signed the Voting Rights Act into law. Only months earlier Vice President Hubert Humphrey had informed King that he doubted that Congress would enact such a law so soon after the Civil Rights Act. The speed with which the Voting Rights Act passed into law is therefore a tribute to the remarkable ability of King to provoke public awareness of the race issue, creating the broad popular consensus that compelled federal government action.

"There is no more civil rights movement," James Bevel proudly proclaimed to news reporters. "President Johnson signed it out of existence when he signed the Voting Rights Bill." The complacency of black activists was starkly exposed by the riot that erupted in the Watts ghetto of Los Angeles on 11 July 1965. The Watts riot was the worst outbreak of urban unrest since World War II. In its wake, thirty-four people lay dead, nearly four hundred were injured, and a further four thousand were under arrest. Damage to property was estimated at $45 million. King traveled to Los Angeles to help restore calm and order in the African-American community. When he arrived, he was shocked to discover that many younger blacks claimed never to have heard of him. "We won," exclaimed one of the rioters to the SCLC leader. "How can you say you won," replied King, "when thirty four people are dead, your community is destroyed . . . ?" "We won," retorted the rioter, "because we made them pay attention to us."

The Watts riot exposed the limitations of the black protest movement led by King. Civil rights activists had invested their energies in the struggle to secure the constitutional rights of African Americans in the southern states. The plight of northern blacks had been largely overlooked. During the Great Migration of the 1920s, African Americans fled in ever increasing numbers from the twin evils of racism and economic depression in the South to start a new life in the North. The influx of thousands of African Americans into northern cities accelerated during World War II as unprecedented job opportunities opened up owing to chronic labor shortages in the defense industries. By the 1960s approximately 50 percent of the black population lived in the North. In the northern states, no laws reduced African Americans to a status of second-class citizenship, but persistent prejudice resulted in widespread unemployment, police brutality, and political neglect. In 1964 some 15 percent of white families in the United States lived below the federal poverty line; the figure for African-American families was 37 percent. The Watts riot awakened King to the harsh economic realities of the northern inner cities. It was time, he understood, to lead the movement out of the South.

King launched his northern offensive in early 1966. His target was the country's second-largest city, Chicago. The civil rights leader was optimistic that his plans to eradicate slum conditions and promote open housing would be welcomed by the liberal establishment, since they accorded with the aims of Johnson's War on Poverty. "Chicago represents all the problems that you can find in the major urban areas of our country," asserted King. "If we can break the system in Chicago, it can be broken anywhere in the country." The system, however, could not be broken.

From the outset, the SCLC campaign failed to establish political momentum. In the South, King had inspired an army of nonviolent soldiers to take battle against the forces of white racism. In Chicago he was met by the cynicism and apathy of the ghetto masses. The SCLC had relied in all its previous campaigns upon the organizational resources and ideological influence of the church. Outside the Bible Belt, the church did not command the same authority and respect and could not be used so effectively as a movement center. King also was outmaneuvered by Chicago's mayor, Richard Daley. In Birmingham and Selma, King had relied upon a violently racist opposition to expose the injustices of the Jim Crow caste system. By contrast, Daley publicly appeared to sympathize with the political objectives of the SCLC campaign. Although the mayor failed to fulfill his promises, his actions succeeded in defusing any dramatic political confrontation between black protesters and city authorities. Moreover, when a riot erupted in the West Side ghetto on 12 July, Daley seized the opportunity to accuse King of stirring up dissent.

Later that month the SCLC launched a series of confrontational marches into white neighborhoods. The marches exposed the realities of northern racism as protesters were met by thousands of violently angry white residents. At the same time, white liberals accused the SCLC of unnecessarily provocative tactics, especially after it announced a march into Cicero, a notoriously racist white suburb. King was compelled to accept a negotiated settlement that committed the city to end housing discrimination. With no timetable for implementation, however, the "Summit Agreement" proved a hollow victory. In November 1967, long after King had abandoned Chicago, Daley won a fourth term of office with 80 percent of the black vote.

The SCLC leader never recovered from the political setback in Chicago. During the last two years of his life King espoused an increasingly radical critique of American society. King realized in the wake of the Chicago campaign that he had underestimated the strength of northern racism. The reality of white prejudice posed not a regional but a national problem. In the past, King had individualized the problem of racism, perceiving it as an irrational hatred toward African Americans on the part of a minority of whites. Racial equality therefore could be accomplished within the existing economic and political structures of American society. The failure of the Chicago campaign convinced King that it was the capitalist system itself that confined African Americans to the poverty and despair of the ghetto. This newfound radicalism, however, stood at odds with the white conservative backlash that swept the country in the late 1960s. King's opposition to the Vietnam War was met with a particularly hostile public reaction.

King made a personal appeal for negotiations to end the war as early as August 1965, but he soon withdrew into a tactical silence when his closest advisers warned him not to alienate the Johnson administration. The civil rights leader suffered an acute crisis of conscience for another eighteen months. As an exponent of nonviolence, how could he refuse to condemn a war in which not only soldiers but also innocent civilians were slaughtered? His political caution also had failed to protect the civil rights movement from the increasing indifference of the federal government. Johnson promised the American people that they could have both "guns and butter," but the massive escalation of military expenditure seriously curtailed funding for Great Society programs, crushing the expectations of impoverished inner-city blacks. "In a real sense," declared King, "the Great Society has been shot down on the battlefields of Vietnam." The war also witnessed a disproportionate number of African Americans being drafted into the army. Although blacks made up only 11 percent of the population, they represented 20 percent of conscripts.

King broke his silence in early 1967 with a series of blistering assaults on American foreign policy. As predicted, the speeches were politically disastrous. The press and political establishment turned on King, accusing him of interfering in affairs about which he had little or no expert knowledge. *Life* magazine denounced his criticisms of the war effort as "demagogic slander that sounded like a script for Radio Hanoi." The speeches also widened the fault lines within the civil rights coalition, as more conservative black leaders, such as Roy Wilkins and Whitney Young, accused King of disloyalty.

The civil rights movement was already on the point of collapse as a result of the emergence of Black Power. This radical strain of protest first had an impact on the public consciousness during James Meredith's March Against Fear in June 1966. It represented an explicit challenge to the nonviolent tactics and integrationist objectives of the mainstream civil rights leadership. While King embraced Black Power's emphasis on racial pride, he otherwise dismissed it as a "nihilistic philosophy." His animus was directed in particular toward the glamourization of violence. During the "long, hot summer" of 1967, urban race riots resulted in eighty-three deaths. King believed that by promoting the riots as legitimate acts of protest, Black Power created political ammunition for white conservatives and a self-

destructive mentality among African Americans. With the emergence of Black Power, the simmering tensions between radical and conservative elements within the civil rights coalition boiled over into mutual public animosity. King, who had acted as a mediator between these conflicting interests, found that the "vital center" he occupied had been irreparably eroded.

In December 1967 King announced plans for a "Poor People's Campaign." Under the auspices of the SCLC, thousands of impoverished citizens, black and white, would converge on Washington to demand a "Bill of Rights for the Disadvantaged." SCLC insiders again questioned the wisdom of the campaign. In the current incendiary racial climate, they were concerned that such a provocative demonstration could spill over into violence. King would not live to assess the legitimacy of these criticisms.

On 18 March 1968 the SCLC leader addressed a rally in Memphis, Tennessee, to express support for sanitation workers, who were striking for union recognition. Ten days later he led a sympathy march to city hall. The march descended into chaos, as young militants known as "the Invaders" stirred unrest, which led to the smashing and looting of storefronts. Police responded by firing tear gas and beating the blinded protesters. It was the first time that a march led by King had collapsed into violent disorder. Although he was profoundly depressed by the experience, King was in part to blame. The precipitous nature of his intervention in the strike meant that the SCLC was poorly prepared. King nonetheless was persuaded to return to Memphis for another rally. "Like anybody I would like to live a long life," King proclaimed. "I've seen the Promised Land. I may not get there with you. But I want you to know tonight that we as a people will get to the Promised Land." His words proved tragically prophetic. The following night, as he stood on the balcony of the Lorraine Motel, King was shot dead by James Earl Ray. King originally was buried in South View Cemetery in Atlanta. He later was reinterred at the Martin Luther King, Jr., Center for Nonviolent Social Change in Atlanta.

Black anger erupted on the streets. As many as 169 cities suffered race riots in the aftermath of the assassination. The Poor People's Campaign also collapsed into disarray. Some commentators have argued that the passage of the 1968 Civil Rights Act owed to the outpouring of public grief, but this has not been established conclusively. This Civil Rights Act was, in any case, a less than fitting tribute to the slain civil rights leader. Although in principle it outlawed housing discrimination, without adequate enforcement mechanisms the new law accomplished little.

It is impossible to determine what King would have achieved had he survived the assassin's bullet. Haunted by political setbacks and hounded by a systematic campaign of Federal Bureau of Investigation (FBI) harassment, he faced an uncertain future. The FBI campaign against King certainly exacted a considerable psychological toll. The FBI leader J. Edgar Hoover pursued the civil rights leader relentlessly once he secured authorization in late 1962 for the wiretapping of King's telephones. Although the FBI failed to establish credible evidence that King was an instrument of the Communist Party, the wiretaps did reveal a series of extramarital liaisons. Public disclosure of this evidence would have seriously undermined King's credibility as a moral leader, a fact that the agency used in a deliberate attempt at blackmail.

Despite the setbacks he faced in his later years, King's greatness as a civil rights leader is incontestable. In later years the literature on the civil rights movement has moved beyond its initially narrow focus on King to emphasize the important contributions of other individuals and organizations. This should not conceal, however, his inestimable contribution to the black liberation struggle. King imbued the civil rights movement with a sense of historical urgency, leading by example in public acts of confrontation against the forces of white racism and forcing an often reluctant federal government to accelerate the process of civil rights reform.

★

Autobiographical works include James M. Washington, ed., *A Testament of Hope: The Essential Writings of Martin Luther King, Jr.* (1986), and Clayborne Carson, ed., *The Autobiography of Martin Luther King* (1998). Biographies of King include David L. Lewis, *King: A Critical Biography* (1970); David J. Garrow, *Bearing the Cross: Martin Luther King, Jr., and the Southern Christian Leadership Conference* (1986); Adam Fairclough, *To Redeem the Soul of America: The Southern Christian Leadership Conference and Martin Luther King, Jr.* (1987); and Taylor Branch, *Parting the Waters: America in the King Years, 1954–63* (1988) and *Pillar of Fire: America in the King Years, 1963–65* (1998).

CLIVE WEBB

KIRK, Grayson Louis (*b.* 12 October 1903 near Jeffersonville, Ohio; *d.* 21 November 1997 in Bronxville, New York), educator, university administrator, and president of Columbia University from 1953 to 1968, who earned national notoriety in 1968 with his infamous decision to call in riot police to quell a massive student uprising at Columbia.

Kirk was born on a farm in rural Ohio to Traine Caldwell Kirk, a farmer, and Phoebe Nora Eichelberger, a schoolteacher. After receiving a bachelor's degree in 1924 from Miami University in Oxford, Ohio, where he served as principal of a local high school during his senior year, Kirk briefly considered a career as a newspaper correspondent. Instead, he pursued further education in political science,

Grayson L. Kirk. AP/WIDE WORLD PHOTOS

earning a master's degree from Clark University in 1925, and in 1930 a doctorate from the University of Wisconsin, where he began his teaching career. On 17 August 1925 he married Marion Louise Sands; they had one son.

Kirk cemented his reputation as an astute scholar of international relations with the publication of his first book, *Philippine Independence* (1936), an examination of U.S.-Philippine relations. The *New York Times* hailed it as "an expert and brilliant analysis," sentiments that were repeated for *Contemporary International Politics* (written with W. R. Sharp, 1940), *The Monroe Doctrine Today* (1941), and *The Study of International Relations in American Colleges and Universities* (1947). In 1940 Kirk left the University of Wisconsin to join the faculty at Columbia University. When the United States entered World War II he reduced his teaching duties to serve in a number of positions within the U.S. State Department. He participated in the Dumbarton Oaks Conference in 1944 and the San Francisco Conference in 1945, where he helped write the charter of the United Nations. With the war's end, Kirk returned to Columbia but moved from teaching to administration. In 1949 he was chosen provost and in 1950 became acting president of the university while Columbia president Dwight Eisenhower served as Supreme Allied Commander in Europe. When Eisenhower was elected president of the United States in 1952, Kirk seemed his obvious successor.

As president of Columbia, the portly, pipe-smoking Kirk substantially transformed the university. More than any preceding president, he compiled an astounding record of fund-raising successes. During his fifteen-year tenure Kirk quadrupled the university's endowments, created six new academic institutes, cultivated a science faculty that won four Nobel Prizes, built more than a dozen buildings, and doubled the number of volumes in the libraries. Nonetheless, his fund-raising triumphs could not compensate for his poor relations with students and faculty, both of whom saw him as an imperious authoritarian.

Ideologically, Kirk remained isolated from Columbia's student population. While he came out against the Vietnam War in 1968, his reasons were far removed from those of antiwar protesters. Instead, he argued that the United States should extricate itself from the conflict because civil disobedience encouraged disrespect for the law, and violence had "almost achieved respectability." While radical students were becoming increasingly distrustful of government, Kirk encouraged university-government relations, most particularly through his membership in the Institute for Defense Analyses (IDA), a consortium of universities engaging in government research. Nor did he see harm in corporate partnerships. In 1967 he came under fire for using sales of a cigarette filter to support the university. These tactics were bound to cause conflict with Columbia students, whose leftist leaders, including the dynamic Mark Rudd, president of the Columbia chapter of Students for a Democratic Society (SDS), resented the administration's complicity with defense research and capitalism. The particular actions of Kirk and Columbia were secondary. As Rudd put it, "the issue is not the issue." For leftist students, the university was merely symbolic of larger social problems.

The breaking point came with the university's plan to build a gymnasium in Morningside Park, a public area near the campus in Harlem. This multimillion-dollar facility, which included a smaller gym for the Harlem community, would have effectively usurped the park from the neighborhood's low-income African-American residents and seemed representative of what many saw as the university's racism and near colonial disregard for the community. Student protests against the plan yielded no response from Kirk, except for a ban on indoor student protests.

On 23 April 1968 Rudd led a group of approximately 150 people, including white and African-American students and a number of nonstudents, in a protest against the gym and Columbia's support of IDA. The group, which grew throughout the next day, seized five university buildings by 25 April, including Kirk's office, and took three administrators hostage. The protesters refused to leave the buildings without a promise of amnesty, and campus gates were locked while the faculty debated its options. Although Kirk proclaimed at a news conference on 25 April that the university "at almost all costs . . . wish[es] to avoid physical confrontation," on the night of 29 to 30 April the administration requested that police end the seizure. While the African-American protesters marched calmly from their buildings to be arrested, others resisted police efforts. By 30 April, although the university was back under the administration's control, 600 students had been arrested, and evidence of excessive police force was receiving public attention, causing sentiment to swell in support of the protesters.

A student strike was immediately called, effectively shutting down the campus again. The strikers' demands included halting construction of the gym, amnesty for the protesters, and the resignation of Kirk, who had become their nemesis. In late May violence erupted once more, as police force was used to end protests against the suspension of four students. While Kirk proclaimed that he would not "resign under fire, because that would be a victory for those who are out to destroy the university," he announced his retirement in August, saying that campus events prevented him from fulfilling his duties. In October the Cox Commission, created to evaluate the campus uprising, placed a significant measure of blame on the Kirk administration and its heavy-handed tactics. For radical students across the country, Columbia represented a major victory—the longest student protest to that time, the first at an Ivy League university, and one that had resulted in a major shift in administration.

After his retirement Kirk faded from public view, dying of natural causes at his home. Although he improved Columbia in many ways during his term as president, Kirk is best remembered as a symbol of the generation gap of the 1960s. His personal views clashed directly with youthful radicalism, which resented and criticized universities as repressive institutions supporting imperialism and oppression both at home and abroad. Kirk's decision to use police force emphasized this gap. While many people at the time criticized his actions and supported the students, Kirk's response to the protesters was emblematic of a growing conservatism in the late 1960s. The reaction of this conservative wing to the protests made by privileged students was to advocate a return to law and order, symbolized best by the administrations of the Republican presidents Richard M. Nixon and Ronald W. Reagan.

★

Biographical information on Kirk can be found in *Current Biography* (1951); Lester A. Sobel, ed., *Facts on File Yearbook 1968*; and *Proceedings of the American Philosophical Society* (Dec. 1999). An obituary is in the *New York Times* (22 Nov. 1997).

MARY RIZZO

KISSINGER, Henry Alfred (*b*. 27 May 1923 in Fürth, Germany), diplomat, political scientist, and principal architect of American foreign policy at the end of the 1960s.

Kissinger, born Heinz Alfred Kissinger, was the first of two sons of Louis Kissinger, a teacher, and Paula Stern, a homemaker. He grew up in a predominantly Jewish community in southern Germany. In 1938 he fled Nazi persecution with his parents and younger brother, Walter, resettling in the Washington Heights neighborhood of Manhattan in New York City. He started college at City College of New York before being drafted and becoming a naturalized citizen in 1943. He spent five years in the army, including three years in occupied Germany, before returning to the United States to continue his studies. He attended Harvard University, earning a B.A. in 1950, an M.A. in 1952, and a Ph.D. in 1954, all in government. While at Harvard he married Anneliese Fleischer, on 6 February 1949 (divorced August 1964); they had two children. In 1974 he married Nancy Maginnes; they have no children.

His studies in government were preparation for a life in international affairs. He spent much of his time as a graduate student and postgraduate networking with important global officials. He edited the foreign affairs journal *Confluence* (1952–1958), worked for the Council on Foreign Relations (1952–1959), and published *Nuclear Weapons and Foreign Policy* (1957), a fourteen-week best-seller. Harvard employed him as a lecturer—a position that was considered a fast track to tenure—and as assistant director of the Center for International Affairs (CFIA), working under Robert Bowie.

Kissinger spent most of the 1960s as a foreign policy

theorist rather than a practitioner. He gained tenure at Harvard in 1959 as an assistant professor and was promoted to full professor in 1962. He was a popular teacher, though he taught only part-time. His classes were well attended as students gravitated to his charismatic teaching style. Kissinger continued his work for the CFIA as a secondary role at Harvard and ran the summer Harvard International Seminar (beginning in 1952) as well. He used these positions to network with politicians and policy makers as he angled for a larger role in government affairs. He also published his ideas, almost exclusively in *Foreign Affairs* magazine, hoping to bring his ideas for conducting foreign policy to the attention of those who made it.

While he was not a full-time official, Kissinger did serve as a foreign-affairs consultant in various capacities for most of the 1960s. In 1961 McGeorge Bundy hired Kissinger as a national-security consultant, based largely on his limited war/flexible response theory, outlined in his book *Necessity for Choice: Prospects of American Foreign Policy* (1961). The timing of the publication with President John F. Kennedy's election was not coincidental—some considered it a job application. Kissinger resigned a year later because he disagreed with the plan to create a multilateral force within the North Atlantic Treaty Organization. His disagreement became the subject of his next book, *The Troubled Partnership: A Reappraisal of the Atlantic Alliance* (1965). Other agencies he assisted include the Arms Control Disarmament Agency (1962–1967) and the Rand Corporation (1962–1968). Kissinger also consulted with New York's governor, Nelson Rockefeller, on foreign policy matters for his 1964 and 1968 presidential campaigns.

Kissinger got his chance to be a practitioner when Pres-

Henry Kissinger. CORBIS CORPORATION (BELLEVUE)

ident Richard Nixon hired him in 1969 as a national security assistant and executive secretary of the National Security Council, at the urging of Henry Cabot Lodge, the U.S. ambassador to South Vietnam. Although Kissinger and Nixon had met only once, they quickly developed a close and effective working relationship. Kissinger believed that foreign policy should be based on power, particularly a balance of power between select nations. He also understood that power, not personality or feelings, best directed foreign affairs.

Under Nixon and Kissinger, foreign policy came mostly from the National Security Office, circumventing the State Department and its bureaucracy. Freed from constraints, Kissinger devoted his office to changing America's overall approach to cold war diplomacy. Instead of competing against the Soviet Union and China, he sought ways to cooperate and ease tensions (détente). Some of his early successes with this approach were the opening of the Strategic Arms Limitation Talks (SALT) in 1969 and the first arms agreement with the Soviets, SALT I (1972). Détente also opened the door for Nixon's historic visit to China in 1972 and the normalizing of relations between the United States and China (an idea Kissinger first had proposed to Rockefeller during his 1968 campaign).

For all his successes, there was the Vietnam War. His first involvement had been when Lodge, who was then ambassador to Vietnam, invited Kissinger to visit in 1965. Kissinger believed in the overall effort, preventing the spread of Communism to other countries in Asia, but not in the tactics employed. He also understood that while the United States might not win the war, it could not withdraw but had to negotiate an end. He first proposed this idea in an article in *Look,* "What Should We Do Now" (9 August 1966), which became the basis of his diplomatic efforts in Vietnam. In June 1967 he arranged secret negotiations with North Vietnam (code name Pennsylvania) through a Paris acquaintance.

While these negotiations faltered, they provided the opportunity for Kissinger to conduct the secret Paris Peace Talks (1968–1972) to achieve Nixon's "peace with honor" campaign promise. He attempted to negotiate from a position of power, conducting secret bombings of North Vietnam, Cambodia, and Laos and secret invasions of Cambodia and Laos. The negotiations led to the Paris Peace Accords, signed 25 January 1973. The accords earned the 1973 Nobel Peace Prize for Kissinger and North Vietnam's negotiator Le Duc Tho, even though the peace they achieved proved tenuous.

Many of Kissinger's contemporaries were critical of his methods, even when praising the results. His power-based policies led some to feel that he was amoral and ignored developing countries and human rights issues. Nixon and

Kissinger angered the State Department and Congress by shifting policy making to the National Security Council, effectively removing policy from congressional oversight. Kissinger appeared to have difficulty with the nuances of America's open democratic system. Leslie Gelb, Kissinger's student at Harvard, wrote that Kissinger was "devious with peers, domineering with subordinates, obsequious to his superiors."

For all his critics, Kissinger was highly popular and an effective policy maker. A 1973 Gallup Poll listed him as the most admired man in America, likely a result of his wit and charm with the public and the press. In 1973 Nixon named Kissinger secretary of state, the first foreign-born person to hold the position. He held the office until 1977, when he returned to teaching and consulting. During the 1970s Kissinger left his imprint on American foreign policy with his efforts in the Middle East, Southeast Asia, the Soviet Union, and China, but it was during the 1960s that he refined and tested the theories that made him one of the most influential men in American foreign policy.

★

Kissinger recorded his official life in his memoirs, *White House Years* (1979) and *Years of Upheaval* (1982). Full-length biographies include David Landau, *Kissinger: The Uses of Power* (1972); Seymour Hersh, *The Price of Power: Kissinger in the Nixon White House* (1983); and Walter Isaacson, *Kissinger: A Biography* (1992). See also Michael Roskin, "Henry A. Kissinger and the Global Balance of Power," in Frank G. Merli and Theodore A. Wilson, eds., *Makers of American Diplomacy: From Benjamin Franklin to Henry Kissinger* (1974), for an in-depth look at Kissinger in the 1960s.

MICHAEL C. MILLER

KLEIN, Anne (*b.* 3 August 1921 or 1923 in New York City; *d.* 19 March 1974 in New York City), fashion designer whose well-tailored and interchangeable sportswear elevated that look as high style and complemented the status of the social change of women during the 1960s.

Klein was born Hannah Golofsky, one of three daughters of Morris, a businessman, and Esther Golofsky, a housewife. Klein was small-boned and petite (five feet, three inches), with a strong sense of style and sophistication. By the time she was fifteen, she was already selling freelance sketches to wholesale garment manufacturers. She studied fine arts and drawing at the Girls' Commercial High School in Brooklyn, New York, and at Traphagen School of Fashion.

Even as a teenager she never cared for garments that were then available for short, small-boned women. In later interviews, Klein described how such garments appeared too "cutesy" and often were "smothered in rhinestones and ruffles." She simply could not walk into a department store that sold expensive dresses and buy something that would fit her without elaborate and expensive alterations. Her subsequent career first revolutionized the garment industry with respect to petite women and then invented well-tailored and interchangeable sportswear for American women of all sizes.

The major influence on Klein was another petite designer, the legendary Parisian Coco Chanel. Chanel was the first designer to adapt the traditional garments of men (shirts, jackets, trousers, and suits) for women. From the 1920s through the 1940s, the American designer Claire McCardell employed Chanel's ideas in designs for taller, sophisticated Hollywood actresses, most notably Greta Garbo and Katharine Hepburn. Anne Klein adapted Chanel's ideas as well as the well-tailored construction and crisp silhouette of Parisian couture. She brought elegant sophistication to what came to be called "junior" size clothing.

Klein sketched and designed for various wholesale dress manufacturers through 1948. That year she was the head designer for Junior Sophisticates, owned by Ben Klein. They married in 1948 and had no children. She caused a revolution in stylizing the small, or junior-size, American woman with a wardrobe that became known as "sportswear." Until 1965 when she left the firm, Klein's designs for Junior Sophisticates created an unprecedentedly flexible wardrobe that provided comfort and style. Clients could wear blazers, trousers, and coordinated separates. Affordable everyday garments could be remixed for evening occasions without the runaway prices of haute couture. After divorcing Ben Klein in 1958, Klein married Matthew ("Chip") Rubenstein in 1963; they had no children. He persuaded her to open a freelance design studio. She did in 1965, and Anne Klein and Company continued her mix-and-match sportswear for women of all sizes. Her collections combined her designs for various manufacturers, and then those garments were sold in over 3,500 stores nationwide.

The first Anne Klein and Company collection became a stunning success, and the company was immediately launched to critical praise and with high profits. For this 1965 fall collection she combined unexpected pairings of cloth fabrics with leather and suede garments for Mallory, a woman's wear manufacturer. Silk culottes were matched with suede blazers dyed in shockingly bright colors. Waists were low and often belted, and skirts were pleated or slightly flared. "We're looking for a truly American look," she explained to the store buyers. "I'm getting sort of fed up with the American look coming from abroad." American West skirt silhouettes were transformed into full-length

suede coats. Levi designs were changed into leather pants dyed in bright yellows, pinks, and greens. A soft white crepe shirt was matched with bell-bottom suede pants laced up the back. Always interested in the complete look, Klein also designed the shoes made by Palizzio.

Klein was also an inventor, and she patented innovative garments. For her spring 1965 collection, she showed the "raincape," manufactured by Dolphin Rainwear. This tent-like garment covered the body from the top of the head to the knee. For the 1966 collection, she devised a special girdle to be worn under Mary Quaint's miniskirts. That year she also invented snaps for doll clothes and children's wear. With various assistants (especially Donna Karan, who became a designer in her own right), Anne Klein and Company wholesaled complete looks, from shoes to dresses to coats to accessories for women. Among Klein's retail clients from 1966 through 1969 were firms that wanted her crisp sportswear look to revitalize tired and out-of-date wardrobe lines. Charles Revson had her firm refreshen his Evan Picone and Dynasty collections. Similarly, Klein's company updated Pierre Cardin coats.

In 1966 the company began redesigning various projects beyond fashion. Prompted by her husband's interest in shopping bags and boxes, her firm devised a new shirt box with exterior floral patterns and filled with variously colored and patterned tissue paper. The new design allowed shirt patterns to stand out. Fieldcrest asked Klein in 1966 to redesign towels. Elaborate towel borders were moved so that when towels were displayed on a store rack the design could be seen. By 1968 her company was redesigning automobile and airplane interiors.

Klein was also continuously involved with the fashion world. For the 1966 through 1969 seasons, her fall collections combined garments in suede and leather for Mallory with that company's knitwear. Over these garments, Modelia coats were shown. In 1967 she designed a gray thigh-length suede tunic to be worn over tight brown leather pants. Klein called the pants "Little Johns." That year she also showed knee socks with short leather pantsuits and side-wrapped leather skirts with a high-rising midriff and a calf-length hem. From 1966 through the early 1970s Anne Klein and Company designed the Danskin line of tights and tops for women and children. In 1968 the firm branched out to design menswear for Hadley, including day to evening sweaters and straight-leg and bell-bottom trousers and knickers. That year Klein told a reporter that the firm's goal was to provide clothing that was simple and chic as well as diverse yet matchable.

Klein's sportswear—fashion in parts—mixed and matched garments for day or night while remaining simplified with expert tailoring. From Mallory leathers to Gant knitwear to Blousecraft garments, Anne Klein and Company created during the 1960s a flexible wardrobe at affordable prices. With four other American designers in 1973, the sportswear look was seen in Paris and created a style revolution in Europe.

Klein won the prestigious Coty Fashion Award in 1955 and 1971, and she was elected to the Coty Fashion Hall of Fame in 1971. After Klein's death from cancer in 1974, Anne Klein and Company continued her legacy: to create for the no-nonsense American woman perfected designs in sportswear that combined evening wear chic with day wear comfort. Her mix-and-match concept became a fixture during the 1960s for women of all sizes. "I've tried to clothe a woman so life is a little freer for her," she said in 1968, "so her clothes can be an enjoyment, not a drag." Klein's garments complemented the social revolution of 1960s American women, whose diversified lives were clothed in a sophisticated yet practical comfort and style.

★

There is no biography of Klein. The Fashion Institute of Technology's exhibition catalogue *50 Years of American Women in Fashion* (1981) includes her designs. Also see Caroline R. Milbank, *New York Fashion: The Evolution of American Style* (1989). An obituary is in the *New York Times* (20 Mar. 1974).

PATRICK S. SMITH

KLEIN, Calvin (*b.* 19 November 1942 in New York City), legendary fashion designer who, in the later 1960s, pioneered casual chic in sportswear with high-quality natural fibers, slim silhouettes, and neutral or earthen colors.

Klein was the second of three children of Leo, a grocer, and Flo (Stern) Klein, a supermarket cashier. The family lived along the Mosholu Parkway section of the Bronx in New York City, a neighborhood populated by garment workers or proprietors of small local shops. His maternal grandmother, Molly Stern, was a seamstress for the dress designer Hattie Carnegie, and his mother was a fashion-conscious clotheshorse who often took her son to a local Loehmann's, where she bought designer labels at discount prices. At Loehmann's, Klein would closely examine the garments to see how they were constructed. From early childhood he sketched, often comic-book characters or women in fancy gowns. For one early birthday, his grandmother Molly gave Klein a sewing machine, and he designed and sewed an entire wardrobe for the dolls of his younger sister and her friends.

From kindergarten through ninth grade, Klein attended Public School 80, where he excelled in art and always carried a sketchbook. His mother always made sure that the young Klein was impeccably groomed and dressed. He was the neighborhood trendsetter, even in kindergarten, where he wore light-colored shirts with a bow tie. By age twelve

he was taking life drawing and sketching lessons on weekends at the Art Students League in Manhattan.

Klein then attended the High School of Industrial Arts in Manhattan. It specialized in various trades, and Klein majored in fashion illustration. Among his classmates there were the fashion illustrator Antonio and the poet-photographer Gerard Malanga. After graduating in 1960 Klein took a summer job at a Bronx amusement park and then entered the Fashion Institute of Technology (FIT). After studying for one year at FIT, Klein was discouraged with his talents and became a copyboy in the art department of *Women's Wear Daily,* the bible of the fashion industry. For six months he tried to become an illustrator for the publication, but no one there was interested in his sketches. He did learn, though, about fashion as an industry.

Klein reentered FIT, where his acquired tastes for his later career were formed. His passion for expensive fabrics tended toward natural yarns of cotton and silk. "I hate polyester!" he would often tell later interviewers. Also, his preference for assignments emphasized his later trademark muted shades of browns and beiges. After his graduation from FIT in 1962 and several odd jobs in New York City's fashion district, Klein became a sketcher and then a design apprentice for Dan Millstein, whose plush showroom building is now occupied by Calvin Klein, Inc. He learned the nuts and bolts of manufacturing garments, including quality control and rapport with buyers. Millstein introduced Klein to haute couture by taking him to Europe to view the Paris collections. In 1964 Klein married Jayne Center, and they had a daughter (who was briefly kidnapped for ransom in 1978).

In 1965 Klein began work at Louis Shlansky's Halldon Ltd., a fake-fur coat manufacturer. Klein designed moderately priced coats in tweeds, gabardine, and wool twills. Klein's design room was right off Shlansky's showroom, and he was introduced to all the merchandise buyers. Klein's work began appearing in industrial publications, including the influential *Tobe Report,* which in 1967 noted that Klein was "one of the more aggressive and imaginative young coat and suit designers." That year Klein began to formulate samples for his own line of women's garments. Klein has always been primarily an idea man. Until then, he had little actual practice in constructing and tailoring clothes, but he learned the tricks of those trades over weekends for several months from Shansky's pattern maker, Abe Morenstein. Also that year he was offered a position with the sportswear firm of Bobbie Brooks.

Klein was advised against the move by Barry Schwartz. Schwartz and Klein had been inseparable best friends since they were five years old and dreamed of getting rich together. While Klein attended FIT, Schwartz studied business at New York University and then worked in his family's supermarket business. In 1968 Schwartz persuaded Klein to become partners with him in what was initially called Calvin Klein Ltd. The company operated first out of a small suite of a Seventh Avenue hotel and then bought out Millstein and moved into his building at 205 West Thirty-ninth Street.

During the late 1960s American fashion *as fashion* was at a low ebb. The fads then were dressing down, hippie style, or the "mod" look of miniskirt and plastic boots. Klein wanted a classic look in which garments would have muted pastel shades and crisp, precise lines and silhouettes. In 1969, while still located at his hotel suite, Klein had few orders. By sheer luck, the vice president of the chic department store Bonwit Teller, Donald O'Brien, happened to see a rack of Klein's garments near the hotel's elevator. That chance occurrence led Klein to show his garments to Mildred Custin, the president of Bonwit. That encounter became legendary in fashion history. Not only did she offer Klein his first substantial order of $50,000 retail, but she also agreed to give him $10 more per garment if they were of the same high quality as the samples. Custin wanted his clothes exclusively, but Klein was able to convince her that other stores also were interested. Shortly after Bonwit's order, a scout for the buying service William Van Buren and a buyer for the chic Washington, D.C., chain Garfinckel's also placed orders. Klein's career was launched.

By the end of Klein's first year in business, his shipping orders exceeded a million dollars. Until 1972 he designed two-piece suits and coats; that year he began sportswear that translated Parisian couture into trimmer proportions more appropriate for American women. He began licensing deals in 1974. That year he and his wife divorced. He married Kelly Rector on 26 September 1986. In 1978 Klein began his menswear collections. Since the late 1960s Klein's garments have pioneered casual chic at a time when American high fashion was in a slump brought about by younger women wearing informal clothes. His clothes, first for women and then for men, became known for high-quality natural fibers, elegant and trim lines, and subdued earth tones or neutral colors. "I design for the new look," Klein once commented, "but with an everlasting feeling."

★

A biography of Klein is Steven Gaines and Sharon Churcher, *Obsession: The Lives and Times of Calvin Klein* (1994). See also John Fairchild, *Chic Savages* (1989), and Barbaralee Diamonstein, *Fashion: The Inside Story* (1985).

PATRICK S. SMITH

KOHL, Herbert R. (*b.* 22 August 1937 in New York City), progressive educator, author, and social activist who, beginning in the 1960s, promoted reform of teaching methods and school systems to encourage all children, regardless of their race or social environment.

Kohl, the only child of Samuel Kohl, a building contractor, and Marion (Jacobs) Kohl, a homemaker, was brought up in a two-family house shared with his Yiddish-speaking paternal grandparents. He graduated from the Bronx High School of Science in 1954, where he had been president of the Student Organization and the New York City Inter-City GO (General Organization) Council. While still in high school, Kohl tutored a teacher's son and participated in a public forum on school reform. At Harvard he majored in philosophy and mathematics, graduating in 1958 Phi Beta Kappa and magna cum laude. He then studied at University College, Oxford, from 1958 to 1959 as a Henry fellow, and at Columbia University Teachers College as a Woodrow Wilson fellow, earning an M.A. in 1962, with further graduate work in 1965 and 1966. In 1963 he married Judith Murdock, a weaver, teacher, and writer; they had three children.

After substitute teaching in two public elementary schools from 1961 to 1962, Kohl embarked on his full-time teaching career when he was assigned in September 1963 to Public School 103 in East Harlem, New York. His book *36 Children* (1967) is his record of how he and the African-American children in his sixth-grade class mutually struggled to teach, learn, and survive in that first year. The book reveals Kohl's immersion in the systemic obstacles that hinder effective learning, particularly for "ghetto kids." Although many of Kohl's actions and ways of earning trust,

Herbert Kohl. MR. JERRY BAUER

including involvement with families and the community, met with bureaucratic criticism, *36 Children*, with its many samples of student writing and art, gained him praise as an innovative educator. The following year (1963), Kohl observed, "The need to shape learning on the basis of the complex interaction of academic content and current social reality was forced on me . . . as I voyaged with my students through school boycotts, freedom schools, protest demonstrations, and the assassination of a president."

Although perceived as threatening to entrenched authority and traditional methods, Kohl's book *The Open Classroom: A Practical Guide to a New Way of Teaching* (1969) also gained national recognition. In it he guides and supports teachers to develop an open environment and "workable alternatives to authoritarian power." The book is written in Kohl's conversational and pragmatic style, which includes his own misgivings and errors. During this same period, from 1962 to 1968, Kohl set up a storefront learning center in East Harlem, worked as a research assistant at Horace Mann–Lincoln Institute, and helped reorganize a Manhattan high school. In 1966 and 1967, as cofounder and director of the Teachers and Writers Collaborative in New York City, he proposed strategies for teaching writing so that teachers and students alike would become more open to learning. In 1968 Kohl began writing a column for *Teacher* magazine and won a National Endowment for the Arts grant for his essay "Teaching the Unteachable," which was published first in the *New York Review of Books* and later as a book.

Kohl moved to Berkeley, California, in 1968, and acted as visiting assistant professor of English education at the University of California, as a kindergarten teacher, and a consultant on curriculum and alternative schools. With support from the Carnegie Corporation, Kohl served as teacher and director from 1969 to 1972 at Other Ways, an alternative public high school. It failed because, in Kohl's words, "the adults were not able to live their ideas." The desire to develop children's abilities in the face of complex and adverse social conditions has been Kohl's lifelong struggle, not just an issue of the 1960s. To this end, in 1972 he established the Center for Open Learning and Teaching, a multicultural center that prepares candidates to become California teachers. Teaching from kindergarten to graduate school, participating in seminars, establishing workshops, giving speeches across the country from New York to Alaska, and writing, Kohl continued to be involved in issues of social justice, writing, theater, and poetry as essential to children's lives.

In the late 1960s Kohl and his wife met Myles Horton, founder of the Highlander Folk School in Monteagle, Tennessee, a school for adults that first focused on trade unions, then civil rights. The Kohls assisted Horton with his autobiography, *The Long Haul* (1970), which won the Robert

F. Kennedy Book Award. The Kohls also collaborated on *View from the Oak,* a book about ethology (the study of animal behavior, especially animal perception), which won the 1977 National Book Award for children's literature. Kohl's other publications from the 1970s and 1980s include *Reading: How To—A People's Guide to Alternative Ways of Teaching and Testing Reading* (1973), *Growing with Your Children* (1978), and *Growing Minds: On Becoming a Teacher* (1984). In 1984 the family lived in London, where Kohl was director of software development for *Scientific Magazine*. He became program director of the Fund for New York City Public Education under an Erin Diamond grant (1992–1996), and following that (1997–1999) he was senior fellow at the Open Society Institute in New York City, part of the Soros Foundation Network.

Having learned at the beginning of his teaching career in the 1960s that "survival is always an issue for an innovator," Kohl believes in Martin Luther King, Jr.'s idea of maladjustment. He discusses this concept, as well as "not-learning" and "hope-mongering," in the five essays of *"I Won't Learn from You": And Other Thoughts of Creative Maladjustment* (1994). *The Discipline of Hope: Learning from a Lifetime of Teaching* (1998) also combines Kohl's personal experience and theories to inspire teachers to provide "schools of hope . . . places where children are honored and well served." Since 1977 Kohl's activities have been based at the Coastal Ridge Research and Education Center in Point Arena, California, an 11.5-acre site on which Kohl and his wife also live. This learning, research, and retreat center also serves as a progressive education think tank. Kohl also directs the Center for Teaching Excellence and Social Justice of the University of San Francisco's School of Education, an advanced teacher preparation program dedicated to training "progressive reform-minded teachers" for America's inner cities.

Innovative educator, champion of social justice, and prolific author, Kohl has extended the community-based educational and civil rights issues of the 1960s throughout his life. Stressing the inherent learning ability and dignity of every child, he has sought to change educational and social systems to eliminate racism and a sense of failure, encouraging instead trust and hope for both young people and teachers. Having taught at all levels and in urban ghettos, Kohl has applied his experience to the development of open classrooms, teacher training programs, writing and theater projects, and just policies. His philosophy, methods, and writing share the joy and struggle of teaching.

★

In *Thirty-Six Children* (1967), Kohl conveys his emotional and professional growth as a beginning teacher along with that of his thirty-six sixth graders in East Harlem. The preface and five essays in *"I Won't Learn from You": And Other Thoughts on Creative*

Maladjustment (1994) integrate material on Kohl's childhood and adolescence in the Bronx with his philosophy of teaching. *The Discipline of Hope* (1998) also includes observations on Kohl's personal and family life and teaching experience in support of his axiom of the necessity of hope in education. *Current Biography 1965–1968* lists dates, publications, and discussion of some of Kohl's books.

RACHEL SHOR

KOHLER, Foy David (*b.* 15 February 1908 in Oakwood, Ohio; *d.* 23 December 1990 in Jupiter, Florida), diplomat and U.S. ambassador to Moscow during the 1962 Cuban Missile Crisis.

The son of Leander David Kohler and Myrtle McClure, Kohler grew up in Ohio and attended the University of Toledo from 1924 to 1927. During this time, he worked as a bank teller and then transferred to Ohio State University, where he earned his B.S. degree in 1931. Kohler married Phyllis Penn on 7 August 1935; they had no children. Kohler spent the bulk of his career, from 1931 to 1967, as a foreign service officer under the U.S. Department of State, with initial postings in Windsor, Ontario (1932 to 1933); Bucharest (1933–1935); Belgrade (1935); Athens (1936–1941); and Cairo (1941). Kohler served in Washington, D.C., as country specialist (1941–1944) and assistant chief of the Division for Near Eastern Affairs (1944 to 1945), and then underwent graduate study at the National War College (1946) and at Cornell University, where he learned to speak Russian.

Kohler's first posting to the Soviet Union, and his first direct experience of cold war politics, came when the state department sent him to Moscow. There he served as first secretary and counselor, from 1947 to 1948, and as minister plenipotentiary, from 1948 to 1949, at the U.S. embassy. Kohler also worked as director of *Voice of America* broadcasts (1949–1952); member of a state department policy planning staff (1952 to 1953); counselor with the U.S. embassy in Ankara, Turkey (1953–1956); an observer with the International Cooperation Administration (1956–1958); and deputy assistant secretary of state for European affairs (1958 to 1959).

The high point of Kohler's career began with his appointment as assistant secretary of state for European affairs in 1959. While serving in this capacity, he was present in Moscow with Vice President Richard M. Nixon when the latter engaged in the famous "kitchen debate" with the Soviet leader Nikita S. Khrushchev. The occasion was the U.S. Trade and Cultural Fair in Moscow's Sokolniki Park, and Nixon and Khrushchev were viewing a model American kitchen when an angry exchange began. Khrushchev

claimed that the Soviets would surpass the United States technologically, to which Nixon replied, "You don't know everything." The comment was not particularly inspired, but much of what followed, as Nixon and Khrushchev argued over the relative merits of capitalism and Communism, showed the future president's debating skills to advantage. One of the items on display happened to be the first video recorder, manufactured by a company called Ampex, which captured the debate on film. Aired on U.S. television, the debate added greatly to Nixon's prestige among Americans.

Kohler himself later remembered Khrushchev with admiration. "You couldn't help but like him just as an individual," he once said. "He was a shrewd peasant, and he loved to trade repartee. He had a quick wit." Though personally impressed with the Soviet leader, Kohler was no less anticommunist than Nixon and remained under no illusions as to Khrushchev's ideological beliefs. "It's true," he noted, "that Khrushchev—especially with his de-Stalinization speech—shook up the society and greatly eased the terror that prevailed under Stalin. On the other hand, Khrushchev was a true believer in Bolshevism."

His knowledge of Khrushchev's character would stand Kohler in good stead when, in 1962, President John F. Kennedy appointed him U.S. ambassador to the Soviet Union. The challenges of the job did not take long to make themselves known. In October 1962 Khrushchev's regime began building missile sites in Cuba, precipitating the greatest crisis of the cold war. Throughout the tense days of the Cuban Missile Crisis, Kohler served as an intermediary in negotiations, and the Kennedy administration relied on his insights regarding his hosts.

For example, on 16 October, at the height of the crisis, Kohler met with Khrushchev, who conveyed his anger at the strident U.S. response to "defensive" Soviet activity in Cuba. In this way, Kohler served as a listener for his own government and as both a sounding board and whipping boy for Khrushchev, who no doubt diffused his fury somewhat by having the opportunity to harangue a U.S. official. The Soviet leader's anger was perhaps in part a reaction to fear, since he rightly recognized that the two superpowers were on the brink of World War III. Later, on 7 November, after the crisis had passed, Kohler sent a cable to Washington reporting that "there seems to me no doubt that events of [the] past ten days have really shaken [the] Soviet leadership." One Soviet military official, he reported, "told my wife he was now willing to believe in God."

The remainder of Kohler's four years in Moscow was, in comparison to the two weeks of the Cuban Missile Crisis, uneventful. In large part because of the crisis, the Soviet leadership replaced Khrushchev with Leonid I. Brezhnev, who had little interest in engaging in repartee with the U.S. ambassador. At the same time, Brezhnev was less of a hot-

Foy Kohler *(left)*, meeting with President John F. Kennedy in February 1963. © BETTMANN/CORBIS

head than Khrushchev and by the late 1960s began sending indications that he was prepared to engage in relatively peaceful, if unfriendly, coexistence with the United States.

Kohler returned to the United States in 1966 and briefly served as deputy undersecretary of state for political affairs before retiring in 1967 with the rank of career ambassador. In 1968 he became a professor of international studies at the University of Miami's Center for Advanced International Studies. During the eleven years that followed, he published almost a dozen books, beginning with *Understanding the Russians: A Citizen's Primer* (1970). He retired from the University of Miami in 1979 and died of heart ailments following a long illness.

With his posting to Moscow, Kohler found himself in the thick of the cold war, both as a battle of words and potentially as a battle of weapons. True to his gift as a diplomat, he remained unobtrusive, and his greatest accomplishments undoubtedly went unpublished, perhaps even in government records. It is testament enough to Kohler's success, however, that he served in one of the most difficult positions the U.S. Department of State had to offer and at one of the greatest times of international crisis that the United States has ever faced.

★

Kohler's dispatches from Moscow are part of the Avalon Project at Yale Law School in New Haven, Connecticut. Some biographical details can be obtained from the record of hearings in Congress, conducted between 27 September and 4 October 1966, on the nomination of Kohler and others to various posts in the U.S. State Department. Kohler was also the subject of a documentary, *Our Man in Moscow,* made by WTOL-TV in Toledo in

1964. Obituaries are in the *New York Times, Washington Post, Los Angeles Times, Chicago Tribune,* and *USA Today* (all 26 Dec. 1990).

JUDSON KNIGHT

KOONTZ, Elizabeth Duncan ("Libby") (*b.* 3 June 1919 in Salisbury, North Carolina; *d.* 6 January 1989 in Salisbury, North Carolina), educator and first African-American president of the National Education Association.

Koontz was the youngest of Lena Bell (Jordan) Duncan and Samuel E. Duncan's seven children. Samuel Duncan was principal of Dunbar High School in East Spencer and also taught at Livingstone College. He died when Koontz was nine, leaving the large family in the hands of Lena Duncan, a teacher at Dunbar Elementary School. Already able to read and write, Koontz began elementary school at the age of four. As an elementary school student, Koontz excelled, even helping to check the lessons of illiterate adults whom her mother was teaching to read. Koontz graduated as class salutatorian from Salisbury's segregated Price High School (1935), then graduated with honors from Livingstone College, with a B.A. in English and elementary education (1938). She received her master's degree from Atlanta University in 1941. In 1947 she married Harry Koontz, a math instructor. They had no children.

"Teaching is the mother profession," Koontz said in a 1969 speech before the American Association of Colleges for Teacher Education. "Without teaching," she continued, "there would be no other professions." For thirty years Koontz dedicated herself to the profession, teaching in the following North Carolina schools: Harnett County Training School (1938–1940); Aggrey Memorial School, Landis (1940–1941); Fourteenth Street School, Winston-Salem (1941–1945); Price High School, Salisbury (1949–1965); and Price Junior-Senior High School, Salisbury (1965–1968).

Koontz became actively involved in local and state teachers' organizations for African Americans and in the North Carolina Teachers Association. From 1959 to 1963 she served as president of the North Carolina Association of Classroom Teachers (NCACT). Under her leadership NCACT boasted many accomplishments, including the publication of its first edition of *Guidelines for Local Associations of Classroom Teachers* (1961) and the passage of a resolution against segregated accommodations at the southeast regional meetings of the National Education Association's (NEA) Department of Classroom Teachers (DCT).

In 1960 Koontz was elected secretary of the NEA-DCT (becoming the first African American to serve in the office). After two years as secretary, followed by one year as vice president and one as president-elect, Koontz became the association's president. During her tenure as president (1965–1966), NEA-DCT represented 825,000 teachers nationwide. In 1962 the North Carolina governor, Terry Stanford, named Koontz to the Commission on the Status of Women. In 1964 Koontz was one of sixteen Americans selected to visit the Soviet Union to discuss ways to improve binational relations. In 1965 Koontz was appointed by President Lyndon B. Johnson to the National Advisory Council on the Education of Disadvantaged Children.

Koontz's professional affiliations included life membership in the NEA, the NEA Council for Exceptional Children, the North Carolina Association of Educators, Phi Beta Kappa, the North Carolina Council on Human Relations, the National Academy of Public Administration, the National Black Child Development Institute, the North Carolina Negro Teachers Association (later "Negro" was dropped), the Women's Equity Action League, the National Commission on Working Women, and the National Organization of Women. She served on *Education Digest*'s editorial board and on the Sex Information and Education Council's board of directors.

In Dallas, Texas, on 6 July 1968, Koontz became the first African-American president of the NEA. In her inaugural speech, "A Time for Educational Statesmanship," Koontz proclaimed, "The education profession has a date with reality, and I intend to see that we keep it." This reality included giving teachers certain benefits and freedoms, including the "time and freedom to practice this same democracy they teach." During her tenure as NEA president, Koontz unceasingly spoke out against teachers' oppression in the educational system. She also rallied to ease racial tensions in schools, worked to bring curricula up to date,

and sought to increase school financing and teachers' salaries.

After a commanding year of leadership, Koontz resigned from the NEA to accept President Richard M. Nixon's request that she head the Women's Bureau of the United States Department of Labor. She was the bureau's first black director. In this position Koontz became a major force in the women's rights movement, especially for minority women. She fought for equal access to positions in all fields, higher salaries for women, and improved working conditions for domestic workers (a field that had been occupied traditionally by minority women). As director of the U.S. Department of Labor's Women's Bureau, and throughout her career, Koontz insisted that education was the key for both women and men in acquiring meaningful, productive employment. Koontz was rewarded with honorary degrees from approximately three dozen American colleges and universities, including an honorary doctor of humane letters from her alma mater, Livingstone College, in May 1967. In that same year, 18 April was officially designated "Libby Koontz Day" in Salisbury, North Carolina. She received honorary memberships from the American Home Economics Association, the Zeta Phi Beta Society, and the Altrusa Club. In 1968 the Association for the Study of Negro Life and History bequeathed Koontz its highest honor, the Distinguished Service Award. In 1969 Koontz received, at the NEA's Human Rights Awards Dinner, the H. Council Trenholm Memorial Award.

Beyond the 1960s Koontz received many more honors, including being one of five women honored by the American Newspapers Women's Club for distinguished service in international affairs (1975). The award was presented by President Gerald Ford. She also accepted a number of other appointments in the field of women's advocacy, such as her 1978 appointment by President Jimmy Carter to the National Advisory Committee for Women. Her last professional position, from which she retired in 1982, was as assistant superintendent for the Department of Public Instruction.

Koontz died of a heart attack and was buried at Union Hill Cemetery in her hometown of Salisbury. Koontz is remembered as a humanitarian and an advocate for youth, minorities, women, and teachers. "We were taught as early as I can recall to share and to help each other," Koontz, in 1968, recalled of her family life. This tradition was well instilled in Koontz, who dedicated her life to helping others.

★

Information about Koontz can be found in *Current Biography Yearbook* (1969 and 1989) and Percy E. Murray, "Elizabeth Duncan Koontz," in *Black Women in America: An Historical Encyclopedia*. An obituary is in the *Washington Post* (7 Jan. 1989).

CANDICE MANCINI-KNIGHT

KOSINSKI, Jerzy Nikodem (*b.* 14 June 1933 in Lodz, Poland; *d.* 3 May 1991 in New York City), writer, celebrity intellectual, and international spokesperson whose autobiographical novels in the 1960s created controversy and broke ground in style and lurid contents.

Kosinski's life presents two sagas: the building of a legend, climaxing in the 1960s, and the collapse of the legend during the 1980s. Kosinski spread exaggerated stories about his past and insisted on the truth of many fictional events in his books, which earlier sources accepted uncritically and which still contribute to confusion about his life. His parents, Moses (Mojzesz) and Elzbieta (Liniecka) Lewinkopf, were well off, resourceful and cultured—though Elzbieta was an amateur musician, not a concert pianist as her son maintained, and Moses was a manager skilled in languages but not a professor of linguistics. The Lewinkopfs, secularized Jews, recognized the Nazi threat to their native Poland, and in late 1939 they acquired papers changing their last name to Kosinski and the father's first name to Mieczyslaw. Kosinski was their only biological child.

Unlike the protagonist in his novel *The Painted Bird,* Kosinski was not separated from his family during World War II; he did hide out in rural poverty, socially isolated from others who might see that he was circumcised or otherwise guess his true background. The family adopted an infant named Henryk in 1942. In July 1944 the Red Army captured Dabrowa, the Polish town where the Kosinskis had settled, and Kosinski was befriended by two Soviet soldiers. In 1947 the family returned to Lodz, where Kosinski attended high school. He then did some award-winning work in photography with Jerzy Neugebauer. Kosinski attended the University of Lodz from 1950 to 1955, receiving M.A. degrees in history and political science.

Kosinski went to New York City in December 1957, knowing little English but much about influencing people and succeeding in bureaucracies. Through a Ford Foundation Fellowship, he studied at Columbia University (1958–1964) and at the New School for Social Research (1962–1965) for a graduate degree in sociology. During those years three of Kosinski's nonfiction books were published. He also edited and translated a volume of American writings in sociology, intended as a textbook for Polish graduate students. Doubleday published two interview-based studies of Soviet culture, *The Future Is Ours, Comrade* (1960) and *No Third Path* (1962). The former was very well received. The books were highly informed and sympathetic to the Soviet people, yet highly critical of the system— perfect for a cold war American audience. Kosinski, who wrote these two books under the pen name Joseph Novak, offered different explanations for the pseudonym; years later, research revealed that for both books Kosinski employed writing assistance that amounted to translation.

Paradoxically, this self-defined outsider yearned for acceptance by the wealthy and well known, and he worked assiduously to charm them and promote himself. In 1960 he met Mary Hayward Weir, an art collector and the wealthy widow of a steel company chief executive officer; she was in her mid-forties, while he was eighteen years younger. They married on 11 January 1962. Despite Kosinski's flagrant infidelities and her alcoholism, they remained married until 1966 and were friends until her death in 1968. With her, Kosinski traveled through the United States and around the globe, making literary and social contacts.

No Third Path did not succeed as Kosinski had hoped, and he turned to fiction. As early as 1958 Kosinski told altered stories of his childhood. In 1963 he began notes for a novel, augmenting his memories with research in books about folklife and historical context. He also engaged several editors/translators to help with his English. In 1964 the Kosinskis attended a dinner with Dorothy de Santillana, a senior editor at Houghton Mifflin; she was intrigued by Kosinski's stories and was offered a manuscript, which she assumed was a memoir. During the publishing process Kosinski backtracked, and *The Painted Bird* was published in 1965 as autobiographical fiction. That same year, Kosinski became an American citizen.

No matter what its genesis, *The Painted Bird* stands as a literary accomplishment, simple in style and bold in its depiction of sex and violence. Because of horrific events the young protagonist undergoes, some critics found the novel anti-Polish. Actually, it represented Kosinski's view of all humanity, and in later editions the sole reference to Poland is changed to "Eastern Europe." Despite controversy, the book won the Prix du Meilleur Livre Etranger in 1966 and landed Kosinski a Guggenheim Fellowship for 1967–1968.

Steps, Kosinski's second novel, solidified his reputation. Published in 1968, it won the National Book Award in 1969. *Steps* further melds autobiography, self-made legend, and total fiction in its loose, anecdotal tale of seemingly random events in the life of a young man who emigrates from the Soviet Union to the United States. Its sex and violence were even more extreme, but by then the culture had caught up to Kosinski, and taboo-breaking had become laudable, even fashionable. The decade ended with Kosinski on the rise, his work acknowledged and his presence familiar from Park Avenue dinner parties to television's *Tonight Show.* Wesleyan and Princeton Universities gave Kosinski his first academic appointments. On one dark note, Kosinski had been invited to the home of Sharon Tate and Roman Polanski, but did not show up, on the night of 9 August 1969, when all five people in the house were killed by Charles Manson's gang of followers.

Kosinski's reputation would climax with his third novel, *Being There,* published in 1971, which was the basis of a movie starring Peter Sellers in 1979. Kosinski served an important term as president of PEN, a highly prestigious and influential writers' organization, from 1973 to 1975. Later novels, such as *The Devil Tree* (1973), *Blind Date* (1977), and *Passion Play* (1979), were successful, but critics found the style less revolutionary and were suspicious of the increasing occupation with the rich and famous. In the 1980s writings by Jerome Klinkowitz, Geoffrey Stokes, and Eliot Fremont-Smith of the *Village Voice,* and others began to undo the Kosinski legend, adding charges of possible Central Intelligence Agency involvement. Despite signs of overcoming the ordeal—Kosinski married Katherina von Fraunhofer on 15 February 1987 and was becoming increasingly at home in Hollywood—Kosinski killed himself in his New York apartment, using alcohol, barbiturates, and suffocation by a plastic bag.

As the indignation among biographers and critics cools, readers are left with Kosinski's undeniable accomplishments. His position as an intellectual Polish émigré lent him authority during the cold war. His novel *The Painted Bird* became a favorite among counterculture college students. Kosinski, the eternal outsider who traveled everywhere, provides a potpourri of 1960s culture in his life and fiction. Equally at home with sex club denizens and *New York Times* editors, international intellectuals and movie stars, Kosinski lived and recorded many of the joys and terrors of World War II, the cold war, and the counterculture revolution.

★

All studies written before 1982, and many after, are helpful but must be read in light of later research. The best-documented and most balanced source is James Park Sloan, *Jerzy Kosinski: A Biography* (1996). Works of partial utility, including literary critical insight, include Jack Hicks, *In the Singer's Temple: The Romance and Terror of Jerzy Kosinski* (1981), and Norman Lavers, *Jerzy Kosinski* (1982). Barbara Tepa Lupack, ed., *Critical Essays on Jerzy Kosinski* (1998), offers an invaluable collection of reviews and essays.

BERNADETTE LYNN BOSKY

KOUFAX, Sanford ("Sandy") (*b.* 30 December 1935 in New York City), professional baseball player who was the dominant pitcher of the early 1960s until forced into early retirement by illness in 1966.

Born Sanford Braun, Koufax is the son of Jack Koufax, a salesman, and Evelyn Braun, an accountant, who were divorced when Sandy was three. His mother remarried when he was nine, and Sandy was adopted by his stepfather, Irving Koufax, a lawyer. Sandy attended Lafayette High School in Brooklyn where he was voted Boy Athlete of the

Sandy Koufax. CORBIS CORPORATION (BELLEVUE)

Year his senior year, starring in baseball and basketball. He attended the University of Cincinnati on a basketball scholarship, but was persuaded to try out for the baseball team. He was 3–1 as a pitcher for the university, with fifty-one strikeouts and thirty walks in thirty-one innings.

Koufax's pitching speed and strikeout totals attracted interest from a number of major league teams, and in December 1954 he signed a contract with the Brooklyn Dodgers for a $14,000 bonus, which made him a "bonus baby." This designation required the team to include him on their major league roster immediately and to keep him there for the next two years. This retarded Koufax's development since he would have minimal playing time. In 1955, as a nineteen-year-old rookie, he won two games and lost two, but his wins included a shutout and the other was also well pitched. Koufax's control was erratic and he had not really learned to pitch. His skills slowly developed, and by 1958, in the Dodgers first year in Los Angeles, he went 11–11 and was a regular starter for the team.

In 1959 the Dodgers unexpectedly won the pennant, defeating the Milwaukee Braves in a playoff and going on to defeat the Chicago White Sox in the World Series, four games to two. Koufax was only 8–6 with 2 saves but struck out 173 batters in only 153 innings, 18 in a single game, which tied the major league record. In the World Series, he gave up only one run in game five, but lost 1–0. The next year the Dodgers and Koufax both struggled, as they finished in fourth, and he went 8–13.

In 1961 the Dodgers were in the pennant race all year before fading in August and finishing second. Koufax finally became the pitcher that many had predicted he could be. He won 18 games, stuck out a National League (NL) record 269 batters, and pitched 256 innings. The next season (1962) the Dodgers seemed to have the pennant in hand before Koufax was sidelined with a blood clot in his pitching hand. He did end the season 14–7, again striking out eighteen in one game and throwing a no-hitter, but the Dodgers lost the pennant in a playoff with the San Francisco Giants.

From 1963, until Koufax was forced into early retirement after the 1966 season, he was the unquestioned top pitcher in baseball. The Dodgers won pennants in three of those four years. Koufax started this run with a 25–5 record in 1963, hurling his second no-hitter and striking out 306 batters to break his NL mark. He had eleven shutouts (a major league record for a lefthander) and an earned run average of 1.88. He capped the season by winning two games in the World Series as the Dodgers swept the New York Yankees in four games. Koufax was Most Valuable Player in the series, as he set a new strikeout record for a World Series game with fifteen in game one and pitched a 2–1 victory in game four. After the season he also won the Cy Young Award as the best pitcher in baseball, at a time when only one award was given, rather than one in each league as is the case today.

In 1964 the Dodgers fell below .500, but Koufax won nineteen games, lost only five, threw his third no-hitter, and lowered his earned run average to 1.74 for the year. His year would have been even better, but he was sidelined on 17 August for the rest of the season with traumatic arthritis, a preview of the condition that would bring his career to an untimely end. Despite fears that Koufax might not be able to come back from the injury the next year, both he and the Dodgers did so in fine fashion. The Dodgers won the pennant by two games over the Giants, then went on to defeat the Minnesota Twins in seven games in the World Series. Koufax tied the major league record for wins by a lefthander as he went 26–8 with an earned run average of 2.04 and pitched his fourth no-hitter, a perfect game against the Chicago Cubs in September. He also set a new major league record for strikeouts in a season with 382, and had eight shutouts. Before the opening of the World Series, Koufax announced that he would not pitch the opener against the Twins since it fell on Yom Kippur, the holiest day of the year for Jews. His principled stand gained him additional admirers. In the World Series he was 2–1, with both wins shutouts, and was the unanimous winner of the Cy Young Award for the season.

In 1965 Koufax and his teammate Don Drysdale, who had won the Cy Young Award in 1962, stunned the baseball world by staging a joint holdout from signing contracts or reporting to the club until they received the pacts that they thought they deserved. This was before free agency had been won in the courts, so the alternatives for the two players were to sign or not to play. Eventually they signed, both for more than $110,000 each, making them the highest paid pitchers in baseball at the time. The loss of much of spring training had little effect on Koufax as he won 27 games, lost 9, had his best earned run average of 1.73, and struck out 317 batters. The Dodgers won the pennant but in the World Series were swept by the Baltimore Orioles in four games. Koufax pitched and lost game two, the last game he would ever pitch. After the season he again won the Cy Young Award unanimously, but the honor was bittersweet as he announced that his career was over. The arthritis had progressed to the degree that he was unable to continue playing.

Koufax finished his meteoric career with a record of 165–87 and was the youngest person inducted into the Baseball Hall of Fame in 1972 at the age of thirty-six. He was voted the Player of the Decade for the 1960s despite the fact that he only played in seven of the ten years. Koufax married Anne Heath Widmark in 1969, but they were divorced in the early 1980s, after which he married and divorced again in the 1990s. After retiring he worked as a baseball analyst for the National Broadcasting Company (NBC) until 1972, then left baseball until 1979, when he returned as a pitching coach for the Dodgers from 1979 to 1982. He rarely makes public appearances but often assists the Dodgers in spring training each year for a short time. In 1999 he was one of 100 players named to Baseball's All-Century team.

★

Koufax and Ed Linn coauthored an autobiography, *Koufax,* in 1966. Koufax has also been the subject of a number of biographies, including Arnold Hano, *Sandy Koufax: Strikeout King* (1964).

MURRY R. NELSON

KOZOL, Jonathan (*b.* 5 September 1936 in Boston, Massachusetts), educational activist whose book *Death at an Early Age: The Destruction of the Hearts and Minds of Negro Children in the Boston Public Schools* illuminated the realities of education for the underprivileged and whose later works brought to light the plight of the poor, displaced, and disadvantaged.

Kozol grew up a child of privilege, the son of Harry Kozol, a neurologist and psychiatrist, and Ruth (Massell) Kozol, a psychiatric social worker. He graduated from the Noble and Greenough School in Dedham, Massachusetts, and

Jonathan Kozol shown prior to testifying at a Senate hearing on juvenile delinquency in October 1967. © BETTMANN/CORBIS

then from Harvard University summa cum laude, in 1958. He was awarded a Rhodes scholarship and went to Oxford University for further study in English literature. His parents pressured him to pursue an "acceptable" degree, such as a Ph.D. or an M.D. Instead he stumbled first into teaching and then into a successful, but sometimes controversial writing career.

While he was away at Oxford, Kozol experienced the first of a series of events that would shape the course of his life. In an interview with the *Boston Globe* staff writer Mark Feeney, he characterized the atmosphere of Oxford as "immature" and abandoned his studies, moving to Paris to write for four years. In 1963 Kozol left off work on his second novel and returned to Boston, still searching for direction. The following year three civil rights workers were found murdered in Mississippi. Kozol identified with one of the victims, Michael Schwerner, who came from circumstances similar to Kozol's: he was Jewish, middle-class, and from a "good" home. When Kozol found a brochure in Harvard Square calling for volunteer teachers for a program operated out of a church basement in Roxbury, a poor, predominantly black area of Boston, he took a train straight there.

Kozol found teaching rewarding. At the end of the summer he announced that he wanted to teach full time. In 1964 he became a permanent substitute in a fourth-grade class at the Christopher Gibson School in Roxbury, where he met his students in a school auditorium that he shared with three other classes. Having come through the upper-class schools of Newton, Massachusetts, Kozol was unprepared for the abysmal conditions he found in Roxbury, such as a roof that constantly leaked, windows that came loose from their frames, and a basement that reeked of urine.

Kozol was an effective teacher who employed innovative pedagogy to help his students develop an interest in learning. One well-known incident led to his dismissal. In an attempt to help his students develop an appreciation of poetry, he read to them from books by the Harlem Renaissance writer Langston Hughes, rightly assuming that the black face on the cover would help students identify with the poet. The next day, he was fired for veering from the standard curriculum.

Throughout 1965 and 1966 Kozol served as a consultant to the U.S. Office of Economic Opportunity while he transformed his journal from his days at Roxbury into his seminal work, *Death at an Early Age: The Destruction of the Hearts and Minds of Negro Children in the Boston Public Schools* (1967), which he wrote to illuminate the realities he had seen. *Death at an Early Age* sold modestly until it was awarded the National Book Award in 1968, when sales of the book soared and it became required reading for anyone in the field of educational reform. The Boston Public School System (which is home of the renowned Boston Latin School) prided itself on its high standards, but when Kozol exposed the dangerous, substandard conditions faced by black schoolchildren in Roxbury, Boston's public school system became the center of controversy. At a time when civil rights were at the forefront of the American consciousness, many people considered *Death at an Early Age* the first scathing critique of a racially unbalanced educational system.

Some critics found *Death at an Early Age* and Kozol's later works passionate, eloquent, and insightful and posited Kozol as an "advocate for the underprivileged and the disadvantaged." Others took issue with Kozol, calling him "angry," "self-righteous," and "condescending," and accused him of further perpetuating racial stereotypes by painting sympathetic pictures of blacks without offering solutions to inequities within the education system. But solutions were not what Kozol was after; he considered himself a witness rather than a reformer. Throughout the 1970s and 1980s Kozol continued to advocate for the rights of the disadvantaged with *Free Schools* (1972), in which he spoke out for alternative education. The volume served as a guide for others to create and fund free schools on his model. He was married briefly in the 1970s but had no children.

Children of the Revolution: A Yankee Teacher in the Cuban Schools (1978) documented the literacy movement in Cuba, and *Rachel and Her Children: Homeless Families in America* (1988) illuminated the lives of homeless families living in a Manhattan shelter. Kozol also worked as an instructor at various schools and universities, among them,

Columbia, Harvard, and Princeton, and on boards of education in Arizona, Illinois, Connecticut, Rhode Island, and Canada. He contributed to the *Los Angeles Times, The New Yorker,* and other widely read publications.

In 1991 Kozol revisited his experiences in Roxbury and Newton in *Savage Inequalities: Children in America's Schools.* The book concludes that the 1954 Supreme Court ruling in *Brown* v. *Board of Education,* which acknowledged that separate schools were inherently unequal, had done little in nearly four decades to improve conditions at minority schools. *Savage Inequalities* documents the ongoing disparity between schools in disadvantaged neighborhoods and schools in middle-class and upper-class neighborhoods. Kozol argues that as long as funding is left up to individual school districts, which draw monies from property taxes within the district, schools will never be equal. *Savage Inequalities* earned Kozol a 1992 New England Book Award and was a finalist for a National Book Critics Circle Award.

Kozol is a Rhodes Scholar and the recipient of Guggenheim Fellowships (1970 and 1984), Rockefeller Fellowships (1978 and 1983), two Christopher Awards (1988 and 2000), and a Robert F. Kennedy Book Award (1988), among many other honors. *Death at an Early Age* and *Savage Inequalities* became landmark works in the field of educational reform and established Kozol as a vocal activist for the disenfranchised and disadvantaged.

★

No book-length biographies of Kozol exist, but several interviews delve into Kozol's early years and first teaching experiences. They include those in *Educational Leadership,* vol. 50 (Dec. 1992/ Jan. 1993); *TECHNOS Quarterly,* vol. 7 (fall 1998), available online at http://www.techos.net; and the *Boston Globe* (17 May 2000). A prolific writer, he shared some personal experiences in *Death at an Early Age* and *Ordinary Resurrections: Children in the Years of Hope* (2000).

LESLIE BOON

KROC, Raymond Albert ("Ray") (*b.* 5 October 1902 in Oak Park, Illinois; *d.* 14 January 1984 in San Diego, California), flamboyant and legendary entrepreneur who, through pluck and luck, created McDonald's, the world's largest chain of fast-food restaurants and the most recognized brand name on the planet.

The 1960s were more than a golden age for the "Golden Arches"; they were also a decade of professional and personal triumph for McDonald's founder. The oldest of three children, Kroc grew up in a family of modest means. His father, Louis Kroc, was a midlevel executive with American District Telegraph, and his mother, Rose Mary (Hrach)

Kroc, was a part-time piano teacher. Kroc's mother taught him how to perform, and his showmanship helped him become a master salesperson.

In 1917, at the end of his sophomore year, Kroc dropped out of Oak Park High School. Always one who preferred action to academics, he wanted to volunteer for military service in World War I. Too young to serve, he lied about his age and entered a Red Cross ambulance driver training program, but the war ended just before he was sent to France. After the armistice in 1918, he returned to Oak Park intent on completing high school, but after one frustrating semester he left school for good. Kroc took a position as a traveling salesperson for a ribbon novelty company, while playing piano on the side.

In the early 1920s Kroc sold paper cups for the Lily Tulip Company, beginning his career in the food industry. He worked for Lily on and off for nearly twenty years, becoming the company's Midwest sales manager. In 1941 he started his own business, the Prince Castle Multimixer Company. Manufacturing a mixer capable of making five milkshakes at once, the company prospered until the early 1950s, when the growing popularity of soft-ice-cream stands signaled the decline of the drugstore soda fountain and the classic malted milkshake.

One obscure restaurant, however, bucked the trend. In 1954 Kroc's Prince Castle Company repeatedly received calls from restaurant owners wanting to buy "a mixer like the one used at McDonald's" in San Bernardino, California. His curiosity piqued, Kroc did some checking and was astonished to learn that McDonald's restaurant had not one multimixer but eight. He had to know why the brothers Richard and Maurice ("Mac") McDonald, the owners of the restaurant, needed the capacity to make forty milkshakes at once. Kroc went to San Bernardino and found the prototype of the fast-food restaurant of the future.

The McDonald brothers had developed a restaurant designed to attract the young families of the post–World War II era. There was a limited menu of assembly-line–produced foods sold in a self-service, squeaky-clean drive-in: no pay phones, carhops, vending machines, or other accoutrements that often turned a typical 1950s hamburger joint into a teenage hangout. Service was fast, the prices reasonable, the quality high, the surroundings spotless, and the food predictability consistent. Kroc encouraged the brothers to franchise their name and unique assembly-line system, but they lacked the ambition to take on such an effort. At the age of fifty-two Kroc offered to become their franchising agent.

Kroc and the McDonald brothers finally reached a formal agreement on 2 March 1955, and McDonald's Systems was incorporated. Just over a month later, on 15 April 1955, a model McDonald's Restaurant, complete with the trademark "Golden Arches," opened in Des Plaines, Illinois.

Ray Kroc. THE LIBRARY OF CONGRESS

(The store is still there today and operates as a museum.) The first day's receipts were $366.12, a handsome sum, considering that a hamburger sold for fifteen cents, fries for ten cents, a milkshake for twenty cents, and a cup of coffee for a nickel.

The Des Plaines site was a showcase store used to entice potential franchisees to buy a restaurant. Initially, growth was slow, in part because the agreement with the McDonald brothers required each franchisee to return 1.9 percent of gross sales to McDonald Systems, Inc. Of that total, 0.5 percent was paid to Dick and Mac McDonald, while the remaining 1.4 percent went to Kroc's company. While McDonald's was poised for growth, this was not enough to finance it, and the company lacked the capital to make growth happen. Enter Harry J. Sonneborn, a well-paid executive with a competing franchise, Tastee-Freeze, who in 1956 went to work for Kroc at a starting salary of $100 per week.

Attracted to McDonald's by its growth potential, Sonneborn created a leaseback system that quickly generated the money Kroc needed to expand McDonald's. The Sonneborn plan worked, and McDonald's, which had only thirty-one stores by the end of 1957, had 228 restaurants in

operation by 1960. During this time, Kroc lived on his income from Prince Castle sales. In 1961, when he sold that company, he drew a salary from McDonald's Corporation.

In 1961 Kroc started the forerunner of Hamburger University, probably the one innovation that most helped McDonald's become an unqualified success in the crowded field of franchisers. The original agreement with the McDonald brothers required each new franchise operator to follow the McDonald's system religiously. This meant that every detail—store design, signage, menu, pricing—had to be duplicated without deviation. Hamburger University, later called McDonald's University in Elk Grove, Illinois, taught owners and managers the McDonald's system, ensuring the consistency needed for commercial success. No freelancing was allowed. As Kroc once said, "The organization can't trust the individual; the individual must always trust the organization." Kroc's dictum was less about autocracy and more about preventing the mistakes that harm a franchise's profitability. Many of McDonald's innovations, however, originated from individual operators.

In the early 1960s, for instance, a franchise in Cincinnati asked the corporation to develop a meatless menu item for Fridays, to satisfy the wants of practicing Catholics (who did not eat meat on Fridays) in the area. Kroc, who often was taken with the power of his own ideas, came up with the Hulaburger—two slices of cheese wrapped around a slice of grilled pineapple on a toasted bun. The sandwich was an instant flop, but the stores in Cincinnati solved the problem by creating the Filet-O-Fish, and the fish sandwich became a standard menu item at McDonald's. "Ronald McDonald," originally portrayed by Willard Scott, the television weatherman, began as "Donald McDonald" at a Washington, D.C., store in 1963 and became the company's spokesperson in 1966. Even the chain's most famous sandwich, the Big Mac, began as a novelty item at a store in Pittsburgh in the mid-1960s. The sandwich is not only McDonald's signature menu item; it also inspired one of the most memorable jingles in advertising history: "Twoallbeefpattiesspecialsaucelettucecheesepicklesonionsonasesameseedbun."

The relationship between the McDonald brothers and Kroc was always strained. The tensions began in 1955, when Kroc wanted to open the Des Plaines restaurant. It transpired that the brothers already had sold the franchise rights to northern Illinois, so before Kroc could build the Des Plaines restaurant in his own neighborhood, he had to buy back the rights. In 1961 Kroc, who wanted unfettered control of the McDonald's name and system, asked the brothers to name their price. They demanded what was then the astronomical sum of $2.7 million in cash—$1 million for Dick, $1 million for Mac, and $700,000 for Uncle Sam. In 1962 a reluctant Kroc agreed, only to discover that his ownership of McDonald's did not extend to the original restaurant in San Bernardino. Miffed at what he considered less than ethical behavior, Kroc exacted his revenge. In 1963 he opened a McDonald's restaurant virtually across the street from the original San Bernardino store, then called the Big M, because the brothers could not legally use the name McDonald's. Within a year, the Big M was out of business, and Kroc finally had complete control of McDonald's, the name, the system, and soon the empire.

Acquiring ownership of McDonald's was a huge career risk for Kroc, but it was financially rewarding. With Sonneborn as president and Kroc as chairperson of the board, McDonald's had more than 700 restaurants in forty-four states by 1965. The time was right for McDonald's to go public, which it did in April of that year. Within days Kroc became a multimillionaire, and at the time of his death, Kroc's personal fortune was estimated at $500 million. Taking McDonald's public was the most significant accomplishment of Kroc's business career.

Kroc was married three times. His first marriage was to Ethel Fleming in 1922; they had one daughter and divorced in 1961. In 1957 Kroc met Joan ("Joni") Smith, an electric organist at a nightclub in Saint Paul, Minnesota. Kroc proposed that Smith and he get divorces so that they could marry each other. Initially, Smith agreed, but she later had second thoughts and changed her mind. Kroc was crushed. In 1962 Kroc moved to California to revitalize McDonald's West Coast business, where imitators had slowed growth to a trickle. He met Jane Dobbins Green, a secretary to John Wayne, and after a whirlwind fourteen-day courtship, the two were married. Seven years later, while he was at a McDonald's convention in San Diego, Kroc again met Joni Smith, who was attending the convention with her husband, a McDonald's manager. The spark that had attracted Kroc and Smith to each other burned as intensely as ever, and they again agreed to divorce their mates and marry. This time they followed through with their plan. They married on 8 March 1969 and remained together until Ray's death nearly fifteen years later.

By the end of the 1960s McDonald's had more than two thousand stores and was still growing rapidly. Kroc was out of his element in the rarefied corporate atmosphere that the company now occupied. He was an entrepreneur, not a manager. He thrived on the smell of the greasepaint and the roar of the crowd, not the proverbial bottom line. Within a few short years his role as strategist morphed into that of corporate cheerleader. He and his wife turned their interests elsewhere, purchasing the San Diego Padres professional baseball team in 1974. In 1976 they also established the Kroc Foundation, which supports medical research in diabetes (from which Kroc himself suffered), arthritis, and multiple sclerosis. The Kroc family is also a major benefactor for many nonprofit organizations in the Chicago area, such as the Children's Memorial Hospital,

the Lincoln Park Zoo, and the Harvard Congregational Church in Oak Park.

Kroc died of a heart attack at the age of eighty-one. He is interred at the El Camino Memorial Park in La Jolla, California. At the time of Kroc's death in 1984, McDonald's annual sales exceeded $8 billion. At a memorial service for Kroc on 20 January 1984, Fred Turner, president of McDonald's from 1967 to 1977, said of his longtime friend: "Ray touched us. . . . He was positive, not negative. He was a giver, not a taker. He was the best boss in the world, a best friend, a second father, a perfect partner, and an inspiration."

★

Kroc's autobiography, written with Robert Anderson, is *Grinding It Out: The Making of McDonald's* (1977). Biographical information is also in Max Boas and Steve Chain, *Big Mac: The Unauthorized Story of McDonald's* (1976); Janice Claire Simpson, *Ray Kroc: Big Mac Man* (1978); and John F. Love, *McDonald's: Behind the Arches* (1986). The McDonald's Web site has executive biographies and historical photographs tracing the history of the company at http://www.mcdonalds.com/corporate/info/history/. There are several videos available about Kroc and McDonald's, including *Biography: Ray Kroc, Fast Food McMillionaire* (1998). Obituaries are in the *Chicago Tribune* and the *New York Times* (both 15 Jan. 1984).

JAMES CICARELLI

KRULAK, Victor Harold (*b.* 7 January 1913 in Denver, Colorado), Marine Corps lieutenant general, counterinsurgency specialist, and commander of the Marine Corps' Pacific Fleet during much of the 1960s.

Krulak, son of Morris and Bessie M. Ball, first dreamed of a career in the military when, as a teenager, he watched the warships steam in and out of San Diego Bay. He secured an appointment to the U.S. Naval Academy, and it was at Annapolis, Maryland, that he earned his scarcastic nickname, "Brute," because of his five-foot, five-inch, 115-pound frame. Upon graduation in 1930 he chose service in the marines over the navy because he felt that the marines offered a greater challenge.

Krulak had a long and distinguished career in the marines. Before and during World War II, he helped create the marine amphibious doctrines. After the war, he worked with a group of marine officers largely responsible for the creation of the National Security Act of 1947, which saved the Marine Corps from being dismantled after World War II. Early in his career he married Amy Chandler (1 June 1936), and they had three children. In July 1956 he earned his first star, becoming the youngest general in marine history.

In 1962 President John F. Kennedy appointed Krulak to the Joint Chiefs of Staff (JCS) as special assistant for counterinsurgency and special activities; he thus became the Marine Corps' lead in Kennedy's call for the military to adopt counterinsurgency training. In this role Krulak made several trips to Vietnam between 1962 and 1964. He used these trips, combined with numerous discussions with the British counterinsurgency expert Sir Robert Thompson, to formulate his ideas on how the war in Vietnam should be fought. During his many visits, he also came to know South Vietnam's President Ngo Dinh Diem and urged the United States to continue supporting him, contrary to the opinion of his travel partner, Joseph Mendenhall of the State Department.

Krulak worked closely with Secretary of Defense Robert McNamara and Presidents Kennedy and Lyndon B. Johnson on Southeast Asian matters. He developed American doctrine on counterinsurgency warfare and created a program to track the United States' progress in South Vietnam. Many of his contemporaries considered him one of the three most powerful military men in the country at the time, because of the unfettered access he had to the White House. On 1 March 1964 Krulak became the commanding general of Fleet Marine Force, Pacific (FMFP). In this role he was responsible for all aspects of marine deployment in Vietnam, from equipment to training, except operational deployment. General William C. Westmoreland, commanding general of Military Assistance Command, Vietnam (MACV), had operational control of all American military in Vietnam. Krulak and Westmoreland developed different concepts on how best to fight the war, and in many ways their conflict served to define Krulak's wartime career.

Upon assuming command, Krulak immediately began to implement the doctrines he had developed as the nation's counterinsurgency expert, coming up with his "inkblot" formula. The formula involved securing and protecting populous areas and destroying the Communists' logistics by bombing roads, rail lines, and ports; mining the harbors; and engaging in large-unit battles only when the situation favored American troops. The secure areas were the inkblots that slowly spread as American and South Vietnamese forces secured more areas. Krulak's plan contradicted the "search and destroy" war of attrition strategy employed by Westmoreland. Krulak became increasingly frustrated with MACV's strategy. In 1966 he wrote a seventeen-page report outlining his concept and, using the influence he had gained while serving in Washington, D.C., brought his ideas to McNamara and Johnson. Both men, however, feared that Krulak's plan would lengthen the war and could possibly force the Soviets or the Chinese into a larger role.

Despite the fact that his overall concept was dismissed,

Krulak continued to battle the operational war planners at MACV and urge the marines in other directions. In October 1966, at Westmoreland's insistence, the marines formed a base at the remote location of Khe Sanh, North Vietnam. Krulak objected to the base, arguing that Khe Sanh was too remote to be an effective border post and was a waste of marine personnel and materiel. Krulak's objections were justified when the base was deemed strategically unimportant and abandoned in June 1968, less than two years after it was established and less than four months after it made international headlines during the Tet Offensive, a major attack launched by North Vietnam on cities in South Vietnam.

In May 1968 Krulak again became a vocal opponent of part of the war policy when Secretary of Defense Clark Clifford pushed for implementation of the single-management plan over all American air units. Krulak, while not completely disagreeing with the concept, believed that the plan would severely limit the marine air units in supporting marine ground operations. During a series of meetings in Saigon, South Vietnam, and Honolulu, Hawaii, Krulak worked to create alternatives. One of his final acts as commander, FMFP, was to draft the plan that gave MACV its "official" single manager, while the marines maintained operational control over 70 percent of its air units.

During the summer of 1968 many considered Krulak the top choice for commandant of the Marine Corps. A group of fellow officers petitioned for his appointment, and his wife secretly bought a set of four stars that he would be entitled to wear. President Johnson, however, chose another candidate, Leonard F. Chapman. Krulak retired from active duty in May 1968 and from the marines in June, after serving thirty-eight years. In 1995 the stars purchased by his wife finally went into service when President Bill Clinton selected their son Charles to serve as commandant of the Marine Corps (all three sons were naval academy graduates). Charles is now a retired U.S. Marine Corps general.

Critics of the United States' strategy in Vietnam believed the military had another option in Krulak's plan. Some even stated that the United States could have won the war had Krulak's plan been adopted. Krulak understood that the only difference between army strategy and marine strategy was emphasis, not substance. When enemy and civilians intermingle, he believed, one cannot shoot everyone, and one needs to stress pacification, not open battle. Krulak's plan, however, had its faults. Critics thought that it was not a complete concept and had many gaps in coverage. Moreover, the process in his plan would have lengthened the war interminably and perhaps turned it into an occupation. After retiring from the marines, Krulak went to work as the director of news policy for Copley News Service in San Diego, where he resided at the beginning of the twenty-first century. He continued to be critical of U.S.

strategy in his news writing and in his semi-autobiographical book, *First to Fight* (1984).

★

Krulak's papers and a 1969 oral history interview relating to his marine career reside at the Marine Corps History Center in Washington, D.C. Krulak included so much of his own experiences in his book, *First to Fight: An Inside View of the United States Marine Corps* (1984), that it can be considered a memoir. The only full-length biography of Krulak is Richard H. Hoy's master's thesis, "Victor H. Krulak: A Marine's Biography" (San Diego State University, 1974). The History Center also published the official multivolume marine history of the Vietnam War, *U.S. Marines in Vietnam,* which provides background on his career, particularly Jack Shulimson's volume, *The Defining Year, 1968* (1997).

MICHAEL C. MILLER

KUBRICK, Stanley (*b.* 26 July 1928 in New York City; *d.* 7 March 1999 in Hertfordshire, England), influential film director who declared independence from the Hollywood studio system, relocated to England in the early 1960s, and became a recognized innovator of film genres, aesthetics, narrative strategies, and the cinematic process, challenging Hollywood mores.

Kubrick was one of two children of Jacques Kubrick, a physician, and Gertrude Perveler, a homemaker. He was raised in the Bronx, New York City, in a middle-class Jewish family. Kubrick's father introduced his son to still photography and chess, disciplines that would inspire and

influence his iconoclastic vision as one of the twentieth-century's premier film directors.

As an adolescent Kubrick immersed himself in photography, developing photos in a friend's apartment darkroom. At William Howard Taft High School he invariably had a camera around his neck and took pictures for school publications. A poor student, Kubrick managed to receive the necessary credits to graduate when mentored by an art teacher who convinced him to view photography as an art. While at Taft, Kubrick sold a photograph to *Look* magazine that dramatically displayed the impact of President Franklin D. Roosevelt's death, and after graduation he became the youngest member of photography staff at the magazine. At the age of nineteen he married Toba Metz; they divorced in 1952. Kubrick married his second wife Ruth Sobotka on 15 January 1955. As a photojournalist Kubrick became interested in visual storytelling, and although he had no formal training, he directed, edited, and photographed an independent short *Day of the Fight* (1951), based on a photo story of boxer Walter Cartier that he had shot for *Look*. Kubrick's self-apprenticeship continued with *The Flying Padre* (1951), a human-interest story about a priest who flies his plane across New Mexico to serve his parish, and *The Seafarers* (1952), an industrial documentary for the Seafarers International Union and his first color film.

The first feature film directed by Kubrick, *Fear and Desire,* was released in 1953. The independent production was written by Howard O. Sackler, who later won a Pulitzer Prize for *The Great White Hope*. The film was financed by

Stanley Kubrick during the filming of *Dr. Strangelove*, 1963. UNDERWOOD & UNDERWOOD/CORBIS

Kubrick's uncle and shot in black and white on location in the San Gabriel Mountains outside of Los Angeles, with a small Mexican crew. The autodidact continued his self-taught approach by photographing and editing *Fear and Desire* himself. Although clearly amateurish, the film evidences Kubrick's dark vision and worldview. This existential drama was the first of many of the director's excursions into the grim reality and absurdity of war. His second feature, *Killer's Kiss* (1955), written with Sackler, is a New York guerrilla production about a down-and-out fighter. In it, Kubrick experimented with narrative structure and captured the noir atmosphere of New York in the 1950s.

In the mid-1950s, Kubrick met James B. Harris, an aspiring producer, and they formed Harris-Kubrick Pictures. Their first production, generally considered the first true Kubrick film, was *The Killing* (1956), which featured prominent B-movie actors and a complex nonlinear narrative structure decades before the concept became fashionable. In the film Kubrick developed his signature dolly shot, which explored the notion of time and space.

In the second of three Harris-Kubrick productions, they teamed with Kirk Douglas to make *Paths of Glory* (1957), a critically acclaimed antiwar film that revealed the sacrifice of three French soldiers during World War I as a result of the machinations of a maniacal general. The relentless dolly shots that follow Douglas reviewing his doomed troops in the trenches, and the hand-held camera (operated by Kubrick) that puts the viewer in the middle of an aimless charge for a hopeless mission, captured the grim reality of war stripped of all Hollywood artifice.

The 1960s were Kubrick's most creative period and brought him international recognition as an auteur. The decade began with a turning point in Kubrick's career, the release of *Spartacus* (1960), produced under the Hollywood system. *Spartacus* marks the only time Kubrick worked as a hired hand and did not have artistic control over a film. The assignment was part of a multipicture deal with Douglas and his Bryna production company. Although the film is one of the most intelligent and emotional of the gladiator genre, it was a painful lesson to Kubrick. He vowed never again to subject himself to working in Hollywood and demanded total artistic and fiscal control over his work.

The final Harris-Kubrick production was an adaptation of the scandalous Vladimir Nabokov novel *Lolita*. Kubrick had made films in both New York and Hollywood. New York lacked the necessary facilities, and although Hollywood had the talent and resources, the conventions of the industry were a threat to Kubrick's independence. *Lolita* (1962) was produced in England under the Eddy plan, which offered financial assistance if a percentage of the cast and crew were English. This environment gave Kubrick the solitude and freedom to make the film in his idiosyncratic and meticulous manner.

Lolita was a landmark exploration into the dark human region of sexual depravity and obsession. The novel had been banned and ostracized, and the feat of visualizing Nabokov's tale of an older man's fixation with a thirteen-year-old girl seemed impossible in an industry monitored by a strict Motion Picture Code and the all-powerful Catholic Church. By telling the story with innuendo and sophisticated subtext, Kubrick made it past the censors and drew attention as a filmmaker who delved into the fringes and shadows of American life.

Kubrick and his third wife, painter Christiane Harlan, whom he married in 1958, were still living in a New York apartment with her daughter from a previous marriage and their two daughters, but England was becoming Kubrick's filmmaking home, a place where he could work with first-rate craftspeople and facilities without interference from meddling studio powers.

After three films Harris-Kubrick Pictures disbanded amicably. Kubrick wanted even more control over his work by producing them himself, and Harris felt the urge to direct. Kubrick had long been interested in the subject of nuclear war. During the iciest phase of the cold war, he acquired the film rights to *Red Alert* by Peter George, a serious novel about a nuclear confrontation between the United States and the Soviet Union. After extensive research Kubrick decided to transform the drama into a black comedy. To push the envelope, he collaborated with hipster Terry Southern, whose diabolical sense of humor explored a new satiric and outrageous terrain.

The irreverent presentation of global annihilation put on the screen in *Dr. Strangelove, or: How I Learned to Stop Worrying and Love the Bomb* (1964) was a benchmark in absurdist humor. The meticulous details of the bomber cockpit, military base, and war room were a platform for the outrageous characters and behavior that brought the world over the brink. Kubrick employed the innovative genius of the actor Peter Sellers, who played three roles, to make fun of humankind's greatest fear, and the film struck a harmonious chord with the 1960s zeitgeist of challenging and taunting the establishment. *Dr. Strangelove* brought Kubrick international acclaim and Academy Award nominations for best director, screenplay, and picture.

Kubrick's most significant and lasting contribution to the cinema began in 1964 when he extended noted science fiction writer Arthur C. Clarke an offer to collaborate on "a really good sci-fi movie." This project, which became the film *2001: A Space Odyssey* (released in 1968 after four years of production), was an accomplishment that continues to resonate beyond the year in which the story was set. The nontraditional narrative begins with "The Dawn of Man" and concludes with the rebirth of an U.S. astronaut who passes through a "Star Gate" into a universe beyond our discovery. Kubrick broke all the Hollywood rules for the genre and established precedents in the production, aesthetic, narrative, and technical properties of motion picture creation.

To write the screenplay, Clarke and Kubrick first collaborated on a novel, which was then adapted into the project's scenario. Kubrick's intensive research into space travel involved the contributions of scientific, military, and aviation corporations to determine what space travel would achieve by 2001. The mountains of research were turned into an inventive production design and special effects that were beyond the cinematic technology of the time. Kubrick and his team of four special-effects supervisors invented their own technology decades before digital application was available to filmmakers. Front-screen projection, detailed mattes, multiple-screen film production, a centrifuge, and an invention named the Split Scan machine were developed and refined to create images of the time before man, life in outer space, and beyond. The minimalist plot and the merging of image and sound to achieve "The Ultimate Trip" features two astronauts and a talking computer named HAL, who is more emotionally and psychologically complex than the humans. This presentation challenged the traditional three-act structure with a nonnarrative mediation that used little dialogue to create a cinematic experience with images and sound. With the promise of rebirth and afterlife, Kubrick's film about the dangers of mechanization and dehumanization features, in the 1960s Aquarian tradition, his most hopeful ending. *2001: A Space Odyssey* is a crown jewel in the counterculture of the decade.

During the 1960s Kubrick developed the analytical and meticulous working methods that distinctly defined his filmmaking. His projects had a long gestation period, as Kubrick searched for the obsessional state that would propel him into the next endeavor. His research was intensive; all possibilities were considered, analyzed, and tested. During shooting Kubrick would call for take after take, often saying no more than "Let's go again." His involvement in all areas of development, preproduction, and postproduction was complete and included marketing, advertising, and the selection of theaters to screen his films. Kubrick even sent trusted colleagues to key venues to check the projection equipment.

In 1971 Kubrick entered into a deal with Warner Brothers, who financed and distributed his films until his death. *A Clockwork Orange* (1971), based on a novel by Anthony Burgess, set off a firestorm by challenging the limits of screen violence. *Barry Lyndon* (1975), a perfect recreation of Thackeray's eighteenth century, is frequently cited as the most beautifully rendered period film ever made. *The Shining* (1980), based on a Stephen King novel, transformed a haunted hotel into a major character, a place where writer's

block and a dysfunctional family make for Grand Guignol horror. *Full Metal Jacket* (1987) is a Vietnam film about how the U.S. Marines turn boys into fighting machines, and *Eyes Wide Shut* (1999) explores the sexual obsessions and jealousy of a young married couple viewed through the prism of a dream world where all the characters are awake. Before the completion of the film, Kubrick died of natural causes at his home in England.

Kubrick's legacy is as a twentieth-century film director who forged commerce and art issues from his artistic integrity; consistent, thematic worldview; distinctive visual style; and a body of work that is diverse in both subject matter and narrative approach. His dedication to the art of filmmaking has inspired moviemakers worldwide to create films that represent the vice and vision of the director, expressed through nontraditional narrative techniques and the inventive use of the cinematic crafts.

★

Kubrick's papers are in the possession of his family in England. Some materials concerning his films released by Warner Brothers are in the Warner Brothers Collection at the University of Southern California, Los Angeles. There are two full-scale biographies of Kubrick: Vincent LoBrutto, *Stanley Kubrick: A Biography* (1997), and John Baxter, *Stanley Kubrick: A Biography* (1997). Alexander Walker, Sybil Taylor, and Ulrich Ruchti, *Stanley Kubrick, Director: A Visual Analysis* (rev. ed. 1999); Norman Kagan, *The Cinema of Stanley Kubrick* (3rd ed. 2000); Thomas Allen Nelson, *Kubrick: Inside a Film Artist's Maze,* (rev. ed. 2000); Michael Ciment, *Kubrick: The Definitive Edition,* translated by Gilbert Adair (2001); and Mario Falsetto, *Stanley Kubrick: A Narrative and Stylistic Analysis (*rev. ed. 2001), contain analytical and critical insights into Kubrick's films. Gene D. Phillips, author of the excellent *Stanley Kubrick: A Film Odyssey* (1975), is also the editor of *Stanley Kubrick Interviews* (2001). Obituaries are in the *New York Times* and *Hollywood Reporter* (both 8 Mar. 1999).

VINCENT LOBRUTTO

KUNSTLER, William Moses (*b.* 7 July 1919 in New York City; *d.* 4 September 1995 in New York City), flamboyant defense attorney for a broad range of civil rights workers, draft resisters, and political radicals who shared his belief that America was an unjust society in need of revolutionary transformation of its power structure and legal system.

Kunstler was the eldest of two sons and a daughter born to Monroe Bradford Kunstler, a proctologist, and Frances (Mandelbaum) Kunstler, a homemaker. Although he later claimed he was always a rebel and outsider, his youth and early career were conventionally middle class. He attended DeWitt Clinton High School and in 1941 graduated from Yale with a B.A. in French and membership in Phi Beta

William Kunstler, March 1970. © BETTMANN/CORBIS

Kappa. Enlisting in the army two months before Pearl Harbor and assigned to the Signal Corps, he served with the U.S. Eighth Army in the Pacific, rising to the rank of major by the war's end.

Kunstler returned home to his young wife, Lotte Rosenberger, a distant cousin whom he had married in 1943. (They had two daughters and divorced in 1976, the year in which he married Margaret Ratner, with whom he also had two daughters.) In 1946 he entered Columbia University Law School in a special two-year program for veterans. Admitted to the New York bar in 1948, he joined his brother as a partner in Kunstler and Kunstler, specializing in matrimonial, estate, and family law. As the practice flourished he moved to the suburbs and began the middle-class routine of commuting, work, and family that soon bored him and led him to pursue new interests. He wrote book reviews for New York City papers and articles for national magazines. He published two books, *The Law of Accidents* (1954) and *First Degree* (1960), and lectured at New York Law School, but after a decade in the law he remained restless and uncertain about his professional life.

That uncertainty disappeared in the tumultuous 1960s, when Kunstler renewed his faith in the law as a vehicle for change. In June 1961 he flew to Mississippi as a representative of the American Civil Liberties Union to defend the Freedom Riders, young blacks and whites who were riding interstate buses in order to force integration of segregated transportation facilities in the South and who had been arrested for violating state and local laws. Kunstler's initial triumph—and a measure of his legal skills—was his discovery of an obscure federal statute from the Reconstruction

era that permitted moving certain cases from state to federal courts if race was involved. He successfully argued in federal court in favor of the statute's application in the South, thereby preventing local courts from taking racially motivated action against civil rights workers.

From the summer of 1961 onward, Kunstler played a major part in cases seeking to desegregate schools and public facilities across the South as counsel to the Congress of Racial Equality and as special counsel to the Reverend Martin Luther King, Jr., and the Southern Christian Leadership Conference. Back in New York, he successfully challenged federal rules governing jury selection in the Southern District of New York (Westchester County, Manhattan, and the Bronx) on the grounds that the rules "systematically" excluded minorities. Returning to the South, he secured a circuit court ruling that overturned the convictions of black ministers involved in bus boycotts in Birmingham, Alabama.

Like others in the movement Kunstler was shaken in late 1963 by a series of murders of black children and civil rights leaders in the South and by the indiscriminate beatings and illegal arrests carried out by the region's local and state police. Believing that legislative and federal relief was ineffective, Kunstler by 1965 abandoned his centrist legal views to embrace a far left radicalism. He was convinced that American society and its legal system had been corrupted by a racism so pervasive and so entrenched that all blacks and most ethnic minorities were denied equal opportunity and social justice. He declared it his responsibility as a lawyer to expose the corrupted system and to defend the underclasses from the overweening power of the state.

When the civil rights movement divided sharply in mid-decade between the integrationists like King, who argued for nonviolent tactics and legislative relief, and radical young men and women like the Black Panthers, who supported black separatism and advocated armed resistance to white oppression, Kunstler was drawn to the radical side, linking the black struggle to the white radical groups operating on both coasts in opposition to the war in Vietnam. He announced that he would take only those clients "whose goals I share."

In the turbulent years after 1965 he crisscrossed the country dozens of times, often alone but sometimes with a team of lawyers, to aid clients whose ideologies ranged from anarchism to pacifism. He became a familiar figure on television: a tall, angular provocateur with flowing dark brown hair, glasses pushed up on the forehead, and a tendency toward making inflammatory statements that regularly provoked his opponents to rage. His radical image was fixed in the public mind during the notorious Chicago Seven conspiracy trial from 1969 to 1970, when he defended seven radical protesters who had disrupted the 1968 Democratic National Convention. His clients, who said they rejected the authority of the federal court, disrupted the proceedings with foul language and wild behavior. Kunstler openly ridiculed Julius J. Hoffman, the presiding judge, challenged every ruling, and argued that the trial was a disgrace. Held in contempt on twenty-four occasions, Kunstler was sentenced to prison (without trial) for four years and thirteen days but was released on appeal and later exonerated. The jury refused to convict the seven of conspiracy but held five of them guilty of incitement.

Kunstler wrote four books in the 1960s: *Beyond a Reasonable Doubt?* (1961), about the trial of Caryl Chessman, whose execution in California stirred up international protests against the death penalty; *The Case for Courage: Ten Lawyers Who Risked Their Careers in the Cause of Justice* (1964); *The Minister and the Choir Singer* (1964), about a murder trial in 1922; and *Deep in My Heart* (1966), a memoir of his years with King.

In 1971 Kunstler was one of the independent observers called for by black inmates at Attica prison in New York during their bloody standoff with prison guards, and he later represented a number of them in court. For the next twenty-four years, until his death from heart disease, he continued to defend social outcasts and pariahs, winning the majority of his cases through hard work and skillful application of the law rather than with the histrionics for which he was famous. Kunstler's body was cremated and the remains scattered at an undisclosed location in the Catskill Mountains.

★

Kunstler's personal papers are held by his widow, Margaret Ratner. His autobiography, *My Life as a Radical Lawyer,* coauthored with Sheila Isenberg (1994), should be used with caution, given his penchant for exaggeration and invention in his legal career. A relatively balanced account of Kunstler's life is David J. Langum, *William M. Kunstler: The Most Hated Lawyer in America* (1999). See also J. Anthony Lukas, *The Barnyard Epithet and Other Obscenities: Notes on the Chicago Conspiracy Trial* (1970); and "An Interview with William Kunstler," in Jonathan Black, ed., *Radical Lawyers: Their Role in the Movement and in the Courts* (1971). An obituary is in the *New York Times* (5 Sept. 1995).

ALLAN L. DAMON

L

LANSDALE, Edward Geary (*b*. 6 February 1908 in Detroit, Michigan; *d*. 23 February 1987 in McLean, Virginia), U.S. Air Force intelligence officer famous as a counterinsurgency expert.

Lansdale was the first of four sons of Henry Lansdale, an automobile parts company executive, and Sarah Frances Philips. He attended the University of California at Los Angeles, but left in 1931 without earning a degree, and in 1935 embarked on an advertising career. In 1932 he married Helen Batcheller; they had two sons. During World War II, Lansdale served in the U.S. Army, working with the Military Intelligence Service and the Office of Strategic Services. Lansdale remained in the service after the war, transferring to the U.S. Air Force in 1947, and eventually rising to the rank of major general in 1963. In 1950, while assigned to the Office of Policy Coordination, a top-secret intelligence agency that engaged in covert operations, Lansdale was sent to the Philippines, which was beset by the Communist-led Hukbalahap insurgency. Under the guise of an adviser to the Philippine army, he developed a counterinsurgency program that defeated the Huks through a skillful combination of social and political reform, psychological warfare, and prudent military operations.

In 1954 Lansdale was named head of the Central Intelligence Agency (CIA) military mission in Saigon, Vietnam, although he was never an employee of the agency. During the next two years, he worked closely with Ngo Dinh Diem, prime minister of the State of Vietnam and later president of the Republic of Vietnam, to turn South Vietnam into a non-Communist nation. Lansdale used psychological warfare techniques to persuade more than 1 million refugees to leave North Vietnam for South Vietnam. He also planned reforms, helped neutralize the opposition to Diem in South Vietnam from religious sects and the Saigon underworld, derailed a coup by a powerful general, and engineered Diem's elevation to the presidency. Lansdale was one of the few people Diem trusted outside his family circle, while Lansdale saw Diem as the only alternative to a Communist triumph in South Vietnam. To the dismay of many U.S. officials, their relationship bypassed formal diplomatic channels, but Lansdale's accomplishments in the Philippines and Vietnam protected him from his critics. Lansdale received orders to return to the United States at the end of 1956, arriving in Washington, D.C., in January 1957. During the next years he served in the Office of Special Operations in the Department of Defense and as chief Pentagon representative on the U.S. Intelligence Board, which was responsible for formulating national covert intelligence policy. In 1960 he became part of U.S. efforts to bring down the Communist government of Fidel Castro in Cuba. The CIA looked to military action, but Lansdale spoke out against military operations in meetings of the intelligence board, arguing that the CIA's plan to land a brigade of Cuban exiles on the Cuban coast was fatally flawed. The CIA, however, was committed to an over-the-beach invasion, leading to the disaster at the Bay of Pigs in April 1961.

In the fall of 1961 President John F. Kennedy named Lansdale executive director of the newly created Special Group, Augmented. Charged with unseating Castro, the group conducted operations under the code name Mongoose. Lansdale proposed to build up a movement among anti-Castro elements in Cuba that would mount an insurrection. The plan, however, was based on wishful thinking. There was no evidence to suppose that Cuba was on the brink of revolt, and Lansdale had no real idea of how to bring one about. Moreover, the CIA showed little interest in the plan and still looked to military intervention to resolve the Castro problem. Ultimately, Mongoose came to center on sabotage missions in Cuba and attempts to assassinate Castro, which Lansdale later said were carried out without his knowledge and served only to prompt the Soviet Union to increase its support of Castro.

Meanwhile, Lansdale had again become involved with Vietnam. At the beginning of 1961 he traveled to South Vietnam to assess the war against Communist insurgents. Questioning the emphasis on military force that Diem's U.S. advisers advocated, he contended that the key to counterinsurgency was to attract the support of the people through civic action, a responsive government, and professional behavior by military forces. Furthermore, while recognizing that Diem had a weak political base, he believed that with sensitive handling he could be guided to adopt policies that would win the "hearts and mind" of the population. Impressed with Lansdale's experience as an Asian hand and his views on the war, Kennedy in February 1961 considered naming him ambassador to South Vietnam. But Secretary of Defense Robert McNamara and Secretary of State Dean Rusk, convinced Lansdale was too much of a lone wolf, vetoed his appointment.

In the fall of 1961 Lansdale participated in a mission to Saigon headed by General Maxwell Taylor, Kennedy's special military adviser, and Walt Rostow, a Kennedy foreign-policy adviser. The Taylor-Rostow report urged a greater U.S. military commitment to the defense of South Vietnam. Presenting the threat to South Vietnam largely in terms of aggression by North Vietnam, it called for more firepower and mobility for South Vietnamese troops, the assignment of U.S. combat troops to South Vietnam, and possible air attacks against North Vietnam. Lansdale, in contrast, emphasized the insurgency within South Vietnam and the need to focus on the political aspects of the war. Kennedy was not prepared to adopt most of the Taylor-Rostow recommendations. But for Lansdale the report was an indication of his waning influence on Vietnam strategy, as policy makers increasingly looked to a military solution. Having few supporters in the Washington bureaucracy, Lansdale retired from the air force on 30 October 1963.

Edward Lansdale. CORBIS CORPORATION (BELLEVUE)

From 1965 to 1968 Lansdale served in Vietnam as special assistant to ambassadors Henry Cabot Lodge, Jr., and Ellsworth Bunker on pacification issues. Arguing that President Lyndon B. Johnson's escalation of the war would overwhelm South Vietnam and take the initiative away from the South Vietnamese government and army, Lansdale criticized the conventional military operations conducted by U.S. forces and urged that greater emphasis be placed on political and social reform. But lacking clearly defined authority and specific programs to administer, he had little impact on the war effort. In retirement Lansdale lectured on Vietnam and occasionally advised the Pentagon on guerrilla war issues. His first wife died in 1972, and he married Patrocinio Kelly Yapcinco on 4 July 1973. Lansdale died of heart failure and was buried at Arlington National Cemetery.

Lansdale stands out for his advocacy of nonconventional means to defeat Communist insurgencies in Third World countries. Whether Lansdale's approach would have produced a better outcome to the Vietnam War is difficult to say, but it was as valid as the costly war of attrition the United States fought for so many years.

★

Lansdale's papers are deposited with the Hoover Institution on War, Revolution, and Peace at Stanford University. His memoir is *In the Midst of Wars: An American's Mission to Southeast Asia* (1972). Cecil B. Curry, *Edward Lansdale: The Unquiet Amer-*

ican (1988), is an admiring biography. Lansdale's activities in Southeast Asia are also portrayed in two novels that appeared in the 1950s. The first, Graham Greene, *The Quiet American* (1955), reviled a Lansdale-like character, although both Greene and Lansdale denied the connection. The second, William Lederer and Eugene Burdick, *The Ugly American* (1958), extolled a Lansdale-like character and was on the best-seller list for more than a year. An obituary is in the *New York Times* (24 Feb. 1987).

JOHN KENNEDY OHL

LASCH, Robert Christopher (*b.* 1 June 1932 in Omaha, Nebraska; *d.* 14 February 1994 in Pittsford, New York), educator, historian, and social critic best known for his reevaluation of liberalism during the 1960s and for his subsequent contention that the absorption with self, which he called "narcissism," lay at the heart of contemporary American culture.

The son of Robert Lasch, a writer and columnist for the *Omaha World Herald,* the *Chicago Sun-Times,* and the *St. Louis Post-Dispatch*, and Zora Schaupp, a part-time social worker with a Ph.D. in philosophy, Lasch was exposed early in his life to the midwestern progressivism that influenced his mature thought. While a student at Barrington

Christopher Lasch. ASSOCIATED PRESS AP

High School in Barrington, Illinois, where he had moved with his parents and his sister in 1942, Lasch campaigned for Henry Wallace, the Progressive Party candidate for president in 1948. Upon graduation from high school in 1950, Lasch declined a scholarship from the University of Chicago to attend Harvard, from which he received a B.A. degree in 1954. He then began graduate study in history at Columbia University, earning an M.A. degree in 1955, and a Ph.D. in 1961, after the completion of a doctoral dissertation under the direction of William E. Leuchtenburg.

On 30 June 1956 Lasch married Nell Commager, the daughter of the eminent historian Henry Steele Commager. The couple had four children. An instructor at Williams College in Williamstown, Massachusetts, between 1957 and 1959, Lasch became assistant professor of history at Roosevelt University in Chicago in 1960, before moving on to the University of Iowa, where he remained until 1966. That year Lasch was appointed professor of history at Northwestern University, but left in 1970 to take a position at the University of Rochester in Rochester, New York. Named Don Alonzo Watson Professor of History in 1979, Lasch became chairman of the department in 1985, an office that he held until his death. Lasch inaugurated his distinguished scholarly career in 1962, with the publication of *The American Liberals and the Russian Revolution.* Analyzing liberal attitudes toward the Bolshevik Revolution of 1917, Lasch condemned the often willful naïveté that permitted intellectuals to discount or ignore Soviet oppression and brutality and thereby convince themselves that the Communists had fashioned a heaven on earth. As Louis Menand has noted, however, Lasch directed his comments as much to the liberals of his own day. When Lasch described liberalism in America as a "messianic creed," Menand declared, "he was describing . . . not only the liberalism of 1919—of Woodrow Wilson and Walter Lippmann—but the liberalism of the Kennedy administration as well." Lasch continued his onslaught against liberalism in his next book, *The New Radicalism in America, 1899–1963: The Intellectual as a Social Type.*

The New Radicalism, which appeared in 1965, confirmed Lasch's scholarly and critical reputation. A series of essays examining the lives, careers, and ideas of figures as diverse as the social reformer Jane Addams, the essayist and literary critic Randolph Bourne, the journalist and social reformer Lincoln Steffens, the promoter of art and social causes Mabel Dodge Luhan, and the novelist Norman Mailer, the New Radicalism, Lasch wrote, reveals "the estrangement of intellectuals" from social and political convention. Frequently troubled by unsatisfying personal relationships, intellectuals compensate by engaging in social, political, and moral reform. In interviews that he gave during the last months of his life, Lasch said that he at last had discovered the theme of *The New Radicalism.* The book was about intellectuals who want to be something other than intellectuals—"movers and shakers, or the power behind the throne, or revolutionaries, or Indians or members of some allegedly simple culture that enjoyed a direct, unmediated connection with nature."

Although the book did not bring Lasch the public acclaim that he would garner from later publications, *The New Radicalism* created a sensation in the history profession. In a letter to Lasch dated 5 July 1965, William Leuchtenburg wrote that *The New Radicalism* was a "brilliant . . . unconventional book, because it is based not on massing evidence but on *thinking* about history, an endeavor that had largely gone out of fashion." Richard Hofstader, another of Lasch's mentors at Columbia, agreed. "The steady flow of marginal insight, about the people you've chosen, the intellectual life as a vocation, and the development of our culture," he wrote to Lasch, explain why the book could be read with profit "by someone who happens not to agree with your central point, and why I think you will still find people reading it when you are an old man."

Lasch, of course, had his critics. In a caustic review, Arthur Mann, skeptical that Lasch could connect figures as different in time, circumstance, and personality as Jane Addams and Norman Mailer in an overarching interpretation of liberalism, pronounced *The New Radicalism* "flawless in its failure." Writing in the *Partisan Review,* Norman Birnbaum maintained that Lasch's analysis "of the source of the intellectuals' discontents is quite unconvincing. He is uncertain whether capitalism, industrialism or mass society is responsible for the intellectuals' plight, and these highly schematic terms are not used anywhere critically."

Liberal and radical thinkers leveled a more overtly political criticism against the book. William Phillips complained that Lasch included nothing about "the Socialists, the IWW [International Workers of the World], the Communists, . . . the civil rights movement, Marxism, the pacifists, the anarchists, [and] Students for a Democratic Society," while Arthur M. Schlesinger, Jr., reproved Lasch for disparaging intellectuals' attachment to the Kennedy administration. Lasch's friend, the radical historian and activist Staunton Lynd, objected that Lasch was compromising "the validity of radical action by exploring its psychic origins." In the midst of their long and increasingly acrimonious exchange of letters, Lasch told Lynd, "I continue to be disturbed by your willingness to exchange analysis for propaganda. . . . To you the radical tradition is sacred and must not be analyzed, except to murmur approvingly."

The controversies that *The New Radicalism* excited only enhanced its value for the generation of young scholars who came of age during the 1960s. Robert B. Westbrook confirmed its impact, acknowledging that "*The New Radicalism* was . . . the book that made Lasch a figure of commanding importance for the generation of historians that

followed his." *The New Radicalism*, along with the essays that Lasch published in the *New York Review of Books,* provided guidance and insight to those struggling to make sense of that turbulent decade. In 1969 Lasch collected many of these influential pieces in *The Agony of the American Left,* in which he extended his critique of liberal and radical intellectuals. Chastising them for their misplaced emphasis on personal liberation and their superficial commitment to revolution, he observed that by the end of the 1960s many, perhaps most, liberal and radical intellectuals had realized their ambitions for advancement by making their peace with corporate capitalism and using the schools and other institutions to disseminate its materialistic ethos. They endeavored to make themselves important, Lasch asserted, by presuming to instruct ordinary men and women about how to live in the complex and bewildering world that the intellectuals themselves had helped create and sustain.

At a time of social and political upheaval and cultural experimentation, Lasch, though firmly entrenched on the Left, championed such exemplary bourgeois values as hard work, parental authority, and moral discipline. He steadfastly refused to acquiesce to the demands that came from various factions within the New Left to forsake marriage and the family, to escape the restrictions of traditional gender roles, to abdicate all moral responsibility, and to substitute instinct for intellect. Disenchanted with conservatism, Lasch nonetheless issued a wholesale indictment of the political and social thought of the 1960s.

Concern with the responsibilities and failures of intellectual elites past and present had dominated Lasch's writing for nearly a decade. By the 1970s he expanded the focus of his work in an effort to clarify how the malfeasance of intellectuals contributed to the disintegration of the family, the abandonment of community, the atomization of society, and the apathy toward public life, which he saw as the legacy of the 1960s. In his three most acclaimed, provocative, and controversial books, *Haven in a Heartless World: The Family Besieged* (1977), *The Culture of Narcissism: American Society in an Age of Diminishing Expectations* (1979), and *The Minimal Self: Psychic Survival in Troubled Times* (1984), Lasch investigated the social, political, moral, and psychic consequences that followed from a preoccupation with things and an absorption with self.

Intellectual elites allied with the forces of corporate capitalism, Lasch maintained in *Haven in a Heartless World,* had subverted the family. The widespread acceptance of easy divorce, single parenthood, and day care, which members of the elite celebrated as evidence of individualism, diversity, and liberation, were in reality indications of social disarray. In *The Culture of Narcissism,* Lasch continued his attack, assailing the emphasis on self-gratification. His thesis intrigued President Jimmy Carter, who in 1979 consulted Lasch on "America's crisis of confidence" before delivering the lamentable "malaise speech," in which the president complained that apathy and selfishness had eroded "the very heart and soul of our national will." Carter's political opponents changed that he was blaming the problems of his administration on the American people. *The Minimal Self,* a sequel of sorts to *The Culture of Narcissism,* represented Lasch's attempt not only to explicate previous arguments, but also to unmask and discredit the optimistic prophets of easy cultural salvation.

During the last decade of his life Lasch returned to a consideration of "the intellectual as a social type." In *The True and Only Heaven: Progress and Its Critics* (1991), and the posthumously published *Revolt of the Elites and the Betrayal of Democracy* (1995), he censured liberals and radicals for their misguided faith in the inevitability of progress, detailed the erosion of the middle class, evaluated the antidemocratic implications of the global economy, and admonished elites for their revolt against the authenticity of ordinary life. With the assistance of his daughter Elisabeth Lasch-Quinn, who is also a historian, Lasch devoted his final year to assembling a selection of essays on women and society, published in 1997 as *Women and the Common Life: Love, Marriage, and Feminism.* Lasch died of renal cancer in 1994, and is buried in Pittsford, New York. Original, erudite, and courageous, Lasch diagnosed, but proposed few remedies for, the absurdity that he thought plagued modern life.

★

There is no biography of Lasch, but his papers are in the Department of Rare Books, Special Collections, and Preservation, Rush Rhees Library, University of Rochester. Interviews with Lasch include Casey Blake and Christopher Phelps, "History as Social Criticism: Conversations With Christopher Lasch," *Journal of American History* 80, no. 4 (Mar. 1994): 1,310–1,332; and Richard Wightman Fox, "An Interview with Christopher Lasch," *Intellectual History Newsletter* 16 (Sept. 1994). Essays on Lasch's life and thought include Louis Menand, "Man of the People," *New York Review of Books* (11 Apr. 1991); James Seaton, "The Gift of Christopher Lasch," *First Things* 45 (Aug.–Sept. 1994); Robert Coles, "Remembering Christopher Lasch," *New Oxford Review* (Sept. 1994); Jean Bethke Elshtain, "The Life and Work of Christopher Lasch: An American Story," *Salmagundi* (spring–summer 1995): 146–161, and "Limits and Hope: Christopher Lasch and Political Theory," *Social Research* 66 (summer 1999); Jackson Lears, "The Man Who Knew Too Much," *New Republic* (Oct. 1995); and Arthur A. Molitierno, "The Authentic Negative Voice of Democracy: Christopher Lasch's Last Will and Testament," *Midwest Quarterly* 41 (winter 2000): 129–144. Essential for understanding Lasch's influence on the history profession and social thought during the 1960s is Robert B. Westbrook, "Christopher Lasch, *The New Radicalism,* and the Vocation of Intellectuals,"

Reviews in American History 23 (Mar. 1995): 176–191. Obituaries are in the *New York Times* (15 Feb. 1994), *Washington Post* (16 Feb. 1994), (London) *Times* (26 Feb. 1994), and *New Republic* (7 Mar. 1994).

MARK G. MALVASI

LAUREN, Ralph (*b.* 14 October 1939 in New York City), designer who pioneered "lifestyle" fashion beginning in the late 1960s as well as the first designer to package, license, and control his own brand of clothes (Polo) in his own chain of stores.

Lauren, born Ralph Lifshitz, is the youngest of four children of Frank, a housepainter and muralist, and Frieda Lifshitz, a housewife. His Russian immigrant family lived in the Mosholu Parkway section of the Bronx, a lower-middle-class area of New York City. He attended Public School (P.S.) 80 and later designed the school's logo. In his spare time he played baseball and said that he wanted to be a professional athlete. When not playing sports Lauren watched Hollywood movies, idolizing Cary Grant and Fred Astaire because of their elegant style and grace. "I was always interested in the look of Cary Grant and Fred Astaire," Lauren once commented. "They were my inspiration." So, too, was the dapper elegance of the Duke of Windsor. While his friends listened to Elvis Presley, Lauren preferred Frank Sinatra. Lauren later translated the easy elegance and uncomplicated effortlessness of his idols into his own confected empire of lifestyle merchandizing.

Unlike many fashion designers, Lauren did not sketch clothes as a child or go to fashion school. He was, however, a dandy. "From the time I was twelve years old I looked cool," he once said. "Whatever I had on, other kids would say, 'Hey, where'd you get that?'" He attended the Boy's Talmudical Academy in 1953 and then DeWitt Clinton High School in the Bronx, from which he graduated in 1957. During this period he also worked part-time as a stock boy at the customer return counter of Alexander's, a department store in Manhattan. Apparently, he spent most of his paycheck on clothes. While his motorcycle buddies wore leather jackets at school dances, Lauren wore buttoned-down shirts with tennis sweaters. In 1955 he and his two brothers legally changed their family name to Lauren.

Lauren stayed on at Alexander's after graduating from high school in 1957 and became a full-time salesperson. At night he took business courses for two years at the City College of New York, but he found the classes boring. After serving in the U.S. Army Reserves for six months, he worked as a salesperson at the fashionable menswear store Brooks Brothers (1962) as well as working as an assistant buyer for Allied Stores (1963), but he was determined to

Ralph Lauren *(left)*, with fellow designer Bill Blass, 1965. HULTON ARCHIVE

break into designing. Lauren applied as a designer to Brooks Brothers and to other manufacturers of menswear, only to be turned down. "I had no portfolio and no sketches," he once commented. "All I had was taste." Indeed, he loved the collegiate look of the New England old money heritage, which he later assimilated, packaged, and licensed. Lauren was inspired most by Brooks Brothers' merchandise and its merchandizing. He once said that his first suit was bought at Brooks Brothers: "I was as Brooksy as you can get." In an interview he described his admiration for the company and his mission to keep the fashion flame alive: "Brooks Brothers was the foundation, and I revived it." What impressed him was the image of the Brooks Brothers brand and the confidence of customers in the quality of the clothes. Affluent men would simply enter a Brooks Brothers' store and ask for so many shirts in so many colors. "They'd do it every year," Lauren commented. "I recognized a certain mentality and security about them." Lauren realized that men's sense of fashion was formed by default, not by trends. If he did not understand the mechanics of constructing fashion, it did not stop him, because he knew that men wanted reliability and taste above all else.

In 1964 he worked in sales for Abe Rivertz and Co., a Boston tie maker that sold its products to New York stores like Brooks Brothers. On 30 December 1964 he married Ricky Low Beer, a receptionist; they have three children. Hoping to branch out, Lauren asked his company's president if he could design its ties, a puzzling question during the early 1960s. The tie business was highly conservative, and its manufacturing firms took weeks to decide on changes of patterns or widths. If a tie width did change, it would be only in eighths of an inch. Moreover, tie fabric suppliers decided on fabric, pattern, and width, whereas the manufacturers determined minimal color changes. For four years Lauren was permitted to make "design" choices of color changes, while continuing in sales and discussing the detailing of men's shirts and jackets with professional tailors. He also spent time looking for a financial backer for his interest in making wide, elegant ties reminiscent of those worn during the 1940s.

In 1967 Lauren began working for Beau Brummell Ties, Inc. In his spare time he continued to design ties, now with unusual fabrics and with widths measuring four to five inches instead of the standard three inches. Wide ties had been introduced in London a few years earlier, with bright colors and bold Carnaby Street patterns (named after a fashion mecca in London); Lauren's designs were also wide but had conservative Ivy League patterns. Moreover, Bill Blass, who entered menswear in 1967, was introducing brightly colored shirts and boldly patterned jackets. Lauren presented models of his new ties to Beau Brummell, whose executives understood that conservative menswear was undergoing a revolution. The company decided to make a limited test run of Lauren's designs, and several were manufactured and sold well at small specialty stores and then at chic department stores like Bloomingdale's. Lauren's designs also sold at double the price of standard ties ($3.50), and the labels significantly proclaimed, "designed by Ralph Lauren."

In 1968 Lauren finally secured a loan from Norman Hilton, a clothing company executive. With that loan Lauren began Polo Fashions. It was first a division of Beau Brummell Ties and then, later that year, became a separate company. The Polo brand label, a mallet-wielding rider astride a galloping horse, suggested sporty, affluent taste. Lauren wanted to build his business quickly, and he hired Michael Cifarelli, a leading conservative pattern maker and designer. Later that year Polo brought out shirts with larger collars to accommodate the wider ties. Suit jackets with wider lapels appeared in 1969. Cifarelli originally cut patterns with regular square shoulders, but Lauren insisted that the shoulders should be "unconstructed" soft shoulders that were rounder and softer and with a longer lapel and high pockets, as well as a minimum of fabric stiffening. Designed for lawyers and stockbrokers of what Lauren called the "New Establishment," this construction provided comfort and a more natural look and feel. His evening suit designs also included what Lauren called a "Churchill" suit, which was a battle jacket style to be worn with a scarf instead of a tie. An "informal formal" dinner suit included red and black checkered pants, and a "walking" suit was a navy blue mid-length jacket with navy pants. Other Polo men's products for 1969 included belts, boots, scarves, and a portfolio briefcase to replace the traditional attaché case.

Lauren then persuaded Bloomingdale's to include a Polo boutique in its men's department. Lauren's line was, in reality, a grouping of varied lines of ties, shirts, and jackets that were orchestrated to define an Ivy League look that surpassed Brooks Brothers. Lauren had created lifestyle marketing, in which garments for sportswear or eveningwear were sold together. His precedent-setting work won the 1970 Coty Menswear Award. Lauren has won seven COTY Awards in all, more than any other designer, and he was inducted into the COTY Hall of Fame in 1986. He launched a line of women's clothing in 1971, and sales skyrocketed after they were featured by the actress Diane Keaton in Woody Allen's movie *Annie Hall* (1977). Lauren opened his first independent retail outlet in 1971 on the trendy Rodeo Drive in Beverley Hills, California. By 1997 his company had more than 100 stores, 1,300 boutiques in department stores, and annual sales in excess of $5 billion.

Lauren has shown customers how to look, dress, and live well by using himself and his wife as models. He pioneered "lifestyle" merchandising in clothes and later in household products. During the 1970s he was the first fashion designer to have his own chain of stores, and he was the first American designer to capitalize on the value of myth and folklore in fashion. By packaging, licensing, and controlling the image of Polo, he appropriated the American Ivy League image and sold it internationally.

★

A biography of Lauren is Jeffrey A. Trachtenberg, *Ralph Lauren: The Man Behind the Mystique* (1988). Biographical information is also in Ann Stegemeyer, *Fairchild's Who's Who in Fashion* (1980); Georgina O'Hara, *The Encyclopedia of Fashion from 1840 to the 1980s* (1986); and Anne Canadeo, *Ralph Lauren: Master of Fashion* (1992). See also Barbaralee Diamonstein, *Fashion: The Inside Story* (1985). Articles about Lauren and fashion are "Ralph Lauren: Success American Style," *Vogue* (Aug. 1982); "Selling a Dream of Elegance and the Good Life," *Time* (1 Sept. 1986); "Ralph Lauren, Suiting Himself," *Washington Post* (24 May 1992); and "Ralph Lauren: The Emperor Has Clothes," *Fortune* (11 Nov. 1996).

PATRICK S. SMITH

LEARY, Timothy Francis (*b.* 22 October 1920 in Springfield, Massachusetts; *d.* 31 May 1996 in Beverly Hills, California), Harvard psychology professor whose experiments with psychedelic drugs led him to proclaim them as a panacea.

Leary was the only child of U.S. Army Captain Timothy Leary, a dentist, and Abigail Ferris, a teacher. He attended Holy Cross from 1938 to 1939, then the U.S. Military Academy at West Point from 1940 to 1941, leaving both institutions before graduating because of discipline problems. Leary graduated from the University of Alabama with a B.A. in 1943. After serving in the U.S. Army as a psychologist in the Medical Corps, he obtained a doctorate in psychology in 1950 from the University of California at Berkeley, where he was an assistant professor from 1950 to 1955. After a stint as director of psychiatric research for the Kaiser Foundation from 1955 to 1958, during which he devised a personality evaluation that was used by many organizations, in 1959 Leary became a lecturer at Harvard University's Center for Personality Research. He married Marianne Busch, a college instructor, in 1944. The couple had a daughter and a son; Marianne died in 1955. Leary would remarry several times, including to one woman twice (actress Rosemary Woodruff, whom he wed in 1967 and 1995).

Leary wanted to apply scientific paradigms to the study of psychology, including the use of chemicals to change consciousness. In 1960, while in Mexico, Leary tried psilocybe mushrooms, undergoing a profound and life-changing experience. He returned to Harvard and, with associates Richard Alpert (later known as Ram Dass) and Ralph Metzner, began to experiment with psilocybin (a synthetic version of the mushroom) and the similar drug mescaline. In 1961 he began experimenting with LSD (d-lysergic acid diethylamide). Using student and prisoner volunteers, Leary found LSD useful in the treatment of alcoholism and schizophrenia.

Harvard was displeased with the controversy over these experiments, and it dismissed Leary and Alpert in 1963. After a brief attempt to settle in Mexico, from which the government expelled them, they went on to found the International Foundation for Internal Freedom (IFIF), which operated in Millbrook, New York. Here Leary attempted to introduce the drug to other intellectual leaders, with varying results. (Allen Ginsberg was wildly enthusiastic; Arthur Koestler was not.)

Leary's enthusiasm for LSD and other psychedelics was so great that he began publicizing them. By 1963 LSD was known to avant-garde elements all over the nation's campuses and artistic communities. In a few years its recreational use would be a fad.

Leary also noticed the similarity between his experiences and the ideas of Eastern religion. In 1964 he, Alpert, and Metzner published *The Psychedelic Experience,* which used the *Tibetan Book of the Dead* as a paradigm for the death and rebirth experience often associated with the use of psychedelics, and in 1965 Leary visited India and converted to Hinduism. The following year he founded the League for Spiritual Discovery, a religious organization that would use LSD as a sacrament, just as the Native American Church used the psychedelic peyote.

By this time Leary had become a celebrity, and the controversies were swirling. Not only was LSD popular among hippies and creative artists of all sorts, but even such establishment figures as the military planner Herman Kahn and the publisher Henry Luce and his wife, the playwright and public official Clare Boothe Luce, said that the drug had expanded their minds. On the other side, activists of the political New Left charged Leary with offering a hedonistic distraction from civil rights and the Vietnam War, while more conservative sorts simply said that he was giving children drugs that would drive them crazy.

Neither of these critical views was entirely mistaken. Certainly the widespread experimentation with powerful chemicals, often contaminated by other substances, by inexperienced users was leading to some bad experiences and even long-term effects, though not as many as the media suggested. It must also be said that Leary, in the throes of

Timothy Leary. ARCHIVE PHOTOS, INC.

enthusiasm, did not always present a consistent, reasoned position. Sometimes he seemed to be urging revolution, psychological or political; other times he seemed to be peddling a new snake oil that would provide spiritual enlightenment *and* more and better orgasms.

Because Leary advocated violating drug laws, attempts were made to catch him doing just that. The most famous of these, a police raid of IFIF headquarters led by G. Gordon Liddy, failed to find anything to arrest him for, but he was caught bringing a minute quantity of marijuana into the country from Mexico and sentenced to ten years in jail. That conviction was overturned, but in 1970 Leary began serving a ten-year sentence on similar charges at the state prison in San Luis Obispo, California, where, like all incoming convicts, he was asked to fill out the personality evaluation he had designed. After an escape, aided by the radical Weather Underground, he eventually was recaptured in Afghanistan and returned to California to serve out his sentence.

Paroled in 1976, Leary turned from drug advocacy to a more science-based approach to human development, which he called SMI^{2}LE, for Space Migration, Increased Intelligence, and Life Extension. He welcomed the arrival of personal computers and became a software designer.

In the 1990s the mass media began treating Leary with affection, as an interesting thinker or, at worst, a lovably eccentric old uncle. Perhaps one reason for the change was the obvious fact that his well-publicized adventures in mind alteration had not left him *non compos mentis.*

In 1995 Leary learned that he had terminal prostate cancer and faced death as the last, greatest adventure. There was some talk of having his body, or at least his head, frozen to await improvements in medical technology, but when the cancer finally killed him in 1996, he was cremated. The next year his ashes were launched into orbit around Earth, with those of *Star Trek* creator Gene Roddenberry and others.

There are those who say that Leary's great mistake was to make LSD a public fad, rather than patiently introducing it through health professionals, and in his last years he came to agree with them. The harm caused by his decision included not only the destructive effects of bad trips and excessive, unsupervised use of the drug, but the loss of the healing potential Leary, Stanislav Grof, and others found in the use of LSD in controlled, therapeutic conditions. The panic of the mid-1960s led to laws forbidding even its most benign uses, laws that are still in effect today. Nevertheless, Leary opened doors, not all of which should have remained shut, and there still many who feel that their lives were enriched by the chemical he offered them.

★

Leary's autobiography, *Flashbacks,* was first published in 1983, then in a revised version, with an introduction by William S. Burroughs, in 1990. Book-length studies of the LSD movement and Leary's role in it include Michael Hollingshead, *The Man Who Turned On the World* (1973); Martin A. Lee and Bruce Shlain, *Acid Dreams* (1985); and Jay Stevens, *Storming Heaven: LSD and the American Dream* (1987). An obituary by Laura Mansnerus was published on the front page of the *New York Times* (1 June 1996).

ARTHUR D. HLAVATY

LEE, (Nelle) Harper (*b.* 28 April 1926 in Monroeville, Alabama), author of the critically acclaimed novel *To Kill a Mockingbird* (1960), which explores issues of racism and prejudice and which is widely considered one of the most influential novels of the twentieth century.

Lee was the youngest of three children of lawyer Amasa Coleman Lee and Frances (Finch) Lee and grew up in Monroeville. She became interested in writing when she was seven years old. Lee went to public school in Monroeville and then spent the 1944–1945 school year at Huntingdon College in Montgomery, Alabama, before attending the University of Alabama from 1945 to 1949. She spent one of these years as an exchange student at Oxford University in England. Although she pursued a law degree at the University of Alabama, she left in 1950, six months before graduating, and moved to New York City to become a writer. Lee was never married and had no children.

In New York Lee worked as an airline reservation clerk and wrote in her free time. A literary agent who read her work suggested that she expand one of her stories into a novel. With this encouragement, as well as financial help from friends, she quit her job and began writing full time, developing the story into her novel *To Kill a Mockingbird.* She submitted the novel to Lippincott in 1957 and, after much rewriting, it was published in 1960. Within a year it had sold 500,000 copies and been translated into ten languages.

The novel, set in the 1930s, stars Jean "Scout" Finch, the tomboy daughter of Atticus Finch, a small-town Alabama lawyer. Atticus is defending Tom Robinson, an African-American man who is falsely accused of raping a white girl. As the trial approaches, the situation becomes increasingly tense and dangerous. Racists threaten Tom Robinson's life as well as those of Atticus and his family, and in the end, although Atticus proves Robinson to be innocent, racial prejudice is so ingrained in the jurors and in society that they find him guilty.

At the same time, Scout is fascinated by a mysterious neighbor, Arthur "Boo" Radley, a reclusive man who is

Harper Lee. AP/WIDE WORLD PHOTOS

feared by many people in the town. Gradually Scout and her friends make contact with him; he turns out to be a kind but shy man and ultimately saves Scout's life when she is attacked by the father of the girl who was raped.

Both of these plot threads emphasize the necessity of understanding and accepting different kinds of people, even when that acceptance runs counter to social and legal custom. They also examine the depth of prejudice and hatred that can lie in the hearts of ordinary people in all walks of life, and how quickly such feelings can lead to violence.

The events in the book bear a striking similarity to those of the Scottsboro trial, in which nine African-American men were accused of raping a white girl. Although the evidence did not support this claim, and although another girl later confessed that the story was made up and that the rape never occurred, eight of the men were sentenced to death in 1931. The executions were suspended, and a series of retrials began, lasting until 1938. Four defendants were released in 1937. In 1938 one defendant, previously sentenced to death, received life imprisonment instead. Three others received jail sentences from seventy-five to ninety-nine years; one received a twenty-year sentence. Those in prison were paroled in the 1940s and through 1950, largely because of the work of activists on their behalf. It was not until 1976 that one of the defendants, who had fled from Alabama in 1946, was officially pardoned.

Themes of prejudice versus acceptance, as well as social justice, were on the minds of all Americans at the time the book was published, when the fight for civil rights and integration of African Americans was at its peak. Laws and customs dictating segregation of whites and African Americans had lasted for decades and were ingrained into society, most notably in the South. For example, throughout most of the twentieth century, African Americans were not allowed to use the same doctors, dentists, restaurants, restrooms, drinking fountains, public swimming pools, and other facilities that whites used. In many cases, they did not have these facilities at all. They went to separate and inferior schools and were not allowed to attend state colleges or universities. The only jobs available to them were menial and low-paying, many of them did not learn to read, and they were discouraged from voting because they did not meet qualifications, which were specifically designed to shut them out.

After World War II civil rights activists began challenging these laws and customs. In 1954 the United States Supreme Court ruled that racial segregation of schools was illegal. In 1955, in Montgomery, African Americans began refusing to sit in their traditional place, at the back of city buses, boycotting services until they were allowed to sit wherever they wanted. And in 1956 African-American leaders began challenging laws that prevented black students from enrolling at the state university. Challenges like these served both to inspire further civil rights actions and to provoke furious and often violent actions against African Americans and those who defended their civil rights. This civil rights battle continued throughout the 1960s.

In 1961 *To Kill a Mockingbird* won the Pulitzer Prize for fiction, as well as the Brotherhood Award of the National Conference of Christians and Jews. It was selected by the Literary Guild and the Book-of-the-Month Club. In 1962 it won the Paperback of the Year award and was made into an Academy Award–winning film.

In the early 1960s Lee published several short pieces about personal experiences, as well as an article, "Love— In Other Words." She has continued to write since but has not published any work. However, even if she never publishes another story or novel, her reputation as an influential American author is secure. As Claudia Durst Johnson wrote in *Understanding To Kill a Mockingbird,* the book "is . . . one of the most widely read . . . and influential books in American literature. It has made a significant difference in the lives of individuals and in the culture."

★

Claudia Durst Johnson's *Understanding To Kill a Mockingbird* (1994) includes a detailed analysis of the novel as well as documents on its social and political context. For more information about Lee see Dorothy Jewell Altman, "Harper Lee," in *Dictionary of Literary Biography,* Volume 6: *American Novelists Since World War II, Second Series* (1980).

KELLY WINTERS

LeMAY, Curtis Emerson (*b.* 15 November 1906 in Columbus, Ohio; *d.* 1 October 1990 on March Air Force Base, near Riverside, California), U.S. army and air force officer who established the ability of bombers to locate small targets at sea, created pattern bombing, oversaw the development of modern jet aircraft for the air force, and served as U.S. Air Force chief of staff from 1961 to 1965.

LeMay was the son of Erving LeMay, an occasional ironworker who often worked odd jobs, and Arizona (Carpenter) LeMay, who was a teacher when she met Erving in 1902. Erving had trouble keeping jobs, and the family relocated as he wandered the United States seeking work. LeMay resolved to become a pilot when, as a boy, he saw an airplane flying overhead.

LeMay hoped to join the U.S. Army Air Corps. However, in 1924 he failed to gain an appointment to the U.S. Military Academy at West Point and instead enrolled at Ohio State University, where he joined the Reserve Officer Training Corps (ROTC). He worked in a steel foundry to pay his way through college. In 1928, not yet having completed college, he enlisted in the Ohio National Guard, and

Curtis E. LeMay. THE LIBRARY OF CONGRESS

into an asset. On 7 January 1945 he became head of the 21st Bomber Command in Guam. He sent bombers on massive, low-level daylight raids, dropping incendiary bombs in dense packs on industrial centers of Japanese cities, markedly diminishing Japan's ability to produce armaments. LeMay was convinced that his tactics were forcing Japan to the point of surrender, but he made no comment about orders to drop atomic bombs on Japan.

In the National Security Act of 1947 the U.S. Air Force was established. LeMay was assigned command of U.S. air forces in Europe. On 26 June 1948 the Soviet Union blocked access by land to West Berlin. LeMay advocated forcing open the route from West Germany to West Berlin but was overruled. Instead he organized "Operation Vittles," an airlift of supplies to West Berliners; on 30 September 1948 the Soviets gave up their blockade.

In October 1948 LeMay was given command of the Strategic Air Command (SAC), which was supposed to protect the United States from attack. He found a badly organized and demoralized organization equipped with outdated aircraft. His reorganization of SAC into one of the world's premier military commands is considered LeMay's greatest achievement. By the mid-1950s SAC had bombers, and 80 percent of its nuclear bombs were in the air at all times.

On 4 April 1957 LeMay was appointed U.S. Air Force vice-chief of staff and assumed his new duties in July, in Washington, D.C. There he oversaw the day-to-day operations of the air force, while General Thomas D. White, the chief of staff, concentrated on his duties for the Joint Chiefs of Staff. While vice-chief, LeMay's efforts to develop new, more advanced aircraft for the air force met with initial success, with the building of prototypes of the B-70 bomber approved by Congress and President Dwight D. Eisenhower.

President Kennedy appointed LeMay his air force chief of staff in 1961. Almost immediately LeMay had problems with the new secretary of defense, Robert McNamara. McNamara had run the Ford Motor Company and had a reputation for being an outstanding manager of resources. He wanted to cut costs in the military and to begin by eliminating the B-70, the intended replacement for the B-52. Both the navy and air force wanted new jet fighters, and in spite of the very different needs of the two services, McNamara decided that instead of two new jet fighters he would approve only one, to be used by both services.

In 1961 LeMay believed the Soviet Union had outpaced America's jet fighters; if there were an air war involving fighters, he thought the United States could lose to the Soviet Union. He believed that to ensure peace, the United States should always have clearly superior armaments to discourage Soviet aggression. Kennedy, McNamara, and Maxwell Taylor, chairman of the Joint Chiefs of Staff, disagreed, adopting a policy of parity with the Soviet Union. On the other hand, the House of Representatives, although

in 1930 he was commissioned a second lieutenant in the artillery. LeMay served at Fort Knox, Kentucky, for a time, then was assigned to Columbus, Ohio, where he finished his studies at Ohio State, earning a bachelor's degree in engineering in 1932. On 9 June 1934 he married Helen Estelle Maitland; they had one daughter.

In 1937 LeMay was chosen to lead a small squadron of B-17 heavy bombers on a flight to South America to demonstrate the United States' ability to defend that continent. In March 1941 he attained the rank of major and was assigned to pioneer air routes in England, Africa, and South America. When the United States entered World War II, LeMay was promoted to lieutenant colonel and given the command of the 305th Bombardment Group. He trained the group and personally led them in attacks on Germany. While in command of the 305th, LeMay developed the pattern attack strategy that all U.S. bomber groups would eventually embrace. On 2 March 1944 he became a major general; at thirty-seven years old he was the youngest person to have held that rank since Ulysses S. Grant.

On 13 August 1944 LeMay was assigned to the China-Burma-India war theater, where he was in charge of the new B-29 Superfortress. This heavy bomber had been plagued by defects, but LeMay reengineered it, turning it controlled by Democrats (the party of Kennedy), agreed with LeMay and appropriated all the money needed to develop and deploy the B-70. McNamara refused to spend most of the money appropriated. This happened every year during LeMay's two terms as Air Force Chief of Staff.

McNamara tended to reduce issues to numbers—the losses of lives that would be acceptable in different sorts of conflicts. LeMay foresaw U.S. pilots flying inferior aircraft against a better-armed enemy and was angered by McNamara's attitude. He and other members of the Joint Chiefs of Staff became worried that they were not being fully informed about events. The Bay of Pigs disaster of 17–19 April 1961 had been partly blamed on them, even though they were not told about it until three days before it began. McNamara had implied that LeMay was at fault.

Given the antagonism between LeMay and McNamara, LeMay expected to retire after his 1961–1963 term ended. Yet it was the navy chief of staff, LeMay's close ally in the Joint Chiefs of Staff, who was dismissed. Strong support for LeMay in Congress and among servicemen made it politically expedient to keep him where he was. Matters between LeMay and the administration worsened, even after Lyndon B. Johnson became president following Kennedy's assassination in November 1963. LeMay opposed committing ground troops to the Vietnam War; he believed that air power properly used could eliminate North Vietnam's war supplies and end the fighting. The policy of gradual escalation adopted by the administration seemed to be absolute folly to LeMay. Even so, the only time he publicly criticized the administration was when he was under oath before Congress in response to direct questions. McNamara told him to lie; Lemay responded that he had a constitutional duty to answer truthfully questions put to him by Congress while he was under oath.

In 1964 rumors circulated that LeMay advocated bombing North Vietnam "back into the Stone Ages" and launching nuclear weapons at Hanoi. Although these rumors appear in many reference works about LeMay, he never promoted either of them. Since LeMay was known for his tactless bluntness of speech, such remarks were attributed to him without substantiation. Meanwhile, LeMay found himself in a scandal. While Kennedy was still president, the awarding of the contract for the new jet fighter for both the navy and air force had come down to General Dynamics and Boeing. The armed services committee for studying the planes proposed by the two companies recommended Boeing's plane. The administration told them to redo their studies and make a new recommendation. They did, and they again recommended Boeing. This was repeated two more times, with Boeing consistently recommended because its aircraft would be more versatile than that of General Dynamics and hundreds of millions of dollars cheaper

to develop. McNamara eventually chose General Dynamics and hinted that the military committee did not know what it was doing. Congress began an investigation into the matter and discovered many irregularities in the awarding of the contract, noting especially that General Dynamics would build its plane in Texas, which had numerous political connections to the administration, whereas Boeing would build its plane in Kansas. LeMay believed that McNamara was telling him to send pilots into combat with an inferior aircraft design.

LeMay's career ended in 1965 when he was not reappointed to his chief of staff position, and he retired as the longest-serving four-star general in U.S. history. Settling in southern California near his daughter and her family, he became a corporate executive. In 1968 Governor George Wallace of Alabama ran for president on the American Independent Party ticket. Twice LeMay was asked to join the ticket as the vice-presidential candidate and twice he declined, but he was very worried by how badly the war in Vietnam was being conducted and eventually agreed to run with Wallace in 1968, despite Wallace's racist views. His candidacy was a disaster for all concerned; LeMay said exactly what was on his mind, offending nearly everyone, and during a press conference with Wallace his hawkish statements seriously damaged an already floundering campaign.

After the election LeMay lived quietly, enjoying the company of his family. He died of a heart attack and was buried in the U.S. Air Force Academy Cemetery in Colorado Springs, Colorado. LeMay was probably the greatest air power strategist of the twentieth century. His innovations in strategy and tactics quite likely helped speed the end of World War II. LeMay molded SAC into a fighting force that served as an important deterrent to attacks on the United States during the cold war. During the 1960s he fought for and won a significant pay rise for all in the armed forces, and though he failed in his fight for significant improvements in armaments, he served as an example of integrity during an unhappy era in U.S. history.

★

Most of LeMay's papers are held in the Manuscripts Division of the Library of Congress. The National Air and Space Museum in Washington, D.C., and the Air Force Academy Library in Colorado Springs, Colorado, also have significant collections of his papers. LeMay and MacKinlay Kantor collaborated on LeMay's autobiography, *Mission with LeMay* (1965), which suffers somewhat from the fact that many of LeMay's exploits were still classified as secret when the book was published. Thomas M. Coffey, *Iron Eagle: The Turbulent Life of General Curtis LeMay* (1986), the standard biography, offers a detailed and lucid account of LeMay's service during the Kennedy and Johnson administrations. An obituary is in the *New York Times* (2 Oct. 1985).

KIRK H. BEETZ

LEMMON, John Uhler, III ("Jack") (*b.* 8 February 1925 in Newton, Massachusetts; *d.* 27 June 2001 in Los Angeles, California), two-time Academy Award–winning actor who often portrayed ordinary men in extraordinary circumstances.

Lemmon was born in an elevator between the fifth and sixth floors of the Wellesley-Newton Hospital, when his mother, Mildred LaRue Noel, refused to leave a game of bridge in which she felt she had a winning hand. His father was John Uhler Lemmon, Jr., the general sales manager and vice president of the Doughnut Corporation of America. Both of Lemmon's parents enjoyed singing and soft-shoe dancing. They placed their only child, when he was four years old, in a local production of *There's Gold in Them Thar Hills.* His theatrical debut included only one line—"Ha, I hear a pistol shot!"

Shy and sickly, Lemmon had missed a full year of schooling by the age of eight. When a friend could not appear in a school play, he put on his friend's oversized cowboy hat and cape and went on for him. The cheers and laughter of his schoolmates, he later recalled, "hooked me on acting," and it quickly became a "lifelong passion." He took up running and his health improved. At thirteen he was sent to the Phillips Academy in Andover, Massachusetts, where he taught himself to play the piano and enter-

Jack Lemmon, 1962. THE KOBAL COLLECTION

tained friends with comedy routines. Though he wanted to study drama at Yale, his father prevailed on him to take business classes at Harvard University, beginning in 1943.

Lemmon chronically cut classes to involve himself in the Hasty Pudding Theater Club, a Harvard theatrical troupe. Eventually he was elected its president. Placed on academic probation, he was billed as "Timothy Orange" so that he could appear in his own production, *The Bottom's Fallen Out of Everything but You.* In 1945 Lemmon was commissioned an ensign in the U.S. Navy, and spent seven months as a communications officer on the U.S.S. *Champlain,* an aircraft carrier. He graduated from Harvard in 1947 and on $300 borrowed from his father went to New York City. There he performed on radio soap operas and, between 1948 and 1952, on television. He costarred with the actress Cynthia Stone in four short-lived series, and the two were married on 7 May 1950.

Lemmon was offered a contract with Columbia after being spotted by a talent scout in the 1953 Broadway revival of *Room Service.* He began his film career opposite Judy Holliday in *It Should Happen to You!* (1954). The following year he won an Oscar for his portrayal of Ensign Pulver in *Mister Roberts.* Fans and critics considered Lemmon a comedian, but he objected. Although he wanted to play in dramas, Columbia would not consider the idea. His Oscar-nominated work in drag for the director Billy Wilder's hugely successful *Some Like It Hot* (1959) seemed to seal his fate in screen comedy.

Lemmon was not altogether satisfied with his success as he entered the 1960s. His marriage to Stone (which had produced a son, Christopher) ended in divorce in 1956. The actor sought more meaningful material and found it in *The Apartment* (1960), Wilder's wickedly perceptive take on corporate life in America. Lemmon's C. C. Baxter is a middle-management employee of an insurance company who "gets ahead" when bosses borrow his apartment for extramarital affairs. The film, along with Wilder's script and direction, all won Oscars, and Lemmon was nominated as best actor. Wilder thought Lemmon "the most consummate and appealing actor since the early Charlie Chaplin." Most actors, he told interviewers, "can show you one or two things and they've emptied their shelves. Jack Lemmon is Macy's and Tiffany's and the Sears and Roebuck Catalogue." Lemmon thought Wilder "grew a rose in a garbage pail" by showing the possibility of true love in "the age of the aspirin."

Lemmon hoped to deepen the impression that he was ready for dramatic roles by returning to Broadway in *Face of a Hero* (1960). He received good notices, but the play closed after only four weeks. Back at Columbia, *The Wackiest Ship in the Army* (1961) and *The Notorious Landlady* (1962), his third film with Kim Novak, confirmed Lemmon's status as a top-ten box office draw but did little to challenge him or his audience.

For nearly two years he and the director Blake Edwards had been trying to interest a Hollywood studio in J. P. Miller's *Days of Wine and Roses* (1962), the tragic tale of a public relations man and his wife, whose lives are destroyed by alcoholism. Warner Brothers reluctantly agreed to make the picture on a small budget. The results were an award-winning film that catapulted Lemmon into the first rank of Hollywood stars. His performance as Joe Clay, who tears up a greenhouse in a drunken rage and loses his mind while strait-jacketed in a detoxification center, shocked audiences and thrilled critics. The *New Yorker* found Lemmon's performance a revelation, alternately "dazzling, funny, anguished, indignant, rueful, affectionate and cruel." A critic in the *Saturday Review* expressed the hope that the film would help Hollywood realize that "Lemmon is not only one of our ablest young comedians, but actually one of the screen's finest all-around performers."

Lemmon reteamed with Wilder for *Irma La Douce* (1963), and while filming in France in 1962 married his long-time love, actress Felicia Farr. They had one daughter, Courtney. Lemmon sped through two well-received but unremarkable comedies—*Under the Yum Yum Tree* (1963) and *Good Neighbor Sam* (1964)—to complete his contract with Columbia. Now able to finally freelance, he was at first uncharacteristically cautious. Roles as the harried husband in *How to Murder Your Wife* (1965) and the evil professor in Edwards's *The Great Race* (1965) did little to enlarge or diminish his reputation.

His next film for Wilder, however, quickly became a fan favorite. In *The Fortune Cookie* (1966) Lemmon is television cameraman Harry Hinkle, who fakes an injury while covering a football game in order to collect a quarter-million dollars in insurance money. His former brother-in-law, "Whiplash" Willie Gingrich, supremely played by Walter Matthau, is behind the fraud and the fun. When Matthau suffered a heart attack midway through the production, Lemmon and Wilder shut the film down and awaited his return. The result was an Academy Award for Matthau and the birth of one of the funniest teams in Hollywood history.

The Odd Couple (1968), Lemmon's and Matthau's next collaboration, and their most memorable, was based on Neil Simon's stage play that starred Matthau and Art Carney. Lemmon solidified his screen persona as the overwrought everyman with his performance as Felix Ungar. Matthau's finely tuned Oscar Madison, the casually indifferent, endlessly sloppy sports writer, was equally unforgettable. The plot involves two fast friends, one divorced and the other about to be, who put civility to the test when they try living together in Madison's mid-Manhattan apartment. Critics and fans found the results riotous. The scene of Lemmon loudly clearing his sinuses as a bewildered Matthau looks on is a comedy classic, as is a shouting match between Felix and Oscar that finally finishes when a sticky plate of spaghetti is hurled against a wall.

The admiration between the two stars was immediate, deep, and permanent. Matthau observed that "Lemmon's characters allow us to see the world through the eyes of someone we know, someone he hints we may even be." Lemmon loved Matthau's improvisational quality that unexpectedly enriched scenes from take to take. The two actors fed off one another in transcending their material. Lemmon said, "When Walter and I really get it going there's three stars in the picture—me, Walter and the two of us together." Simon believed the contradiction of their characters made them particularly appealing. Their relationship "is like a marriage," he noted. "They fight but the audience knows they want to hold on to one another. The way Jack and Walter play it—the love shows through."

Lemmon's next Neil Simon character became a cult classic, even though critics are still divided as to whether *The Out-of-Towners* (1970) is worthy of all the excitement. The story follows the tortured path of George and Gwen Kellerman from their quiet suburban home in Dayton, Ohio, to their nightmare encounter with New York City. What follows is a survey of all that had gone wrong with the American city of the 1960s. Their plane is rerouted, their luggage lost, and their train's dining car is closed. They finally arrive during a downpour. There is a transportation strike and a sanitation strike, and their hotel reservation is lost. They are mugged, thrown out of church, and even have their last cracker-jack box taken from them, but only after George chips a front tooth on a nut. At its release, New York critics were nearly unanimous in deriding Simon's "excruciating" script and Lemmon's "stupidly stubborn" character. What the *New York Times* called "witlessly uncomfortable," the *New York Daily News* described as "desperately hilarious." Simon saw Lemmon's "complete conviction" capturing "the common man's battle against what modern living puts upon him." He is pushed beyond what would seem endurable but refuses to surrender. That is why Lemmon was "my voice and the voice of many" in his battle with modernity. "He played the character like an instrument," Simon said, "and made it into a Stradivarius."

Lemmon directed Matthau in *Kotch* (1971), the largely successful, if highly sentimental, story of a garrulous old man who is a nuisance to his son and daughter-in-law. *Save the Tiger* (1973) was his Oscar-winning account of Harry Stoner, a middle-aged dress manufacturer who sets fire to his factory. Behind the act is a formerly decent man in indecent times who comforts himself in the rationalization, "it's only arson if you're caught." For Lemmon the part was an opportunity "to go beyond entertainment in making people stop and think what they would not have thought had they not seen the film." In his twentieth year in films, he had come to see that as "a great gift."

The quarter-century that followed affirmed Lemmon's rank as a star of the first magnitude whose characters, in Lemmon's view, "had to make a fundamental choice" between doing what they knew to be right or what was expedient, even when virtue came at a considerable cost. Roles included that of Mel, an out-of-work executive who remembers every insult and is brutalized by affluence, in Simon's *The Prisoner of Second Avenue* (1975); Jack Godell, the nuclear engineer who stands alone, risking his own career, when he senses that unsafe conditions might lead to a meltdown, in *The China Syndrome* (1979); and Ed Horman, who in *Missing* (1982) takes on the American government in seeking the whereabouts of his son, who disappeared in a Chilean coup surreptitiously backed by Washington. A decade later he played Sheldon "the Machine" Levene, a pathetic real-estate salesman in *Glengarry Glen Ross* (1992). His reunion with Matthau in *Grumpy Old Men* (1993) was a box office bonanza and led to a string of Lemmon-Matthau collaborations, among them *Grumpier Old Men* (1995) and *The Old Couple II* (1998).

Lemmon was a long-time friend of liberal causes, particularly the environment. A number of younger actors, including Kevin Spacey, Alec Baldwin, and Matthew Broderick, all said that no one had been more helpful to them than Lemmon. Shortly before his death of complications from cancer, Lemmon said that his acting had long been shaped by the French writer Albert Camus's idea that "if man understood the enigma of life there would be no need for the arts." When Lemmon died, headlines heralded the passing of the "American Everyman," the great landscape painter of cinema's second half-century, whose brushstrokes captured the striving, uncertain success and ultimate sadness of postmodern man.

★

Biographies of Lemmon include Don Widener, *Lemmon: A Biography* (1975); Will Holtzman, *Jack Lemmon* (1977); Michael Freedland, *Jack Lemmon* (1985); and Joe Baltake, *Jack Lemmon: His Films and Career* (1986). Major articles include Joe Baltake, "Jack Lemmon Has the Potential to Succeed Bob Hope or Fredric March," *Films in Review* (Jan. 1970). Obituaries are in the *New York Times* and *Los Angeles Times* (both 29 June 2001).

BRUCE J. EVENSEN

LEONARD, Sheldon (*b.* 22 February 1907 in New York City; *d.* 10 January 1997 in Beverly Hills, California), actor, producer, director and cocreator of television series, including *The Andy Griffith Show* and *The Dick Van Dyke Show.*

Born Sheldon Leonard Bershad, Leonard was the oldest son of Frank Bershad, a salesman of watchbands, electric mousetraps, and other odds and ends, and Anna Levitt, whose father had once served as a scribe in the court of Czar Nicholas II. Raised in the Bronx and lower Manhattan, Leonard took to acting early, starring in a number of high school productions. After graduating from Syracuse University, he landed a job with a brokerage firm on Wall Street, only to lose it after the stock market crash of October 1929. Following his wedding to Frankie Bober in 1931 (they would remain married until his death sixty-six years later), Leonard returned to acting and appeared in several Broadway productions during the 1930s. Because of his dark, brooding countenance, muscular build, and thick "New Yawk" accent, he was frequently cast as a villain, gangster, or other "heavy."

In 1939 Leonard made his film debut in *Another Thin Man* and, over the next two decades, appeared in more than fifty motion pictures, becoming one of the best "character actors" in the business. His performances in such movies as *Tall, Dark, and Handsome* (1941), *To Have and Have Not* (1945), and *Guys and Dolls* (1955) have often been described as "Runyonesque" and "quietly menacing." His turn as Nick the bartender in the Frank Capra classic *It's a Wonderful Life* (1946) is arguably his most memorable role.

During the 1950s Leonard accepted fewer acting jobs and, instead, began to focus his considerable skills and energy upon the new medium of television. In 1953 he became director for the Danny Thomas vehicle, *The Danny Thomas Show* (also known as *Make Room for Daddy*). He was later promoted to producer, and stayed with the show until its end in 1965. In addition, Leonard was associated, as either producer or director (or both), with a number of other shows, including *Lassie* (1954–1971), *The Jimmy Durante Show* (1954–1957), and *The Real McCoys* (1957–1963), earning plaudits from both his peers and the press for his work.

By the 1960s Thomas and Leonard had formed a partnership that would leave an indelible mark upon television, comedy, and American popular culture. Their company, T and L Productions, was responsible for two of the most critically acclaimed series of all time, *The Andy Griffith Show* and *The Dick Van Dyke Show,* along with such minor classics as *My Favorite Martian; Gomer Pyle, U.S.M.C.;* and *The Bill Dana Show.* The formula for these programs, or what some termed the "T and L trademark," was simple: good writing, believable characters, and stories that dealt

Sheldon Leonard *(right)*, with his wife, September 1963. JACK ALBIN/GETTY IMAGES

with modern relationships without either cynicism or mindless slapstick.

The Dick Van Dyke Show, the brainchild of comedian Carl Reiner, debuted on 3 October 1961. It centered upon the private and professional lives of television comedy writer Robert Petrie, played by the irrepressible Van Dyke. Anticipating later comedies, such as *Taxi, Cheers,* and *Friends,* the show featured a talented ensemble cast, whose efforts to navigate a sometimes harrowing urban landscape resulted in what many consider some of television's funniest moments. The success of *The Dick Van Dyke Show* has been largely attributed to Leonard's unparalleled knack for recognizing comic genius (it was Leonard, after all, who suggested Van Dyke for the role of Petrie over Reiner, who stayed on as writer and featured performer) and for demanding solid work, week in and week out, from the show's gifted team of writers.

Premiering a year before *The Dick Van Dyke Show, The Andy Griffith Show* seemed light years removed from the urbanity and glitz of Leonard's other creations. Chronicling the exploits of a southern sheriff Andy Taylor (Griffith), and his bungling yet well-intentioned deputy Barney Fife (Don Knotts), the show sympathetically and hilariously portrayed small-town American life without resorting to outdated stereotypes and exploitative humor. In an era when abusive and bigoted southern lawmen were making headlines, Sheriff Taylor appeared as a gentle voice of reason, treating even the town drunk Otis with dignity and respect. Leonard, who had recognized immediately the co-

medic potential of Griffith, and who, along with the star and Aaron Ruben, devised a majority of the storylines, told an interviewer years later: "I think the *Andy Griffith Show* maintained a higher level of quality than almost any other show I can think of . . . the performance, the direction, the editing, and the scoring were of a quality that has seldom been equaled." Considering the ever-growing popularity of the show in syndication, few could argue with this.

By the mid-1960s, following a full decade of mainstream success in the television industry, Leonard moved on to more risky projects. In the fall of 1965, his espionage thriller *I Spy,* starring Robert Culp and the comedian Bill Cosby, appeared on the National Broadcasting Company (NBC). The series, which concerned the frenetic lives of two government agents, Kelly Robinson and Alexander Scott, appeared in a field flooded by similar programs. But what set *I Spy* apart from its competitors was its wry sense of humor, its exotic locales, and the fact that one of its leading men was African American—an unprecedented casting decision that Leonard feared would doom the show in the eyes of network executives and viewers below the Mason-Dixon line. He could not have been more wrong. *I Spy* became a critical and popular success, earning its stars and creator innumerable awards and wide acclaim.

During the latter half of the 1960s and early 1970s, Leonard produced a number of short-lived series, including *Good Morning, World* (1967); *My Friend Tony* (1969); the inventive and critically acclaimed *My World and Welcome to It* (1969–1970); *Shirley's World* (1971–1972); and *The*

Don Rickles Show (1972). In 1975 he returned to acting, playing the role of Eddie Smith, a hard-nosed sports promoter and former gambler, in the Columbia Broadcasting System (CBS) series *Big Eddie.* Although Leonard never again topped the success of *The Andy Griffith Show* or *The Dick Van Dyke Show,* his position as one of television's most innovative and talented producers and directors was secure. On 3 October 1992 he was inducted into the Television Academy Hall of Fame, along with friend Andy Griffith and others. Leonard died at the age of eighty-nine and is buried at the Hillside Cemetery in Culver City, California.

★

For further reading, see Leonard's autobiography, *And the Show Goes On: Broadway and Hollywood Adventures* (1995); Richard Kelly, *The Andy Griffith Show* (1981); and Vince Waldron, *The Official Dick Van Dyke Show Book* (1994).

GARY SPRAYBERRY

LEWIS, (Joseph) Anthony (*b.* 27 March 1927 in New York City), two-time Pulitzer Prize–winning journalist, United States Supreme Court and Department of Justice correspondent for the *New York Times* Washington bureau in the early 1960s, and chief of the London bureau in the latter part of the 1960s.

Anthony Lewis, May 1963. ASSOCIATED PRESS AP

The son of Kassel Lewis, a textile executive, and Silvia Surut, Lewis was editor of a student publication at New York's Horace Mann High School. In 1944 he entered Harvard, majoring in English, and was managing editor of the *Harvard Crimson,* the daily school newspaper. He served three months in the U.S. Navy during World War II but was discharged because of eye problems. He graduated with an A.B. from Harvard in 1948. In 1952 he worked as a researcher for the Democratic governor of Illinois, Adlai Stevenson. On 8 July 1951 he married Linda Joan Rannells, whom he later divorced. The couple had three children.

In 1952 Lewis joined the *Washington Daily News* staff and in 1955 won a Pulitzer Prize for journalism for his articles on employee security in the government. Communism among civil service employees was an important issue in that era. Just after the Pulitzer Prize was announced, Lewis was recruited by James Reston, then Washington bureau chief, to join the staff of the *New York Times.* Lewis's beat became the Justice Department and the Supreme Court. In the 1960s the focus of both agencies was the civil rights movement, as the Supreme Court led the way in securing rights for the black minority.

In 1964 Lewis edited a compilation of articles by *New York Times* journalists, *Portrait of a Decade: The Second American Revolution, A First Hand Account of the Struggle for Civil Rights from 1954–1964.* Lewis painted a picture of

the South in turmoil—President Dwight Eisenhower using troops to admit students to high school in Little Rock, Arkansas; fire bombings of churches in Alabama; and the murder of a black student admitted to the University of Mississippi. In the book's view, matters on an economic and social level were getting worse even as the Supreme Court was fleshing out improved legal rights. Moreover, there was no need for the North to be smug—Lewis inserted an article depicting the suburbs of Chicago in turmoil over the influx of blacks. There was also an article by the poet LeRoi Jones (later called Amiri Baraka), then unknown, attacking the depiction of American blacks as happy with their lot. The only positive institution emerging from the pages was the United States Supreme Court— with the voice of the civil rights leader the Reverend Martin Luther King, Jr., in the background.

In 1962 the Supreme Court announced its decision in *Baker* v. *Carr,* in which it ruled that legislative districts in the popular branches of state legislatures must be of essentially equal size in population. The ruling was later expanded to virtually all U.S. legislative bodies except the U.S. Senate. Lewis released a Pulitzer Prize–winning article on the decision titled "Historic Change in Supreme Court" that "opened the doors of the federal courts to legal attacks on the apportionment of seats in state legislatures." Lewis saw the decision as part of a "revolution in constitutional doctrine in recent years" involving "criminal proceedings" and "racial segregation." The Supreme Court's focus was no longer on economic issues. "The conclusion is that the Supreme Court has tended in recent years to act as the instrument of national moral values that have not been able to find other governmental expression." Lewis concluded with respect to the Court: "Its great success has been as a moral goad to the political process—when it has urged politicians to do what they have avoided doing but knew in their hearts they should . . . the Court is taking up the role of conscience to the country."

Lewis's most enduring popular work was *Gideon's Trumpet* (1964). Clarence Earl Gideon, a down-on-his-luck defendant in a routine Florida burglary trial, quietly requested defense counsel but was turned down because the state of Florida at that time did not provide an attorney to a defendant unless the case involved the death penalty. Gideon was found guilty, mostly on the basis of questionable eyewitness testimony, and was sentenced to a Florida penitentiary. He sought review by the United States Supreme Court, urging that he had been entitled to counsel.

Much of Lewis's book details the long odds that Gideon's plea to the Supreme Court would ever get a full hearing. By what Lewis described as a near miracle, the Court heard his case and assigned Arthur Goldberg, later a justice himself, as Gideon's attorney. Lewis accounted in detail Goldberg's briefing and argument of his case as well as the preparations of the lawyer assigned by Florida to defend the matter. After argument and internal battling in the Court, Gideon prevailed, as the Supreme Court announced that all defendants in the United States facing deprivation of liberty would be entitled to an assigned counsel to defend them if they desired an attorney and were unable to afford one. As Lewis wrote, like the Gideon of the Old Testament, he blew his trumpet and the walls fell down. He also followed up the story: Gideon was retried with competent counsel and found not guilty. Lewis then conducted an extensive study of the efforts of states to provide counsel for defendants in non-capital cases. While such lawyers are underpaid and overworked, once again the 1960s ethos of placing social problems in the hands of the legal community is in evidence.

In 1964 Lewis became the *New York Times* London bureau chief and within three months was writing the obituary for Sir Winston Churchill, the former statesman and prime minister. His bureau covered Harold Wilson's short career as prime minister, the slow decline of the British Empire, and Charles's investiture as Prince of Wales. In the meantime Lewis continued to pursue American legal topics; among other works, he wrote an introduction to the *Times* publication of the Warren Commission report on the assassination of President John F. Kennedy. In 1972 Lewis left the London bureau and was posted to Boston. He married Margaret H. Marshall on 23 September 1984.

In 1991 Lewis returned to the *Times* v. *Sullivan* case that he had covered in the 1960s. That case provided that only recklessly false statements about public figures would be subject to libel suits. Lewis documented the changes in how lawyers, the courts, and the media reacted to libel complaints in a book entitled *Make No Law: The Sullivan Case and the First Amendment* (1992).

★

Lewis's works include a large number of opinion/editorial pieces and dispatches to the *New York Times* and *Washington Daily News*. His books include *Gideon's Trumpet* (1964) and *Portrait of a Decade: The Second American Revolution* (1964). For biographical information on Lewis see *Current Biography* (1955) and the *New York Times* (3 May 1955).

JOHN DAVID HEALY

LEWIS, Jerry (*b.* 16 March 1926 in Newark, New Jersey), comedian, actor, philanthropist, filmmaker, and auteur who morphed during the 1960s from a nerdy sidekick into an *artiste,* the darling of French intelligentsia and their "Sacred Monster."

Lewis, born Jerome (some sources say Joseph) Levitch, was the only child of Daniel Levitch, an actor, and Rae Brodsky, a pianist and actor. Lewis's parents were a show business

Jerry Lewis. THE KOBAL COLLECTION

couple that performed professionally as Danny and Rae Lewis. Young Lewis made his debut at a benefit in the Catskills in 1932 with a poignant rendition of "Brother, Can You Spare a Dime?" He was just six years old. Hooked on entertainment, Lewis left Irvington High School at the age of sixteen. He developed a "bit" that was part Charlie McCarthy (the dummy prop of the comedian Edgar Bergen) and part Al Jolson (a vaudeville performer and early movie star), in which he would mime to music with exaggerated, spastic movements. Though nurtured in the Borscht Belt environs of Jewish humor in upstate New York, the young comic quite deliberately de-emphasized his background in order to reach a wider audience. Although eager to serve in World War II, Lewis was declared unfit for service because of a perforated eardrum and a heart murmur.

After a floundering apprenticeship as a "hack" comic, Lewis hit pay dirt in the summer of 1946 at Atlantic City, New Jersey, when he joined the actor and singer Dean Martin to form America's most dynamic comedic duo since Bud Abbott and Lou Costello. Based on the best Borscht Belt tradition of doing anything for a laugh, the comic and the crooner fed off each other's shtick. They became an instant hit. Jew and Italian, putz and playboy, the duet played to packed audiences in nightclubs and theaters, especially New York's Paramount. They moved on to box-office bonanzas in Hollywood and enormous success on television, America's "tube of plenty." Together they starred in seventeen films, which earned millions for Paramount Pictures. According to the biographer Nick Tosches, Lewis and Martin's ability to cross boundaries—between masculine and feminine, straight and gay, adult and child—provided a much-needed escape from cold war anxieties, while sustaining male camaraderie forged during World War II. Lewis conceded that he "kept the child in me alive. I'm nine and I've always been nine since 1935 and I will always be nine."

Lewis married the nightclub singer Patti Palmer, six years his senior, on 3 October 1944. They had five sons and adopted another, but their marriage—plagued by the comic's imperious manner and frequent infidelities—ended in divorce in 1982. One year later, on 13 February 1983, Lewis married Sandra ("San Dee") Pitnick, with whom he had been romantically linked. They adopted a daughter in 1992.

In 1956 a discontented Martin bolted after their last film, *Hollywood or Bust.* On 25 July 1956 Lewis and Martin made their final stage appearance at the Copacabana club in New York City, ten years to the day after their first team performance. After the split Martin thrived as a singer and actor, while his erstwhile partner was "All Alone" by the Irving Berlin telephone. Lewis refocused his energies as an actor, writer, director, and singer. Prodded by the singer

Judy Garland, Lewis even sang solo. In fact, his first recording, *Jerry Lewis Just Sings* (1956), was a best-selling album, and his single "Rock-a-Bye Your Baby" sold more than a million copies in the late 1950s. Inspired by the songs of Jolson and the films of Charlie Chaplin, the young artist branched out in the halcyon 1960s to essay the varied roles of a "Renaissance man."

Lewis's career peaked during the 1960s. He made seventeen films, including several gems, namely, *The Bellboy* and *Cinderfella* (1960), *The Ladies Man* and *The Errand Boy* (1961), and *The Patsy* (1964). Chaplin hailed *The Bellboy* as a work of genius. It paid homage to the silent movie clowns Chaplin and Buster Keaton. Drawing on his Catskills experience, Lewis identified with the silent working class and crafted a comic character—Stanley—in opposition to an oppressive society. The other movies proved less popular and profitable, with the exception of *The Nutty Professor* (1963), which showed his talents as writer, director, and performer. Derived from the polar personas of Dr. Jekyll and Mr. Hyde, the film projected two sides of Lewis's personality, the introverted intellectual Julius Kelp and the chemically charged, ebullient Buddy Love. Although most fans believed that the movie caricatured his former partner, Dean Martin, Lewis claimed that it actually highlighted his own dark side.

By the mid-1960s Lewis was up against the creative wall. An ambitious attempt to emulate the British actor Sir Alec Guinness (in *Kind Hearts and Coronets,* 1949), by impersonating seven characters in search of a legacy in *The Family Jewels* (1965), flopped. In that same year Lewis suffered a freak accident in an appearance on *The Andy Williams Show,* which resulted in a linear skull fracture. This injury precipitated severe disability and constant pain—alleviated only by powerful painkillers. Lewis admitted later that he suffered from a long-term drug dependency on Percodan, an addiction he finally broke in 1979. In 1965 Lewis left Paramount for Columbia Pictures, where he continued to write, direct, and produce films that earned diminishing profits. Evidently, Lewis was out of synch with 1960s youth culture. Lewis tried in vain to stay current, even singing with his rock star son Gary, but the older Lewis could not keep the beat of Gary Lewis and the Playboys.

Lewis's burst of creativity in the 1960s endeared him to the mandarins of French culture. The moviemaker Jean Luc Godard "dug" his movies, as the slang of the day put it. Jack Lang dubbed him "a child's friend and a model for adults." Lewis even taught a graduate course in film direction at the University of Southern California (USC) in 1967, where he was a professor of cinema arts. Hundreds of students flocked to this course; among them, the filmmakers George Lukas, Francis Ford Coppola, Randy Klieser, Peter Bogdanovich, and Steven Spielberg. Out of this heady experience issued a text, aptly titled: *The Total*

Film-Maker (1971). Lewis also helped raise enormous sums for charity. He is a spokesperson for the Muscular Dystrophy Association (MDA), a charity that he has been involved with since the 1940s. In 1966 Lewis began annual television appeals for MDA that were broadcast over the Labor Day weekend. The MDA Telethon yearly netted increasing amounts of money: $1.25 million in 1967, $1.4 million in 1968, $2.04 million in 1969, and $5.09 million at the decade's end.

Lionized abroad, Lewis floundered at home. In January 1957 he launched a series of specials for the National Broadcasting Company (NBC) dubbed *The Jerry Lewis Show*. Only moderately successful, they were superceded by a disastrous switch to the American Broadcasting Company (ABC) in 1963. A hybrid of talk and variety, the two-hour *The Jerry Lewis Show* appeared live on Saturday evenings. After thirteen shows the series ended on 25 December 1963. Lewis blamed the sponsors and affiliates. A comeback attempt on ABC on 12 September 1967 proved equally dismal. A stage version of *Hellzapoppin'* in 1976 never reached Broadway. Most painful, however, was the failure of his pet film project, *The Day the Clown Cried* (1972), which remained incomplete and unreleased. Evidently seeking to reconnect with his Jewish roots and to regain his golden touch at the movie box office, Lewis unhappily succumbed to bathos, banality, and litigation.

Lewis's work for the MDA earned him a nomination, courtesy of Congressman Les Aspin, for the Nobel Peace Prize in 1977. Frank Krutnick insightfully locates the roots of Lewis's philanthropy. Empowered and impassioned with the rhetoric of love, often absent from his formative years, Lewis is the mediating father figure who "rages, cries, pleads, and cajoles on behalf of the victim-child against the villain of disease." Lewis transforms fear and guilt into love—a precious kind of love that is measured in money. On 3 September the 2001 MDA Telethon raised $56.7 million for medical research. The telethon was carried on more than two hundred television stations and viewed by more than seventy-five million people in the United States, Canada, and Puerto Rico.

Lewis's artistic regeneration began after a near fatal heart attack in December 1982, with a stunning performance in Martin Scorcese's *The King of Comedy* (1983). In a strikingly understated performance, he played Jerry Langford, who personified the many faces—in the apposite French designation—of the "Sacred Monster." His impersonation of Applegate, the Devil, in the 1995–1997 stage revival of *Damn Yankees* also elicited rave reviews. Lewis's films garnered more than $800 million at a time when most ticket prices were less than one dollar. Remakes of his best films, plus his prolific output of sixty-three films as an actor, seventeen as a director, fourteen as a producer, and eleven as a writer assure Lewis a place in our national pantheon.

★

Lewis's autobiography, written with Herb Gluck, is *Jerry Lewis in Person* (1984). A collection of Lewis's insights on filmmaking is in his book *The Total Film-Maker* (1971). Biographies of Lewis include Richard Gehman, *That Kid—The Story of Jerry Lewis* (1964); Patti Lewis, *I Laffed Till I Cried: Thirty-Six Years of Marriage to Jerry Lewis* (1993); and Shawn Levy, *King of Comedy: The Life and Art of Jerry Lewis* (1996). Biographical information is also in Nick Tosches's biography of Dean Martin, *Dino: Living High in the Dirty Business of Dreams* (1992); James L. Neibaur and Ted Okuda, *The Jerry Lewis Films: An Analytical Filmography of the Innovative Comic* (1995); Frank Krutnik, *Inventing Jerry Lewis* (2000); and Rae Beth Gordon, *Why the French Love Jerry Lewis: From Cabaret to Early Cinema* (2001).

JOSEPH DORINSON

LEWIS, John Robert (*b.* 21 February 1940 near Troy, Alabama), leader of the Nashville, Tennessee, sit-in demonstrations, freedom rider, and head of the Student Nonviolent Coordinating Committee, who was involved in nearly all phases of the southern civil rights movement from 1960 to 1966.

The third of ten children born to Eddie and Willie Mae Lewis, Lewis was raised on a 110-acre cotton and peanut

John Lewis. AP/WIDE WORLD PHOTOS

farm in Pike County, Alabama. As a boy he dreamed of being a preacher. In 1957 he enrolled at the American Baptist Theological Seminary in Nashville. His interest in civil rights was enhanced when he attended workshops in nonviolence conducted by James Lawson, a Methodist divinity student who had gone to India to study the tactics of the Indian activist Mahatma Gandhi. On 13 February 1960 Lewis was one of 124 well-dressed and highly disciplined students who sat in at segregated downtown Nashville lunch counters, insisting that they be served. Lewis viewed his participation as a manifestation of his religious beliefs: "it was like being involved in a Holy Crusade," he recalled. "I really felt that what we were doing was so in keeping with the Christian faith." The nonviolent students continued their protest for four months until Mayor Ben West publicly conceded that segregation was morally wrong. A few days later lunch counters quietly desegregated.

Lewis was one of the southern sit-in leaders who attended an Easter weekend conference at Shaw University in Raleigh, North Carolina, in 1960 to discuss ways to sustain and expand their movement. Out of that meeting the Student Nonviolent Coordinating Committee (SNCC) was formed. Lewis received a B.A. from American Baptist Theological Seminary in 1961 and would later receive a second B.A. from Fisk University in 1967.

In May 1961 Lewis joined an interracial band of nonviolent activists organized by the Congress of Racial Equality. They planned to ride from Washington, D.C., to New Orleans to test compliance with a Supreme Court ruling that declared segregated transportation facilities unconstitutional. In Rock Hill, South Carolina, angry whites assaulted Lewis and other riders. Outside of Anniston, Alabama, their bus was firebombed. When they arrived in Birmingham, Alabama, the so-called freedom riders were savagely beaten by a white mob. Lewis had left the group in South Carolina but rejoined the journey for its next leg from Birmingham to Montgomery, Alabama, where another mob lay in wait. Lewis was hit over the head with a wooden crate and knocked unconscious, but he later continued to Jackson, Mississippi, where he was arrested and sentenced to sixty days in jail.

In 1963 Lewis left college to work full-time as a freedom fighter. He soon was elected SNCC's chairman, a position he held for the next three years during the height of the civil rights movement.

As SNCC's spokesman, Lewis was among the "Big Six" civil rights leaders who planned the 1963 March on Washington. He delivered one of the major addresses at the rally in front of the Lincoln Memorial on 28 August. The original version of his oration strongly criticized President John F. Kennedy's timid commitment to civil rights: "In good conscience, we cannot support the administration's civil rights bill for it is too little, and too late." When other, more moderate leaders objected to the harsh tone of his remarks, Lewis was forced to excise the most critical passages.

Lewis was an early advocate of the 1964 Mississippi Freedom Summer, which brought 800 volunteer civil rights workers to the most violent southern state. In August he worked on behalf of the Mississippi Freedom Democratic Party (formed to circumvent the segregationist-dominated mainstream Democratic Party in Mississippi) by attempting to seat their delegates at the Democratic National Convention in Atlantic City, New Jersey. In early 1965 Lewis was in Selma, Alabama, campaigning for voting rights. On 7 March 1965 Lewis and the Southern Christian Leadership Conference activist Hosea Williams led a column of some 600 demonstrators intending to march from Selma to the state capitol in Montgomery to protest the killing of Jimmy Lee Jackson in Marion, Alabama. As the marchers crossed the Edmund Pettus Bridge, a force of 200 state troopers and sheriff's deputies blocked the road. When ordered to turn back, the marchers refused to disperse and the lawmen attacked with tear gas and clubs. Lewis was one of the first to fall, knocked to the pavement with a fractured skull and concussion. The brutal scene was rapidly transmitted around the world by television and became known as "Bloody Sunday." The resulting outrage was instrumental in securing passage of the Voting Rights Act five months later.

In the summer of 1966 the civil rights movement headed in a new, more militant direction. Lewis was criticized for participating in the planning of the White House Conference on Civil Rights and was voted out as SNCC's chairman. His replacement by Stokely Carmichael, the leading advocate of Black Power, signaled the group's shift in the direction of extremism. Shortly afterwards Lewis resigned from SNCC, expressing concern that the organization had strayed from its nonviolent roots.

Lewis remained active in the civil rights movement, working first for the Field Foundation and later for the Southern Regional Council. From 1970 to 1977 he headed the Voter Education Project, which added millions of African Americans to the voter rolls. In 1977 he joined the administration of President Jimmy Carter as director of ACTION, the agency that coordinated federal volunteer programs including the Peace Corps and VISTA. In 1981 Lewis was elected to the Atlanta City Council, and in 1986 he was elected to the U.S. House of Representatives from Georgia's Fifth Congressional District in Atlanta. He later sat on the House Ways and Means Committee and served as chief deputy minority whip.

Lewis married Lillian Miles in 1968. They had one son, John Miles Lewis.

One of the genuine heroes of the southern civil rights movement, Lewis was jailed more than forty times and was the victim of several vicious beatings, yet his faith in non-violence never wavered. His great personal courage and quiet leadership earned him the respect and admiration of his colleagues in the movement, even those who disagreed with his politics. Furthermore, his rise from a sharecropper's cabin to the halls of Congress is an inspirational American success story.

★

John Lewis with Michael D'Orso, *Walking with the Wind: A Memoir of the Movement* (1998), is the best single source on Lewis's career. David Halberstam, *The Children* (1998), profiles the lives of Lewis and seven other Nashville protest leaders. Clayborne Carson, *In Struggle: SNCC and the Black Awakening of the 1960s* (1981), places Lewis's role within SNCC in perspective. Lewis is also prominently featured in several segments of the 1987 Public Broadcasting System documentary series *Eyes on the Prize*.

PAUL T. MURRAY

LEWIS, Oscar (*b.* 25 December 1914 in New York City; *d.* 16 December 1970 in New York City), gifted anthropologist, educator, and author and an inspired innovator in anthropological methods whose controversial work on the "culture of poverty" theory greatly influenced political policy makers in the United States during the 1960s.

Lewis was born Yehezkiel Lefkowitz, the youngest of five children born to Polish émigrés Chaim Leb ("Herman") Lefkowitz, a rabbi and cantor, and Broche ("Bertha") Biblowitz Lefkowitz, a homemaker. During the early 1920s Lewis's family moved to a small farm in Liberty, New York. Lewis spent much of his early childhood in the countryside. He enjoyed sports and music. Lewis had a rich, opera-quality voice and took music lessons until late in his life. He entered City College of New York in 1930 and earned a bachelor's degree in history in 1936. He enrolled at Columbia University that same year for doctoral studies and met the anthropologist Ruth Benedict. Under her tutelage, Lewis developed into an outstanding anthropologist. Other noted anthropologists who influenced Lewis were Franz Boas, Ralph Linton, and Margaret Mead. Lewis legally changed his surname during graduate school.

In 1937 Lewis married Ruth Maslow, who became his lifetime research partner and the mother of their two children. In 1939 Lewis and his wife went on their first field investigation, among the Blackfoot tribe in Alberta, Canada. In 1940 Lewis's dissertation, *The Effects of White Contact upon Blackfoot Culture, with Special Reference to the Role of the Fur Trade,* won an American Philosophical Society award and was published by the American Ethnological Society. Lewis joined the faculty at the University of Illinois, Urbana, in 1948, where he was instrumental in establishing the anthropology department, which he

600

Oscar Lewis. © BETTMANN/CORBIS

headed until his death in 1970. Lewis conducted field research in Spain, Mexico, India, Puerto Rico, New York City, and Cuba, broadening his cross-cultural knowledge.

In 1943 Lewis visited Mexico as a representative of the Inter-American Indian Institute to study the peasant village of Tepoztlán, first analyzed by Robert Redfield in 1926. The resulting book, *Life in a Mexican Village: Tepoztlán Restudied* (1951), presented different conclusions from Redfield's. It brought Lewis considerable attention and generated long-lasting controversy among many critics. Despite the controversy, this book is considered his most important contribution to anthropology. Lewis soared into greater prominence in the politically volatile 1960s particularly because of his writings on the "culture of poverty" theory and his innovative methods of research. It was during the time of his Tepoztlán project that Lewis began to develop his field method for doing family case studies through tape-recorded interviews and household observation, as opposed to documenting "traditional" obscure tribal life.

Lewis was concerned about peasant communities in relation to cultural and social change and family life. Much of his work describes the lives of poor Hispanics in Latin America and the United States. He also became involved in urban studies, as he noted that the Tepoztecans who migrated to the city lived in culturally similar slum neighborhoods. This prompted him to advance his controversial "culture of poverty" theory. This theory, as Lewis initially expressed it, views the poor as living in a separate subculture within the national culture. Lewis maintained that the characteristics of this subculture as a way of life are perpetuated through the family from generation to generation and transcend national differences.

In 1959 and into the 1960s Lewis published many works of family case studies. *Five Families: Mexican Case Studies in the Culture of Poverty* (1959) showed the variation of family life resulting from differences in socioeconomic status. *The Children of Sánchez* (1961) provided an inside view of one poor family living in a slum neighborhood of a rapidly changing city. These and subsequent books were based on extensive tape-recorded interviews in which his subjects spoke for themselves. The popularity of his books, though heavily criticized, brought the reality of poverty to countless readers. Lewis, having known poverty himself, viewed his work among the poor of Latin America and elsewhere as both anthropological and supportive of social change.

Other books published during the 1960s were *Pedro Martinez: A Mexican Peasant and His Family* (1964), *La Vida: A Puerto Rican Family in the Culture of Poverty—San Juan and New York* (1966), *A Study of Slum Culture: Background for La Vida* (1968), and *A Death in the Sánchez Family* (1969). Perhaps Lewis's best-known and most controversial book was *La Vida,* which is a case study of poverty in four generations of the Rios family living in Puerto Rican ghettos and in New York; it won the National Book Award for nonfiction. Two of Lewis's books, however, came under serious attack. Charges that *The Children of Sánchez* slandered the Mexican nation soured into a national scandal, which subsided only after an investigation conducted by the attorney general of Mexico led to dismissal of all charges. The second book, *La Vida,* was criticized by Puerto Rican civic leaders for misrepresenting their way of life.

Lewis's "culture of poverty" theory was given widespread exposure in the United States by Michael Harrington in *The Other America* (1962) as well as by a series of other studies leading the drive against squalor. A compelling objective of Lewis's work was to provide a better understanding of the plight of the poor and their lifestyles to those entrusted with major responsibility for forming antipoverty programs. Lewis's work profoundly influenced Democratic policy makers as they launched the War on Poverty as part of President Lyndon B. Johnson's Great Society reforms. Lewis became a consultant to Project Head Start and engaged in a public dialogue with Senator Robert Kennedy about the causes of poverty in America.

In 1969 and 1970 Lewis went to Cuba, having received permission from the Cuban leader Fidel Castro to study cultural change in a revolutionary system. The project was aborted midway when Cuban State Security accused Lewis of espionage. After leaving Cuba, Lewis died in New York City at the Polyclinic Hospital of a heart attack and was buried in Montefiore Cemetery in Farmingdale, New York. Following his death, Lewis's wife, Ruth, and the political scientist Susan Rigdon used his oral history data from Cuba to publish his last work, *Living the Revolution: An Oral History of Contemporary Cuba* (1977).

Lewis is best remembered in anthropology as a compassionate, innovative, and impressive field worker with a great gift for establishing rapport. His books, produced from tape-recorded biographies and many years of research, provide rich documentation of family life and are notable for their innovative presentations in anthropological method. Although Lewis left much unfinished work when he died, as an important social scientist of his generation, he nevertheless succeeded in bringing widespread public attention to the plight of the rural and urban poor as he strove to expose the roots of poverty. On the other hand, his work became the focus of ongoing political controversy and critical debates in academic circles throughout the last decade of his life.

★

There is no book-length biography of Lewis. A major collection of Lewis's papers, tapes, and field data is in the Archives of the University of Illinois Graduate Library. Lewis's book *Anthropological Essays* (1970) contains reprints of his doctoral thesis and most of his major articles. Lewis's "Culture of Poverty" thesis is in *Scientific American* 215 (1966): 19–25. Susan M. Rigdon, *The Culture Facade: Art, Science, and Politics in the Work of Oscar Lewis* (1988), provides biographical information that includes correspondence. There are numerous other useful biographical pieces on Lewis, including the entry in *Current Biography Yearbook* (1968); Douglas Butterworth's obituary essay "Oscar Lewis, 1914–1970," *American Anthropologist* 74 (1972): 747–757; Sol Tax's essay in David L. Sills, ed., *International Encyclopedia of the Social Sciences,* vol. 18 (1979): 446–450; and Rigdon's essay in *American National Biography* 13 (1999). Additional information on Lewis can be found in Charles Valentine, *Culture and Poverty: Critique and Counter-Proposals* (1968), and E. B. Leacock, ed., *The Culture of Poverty: A Critique* (1971). Extensive reviews of three of Lewis's books are in *Current Anthropology* 8 (1967): 480–501. An obituary is in the *New York Times* (18 Dec. 1970).

HOPE E. YOUNG

LIBBY, Willard Frank (*b.* 17 December 1908 in Grand Valley, Colorado; *d.* 8 September 1980 in Los Angeles, California), chemist and Nobel Prize winner whose technique of carbon-14 (radiocarbon) dating provides an extremely valuable tool for archeologists, anthropologists, and earth scientists.

Libby was one of five children born to farmers Ora Edward Libby and Eva May Rivers. After attending high school near Sebastopol, California, Libby enrolled in the University of California, Berkeley in 1927, earned a B.S. in chemistry in 1931. He continued his graduate studies at that institution under the direction of Dr. Wendell H. Latimer and earned a Ph.D. in chemistry in 1933. Libby received the rare distinction of being offered a faculty appointment directly upon receiving the Ph.D., and he was a faculty member at Berkeley from 1933 to 1941 as assistant, and then associate professor of chemistry. Libby married Leonor Lucinda Hickey on 9 August 1940; they had twin daughters and divorced in 1966. He married Leona Woods Marshall, a professor of environmental engineering at UCLA, in 1966.

In 1941 Libby received a Guggenheim Memorial Foundation Fellowship (he would later hold two more, in 1951 and 1959) and elected to do his work at Princeton University. The fellowship was interrupted for tasks related to World War II, and he went to Columbia University in New York City to concentrate on the Manhattan Project, an ultrasecret government project to develop an atomic bomb. He worked on that project from 1942 to 1945 and during that time helped develop a gas-diffusion method for separating uranium isotopes, an essential step in the creation of the atomic bomb. From 1945 to 1954 Libby worked with the Institute for Nuclear Studies at the University of Chicago as professor of chemistry. There, his prewar invention of the screen-wall counter for measuring low-level radioactivity made possible the determination, in 1946, of the atmospheric radioactive isotopes hydrogen-3 (tritium) and carbon-14 produced by cosmic radiation.

Newly formed carbon-14 has high energy at the moment of its formation so that it rapidly oxidizes to carbon dioxide, which spreads out and distributes itself evenly in the atmosphere. All plants and animals incorporate traces of it into their bodies as they breathe and eat. After an organism dies, this internal carbon-14 breaks down at a constant rate as it is converted into nitrogen by the emission of an electron, which can be detected by a sensitive apparatus. If it is assumed that the intensity of cosmic radiation has been constant during the last few tens of thousands of years, as Libby proposed, then there is an unchanging amount of carbon-14 in the world, and the formation of new carbon-14 atoms is offset by the decay of old ones. Libby reasoned that a determination of the carbon-14 content of anything derived from plant or animal tissue gives a good measure of the time that has elapsed since the plant or animal died.

In 1947 Libby developed the carbon-14, or radiocarbon, dating technique, used to date material derived from formerly living organisms as old as 50,000 years by measuring the small amounts of radioactivity from the carbon-14 present in organic materials. Carbon-14 dating has become the single most important advance in the field of archeology. This technique has been used to determine the age of ancient ruins and artifacts, mummies and monuments, among them, the Shroud of Turin (alleged to be the burial sheet of Christ), the Dead Sea Scrolls, and the Iceman (the frozen mummy found in the Italian Alps in 1991). In 1952 Libby published the monograph *Radiocarbon Dating,* presenting the details of his work in this field. Later he employed his work on tritium to determine the recent history of water, opening a new field of research in vulcanology, limnology, and the circulation of oceans. Although Libby's pioneer work in radiocarbon dating took place in the mid-1940s, most of the recognition for his developments came in the late 1950s, culminating in the Nobel Prize for chemistry in 1960.

In 1954 Libby became the first chemist named to serve on the U.S. Atomic Energy Commission, a position he held until 1959. While there, he headed President Dwight D. Eisenhower's international Atoms for Peace project and studied the effects of radioactive fallout. The radioactive fallout program yielded new information that led to the tracing of such elements as strontium-90 through the biosphere, and identifying the pathways for their incorporation into plants, ingestion by herbivores, and ultimate appearance in milk. Libby also actively encouraged the development of nuclear reactors to produce power and helped organize the International Atomic Energy Agency. From 1954 to 1959 he also worked as a research associate in the Geophysical Laboratory of Washington's Carnegie Institution.

Libby resigned from the Atomic Energy Commission in 1959 and became professor of chemistry at the University of California, Los Angeles (UCLA), where he was director of the Institute of Geophysics and Planetary Physics from 1962 to 1976 and professor emeritus from 1976 until his death in 1980. He was the prime mover in the establishment of the space research program at UCLA. Some of his awards include the Research Corporation Award (1951), the Columbia University Chandler Medal (1954), the American Chemical Society Award for Nuclear Applications in Chemistry (1956), the Elliot Cresson Medal of the Franklin Institute (1957), the Willard Gibbs Medal from the American Chemical Society (1958), the Albert Einstein Medal Award (1959), and the Day Medal of the Geological Society of America (1961). He was elected to the National Academy of Sciences, the Royal Swedish Academy of Science, the Heidelberg Academy of Sciences, and the Bolivian Society of Anthropology.

A frequent appointee to federal and state bodies, Libby gave hundreds of expository public lectures on both science and national science policy. During the 1960s he was a member of California governor Ronald W. Reagan's Air Resources Board and Earthquake Council, President Rich-

Willard F. Libby. THE LIBRARY OF CONGRESS

ard M. Nixon's Task Force on Air Pollution, and the U.S.–Japanese Commission on Scientific Cooperation. Rumors in 1968 that he would be named as science adviser to President Nixon drew protests from many of his colleagues, who found Nixon's political conservatism too extreme.

In the early 1970s Libby's concern for environmental issues led him to institute a new graduate curriculum devoted to training environmental chemists, the first of its kind. As one of the prime movers in the California Air Resources Board, Libby's main concern became the reduction of noxious automobile exhaust fumes. Libby died of a blood clot in the lung, complicated by pneumonia.

★

Libby's papers are in the Department of Special Collections at the UCLA Library. See also his Collected Papers (1981), Rainer Berger and Leona Marshall Libby, eds. For more information, see Theodore Berland, *The Scientific Life* (1962). An obituary is in the *New York Times* (10 Sept. 1980).

MARIA PACHECO

LICHTENSTEIN, Roy (*b.* 27 October 1923 in New York City; *d.* 29 September 1997 in New York City), painter, sculptor, and printmaker who was one of the foremost artists of the pop art movement.

Lichtenstein was the eldest of two children of Milton Lichtenstein, a realtor, and Beatrice (Werner) Lichtenstein, a homemaker. He first attended public school and then a private school in Manhattan, the Benjamin Franklin High School for Boys, graduating in June 1940. Attending the School of Fine Arts at Ohio State University from 1940 to 1943 and again from 1946 to 1949, he was influenced by Professor Hoyt L. Sherman, who had students draw from memory images that had just been projected through lantern slides. Lichtenstein graduated from the university with a B.F.A. in 1946 and an M.F.A. in 1949. From 1943 to 1946 Lichtenstein served in the U.S. Army in the engineering battalion of the Sixty-ninth Infantry Division, drawing maps to aid the Allied advance across Europe. He was discharged with the rank of private first class.

From 1952 to 1955 Lichtenstein worked in a variety of styles and mediums, including expressionism, abstraction, and painted wood constructions—all with a distinctly American subject matter. In 1957 he made his first proto-pop work, a lithograph entitled *The Ten Dollar Bill*. From 1957 to 1960, while teaching as an assistant professor at the State University of New York at Oswego, Lichtenstein made renderings of the cartoon characters Mickey Mouse, Donald Duck, and others. From 1960 to 1964 he was an assistant professor at Douglass College of Rutgers University in New Brunswick, New Jersey, and while there he attended the avant-garde artist Allen Kaprow's "happenings," which featured audience participation and welcomed spontaneous developments. There he met the artists Claes Oldenburg, Jim Dine, Lucas Samaras, and George Segal.

In 1960 Lichtenstein's painting *Look, Mickey, I've Hooked a Big One* was his first work taken directly from the panel of a comic strip, a picture of Donald Duck tug-

Roy Lichtenstein. CORBIS CORPORATION (NEW YORK)

ging at a fishing pole with its hook caught in his jacket. Most of his paintings of the 1962–1964 period were based on panels of comic strips dealing with pulp romance and combat in war. He liked to work in series. In 1964 he produced ceramic sculptures of girls' heads, derived from teen comics, and precariously balanced cups as well as painted landscapes of sunsets, sunrises, seascapes, and a series of paintings of Greek temples. In 1965–1966 he created another series of paintings of brushstrokes and explosions. Paintings of monumental architecture continued from 1964 to 1969. At the end of the decade Lichtenstein made paintings based on other paintings or parts of paintings by past masters, such as Paul Cezanne, Pablo Picasso, Henri Matisse, Piet Mondrian, and Claude Monet. His *Haystacks* (1968) and *Cathedral* series of 1969 were facsimiles of famous works of Monet dating to the 1890s.

In 1961 Lichtenstein joined the prominent Leo Castelli Gallery in New York. The next year he was included in the New Paintings/Common Objects exhibition at the Pasadena Art Museum, the first museum exhibition to feature pop art, and in the New Realists exhibition at the Sidney Janis Gallery in New York along with many other pop artists. In 1963 he was given a year of absence from Rutgers University (he resigned the next year to devote himself to making art full-time) and moved to Twenty-sixth Street in

New York City. That year he was one of ten artists commissioned by the architect Philip Johnson to make works for his circular theater at New York's World Fair, and he was given a solo exhibition at the Galerie Sonnabend in Paris. Thereafter, he was recognized as a major American artist. In April 1967 Lichtenstein was given his first museum retrospective, at the Pasadena Art Museum, and his first New York retrospective was held at the Guggenheim Museum in September 1969. In 1969 he spent two weeks at the Universal Film Studios in Los Angeles as artist in residence to make a seascape film for the art and technology exhibition at the Los Angeles County Museum.

On 12 June 1949 Lichtenstein married Isabel Wilson, whom he had met in Cleveland, where she was codirector of the Ten-Thirty Gallery. They had two sons and divorced in 1965. On 1 November 1968 he married Dorothy Herzka, and they settled in Southampton, Long Island, in 1970. They had no children.

Pop art uses as its subject matter new, mass-produced, instantly recognizable consumer objects, and its end product is often cool and hard to the touch. As an art form it is one of the major reactions against abstract expressionism, which is wholly or mostly nonobjective, painterly in style, and improvisational in approach. Lichtenstein's comic-strip paintings are enlargements of one frame of a comic strip. They feature strong comic-book colors, even the mechanically regular Ben-day dotted textures (named after the printer Benjamin Day), but there are modifications. The paintings omit superfluous wording and excess detailing to produce a leaner, more pared-down image. Lichtenstein insisted that "what I do is form, whereas the comic strip is not formed in the sense that I'm using the word; the comics have shapes but there has been no effort to make them intensely unified." His renderings of brushstrokes that are isolated from their larger context, set forth on a gigantic scale—his *Big Painting #6* (1965) measures seven feet, eight-and-a-half inches by ten feet, nine inches—can be construed as an affront to the humanistic underpinnings of abstract expressionism.

Lichtenstein sought to make bombastic that which intrinsically was commonplace and secondary, while bypassing that which was original and aesthetically meritorious. His *Rouen Cathedral* series was given the appearance not of Monet's originals but of the cheap, garish posters typically displayed in travel agents' offices. His art had to do with tastelessness, with the second-rate, with the erosion of quality. Not so much as an excuse but as a self-validation, the artist asserted, "I have the feeling that these flat images conform far more to what really goes on inside our heads than those false depths" of the abstract expressionists. The idea behind Lichtenstein's art was paramount. His art can be taken simultaneously as clever humor, bold form, and subtle social commentary.

While continuing to work with series of paintings, Lichtenstein explored new subjects after the 1960s. These included the *Mirrors* in 1970–1972, the *Entablatures* in 1971–1972 and 1974–1976, and the *Mirrors and Entablatures* in the early 1980s. In the 1970s he made paintings composed of a variety of borrowings from several artists. His reputation as a major artist following abstract expressionism held firm. On 26 April 1977 Lichtenstein won the Skowhegan Medal for painting. In 1981 a retrospective of his work from the 1970s, organized by the St. Louis Museum, traveled through the United States, Europe, and Japan. In his comic-strip paintings, in his works based on paintings of earlier modern masters, and in his series of *Brushstrokes,* Lichtenstein set forth an iconography of pop art as enduring as the most familiar works of Andy Warhol, James Rosenquist, and Robert Indiana. Lichtenstein died at the age of seventy-three at New York University Medical Center in Manhattan from complications of pneumonia.

★

Biographies on Lichtenstein include John Coplans, ed., *Roy Lichtenstein* (1972); Diane Waldman, *Roy Lichtenstein* (1993), a comprehensive and scholarly book; and Janis Hendrickson, *Roy Lichtenstein* (1996). For works on Lichtenstein's art see Jack Cowart, *Lichtenstein 1970–1980* (1981), which has good illustrations, including some of colored pencil sketches and aluminum and bronze pieces; Lawrence Alloway, *Roy Lichtenstein* (1983); and Lou Ann Walker, *Roy Lichtenstein: The Artist at Work* (1994). Interviews with Lichtenstein are in "An Interview with Roy Lichtenstein," *Artforum* (Oct. 1963), and "Talking with Roy Lichtenstein," *Artforum* (May 1967). Obituaries are in the *New York Times, Los Angeles Times, Detroit Free Press,* and *USA Today* (all 30 Sept. 1997); the *Times* (London) and *Washington Post* (both 1 Oct. 1997); and the *Chicago Tribune* (3 Oct. 1997).

ABRAHAM A. DAVIDSON

LINDSAY, John Vliet (*b.* 24 November 1921 in New York City; *d.* 19 December 2000 in Hilton Head, South Carolina), lawyer, politician, and controversial Republican mayor of New York City from 1966 to 1973 who was hailed as an "urban messiah" during his first term.

Lindsay had a twin brother and was one of five children born to George Nelson Lindsay, an investment banker of English descent, and Florence Eleanor Vliet, a woman of Dutch descent who instilled in her children a love for cultural pursuits. Lindsay's grandfather was a brick manufacturer from the Isle of Wight who immigrated to the United States in 1881. Lindsay grew up as an Episcopalian and

John Lindsay. ARCHIVE PHOTOS, INC.

attended Saint Paul's School in Concord, New Hampshire. In 1943 he studied history and earned a B.A. from Yale University, graduating in only three years in an accelerated program. Later that year, Lindsay became an ensign officer in the U.S. Naval Reserve. During World War II, he earned five battle stars as a gunnery officer aboard a destroyer. In 1948 Lindsay earned a law degree from Yale and was admitted to the New York bar. He began working for the law firm of Webster, Sheffield, Fleischmann, Hitchcock, and Christie. On 18 June 1949 he married a former schoolteacher, Mary Anne Hutchison; the couple had three daughters and a son.

Lindsay was a natural for politics. Six feet, four inches tall and charismatic, handsome, and photogenic, he flashed his winning smile whenever the media were present. It was not long before he was running for Congress. He won the election in 1958 and was reelected for three succeeding terms, in 1960, 1962, and 1964. Although he came from Manhattan's affluent Seventeenth Congressional District, Lindsay was considered a liberal Republican in the 1960s because he supported civil rights and fought for more lenient immigration policies. He also sought medical insurance for the elderly. Because of his support for African-American communities, many in his party judged his policies as too pro black.

At times Lindsay chose not to go along with the Republican Party dictates. Pressuring him had no effect; he made up his own mind on issues. He criticized Governor Nelson Rockefeller, even though Rockefeller was a fellow Republican, and he supported enlarging the House Rules Committee, even though the idea was the brainchild of a Democratic president. He also helped to set up the federal Department of Urban Affairs in 1960, which his party did not want. Further irritating his colleagues, Lindsay in 1964 refused to endorse the Republican presidential candidate, Senator Barry Goldwater. Lindsay's frequent opposition to party politics had its drawbacks. He soon found his upward political climb blocked in Congress, so he decided to run for the mayor of New York City. He won the election and took office in 1966. Lindsay was the first Republican mayor since 1941 and one of the youngest ever to assume the title.

At first, Lindsay's arrival was welcomed. His renown was enhanced by his easy media presence. Soon, however, the exigencies of office began to erode his popularity. The first major challenge was the transit workers' strike. For thirteen days, New York City buses and subways were at a standstill. Before he could get them moving again, Lindsay had to agree to give workers sizable raises and benefits, which caused a strain on the city budget. Budget woes continued to grow. During Lindsay's administration, welfare spending and city workers' pension expenses nearly doubled. When the city went bankrupt in 1975, many pointed to Lindsay as the culprit who had begun the downward spiral.

Not all of Lindsay's actions were criticized as failures, however. His reorganization and consolidation of fifty city departments and agencies increased efficiency. He promoted arts and culture, revived Central Park, and created the Brooklyn Bridge bicycle path. He also helped to still racial clashes in an era when this kind of strife was almost ubiquitous in cities. In 1967 and 1968 Lindsay began to walk through the ghettos of Harlem. These walks helped to preserve racial peace during a time when riots and violence were commonplace; they were a key factor in keeping New York City from experiencing the worst of the urban crises that swept the country during the 1960s. Lindsay became famous for his trips through the black neighborhoods of Brooklyn, with children following after him. Although critics have called them mere political maneuvers, Lindsay's trips into troubled areas did seem to convey that he was genuinely concerned with the welfare of New York City's poor.

Nonetheless, Lindsay was responsible for increasing racial tensions, albeit unintentionally, when he supported a decentralized school system. Soon African-American and Jewish communities were at odds, because the decision to hire teachers was made locally and therefore each community strove to hire its own. The resulting conflict led to a teacher's strike and continued ill feelings in both the Jew-

ish and African-American communities in the years to come. Budget problems continued to be a thorn in Lindsay's side. The Vietnam War was a further drain on New York City's budget, a situation that Lindsay deplored. Because of budget shortfalls, he had to start an income tax in 1966, double subway fares, and seek more state and federal financial assistance.

Lindsay's political triumphs seemed to be over once the 1960s ended. In 1971 Lindsay ran in the presidential primaries as a Democratic candidate. He withdrew when he lost the support of two states, however. Soon after, he gave up his career aspirations. In 1973 Lindsay retired from political office. He and his family vacationed in Europe for a year before Lindsay returned to New York City and began working for his old law firm. For a time, he also was a television commentator for American Broadcasting Company's *Good Morning America*. During his time as mayor, Lindsay wrote two books: *Journey into Politics* (1966), which dealt with his career in Congress, and *The City* (1970), which covered his struggles in New York City. In 1976 he published his first novel, *The Edge*. The story line revolves around a congressman fighting against national martial law.

Although he had retired from political office, Lindsay was not completely out of the picture. In 1981 New York City Mayor Ed Koch appointed Lindsay to the post of city trade representative. That same year Lindsay was the chair of a committee in charge of reducing court overcrowding. He also became the chair of the Port Authority board. In 1984 Lindsay became the chair of the Lincoln Center for the Performing Arts, a position he held until a heart operation in 1988 forced him to retire. After fighting Parkinson's disease for many years, Lindsay died of complications from the disease coupled with pneumonia on 19 December 2000 in Hilton Head. During the pivotal 1960s he had been a controversial mayor; in death he was remembered as a compassionate man, hated by conservatives and loved by liberals.

★

A biographical essay on Lindsay can be found in the *Encyclopedia of World Biography,* 2nd ed. (1998). Vincent J. Cannato, *The Ungovernable City: John Lindsay and His Struggle to Save New York* (2001), covers the irony of Lindsay's successes and failures. See also the following reviews of Cannato's book: John Podhoretz, *National Review* (17 Sept. 2001); Andrew White, *The American Prospect* (22 Oct. 2001); and Michael Barone, *The Public Interest* (spring 2002). Articles about Lindsay include "Lindsay's Compassion Did Not Help," *Newsday* (17 Jan. 2001), and Fred Siegel, "Succeeding Guiliani," *Commentary* (Jan. 2002). Obituaries are in the *New York Times* and *Washington Post* (both 21 Dec. 2000), and the *Nation* (22 Jan. 2001).

A. E. SCHULTHIES

LING, James Joseph (*b.* 31 December 1922 in Hugo, Oklahoma), Texas-based business executive and conglomerateur who, through a series of daring and controversial acquisitions, built one of the largest single corporate entities of the 1960s, Ling-Temco-Vought (LTV), which was eventually the target of federal antitrust action.

Mary (Jones) and Henry William Ling gave their son a Bavarian ancestry and a Catholic upbringing. Ling's mother passed away when he was eleven, and a few years later his father left his six children and his railroad job to join a Carmelite monastery. Ling grew up working on his own in the oil fields of Texas and never completed his high school education. He married a young Dallas woman in 1939, while he was still in his teens, and they had three children. He picked up practical training in electrical contracting when he joined the navy in 1944, and he started Ling Electric Company with the $2,000 from the sale of his house when he returned to Dallas in 1946. Ling continually sought to expand the tiny contracting business through the sale of common stock, personally handing out the firm's prospectus at the state fair. With the proceeds Ling purchased undervalued corporations, snapping up eight different contracting firms and one electronics producer. By

James J. Ling. © BETTMANN/CORBIS

1958 Ling had built a small but powerful firm grossing nearly $7 million.

By 1960 Ling had purchased the audio equipment manufacturer Altec Lansing and merged the resulting Ling–Altec Electronics with a government defense contractor, Temco Electronics and Missile Company. At the end of the year the newly established Ling-Temco reported sales of $148 million. While the merger with Temco had been largely amiable, Ling now initiated a hostile takeover of Chance Vought, another defense aerospace company. Chance Vought fought back, but by March 1961 Ling and his company owned 39 percent of the available stock and offered stockholders a price considerably above market value for additional shares. At the end of 1962 the consolidated Ling-Temco-Vought (LTV) brought in sales of more than $325 million.

Ling then moved to reorganize his corporate behemoth. Calling his plan Project Redeployment, Ling attempted to sell, streamline, or restructure debt in the disparate parts of the vast empire. Ling's complicated stock deals and management reorganizations confused some but allowed Ling the opportunity to initiate Project Touchdown: the ambitious takeover of Wilson and Company. In 1967 Wilson was worth about a billion dollars, more than twice as much as LTV as a whole. But the corporation was undervalued, and Ling raised $80 million from investors in Europe and the United States. With that cash Ling bought control of Wilson and then acquired the rest of the company in a huge stock swap. He split Wilson into the meatpacking section (which investors dubbed "Meat Ball"), the sporting goods section ("Golf Ball"), and the pharmaceuticals section ("Goof Ball"), which together received around $250 million in increased market valuation from public investment.

With this acquisition Ling truly rose to national attention, and glowing articles about him began to appear in mainstream magazines. *Fortune*'s Stanley H. Brown called Ling "part prestidigitator, part brooding genius, and part wunderkind" in a January 1967 article. *Newsweek*'s October 1967 profile dubbed him "Ling the Merger King," while *Business Week* lavishly praised him in their March 1967 cover story. Most journalistic coverage of Ling emphasized his dynamism, his inclination to military or sporting analogies, or his then astronomically expensive $3 million Dallas mansion (where he lived with his second wife, Dorothy Hill, whom he married after divorcing his first wife in 1954, and his stepson). Many described him as a physically imposing man with an intense gaze and a compact physique perhaps better suited to football but instead stuffed into a button-down shirt and Ivy League suit.

After the successful acquisition and "redeployment" of Greatamerica Corporation, which was split into its component parts (National Car Rental, Braniff Airlines, and a banking/insurance firm), Ling was able to offer an unprecedented $425 million cash for the venerable Pittsburgh steelmaker Jones and Laughlin. Once the deal was completed, excited investors bid the LTV stock price up to a stratospheric $135. At this point LTV was the fourteenth largest corporation in the United States, with about $2.8 billion in sales for 1968. Despite its size LTV was not a monopoly or a trust like Standard Oil. Ling had not built a corporate empire based on vertical combination (the acquisition of suppliers and distributors) or horizontal combination (the acquisition of competing firms). LTV was not a combination but a conglomeration: a grouping of largely unrelated firms under the loose control of a single parent company.

Although the conglomerate could not control or manipulate a single market like a monopoly, the sheer size of the corporation made many observers concerned about the concentration of power. A *Saturday Evening Post* story from November 1968 stated in its headline that "It Is Theoretically Possible for the Entire United States to Become One Vast Conglomerate Presided Over by Mr. James J. Ling." While the general public fretted about the impersonal size of the corporate giant, the financial world grew concerned about the viability of this vast organization and whether it would be able to absorb and "redeploy" the debts and assets of the corporations it had acquired. But LTV's most powerful critic was the federal government, which surprised many in the business world by choosing to take antitrust action against LTV. The Justice Department under President Richard M. Nixon announced its case against LTV in early 1969, driving the LTV stock price into the basement. Though LTV eventually settled the federal suit, a plunging stock market and accumulating debts dragged LTV stock down to $7.125, and Ling was forced to cede control of the company.

For some Americans of the 1960s Ling was a model of executive action, lauded for his assertiveness and mastery of the corporate world. For others Ling was an archetypal self-made man who came from humble beginnings to single-handedly create a multibillion-dollar corporation. But for critics he represented a disturbing trend toward the corporate conglomerate: vast institutions driven by their own logic, largely disconnected from the actual marketplace, and pledged to a naked avarice openly detested by the anticorporate generation of the 1960s. In all of these aspects Ling foreshadowed the charismatic chief executive officers, corporate raiders, and merger kings of later decades.

While his methods lived on, Ling never reached the same level of financial control or popular acclaim he enjoyed during the decade of the 1960s. Even as LTV entered bankruptcy in April 2002, Ling continued to structure financial deals from his Dallas office. Ling has been involved in various charities, including the National Jewish Hospital and Research Center in Denver, the boards of trustees of numerous Texas institutions of higher education, and many Dallas-area cultural organizations.

★

Biographies or other works on Ling include Stanley H. Brown, *Ling: The Rise, Fall, and Return of a Texas Titan* (1972), and "Jimmy Ling's Wonderful Growth Machine," *Fortune* (Jan. 1967). See also "LTV Blitzes Its Way into Ranks of Giants," *Business Week* (18 Mar. 1967); "Ling the Merger King," *Newsweek* (9 Oct. 1967); Don A. Schanche, "It Is Theoretically Possible for the Entire United States to Become One Vast Conglomerate Presided Over by Mr. James J. Ling," *Saturday Evening Post* (2 Nov. 1968); and Claire Poole, "Merge Ahead," *Texas Monthly* (Aug. 2000).

JAMES LONGHURST

LIPPMANN, Walter   (*b.* 23 September 1889 in New York City; *d.* 14 December 1974 in New York City), Pulitzer Prize–winning journalist and author, one of the most respected and politically influential writers in the United States, and author of the popular syndicated column *Today and Tomorrow,* in which he analyzed world events, from 1931 to 1967.

Lippmann, the only child of Jacob and Daisy (Baum) Lipp-

Walter Lippmann. ARCHIVE PHOTOS, INC.

mann, was born to privilege. He grew up in a wealthy German-Jewish family. His parents took him to Europe most summers and exposed him to culture and famous people. As a small boy he shook hands with President William McKinley and Admiral George Dewey. Jacob Lippmann was a clothing manufacturer in a business started by his father when he came to the United States in 1848. Daisy Lippmann was educated at Hunter College.

Lippmann received his early education at Dr. Julius Sachs School for Boys in New York City, followed by the Sachs Collegiate Institute, from which he graduated in 1906, where he was groomed to attend Harvard University. At Harvard, Lippmann received praise for his academics and his writing. He wrote for both the political *Harvard Illustrated* and the more literary *Harvard Monthly*. He saw poverty for the first time when he joined other Harvard students to help victims of a slum fire in Chelsea, Massachusetts. With his social conscience aroused, Lippmann and eight other students formed the Socialist Club. He earned his A.B. with honors from Harvard in 1910.

His parents' wealth came in part from inherited real estate that included some tenements in the Lower East Side of New York City. In 1921 Lippmann urged his father to fix or sell them and when he would not, Lippmann no longer accepted money from his father. Lippmann always maintained a social conscience, but his political leanings were based on the candidate he felt he could support, which through the years included many world leaders and U.S. presidents, including John F. Kennedy, and, for a while, Lyndon B. Johnson in the 1960s.

In 1931 Lippmann was invited to write a column for the *New York Herald Tribune,* which, after some misgivings, he called *Today and Tomorrow*. Lippmann wrote that column until 1967, although he left the *Herald Tribune* in 1957 for the *Washington Post*. He started a similar column in *Newsweek* in 1963. Millions of readers were kept informed on national and world events through more than four thousand nationally syndicated columns written by Lippmann.

Lippmann's column brought him fame from its style as a political column devoted entirely to opinion. Influence also helped make Lippmann a powerful public figure. Lippmann traveled in grand style every year, usually conferring with heads of state along the way. Leaders often sought to meet with him. In his engagement book he wrote on one of his later trips: "saw the King, the prime minister, etc.—the usual people."

When Lippmann turned seventy he was honored by the National Press Club with even more people in attendance than had come to hear the Soviet leader Nikita Khrushchev the previous week. Although Lippmann had little regard for television, he was persuaded by the Columbia Broadcasting System (CBS) to grant a one-hour taped interview

to the newscaster Howard K. Smith. The program ran on 11 August 1960. Public response was far more than CBS expected. The network ultimately ran six more interviews, which were later published in book form.

In 1958 and again in 1961 Lippmann met with Khrushchev in Russia to discuss crucial aspects of the East-West conflict. He won a Pulitzer Prize for each of the *Today and Tomorrow* columns in which he published accounts of the meetings. The special citation for the 1958 column was for "the wisdom, perception and high sense of responsibility with which he has commented for many years on national and international affairs." In 1962 the award was for "wise and responsible international reporting."

Lippmann supported Kennedy for president in 1960, and once he was in office they consulted regularly. When Kennedy was assassinated Lippmann was shocked for days but recognized the immediate need for the country to get behind Johnson. He praised Johnson's inaugural address with its promise of a "Great Society" and called the president "a bold innovator." Although Lippmann was not immediately attracted to Johnson personally, he succumbed for a time to the famous Johnson flattery campaign. Lippmann received the Presidential Medal of Freedom in 1964 "for profound interpretation of his country and the affairs of the world."

In February 1965 Lippmann supported Johnson when he ordered the bombing of military sites in North Vietnam in retaliation for the killing of several American "advisers" sent to Vietnam by Kennedy in 1963. He believed air strikes put the United States in "a better bargaining position for negotiations." But in mid-March 1965 Lippmann was having serious doubts about Johnson's approach to the Vietnam question. Although he did not object to the use of the military on principle, Lippmann could see no justification for the country's getting involved in a land war in Asia, and he kept pushing Johnson for a "peace offensive." Lippmann understood something of combat; he had served as an army captain with a propaganda team in Europe in World War I.

Lippmann's objections to how Johnson was handling the Vietnam War were the undoing of their relationship. He described Johnson's Vietnam policy as it was unfolding by the end of 1965 as a "historic mistake" and began criticizing Johnson in personal and uncompromising language as he began to see what he perceived as the outlines of American imperialism in the administration's policies. In 1967 Lippmann wrote, "We are seeing how a war waged without hope of military decision degenerates into savagery." In his later years Lippmann's usual optimism waned, driven in part by the seemingly interminable Vietnam War. He wrote his final article for *Today and Tomorrow* on 25 May 1967, and the final one for *Newsweek* on 11 January 1971.

Lippmann was married twice, first to Faye Albertson on 24 May 1917. They had one foster daughter. The couple divorced in 1937 when Lippmann became involved with Helen Byrne Armstrong, the wife of a close friend; after Armstrong divorced her husband, she and Lippmann married on 26 March 1938. After a disabling illness lasting several years, Lippmann died of cardiac arrest at the age of sixty-five. He was cremated, and his ashes were scattered off the coast of Maine, a state where for many years he had taken refuge to think and write.

★

Lippmann's papers are at the Yale University Library, New Haven, Connecticut. The authorized biography is Ronald Steel, *Walter Lippmann and the American Century* (1980). See also Marquis Childs and James Reston, *Walter Lippmann and His Times* (1959), and Barry D. Riccio, *Walter Lippmann—Odyssey of a Liberal* (1996). For his writings in the 1960s see Clinton Rossiter and James Lave, eds., *The Essential Lippmann: A Political Philosophy for Liberal Democracy* (1963), and *Conversations with Walter Lippmann,* a CBS Reports television program with introduction by Edward Weeks (1965). An obituary is in the *New York Times* (15 Dec. 1974).

M. C. NAGEL

Sonny Liston. CORBIS CORPORATION (BELLEVUE)

LISTON, Charles ("Sonny") (*b.* 8 May 1932 in Saint Francis County, Arkansas; *d.* 30 December 1970 in Las Vegas, Nevada), boxing heavyweight champion from 1962 to 1964, defeated by Muhammad Ali's stunning one-round thumping on 25 May 1965 in one of the greatest upsets in boxing history.

Liston's early years almost mirror those of the younger boxer Mike Tyson. Biographer Michael McLean describes this period of Liston's life as "brutal and impoverished." Comparisons too can be made with another heavyweight champion, Joe Louis, who grew up—one of eight children—"dirt poor" in Alabama. Liston was one of twenty-five children born within two marriages. His father, Tobe Liston, farmed on rented land. Tobe Liston's second wife, Helen Baskin, was Liston's mother. Home was no more than a run-down shack on Morledge Plantation, Arkansas. Liston received very little formal education, and growing up for him meant being one of his father's farm laborers. The *American National Biography* profile of Liston is both harrowing and grim. In his adult years Liston remembered a father who "whipped and verbally degraded him almost daily." His mother fled Arkansas and relocated in St. Louis, Missouri, where Liston joined her in 1945.

By 1950 Liston had fallen into a life of crime. He had amassed six arrests for mugging and then was convicted on two counts of robbery and larceny. He received a five-year sentence in the Missouri State Penitentiary but served only two years; he was paroled on 30 October 1952. Liston put those two years to excellent use; with a height of six feet, four inches, a 210-pound build, and a mean temper and combative personality, Liston quickly became his prison's premier boxer. He was mentored by the prison chaplain, Father Alois Stevens, who eventually signed up Frank W. Mitchell, publisher of the newspaper *St. Louis Argus,* as Liston's manager.

Liston's amateur career was short but mostly successful. He won the 1953 Midwestern Golden Gloves heavyweight championship in Chicago. His first professional fight took place on 2 September 1953 in St. Louis.

Liston's boxing career from 1953 to 1960 possessed two key characteristics. First, Liston was a very aggressive and hard-hitting boxer. Finesse, skill, and speed were not his strengths. He went into the ring to knock out opponents. He won fourteen of his first fifteen fights. In 1958 *Ring* magazine ranked him as the ninth place contender for the heavyweight title. In 1960 he had moved up to being the number one challenger. Second, Liston never avoided controversy. In the mid-1950s he was comanaged by gangland leader John Vitale. In December 1956 he returned to prison after assaulting a police officer. Upon his release he continued to be successful as a boxer, but Vitale linked him up with Frank "Blinky" Palermo, a Mafia figure. Paradoxically, this event advanced Liston's career, as Palermo's underworld connections facilitated better fights for Liston. By the start of 1961, and following the defeats of other contenders such as Mike DeJohn, Cleveland Williams, Nino Valdes, Zora Folley, Roy Harris, and Eddie Machen, Liston was seen to be America's most feared and revered boxer. Possessing an intimidating, invincible demeanor, Liston was able to overwhelm his opponents physically and psychologically. McLean captures Liston's persona, writing that he lacked "any real ring refinement" but "was known for his intimidating scowl . . . brute strength and a left hand from hell."

Liston's campaign to win the world heavyweight championship in the early 1960s has to be viewed in light of the criminal mosaic that was professional boxing. Professional boxing has always been heavily corrupt, and by the start of the 1960s the Senate Subcommittee on Antitrust and Monopoly, chaired by Estes Kefauver, focused on its monopolistic practices. Eventually, the various investigations seemed more akin to public crusades against organized crime.

The sports historian Jeffrey T. Sammons highlights the extent of the criminal clique that supported and sustained Liston. Sammons argues that the criminal control of Liston was a disgrace and that it exacerbated professional boxing's already tarnished image. The New York State Athletic Commission in 1962 refused to sanction Liston's contention for Floyd Patterson's heavyweight title. Nevertheless, the Illinois State Athletic Commission approved the fight, which took place on 25 September 1962 at Comiskey Park in Chicago. Liston knocked out Patterson in round one. According to Sammons, "the underworld . . . owned the heavyweight championship," and Liston's victory, however stunning, savage, and swift, was a testament to "criminal infiltration in sport." A Patterson rematch on 22 July 1963 in Las Vegas helped solidify Liston's reputation as a pugilistic destroyer. Yet again he flattened Patterson in the first round.

The emergence of a young, brash fighter named Cassius Clay, also known as the "Louisville Lip" and finally as Muhammad Ali, made for what boxing aficionados felt could be a "Fight of the Century." The majority of boxing journalists felt that Liston had too much power, anger, and menace for Ali, the boyish and charming 1960 Olympic light heavyweight champion.

The 25 February 1964 bout in Miami Beach, Florida, saw a quick, confident, and almost ethereal Ali dance his way around, and away, from Liston. But the fight's conclusion was abrupt. At the start of the seventh round, Liston refused to leave his corner because of a shoulder injury. The singular conclusion to the fight resulted in several investigations, including one carried out by the U.S. Senate. While no irregularities were found, Sammons points out that on the night of the fight Liston's odds went down from ten-to-one to four-to-one and that a lot of money had been wagered on Ali.

The 25 May 1965 rematch in Lewiston, Maine, was even more surreal, with Liston slipping to the floor in round one after being caught by a glancing rather than damaging blow. As McLean notes, "Rumors of a fix quickly ensued, and Liston's reputation was ruined." To this day there is no hard evidence that Liston "took a dive." But Sammons's detailed analysis reveals that criminal connections abounded. The possibility of a fixed fight is not unlikely. Nick Tosches, in his definitive biography of Liston, writes that the fight "was a shambles."

Liston continued fighting throughout the 1960s, but his boxing career never rebounded after the Ali fiascoes. His last fight was in New Jersey on 27 June 1970. Although he had married Geraldine Chambers on 3 September 1957 and had a daughter with her, his life never achieved either stability or security. He never emerged from his street fighting, alcohol abuse, driving problems, and petty drug crimes. Liston was found dead in his Las Vegas home at the age of thirty-eight. The confusion of his life was compounded by uncertainty over his death. It may have been from heart failure, or it may have been from a drug overdose. Liston is buried in Paradise Memorial Gardens in Las Vegas.

Ali ridiculed Liston, calling him "ugly bear." Liston had easily crushed Floyd Patterson, but few boxing authorities thought highly of Patterson's ability. Liston's dismal showings against Ali, however, do not seem to represent a talented boxer who, once upon a time, seemed invincible. Liston's contribution to social history was inconsequential. In fact, the *American National Biography* concludes a piece on Liston with the observation that "his arrival as heavyweight champion coincided with the civil rights revolution and most African Americans deplored him as a setback to their cause."

★

The Nick Tosches biography, *The Devil and Sonny Liston* (2000), is full of vivid comments and quotes on Liston's tragic life. Michael McLean's excellent mini-biography on Liston can be found in the *Scribner Encyclopedia of American Lives, Sports Figures* (2002). Lucket V. Davis's article on Liston is in the *American National Biography* (1999), volume one, and related Liston material is available in the *Boxing Hall of Fame Boxing Register* (1999). There is also a useful article on Liston in Arthur Ashe, *A Hard Road to Glory: A History of the African-American Athlete* (1988). Jeffrey T. Sammons, *Beyond the Ring: The Role of Boxing in American Society* (1988), remains the best source on Liston, his boxing career, and the interpenetration of race, sport, and American culture in the 1960s. An obituary is in the *New York Times* (7 Jan. 1971).

Scott A. G. M. Crawford

LODGE, Henry Cabot, Jr. (*b.* 5 July 1902 in Nahant, Massachusetts; *d.* 27 February 1985 in Beverly, Massachusetts), U.S. senator; ambassador to the United Nations (1953–1960), South Vietnam (1963–1964 and 1965–1967), and West Germany (1968–1969); Republican candidate for U.S. vice president (1960); special envoy to the Vatican; and chief negotiator at Vietnam peace talks in Paris.

Lodge's parents were George Cabot Lodge, a poet, and Mathilda Elizabeth Frelinghuysen (Davis) Lodge. When George Cabot Lodge died in 1909, his family was taken in by his father, Henry Cabot Lodge, Sr., who was a U.S. senator from Massachusetts from 1893 to 1924. Lodge was the oldest of three children. His younger brother John Davis Lodge eventually became governor of Connecticut. As children, Lodge, called "Cabot," and his siblings were taught their responsibility to use the privileges given them by wealth and high social standing in service to their nation and its people.

Henry Cabot Lodge, Jr., July 1964. Ted Streshinsky/Corbis

Lodge's education was haphazard but broad, including schooling for two years in Paris. He attended preparatory school at Middlesex School in Concord, Massachusetts, graduating in 1920. He then attended Harvard University, finishing his course work in only three years, taking a year off, and then graduating in 1924 with a degree in Romance languages. On 1 July 1926 he married the daughter of a physician, Emily Esther Sears; in later years they had two sons. That same year he joined the U.S. Army Reserve.

From 1923 to 1925 he worked as a reporter for the *Boston Transcript,* until accepting a job for the *New York Herald Tribune,* where he was primarily a political reporter until 1932. His January 1930 article "Our Failure in the Philippines" in *Harper's* suggested that the United States was misgoverning the islands. His 1932 book *Cult of Weakness* argued that American pacifism was weakening American foreign policy. That year he was elected to the General Court (assembly) of Massachusetts, then reelected in 1934. In 1936 he was elected to the U.S. Senate.

In the Senate he proved to be a moderate on domestic matters, supporting President Franklin D. Roosevelt's efforts to enhance the minimum wage and establish a five-day workweek for American wage earners. In 1939 he not only supported Social Security but also tried to amend the law to increase the size of payments to the elderly. On matters of foreign policy, he favored a buildup of the U.S. military and favored the draft. Although he was opposed to U.S. membership in the League of Nations and in 1940 opposed aiding the British in World War II, in 1941 he supported Roosevelt's Lend-Lease program of American ships to Britain.

He was still in the U.S. Army Reserve when the empire of Japan attacked Pearl Harbor, drawing the United States directly into World War II. He took a leave of absence from the Senate and saw combat as an officer in America's tank corps in North Africa. He was promoted to major, then was sent to the United States to report to the government on what he had observed. His return to duty was blocked in July 1942 by the Secretary of War, Henry L. Stimson; Stimson believed that Lodge could better serve his country in the Senate.

Lodge soon became restive, and in February 1944 he resigned from the Senate and was sent to Italy to become deputy chief of staff of America's Fourth Corps, leaving the army on December 1945 as a lieutenant colonel. In 1946 he was reelected to the Senate. His experiences in World War II had convinced him that America needed to be actively engaged in foreign affairs, and he became an advocate for the United Nations. President Harry S Truman appointed Lodge as a delegate to the United Nations in 1950.

It is possible that by 1952 Lodge had tired of being a senator, devoting little time to his own campaign. Instead, he focused on getting Dwight D. Eisenhower elected president of the United States. John Kennedy defeated Lodge for the Senate seat, but Eisenhower won the presidency. He then appointed Lodge as America's ambassador to the United Nations and gave Lodge cabinet rank. Lodge served in the United Nations from 1953 to 1960.

In 1960 the Republicans nominated Lodge for vice president of the United States, with Richard Nixon the nominee for president. Lodge's indifferent campaigning indicated that he had lost his enthusiasm for elective office. He and Nixon lost the election by a very narrow margin to John F. Kennedy and Lyndon B. Johnson, and Lodge's political career appeared to be over. After the election he took a job with the Atlantic Institute, an organization that promoted international cooperation.

In 1963 President Kennedy appointed Lodge to be America's ambassador to South Vietnam. When Lodge arrived in Saigon, capital of South Vietnam, the nation was in turmoil. The North Vietnamese were making military inroads into their neighbor; a Communist-inspired insurgency called the Vietcong was trying to make South Vietnam into an independent Communist state; and South Vietnamese dictator Ngo Dinh Diem was stripping opponents of their legal rights. Periodically a Buddhist monk would publicly burn himself alive in protest of the Roman Catholic Diem's restrictive policies. Lodge soon realized that Diem could not remain in power much longer and that Diem's policies were driving South Vietnamese citizens to support the Communists. In late summer 1963 South Vietnamese military officers organized a coup against Diem, and on 1 November 1963 they took action. Diem telephoned Lodge and asked whether the United States would help him. Lodge suggested he should flee while he could. Diem said that he would resist, and he was gunned down in his car soon thereafter.

Kennedy was assassinated on 22 November 1963, and Lodge told the new president, Lyndon Johnson, that South Vietnam would surely fall without considerable aid from America. Johnson foresaw the whole of Indochina falling into Communism if South Vietnam fell, and at the urging of Lodge and others, he considered committing American troops to the war. In 1964 Lodge left his post as ambassador.

In the meantime, the New Hampshire presidential primary was held. Friends and Lodge's brother urged voters to write in Lodge's name rather than vote for the leaders in the race, Nelson Rockefeller and Barry Goldwater. Lodge's victory was stunning; he had not even campaigned or shown any interest in running. Yet, he truly had had enough of campaigning, and he declared himself uninterested in becoming the president, even though he seemed likely to win the Republican nomination if he wanted it.

In 1965 President Lyndon B. Johnson, fresh from being elected president, reappointed Lodge ambassador to Vietnam. Lodge believed that a Communist takeover of South Vietnam would be a catastrophe for the South Vietnamese people and for their neighbors throughout Indochina. Thus, he was in favor of America's commitment of troops to the ground war, and he worked hard to coordinate cooperation between the American and the South Vietnamese armies. Part of his labor involved an intense effort to prepare the South Vietnamese to carry on the fighting themselves without American help; there were numerous examples of exceptional courage on the part of South Vietnamese soldiers. Yet, the continued corrupt behavior of the South Vietnamese government was discouraging. By the time he left his post in 1967 he was changing his mind about what could be done in South Vietnam, and in 1968 he concluded that the Vietnam War was unwinnable.

From 1968 to 1969 Lodge served as ambassador to West Germany, normally an enjoyable posting, but he spent much of his time laying the groundwork for a negotiated settlement of the war in Vietnam. In the United States, President Johnson withdrew from the race for reelection in favor of his vice president, Hubert Humphrey. In November 1968 Richard Nixon narrowly defeated Humphrey. In 1969 Nixon made Lodge America's chief delegate to the Paris peace talks for the Vietnam War. Although Lodge had been a brilliant negotiator in the United Nations, he made little headway with the intransigent delegates from North Vietnam, who argued over every petty detail, even the shape and size of the table where the delegates were to sit. Lodge soon left the peace talks, and he was appointed to be envoy to the Vatican by Nixon in 1970, a post he held until 1977. Thereafter, he lived in retirement in Beverly, Massachusetts. Lodge died of congestive heart failure following a lengthy illness. He is buried at Mount Auburn Cemetery in Cambridge, Massachusetts.

Americans of all political persuasions admired Lodge as a statesman who served his country well in war and peace. As a senator, he helped to guide important social legislation through Congress. As an ambassador to the United Nations, he helped the United States establish itself as a great power in foreign affairs. In South Vietnam he miscalculated the difficulties America would encounter if it intervened, contributing to the disaster that followed after he left. By selflessly serving two Democratic presidents, Kennedy and Johnson, he sacrificed his chances of ever becoming president of the United States, had he wanted to.

★

The largest collection of Lodge's papers belongs to the Massachusetts Historical Society. Lodge's memoirs, *The Storm Has Many Eyes: A Personal Narrative* (1973) and *As It Was: An Inside View of Politics and Power in the '50s and '60s* (1976), are frank accounts, especially regarding the blunders behind the Vietnam War. Anne E. Blair, *Lodge in Vietnam: A Patriot Abroad* (1995), tells of Lodge's efforts to save South Vietnam from Communism.

A good obituary is William E. Smith, "A Brahmin's Life of Service," *Time* (11 Mar. 1985).

KIRK H. BEETZ

LOMBARDI, Vincent Thomas ("Vince") (*b.* 11 June 1913 in New York City; *d.* 3 September 1970 in Washington, D.C.), coach of the Green Bay Packers football dynasty in the 1960s who was honored by having the Super Bowl trophy named the Lombardi Trophy.

Lombardi was the oldest of five children of the Italian immigrants Henry ("Harry") Lombardi, a butcher and meat wholesaler, and Matilda (Izzo) Lombardi, a homemaker. Lombardi attended Saint Francis Preparatory School in Brooklyn, where he made All-City as a football running back. Lombardi played offensive and defensive guard on the legendary "Seven Blocks of Granite" line at Fordham University in 1935 and 1936 under the head coach Jim Crowley and the assistant coach Frank Leahy. Although only five feet, nine inches tall and weighing between 170 and 175 pounds, Lombardi compensated for his relatively small size with the ferocity of his play. In 1937 he graduated magna cum laude with a B.S. in business administration.

Lombardi taught chemistry, Latin, and physics from 1939 to 1947 at Saint Cecelia's Prep School in Englewood, New Jersey, and coached the football team to six state titles and the basketball team to one state title. He married Marie Planitz on 31 August 1940; they had two children. After serving as freshman football coach in 1947 and varsity offensive coach in 1948 at Fordham University, Lombardi coached the offensive line at the U.S. Military Academy at West Point (Army) from 1949 to 1953 under the head coach Earl ("Red") Blaik. From 1954 to 1958 he was offensive coordinator for the New York Giants of the National Football League (NFL) under the coach Jim Lee Howell. Lombardi developed a powerful rushing attack based on the single wing formation. New York overwhelmed the Chicago Bears, 47–7, in the 1956 NFL title game and lost a classic overtime contest, 23–17, to the Baltimore Colts in the 1958 NFL championship game.

In January 1959 the Green Bay Packers named Lombardi head coach and general manager. The Packers, at one time a dominant NFL team, had triumphed only once and tied once in 1958, finishing with a 1–10–1 record. Lombardi revived the sagging Packer franchise, the NFL's only surviving team that was publicly owned by the town in which it played. He handled all phases of team operations, including setting salaries, hiring and firing personnel, and designing uniforms. Lombardi stressed football fundamentals, notably blocking and tackling. He believed that the team that blocked better usually won the game. Lombardi

Vince Lombardi. ARCHIVE PHOTOS, INC.

pitted strength against strength and taught zone blocking to facilitate more efficient "runs to daylight." He relied primarily on the single wing formation and preferred a running attack to the forward pass.

Not a true innovator, Lombardi adopted techniques from his loving, perfectionist father, his years at Saint Cecelia's, his belief in the hierarchical system of the Roman Catholic Church, and the lessons he learned from coaches at Fordham and West Point. He utilized the power sweep learned from Crowley and Leahy at Fordham, the passing game learned from the assistant coach Sid Gillman at Army, and execution and organization learned from Blaik at Army. Lombardi, a motivational expert, gave the Packers self-confidence and an intense desire to win. "Winning isn't everything," he said. "It's the only thing." "Fatigue," Lombardi claimed, "makes cowards of us all." Lombardi considered coaching to be teaching, and he worked to achieve excellence by endless repetition and by motivating each of his players. The devout Roman Catholic who once aspired to become a priest implored his players to concentrate on God, family, and the Green Bay Packers. A stern disciplinarian, he set rigid rules to govern the daily lives of his players. Lombardi portrayed strength, precision, intelligence, and excellence, qualities inculcated in his Packers.

He held exhausting training camps and grueling practices and engaged in meticulous film study.

Lombardi built the Packers into a formidable dynasty, making him a folk hero. He inherited talent upon his arrival but needed time to develop it. He molded the offense, moving the reserve Bart Starr to first-string quarterback, the reserve Jim Taylor to starting fullback, and the part-time quarterback Paul Horning to full-time running back. The end Ron Kramer, the guard Jerry Kramer, the tackle Forrest Gregg, and the center Jim Ringo made the offensive unit more potent. The offense executed a fundamental power sweep nearly flawlessly. Horning swept around end with Kramer pulling out to lead the formation. Lombardi delighted in using such variations as the halfback option pass by Horning. He also popularized the idea of permitting the runner to "run to daylight," or to choose his own route according to the actions of his blockers. Taylor blasted over Gregg on a weak-side slant. Starr threw deep to the end Max McGee after sucking in the defense with play action on third down and short-yardage situations.

Green Bay quickly showed remarkable progress under Lombardi, winning their first three games, losing their next five, and winning their last four for their first winning season since 1947. Besides drafting the end Boyd Dowler, the Packers acquired the defensive tackle Henry Jordan from Cleveland, the safety Emlen Tunnell from the New York Giants, and the guard Fred ("Fuzzy") Thurston from Baltimore. Thurston joined Jerry Kramer to form a tandem of outstanding offensive guards. The linebackers Ray Nitschke and Dan Currie strengthened the defense. For the Packers' 7–5 season in 1959, Lombardi was named NFL Coach of the Year.

In 1960 Green Bay won eight of twelve games and the Western Conference title. The Packers drafted the halfback Tom Moore, acquired the defensive end Willie Davis from Cleveland, and signed the free-agent safety Willie Wood. Horning set an NFL scoring record with 176 points, while Davis, Jordan, and Wood joined an increasingly potent defense. In the 1960 NFL championship game, the veteran Philadelphia Eagles bested the Packers, 17–13. Lombardi's Packers never lost another NFL title game. The team became profitable, enabling Lombardi to upgrade Green Bay's City Stadium and the training facilities.

Green Bay repeated as Western Conference champions in 1961 with an 11–3 record. Starr firmly controlled the reins at quarterback. Horning commuted from military service at Fort Riley, Kansas, but still scored 146 points. Taylor rushed for 1,307 yards, while Ron Kramer, a pioneer tight end, made thirty-five receptions. The Packers added three rookies to the team, including the defensive tackle Ron Kostelnik, the cornerback Herb Adderley, and the running back Elijah Pitts. The Packers resoundingly defeated Lombardi's old team, the New York Giants, 37–0, in the 1961 NFL championship game at City Stadium.

Green Bay dominated the NFL with a 13–1 record in 1962, winning the Western Conference crown for the third consecutive year. The Packers led the NFL offensively in most points scored and defensively in fewest points permitted. Tom Moore filled in for the injured Horning at halfback, while Ron Kramer became the new kicker. A Thanksgiving Day 26–14 loss to the Detroit Lions denied the Packers a perfect season. Lombardi's squad defeated the New York Giants for the second straight year in the NFL title game, winning 16–7 in a bitterly cold Yankee Stadium.

Green Bay, now known as Title Town, U.S.A., enjoyed another great season with an 11–2–1 mark in 1963, finishing a half game behind the Chicago Bears in the Western Conference. Commissioner Pete Rozelle had suspended Horning indefinitely for betting on NFL games, so Lenny Moore and Pitts filled in for Horning in the backfield. The Packers lost their home opener, 10–3, to the Bears; won eight consecutive games; and then were trounced by the Bears, 26–7. Horning returned in 1964, but the Packers still finished second in the Western Conference, this time to the Colts, with an 8–5–1 record.

Lombardi rebuilt his aging team in 1965, bringing in the kicker Don Chandler from the New York Giants, acquiring the flanker Carroll Dale from the Los Angeles Rams, and promoting the tight end Marv Fleming and the linebacker Dave Robinson to starting roles. The Packers returned to their former glory with a 10–3–1 mark. Green Bay defeated the Baltimore Colts, 13–10, on Don Chandler's field goal in overtime to win the Western Conference title and triumphed over the defending league champion Cleveland Browns, 23–12, at snowy Lambeau Field in January 1966 to reclaim the NFL title. (City Stadium had been renamed Lambeau Field on 11 September 1965 after the death of Curly Lambeau, who founded the Packers' franchise.) Nitschke spearheaded the Packer defense in holding the fullback Jim Brown, the league's leading rusher, to fifty yards rushing.

Green Bay won another Western Conference title with a 12–2 record in 1966. The quarterback Starr led the NFL in passing and was intercepted only three times. The defense led the NFL, giving up just 163 points. Green Bay lost only to the San Francisco 49ers and the Minnesota Vikings by a total of four points. The Packers defeated the Dallas Cowboys, 34–27, for their fourth NFL championship and the American Football League champion Kansas City Chiefs, 35–10, in historic Super Bowl I on 15 January 1967. Starr won the game's Most Valuable Player (MVP) award after completing sixteen passes for 250 yards and two touchdowns.

In 1967 the NFL realigned because of expansion, and Green Bay joined the Central Division with its traditional rivals Chicago, Detroit, and Minnesota. Lombardi coached the injury-riddled Packers to a 9–4–1 mark and the Central Division crown. In a 55–7 victory over Cleveland, Green Bay scored an NFL record thirty-five points in the first quarter. Travis Williams returned four kickoffs for touchdowns. The Packers won a third consecutive Western Conference championship by upsetting the Los Angeles Rams, 28–7, in Milwaukee's County Stadium. Green Bay rallied to defeat the Dallas Cowboys, 21–17, in a classic NFL championship game called the "Ice Bowl," played at a temperature of minus thirteen degrees, with a wind-chill factor of minus fifty-eight, at Lambeau Field. Starr's quarterback sneak from one yard out with just thirteen seconds remaining decided the game. The play, recaptured in Ron Kramer's book *Instant Replay*, enabled the Packers to become the only modern team to win three straight NFL championships. In Super Bowl II, on 14 January 1968, Green Bay dominated the American Football League champion Oakland Raiders, 33–14. Starr repeated as Super Bowl MVP, completing thirteen passes for 202 yards and one touchdown.

Lombardi resigned as the Packers head coach in February 1968 but remained as general manager. Phil Bengston, the long-time defensive coach, replaced Lombardi as head coach. Lombardi was exhausted by the tensions of coaching and claimed that the demands of the two jobs were too great. In nine years as head coach, Lombardi had built Green Bay into a sports dynasty and national symbol of excellence. He had compiled a regular season record of 98–30–4 and a postseason record of 9–1. He found the season away from coaching very difficult. "I miss the fire on Sunday, and the close camaraderie of the team," he remarked.

In February 1969 Lombardi joined the Washington Redskins as executive vice president, head coach, general manager, and 5 percent owner. The Redskins had finished just 5–9 in 1968. Lombardi guided Washington, led by their star quarterback Sonny Jurgensen and the linebacker Sam Huff, to a 7–5–2 record in 1969 and their first wining season in fourteen years. His mark mirrored that of his first year at Green Bay a decade earlier. In 1970 preseason drills Lombardi became ill. Doctors diagnosed colon cancer that June and treated him at Georgetown University Hospital. Lombardi died from cancer at the age of fifty-seven. His funeral was held in New York City, and he is buried at Mount Olivet Cemetery in Middletown, New Jersey. He received the NFL Distinguished Service Award in 1970 and was elected to the Pro Football Hall of Fame in 1971. In 2000 ESPN named Lombardi Coach of the Century.

Lombardi, who symbolized authority and discipline, ranks among the most legendary NFL coaches and greatest winners in sport history. The disciplinarian became a symbol of excellence for athletes and business professionals, demanding fair play, striving for perfection, and working hard. He treated veterans and rookies alike and conducted player sessions as strictly business. "Lombardi," Jerry Kramer recalled, "was a cruel, kind, tough, gentle, miserable, wonderful man whom I often hate and often love and always respect."

Lombardi symbolized professional football's success and also represented order and stability in a troubled time. He spoke of the older values of hard work, discipline, loyalty to family and team, duty to God, and respect for one's family. Lombardi openly criticized individualism that lacked personal responsibility and attempted to direct the outside interests of his players. He aligned with professional football's management in its developing quarrels with players over rights and benefits.

Lombardi always struggled to separate his private and professional lives. Devoted to family and close friends, the devout Roman Catholic attended mass daily. He was shy, wary of the press, and difficult to approach, but many players spoke of him with affection and respect. No NFL coach with at least ten seasons compiled a better record. Lombardi finished with a 105–35–6 mark and a .740 winning percentage during the regular season and a 9–1 mark in the playoffs. He guided his teams to six Western Conference crowns, five NFL championships, and two Super Bowl titles. The street on which the Packer offices are located was renamed Lombardi Avenue, while the Super Bowl trophy awarded annually is called the Lombardi Trophy.

★

Lombardi's autobiographical works are *Run to Daylight* (1968) and the posthumously published *Vince Lombardi on Football* (1973). The best biography of Lombardi is David Maraniss, *When Pride Still Mattered: A Life of Vince Lombardi* (1999). Other biographies include Jerry Kramer, ed., *Lombardi: Winning Is the Only Thing* (1970), recounting the Green Bay Packers glory days; Tom Dowling, *Coach: A Season with Lombardi* (1970), reviewing Lombardi's year with the Washington Redskins; Robert W. Wells, *Vince Lombardi: His Life and Times* (1971); John Wiebusch, ed., *Lombardi* (1971); Michael O'Brien, *Vince: A Personal Biography of Vince Lombardi* (1987); Mike Bynum, ed., *Vince Lombardi: Memories of a Special Time* (1988), and *Lombardi: A Dynasty Remembered* (1994); Gary R. George, ed., *Winning Is a Habit: Vince Lombardi on Winning, Success, and the Pursuit of Excellence* (1997); and Vince Lombardi, Jr., *What It Takes to Be Number One: Vince Lombardi on Leadership* (2000). Biographical information is also in the official Vince Lombardi website at <http://www.vincelombardi.com>. Obituaries are in the *Evening Bulletin* (Philadelphia) (3 Sept. 1970), the *New York Times* (4 Sept. 1970), and *Time* (14 Sept. 1970).

DAVID L. PORTER

LOWELL, Robert Traill Spence, IV ("Cal") (*b*. 1 March 1917 in Boston, Massachusetts; *d*. 12 September 1977 in New York City), poet, playwright, and teacher known for his complex, confessional style, whose widely publicized protests against the Vietnam War and campaign for the peace candidate Eugene McCarthy propelled him into the political turmoil of the 1960s.

Lowell was the only child of Robert Traill Spence Lowell III, a U.S. naval officer and executive at Lever Brothers, and Charlotte Winslow Lowell, a Boston socialite; both parents were descendents of distinguished New England families. Lowell attended Saint Mark's preparatory school, where his slovenly appearance and bullying earned him his lifelong sobriquet "Cal," short for both the beastly Caliban of Shakespeare's *The Tempest* and the Roman despot Caligula. Lowell entered Harvard in 1935 but after two years transferred to Kenyon College in Ohio. He married writer Jean Stafford on 2 April 1940 before graduating in June. His first book, *Land of Unlikeness*, was published in 1944; his second, *Lord Weary's Castle* (1946), won the 1947 Pulitzer Prize for poetry. In June 1948 he divorced Stafford and on 28 July 1949 married the writer Elizabeth Hardwick, with whom he had a daughter. During this time Lowell began suffering from a series of mental breakdowns

Robert Lowell. AP/WIDE WORLD PHOTOS

due to bipolar disorder, which would plague him the rest of his life.

Life Studies (1959) was a landmark in Lowell's poetic development. Unlike his earlier poetry, which was highly stylized and remote, *Life Studies* is looser in structure and more personal in tone, drawing on the poet's own life experiences—childhood memories, marital woes, and mental breakdowns. Such poems as the justly famous "Skunk Hour" evoke an almost unbearable existential anguish. Described as a "heartbreaking statement of the human condition" by friend and poet William Carlos Williams, it initiated the "confessional" school of poetry and won the National Book Award in 1960.

In September of that year the Lowells moved from Boston, where Lowell had been teaching at Boston University, to New York City. They settled into an apartment at 15 West Sixty-seventh Street on Manhattan's Upper West Side, where they lived for the next ten years. Unfortunately, Lowell's illness resurfaced, and he became wildly infatuated with Sandra Hochman, a young poet. Drinking heavily and threatening to leave his wife, he was admitted to the Neurological Institute at the Columbia-Presbyterian Medical Center. Upon his release Lowell completed work on *Imitations* (1961), a collection of loose translations of works by various poets that won the Bollingen Prize in poetry for translation in 1962. During this time Lowell was also working on his drama, *The Old Glory* (1965), a trilogy of plays—"Benito Cereno," "My Kinsman, Major Molineux," and "Endecott and the Red Cross"—based on short stories by Herman Melville and Nathaniel Hawthorne.

During the early 1960s Lowell became increasingly involved in politics. A staunch liberal who had been dismayed by the "tranquilized" era under President Dwight D. Eisenhower, he was buoyed by the election of John F. Kennedy and attended his inauguration in 1960. On 11 May 1962 he, along with other artists and intellectuals whose favor the administration courted, attended a glamorous White House dinner in honor of André Malraux, the French Minister of Culture, and Lowell was suitably impressed. Still, the Bay of Pigs fiasco of the previous spring—in which U.S.-backed Cuban exiles attempted to invade the island—and the intensifying cold war troubled Lowell. In February 1963 he assumed a teaching position at Harvard to which he commuted from New York two days a week. He also assisted his wife in the founding of the *New York Review of Books,* intended to fill the gap left by the loss of the *New York Times Book Review* during a prolonged newspaper strike. The trauma of Kennedy's assassination in November, however, resulted in another breakdown, and Lowell was admitted to the Institute for Living, a psychiatric hospital in Hartford, Connecticut.

For the Union Dead was published in the fall of 1964. The title poem is Lowell's scathing indictment of contemporary decline, nuclear peril, and racial injustice in America. The volume was widely praised, and the critics now heralded Lowell as *the* American poet. In addition, *The Old Glory* premiered on 1 November at the American Place Theater in Manhattan to favorable reviews. It won five Obie Awards for the 1964–1965 season, including one for best off–Broadway play. Such heady success, however, pushed Lowell over the edge yet again. In January 1965 he began a relationship with a Latvian dancer, Vija Vetra, precipitating another stay at the Institute for Living.

In June 1965 Lowell made headlines by declining President Lyndon B. Johnson's invitation to a White House Festival of the Arts, a ploy designed by the administration to quell the protests that had erupted on campuses across the country as the war in Vietnam escalated. Lowell had initially accepted but then reneged. Instead he wrote an open letter to Johnson excoriating his foreign policy and expressing his fears that America was in danger of "becoming an explosive and suddenly chauvinistic nation, and may even be drifting on our way to the last nuclear ruin." Lowell's letter ran on the front page of the *New York Times* on 3 June 1965. The next day twenty other artists and writers joined his rebuff, leaving the festival in shambles.

An awkwardly handsome man, Lowell now emerged as an important public figure whose voice was one to be listened to in political debate. He stood six feet tall with thick black hair graying at the temples and quizzical blue eyes behind black, horn-rimmed glasses. The poems he composed that summer and that later appeared in *Near the Ocean* (1967) reflect his many political concerns. "Waking Early Sunday Morning," a key political poem of the 1960s, laments the endless cycles of violence perpetuated by corrupt governments, while "Central Park" portrays a nation torn by "fear and poverty," racial unrest, and police brutality. Lowell was also working on a translation of Aeschylus's *Prometheus Bound,* in which a vindictive Zeus unleashing thunderbolts on hapless mortals seems chillingly reminiscent of Johnson dropping bombs on Vietnam. In the spring of 1967 the Yale Drama School received a $25,000 grant from the National Endowment for the Humanities for a production of *Prometheus Bound: Derived from Aeschylus* (1969), with $10,000 going to Lowell. Enraged that a government agency had granted money to the poet who had publicly humiliated him, Johnson tried, but failed, to revoke the grant. The play premiered to mixed reviews on 9 May 1967. Lowell spent the rest of the year campaigning vigorously against the war. On 20 October he traveled to Washington, D.C., along with the author Norman Mailer and others to take part in a protest against the government's "immoral authority." Lowell, who had been jailed as a conscientious objector during World War II,

spoke eloquently in defense of the assembled draft-resisters and their sympathizers from the steps of the Department of Justice and later marched on the Pentagon.

Lowell returned to New York and resumed work on a series of blank verse sonnets he had begun in June 1967, which would be published as *Notebook 1967–68* (1969). Lowell produced the sonnets at a remarkable rate: by Christmas 1967 he had written more than seventy and over the course of the next year produced an average of four per week. Inspired by the example of John Berryman's *Dream Songs,* everything became grist for Lowell's poetic mill—headlines, historical figures, sex, memories, conversational fragments, politics, banalities—as he strove to create a sprawling epic of his own consciousness and times. Lowell later revised and republished the volume as *Notebook* (1970) and still later revised, reorganized, and expanded it into three volumes: *History, For Lizzie and Harriet,* and the 1974 Pulitzer Prize–winning *The Dolphin*—all published in 1973.

In the fall of 1967 Lowell began campaigning for Senator Eugene McCarthy, who had challenged Johnson for the Democratic presidential nomination. Running on an antiwar platform, underdog McCarthy captured an astonishing 42 percent of the vote to Johnson's 49 percent in the New Hampshire primary, prompting Senator Robert F. Kennedy to enter the race. Although Lowell was intrigued by the Kennedy mystique, he remained loyal to McCarthy. After McCarthy's loss to Kennedy in the pivotal California primary and Kennedy's assassination on 5 June 1968, however, Lowell lost interest, although he continued campaigning for McCarthy up through the disastrous Democratic National Convention in Chicago that August, in which police and protesters battled in the streets.

Disillusioned with America, Lowell accepted a teaching position at the University of Essex in England beginning in October 1970. There he became romantically involved with the writer Lady Caroline Blackwood. They had a son on 28 September 1971, and in October 1972 the couple flew to Santo Domingo, where Lowell secured a divorce from Hardwick and married Blackwell. In his final years Lowell suffered increasingly from failing health and severe bouts of depression, and as his marriage to Blackwood grew strained, he drifted back toward Hardwick. He died of congestive heart failure at age sixty in a taxi on his way to visit her in Manhattan. He is buried in Stark Cemetery in Dunbarton, New Hampshire.

Lowell was arguably the greatest American poet of his generation and a unique chronicler of the American scene during the turbulent 1960s. The poet Richard Tillinghast has observed, "Lowell straddled the poetry scene of his day like a colossus," and other critics have spoken of the era as the "Age of Lowell." The personal or "confessional" style of *Life Studies* set the tone for a generation of younger poets such as Sylvia Plath and Anne Sexton. Although the polemics of Lowell's plays now seem dated, his "public" poetry of the mid-1960s remains an artful and compelling commentary on the political, social, and ideological upheavals of the decade. As important as Lowell's literary achievement is his example of the poet as public spokesman and political activist. Through his highly visible protests, Lowell braved the glare of public scrutiny for the sake of his moral convictions and inexorably altered the poetry and politics of America.

★

The Houghton Library at Harvard University, the Harry Ransom Humanities Research Center at the University of Texas at Austin, and the Berg Collection of the New York Public Library are major repositories of Lowell papers. In-depth biographies are Ian Hamilton, *Robert Lowell: A Biography* (1982), the first and best account of Lowell's turbulent career, and Paul Mariani's more sympathetic *Lost Puritan: A Life of Robert Lowell* (1994). Richard Tillinghast, *Robert Lowell's Life and Work: Damaged Grandeur* (1995), is an informative critical memoir. Norman Mailer, *Armies of the Night: History as a Novel, the Novel as History* (1968), features an informative portrait of Lowell during the protests of the 1960s. Richard J. Fein, *Robert Lowell* (1970), is a handy introduction that contains some biographical material. Jeffrey Meyers, ed., *Robert Lowell, Interviews and Memoirs* (1988), is a useful resource on the poet's life and times. *Voices and Visions: Robert Lowell, A Mania for Phrases* (1988), a fifty-six-minute documentary film, contains readings by and interviews with the poet interspersed with illustrative footage. An obituary is in the *New York Times* (13 Sept. 1977).

MICHAEL MCLEAN

LOWENSTEIN, Allard Kenneth (*b.* 16 January 1929 in Newark, New Jersey; *d.* 14 March 1980 in New York City), political activist and congressman from New York in the 1960s who supported the civil rights movement and opposed the Vietnam War.

Lowenstein was born in Newark but grew up in Harrison and Scarsdale, Westchester County, New York. He was the youngest of three boys and had a younger sister. His father, Gabriel Abraham Lowenstein, was a physician and biochemist who taught at the Columbia University College of Physicians and Surgeons before becoming a prominent New York City restaurateur. His mother, Augusta Goldberg, died when he was a year old, and his father remarried. Not until his thirteenth birthday did Lowenstein learn that Florence Lowenstein was actually his stepmother.

Following his 1945 graduation from the Horace Mann School in New York City, Lowenstein attended the University of North Carolina at Chapel Hill, where he challenged the university's discriminatory policies toward Jewish students. He was also an admirer of the school's liberal president, Frank Porter Graham. In 1949 Graham was appointed to fill a vacancy in the United States Senate, and following his graduation that same year Lowenstein moved to Washington, D.C., and worked for the senator.

After Graham was unsuccessful in retaining his Senate seat in 1950, Lowenstein served as president of the United States National Student Association from 1950 to 1951. He entered Yale University Law School in 1952 and was the national chairman of Students for Stevenson during Adlai Stevenson's presidential bid. Lowenstein received his law degree from Yale in 1954 and served two years as an enlisted man in the U.S. Army. From 1956 to 1957 he was an educational consultant to the American Association for the United Nations, working closely with one of his political idols, Eleanor Roosevelt. Following a year laboring in the offices of Minnesota Senator Hubert H. Humphrey, Lowenstein returned to the United Nations, for which he traveled to Southwest Africa (Namibia) and prepared a report, later published as *Brutal Mandate: Journey to South-West Africa* (1962), on conditions of apartheid in that region under the control of South Africa.

Lowenstein began to be called a "Pied Piper" who motivated college students to become politically active when, in 1961, he was appointed assistant dean of men and a political science lecturer at Stanford University. Although he was at Stanford for only a single academic year, Lowenstein established a following among students, often referred to as "Al People," who would join him in the civil rights struggles of the 1960s. His ability to attract the support of young male students also revealed a degree of sexual ambiguity. Lowenstein would hug and sleep with some of his young male devotees, but he evidently avoided genital sex. Of Lowenstein's sexuality, his biographer William Chafe asserts, "His closest companions were men, and from adolescence onward he struggled with the issue of whether or not he might be homosexual. In his appeal to the young, he often inspired devotion and worship. Yet these same emotions could turn to hatred and alienation when the magic of the moment, as the intensity of the crusade, had passed."

In the fall of 1962 Lowenstein began a two-year tenure in the political science department at North Carolina State University in Raleigh, where he actively encouraged integration efforts. The charismatic teacher attracted numerous northern students to the South to participate in the civil rights movement and register black voters. He helped organize the Mississippi Freedom Vote, the predecessor of the Mississippi Freedom Democratic Party, which chal-

Allard Lowenstein. CORBIS CORPORATION (BELLEVUE)

lenged the white power structure of the state's traditional Democratic Party. He also served as an adviser to Dr. Martin Luther King, Jr. Lowenstein sought to maintain an alliance between the National Association for the Advancement of Colored People, with whom he had close ties, and more radical elements within the Student Nonviolent Coordinating Committee (SNCC). Many young African Americans in SNCC resented what they deemed his efforts to dominate the civil rights struggle in Mississippi. For example, Lowenstein urged that the committee reject the support of the National Lawyers' Guild and Southern Conference Education Fund because these organizations were tainted by ties to the American Communist Party. His final break with SNCC occurred at the 1964 Democratic National Convention, when Lowenstein urged that the Mississippi Freedom Democratic Party delegation accept a compromise on the matter of seating and credentials. Although he was an insurgent who questioned the political establishment, Lowenstein was a liberal rather than a radical, preferring to work for change within the system.

Returning to New York City, Lowenstein was defeated in 1966 when he attempted to garner the Democratic congressional nomination for Manhattan's Nineteenth District. In the same year he married Jennifer Lyman. They had three children but divorced in 1979. From 1967 to 1968 Lowenstein taught political science at the City University of New York. After serving as a civilian observer for 1967 elections in South Vietnam, he returned to the United States and founded the Conference of Concerned Democrats and the Coalition for a Democratic Alternative, organizations opposed to President Lyndon B. Johnson's reelection and policies in Vietnam.

Failing in his efforts to get senators Robert Kennedy and George McGovern to oppose Johnson, Lowenstein announced that he would support the antiwar candidacy of Minnesota senator Eugene McCarthy, who challenged Johnson in the Democratic primaries. With the endorsement of Lowenstein, thousands of young people campaigned for McCarthy, who shocked the president by capturing twenty of twenty-four delegates in the March 1968 New Hampshire presidential primary. Johnson responded to this stunning turn of events by withdrawing from the race. With Johnson out of the race, Kennedy, for whom Lowenstein had great admiration, entered it. Lowenstein, however, remained loyal to McCarthy.

Lowenstein may have succeeded in toppling Johnson, but the system was resilient. Kennedy defeated McCarthy in the California primary, but his candidacy was cut short by an assassin's bullet in June 1968. When it appeared that Johnson's vice president, Hubert Humphrey, would gain the Democratic nomination at the party's Chicago convention, Lowenstein formed the Coalition for an Open Convention. His labors to thwart Humphrey's nomination were unsuccessful, and he eventually agreed to support Humphrey's candidacy after the Johnson administration consented to a bombing halt in North Vietnam.

In the fall of 1968 Lowenstein put most of his energies into a congressional contest in the heavily Republican Fifth Congressional District, located in New York's Nassau County. Using his Pied Piper appeal to the "Al People," he had his enthusiastic supporters canvass almost every home in the district in an effort to dispel allegations that he was a radical. Urging an end to the Vietnam War, Lowenstein upset Republican Mason L. Hampton by the narrow margin of 99,193 votes to 96,427. In Congress, Lowenstein voted for tax relief and to abolish the House Un-American Activities Committee. He opposed the Safeguard Antiballistic Missile, the District of Columbia anti-crime bill, increased military appropriations, and a proposal to abolish aid to students involved with campus unrest. The congressman also established advisory councils on such issues as housing, jet noise, transportation, and wetlands preservation.

The Republican-controlled New York state legislature undermined Lowenstein's reelection bid in 1970 by gerrymandering the Fifth Congressional District to exclude many Jewish and liberal Democratic voters. This contributed to Lowenstein's narrow defeat by Republican Norman F. Lent.

Following his electoral disappointment, Lowenstein joined the faculty of the Yale University School of Urban Studies, but he was hardly finished with politics. In 1971 he headed a national nonpartisan voter registration drive among young people, and served two terms as chair of Americans for Democratic Action. In the late 1970s he worked as U.S. representative to the United Nations Commission on Human Rights, denouncing the system of apartheid in Rhodesia and South Africa. Lowenstein's dream of returning to Congress was thwarted by electoral setbacks in 1972, 1974, 1976, and 1978. He continued to teach and lecture, remaining a gadfly on issues of peace and racial justice, and allegedly earning seventh place on President Richard M. Nixon's enemies list.

Lowenstein's life ended abruptly when he was murdered in his New York law office by Douglas Sweeney, who was suffering from mental illness. Sweeney had first met Lowenstein at Stanford in 1961, becoming an enthusiastic supporter of the political Pied Piper. The two had a falling out, however, over what Sweeney perceived as Lowenstein's betrayal of SNCC in 1964. He also apparently blamed Lowenstein for the death of his stepfather, who was being sued by a company represented by the New York attorney. Lowenstein was hit in the chest by five bullets, and doctors at Saint Clare's Hospital were unable to save his life. Edward Kennedy, whose 1980 presidential bid Lowenstein was supporting, rushed to the hospital, declaring that Lowenstein was a "powerful lobby for progressive principles" and a man who truly made "a difference." During the radical 1960s Lowenstein had labored to keep the tradition of American liberalism alive. He is buried at Arlington National Cemetery in Arlington, Virginia.

★

Lowenstein's papers are available at the Southern Historical Collection, Wilson Library, University of North Carolina at Chapel Hill. A collection of his speeches and writings may be found in Gregory Stone and Douglas Lowenstein, eds., *Lowenstein: Acts of Courage and Belief* (1983). Important biographical treatments of Lowenstein may be found in Richard Cummings, *The Pied Piper: Allard K. Lowenstein and the Liberal Dream* (1985), and William H. Chafe, *Never Stop Running: Allard Lowenstein and the Struggle to Save American Liberalism* (1993). For a critical account of Lowenstein and Sweeney by a former associate, see David Harris, *Dreams Die Hard* (1992). An obituary is in the *New York Times* (15 Mar. 1980).

RON BRILEY

LUMET, Sidney (*b.* 25 June 1924 in Philadelphia, Pennsylvania), actor, producer, and television and film director who honed his craft during the golden age of live television and, during the 1960s, began his career as a New York City–based feature filmmaker noted for his expertise with actors and the efficiency and economy of his productions, which often addressed social, moral, political, and ethical issues.

Lumet was the son of Polish immigrants Baruch Lumet, a professional actor in Warsaw, Poland, and Eugenia Wermus Lumet, a dancer; both were veterans of New York's Yiddish theater.

Lumet made his acting debut at the age of four on the radio show *The Rabbi from Brooklyn,* which Baruch Lumet wrote and directed. In 1928 the five-year-old Lumet appeared on the Yiddish stage alongside his father. As a child and adolescent he read Karl Marx, had a membership in the Young Communist League, and met the playwright Maxwell Anderson, the composer Kurt Weill, and the painter Marc Chagall. Lumet served in the U.S. Army Signal Corps from 1942 to 1946.

Lumet studied with Sandford Meisner at the American Playhouse and was creatively active playing juvenile roles. He was expelled from the newly formed Actor's Studio for rejecting its single acting technique philosophy. Along with other dissidents, Lumet formed the Actor's Workshop, where he conducted a course in the history of drama beginning with contemporary work and tracing back to the Greeks.

Lumet taught acting at the High School of Performing Arts and learned stage directing with productions of Moliere's *Bourgeois Gentleman* and *Doctor's Dilemma* and Albert Camus's *Caligula*. At the age of twenty-six he was offered an assistant director position in the television division of the Columbia Broadcasting System (CBS). This training ground refined Lumet's skills with actors as he learned the language and purpose of the camera, lenses, composition, blocking, and editing. He directed a staggering five hundred live television dramas at the height of the popularity of this medium. Lumet built one of the most impressive resumes of the era, directing 150 episodes of the

Sidney Lumet *(left)*, with his wife, Gloria Vanderbilt, April 1960. © BETTMANN/CORBIS

CBS series *Danger,* twenty-six episodes of *You Are There,* and working on assignments for *Omnibus, Best of Broadway, Alcoa Theater,* and *Goodyear Playhouse.*

Lumet was married to Rita Gam from 1949 to 1954 and Gloria Vanderbilt from 1956 to 1963. On 23 November 1963 he married Gail Jones, with whom he had two children; the couple divorced in 1978. Lumet married Mary Gimbel in 1980.

In 1957 the actor Henry Fonda gave Lumet the opportunity to direct *Twelve Angry Men,* a theatrical film he was producing. The low-budget New York production was completed in just nineteen days for $343,000. The conscience of the Reginald Rose script and exploration of democracy at work in the criminal judicial system kindled Lumet's lifelong interest in the moral spectrum of justice.

In the 1960s *Twelve Angry Men* led to the flowering of a new American cinema. Lumet's training taught him to pre-plan every shot and to work on his feet with intelligence and visual acuity. His political upbringing and sensitivity to social causes merged with his background in the theater to produce a morality that represented the prevailing consciousness of artists of the decade.

Lumet immediately understood the importance of an independent and ethical film artist. Bringing in low-budget

films on schedule guaranteed his freedom, because it allowed him to make many films that expressed his fervent views on socially responsible issues. He embraced the philosophy that writers and actors were messengers who could deliver society's truths and create a forum for difficult topics that demanded a cinematic voice.

Tapping into his familiarity with theater, Lumet's first three films of the 1960s were adaptations of Tennessee Williams, Eugene O'Neill, and Arthur Miller plays. *The Fugitive Kind* (1960) is a rendering of Williams's overheated *Orpheus Descending* (1957) and is notable for Marlon Brando's electric performance. Shot in sequence, *Long Day's Journey into Night* (1962) successfully exploits the all-star cast of Katharine Hepburn, Ralph Richardson, Jason Robards, and Dean Stockwell as the Tyrone family, and it is faithful to the play's script. *A View from the Bridge* (1962) is Arthur Miller's play of forbidden love and betrayal, set in Brooklyn, New York.

After examining the power of sexuality and complex relationships among very different families, Lumet moved into the center of the most-feared global horror of the 1960s, depicted in *Fail Safe* (1964). The film probed the dangers of the nuclear weapons race between the United States and the Soviet Union. Working again with Henry Fonda, who portrayed the president of the United States, Lumet emphasized the moral agony of a single man. The president is forced by his core values and the enormity of his responsibility to make a decision that not only will annihilate thousands of people he represents, but also will destroy the very lives of his own family. *The Pawnbroker* (1965) examines the pain and guilt of a Holocaust survivor who struggles with an inability to express emotion. Flash cuts of life in the concentration camp enhance Rod Steiger's emotionally shattering performance.

Lumet was a New York City filmmaker who placed his city at the heart of the drama. *Fail Safe* concludes with a montage of the vibrant metropolis just seconds before it is sacrificed for the sins of the military-industrial complex. *The Pawnbroker* chronicles the effects of moral and urban decay of a New York that was home to many who could not live down the past and confront the issues of a decade of changing values and mores. *The Hill* (1965) explores injustice in a military prison. *The Group* (1965) is an adaptation of the Mary McCarthy novel that focuses on the social and psychological lives of eight women from Ivy League backgrounds. *The Deadly Affair* (1967) is a dark adaptation of the John Le Carre novel of espionage. In 1968 Lumet brought Anton Chekov's *Seagull* to the screen. *Bye Bye Braverman* (1968) is a comedy concerning third-string literary intellectuals who attend the funeral of a forty-one-year-old colleague. In this film, decades before Steven Spielberg's *Schindler's List* (1993), Lumet brought the emotional and physical horror of the Holocaust to the screen and satirized the intellectual culture of Jews, a subject about which he had intimate knowledge. Unlike the moguls who created Hollywood, Lumet was not afraid to deal with his Jewish heritage. Lumet closed the decade with *The Appointment* (1969), a story of obsessive jealousy that destroys a woman's spirit. In the subsequent three decades Lumet dedicated himself to considerations of law enforcement, police corruption, and judicial ethics in *Serpico* (1974), *Dog Day Afternoon* (1975), *Prince of the City* (1981), *The Verdict* (1982), and *Q and A* (1990).

Lumet directed theatrical adaptations of *Equus* (1977), *The Wiz* (1978), and *Deathtrap* (1982), and the political dramas *Daniel* (1983), a fictional account of the Rosenberg spy case, and *Running on Empty* (1988), which explored the family tensions of underground 1960s radicals.

Lumet's contribution to 1960s filmmaking was a commitment to honest and heartfelt performances realized through a visceral cinematic technique. He probed our sense of right and wrong in a world that since the 1960s has had an increasingly complex social, ethical, and political context.

★

Sidney Lumet, *Making Movies* (1995), is a moviemaking primer that gives insight into the director's distinctive methods. Jay Boyer, *Sidney Lumet* (1993), and Frank R. Cunningham, *Sidney Lumet: Film and Literary Vision* (rev. ed., 2001), are probing critical studies of the filmmaker's work.

VINCENT LoBRUTTO

LURIA, Salvador Edward (*b.* 13 August 1912 in Turin, Italy; *d.* 6 February 1991 in Lexington, Massachusetts), geneticist, administrator, and writer who won the 1969 Nobel Prize in physiology or medicine for his work on viral and bacterial genetics.

Luria was the son of David Luria, an accountant who managed a printing business, and Ester Sacerdote, a homemaker. The Lurias were members of one of the most prominent Jewish families in Turin, and Salvatore (as his name was originally spelled) attended the Liceo d'Azeglio, one of the most prestigious high schools in northern Italy. Afterward he studied at the University of Turin medical school, where he took his degree with honors in 1935. He was then drafted into the Italian army as a medical officer. After he was discharged in 1937, Luria decided against a career in medicine and undertook more theoretical studies on radiology, physics, and mathematics in Enrico Fermi's laboratory at the Physics Institute of the University of Rome.

It was in Rome that Luria began the work that would lead to major discoveries about DNA (deoxyribonucleic acid) in the 1960s, and ultimately to his being awarded a Nobel Prize in 1969. (DNA is present in the chromosomes of all cell nuclei; the distinctive double helical strand is the chemical basis of heredity and carries genetic information for most living things.) Inspired by the work of the physicist Max Delbrück, he became interested in bacteriophage (phage), viruses that infect and kill bacteria. Luria went to France in 1938 when the situation for Italian Jews deteriorated after Italy became more closely tied with Nazi Germany. He briefly did research in Paris, and then, as the German Army approached the city, fled to New York in 1940 and obtained a position at Columbia University. In the early 1940s, funded by a Guggenheim Fellowship, he worked with Delbrück at Vanderbilt University and then accepted a faculty position in the microbiology department at Indiana University in Bloomington. There he met and married Zella Hurwitz, a psychologist, on 18 April 1945. They had one son, Daniel, who became a political economist. In 1947 Luria became a naturalized citizen of the United States.

At Bloomington, Luria discovered that bacteria, like higher organisms, can mutate or change genetically, and he developed a test to detect such mutations. He exposed bacteria to phage and then identified strains that continued

Salvador E. Luria. ARCHIVE PHOTOS, INC.

By the 1960s Luria was busy building the MIT Department of Microbiology into one of the best in the United States. Deciding that phage research had gone as far as it could, he set his sights on different problems and became interested in cell membranes. He held a series of influential research conferences to draw attention to the field, and studied a class of proteins called colicins. Colicin produced by one type of bacteria can kill bacteria of other strains. Luria and his associates found that colicin works by creating a hole in the bacterial membrane and causing a fatal leakage of salts.

By the 1960s the scientific community had come to appreciate the work of the phage group. It was clear that work on phage had opened up a new era in biochemistry and molecular biology. It also was evident that DNA was the genetic molecule, and the work of the phage group in making that obvious was finally appreciated. In 1962 one of Luria's students, James Watson, received the Nobel Prize along with Francis Crick for discovering the structure of DNA. It was just a matter of time before Luria's earlier work on mutations in the DNA in bacteria and phage would also be recognized. Finally, in 1969, Luria was awarded the Nobel Prize in physiology or medicine along with the other two founders of the phage group, Delbrück and Hershey. The consensus by scientific observers at the time was that this award was long overdue, but the phage group's work was so revolutionary when it was first performed that its significance was fully appreciated only in the light of later work.

In 1972 Luria was asked by the president of MIT to create a Center for Cancer Research, and he recruited a stellar group of scientists, thus putting the center on a firm footing before his retirement in 1985. In 1984 Luria published his autobiography, *A Slot Machine, A Broken Test Tube,* the last of a series of books he wrote before his death from a heart attack in 1991 at his home in Lexington, Massachusetts. These include a textbook on viruses written in the 1950s and two books on biology written in the 1970s. One of these, *Life: The Unfinished Experiment* (1973) received the National Book Award in 1974.

A friendly and witty man, Luria had other interests besides science. He studied sculpture while on sabbatical in France in the 1960s and continued to create works for several years. Toward the end of his life he taught a world literatures course at MIT. Throughout his career Luria was interested in liberal political causes. He was active in the peace movement, being a critic of the Vietnam War and of U.S. defense spending.

Luria is considered one of the most influential molecular biologists of the twentieth century because of the breadth of his interests and the quality of his discoveries. He opened up several new fields, including phage research, as well as the study of mutations at the molecular level, the

to grow, indicating that they had mutated to become resistant to the damaging effects of the phage. Luria later discovered that phage can mutate. This work, along with that of two other phage researchers, Delbrück and Alfred Day Hershey, brought the study of genetics down to the molecular level. The trio began what came to be called the "phage group," and had a profound impact on genetic research of the 1960s. (The phage group was a group of researchers associated with the Cold Spring Harbor Laboratory, Long Island, New York. Today's comparatively sophisticated understanding of viruses is based on the work the phage group did in the 1960s.)

In 1950 Luria moved to the University of Illinois, where he remained until becoming professor and chair of the Massachusetts Institute of Technology (MIT) Department of Microbiology in 1959. At Illinois, Luria found that phage damaged by radiation can be "reactivated" by exchanging genes with other phage. He then accidentally discovered the process of restriction, where DNA is broken down into small pieces by protein catalysts called enzymes. Restriction enzymes later were crucial tools in what became known as genetic engineering, since they allowed biochemists to cut DNA and then take the pieces and insert them into other organisms. This ultimately led to the creation of genetically modified plants and animals.

repair of radiation damage, and the enzymes needed for genetic engineering. His Nobel Prize capped a career that put him at the center of the most important discoveries in mid-century biochemistry.

★

Luria's papers are located at the American Philosophical Library in Philadelphia, Pennsylvania. Biographies of Luria include his autobiography, *A Slot Machine, A Broken Test Tube* (1984). See also "Salvador Edward Luria," in *Modern Scientists and Engineers* (1980) and James Watson, "Memoirs: Salvador E. Luria," in *Proceedings of the American Philosophical Society* (1999). Obituaries are in the *New York Times* (7 Feb. 1991) and the *Washington Post* (8 Feb. 1991).

MAURA C. FLANNERY